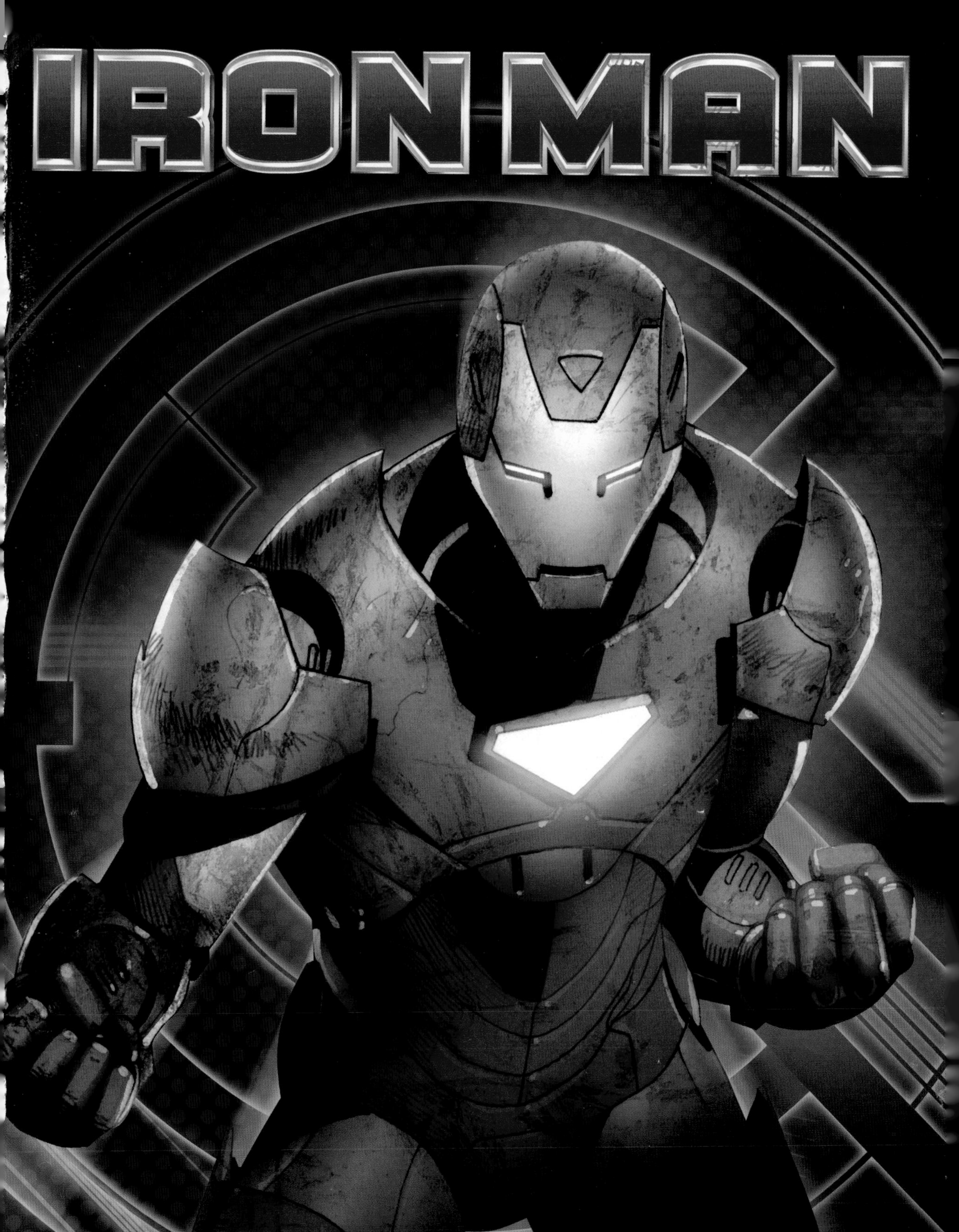

IRON MAN

INVINCIBLE IRON MAN VOL. 1. Contains material originally published in magazine form as INVINCIBLE IRON MAN #1-19. Second printing 2010. ISBN# 978-0-7851-4295-9. Published by MARVEL WORLDWIDE, INC., a subsidiary of MARVEL ENTERTAINMENT, LLC. OFFICE OF PUBLICATION: 417 5th Avenue, New York, NY 10016. Copyright © 2009 and 2010 Marvel Characters, Inc. All rights reserved. $39.99 per copy in the U.S. (GST #R127032852); Canadian Agreement #40668537. All characters featured in this issue and the distinctive names and likenesses thereof, and all related indicia are trademarks of Marvel Characters, Inc. No similarity between any of the names, characters, persons, and/or institutions in this magazine with those of any living or dead person or institution is intended, and any such similarity which may exist is purely coincidental. **Printed in the U.S.A.** ALAN FINE, EVP - Office of the President, Marvel Worldwide, Inc. and EVP & CMO Marvel Characters B.V.; DAN BUCKLEY, Chief Executive Officer and Publisher - Print, Animation & Digital Media; JIM SOKOLOWSKI, Chief Operating Officer; DAVID GABRIEL, SVP of Publishing Sales & Circulation; DAVID BOGART, SVP of Business Affairs & Talent Management; MICHAEL PASCIULLO, VP Merchandising & Communications; JIM O'KEEFE, VP of Operations & Logistics; DAN CARR, Executive Director of Publishing Technology; JUSTIN F. GABRIE, Director of Publishing & Editorial Operations; SUSAN CRESPI, Editorial Operations Manager; ALEX MORALES, Publishing Operations Manager; STAN LEE, Chairman Emeritus. For information regarding advertising in Marvel Comics or on Marvel.com, please contact Ron Stern, VP of Business Development, at rstern@marvel.com. For Marvel subscription inquiries, please call 800-217-9158. **Manufactured between**

THE INVINCIBLE
IRON MAN

WRITER: **MATT FRACTION**
ARTIST: **SALVADOR LARROCA**
COLORS: **FRANK D'ARMATA & STEPHANE PERU**
LETTERS: **CHRIS ELIOPOULOS & VC'S JOE CARAMAGNA**
ASSISTANT EDITOR: **ALEJANDRO ARBONA**
EDITORS: **WARREN SIMONS & RALPH MACCHIO**

DEDICATED TO STEPHANE PERU (1981-2008)

COVER ARTIST: **SALVADOR LARROCA**

COLLECTION EDITOR: **MARK D. BEAZLEY**
ASSISTANT EDITOR: **ALEX STARBUCK**
ASSOCIATE EDITOR: **JOHN DENNING**
EDITOR, SPECIAL PROJECTS: **JENNIFER GRÜNWALD**
SENIOR EDITOR, SPECIAL PROJECTS: **JEFF YOUNGQUIST**
SENIOR VICE PRESIDENT OF SALES: **DAVID GABRIEL**
PRODUCTION: **JERRY KALINOWSKI**
JACKET DESIGN: **SPRING HOTELING**
BOOK DESIGNER: **RODOLFO MURAGUCHI**

EDITOR IN CHIEF: **JOE QUESADA**
PUBLISHER: **DAN BUCKLEY**
EXECUTIVE PRODUCER: **ALAN FINE**

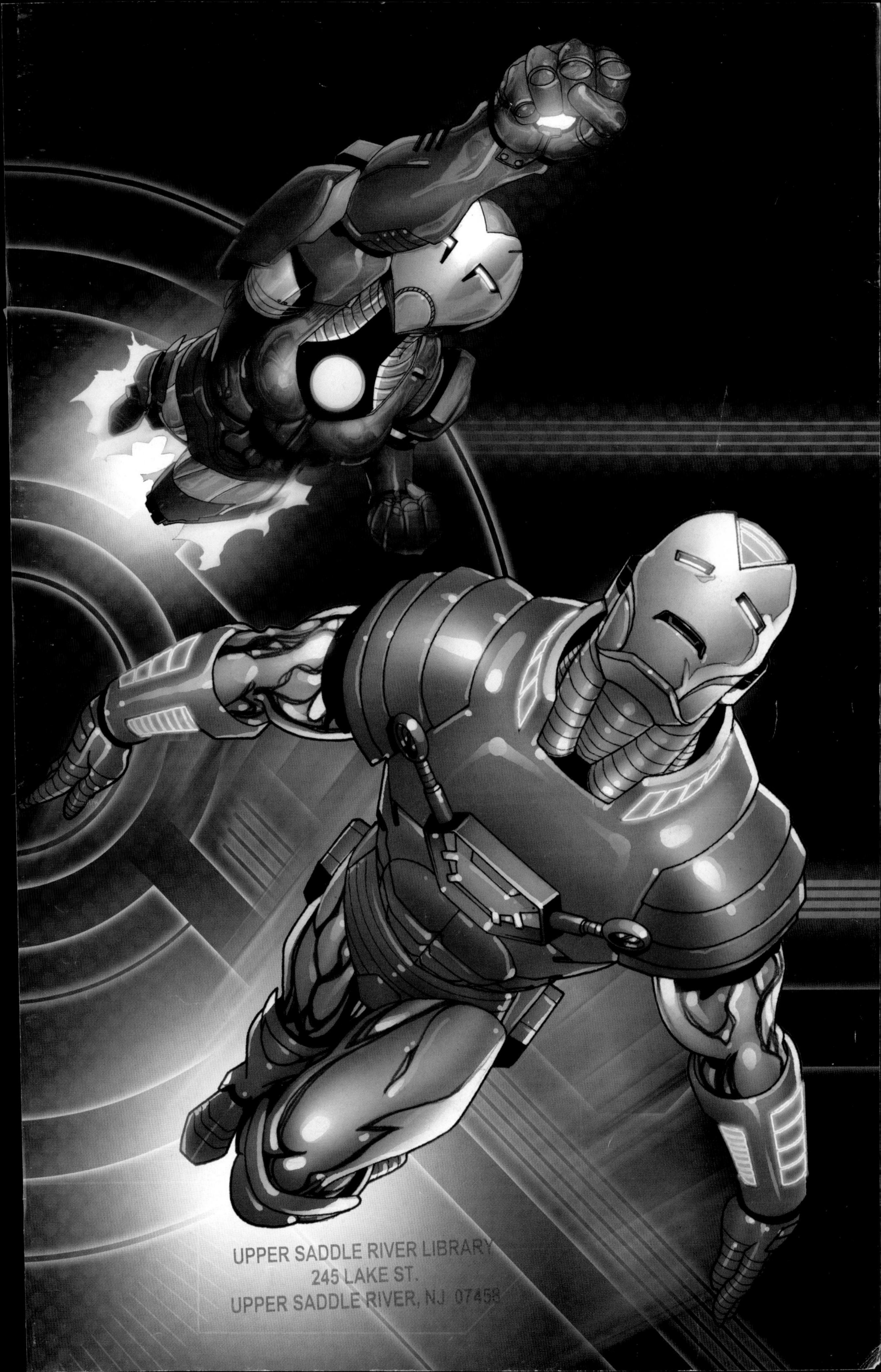

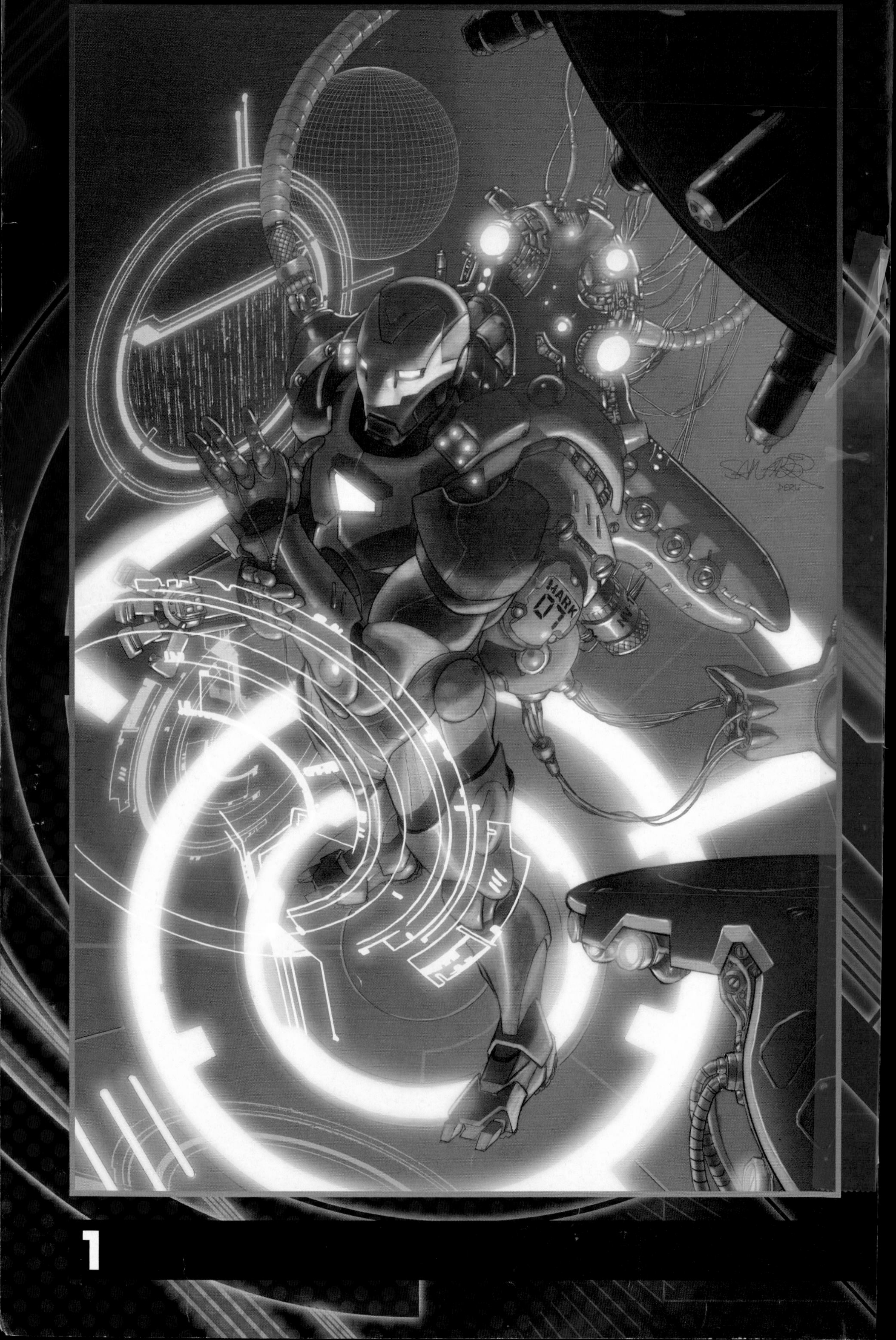
MARK
07

1

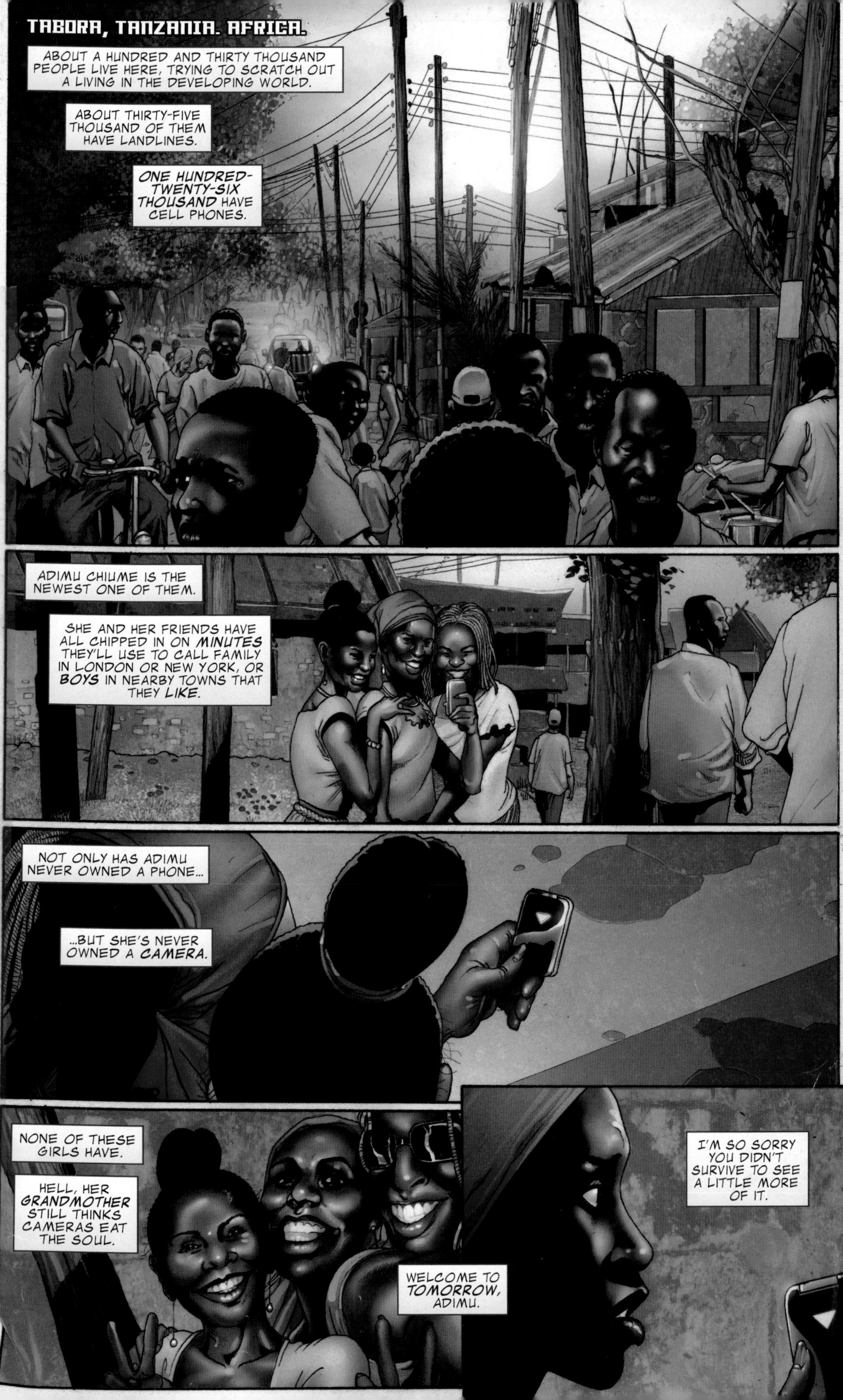
TABORA, TANZANIA. AFRICA.
ABOUT A HUNDRED AND THIRTY THOUSAND PEOPLE LIVE HERE, TRYING TO SCRATCH OUT A LIVING IN THE DEVELOPING WORLD.
ABOUT THIRTY-FIVE THOUSAND OF THEM HAVE LANDLINES.
ONE HUNDRED-TWENTY-SIX THOUSAND HAVE CELL PHONES.
ADIMU CHIUME IS THE NEWEST ONE OF THEM.
SHE AND HER FRIENDS HAVE ALL CHIPPED IN ON MINUTES THEY'LL USE TO CALL FAMILY IN LONDON OR NEW YORK, OR BOYS IN NEARBY TOWNS THAT THEY LIKE.
NOT ONLY HAS ADIMU NEVER OWNED A PHONE...
...BUT SHE'S NEVER OWNED A CAMERA.
NONE OF THESE GIRLS HAVE.
HELL, HER GRANDMOTHER STILL THINKS CAMERAS EAT THE SOUL.
WELCOME TO TOMORROW, ADIMU.
I'M SO SORRY YOU DIDN'T SURVIVE TO SEE A LITTLE MORE OF IT.

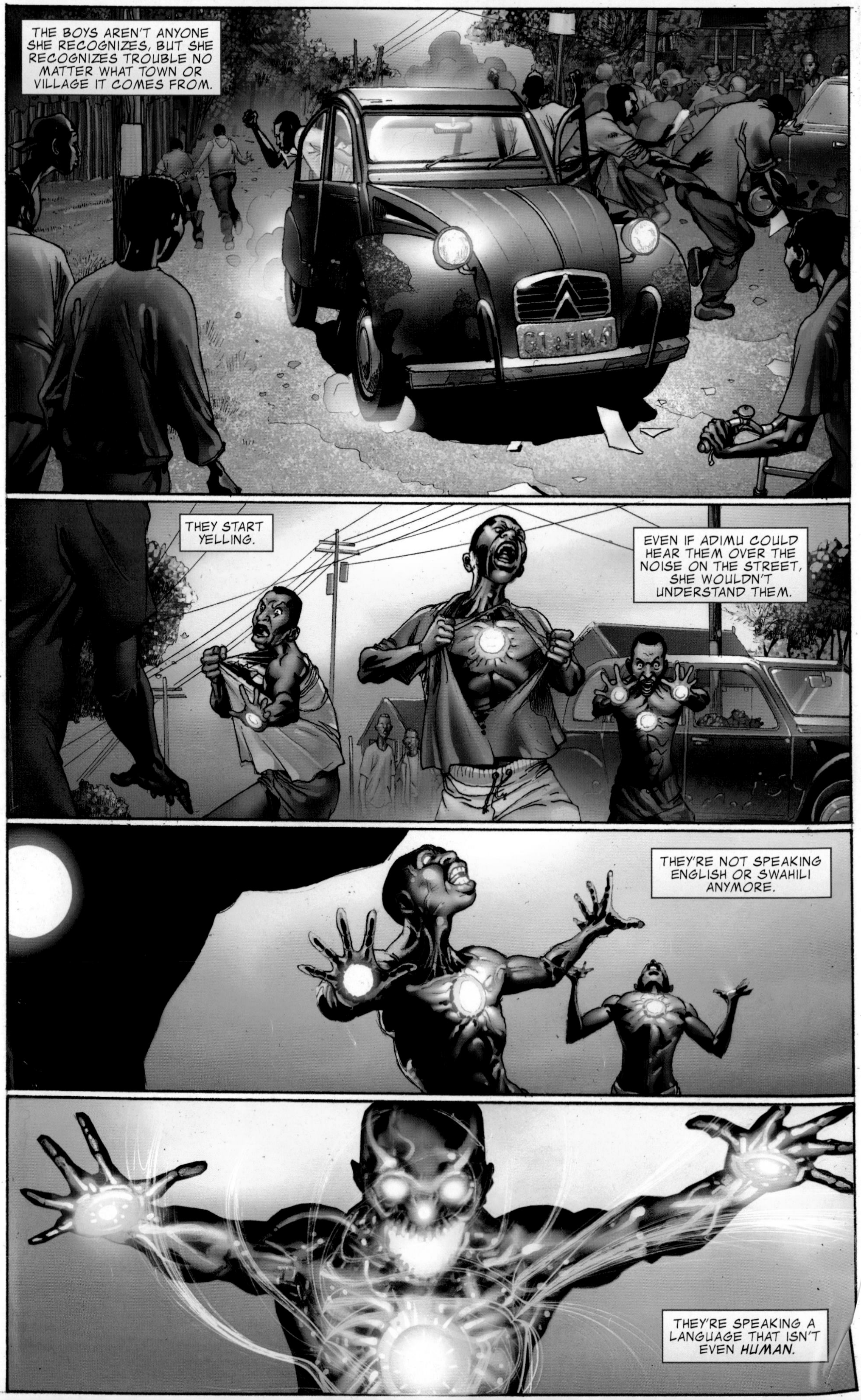

THE BOYS AREN'T ANYONE SHE RECOGNIZES, BUT SHE RECOGNIZES TROUBLE NO MATTER WHAT TOWN OR VILLAGE IT COMES FROM.
THEY START YELLING.
EVEN IF ADIMU COULD HEAR THEM OVER THE NOISE ON THE STREET, SHE WOULDN'T UNDERSTAND THEM.
THEY'RE NOT SPEAKING ENGLISH OR SWAHILI ANYMORE.
THEY'RE SPEAKING A LANGUAGE THAT ISN'T EVEN *HUMAN*.

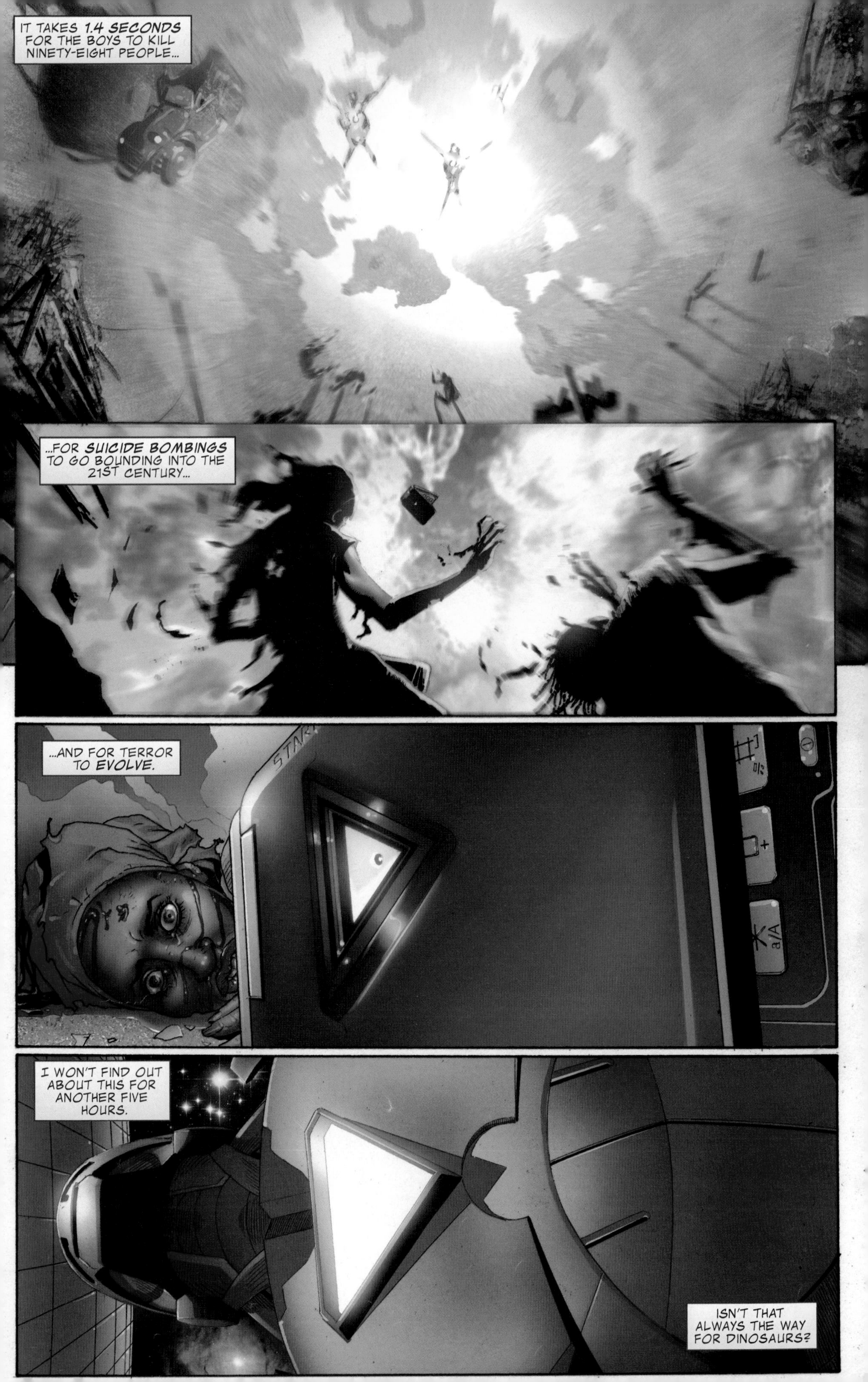
IT TAKES 1.4 SECONDS FOR THE BOYS TO KILL NINETY-EIGHT PEOPLE...
...FOR SUICIDE BOMBINGS TO GO BOUNDING INTO THE 21ST CENTURY...
...AND FOR TERROR TO EVOLVE.
STARK
I WON'T FIND OUT ABOUT THIS FOR ANOTHER FIVE HOURS.
ISN'T THAT ALWAYS THE WAY FOR DINOSAURS?

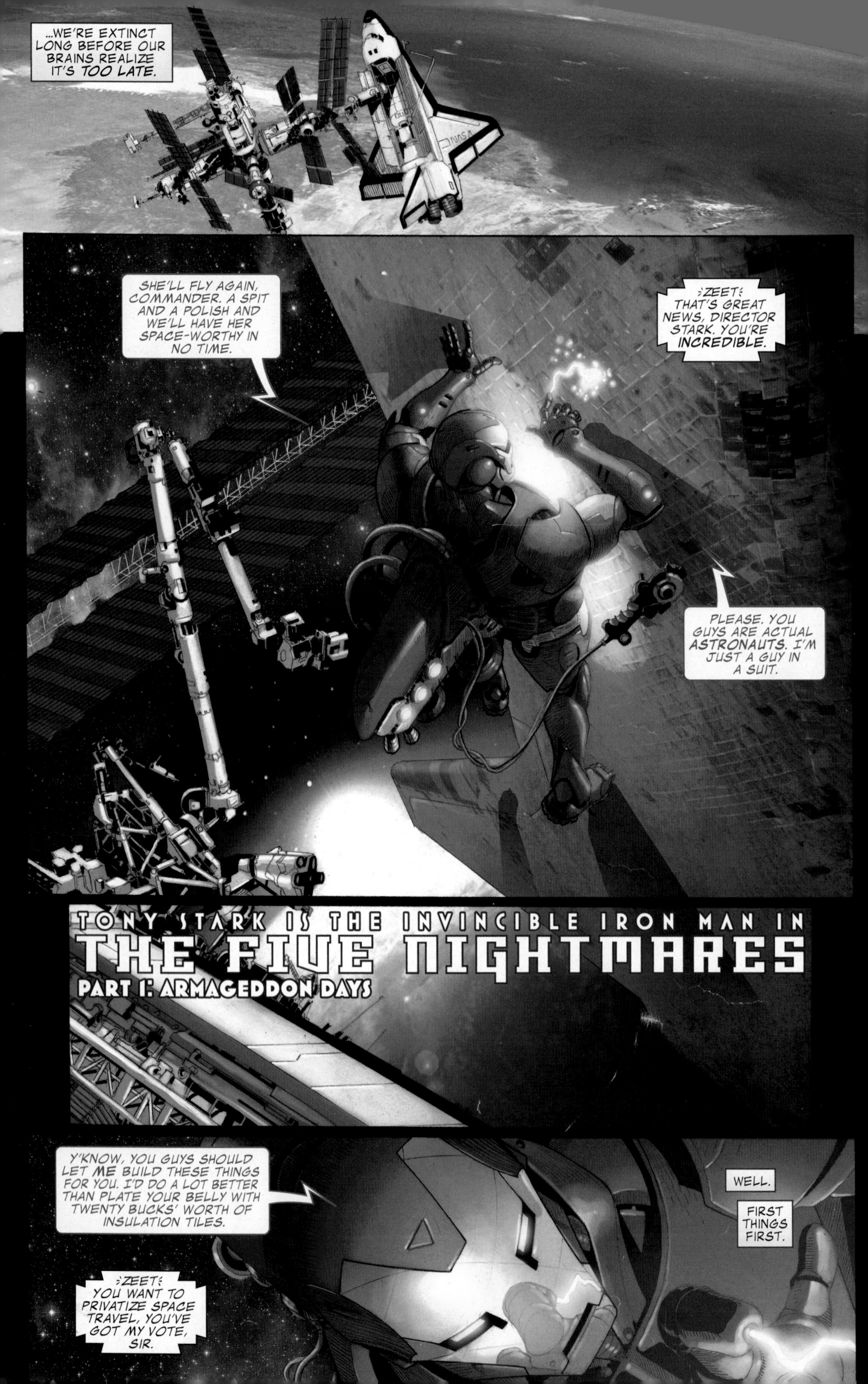
...WE'RE EXTINCT LONG BEFORE OUR BRAINS REALIZE IT'S TOO LATE.
SHE'LL FLY AGAIN, COMMANDER. A SPIT AND A POLISH AND WE'LL HAVE HER SPACE-WORTHY IN NO TIME.
ZEET THAT'S GREAT NEWS, DIRECTOR STARK. YOU'RE INCREDIBLE.
PLEASE. YOU GUYS ARE ACTUAL ASTRONAUTS. I'M JUST A GUY IN A SUIT.
TONY STARK IS THE INVINCIBLE IRON MAN IN
THE FIVE NIGHTMARES
PART 1: ARMAGEDDON DAYS
Y'KNOW, YOU GUYS SHOULD LET ME BUILD THESE THINGS FOR YOU. I'D DO A LOT BETTER THAN PLATE YOUR BELLY WITH TWENTY BUCKS' WORTH OF INSULATION TILES.
ZEET YOU WANT TO PRIVATIZE SPACE TRAVEL, YOU'VE GOT MY VOTE, SIR.
WELL.
FIRST THINGS FIRST.

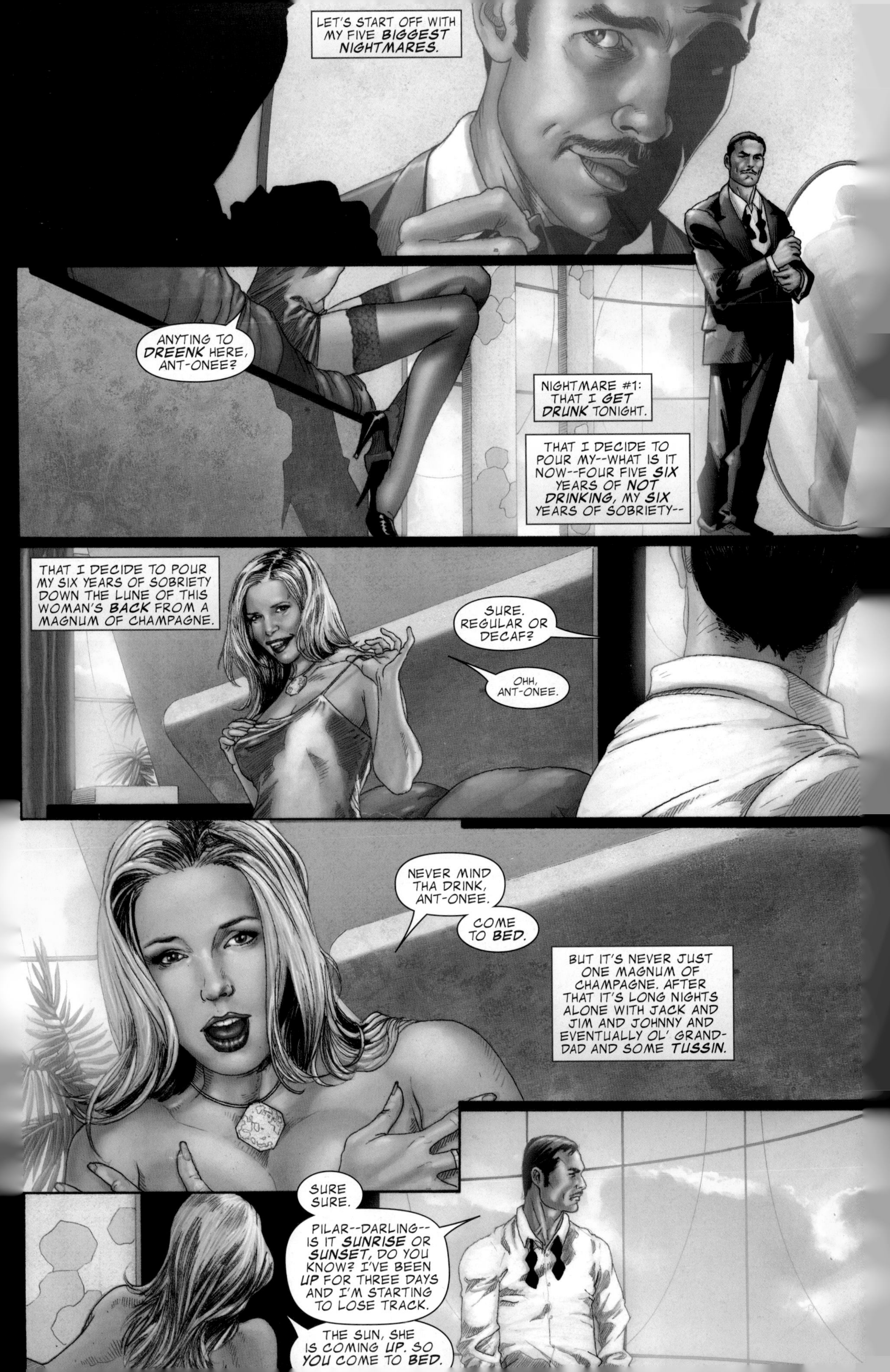
LET'S START OFF WITH MY FIVE BIGGEST NIGHTMARES.
ANYTING TO DREENK HERE, ANT-ONEE?
NIGHTMARE #1: THAT I GET DRUNK TONIGHT.
THAT I DECIDE TO POUR MY--WHAT IS IT NOW--FOUR FIVE SIX YEARS OF NOT DRINKING, MY SIX YEARS OF SOBRIETY--
THAT I DECIDE TO POUR MY SIX YEARS OF SOBRIETY DOWN THE LUNE OF THIS WOMAN'S BACK FROM A MAGNUM OF CHAMPAGNE.
SURE. REGULAR OR DECAF?
OHH, ANT-ONEE.
NEVER MIND THA DRINK, ANT-ONEE.
COME TO BED.
BUT IT'S NEVER JUST ONE MAGNUM OF CHAMPAGNE. AFTER THAT IT'S LONG NIGHTS ALONE WITH JACK AND JIM AND JOHNNY AND EVENTUALLY OL' GRAND-DAD AND SOME TUSSIN.
SURE SURE.
PILAR--DARLING--IS IT SUNRISE OR SUNSET, DO YOU KNOW? I'VE BEEN UP FOR THREE DAYS AND I'M STARTING TO LOSE TRACK.
THE SUN, SHE IS COMING UP. SO YOU COME TO BED.

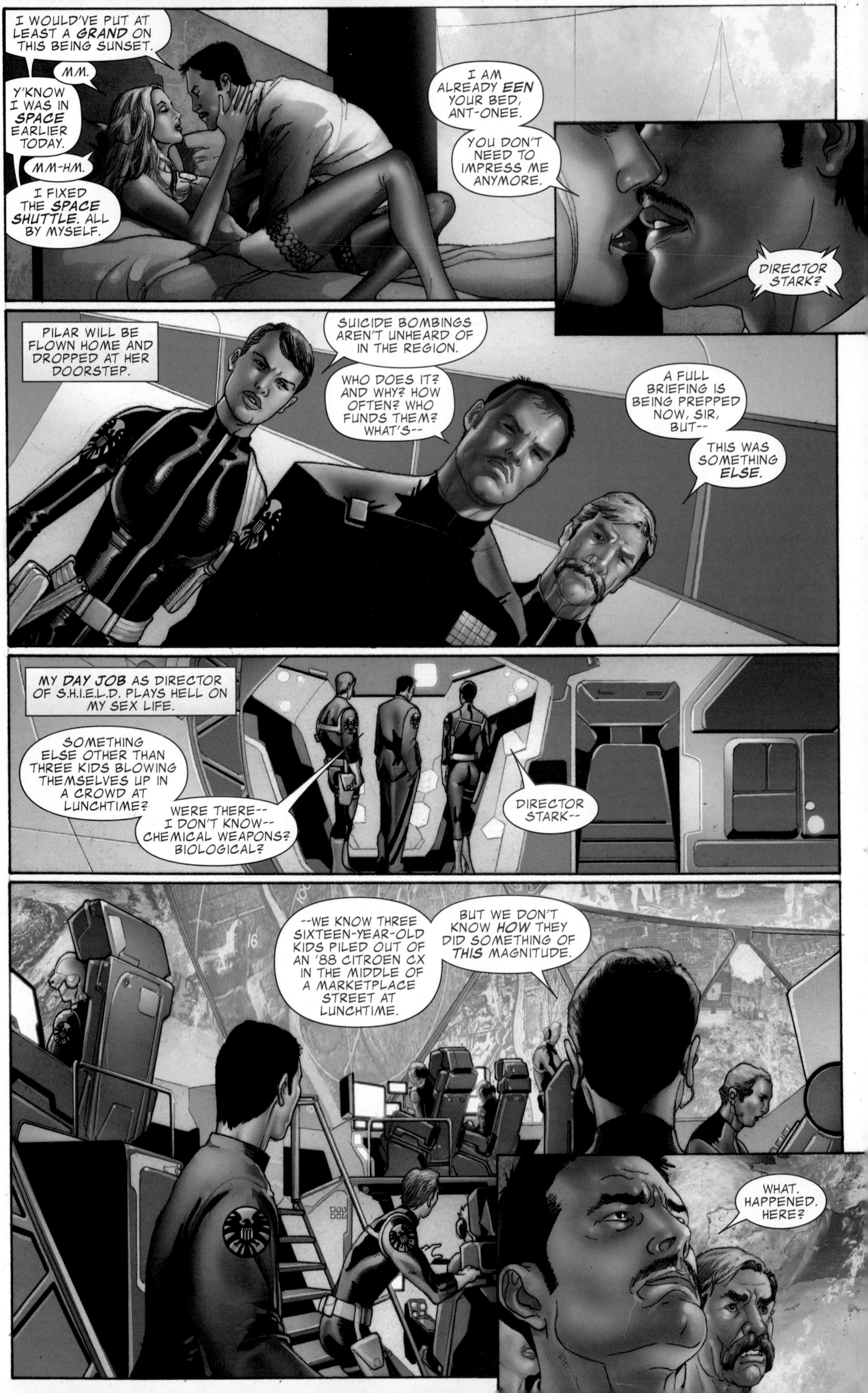
I WOULD'VE PUT AT LEAST A GRAND ON THIS BEING SUNSET.
MM.
Y'KNOW I WAS IN SPACE EARLIER TODAY.
MM-HM.
I FIXED THE SPACE SHUTTLE. ALL BY MYSELF.
I AM ALREADY EEN YOUR BED, ANT-ONEE.
YOU DON'T NEED TO IMPRESS ME ANYMORE.
DIRECTOR STARK?
PILAR WILL BE FLOWN HOME AND DROPPED AT HER DOORSTEP.
SUICIDE BOMBINGS AREN'T UNHEARD OF IN THE REGION.
WHO DOES IT? AND WHY? HOW OFTEN? WHO FUNDS THEM? WHAT'S--
A FULL BRIEFING IS BEING PREPPED NOW, SIR, BUT--
THIS WAS SOMETHING ELSE.
MY DAY JOB AS DIRECTOR OF S.H.I.E.L.D. PLAYS HELL ON MY SEX LIFE.
SOMETHING ELSE OTHER THAN THREE KIDS BLOWING THEMSELVES UP IN A CROWD AT LUNCHTIME?
WERE THERE-- I DON'T KNOW-- CHEMICAL WEAPONS? BIOLOGICAL?
DIRECTOR STARK--
--WE KNOW THREE SIXTEEN-YEAR-OLD KIDS PILED OUT OF AN '88 CITROEN CX IN THE MIDDLE OF A MARKETPLACE STREET AT LUNCHTIME.
BUT WE DON'T KNOW HOW THEY DID SOMETHING OF THIS MAGNITUDE.
WHAT. HAPPENED. HERE?

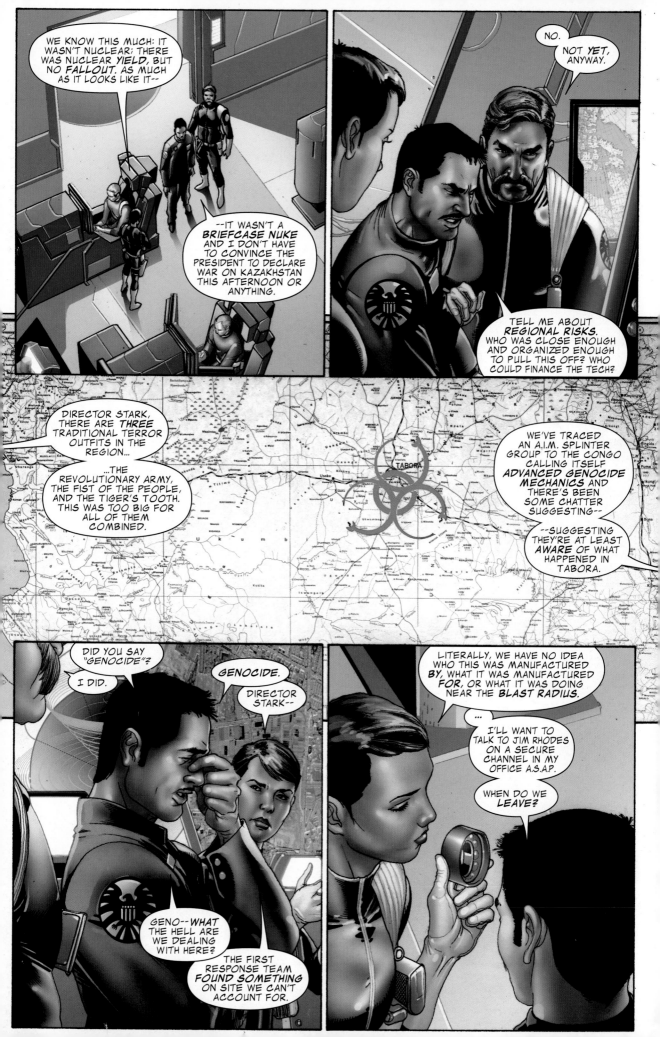

WE KNOW THIS MUCH: IT WASN'T NUCLEAR; THERE WAS NUCLEAR *YIELD*, BUT NO *FALLOUT*. AS MUCH AS IT LOOKS LIKE IT--

--IT WASN'T A *BRIEFCASE NUKE* AND I DON'T HAVE TO CONVINCE THE PRESIDENT TO DECLARE WAR ON KAZAKHSTAN THIS AFTERNOON OR ANYTHING.

NO.

NOT *YET*, ANYWAY.

TELL ME ABOUT *REGIONAL RISKS.* WHO WAS CLOSE ENOUGH AND ORGANIZED ENOUGH TO PULL THIS OFF? WHO COULD FINANCE THE TECH?

DIRECTOR STARK, THERE ARE *THREE* TRADITIONAL TERROR OUTFITS IN THE REGION...

...THE REVOLUTIONARY ARMY, THE FIST OF THE PEOPLE, AND THE TIGER'S TOOTH. THIS WAS TOO BIG FOR ALL OF THEM COMBINED.

WE'VE TRACED AN A.I.M. SPLINTER GROUP TO THE CONGO CALLING ITSELF *ADVANCED GENOCIDE MECHANICS* AND THERE'S BEEN SOME CHATTER SUGGESTING--

--SUGGESTING THEY'RE AT LEAST *AWARE* OF WHAT HAPPENED IN TABORA.

DID YOU SAY "GENOCIDE"?

I DID.

GENOCIDE.

DIRECTOR STARK--

GENO--*WHAT* THE HELL ARE WE DEALING WITH HERE?

THE FIRST RESPONSE TEAM *FOUND SOMETHING* ON SITE WE CAN'T ACCOUNT FOR.

LITERALLY, WE HAVE NO IDEA WHO THIS WAS MANUFACTURED *BY*, WHAT IT WAS MANUFACTURED *FOR*, OR WHAT IT WAS DOING NEAR THE *BLAST RADIUS.*

...

I'LL WANT TO TALK TO JIM RHODES ON A SECURE CHANNEL IN MY OFFICE A.S.A.P.

WHEN DO WE *LEAVE?*

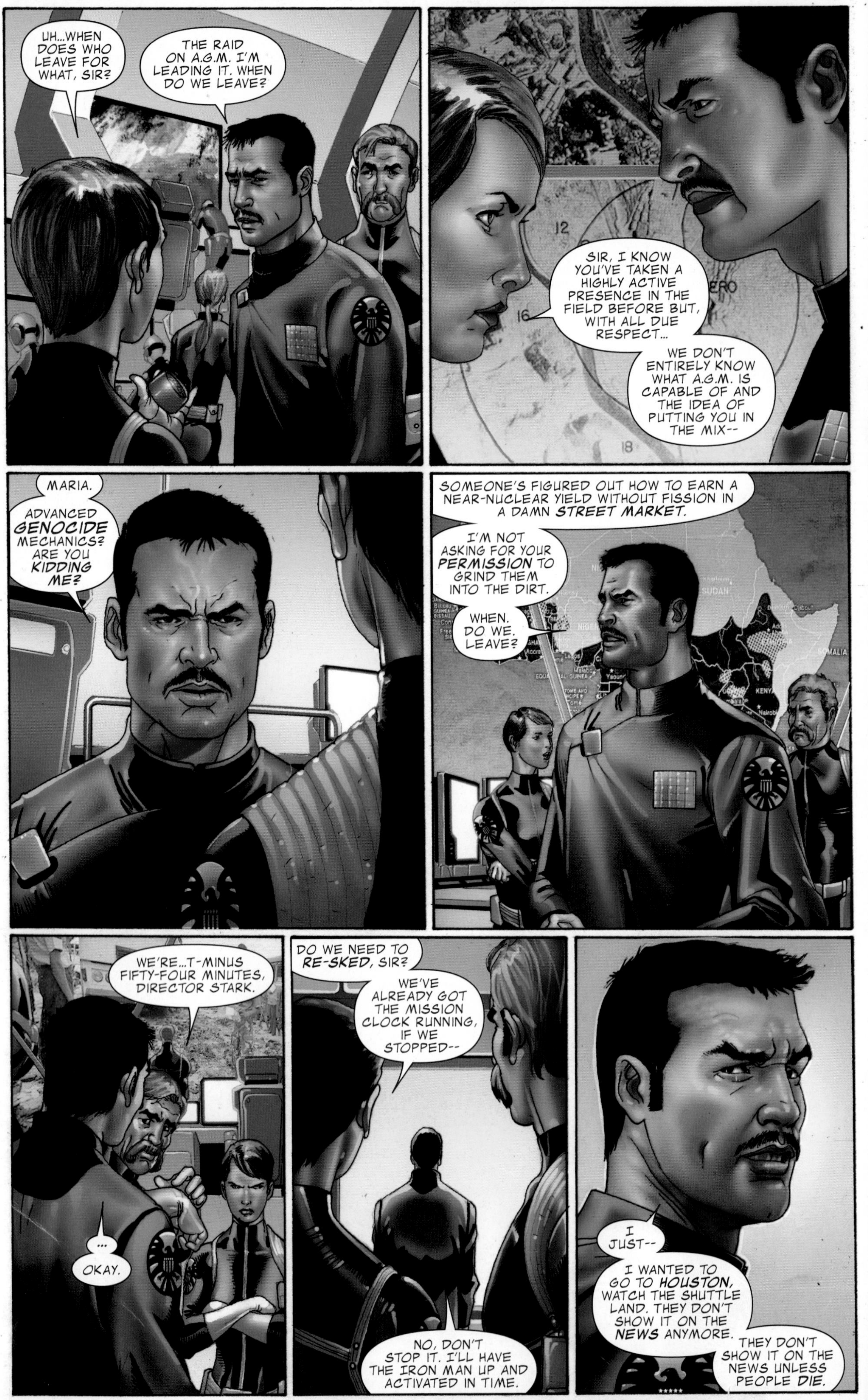
UH...WHEN DOES WHO LEAVE FOR WHAT, SIR?
THE RAID ON A.G.M. I'M LEADING IT. WHEN DO WE LEAVE?
SIR, I KNOW YOU'VE TAKEN A HIGHLY ACTIVE PRESENCE IN THE FIELD BEFORE BUT, WITH ALL DUE RESPECT...
WE DON'T ENTIRELY KNOW WHAT A.G.M. IS CAPABLE OF AND THE IDEA OF PUTTING YOU IN THE MIX--
MARIA.
ADVANCED GENOCIDE MECHANICS? ARE YOU KIDDING ME?
SOMEONE'S FIGURED OUT HOW TO EARN A NEAR-NUCLEAR YIELD WITHOUT FISSION IN A DAMN STREET MARKET.
I'M NOT ASKING FOR YOUR PERMISSION TO GRIND THEM INTO THE DIRT.
WHEN. DO WE. LEAVE?
WE'RE...T-MINUS FIFTY-FOUR MINUTES, DIRECTOR STARK.
...
OKAY.
DO WE NEED TO RE-SKED, SIR?
WE'VE ALREADY GOT THE MISSION CLOCK RUNNING, IF WE STOPPED--
NO, DON'T STOP IT. I'LL HAVE THE IRON MAN UP AND ACTIVATED IN TIME.
I JUST--
I WANTED TO GO TO HOUSTON, WATCH THE SHUTTLE LAND. THEY DON'T SHOW IT ON THE NEWS ANYMORE.
THEY DON'T SHOW IT ON THE NEWS UNLESS PEOPLE DIE.

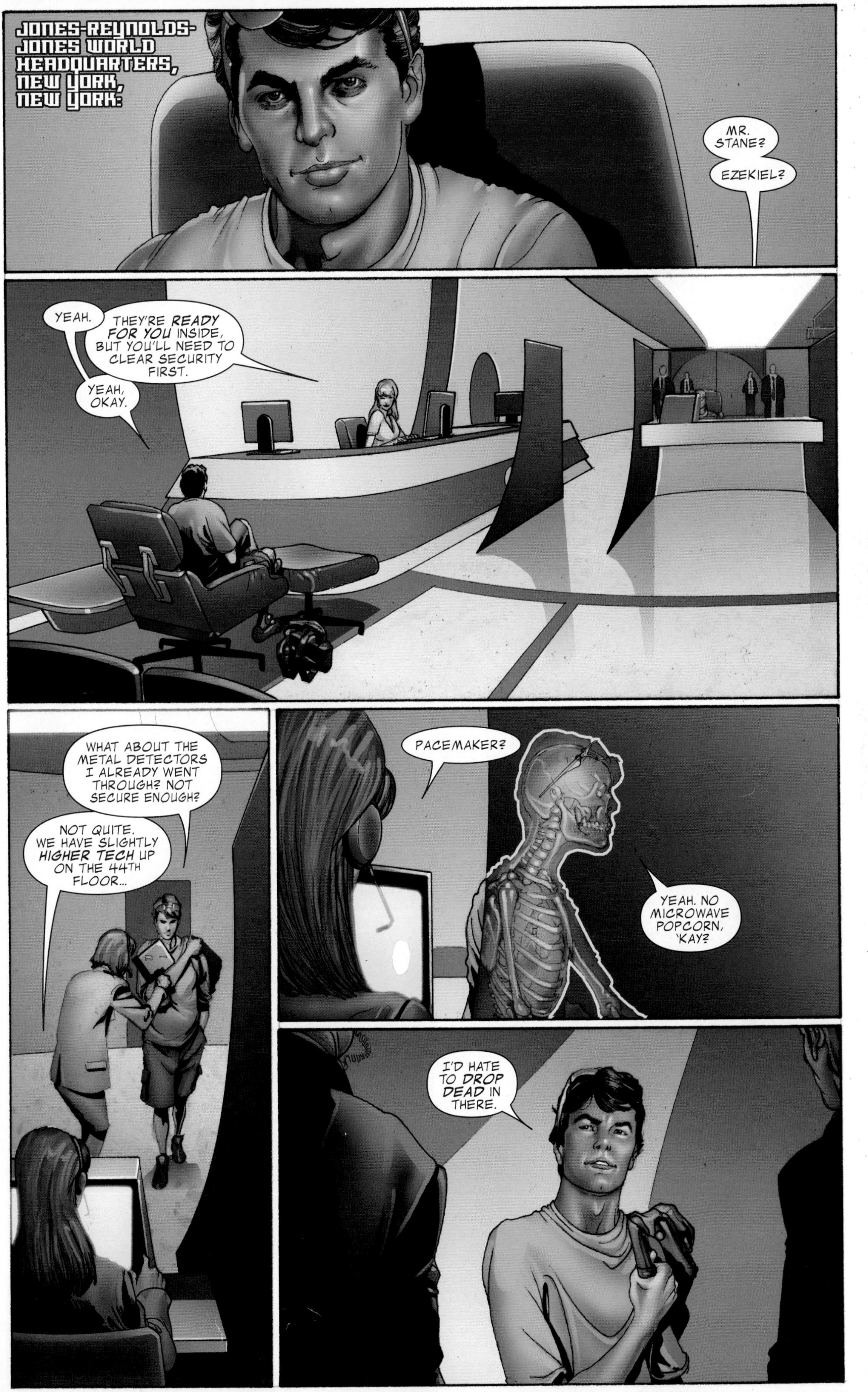
JONES-REYNOLDS-JONES WORLD HEADQUARTERS, NEW YORK, NEW YORK:
MR. STANE?
EZEKIEL?
YEAH.
THEY'RE READY FOR YOU INSIDE, BUT YOU'LL NEED TO CLEAR SECURITY FIRST.
YEAH, OKAY.
WHAT ABOUT THE METAL DETECTORS I ALREADY WENT THROUGH? NOT SECURE ENOUGH?
NOT QUITE. WE HAVE SLIGHTLY HIGHER TECH UP ON THE 44TH FLOOR...
PACEMAKER?
YEAH. NO MICROWAVE POPCORN, 'KAY?
I'D HATE TO DROP DEAD IN THERE.

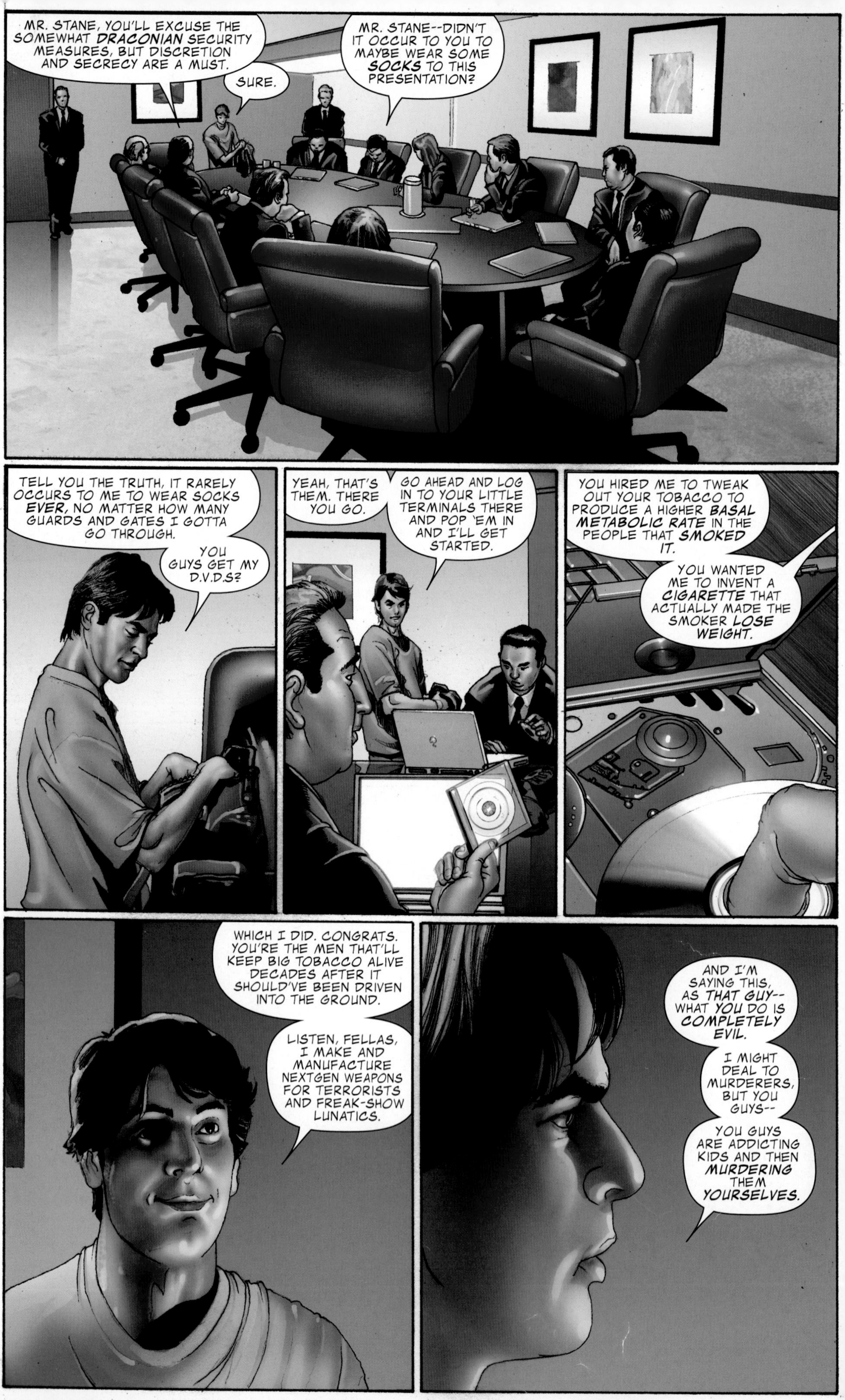
MR. STANE, YOU'LL EXCUSE THE SOMEWHAT DRACONIAN SECURITY MEASURES, BUT DISCRETION AND SECRECY ARE A MUST.
SURE.
MR. STANE--DIDN'T IT OCCUR TO YOU TO MAYBE WEAR SOME SOCKS TO THIS PRESENTATION?
TELL YOU THE TRUTH, IT RARELY OCCURS TO ME TO WEAR SOCKS EVER, NO MATTER HOW MANY GUARDS AND GATES I GOTTA GO THROUGH.
YOU GUYS GET MY D.V.D.S?
YEAH, THAT'S THEM. THERE YOU GO.
GO AHEAD AND LOG IN TO YOUR LITTLE TERMINALS THERE AND POP 'EM IN AND I'LL GET STARTED.
YOU HIRED ME TO TWEAK OUT YOUR TOBACCO TO PRODUCE A HIGHER BASAL METABOLIC RATE IN THE PEOPLE THAT SMOKED IT.
YOU WANTED ME TO INVENT A CIGARETTE THAT ACTUALLY MADE THE SMOKER LOSE WEIGHT.
WHICH I DID. CONGRATS. YOU'RE THE MEN THAT'LL KEEP BIG TOBACCO ALIVE DECADES AFTER IT SHOULD'VE BEEN DRIVEN INTO THE GROUND.
LISTEN, FELLAS, I MAKE AND MANUFACTURE NEXTGEN WEAPONS FOR TERRORISTS AND FREAK-SHOW LUNATICS.
AND I'M SAYING THIS, AS THAT GUY--WHAT YOU DO IS COMPLETELY EVIL.
I MIGHT DEAL TO MURDERERS, BUT YOU GUYS--
YOU GUYS ARE ADDICTING KIDS AND THEN MURDERING THEM YOURSELVES.

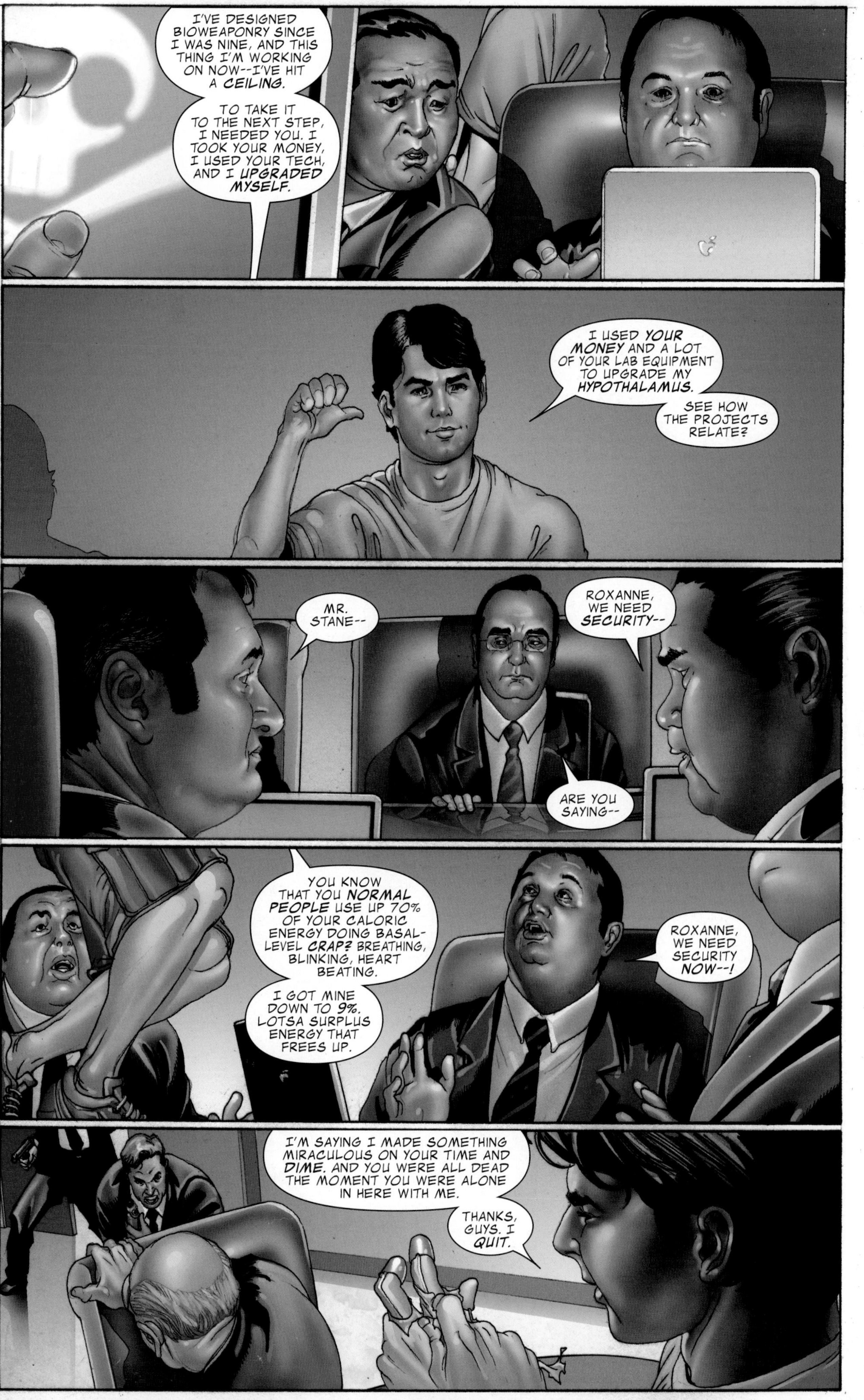
I'VE DESIGNED BIOWEAPONRY SINCE I WAS NINE, AND THIS THING I'M WORKING ON NOW--I'VE HIT A CEILING.
TO TAKE IT TO THE NEXT STEP, I NEEDED YOU. I TOOK YOUR MONEY, I USED YOUR TECH, AND I UPGRADED MYSELF.
I USED YOUR MONEY AND A LOT OF YOUR LAB EQUIPMENT TO UPGRADE MY HYPOTHALAMUS.
SEE HOW THE PROJECTS RELATE?
MR. STANE--
ROXANNE, WE NEED SECURITY--
ARE YOU SAYING--
YOU KNOW THAT YOU NORMAL PEOPLE USE UP 70% OF YOUR CALORIC ENERGY DOING BASAL-LEVEL CRAP? BREATHING, BLINKING, HEART BEATING.
I GOT MINE DOWN TO 9%. LOTSA SURPLUS ENERGY THAT FREES UP.
ROXANNE, WE NEED SECURITY NOW--!
I'M SAYING I MADE SOMETHING MIRACULOUS ON YOUR TIME AND DIME. AND YOU WERE ALL DEAD THE MOMENT YOU WERE ALONE IN HERE WITH ME.
THANKS, GUYS. I QUIT.

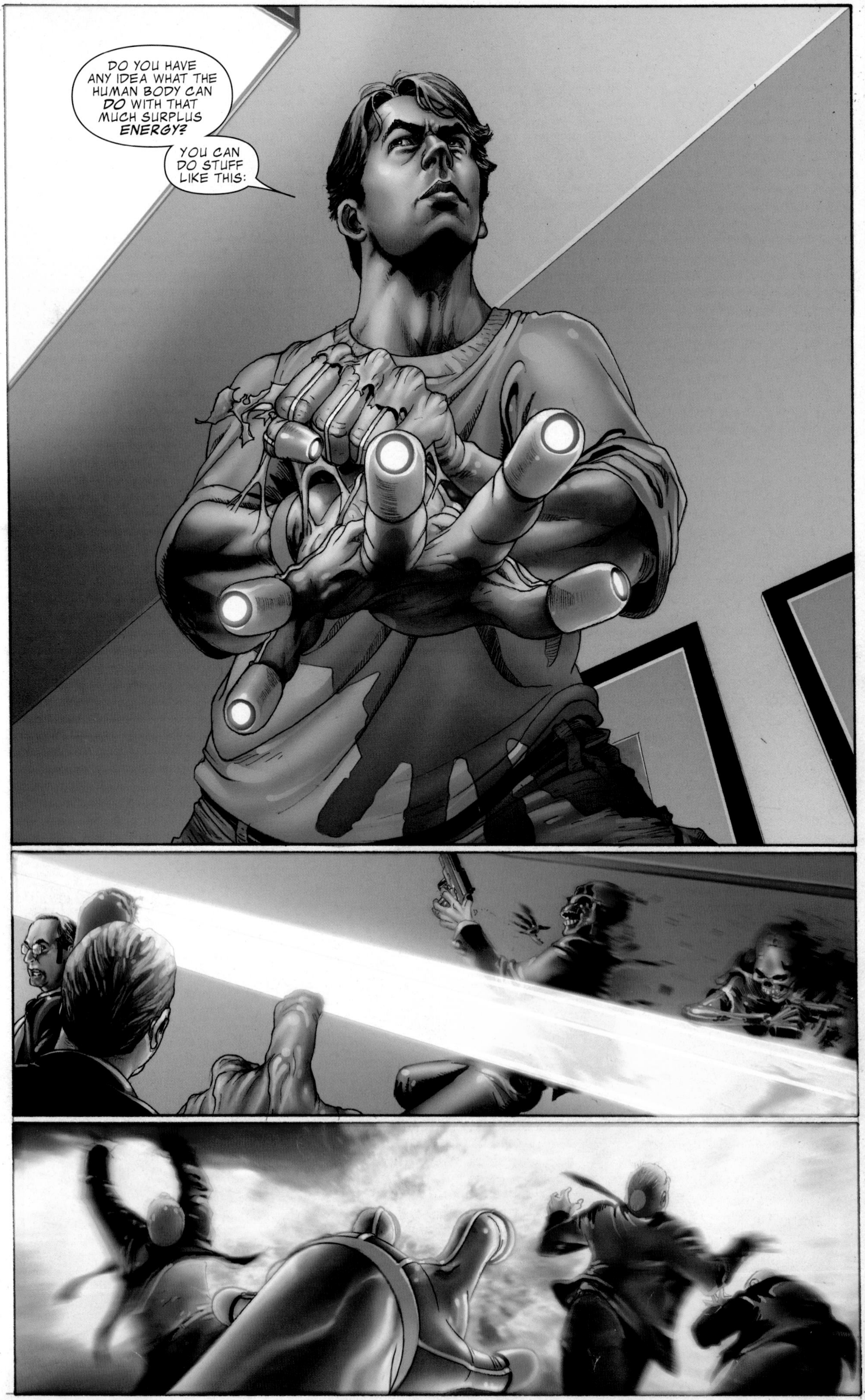
DO YOU HAVE ANY IDEA WHAT THE HUMAN BODY CAN DO WITH THAT MUCH SURPLUS ENERGY?
YOU CAN DO STUFF LIKE THIS:

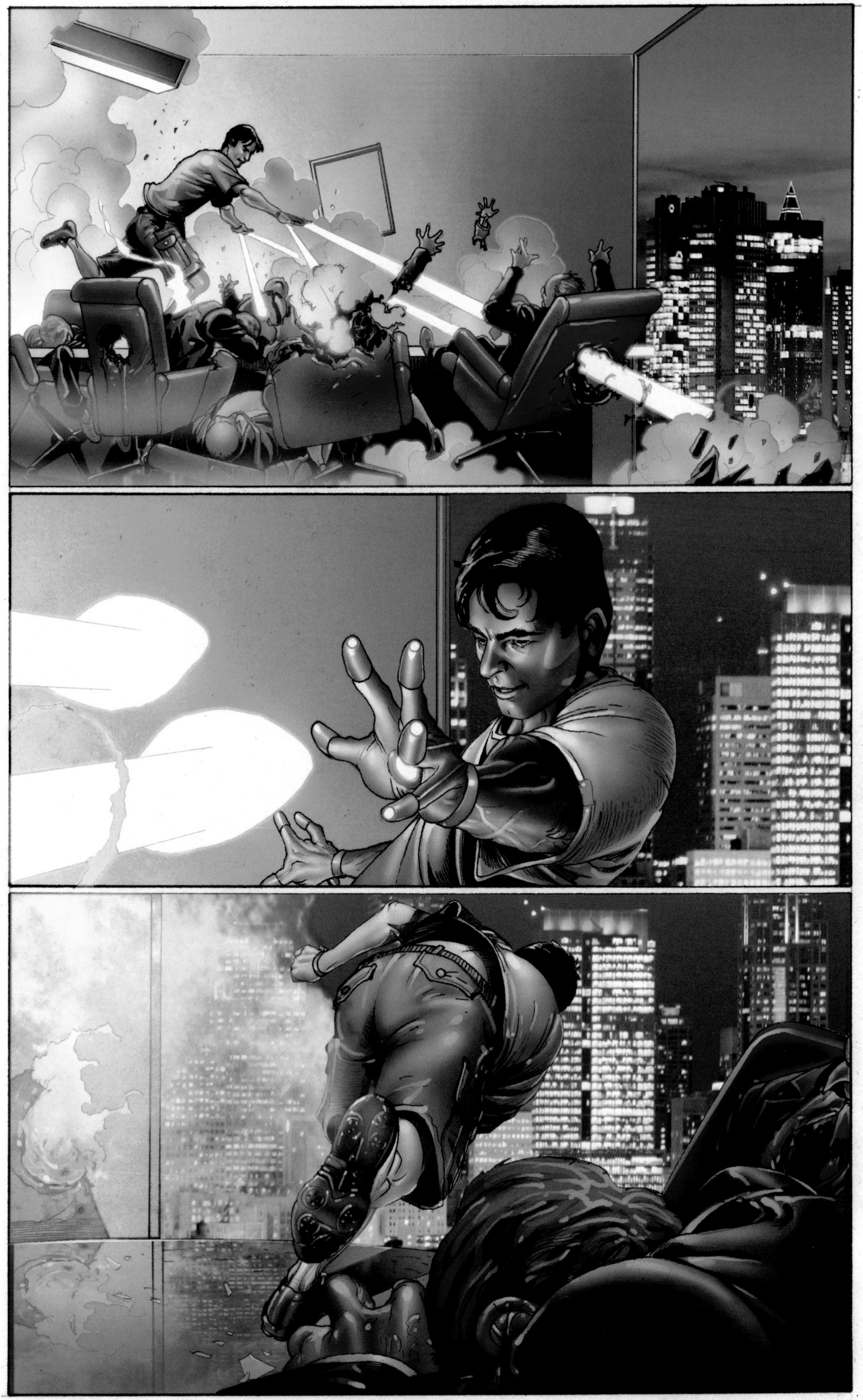

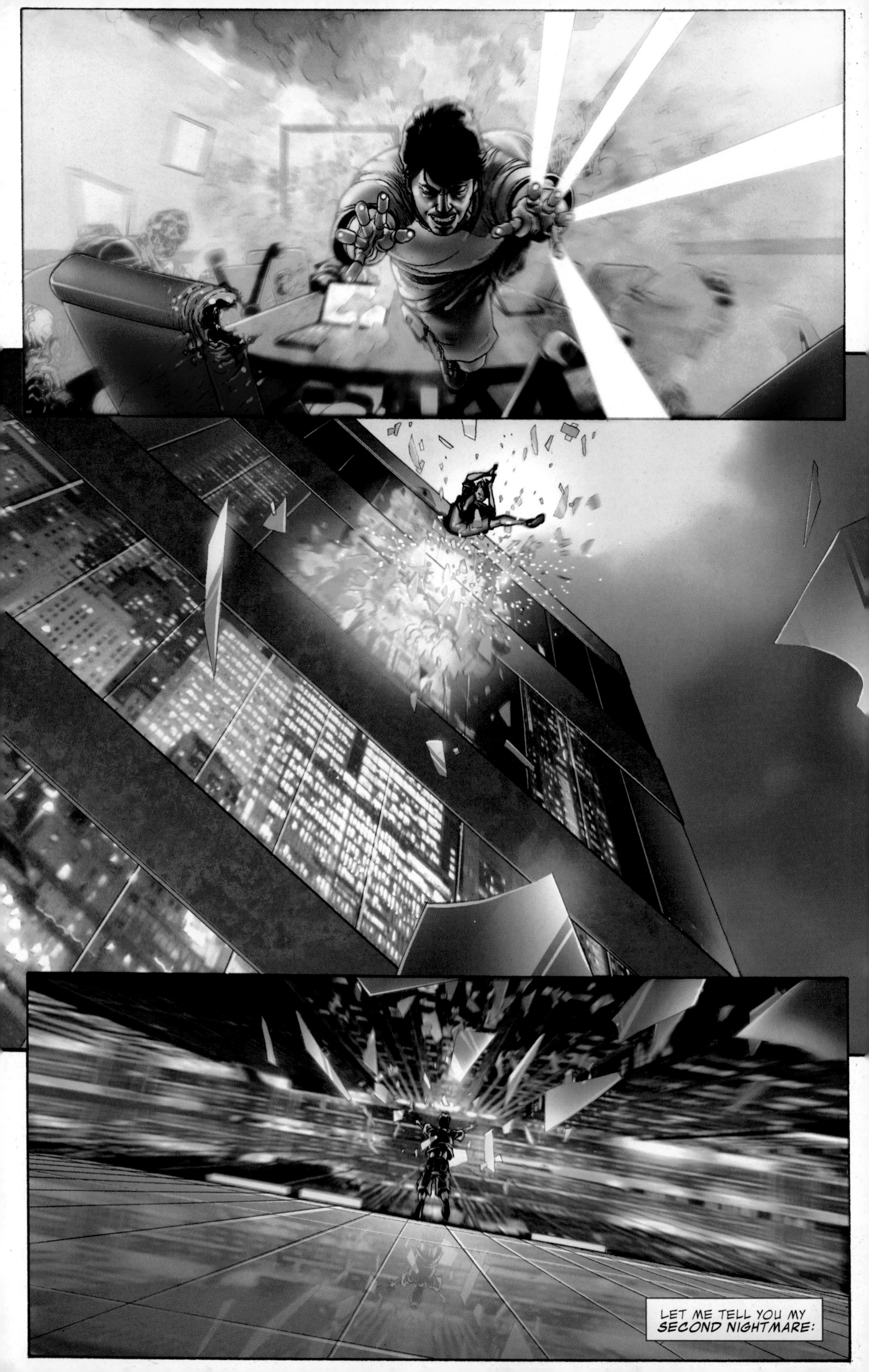
LET ME TELL YOU MY
SECOND NIGHTMARE:

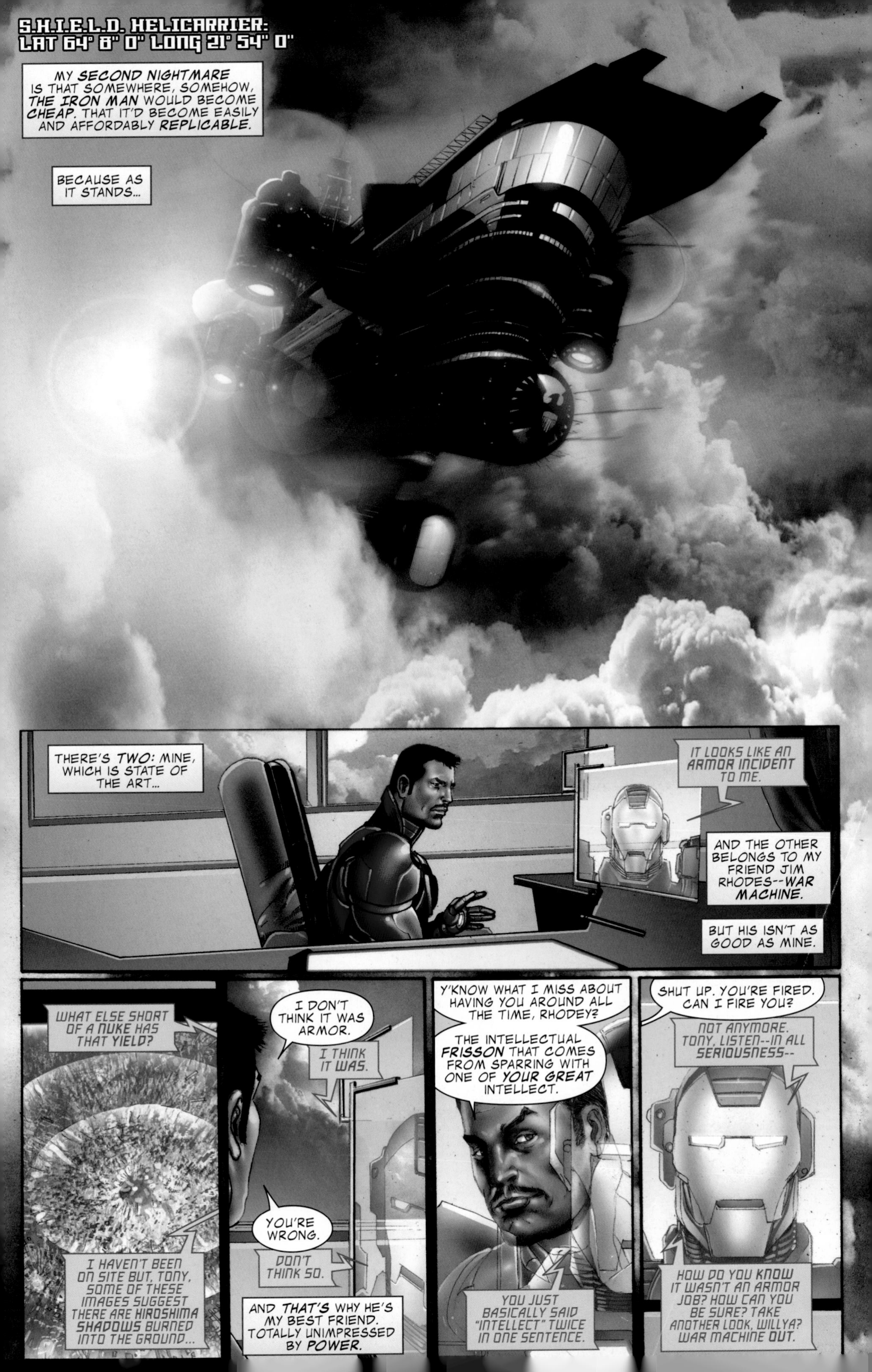
S.H.I.E.L.D. HELICARRIER:
LAT 64° 8" 0" LONG 21° 54" 0"
MY SECOND NIGHTMARE IS THAT SOMEWHERE, SOMEHOW, THE IRON MAN WOULD BECOME CHEAP. THAT IT'D BECOME EASILY AND AFFORDABLY REPLICABLE.
BECAUSE AS IT STANDS...
THERE'S TWO: MINE, WHICH IS STATE OF THE ART...
IT LOOKS LIKE AN ARMOR INCIDENT TO ME.
AND THE OTHER BELONGS TO MY FRIEND JIM RHODES--WAR MACHINE.
BUT HIS ISN'T AS GOOD AS MINE.
WHAT ELSE SHORT OF A NUKE HAS THAT YIELD?
I HAVEN'T BEEN ON SITE BUT, TONY, SOME OF THESE IMAGES SUGGEST THERE ARE HIROSHIMA SHADOWS BURNED INTO THE GROUND...
I DON'T THINK IT WAS ARMOR.
I THINK IT WAS.
YOU'RE WRONG.
DON'T THINK SO.
AND THAT'S WHY HE'S MY BEST FRIEND. TOTALLY UNIMPRESSED BY POWER.
Y'KNOW WHAT I MISS ABOUT HAVING YOU AROUND ALL THE TIME, RHODEY?
THE INTELLECTUAL FRISSON THAT COMES FROM SPARRING WITH ONE OF YOUR GREAT INTELLECT.
YOU JUST BASICALLY SAID "INTELLECT" TWICE IN ONE SENTENCE.
SHUT UP. YOU'RE FIRED. CAN I FIRE YOU?
NOT ANYMORE. TONY, LISTEN--IN ALL SERIOUSNESS--
HOW DO YOU KNOW IT WASN'T AN ARMOR JOB? HOW CAN YOU BE SURE? TAKE ANOTHER LOOK, WILLYA? WAR MACHINE OUT.

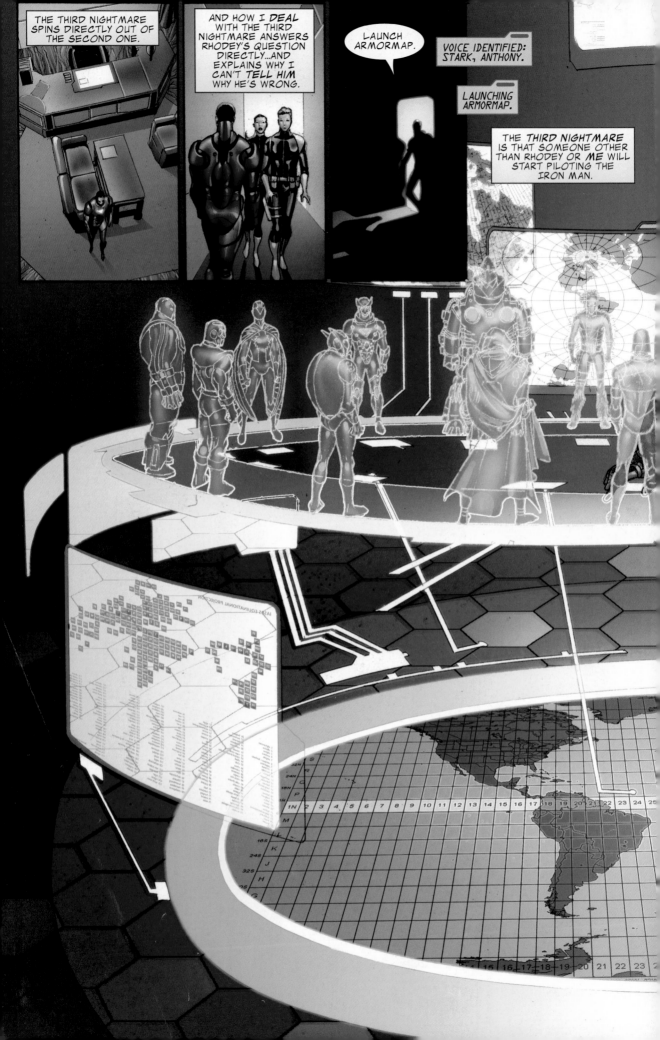

THE THIRD NIGHTMARE SPINS DIRECTLY OUT OF THE SECOND ONE.

AND HOW I *DEAL* WITH THE THIRD NIGHTMARE ANSWERS RHODEY'S QUESTION DIRECTLY...AND EXPLAINS WHY I CAN'T *TELL HIM* WHY HE'S WRONG.

LAUNCH ARMORMAP.

VOICE IDENTIFIED: STARK, ANTHONY.

LAUNCHING ARMORMAP.

THE *THIRD NIGHTMARE* IS THAT SOMEONE OTHER THAN RHODEY OR *ME* WILL START PILOTING THE IRON MAN.

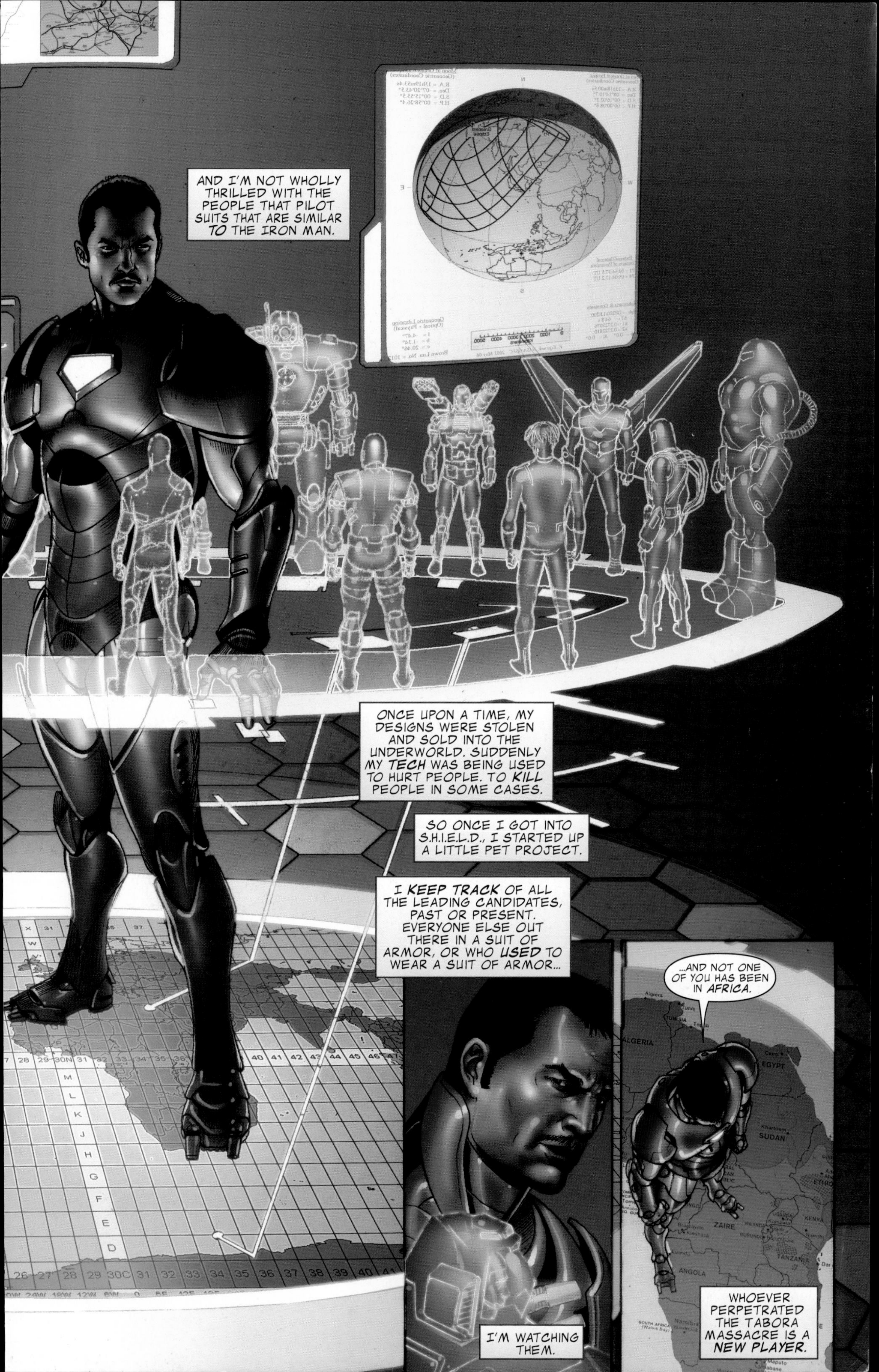
AND I'M NOT WHOLLY THRILLED WITH THE PEOPLE THAT PILOT SUITS THAT ARE SIMILAR TO THE IRON MAN.
ONCE UPON A TIME, MY DESIGNS WERE STOLEN AND SOLD INTO THE UNDERWORLD. SUDDENLY MY TECH WAS BEING USED TO HURT PEOPLE. TO KILL PEOPLE IN SOME CASES.
SO ONCE I GOT INTO S.H.I.E.L.D., I STARTED UP A LITTLE PET PROJECT.
I KEEP TRACK OF ALL THE LEADING CANDIDATES, PAST OR PRESENT. EVERYONE ELSE OUT THERE IN A SUIT OF ARMOR, OR WHO USED TO WEAR A SUIT OF ARMOR...
I'M WATCHING THEM.
...AND NOT ONE OF YOU HAS BEEN IN AFRICA.
ALGERIA
EGYPT
SUDAN
ZAIRE
ANGOLA
TANZANIA
WHOEVER PERPETRATED THE TABORA MASSACRE IS A NEW PLAYER.

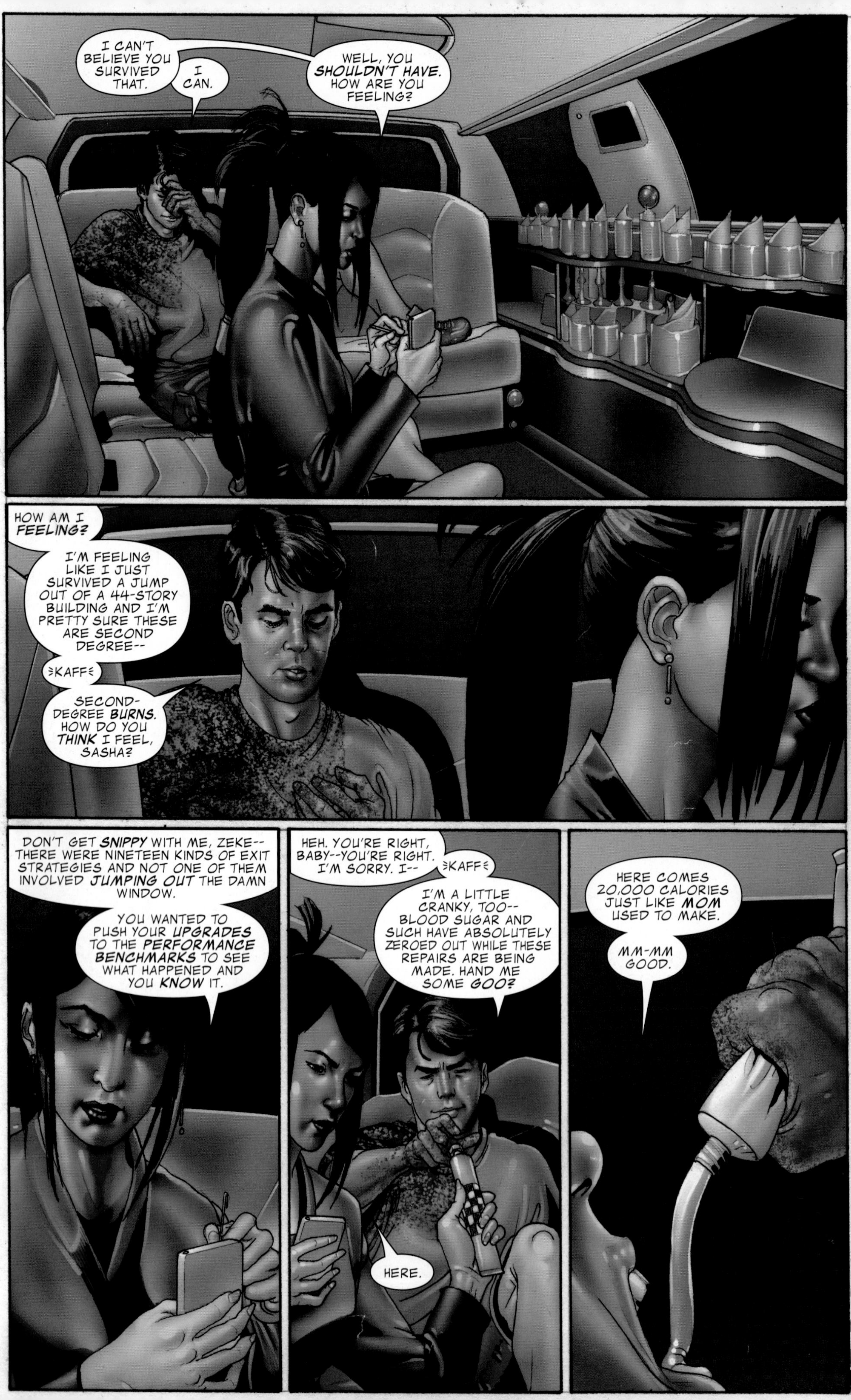
I CAN'T BELIEVE YOU SURVIVED THAT.
I CAN.
WELL, YOU SHOULDN'T HAVE. HOW ARE YOU FEELING?
HOW AM I FEELING?
I'M FEELING LIKE I JUST SURVIVED A JUMP OUT OF A 44-STORY BUILDING AND I'M PRETTY SURE THESE ARE SECOND DEGREE--
KAFF
SECOND-DEGREE BURNS. HOW DO YOU THINK I FEEL, SASHA?
DON'T GET SNIPPY WITH ME, ZEKE--THERE WERE NINETEEN KINDS OF EXIT STRATEGIES AND NOT ONE OF THEM INVOLVED JUMPING OUT THE DAMN WINDOW.
YOU WANTED TO PUSH YOUR UPGRADES TO THE PERFORMANCE BENCHMARKS TO SEE WHAT HAPPENED AND YOU KNOW IT.
HEH. YOU'RE RIGHT, BABY--YOU'RE RIGHT. I'M SORRY. I--
KAFF
I'M A LITTLE CRANKY, TOO--BLOOD SUGAR AND SUCH HAVE ABSOLUTELY ZEROED OUT WHILE THESE REPAIRS ARE BEING MADE. HAND ME SOME GOO?
HERE.
HERE COMES 20,000 CALORIES JUST LIKE MOM USED TO MAKE.
MM-MM GOOD.

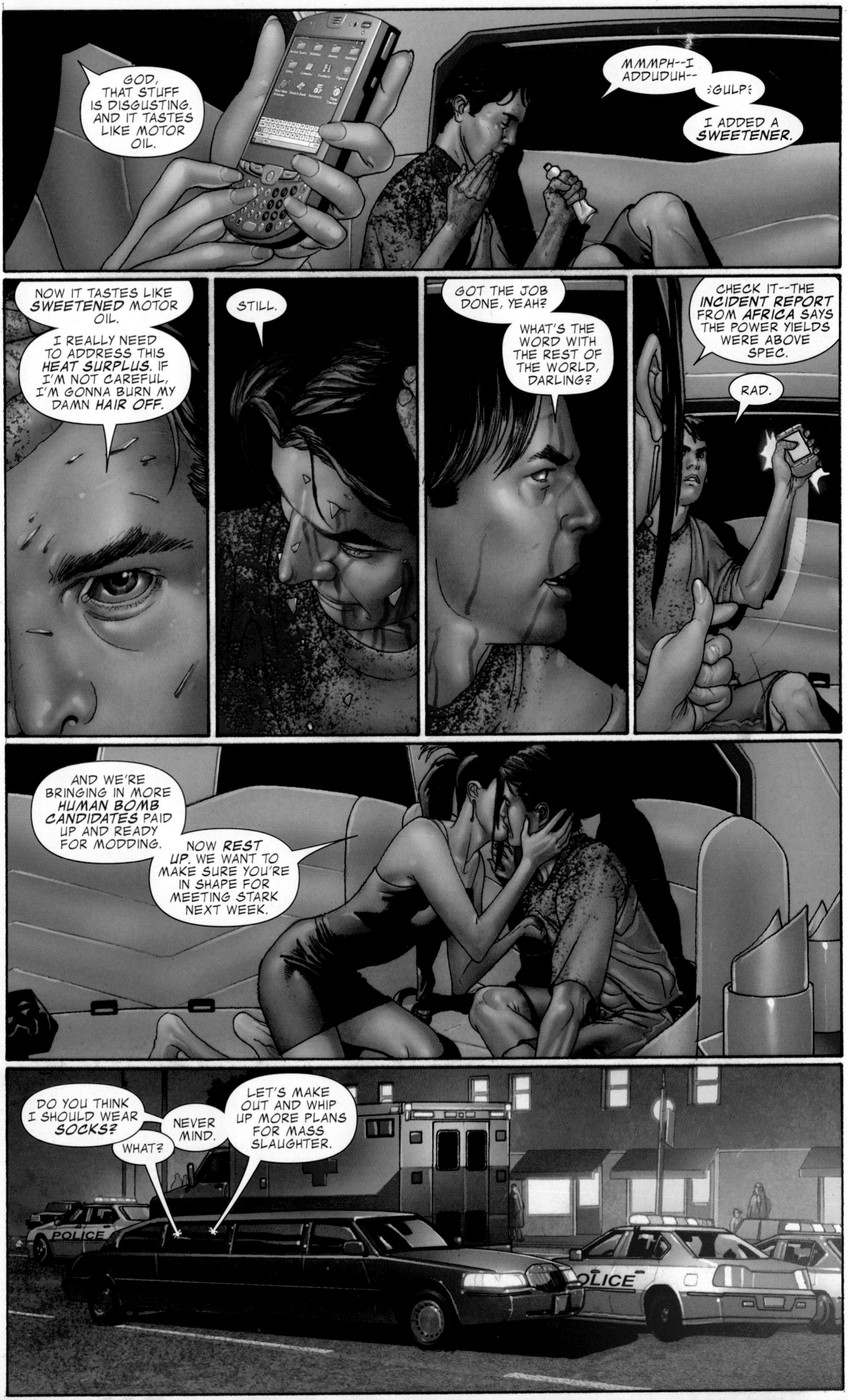
GOD, THAT STUFF IS DISGUSTING. AND IT TASTES LIKE MOTOR OIL.
MMMPH--I ADDUDUH--
GULP
I ADDED A SWEETENER.
NOW IT TASTES LIKE SWEETENED MOTOR OIL.
I REALLY NEED TO ADDRESS THIS HEAT SURPLUS. IF I'M NOT CAREFUL, I'M GONNA BURN MY DAMN HAIR OFF.
STILL.
GOT THE JOB DONE, YEAH?
WHAT'S THE WORD WITH THE REST OF THE WORLD, DARLING?
CHECK IT--THE INCIDENT REPORT FROM AFRICA SAYS THE POWER YIELDS WERE ABOVE SPEC.
RAD.
AND WE'RE BRINGING IN MORE HUMAN BOMB CANDIDATES PAID UP AND READY FOR MODDING.
NOW REST UP. WE WANT TO MAKE SURE YOU'RE IN SHAPE FOR MEETING STARK NEXT WEEK.
DO YOU THINK I SHOULD WEAR SOCKS?
WHAT?
NEVER MIND.
LET'S MAKE OUT AND WHIP UP MORE PLANS FOR MASS SLAUGHTER.
POLICE
POLICE

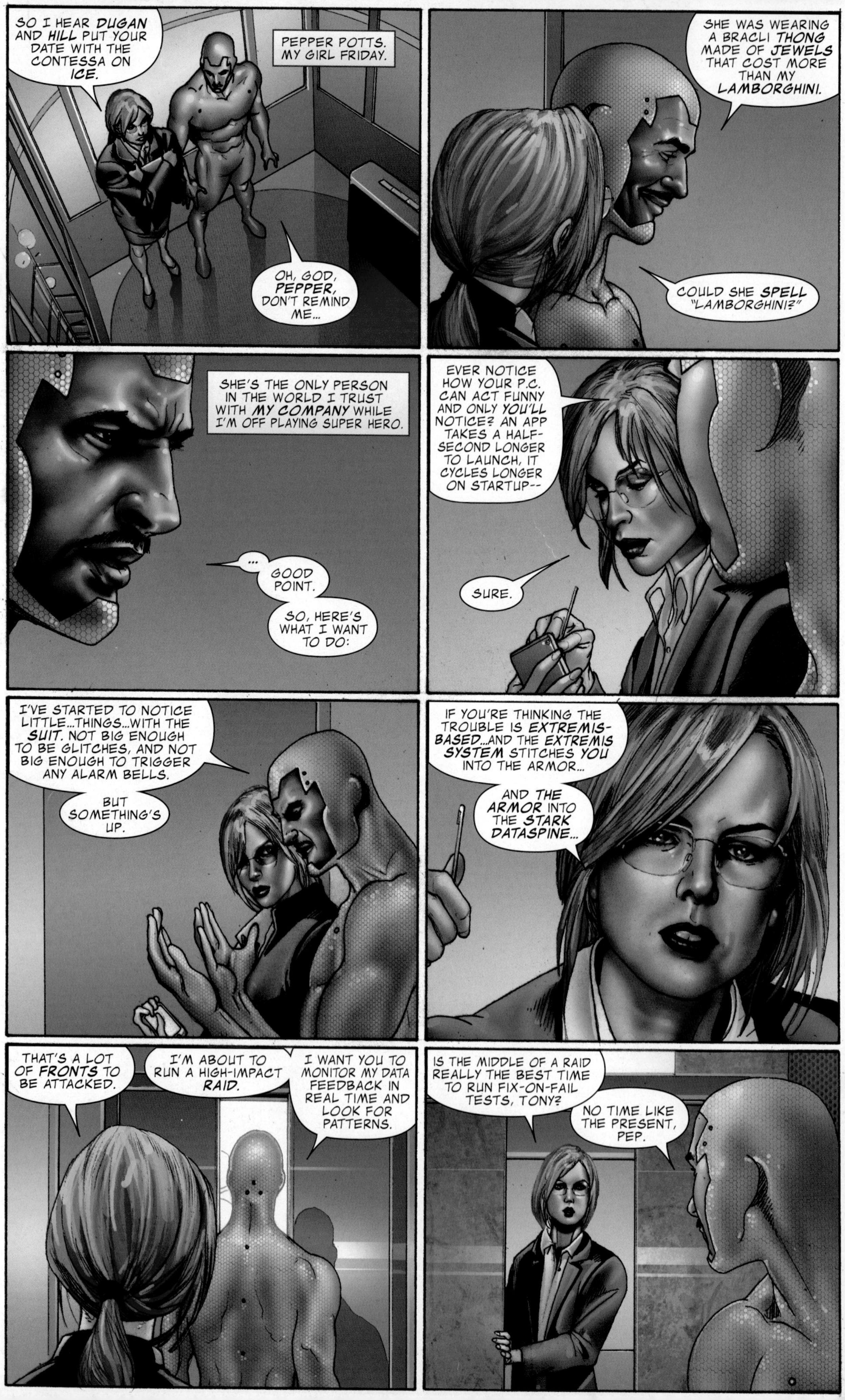
SO I HEAR DUGAN AND HILL PUT YOUR DATE WITH THE CONTESSA ON ICE.
PEPPER POTTS. MY GIRL FRIDAY.
OH, GOD, PEPPER, DON'T REMIND ME...
SHE WAS WEARING A BRACLI THONG MADE OF JEWELS THAT COST MORE THAN MY LAMBORGHINI.
COULD SHE SPELL "LAMBORGHINI?"
SHE'S THE ONLY PERSON IN THE WORLD I TRUST WITH MY COMPANY WHILE I'M OFF PLAYING SUPER HERO.
...
GOOD POINT.
SO, HERE'S WHAT I WANT TO DO:
EVER NOTICE HOW YOUR P.C. CAN ACT FUNNY AND ONLY YOU'LL NOTICE? AN APP TAKES A HALF-SECOND LONGER TO LAUNCH, IT CYCLES LONGER ON STARTUP--
SURE.
I'VE STARTED TO NOTICE LITTLE...THINGS...WITH THE SUIT. NOT BIG ENOUGH TO BE GLITCHES, AND NOT BIG ENOUGH TO TRIGGER ANY ALARM BELLS.
BUT SOMETHING'S UP.
IF YOU'RE THINKING THE TROUBLE IS EXTREMIS-BASED...AND THE EXTREMIS SYSTEM STITCHES YOU INTO THE ARMOR...
AND THE ARMOR INTO THE STARK DATASPINE...
THAT'S A LOT OF FRONTS TO BE ATTACKED.
I'M ABOUT TO RUN A HIGH-IMPACT RAID.
I WANT YOU TO MONITOR MY DATA FEEDBACK IN REAL TIME AND LOOK FOR PATTERNS.
IS THE MIDDLE OF A RAID REALLY THE BEST TIME TO RUN FIX-ON-FAIL TESTS, TONY?
NO TIME LIKE THE PRESENT, PEP.

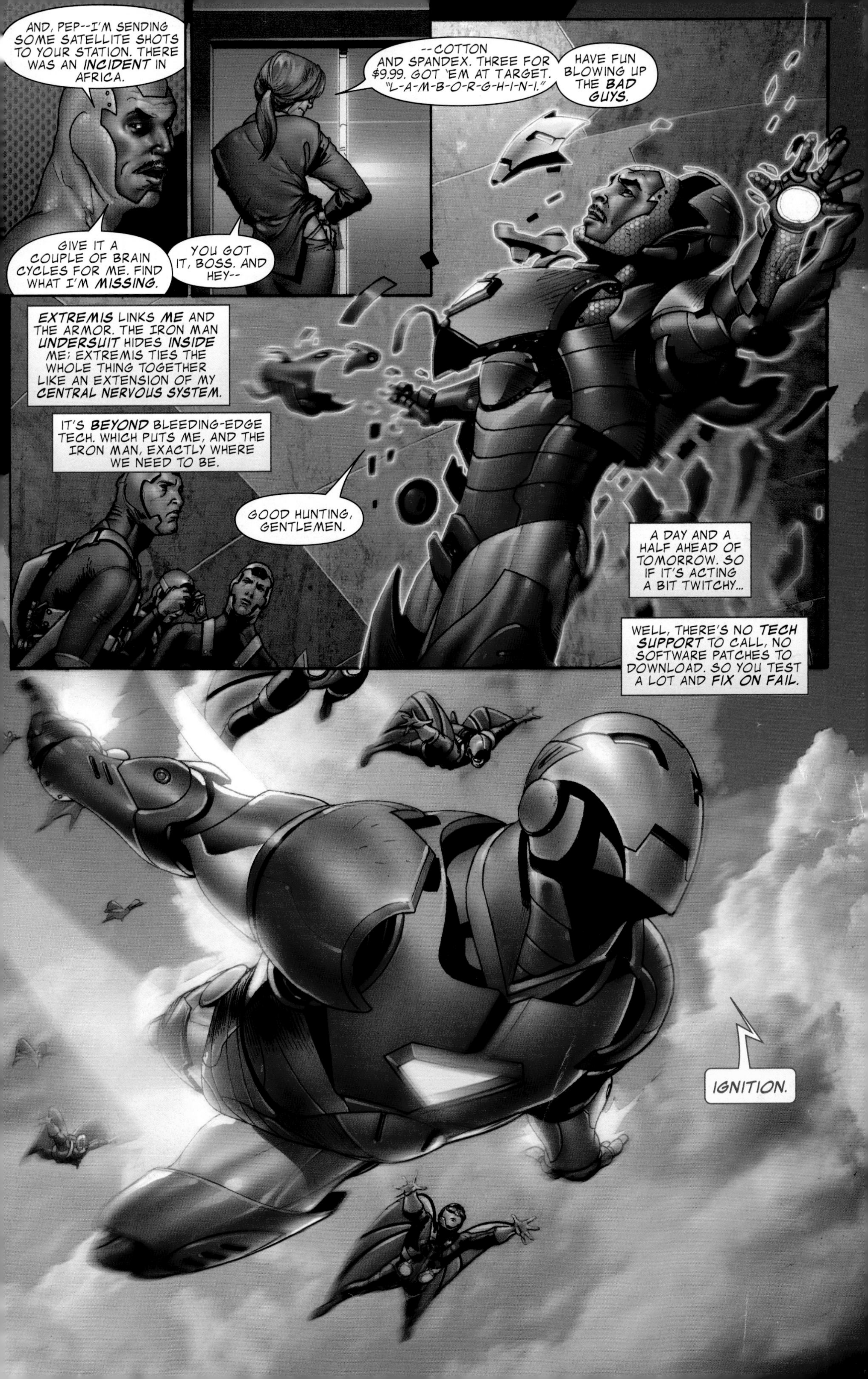
AND, PEP--I'M SENDING SOME SATELLITE SHOTS TO YOUR STATION. THERE WAS AN INCIDENT IN AFRICA.
GIVE IT A COUPLE OF BRAIN CYCLES FOR ME. FIND WHAT I'M MISSING.
YOU GOT IT, BOSS. AND HEY--
--COTTON AND SPANDEX. THREE FOR $9.99. GOT 'EM AT TARGET. "L-A-M-B-O-R-G-H-I-N-I."
HAVE FUN BLOWING UP THE BAD GUYS.
EXTREMIS LINKS ME AND THE ARMOR. THE IRON MAN UNDERSUIT HIDES INSIDE ME; EXTREMIS TIES THE WHOLE THING TOGETHER LIKE AN EXTENSION OF MY CENTRAL NERVOUS SYSTEM.
IT'S BEYOND BLEEDING-EDGE TECH. WHICH PUTS ME, AND THE IRON MAN, EXACTLY WHERE WE NEED TO BE.
GOOD HUNTING, GENTLEMEN.
A DAY AND A HALF AHEAD OF TOMORROW. SO IF IT'S ACTING A BIT TWITCHY...
WELL, THERE'S NO TECH SUPPORT TO CALL, NO SOFTWARE PATCHES TO DOWNLOAD. SO YOU TEST A LOT AND FIX ON FAIL.
IGNITION.

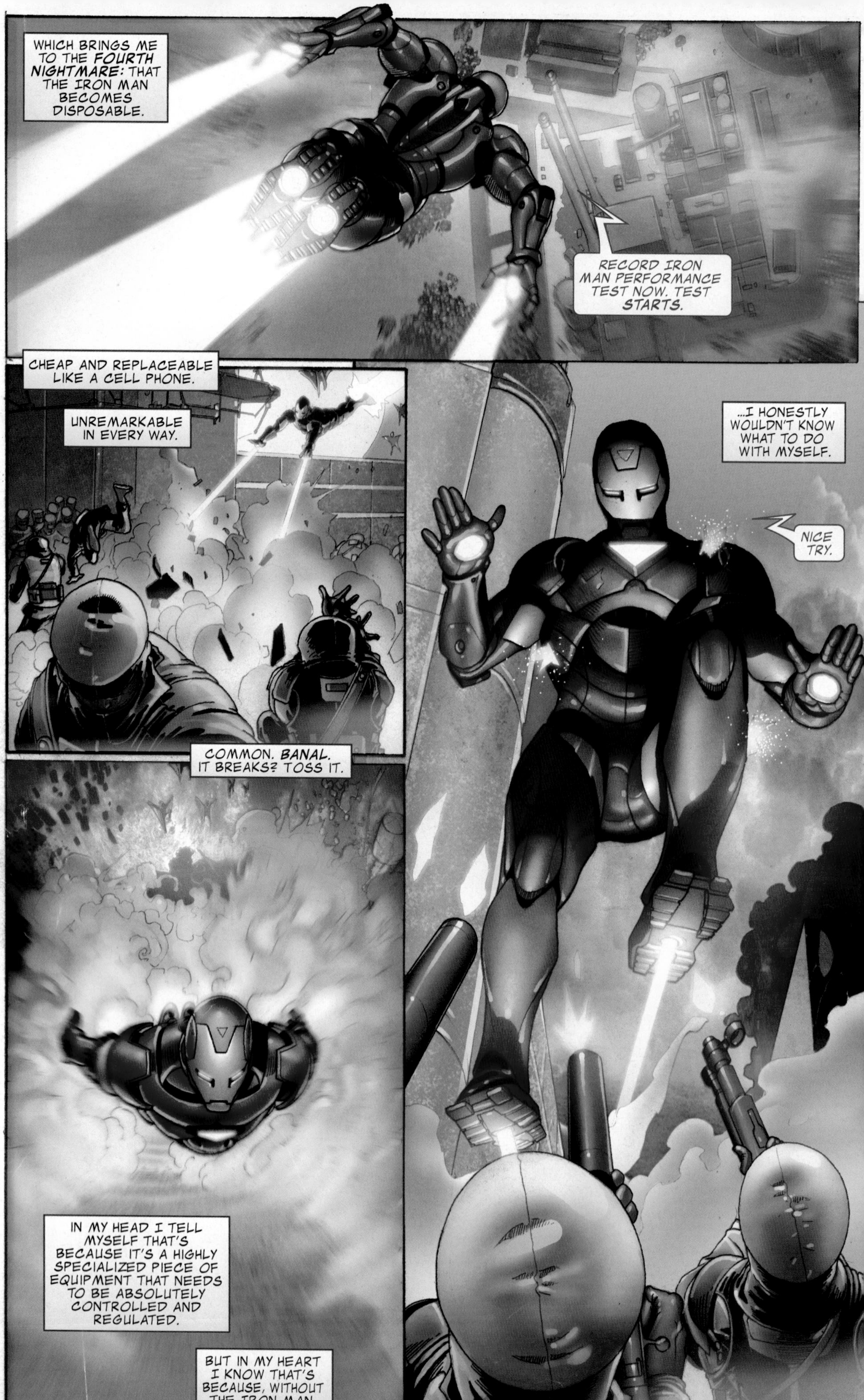
WHICH BRINGS ME TO THE **FOURTH NIGHTMARE:** THAT THE IRON MAN BECOMES DISPOSABLE.
RECORD IRON MAN PERFORMANCE TEST NOW. TEST *STARTS.*
CHEAP AND REPLACEABLE LIKE A CELL PHONE.
UNREMARKABLE IN EVERY WAY.
COMMON. *BANAL.* IT BREAKS? TOSS IT.
IN MY HEAD I TELL MYSELF THAT'S BECAUSE IT'S A HIGHLY SPECIALIZED PIECE OF EQUIPMENT THAT NEEDS TO BE ABSOLUTELY CONTROLLED AND REGULATED.
BUT IN MY HEART I KNOW THAT'S BECAUSE, WITHOUT THE IRON MAN...
...I HONESTLY WOULDN'T KNOW WHAT TO DO WITH MYSELF.
NICE TRY.

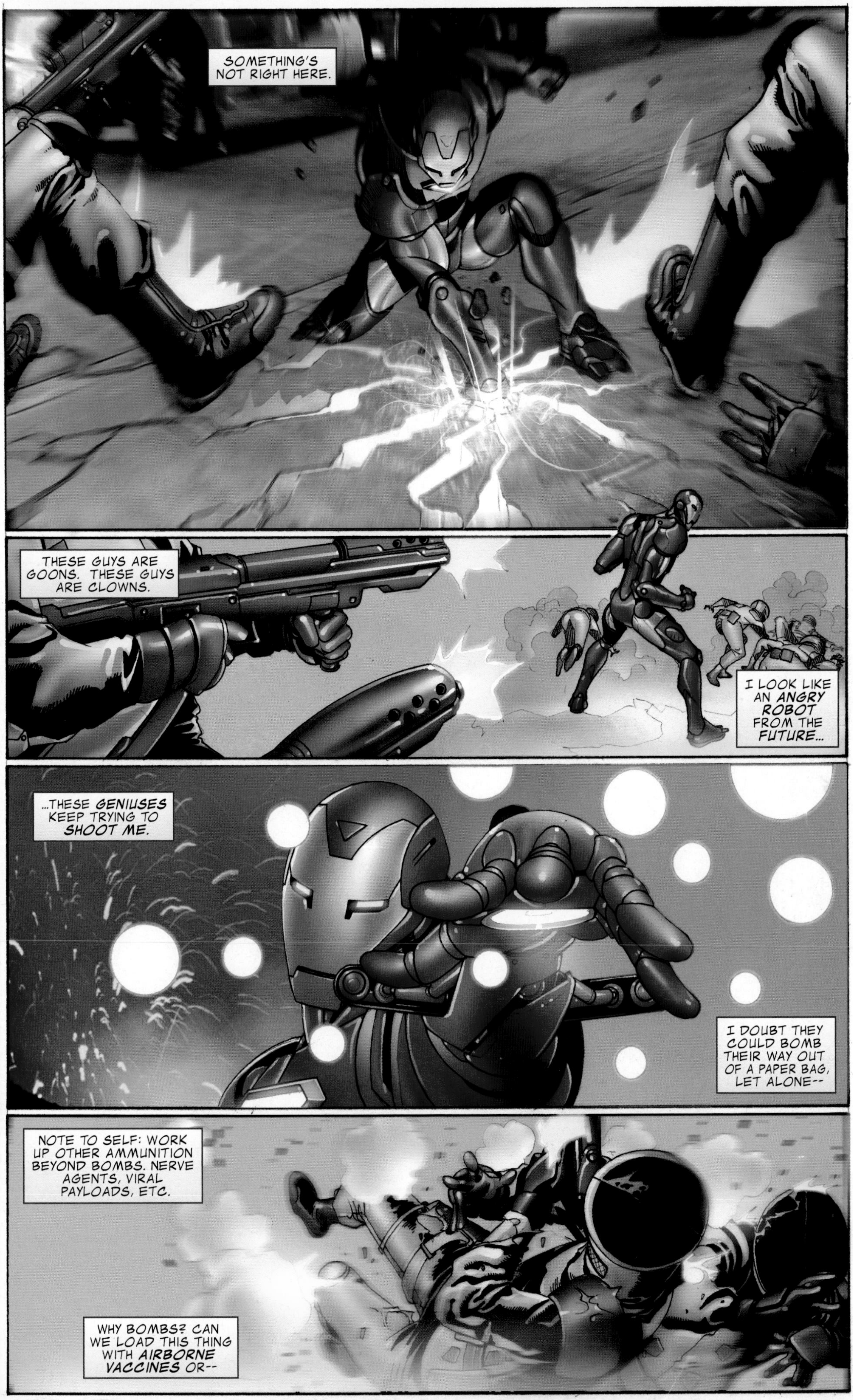
SOMETHING'S NOT RIGHT HERE.
THESE GUYS ARE GOONS. THESE GUYS ARE CLOWNS.
I LOOK LIKE AN ANGRY ROBOT FROM THE FUTURE...
...THESE GENIUSES KEEP TRYING TO SHOOT ME.
I DOUBT THEY COULD BOMB THEIR WAY OUT OF A PAPER BAG, LET ALONE--
NOTE TO SELF: WORK UP OTHER AMMUNITION BEYOND BOMBS. NERVE AGENTS, VIRAL PAYLOADS, ETC.
WHY BOMBS? CAN WE LOAD THIS THING WITH AIRBORNE VACCINES OR--

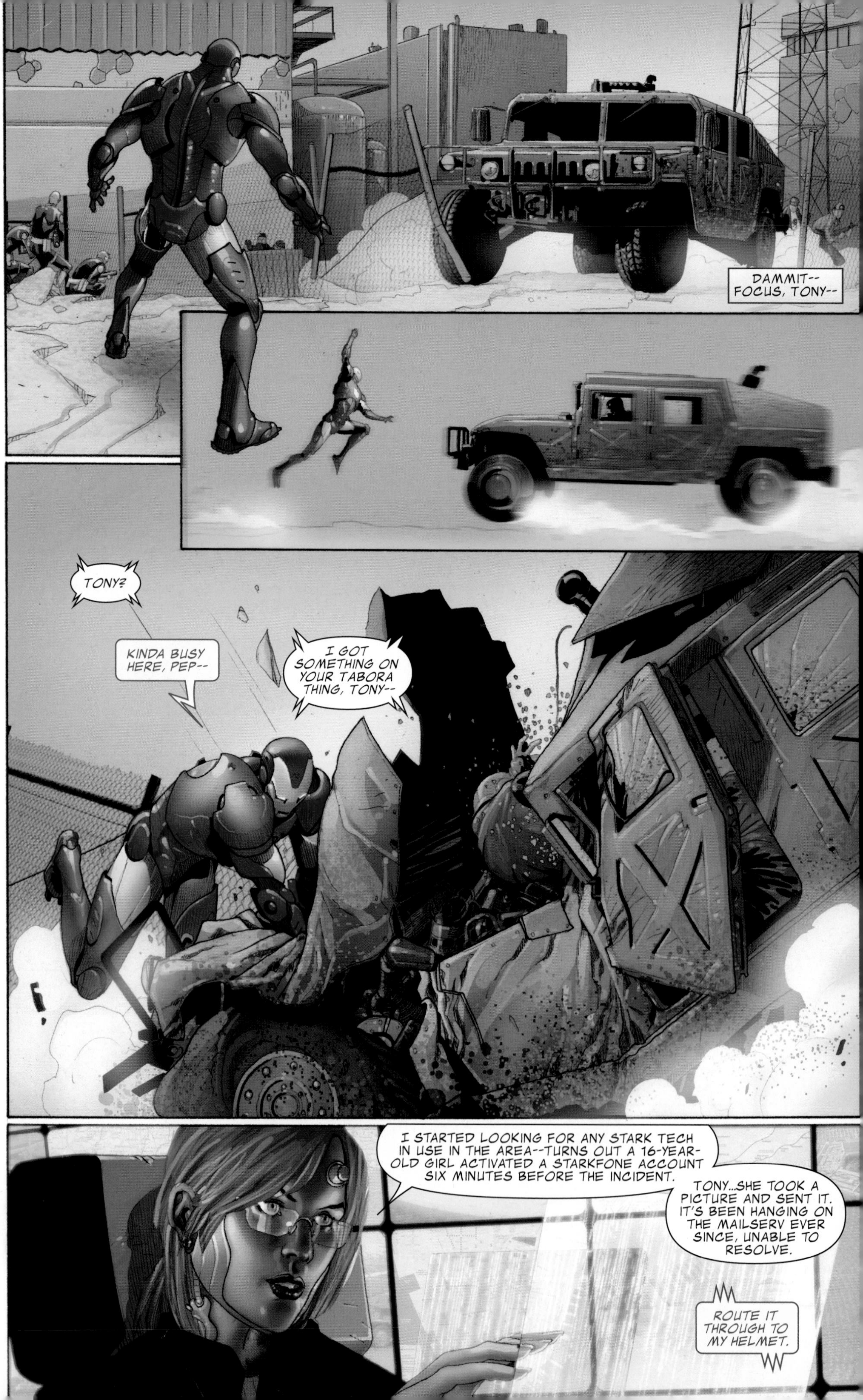
DAMMIT--
FOCUS, TONY--
TONY?
KINDA BUSY HERE, PEP--
I GOT SOMETHING ON YOUR TABORA THING, TONY--
I STARTED LOOKING FOR ANY STARK TECH IN USE IN THE AREA--TURNS OUT A 16-YEAR-OLD GIRL ACTIVATED A STARKFONE ACCOUNT SIX MINUTES BEFORE THE INCIDENT.
TONY...SHE TOOK A PICTURE AND SENT IT. IT'S BEEN HANGING ON THE MAILSERV EVER SINCE, UNABLE TO RESOLVE.
ROUTE IT THROUGH TO MY HELMET.

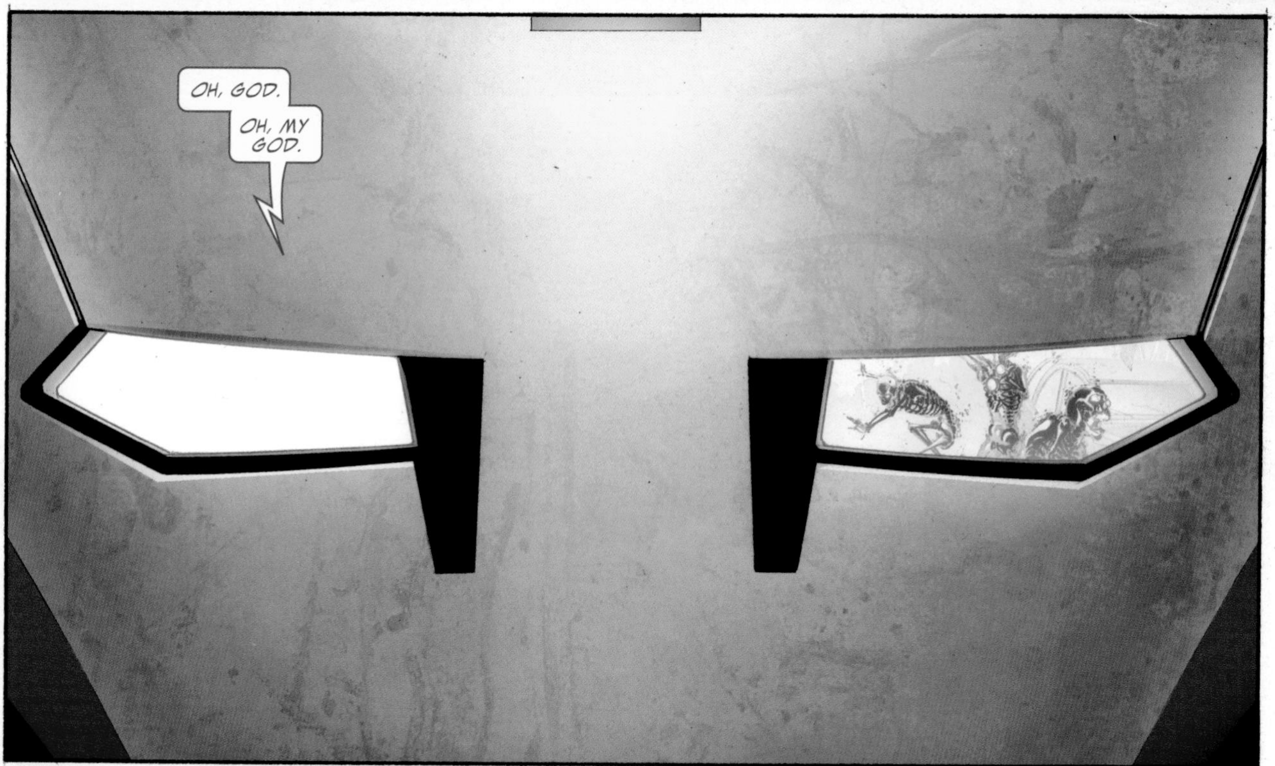
OH, GOD.
OH, MY GOD.

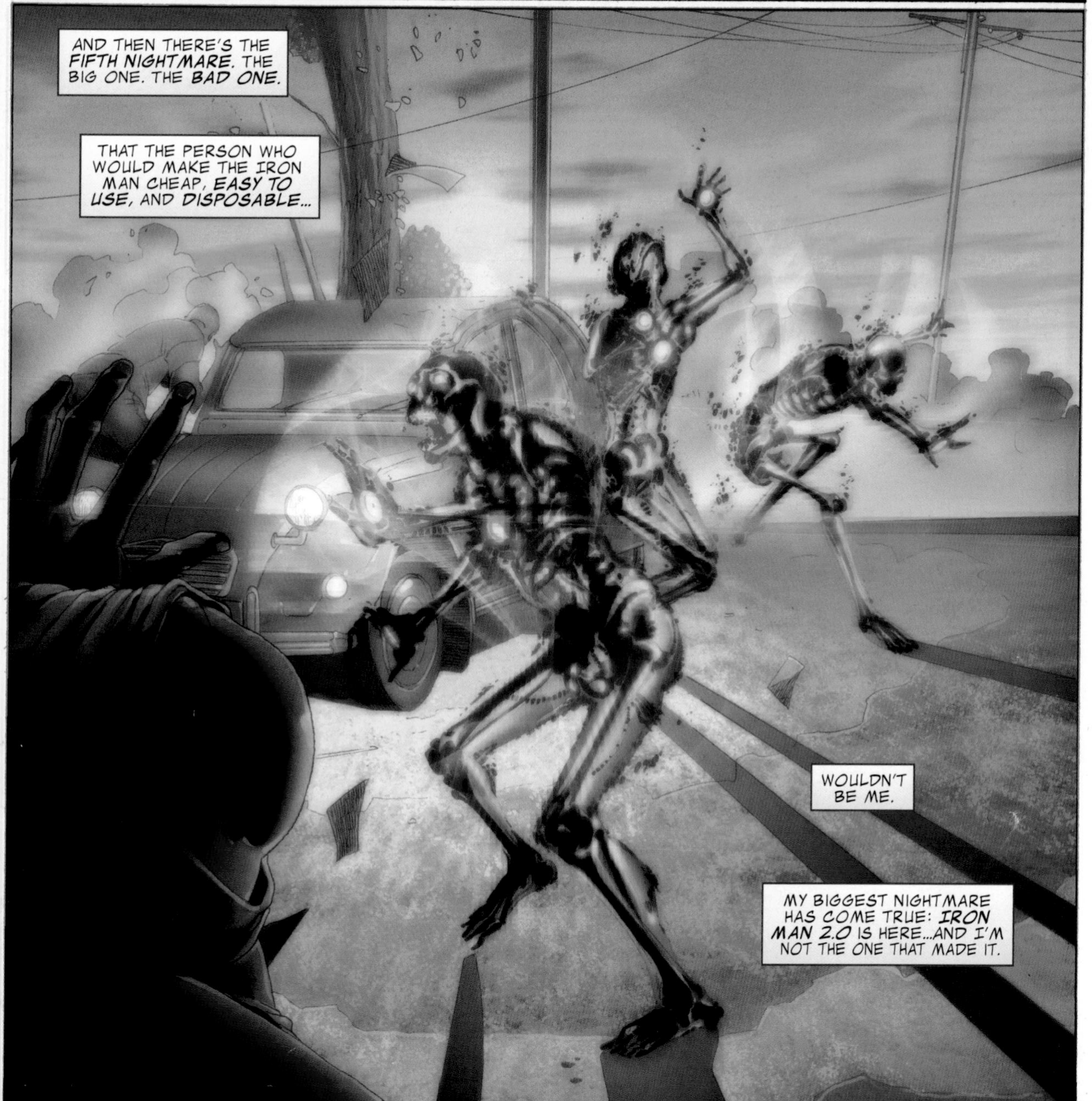
AND THEN THERE'S THE FIFTH NIGHTMARE. THE BIG ONE. THE BAD ONE.
THAT THE PERSON WHO WOULD MAKE THE IRON MAN CHEAP, EASY TO USE, AND DISPOSABLE...
WOULDN'T BE ME.
MY BIGGEST NIGHTMARE HAS COME TRUE: IRON MAN 2.0 IS HERE...AND I'M NOT THE ONE THAT MADE IT.

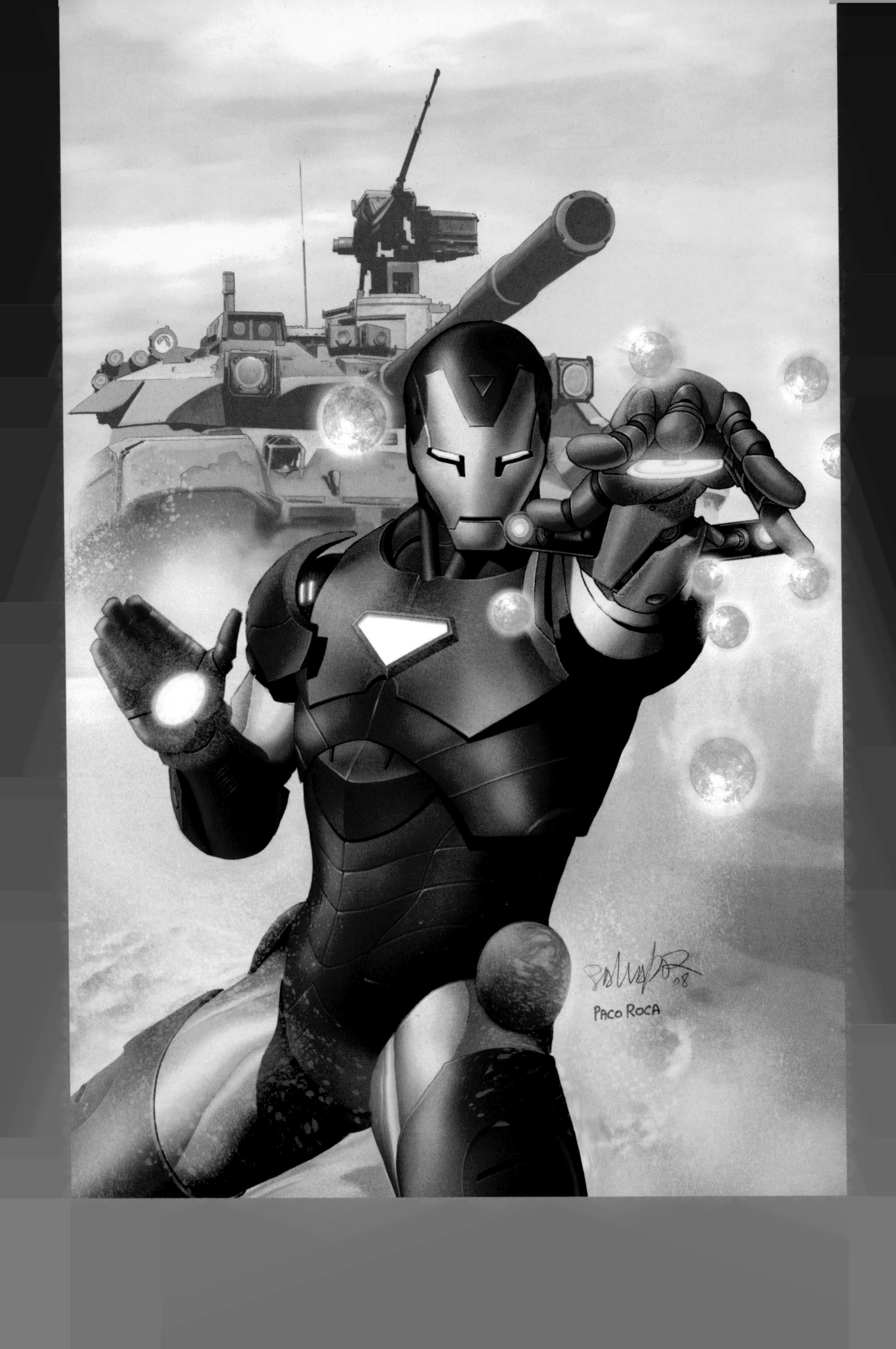
PACO ROCA

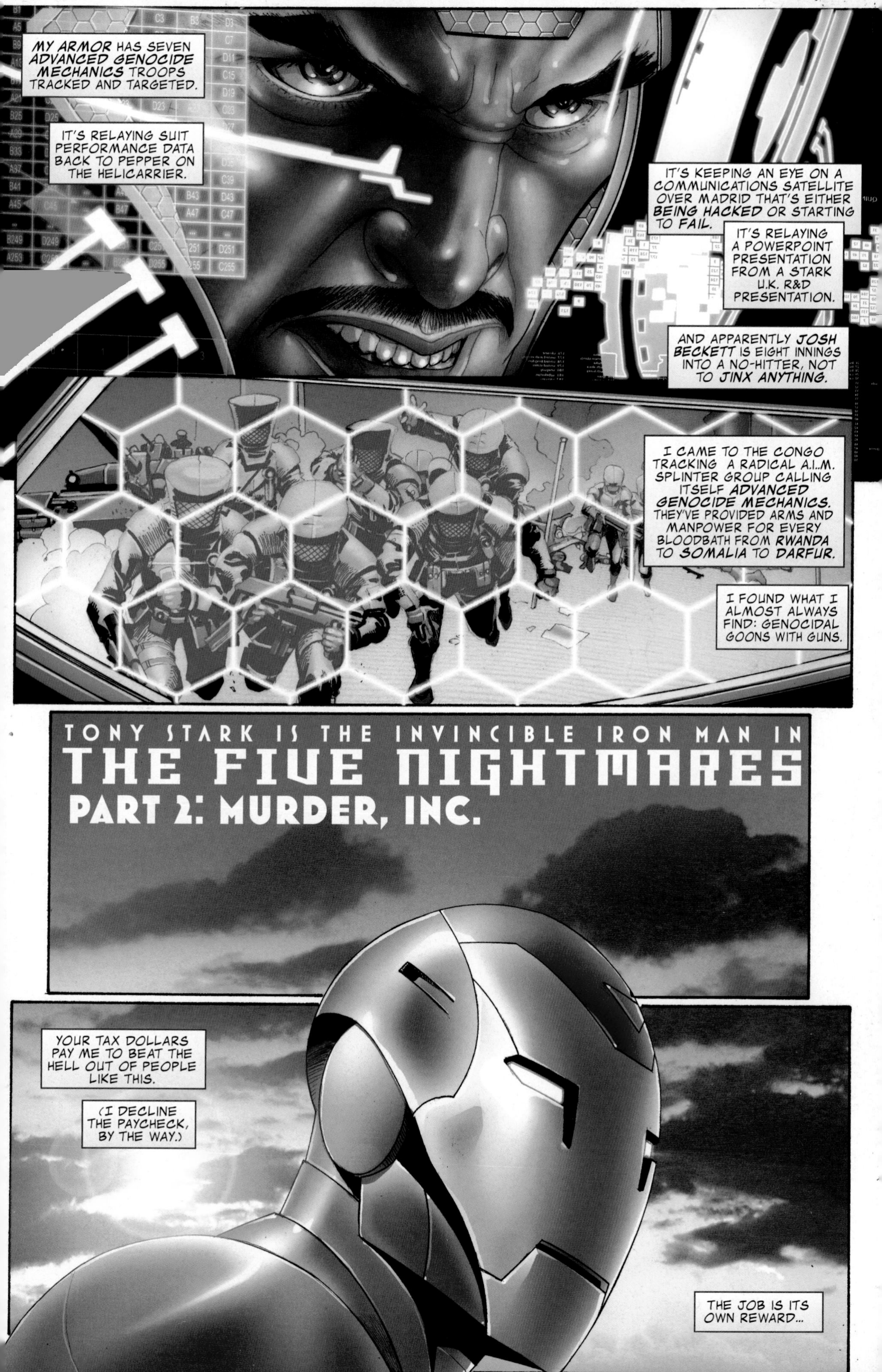

MY ARMOR HAS SEVEN ADVANCED GENOCIDE MECHANICS TROOPS TRACKED AND TARGETED.
IT'S RELAYING SUIT PERFORMANCE DATA BACK TO PEPPER ON THE HELICARRIER.
IT'S KEEPING AN EYE ON A COMMUNICATIONS SATELLITE OVER MADRID THAT'S EITHER BEING HACKED OR STARTING TO FAIL.
IT'S RELAYING A POWERPOINT PRESENTATION FROM A STARK U.K. R&D PRESENTATION.
AND APPARENTLY JOSH BECKETT IS EIGHT INNINGS INTO A NO-HITTER, NOT TO JINX ANYTHING.
I CAME TO THE CONGO TRACKING A RADICAL A.I.M. SPLINTER GROUP CALLING ITSELF ADVANCED GENOCIDE MECHANICS. THEY'VE PROVIDED ARMS AND MANPOWER FOR EVERY BLOODBATH FROM RWANDA TO SOMALIA TO DARFUR.
I FOUND WHAT I ALMOST ALWAYS FIND: GENOCIDAL GOONS WITH GUNS.
TONY STARK IS THE INVINCIBLE IRON MAN IN
THE FIVE NIGHTMARES
PART 2: MURDER, INC.
YOUR TAX DOLLARS PAY ME TO BEAT THE HELL OUT OF PEOPLE LIKE THIS.
(I DECLINE THE PAYCHECK, BY THE WAY.)
THE JOB IS ITS OWN REWARD...

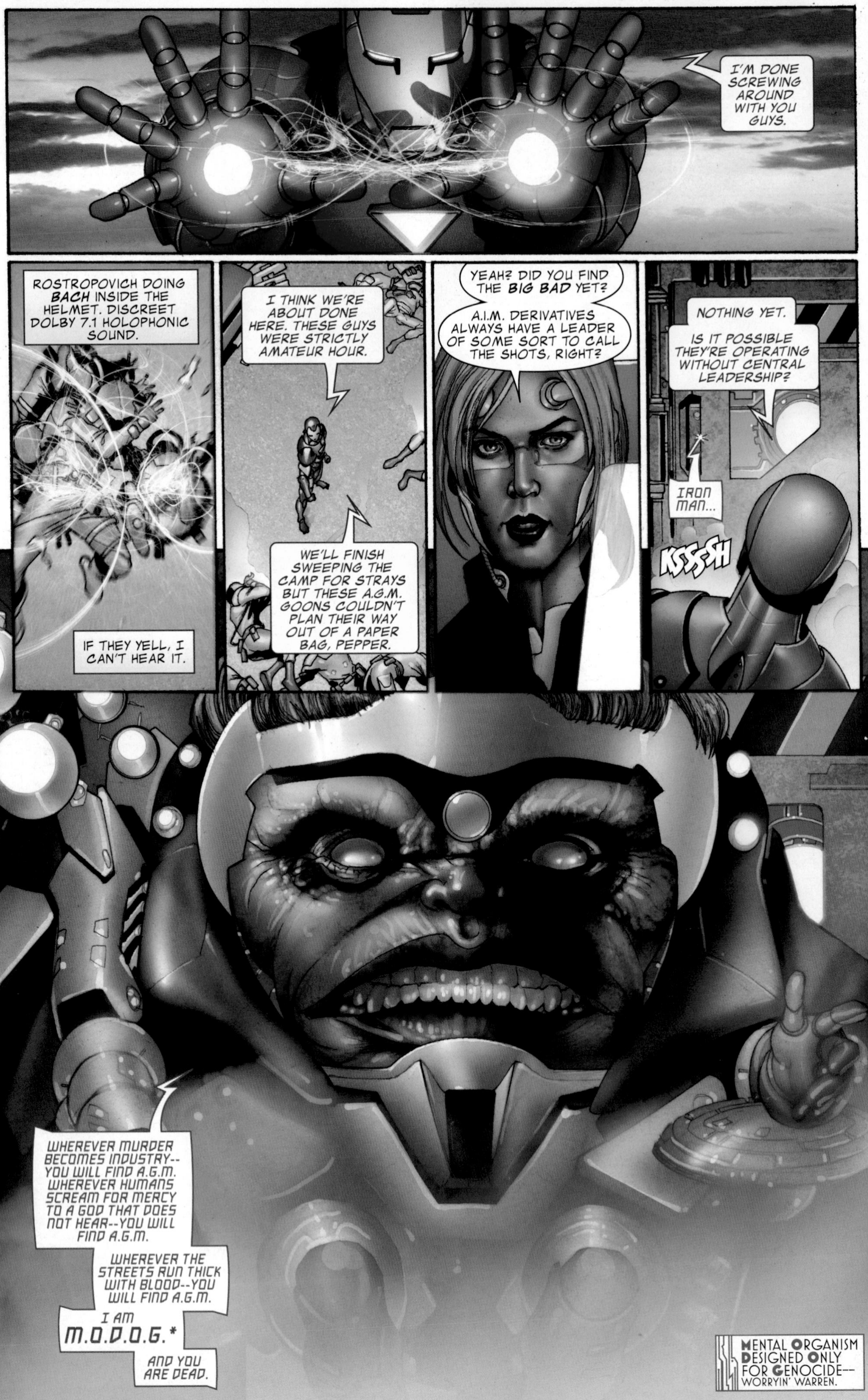
I'M DONE SCREWING AROUND WITH YOU GUYS.
ROSTROPOVICH DOING BACH INSIDE THE HELMET. DISCREET DOLBY 7.1 HOLOPHONIC SOUND.
IF THEY YELL, I CAN'T HEAR IT.
I THINK WE'RE ABOUT DONE HERE. THESE GUYS WERE STRICTLY AMATEUR HOUR.
WE'LL FINISH SWEEPING THE CAMP FOR STRAYS BUT THESE A.G.M. GOONS COULDN'T PLAN THEIR WAY OUT OF A PAPER BAG, PEPPER.
YEAH? DID YOU FIND THE BIG BAD YET?
A.I.M. DERIVATIVES ALWAYS HAVE A LEADER OF SOME SORT TO CALL THE SHOTS, RIGHT?
NOTHING YET.
IS IT POSSIBLE THEY'RE OPERATING WITHOUT CENTRAL LEADERSHIP?
IRON MAN...
KSSSSH
WHEREVER MURDER BECOMES INDUSTRY-- YOU WILL FIND A.G.M. WHEREVER HUMANS SCREAM FOR MERCY TO A GOD THAT DOES NOT HEAR--YOU WILL FIND A.G.M.
WHEREVER THE STREETS RUN THICK WITH BLOOD--YOU WILL FIND A.G.M.
I AM M.O.D.O.G.*
AND YOU ARE DEAD.
*MENTAL ORGANISM DESIGNED ONLY FOR GENOCIDE-- WORRYIN' WARREN.

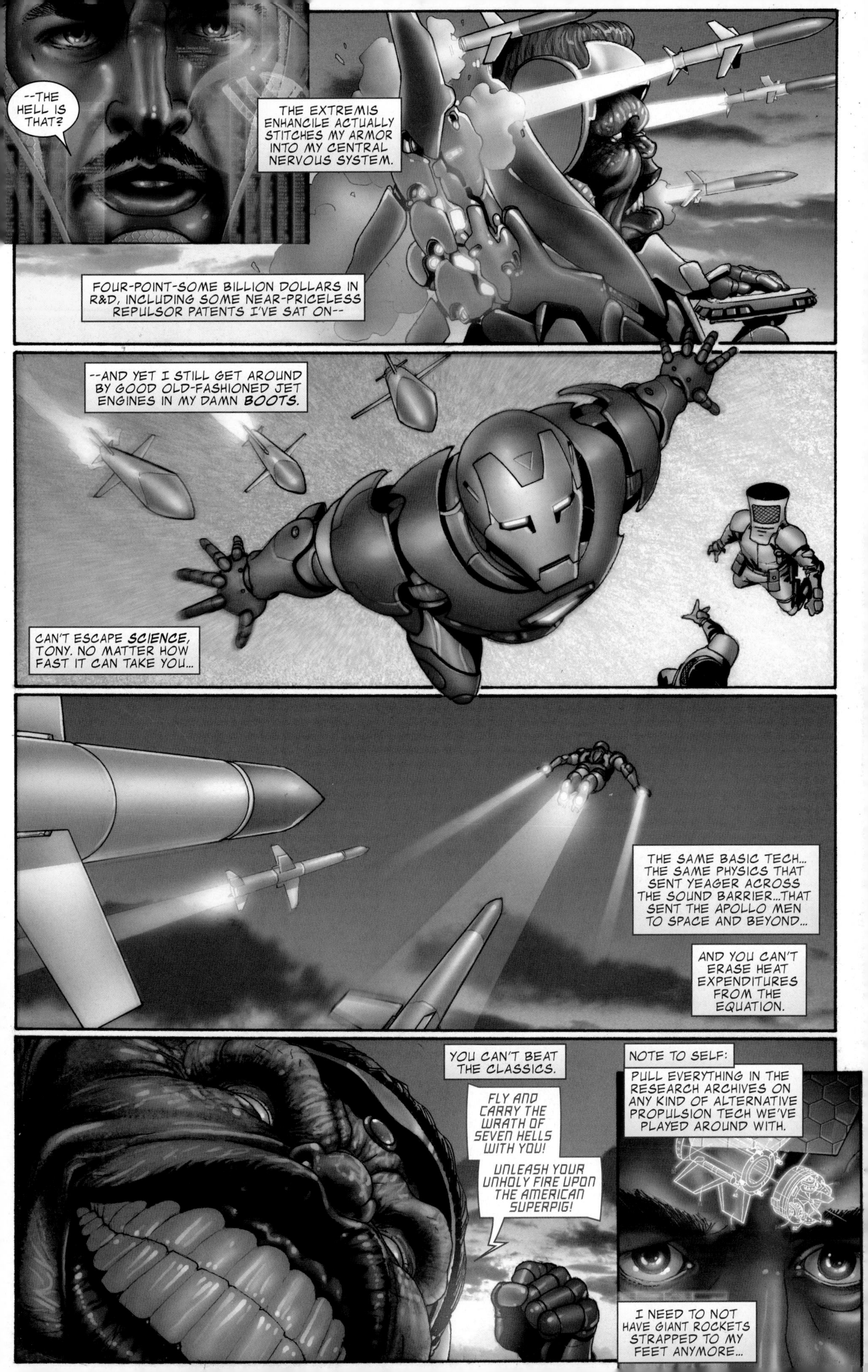
--THE HELL IS THAT?
THE EXTREMIS ENHANCILE ACTUALLY STITCHES MY ARMOR INTO MY CENTRAL NERVOUS SYSTEM.
FOUR-POINT-SOME BILLION DOLLARS IN R&D, INCLUDING SOME NEAR-PRICELESS REPULSOR PATENTS I'VE SAT ON--
--AND YET I STILL GET AROUND BY GOOD OLD-FASHIONED JET ENGINES IN MY DAMN BOOTS.
CAN'T ESCAPE SCIENCE, TONY. NO MATTER HOW FAST IT CAN TAKE YOU...
THE SAME BASIC TECH... THE SAME PHYSICS THAT SENT YEAGER ACROSS THE SOUND BARRIER...THAT SENT THE APOLLO MEN TO SPACE AND BEYOND...
AND YOU CAN'T ERASE HEAT EXPENDITURES FROM THE EQUATION.
YOU CAN'T BEAT THE CLASSICS.
FLY AND CARRY THE WRATH OF SEVEN HELLS WITH YOU!
UNLEASH YOUR UNHOLY FIRE UPON THE AMERICAN SUPERPIG!
NOTE TO SELF:
PULL EVERYTHING IN THE RESEARCH ARCHIVES ON ANY KIND OF ALTERNATIVE PROPULSION TECH WE'VE PLAYED AROUND WITH.
I NEED TO NOT HAVE GIANT ROCKETS STRAPPED TO MY FEET ANYMORE...

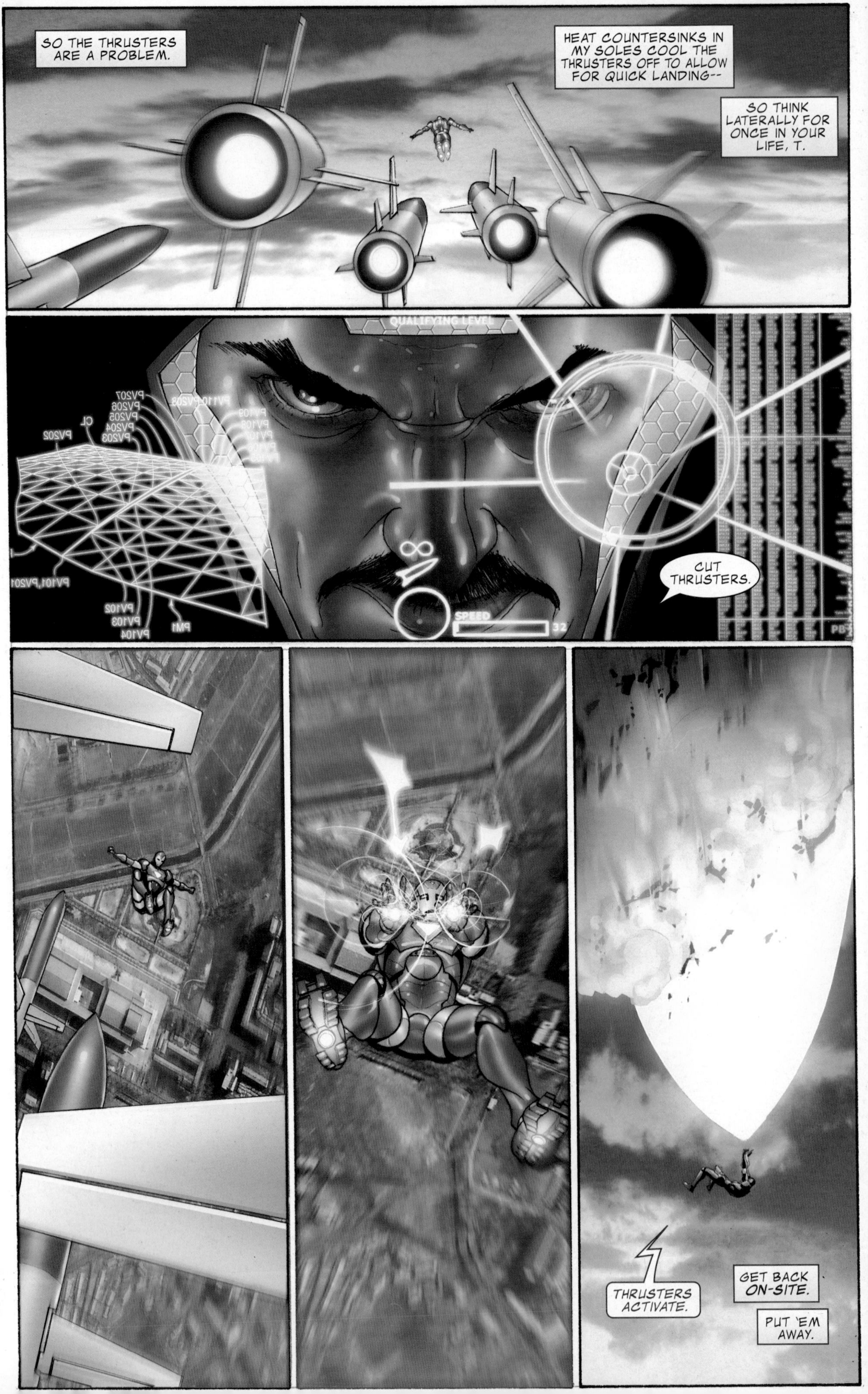
SO THE THRUSTERS ARE A PROBLEM.
HEAT COUNTERSINKS IN MY SOLES COOL THE THRUSTERS OFF TO ALLOW FOR QUICK LANDING--
SO THINK LATERALLY FOR ONCE IN YOUR LIFE, T.
QUALIFYING LEVEL
CUT THRUSTERS.
SPEED
32
THRUSTERS ACTIVATE.
GET BACK ON-SITE.
PUT 'EM AWAY.

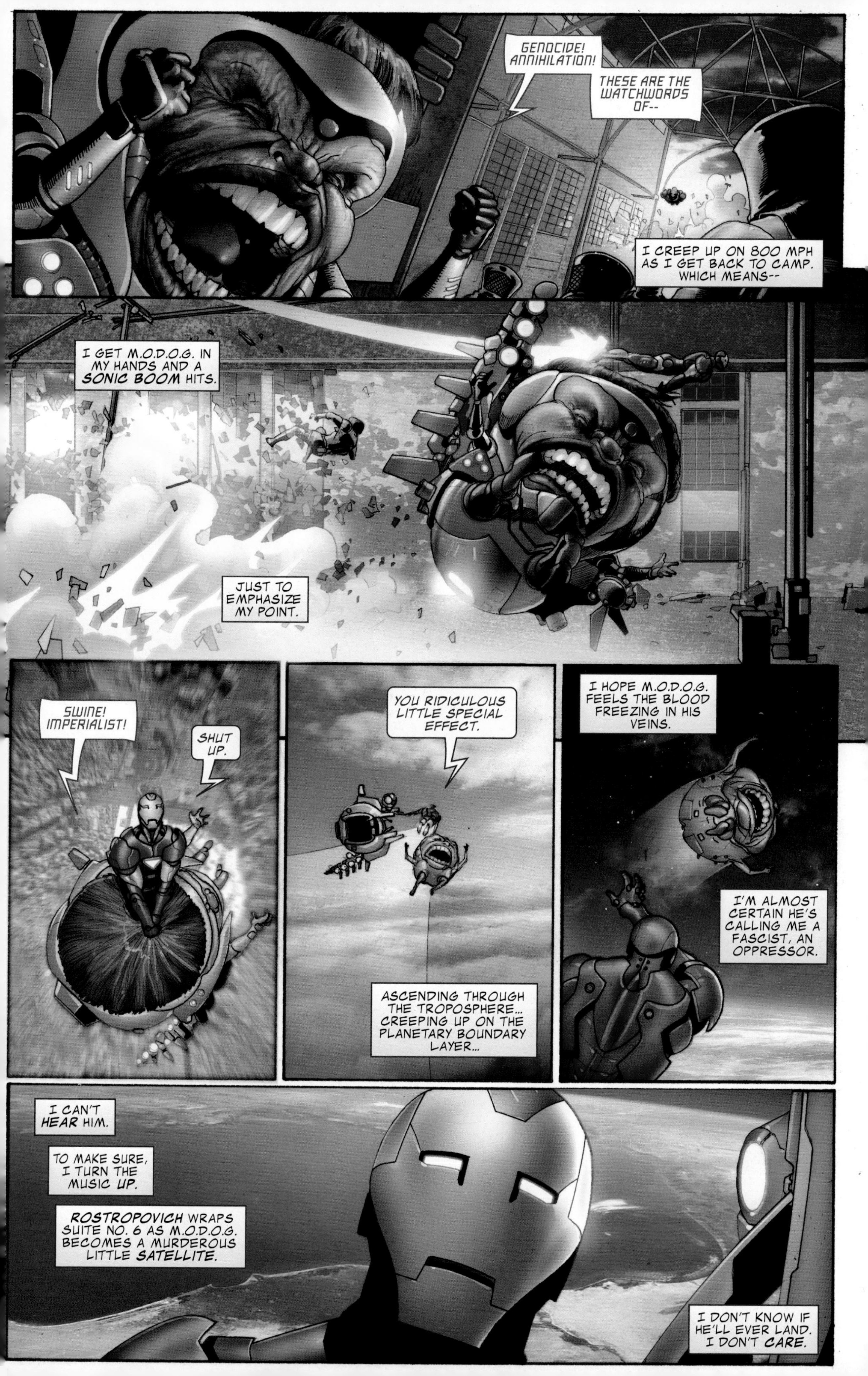
GENOCIDE! ANNIHILATION!
THESE ARE THE WATCHWORDS OF--
I CREEP UP ON 800 MPH AS I GET BACK TO CAMP. WHICH MEANS--
I GET M.O.D.O.G. IN MY HANDS AND A SONIC BOOM HITS.
JUST TO EMPHASIZE MY POINT.
SWINE! IMPERIALIST!
SHUT UP.
YOU RIDICULOUS LITTLE SPECIAL EFFECT.
ASCENDING THROUGH THE TROPOSPHERE... CREEPING UP ON THE PLANETARY BOUNDARY LAYER...
I HOPE M.O.D.O.G. FEELS THE BLOOD FREEZING IN HIS VEINS.
I'M ALMOST CERTAIN HE'S CALLING ME A FASCIST, AN OPPRESSOR.
I CAN'T HEAR HIM.
TO MAKE SURE, I TURN THE MUSIC UP.
ROSTROPOVICH WRAPS SUITE NO. 6 AS M.O.D.O.G. BECOMES A MURDEROUS LITTLE SATELLITE.
I DON'T KNOW IF HE'LL EVER LAND. I DON'T CARE.

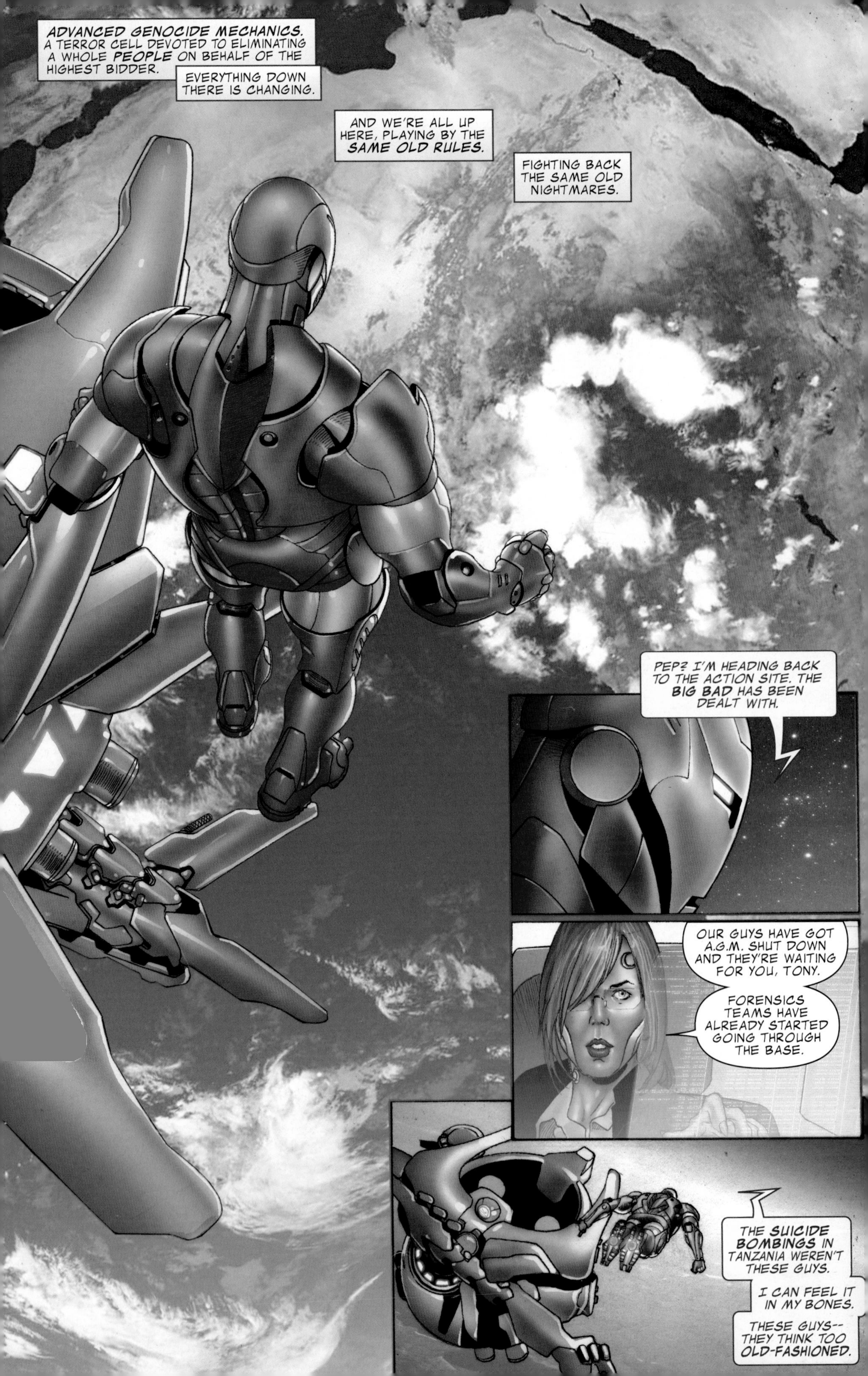
ADVANCED GENOCIDE MECHANICS. A TERROR CELL DEVOTED TO ELIMINATING A WHOLE PEOPLE ON BEHALF OF THE HIGHEST BIDDER.
EVERYTHING DOWN THERE IS CHANGING.
AND WE'RE ALL UP HERE, PLAYING BY THE SAME OLD RULES.
FIGHTING BACK THE SAME OLD NIGHTMARES.
PEP? I'M HEADING BACK TO THE ACTION SITE. THE BIG BAD HAS BEEN DEALT WITH.
OUR GUYS HAVE GOT A.G.M. SHUT DOWN AND THEY'RE WAITING FOR YOU, TONY.
FORENSICS TEAMS HAVE ALREADY STARTED GOING THROUGH THE BASE.
THE SUICIDE BOMBINGS IN TANZANIA WEREN'T THESE GUYS.
I CAN FEEL IT IN MY BONES.
THESE GUYS-- THEY THINK TOO OLD-FASHIONED.

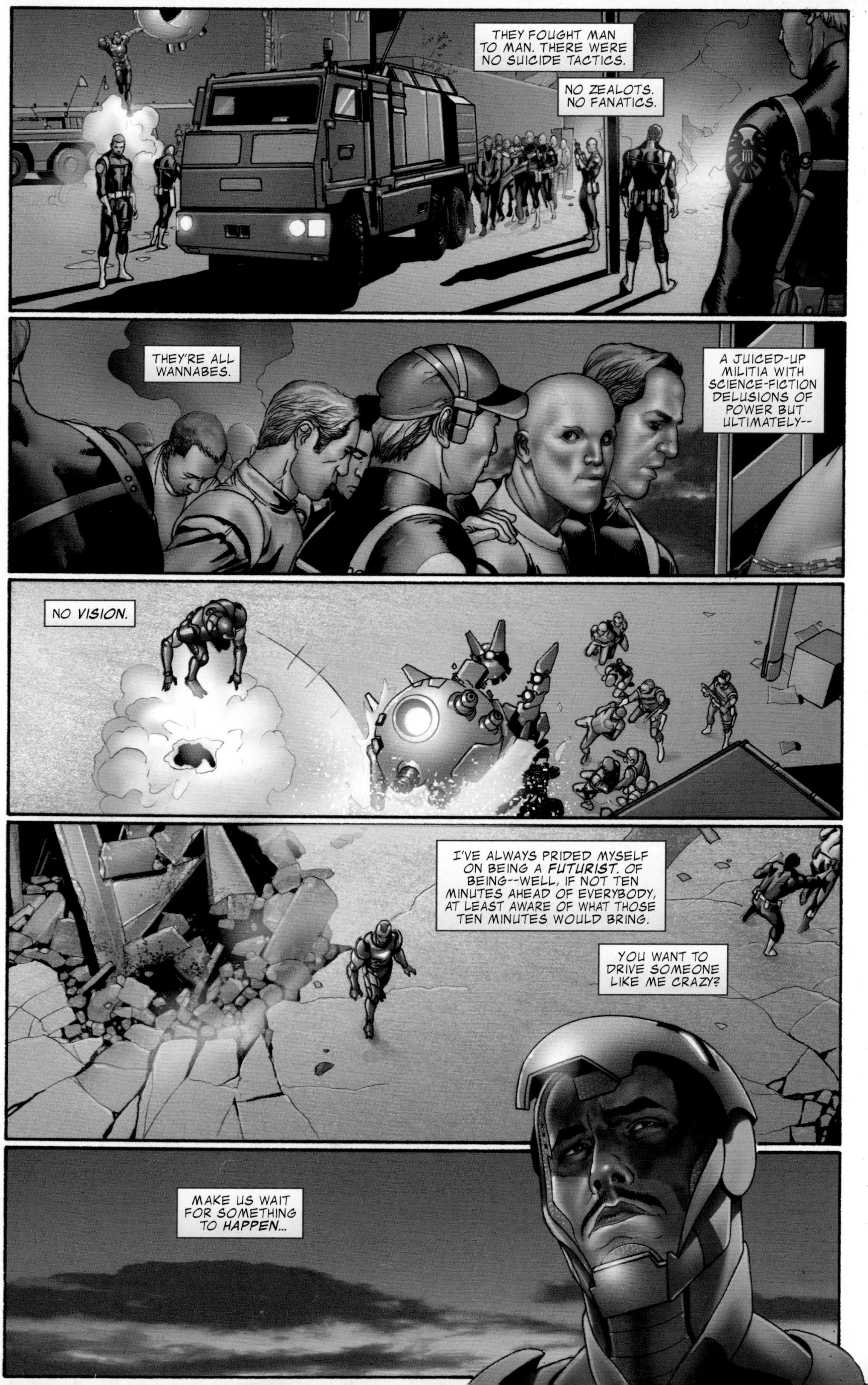
THEY FOUGHT MAN TO MAN. THERE WERE NO SUICIDE TACTICS.
NO ZEALOTS. NO FANATICS.
THEY'RE ALL WANNABES.
A JUICED-UP MILITIA WITH SCIENCE-FICTION DELUSIONS OF POWER BUT ULTIMATELY--
NO VISION.
I'VE ALWAYS PRIDED MYSELF ON BEING A FUTURIST. OF BEING--WELL, IF NOT TEN MINUTES AHEAD OF EVERYBODY, AT LEAST AWARE OF WHAT THOSE TEN MINUTES WOULD BRING.
YOU WANT TO DRIVE SOMEONE LIKE ME CRAZY?
MAKE US WAIT FOR SOMETHING TO HAPPEN...

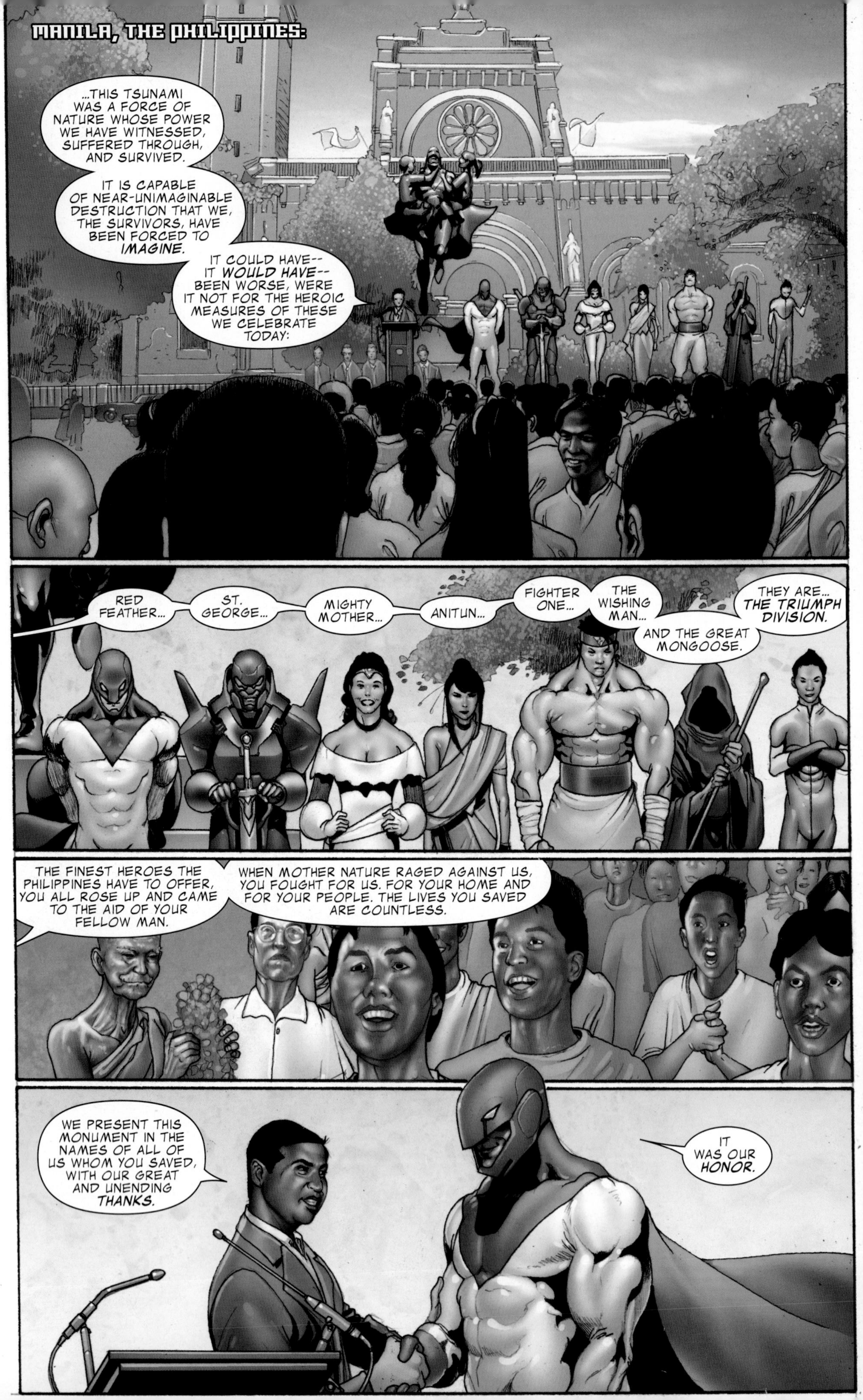
MANILA, THE PHILIPPINES:
...THIS TSUNAMI WAS A FORCE OF NATURE WHOSE POWER WE HAVE WITNESSED, SUFFERED THROUGH, AND SURVIVED.
IT IS CAPABLE OF NEAR-UNIMAGINABLE DESTRUCTION THAT WE, THE SURVIVORS, HAVE BEEN FORCED TO IMAGINE.
IT COULD HAVE-- IT WOULD HAVE-- BEEN WORSE, WERE IT NOT FOR THE HEROIC MEASURES OF THESE WE CELEBRATE TODAY:
RED FEATHER...
ST. GEORGE...
MIGHTY MOTHER...
ANITUN...
FIGHTER ONE...
THE WISHING MAN...
AND THE GREAT MONGOOSE.
THEY ARE... THE TRIUMPH DIVISION.
THE FINEST HEROES THE PHILIPPINES HAVE TO OFFER, YOU ALL ROSE UP AND CAME TO THE AID OF YOUR FELLOW MAN.
WHEN MOTHER NATURE RAGED AGAINST US, YOU FOUGHT FOR US. FOR YOUR HOME AND FOR YOUR PEOPLE. THE LIVES YOU SAVED ARE COUNTLESS.
WE PRESENT THIS MONUMENT IN THE NAMES OF ALL OF US WHOM YOU SAVED, WITH OUR GREAT AND UNENDING THANKS.
IT WAS OUR HONOR.

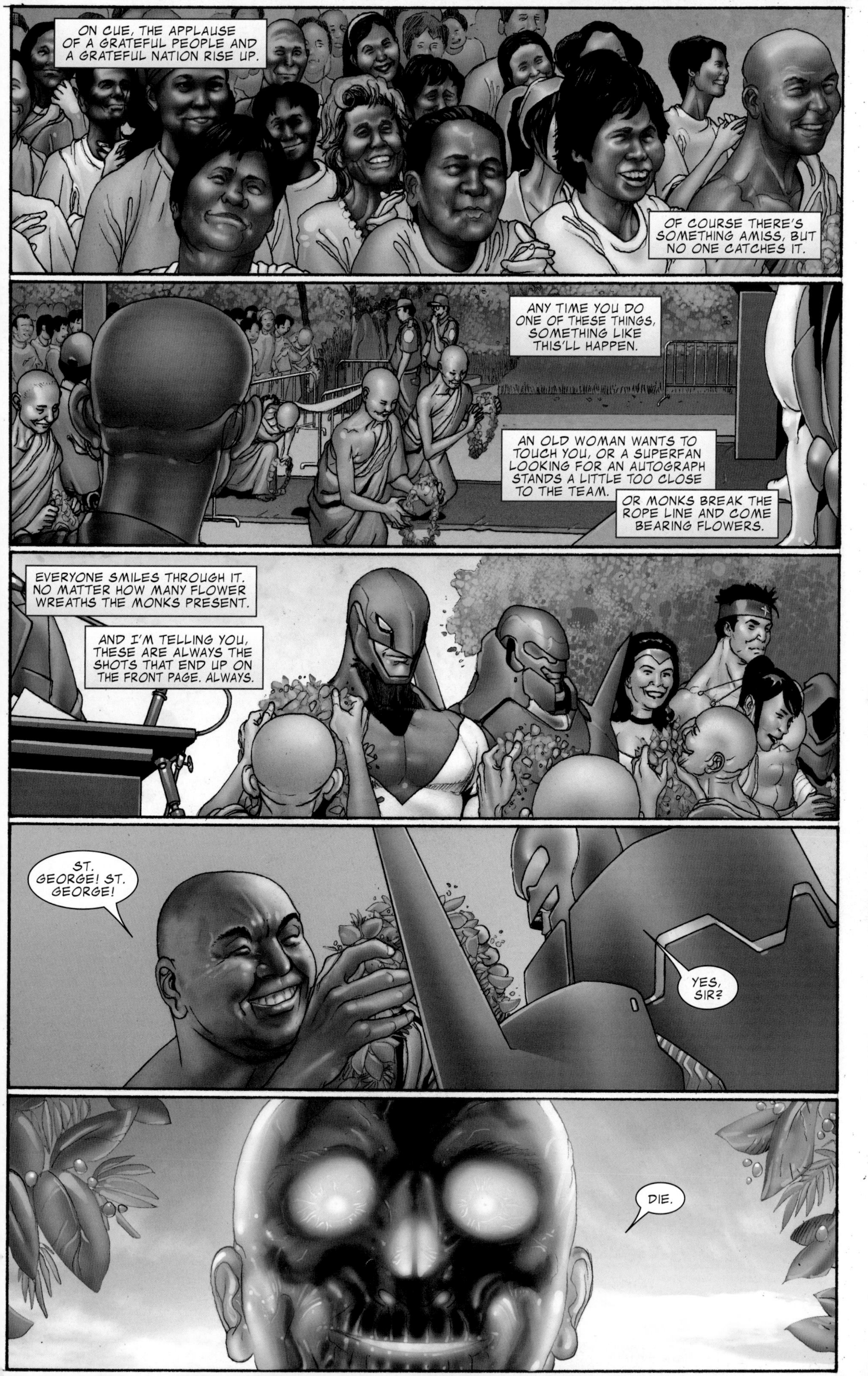
ON CUE, THE APPLAUSE OF A GRATEFUL PEOPLE AND A GRATEFUL NATION RISE UP.
OF COURSE THERE'S SOMETHING AMISS, BUT NO ONE CATCHES IT.
ANY TIME YOU DO ONE OF THESE THINGS, SOMETHING LIKE THIS'LL HAPPEN.
AN OLD WOMAN WANTS TO TOUCH YOU, OR A SUPERFAN LOOKING FOR AN AUTOGRAPH STANDS A LITTLE TOO CLOSE TO THE TEAM.
OR MONKS BREAK THE ROPE LINE AND COME BEARING FLOWERS.
EVERYONE SMILES THROUGH IT. NO MATTER HOW MANY FLOWER WREATHS THE MONKS PRESENT.
AND I'M TELLING YOU, THESE ARE ALWAYS THE SHOTS THAT END UP ON THE FRONT PAGE. ALWAYS.
ST. GEORGE! ST. GEORGE!
YES, SIR?
DIE.

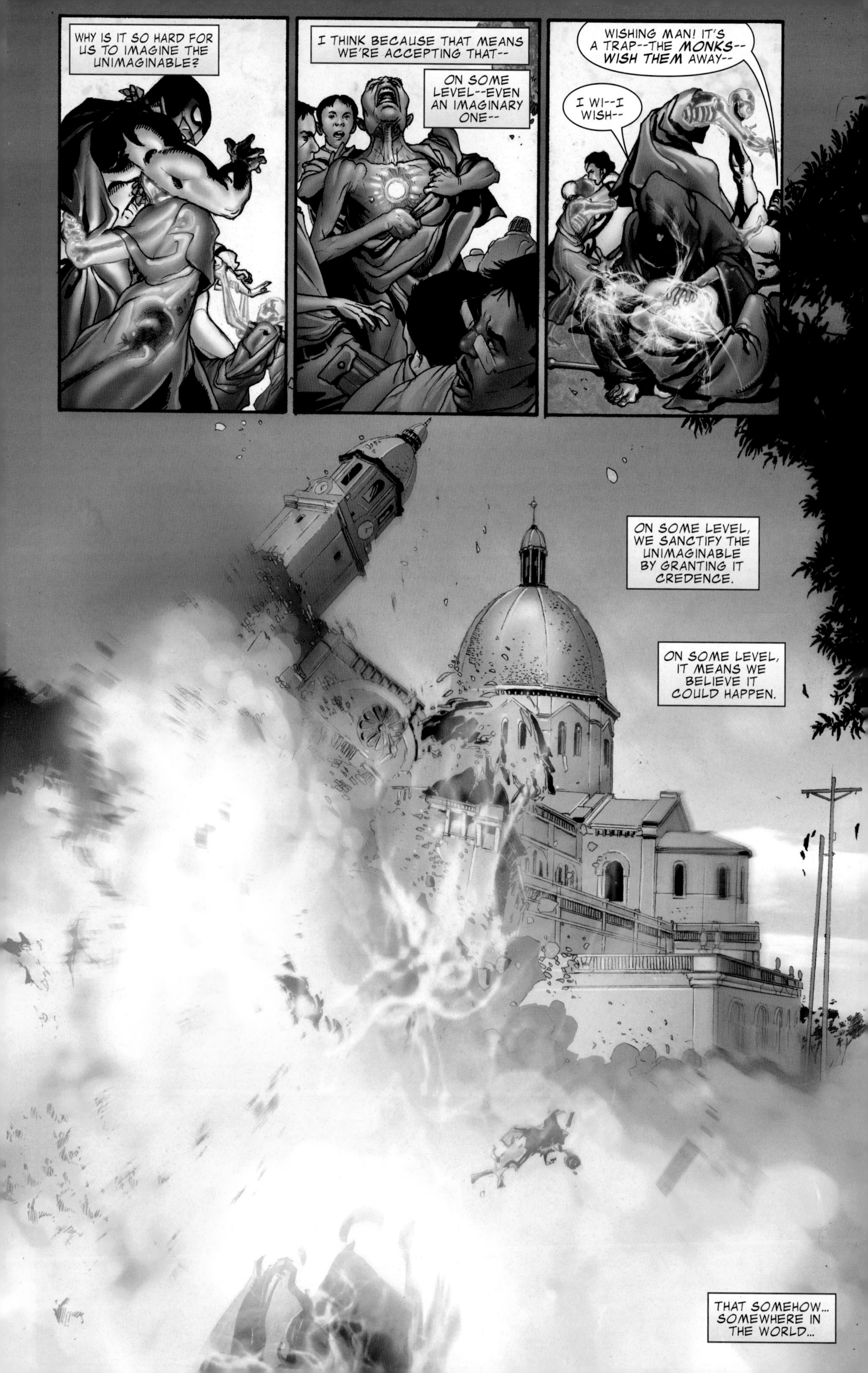
WHY IS IT SO HARD FOR US TO IMAGINE THE UNIMAGINABLE?
I THINK BECAUSE THAT MEANS WE'RE ACCEPTING THAT--
ON SOME LEVEL--EVEN AN IMAGINARY ONE--
WISHING MAN! IT'S A TRAP--THE MONKS--WISH THEM AWAY--
I WI--I WISH--
ON SOME LEVEL, WE SANCTIFY THE UNIMAGINABLE BY GRANTING IT CREDENCE.
ON SOME LEVEL, IT MEANS WE BELIEVE IT COULD HAPPEN.
THAT SOMEHOW... SOMEWHERE IN THE WORLD...

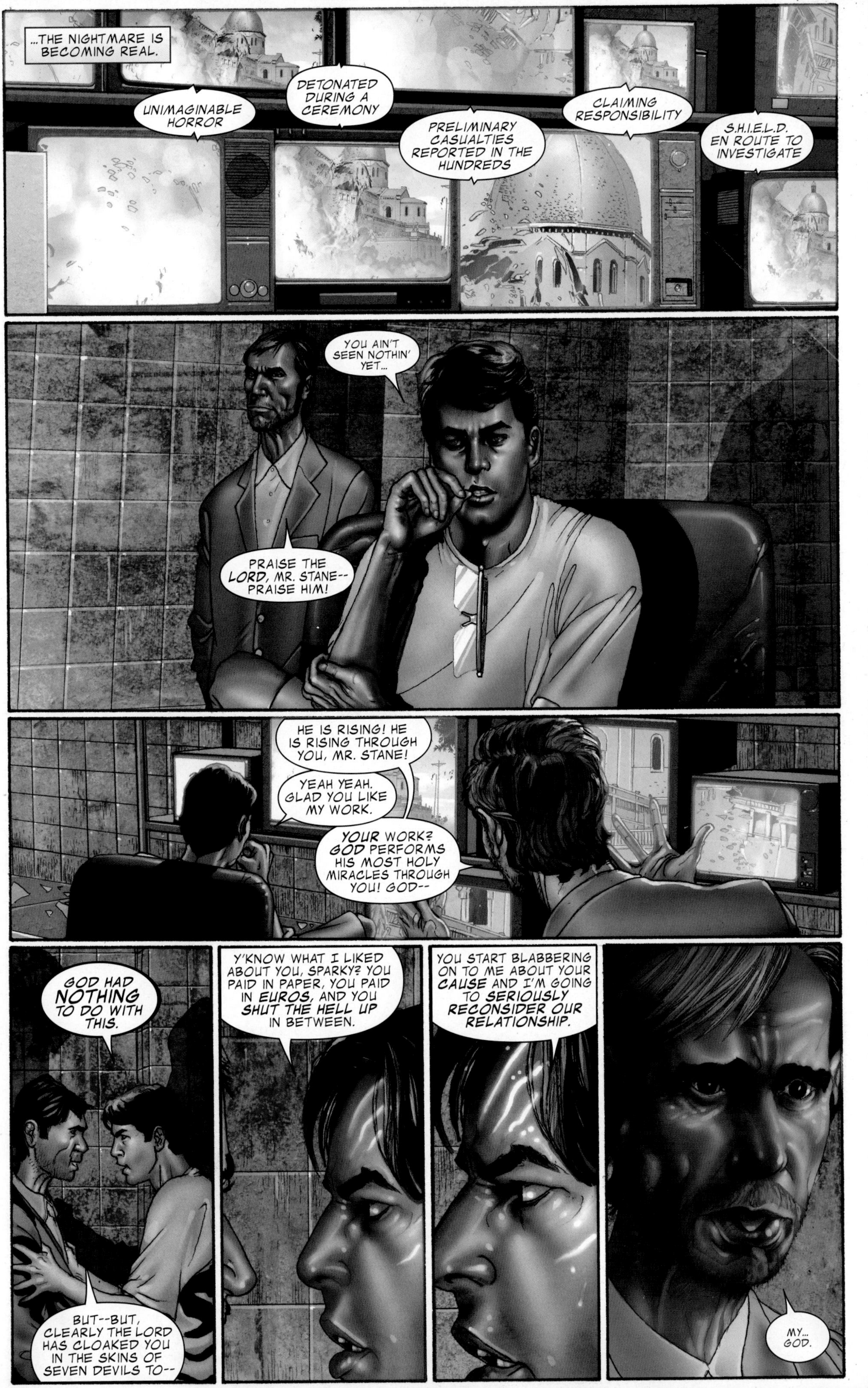
...THE NIGHTMARE IS BECOMING REAL.
UNIMAGINABLE HORROR
DETONATED DURING A CEREMONY
PRELIMINARY CASUALTIES REPORTED IN THE HUNDREDS
CLAIMING RESPONSIBILITY
S.H.I.E.L.D. EN ROUTE TO INVESTIGATE
YOU AIN'T SEEN NOTHIN' YET...
PRAISE THE LORD, MR. STANE-- PRAISE HIM!
HE IS RISING! HE IS RISING THROUGH YOU, MR. STANE!
YEAH YEAH. GLAD YOU LIKE MY WORK.
YOUR WORK? GOD PERFORMS HIS MOST HOLY MIRACLES THROUGH YOU! GOD--
GOD HAD NOTHING TO DO WITH THIS.
BUT--BUT, CLEARLY THE LORD HAS CLOAKED YOU IN THE SKINS OF SEVEN DEVILS TO--
Y'KNOW WHAT I LIKED ABOUT YOU, SPARKY? YOU PAID IN PAPER, YOU PAID IN EUROS, AND YOU SHUT THE HELL UP IN BETWEEN.
YOU START BLABBERING ON TO ME ABOUT YOUR CAUSE AND I'M GOING TO SERIOUSLY RECONSIDER OUR RELATIONSHIP.
MY... GOD.

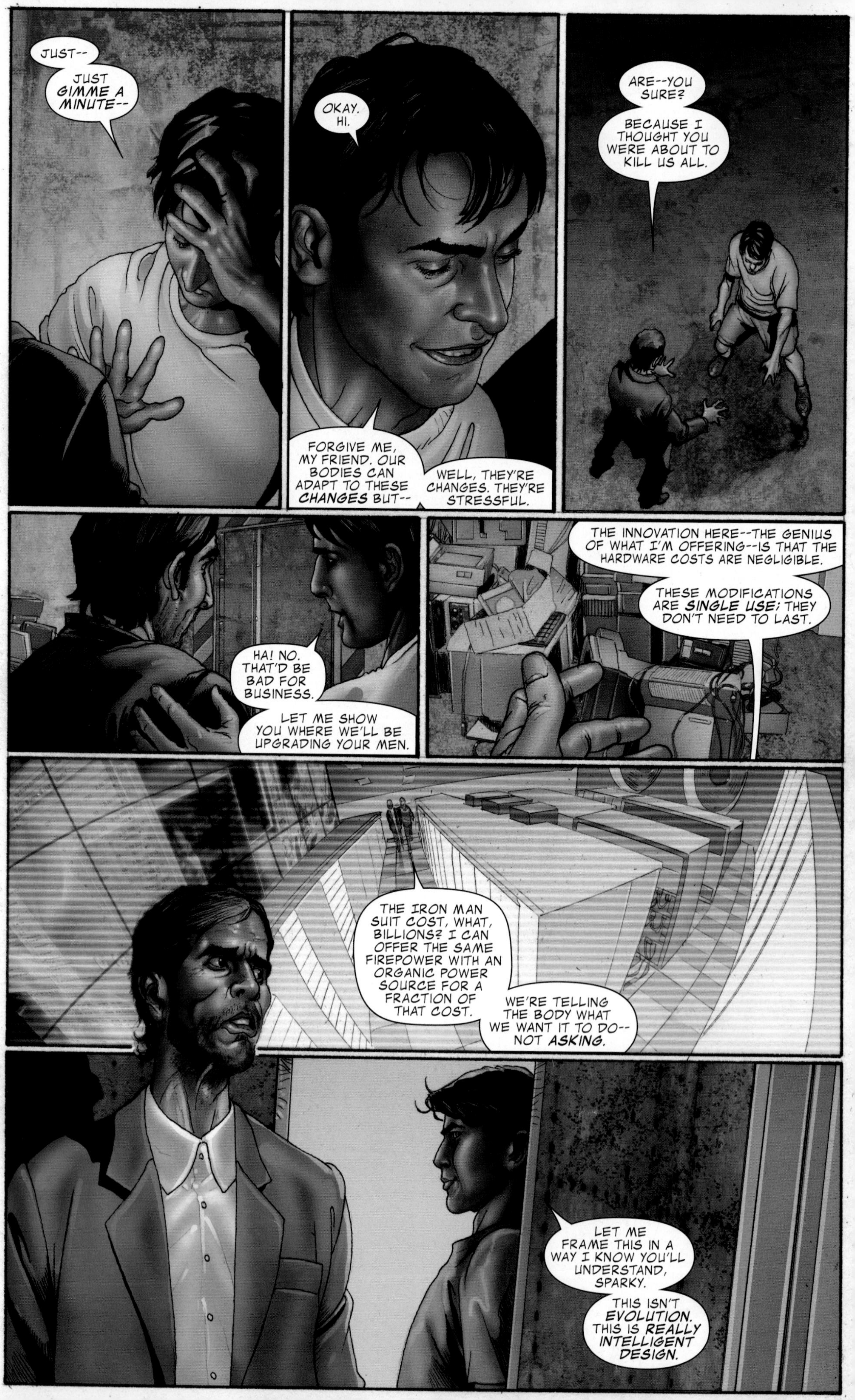
JUST--
JUST GIMME A MINUTE--
OKAY. HI.
FORGIVE ME, MY FRIEND. OUR BODIES CAN ADAPT TO THESE CHANGES BUT--
WELL, THEY'RE CHANGES. THEY'RE STRESSFUL.
ARE--YOU SURE?
BECAUSE I THOUGHT YOU WERE ABOUT TO KILL US ALL.
HA! NO. THAT'D BE BAD FOR BUSINESS.
LET ME SHOW YOU WHERE WE'LL BE UPGRADING YOUR MEN.
THE INNOVATION HERE--THE GENIUS OF WHAT I'M OFFERING--IS THAT THE HARDWARE COSTS ARE NEGLIGIBLE.
THESE MODIFICATIONS ARE SINGLE USE; THEY DON'T NEED TO LAST.
THE IRON MAN SUIT COST, WHAT, BILLIONS? I CAN OFFER THE SAME FIREPOWER WITH AN ORGANIC POWER SOURCE FOR A FRACTION OF THAT COST.
WE'RE TELLING THE BODY WHAT WE WANT IT TO DO--NOT ASKING.
LET ME FRAME THIS IN A WAY I KNOW YOU'LL UNDERSTAND, SPARKY.
THIS ISN'T EVOLUTION. THIS IS REALLY INTELLIGENT DESIGN.

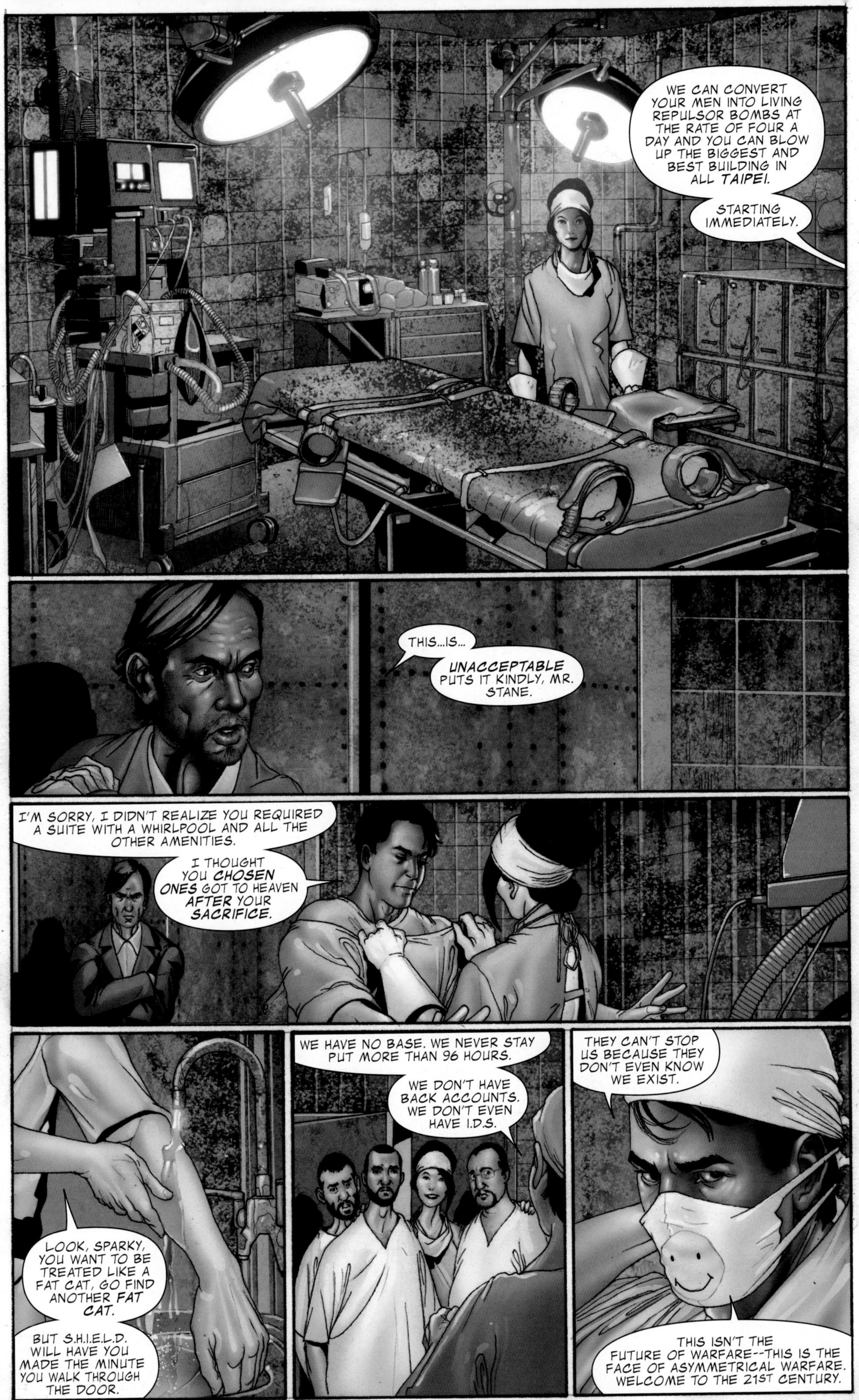
WE CAN CONVERT YOUR MEN INTO LIVING REPULSOR BOMBS AT THE RATE OF FOUR A DAY AND YOU CAN BLOW UP THE BIGGEST AND BEST BUILDING IN ALL TAIPEI.
STARTING IMMEDIATELY.
THIS...IS...
UNACCEPTABLE PUTS IT KINDLY, MR. STANE.
I'M SORRY, I DIDN'T REALIZE YOU REQUIRED A SUITE WITH A WHIRLPOOL AND ALL THE OTHER AMENITIES.
I THOUGHT YOU CHOSEN ONES GOT TO HEAVEN AFTER YOUR SACRIFICE.
LOOK, SPARKY, YOU WANT TO BE TREATED LIKE A FAT CAT, GO FIND ANOTHER FAT CAT.
BUT S.H.I.E.L.D. WILL HAVE YOU MADE THE MINUTE YOU WALK THROUGH THE DOOR.
WE HAVE NO BASE. WE NEVER STAY PUT MORE THAN 96 HOURS.
WE DON'T HAVE BACK ACCOUNTS. WE DON'T EVEN HAVE I.D.S.
THEY CAN'T STOP US BECAUSE THEY DON'T EVEN KNOW WE EXIST.
THIS ISN'T THE FUTURE OF WARFARE--THIS IS THE FACE OF ASYMMETRICAL WARFARE. WELCOME TO THE 21ST CENTURY.

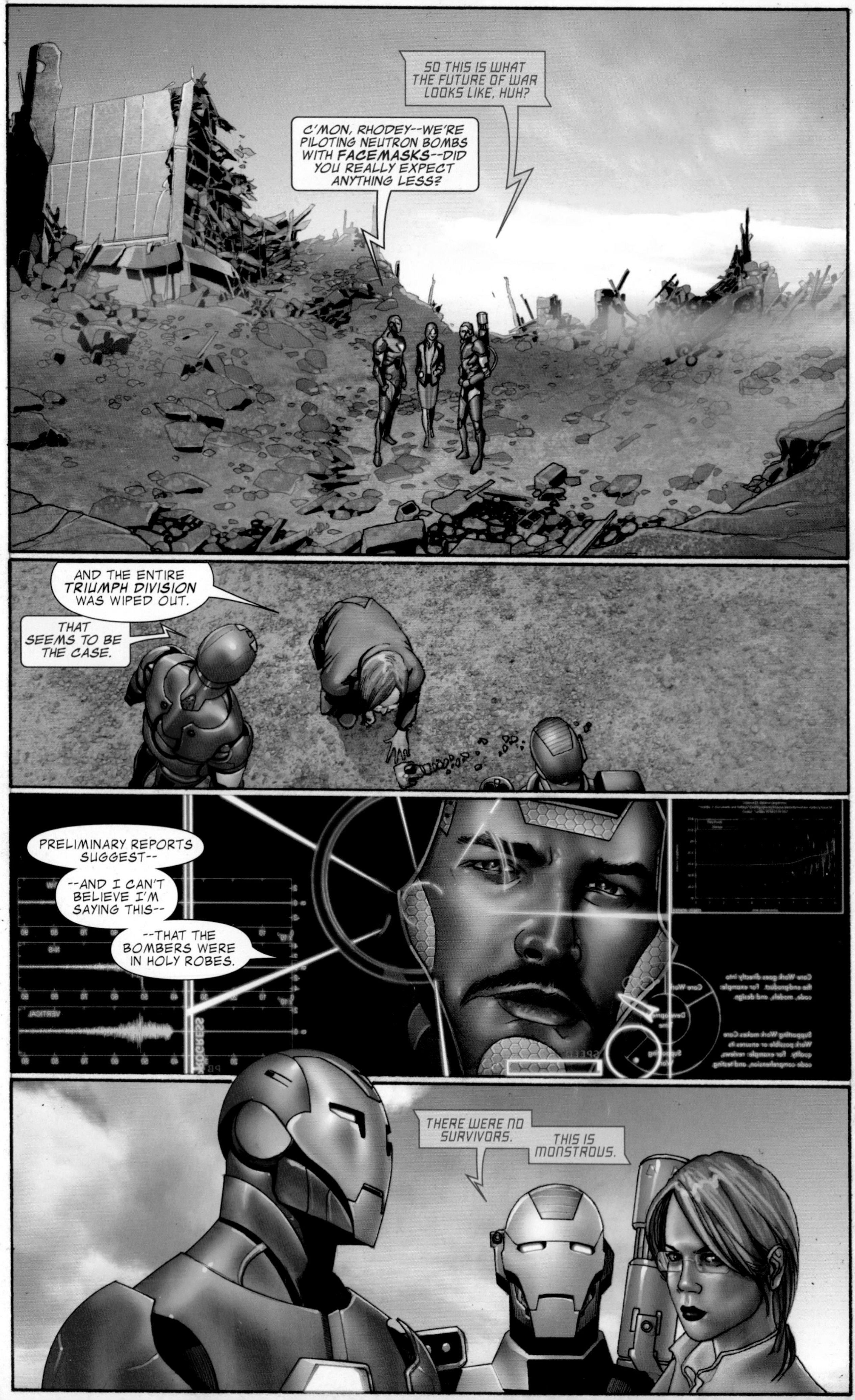
SO THIS IS WHAT THE FUTURE OF WAR LOOKS LIKE, HUH?
C'MON, RHODEY--WE'RE PILOTING NEUTRON BOMBS WITH FACEMASKS--DID YOU REALLY EXPECT ANYTHING LESS?
AND THE ENTIRE TRIUMPH DIVISION WAS WIPED OUT.
THAT SEEMS TO BE THE CASE.
PRELIMINARY REPORTS SUGGEST--
--AND I CAN'T BELIEVE I'M SAYING THIS--
--THAT THE BOMBERS WERE IN HOLY ROBES.
THERE WERE NO SURVIVORS.
THIS IS MONSTROUS.

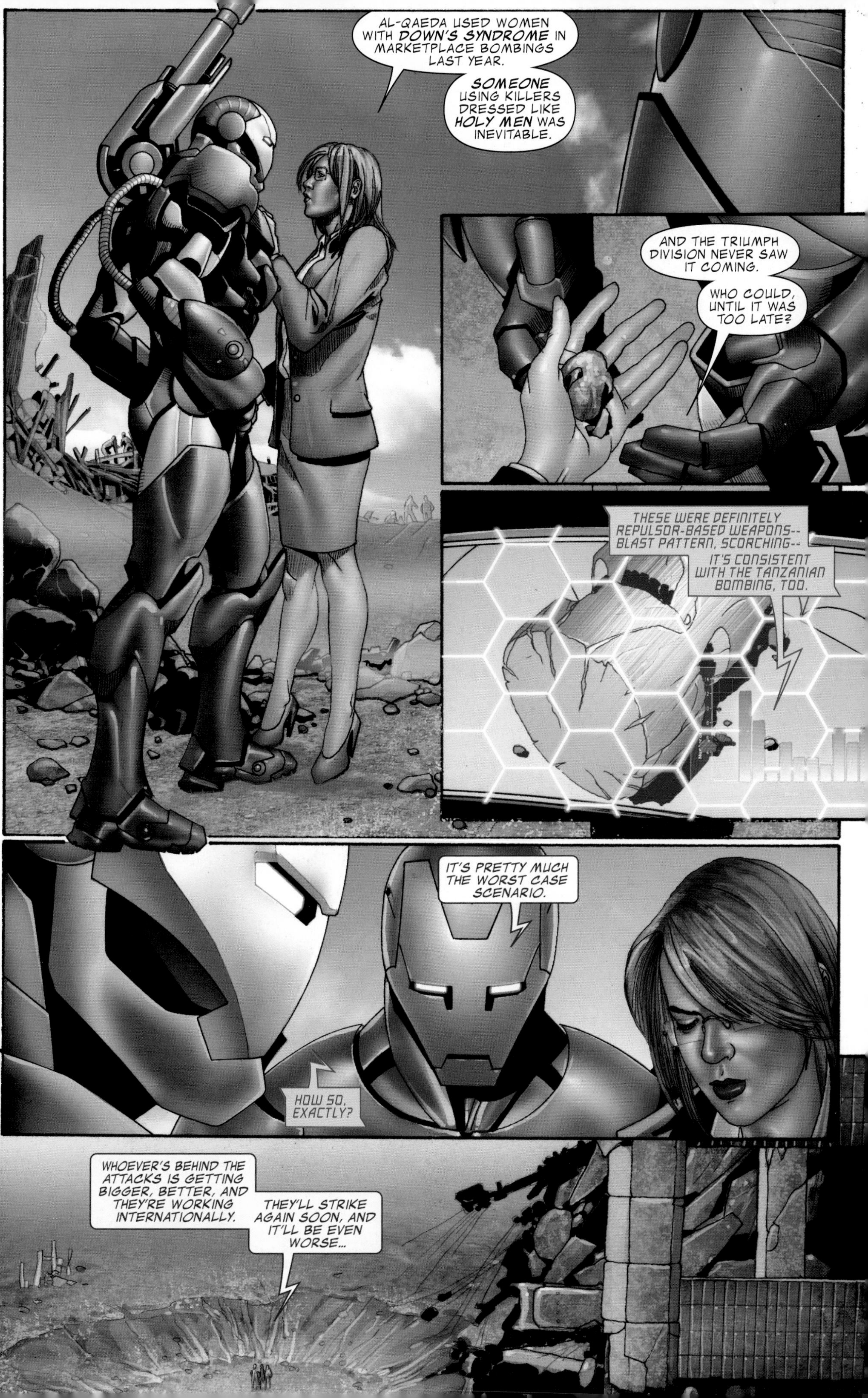
AL-QAEDA USED WOMEN WITH DOWN'S SYNDROME IN MARKETPLACE BOMBINGS LAST YEAR.
SOMEONE USING KILLERS DRESSED LIKE HOLY MEN WAS INEVITABLE.
AND THE TRIUMPH DIVISION NEVER SAW IT COMING.
WHO COULD, UNTIL IT WAS TOO LATE?
THESE WERE DEFINITELY REPULSOR-BASED WEAPONS-- BLAST PATTERN, SCORCHING--
IT'S CONSISTENT WITH THE TANZANIAN BOMBING, TOO.
IT'S PRETTY MUCH THE WORST CASE SCENARIO.
HOW SO, EXACTLY?
WHOEVER'S BEHIND THE ATTACKS IS GETTING BIGGER, BETTER, AND THEY'RE WORKING INTERNATIONALLY.
THEY'LL STRIKE AGAIN SOON, AND IT'LL BE EVEN WORSE...

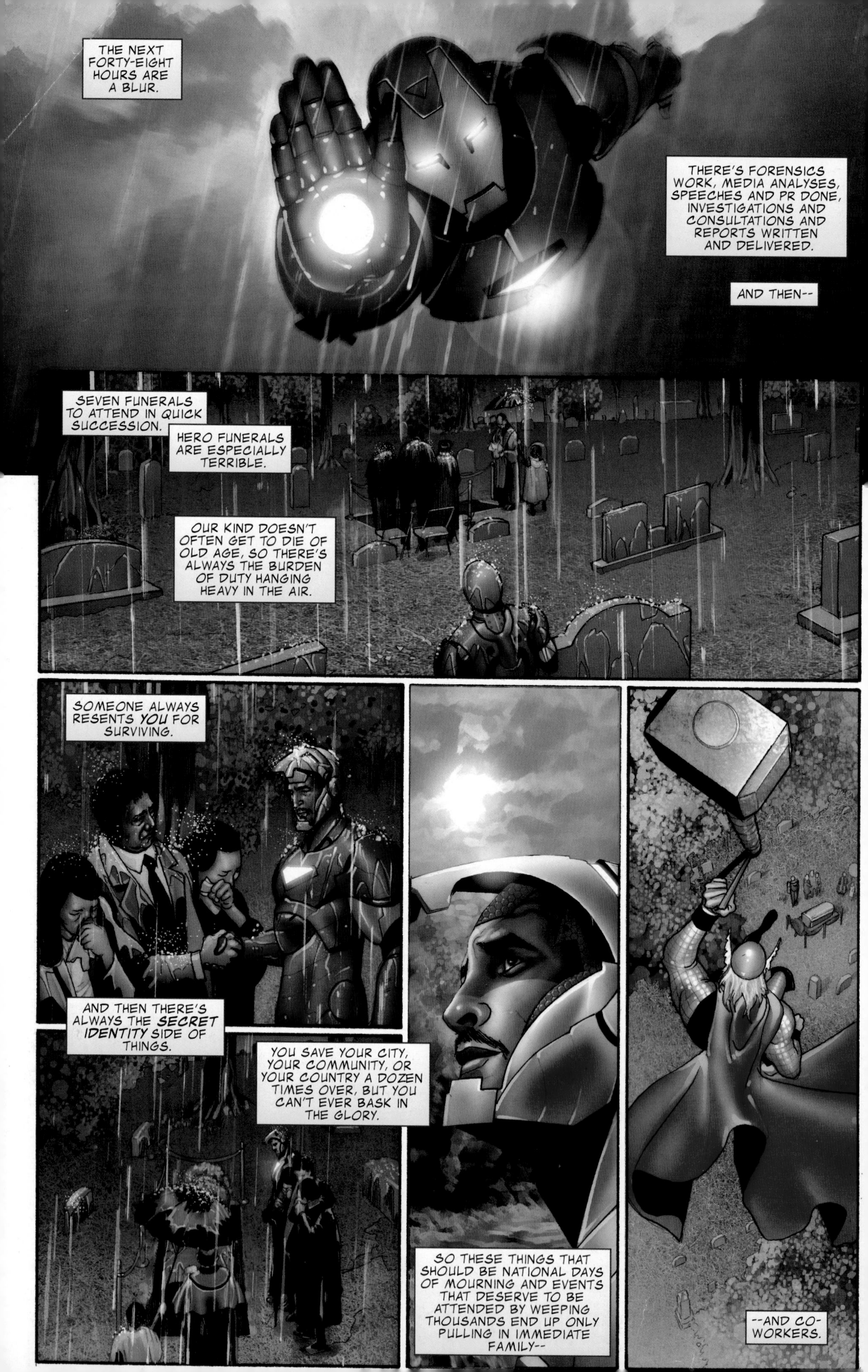
THE NEXT FORTY-EIGHT HOURS ARE A BLUR.
THERE'S FORENSICS WORK, MEDIA ANALYSES, SPEECHES AND PR DONE, INVESTIGATIONS AND CONSULTATIONS AND REPORTS WRITTEN AND DELIVERED.
AND THEN--
SEVEN FUNERALS TO ATTEND IN QUICK SUCCESSION.
HERO FUNERALS ARE ESPECIALLY TERRIBLE.
OUR KIND DOESN'T OFTEN GET TO DIE OF OLD AGE, SO THERE'S ALWAYS THE BURDEN OF DUTY HANGING HEAVY IN THE AIR.
SOMEONE ALWAYS RESENTS YOU FOR SURVIVING.
AND THEN THERE'S ALWAYS THE SECRET IDENTITY SIDE OF THINGS.
YOU SAVE YOUR CITY, YOUR COMMUNITY, OR YOUR COUNTRY A DOZEN TIMES OVER, BUT YOU CAN'T EVER BASK IN THE GLORY.
SO THESE THINGS THAT SHOULD BE NATIONAL DAYS OF MOURNING AND EVENTS THAT DESERVE TO BE ATTENDED BY WEEPING THOUSANDS END UP ONLY PULLING IN IMMEDIATE FAMILY--
--AND CO-WORKERS.

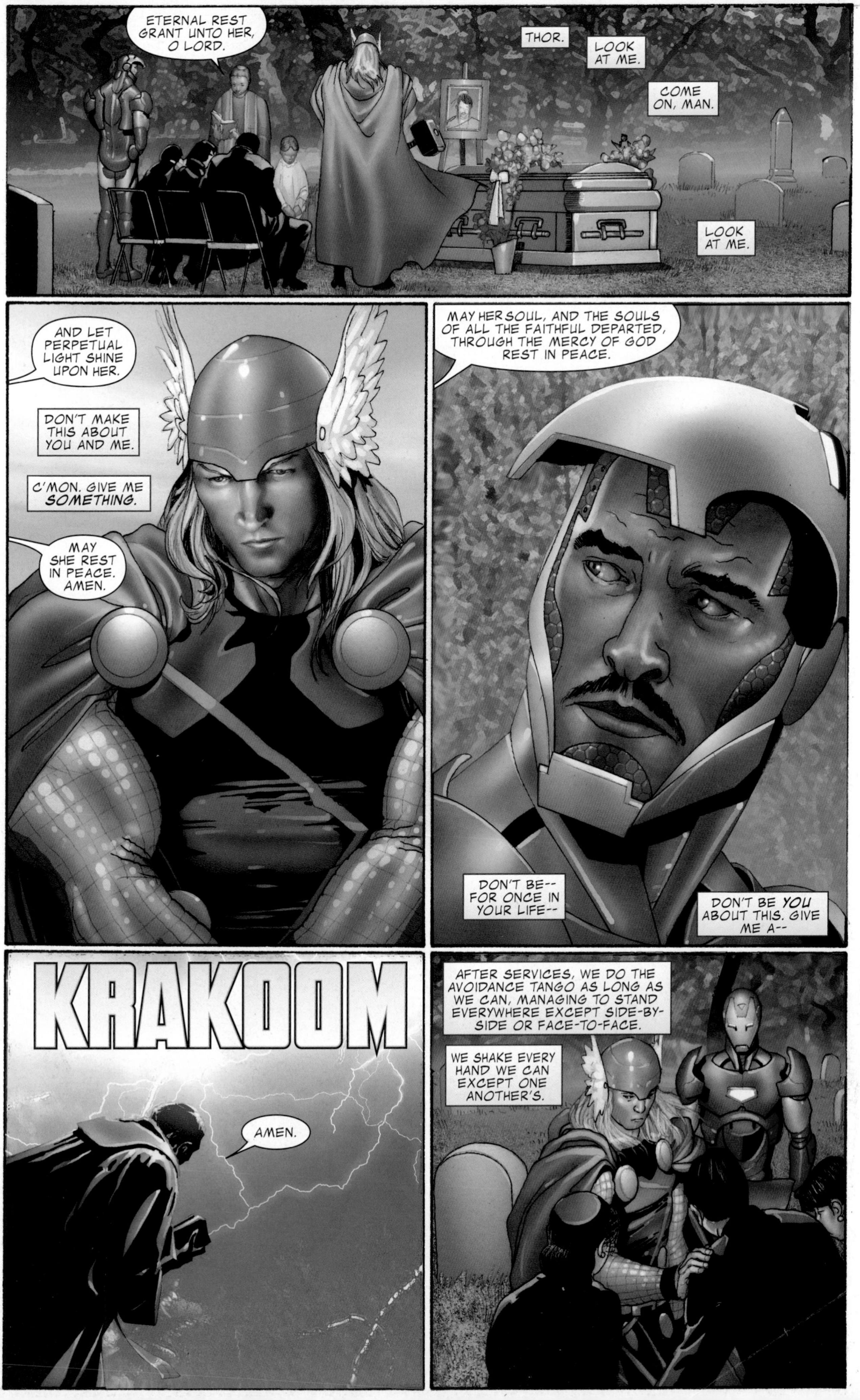
ETERNAL REST GRANT UNTO HER, O LORD.
THOR.
LOOK AT ME.
COME ON, MAN.
LOOK AT ME.
AND LET PERPETUAL LIGHT SHINE UPON HER.
DON'T MAKE THIS ABOUT YOU AND ME.
C'MON. GIVE ME SOMETHING.
MAY SHE REST IN PEACE. AMEN.
MAY HER SOUL, AND THE SOULS OF ALL THE FAITHFUL DEPARTED, THROUGH THE MERCY OF GOD REST IN PEACE.
DON'T BE-- FOR ONCE IN YOUR LIFE--
DON'T BE YOU ABOUT THIS. GIVE ME A--
KRAKOOM
AMEN.
AFTER SERVICES, WE DO THE AVOIDANCE TANGO AS LONG AS WE CAN, MANAGING TO STAND EVERYWHERE EXCEPT SIDE-BY-SIDE OR FACE-TO-FACE.
WE SHAKE EVERY HAND WE CAN EXCEPT ONE ANOTHER'S.

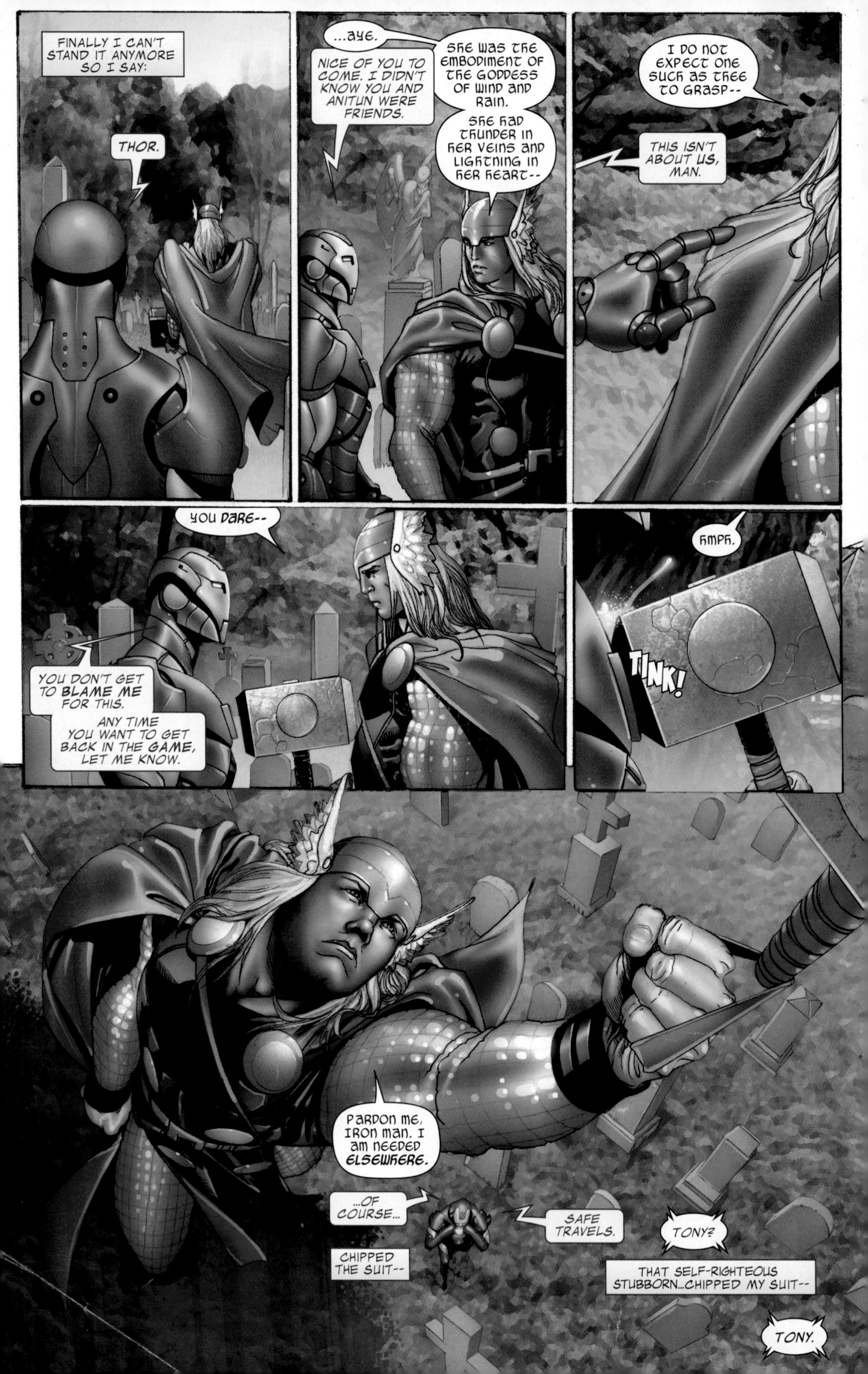
FINALLY I CAN'T STAND IT ANYMORE SO I SAY:
THOR.
...AYE.
NICE OF YOU TO COME. I DIDN'T KNOW YOU AND ANITUN WERE FRIENDS.
SHE WAS THE EMBODIMENT OF THE GODDESS OF WIND AND RAIN.
SHE HAD THUNDER IN HER VEINS AND LIGHTNING IN HER HEART--
I DO NOT EXPECT ONE SUCH AS THEE TO GRASP--
THIS ISN'T ABOUT US, MAN.
YOU DARE--
YOU DON'T GET TO BLAME ME FOR THIS.
ANY TIME YOU WANT TO GET BACK IN THE GAME, LET ME KNOW.
HMPH.
TINK!
PARDON ME, IRON MAN. I AM NEEDED ELSEWHERE.
...OF COURSE...
SAFE TRAVELS.
CHIPPED THE SUIT--
TONY?
THAT SELF-RIGHTEOUS STUBBORN...CHIPPED MY SUIT--
TONY.

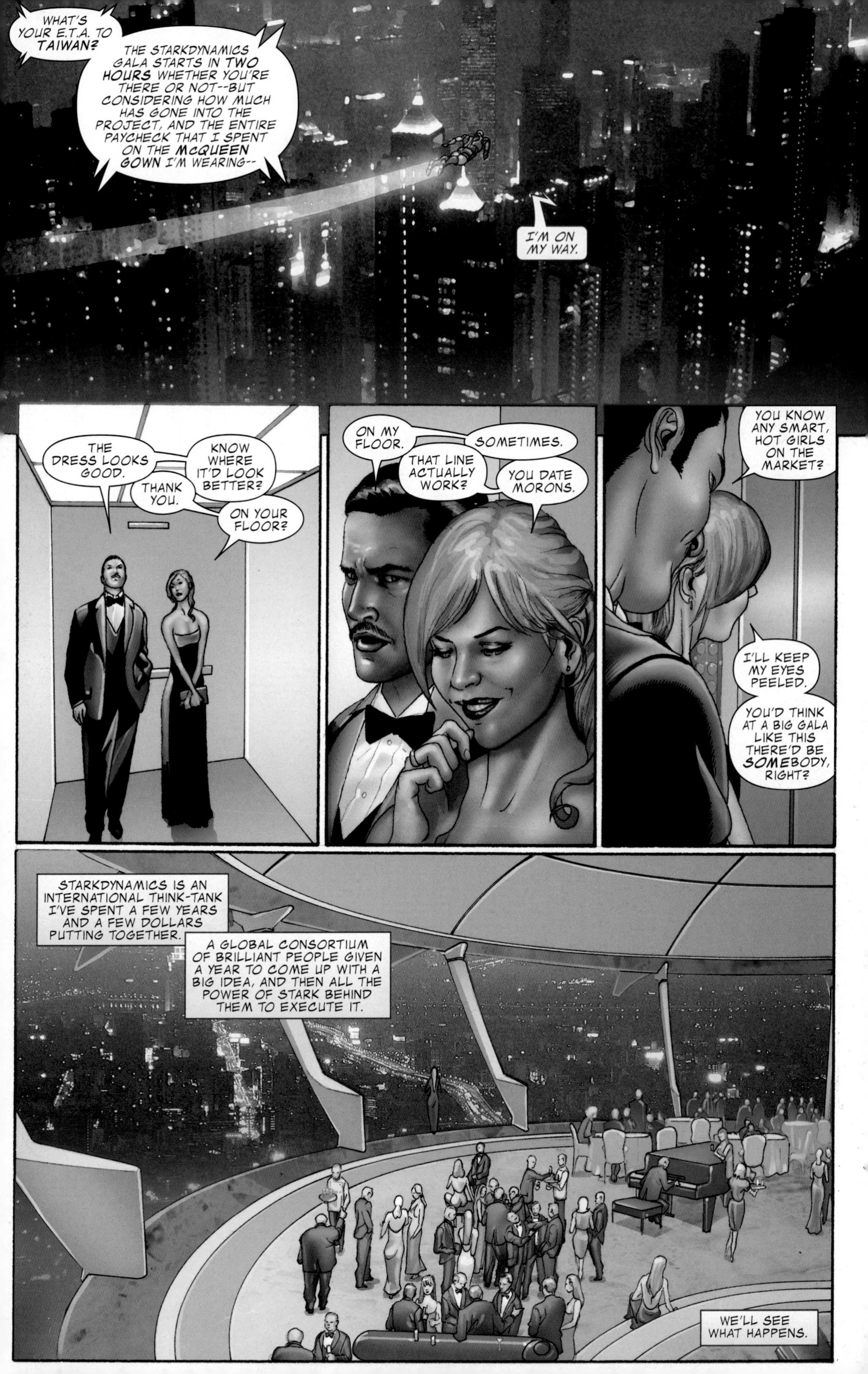
WHAT'S YOUR E.T.A. TO TAIWAN?
THE STARKDYNAMICS GALA STARTS IN TWO HOURS WHETHER YOU'RE THERE OR NOT--BUT CONSIDERING HOW MUCH HAS GONE INTO THE PROJECT, AND THE ENTIRE PAYCHECK THAT I SPENT ON THE McQUEEN GOWN I'M WEARING--
I'M ON MY WAY.
THE DRESS LOOKS GOOD.
THANK YOU.
KNOW WHERE IT'D LOOK BETTER?
ON YOUR FLOOR?
ON MY FLOOR.
THAT LINE ACTUALLY WORK?
SOMETIMES.
YOU DATE MORONS.
YOU KNOW ANY SMART, HOT GIRLS ON THE MARKET?
I'LL KEEP MY EYES PEELED.
YOU'D THINK AT A BIG GALA LIKE THIS THERE'D BE SOMEBODY, RIGHT?
STARKDYNAMICS IS AN INTERNATIONAL THINK-TANK I'VE SPENT A FEW YEARS AND A FEW DOLLARS PUTTING TOGETHER.
A GLOBAL CONSORTIUM OF BRILLIANT PEOPLE GIVEN A YEAR TO COME UP WITH A BIG IDEA, AND THEN ALL THE POWER OF STARK BEHIND THEM TO EXECUTE IT.
WE'LL SEE WHAT HAPPENS.

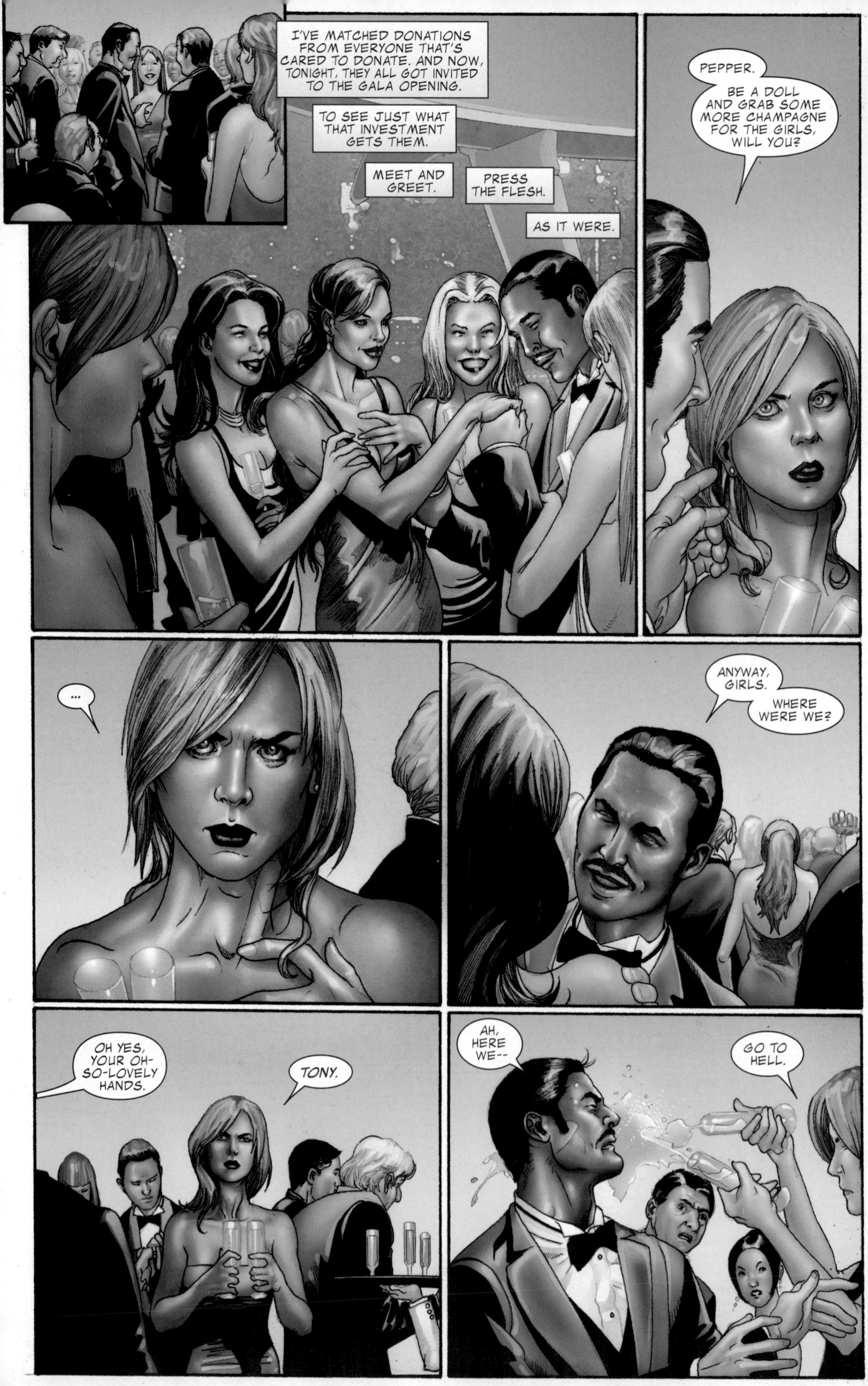
I'VE MATCHED DONATIONS FROM EVERYONE THAT'S CARED TO DONATE. AND NOW, TONIGHT, THEY ALL GOT INVITED TO THE GALA OPENING.
TO SEE JUST WHAT THAT INVESTMENT GETS THEM.
MEET AND GREET.
PRESS THE FLESH.
AS IT WERE.
PEPPER.
BE A DOLL AND GRAB SOME MORE CHAMPAGNE FOR THE GIRLS, WILL YOU?
...
ANYWAY, GIRLS.
WHERE WERE WE?
OH YES, YOUR OH-SO-LOVELY HANDS.
TONY.
AH, HERE WE--
GO TO HELL.

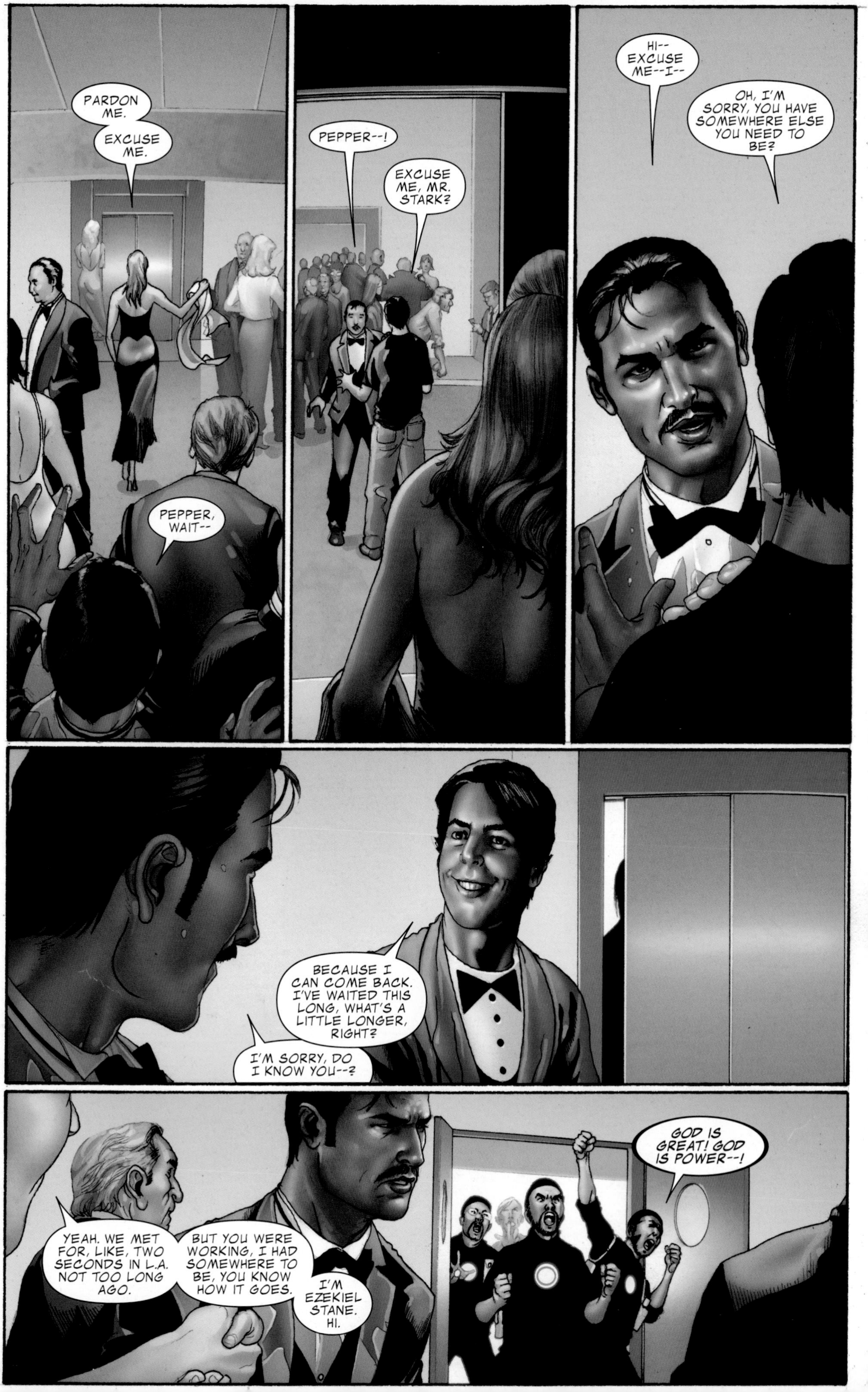

PARDON ME.
EXCUSE ME.
PEPPER, WAIT--
PEPPER--!
EXCUSE ME, MR. STARK?
HI-- EXCUSE ME--I--
OH, I'M SORRY, YOU HAVE SOMEWHERE ELSE YOU NEED TO BE?
BECAUSE I CAN COME BACK. I'VE WAITED THIS LONG, WHAT'S A LITTLE LONGER, RIGHT?
I'M SORRY, DO I KNOW YOU--?
YEAH. WE MET FOR, LIKE, TWO SECONDS IN L.A. NOT TOO LONG AGO.
BUT YOU WERE WORKING, I HAD SOMEWHERE TO BE, YOU KNOW HOW IT GOES.
I'M EZEKIEL STANE. HI.
GOD IS GREAT! GOD IS POWER--!

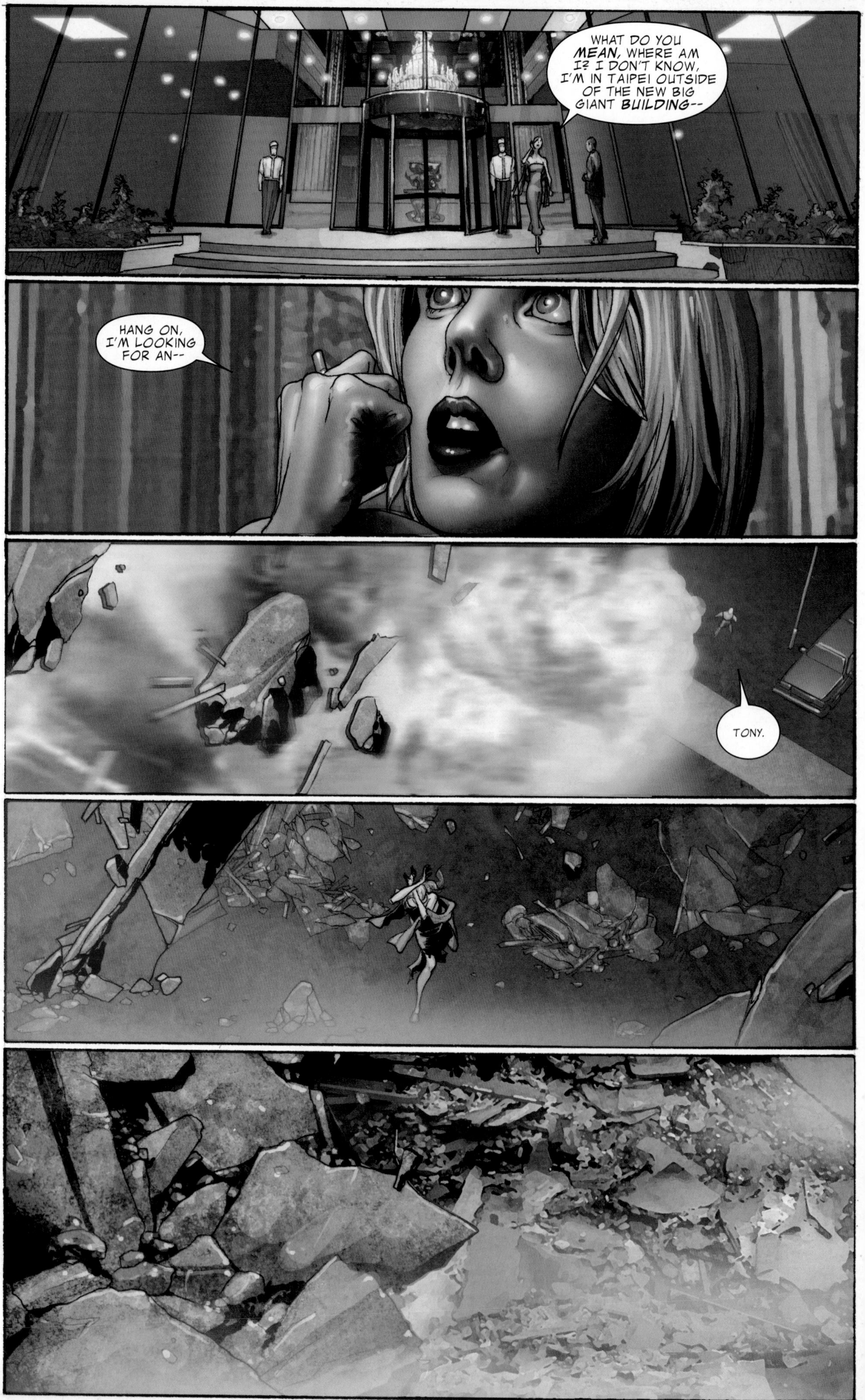
WHAT DO YOU MEAN, WHERE AM I? I DON'T KNOW, I'M IN TAIPEI OUTSIDE OF THE NEW BIG GIANT BUILDING--
HANG ON, I'M LOOKING FOR AN--
TONY.

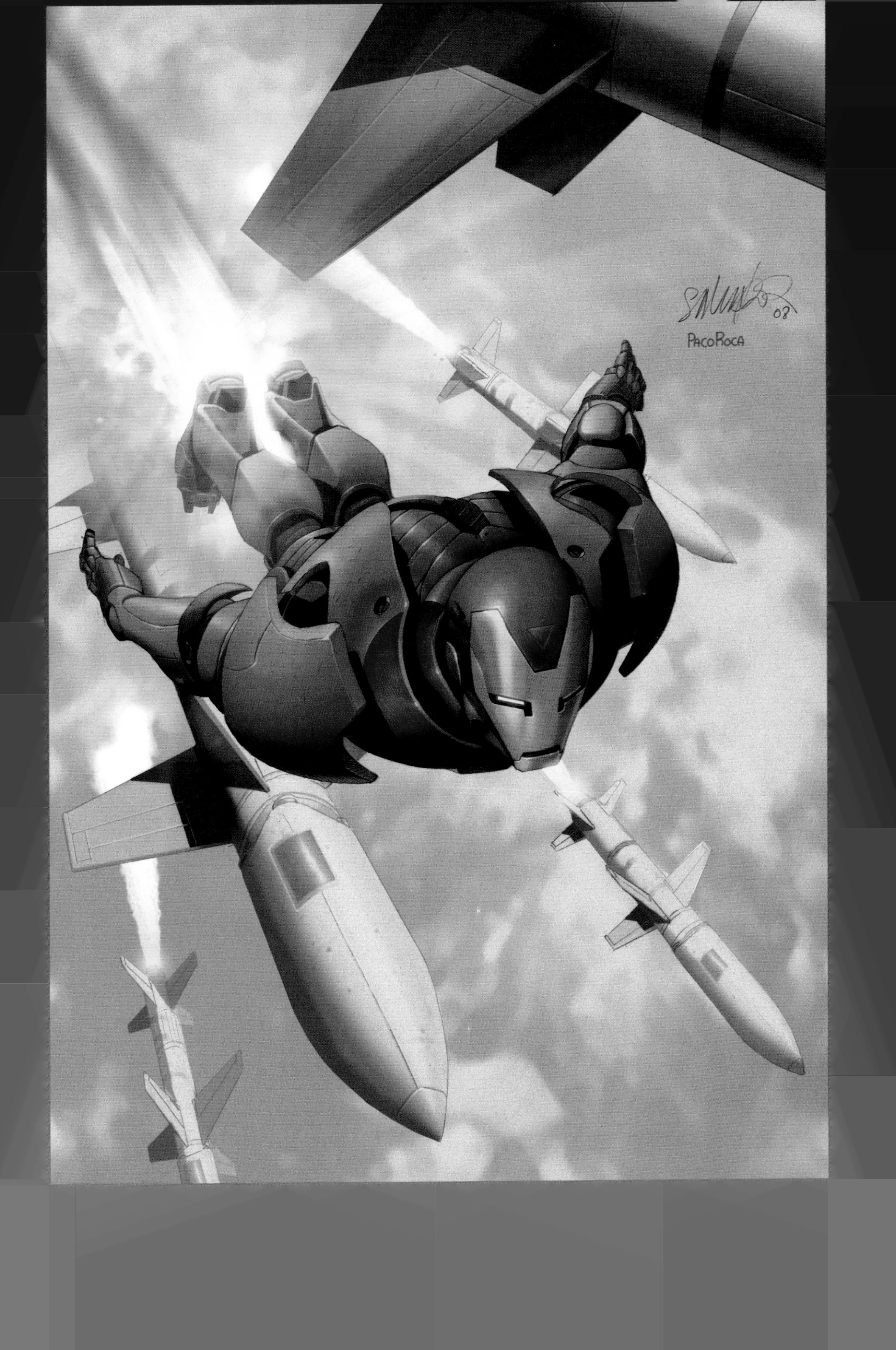
PacoRoca

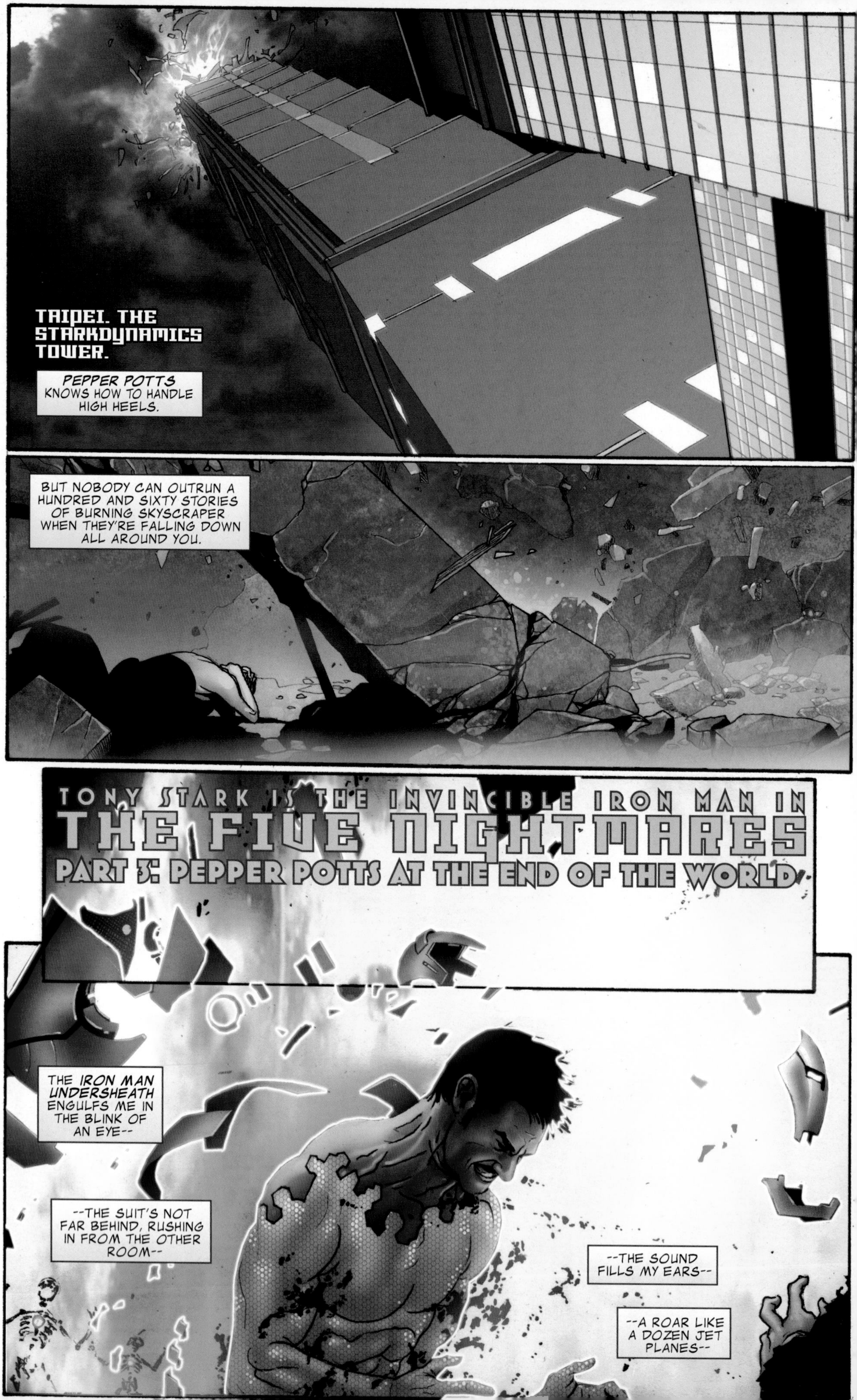
TAIPEI. THE STARKDYNAMICS TOWER.
PEPPER POTTS KNOWS HOW TO HANDLE HIGH HEELS.
BUT NOBODY CAN OUTRUN A HUNDRED AND SIXTY STORIES OF BURNING SKYSCRAPER WHEN THEY'RE FALLING DOWN ALL AROUND YOU.
TONY STARK IS THE INVINCIBLE IRON MAN IN
THE FIVE NIGHTMARES
PART 3: PEPPER POTTS AT THE END OF THE WORLD
THE IRON MAN UNDERSHEATH ENGULFS ME IN THE BLINK OF AN EYE--
--THE SUIT'S NOT FAR BEHIND, RUSHING IN FROM THE OTHER ROOM--
--THE SOUND FILLS MY EARS--
--A ROAR LIKE A DOZEN JET PLANES--

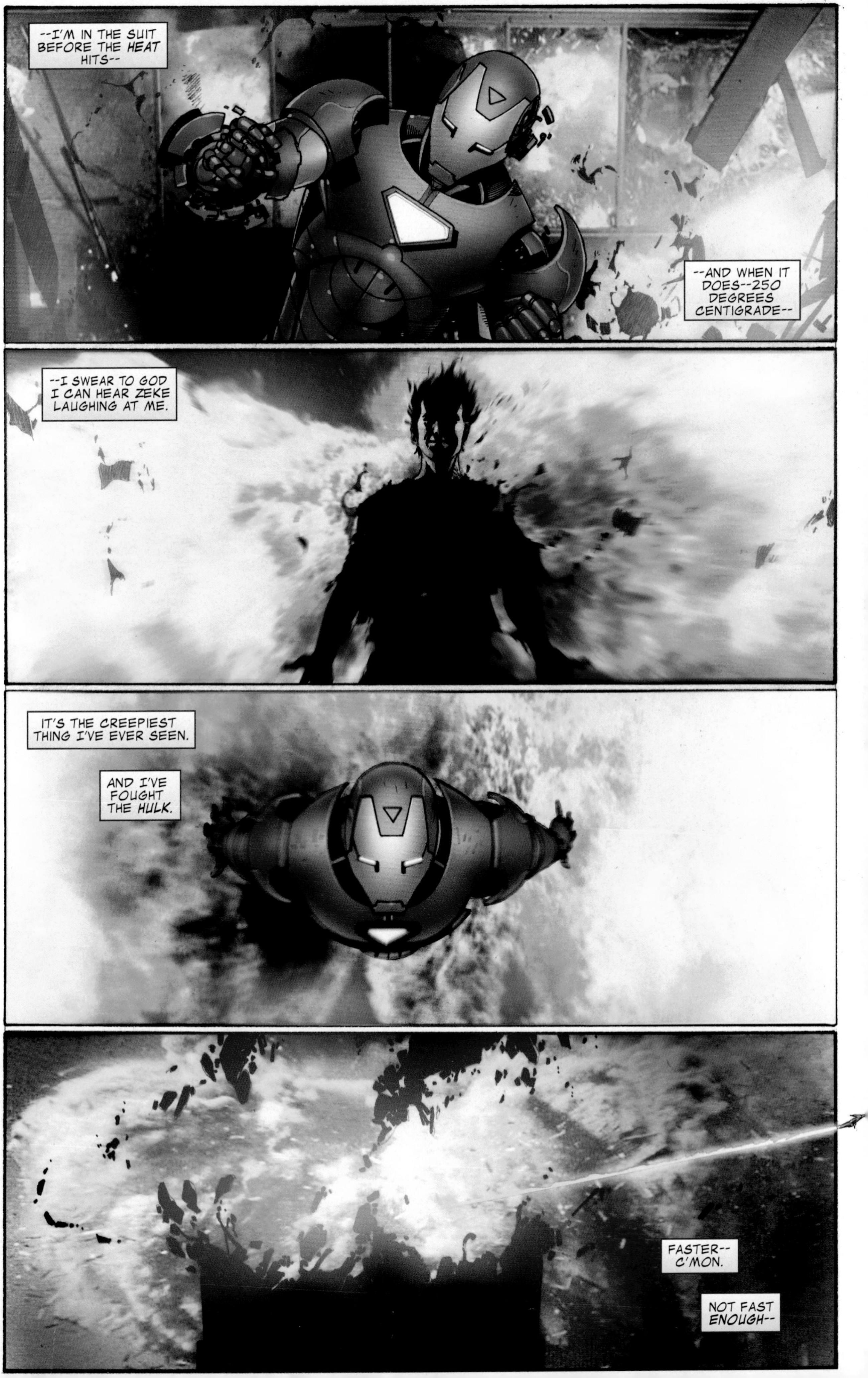
--I'M IN THE SUIT BEFORE THE HEAT HITS--
--AND WHEN IT DOES--250 DEGREES CENTIGRADE--
--I SWEAR TO GOD I CAN HEAR ZEKE LAUGHING AT ME.
IT'S THE CREEPIEST THING I'VE EVER SEEN.
AND I'VE FOUGHT THE HULK.
FASTER-- C'MON.
NOT FAST ENOUGH--

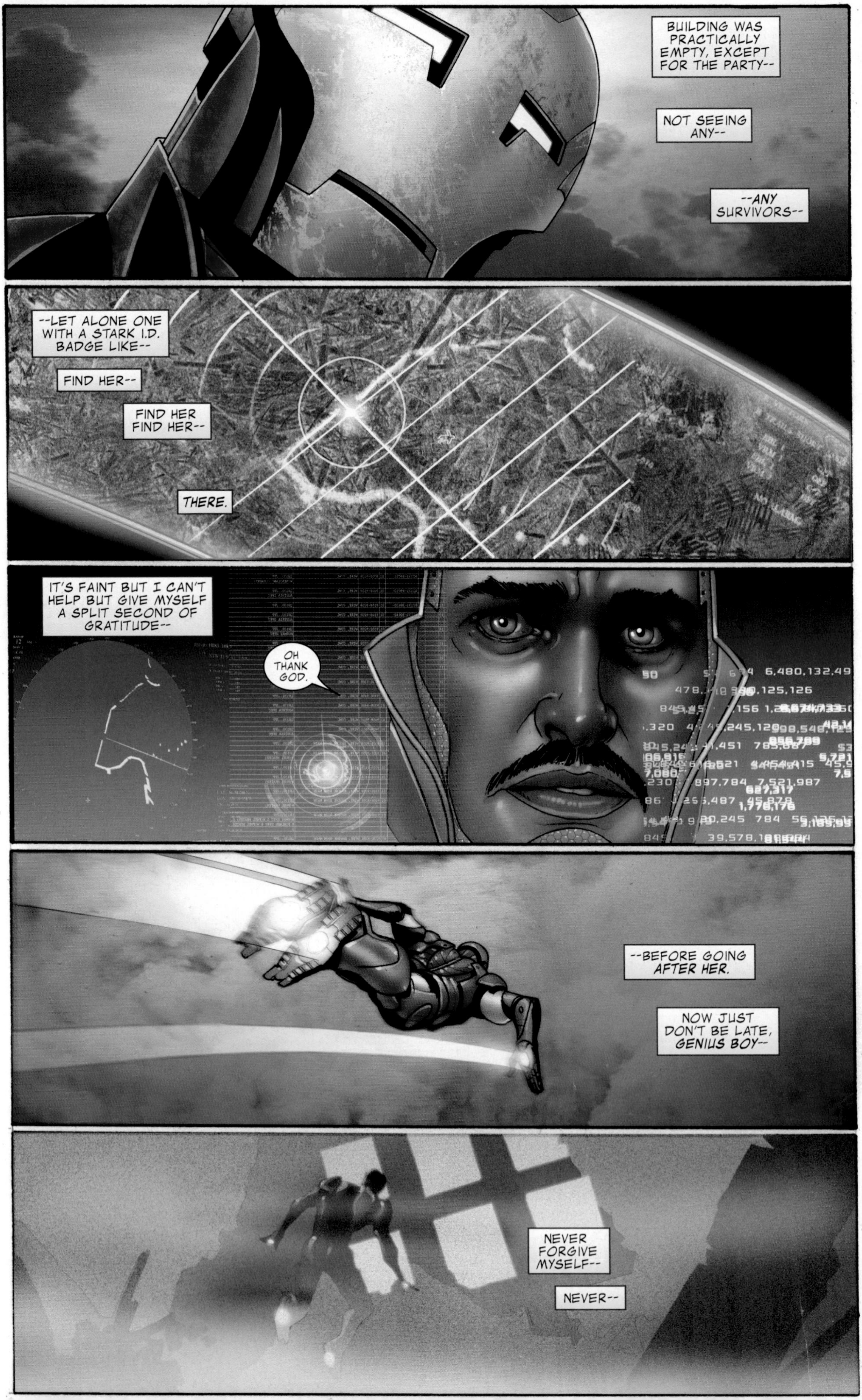
BUILDING WAS PRACTICALLY EMPTY, EXCEPT FOR THE PARTY--
NOT SEEING ANY--
--ANY SURVIVORS--
--LET ALONE ONE WITH A STARK I.D. BADGE LIKE--
FIND HER--
FIND HER FIND HER--
THERE.
IT'S FAINT BUT I CAN'T HELP BUT GIVE MYSELF A SPLIT SECOND OF GRATITUDE--
OH THANK GOD.
--BEFORE GOING AFTER HER.
NOW JUST DON'T BE LATE, GENIUS BOY--
NEVER FORGIVE MYSELF--
NEVER--

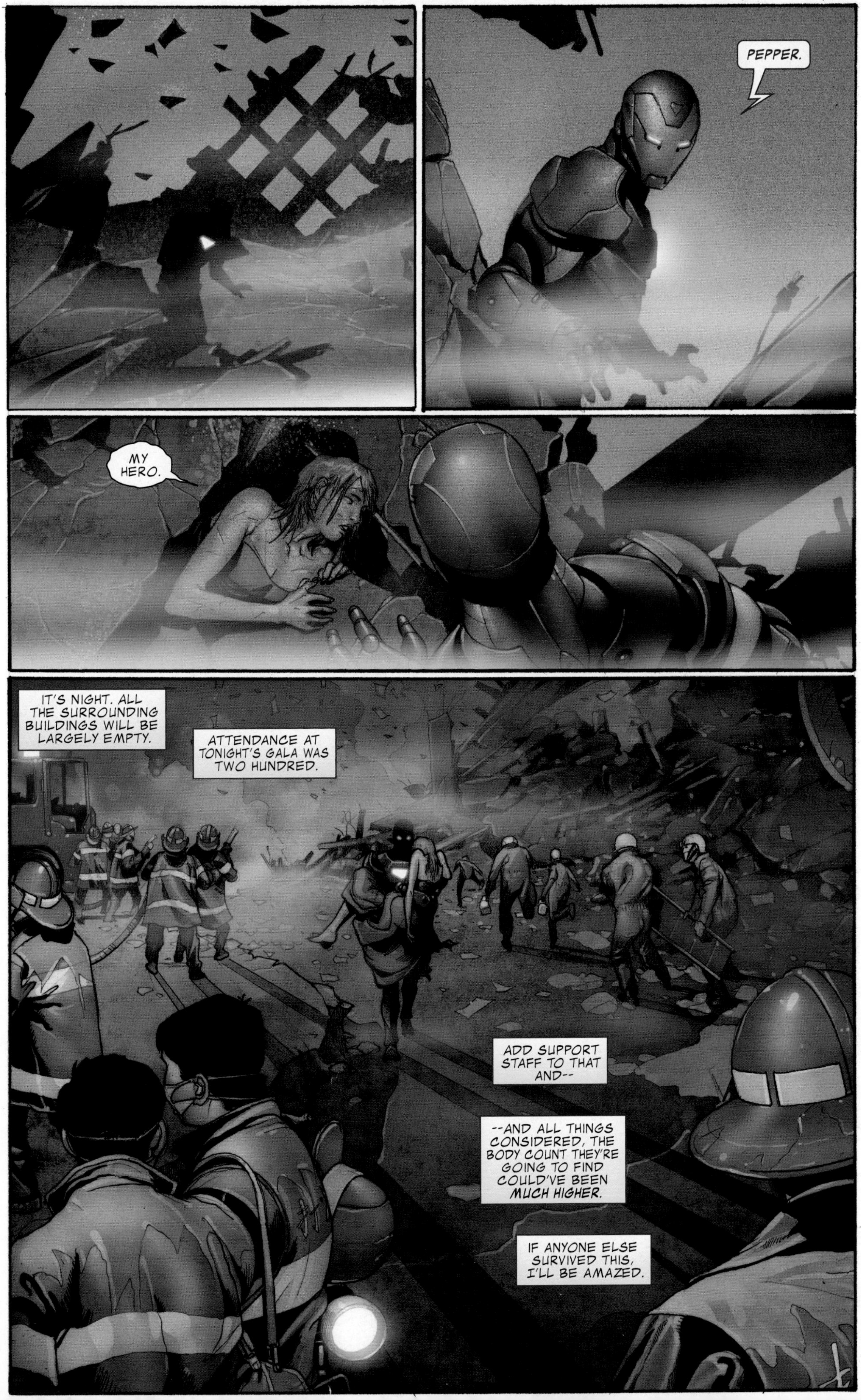
PEPPER.
MY HERO.
IT'S NIGHT. ALL THE SURROUNDING BUILDINGS WILL BE LARGELY EMPTY.
ATTENDANCE AT TONIGHT'S GALA WAS TWO HUNDRED.
ADD SUPPORT STAFF TO THAT AND--
--AND ALL THINGS CONSIDERED, THE BODY COUNT THEY'RE GOING TO FIND COULD'VE BEEN MUCH HIGHER.
IF ANYONE ELSE SURVIVED THIS, I'LL BE AMAZED.

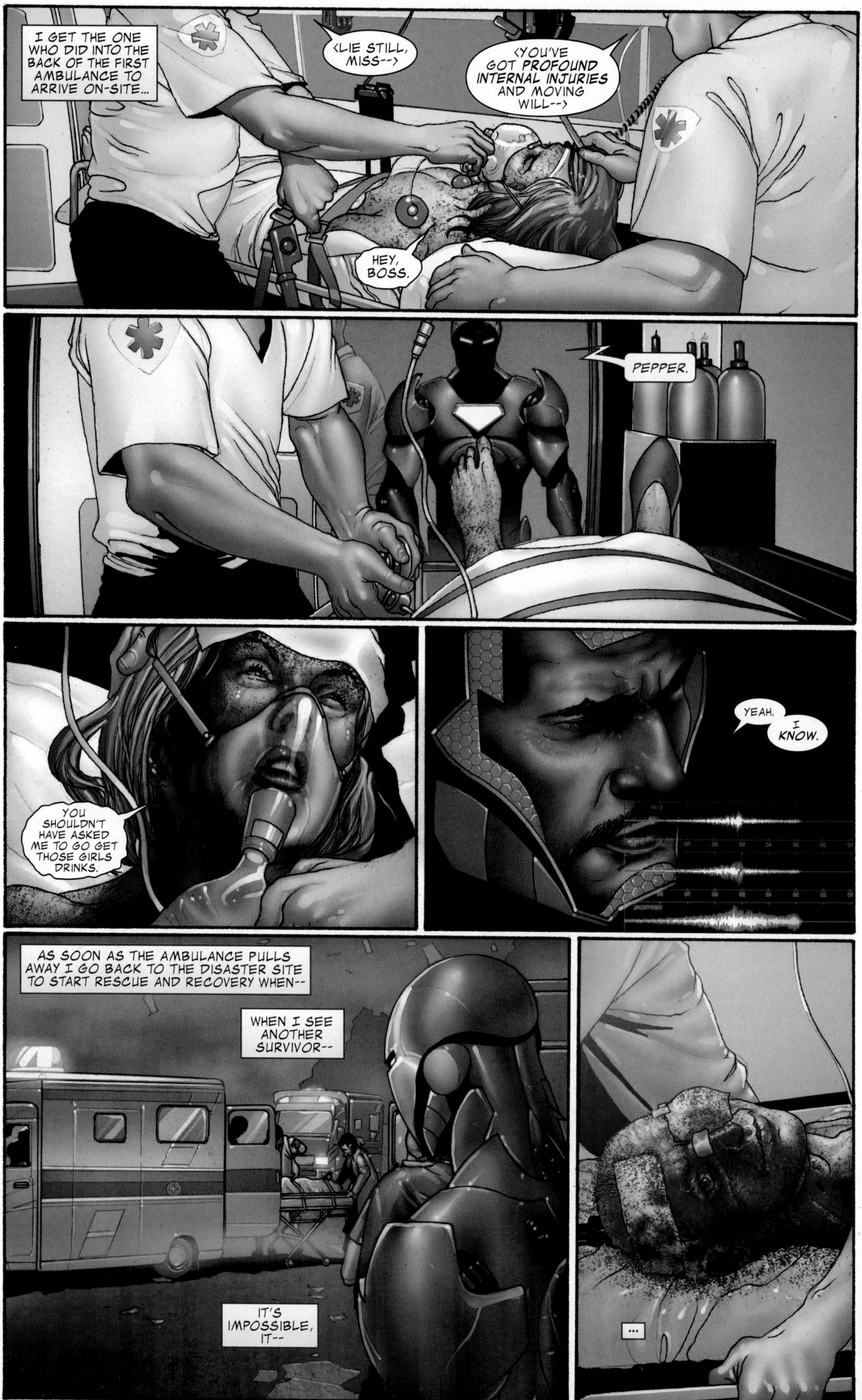
I GET THE ONE WHO DID INTO THE BACK OF THE FIRST AMBULANCE TO ARRIVE ON-SITE...
<LIE STILL, MISS-->
<YOU'VE GOT PROFOUND INTERNAL INJURIES AND MOVING WILL-->
HEY, BOSS.
PEPPER.
YOU SHOULDN'T HAVE ASKED ME TO GO GET THOSE GIRLS DRINKS.
YEAH. I KNOW.
AS SOON AS THE AMBULANCE PULLS AWAY I GO BACK TO THE DISASTER SITE TO START RESCUE AND RECOVERY WHEN--
WHEN I SEE ANOTHER SURVIVOR--
IT'S IMPOSSIBLE, IT--
...

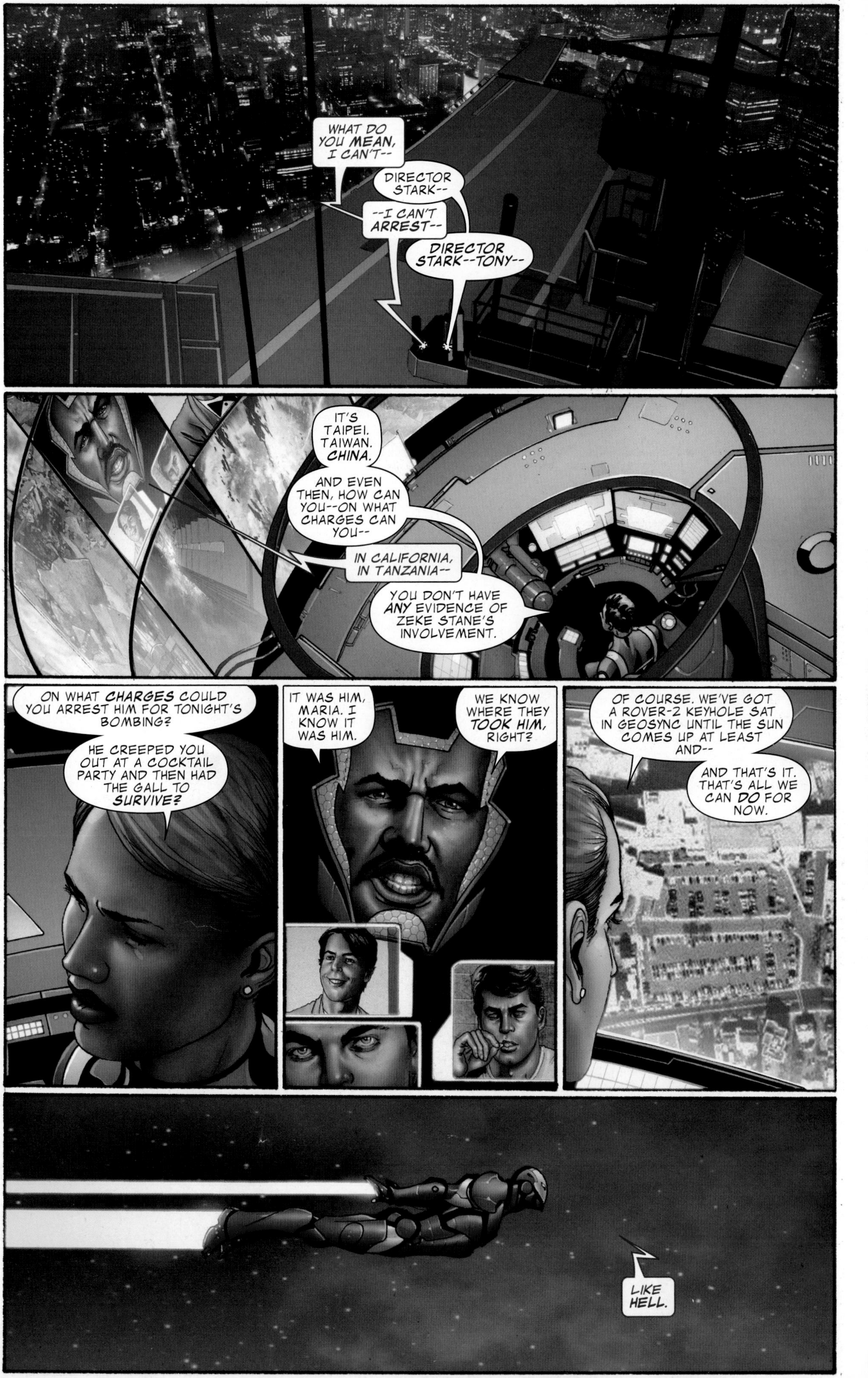
WHAT DO YOU MEAN, I CAN'T--
DIRECTOR STARK--
--I CAN'T ARREST--
DIRECTOR STARK--TONY--
IT'S TAIPEI. TAIWAN. CHINA.
AND EVEN THEN, HOW CAN YOU--ON WHAT CHARGES CAN YOU--
IN CALIFORNIA, IN TANZANIA--
YOU DON'T HAVE ANY EVIDENCE OF ZEKE STANE'S INVOLVEMENT.
ON WHAT CHARGES COULD YOU ARREST HIM FOR TONIGHT'S BOMBING?
HE CREEPED YOU OUT AT A COCKTAIL PARTY AND THEN HAD THE GALL TO SURVIVE?
IT WAS HIM, MARIA. I KNOW IT WAS HIM.
WE KNOW WHERE THEY TOOK HIM, RIGHT?
OF COURSE. WE'VE GOT A ROVER-2 KEYHOLE SAT IN GEOSYNC UNTIL THE SUN COMES UP AT LEAST AND--
AND THAT'S IT. THAT'S ALL WE CAN DO FOR NOW.
LIKE HELL.

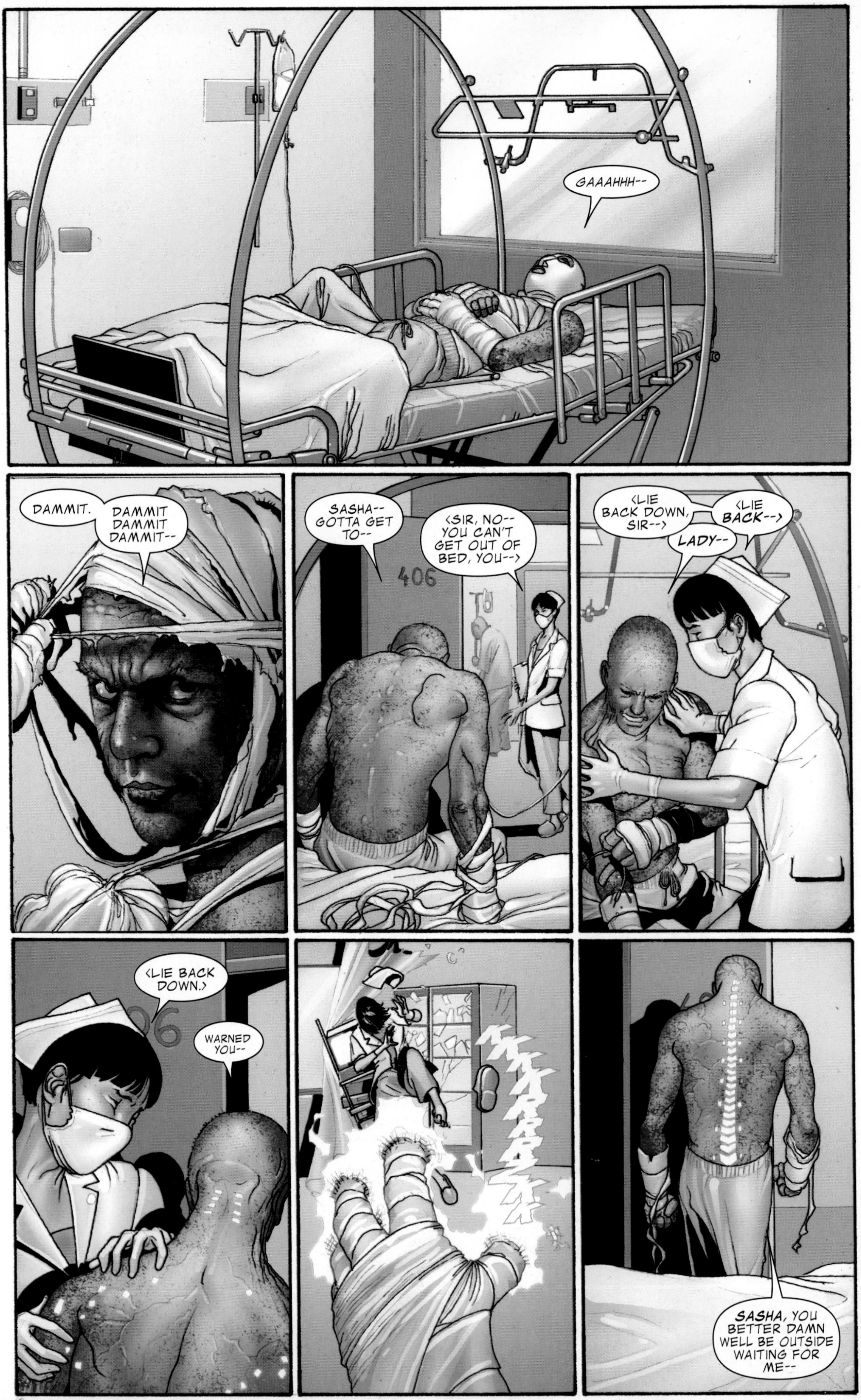
GAAAHHH--
DAMMIT.
DAMMIT DAMMIT DAMMIT--
SASHA-- GOTTA GET TO--
406
<SIR, NO-- YOU CAN'T GET OUT OF BED, YOU-->
<LIE BACK DOWN, SIR-->
<LIE BACK-->
LADY--
<LIE BACK DOWN.>
WARNED YOU--
KKRRAAKK
SASHA, YOU BETTER DAMN WELL BE OUTSIDE WAITING FOR ME--

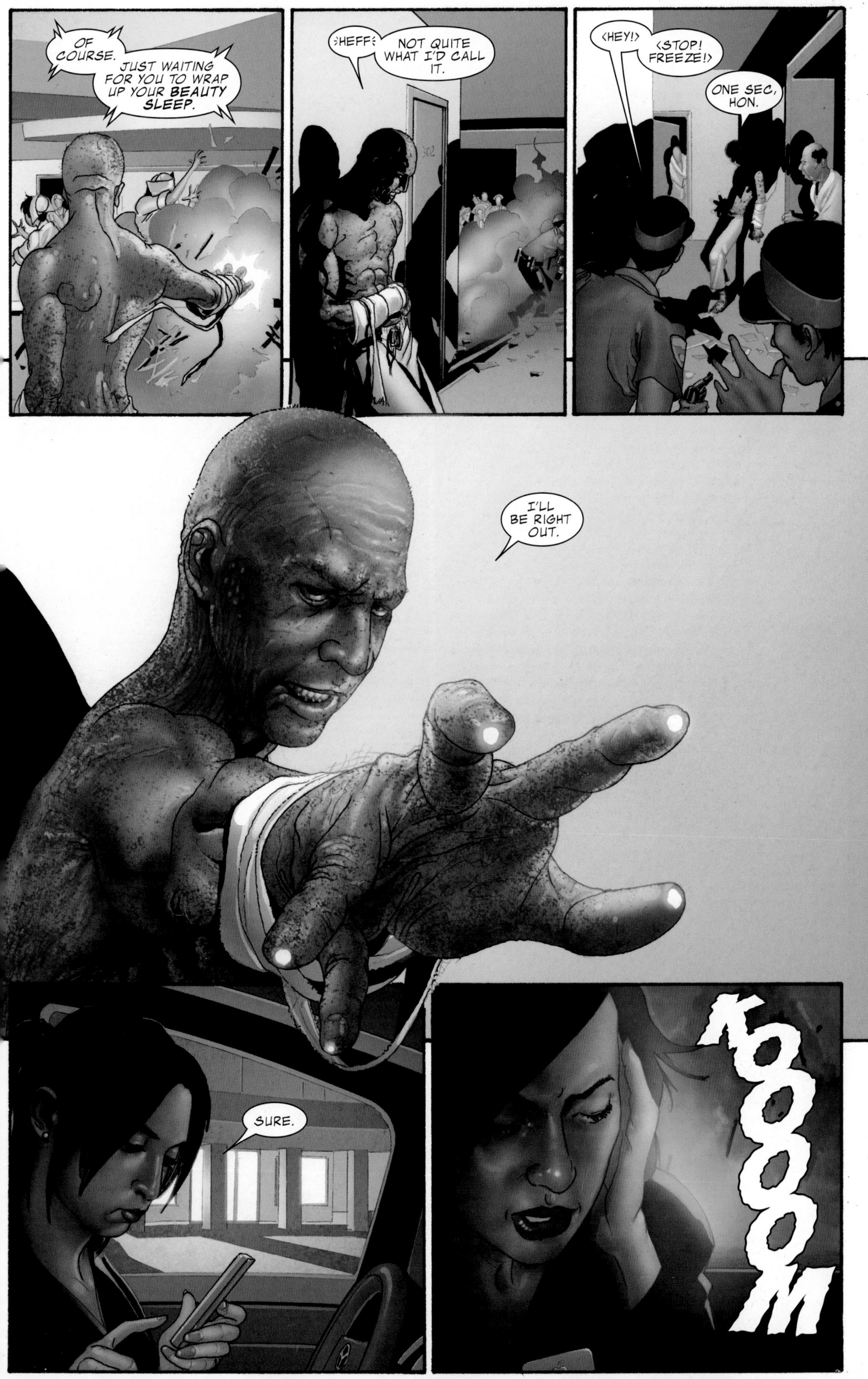
OF COURSE.
JUST WAITING FOR YOU TO WRAP UP YOUR BEAUTY SLEEP.
HEFF
NOT QUITE WHAT I'D CALL IT.
<HEY!>
<STOP! FREEZE!>
ONE SEC, HON.
I'LL BE RIGHT OUT.
SURE.
KOOOM

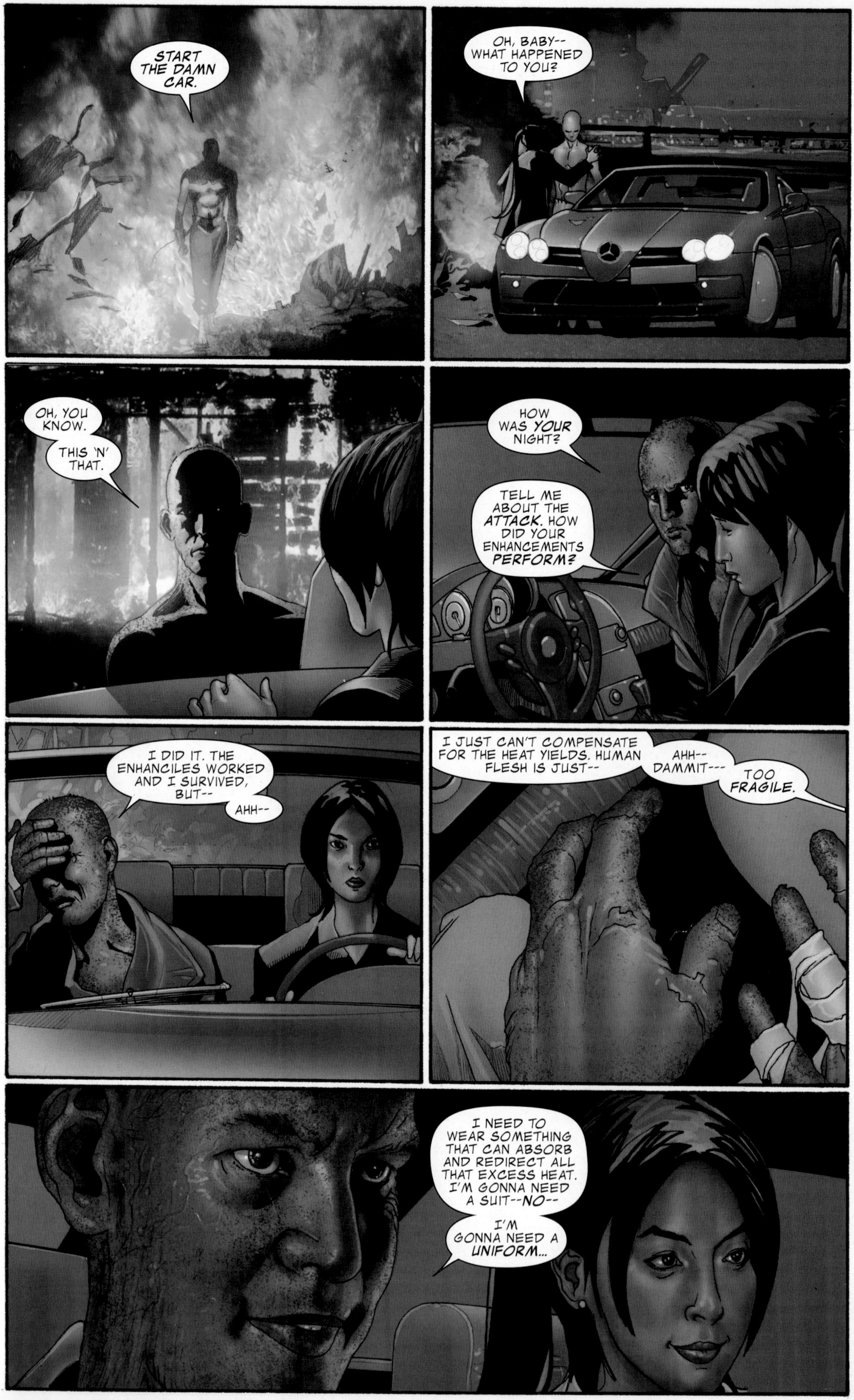
START THE DAMN CAR.
OH, BABY-- WHAT HAPPENED TO YOU?
OH, YOU KNOW.
THIS 'N' THAT.
HOW WAS YOUR NIGHT?
TELL ME ABOUT THE ATTACK. HOW DID YOUR ENHANCEMENTS PERFORM?
I DID IT. THE ENHANCILES WORKED AND I SURVIVED, BUT--
AHH--
I JUST CAN'T COMPENSATE FOR THE HEAT YIELDS. HUMAN FLESH IS JUST--
AHH-- DAMMIT---
TOO FRAGILE.
I NEED TO WEAR SOMETHING THAT CAN ABSORB AND REDIRECT ALL THAT EXCESS HEAT. I'M GONNA NEED A SUIT--NO--
I'M GONNA NEED A UNIFORM...

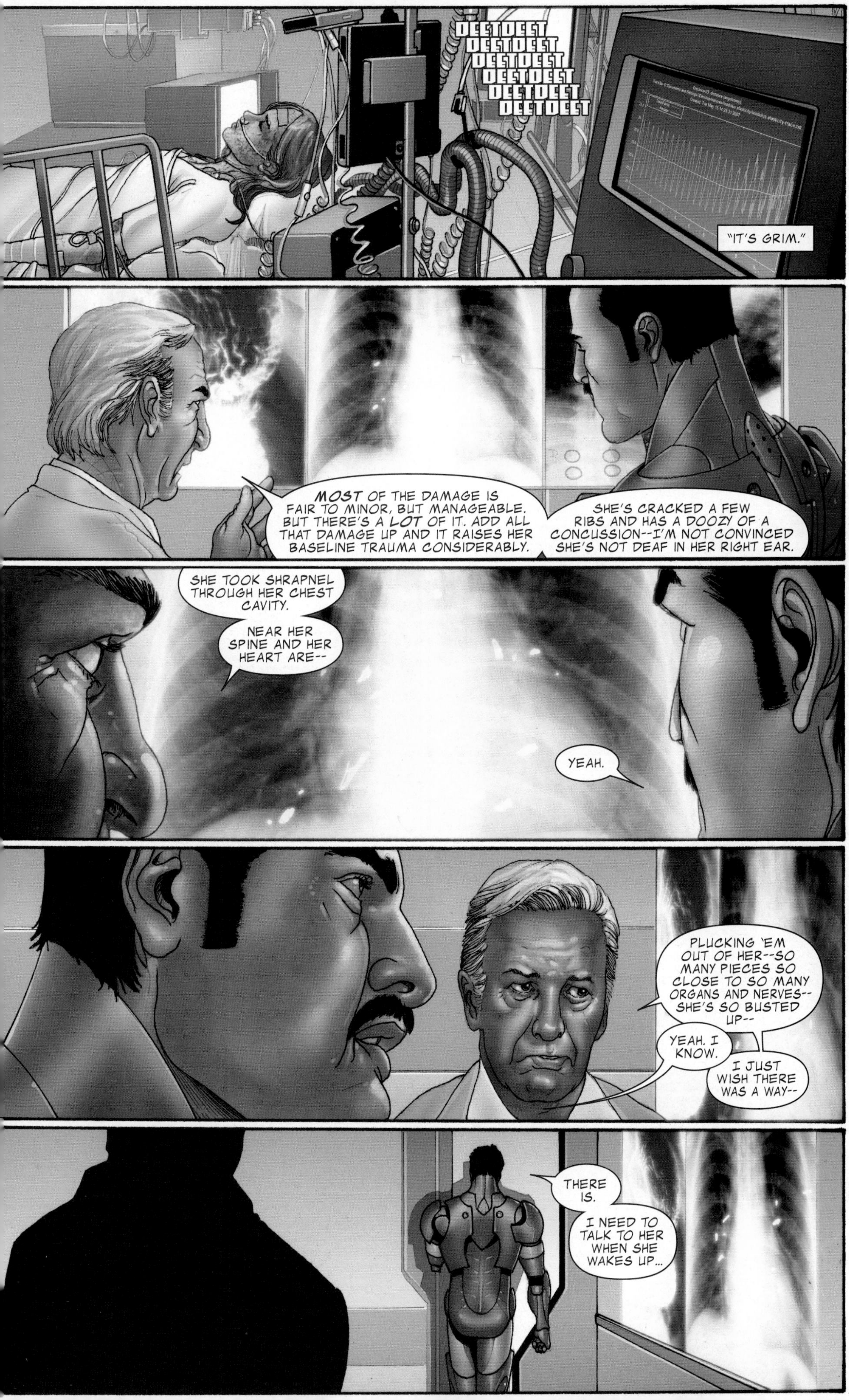
DEETDEET DEETDEET DEETDEET DEETDEET DEETDEET DEETDEET
"IT'S GRIM."
MOST OF THE DAMAGE IS FAIR TO MINOR, BUT MANAGEABLE. BUT THERE'S A LOT OF IT. ADD ALL THAT DAMAGE UP AND IT RAISES HER BASELINE TRAUMA CONSIDERABLY.
SHE'S CRACKED A FEW RIBS AND HAS A DOOZY OF A CONCUSSION--I'M NOT CONVINCED SHE'S NOT DEAF IN HER RIGHT EAR.
SHE TOOK SHRAPNEL THROUGH HER CHEST CAVITY.
NEAR HER SPINE AND HER HEART ARE--
YEAH.
PLUCKING 'EM OUT OF HER--SO MANY PIECES SO CLOSE TO SO MANY ORGANS AND NERVES--SHE'S SO BUSTED UP--
YEAH. I KNOW.
I JUST WISH THERE WAS A WAY--
THERE IS.
I NEED TO TALK TO HER WHEN SHE WAKES UP...

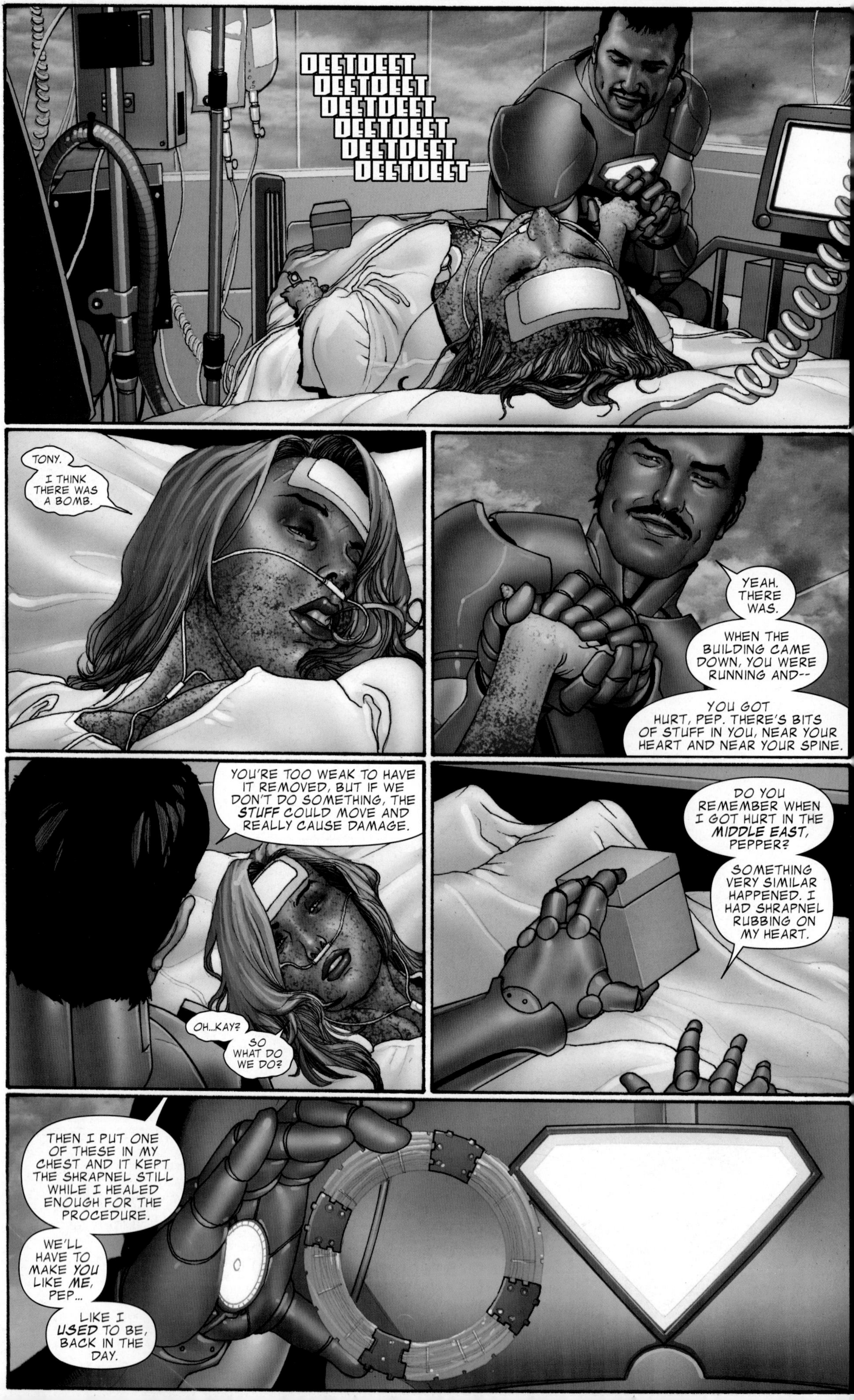
DEETDEET DEETDEET DEETDEET DEETDEET DEETDEET DEETDEET
TONY.
I THINK THERE WAS A BOMB.
YEAH. THERE WAS.
WHEN THE BUILDING CAME DOWN, YOU WERE RUNNING AND--
YOU GOT HURT, PEP. THERE'S BITS OF STUFF IN YOU, NEAR YOUR HEART AND NEAR YOUR SPINE.
YOU'RE TOO WEAK TO HAVE IT REMOVED, BUT IF WE DON'T DO SOMETHING, THE STUFF COULD MOVE AND REALLY CAUSE DAMAGE.
OH...KAY?
SO WHAT DO WE DO?
DO YOU REMEMBER WHEN I GOT HURT IN THE MIDDLE EAST, PEPPER?
SOMETHING VERY SIMILAR HAPPENED. I HAD SHRAPNEL RUBBING ON MY HEART.
THEN I PUT ONE OF THESE IN MY CHEST AND IT KEPT THE SHRAPNEL STILL WHILE I HEALED ENOUGH FOR THE PROCEDURE.
WE'LL HAVE TO MAKE YOU LIKE ME, PEP...
LIKE I USED TO BE, BACK IN THE DAY.

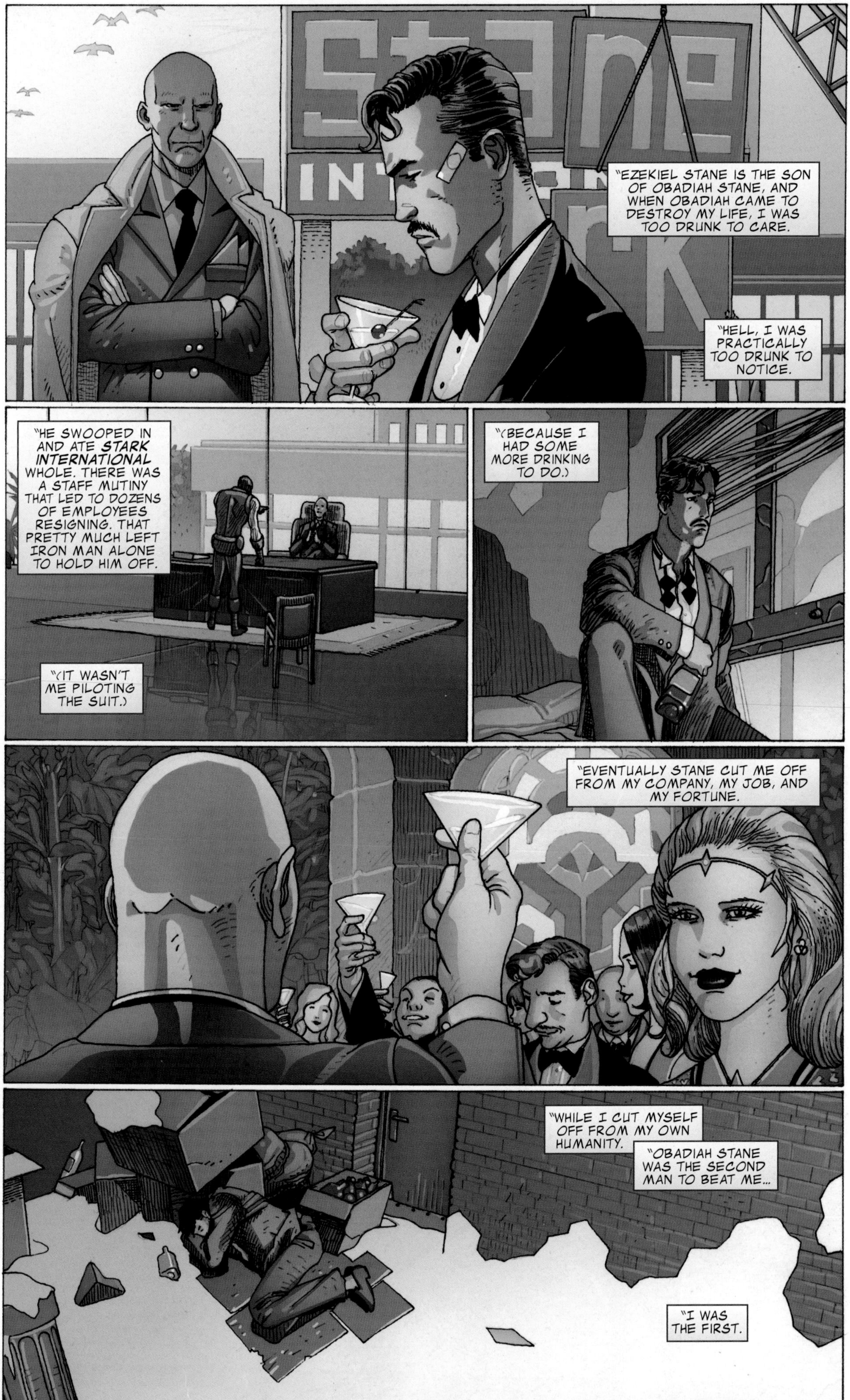
"EZEKIEL STANE IS THE SON OF OBADIAH STANE, AND WHEN OBADIAH CAME TO DESTROY MY LIFE, I WAS TOO DRUNK TO CARE.
"HELL, I WAS PRACTICALLY TOO DRUNK TO NOTICE.
"HE SWOOPED IN AND ATE STARK INTERNATIONAL WHOLE. THERE WAS A STAFF MUTINY THAT LED TO DOZENS OF EMPLOYEES RESIGNING. THAT PRETTY MUCH LEFT IRON MAN ALONE TO HOLD HIM OFF.
"(IT WASN'T ME PILOTING THE SUIT.)
"(BECAUSE I HAD SOME MORE DRINKING TO DO.)
"EVENTUALLY STANE CUT ME OFF FROM MY COMPANY, MY JOB, AND MY FORTUNE.
"WHILE I CUT MYSELF OFF FROM MY OWN HUMANITY.
"OBADIAH STANE WAS THE SECOND MAN TO BEAT ME...
"I WAS THE FIRST.

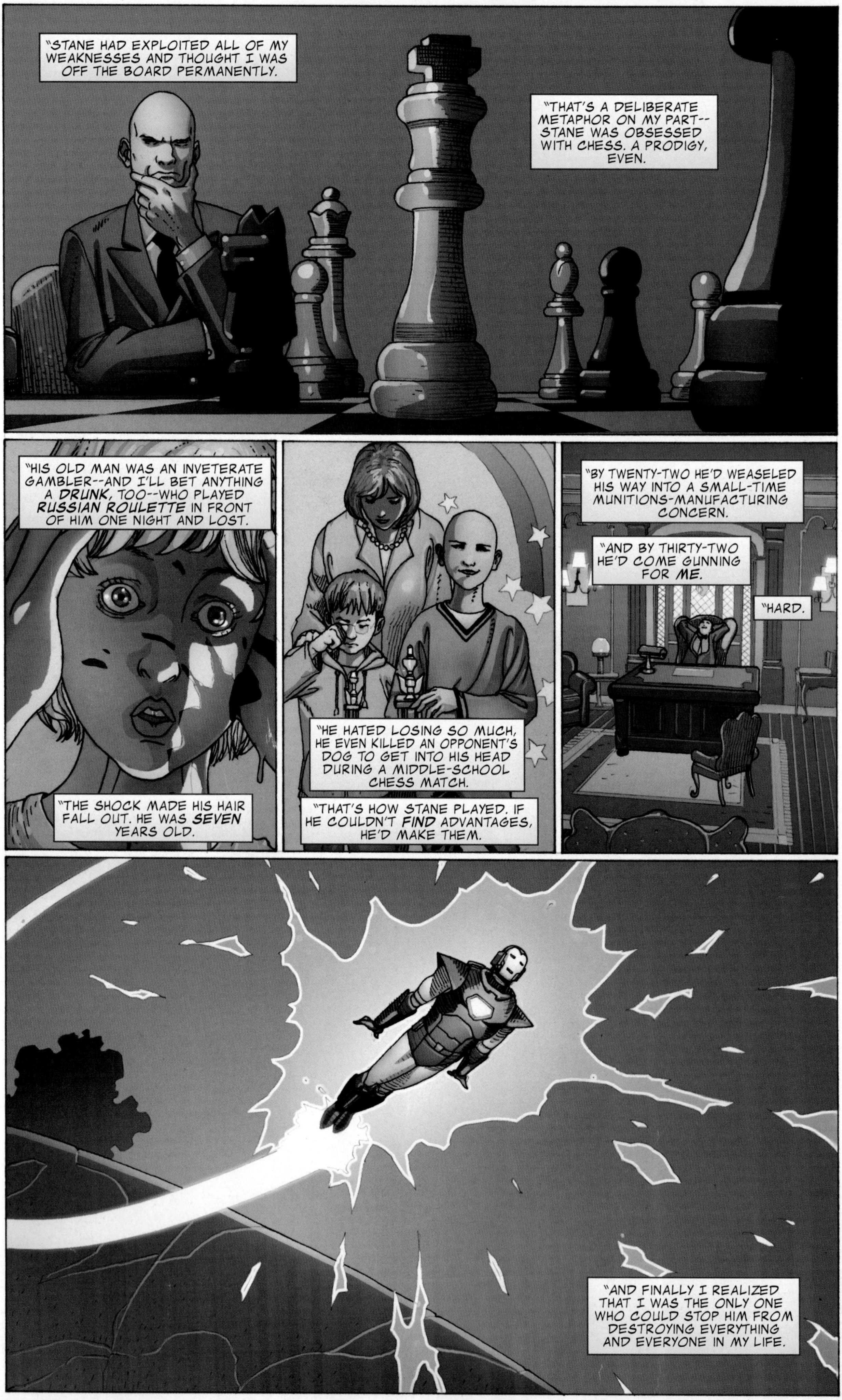
"STANE HAD EXPLOITED ALL OF MY WEAKNESSES AND THOUGHT I WAS OFF THE BOARD PERMANENTLY.
"THAT'S A DELIBERATE METAPHOR ON MY PART--STANE WAS OBSESSED WITH CHESS. A PRODIGY, EVEN.
"HIS OLD MAN WAS AN INVETERATE GAMBLER--AND I'LL BET ANYTHING A DRUNK, TOO--WHO PLAYED RUSSIAN ROULETTE IN FRONT OF HIM ONE NIGHT AND LOST.
"THE SHOCK MADE HIS HAIR FALL OUT. HE WAS SEVEN YEARS OLD.
"HE HATED LOSING SO MUCH, HE EVEN KILLED AN OPPONENT'S DOG TO GET INTO HIS HEAD DURING A MIDDLE-SCHOOL CHESS MATCH.
"THAT'S HOW STANE PLAYED. IF HE COULDN'T FIND ADVANTAGES, HE'D MAKE THEM.
"BY TWENTY-TWO HE'D WEASELED HIS WAY INTO A SMALL-TIME MUNITIONS-MANUFACTURING CONCERN.
"AND BY THIRTY-TWO HE'D COME GUNNING FOR ME.
"HARD.
"AND FINALLY I REALIZED THAT I WAS THE ONLY ONE WHO COULD STOP HIM FROM DESTROYING EVERYTHING AND EVERYONE IN MY LIFE.

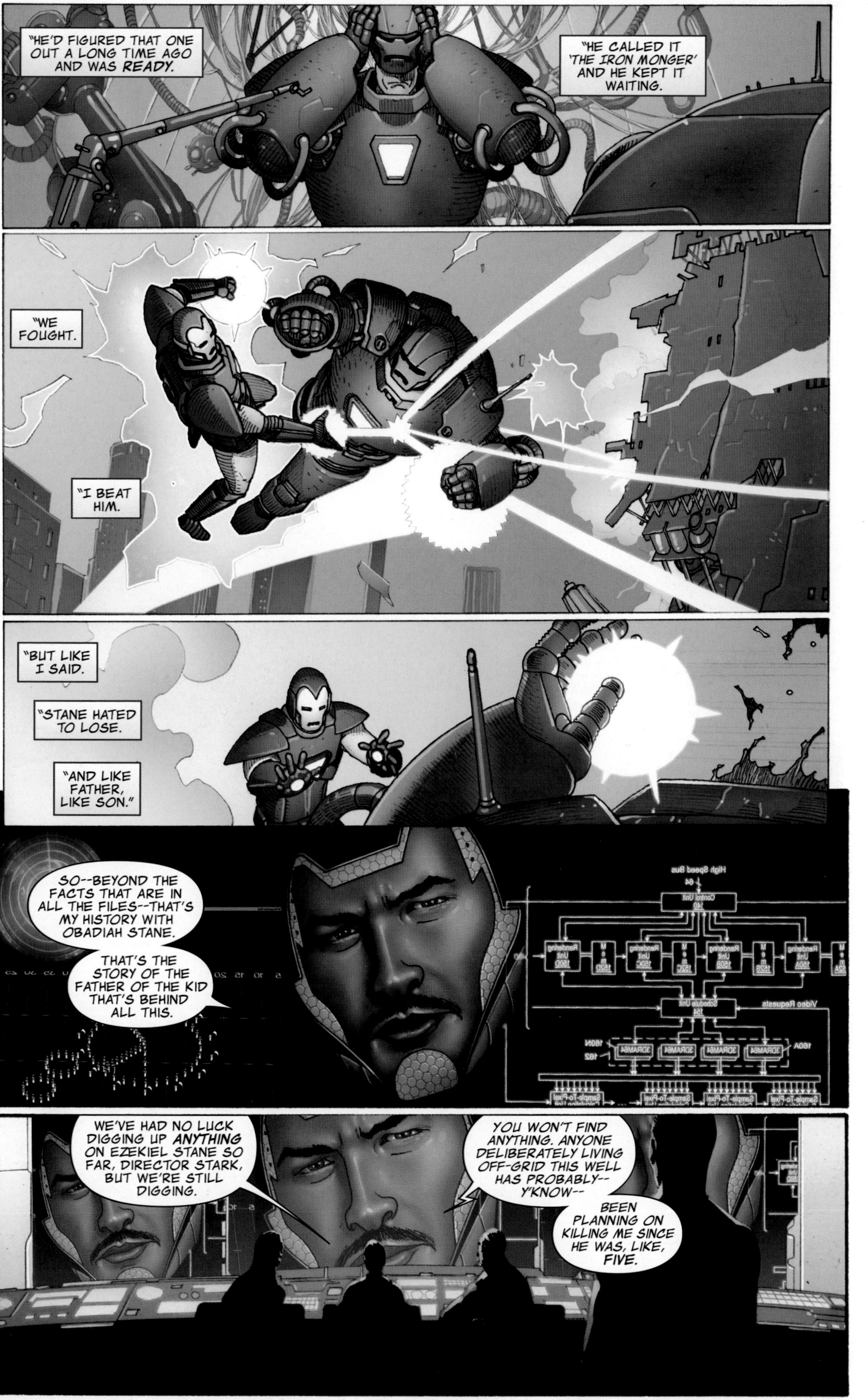
"HE'D FIGURED THAT ONE OUT A LONG TIME AGO AND WAS READY.
"HE CALLED IT 'THE IRON MONGER' AND HE KEPT IT WAITING.
"WE FOUGHT.
"I BEAT HIM.
"BUT LIKE I SAID.
"STANE HATED TO LOSE.
"AND LIKE FATHER, LIKE SON."
SO--BEYOND THE FACTS THAT ARE IN ALL THE FILES--THAT'S MY HISTORY WITH OBADIAH STANE.
THAT'S THE STORY OF THE FATHER OF THE KID THAT'S BEHIND ALL THIS.
WE'VE HAD NO LUCK DIGGING UP ANYTHING ON EZEKIEL STANE SO FAR, DIRECTOR STARK, BUT WE'RE STILL DIGGING.
YOU WON'T FIND ANYTHING. ANYONE DELIBERATELY LIVING OFF-GRID THIS WELL HAS PROBABLY-- Y'KNOW--
BEEN PLANNING ON KILLING ME SINCE HE WAS, LIKE, FIVE.

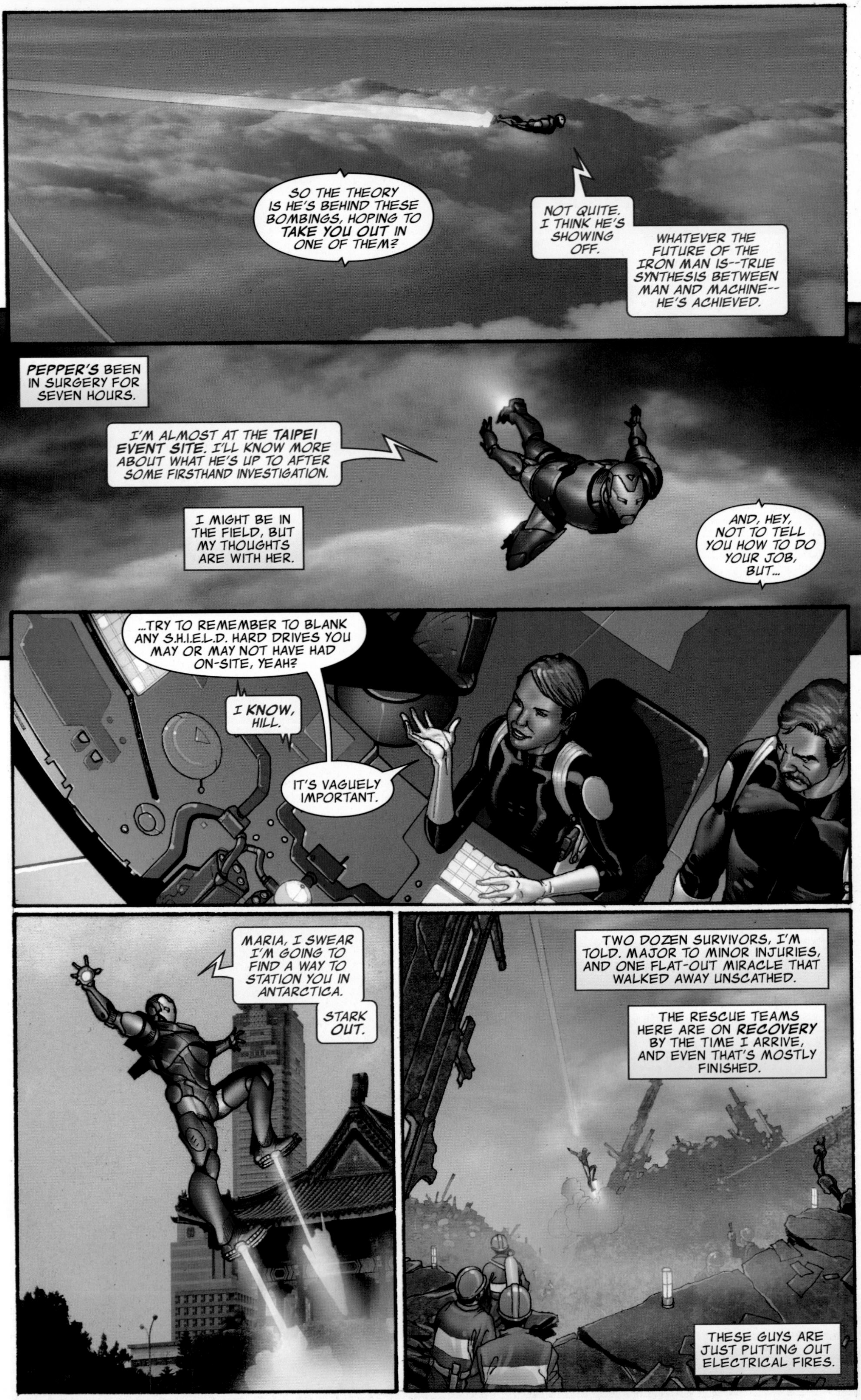
SO THE THEORY IS HE'S BEHIND THESE BOMBINGS, HOPING TO TAKE YOU OUT IN ONE OF THEM?
NOT QUITE. I THINK HE'S SHOWING OFF.
WHATEVER THE FUTURE OF THE IRON MAN IS--TRUE SYNTHESIS BETWEEN MAN AND MACHINE--HE'S ACHIEVED.
PEPPER'S BEEN IN SURGERY FOR SEVEN HOURS.
I'M ALMOST AT THE TAIPEI EVENT SITE. I'LL KNOW MORE ABOUT WHAT HE'S UP TO AFTER SOME FIRSTHAND INVESTIGATION.
I MIGHT BE IN THE FIELD, BUT MY THOUGHTS ARE WITH HER.
AND, HEY, NOT TO TELL YOU HOW TO DO YOUR JOB, BUT...
...TRY TO REMEMBER TO BLANK ANY S.H.I.E.L.D. HARD DRIVES YOU MAY OR MAY NOT HAVE HAD ON-SITE, YEAH?
I KNOW, HILL.
IT'S VAGUELY IMPORTANT.
MARIA, I SWEAR I'M GOING TO FIND A WAY TO STATION YOU IN ANTARCTICA.
STARK OUT.
TWO DOZEN SURVIVORS, I'M TOLD. MAJOR TO MINOR INJURIES, AND ONE FLAT-OUT MIRACLE THAT WALKED AWAY UNSCATHED.
THE RESCUE TEAMS HERE ARE ON RECOVERY BY THE TIME I ARRIVE, AND EVEN THAT'S MOSTLY FINISHED.
THESE GUYS ARE JUST PUTTING OUT ELECTRICAL FIRES.

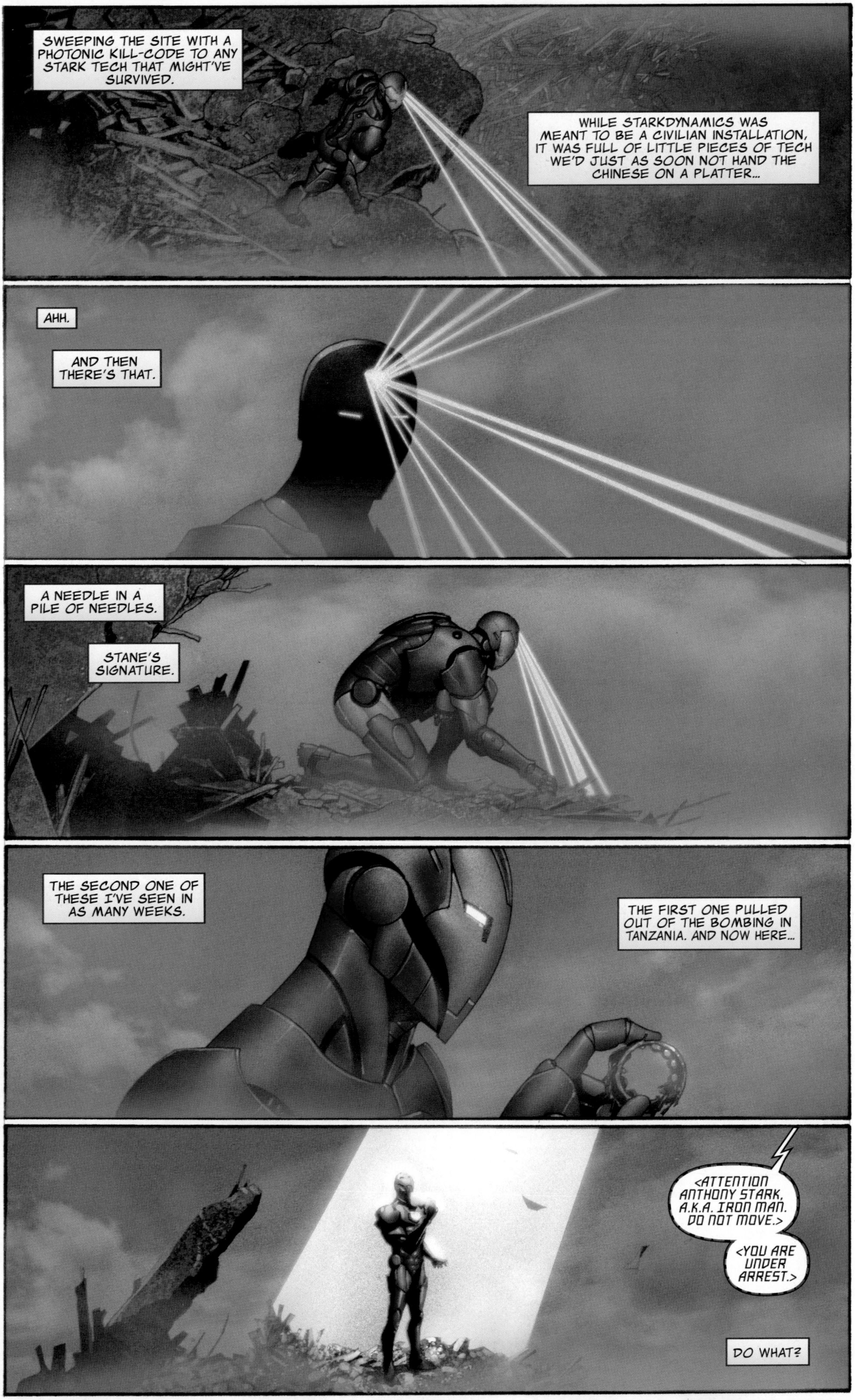
SWEEPING THE SITE WITH A PHOTONIC KILL-CODE TO ANY STARK TECH THAT MIGHT'VE SURVIVED.
WHILE STARKDYNAMICS WAS MEANT TO BE A CIVILIAN INSTALLATION, IT WAS FULL OF LITTLE PIECES OF TECH WE'D JUST AS SOON NOT HAND THE CHINESE ON A PLATTER...
AHH.
AND THEN THERE'S THAT.
A NEEDLE IN A PILE OF NEEDLES.
STANE'S SIGNATURE.
THE SECOND ONE OF THESE I'VE SEEN IN AS MANY WEEKS.
THE FIRST ONE PULLED OUT OF THE BOMBING IN TANZANIA. AND NOW HERE...
<ATTENTION ANTHONY STARK, A.K.A. IRON MAN. DO NOT MOVE.>
<YOU ARE UNDER ARREST.>
DO WHAT?

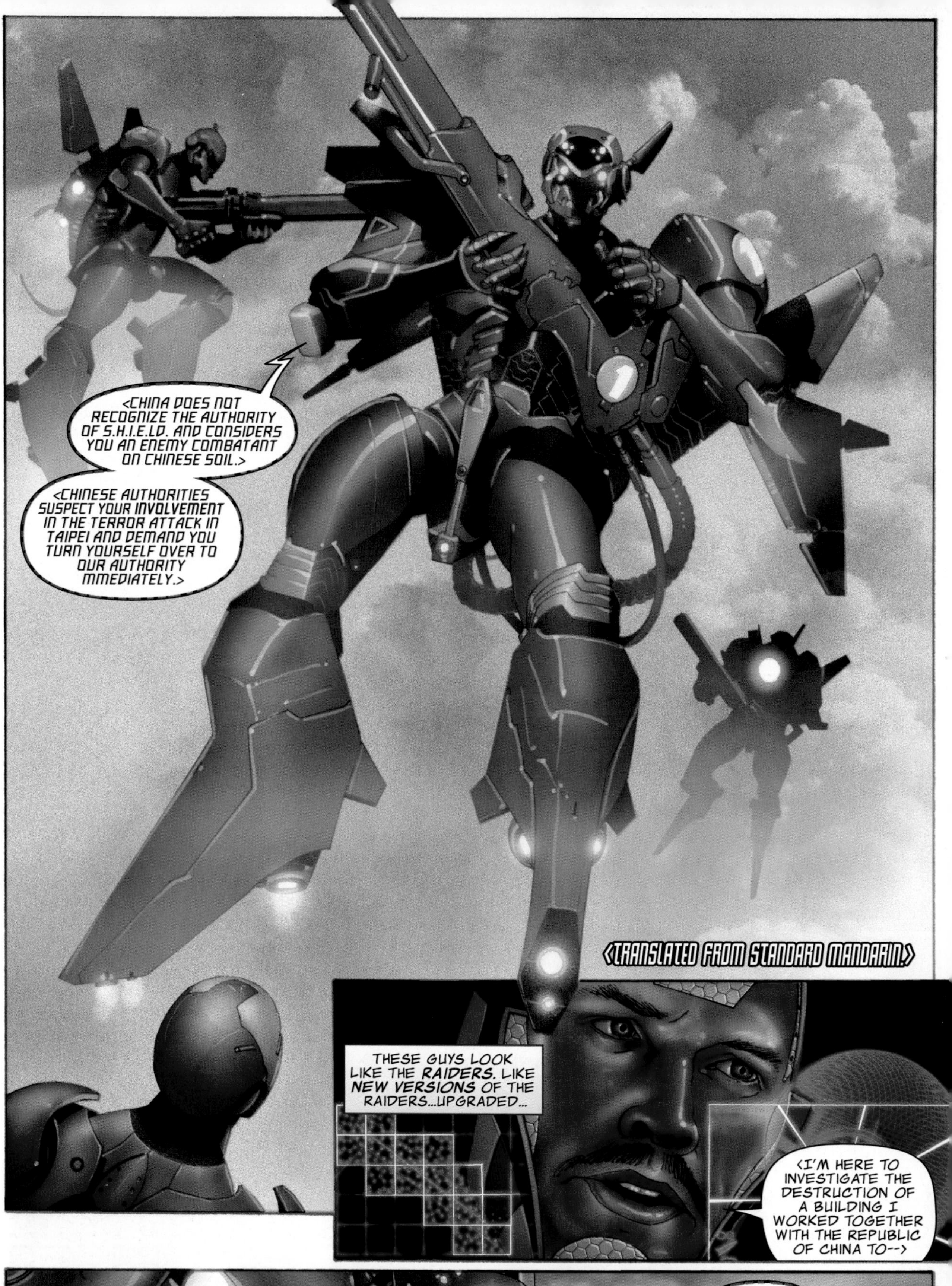
<CHINA DOES NOT RECOGNIZE THE AUTHORITY OF S.H.I.E.L.D. AND CONSIDERS YOU AN ENEMY COMBATANT ON CHINESE SOIL.>
<CHINESE AUTHORITIES SUSPECT YOUR INVOLVEMENT IN THE TERROR ATTACK IN TAIPEI AND DEMAND YOU TURN YOURSELF OVER TO OUR AUTHORITY MMEDIATELY.>
<TRANSLATED FROM STANDARD MANDARIN.>

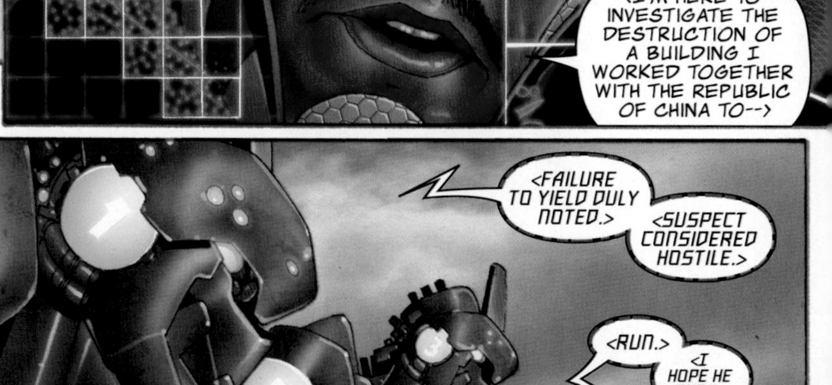
THESE GUYS LOOK LIKE THE RAIDERS. LIKE NEW VERSIONS OF THE RAIDERS...UPGRADED...
<I'M HERE TO INVESTIGATE THE DESTRUCTION OF A BUILDING I WORKED TOGETHER WITH THE REPUBLIC OF CHINA TO-->

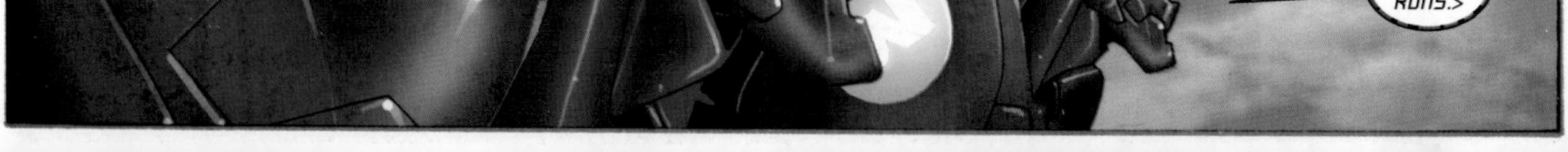
<FAILURE TO YIELD DULY NOTED.>
<SUSPECT CONSIDERED HOSTILE.>
<RUN.>
<I HOPE HE RUNS.>

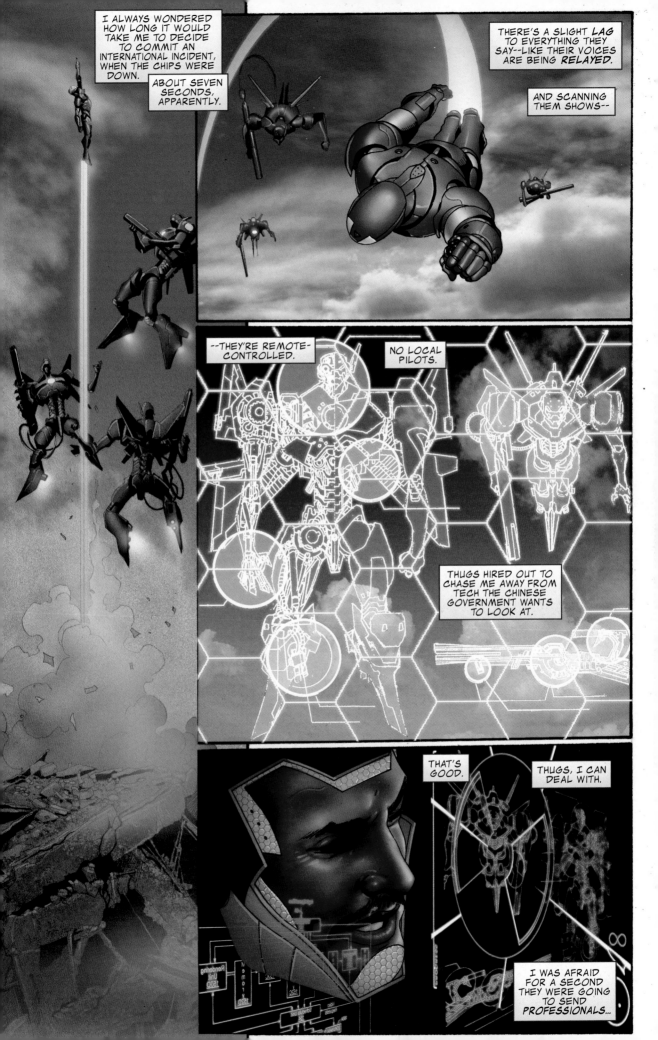

I ALWAYS WONDERED HOW LONG IT WOULD TAKE ME TO DECIDE TO COMMIT AN INTERNATIONAL INCIDENT, WHEN THE CHIPS WERE DOWN.

ABOUT SEVEN SECONDS, APPARENTLY.

THERE'S A SLIGHT *LAG* TO EVERYTHING THEY SAY--LIKE THEIR VOICES ARE BEING *RELAYED.*

AND SCANNING THEM SHOWS--

--THEY'RE REMOTE-CONTROLLED.

NO LOCAL PILOTS.

THUGS HIRED OUT TO CHASE ME AWAY FROM TECH THE CHINESE GOVERNMENT WANTS TO LOOK AT.

THAT'S GOOD.

THUGS, I CAN DEAL WITH.

I WAS AFRAID FOR A SECOND THEY WERE GOING TO SEND PROFESSIONALS...

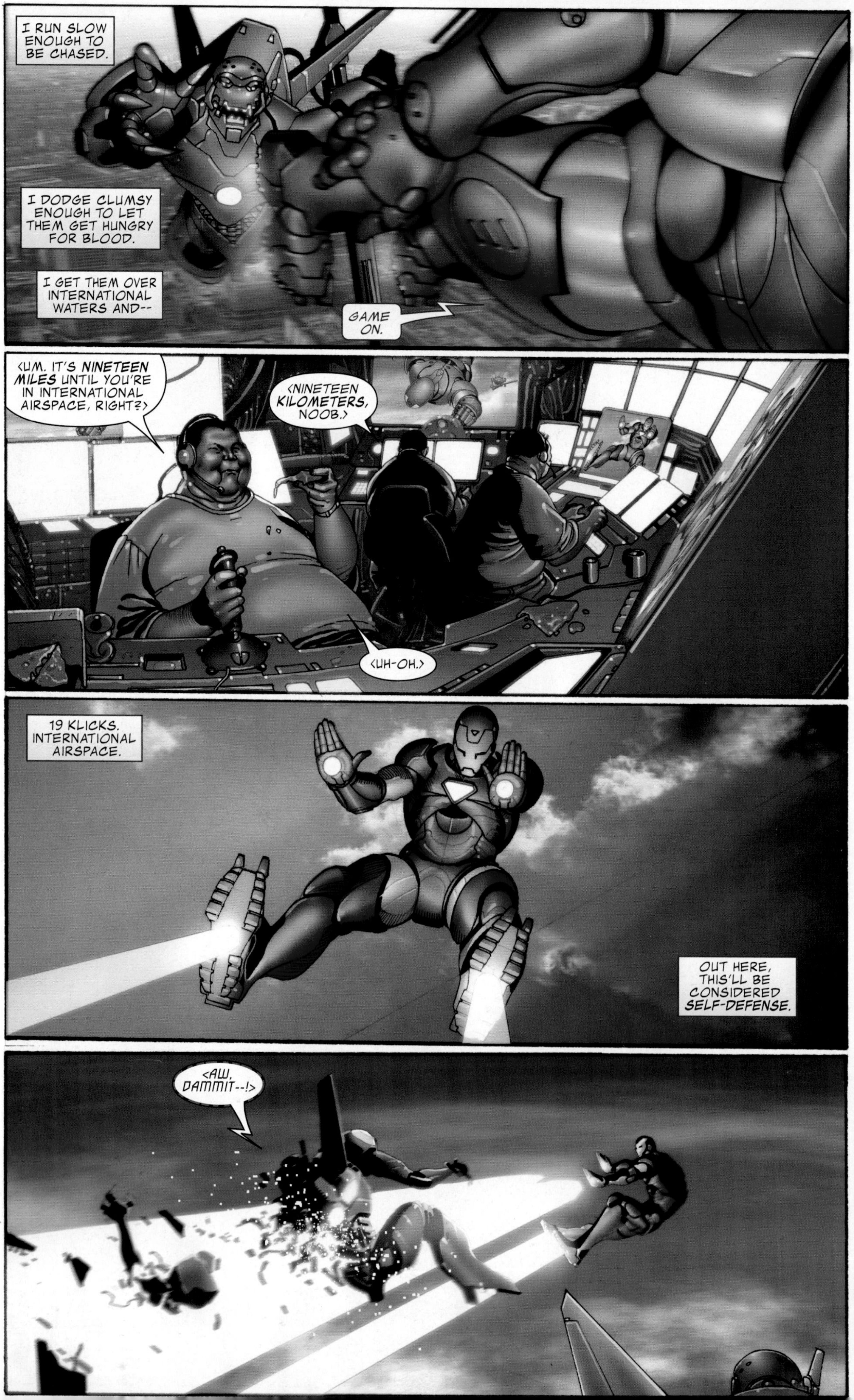

I RUN SLOW ENOUGH TO BE CHASED.
I DODGE CLUMSY ENOUGH TO LET THEM GET HUNGRY FOR BLOOD.
I GET THEM OVER INTERNATIONAL WATERS AND--
GAME ON.
<UM. IT'S NINETEEN MILES UNTIL YOU'RE IN INTERNATIONAL AIRSPACE, RIGHT?>
<NINETEEN KILOMETERS, NOOB.>
<UH-OH.>
19 KLICKS. INTERNATIONAL AIRSPACE.
OUT HERE, THIS'LL BE CONSIDERED SELF-DEFENSE.
<AW, DAMMIT--!>

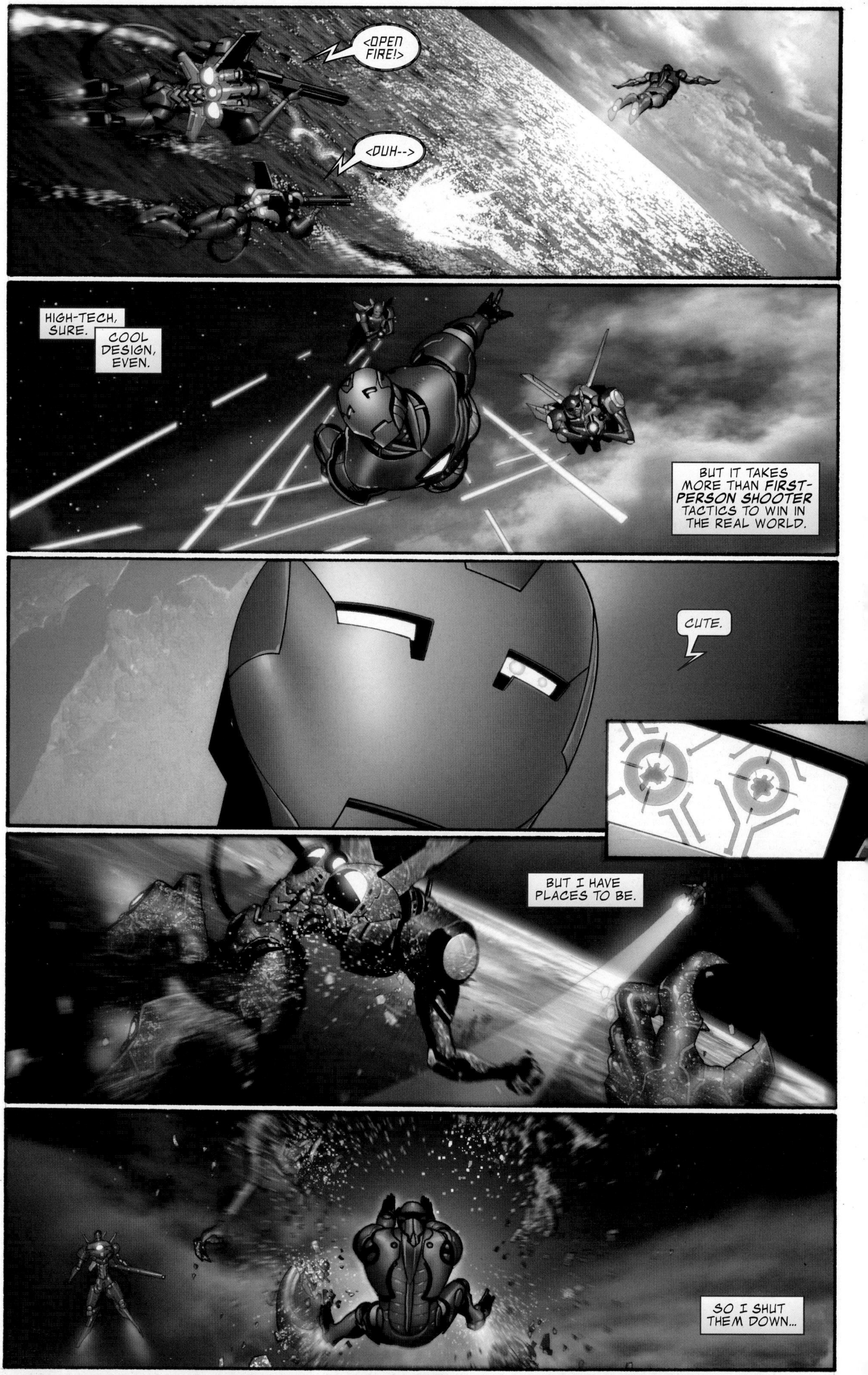
<OPEN FIRE!>
<DUH-->
HIGH-TECH, SURE.
COOL DESIGN, EVEN.
BUT IT TAKES MORE THAN FIRST-PERSON SHOOTER TACTICS TO WIN IN THE REAL WORLD.
CUTE.
BUT I HAVE PLACES TO BE.
SO I SHUT THEM DOWN...

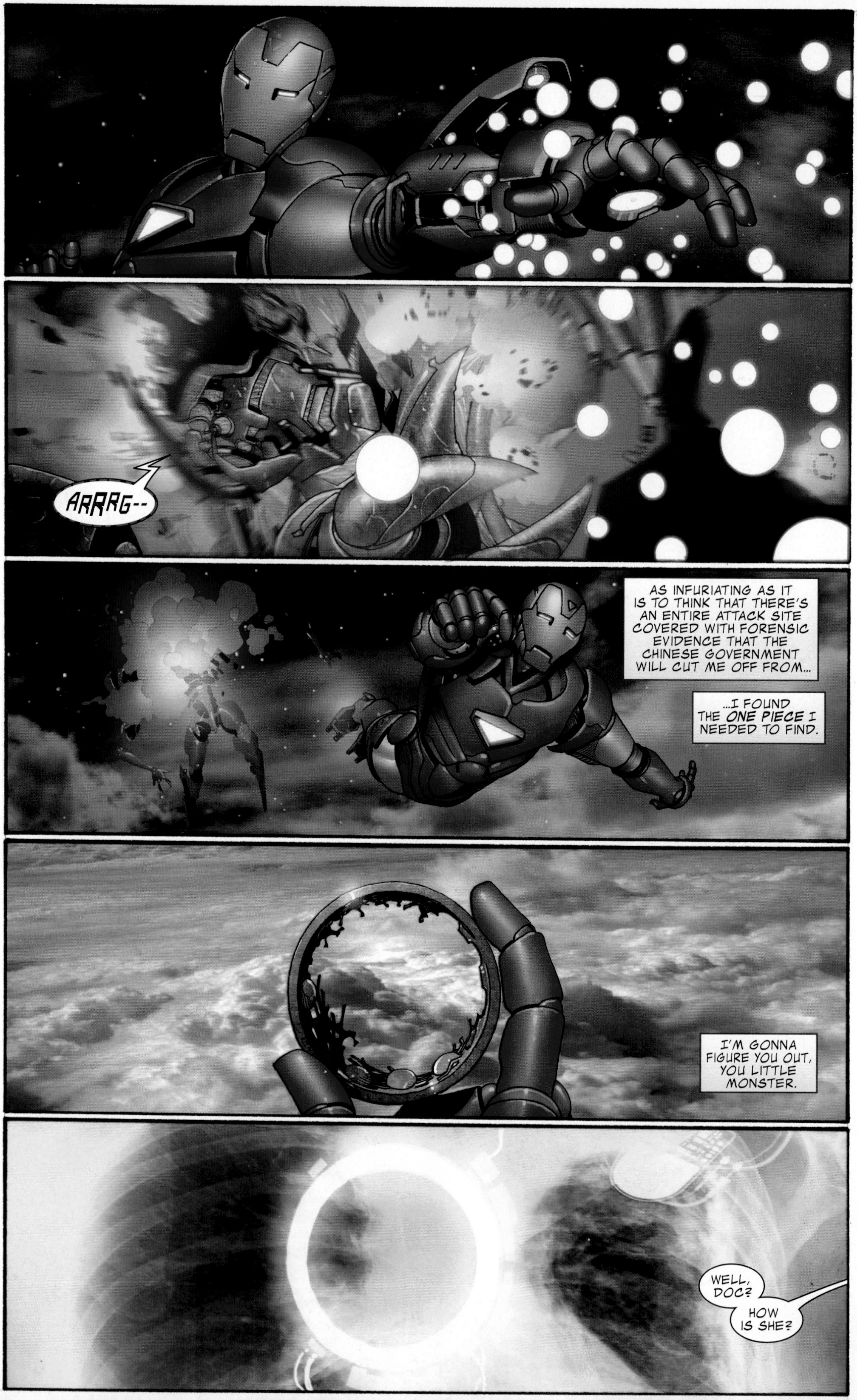

ARRRG--
AS INFURIATING AS IT IS TO THINK THAT THERE'S AN ENTIRE ATTACK SITE COVERED WITH FORENSIC EVIDENCE THAT THE CHINESE GOVERNMENT WILL CUT ME OFF FROM...
...I FOUND THE ONE PIECE I NEEDED TO FIND.
I'M GONNA FIGURE YOU OUT, YOU LITTLE MONSTER.
WELL, DOC?
HOW IS SHE?

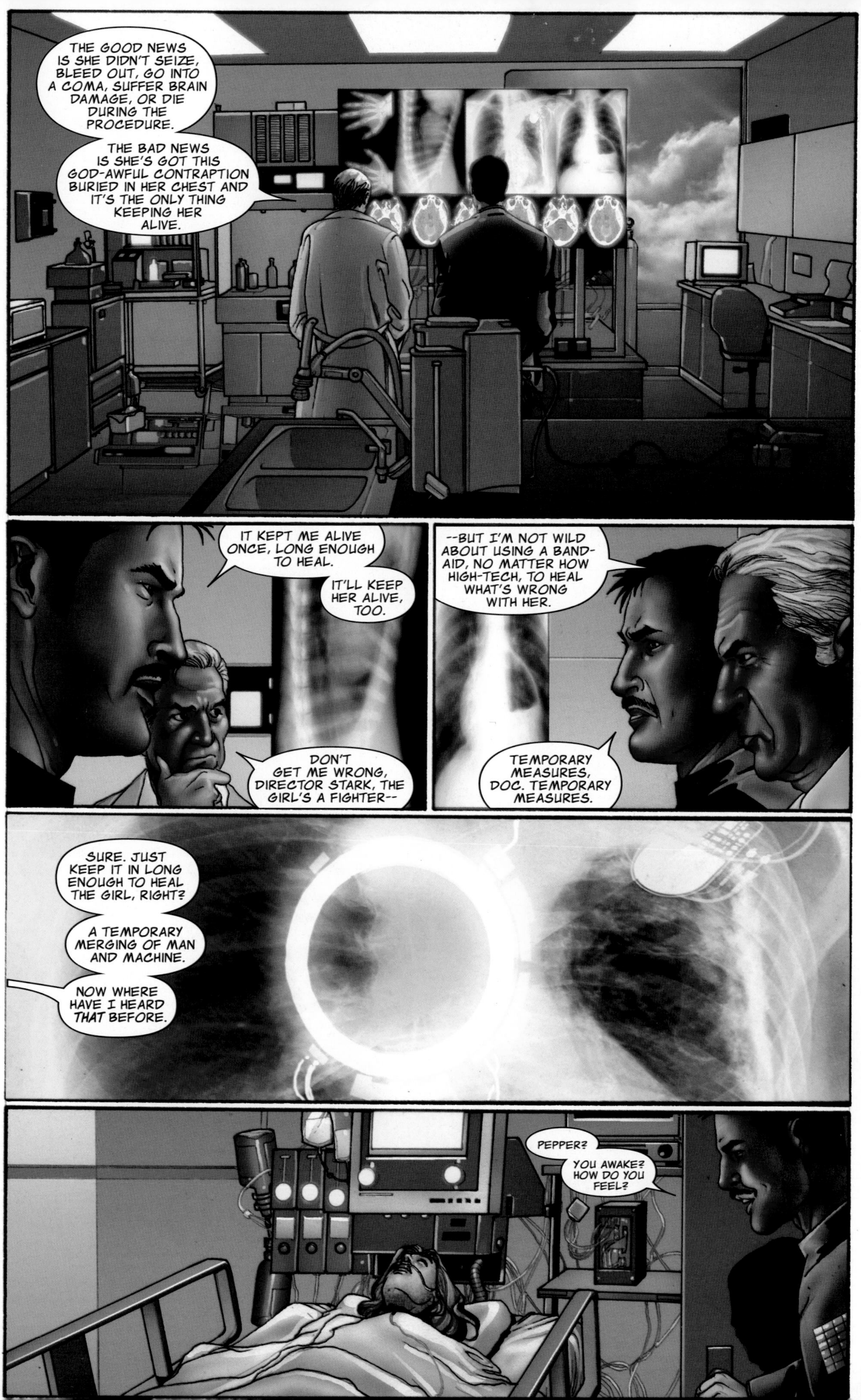
THE GOOD NEWS IS SHE DIDN'T SEIZE, BLEED OUT, GO INTO A COMA, SUFFER BRAIN DAMAGE, OR DIE DURING THE PROCEDURE.
THE BAD NEWS IS SHE'S GOT THIS GOD-AWFUL CONTRAPTION BURIED IN HER CHEST AND IT'S THE ONLY THING KEEPING HER ALIVE.
IT KEPT ME ALIVE ONCE, LONG ENOUGH TO HEAL.
IT'LL KEEP HER ALIVE, TOO.
DON'T GET ME WRONG, DIRECTOR STARK, THE GIRL'S A FIGHTER--
--BUT I'M NOT WILD ABOUT USING A BAND-AID, NO MATTER HOW HIGH-TECH, TO HEAL WHAT'S WRONG WITH HER.
TEMPORARY MEASURES, DOC. TEMPORARY MEASURES.
SURE. JUST KEEP IT IN LONG ENOUGH TO HEAL THE GIRL, RIGHT?
A TEMPORARY MERGING OF MAN AND MACHINE.
NOW WHERE HAVE I HEARD *THAT* BEFORE.
PEPPER?
YOU AWAKE? HOW DO YOU FEEL?

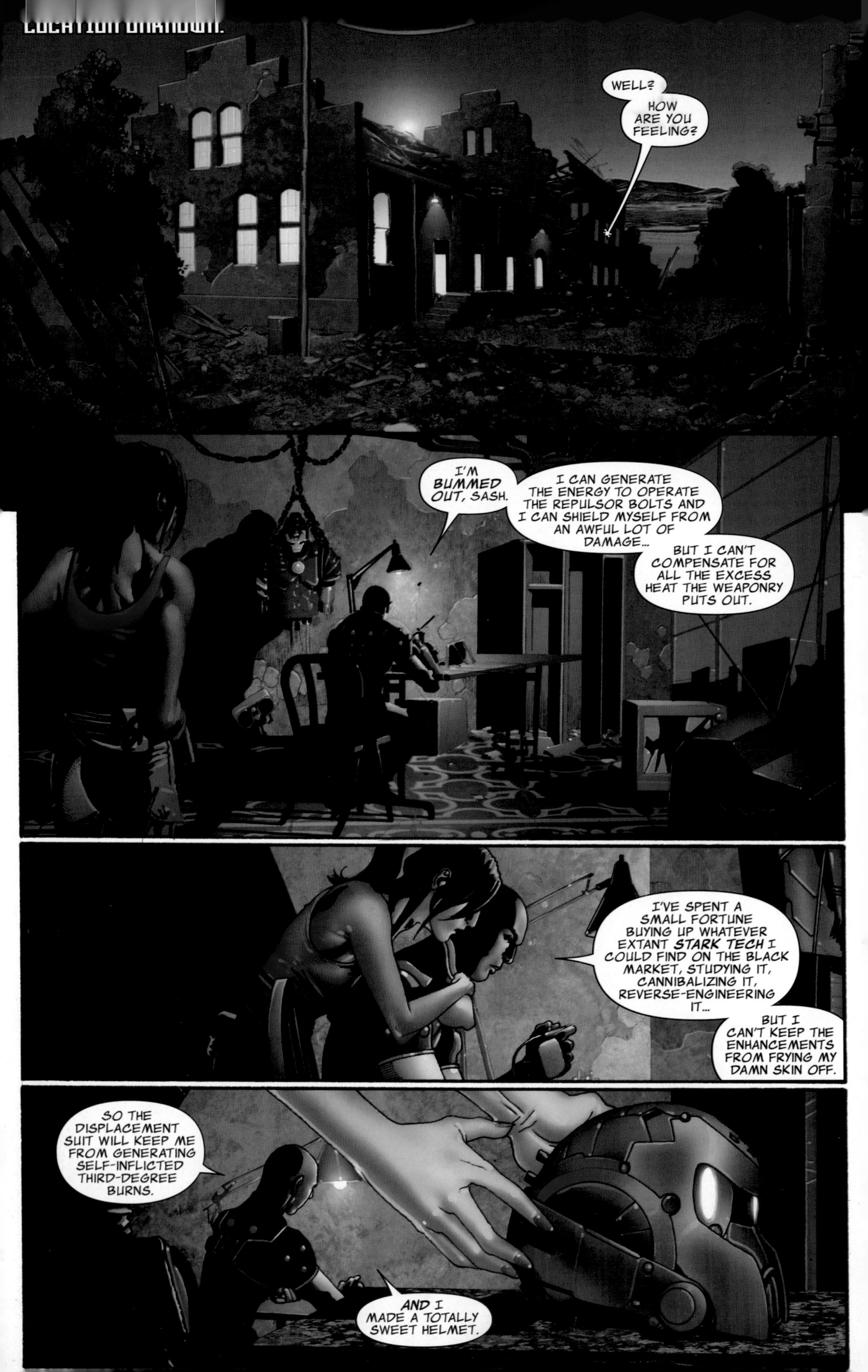
LOCATION UNKNOWN.
WELL?
HOW ARE YOU FEELING?
I'M BUMMED OUT, SASH.
I CAN GENERATE THE ENERGY TO OPERATE THE REPULSOR BOLTS AND I CAN SHIELD MYSELF FROM AN AWFUL LOT OF DAMAGE...
BUT I CAN'T COMPENSATE FOR ALL THE EXCESS HEAT THE WEAPONRY PUTS OUT.
I'VE SPENT A SMALL FORTUNE BUYING UP WHATEVER EXTANT STARK TECH I COULD FIND ON THE BLACK MARKET, STUDYING IT, CANNIBALIZING IT, REVERSE-ENGINEERING IT...
BUT I CAN'T KEEP THE ENHANCEMENTS FROM FRYING MY DAMN SKIN OFF.
SO THE DISPLACEMENT SUIT WILL KEEP ME FROM GENERATING SELF-INFLICTED THIRD-DEGREE BURNS.
AND I MADE A TOTALLY SWEET HELMET.

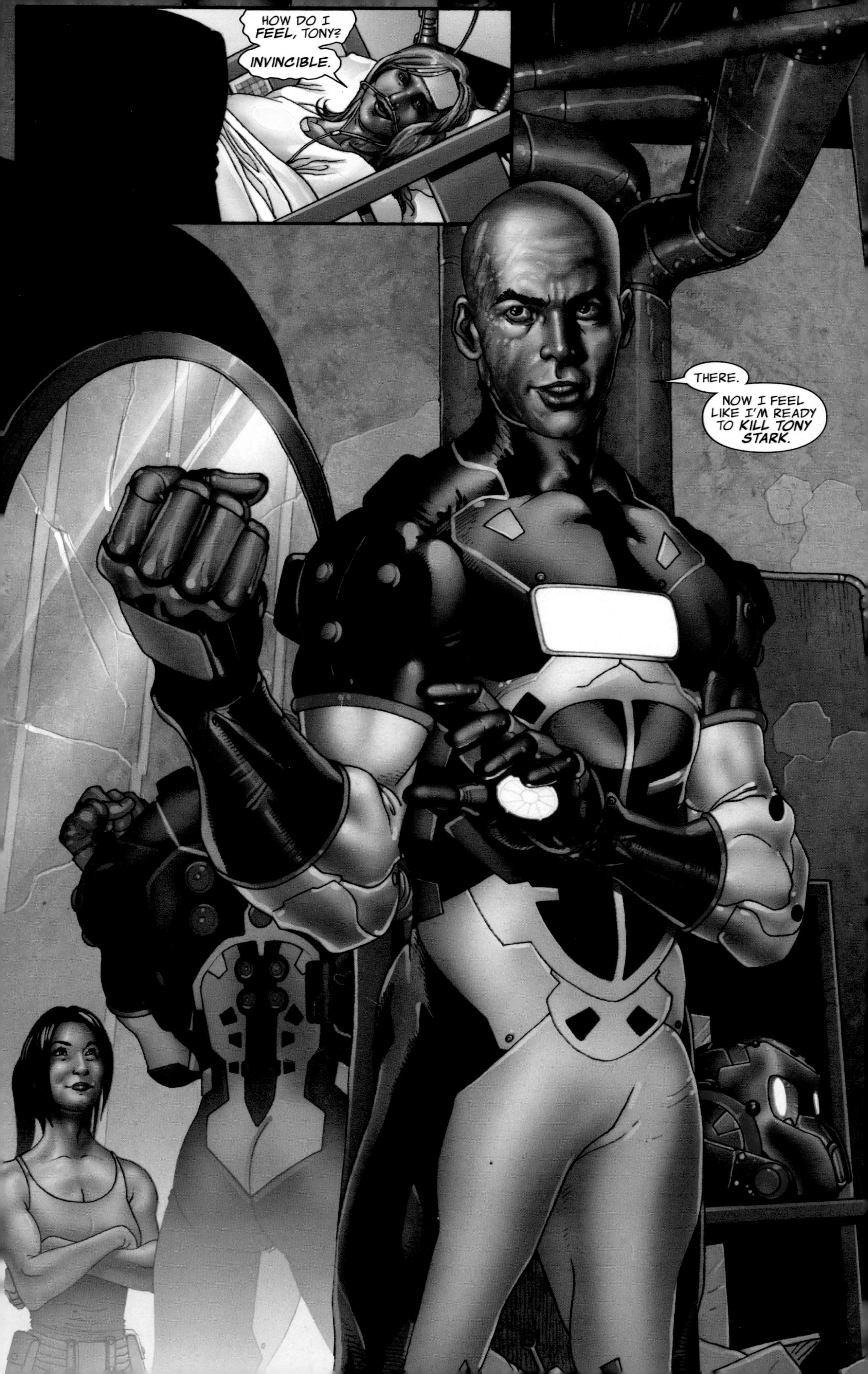
HOW DO I FEEL, TONY?
INVINCIBLE.
THERE.
NOW I FEEL LIKE I'M READY TO KILL TONY STARK.

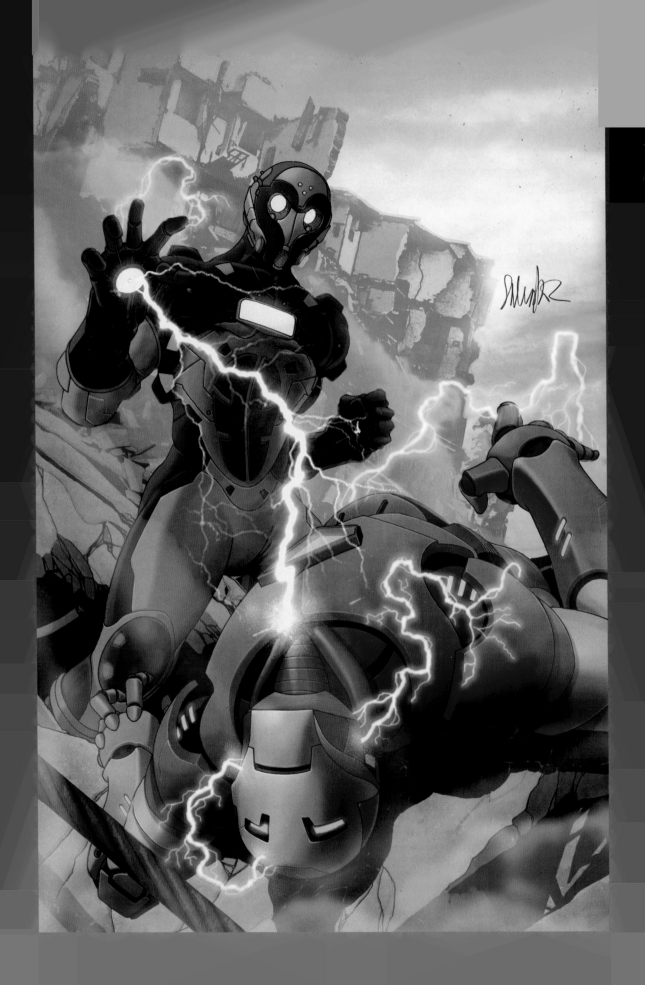

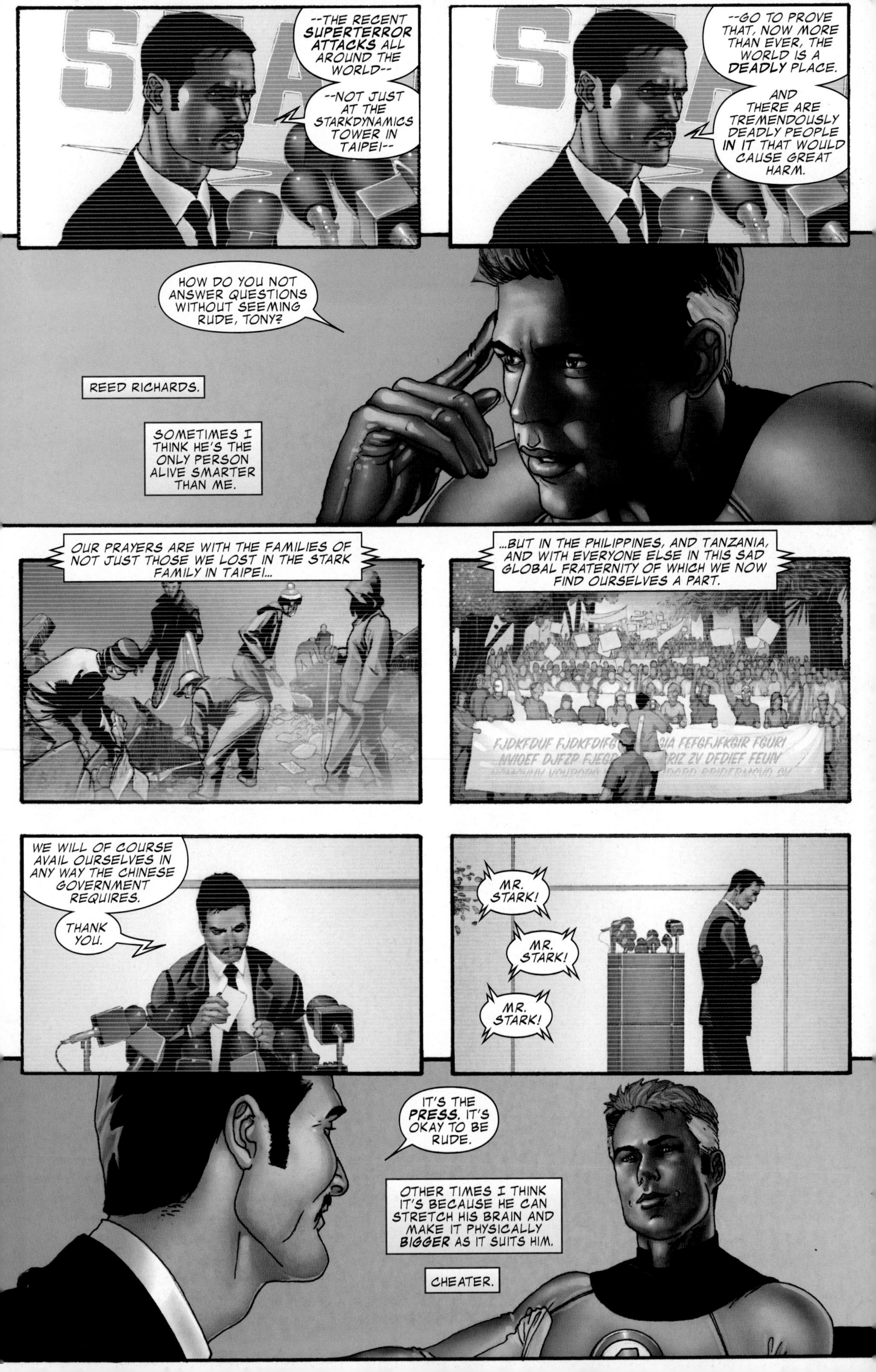
--THE RECENT SUPERTERROR ATTACKS ALL AROUND THE WORLD--
--NOT JUST AT THE STARKDYNAMICS TOWER IN TAIPEI--
--GO TO PROVE THAT, NOW MORE THAN EVER, THE WORLD IS A DEADLY PLACE.
AND THERE ARE TREMENDOUSLY DEADLY PEOPLE IN IT THAT WOULD CAUSE GREAT HARM.
HOW DO YOU NOT ANSWER QUESTIONS WITHOUT SEEMING RUDE, TONY?
REED RICHARDS.
SOMETIMES I THINK HE'S THE ONLY PERSON ALIVE SMARTER THAN ME.
OUR PRAYERS ARE WITH THE FAMILIES OF NOT JUST THOSE WE LOST IN THE STARK FAMILY IN TAIPEI...
...BUT IN THE PHILIPPINES, AND TANZANIA, AND WITH EVERYONE ELSE IN THIS SAD GLOBAL FRATERNITY OF WHICH WE NOW FIND OURSELVES A PART.
WE WILL OF COURSE AVAIL OURSELVES IN ANY WAY THE CHINESE GOVERNMENT REQUIRES.
THANK YOU.
MR. STARK!
MR. STARK!
MR. STARK!
IT'S THE PRESS. IT'S OKAY TO BE RUDE.
OTHER TIMES I THINK IT'S BECAUSE HE CAN STRETCH HIS BRAIN AND MAKE IT PHYSICALLY BIGGER AS IT SUITS HIM.
CHEATER.

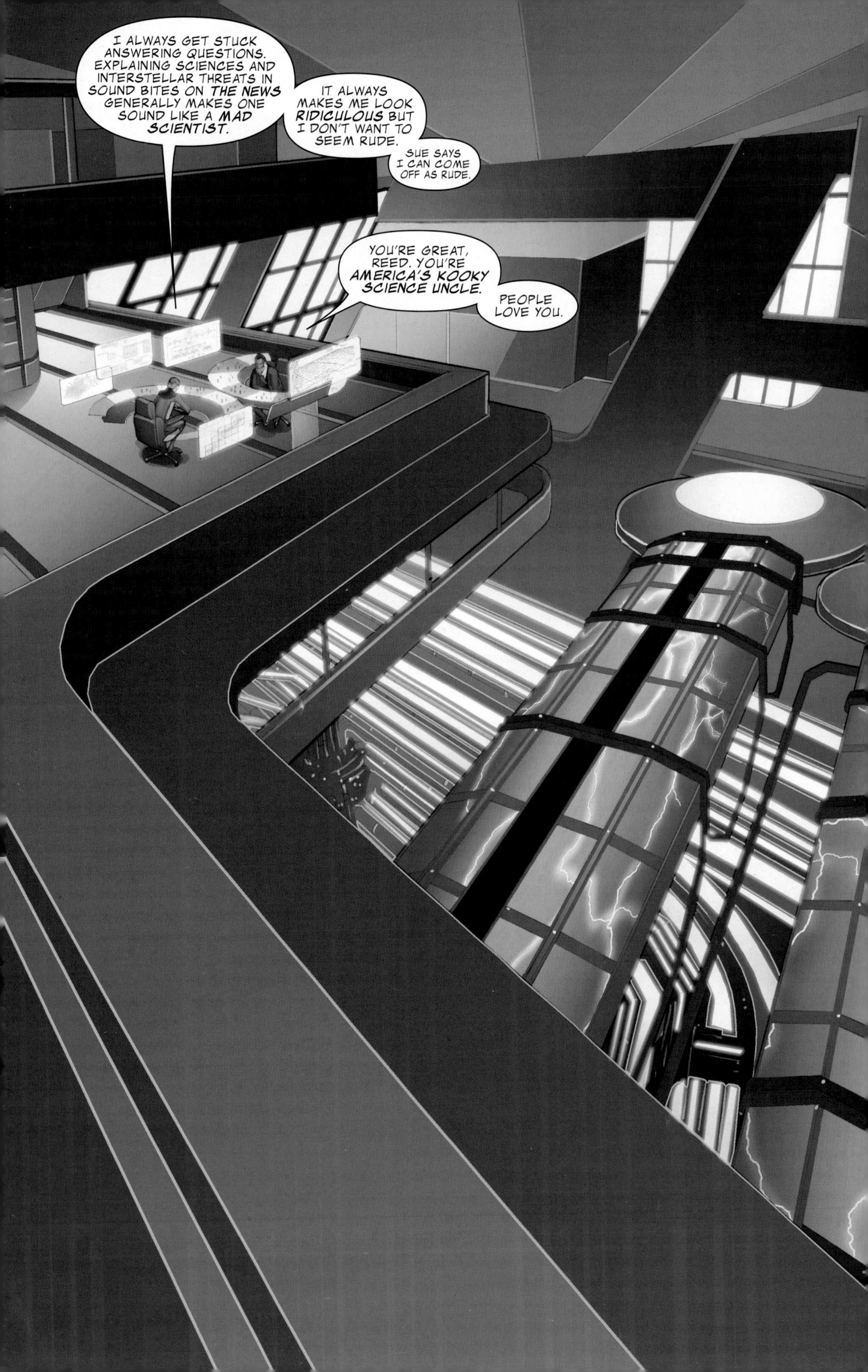
I ALWAYS GET STUCK ANSWERING QUESTIONS. EXPLAINING SCIENCES AND INTERSTELLAR THREATS IN SOUND BITES ON *THE NEWS* GENERALLY MAKES ONE SOUND LIKE A *MAD SCIENTIST*.
IT ALWAYS MAKES ME LOOK **RIDICULOUS** BUT I DON'T WANT TO SEEM RUDE.
SUE SAYS I CAN COME OFF AS RUDE.
YOU'RE GREAT, REED. YOU'RE ***AMERICA'S KOOKY SCIENCE UNCLE.***
PEOPLE LOVE YOU.

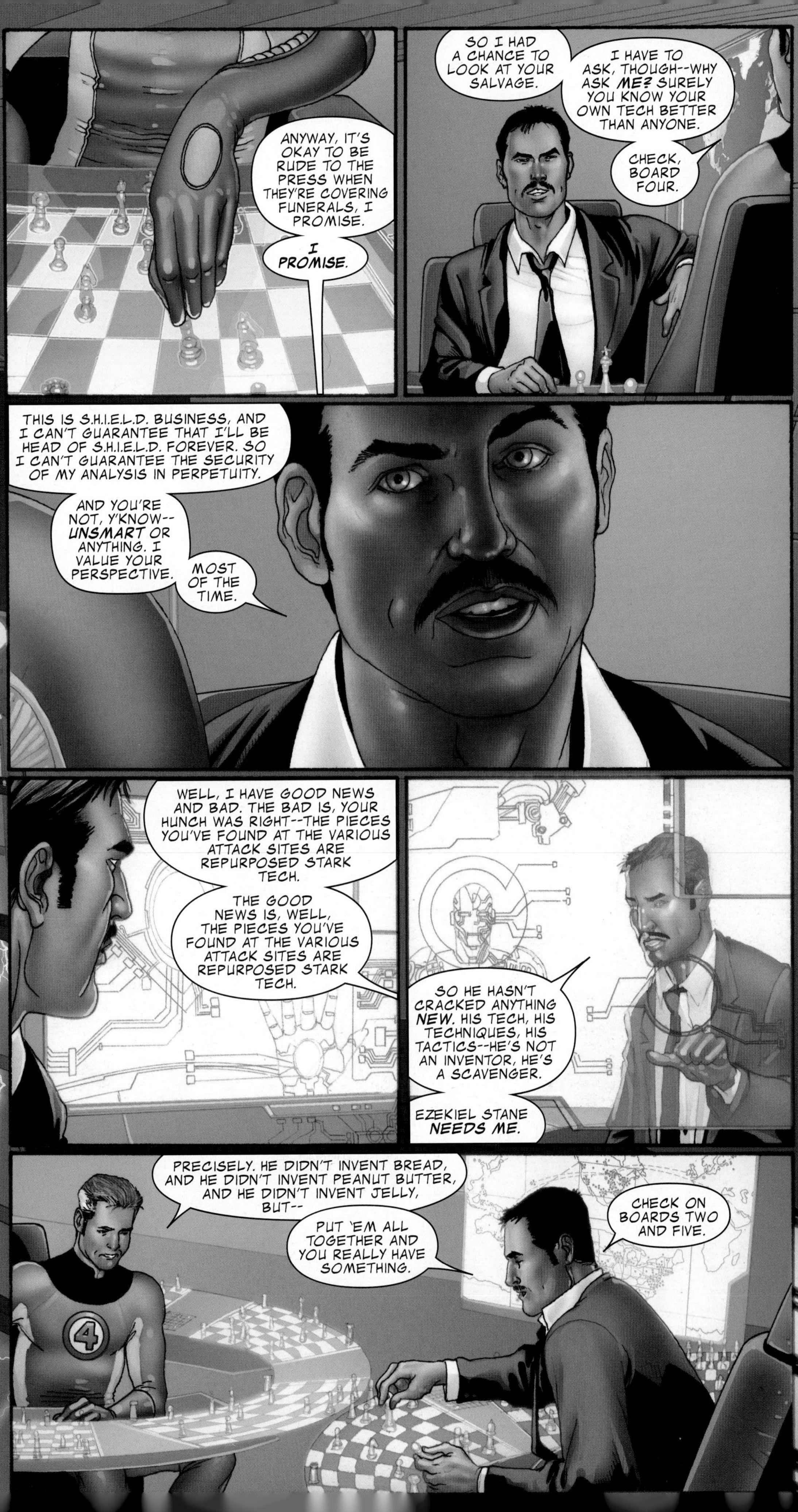
ANYWAY, IT'S OKAY TO BE RUDE TO THE PRESS WHEN THEY'RE COVERING FUNERALS, I PROMISE.
I PROMISE.
SO I HAD A CHANCE TO LOOK AT YOUR SALVAGE.
I HAVE TO ASK, THOUGH--WHY ASK ME? SURELY YOU KNOW YOUR OWN TECH BETTER THAN ANYONE.
CHECK, BOARD FOUR.
THIS IS S.H.I.E.L.D. BUSINESS, AND I CAN'T GUARANTEE THAT I'LL BE HEAD OF S.H.I.E.L.D. FOREVER. SO I CAN'T GUARANTEE THE SECURITY OF MY ANALYSIS IN PERPETUITY.
AND YOU'RE NOT, Y'KNOW-- UNSMART OR ANYTHING. I VALUE YOUR PERSPECTIVE.
MOST OF THE TIME.
WELL, I HAVE GOOD NEWS AND BAD. THE BAD IS, YOUR HUNCH WAS RIGHT--THE PIECES YOU'VE FOUND AT THE VARIOUS ATTACK SITES ARE REPURPOSED STARK TECH.
THE GOOD NEWS IS, WELL, THE PIECES YOU'VE FOUND AT THE VARIOUS ATTACK SITES ARE REPURPOSED STARK TECH.
SO HE HASN'T CRACKED ANYTHING NEW. HIS TECH, HIS TECHNIQUES, HIS TACTICS--HE'S NOT AN INVENTOR, HE'S A SCAVENGER.
EZEKIEL STANE NEEDS ME.
PRECISELY. HE DIDN'T INVENT BREAD, AND HE DIDN'T INVENT PEANUT BUTTER, AND HE DIDN'T INVENT JELLY, BUT--
PUT 'EM ALL TOGETHER AND YOU REALLY HAVE SOMETHING.
CHECK ON BOARDS TWO AND FIVE.
4

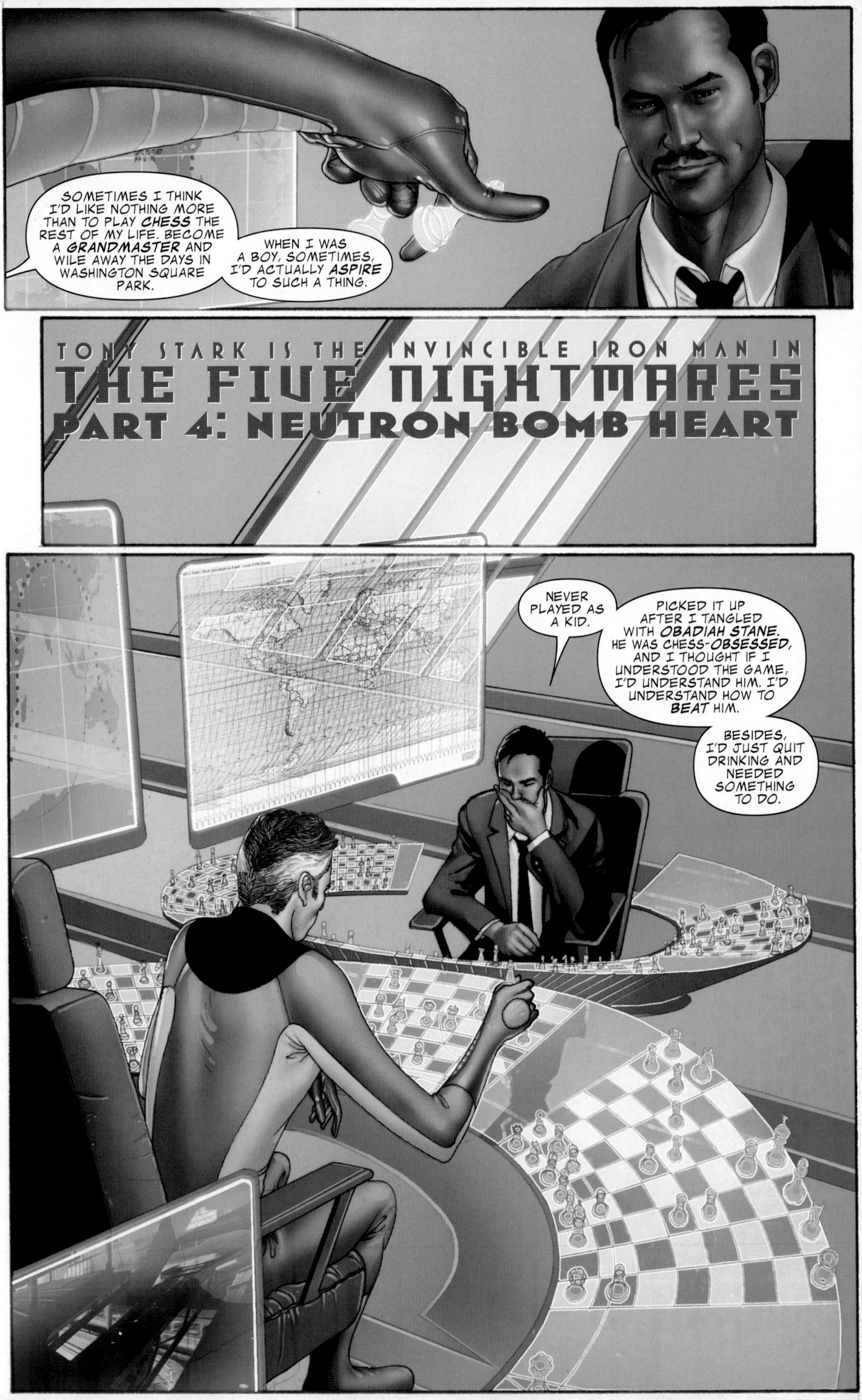
SOMETIMES I THINK I'D LIKE NOTHING MORE THAN TO PLAY CHESS THE REST OF MY LIFE. BECOME A GRANDMASTER AND WILE AWAY THE DAYS IN WASHINGTON SQUARE PARK.
WHEN I WAS A BOY, SOMETIMES, I'D ACTUALLY ASPIRE TO SUCH A THING.
TONY STARK IS THE INVINCIBLE IRON MAN IN
THE FIVE NIGHTMARES
PART 4: NEUTRON BOMB HEART
NEVER PLAYED AS A KID.
PICKED IT UP AFTER I TANGLED WITH OBADIAH STANE. HE WAS CHESS-OBSESSED, AND I THOUGHT IF I UNDERSTOOD THE GAME, I'D UNDERSTAND HIM. I'D UNDERSTAND HOW TO BEAT HIM.
BESIDES, I'D JUST QUIT DRINKING AND NEEDED SOMETHING TO DO.

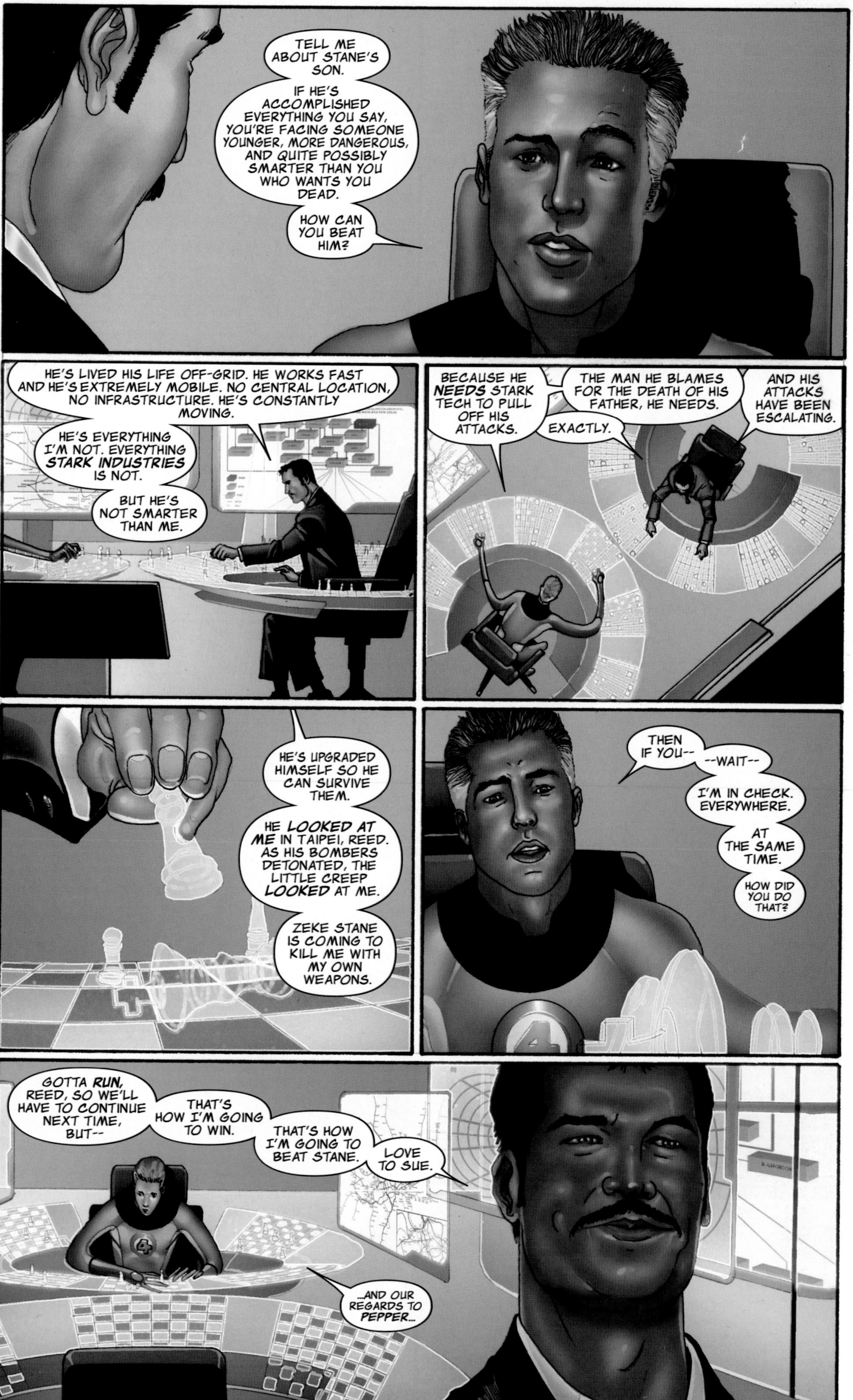
TELL ME ABOUT STANE'S SON.
IF HE'S ACCOMPLISHED EVERYTHING YOU SAY, YOU'RE FACING SOMEONE YOUNGER, MORE DANGEROUS, AND QUITE POSSIBLY SMARTER THAN YOU WHO WANTS YOU DEAD.
HOW CAN YOU BEAT HIM?
HE'S LIVED HIS LIFE OFF-GRID. HE WORKS FAST AND HE'S EXTREMELY MOBILE. NO CENTRAL LOCATION, NO INFRASTRUCTURE. HE'S CONSTANTLY MOVING.
HE'S EVERYTHING I'M NOT. EVERYTHING STARK INDUSTRIES IS NOT.
BUT HE'S NOT SMARTER THAN ME.
BECAUSE HE NEEDS STARK TECH TO PULL OFF HIS ATTACKS.
THE MAN HE BLAMES FOR THE DEATH OF HIS FATHER, HE NEEDS.
EXACTLY.
AND HIS ATTACKS HAVE BEEN ESCALATING.
HE'S UPGRADED HIMSELF SO HE CAN SURVIVE THEM.
HE LOOKED AT ME IN TAIPEI, REED. AS HIS BOMBERS DETONATED, THE LITTLE CREEP LOOKED AT ME.
ZEKE STANE IS COMING TO KILL ME WITH MY OWN WEAPONS.
THEN IF YOU--
--WAIT--
I'M IN CHECK. EVERYWHERE.
AT THE SAME TIME.
HOW DID YOU DO THAT?
GOTTA RUN, REED, SO WE'LL HAVE TO CONTINUE NEXT TIME, BUT--
THAT'S HOW I'M GOING TO WIN.
THAT'S HOW I'M GOING TO BEAT STANE.
LOVE TO SUE.
...AND OUR REGARDS TO PEPPER...

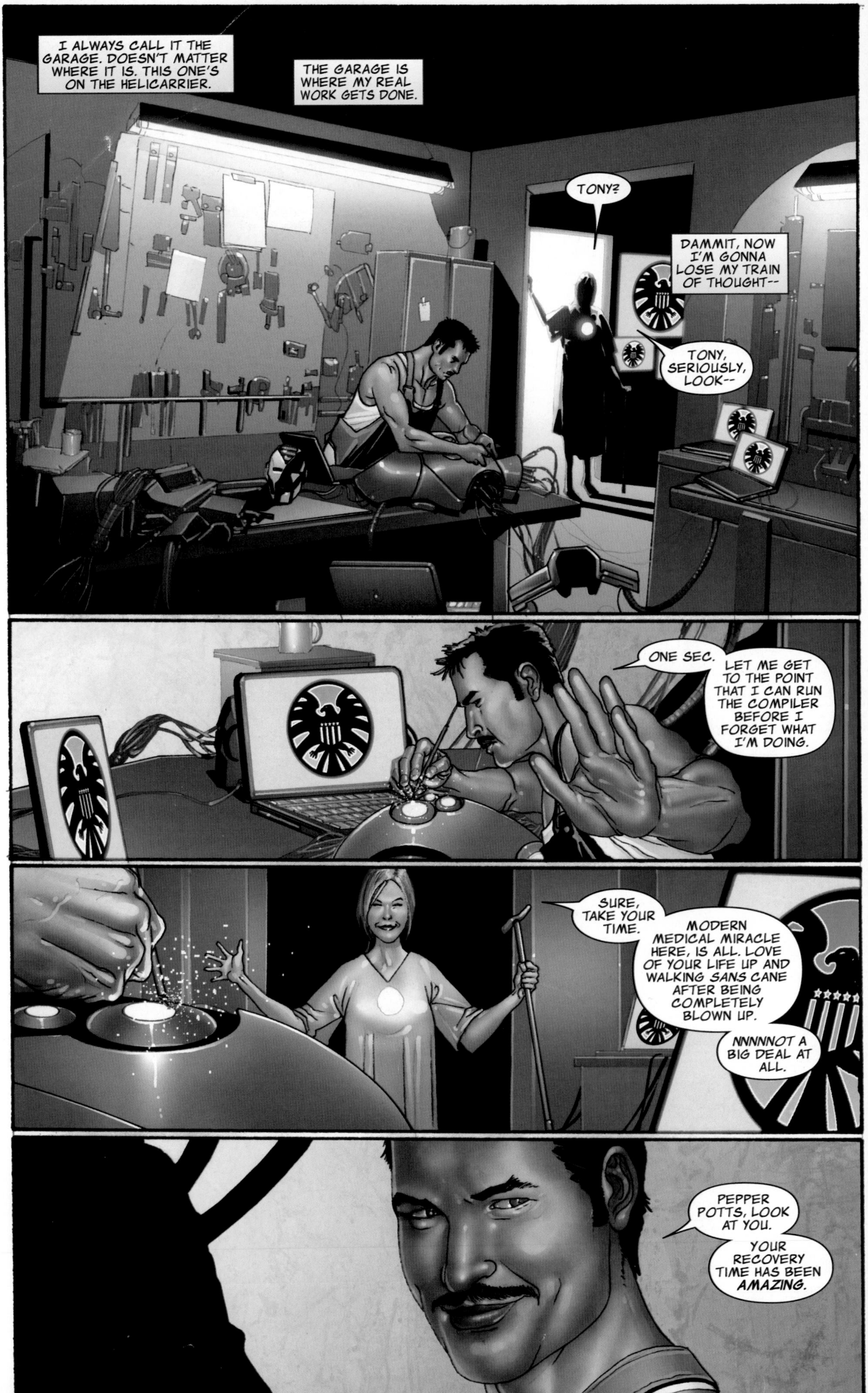
I ALWAYS CALL IT THE GARAGE. DOESN'T MATTER WHERE IT IS. THIS ONE'S ON THE HELICARRIER.
THE GARAGE IS WHERE MY REAL WORK GETS DONE.
TONY?
DAMMIT, NOW I'M GONNA LOSE MY TRAIN OF THOUGHT--
TONY, SERIOUSLY, LOOK--
ONE SEC.
LET ME GET TO THE POINT THAT I CAN RUN THE COMPILER BEFORE I FORGET WHAT I'M DOING.
SURE, TAKE YOUR TIME.
MODERN MEDICAL MIRACLE HERE, IS ALL. LOVE OF YOUR LIFE UP AND WALKING SANS CANE AFTER BEING COMPLETELY BLOWN UP.
NNNNNOT A BIG DEAL AT ALL.
PEPPER POTTS, LOOK AT YOU.
YOUR RECOVERY TIME HAS BEEN AMAZING.

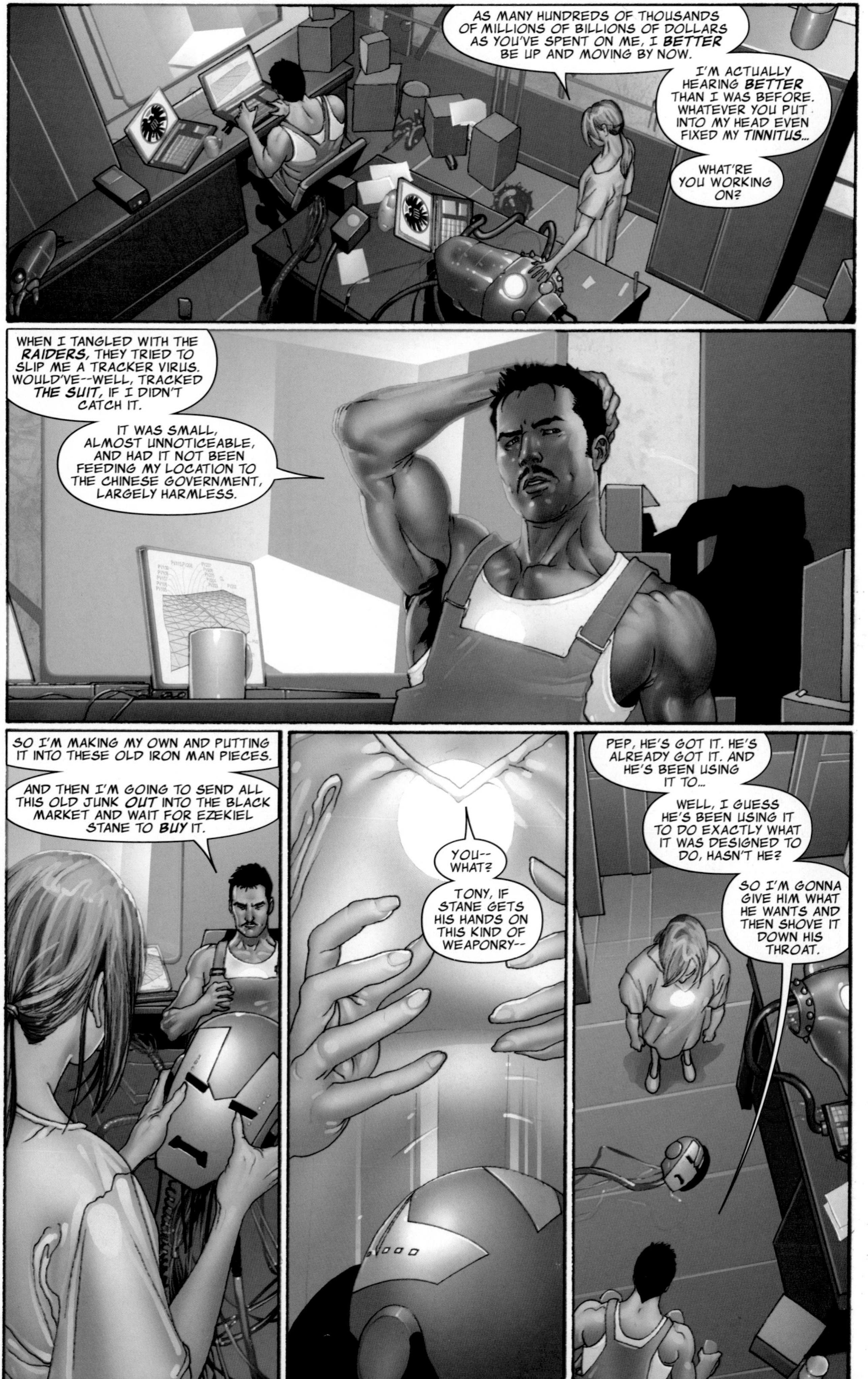
AS MANY HUNDREDS OF THOUSANDS OF MILLIONS OF BILLIONS OF DOLLARS AS YOU'VE SPENT ON ME, I BETTER BE UP AND MOVING BY NOW.
I'M ACTUALLY HEARING BETTER THAN I WAS BEFORE. WHATEVER YOU PUT INTO MY HEAD EVEN FIXED MY TINNITUS...
WHAT'RE YOU WORKING ON?
WHEN I TANGLED WITH THE RAIDERS, THEY TRIED TO SLIP ME A TRACKER VIRUS. WOULD'VE--WELL, TRACKED THE SUIT, IF I DIDN'T CATCH IT.
IT WAS SMALL, ALMOST UNNOTICEABLE, AND HAD IT NOT BEEN FEEDING MY LOCATION TO THE CHINESE GOVERNMENT, LARGELY HARMLESS.
SO I'M MAKING MY OWN AND PUTTING IT INTO THESE OLD IRON MAN PIECES.
AND THEN I'M GOING TO SEND ALL THIS OLD JUNK OUT INTO THE BLACK MARKET AND WAIT FOR EZEKIEL STANE TO BUY IT.
YOU--WHAT?
TONY, IF STANE GETS HIS HANDS ON THIS KIND OF WEAPONRY--
PEP, HE'S GOT IT. HE'S ALREADY GOT IT. AND HE'S BEEN USING IT TO...
WELL, I GUESS HE'S BEEN USING IT TO DO EXACTLY WHAT IT WAS DESIGNED TO DO, HASN'T HE?
SO I'M GONNA GIVE HIM WHAT HE WANTS AND THEN SHOVE IT DOWN HIS THROAT.

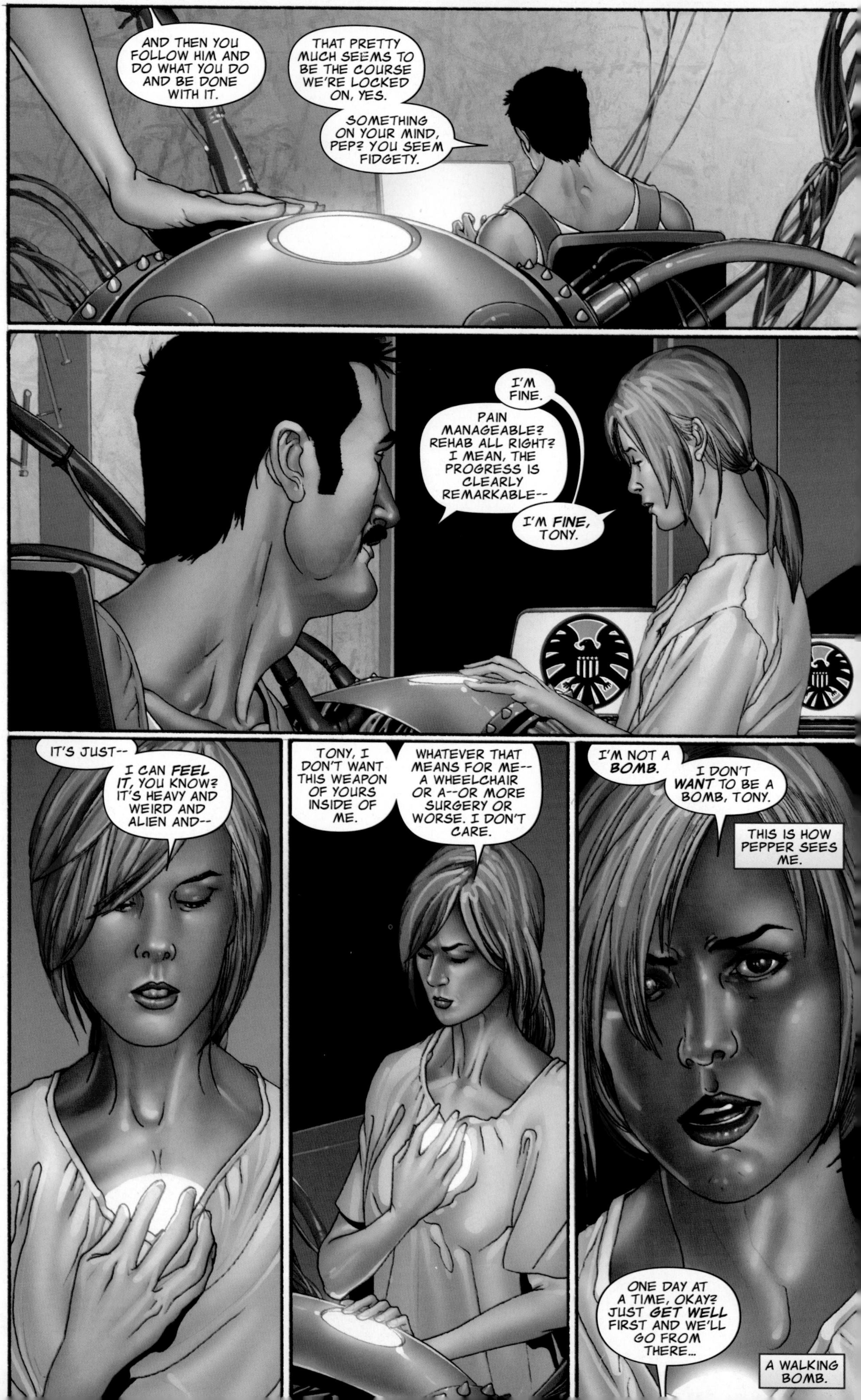

AND THEN YOU FOLLOW HIM AND DO WHAT YOU DO AND BE DONE WITH IT.
THAT PRETTY MUCH SEEMS TO BE THE COURSE WE'RE LOCKED ON, YES.
SOMETHING ON YOUR MIND, PEP? YOU SEEM FIDGETY.
I'M FINE.
PAIN MANAGEABLE? REHAB ALL RIGHT? I MEAN, THE PROGRESS IS CLEARLY REMARKABLE--
I'M FINE, TONY.
IT'S JUST--
I CAN FEEL IT, YOU KNOW? IT'S HEAVY AND WEIRD AND ALIEN AND--
TONY, I DON'T WANT THIS WEAPON OF YOURS INSIDE OF ME.
WHATEVER THAT MEANS FOR ME--A WHEELCHAIR OR A--OR MORE SURGERY OR WORSE. I DON'T CARE.
I'M NOT A BOMB.
I DON'T WANT TO BE A BOMB, TONY.
THIS IS HOW PEPPER SEES ME.
ONE DAY AT A TIME, OKAY? JUST GET WELL FIRST AND WE'LL GO FROM THERE...
A WALKING BOMB.

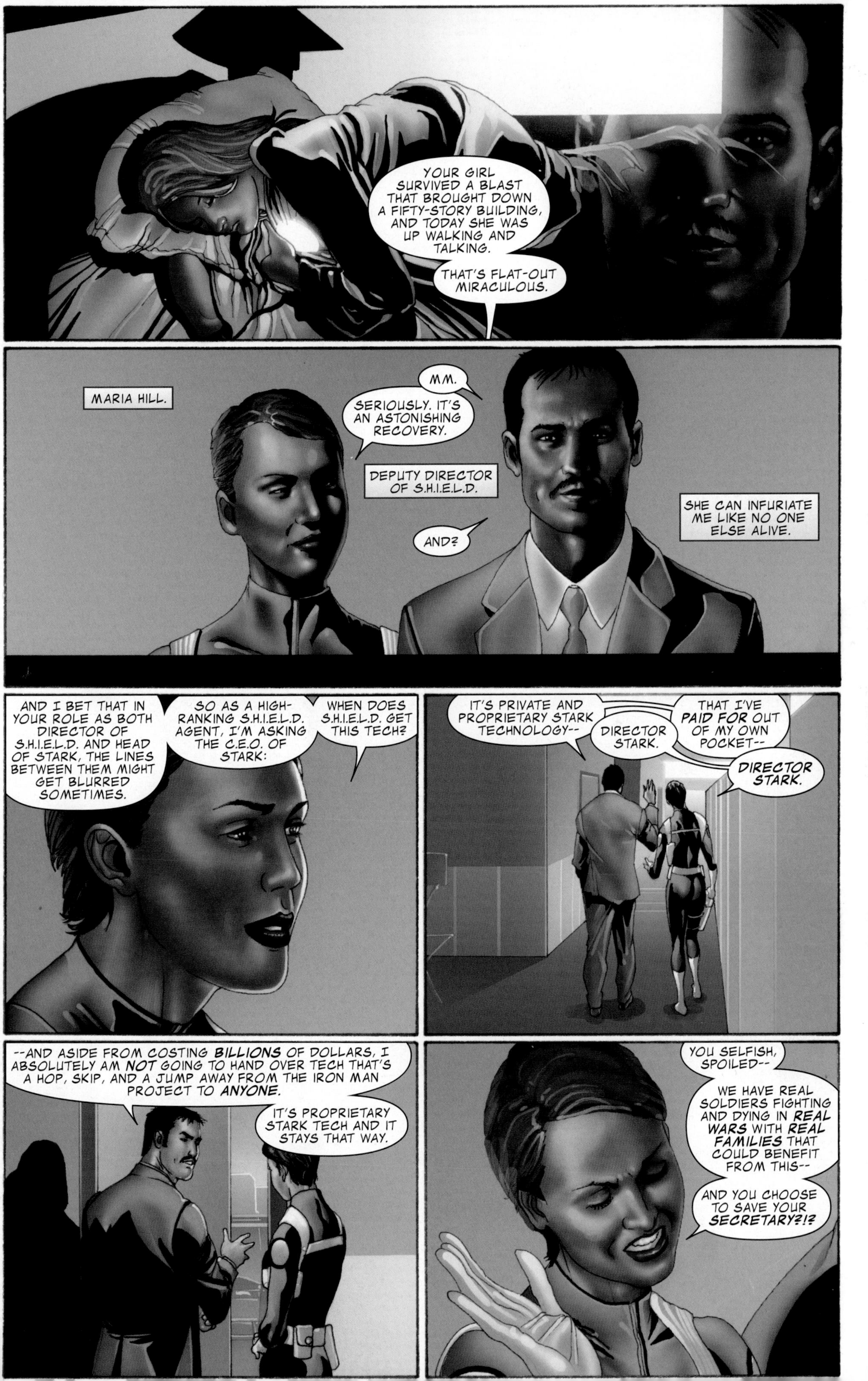
YOUR GIRL SURVIVED A BLAST THAT BROUGHT DOWN A FIFTY-STORY BUILDING, AND TODAY SHE WAS UP WALKING AND TALKING.
THAT'S FLAT-OUT MIRACULOUS.
MARIA HILL.
MM.
SERIOUSLY. IT'S AN ASTONISHING RECOVERY.
DEPUTY DIRECTOR OF S.H.I.E.L.D.
AND?
SHE CAN INFURIATE ME LIKE NO ONE ELSE ALIVE.
AND I BET THAT IN YOUR ROLE AS BOTH DIRECTOR OF S.H.I.E.L.D. AND HEAD OF STARK, THE LINES BETWEEN THEM MIGHT GET BLURRED SOMETIMES.
SO AS A HIGH-RANKING S.H.I.E.L.D. AGENT, I'M ASKING THE C.E.O. OF STARK:
WHEN DOES S.H.I.E.L.D. GET THIS TECH?
IT'S PRIVATE AND PROPRIETARY STARK TECHNOLOGY--
DIRECTOR STARK.
THAT I'VE PAID FOR OUT OF MY OWN POCKET--
DIRECTOR STARK.
--AND ASIDE FROM COSTING BILLIONS OF DOLLARS, I ABSOLUTELY AM NOT GOING TO HAND OVER TECH THAT'S A HOP, SKIP, AND A JUMP AWAY FROM THE IRON MAN PROJECT TO ANYONE.
IT'S PROPRIETARY STARK TECH AND IT STAYS THAT WAY.
YOU SELFISH, SPOILED--
WE HAVE REAL SOLDIERS FIGHTING AND DYING IN REAL WARS WITH REAL FAMILIES THAT COULD BENEFIT FROM THIS--
AND YOU CHOOSE TO SAVE YOUR SECRETARY?!?

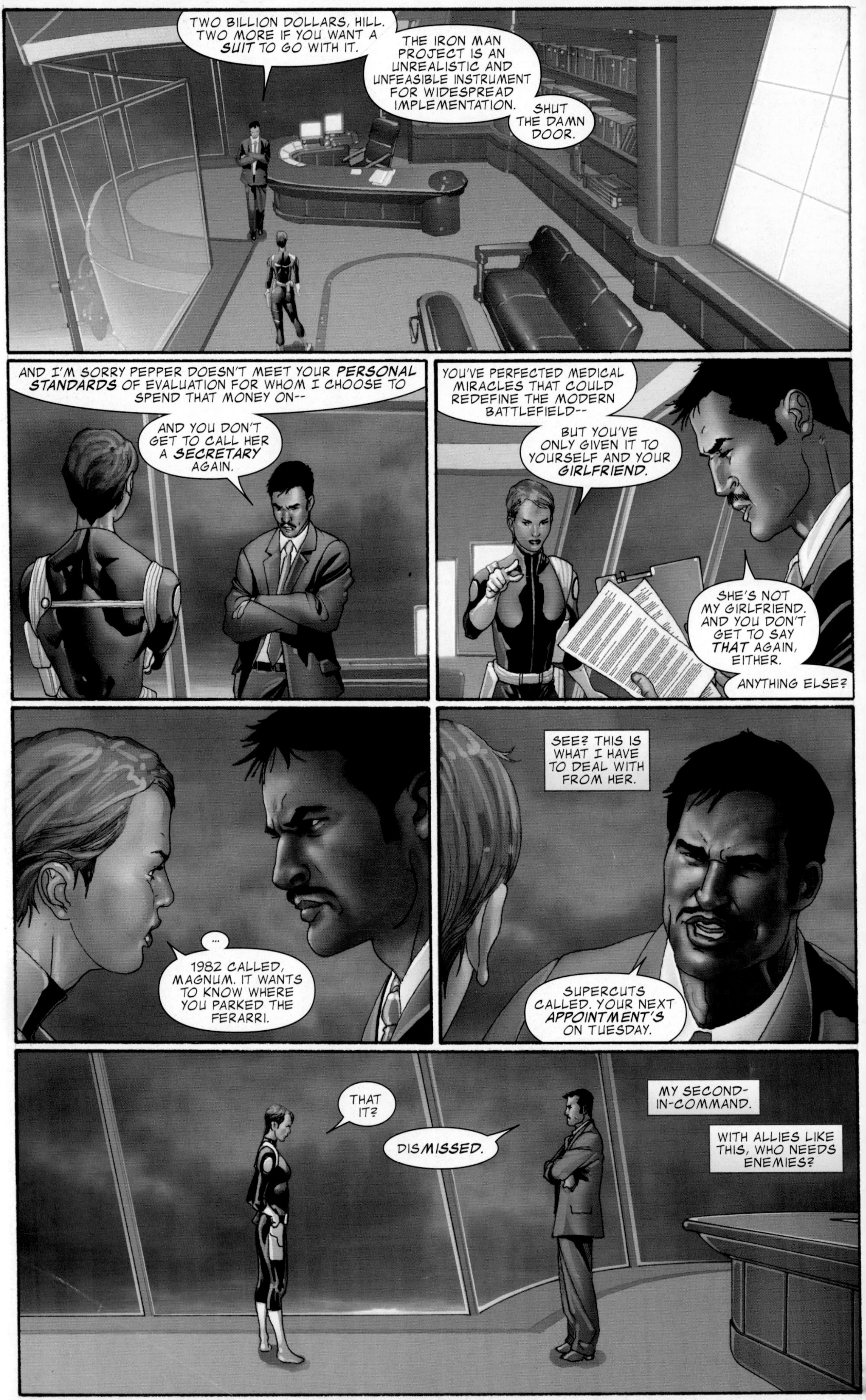
TWO BILLION DOLLARS, HILL. TWO MORE IF YOU WANT A SUIT TO GO WITH IT.
THE IRON MAN PROJECT IS AN UNREALISTIC AND UNFEASIBLE INSTRUMENT FOR WIDESPREAD IMPLEMENTATION.
SHUT THE DAMN DOOR.
AND I'M SORRY PEPPER DOESN'T MEET YOUR PERSONAL STANDARDS OF EVALUATION FOR WHOM I CHOOSE TO SPEND THAT MONEY ON--
AND YOU DON'T GET TO CALL HER A SECRETARY AGAIN.
YOU'VE PERFECTED MEDICAL MIRACLES THAT COULD REDEFINE THE MODERN BATTLEFIELD--
BUT YOU'VE ONLY GIVEN IT TO YOURSELF AND YOUR GIRLFRIEND.
SHE'S NOT MY GIRLFRIEND. AND YOU DON'T GET TO SAY THAT AGAIN, EITHER.
ANYTHING ELSE?
...
1982 CALLED, MAGNUM. IT WANTS TO KNOW WHERE YOU PARKED THE FERARRI.
SEE? THIS IS WHAT I HAVE TO DEAL WITH FROM HER.
SUPERCUTS CALLED. YOUR NEXT APPOINTMENT'S ON TUESDAY.
THAT IT?
DISMISSED.
MY SECOND-IN-COMMAND.
WITH ALLIES LIKE THIS, WHO NEEDS ENEMIES?

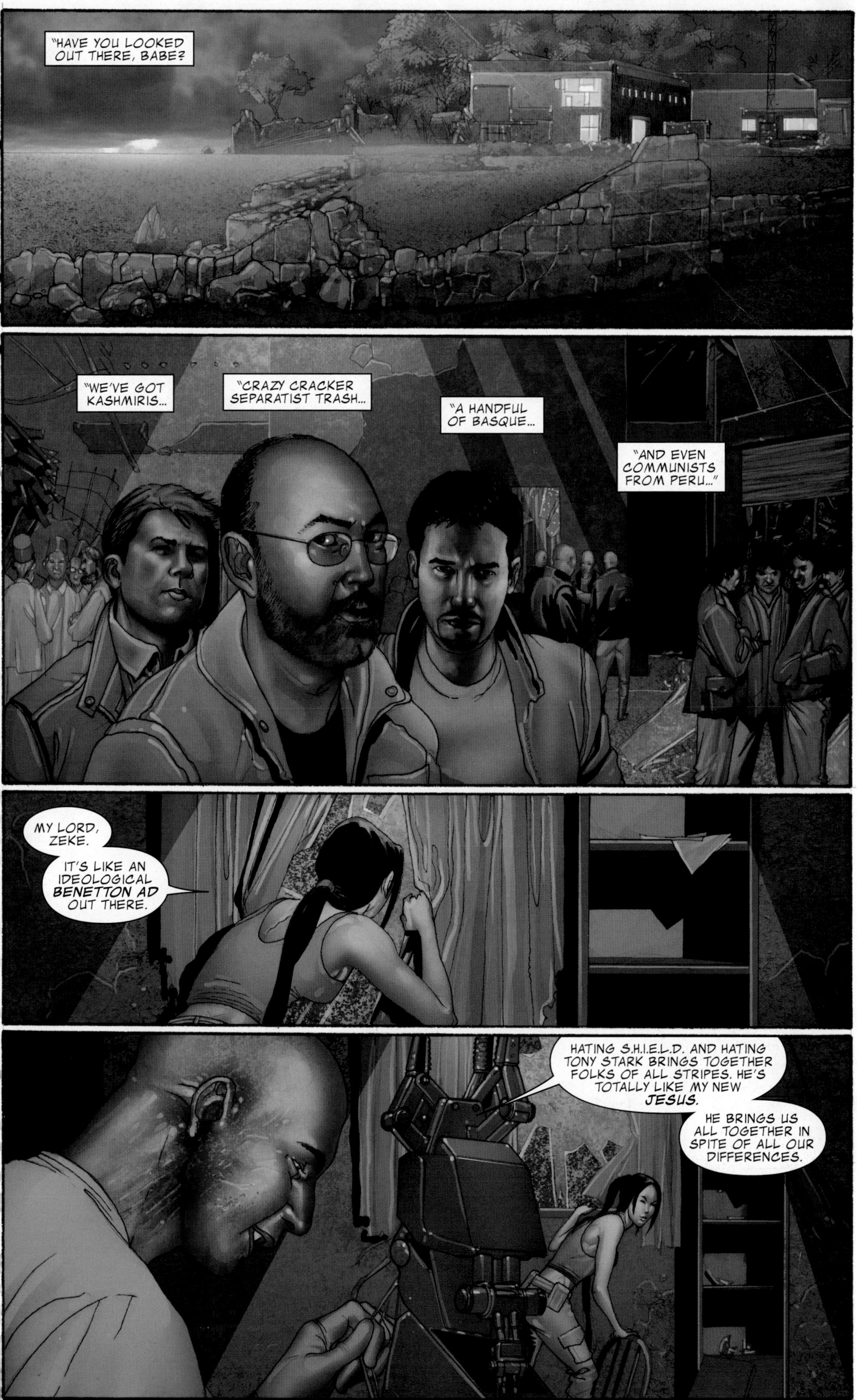
"HAVE YOU LOOKED OUT THERE, BABE?
"WE'VE GOT KASHMIRIS...
"CRAZY CRACKER SEPARATIST TRASH...
"A HANDFUL OF BASQUE...
"AND EVEN COMMUNISTS FROM PERU..."
MY LORD, ZEKE.
IT'S LIKE AN IDEOLOGICAL BENETTON AD OUT THERE.
HATING S.H.I.E.L.D. AND HATING TONY STARK BRINGS TOGETHER FOLKS OF ALL STRIPES. HE'S TOTALLY LIKE MY NEW JESUS.
HE BRINGS US ALL TOGETHER IN SPITE OF ALL OUR DIFFERENCES.

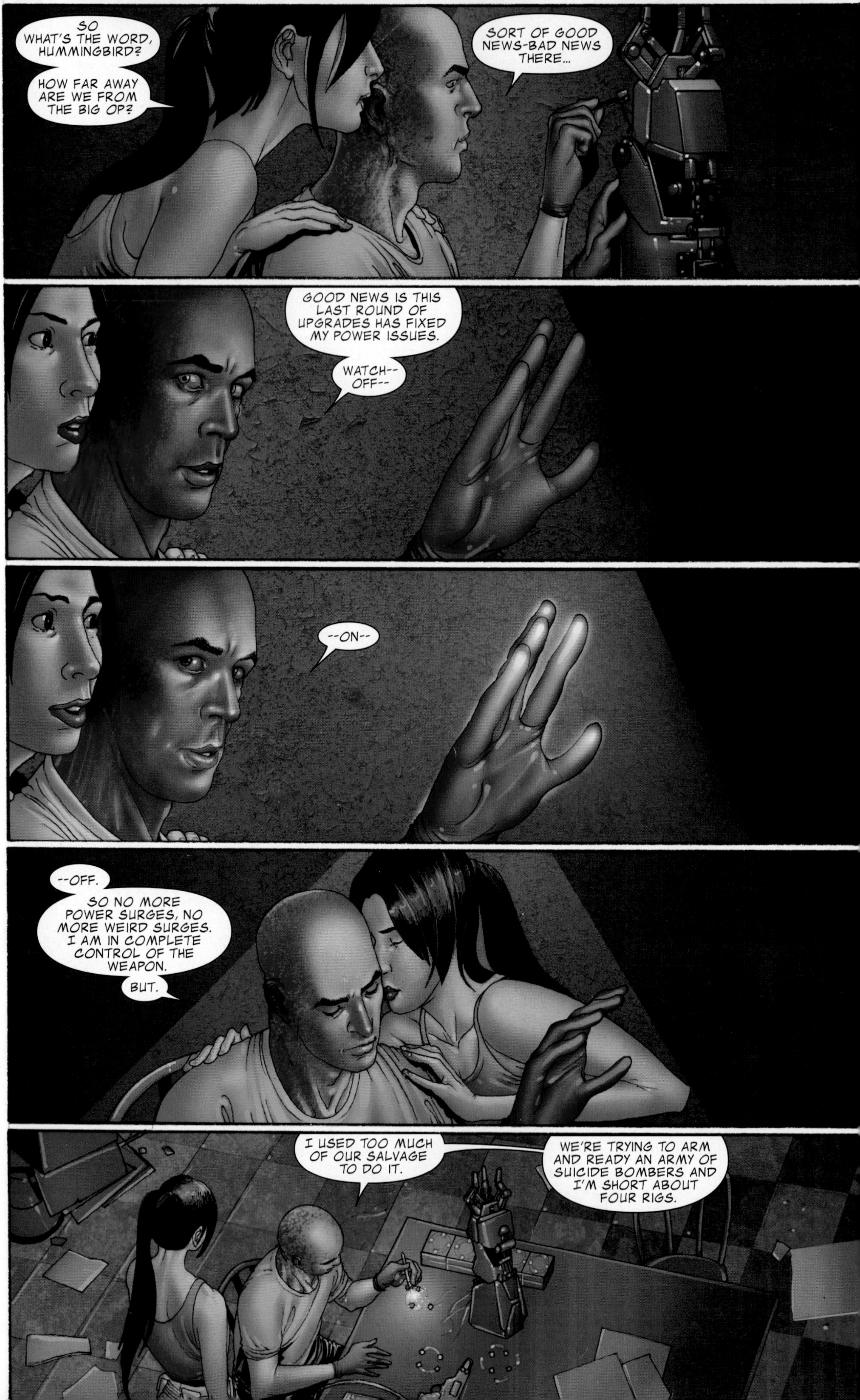
SO WHAT'S THE WORD, HUMMINGBIRD?
HOW FAR AWAY ARE WE FROM THE BIG OP?
SORT OF GOOD NEWS-BAD NEWS THERE...
GOOD NEWS IS THIS LAST ROUND OF UPGRADES HAS FIXED MY POWER ISSUES.
WATCH-- OFF--
--ON--
--OFF.
SO NO MORE POWER SURGES, NO MORE WEIRD SURGES. I AM IN COMPLETE CONTROL OF THE WEAPON.
BUT.
I USED TOO MUCH OF OUR SALVAGE TO DO IT.
WE'RE TRYING TO ARM AND READY AN ARMY OF SUICIDE BOMBERS AND I'M SHORT ABOUT FOUR RIGS.

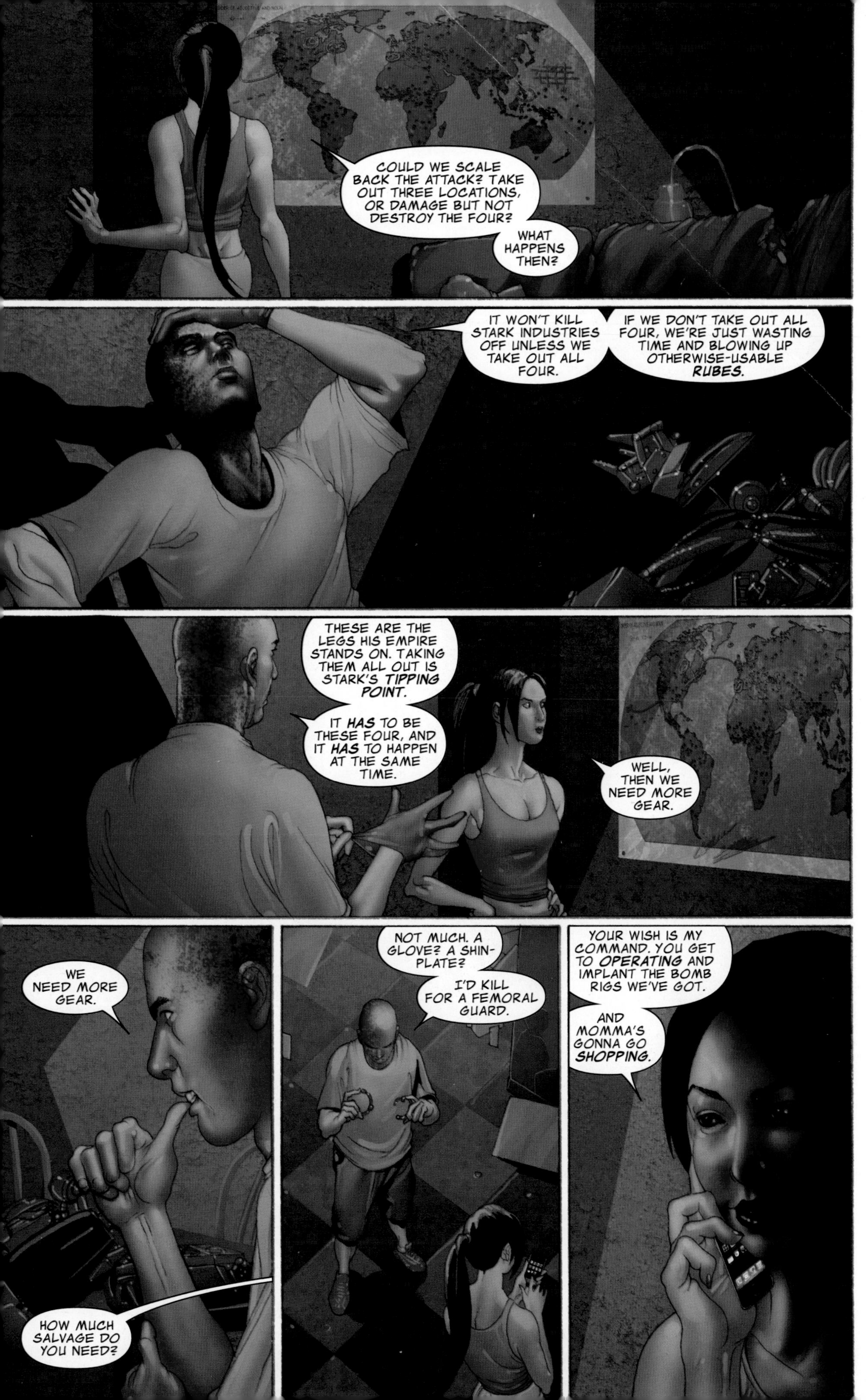
COULD WE SCALE BACK THE ATTACK? TAKE OUT THREE LOCATIONS, OR DAMAGE BUT NOT DESTROY THE FOUR?
WHAT HAPPENS THEN?
IT WON'T KILL STARK INDUSTRIES OFF UNLESS WE TAKE OUT ALL FOUR.
IF WE DON'T TAKE OUT ALL FOUR, WE'RE JUST WASTING TIME AND BLOWING UP OTHERWISE-USABLE RUBES.
THESE ARE THE LEGS HIS EMPIRE STANDS ON. TAKING THEM ALL OUT IS STARK'S TIPPING POINT.
IT HAS TO BE THESE FOUR, AND IT HAS TO HAPPEN AT THE SAME TIME.
WELL, THEN WE NEED MORE GEAR.
WE NEED MORE GEAR.
HOW MUCH SALVAGE DO YOU NEED?
NOT MUCH. A GLOVE? A SHIN-PLATE?
I'D KILL FOR A FEMORAL GUARD.
YOUR WISH IS MY COMMAND. YOU GET TO OPERATING AND IMPLANT THE BOMB RIGS WE'VE GOT.
AND MOMMA'S GONNA GO SHOPPING.

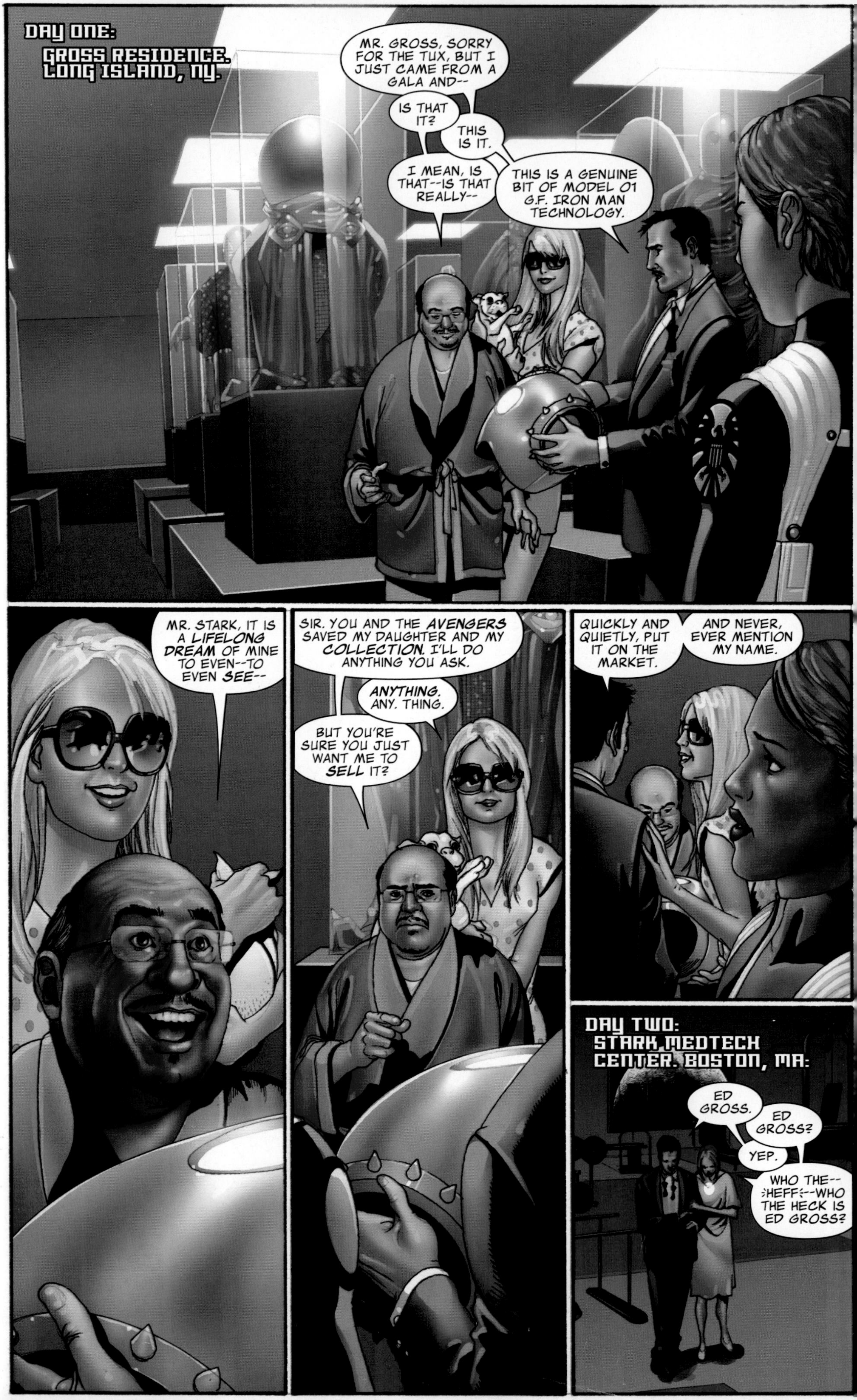
DAY ONE:
GROSS RESIDENCE. LONG ISLAND, NY.
MR. GROSS, SORRY FOR THE TUX, BUT I JUST CAME FROM A GALA AND--
IS THAT IT?
THIS IS IT.
I MEAN, IS THAT--IS THAT REALLY--
THIS IS A GENUINE BIT OF MODEL 01 G.F. IRON MAN TECHNOLOGY.
MR. STARK, IT IS A LIFELONG DREAM OF MINE TO EVEN--TO EVEN SEE--
SIR. YOU AND THE AVENGERS SAVED MY DAUGHTER AND MY COLLECTION. I'LL DO ANYTHING YOU ASK.
ANYTHING. ANY. THING.
BUT YOU'RE SURE YOU JUST WANT ME TO SELL IT?
QUICKLY AND QUIETLY, PUT IT ON THE MARKET.
AND NEVER, EVER MENTION MY NAME.
DAY TWO:
STARK MEDTECH CENTER. BOSTON, MA:
ED GROSS.
ED GROSS?
YEP.
WHO THE-- HEFF--WHO THE HECK IS ED GROSS?

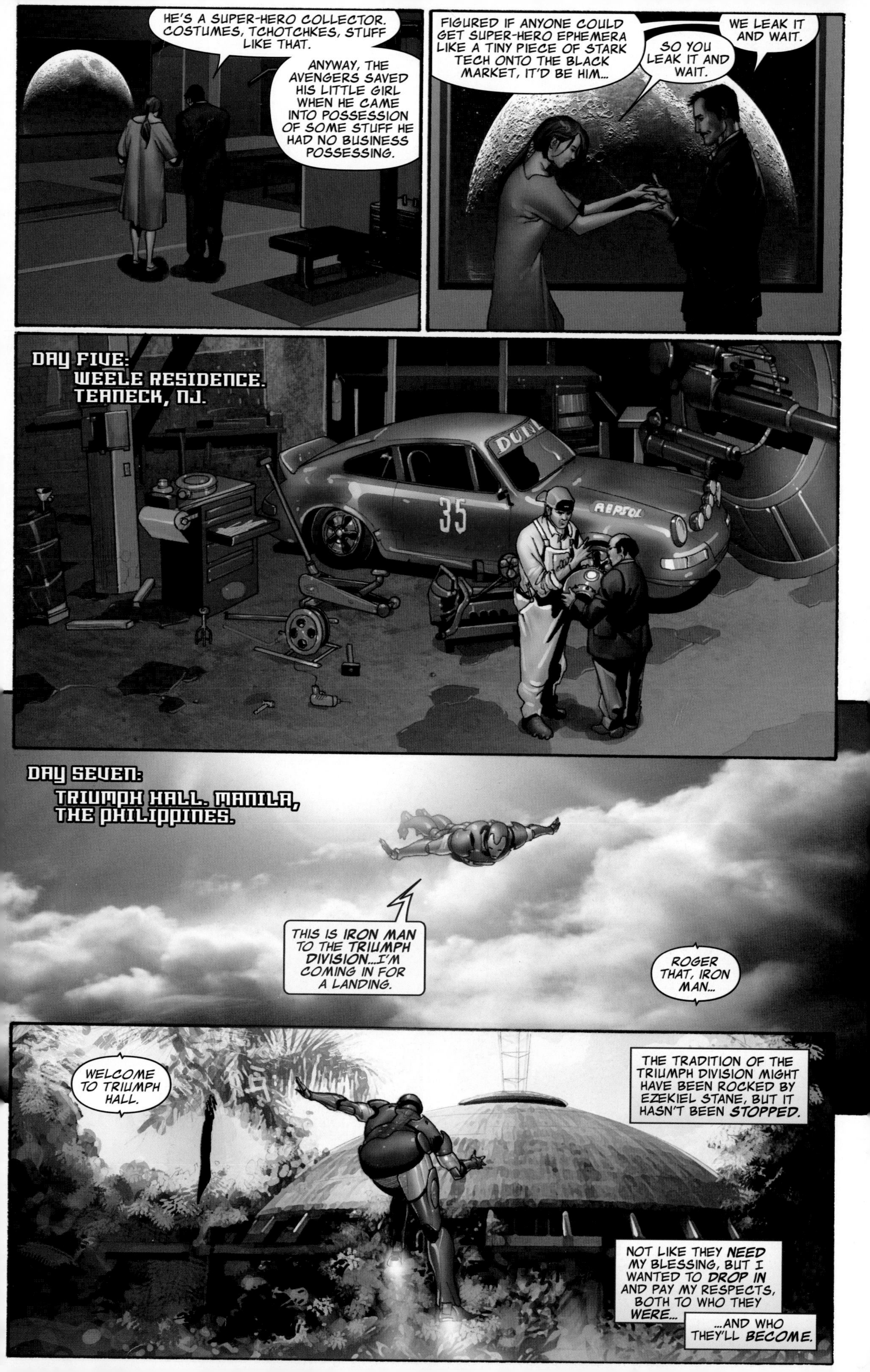

HE'S A SUPER-HERO COLLECTOR. COSTUMES, TCHOTCHKES, STUFF LIKE THAT.
ANYWAY, THE AVENGERS SAVED HIS LITTLE GIRL WHEN HE CAME INTO POSSESSION OF SOME STUFF HE HAD NO BUSINESS POSSESSING.
FIGURED IF ANYONE COULD GET SUPER-HERO EPHEMERA LIKE A TINY PIECE OF STARK TECH ONTO THE BLACK MARKET, IT'D BE HIM...
SO YOU LEAK IT AND WAIT.
WE LEAK IT AND WAIT.
DAY FIVE: WEELE RESIDENCE. TEANECK, NJ.
35
DAY SEVEN: TRIUMPH HALL. MANILA, THE PHILIPPINES.
THIS IS IRON MAN TO THE TRIUMPH DIVISION...I'M COMING IN FOR A LANDING.
ROGER THAT, IRON MAN...
WELCOME TO TRIUMPH HALL.
THE TRADITION OF THE TRIUMPH DIVISION MIGHT HAVE BEEN ROCKED BY EZEKIEL STANE, BUT IT HASN'T BEEN STOPPED.
NOT LIKE THEY NEED MY BLESSING, BUT I WANTED TO DROP IN AND PAY MY RESPECTS, BOTH TO WHO THEY WERE...
...AND WHO THEY'LL BECOME.

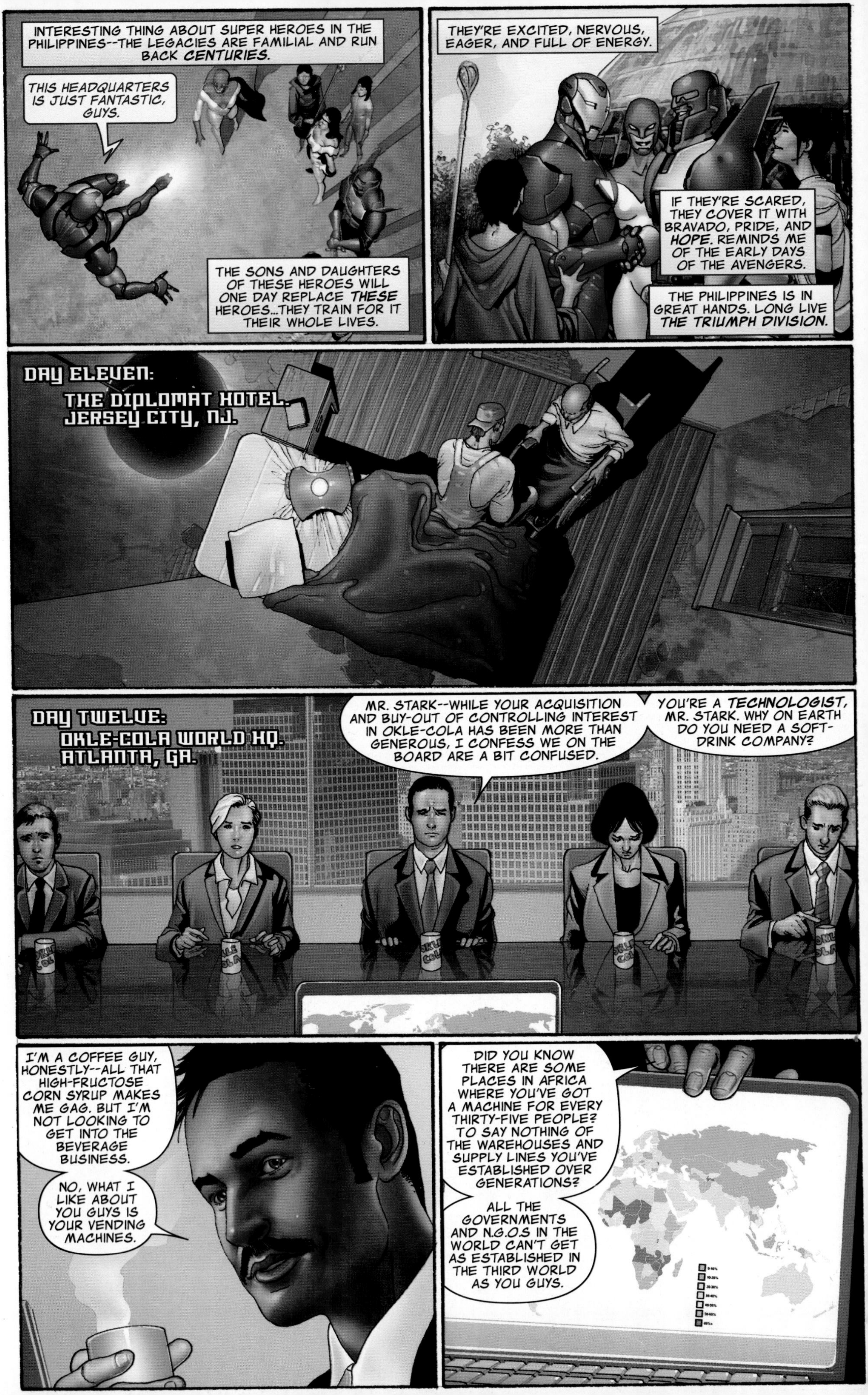
INTERESTING THING ABOUT SUPER HEROES IN THE PHILIPPINES--THE LEGACIES ARE FAMILIAL AND RUN BACK CENTURIES.
THIS HEADQUARTERS IS JUST FANTASTIC, GUYS.
THE SONS AND DAUGHTERS OF THESE HEROES WILL ONE DAY REPLACE THESE HEROES...THEY TRAIN FOR IT THEIR WHOLE LIVES.
THEY'RE EXCITED, NERVOUS, EAGER, AND FULL OF ENERGY.
IF THEY'RE SCARED, THEY COVER IT WITH BRAVADO, PRIDE, AND HOPE. REMINDS ME OF THE EARLY DAYS OF THE AVENGERS.
THE PHILIPPINES IS IN GREAT HANDS. LONG LIVE THE TRIUMPH DIVISION.
DAY ELEVEN:
THE DIPLOMAT HOTEL. JERSEY CITY, NJ.
DAY TWELVE:
OKLE-COLA WORLD HQ. ATLANTA, GA.
MR. STARK--WHILE YOUR ACQUISITION AND BUY-OUT OF CONTROLLING INTEREST IN OKLE-COLA HAS BEEN MORE THAN GENEROUS, I CONFESS WE ON THE BOARD ARE A BIT CONFUSED.
YOU'RE A TECHNOLOGIST, MR. STARK. WHY ON EARTH DO YOU NEED A SOFT-DRINK COMPANY?
I'M A COFFEE GUY, HONESTLY--ALL THAT HIGH-FRUCTOSE CORN SYRUP MAKES ME GAG. BUT I'M NOT LOOKING TO GET INTO THE BEVERAGE BUSINESS.
NO, WHAT I LIKE ABOUT YOU GUYS IS YOUR VENDING MACHINES.
DID YOU KNOW THERE ARE SOME PLACES IN AFRICA WHERE YOU'VE GOT A MACHINE FOR EVERY THIRTY-FIVE PEOPLE? TO SAY NOTHING OF THE WAREHOUSES AND SUPPLY LINES YOU'VE ESTABLISHED OVER GENERATIONS?
ALL THE GOVERNMENTS AND N.G.O.S IN THE WORLD CAN'T GET AS ESTABLISHED IN THE THIRD WORLD AS YOU GUYS.

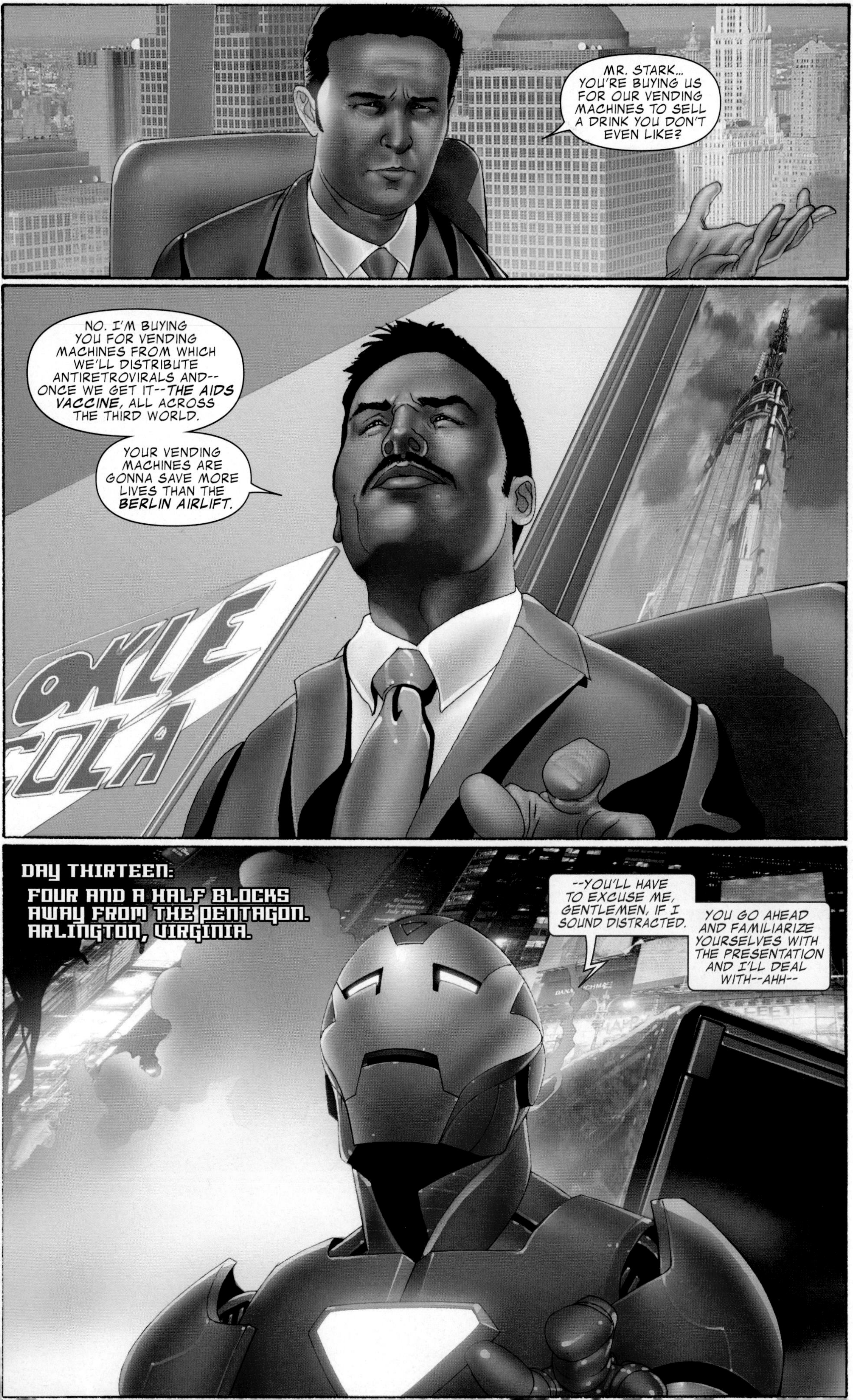
MR. STARK... YOU'RE BUYING US FOR OUR VENDING MACHINES TO SELL A DRINK YOU DON'T EVEN LIKE?
NO. I'M BUYING YOU FOR VENDING MACHINES FROM WHICH WE'LL DISTRIBUTE ANTIRETROVIRALS AND--ONCE WE GET IT--THE AIDS VACCINE, ALL ACROSS THE THIRD WORLD.
YOUR VENDING MACHINES ARE GONNA SAVE MORE LIVES THAN THE BERLIN AIRLIFT.
DAY THIRTEEN:
FOUR AND A HALF BLOCKS AWAY FROM THE PENTAGON. ARLINGTON, VIRGINIA.
--YOU'LL HAVE TO EXCUSE ME, GENTLEMEN, IF I SOUND DISTRACTED.
YOU GO AHEAD AND FAMILIARIZE YOURSELVES WITH THE PRESENTATION AND I'LL DEAL WITH--AHH--

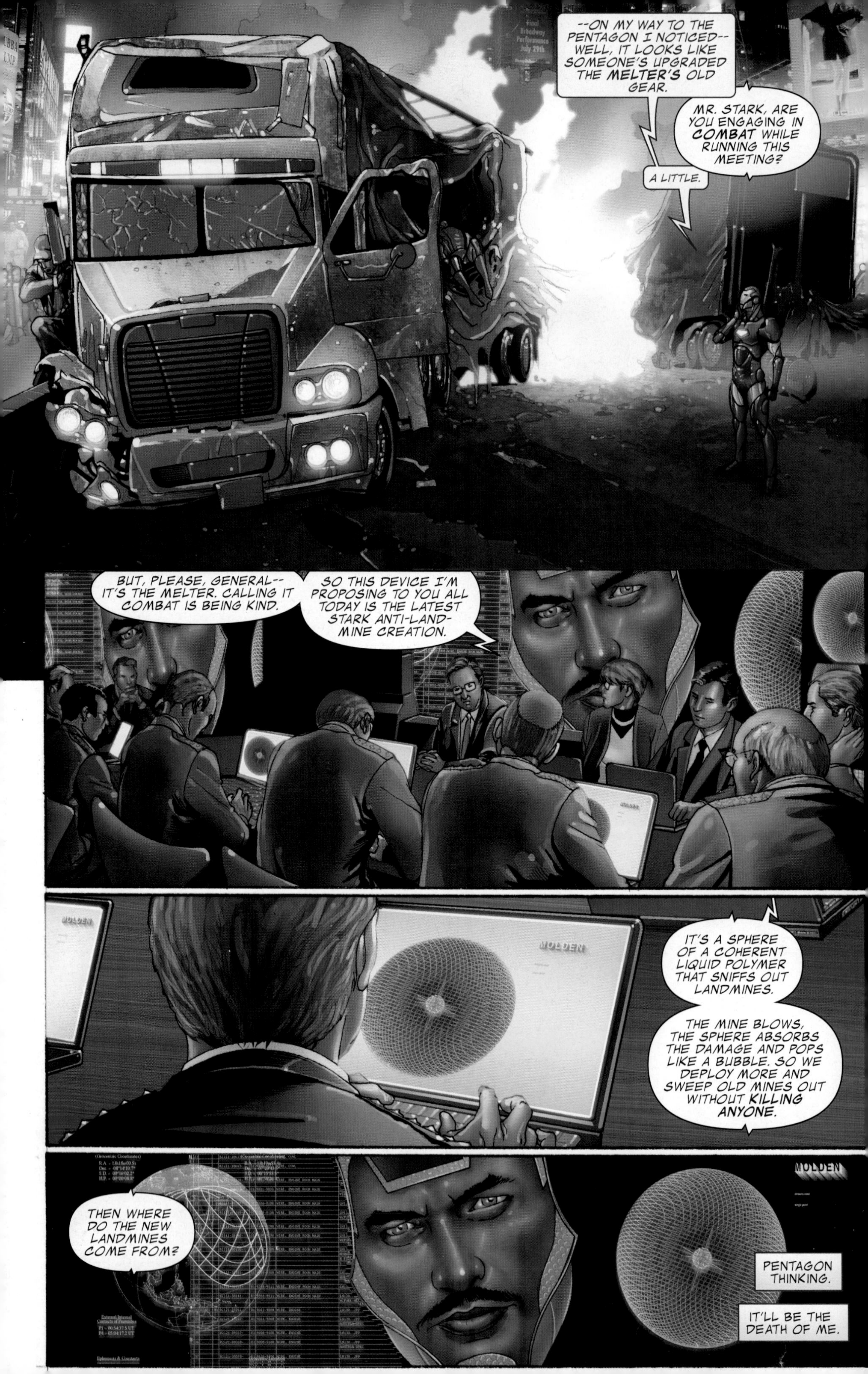

Final Broadway Performance July 29th
--ON MY WAY TO THE PENTAGON I NOTICED--WELL, IT LOOKS LIKE SOMEONE'S UPGRADED THE MELTER'S OLD GEAR.
MR. STARK, ARE YOU ENGAGING IN COMBAT WHILE RUNNING THIS MEETING?
A LITTLE.
BUT, PLEASE, GENERAL--IT'S THE MELTER. CALLING IT COMBAT IS BEING KIND.
SO THIS DEVICE I'M PROPOSING TO YOU ALL TODAY IS THE LATEST STARK ANTI-LAND-MINE CREATION.
MOLDEN
IT'S A SPHERE OF A COHERENT LIQUID POLYMER THAT SNIFFS OUT LANDMINES.
THE MINE BLOWS, THE SPHERE ABSORBS THE DAMAGE AND POPS LIKE A BUBBLE. SO WE DEPLOY MORE AND SWEEP OLD MINES OUT WITHOUT KILLING ANYONE.
THEN WHERE DO THE NEW LANDMINES COME FROM?
MOLDEN
PENTAGON THINKING.
IT'LL BE THE DEATH OF ME.

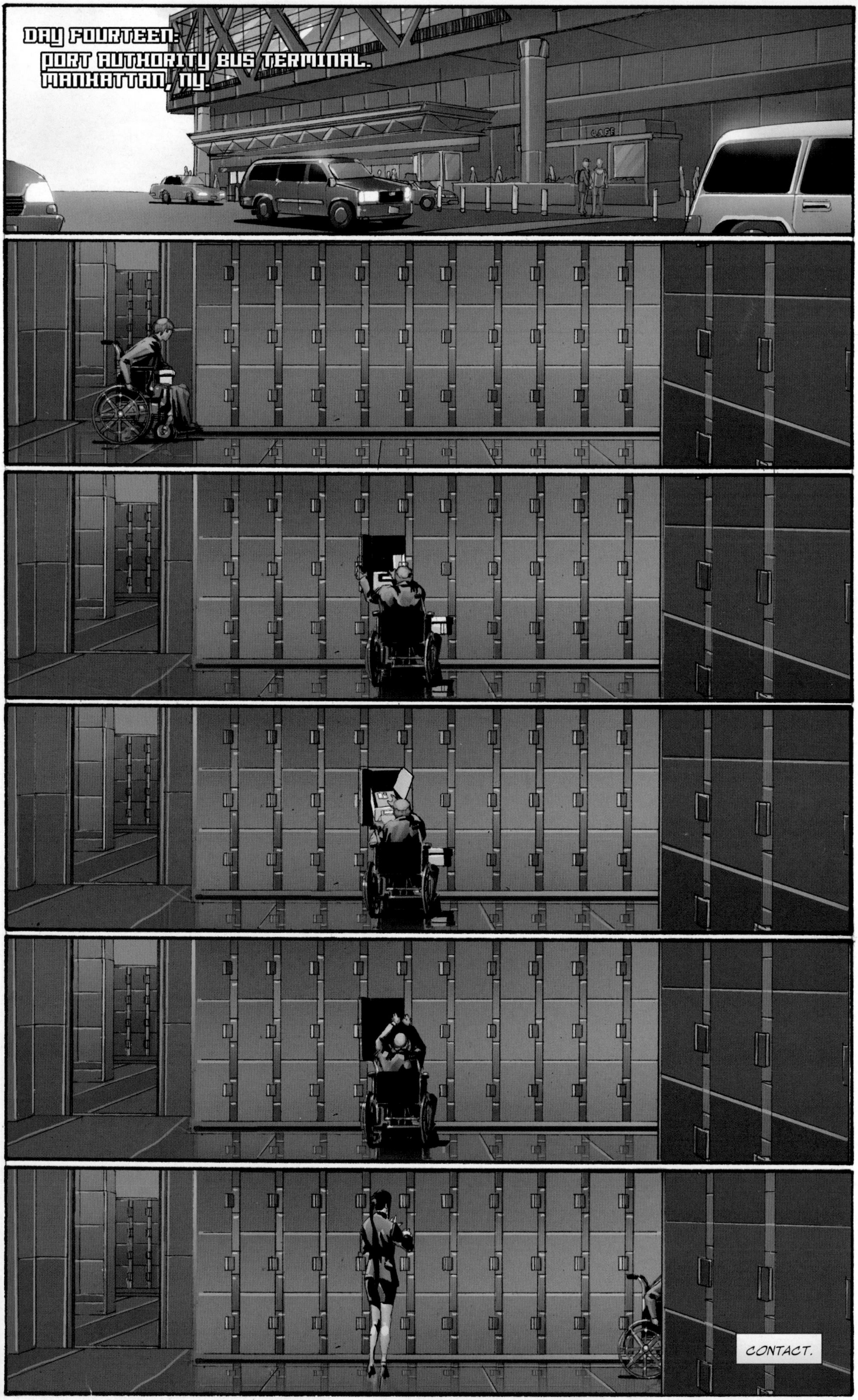
DAY FOURTEEN:
PORT AUTHORITY BUS TERMINAL.
MANHATTAN, NY.
CAFE
CONTACT.

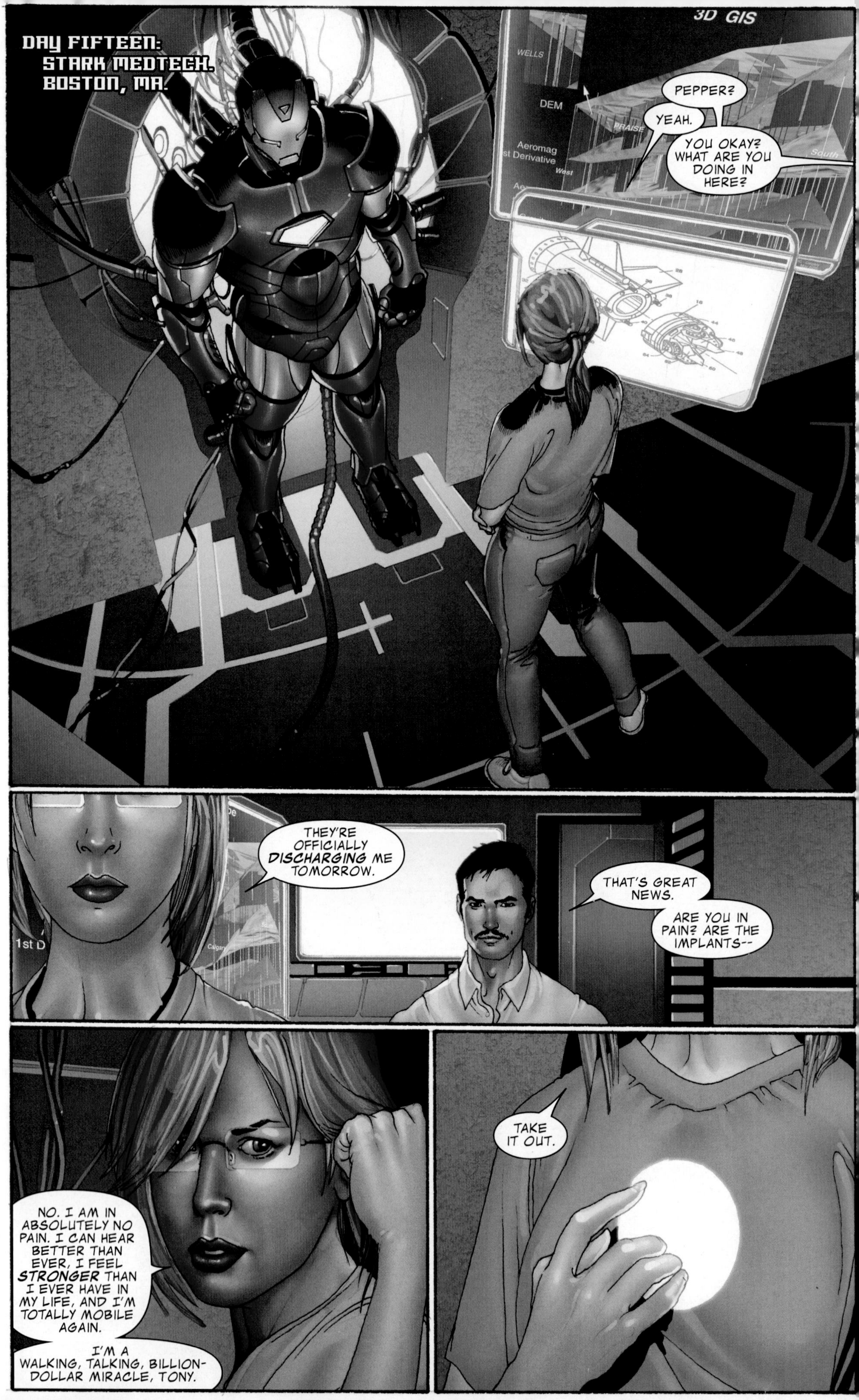
DAY FIFTEEN:
STARK MEDTECH.
BOSTON, MA.
3D GIS
WELLS
DEM
Aeromag
PEPPER?
YEAH.
YOU OKAY? WHAT ARE YOU DOING IN HERE?
THEY'RE OFFICIALLY DISCHARGING ME TOMORROW.
THAT'S GREAT NEWS.
ARE YOU IN PAIN? ARE THE IMPLANTS--
NO. I AM IN ABSOLUTELY NO PAIN. I CAN HEAR BETTER THAN EVER, I FEEL STRONGER THAN I EVER HAVE IN MY LIFE, AND I'M TOTALLY MOBILE AGAIN.
I'M A WALKING, TALKING, BILLION-DOLLAR MIRACLE, TONY.
TAKE IT OUT.

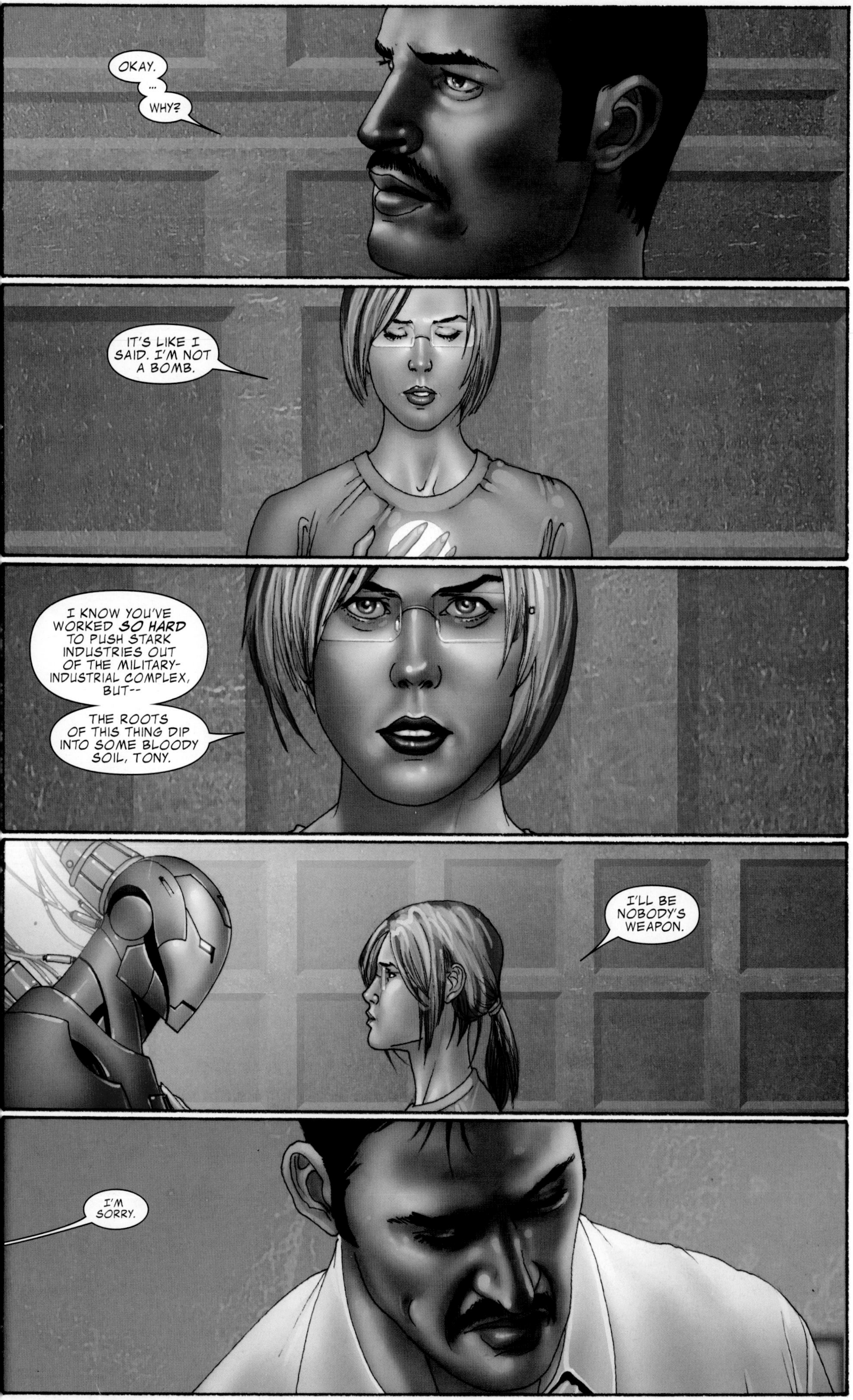
OKAY.
...
WHY?
IT'S LIKE I SAID. I'M NOT A BOMB.
I KNOW YOU'VE WORKED SO HARD TO PUSH STARK INDUSTRIES OUT OF THE MILITARY-INDUSTRIAL COMPLEX, BUT--
THE ROOTS OF THIS THING DIP INTO SOME BLOODY SOIL, TONY.
I'LL BE NOBODY'S WEAPON.
I'M SORRY.

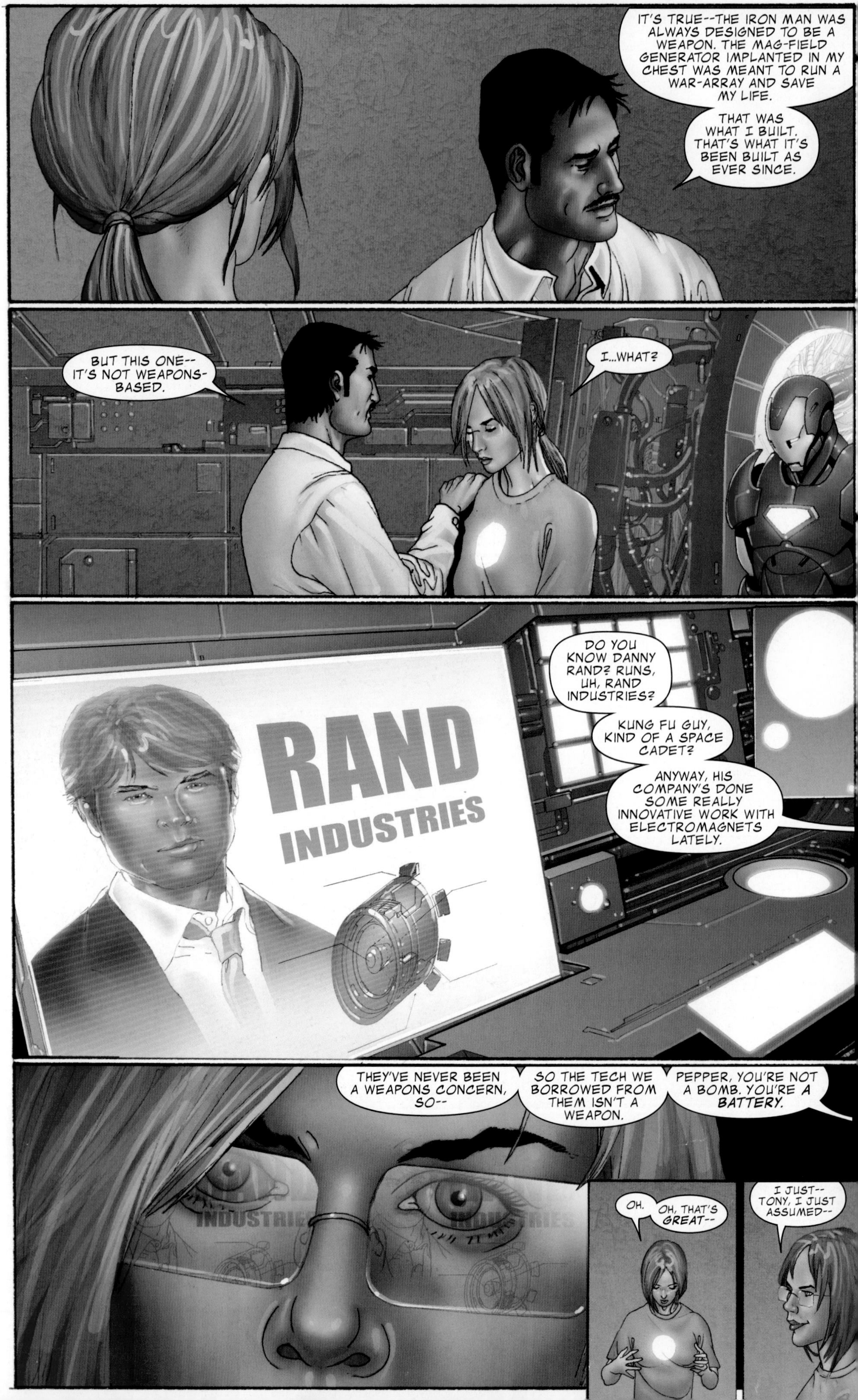
IT'S TRUE--THE IRON MAN WAS ALWAYS DESIGNED TO BE A WEAPON. THE MAG-FIELD GENERATOR IMPLANTED IN MY CHEST WAS MEANT TO RUN A WAR-ARRAY AND SAVE MY LIFE.
THAT WAS WHAT I BUILT. THAT'S WHAT IT'S BEEN BUILT AS EVER SINCE.
BUT THIS ONE-- IT'S NOT WEAPONS-BASED.
I...WHAT?
DO YOU KNOW DANNY RAND? RUNS, UH, RAND INDUSTRIES?
KUNG FU GUY, KIND OF A SPACE CADET?
ANYWAY, HIS COMPANY'S DONE SOME REALLY INNOVATIVE WORK WITH ELECTROMAGNETS LATELY.
RAND
INDUSTRIES
THEY'VE NEVER BEEN A WEAPONS CONCERN, SO--
SO THE TECH WE BORROWED FROM THEM ISN'T A WEAPON.
PEPPER, YOU'RE NOT A BOMB. YOU'RE A *BATTERY.*
OH.
OH, THAT'S *GREAT*--
I JUST-- TONY, I JUST ASSUMED--

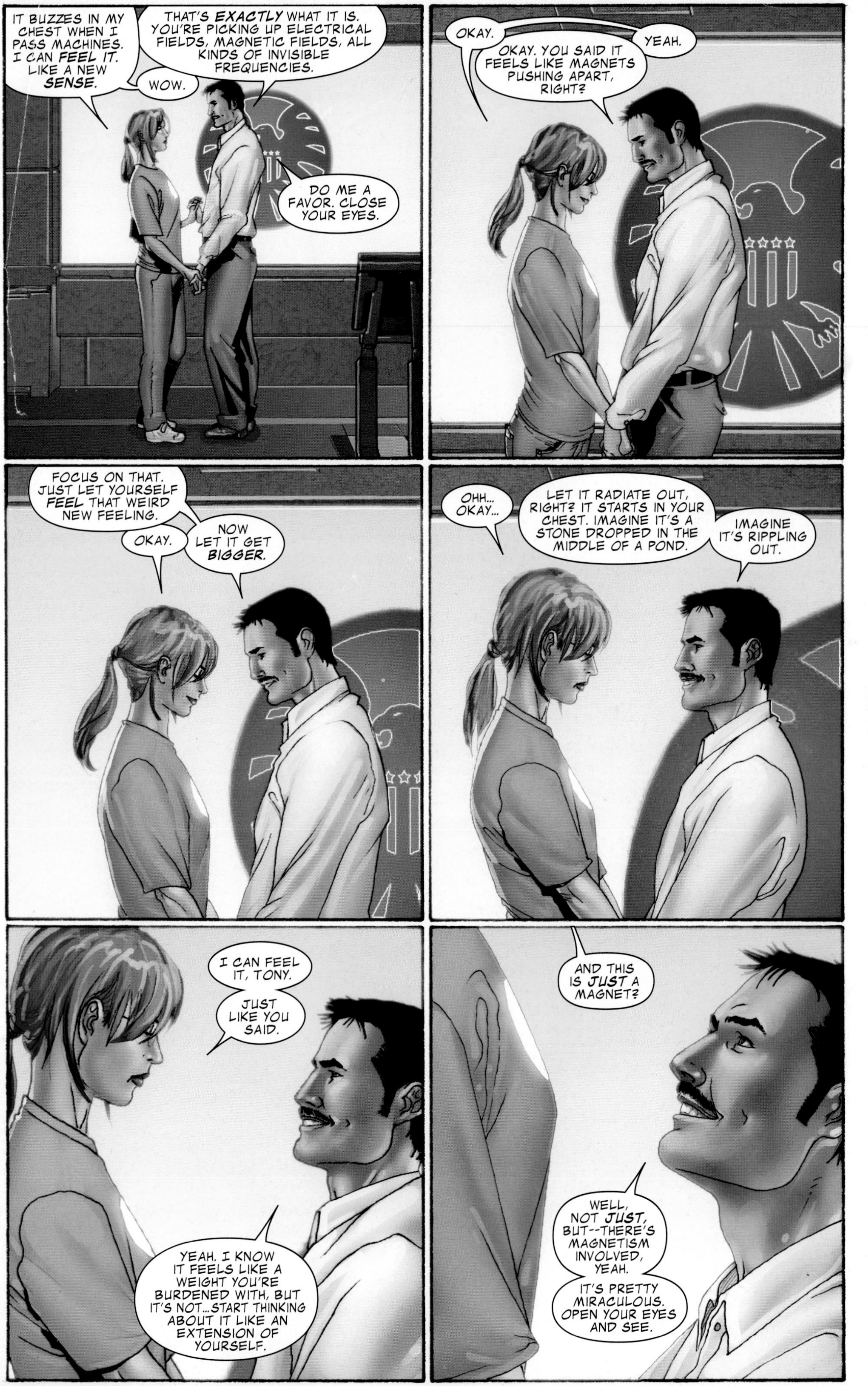
IT BUZZES IN MY CHEST WHEN I PASS MACHINES. I CAN FEEL IT. LIKE A NEW SENSE.
THAT'S EXACTLY WHAT IT IS. YOU'RE PICKING UP ELECTRICAL FIELDS, MAGNETIC FIELDS, ALL KINDS OF INVISIBLE FREQUENCIES.
WOW.
DO ME A FAVOR. CLOSE YOUR EYES.
OKAY.
YEAH.
OKAY. YOU SAID IT FEELS LIKE MAGNETS PUSHING APART, RIGHT?
FOCUS ON THAT. JUST LET YOURSELF FEEL THAT WEIRD NEW FEELING.
OKAY.
NOW LET IT GET BIGGER.
OHH... OKAY...
LET IT RADIATE OUT, RIGHT? IT STARTS IN YOUR CHEST. IMAGINE IT'S A STONE DROPPED IN THE MIDDLE OF A POND.
IMAGINE IT'S RIPPLING OUT.
I CAN FEEL IT, TONY.
JUST LIKE YOU SAID.
YEAH. I KNOW IT FEELS LIKE A WEIGHT YOU'RE BURDENED WITH, BUT IT'S NOT...START THINKING ABOUT IT LIKE AN EXTENSION OF YOURSELF.
AND THIS IS JUST A MAGNET?
WELL, NOT JUST, BUT--THERE'S MAGNETISM INVOLVED, YEAH.
IT'S PRETTY MIRACULOUS. OPEN YOUR EYES AND SEE.

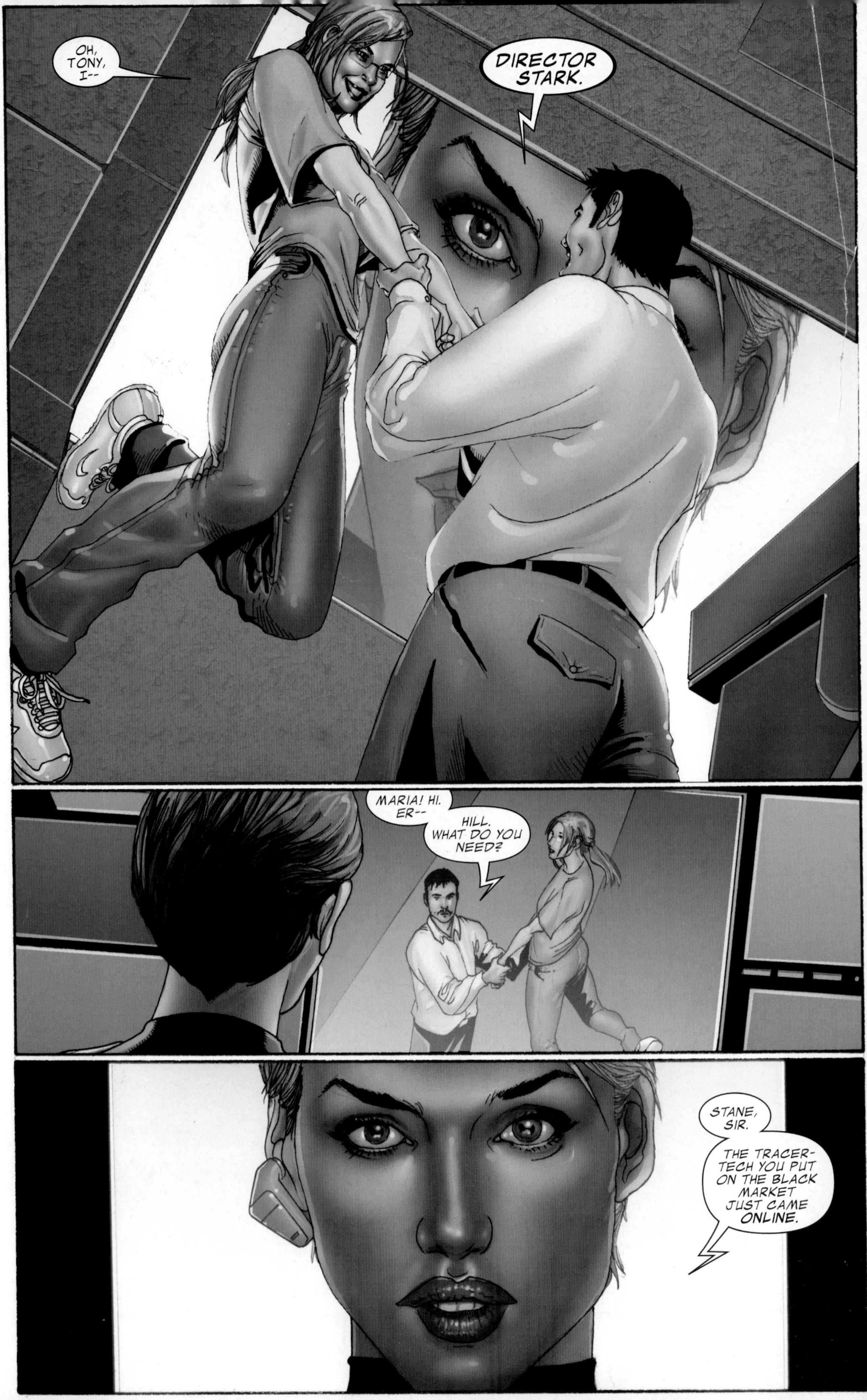
OH, TONY, I--
DIRECTOR STARK.
MARIA! HI. ER--
HILL. WHAT DO YOU NEED?
STANE, SIR.
THE TRACER-TECH YOU PUT ON THE BLACK MARKET JUST CAME ONLINE.

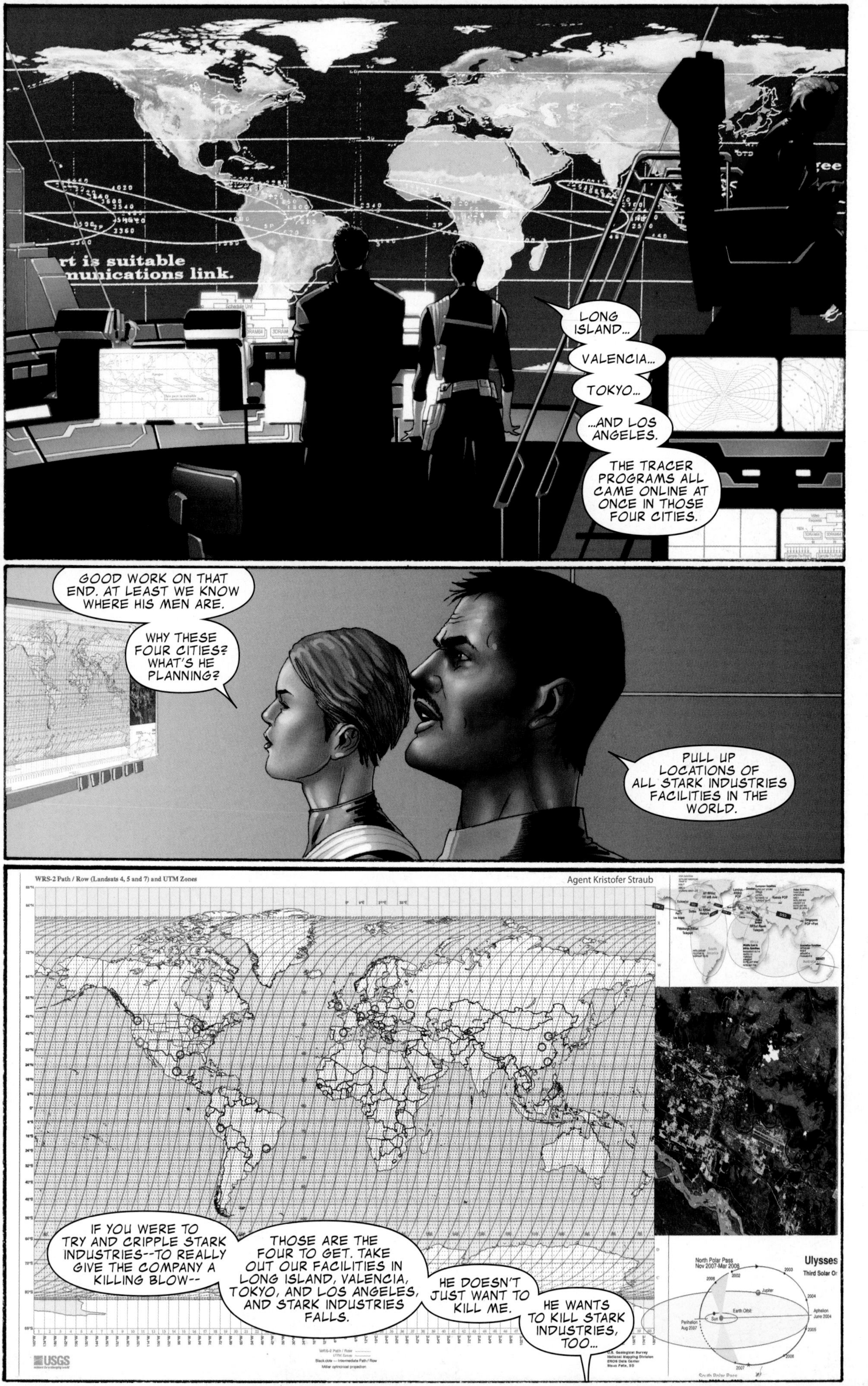

LONG ISLAND...
VALENCIA...
TOKYO...
...AND LOS ANGELES.
THE TRACER PROGRAMS ALL CAME ONLINE AT ONCE IN THOSE FOUR CITIES.
GOOD WORK ON THAT END. AT LEAST WE KNOW WHERE HIS MEN ARE.
WHY THESE FOUR CITIES? WHAT'S HE PLANNING?
PULL UP LOCATIONS OF ALL STARK INDUSTRIES FACILITIES IN THE WORLD.
WRS-2 Path / Row (Landsats 4, 5 and 7) and UTM Zones
Agent Kristofer Straub
North Polar Pass Nov 2007-Mar 2008
Ulysses
IF YOU WERE TO TRY AND CRIPPLE STARK INDUSTRIES--TO REALLY GIVE THE COMPANY A KILLING BLOW--
THOSE ARE THE FOUR TO GET. TAKE OUT OUR FACILITIES IN LONG ISLAND, VALENCIA, TOKYO, AND LOS ANGELES, AND STARK INDUSTRIES FALLS.
HE DOESN'T JUST WANT TO KILL ME.
HE WANTS TO KILL STARK INDUSTRIES, TOO...

5

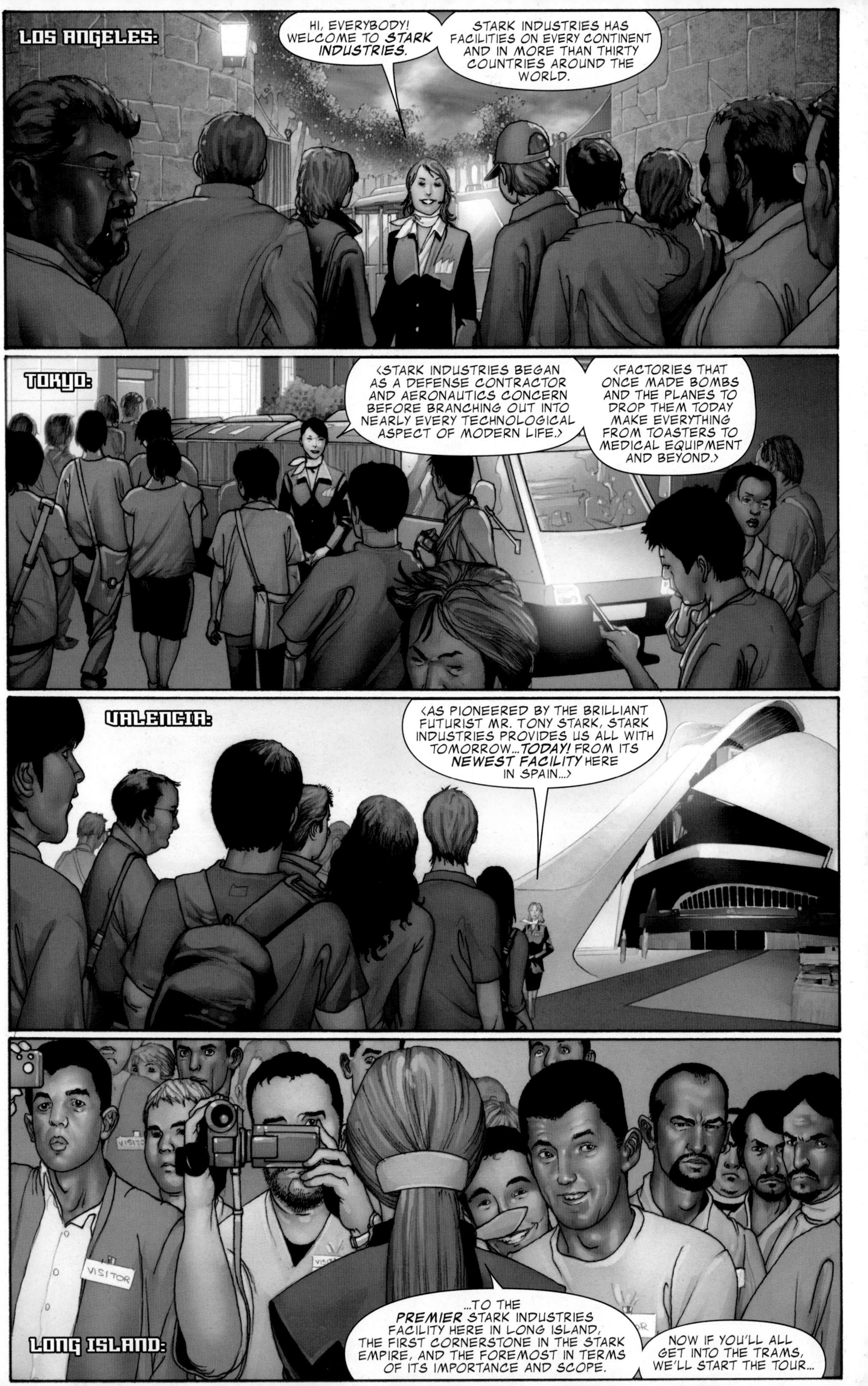
LOS ANGELES:
HI, EVERYBODY! WELCOME TO STARK INDUSTRIES.
STARK INDUSTRIES HAS FACILITIES ON EVERY CONTINENT AND IN MORE THAN THIRTY COUNTRIES AROUND THE WORLD.
TOKYO:
<STARK INDUSTRIES BEGAN AS A DEFENSE CONTRACTOR AND AERONAUTICS CONCERN BEFORE BRANCHING OUT INTO NEARLY EVERY TECHNOLOGICAL ASPECT OF MODERN LIFE.>
<FACTORIES THAT ONCE MADE BOMBS AND THE PLANES TO DROP THEM TODAY MAKE EVERYTHING FROM TOASTERS TO MEDICAL EQUIPMENT AND BEYOND.>
VALENCIA:
<AS PIONEERED BY THE BRILLIANT FUTURIST MR. TONY STARK, STARK INDUSTRIES PROVIDES US ALL WITH TOMORROW...TODAY! FROM ITS NEWEST FACILITY HERE IN SPAIN...>
VISITOR
...TO THE PREMIER STARK INDUSTRIES FACILITY HERE IN LONG ISLAND, THE FIRST CORNERSTONE IN THE STARK EMPIRE, AND THE FOREMOST IN TERMS OF ITS IMPORTANCE AND SCOPE.
NOW IF YOU'LL ALL GET INTO THE TRAMS, WE'LL START THE TOUR...
LONG ISLAND:

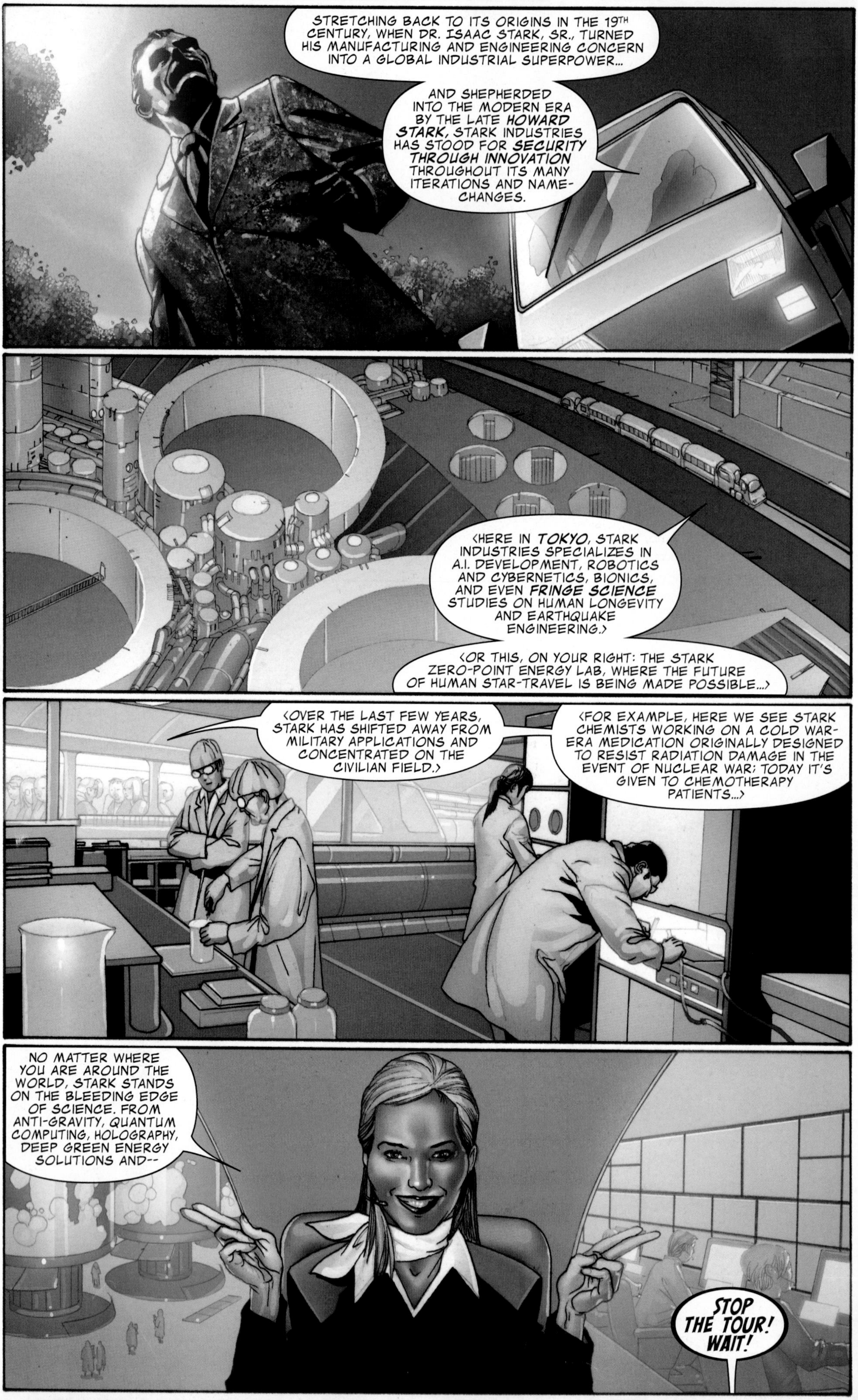
STRETCHING BACK TO ITS ORIGINS IN THE 19TH CENTURY, WHEN DR. ISAAC STARK, SR., TURNED HIS MANUFACTURING AND ENGINEERING CONCERN INTO A GLOBAL INDUSTRIAL SUPERPOWER...
AND SHEPHERDED INTO THE MODERN ERA BY THE LATE HOWARD STARK, STARK INDUSTRIES HAS STOOD FOR SECURITY THROUGH INNOVATION THROUGHOUT ITS MANY ITERATIONS AND NAME-CHANGES.
<HERE IN TOKYO, STARK INDUSTRIES SPECIALIZES IN A.I. DEVELOPMENT, ROBOTICS AND CYBERNETICS, BIONICS, AND EVEN FRINGE SCIENCE STUDIES ON HUMAN LONGEVITY AND EARTHQUAKE ENGINEERING.>
<OR THIS, ON YOUR RIGHT: THE STARK ZERO-POINT ENERGY LAB, WHERE THE FUTURE OF HUMAN STAR-TRAVEL IS BEING MADE POSSIBLE...>
<OVER THE LAST FEW YEARS, STARK HAS SHIFTED AWAY FROM MILITARY APPLICATIONS AND CONCENTRATED ON THE CIVILIAN FIELD.>
<FOR EXAMPLE, HERE WE SEE STARK CHEMISTS WORKING ON A COLD WAR-ERA MEDICATION ORIGINALLY DESIGNED TO RESIST RADIATION DAMAGE IN THE EVENT OF NUCLEAR WAR; TODAY IT'S GIVEN TO CHEMOTHERAPY PATIENTS...>
NO MATTER WHERE YOU ARE AROUND THE WORLD, STARK STANDS ON THE BLEEDING EDGE OF SCIENCE. FROM ANTI-GRAVITY, QUANTUM COMPUTING, HOLOGRAPHY, DEEP GREEN ENERGY SOLUTIONS AND--
STOP THE TOUR! WAIT!

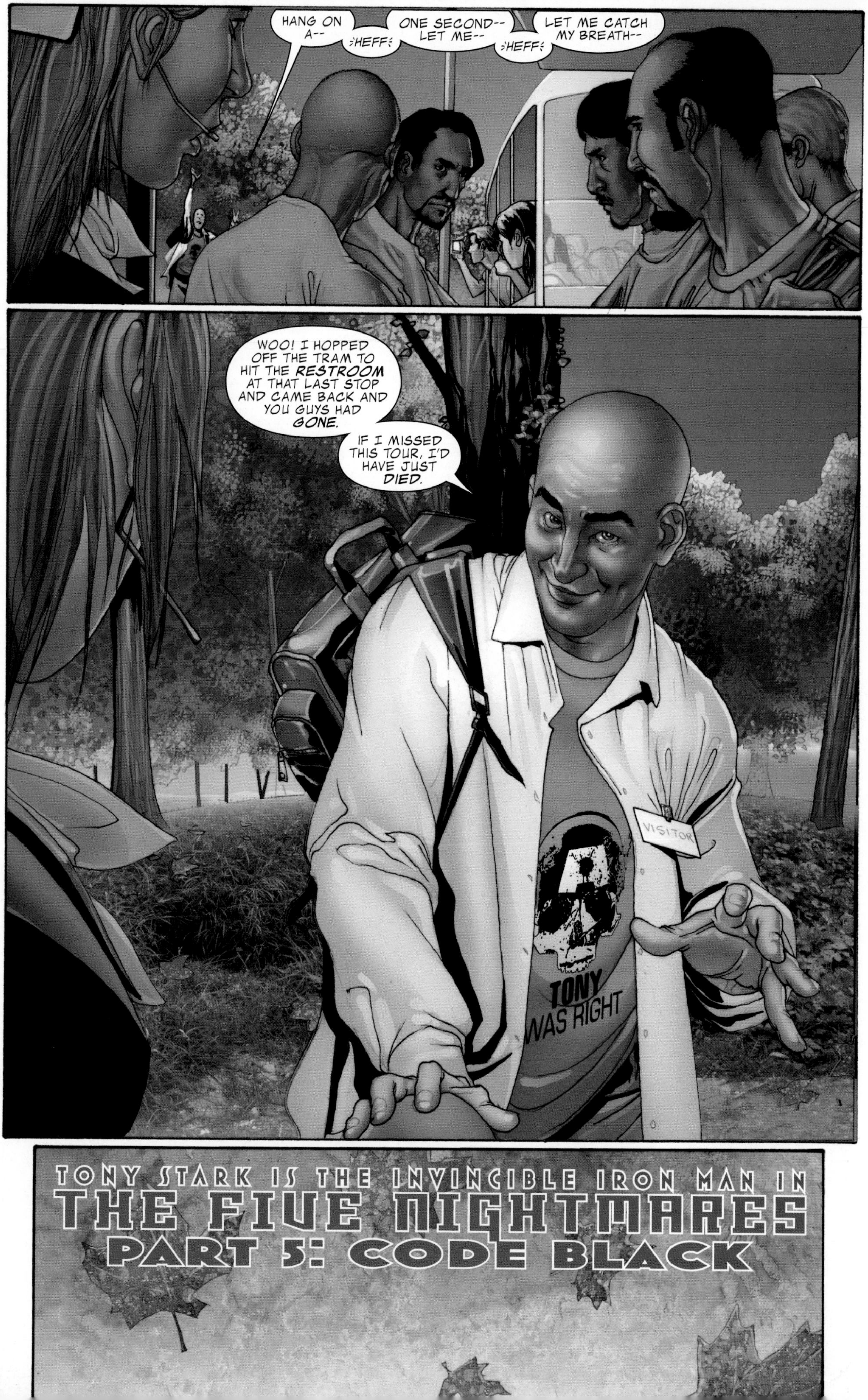
HANG ON A--
HEFF
ONE SECOND-- LET ME--
HEFF
LET ME CATCH MY BREATH--
WOO! I HOPPED OFF THE TRAM TO HIT THE RESTROOM AT THAT LAST STOP AND CAME BACK AND YOU GUYS HAD GONE.
IF I MISSED THIS TOUR, I'D HAVE JUST DIED.
VISITOR
TONY WAS RIGHT
TONY STARK IS THE INVINCIBLE IRON MAN IN
THE FIVE NIGHTMARES
PART 5: CODE BLACK

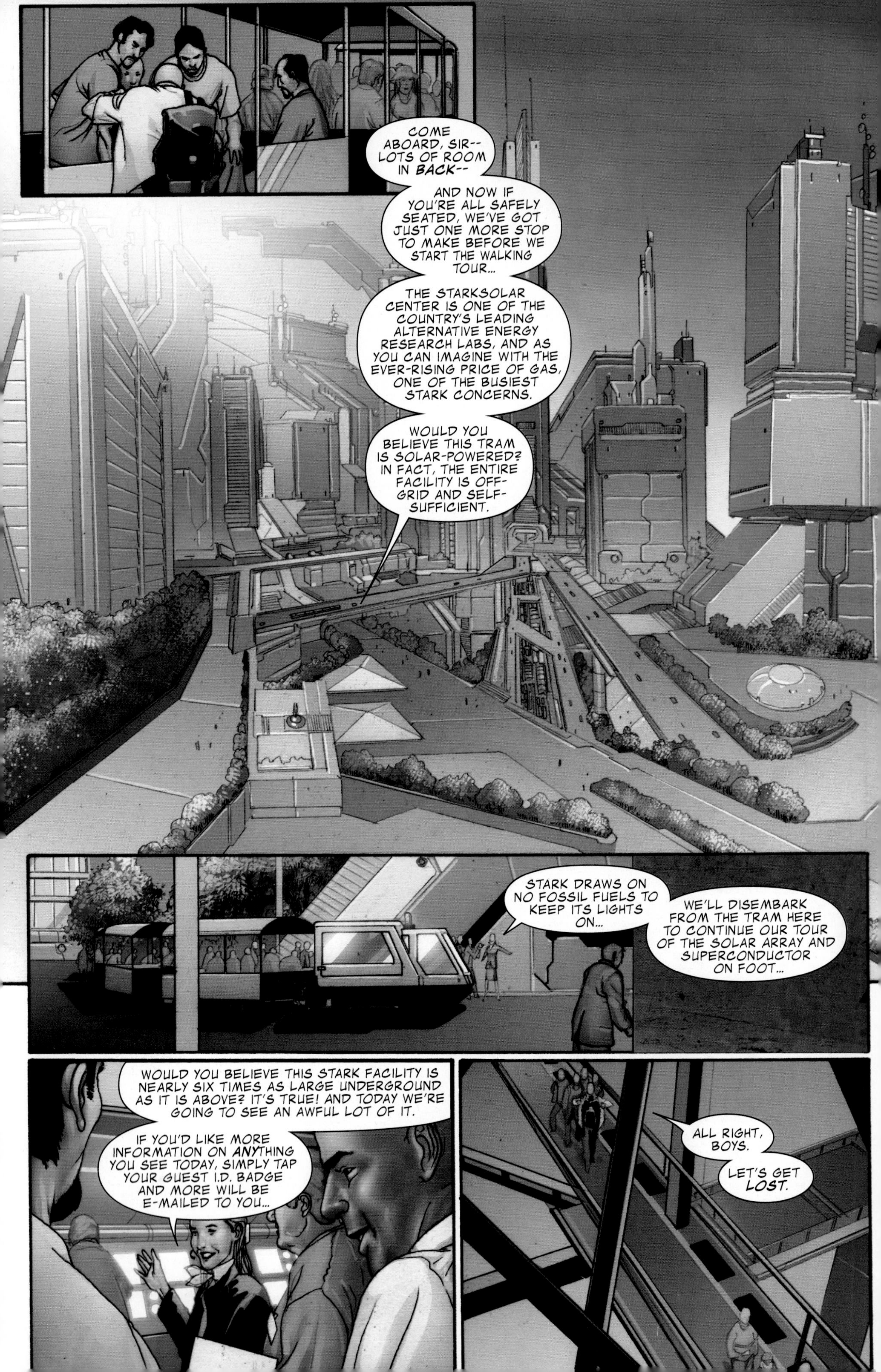
COME ABOARD, SIR-- LOTS OF ROOM IN BACK--
AND NOW IF YOU'RE ALL SAFELY SEATED, WE'VE GOT JUST ONE MORE STOP TO MAKE BEFORE WE START THE WALKING TOUR...
THE STARKSOLAR CENTER IS ONE OF THE COUNTRY'S LEADING ALTERNATIVE ENERGY RESEARCH LABS, AND AS YOU CAN IMAGINE WITH THE EVER-RISING PRICE OF GAS, ONE OF THE BUSIEST STARK CONCERNS.
WOULD YOU BELIEVE THIS TRAM IS SOLAR-POWERED? IN FACT, THE ENTIRE FACILITY IS OFF-GRID AND SELF-SUFFICIENT.
STARK DRAWS ON NO FOSSIL FUELS TO KEEP ITS LIGHTS ON...
WE'LL DISEMBARK FROM THE TRAM HERE TO CONTINUE OUR TOUR OF THE SOLAR ARRAY AND SUPERCONDUCTOR ON FOOT...
WOULD YOU BELIEVE THIS STARK FACILITY IS NEARLY SIX TIMES AS LARGE UNDERGROUND AS IT IS ABOVE? IT'S TRUE! AND TODAY WE'RE GOING TO SEE AN AWFUL LOT OF IT.
IF YOU'D LIKE MORE INFORMATION ON ANYTHING YOU SEE TODAY, SIMPLY TAP YOUR GUEST I.D. BADGE AND MORE WILL BE E-MAILED TO YOU...
ALL RIGHT, BOYS.
LET'S GET LOST.

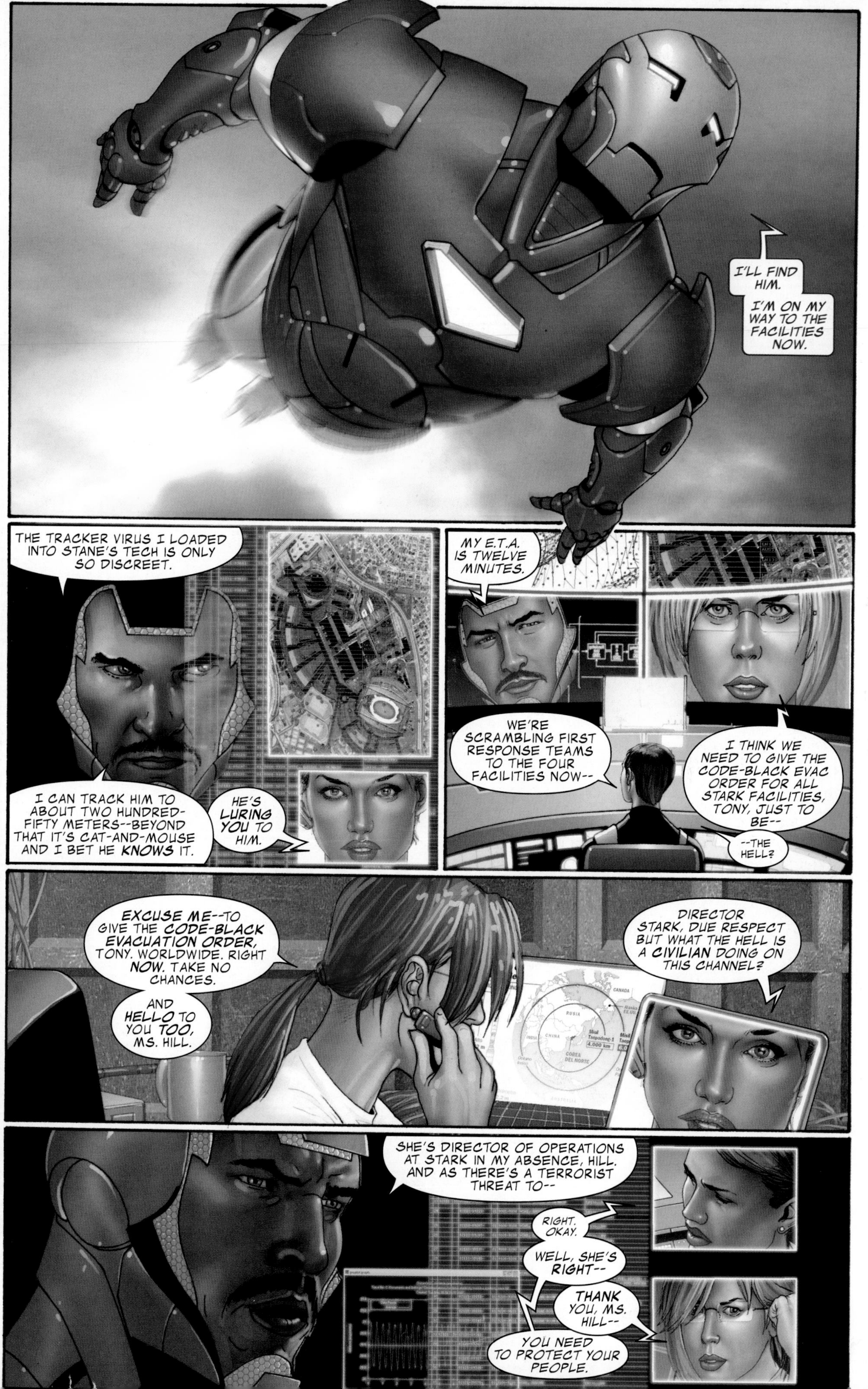
I'LL FIND HIM.
I'M ON MY WAY TO THE FACILITIES NOW.
THE TRACKER VIRUS I LOADED INTO STANE'S TECH IS ONLY SO DISCREET.
I CAN TRACK HIM TO ABOUT TWO HUNDRED-FIFTY METERS--BEYOND THAT IT'S CAT-AND-MOUSE AND I BET HE KNOWS IT.
HE'S LURING YOU TO HIM.
MY E.T.A. IS TWELVE MINUTES.
WE'RE SCRAMBLING FIRST RESPONSE TEAMS TO THE FOUR FACILITIES NOW--
I THINK WE NEED TO GIVE THE CODE-BLACK EVAC ORDER FOR ALL STARK FACILITIES, TONY, JUST TO BE--
--THE HELL?
EXCUSE ME--TO GIVE THE CODE-BLACK EVACUATION ORDER, TONY. WORLDWIDE. RIGHT NOW. TAKE NO CHANCES.
AND HELLO TO YOU TOO, MS. HILL.
DIRECTOR STARK, DUE RESPECT BUT WHAT THE HELL IS A CIVILIAN DOING ON THIS CHANNEL?
SHE'S DIRECTOR OF OPERATIONS AT STARK IN MY ABSENCE, HILL. AND AS THERE'S A TERRORIST THREAT TO--
RIGHT. OKAY.
WELL, SHE'S RIGHT--
THANK YOU, MS. HILL--
YOU NEED TO PROTECT YOUR PEOPLE.

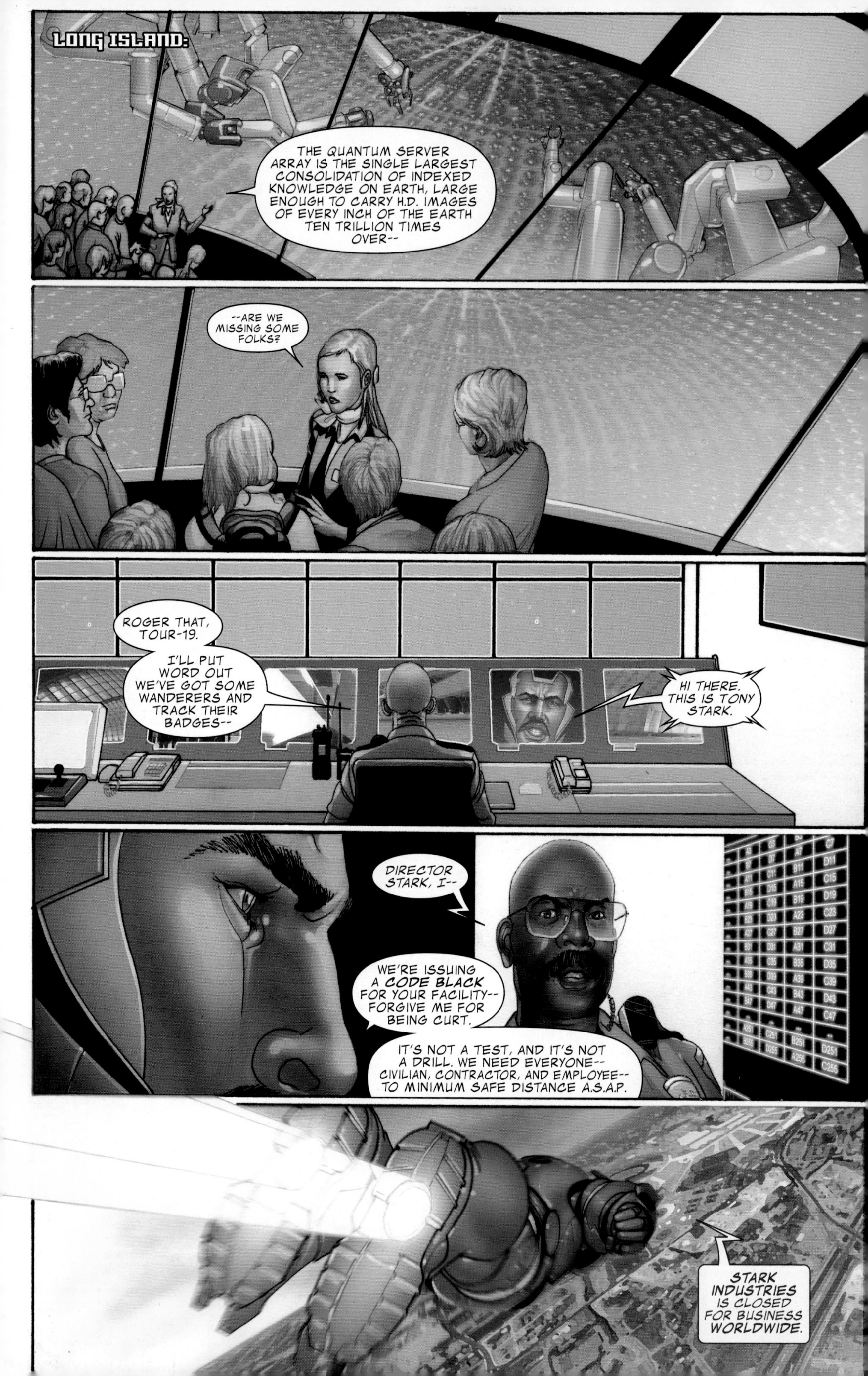
LONG ISLAND:
THE QUANTUM SERVER ARRAY IS THE SINGLE LARGEST CONSOLIDATION OF INDEXED KNOWLEDGE ON EARTH, LARGE ENOUGH TO CARRY H.D. IMAGES OF EVERY INCH OF THE EARTH TEN TRILLION TIMES OVER--
--ARE WE MISSING SOME FOLKS?
ROGER THAT, TOUR-19.
I'LL PUT WORD OUT WE'VE GOT SOME WANDERERS AND TRACK THEIR BADGES--
HI THERE. THIS IS TONY STARK.
DIRECTOR STARK, I--
WE'RE ISSUING A **CODE BLACK** FOR YOUR FACILITY--FORGIVE ME FOR BEING CURT.
IT'S NOT A TEST, AND IT'S NOT A DRILL. WE NEED EVERYONE--CIVILIAN, CONTRACTOR, AND EMPLOYEE--TO MINIMUM SAFE DISTANCE A.S.A.P.
STARK INDUSTRIES IS CLOSED FOR BUSINESS **WORLDWIDE.**

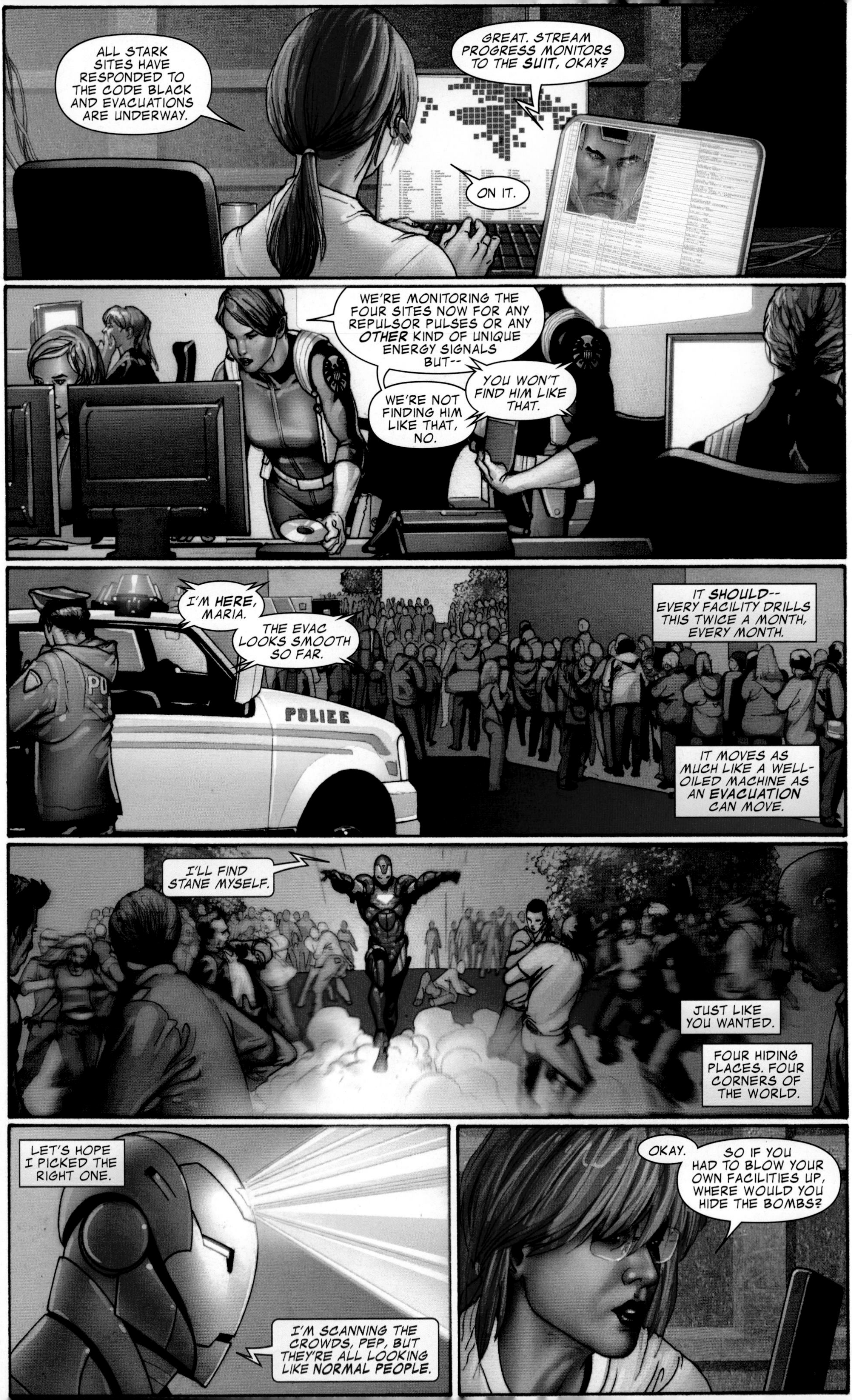
ALL STARK SITES HAVE RESPONDED TO THE CODE BLACK AND EVACUATIONS ARE UNDERWAY.
GREAT. STREAM PROGRESS MONITORS TO THE SUIT, OKAY?
ON IT.
WE'RE MONITORING THE FOUR SITES NOW FOR ANY REPULSOR PULSES OR ANY OTHER KIND OF UNIQUE ENERGY SIGNALS BUT--
YOU WON'T FIND HIM LIKE THAT.
WE'RE NOT FINDING HIM LIKE THAT, NO.
I'M HERE, MARIA.
THE EVAC LOOKS SMOOTH SO FAR.
POLICE
IT SHOULD-- EVERY FACILITY DRILLS THIS TWICE A MONTH, EVERY MONTH.
IT MOVES AS MUCH LIKE A WELL-OILED MACHINE AS AN EVACUATION CAN MOVE.
I'LL FIND STANE MYSELF.
JUST LIKE YOU WANTED.
FOUR HIDING PLACES. FOUR CORNERS OF THE WORLD.
LET'S HOPE I PICKED THE RIGHT ONE.
I'M SCANNING THE CROWDS, PEP, BUT THEY'RE ALL LOOKING LIKE NORMAL PEOPLE.
OKAY.
SO IF YOU HAD TO BLOW YOUR OWN FACILITIES UP, WHERE WOULD YOU HIDE THE BOMBS?

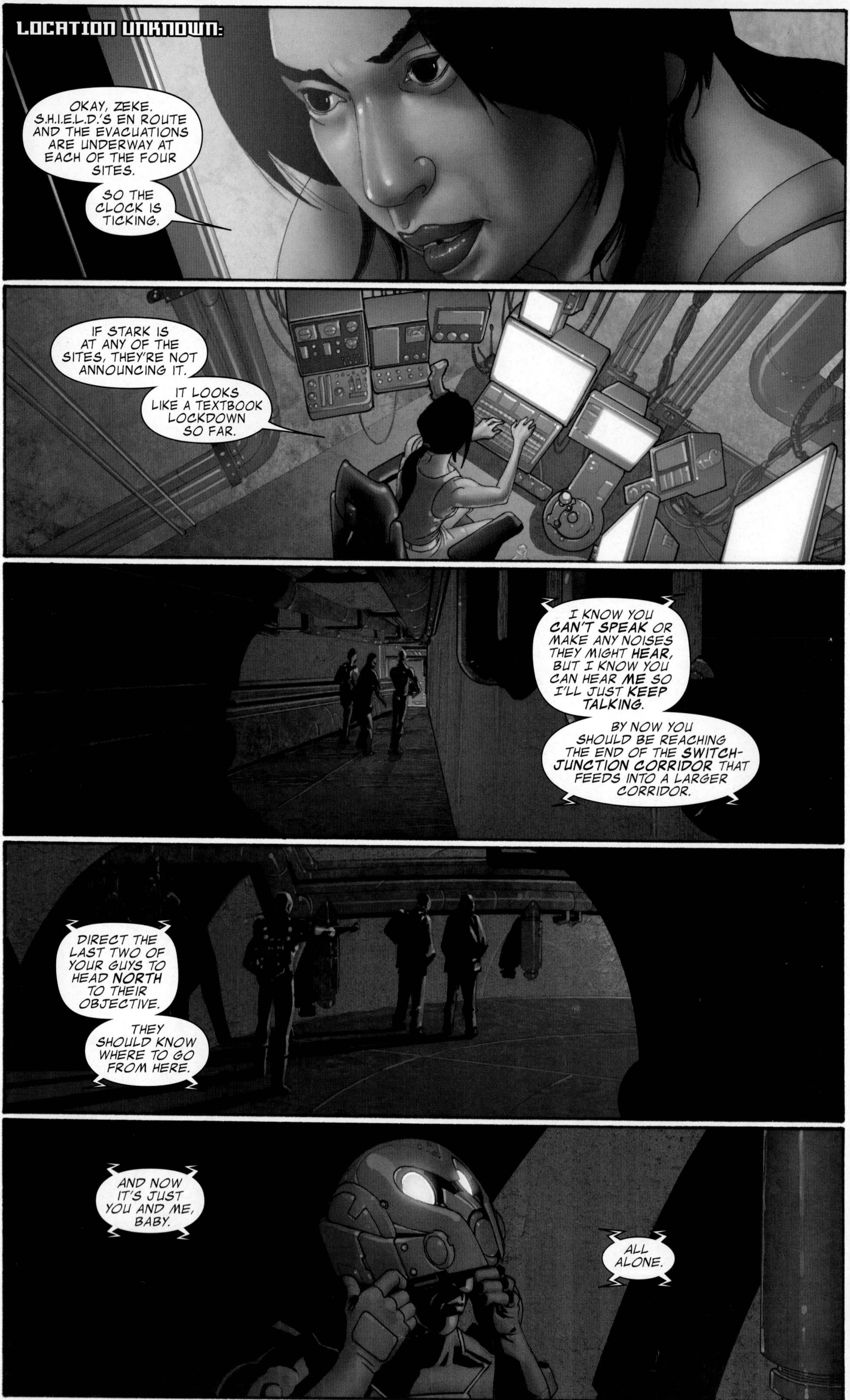
LOCATION UNKNOWN:
OKAY, ZEKE. S.H.I.E.L.D.'S EN ROUTE AND THE EVACUATIONS ARE UNDERWAY AT EACH OF THE FOUR SITES.
SO THE CLOCK IS TICKING.
IF STARK IS AT ANY OF THE SITES, THEY'RE NOT ANNOUNCING IT.
IT LOOKS LIKE A TEXTBOOK LOCKDOWN SO FAR.
I KNOW YOU CAN'T SPEAK OR MAKE ANY NOISES THEY MIGHT HEAR, BUT I KNOW YOU CAN HEAR ME SO I'LL JUST KEEP TALKING.
BY NOW YOU SHOULD BE REACHING THE END OF THE SWITCH-JUNCTION CORRIDOR THAT FEEDS INTO A LARGER CORRIDOR.
DIRECT THE LAST TWO OF YOUR GUYS TO HEAD NORTH TO THEIR OBJECTIVE.
THEY SHOULD KNOW WHERE TO GO FROM HERE.
AND NOW IT'S JUST YOU AND ME, BABY.
ALL ALONE.

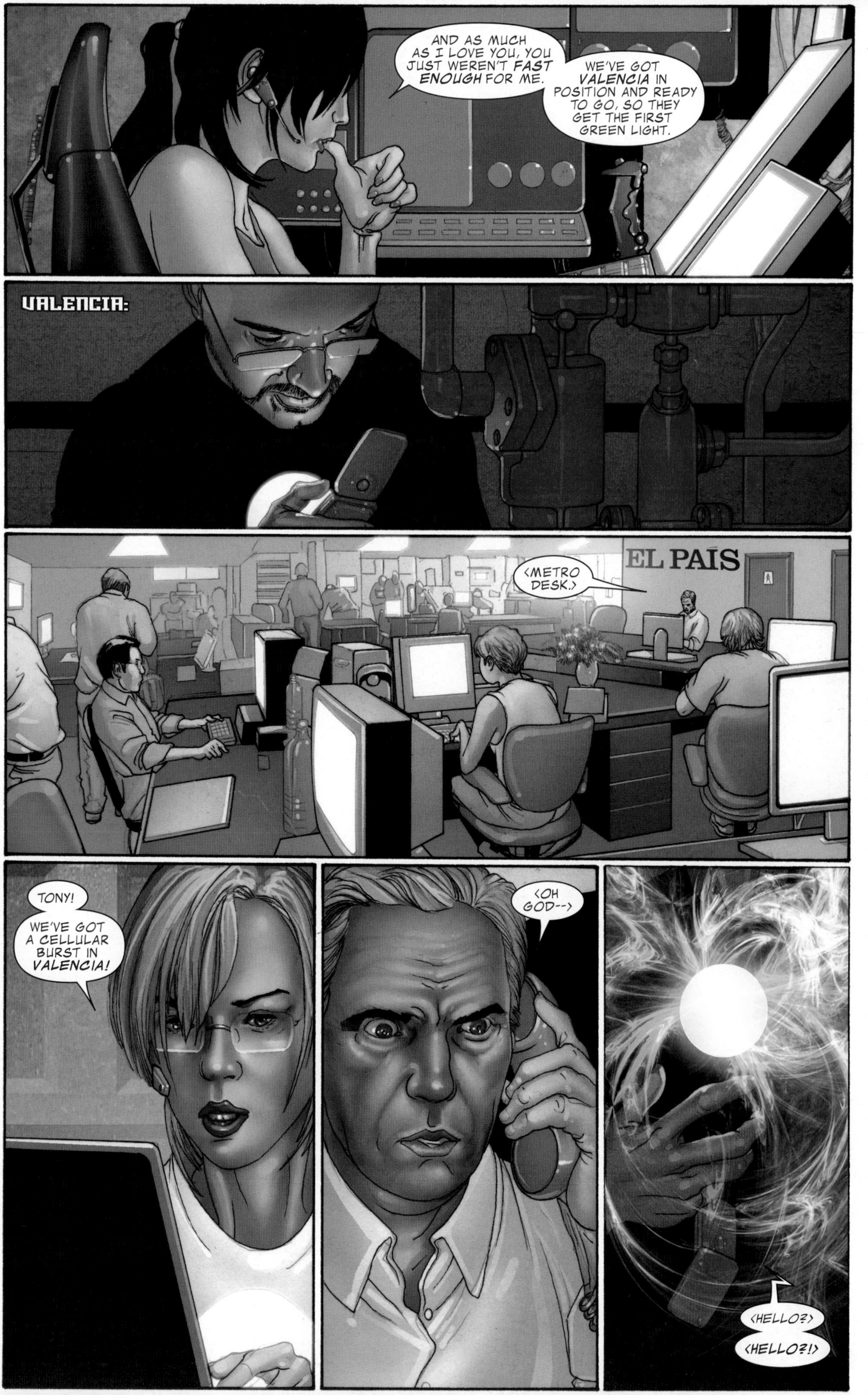
AND AS MUCH AS I LOVE YOU, YOU JUST WEREN'T FAST ENOUGH FOR ME.
WE'VE GOT VALENCIA IN POSITION AND READY TO GO, SO THEY GET THE FIRST GREEN LIGHT.
VALENCIA:
EL PAIS
<METRO DESK.>
TONY!
WE'VE GOT A CELLULAR BURST IN VALENCIA!
<OH GOD-->
<HELLO?>
<HELLO?!>

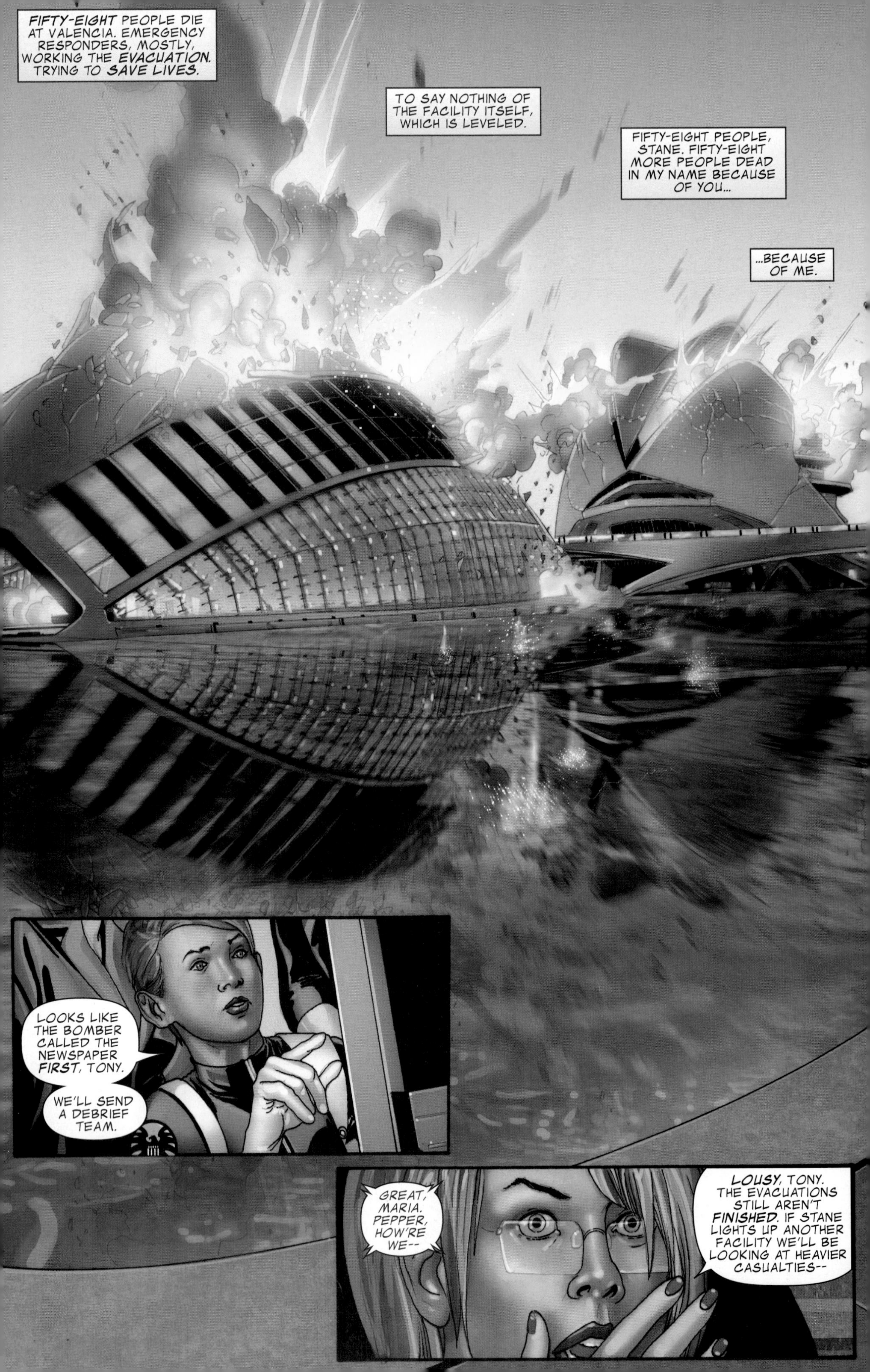
FIFTY-EIGHT PEOPLE DIE AT VALENCIA. EMERGENCY RESPONDERS, MOSTLY, WORKING THE EVACUATION. TRYING TO SAVE LIVES.
TO SAY NOTHING OF THE FACILITY ITSELF, WHICH IS LEVELED.
FIFTY-EIGHT PEOPLE, STANE. FIFTY-EIGHT MORE PEOPLE DEAD IN MY NAME BECAUSE OF YOU...
...BECAUSE OF ME.
LOOKS LIKE THE BOMBER CALLED THE NEWSPAPER FIRST, TONY.
WE'LL SEND A DEBRIEF TEAM.
GREAT, MARIA. PEPPER, HOW'RE WE--
LOUSY, TONY. THE EVACUATIONS STILL AREN'T FINISHED. IF STANE LIGHTS UP ANOTHER FACILITY WE'LL BE LOOKING AT HEAVIER CASUALTIES--

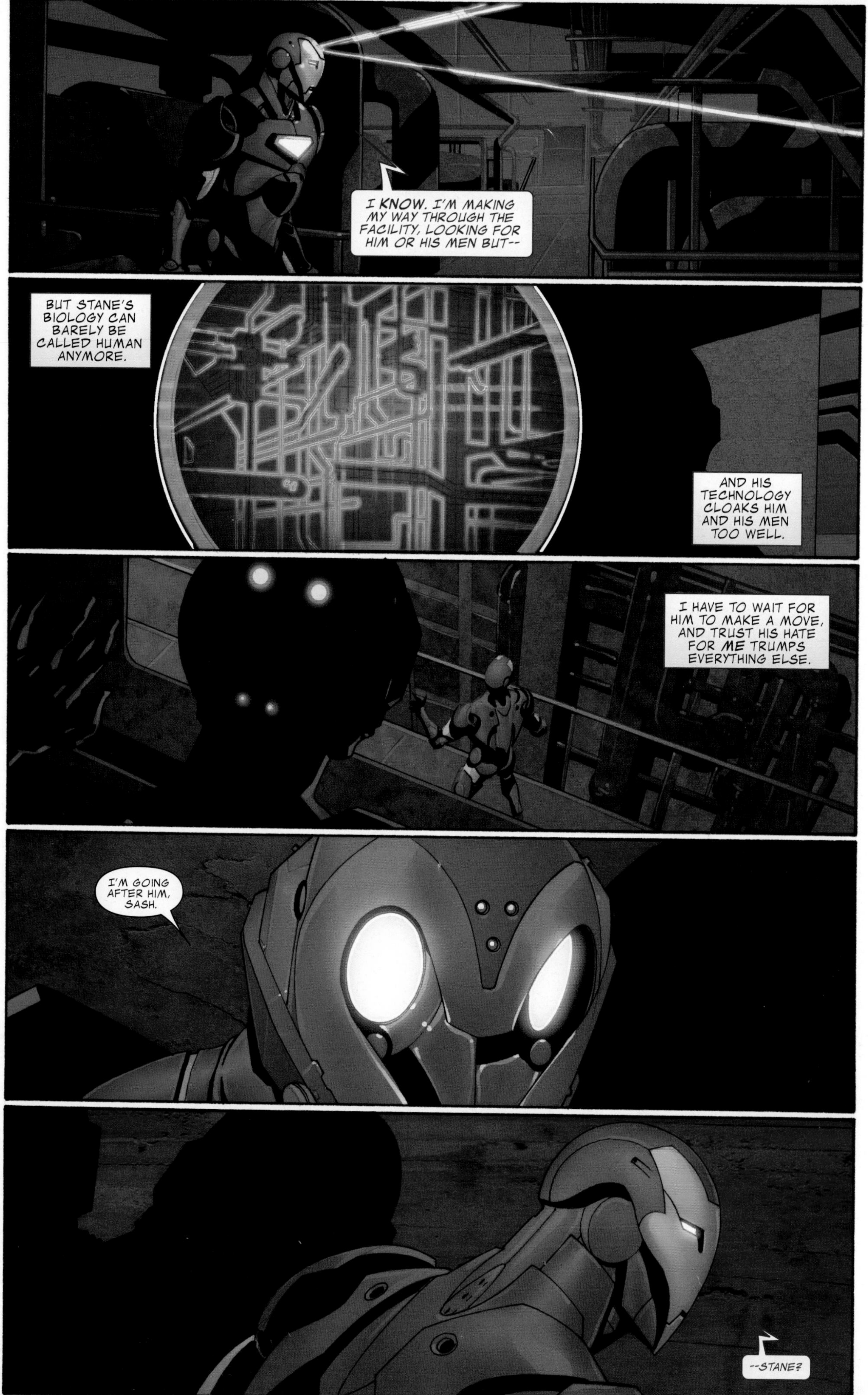

I KNOW. I'M MAKING MY WAY THROUGH THE FACILITY, LOOKING FOR HIM OR HIS MEN BUT--
BUT STANE'S BIOLOGY CAN BARELY BE CALLED HUMAN ANYMORE.
AND HIS TECHNOLOGY CLOAKS HIM AND HIS MEN TOO WELL.
I HAVE TO WAIT FOR HIM TO MAKE A MOVE, AND TRUST HIS HATE FOR ME TRUMPS EVERYTHING ELSE.
I'M GOING AFTER HIM, SASH.
--STANE?

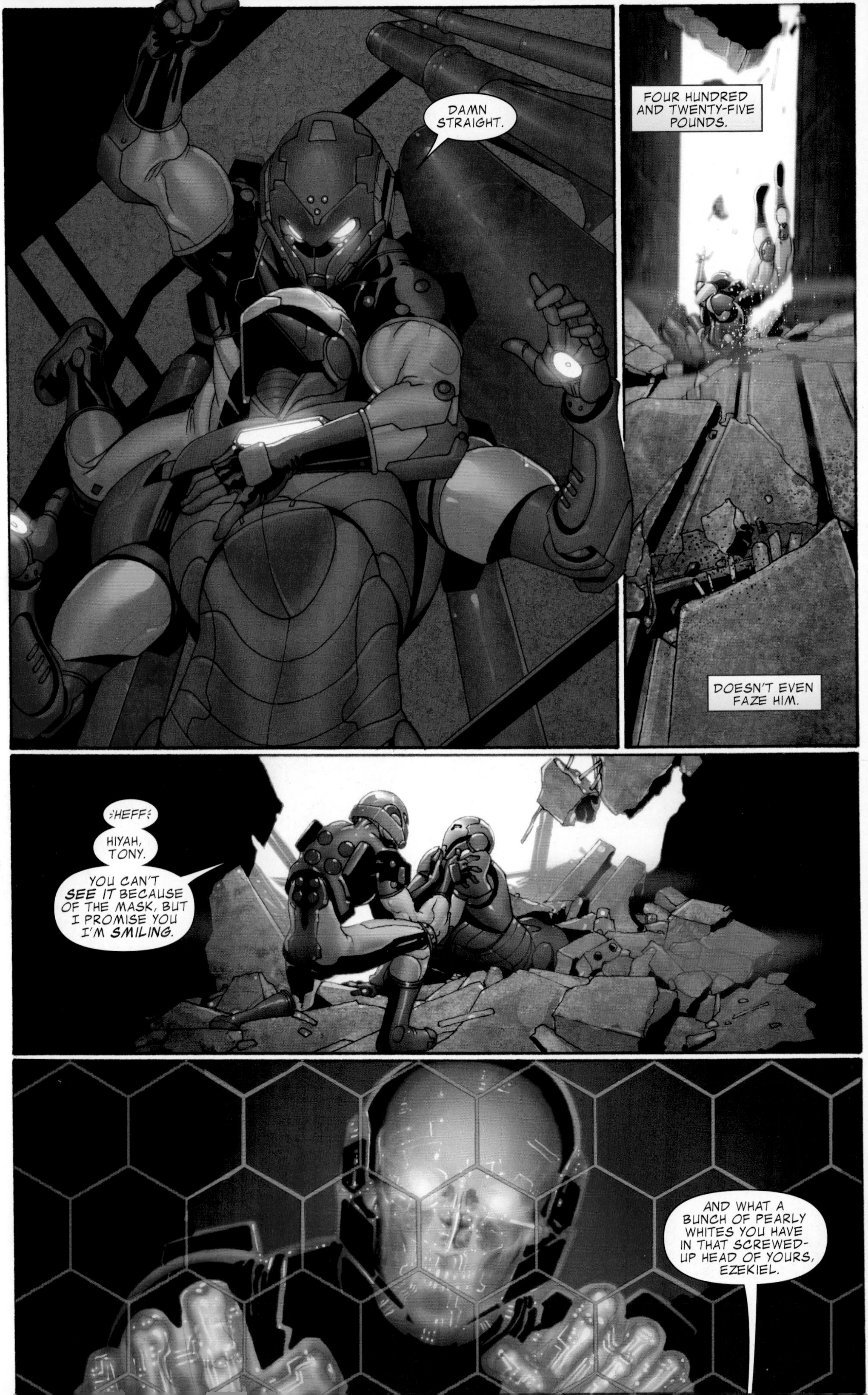
DAMN STRAIGHT.
FOUR HUNDRED AND TWENTY-FIVE POUNDS.
DOESN'T EVEN FAZE HIM.
HEFF
HIYAH, TONY.
YOU CAN'T SEE IT BECAUSE OF THE MASK, BUT I PROMISE YOU I'M SMILING.
AND WHAT A BUNCH OF PEARLY WHITES YOU HAVE IN THAT SCREWED-UP HEAD OF YOURS, EZEKIEL.

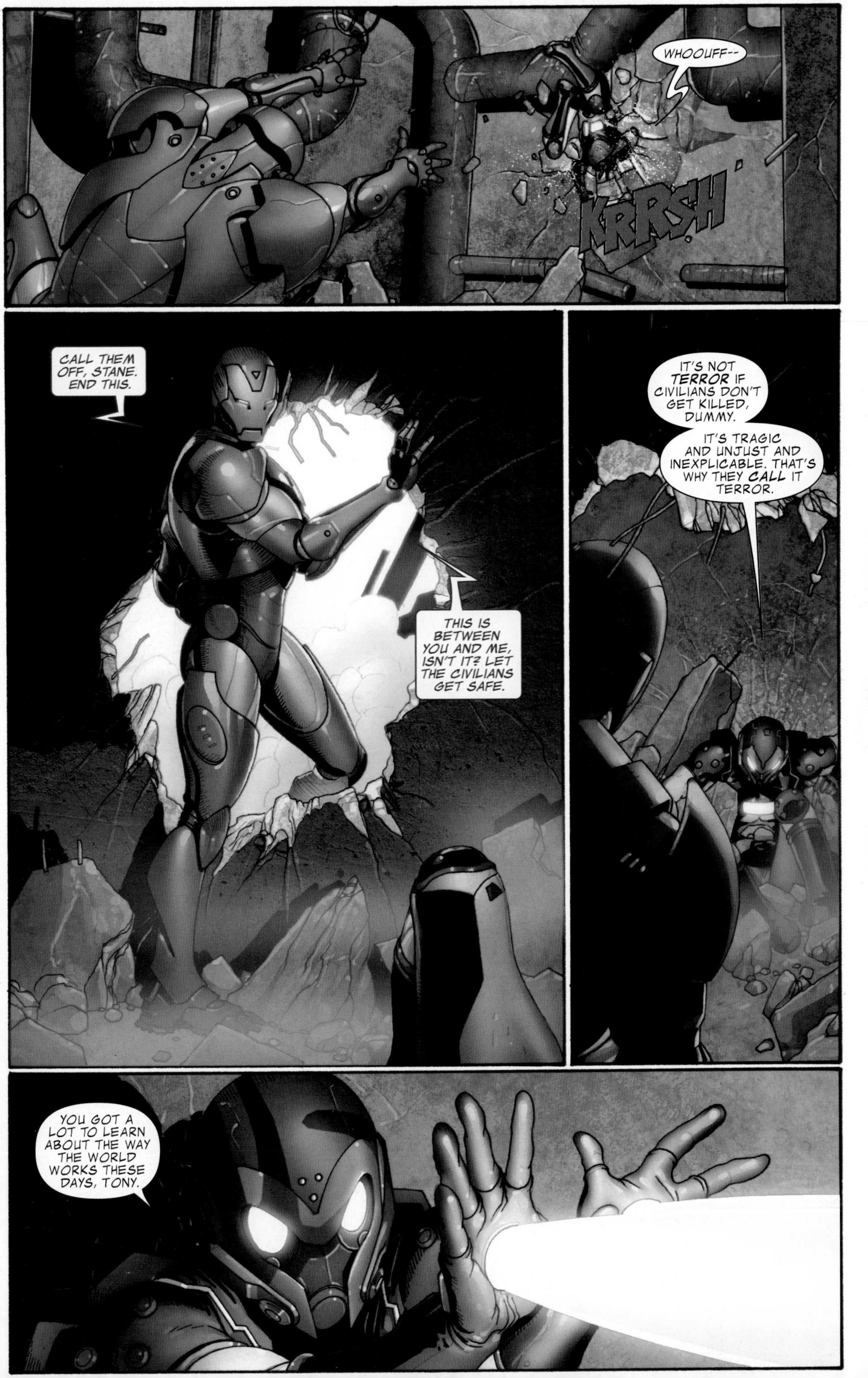
WHOOUFF--
KRRSH
CALL THEM OFF, STANE. END THIS.
THIS IS BETWEEN YOU AND ME, ISN'T IT? LET THE CIVILIANS GET SAFE.
IT'S NOT TERROR IF CIVILIANS DON'T GET KILLED, DUMMY.
IT'S TRAGIC AND UNJUST AND INEXPLICABLE. THAT'S WHY THEY CALL IT TERROR.
YOU GOT A LOT TO LEARN ABOUT THE WAY THE WORLD WORKS THESE DAYS, TONY.

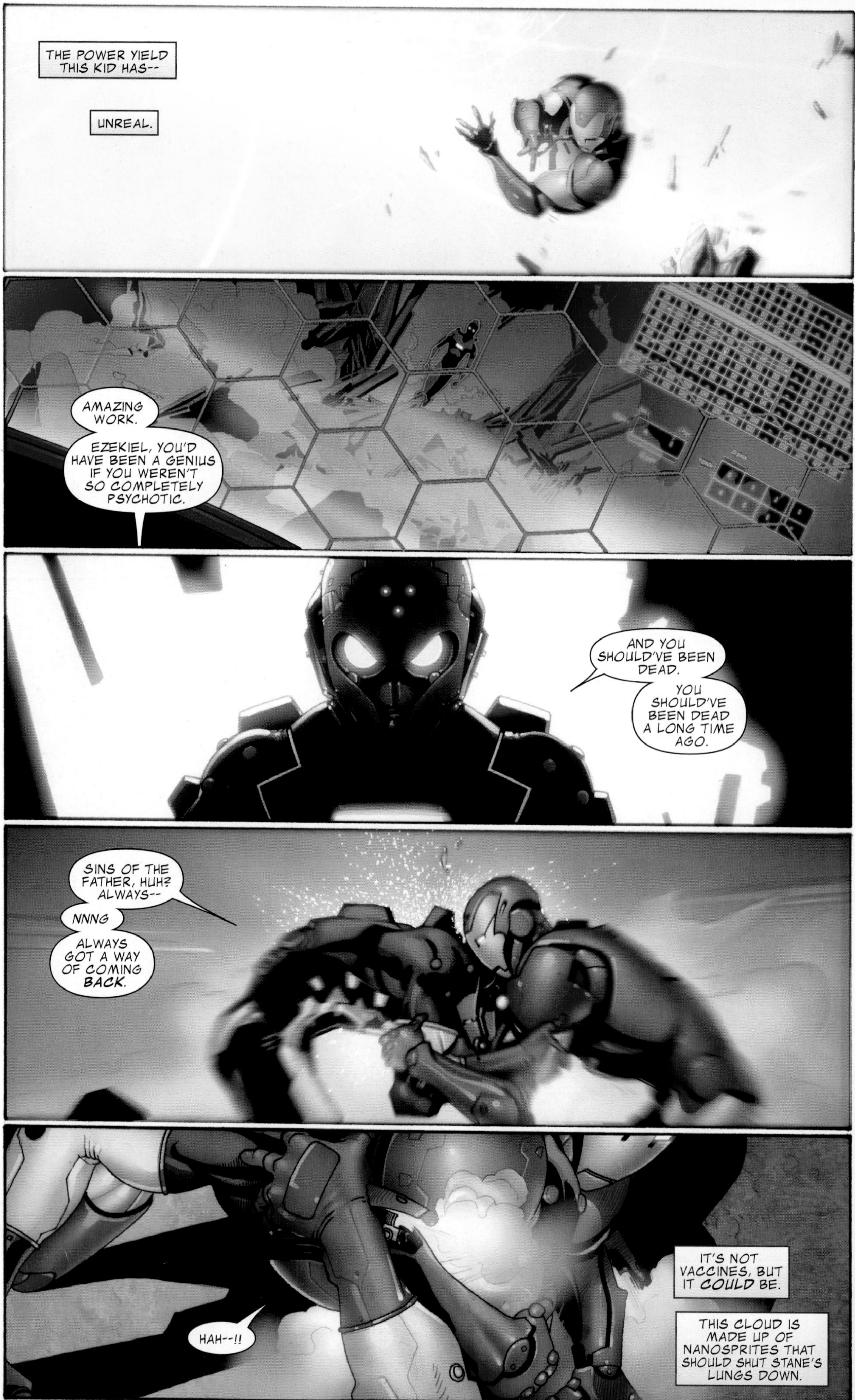

THE POWER YIELD THIS KID HAS--
UNREAL.
AMAZING WORK.
EZEKIEL, YOU'D HAVE BEEN A GENIUS IF YOU WEREN'T SO COMPLETELY PSYCHOTIC.
AND YOU SHOULD'VE BEEN DEAD.
YOU SHOULD'VE BEEN DEAD A LONG TIME AGO.
SINS OF THE FATHER, HUH? ALWAYS--
NNNG
ALWAYS GOT A WAY OF COMING BACK.
IT'S NOT VACCINES, BUT IT COULD BE.
THIS CLOUD IS MADE UP OF NANOSPRITES THAT SHOULD SHUT STANE'S LUNGS DOWN.
HAH--!!

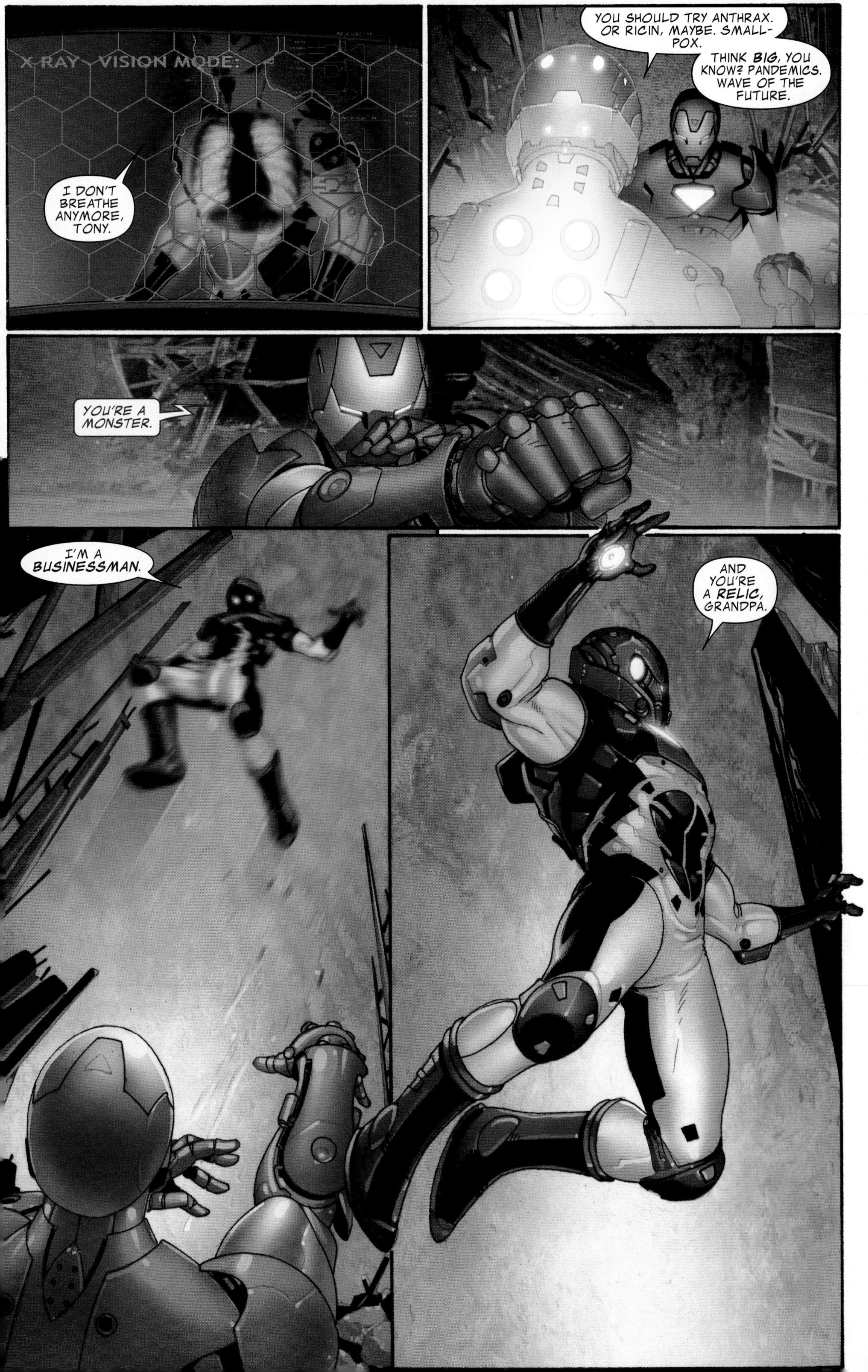
X RAY VISION MODE:
I DON'T BREATHE ANYMORE, TONY.
YOU SHOULD TRY ANTHRAX. OR RICIN, MAYBE. SMALL-POX.
THINK BIG, YOU KNOW? PANDEMICS. WAVE OF THE FUTURE.
YOU'RE A MONSTER.
I'M A BUSINESSMAN.
AND YOU'RE A RELIC, GRANDPA.

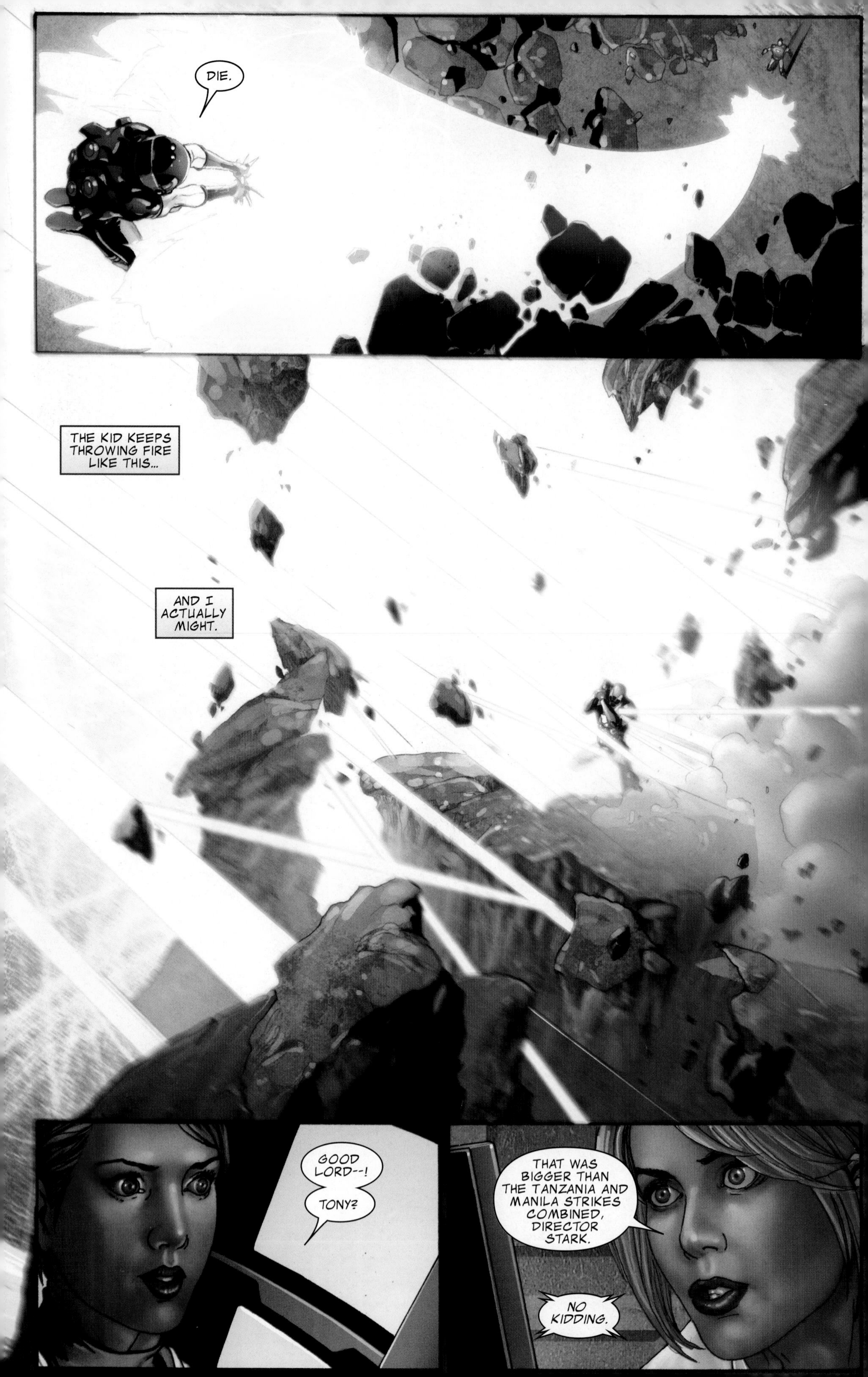

DIE.
THE KID KEEPS THROWING FIRE LIKE THIS...
AND I ACTUALLY MIGHT.
GOOD LORD--!
TONY?
THAT WAS BIGGER THAN THE TANZANIA AND MANILA STRIKES COMBINED, DIRECTOR STARK.
NO KIDDING.

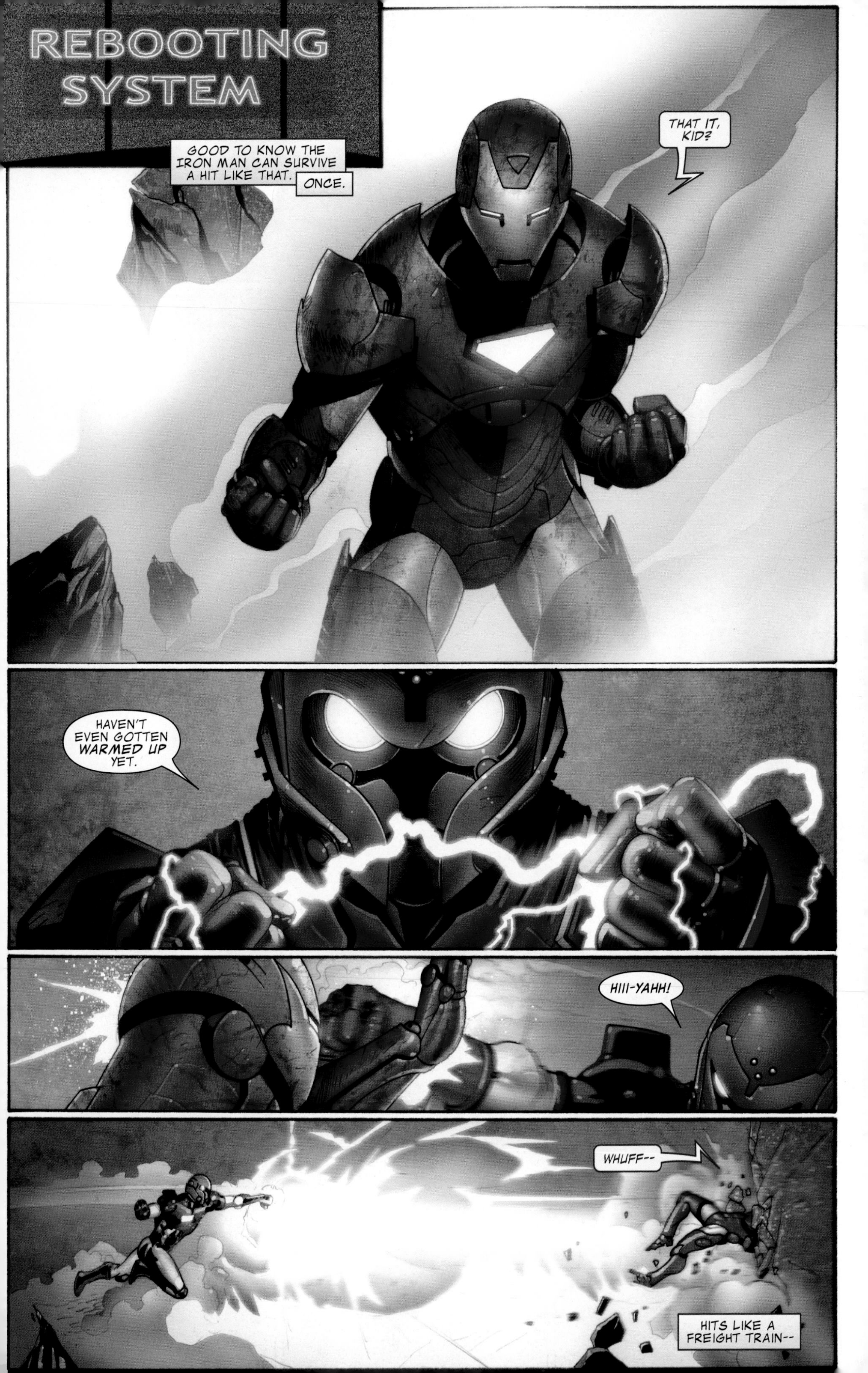
REBOOTING SYSTEM
GOOD TO KNOW THE IRON MAN CAN SURVIVE A HIT LIKE THAT.
ONCE.
THAT IT, KID?
HAVEN'T EVEN GOTTEN WARMED UP YET.
HIII-YAHH!
WHUFF--
HITS LIKE A FREIGHT TRAIN--

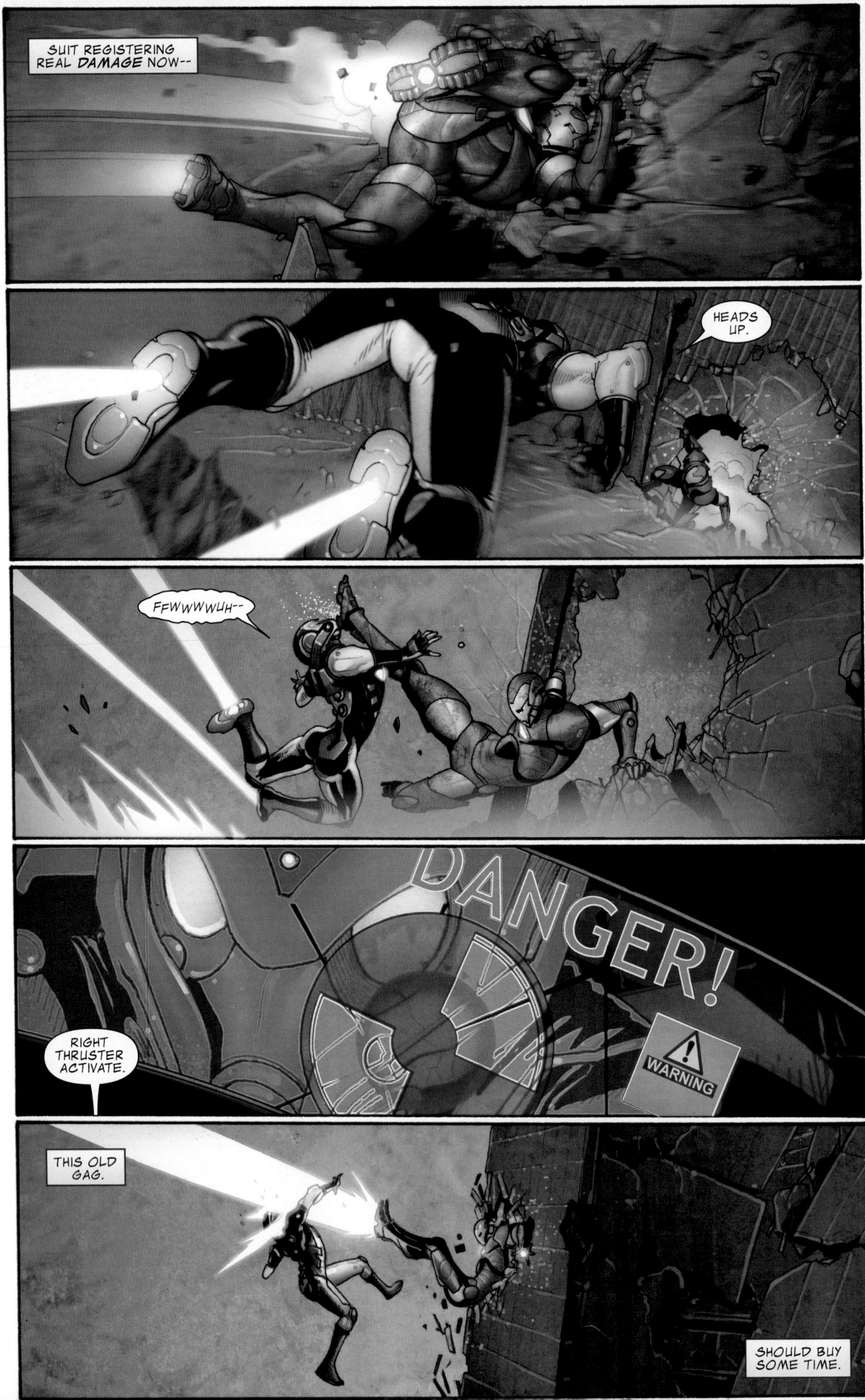
SUIT REGISTERING REAL DAMAGE NOW--
HEADS UP.
FFWWWWUH--
DANGER!
WARNING
RIGHT THRUSTER ACTIVATE.
THIS OLD GAG.
SHOULD BUY SOME TIME.

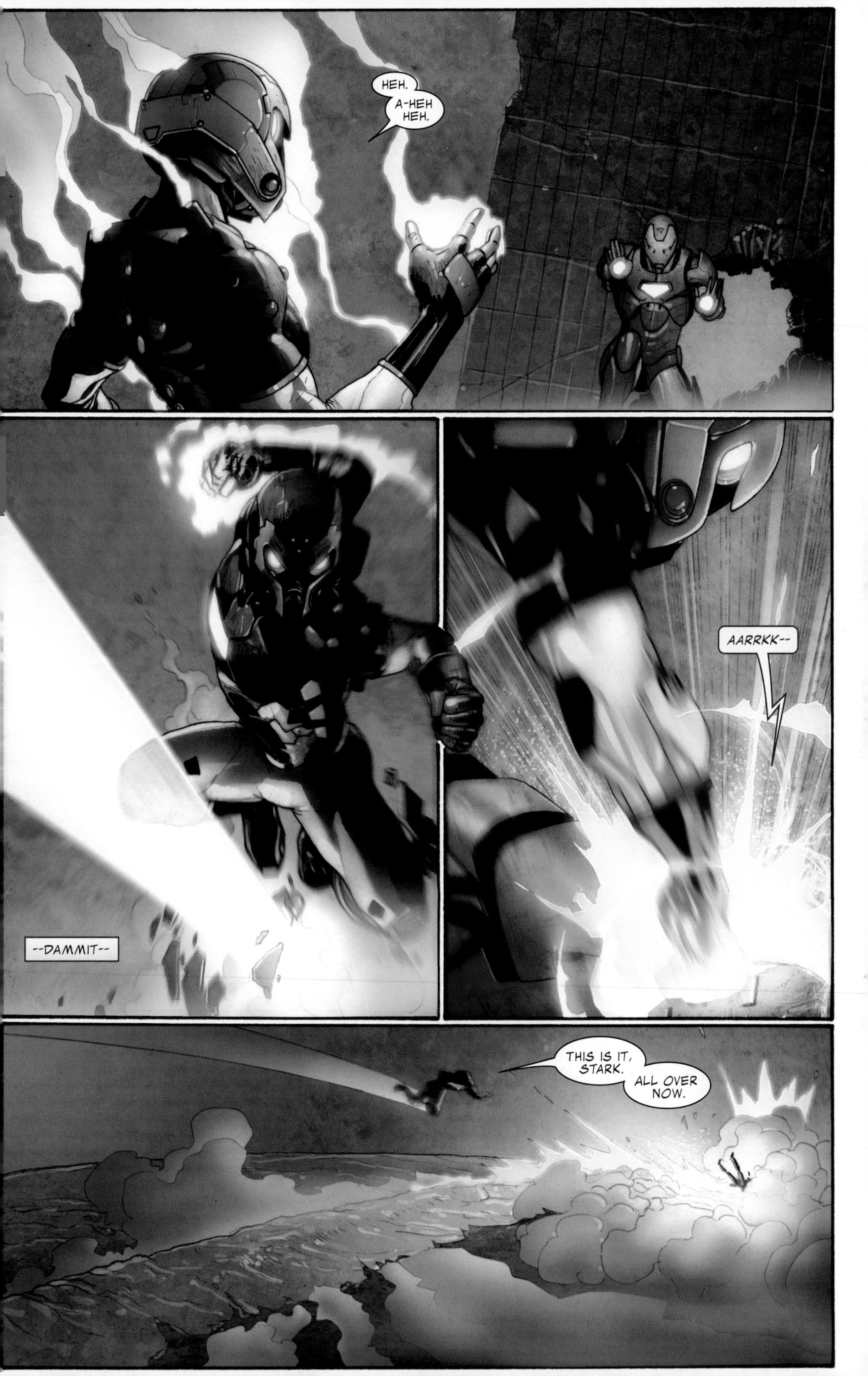
HEH.
A-HEH HEH.
--DAMMIT--
AARRKK--
THIS IS IT, STARK.
ALL OVER NOW.

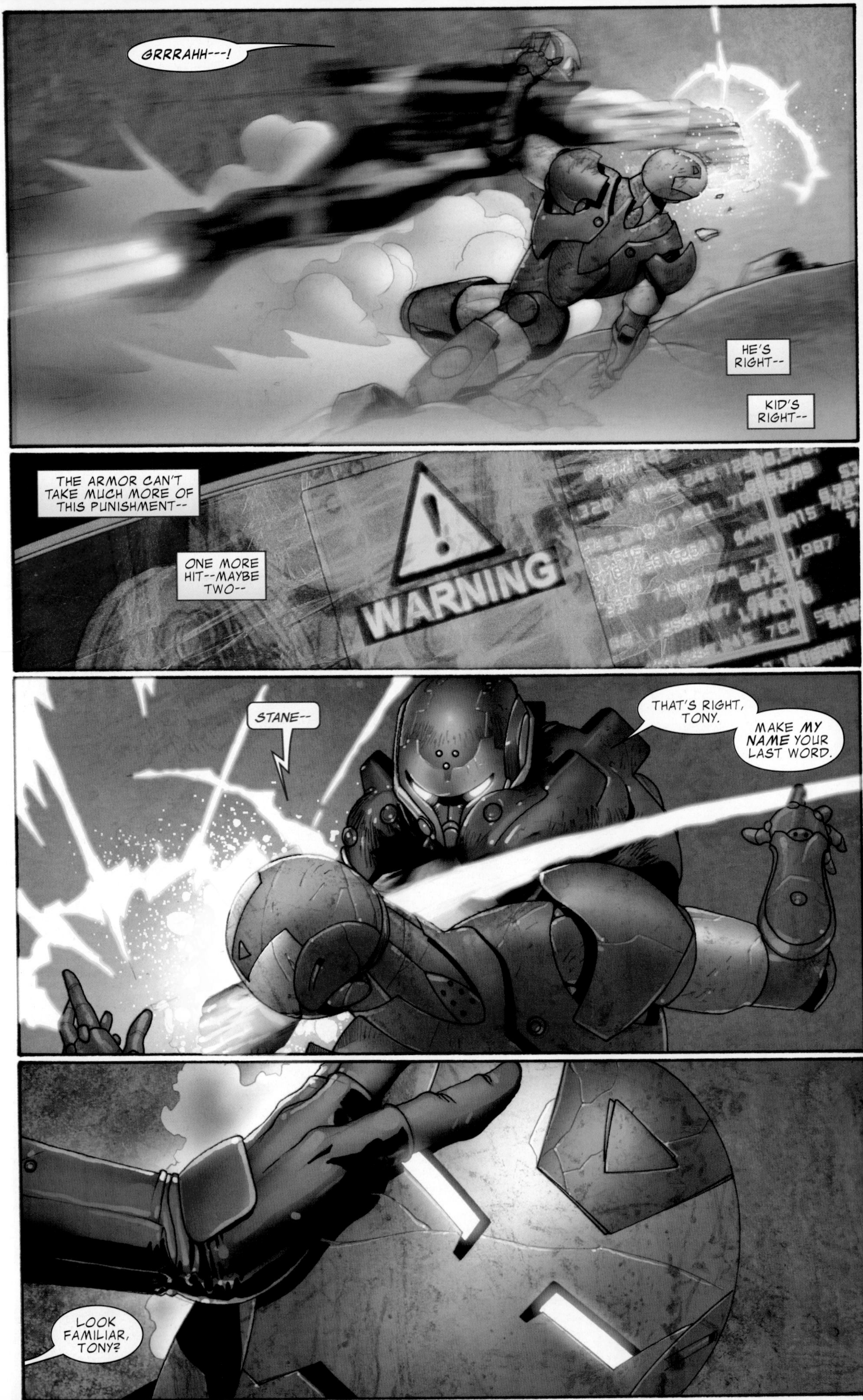
GRRRAHH---!
HE'S RIGHT--
KID'S RIGHT--
THE ARMOR CAN'T TAKE MUCH MORE OF THIS PUNISHMENT--
ONE MORE HIT--MAYBE TWO--
WARNING
STANE--
THAT'S RIGHT, TONY.
MAKE MY NAME YOUR LAST WORD.
LOOK FAMILIAR, TONY?

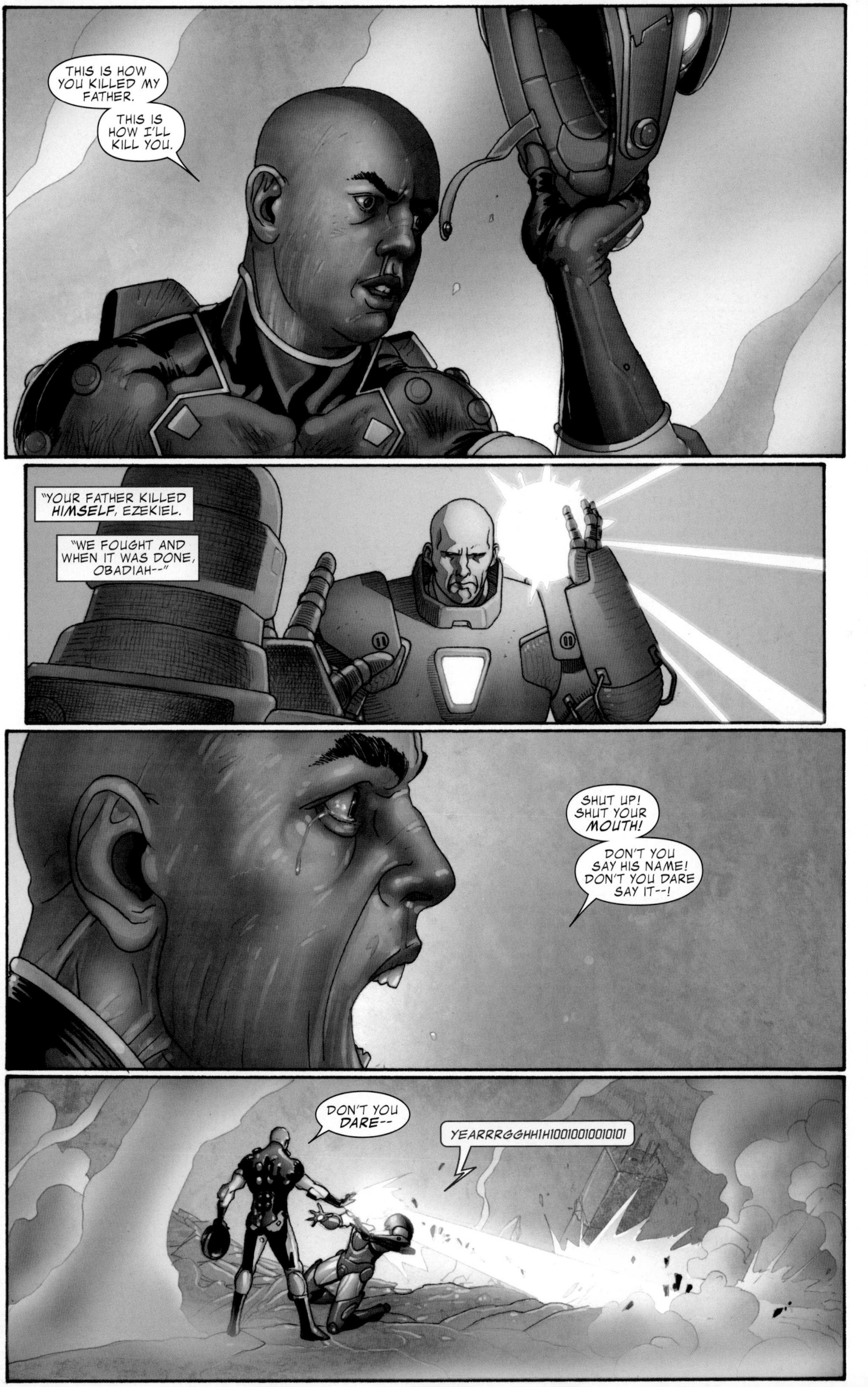
THIS IS HOW YOU KILLED MY FATHER.
THIS IS HOW I'LL KILL YOU.
"YOUR FATHER KILLED HIMSELF, EZEKIEL.
"WE FOUGHT AND WHEN IT WAS DONE, OBADIAH--"
SHUT UP! SHUT YOUR MOUTH!
DON'T YOU SAY HIS NAME! DON'T YOU DARE SAY IT--!
DON'T YOU DARE--
YEARRRGGHH1H1001001001010101

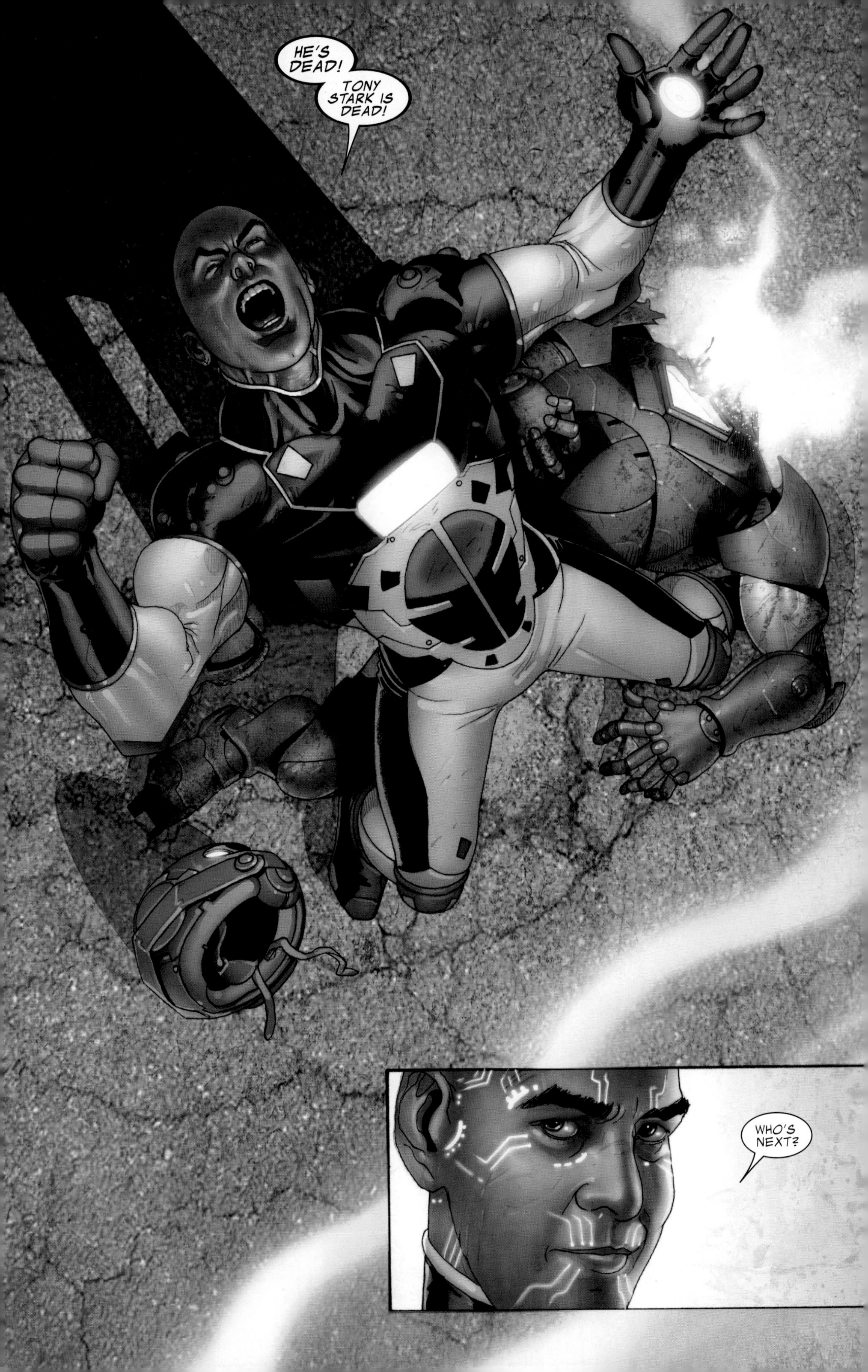
HE'S DEAD!
TONY STARK IS DEAD!
WHO'S NEXT?

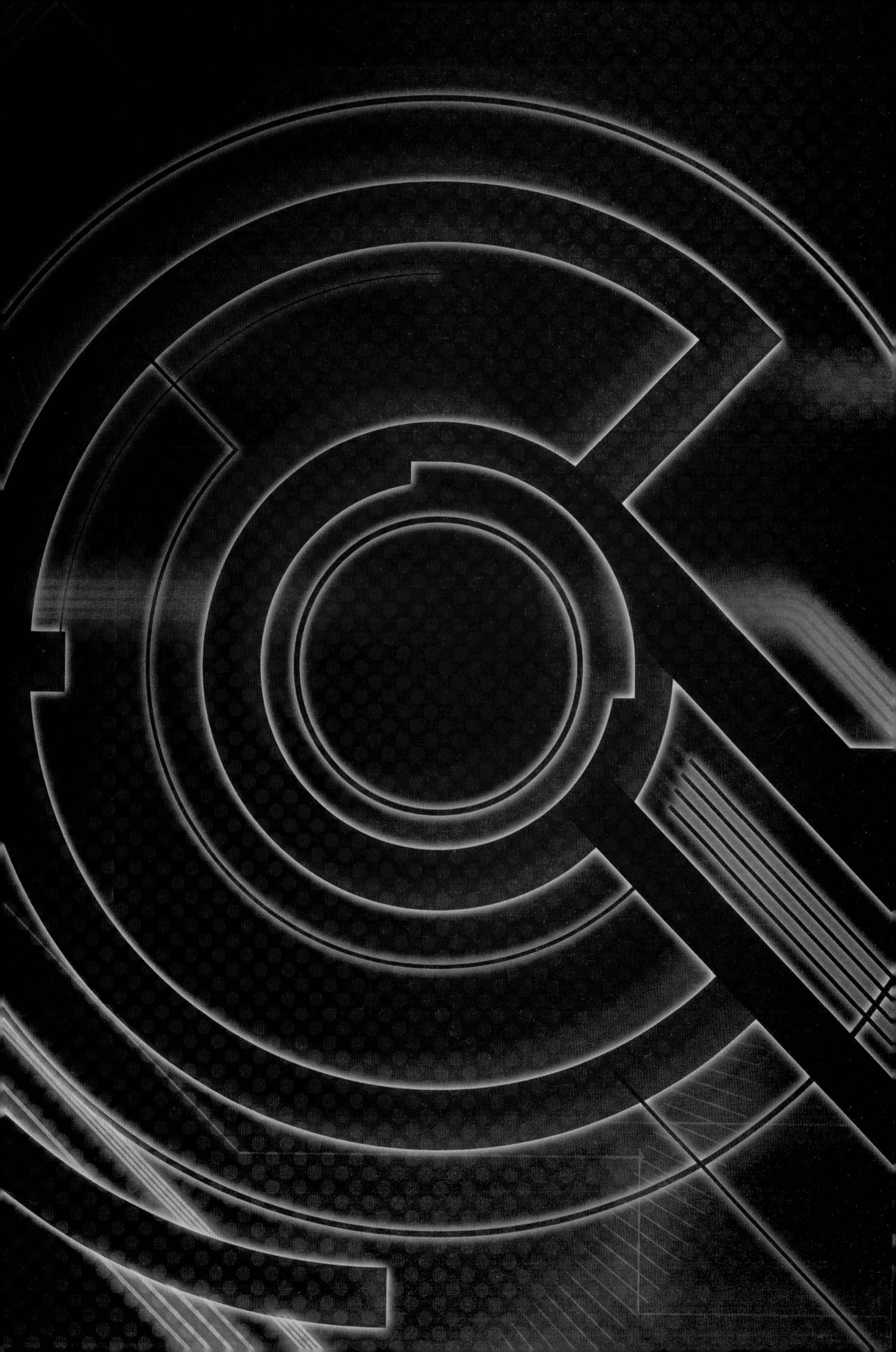

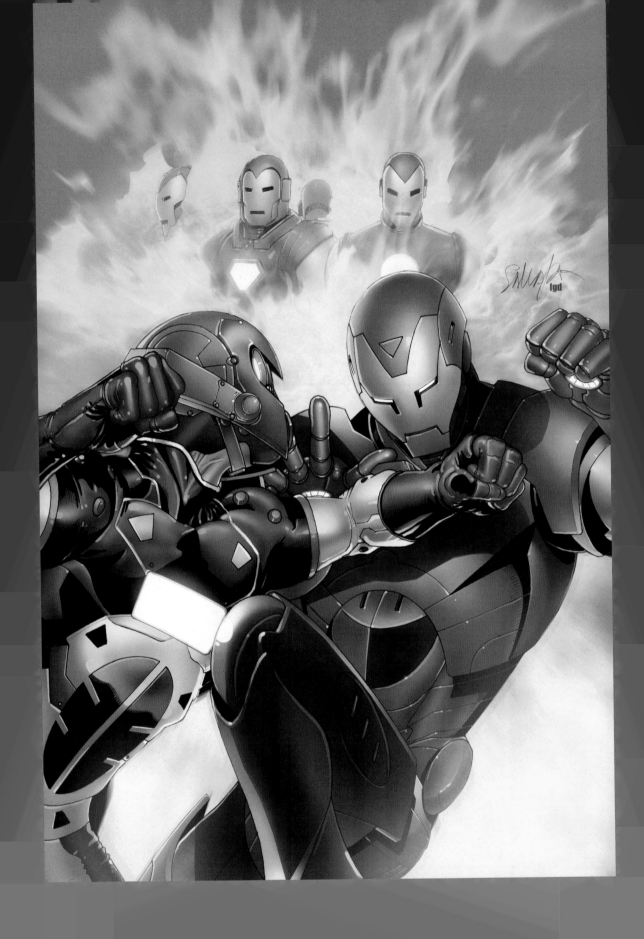

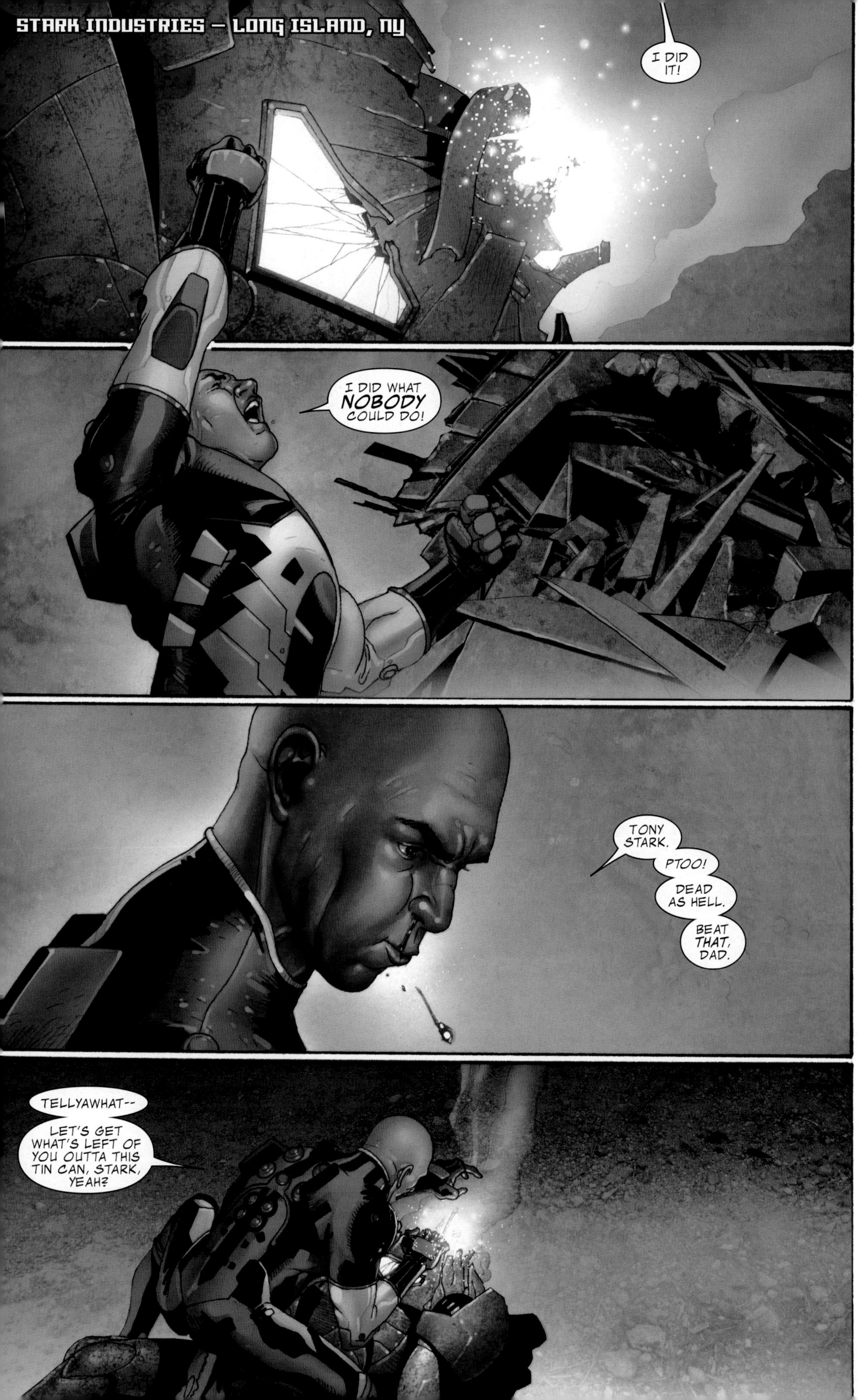
STARK INDUSTRIES — LONG ISLAND, NY
I DID IT!
I DID WHAT NOBODY COULD DO!
TONY STARK.
PTOO!
DEAD AS HELL.
BEAT THAT, DAD.
TELLYAWHAT--
LET'S GET WHAT'S LEFT OF YOU OUTTA THIS TIN CAN, STARK, YEAH?

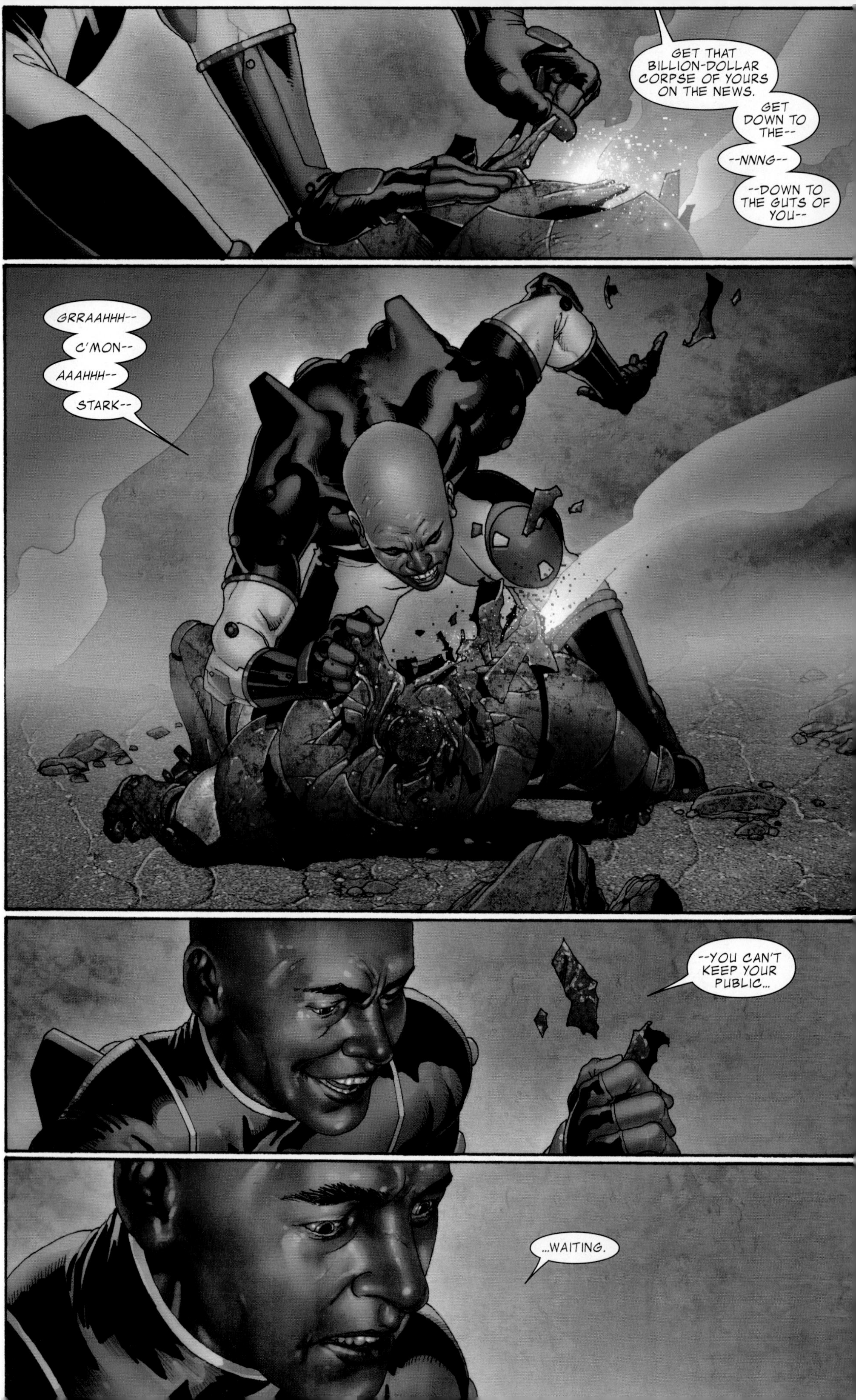
GET THAT BILLION-DOLLAR CORPSE OF YOURS ON THE NEWS.
GET DOWN TO THE--
--NNNG--
--DOWN TO THE GUTS OF YOU--
GRRAAHHH--
C'MON--
AAAHHH--
STARK--
--YOU CAN'T KEEP YOUR PUBLIC...
...WAITING.

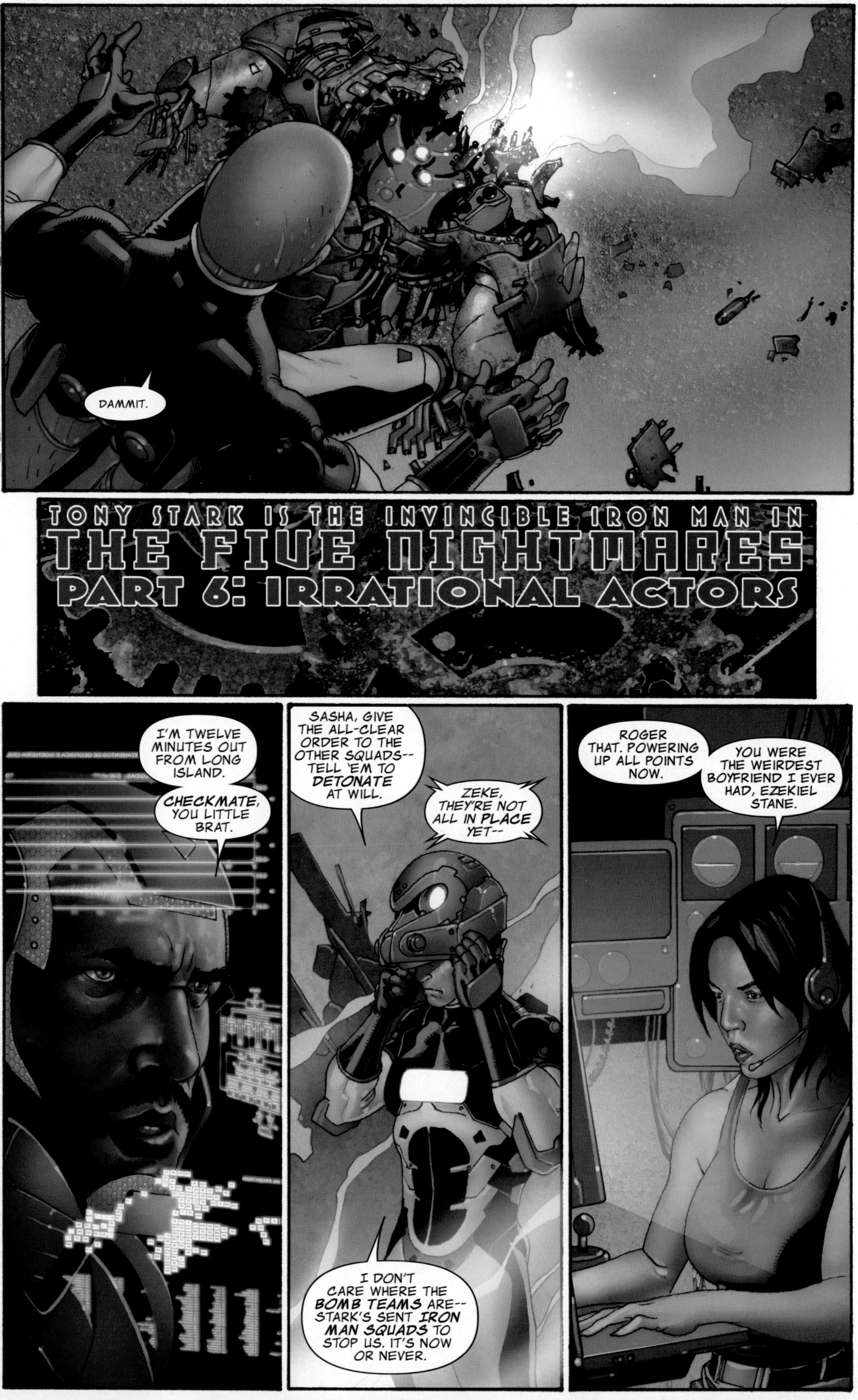

DAMMIT.
TONY STARK IS THE INVINCIBLE IRON MAN IN
THE FIVE NIGHTMARES
PART 6: IRRATIONAL ACTORS
I'M TWELVE MINUTES OUT FROM LONG ISLAND.
CHECKMATE, YOU LITTLE BRAT.
SASHA, GIVE THE ALL-CLEAR ORDER TO THE OTHER SQUADS-- TELL 'EM TO DETONATE AT WILL.
ZEKE, THEY'RE NOT ALL IN PLACE YET--
I DON'T CARE WHERE THE BOMB TEAMS ARE-- STARK'S SENT IRON MAN SQUADS TO STOP US. IT'S NOW OR NEVER.
ROGER THAT. POWERING UP ALL POINTS NOW.
YOU WERE THE WEIRDEST BOYFRIEND I EVER HAD, EZEKIEL STANE.

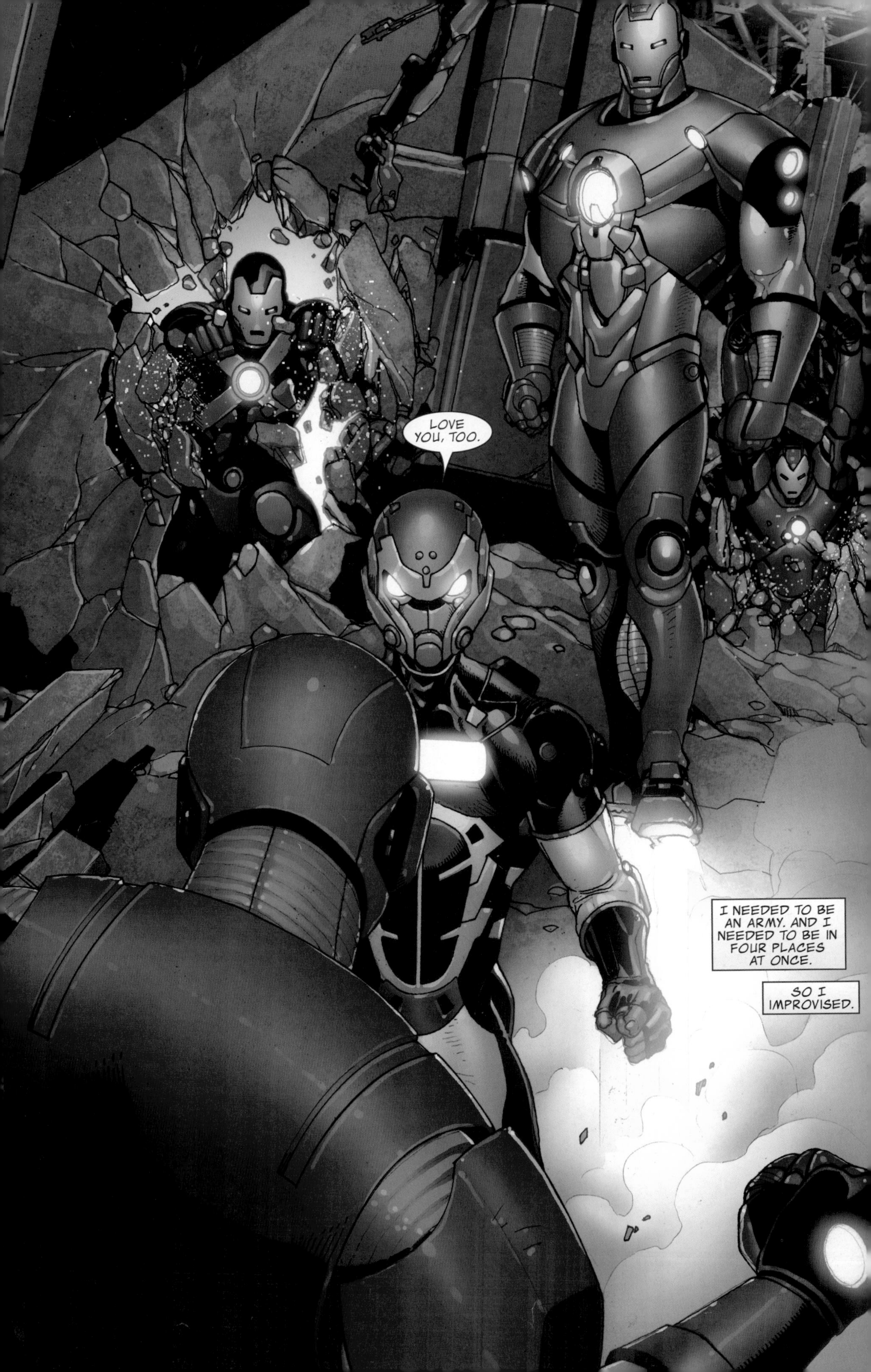
LOVE YOU, TOO.
I NEEDED TO BE AN ARMY. AND I NEEDED TO BE IN FOUR PLACES AT ONCE.
SO I IMPROVISED.

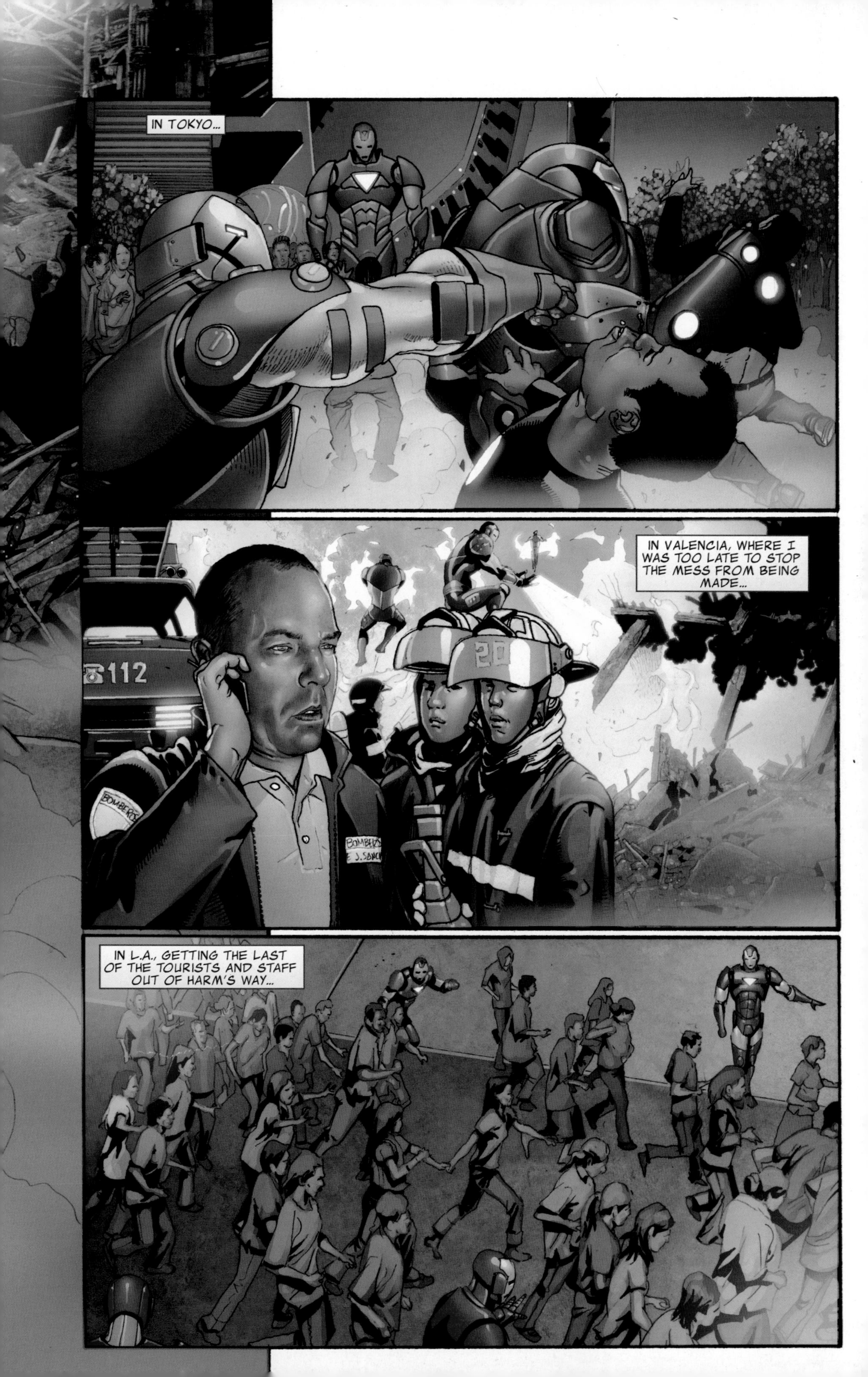
IN TOKYO...
IN VALENCIA, WHERE I WAS TOO LATE TO STOP THE MESS FROM BEING MADE...
112
20
BOMBEROS
BOMBEROS
J. SANCH
IN L.A., GETTING THE LAST OF THE TOURISTS AND STAFF OUT OF HARM'S WAY...

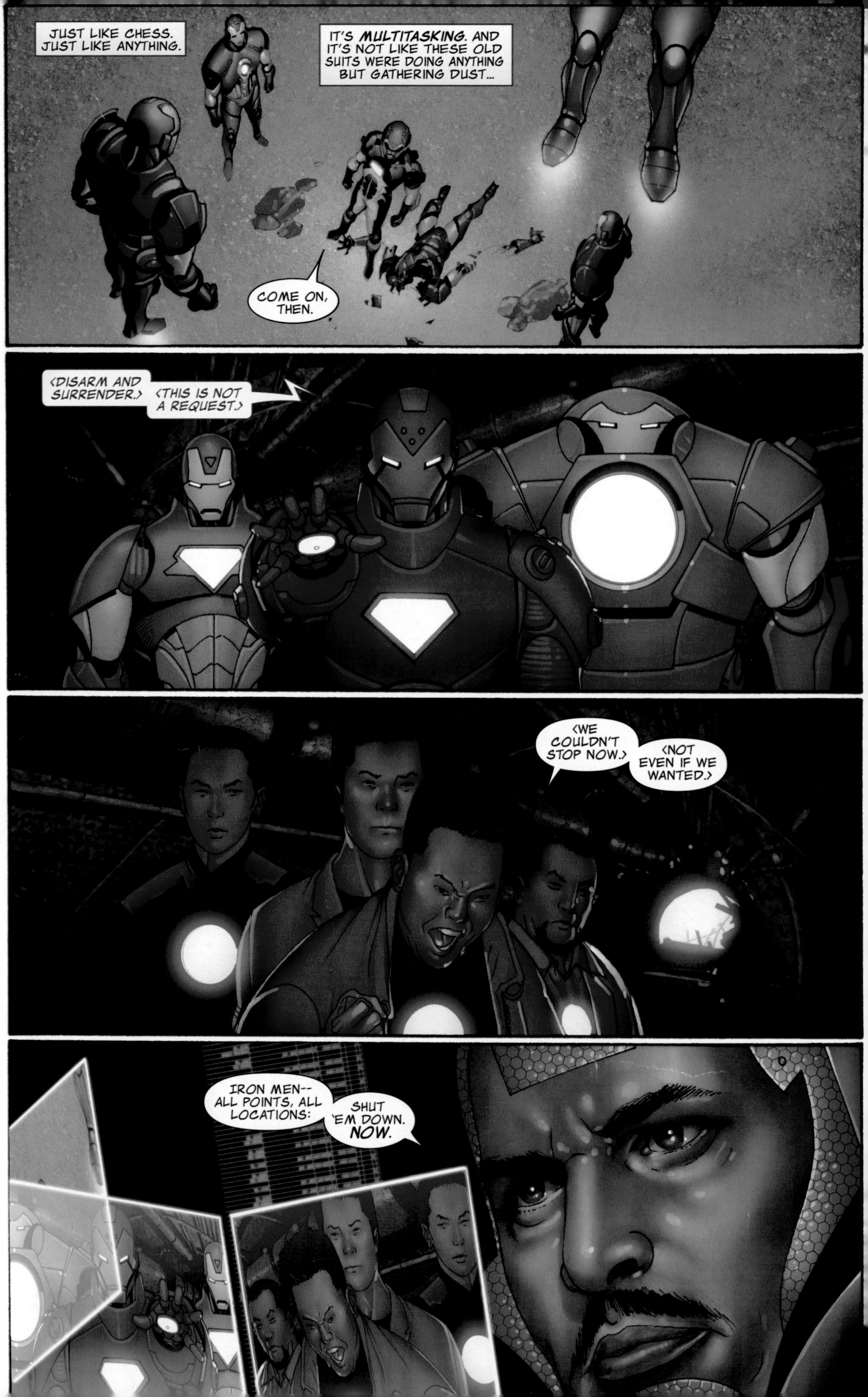
JUST LIKE CHESS. JUST LIKE ANYTHING.
IT'S MULTITASKING. AND IT'S NOT LIKE THESE OLD SUITS WERE DOING ANYTHING BUT GATHERING DUST...
COME ON, THEN.
<DISARM AND SURRENDER.>
<THIS IS NOT A REQUEST.>
<WE COULDN'T STOP NOW.>
<NOT EVEN IF WE WANTED.>
IRON MEN-- ALL POINTS, ALL LOCATIONS:
SHUT 'EM DOWN. NOW.

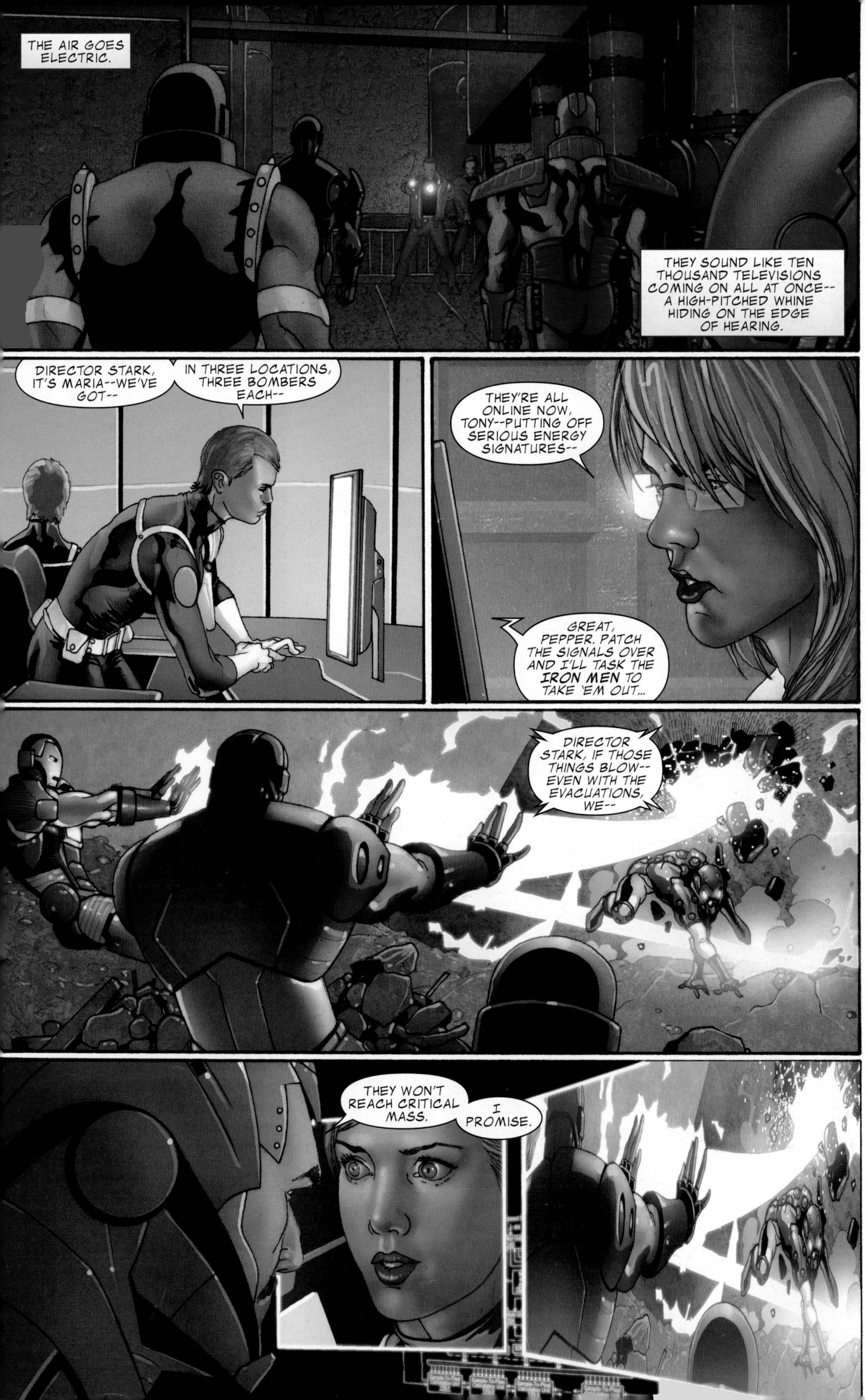
THE AIR GOES ELECTRIC.
THEY SOUND LIKE TEN THOUSAND TELEVISIONS COMING ON ALL AT ONCE-- A HIGH-PITCHED WHINE HIDING ON THE EDGE OF HEARING.
DIRECTOR STARK, IT'S MARIA--WE'VE GOT--
IN THREE LOCATIONS, THREE BOMBERS EACH--
THEY'RE ALL ONLINE NOW, TONY--PUTTING OFF SERIOUS ENERGY SIGNATURES--
GREAT, PEPPER. PATCH THE SIGNALS OVER AND I'LL TASK THE IRON MEN TO TAKE 'EM OUT...
DIRECTOR STARK, IF THOSE THINGS BLOW-- EVEN WITH THE EVACUATIONS, WE--
THEY WON'T REACH CRITICAL MASS.
I PROMISE.

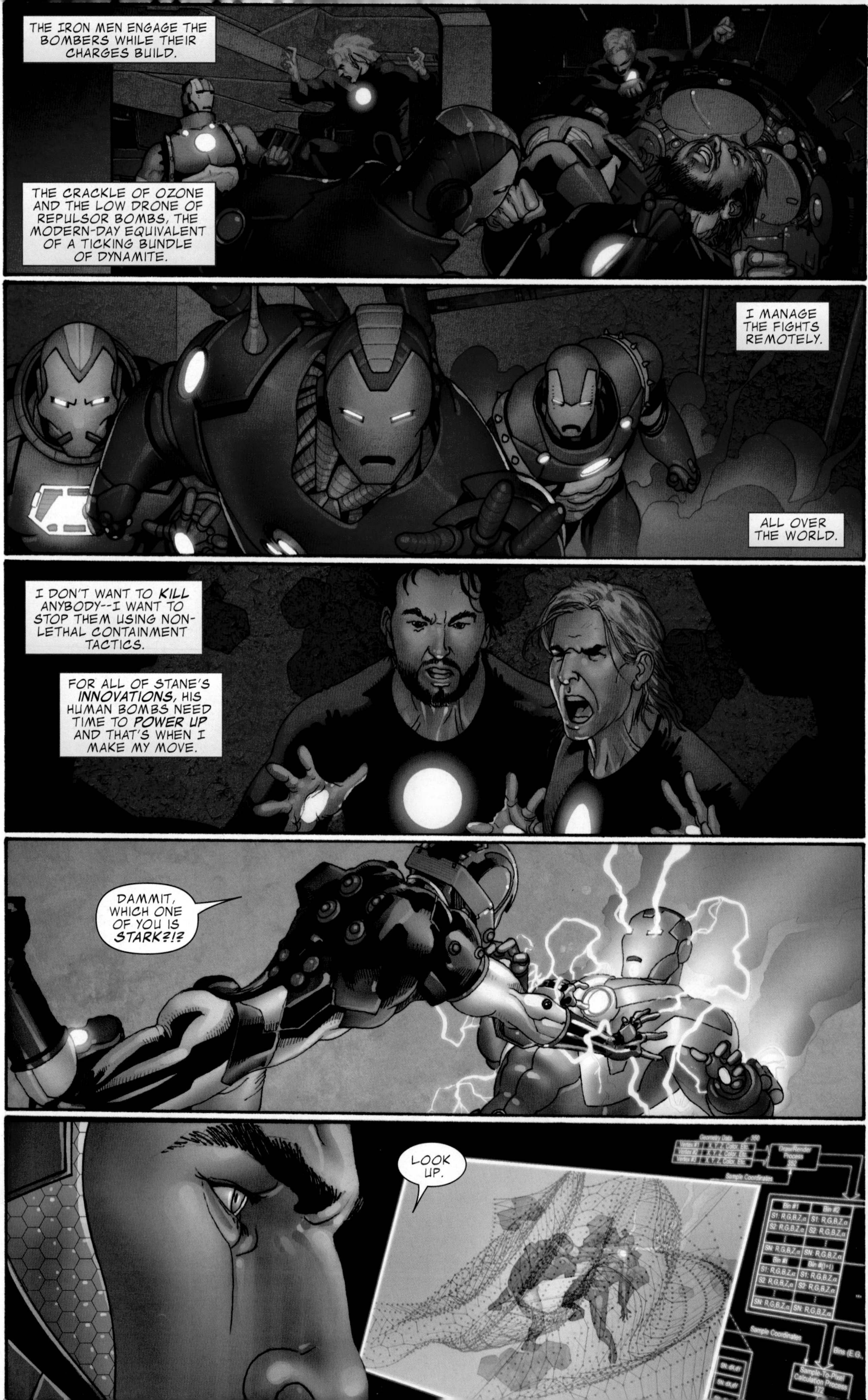
THE IRON MEN ENGAGE THE BOMBERS WHILE THEIR CHARGES BUILD.
THE CRACKLE OF OZONE AND THE LOW DRONE OF REPULSOR BOMBS, THE MODERN-DAY EQUIVALENT OF A TICKING BUNDLE OF DYNAMITE.
I MANAGE THE FIGHTS REMOTELY.
ALL OVER THE WORLD.
I DON'T WANT TO KILL ANYBODY--I WANT TO STOP THEM USING NON-LETHAL CONTAINMENT TACTICS.
FOR ALL OF STANE'S INNOVATIONS, HIS HUMAN BOMBS NEED TIME TO POWER UP AND THAT'S WHEN I MAKE MY MOVE.
DAMMIT, WHICH ONE OF YOU IS STARK?!?
LOOK UP.

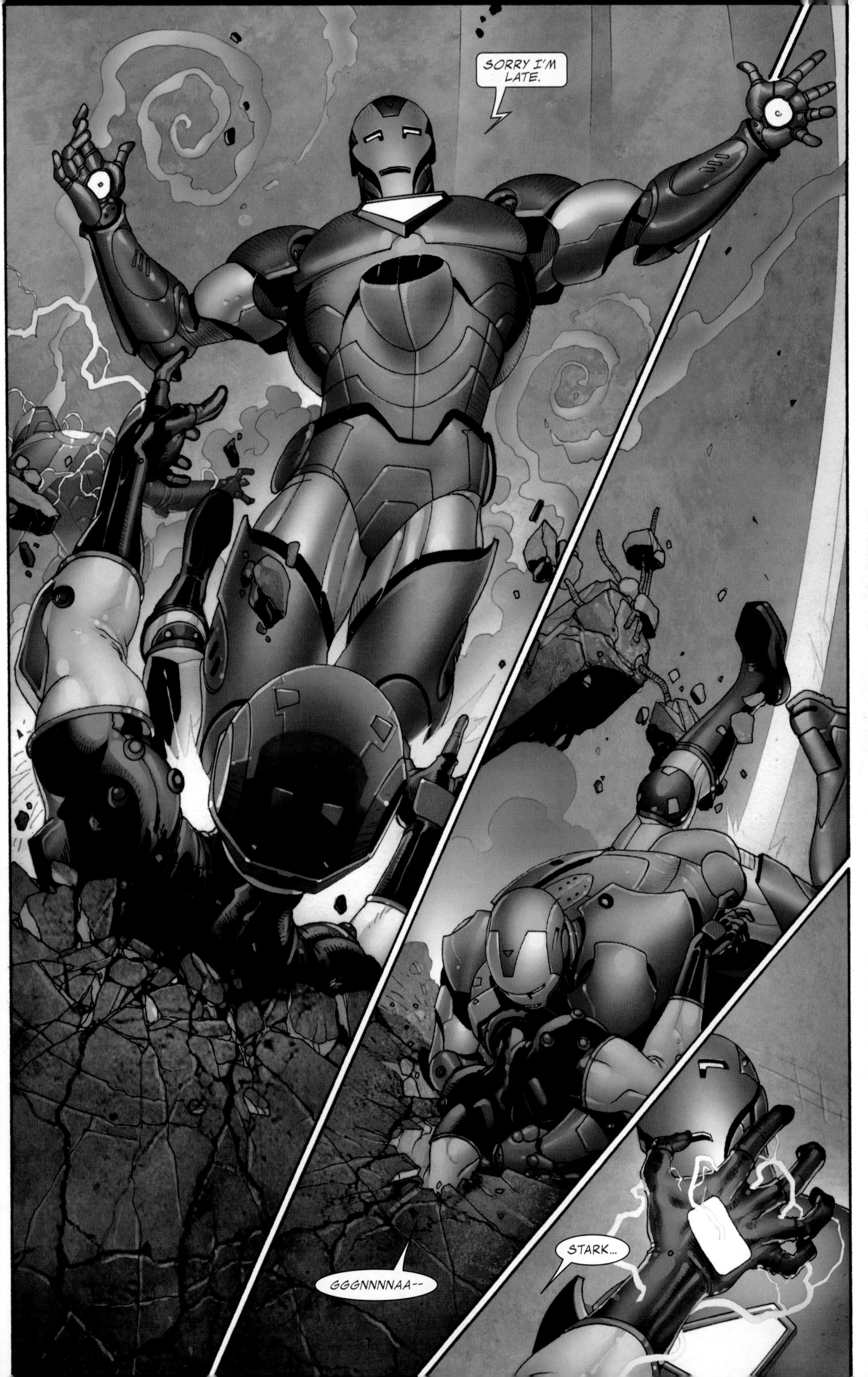
SORRY I'M LATE.
GGGNNNNAA--
STARK...

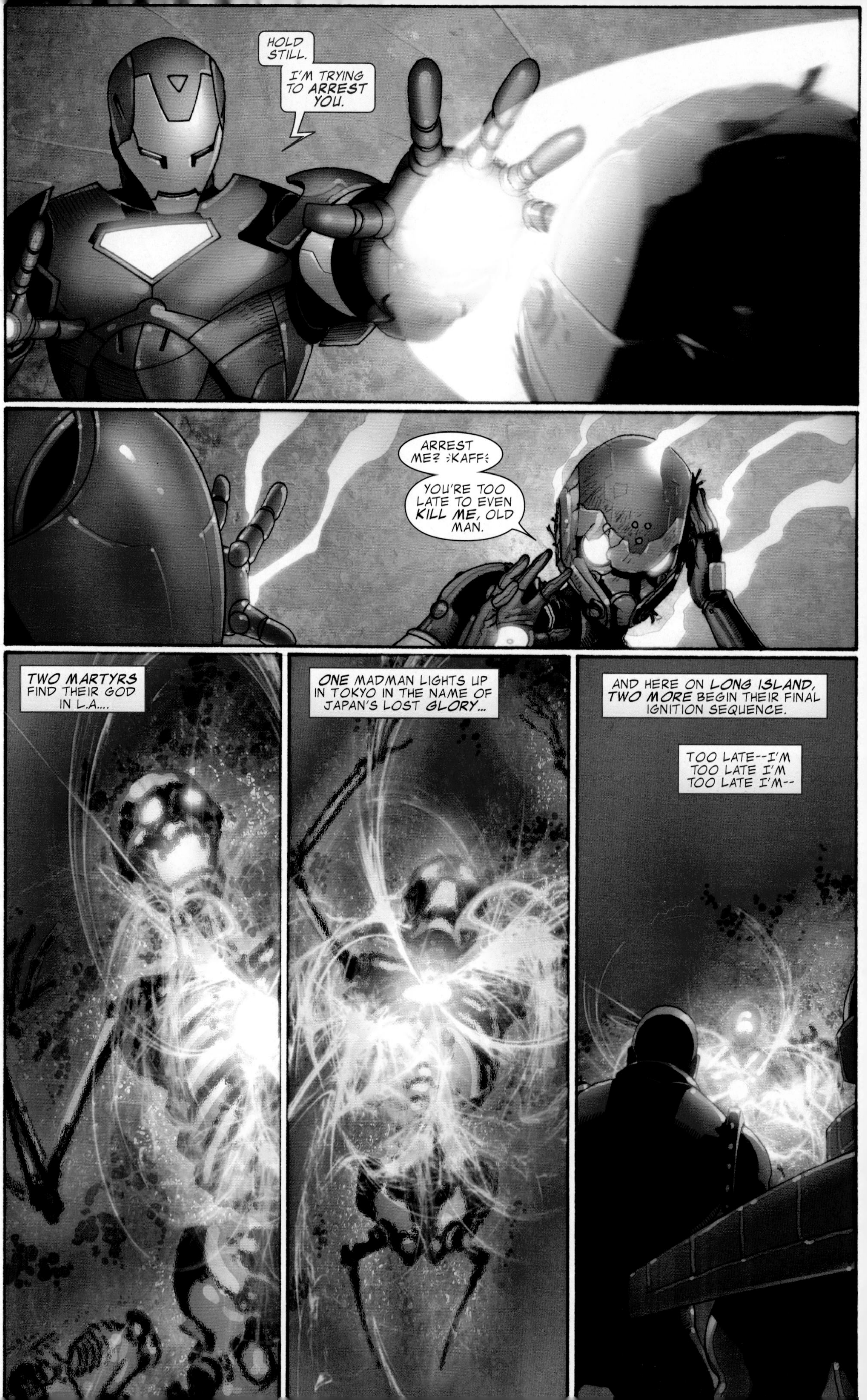
HOLD STILL.
I'M TRYING TO ARREST YOU.
ARREST ME? <KAFF>
YOU'RE TOO LATE TO EVEN KILL ME, OLD MAN.
TWO MARTYRS FIND THEIR GOD IN L.A....
ONE MADMAN LIGHTS UP IN TOKYO IN THE NAME OF JAPAN'S LOST GLORY...
AND HERE ON LONG ISLAND, TWO MORE BEGIN THEIR FINAL IGNITION SEQUENCE.
TOO LATE--I'M TOO LATE I'M TOO LATE I'M--

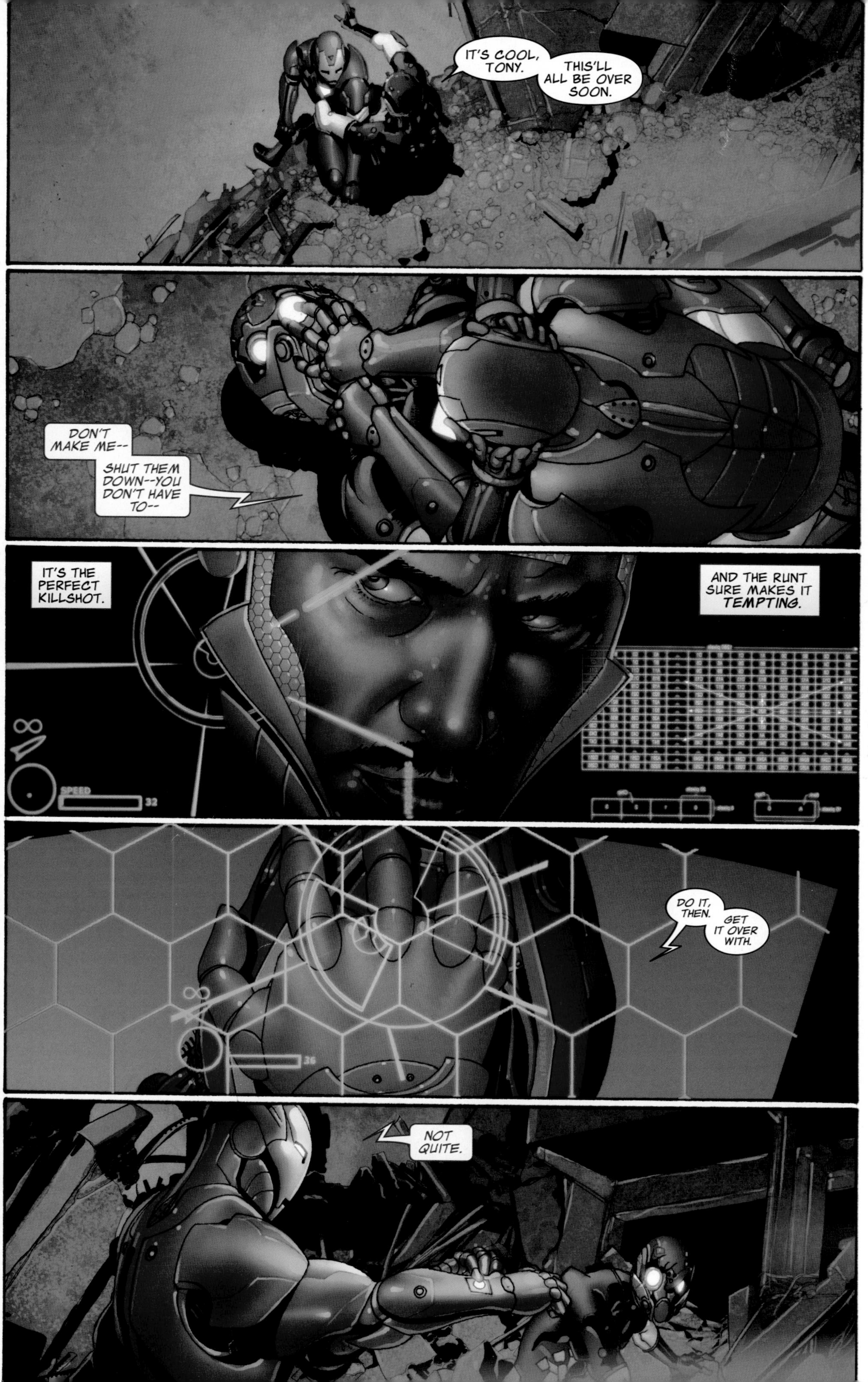
IT'S COOL, TONY.
THIS'LL ALL BE OVER SOON.
DON'T MAKE ME--
SHUT THEM DOWN--YOU DON'T HAVE TO--
IT'S THE PERFECT KILLSHOT.
AND THE RUNT SURE MAKES IT TEMPTING.
SPEED
32
DO IT, THEN.
GET IT OVER WITH.
NOT QUITE.

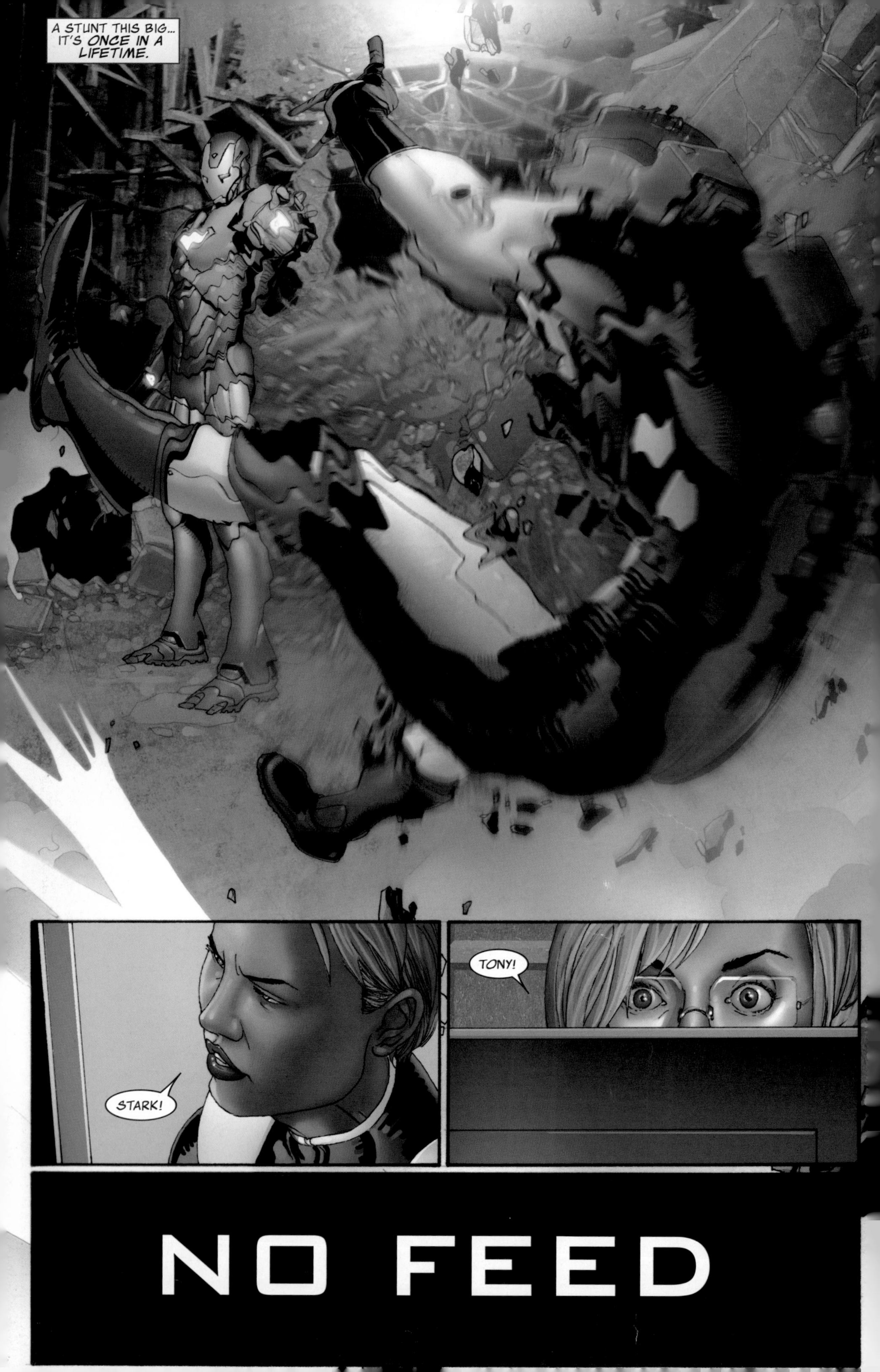
A STUNT THIS BIG... IT'S ONCE IN A LIFETIME.
STARK!
TONY!
NO FEED

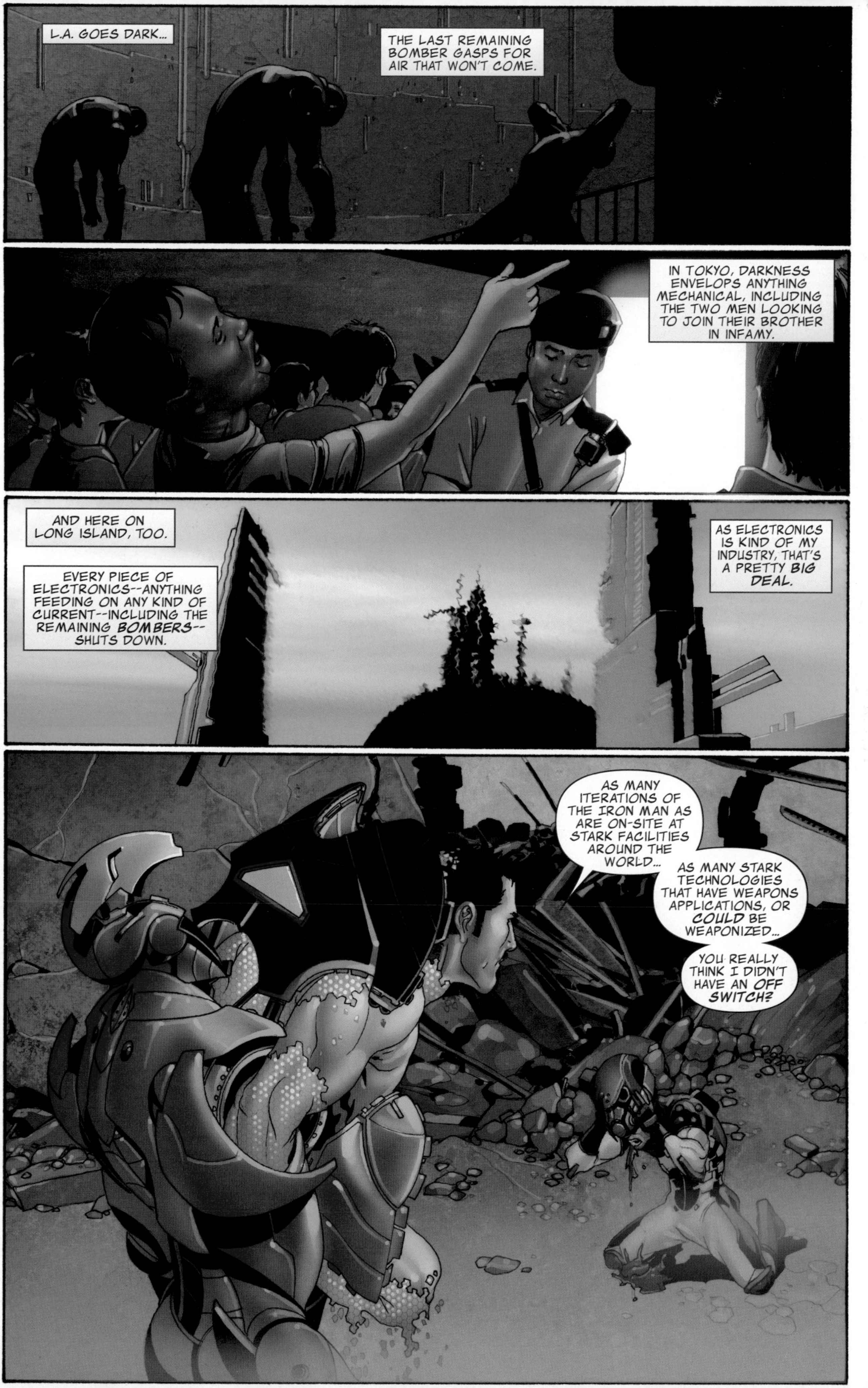

L.A. GOES DARK...
THE LAST REMAINING BOMBER GASPS FOR AIR THAT WON'T COME.
IN TOKYO, DARKNESS ENVELOPS ANYTHING MECHANICAL, INCLUDING THE TWO MEN LOOKING TO JOIN THEIR BROTHER IN INFAMY.
AND HERE ON LONG ISLAND, TOO.
EVERY PIECE OF ELECTRONICS--ANYTHING FEEDING ON ANY KIND OF CURRENT--INCLUDING THE REMAINING BOMBERS--SHUTS DOWN.
AS ELECTRONICS IS KIND OF MY INDUSTRY, THAT'S A PRETTY BIG DEAL.
AS MANY ITERATIONS OF THE IRON MAN AS ARE ON-SITE AT STARK FACILITIES AROUND THE WORLD...
AS MANY STARK TECHNOLOGIES THAT HAVE WEAPONS APPLICATIONS, OR COULD BE WEAPONIZED...
YOU REALLY THINK I DIDN'T HAVE AN OFF SWITCH?

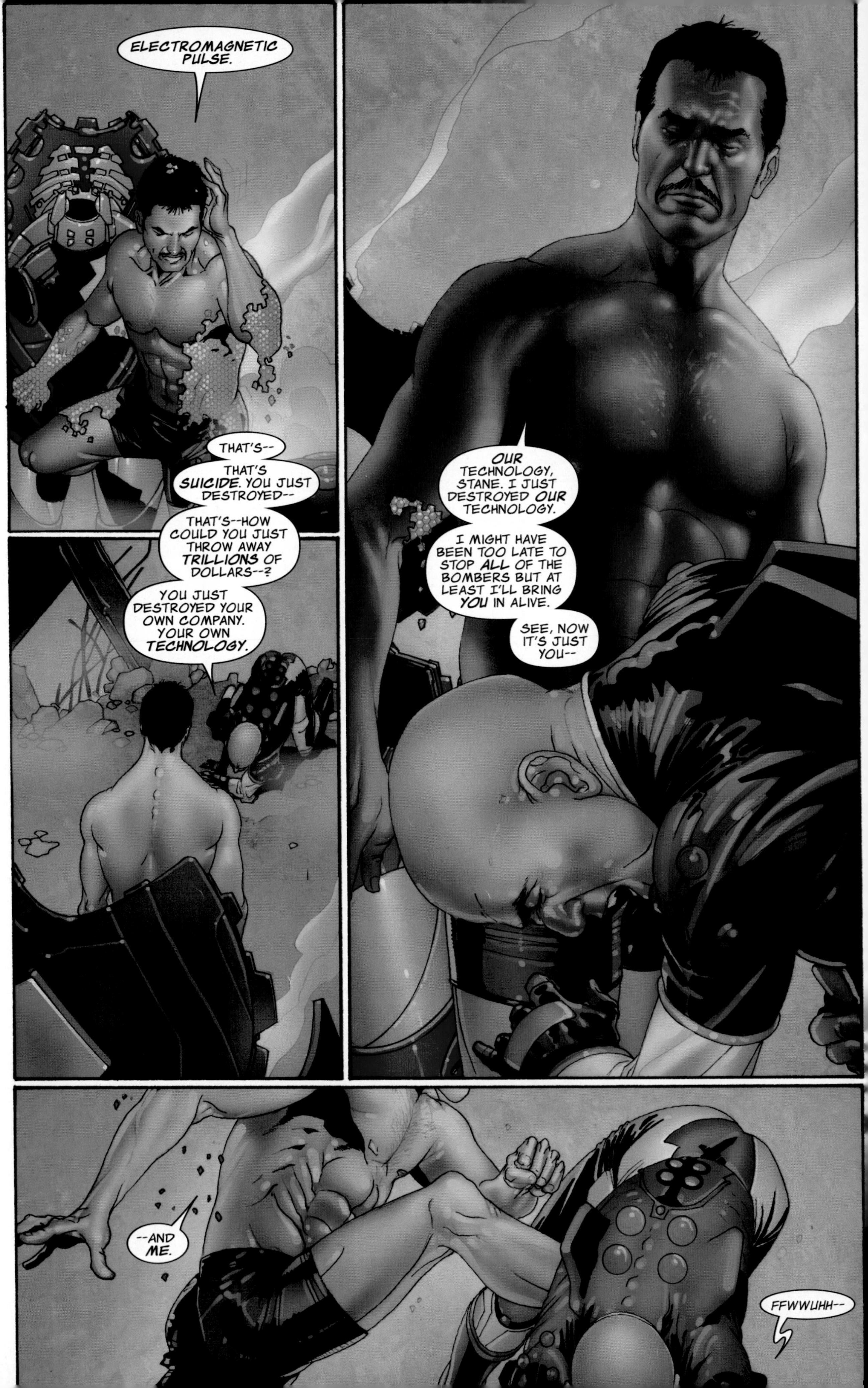
ELECTROMAGNETIC PULSE.
THAT'S--
THAT'S SUICIDE. YOU JUST DESTROYED--
THAT'S--HOW COULD YOU JUST THROW AWAY TRILLIONS OF DOLLARS--?
YOU JUST DESTROYED YOUR OWN COMPANY. YOUR OWN TECHNOLOGY.
OUR TECHNOLOGY, STANE. I JUST DESTROYED OUR TECHNOLOGY.
I MIGHT HAVE BEEN TOO LATE TO STOP ALL OF THE BOMBERS BUT AT LEAST I'LL BRING YOU IN ALIVE.
SEE, NOW IT'S JUST YOU--
--AND ME.
FFWWUHH--

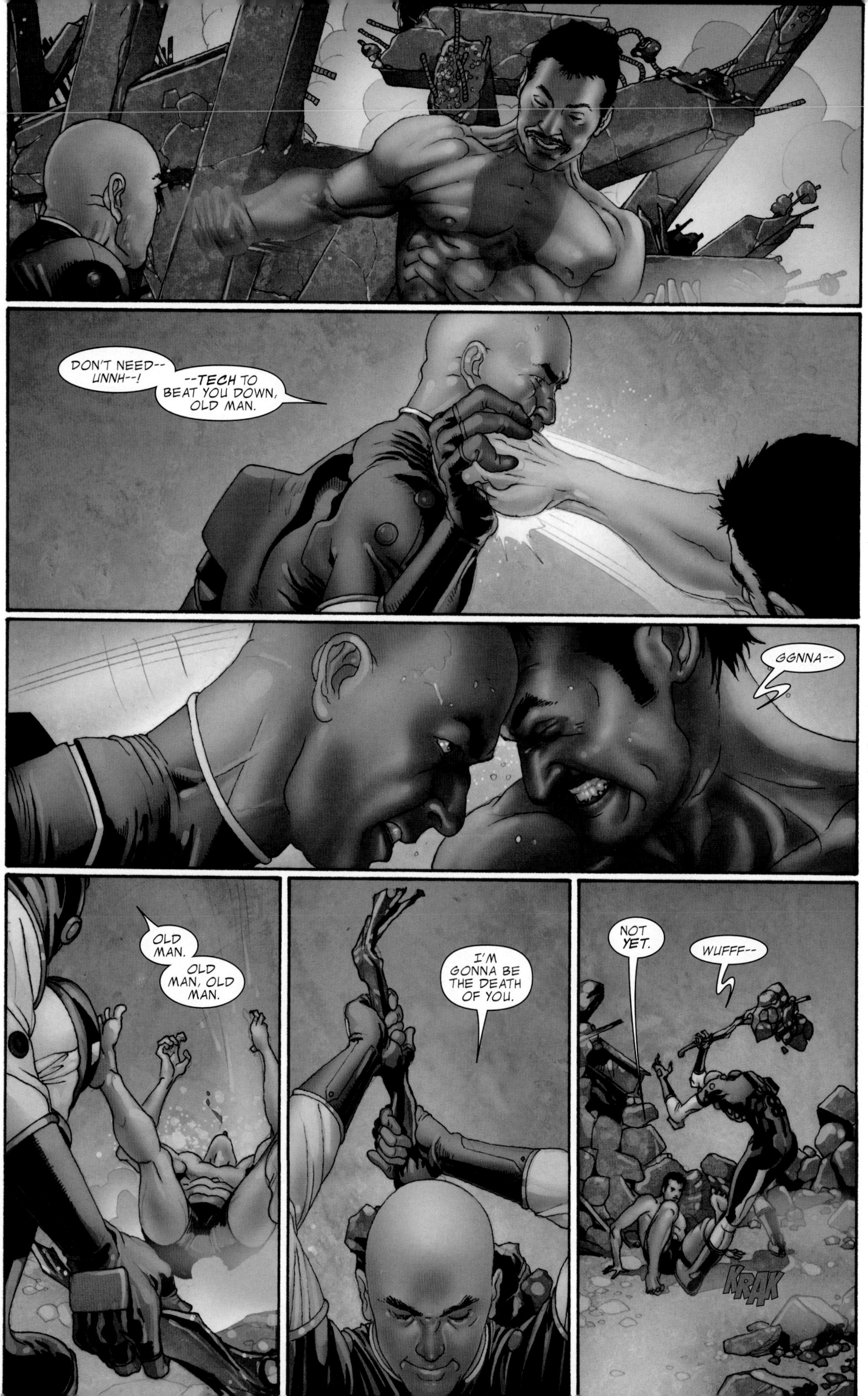
DON'T NEED-- UNNH--!
--TECH TO BEAT YOU DOWN, OLD MAN.
GGNNA--
OLD MAN.
OLD MAN, OLD MAN.
I'M GONNA BE THE DEATH OF YOU.
NOT YET.
WUFFF--
KRAK

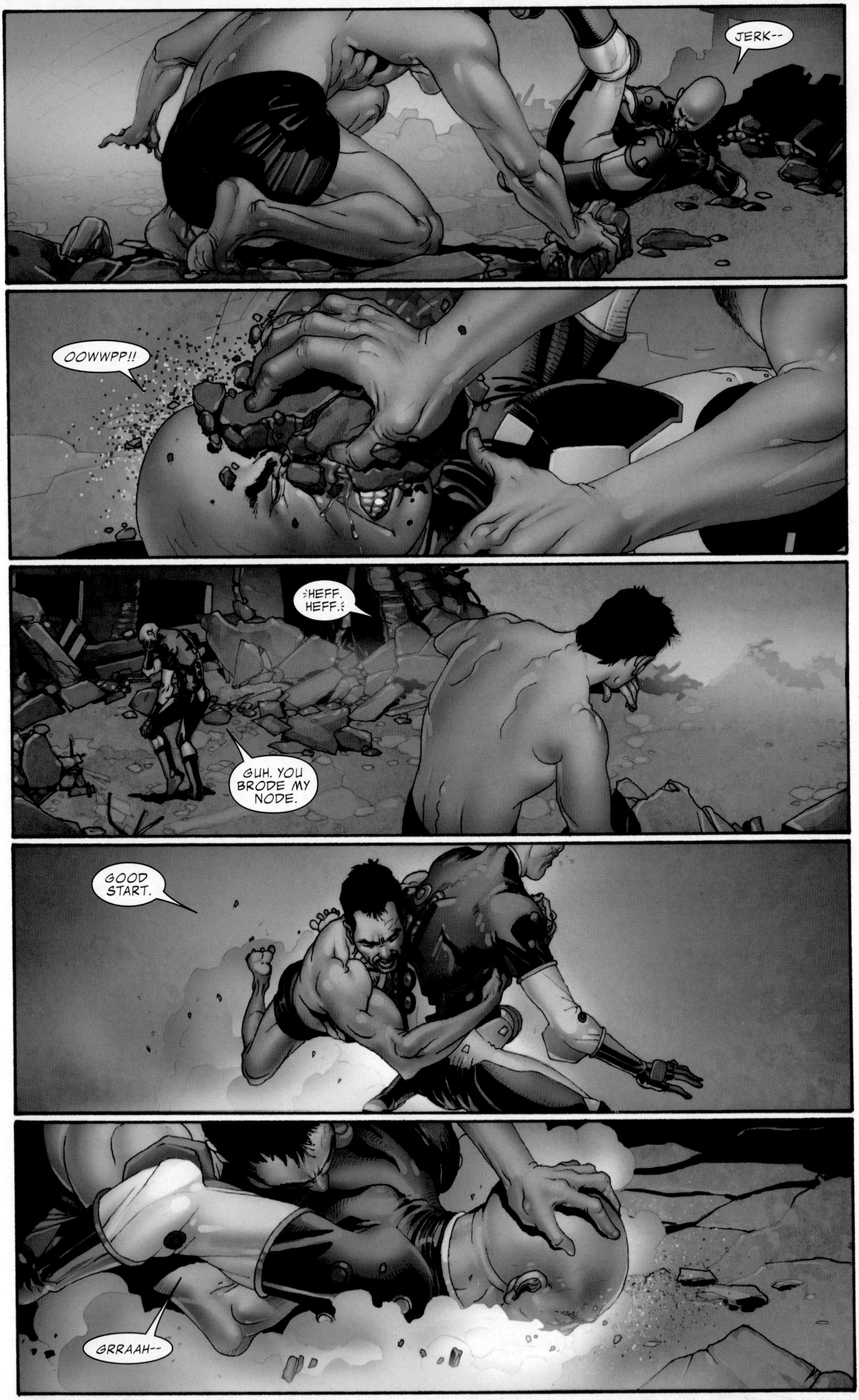
JERK--
OOWWPP!!
HEFF. HEFF.
GUH. YOU BRODE MY NODE.
GOOD START.
GRRAAH--

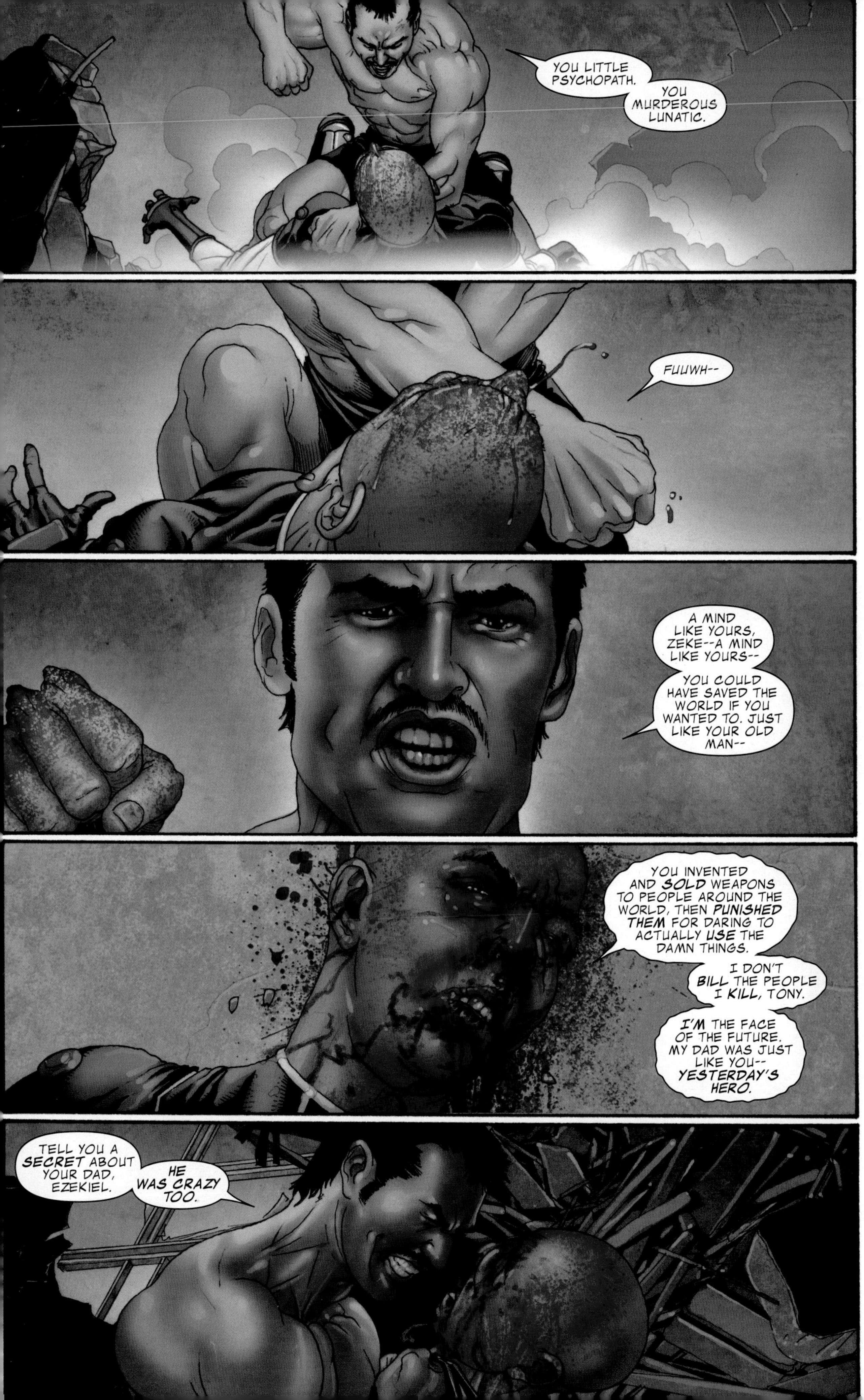
YOU LITTLE PSYCHOPATH.
YOU MURDEROUS LUNATIC.
FUUWH--
A MIND LIKE YOURS, ZEKE--A MIND LIKE YOURS--
YOU COULD HAVE SAVED THE WORLD IF YOU WANTED TO. JUST LIKE YOUR OLD MAN--
YOU INVENTED AND SOLD WEAPONS TO PEOPLE AROUND THE WORLD, THEN PUNISHED THEM FOR DARING TO ACTUALLY USE THE DAMN THINGS.
I DON'T BILL THE PEOPLE I KILL, TONY.
I'M THE FACE OF THE FUTURE. MY DAD WAS JUST LIKE YOU-- YESTERDAY'S HERO.
TELL YOU A SECRET ABOUT YOUR DAD, EZEKIEL.
HE WAS CRAZY TOO.

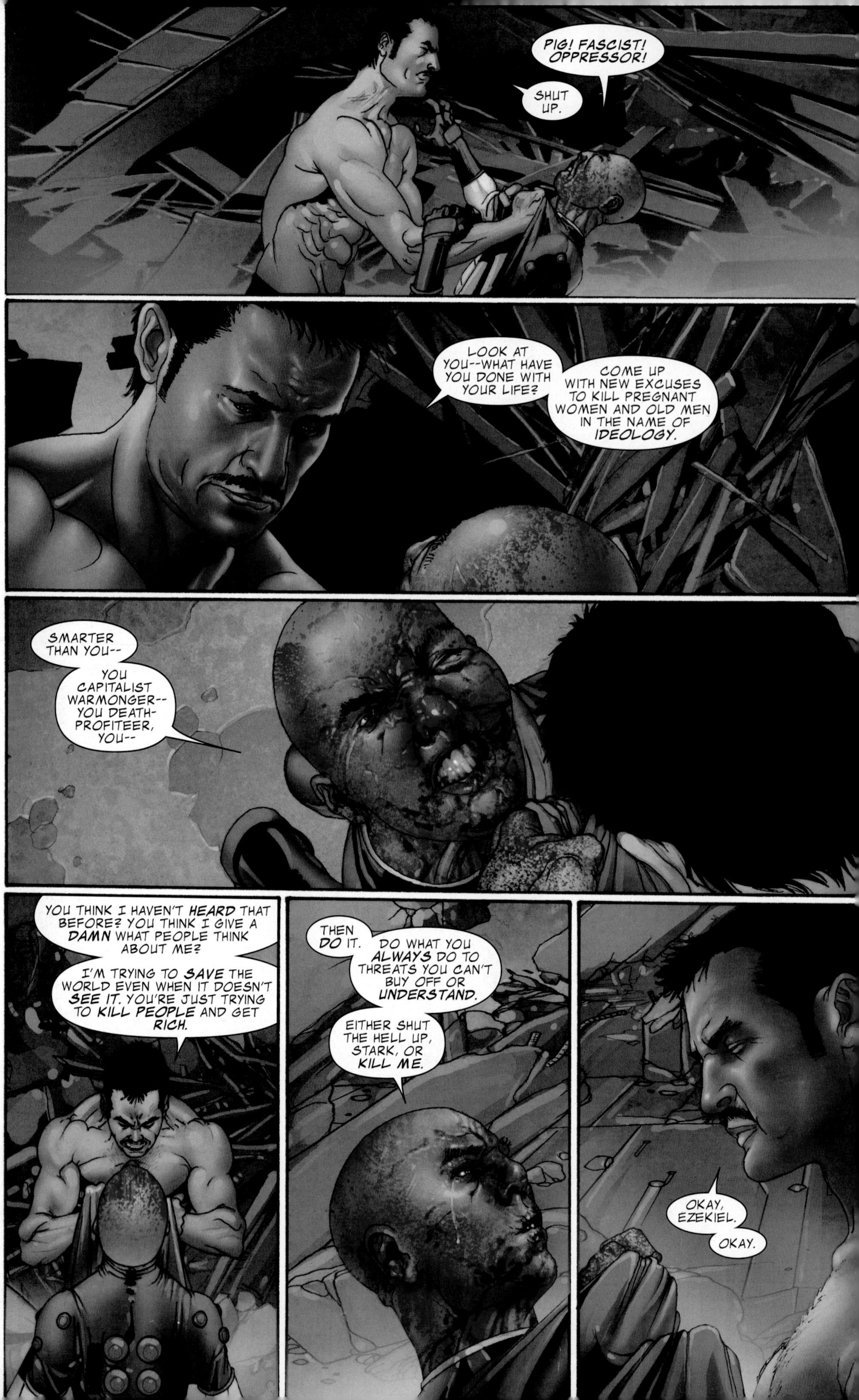
PIG! FASCIST! OPPRESSOR!
SHUT UP.
LOOK AT YOU--WHAT HAVE YOU DONE WITH YOUR LIFE?
COME UP WITH NEW EXCUSES TO KILL PREGNANT WOMEN AND OLD MEN IN THE NAME OF IDEOLOGY.
SMARTER THAN YOU--
YOU CAPITALIST WARMONGER--YOU DEATH-PROFITEER, YOU--
YOU THINK I HAVEN'T HEARD THAT BEFORE? YOU THINK I GIVE A DAMN WHAT PEOPLE THINK ABOUT ME?
I'M TRYING TO SAVE THE WORLD EVEN WHEN IT DOESN'T SEE IT. YOU'RE JUST TRYING TO KILL PEOPLE AND GET RICH.
THEN DO IT.
DO WHAT YOU ALWAYS DO TO THREATS YOU CAN'T BUY OFF OR UNDERSTAND.
EITHER SHUT THE HELL UP, STARK, OR KILL ME.
OKAY, EZEKIEL.
OKAY.

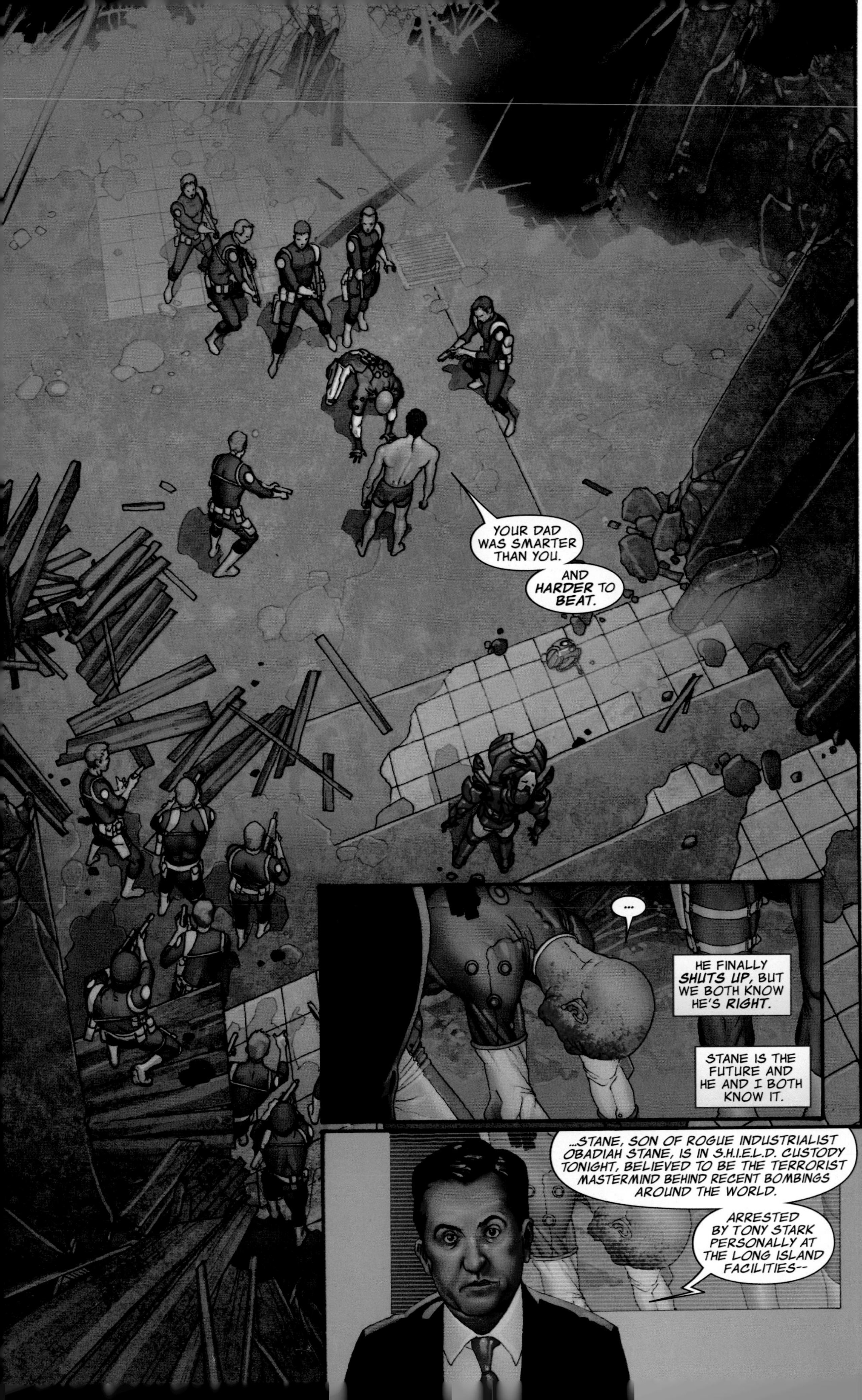
YOUR DAD WAS SMARTER THAN YOU.
AND HARDER TO BEAT.
...
HE FINALLY SHUTS UP, BUT WE BOTH KNOW HE'S RIGHT.
STANE IS THE FUTURE AND HE AND I BOTH KNOW IT.
...STANE, SON OF ROGUE INDUSTRIALIST OBADIAH STANE, IS IN S.H.I.E.L.D. CUSTODY TONIGHT, BELIEVED TO BE THE TERRORIST MASTERMIND BEHIND RECENT BOMBINGS AROUND THE WORLD.
ARRESTED BY TONY STARK PERSONALLY AT THE LONG ISLAND FACILITIES--

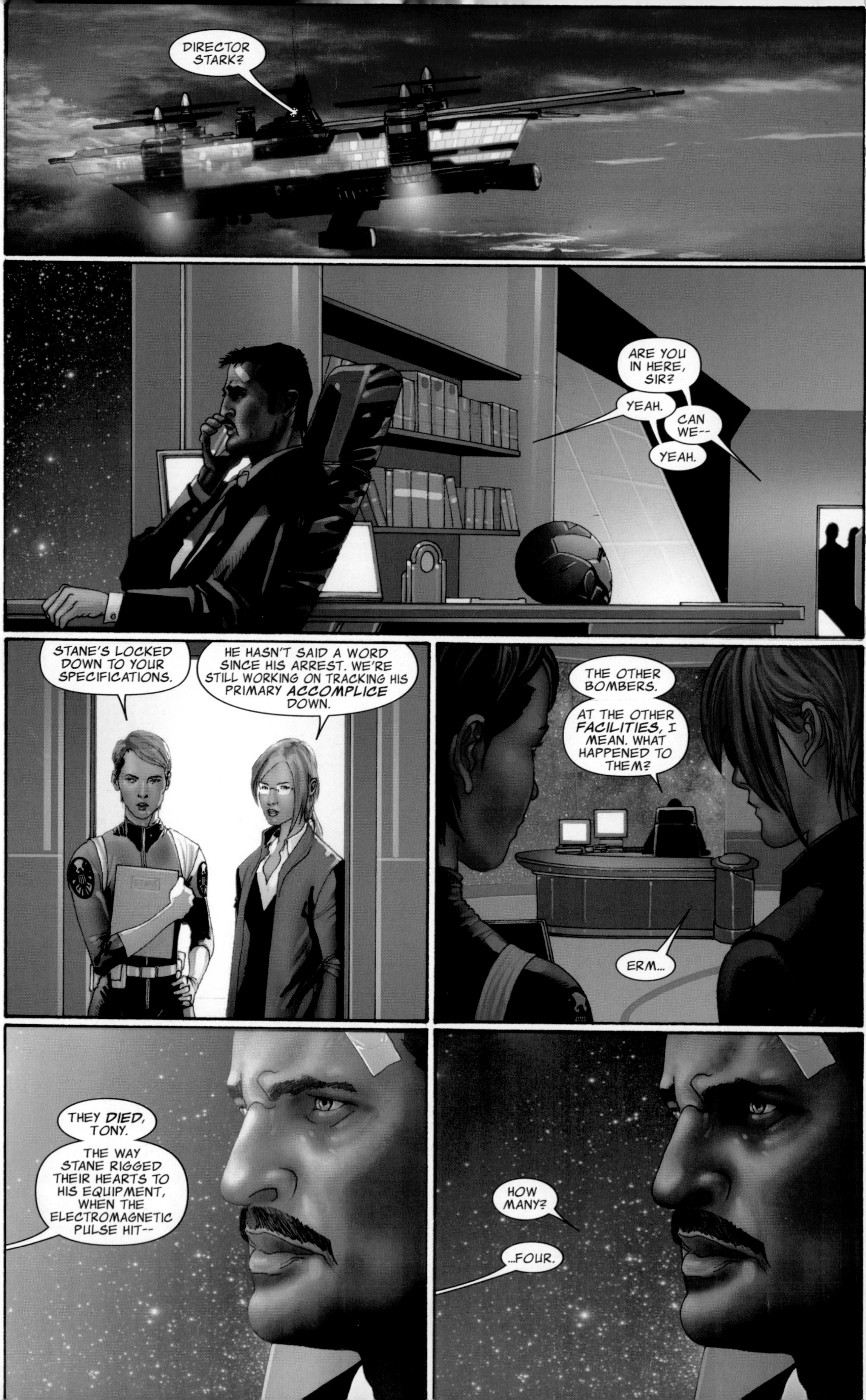
DIRECTOR STARK?
ARE YOU IN HERE, SIR?
YEAH.
CAN WE--
YEAH.
STANE'S LOCKED DOWN TO YOUR SPECIFICATIONS.
HE HASN'T SAID A WORD SINCE HIS ARREST. WE'RE STILL WORKING ON TRACKING HIS PRIMARY ACCOMPLICE DOWN.
THE OTHER BOMBERS.
AT THE OTHER FACILITIES, I MEAN. WHAT HAPPENED TO THEM?
ERM...
THEY DIED, TONY.
THE WAY STANE RIGGED THEIR HEARTS TO HIS EQUIPMENT, WHEN THE ELECTROMAGNETIC PULSE HIT--
HOW MANY?
...FOUR.

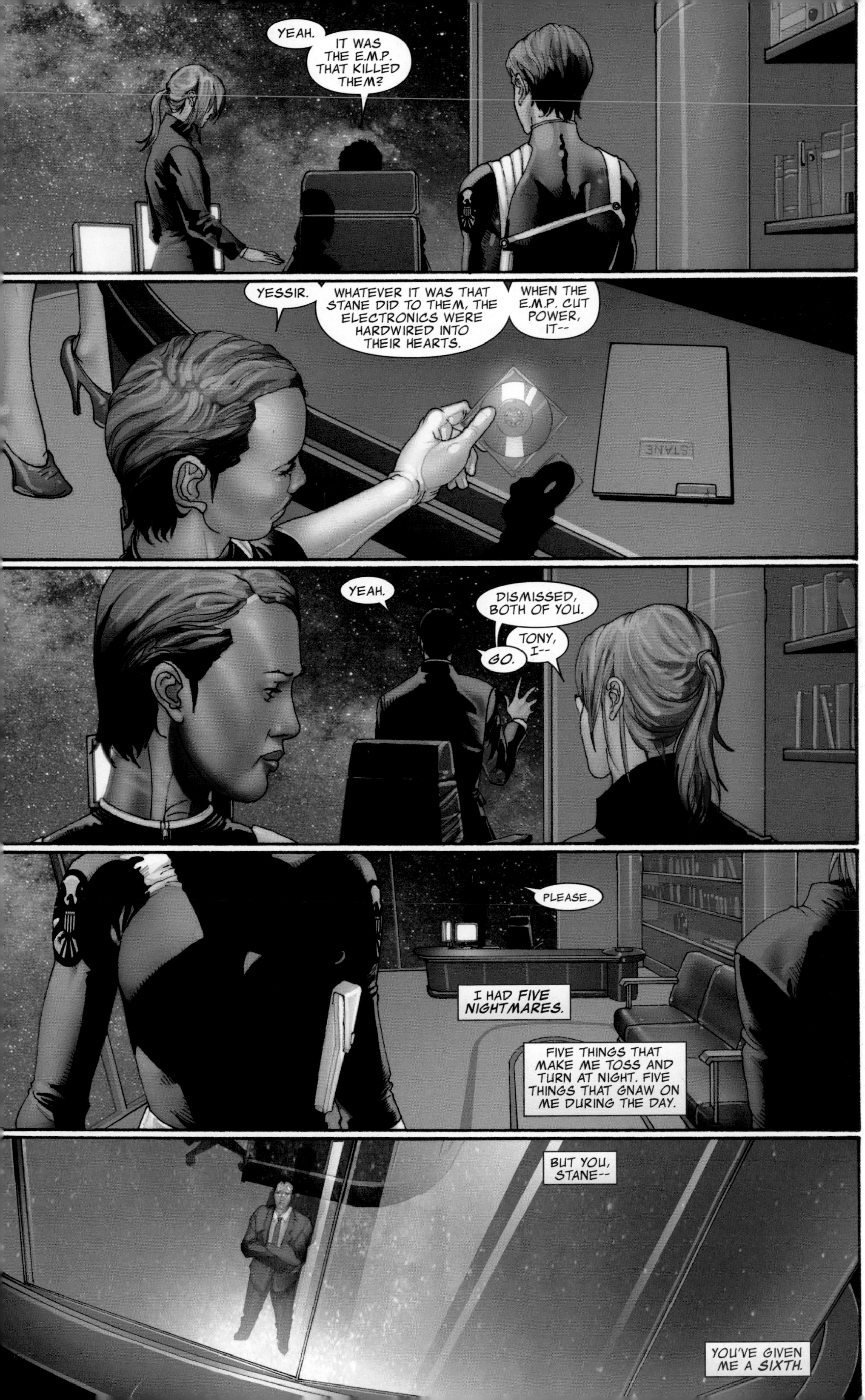
YEAH.
IT WAS THE E.M.P. THAT KILLED THEM?
YESSIR.
WHATEVER IT WAS THAT STANE DID TO THEM, THE ELECTRONICS WERE HARDWIRED INTO THEIR HEARTS.
WHEN THE E.M.P. CUT POWER, IT--
STANE
YEAH.
DISMISSED, BOTH OF YOU.
TONY, I--
GO.
PLEASE...
I HAD FIVE NIGHTMARES.
FIVE THINGS THAT MAKE ME TOSS AND TURN AT NIGHT. FIVE THINGS THAT GNAW ON ME DURING THE DAY.
BUT YOU, STANE--
YOU'VE GIVEN ME A SIXTH.

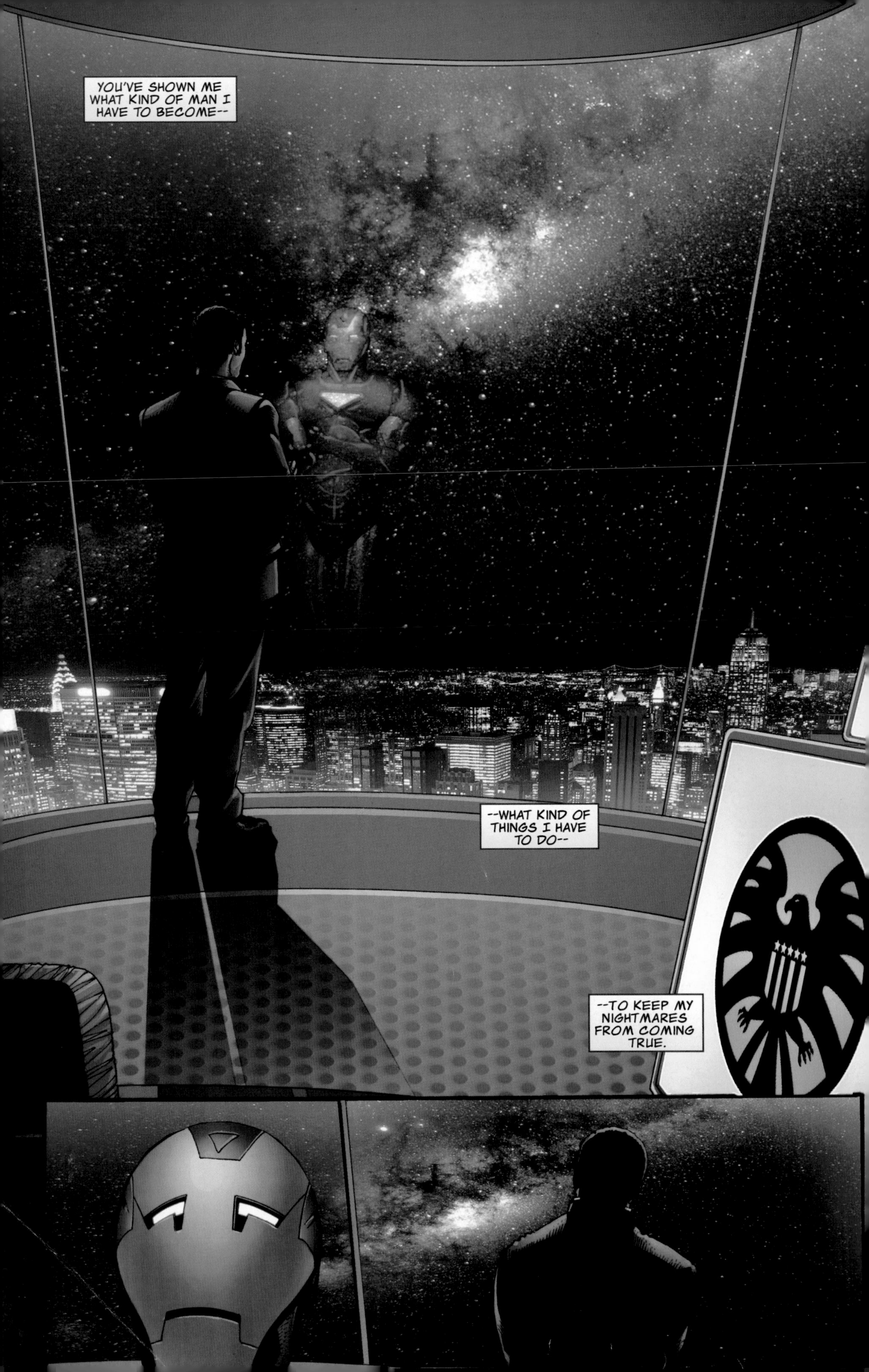
YOU'VE SHOWN ME WHAT KIND OF MAN I HAVE TO BECOME--
--WHAT KIND OF THINGS I HAVE TO DO--
--TO KEEP MY NIGHTMARES FROM COMING TRUE.

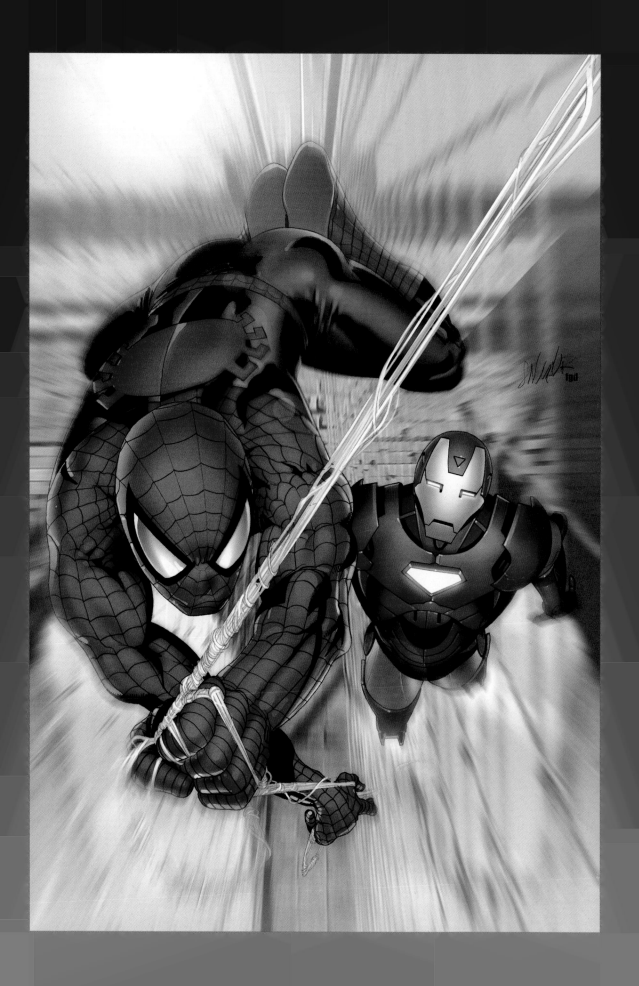

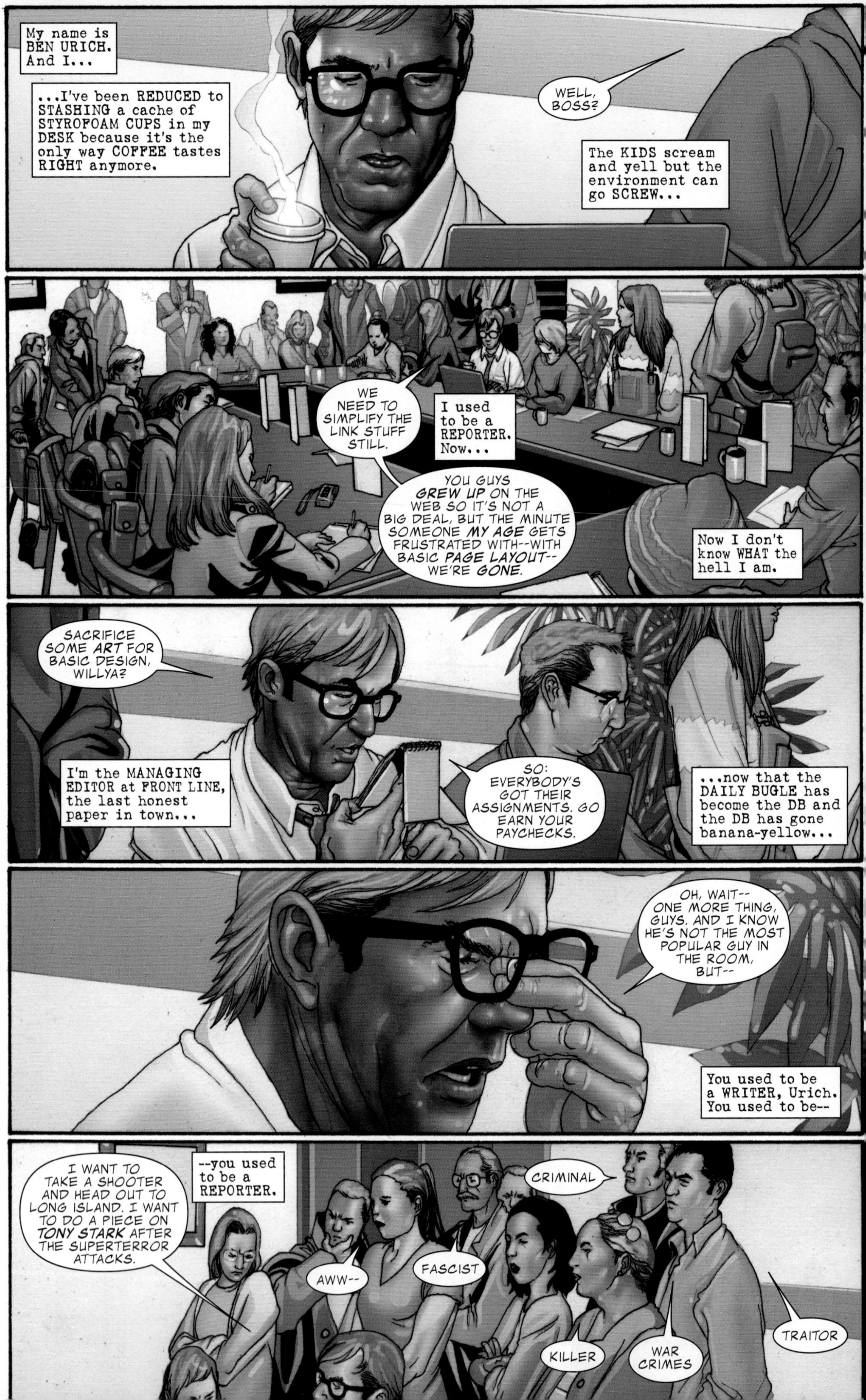
My name is BEN URICH. And I...
...I've been REDUCED to STASHING a cache of STYROFOAM CUPS in my DESK because it's the only way COFFEE tastes RIGHT anymore.
WELL, BOSS?
The KIDS scream and yell but the environment can go SCREW...
WE NEED TO SIMPLIFY THE LINK STUFF STILL.
I used to be a REPORTER. Now...
YOU GUYS GREW UP ON THE WEB SO IT'S NOT A BIG DEAL, BUT THE MINUTE SOMEONE MY AGE GETS FRUSTRATED WITH--WITH BASIC PAGE LAYOUT--WE'RE GONE.
Now I don't know WHAT the hell I am.
SACRIFICE SOME ART FOR BASIC DESIGN, WILLYA?
I'm the MANAGING EDITOR at FRONT LINE, the last honest paper in town...
SO: EVERYBODY'S GOT THEIR ASSIGNMENTS. GO EARN YOUR PAYCHECKS.
...now that the DAILY BUGLE has become the DB and the DB has gone banana-yellow...
OH, WAIT--ONE MORE THING, GUYS. AND I KNOW HE'S NOT THE MOST POPULAR GUY IN THE ROOM, BUT--
You used to be a WRITER, Urich. You used to be--
I WANT TO TAKE A SHOOTER AND HEAD OUT TO LONG ISLAND. I WANT TO DO A PIECE ON TONY STARK AFTER THE SUPERTERROR ATTACKS.
--you used to be a REPORTER.
CRIMINAL
AWW--
FASCIST
TRAITOR
KILLER
WAR CRIMES

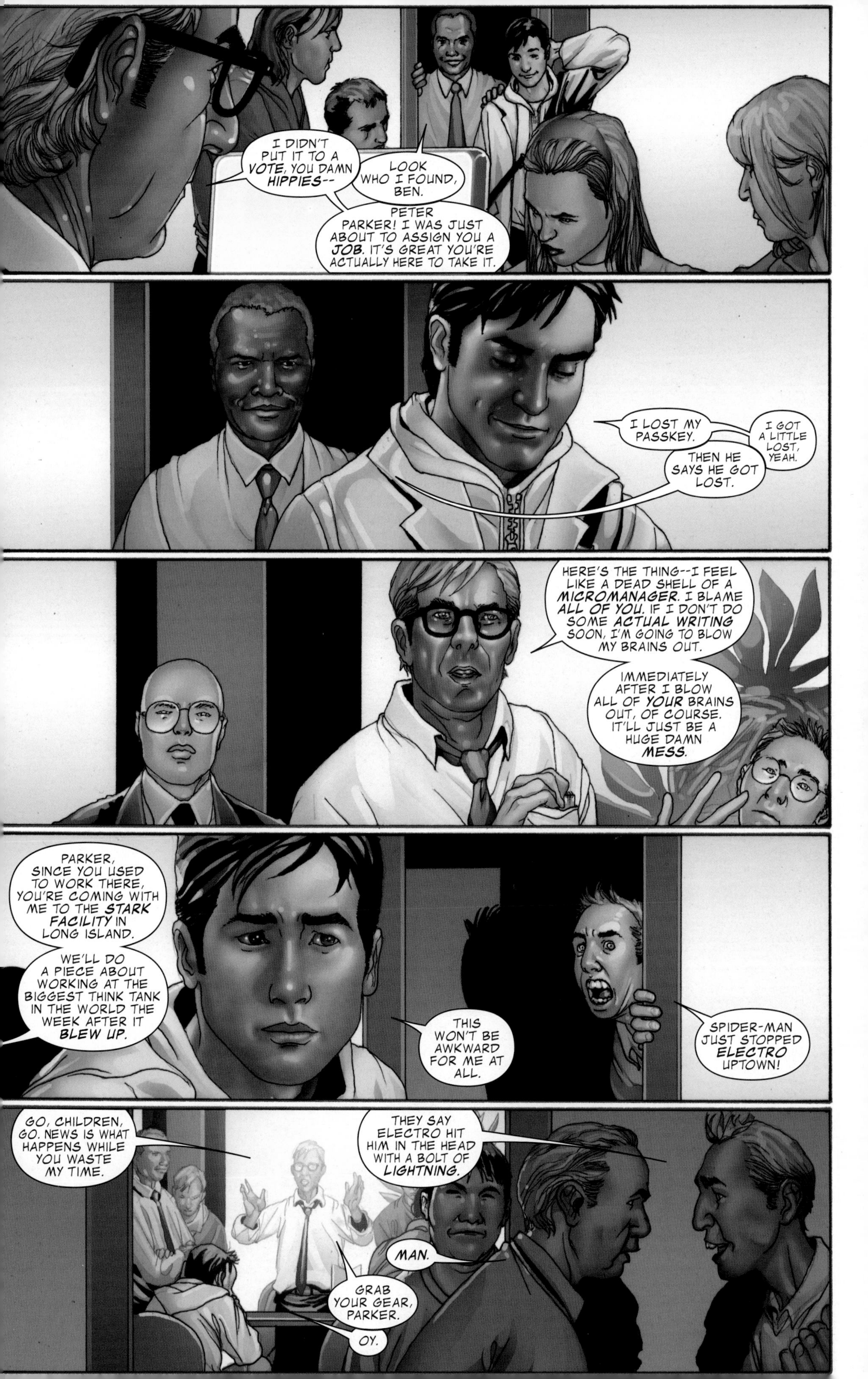
I DIDN'T PUT IT TO A VOTE, YOU DAMN HIPPIES--
LOOK WHO I FOUND, BEN.
PETER PARKER! I WAS JUST ABOUT TO ASSIGN YOU A JOB. IT'S GREAT YOU'RE ACTUALLY HERE TO TAKE IT.
I LOST MY PASSKEY.
THEN HE SAYS HE GOT LOST.
I GOT A LITTLE LOST, YEAH.
HERE'S THE THING--I FEEL LIKE A DEAD SHELL OF A MICROMANAGER. I BLAME ALL OF YOU. IF I DON'T DO SOME ACTUAL WRITING SOON, I'M GOING TO BLOW MY BRAINS OUT.
IMMEDIATELY AFTER I BLOW ALL OF YOUR BRAINS OUT, OF COURSE. IT'LL JUST BE A HUGE DAMN MESS.
PARKER, SINCE YOU USED TO WORK THERE, YOU'RE COMING WITH ME TO THE STARK FACILITY IN LONG ISLAND.
WE'LL DO A PIECE ABOUT WORKING AT THE BIGGEST THINK TANK IN THE WORLD THE WEEK AFTER IT BLEW UP.
THIS WON'T BE AWKWARD FOR ME AT ALL.
SPIDER-MAN JUST STOPPED ELECTRO UPTOWN!
GO, CHILDREN, GO. NEWS IS WHAT HAPPENS WHILE YOU WASTE MY TIME.
THEY SAY ELECTRO HIT HIM IN THE HEAD WITH A BOLT OF LIGHTNING.
MAN.
GRAB YOUR GEAR, PARKER.
OY.

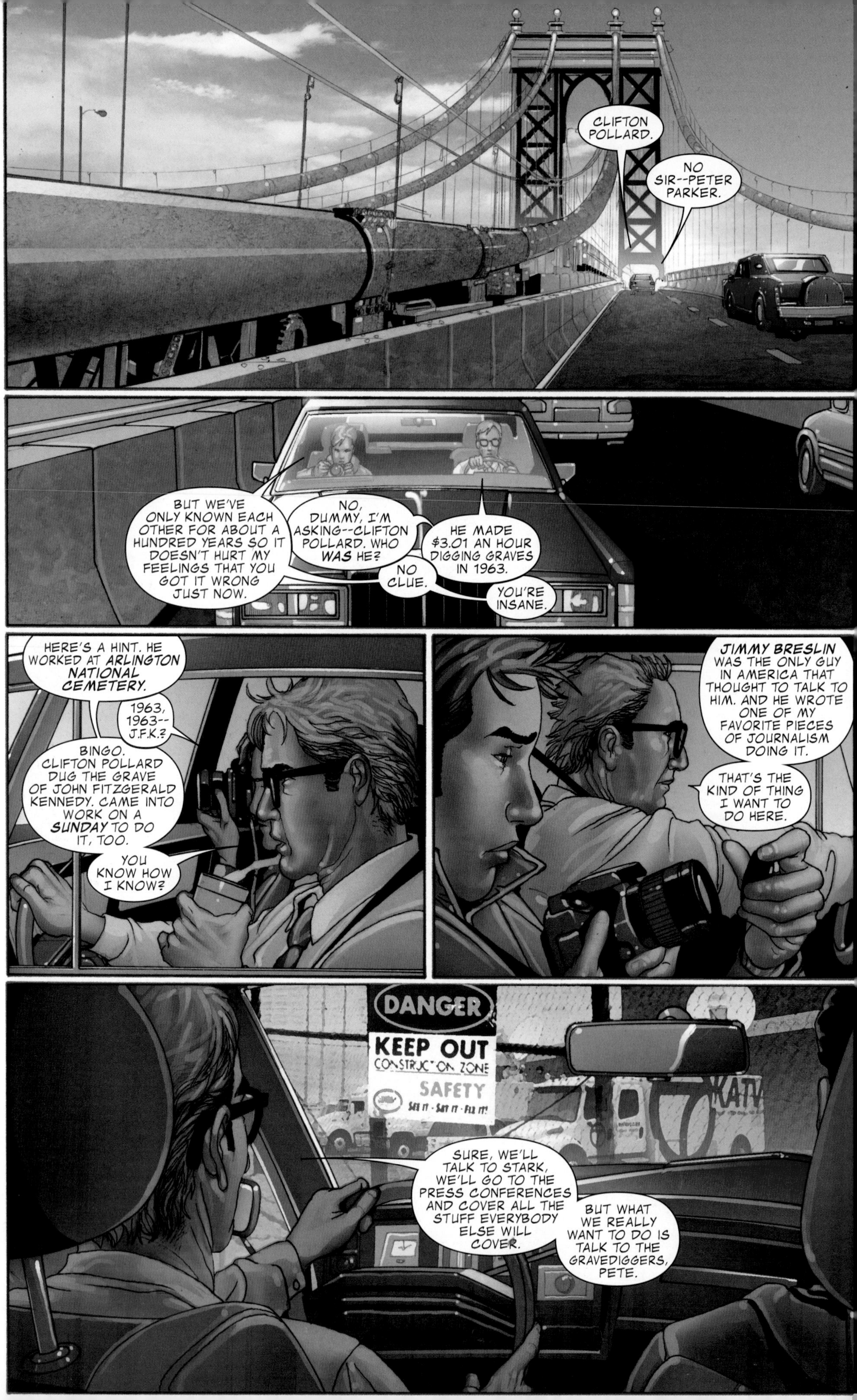
CLIFTON POLLARD.
NO SIR--PETER PARKER.
BUT WE'VE ONLY KNOWN EACH OTHER FOR ABOUT A HUNDRED YEARS SO IT DOESN'T HURT MY FEELINGS THAT YOU GOT IT WRONG JUST NOW.
NO, DUMMY, I'M ASKING--CLIFTON POLLARD. WHO WAS HE?
HE MADE $3.01 AN HOUR DIGGING GRAVES IN 1963.
NO CLUE.
YOU'RE INSANE.
HERE'S A HINT. HE WORKED AT ARLINGTON NATIONAL CEMETERY.
1963, 1963--J.F.K.?
BINGO. CLIFTON POLLARD DUG THE GRAVE OF JOHN FITZGERALD KENNEDY. CAME INTO WORK ON A SUNDAY TO DO IT, TOO.
YOU KNOW HOW I KNOW?
JIMMY BRESLIN WAS THE ONLY GUY IN AMERICA THAT THOUGHT TO TALK TO HIM. AND HE WROTE ONE OF MY FAVORITE PIECES OF JOURNALISM DOING IT.
THAT'S THE KIND OF THING I WANT TO DO HERE.
DANGER
KEEP OUT
CONSTRUC'ON ZONE
SAFETY
SEE IT · SAY IT · FIX IT!
SURE, WE'LL TALK TO STARK, WE'LL GO TO THE PRESS CONFERENCES AND COVER ALL THE STUFF EVERYBODY ELSE WILL COVER.
BUT WHAT WE REALLY WANT TO DO IS TALK TO THE GRAVEDIGGERS, PETE.

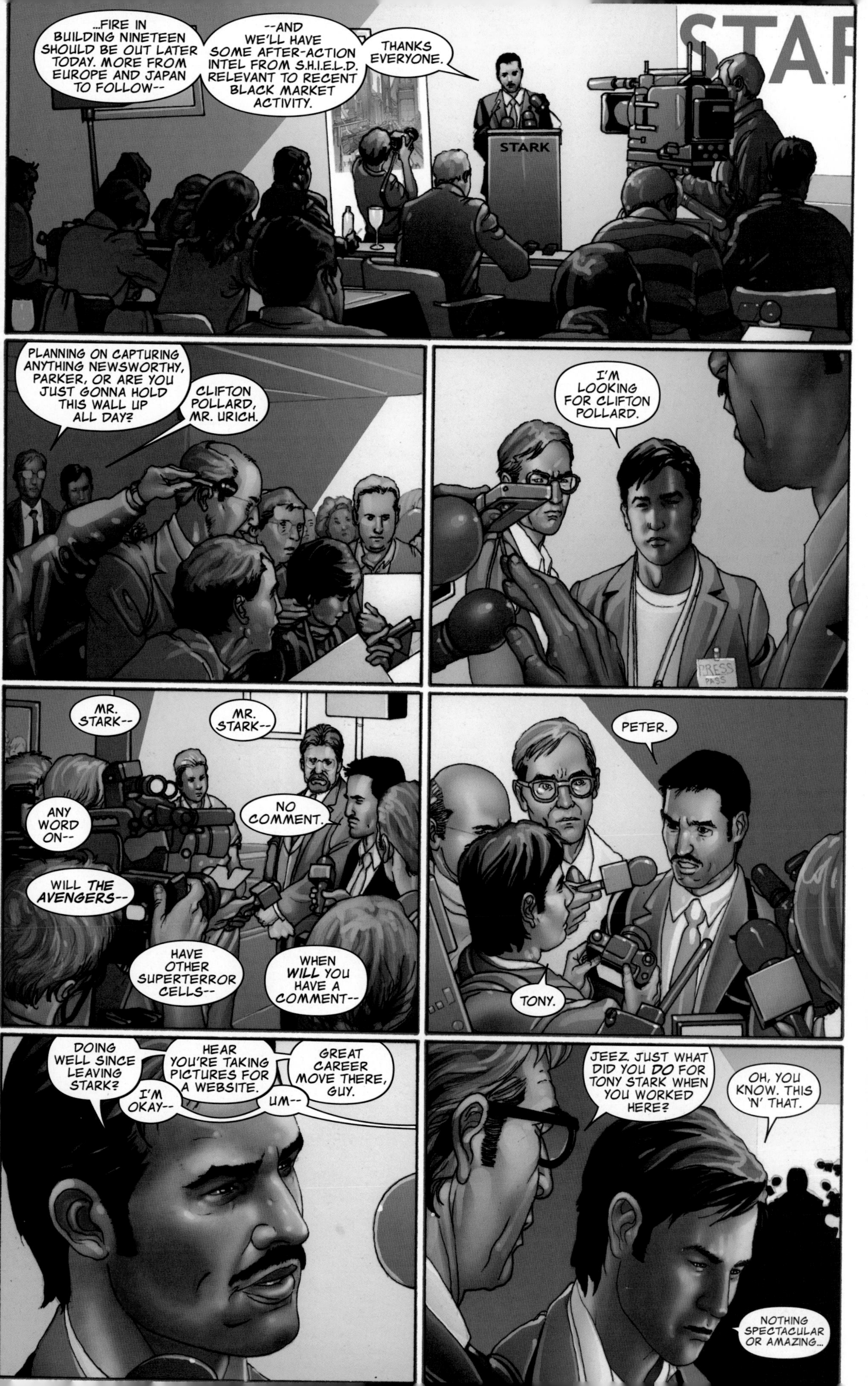
STARK
...FIRE IN BUILDING NINETEEN SHOULD BE OUT LATER TODAY. MORE FROM EUROPE AND JAPAN TO FOLLOW--
--AND WE'LL HAVE SOME AFTER-ACTION INTEL FROM S.H.I.E.L.D. RELEVANT TO RECENT BLACK MARKET ACTIVITY.
THANKS EVERYONE.
STARK
PLANNING ON CAPTURING ANYTHING NEWSWORTHY, PARKER, OR ARE YOU JUST GONNA HOLD THIS WALL UP ALL DAY?
CLIFTON POLLARD, MR. URICH.
I'M LOOKING FOR CLIFTON POLLARD.
PRESS PASS
MR. STARK--
MR. STARK--
ANY WORD ON--
NO COMMENT.
WILL THE AVENGERS--
HAVE OTHER SUPERTERROR CELLS--
WHEN WILL YOU HAVE A COMMENT--
PETER.
TONY.
DOING WELL SINCE LEAVING STARK?
I'M OKAY--
HEAR YOU'RE TAKING PICTURES FOR A WEBSITE.
UM--
GREAT CAREER MOVE THERE, GUY.
JEEZ. JUST WHAT DID YOU DO FOR TONY STARK WHEN YOU WORKED HERE?
OH, YOU KNOW. THIS 'N' THAT.
NOTHING SPECTACULAR OR AMAZING...

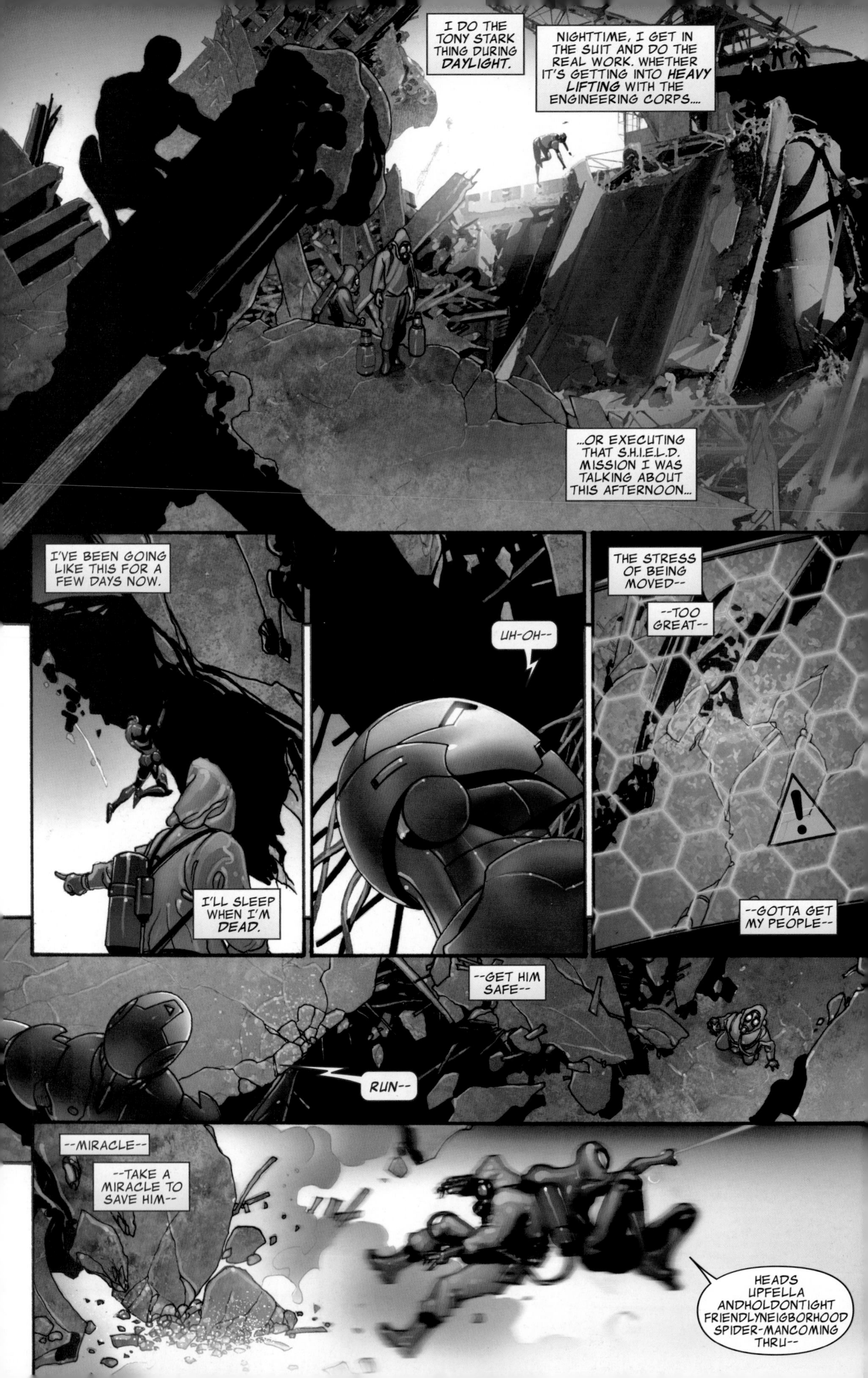
I DO THE TONY STARK THING DURING DAYLIGHT.
NIGHTTIME, I GET IN THE SUIT AND DO THE REAL WORK. WHETHER IT'S GETTING INTO HEAVY LIFTING WITH THE ENGINEERING CORPS....
...OR EXECUTING THAT S.H.I.E.L.D. MISSION I WAS TALKING ABOUT THIS AFTERNOON...
I'VE BEEN GOING LIKE THIS FOR A FEW DAYS NOW.
I'LL SLEEP WHEN I'M DEAD.
UH-OH--
THE STRESS OF BEING MOVED--
--TOO GREAT--
--GOTTA GET MY PEOPLE--
--GET HIM SAFE--
RUN--
--MIRACLE--
--TAKE A MIRACLE TO SAVE HIM--
HEADS UPFELLA ANDHOLDONTIGHT FRIENDLYNEIGBORHOOD SPIDER-MANCOMING THRU--

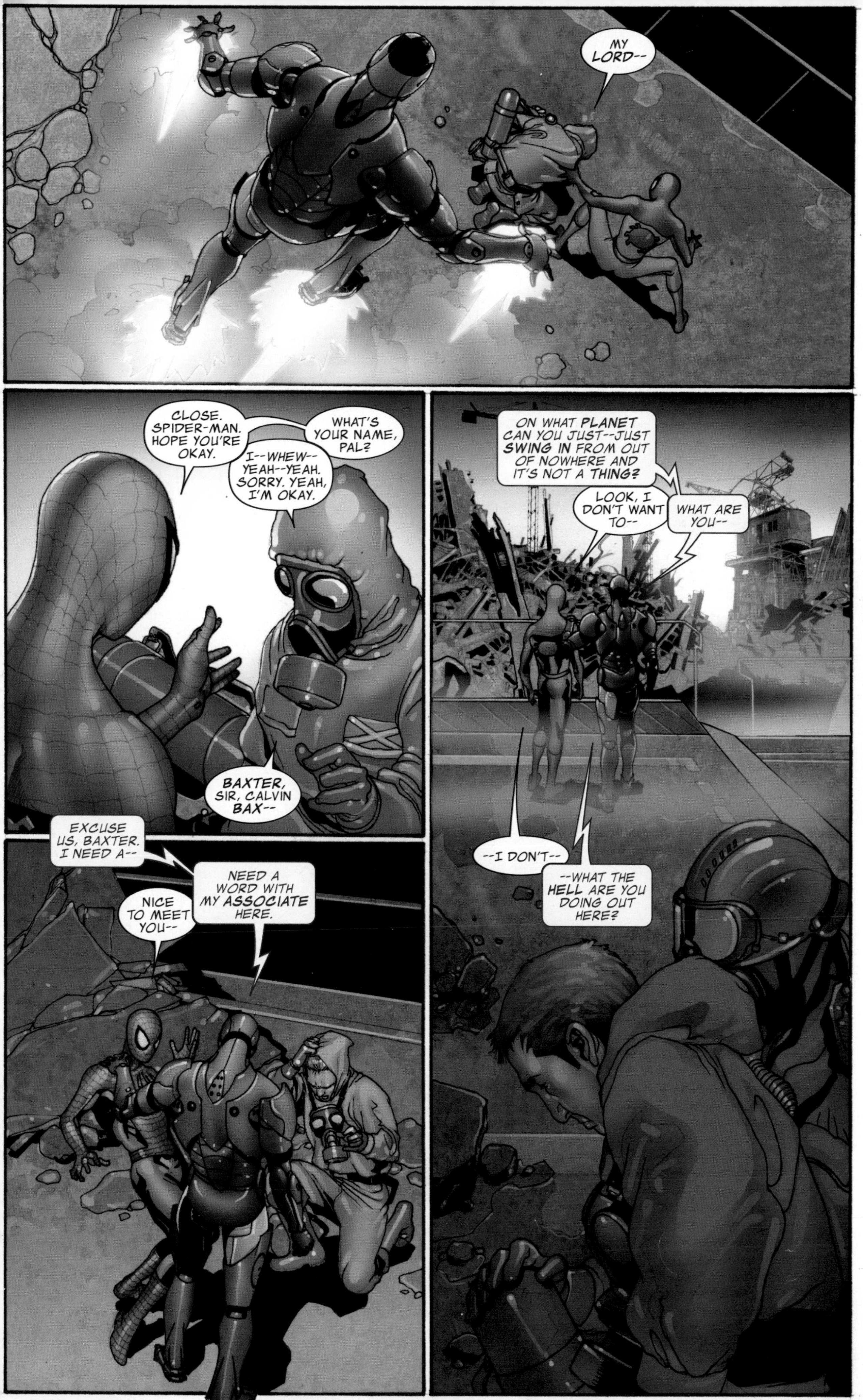
MY LORD--
CLOSE. SPIDER-MAN. HOPE YOU'RE OKAY.
WHAT'S YOUR NAME, PAL?
I--WHEW--YEAH--YEAH. SORRY. YEAH, I'M OKAY.
BAXTER, SIR, CALVIN BAX--
EXCUSE US, BAXTER. I NEED A--
NEED A WORD WITH MY ASSOCIATE HERE.
NICE TO MEET YOU--
ON WHAT PLANET CAN YOU JUST--JUST SWING IN FROM OUT OF NOWHERE AND IT'S NOT A THING?
LOOK, I DON'T WANT TO--
WHAT ARE YOU--
--I DON'T--
--WHAT THE HELL ARE YOU DOING OUT HERE?

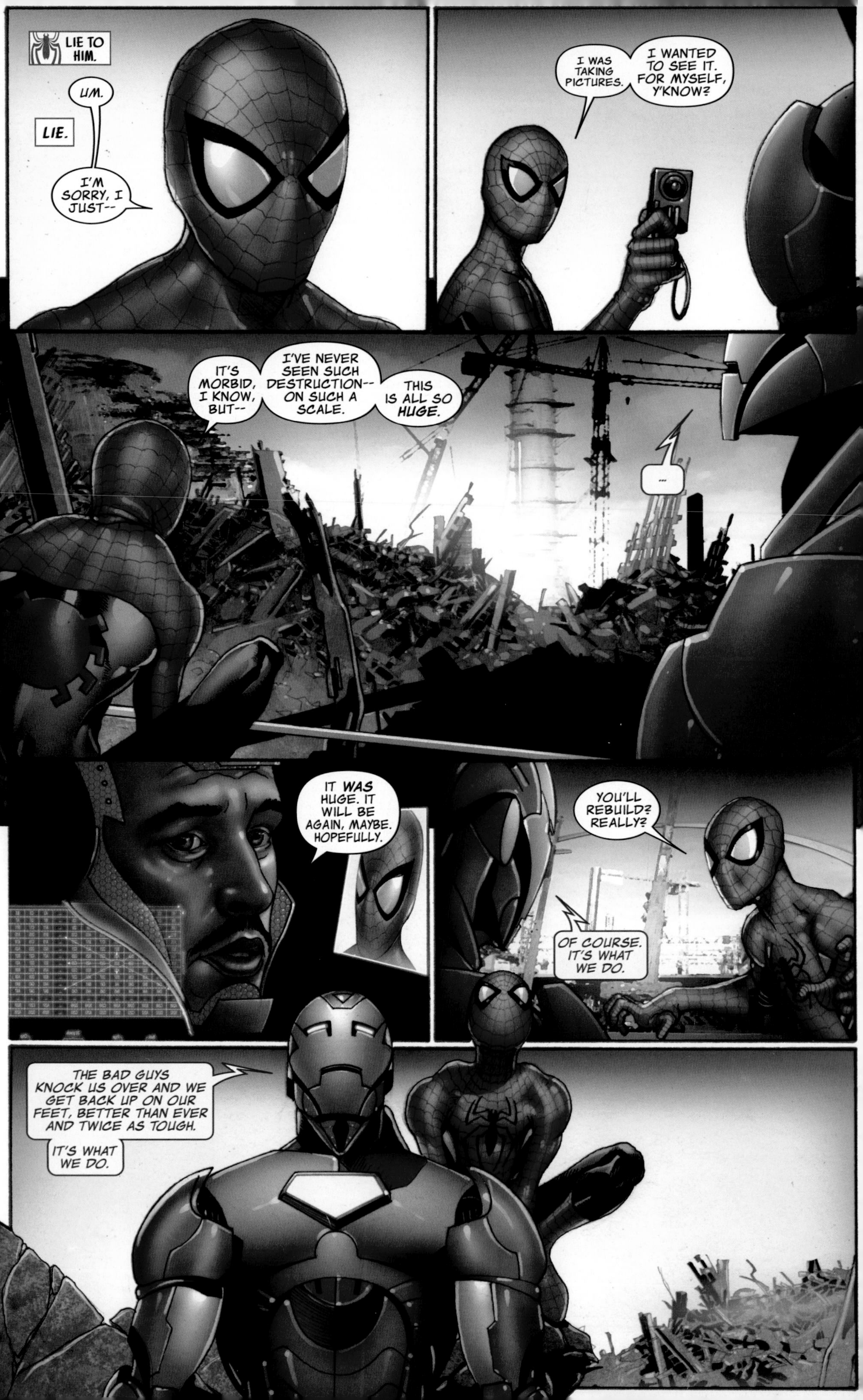

LIE TO HIM.
UM.
LIE.
I'M SORRY, I JUST--
I WAS TAKING PICTURES.
I WANTED TO SEE IT. FOR MYSELF, Y'KNOW?
IT'S MORBID, I KNOW, BUT--
I'VE NEVER SEEN SUCH DESTRUCTION-- ON SUCH A SCALE.
THIS IS ALL SO HUGE.
...
IT WAS HUGE. IT WILL BE AGAIN, MAYBE. HOPEFULLY.
YOU'LL REBUILD? REALLY?
OF COURSE. IT'S WHAT WE DO.
THE BAD GUYS KNOCK US OVER AND WE GET BACK UP ON OUR FEET, BETTER THAN EVER AND TWICE AS TOUGH.
IT'S WHAT WE DO.

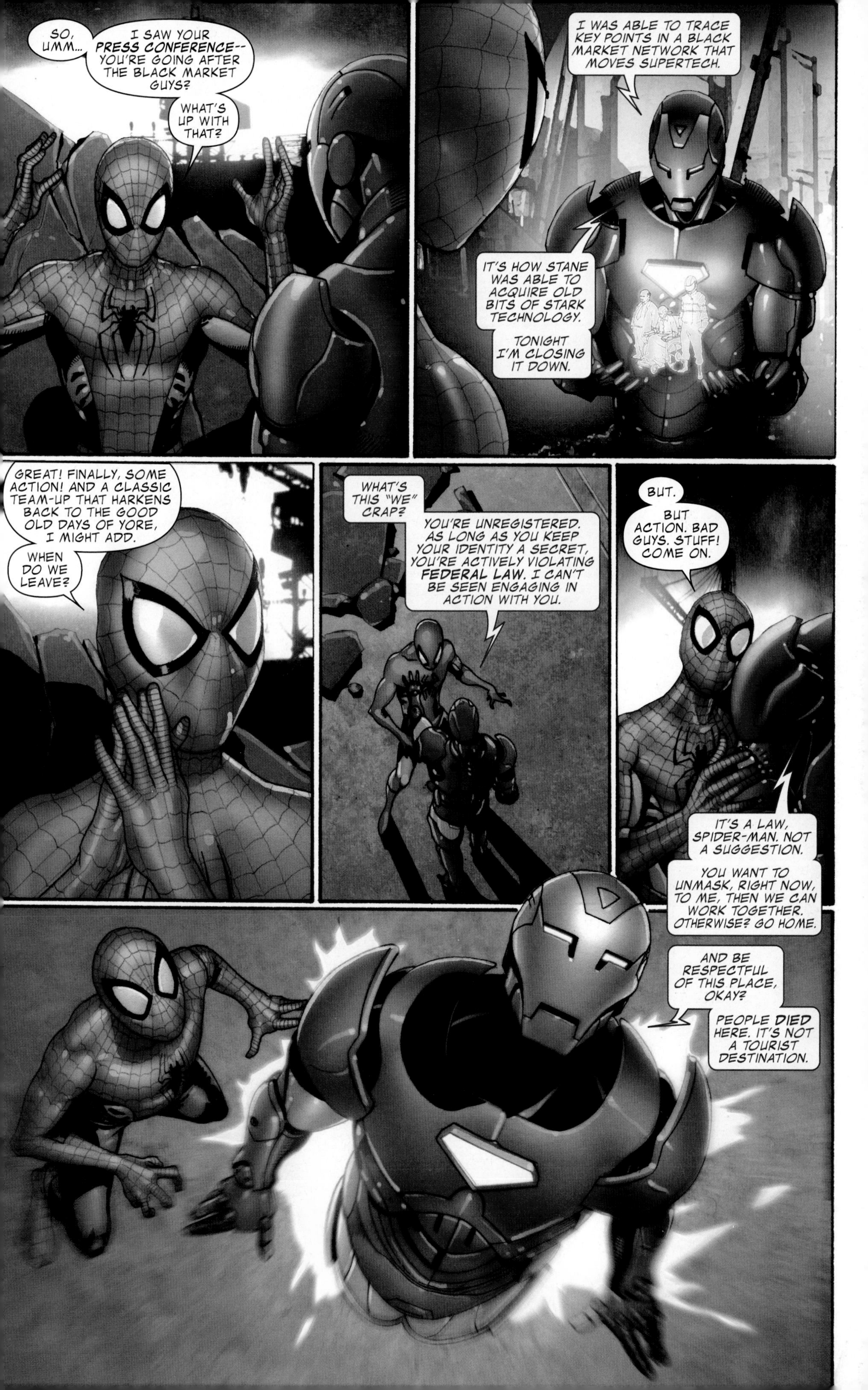

SO, UMM...
I SAW YOUR PRESS CONFERENCE-- YOU'RE GOING AFTER THE BLACK MARKET GUYS?
WHAT'S UP WITH THAT?
I WAS ABLE TO TRACE KEY POINTS IN A BLACK MARKET NETWORK THAT MOVES SUPERTECH.
IT'S HOW STANE WAS ABLE TO ACQUIRE OLD BITS OF STARK TECHNOLOGY.
TONIGHT I'M CLOSING IT DOWN.
GREAT! FINALLY, SOME ACTION! AND A CLASSIC TEAM-UP THAT HARKENS BACK TO THE GOOD OLD DAYS OF YORE, I MIGHT ADD.
WHEN DO WE LEAVE?
WHAT'S THIS "WE" CRAP?
YOU'RE UNREGISTERED. AS LONG AS YOU KEEP YOUR IDENTITY A SECRET, YOU'RE ACTIVELY VIOLATING FEDERAL LAW. I CAN'T BE SEEN ENGAGING IN ACTION WITH YOU.
BUT.
BUT ACTION. BAD GUYS. STUFF! COME ON.
IT'S A LAW, SPIDER-MAN. NOT A SUGGESTION.
YOU WANT TO UNMASK, RIGHT NOW, TO ME, THEN WE CAN WORK TOGETHER. OTHERWISE? GO HOME.
AND BE RESPECTFUL OF THIS PLACE, OKAY?
PEOPLE DIED HERE. IT'S NOT A TOURIST DESTINATION.

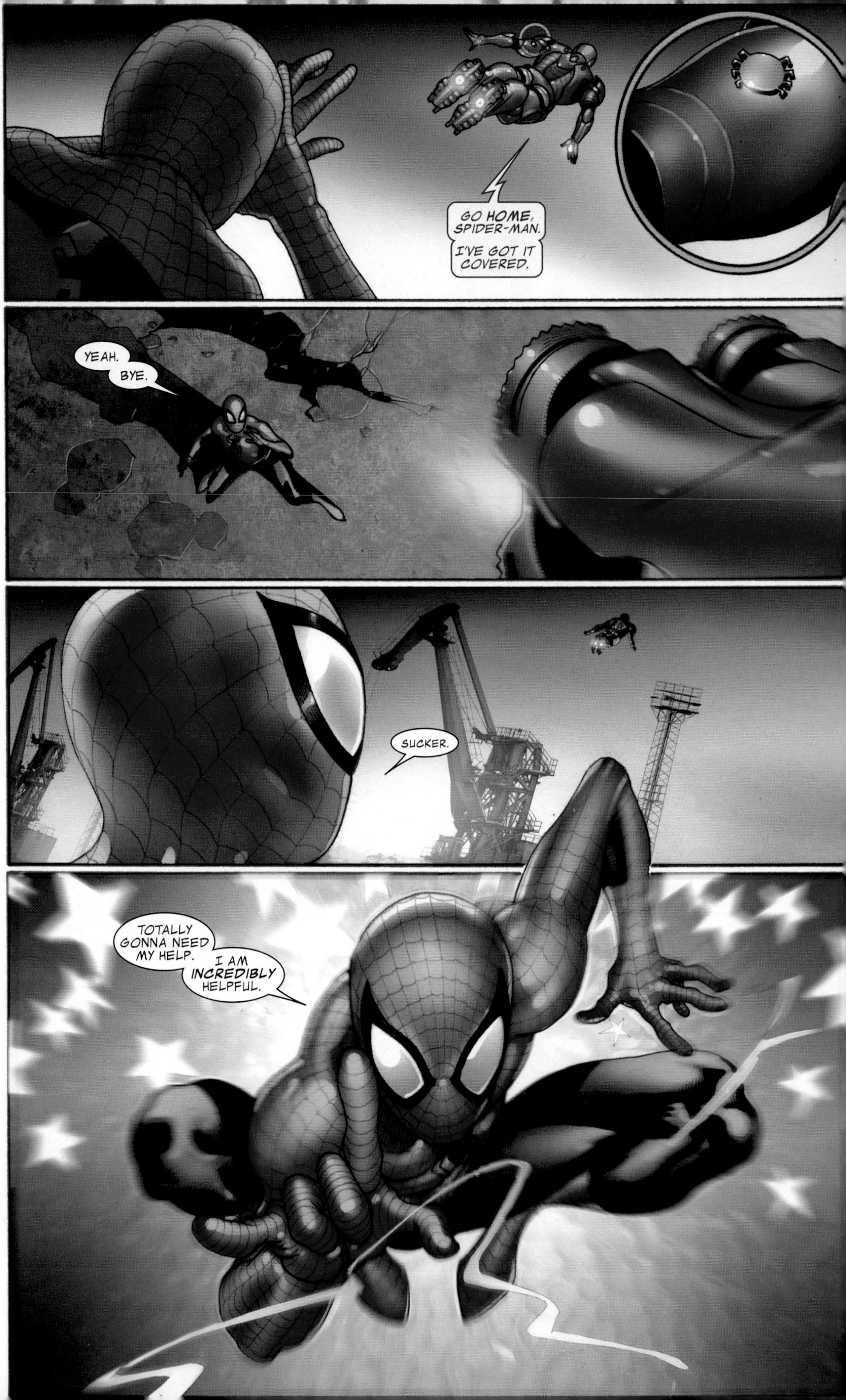
GO HOME, SPIDER-MAN.
I'VE GOT IT COVERED.
YEAH.
BYE.
SUCKER.
TOTALLY GONNA NEED MY HELP.
I AM INCREDIBLY HELPFUL.

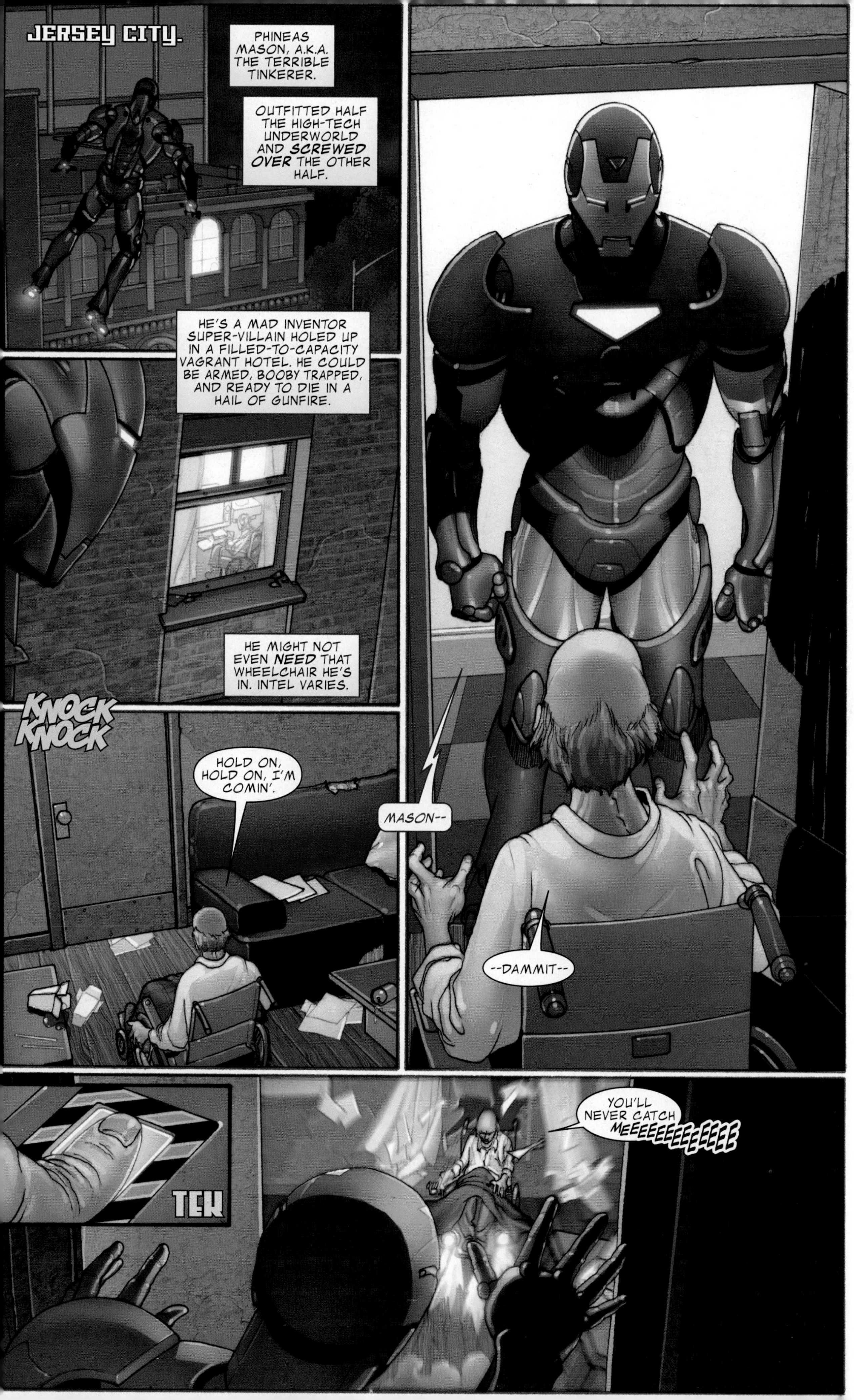
JERSEY CITY.
PHINEAS MASON, A.K.A. THE TERRIBLE TINKERER.
OUTFITTED HALF THE HIGH-TECH UNDERWORLD AND SCREWED OVER THE OTHER HALF.
HE'S A MAD INVENTOR SUPER-VILLAIN HOLED UP IN A FILLED-TO-CAPACITY VAGRANT HOTEL. HE COULD BE ARMED, BOOBY TRAPPED, AND READY TO DIE IN A HAIL OF GUNFIRE.
HE MIGHT NOT EVEN NEED THAT WHEELCHAIR HE'S IN. INTEL VARIES.
KNOCK KNOCK
HOLD ON, HOLD ON, I'M COMIN'.
MASON--
--DAMMIT--
TEK
YOU'LL NEVER CATCH MEEEEEEEEEEEEE

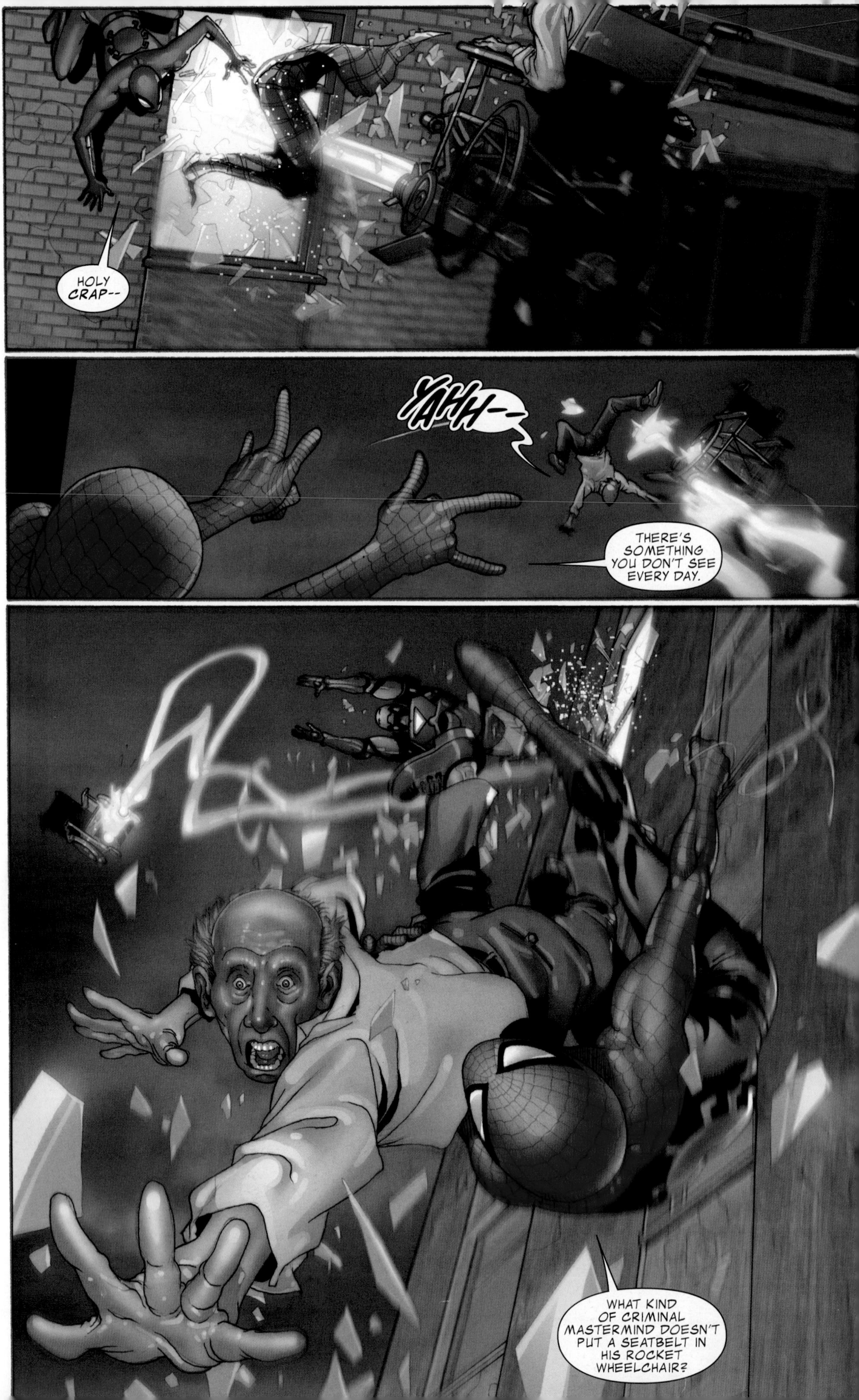
HOLY CRAP--
YAHH--
THERE'S SOMETHING YOU DON'T SEE EVERY DAY.
WHAT KIND OF CRIMINAL MASTERMIND DOESN'T PUT A SEATBELT IN HIS ROCKET WHEELCHAIR?

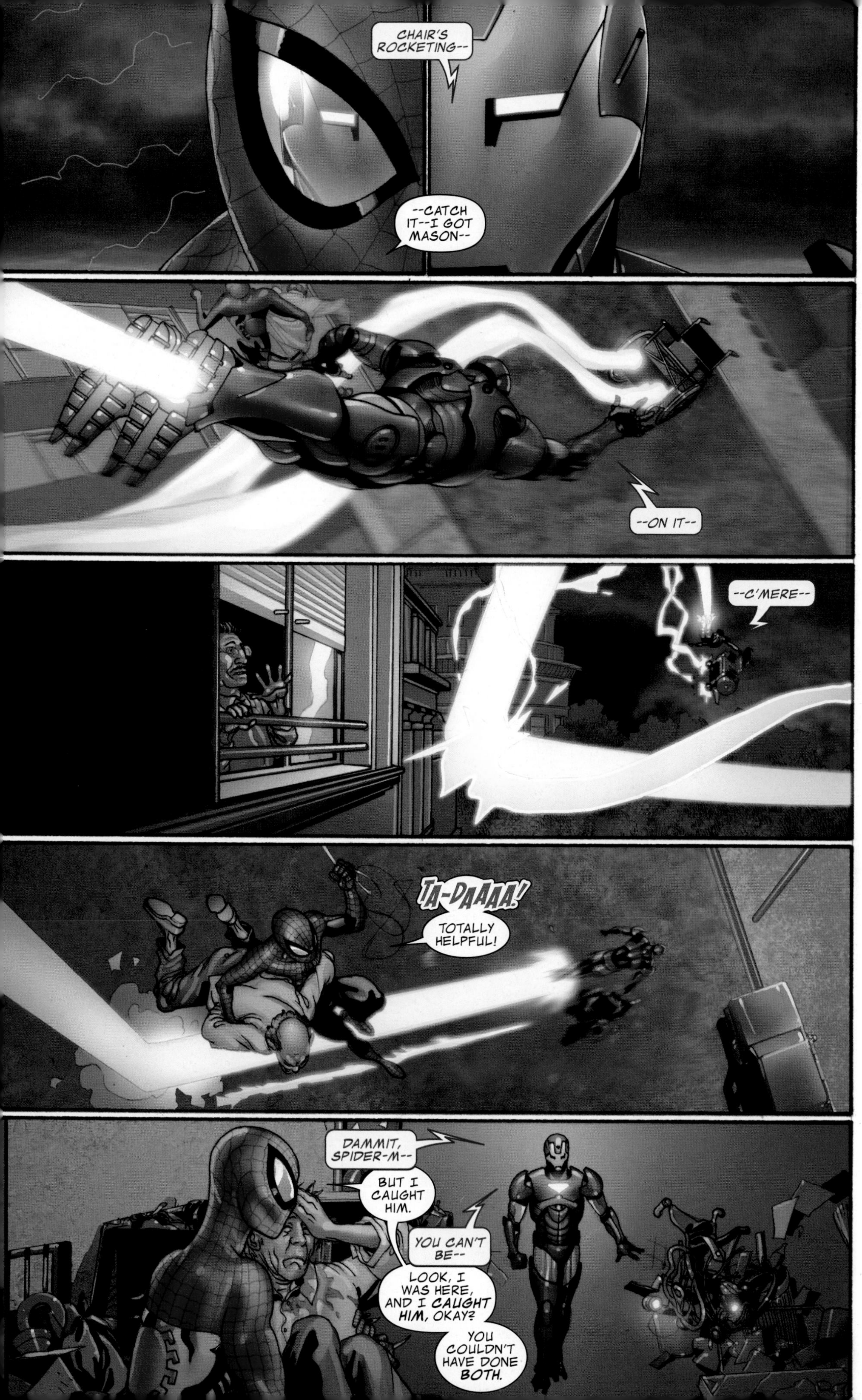
CHAIR'S ROCKETING--
--CATCH IT--I GOT MASON--
--ON IT--
--C'MERE--
TA-DAAAA!
TOTALLY HELPFUL!
DAMMIT, SPIDER-M--
BUT I CAUGHT HIM.
YOU CAN'T BE--
LOOK, I WAS HERE, AND I CAUGHT HIM, OKAY?
YOU COULDN'T HAVE DONE BOTH.

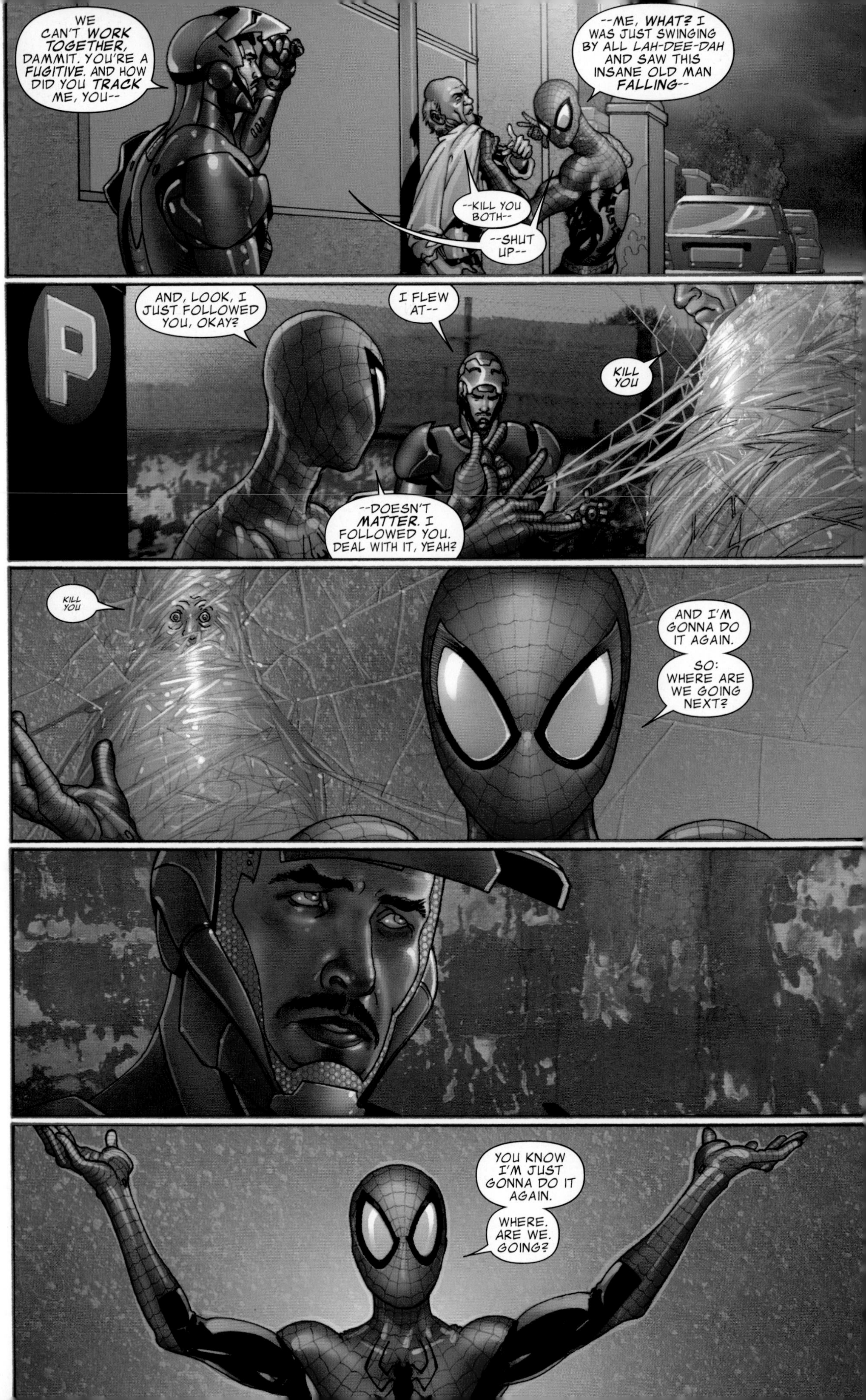

WE CAN'T WORK TOGETHER, DAMMIT. YOU'RE A FUGITIVE. AND HOW DID YOU TRACK ME, YOU--
--ME, WHAT? I WAS JUST SWINGING BY ALL LAH-DEE-DAH AND SAW THIS INSANE OLD MAN FALLING--
--KILL YOU BOTH--
--SHUT UP--
AND, LOOK, I JUST FOLLOWED YOU, OKAY?
I FLEW AT--
KILL YOU
--DOESN'T MATTER. I FOLLOWED YOU. DEAL WITH IT, YEAH?
KILL YOU
AND I'M GONNA DO IT AGAIN.
SO: WHERE ARE WE GOING NEXT?
YOU KNOW I'M JUST GONNA DO IT AGAIN.
WHERE. ARE WE. GOING?

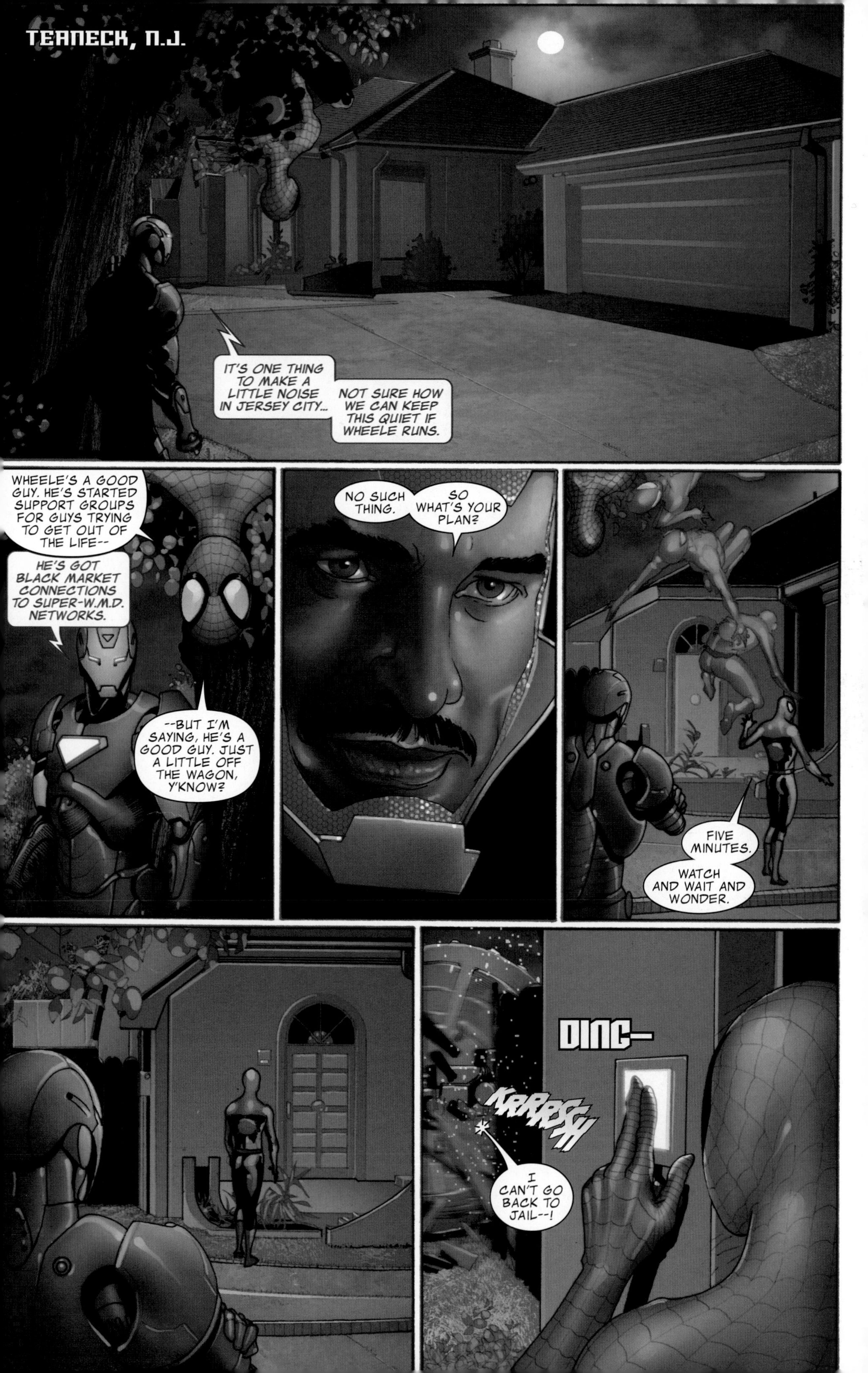
TEANECK, N.J.
IT'S ONE THING TO MAKE A LITTLE NOISE IN JERSEY CITY...
NOT SURE HOW WE CAN KEEP THIS QUIET IF WHEELE RUNS.
WHEELE'S A GOOD GUY. HE'S STARTED SUPPORT GROUPS FOR GUYS TRYING TO GET OUT OF THE LIFE--
HE'S GOT BLACK MARKET CONNECTIONS TO SUPER-W.M.D. NETWORKS.
--BUT I'M SAYING, HE'S A GOOD GUY. JUST A LITTLE OFF THE WAGON, Y'KNOW?
NO SUCH THING.
SO WHAT'S YOUR PLAN?
FIVE MINUTES.
WATCH AND WAIT AND WONDER.
DING--
KRRESH
I CAN'T GO BACK TO JAIL--!

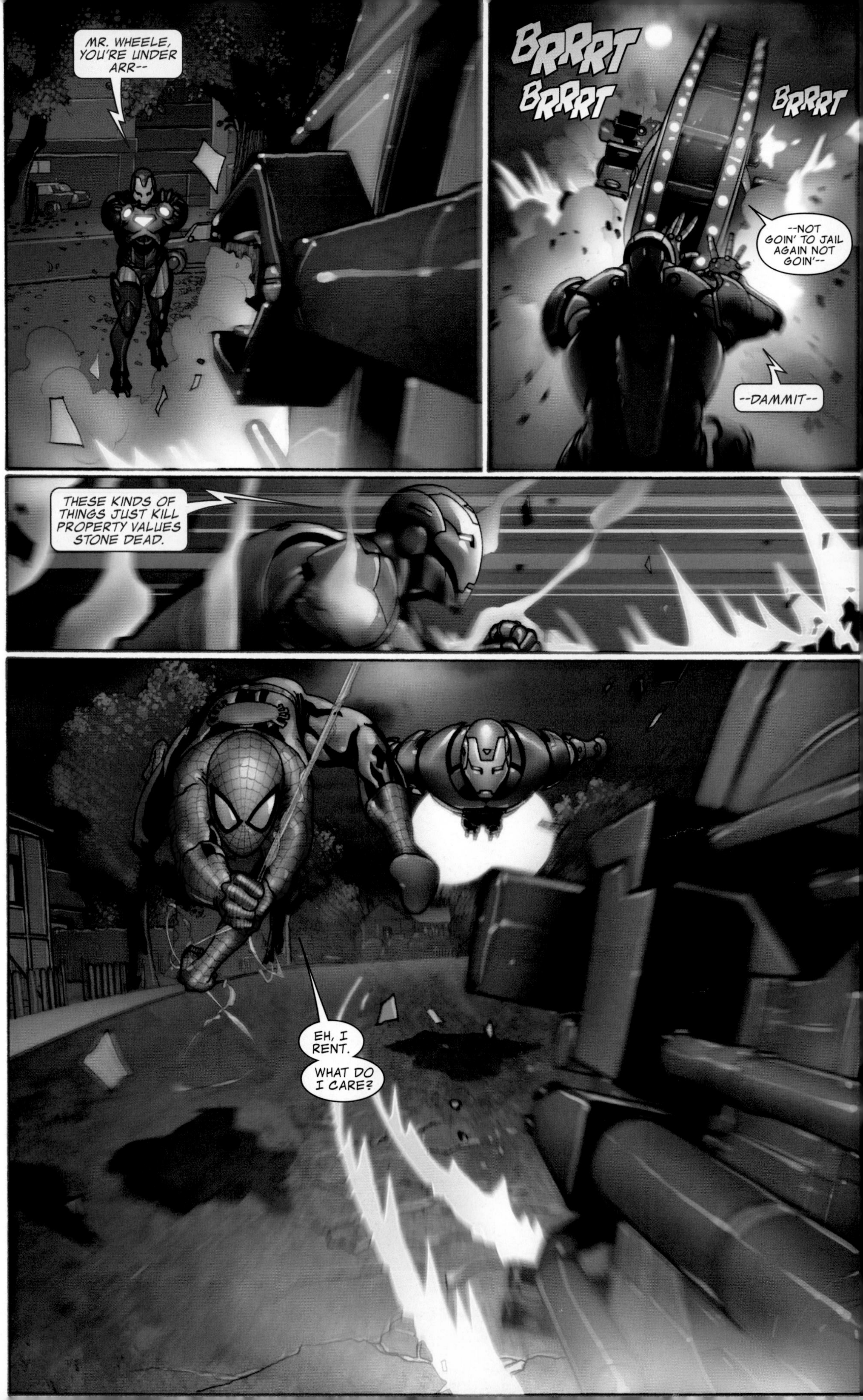
MR. WHEELE, YOU'RE UNDER ARR--
BRRRT
BRRRT
BRRRT
--NOT GOIN' TO JAIL AGAIN NOT GOIN'--
--DAMMIT--
THESE KINDS OF THINGS JUST KILL PROPERTY VALUES STONE DEAD.
EH, I RENT.
WHAT DO I CARE?

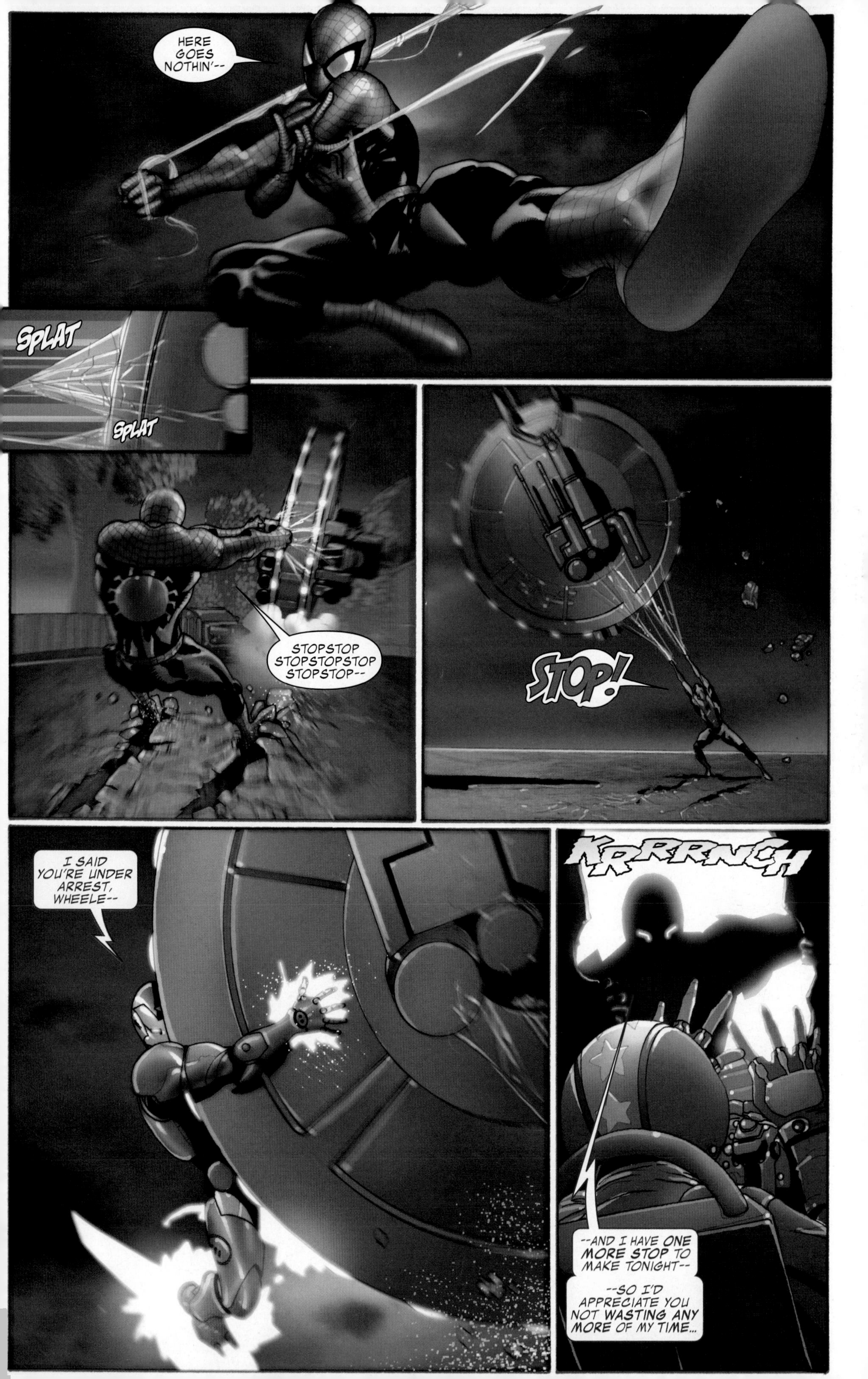
HERE GOES NOTHIN'--
SPLAT
SPLAT
STOPSTOP STOPSTOPSTOP STOPSTOP--
STOP!
I SAID YOU'RE UNDER ARREST, WHEELE--
KRRRNCH
--AND I HAVE ONE MORE STOP TO MAKE TONIGHT--
--SO I'D APPRECIATE YOU NOT WASTING ANY MORE OF MY TIME...

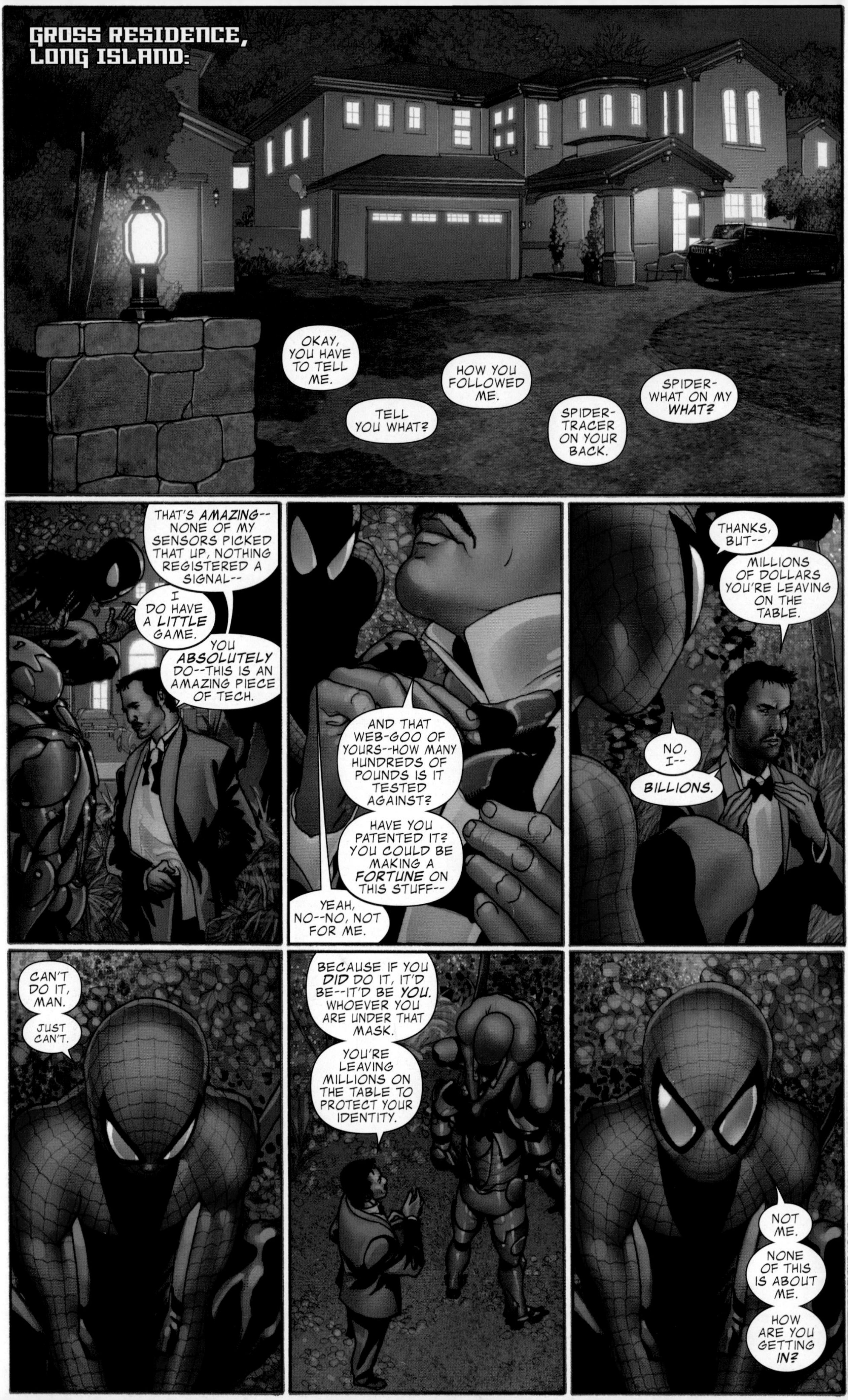
GROSS RESIDENCE, LONG ISLAND:
OKAY, YOU HAVE TO TELL ME.
TELL YOU WHAT?
HOW YOU FOLLOWED ME.
SPIDER-TRACER ON YOUR BACK.
SPIDER-WHAT ON MY WHAT?
THAT'S AMAZING--NONE OF MY SENSORS PICKED THAT UP, NOTHING REGISTERED A SIGNAL--
I DO HAVE A LITTLE GAME.
YOU ABSOLUTELY DO--THIS IS AN AMAZING PIECE OF TECH.
AND THAT WEB-GOO OF YOURS--HOW MANY HUNDREDS OF POUNDS IS IT TESTED AGAINST?
HAVE YOU PATENTED IT? YOU COULD BE MAKING A FORTUNE ON THIS STUFF--
YEAH, NO--NO, NOT FOR ME.
THANKS, BUT--
MILLIONS OF DOLLARS YOU'RE LEAVING ON THE TABLE.
NO, I--
BILLIONS.
CAN'T DO IT, MAN.
JUST CAN'T.
BECAUSE IF YOU DID DO IT, IT'D BE--IT'D BE YOU. WHOEVER YOU ARE UNDER THAT MASK.
YOU'RE LEAVING MILLIONS ON THE TABLE TO PROTECT YOUR IDENTITY.
NOT ME.
NONE OF THIS IS ABOUT ME.
HOW ARE YOU GETTING IN?

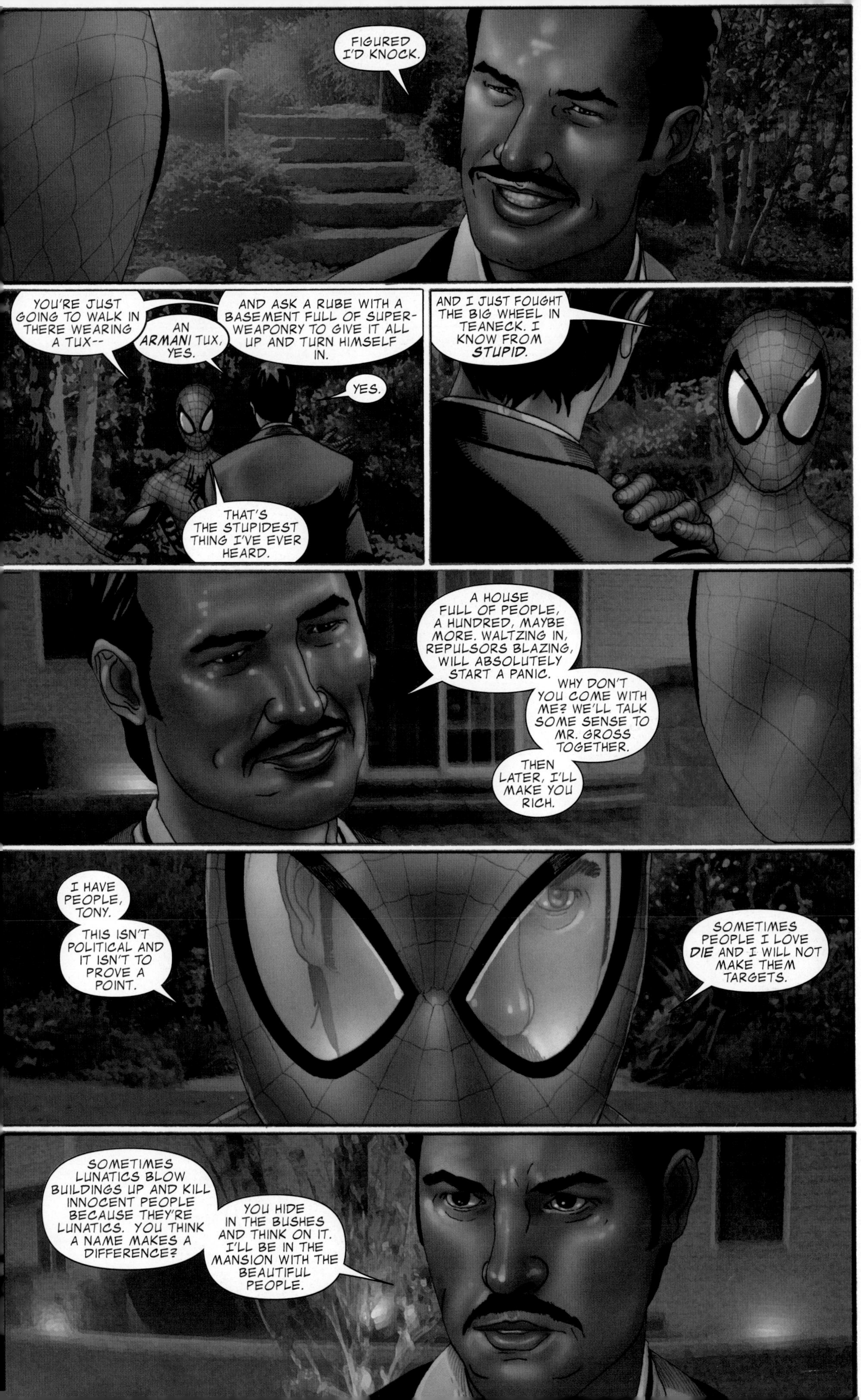
FIGURED I'D KNOCK.
YOU'RE JUST GOING TO WALK IN THERE WEARING A TUX--
AN ARMANI TUX, YES.
AND ASK A RUBE WITH A BASEMENT FULL OF SUPER-WEAPONRY TO GIVE IT ALL UP AND TURN HIMSELF IN.
YES.
THAT'S THE STUPIDEST THING I'VE EVER HEARD.
AND I JUST FOUGHT THE BIG WHEEL IN TEANECK. I KNOW FROM STUPID.
A HOUSE FULL OF PEOPLE, A HUNDRED, MAYBE MORE. WALTZING IN, REPULSORS BLAZING, WILL ABSOLUTELY START A PANIC.
WHY DON'T YOU COME WITH ME? WE'LL TALK SOME SENSE TO MR. GROSS TOGETHER.
THEN LATER, I'LL MAKE YOU RICH.
I HAVE PEOPLE, TONY.
THIS ISN'T POLITICAL AND IT ISN'T TO PROVE A POINT.
SOMETIMES PEOPLE I LOVE DIE AND I WILL NOT MAKE THEM TARGETS.
SOMETIMES LUNATICS BLOW BUILDINGS UP AND KILL INNOCENT PEOPLE BECAUSE THEY'RE LUNATICS. YOU THINK A NAME MAKES A DIFFERENCE?
YOU HIDE IN THE BUSHES AND THINK ON IT. I'LL BE IN THE MANSION WITH THE BEAUTIFUL PEOPLE.

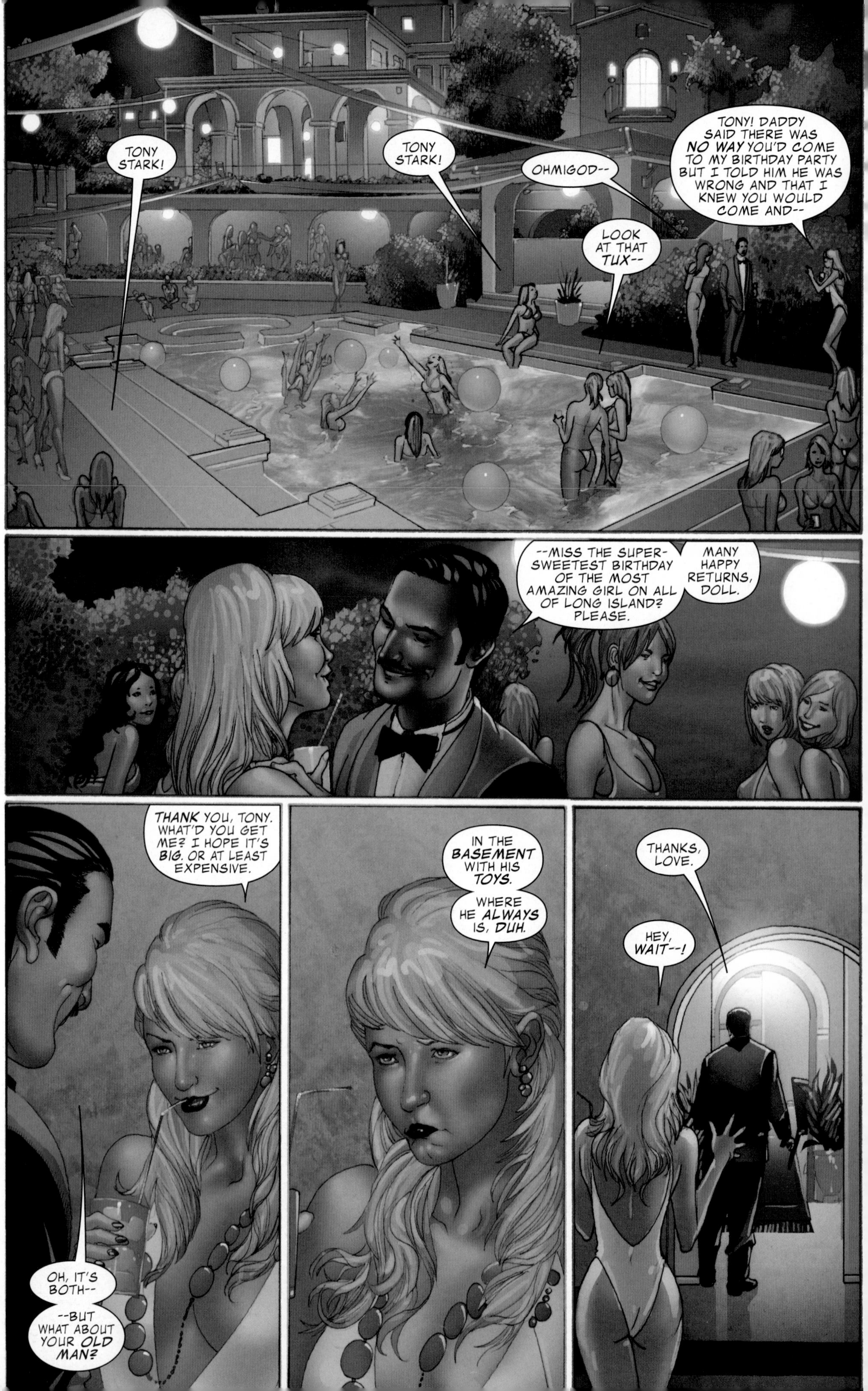
TONY STARK!
TONY STARK!
OHMIGOD--
LOOK AT THAT TUX--
TONY! DADDY SAID THERE WAS NO WAY YOU'D COME TO MY BIRTHDAY PARTY BUT I TOLD HIM HE WAS WRONG AND THAT I KNEW YOU WOULD COME AND--
--MISS THE SUPER-SWEETEST BIRTHDAY OF THE MOST AMAZING GIRL ON ALL OF LONG ISLAND? PLEASE.
MANY HAPPY RETURNS, DOLL.
THANK YOU, TONY. WHAT'D YOU GET ME? I HOPE IT'S BIG. OR AT LEAST EXPENSIVE.
OH, IT'S BOTH--
--BUT WHAT ABOUT YOUR OLD MAN?
IN THE BASEMENT WITH HIS TOYS.
WHERE HE ALWAYS IS, DUH.
THANKS, LOVE.
HEY, WAIT--!

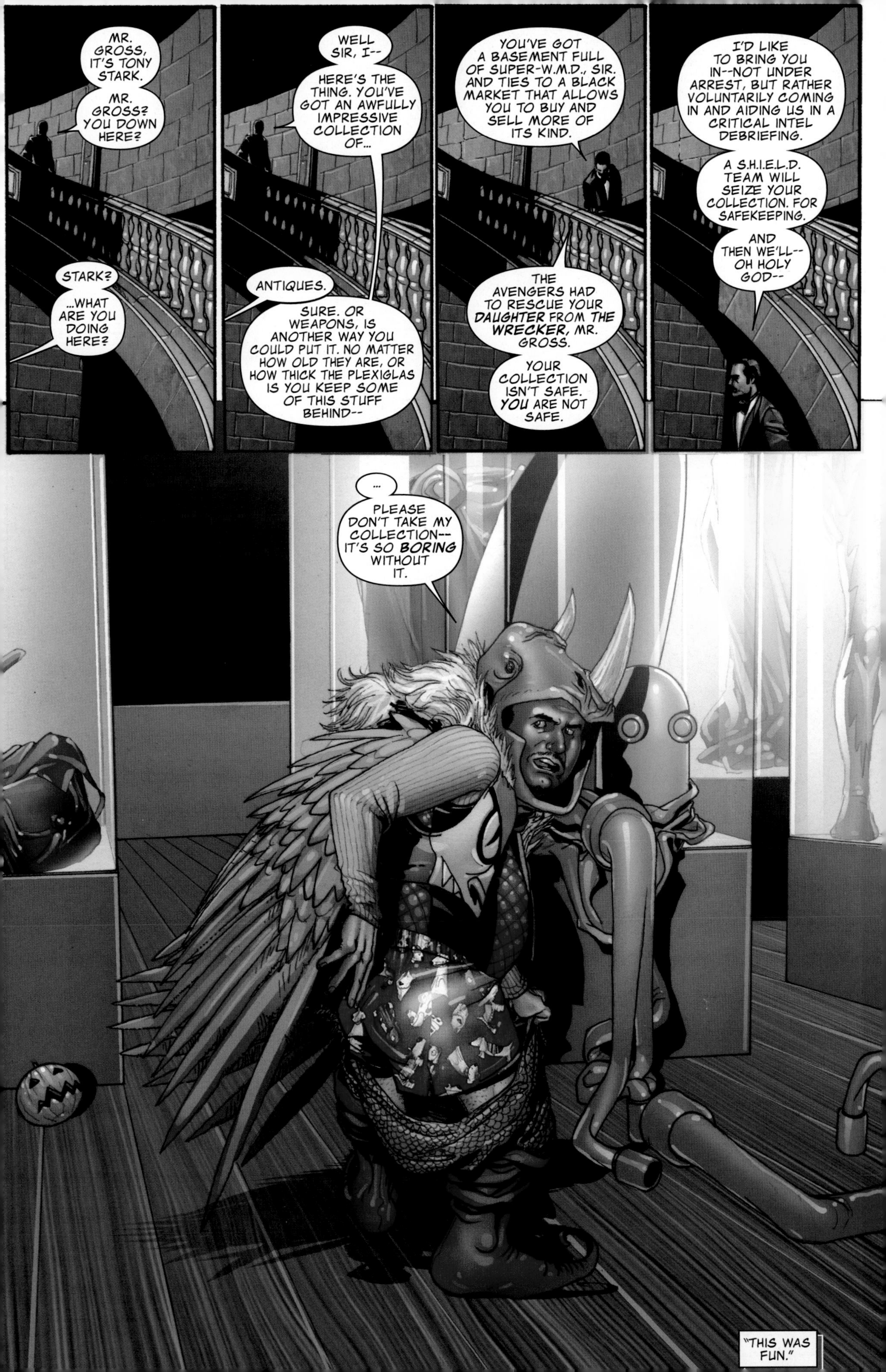
MR. GROSS, IT'S TONY STARK.
MR. GROSS? YOU DOWN HERE?
STARK?
...WHAT ARE YOU DOING HERE?
WELL SIR, I--
HERE'S THE THING. YOU'VE GOT AN AWFULLY IMPRESSIVE COLLECTION OF...
ANTIQUES.
SURE. OR WEAPONS, IS ANOTHER WAY YOU COULD PUT IT. NO MATTER HOW OLD THEY ARE, OR HOW THICK THE PLEXIGLAS IS YOU KEEP SOME OF THIS STUFF BEHIND--
YOU'VE GOT A BASEMENT FULL OF SUPER-W.M.D., SIR. AND TIES TO A BLACK MARKET THAT ALLOWS YOU TO BUY AND SELL MORE OF ITS KIND.
THE AVENGERS HAD TO RESCUE YOUR DAUGHTER FROM THE WRECKER, MR. GROSS.
YOUR COLLECTION ISN'T SAFE. YOU ARE NOT SAFE.
I'D LIKE TO BRING YOU IN--NOT UNDER ARREST, BUT RATHER VOLUNTARILY COMING IN AND AIDING US IN A CRITICAL INTEL DEBRIEFING.
A S.H.I.E.L.D. TEAM WILL SEIZE YOUR COLLECTION. FOR SAFEKEEPING.
AND THEN WE'LL-- OH HOLY GOD--
...
PLEASE DON'T TAKE MY COLLECTION-- IT'S SO BORING WITHOUT IT.
"THIS WAS FUN."

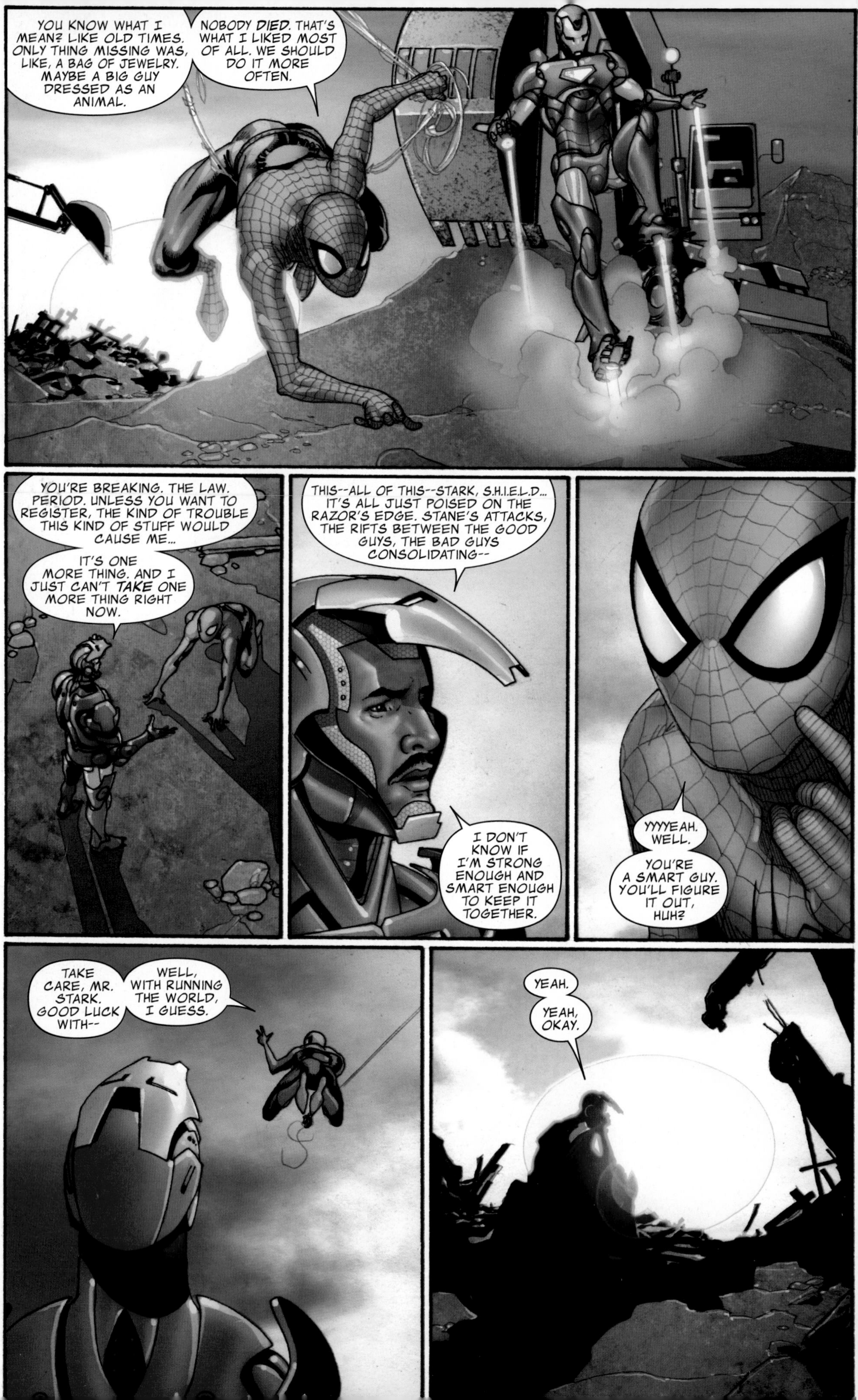
YOU KNOW WHAT I MEAN? LIKE OLD TIMES. ONLY THING MISSING WAS, LIKE, A BAG OF JEWELRY. MAYBE A BIG GUY DRESSED AS AN ANIMAL.
NOBODY DIED. THAT'S WHAT I LIKED MOST OF ALL. WE SHOULD DO IT MORE OFTEN.
YOU'RE BREAKING. THE LAW. PERIOD. UNLESS YOU WANT TO REGISTER, THE KIND OF TROUBLE THIS KIND OF STUFF WOULD CAUSE ME...
IT'S ONE MORE THING. AND I JUST CAN'T TAKE ONE MORE THING RIGHT NOW.
THIS--ALL OF THIS--STARK, S.H.I.E.L.D... IT'S ALL JUST POISED ON THE RAZOR'S EDGE. STANE'S ATTACKS, THE RIFTS BETWEEN THE GOOD GUYS, THE BAD GUYS CONSOLIDATING--
I DON'T KNOW IF I'M STRONG ENOUGH AND SMART ENOUGH TO KEEP IT TOGETHER.
YYYYEAH. WELL.
YOU'RE A SMART GUY. YOU'LL FIGURE IT OUT, HUH?
TAKE CARE, MR. STARK. GOOD LUCK WITH--
WELL, WITH RUNNING THE WORLD, I GUESS.
YEAH.
YEAH, OKAY.

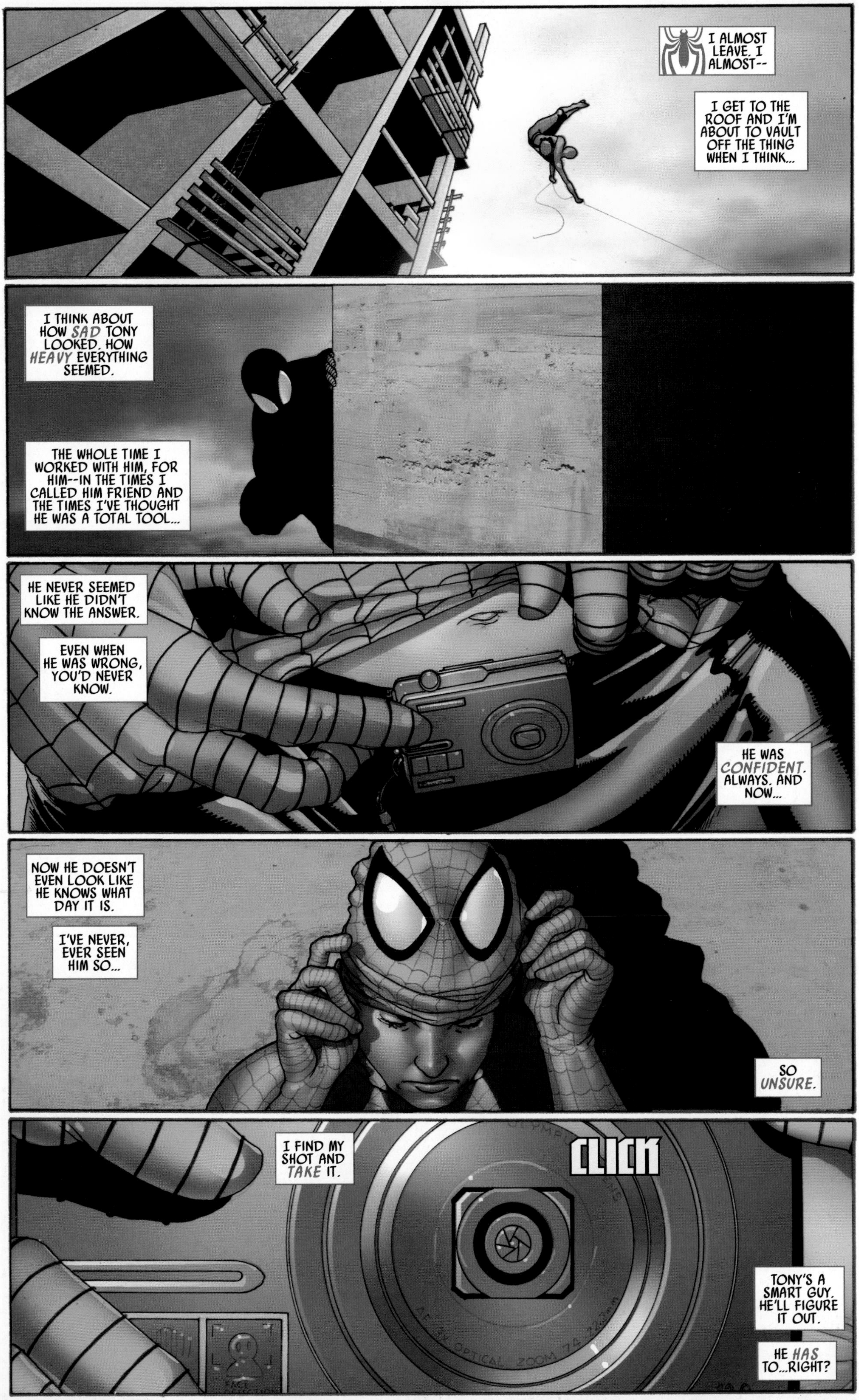

I ALMOST LEAVE. I ALMOST--
I GET TO THE ROOF AND I'M ABOUT TO VAULT OFF THE THING WHEN I THINK...
I THINK ABOUT HOW SAD TONY LOOKED. HOW HEAVY EVERYTHING SEEMED.
THE WHOLE TIME I WORKED WITH HIM, FOR HIM--IN THE TIMES I CALLED HIM FRIEND AND THE TIMES I'VE THOUGHT HE WAS A TOTAL TOOL...
HE NEVER SEEMED LIKE HE DIDN'T KNOW THE ANSWER.
EVEN WHEN HE WAS WRONG, YOU'D NEVER KNOW.
HE WAS CONFIDENT. ALWAYS. AND NOW...
NOW HE DOESN'T EVEN LOOK LIKE HE KNOWS WHAT DAY IT IS.
I'VE NEVER, EVER SEEN HIM SO...
SO UNSURE.
I FIND MY SHOT AND TAKE IT.
CLICK
TONY'S A SMART GUY. HE'LL FIGURE IT OUT.
HE HAS TO...RIGHT?

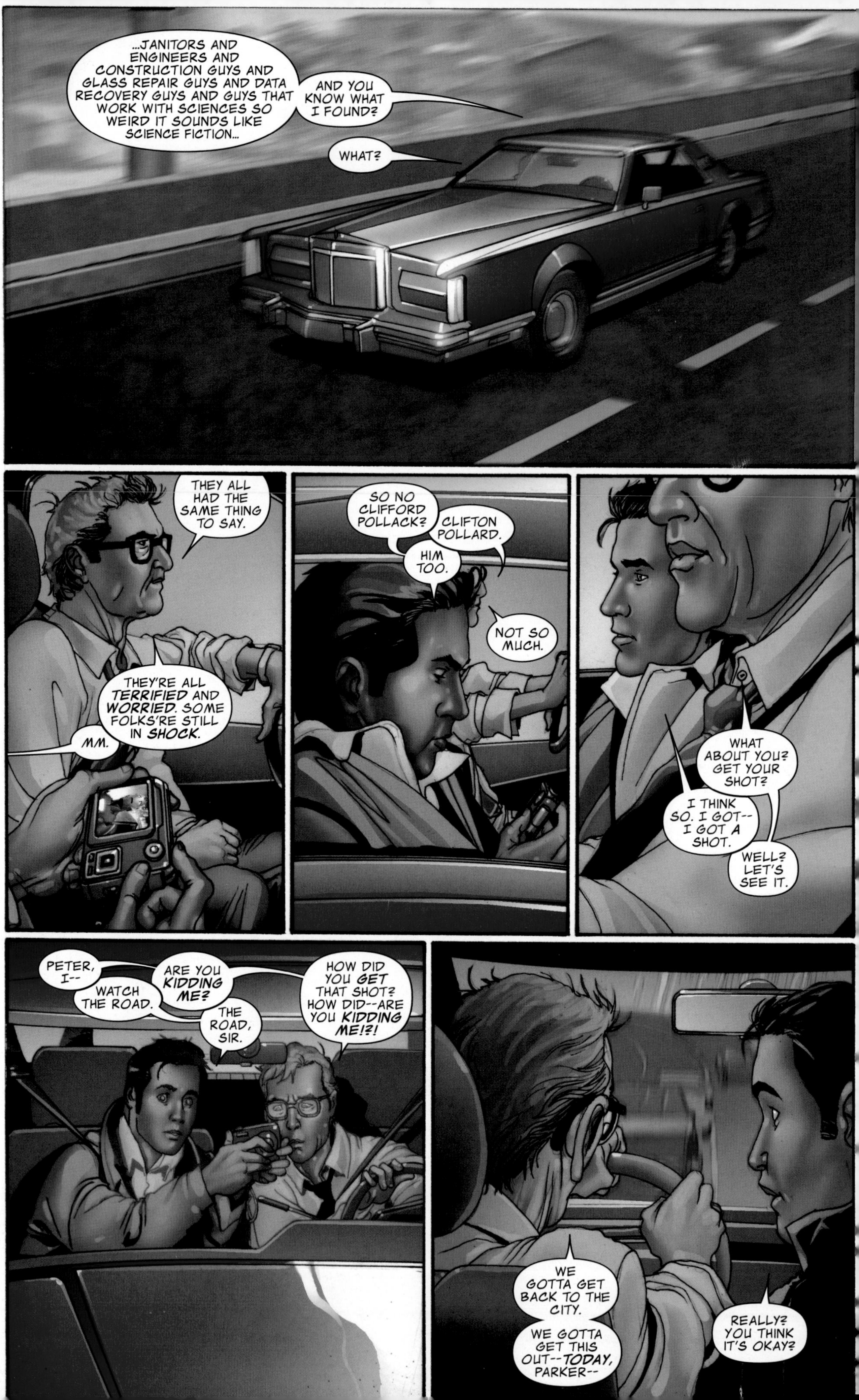
...JANITORS AND ENGINEERS AND CONSTRUCTION GUYS AND GLASS REPAIR GUYS AND DATA RECOVERY GUYS AND GUYS THAT WORK WITH SCIENCES SO WEIRD IT SOUNDS LIKE SCIENCE FICTION...
AND YOU KNOW WHAT I FOUND?
WHAT?
THEY ALL HAD THE SAME THING TO SAY.
THEY'RE ALL TERRIFIED AND WORRIED. SOME FOLKS'RE STILL IN SHOCK.
MM.
SO NO CLIFFORD POLLACK?
CLIFTON POLLARD.
HIM TOO.
NOT SO MUCH.
WHAT ABOUT YOU? GET YOUR SHOT?
I THINK SO. I GOT-- I GOT A SHOT.
WELL? LET'S SEE IT.
PETER, I--
WATCH THE ROAD.
ARE YOU KIDDING ME?
THE ROAD, SIR.
HOW DID YOU GET THAT SHOT? HOW DID--ARE YOU KIDDING ME!?!
WE GOTTA GET BACK TO THE CITY.
WE GOTTA GET THIS OUT--TODAY, PARKER--
REALLY? YOU THINK IT'S OKAY?

FRONT LINE

MORNING EDITION · 50 CENTS　　　　　　　　**WEDNESDAY, NOVEMBER 5, 2008**

THE HEAD THAT WEARS THE CROWN

FEATURE ARTICLE
BY BEN URICH

PHOTOGRAPH BY PETER PARKER

LONG ISLAND–The fires at Stark Industries have been burning for a week now. It smells like burnt fish and hot dust. They tell you it's all the wiring that melted when a high-tech lunatic named Ezekiel Stane tried to wipe Tony Stark, and Stark Industries, off the face of the earth.

And Stark, as anyone with a television can tell you, hasn't slept since the fires started.

The mood at Stark Industries, or what's left of it, is that of a bereaved family, only instead of mourning the passing of a beloved patriarch or doddering old aunt, this is a family dozens of lives smaller, stolen in an instant by an inhuman monster, in an inhumanly monstrous moment of cruelty. There are not words to adequately explain the loss.

Stark employees, as they'll tell you if you give them half a second, tend to work for Stark as long as possible. Every employee I spoke with--from the janitors to the particle physicists--would introduce themselves to me, then rattle off their tenure at Stark like it was their last name.

"I can't imagine a world without Stark Industries."

Continued on pg. 19

TONY STARK AT THE LONG ISLAND FACILITY

MORE HEADLINES

"CLIFTON POLLARD"
THE FIVE NIGHTMARES: EPILOGUE

PREVIOUSLY:

The shape-shifting aliens known as Skrulls infiltrated all aspects of human life, and planted a destructive virus in Stark technology, causing it to fail around the world — from cell phones to toasters to the Extremis armor that made Tony Stark into Iron Man. In the ashes of the invasion, Stark technology is synonymous with failure.

Tony Stark held himself accountable for his failure to prevent the invasion. For his troubles, he was stripped of his roles as leader of the Avengers and director of a now-defunct S.H.I.E.L.D.

Norman Osborn, the man behind the government-sponsored super-villain team, the Thunderbolts, has risen to power in Tony's place. With Stark and S.H.I.E.L.D. out, Osborn now sits at the head of the newly formed peacekeeping agency, H.A.M.M.E.R.

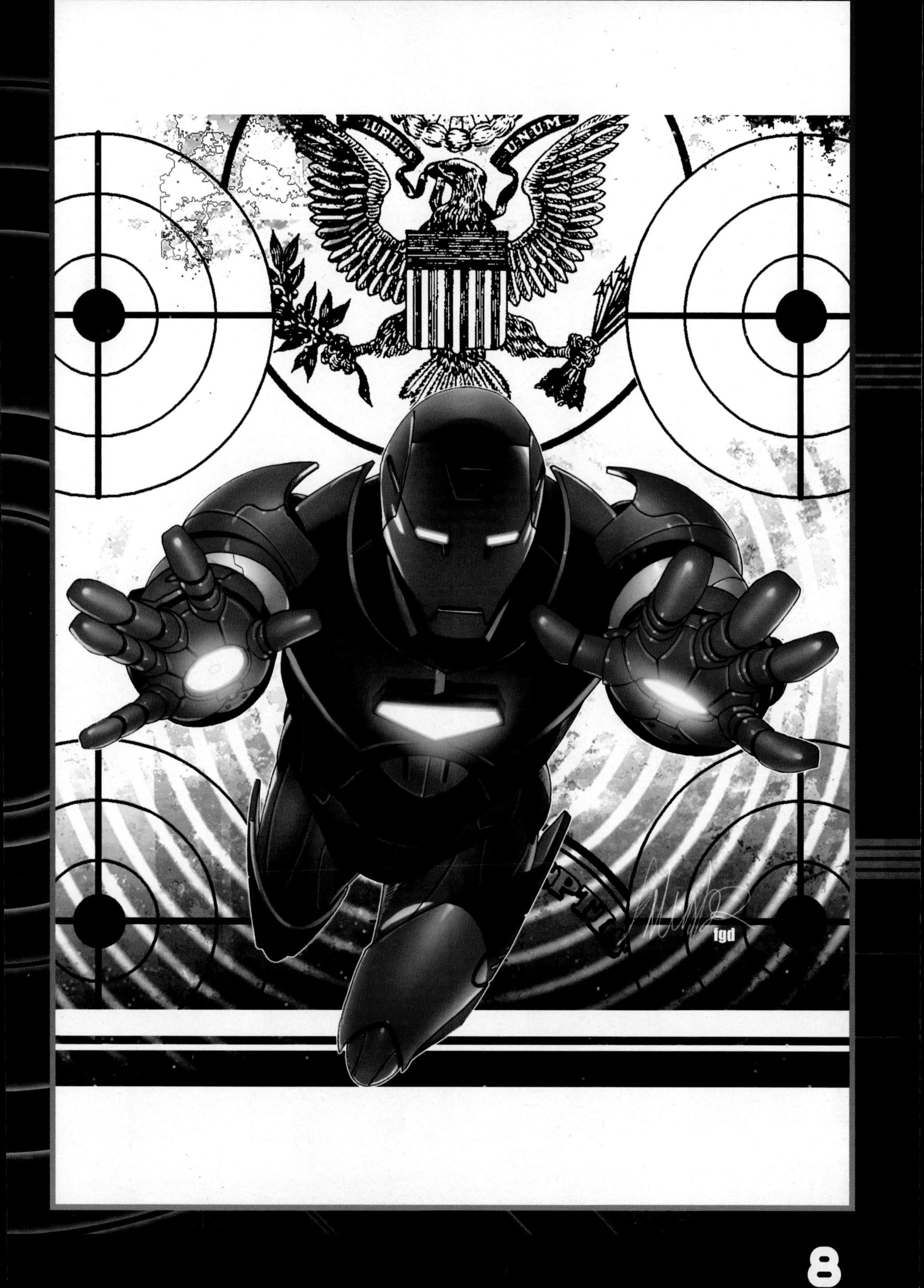
PLURIBUS
UNUM
fgd

8

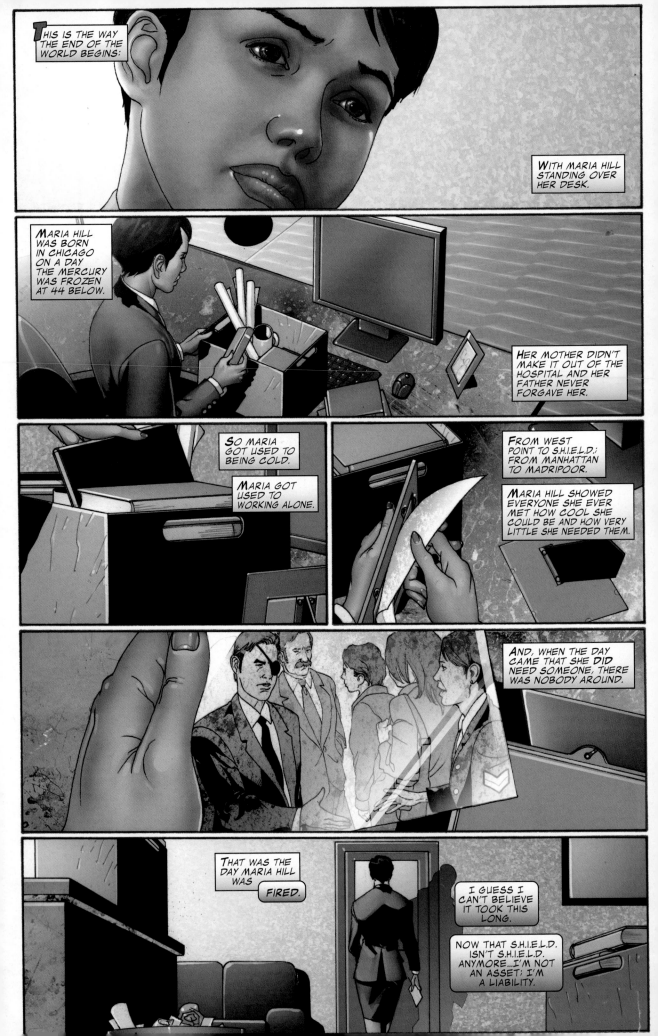

THIS IS THE WAY THE END OF THE WORLD BEGINS:

WITH MARIA HILL STANDING OVER HER DESK.

MARIA HILL WAS BORN IN CHICAGO ON A DAY THE MERCURY WAS FROZEN AT 44 BELOW.

HER MOTHER DIDN'T MAKE IT OUT OF THE HOSPITAL AND HER FATHER NEVER FORGAVE HER.

SO MARIA GOT USED TO BEING COLD.

MARIA GOT USED TO WORKING ALONE.

FROM WEST POINT TO S.H.I.E.L.D.; FROM MANHATTAN TO MADRIPOOR.

MARIA HILL SHOWED EVERYONE SHE EVER MET HOW COOL SHE COULD BE AND HOW VERY LITTLE SHE NEEDED THEM.

AND, WHEN THE DAY CAME THAT SHE DID NEED SOMEONE, THERE WAS NOBODY AROUND.

THAT WAS THE DAY MARIA HILL WAS FIRED.

I GUESS I CAN'T BELIEVE IT TOOK THIS LONG.

NOW THAT S.H.I.E.L.D. ISN'T S.H.I.E.L.D. ANYMORE...I'M NOT AN ASSET; I'M A LIABILITY.

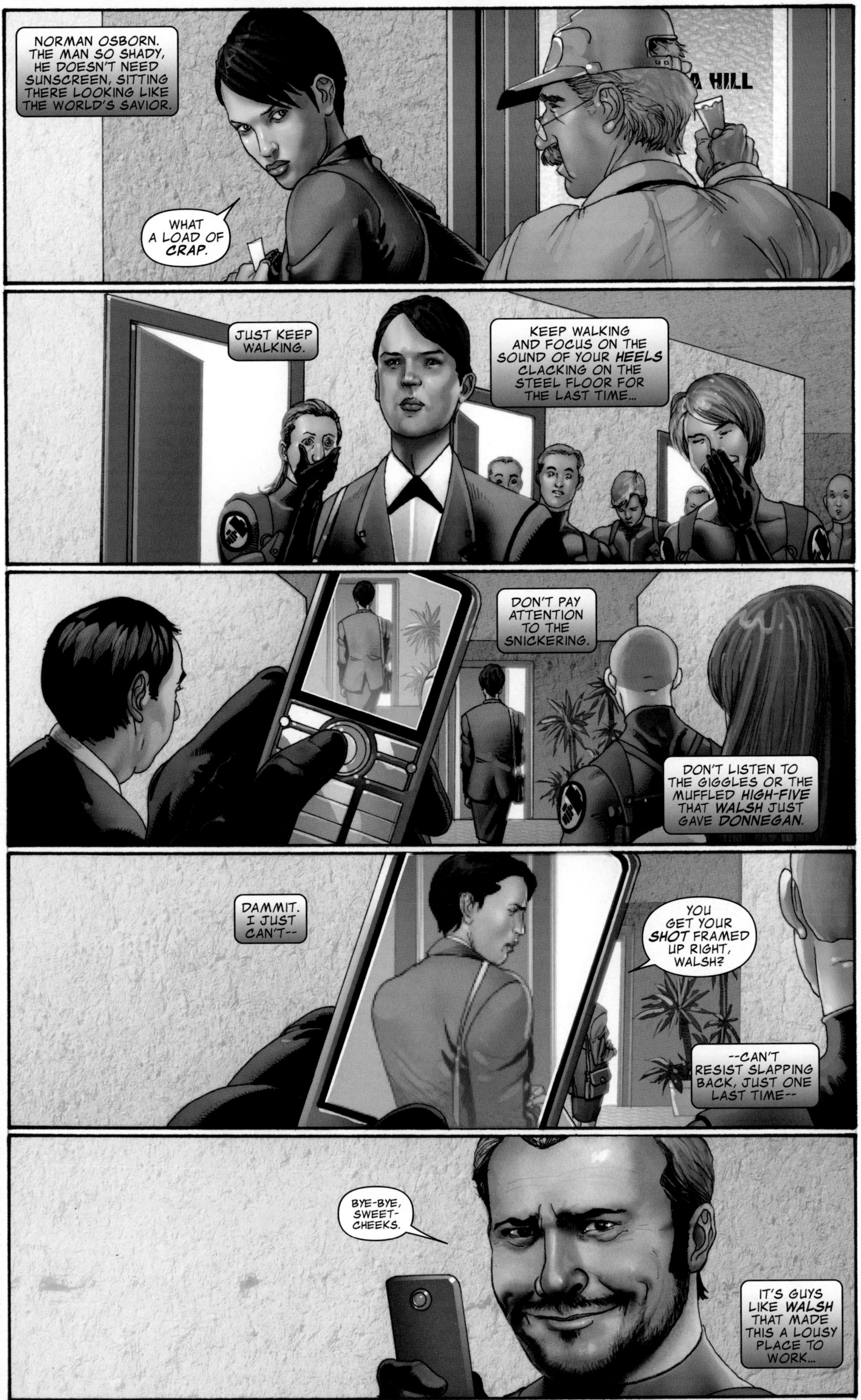

NORMAN OSBORN. THE MAN SO SHADY, HE DOESN'T NEED SUNSCREEN, SITTING THERE LOOKING LIKE THE WORLD'S SAVIOR.
A HILL
WHAT A LOAD OF CRAP.
JUST KEEP WALKING.
KEEP WALKING AND FOCUS ON THE SOUND OF YOUR HEELS CLACKING ON THE STEEL FLOOR FOR THE LAST TIME...
DON'T PAY ATTENTION TO THE SNICKERING.
DON'T LISTEN TO THE GIGGLES OR THE MUFFLED HIGH-FIVE THAT WALSH JUST GAVE DONNEGAN.
DAMMIT. I JUST CAN'T--
YOU GET YOUR SHOT FRAMED UP RIGHT, WALSH?
--CAN'T RESIST SLAPPING BACK, JUST ONE LAST TIME--
BYE-BYE, SWEET-CHEEKS.
IT'S GUYS LIKE WALSH THAT MADE THIS A LOUSY PLACE TO WORK...

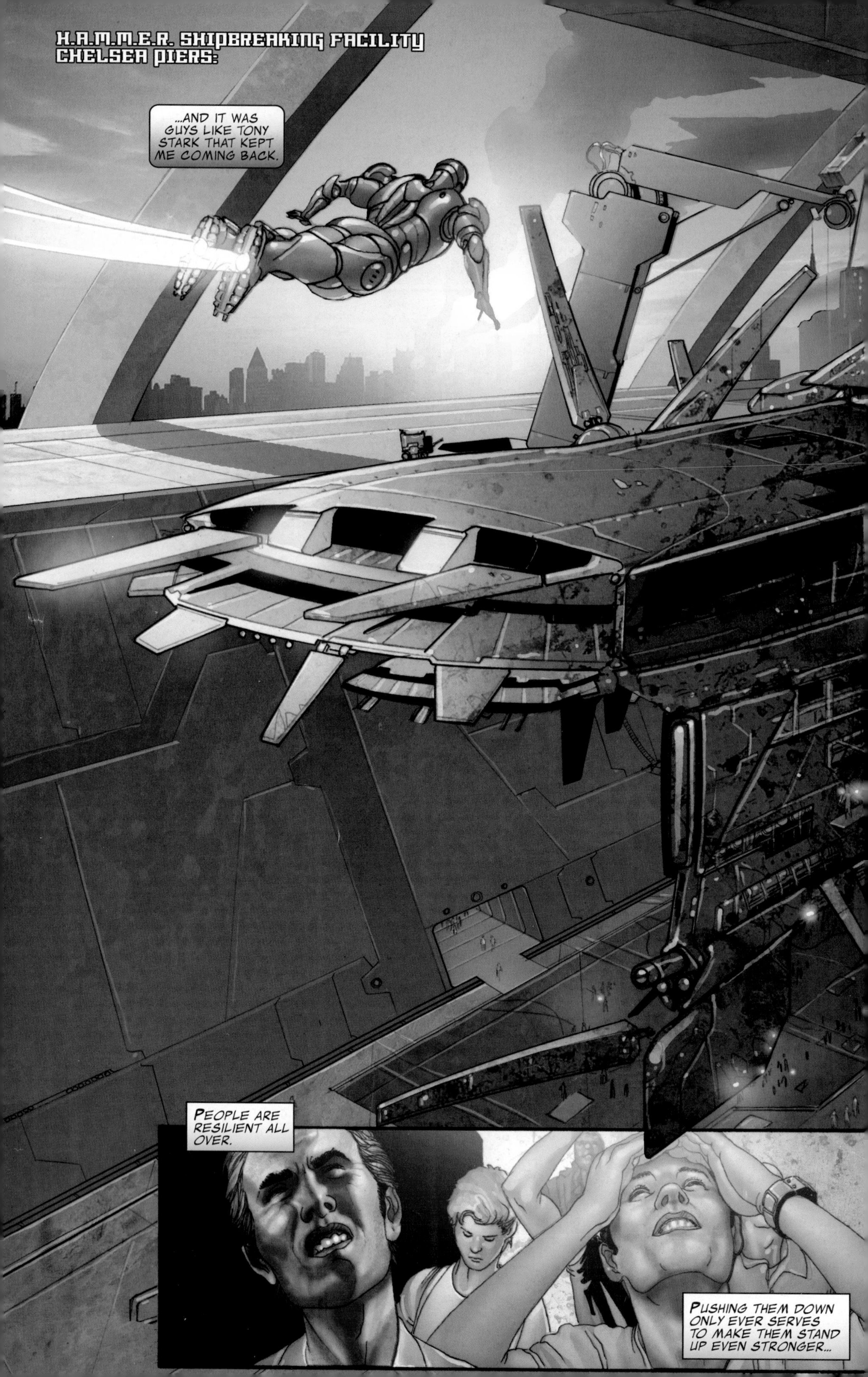
H.A.M.M.E.R. SHIPBREAKING FACILITY
CHELSEA PIERS:
...AND IT WAS GUYS LIKE TONY STARK THAT KEPT ME COMING BACK.
PEOPLE ARE RESILIENT ALL OVER.
PUSHING THEM DOWN ONLY EVER SERVES TO MAKE THEM STAND UP EVEN STRONGER...

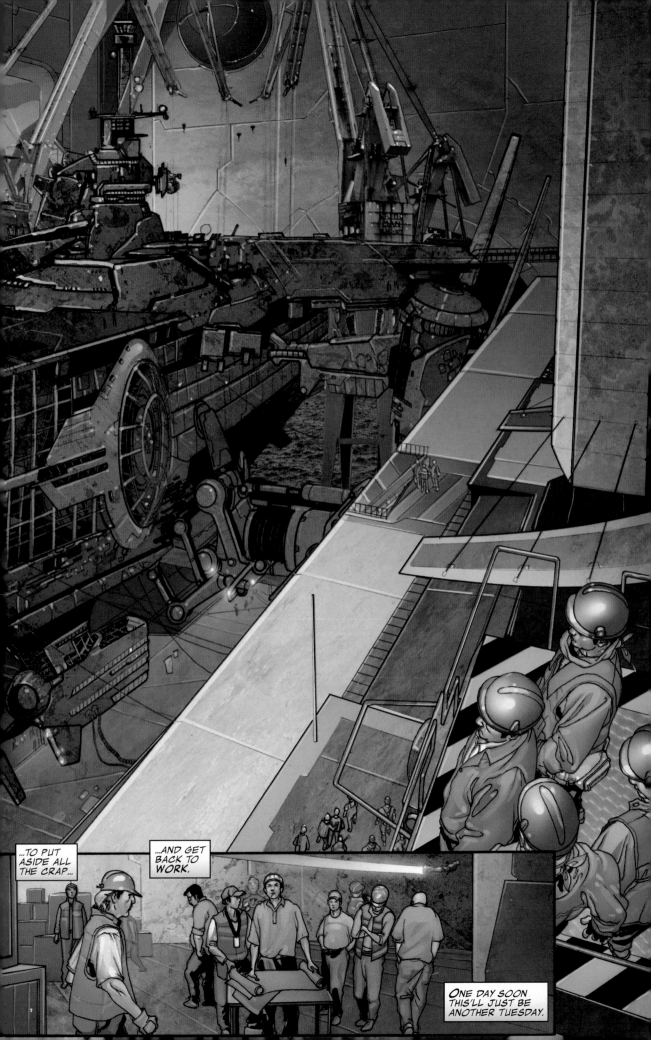

...TO PUT ASIDE ALL THE CRAP...

...AND GET BACK TO WORK.

ONE DAY SOON THIS'LL JUST BE ANOTHER TUESDAY.

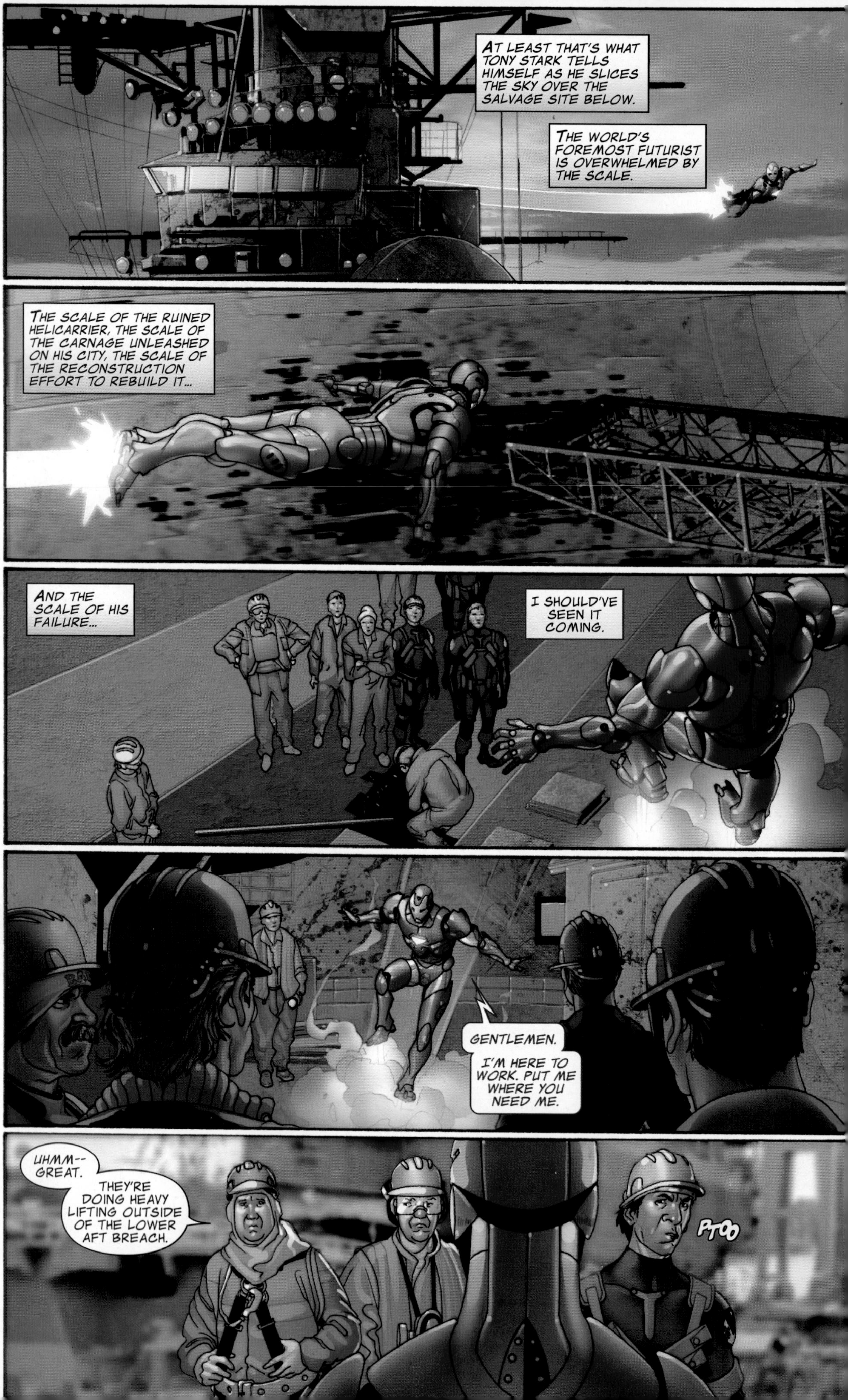
AT LEAST THAT'S WHAT TONY STARK TELLS HIMSELF AS HE SLICES THE SKY OVER THE SALVAGE SITE BELOW.
THE WORLD'S FOREMOST FUTURIST IS OVERWHELMED BY THE SCALE.
THE SCALE OF THE RUINED HELICARRIER, THE SCALE OF THE CARNAGE UNLEASHED ON HIS CITY, THE SCALE OF THE RECONSTRUCTION EFFORT TO REBUILD IT...
AND THE SCALE OF HIS FAILURE...
I SHOULD'VE SEEN IT COMING.
GENTLEMEN.
I'M HERE TO WORK. PUT ME WHERE YOU NEED ME.
UHMM-- GREAT.
THEY'RE DOING HEAVY LIFTING OUTSIDE OF THE LOWER AFT BREACH.
PTOO

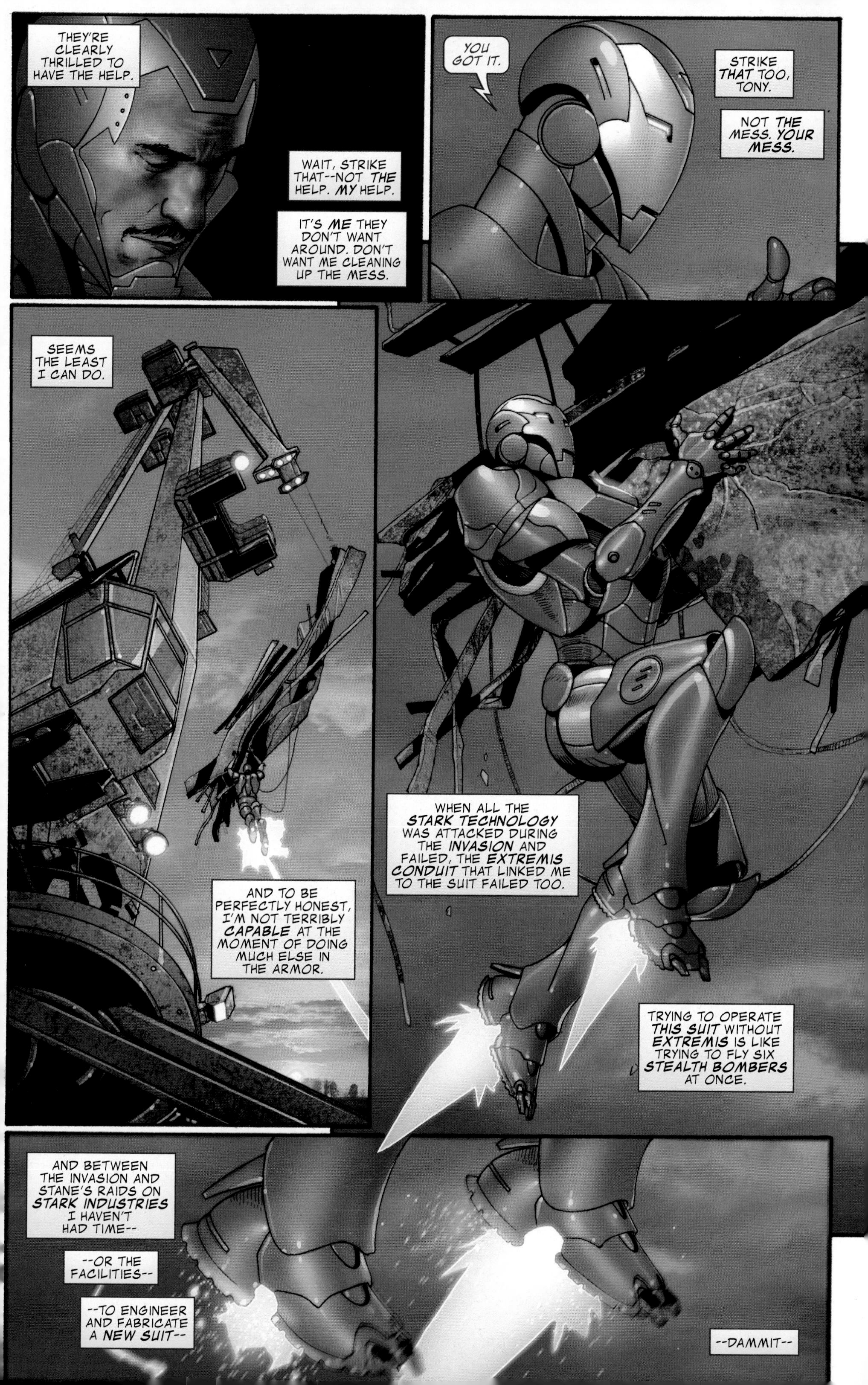
THEY'RE CLEARLY THRILLED TO HAVE THE HELP.
WAIT, STRIKE THAT--NOT THE HELP. MY HELP.
IT'S ME THEY DON'T WANT AROUND. DON'T WANT ME CLEANING UP THE MESS.
YOU GOT IT.
STRIKE THAT TOO, TONY.
NOT THE MESS. YOUR MESS.
SEEMS THE LEAST I CAN DO.
AND TO BE PERFECTLY HONEST, I'M NOT TERRIBLY CAPABLE AT THE MOMENT OF DOING MUCH ELSE IN THE ARMOR.
WHEN ALL THE STARK TECHNOLOGY WAS ATTACKED DURING THE INVASION AND FAILED, THE EXTREMIS CONDUIT THAT LINKED ME TO THE SUIT FAILED TOO.
TRYING TO OPERATE THIS SUIT WITHOUT EXTREMIS IS LIKE TRYING TO FLY SIX STEALTH BOMBERS AT ONCE.
AND BETWEEN THE INVASION AND STANE'S RAIDS ON STARK INDUSTRIES I HAVEN'T HAD TIME--
--OR THE FACILITIES--
--TO ENGINEER AND FABRICATE A NEW SUIT--
--DAMMIT--

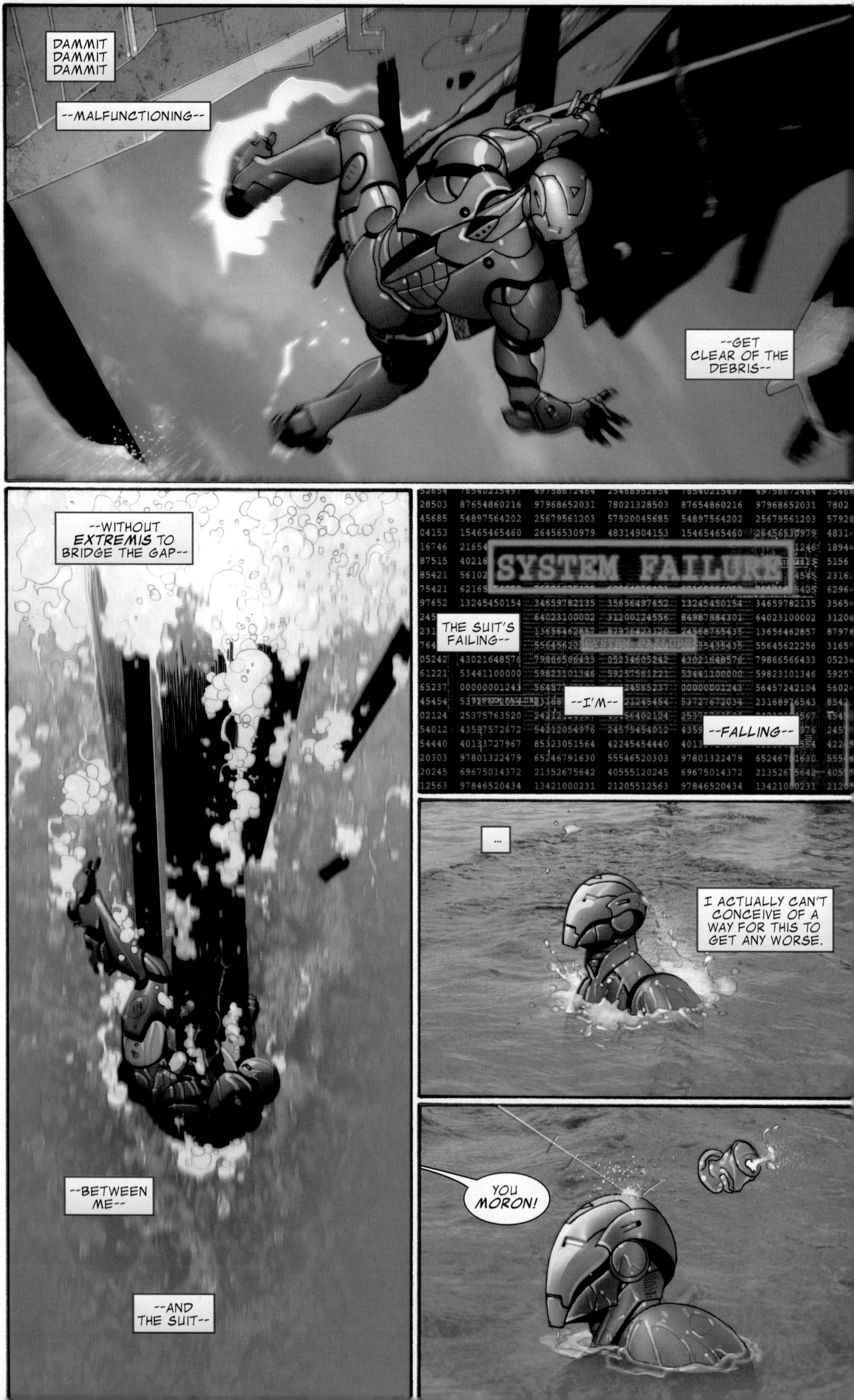
DAMMIT DAMMIT DAMMIT
--MALFUNCTIONING--
--GET CLEAR OF THE DEBRIS--
--WITHOUT EXTREMIS TO BRIDGE THE GAP--
--BETWEEN ME--
--AND THE SUIT--
SYSTEM FAILURE
THE SUIT'S FAILING--
--I'M--
--FALLING--
...
I ACTUALLY CAN'T CONCEIVE OF A WAY FOR THIS TO GET ANY WORSE.
YOU MORON!

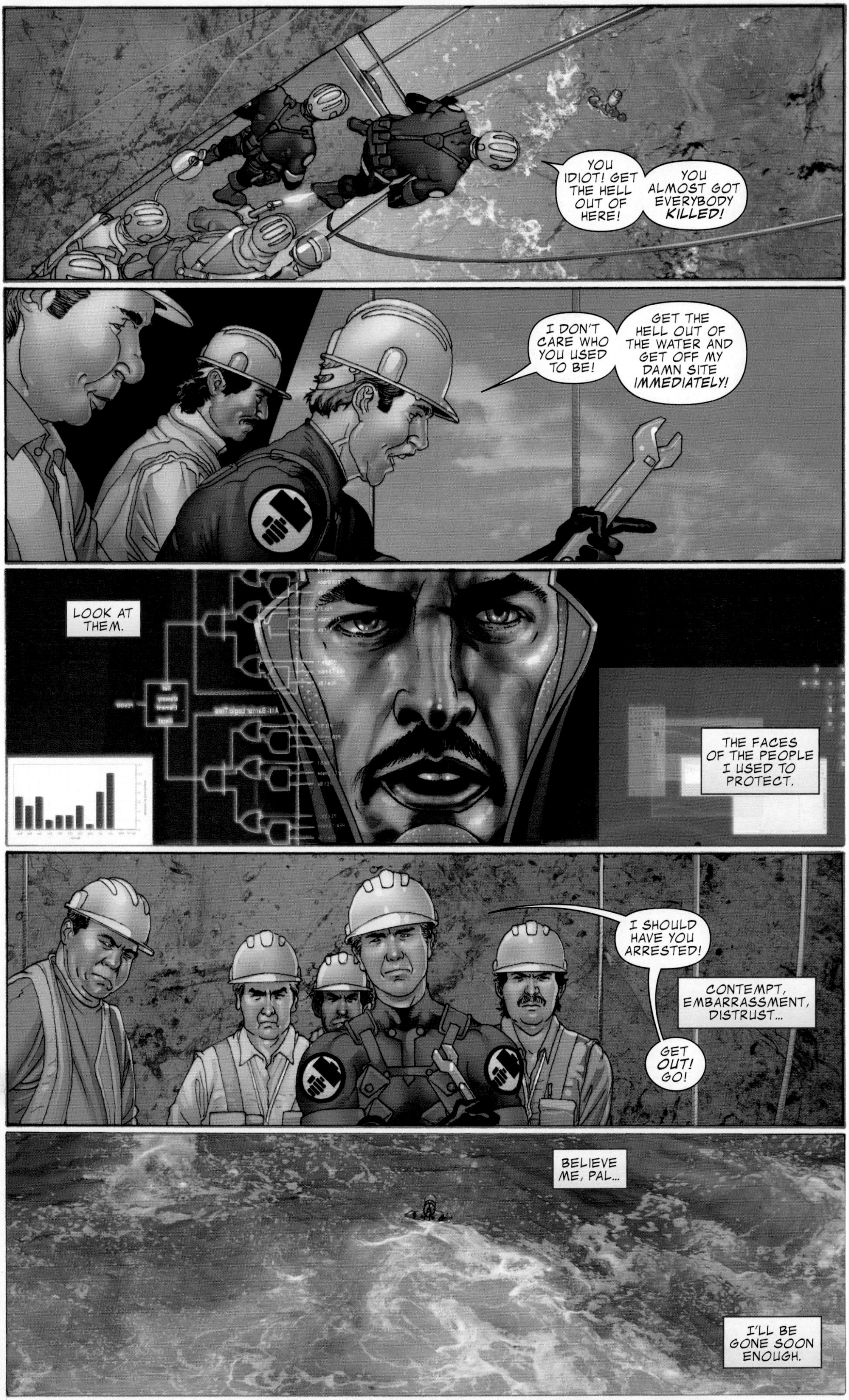
YOU IDIOT! GET THE HELL OUT OF HERE!
YOU ALMOST GOT EVERYBODY KILLED!
I DON'T CARE WHO YOU USED TO BE!
GET THE HELL OUT OF THE WATER AND GET OFF MY DAMN SITE IMMEDIATELY!
LOOK AT THEM.
THE FACES OF THE PEOPLE I USED TO PROTECT.
I SHOULD HAVE YOU ARRESTED!
CONTEMPT, EMBARRASSMENT, DISTRUST...
GET OUT! GO!
BELIEVE ME, PAL...
I'LL BE GONE SOON ENOUGH.

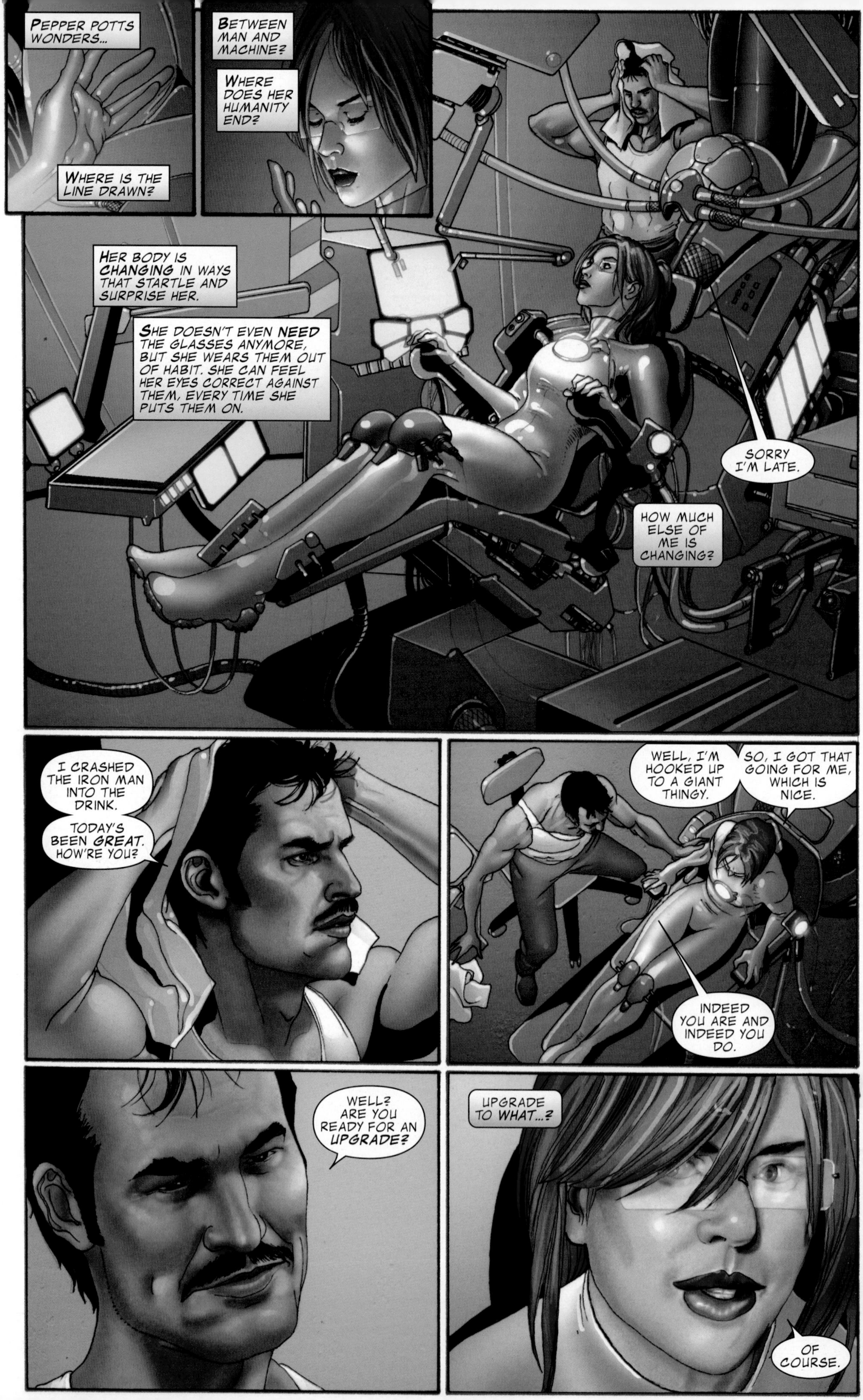
PEPPER POTTS WONDERS...
WHERE IS THE LINE DRAWN?
BETWEEN MAN AND MACHINE?
WHERE DOES HER HUMANITY END?
HER BODY IS CHANGING IN WAYS THAT STARTLE AND SURPRISE HER.
SHE DOESN'T EVEN NEED THE GLASSES ANYMORE, BUT SHE WEARS THEM OUT OF HABIT. SHE CAN FEEL HER EYES CORRECT AGAINST THEM, EVERY TIME SHE PUTS THEM ON.
SORRY I'M LATE.
HOW MUCH ELSE OF ME IS CHANGING?
I CRASHED THE IRON MAN INTO THE DRINK.
TODAY'S BEEN GREAT. HOW'RE YOU?
WELL, I'M HOOKED UP TO A GIANT THINGY.
SO, I GOT THAT GOING FOR ME, WHICH IS NICE.
INDEED YOU ARE AND INDEED YOU DO.
WELL? ARE YOU READY FOR AN UPGRADE?
UPGRADE TO WHAT...?
OF COURSE.

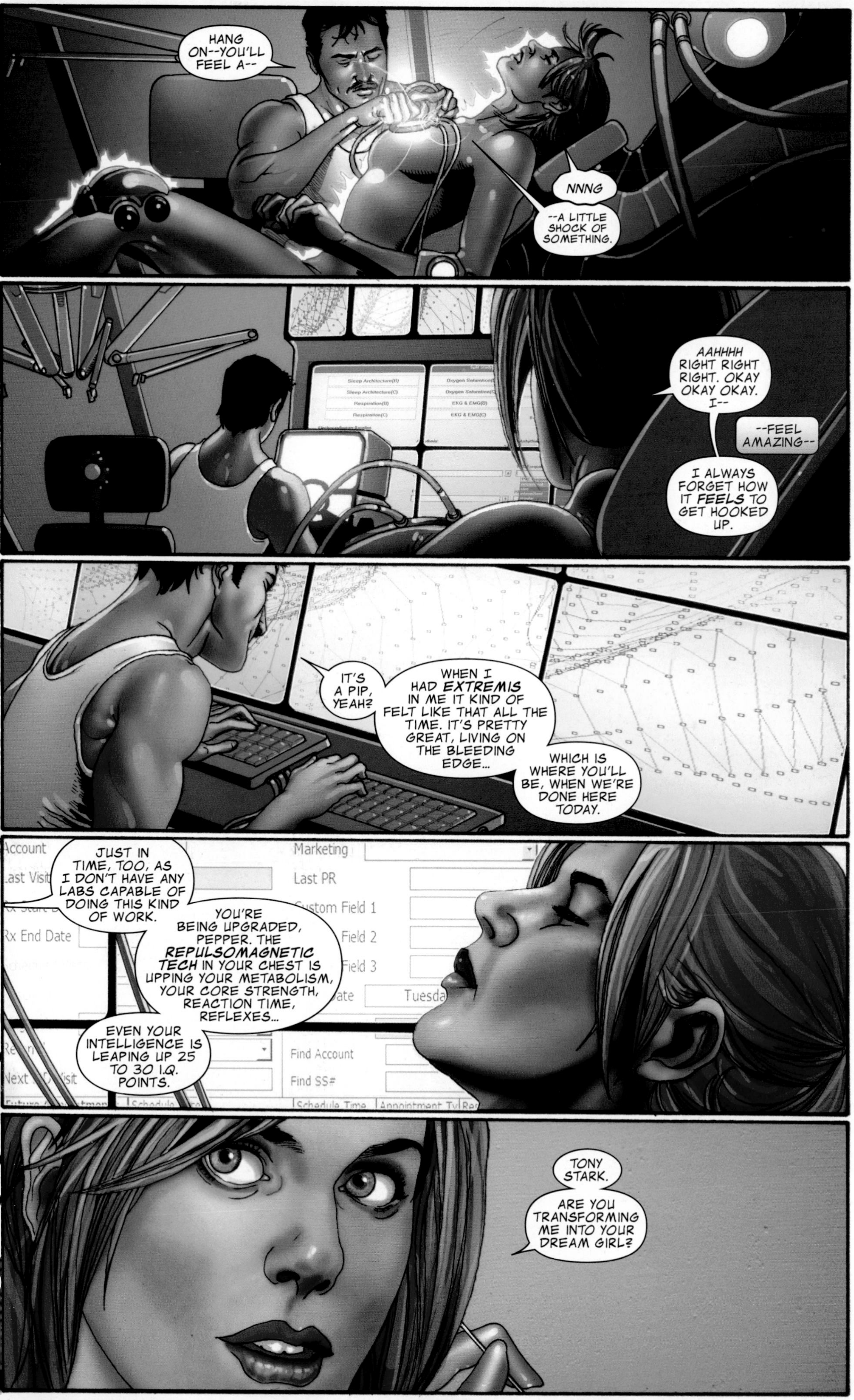
HANG ON--YOU'LL FEEL A--
NNNG
--A LITTLE SHOCK OF SOMETHING.
AAHHHH RIGHT RIGHT RIGHT. OKAY OKAY OKAY. I--
--FEEL AMAZING--
I ALWAYS FORGET HOW IT FEELS TO GET HOOKED UP.
IT'S A PIP, YEAH?
WHEN I HAD EXTREMIS IN ME IT KIND OF FELT LIKE THAT ALL THE TIME. IT'S PRETTY GREAT, LIVING ON THE BLEEDING EDGE...
WHICH IS WHERE YOU'LL BE, WHEN WE'RE DONE HERE TODAY.
JUST IN TIME, TOO, AS I DON'T HAVE ANY LABS CAPABLE OF DOING THIS KIND OF WORK.
YOU'RE BEING UPGRADED, PEPPER. THE REPULSOMAGNETIC TECH IN YOUR CHEST IS UPPING YOUR METABOLISM, YOUR CORE STRENGTH, REACTION TIME, REFLEXES...
EVEN YOUR INTELLIGENCE IS LEAPING UP 25 TO 30 I.Q. POINTS.
TONY STARK.
ARE YOU TRANSFORMING ME INTO YOUR DREAM GIRL?

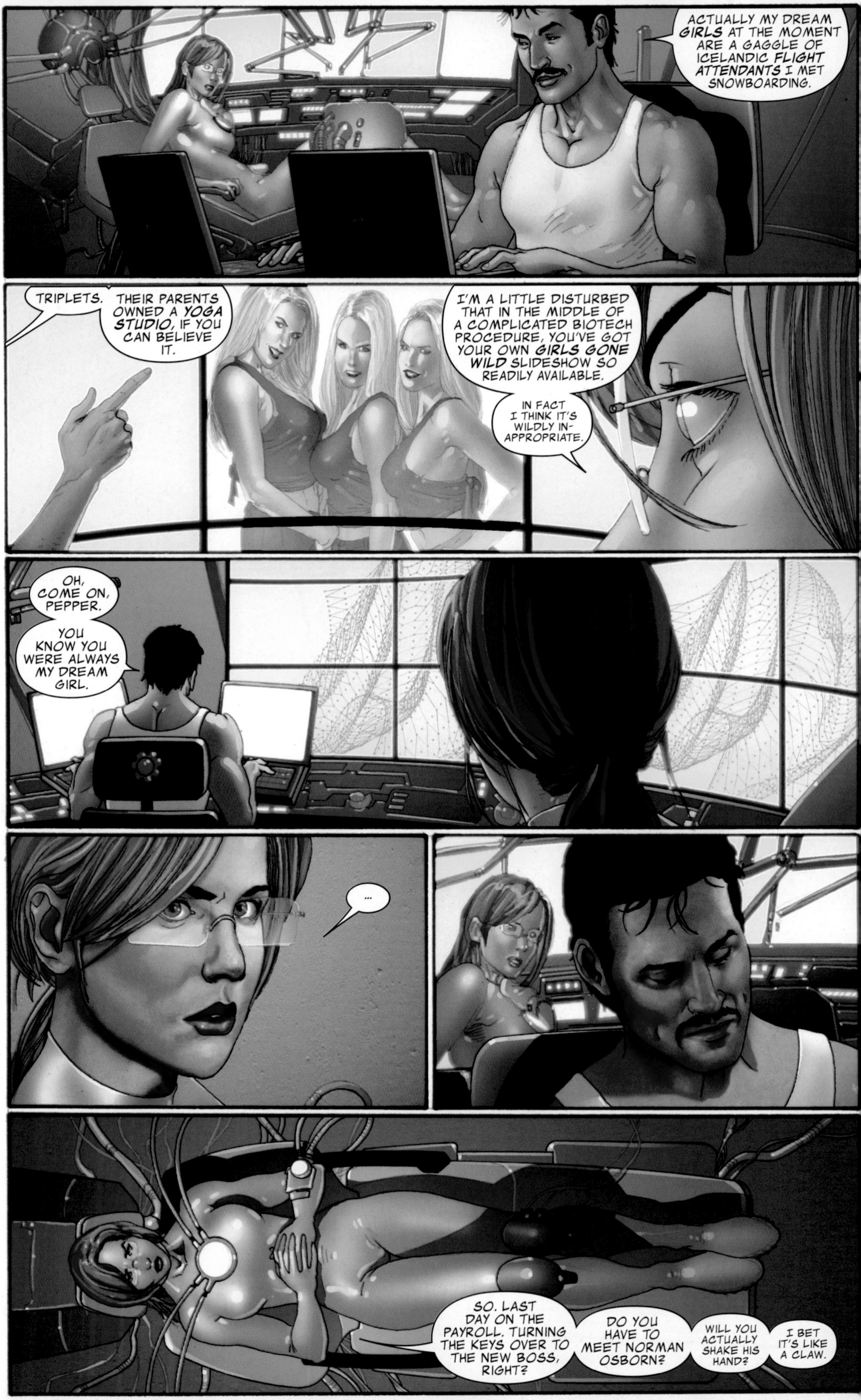
ACTUALLY MY DREAM GIRLS AT THE MOMENT ARE A GAGGLE OF ICELANDIC FLIGHT ATTENDANTS I MET SNOWBOARDING.
TRIPLETS.
THEIR PARENTS OWNED A YOGA STUDIO, IF YOU CAN BELIEVE IT.
I'M A LITTLE DISTURBED THAT IN THE MIDDLE OF A COMPLICATED BIOTECH PROCEDURE, YOU'VE GOT YOUR OWN GIRLS GONE WILD SLIDESHOW SO READILY AVAILABLE.
IN FACT I THINK IT'S WILDLY IN-APPROPRIATE.
OH, COME ON, PEPPER.
YOU KNOW YOU WERE ALWAYS MY DREAM GIRL.
...
SO. LAST DAY ON THE PAYROLL. TURNING THE KEYS OVER TO THE NEW BOSS, RIGHT?
DO YOU HAVE TO MEET NORMAN OSBORN?
WILL YOU ACTUALLY SHAKE HIS HAND?
I BET IT'S LIKE A CLAW.

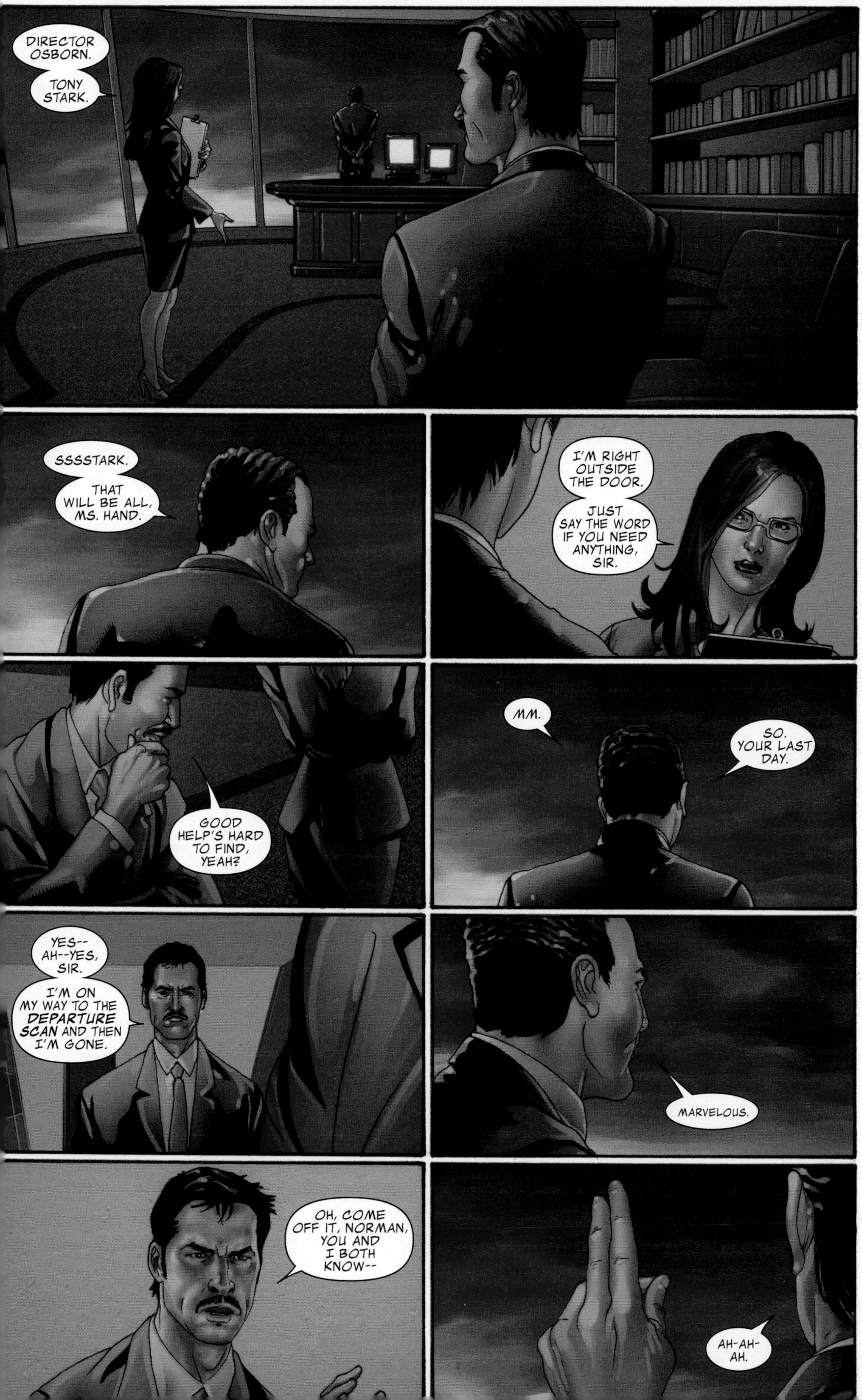
DIRECTOR OSBORN.
TONY STARK.
SSSSTARK.
THAT WILL BE ALL, MS. HAND.
I'M RIGHT OUTSIDE THE DOOR.
JUST SAY THE WORD IF YOU NEED ANYTHING, SIR.
GOOD HELP'S HARD TO FIND, YEAH?
MM.
SO. YOUR LAST DAY.
YES--AH--YES, SIR.
I'M ON MY WAY TO THE DEPARTURE SCAN AND THEN I'M GONE.
MARVELOUS.
OH, COME OFF IT, NORMAN, YOU AND I BOTH KNOW--
AH-AH-AH.

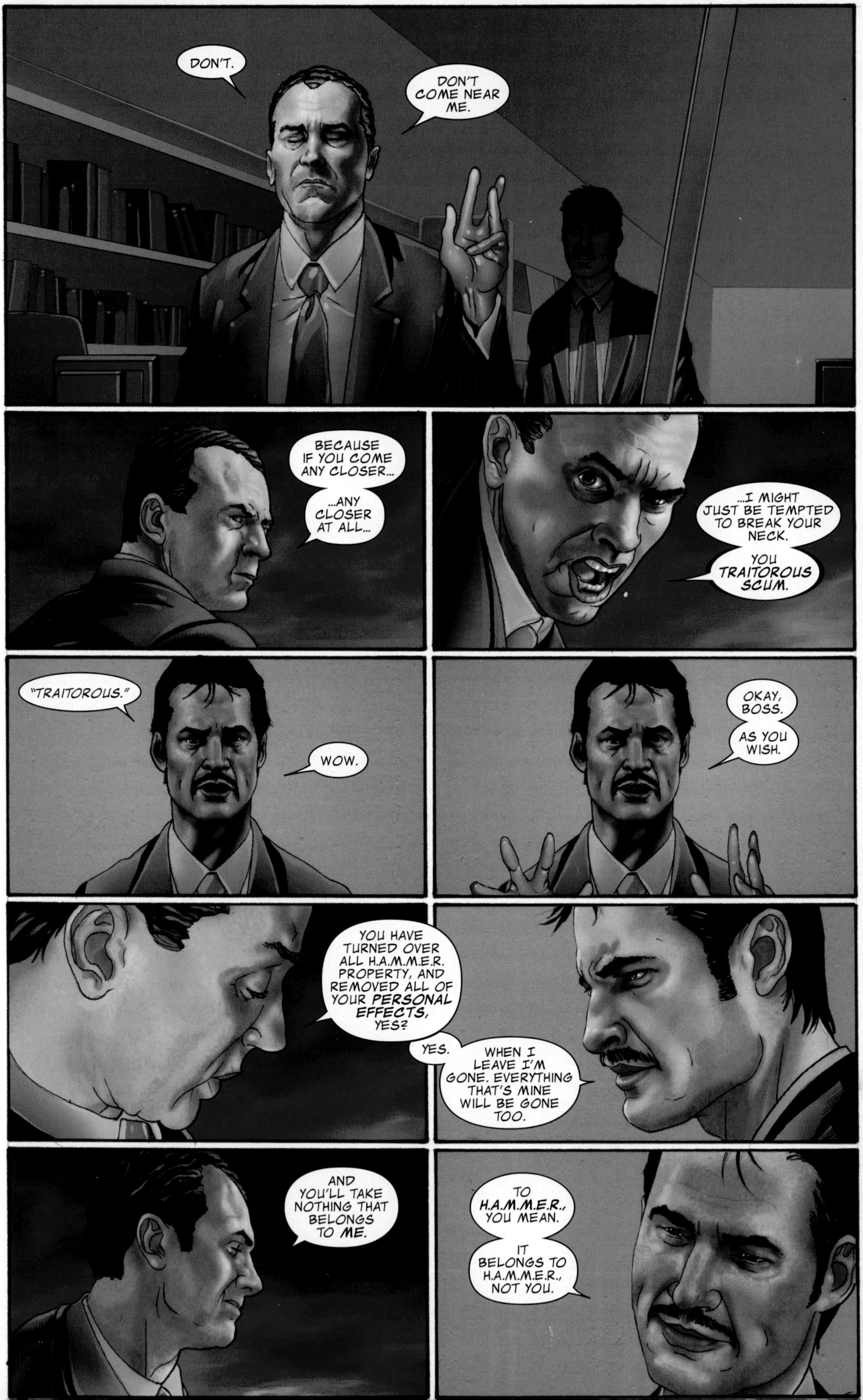
DON'T.
DON'T COME NEAR ME.
BECAUSE IF YOU COME ANY CLOSER...
...ANY CLOSER AT ALL...
...I MIGHT JUST BE TEMPTED TO BREAK YOUR NECK.
YOU **TRAITOROUS SCUM.**
"TRAITOROUS."
WOW.
OKAY, BOSS.
AS YOU WISH.
YOU HAVE TURNED OVER ALL H.A.M.M.E.R. PROPERTY, AND REMOVED ALL OF YOUR ***PERSONAL EFFECTS,*** YES?
YES.
WHEN I LEAVE I'M GONE. EVERYTHING THAT'S MINE WILL BE GONE TOO.
AND YOU'LL TAKE NOTHING THAT BELONGS TO ***ME.***
TO ***H.A.M.M.E.R.,*** YOU MEAN.
IT BELONGS TO H.A.M.M.E.R., NOT YOU.

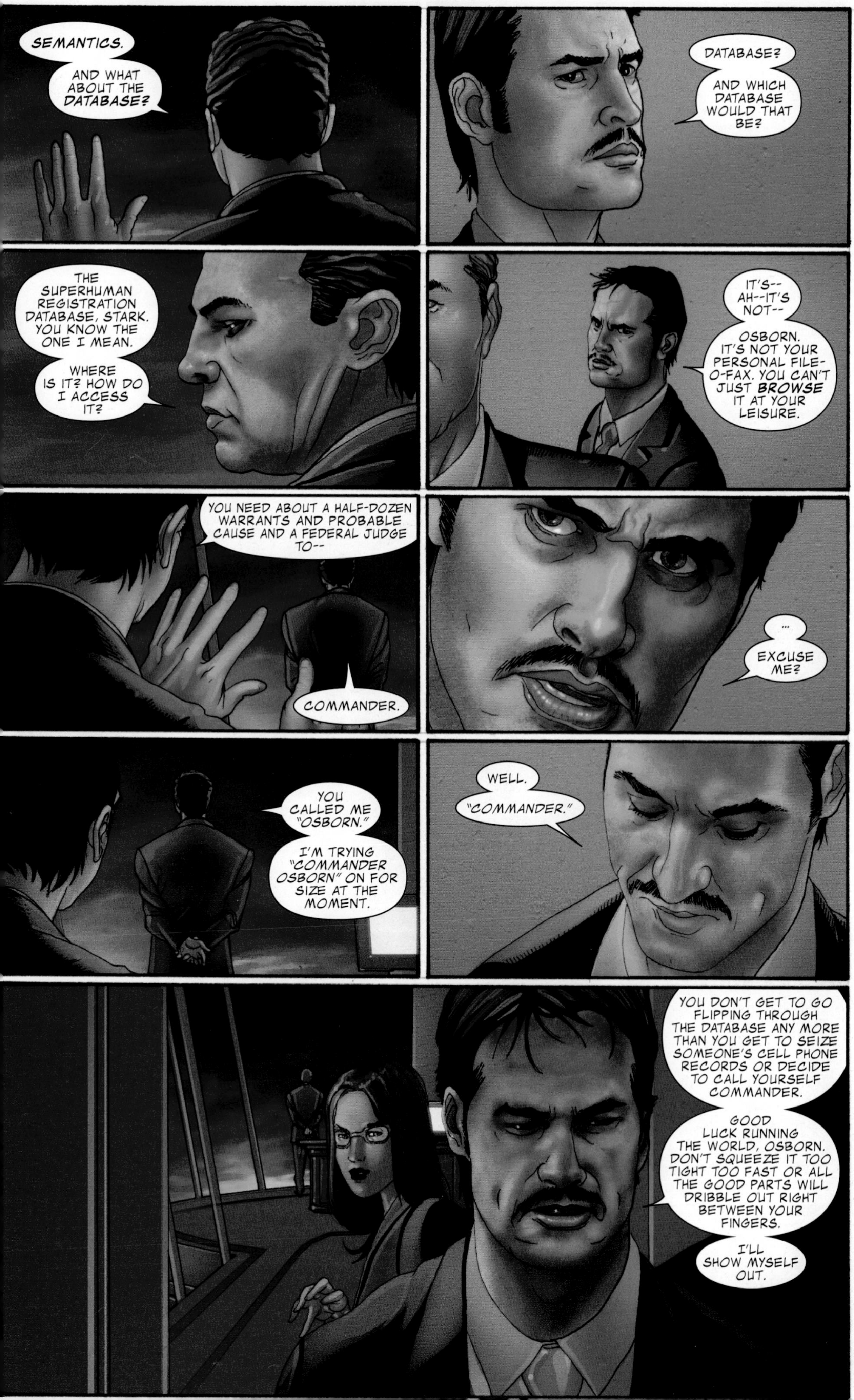
SEMANTICS.
AND WHAT ABOUT THE DATABASE?
DATABASE?
AND WHICH DATABASE WOULD THAT BE?
THE SUPERHUMAN REGISTRATION DATABASE, STARK. YOU KNOW THE ONE I MEAN.
WHERE IS IT? HOW DO I ACCESS IT?
IT'S-- AH--IT'S NOT--
OSBORN. IT'S NOT YOUR PERSONAL FILE-O-FAX. YOU CAN'T JUST BROWSE IT AT YOUR LEISURE.
YOU NEED ABOUT A HALF-DOZEN WARRANTS AND PROBABLE CAUSE AND A FEDERAL JUDGE TO--
COMMANDER.
...
EXCUSE ME?
YOU CALLED ME "OSBORN."
I'M TRYING "COMMANDER OSBORN" ON FOR SIZE AT THE MOMENT.
WELL.
"COMMANDER."
YOU DON'T GET TO GO FLIPPING THROUGH THE DATABASE ANY MORE THAN YOU GET TO SEIZE SOMEONE'S CELL PHONE RECORDS OR DECIDE TO CALL YOURSELF COMMANDER.
GOOD LUCK RUNNING THE WORLD, OSBORN. DON'T SQUEEZE IT TOO TIGHT TOO FAST OR ALL THE GOOD PARTS WILL DRIBBLE OUT RIGHT BETWEEN YOUR FINGERS.
I'LL SHOW MYSELF OUT.

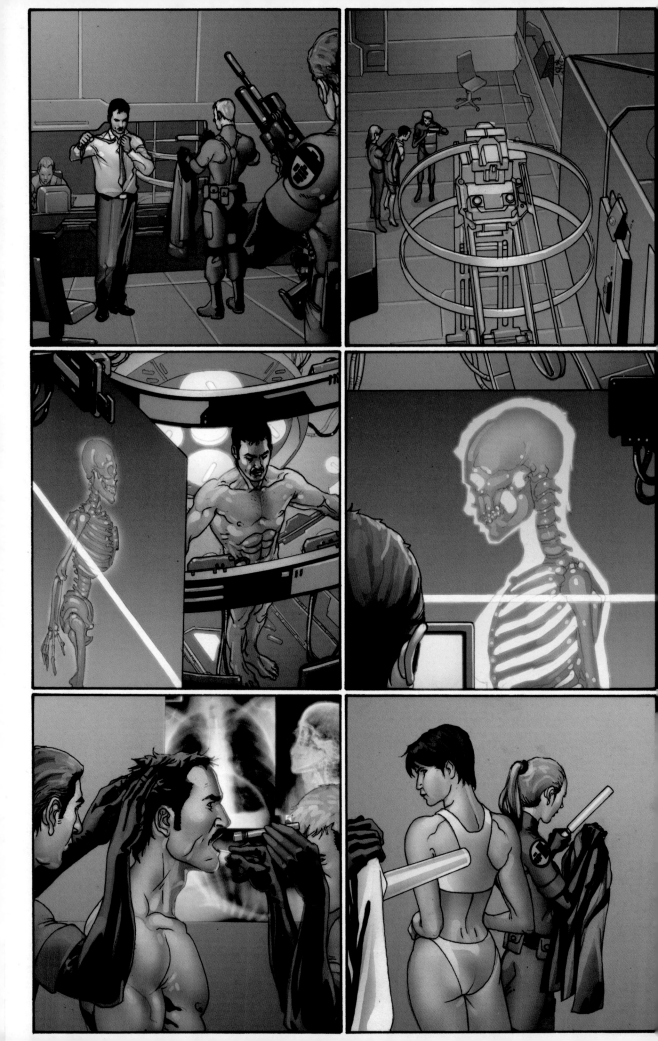

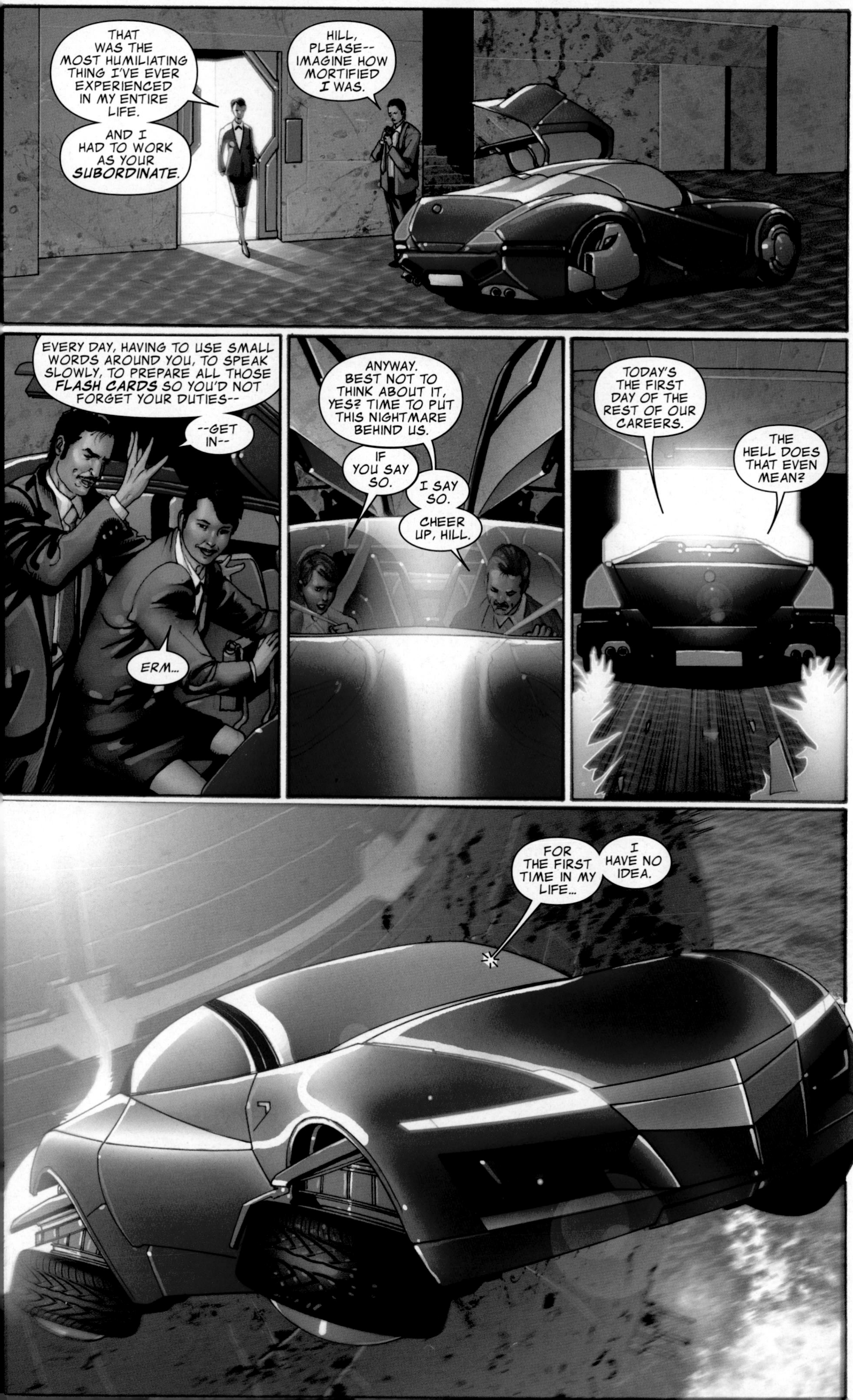
THAT WAS THE MOST HUMILIATING THING I'VE EVER EXPERIENCED IN MY ENTIRE LIFE.
AND I HAD TO WORK AS YOUR SUBORDINATE.
HILL, PLEASE-- IMAGINE HOW MORTIFIED I WAS.
EVERY DAY, HAVING TO USE SMALL WORDS AROUND YOU, TO SPEAK SLOWLY, TO PREPARE ALL THOSE FLASH CARDS SO YOU'D NOT FORGET YOUR DUTIES--
--GET IN--
ERM...
ANYWAY. BEST NOT TO THINK ABOUT IT, YES? TIME TO PUT THIS NIGHTMARE BEHIND US.
IF YOU SAY SO.
I SAY SO.
CHEER UP, HILL.
TODAY'S THE FIRST DAY OF THE REST OF OUR CAREERS.
THE HELL DOES THAT EVEN MEAN?
FOR THE FIRST TIME IN MY LIFE...
I HAVE NO IDEA.

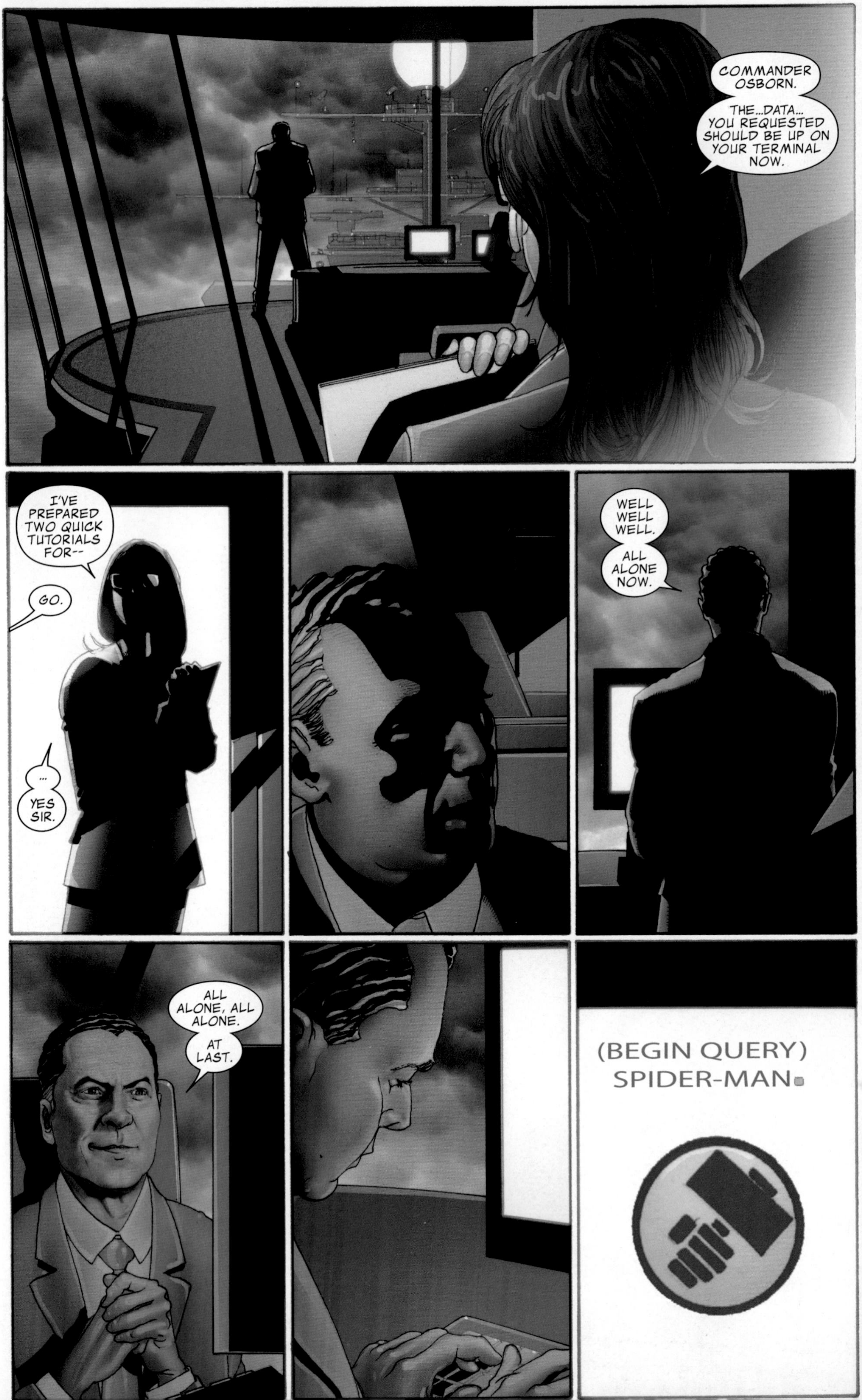
COMMANDER OSBORN.
THE...DATA... YOU REQUESTED SHOULD BE UP ON YOUR TERMINAL NOW.
I'VE PREPARED TWO QUICK TUTORIALS FOR--
GO.
...
YES SIR.
WELL WELL WELL.
ALL ALONE NOW.
ALL ALONE, ALL ALONE.
AT LAST.
(BEGIN QUERY)
SPIDER-MAN

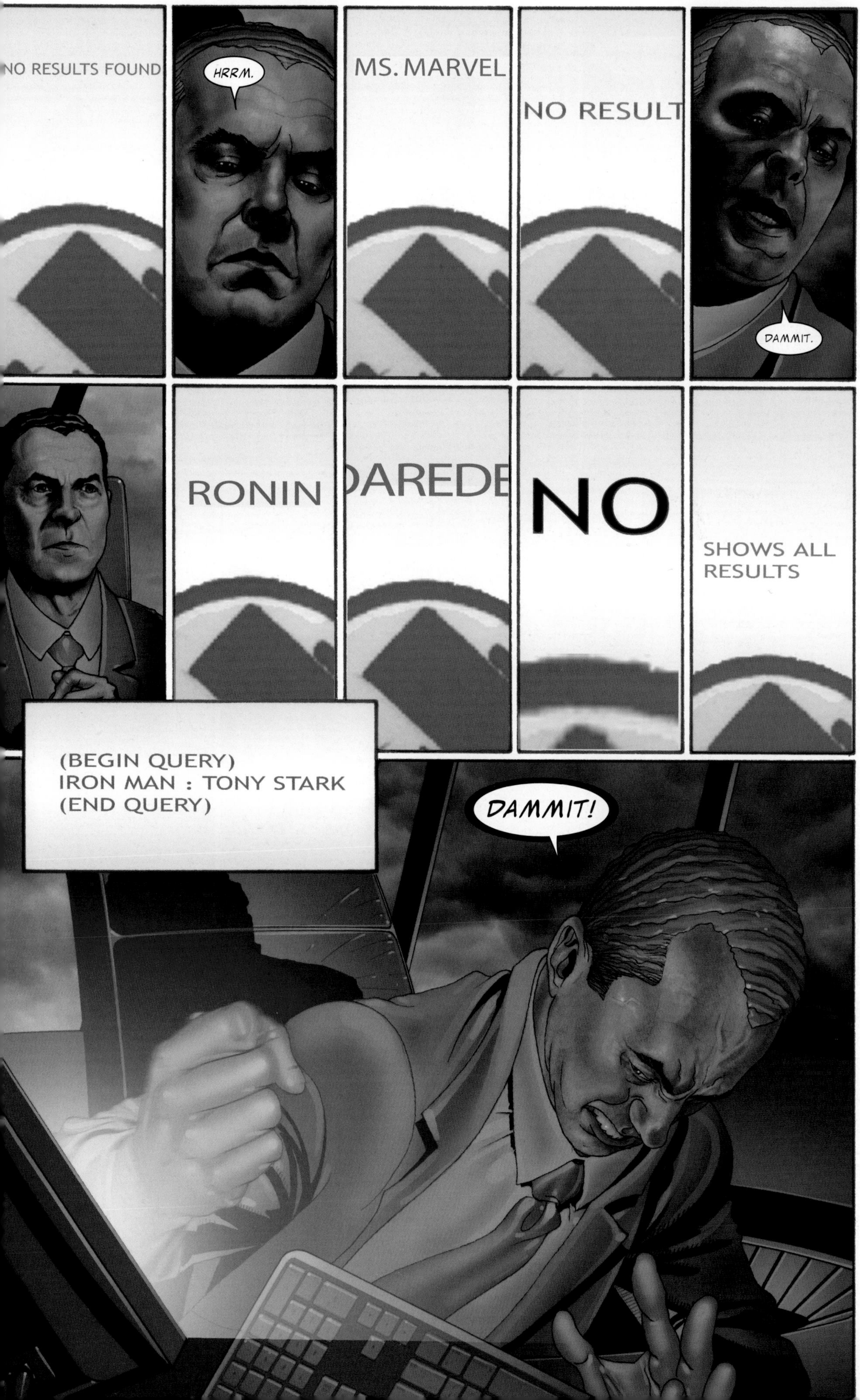
NO RESULTS FOUND
HRRM.
MS. MARVEL
NO RESULT
DAMMIT.
RONIN
DAREDE
NO
SHOWS ALL RESULTS
(BEGIN QUERY)
IRON MAN : TONY STARK
(END QUERY)
DAMMIT!

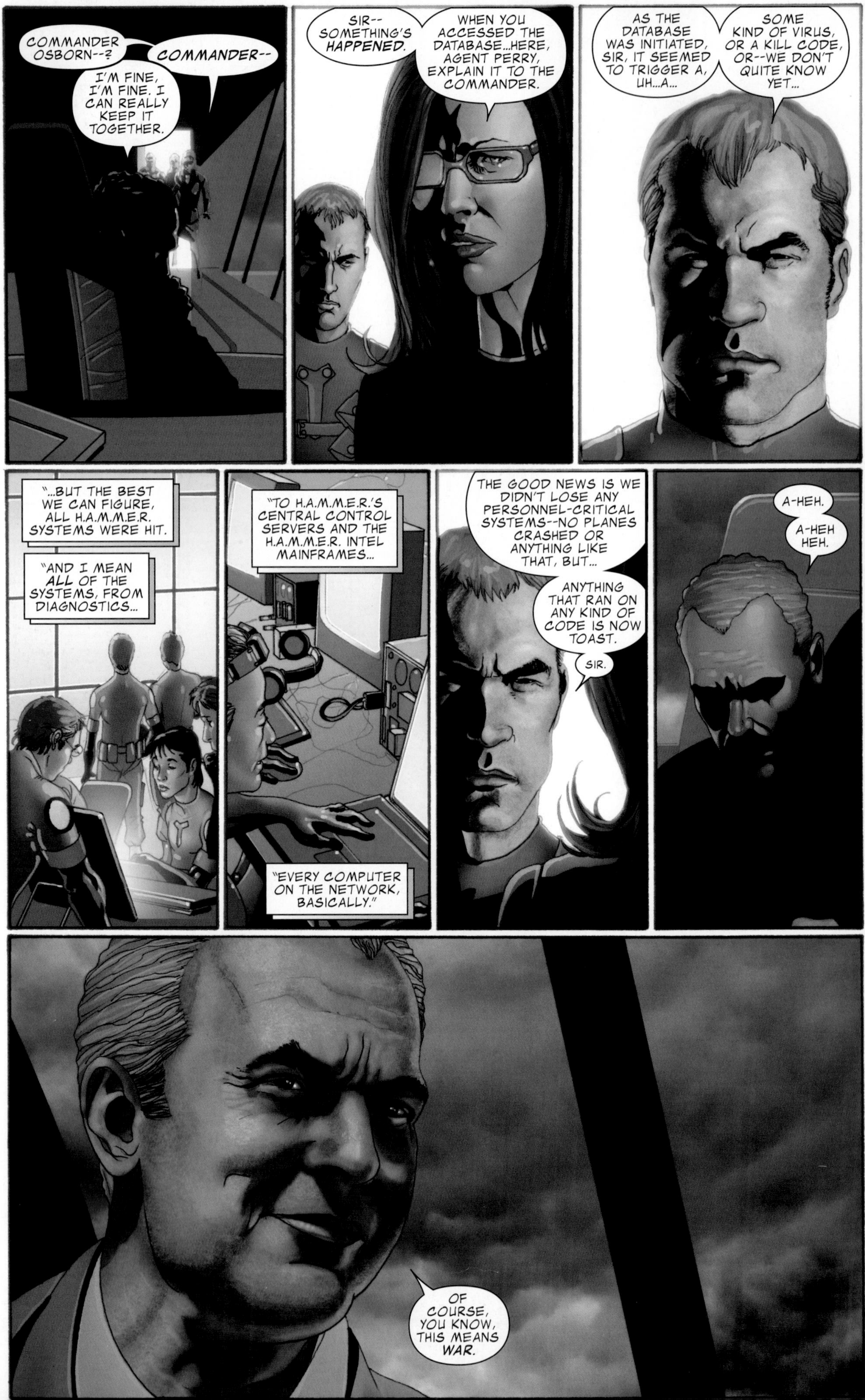
COMMANDER OSBORN--?
COMMANDER--
I'M FINE, I'M FINE. I CAN REALLY KEEP IT TOGETHER.
SIR-- SOMETHING'S HAPPENED.
WHEN YOU ACCESSED THE DATABASE...HERE, AGENT PERRY, EXPLAIN IT TO THE COMMANDER.
AS THE DATABASE WAS INITIATED, SIR, IT SEEMED TO TRIGGER A, UH...A...
SOME KIND OF VIRUS, OR A KILL CODE, OR--WE DON'T QUITE KNOW YET...
"...BUT THE BEST WE CAN FIGURE, ALL H.A.M.M.E.R. SYSTEMS WERE HIT.
"AND I MEAN ALL OF THE SYSTEMS, FROM DIAGNOSTICS...
"TO H.A.M.M.E.R.'S CENTRAL CONTROL SERVERS AND THE H.A.M.M.E.R. INTEL MAINFRAMES...
"EVERY COMPUTER ON THE NETWORK, BASICALLY."
THE GOOD NEWS IS WE DIDN'T LOSE ANY PERSONNEL-CRITICAL SYSTEMS--NO PLANES CRASHED OR ANYTHING LIKE THAT, BUT...
ANYTHING THAT RAN ON ANY KIND OF CODE IS NOW TOAST.
SIR.
A-HEH.
A-HEH HEH.
OF COURSE, YOU KNOW, THIS MEANS WAR.

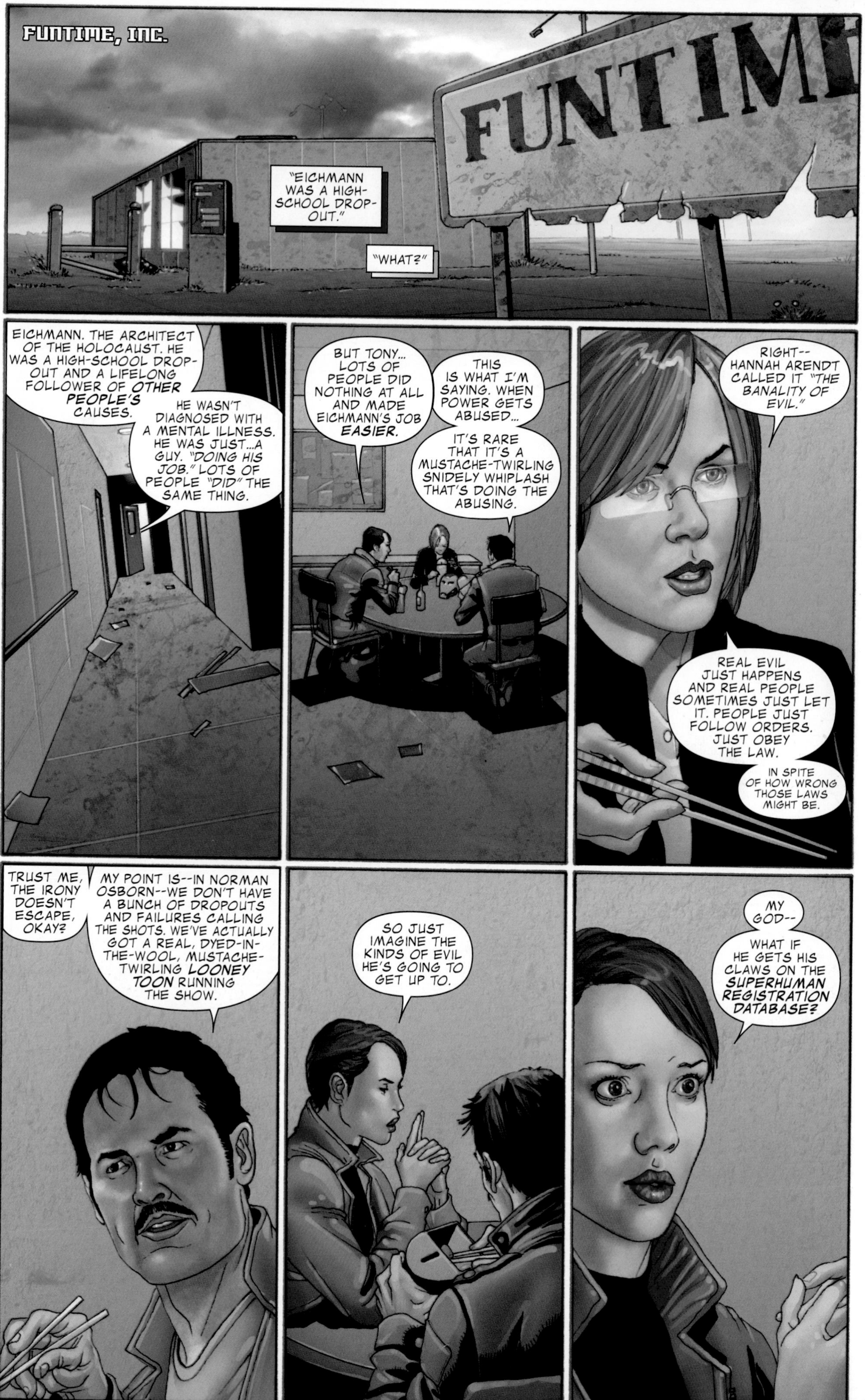

FUNTIME, INC.
FUNTIME
"EICHMANN WAS A HIGH-SCHOOL DROP-OUT."
"WHAT?"
EICHMANN. THE ARCHITECT OF THE HOLOCAUST. HE WAS A HIGH-SCHOOL DROP-OUT AND A LIFELONG FOLLOWER OF OTHER PEOPLE'S CAUSES.
HE WASN'T DIAGNOSED WITH A MENTAL ILLNESS. HE WAS JUST...A GUY. "DOING HIS JOB." LOTS OF PEOPLE "DID" THE SAME THING.
BUT TONY... LOTS OF PEOPLE DID NOTHING AT ALL AND MADE EICHMANN'S JOB EASIER.
THIS IS WHAT I'M SAYING. WHEN POWER GETS ABUSED...
IT'S RARE THAT IT'S A MUSTACHE-TWIRLING SNIDELY WHIPLASH THAT'S DOING THE ABUSING.
RIGHT-- HANNAH ARENDT CALLED IT "THE BANALITY OF EVIL."
REAL EVIL JUST HAPPENS AND REAL PEOPLE SOMETIMES JUST LET IT. PEOPLE JUST FOLLOW ORDERS. JUST OBEY THE LAW.
IN SPITE OF HOW WRONG THOSE LAWS MIGHT BE.
TRUST ME, THE IRONY DOESN'T ESCAPE, OKAY?
MY POINT IS--IN NORMAN OSBORN--WE DON'T HAVE A BUNCH OF DROPOUTS AND FAILURES CALLING THE SHOTS. WE'VE ACTUALLY GOT A REAL, DYED-IN-THE-WOOL, MUSTACHE-TWIRLING LOONEY TOON RUNNING THE SHOW.
SO JUST IMAGINE THE KINDS OF EVIL HE'S GOING TO GET UP TO.
MY GOD--
WHAT IF HE GETS HIS CLAWS ON THE SUPERHUMAN REGISTRATION DATABASE?

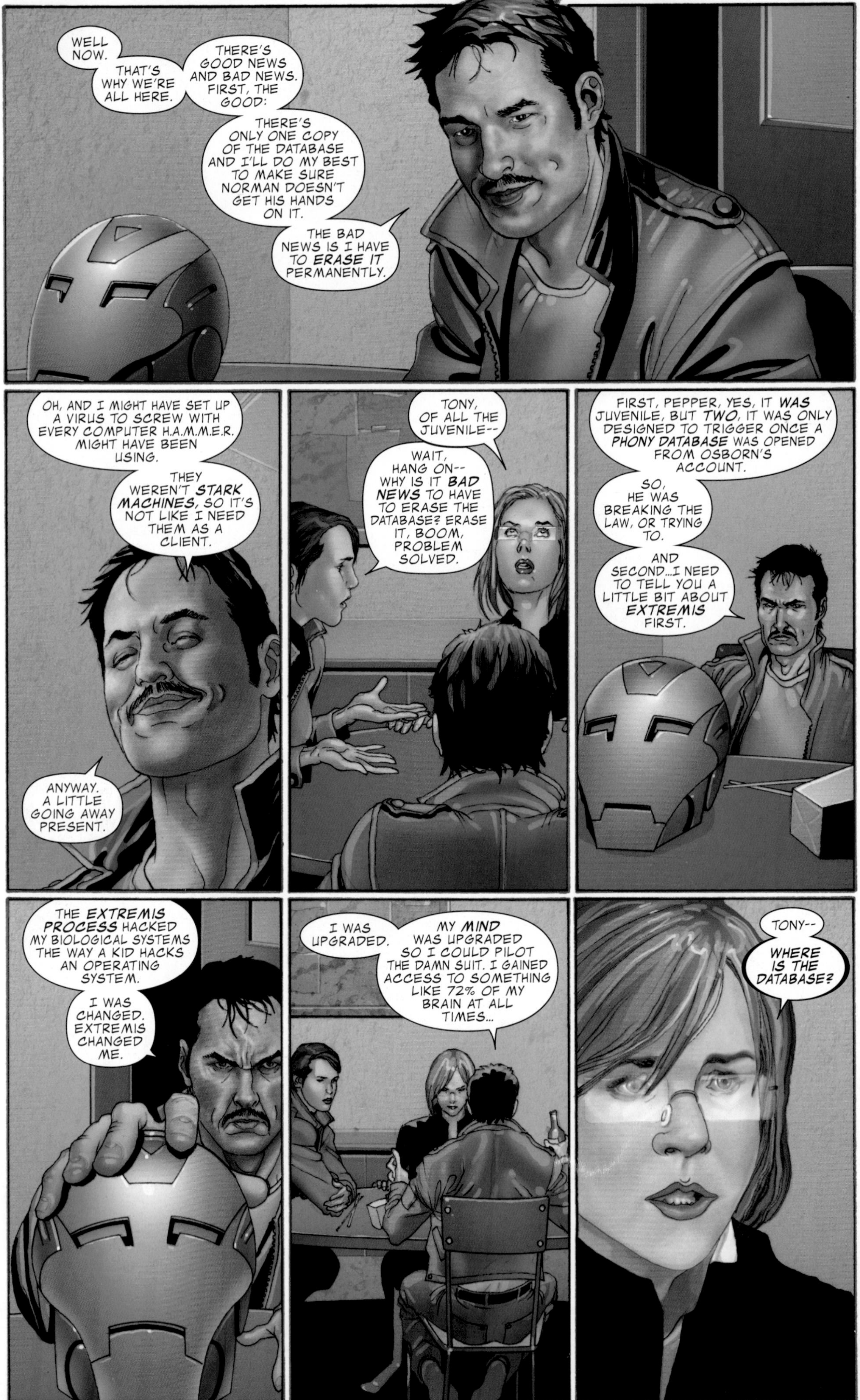
WELL NOW.
THAT'S WHY WE'RE ALL HERE.
THERE'S GOOD NEWS AND BAD NEWS. FIRST, THE GOOD:
THERE'S ONLY ONE COPY OF THE DATABASE AND I'LL DO MY BEST TO MAKE SURE NORMAN DOESN'T GET HIS HANDS ON IT.
THE BAD NEWS IS I HAVE TO ERASE IT PERMANENTLY.
OH, AND I MIGHT HAVE SET UP A VIRUS TO SCREW WITH EVERY COMPUTER H.A.M.M.E.R. MIGHT HAVE BEEN USING.
THEY WEREN'T STARK MACHINES, SO IT'S NOT LIKE I NEED THEM AS A CLIENT.
ANYWAY. A LITTLE GOING AWAY PRESENT.
TONY, OF ALL THE JUVENILE--
WAIT, HANG ON-- WHY IS IT BAD NEWS TO HAVE TO ERASE THE DATABASE? ERASE IT, BOOM, PROBLEM SOLVED.
FIRST, PEPPER, YES, IT WAS JUVENILE, BUT TWO, IT WAS ONLY DESIGNED TO TRIGGER ONCE A PHONY DATABASE WAS OPENED FROM OSBORN'S ACCOUNT.
SO, HE WAS BREAKING THE LAW, OR TRYING TO.
AND SECOND...I NEED TO TELL YOU A LITTLE BIT ABOUT EXTREMIS FIRST.
THE EXTREMIS PROCESS HACKED MY BIOLOGICAL SYSTEMS THE WAY A KID HACKS AN OPERATING SYSTEM.
I WAS CHANGED. EXTREMIS CHANGED ME.
I WAS UPGRADED.
MY MIND WAS UPGRADED SO I COULD PILOT THE DAMN SUIT. I GAINED ACCESS TO SOMETHING LIKE 72% OF MY BRAIN AT ALL TIMES...
TONY--
WHERE IS THE DATABASE?

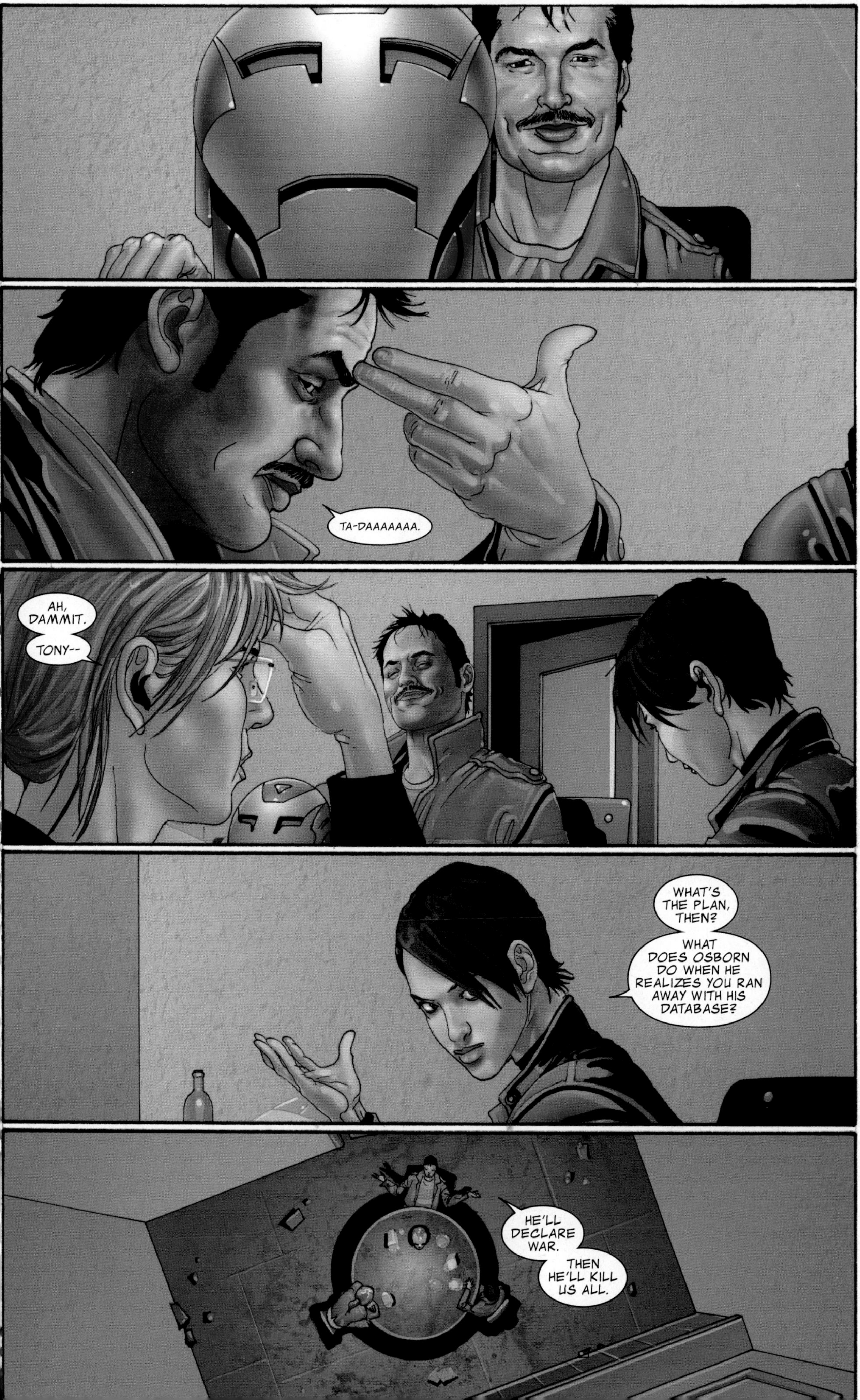
TA-DAAAAAAA.
AH, DAMMIT.
TONY--
WHAT'S THE PLAN, THEN?
WHAT DOES OSBORN DO WHEN HE REALIZES YOU RAN AWAY WITH HIS DATABASE?
HE'LL DECLARE WAR.
THEN HE'LL KILL US ALL.

WORLD'S MOST WANTED

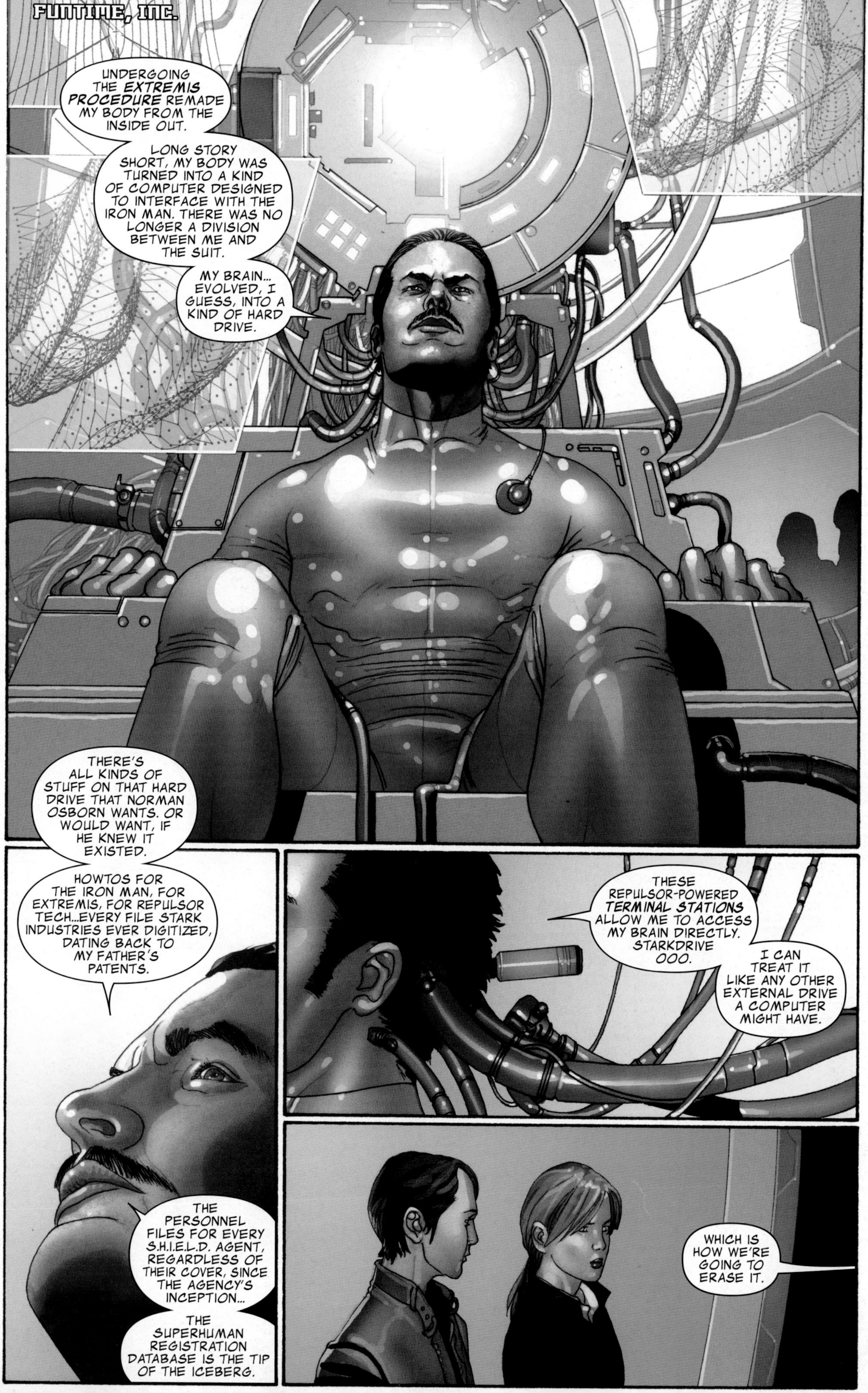
FUNTIME, INC.
UNDERGOING THE EXTREMIS PROCEDURE REMADE MY BODY FROM THE INSIDE OUT.
LONG STORY SHORT, MY BODY WAS TURNED INTO A KIND OF COMPUTER DESIGNED TO INTERFACE WITH THE IRON MAN. THERE WAS NO LONGER A DIVISION BETWEEN ME AND THE SUIT.
MY BRAIN... EVOLVED, I GUESS, INTO A KIND OF HARD DRIVE.
THERE'S ALL KINDS OF STUFF ON THAT HARD DRIVE THAT NORMAN OSBORN WANTS. OR WOULD WANT, IF HE KNEW IT EXISTED.
HOWTOS FOR THE IRON MAN, FOR EXTREMIS, FOR REPULSOR TECH...EVERY FILE STARK INDUSTRIES EVER DIGITIZED, DATING BACK TO MY FATHER'S PATENTS.
THE PERSONNEL FILES FOR EVERY S.H.I.E.L.D. AGENT, REGARDLESS OF THEIR COVER, SINCE THE AGENCY'S INCEPTION...
THE SUPERHUMAN REGISTRATION DATABASE IS THE TIP OF THE ICEBERG.
THESE REPULSOR-POWERED TERMINAL STATIONS ALLOW ME TO ACCESS MY BRAIN DIRECTLY. STARKDRIVE OOO.
I CAN TREAT IT LIKE ANY OTHER EXTERNAL DRIVE A COMPUTER MIGHT HAVE.
WHICH IS HOW WE'RE GOING TO ERASE IT.

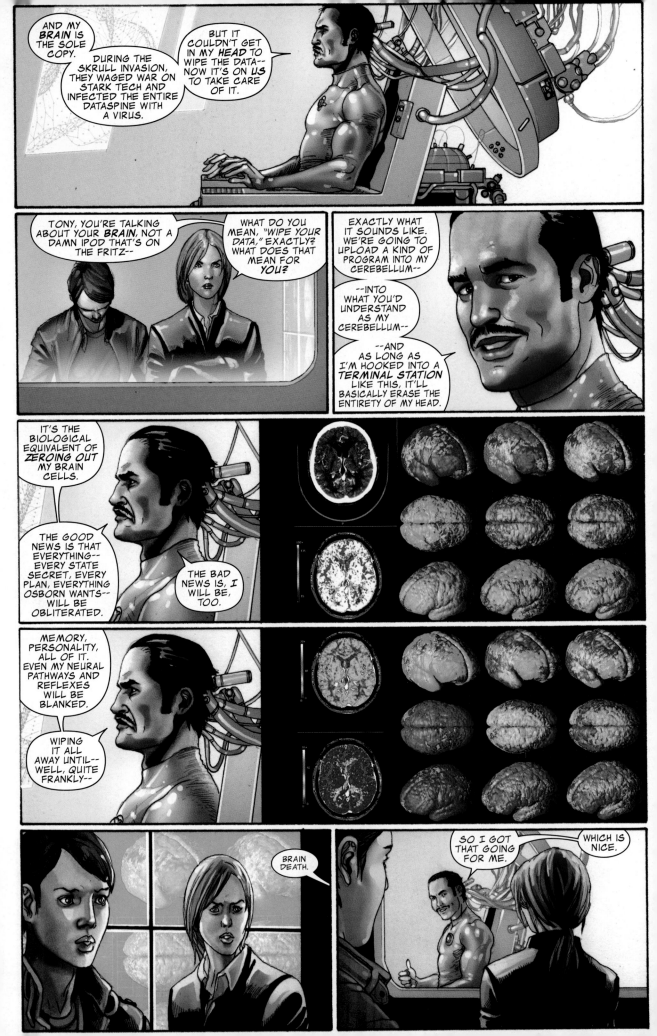

AND MY **BRAIN** IS THE SOLE COPY.

DURING THE SKRULL INVASION, THEY WAGED WAR ON STARK TECH AND INFECTED THE ENTIRE DATASPINE WITH A VIRUS.

BUT IT COULDN'T GET IN MY **HEAD** TO WIPE THE DATA-- NOW IT'S ON **US** TO TAKE CARE OF IT.

TONY, YOU'RE TALKING ABOUT YOUR **BRAIN**, NOT A DAMN IPOD THAT'S ON THE FRITZ--

WHAT DO YOU MEAN, "WIPE YOUR DATA," EXACTLY? WHAT DOES THAT MEAN FOR **YOU**?

EXACTLY WHAT IT SOUNDS LIKE. WE'RE GOING TO UPLOAD A KIND OF PROGRAM INTO MY CEREBELLUM--

--INTO WHAT YOU'D UNDERSTAND AS MY CEREBELLUM--

--AND AS LONG AS I'M HOOKED INTO A **TERMINAL STATION** LIKE THIS, IT'LL BASICALLY ERASE THE ENTIRETY OF MY HEAD.

IT'S THE BIOLOGICAL EQUIVALENT OF **ZEROING OUT** MY BRAIN CELLS.

THE GOOD NEWS IS THAT EVERYTHING-- EVERY STATE SECRET, EVERY PLAN, EVERYTHING OSBORN WANTS-- WILL BE OBLITERATED.

THE BAD NEWS IS, I WILL BE, TOO.

MEMORY, PERSONALITY, ALL OF IT. EVEN MY NEURAL PATHWAYS AND REFLEXES WILL BE BLANKED.

WIPING IT ALL AWAY UNTIL-- WELL, QUITE FRANKLY--

BRAIN DEATH.

SO I GOT THAT GOING FOR ME.

WHICH IS NICE.

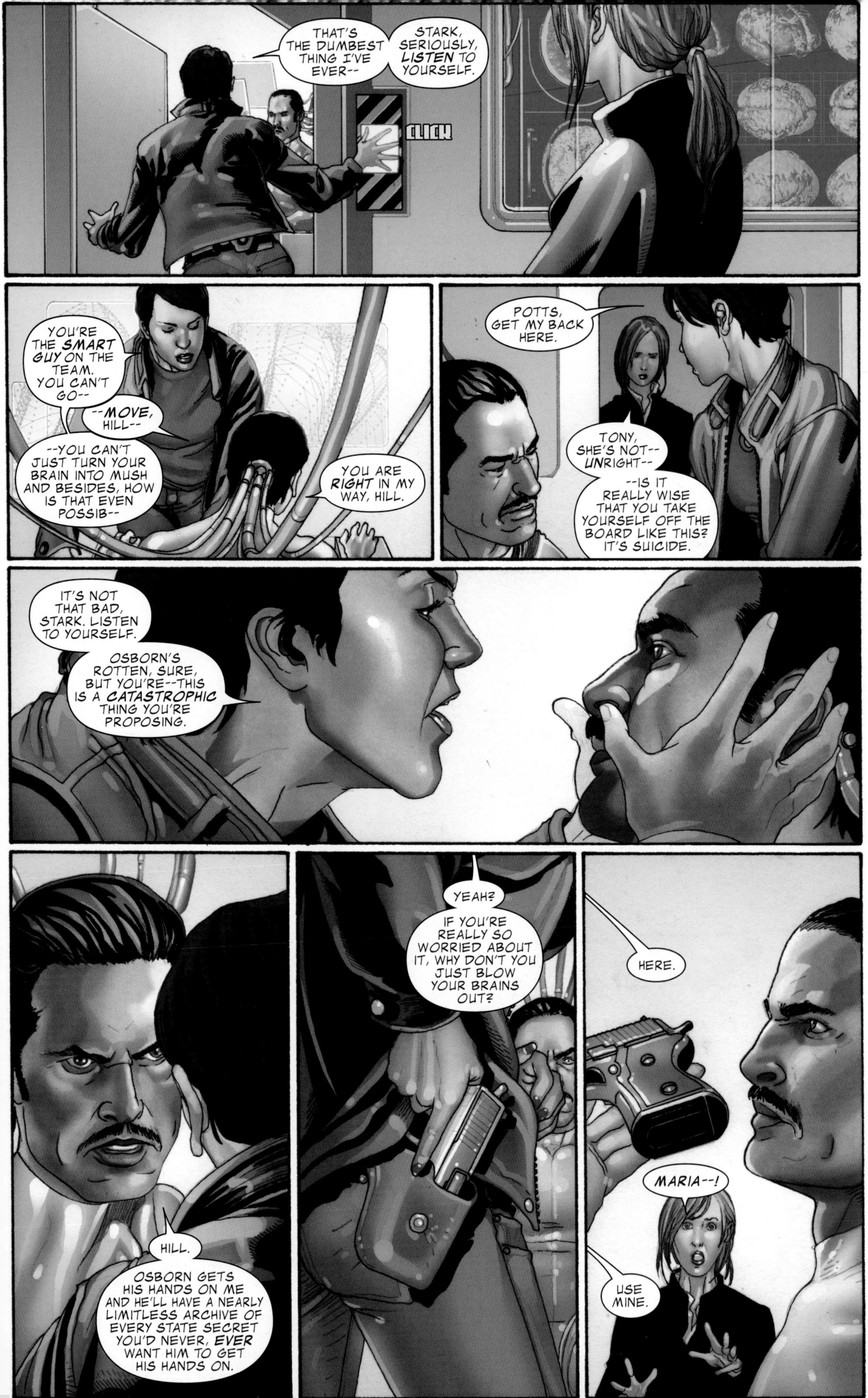
THAT'S THE DUMBEST THING I'VE EVER--
STARK, SERIOUSLY, LISTEN TO YOURSELF.
CLICK
YOU'RE THE SMART GUY ON THE TEAM. YOU CAN'T GO--
--MOVE, HILL--
--YOU CAN'T JUST TURN YOUR BRAIN INTO MUSH AND BESIDES, HOW IS THAT EVEN POSSIB--
YOU ARE RIGHT IN MY WAY, HILL.
POTTS, GET MY BACK HERE.
TONY, SHE'S NOT--UNRIGHT--
--IS IT REALLY WISE THAT YOU TAKE YOURSELF OFF THE BOARD LIKE THIS? IT'S SUICIDE.
IT'S NOT THAT BAD, STARK. LISTEN TO YOURSELF.
OSBORN'S ROTTEN, SURE, BUT YOU'RE--THIS IS A CATASTROPHIC THING YOU'RE PROPOSING.
HILL.
OSBORN GETS HIS HANDS ON ME AND HE'LL HAVE A NEARLY LIMITLESS ARCHIVE OF EVERY STATE SECRET YOU'D NEVER, EVER WANT HIM TO GET HIS HANDS ON.
YEAH?
IF YOU'RE REALLY SO WORRIED ABOUT IT, WHY DON'T YOU JUST BLOW YOUR BRAINS OUT?
HERE.
MARIA--!
USE MINE.

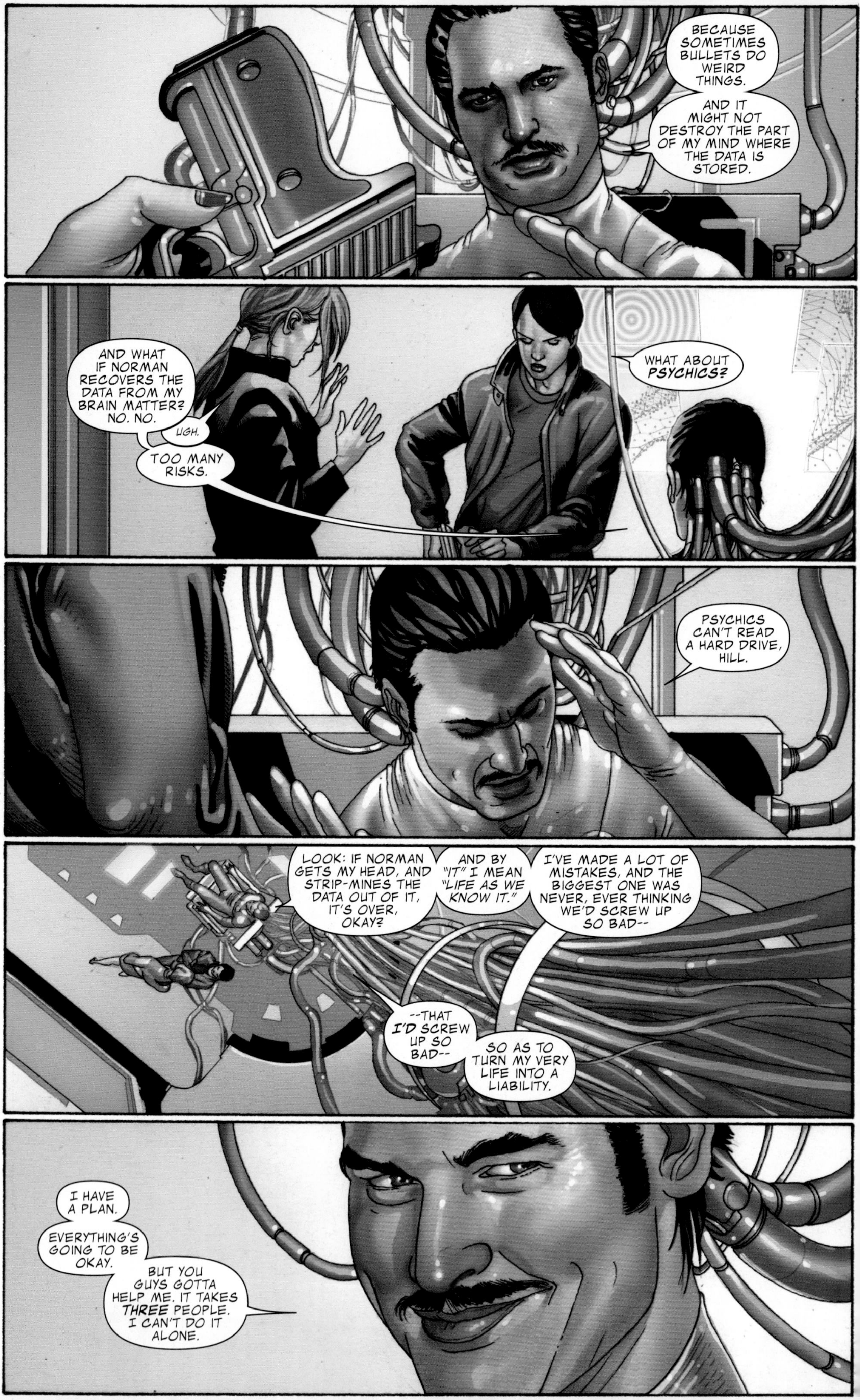
BECAUSE SOMETIMES BULLETS DO WEIRD THINGS.
AND IT MIGHT NOT DESTROY THE PART OF MY MIND WHERE THE DATA IS STORED.
AND WHAT IF NORMAN RECOVERS THE DATA FROM MY BRAIN MATTER? NO. NO.
UGH.
TOO MANY RISKS.
WHAT ABOUT PSYCHICS?
PSYCHICS CAN'T READ A HARD DRIVE, HILL.
LOOK: IF NORMAN GETS MY HEAD, AND STRIP-MINES THE DATA OUT OF IT, IT'S OVER, OKAY?
AND BY "IT" I MEAN "LIFE AS WE KNOW IT."
I'VE MADE A LOT OF MISTAKES, AND THE BIGGEST ONE WAS NEVER, EVER THINKING WE'D SCREW UP SO BAD--
--THAT I'D SCREW UP SO BAD--
SO AS TO TURN MY VERY LIFE INTO A LIABILITY.
I HAVE A PLAN.
EVERYTHING'S GOING TO BE OKAY.
BUT YOU GUYS GOTTA HELP ME. IT TAKES THREE PEOPLE. I CAN'T DO IT ALONE.

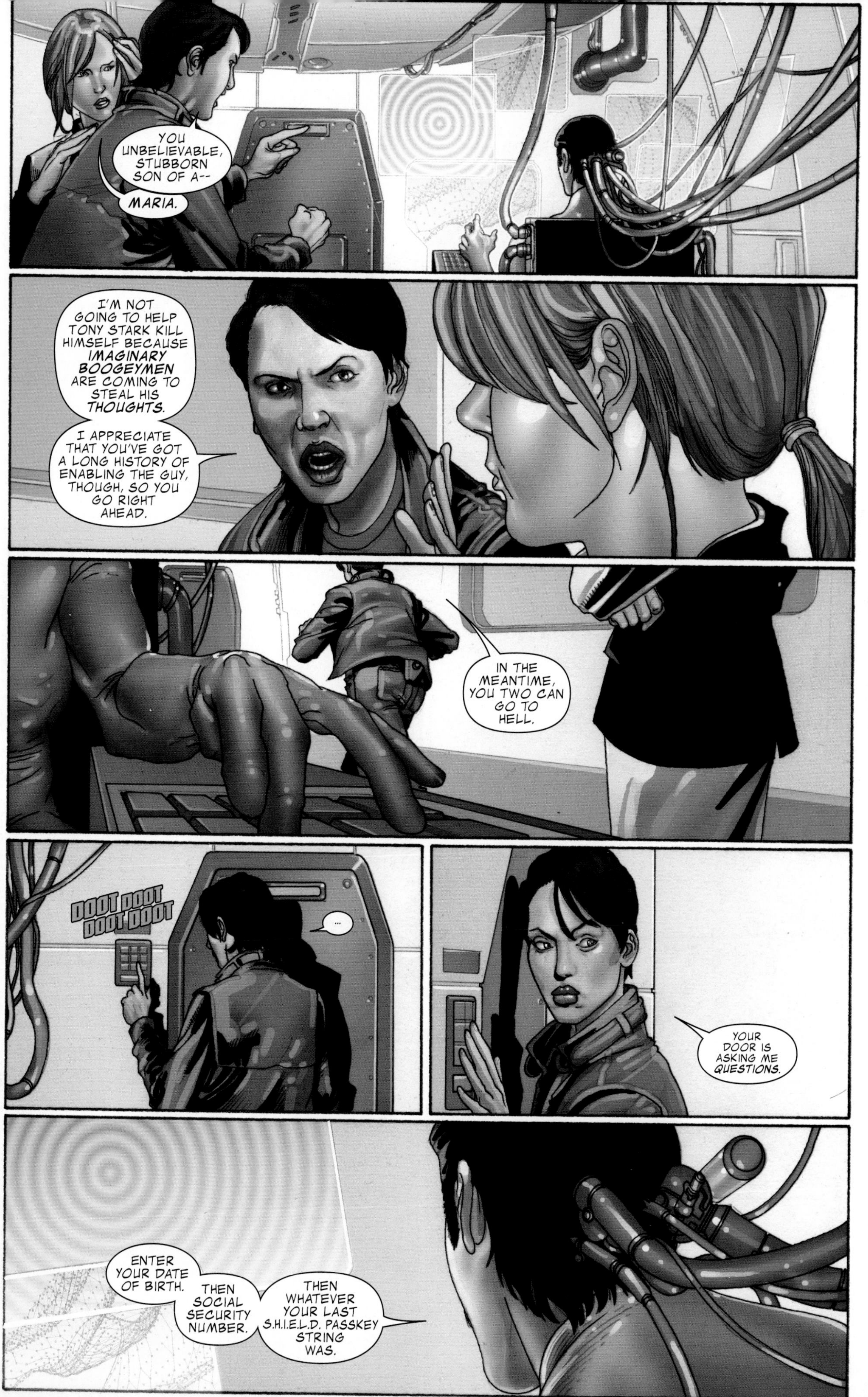

YOU UNBELIEVABLE, STUBBORN SON OF A--
MARIA.
I'M NOT GOING TO HELP TONY STARK KILL HIMSELF BECAUSE IMAGINARY BOOGEYMEN ARE COMING TO STEAL HIS THOUGHTS.
I APPRECIATE THAT YOU'VE GOT A LONG HISTORY OF ENABLING THE GUY, THOUGH, SO YOU GO RIGHT AHEAD.
IN THE MEANTIME, YOU TWO CAN GO TO HELL.
DOOT DOOT DOOT DOOT
...
YOUR DOOR IS ASKING ME QUESTIONS.
ENTER YOUR DATE OF BIRTH.
THEN SOCIAL SECURITY NUMBER.
THEN WHATEVER YOUR LAST S.H.I.E.L.D. PASSKEY STRING WAS.

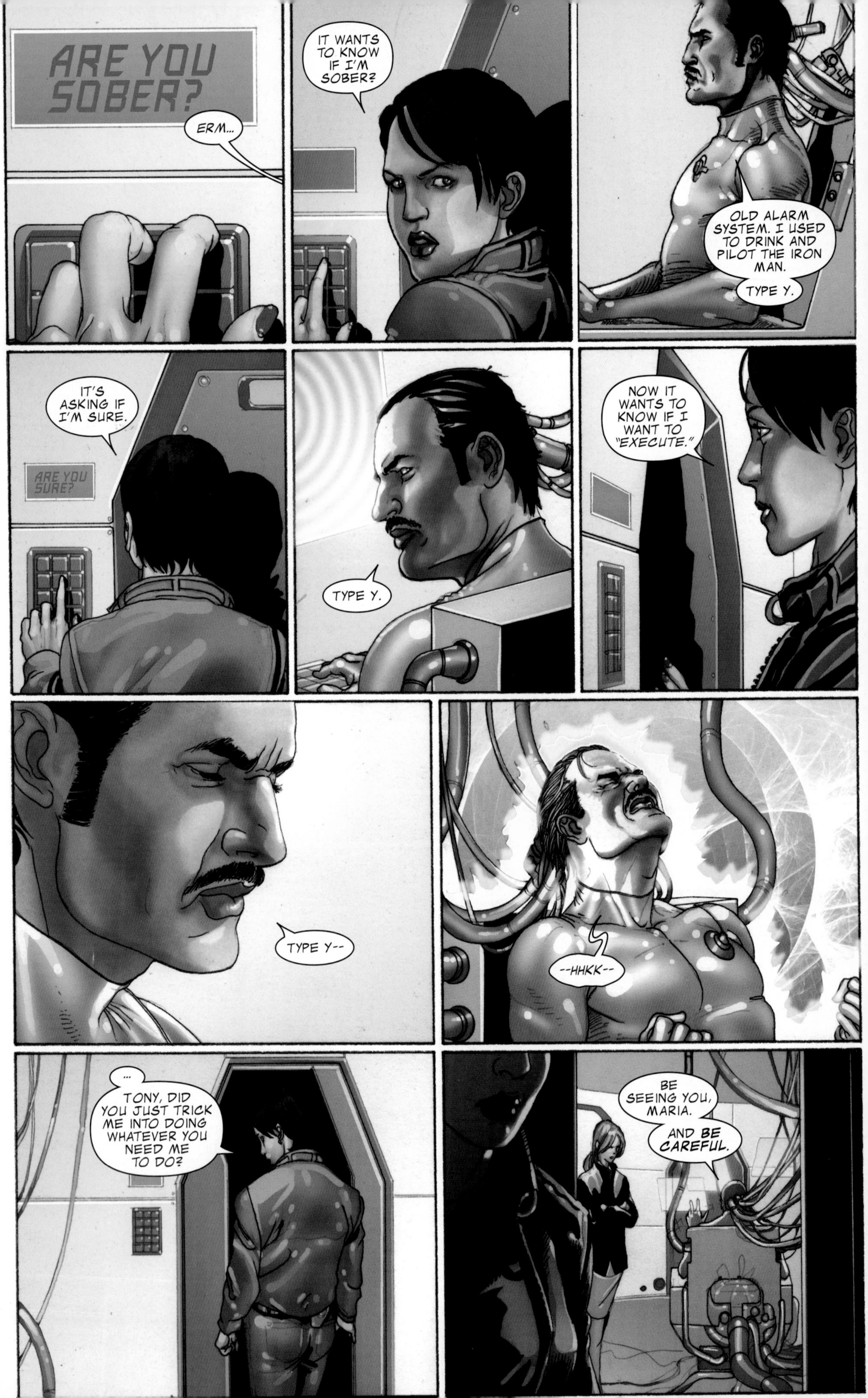
ARE YOU SOBER?
ERM...
IT WANTS TO KNOW IF I'M SOBER?
OLD ALARM SYSTEM. I USED TO DRINK AND PILOT THE IRON MAN.
TYPE Y.
IT'S ASKING IF I'M SURE.
ARE YOU SURE?
TYPE Y.
NOW IT WANTS TO KNOW IF I WANT TO "EXECUTE."
TYPE Y--
--HHKK--
...
TONY, DID YOU JUST TRICK ME INTO DOING WHATEVER YOU NEED ME TO DO?
BE SEEING YOU, MARIA.
AND BE CAREFUL.

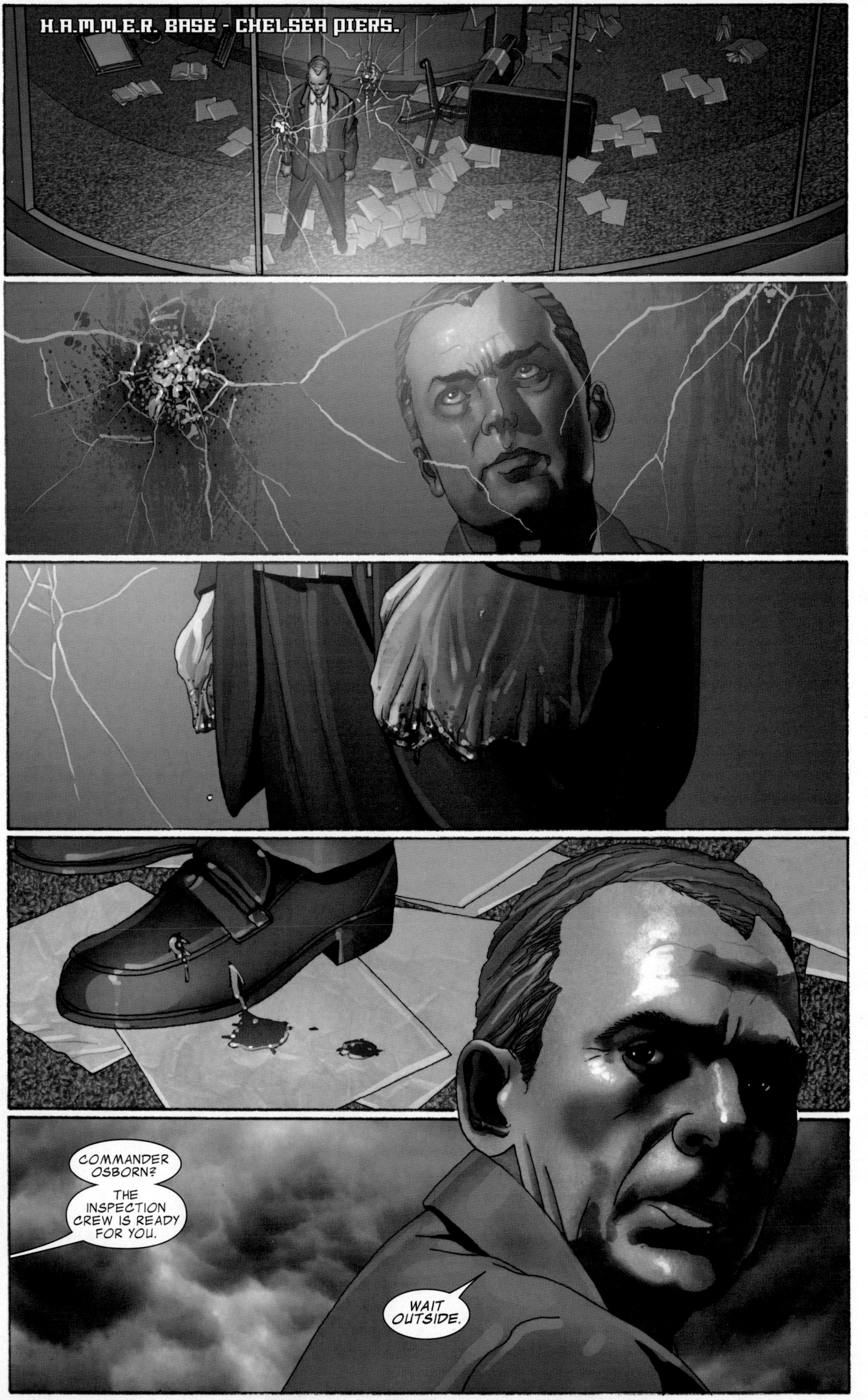
H.A.M.M.E.R. BASE - CHELSEA PIERS.
COMMANDER OSBORN?
THE INSPECTION CREW IS READY FOR YOU.
WAIT OUTSIDE.

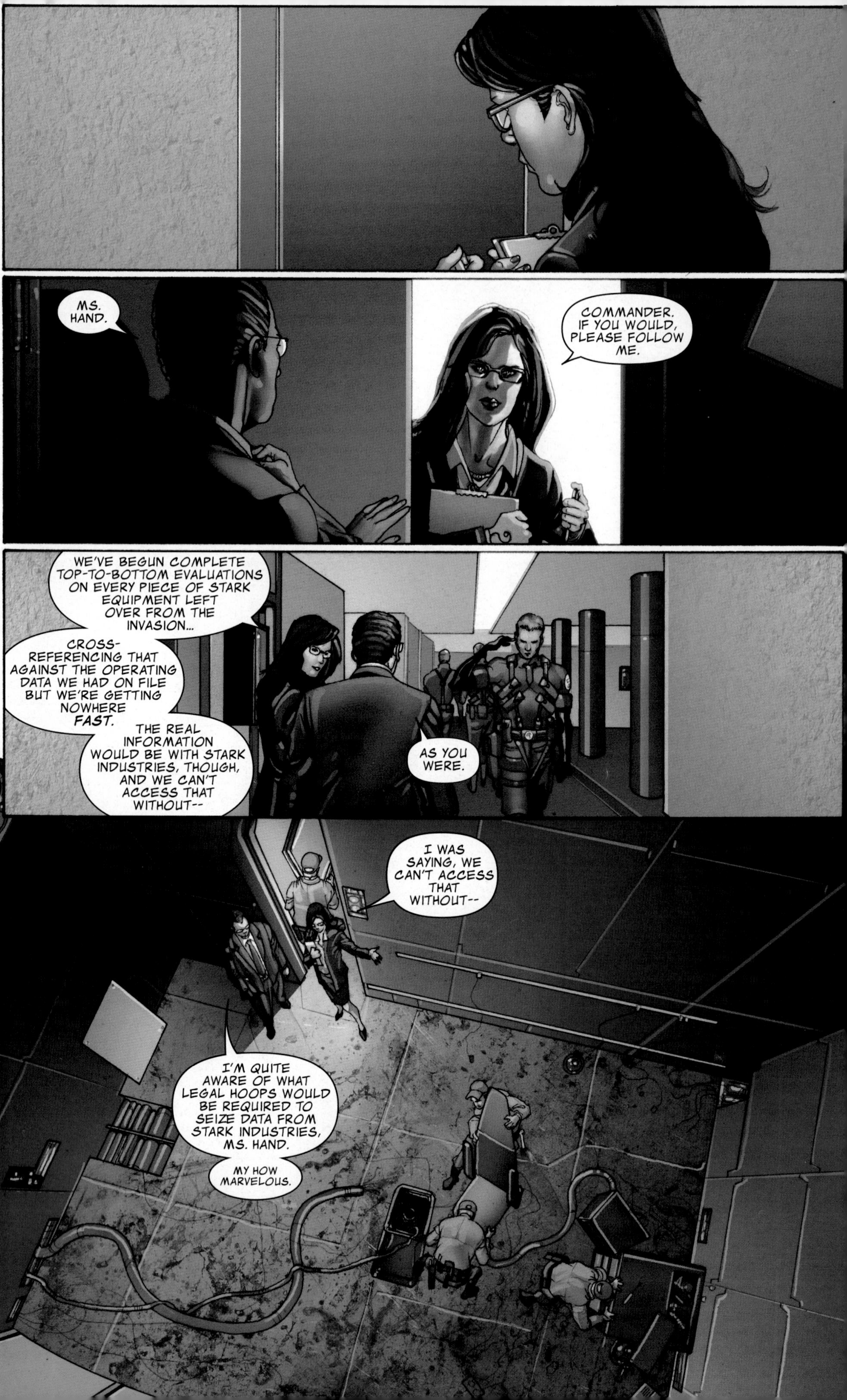
MS. HAND.
COMMANDER. IF YOU WOULD, PLEASE FOLLOW ME.
WE'VE BEGUN COMPLETE TOP-TO-BOTTOM EVALUATIONS ON EVERY PIECE OF STARK EQUIPMENT LEFT OVER FROM THE INVASION...
CROSS-REFERENCING THAT AGAINST THE OPERATING DATA WE HAD ON FILE BUT WE'RE GETTING NOWHERE FAST.
THE REAL INFORMATION WOULD BE WITH STARK INDUSTRIES, THOUGH, AND WE CAN'T ACCESS THAT WITHOUT--
AS YOU WERE.
I WAS SAYING, WE CAN'T ACCESS THAT WITHOUT--
I'M QUITE AWARE OF WHAT LEGAL HOOPS WOULD BE REQUIRED TO SEIZE DATA FROM STARK INDUSTRIES, MS. HAND.
MY HOW MARVELOUS.

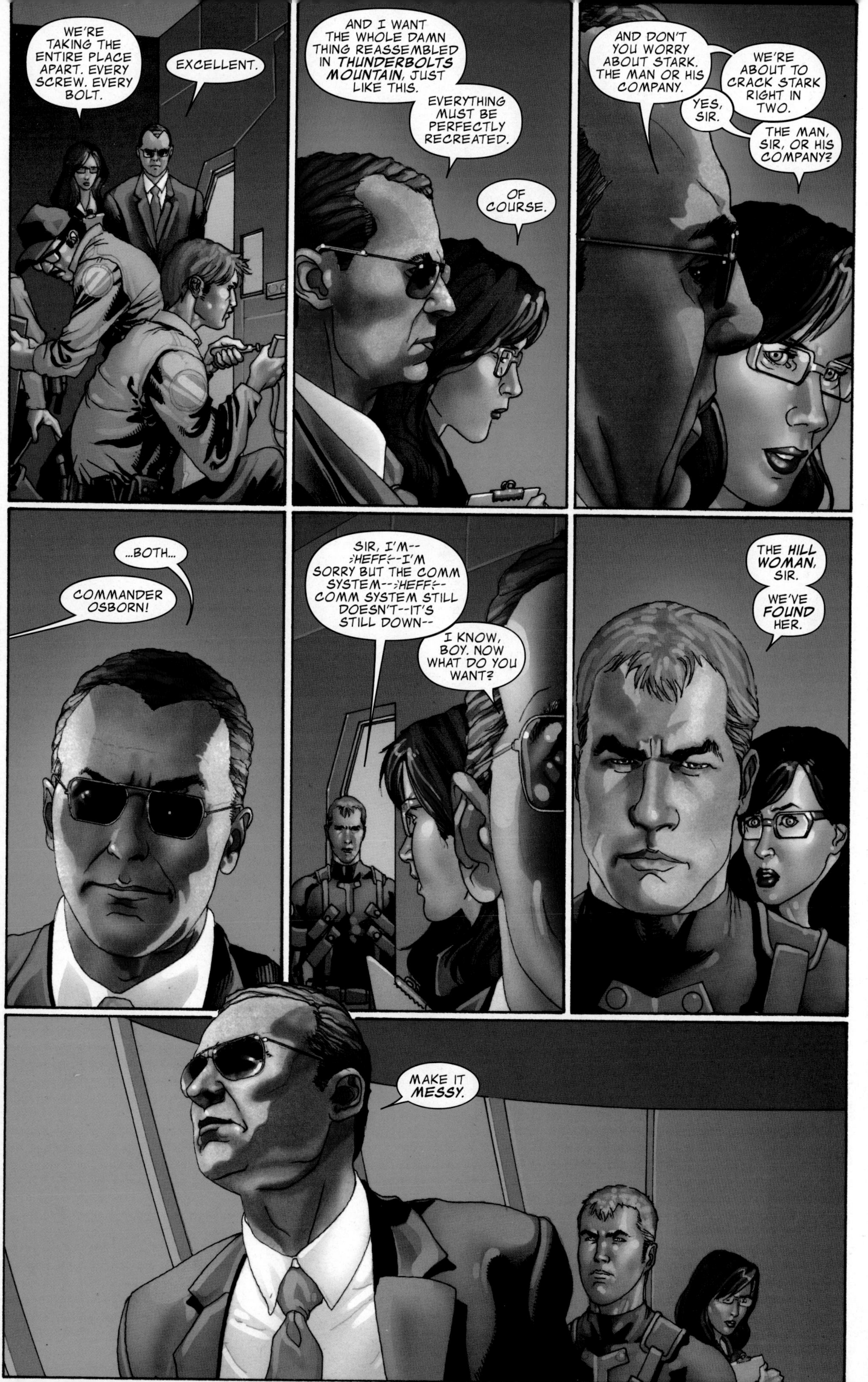
WE'RE TAKING THE ENTIRE PLACE APART. EVERY SCREW. EVERY BOLT.
EXCELLENT.
AND I WANT THE WHOLE DAMN THING REASSEMBLED IN THUNDERBOLTS MOUNTAIN, JUST LIKE THIS.
EVERYTHING MUST BE PERFECTLY RECREATED.
OF COURSE.
AND DON'T YOU WORRY ABOUT STARK. THE MAN OR HIS COMPANY.
WE'RE ABOUT TO CRACK STARK RIGHT IN TWO.
YES, SIR.
THE MAN, SIR, OR HIS COMPANY?
...BOTH...
COMMANDER OSBORN!
SIR, I'M-- >HEFF<--I'M SORRY BUT THE COMM SYSTEM-->HEFF<--COMM SYSTEM STILL DOESN'T--IT'S STILL DOWN--
I KNOW, BOY. NOW WHAT DO YOU WANT?
THE HILL WOMAN, SIR.
WE'VE FOUND HER.
MAKE IT MESSY.

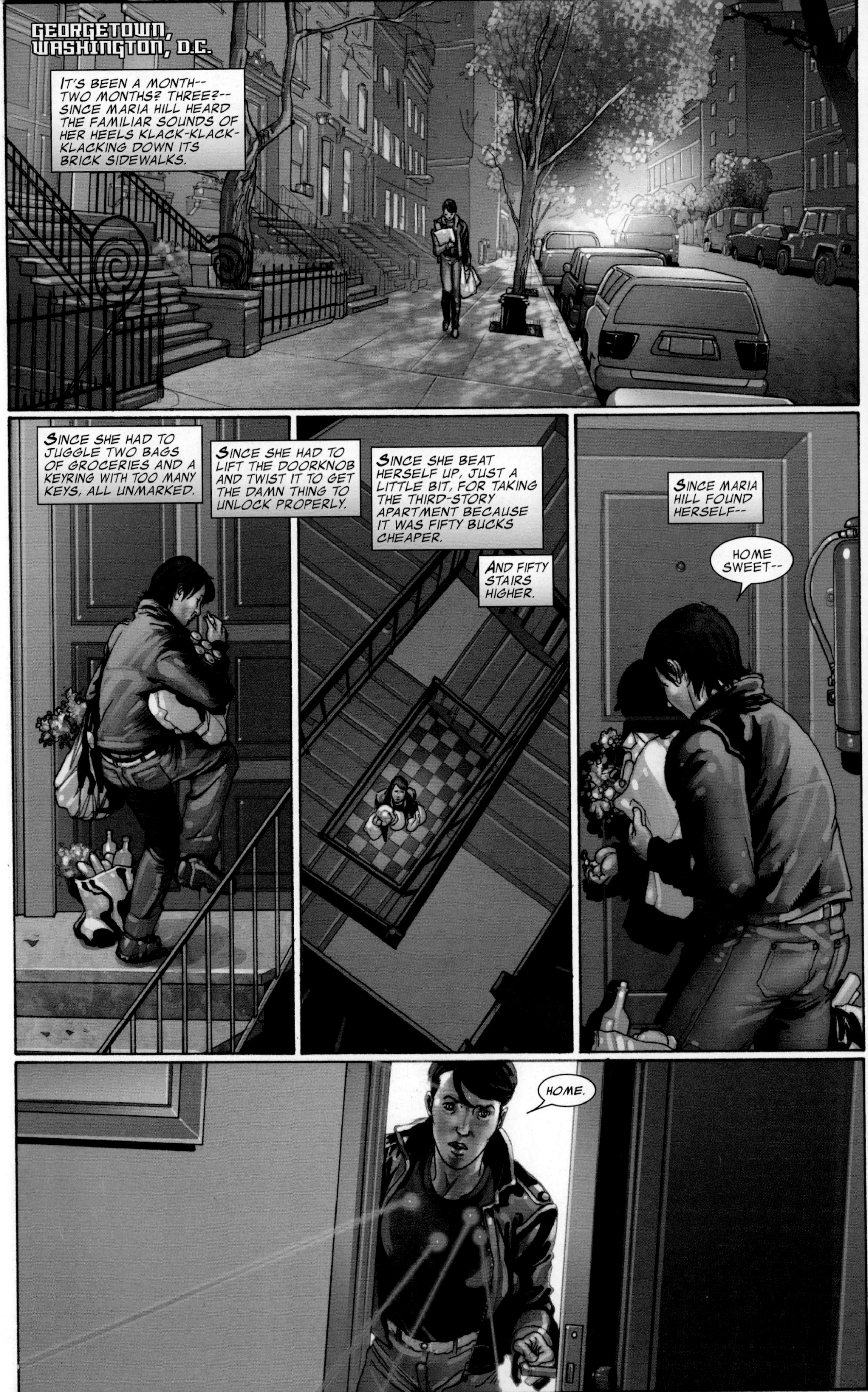
GEORGETOWN, WASHINGTON, D.C.
IT'S BEEN A MONTH-- TWO MONTHS? THREE?-- SINCE MARIA HILL HEARD THE FAMILIAR SOUNDS OF HER HEELS KLACK-KLACK-KLACKING DOWN ITS BRICK SIDEWALKS.
SINCE SHE HAD TO JUGGLE TWO BAGS OF GROCERIES AND A KEYRING WITH TOO MANY KEYS, ALL UNMARKED.
SINCE SHE HAD TO LIFT THE DOORKNOB AND TWIST IT TO GET THE DAMN THING TO UNLOCK PROPERLY.
SINCE SHE BEAT HERSELF UP, JUST A LITTLE BIT, FOR TAKING THE THIRD-STORY APARTMENT BECAUSE IT WAS FIFTY BUCKS CHEAPER.
AND FIFTY STAIRS HIGHER.
SINCE MARIA HILL FOUND HERSELF--
HOME SWEET--
HOME.

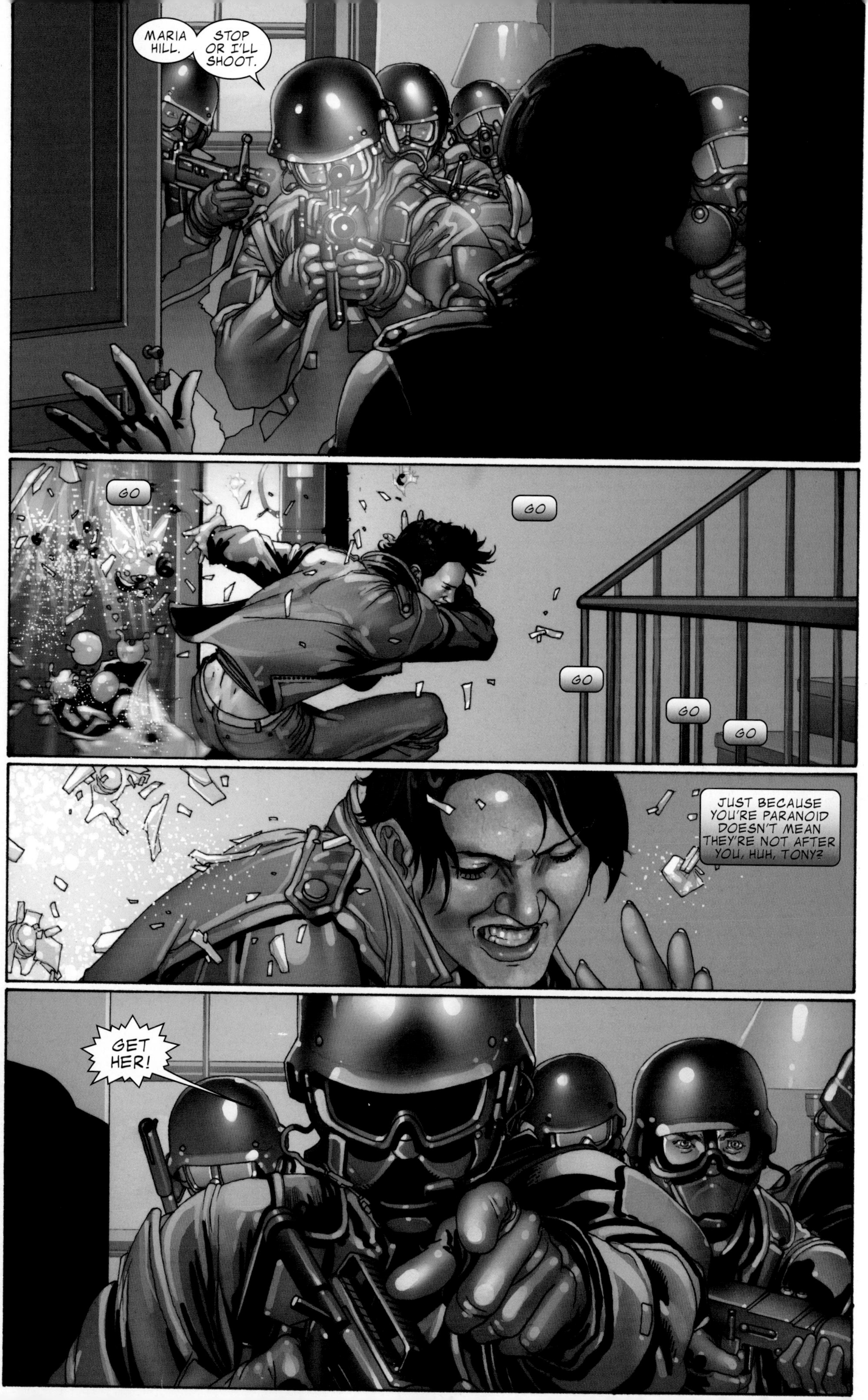
MARIA HILL.
STOP OR I'LL SHOOT.
GO
GO
GO
GO
GO
JUST BECAUSE YOU'RE PARANOID DOESN'T MEAN THEY'RE NOT AFTER YOU, HUH, TONY?
GET HER!

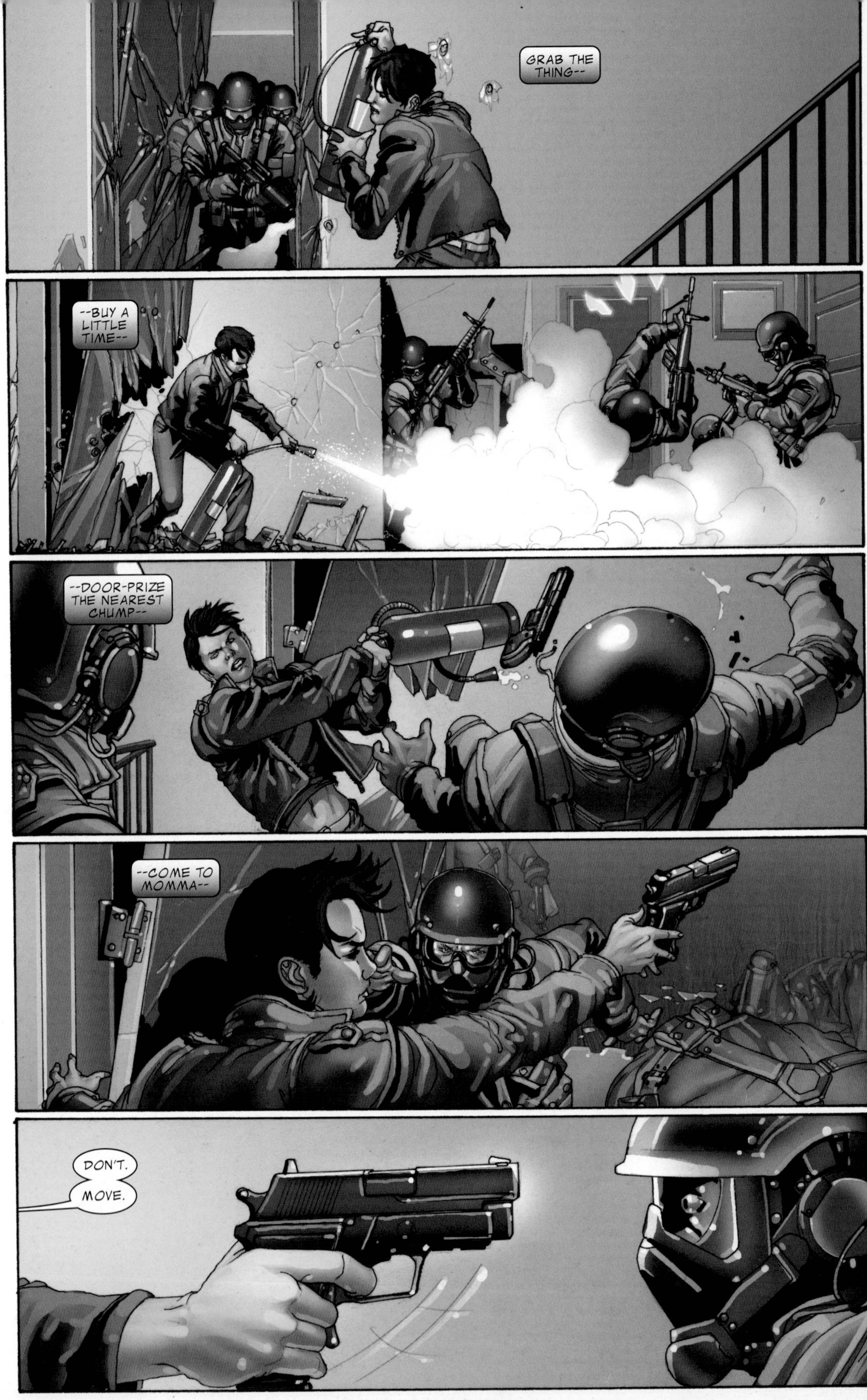
GRAB THE THING--
--BUY A LITTLE TIME--
--DOOR-PRIZE THE NEAREST CHUMP--
--COME TO MOMMA--
DON'T.
MOVE.

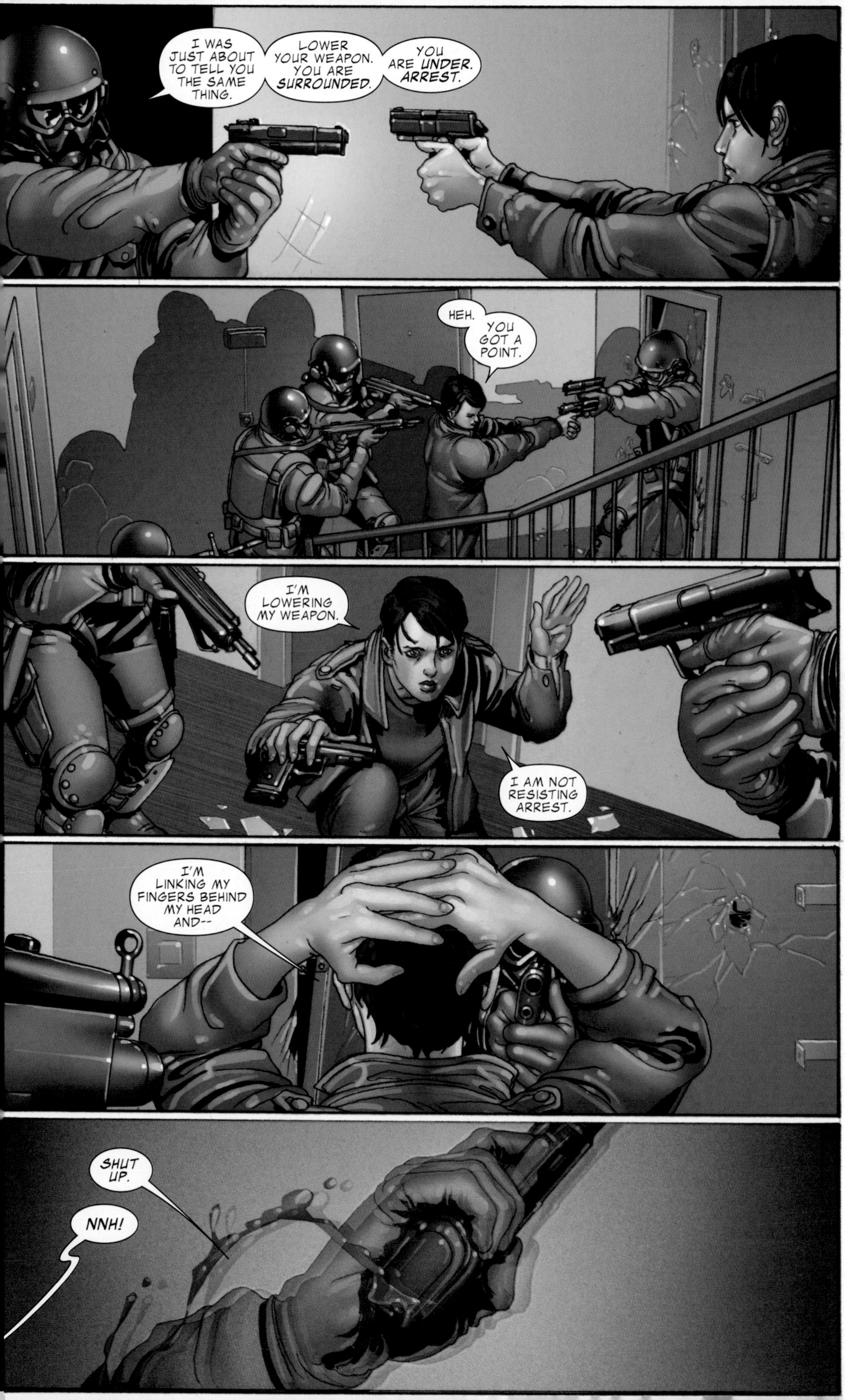
I WAS JUST ABOUT TO TELL YOU THE SAME THING.
LOWER YOUR WEAPON. YOU ARE SURROUNDED.
YOU ARE UNDER. ARREST.
HEH.
YOU GOT A POINT.
I'M LOWERING MY WEAPON.
I AM NOT RESISTING ARREST.
I'M LINKING MY FINGERS BEHIND MY HEAD AND--
SHUT UP.
NNH!

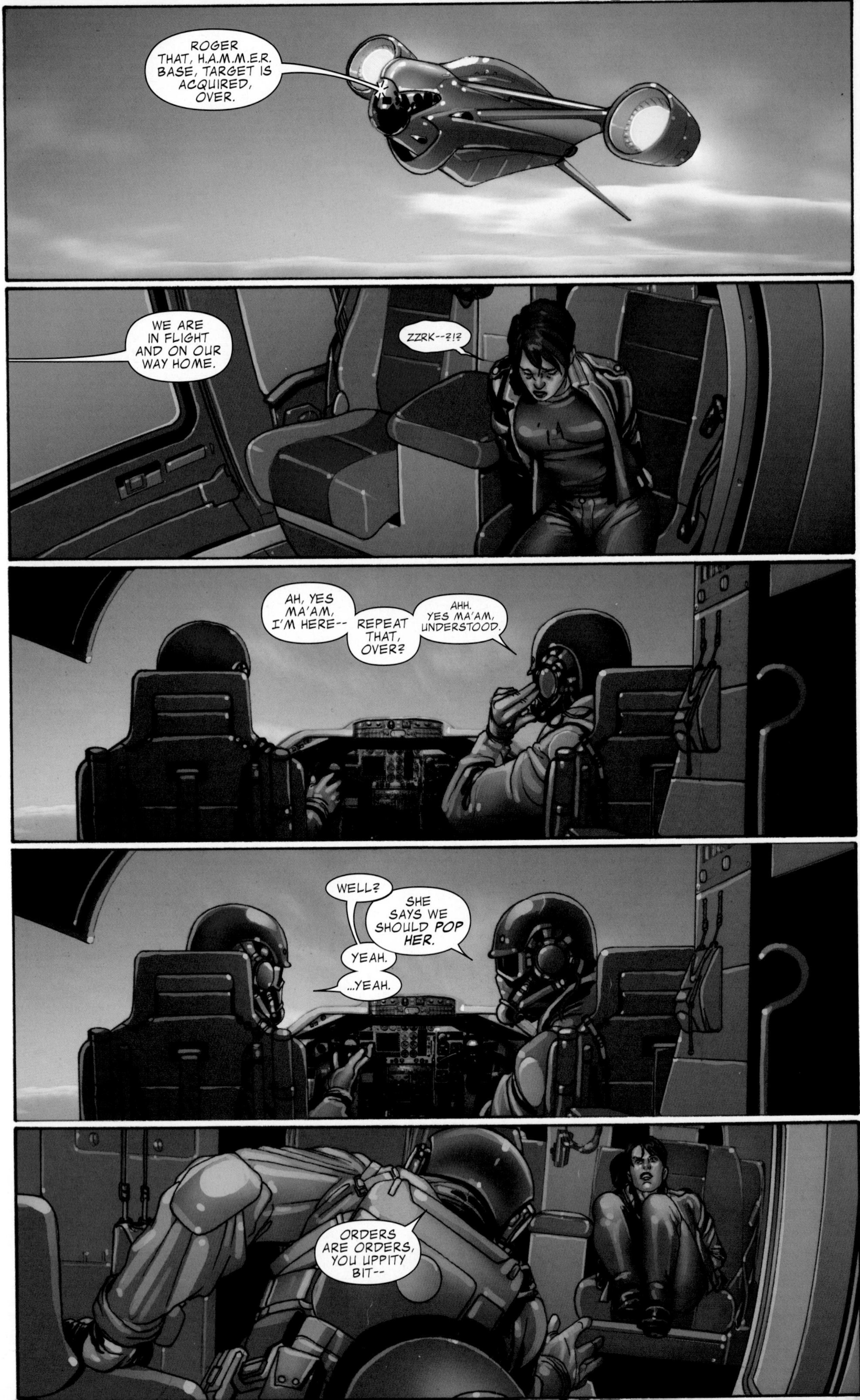
ROGER THAT, H.A.M.M.E.R. BASE, TARGET IS ACQUIRED, OVER.
WE ARE IN FLIGHT AND ON OUR WAY HOME.
ZZRK--?!?
AH, YES MA'AM, I'M HERE--
REPEAT THAT, OVER?
AHH. YES MA'AM, UNDERSTOOD.
WELL?
SHE SAYS WE SHOULD POP HER.
YEAH.
...YEAH.
ORDERS ARE ORDERS, YOU UPPITY BIT--

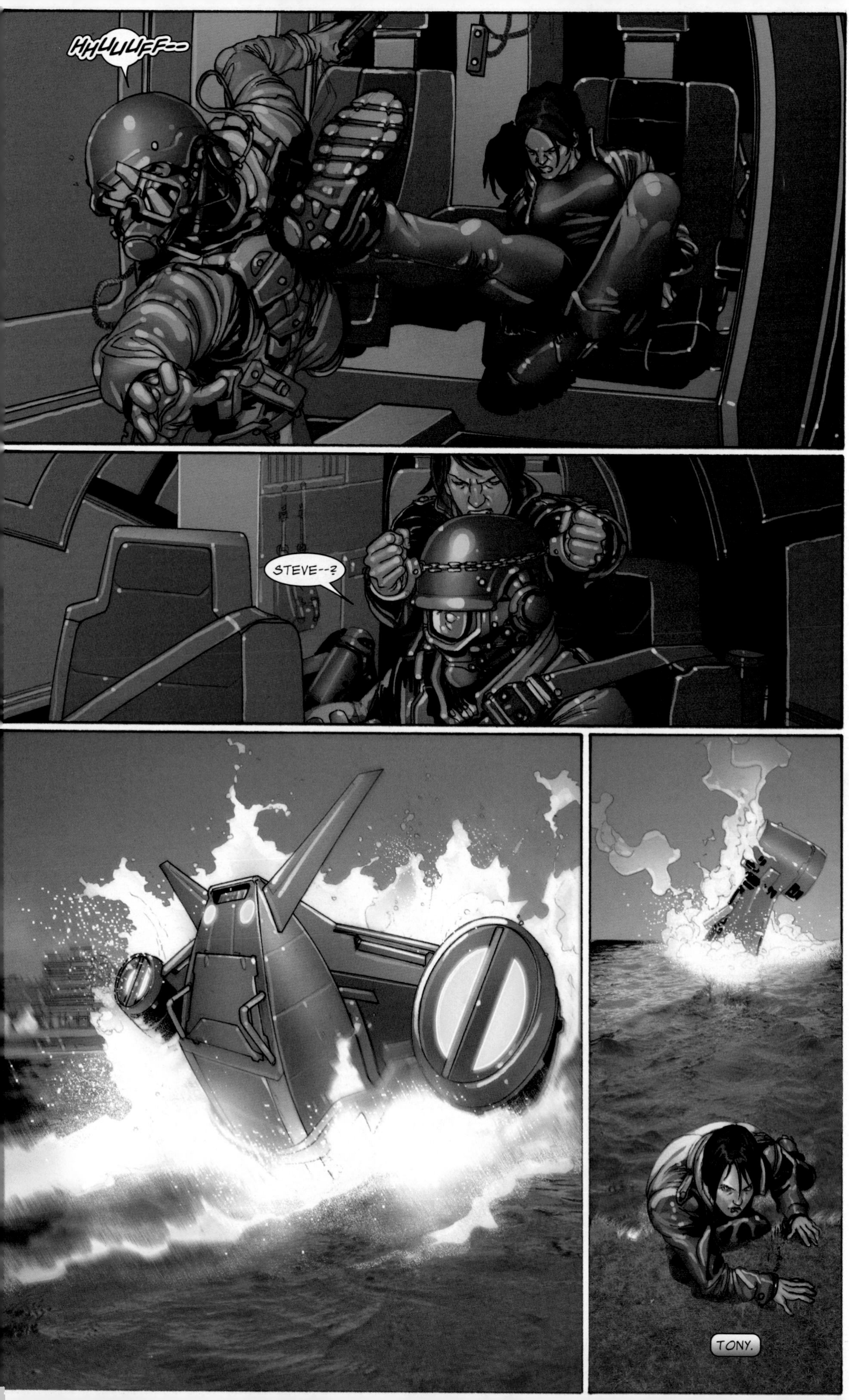
HHUUUFF--
STEVE--?
TONY.

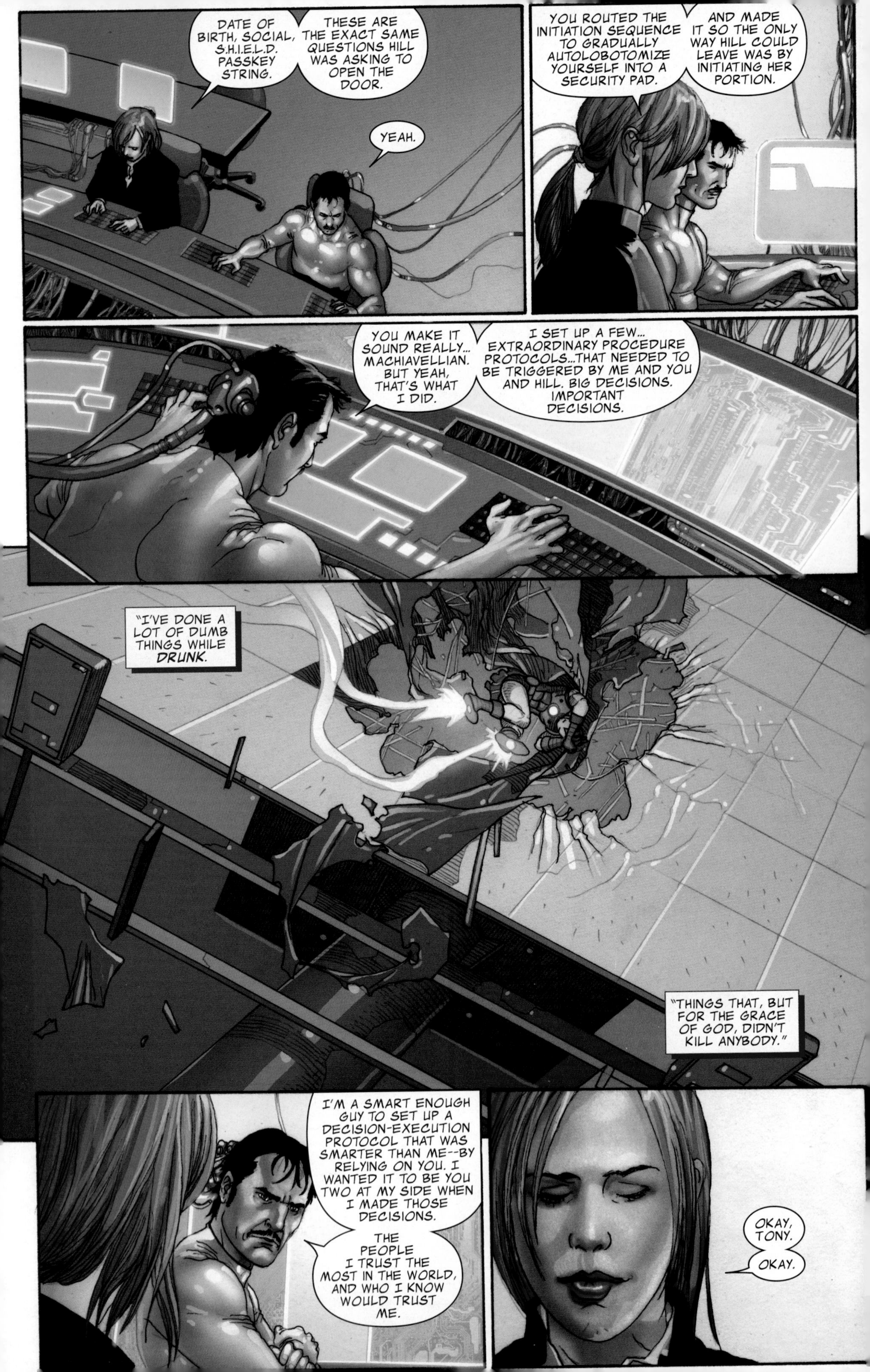
DATE OF BIRTH, SOCIAL, S.H.I.E.L.D. PASSKEY STRING.
THESE ARE THE EXACT SAME QUESTIONS HILL WAS ASKING TO OPEN THE DOOR.
YEAH.
YOU ROUTED THE INITIATION SEQUENCE TO GRADUALLY AUTOLOBOTOMIZE YOURSELF INTO A SECURITY PAD.
AND MADE IT SO THE ONLY WAY HILL COULD LEAVE WAS BY INITIATING HER PORTION.
YOU MAKE IT SOUND REALLY... MACHIAVELLIAN. BUT YEAH, THAT'S WHAT I DID.
I SET UP A FEW... EXTRAORDINARY PROCEDURE PROTOCOLS...THAT NEEDED TO BE TRIGGERED BY ME AND YOU AND HILL. BIG DECISIONS. IMPORTANT DECISIONS.
"I'VE DONE A LOT OF DUMB THINGS WHILE DRUNK.
"THINGS THAT, BUT FOR THE GRACE OF GOD, DIDN'T KILL ANYBODY."
I'M A SMART ENOUGH GUY TO SET UP A DECISION-EXECUTION PROTOCOL THAT WAS SMARTER THAN ME--BY RELYING ON YOU. I WANTED IT TO BE YOU TWO AT MY SIDE WHEN I MADE THOSE DECISIONS.
THE PEOPLE I TRUST THE MOST IN THE WORLD, AND WHO I KNOW WOULD TRUST ME.
OKAY, TONY.
OKAY.

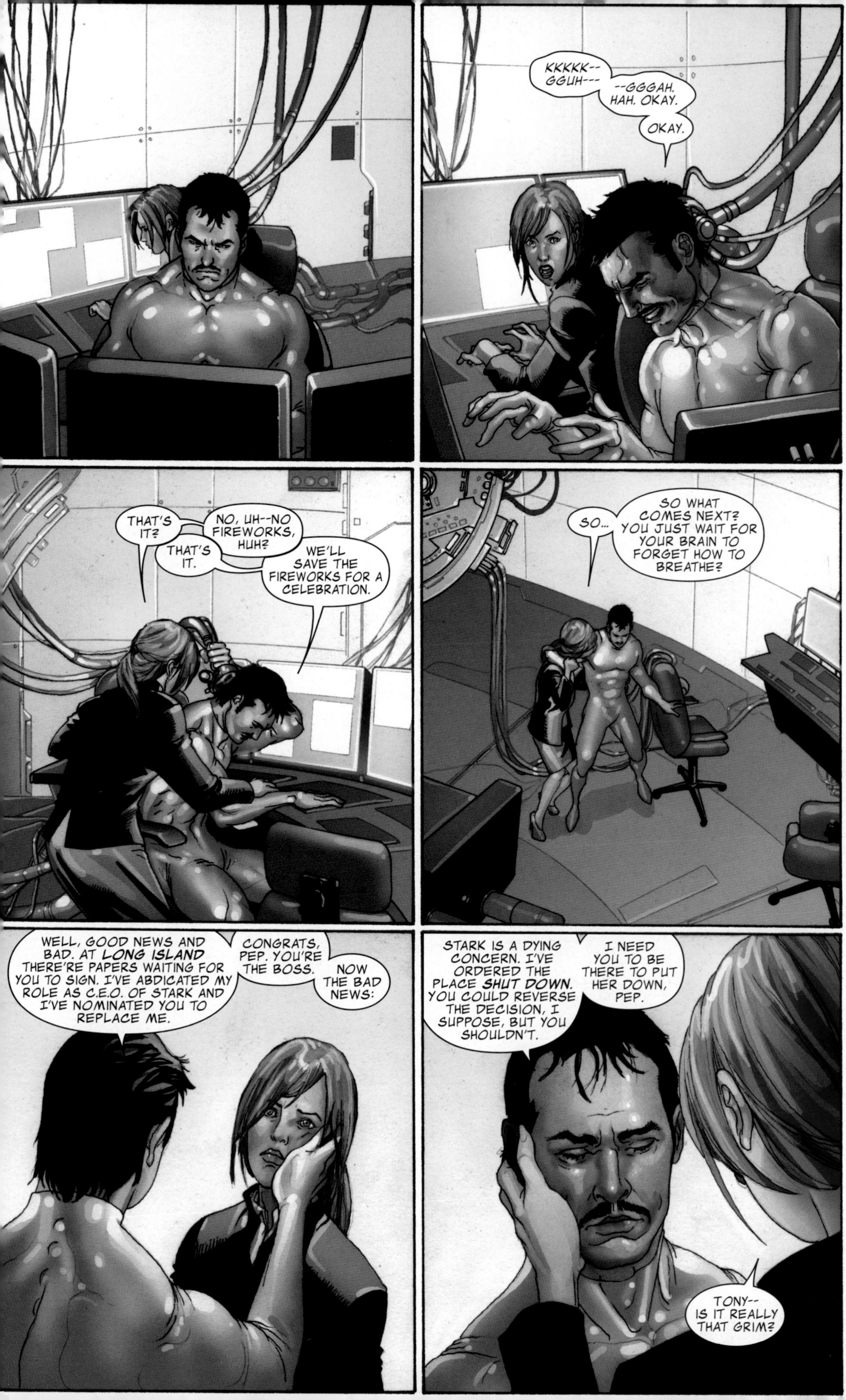
KKKKK-- GGUH---
--GGGAH. HAH. OKAY.
OKAY.
THAT'S IT?
NO, UH--NO FIREWORKS, HUH?
THAT'S IT.
WE'LL SAVE THE FIREWORKS FOR A CELEBRATION.
SO...
SO WHAT COMES NEXT? YOU JUST WAIT FOR YOUR BRAIN TO FORGET HOW TO BREATHE?
WELL, GOOD NEWS AND BAD. AT LONG ISLAND THERE'RE PAPERS WAITING FOR YOU TO SIGN. I'VE ABDICATED MY ROLE AS C.E.O. OF STARK AND I'VE NOMINATED YOU TO REPLACE ME.
CONGRATS, PEP. YOU'RE THE BOSS.
NOW THE BAD NEWS:
STARK IS A DYING CONCERN. I'VE ORDERED THE PLACE SHUT DOWN. YOU COULD REVERSE THE DECISION, I SUPPOSE, BUT YOU SHOULDN'T.
I NEED YOU TO BE THERE TO PUT HER DOWN, PEP.
TONY-- IS IT REALLY THAT GRIM?

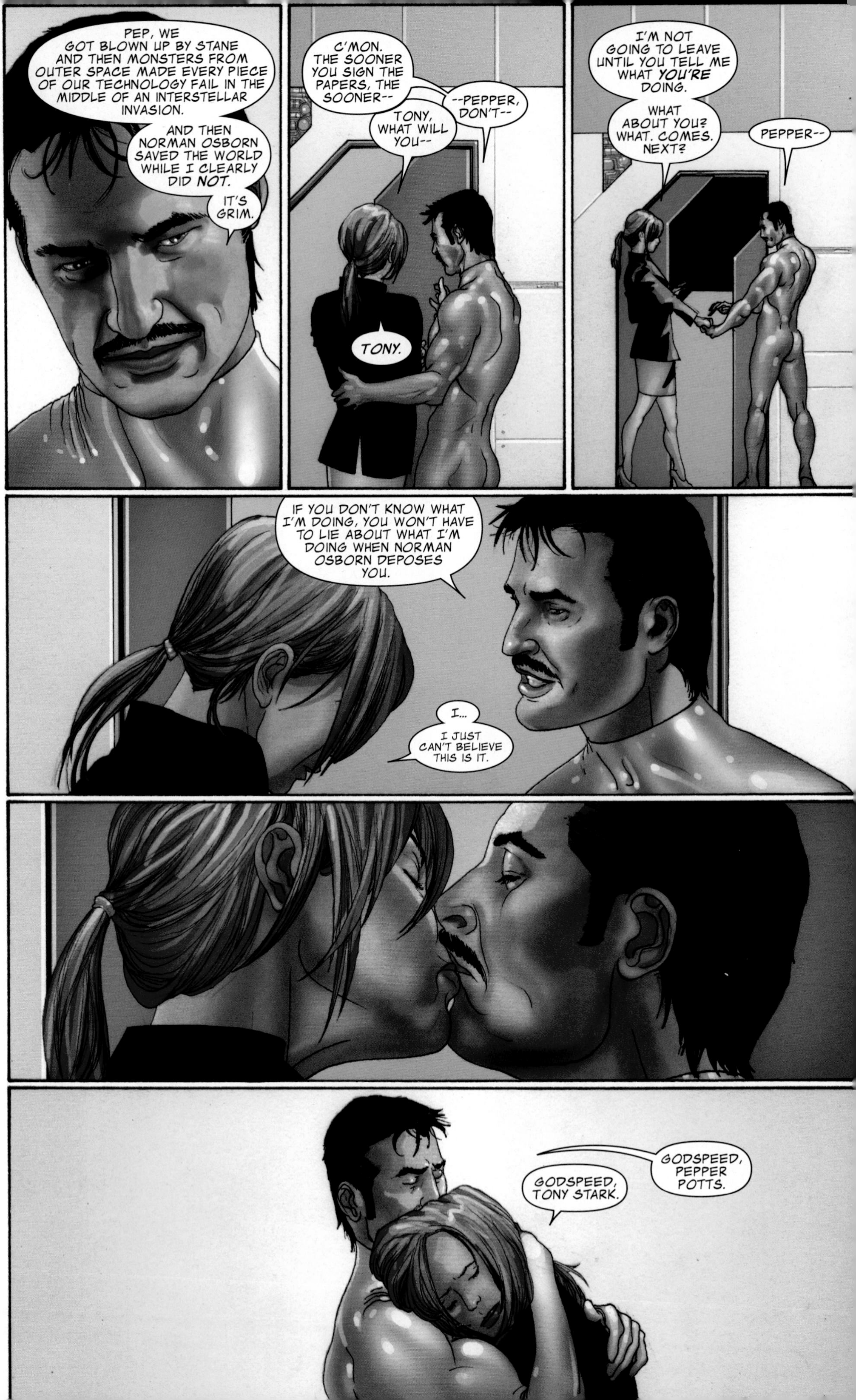
PEP, WE GOT BLOWN UP BY STANE AND THEN MONSTERS FROM OUTER SPACE MADE EVERY PIECE OF OUR TECHNOLOGY FAIL IN THE MIDDLE OF AN INTERSTELLAR INVASION.
AND THEN NORMAN OSBORN SAVED THE WORLD WHILE I CLEARLY DID NOT.
IT'S GRIM.
C'MON. THE SOONER YOU SIGN THE PAPERS, THE SOONER--
--PEPPER, DON'T--
TONY, WHAT WILL YOU--
TONY.
I'M NOT GOING TO LEAVE UNTIL YOU TELL ME WHAT YOU'RE DOING.
WHAT ABOUT YOU? WHAT. COMES. NEXT?
PEPPER--
IF YOU DON'T KNOW WHAT I'M DOING, YOU WON'T HAVE TO LIE ABOUT WHAT I'M DOING WHEN NORMAN OSBORN DEPOSES YOU.
I... I JUST CAN'T BELIEVE THIS IS IT.
GODSPEED, PEPPER POTTS.
GODSPEED, TONY STARK.

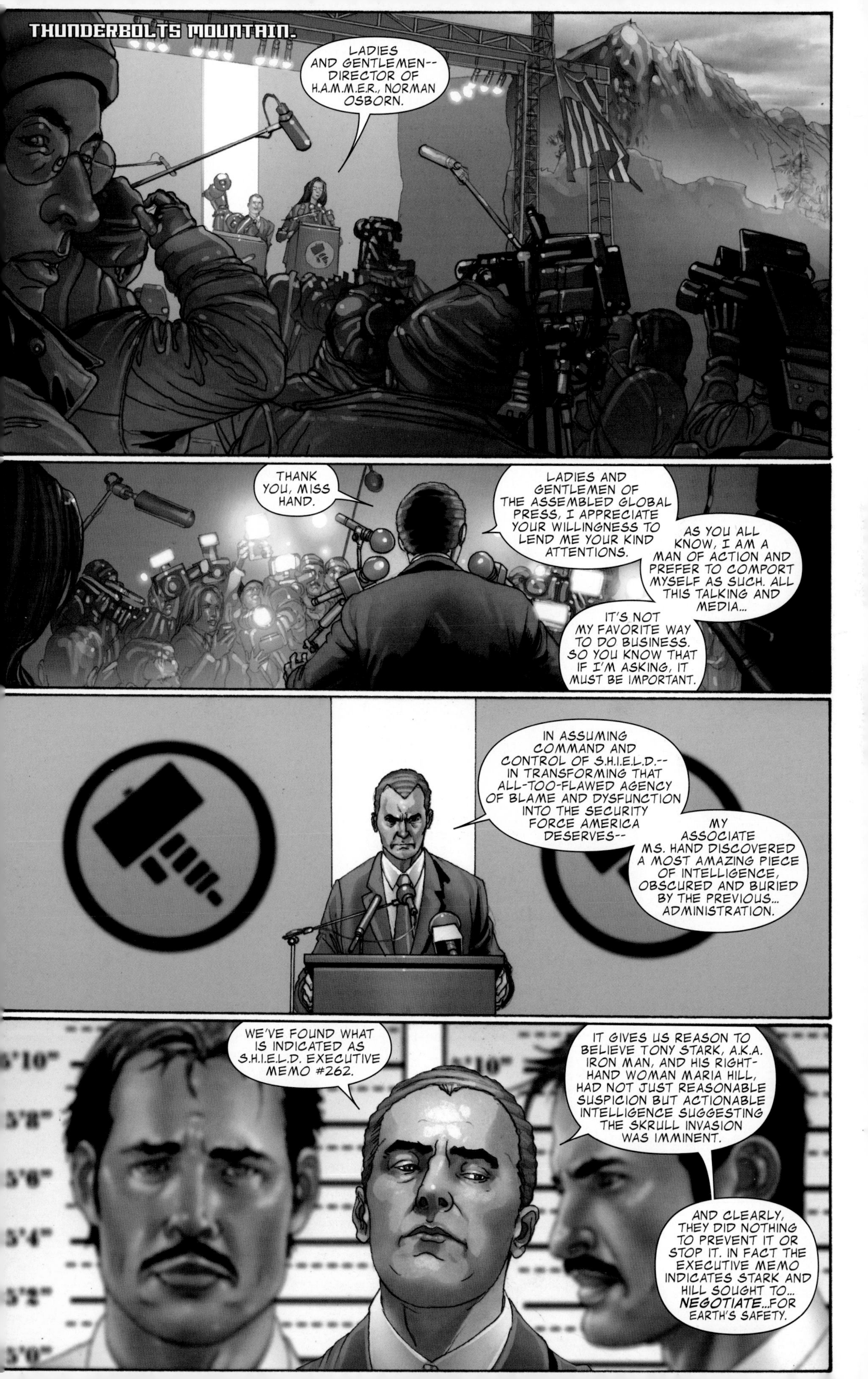
THUNDERBOLTS MOUNTAIN.
LADIES AND GENTLEMEN--DIRECTOR OF H.A.M.M.E.R., NORMAN OSBORN.
THANK YOU, MISS HAND.
LADIES AND GENTLEMEN OF THE ASSEMBLED GLOBAL PRESS, I APPRECIATE YOUR WILLINGNESS TO LEND ME YOUR KIND ATTENTIONS.
AS YOU ALL KNOW, I AM A MAN OF ACTION AND PREFER TO COMPORT MYSELF AS SUCH. ALL THIS TALKING AND MEDIA...
IT'S NOT MY FAVORITE WAY TO DO BUSINESS. SO YOU KNOW THAT IF I'M ASKING, IT MUST BE IMPORTANT.
IN ASSUMING COMMAND AND CONTROL OF S.H.I.E.L.D.--IN TRANSFORMING THAT ALL-TOO-FLAWED AGENCY OF BLAME AND DYSFUNCTION INTO THE SECURITY FORCE AMERICA DESERVES--
MY ASSOCIATE MS. HAND DISCOVERED A MOST AMAZING PIECE OF INTELLIGENCE, OBSCURED AND BURIED BY THE PREVIOUS... ADMINISTRATION.
WE'VE FOUND WHAT IS INDICATED AS S.H.I.E.L.D. EXECUTIVE MEMO #262.
IT GIVES US REASON TO BELIEVE TONY STARK, A.K.A. IRON MAN, AND HIS RIGHT-HAND WOMAN MARIA HILL, HAD NOT JUST REASONABLE SUSPICION BUT ACTIONABLE INTELLIGENCE SUGGESTING THE SKRULL INVASION WAS IMMINENT.
AND CLEARLY, THEY DID NOTHING TO PREVENT IT OR STOP IT. IN FACT THE EXECUTIVE MEMO INDICATES STARK AND HILL SOUGHT TO... NEGOTIATE...FOR EARTH'S SAFETY.

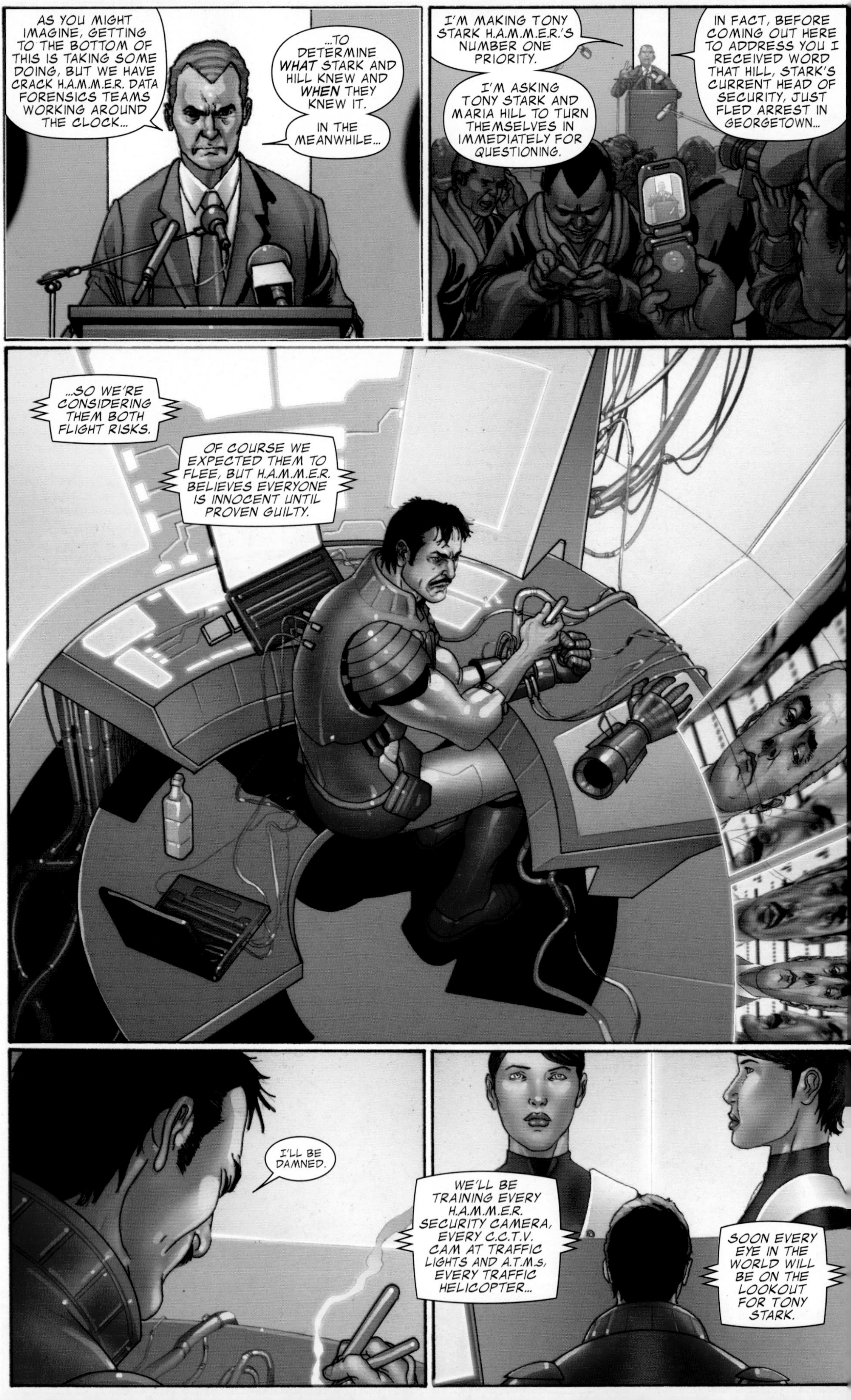
AS YOU MIGHT IMAGINE, GETTING TO THE BOTTOM OF THIS IS TAKING SOME DOING, BUT WE HAVE CRACK H.A.M.M.E.R. DATA FORENSICS TEAMS WORKING AROUND THE CLOCK...
...TO DETERMINE WHAT STARK AND HILL KNEW AND WHEN THEY KNEW IT.
IN THE MEANWHILE...
I'M MAKING TONY STARK H.A.M.M.E.R.'S NUMBER ONE PRIORITY.
I'M ASKING TONY STARK AND MARIA HILL TO TURN THEMSELVES IN IMMEDIATELY FOR QUESTIONING.
IN FACT, BEFORE COMING OUT HERE TO ADDRESS YOU I RECEIVED WORD THAT HILL, STARK'S CURRENT HEAD OF SECURITY, JUST FLED ARREST IN GEORGETOWN...
...SO WE'RE CONSIDERING THEM BOTH FLIGHT RISKS.
OF COURSE WE EXPECTED THEM TO FLEE, BUT H.A.M.M.E.R. BELIEVES EVERYONE IS INNOCENT UNTIL PROVEN GUILTY.
I'LL BE DAMNED.
WE'LL BE TRAINING EVERY H.A.M.M.E.R. SECURITY CAMERA, EVERY C.C.T.V. CAM AT TRAFFIC LIGHTS AND A.T.M.s, EVERY TRAFFIC HELICOPTER...
SOON EVERY EYE IN THE WORLD WILL BE ON THE LOOKOUT FOR TONY STARK.

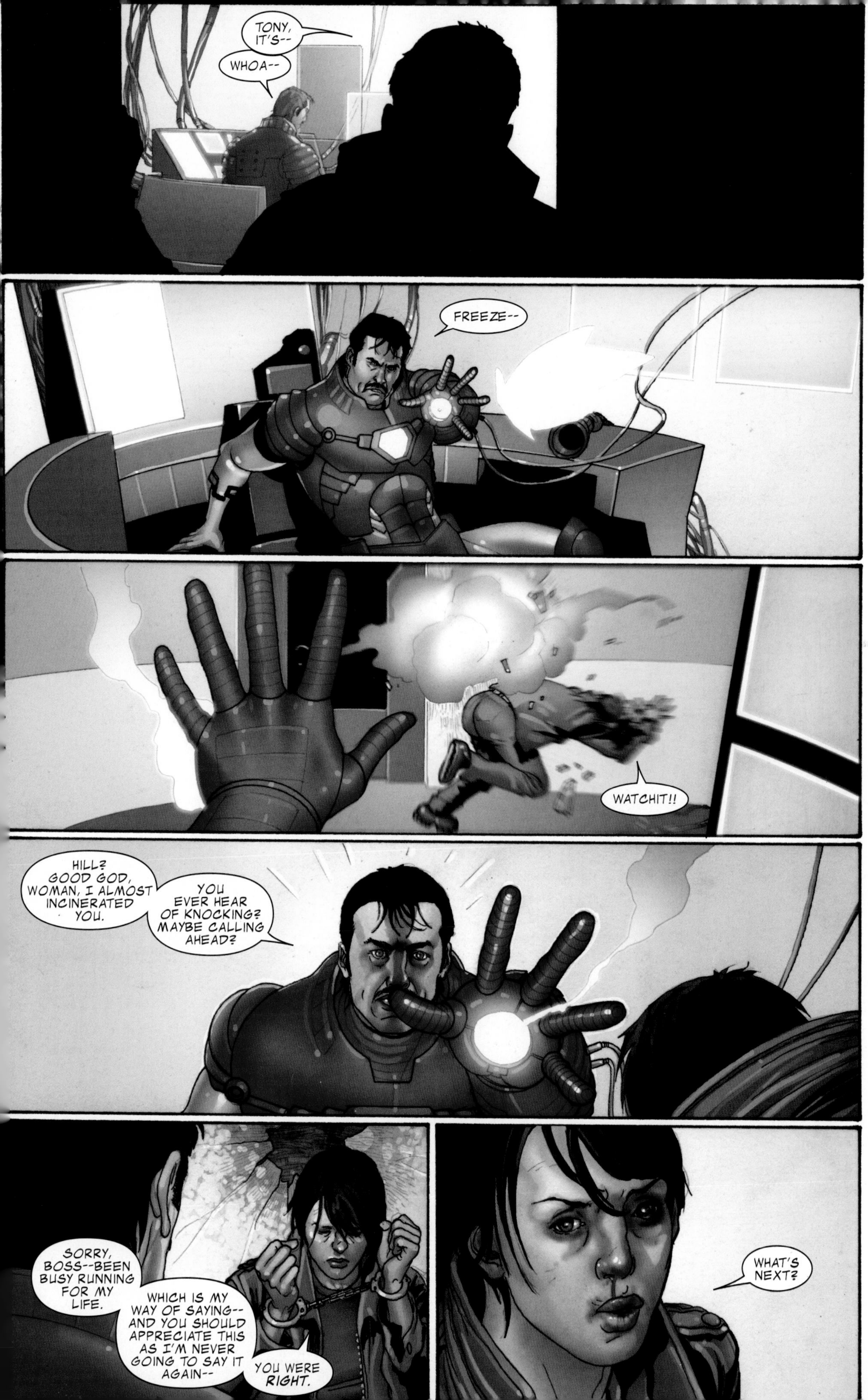
TONY, IT'S--
WHOA--
FREEZE--
WATCHIT!!
HILL? GOOD GOD, WOMAN, I ALMOST INCINERATED YOU.
YOU EVER HEAR OF KNOCKING? MAYBE CALLING AHEAD?
SORRY, BOSS--BEEN BUSY RUNNING FOR MY LIFE.
WHICH IS MY WAY OF SAYING-- AND YOU SHOULD APPRECIATE THIS AS I'M NEVER GOING TO SAY IT AGAIN--
YOU WERE RIGHT.
WHAT'S NEXT?

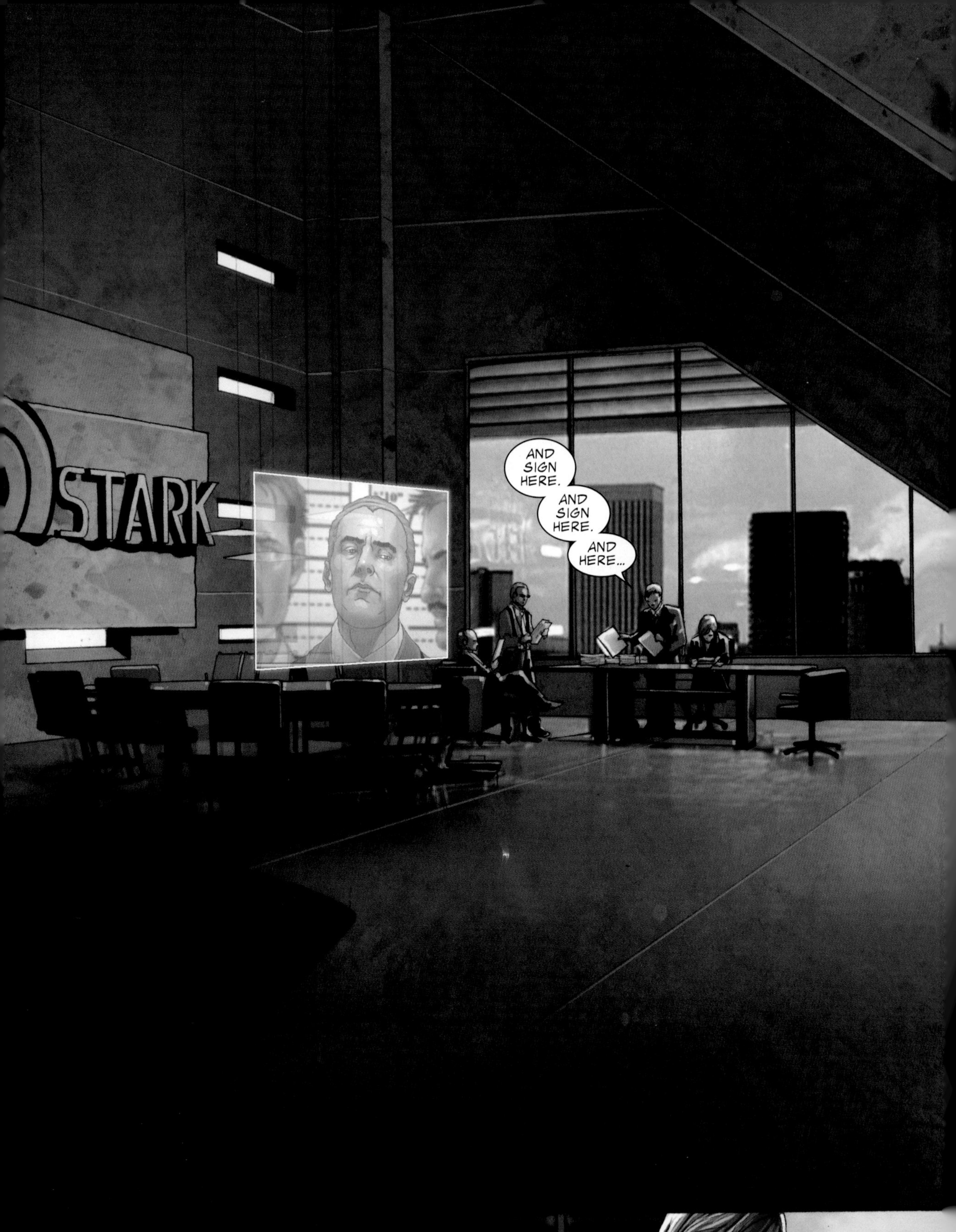
STARK
AND SIGN HERE.
AND SIGN HERE.
AND HERE...

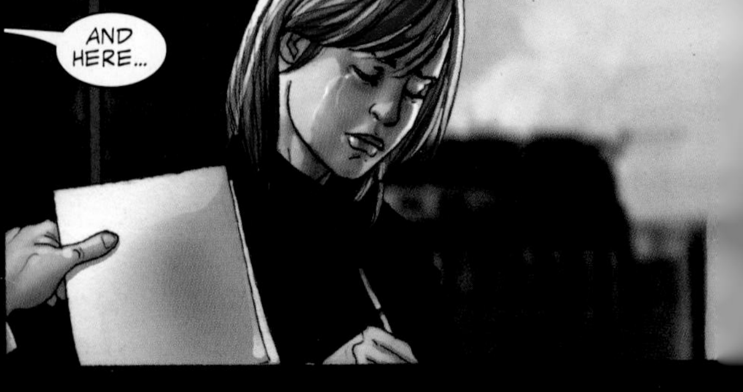
AND HERE...

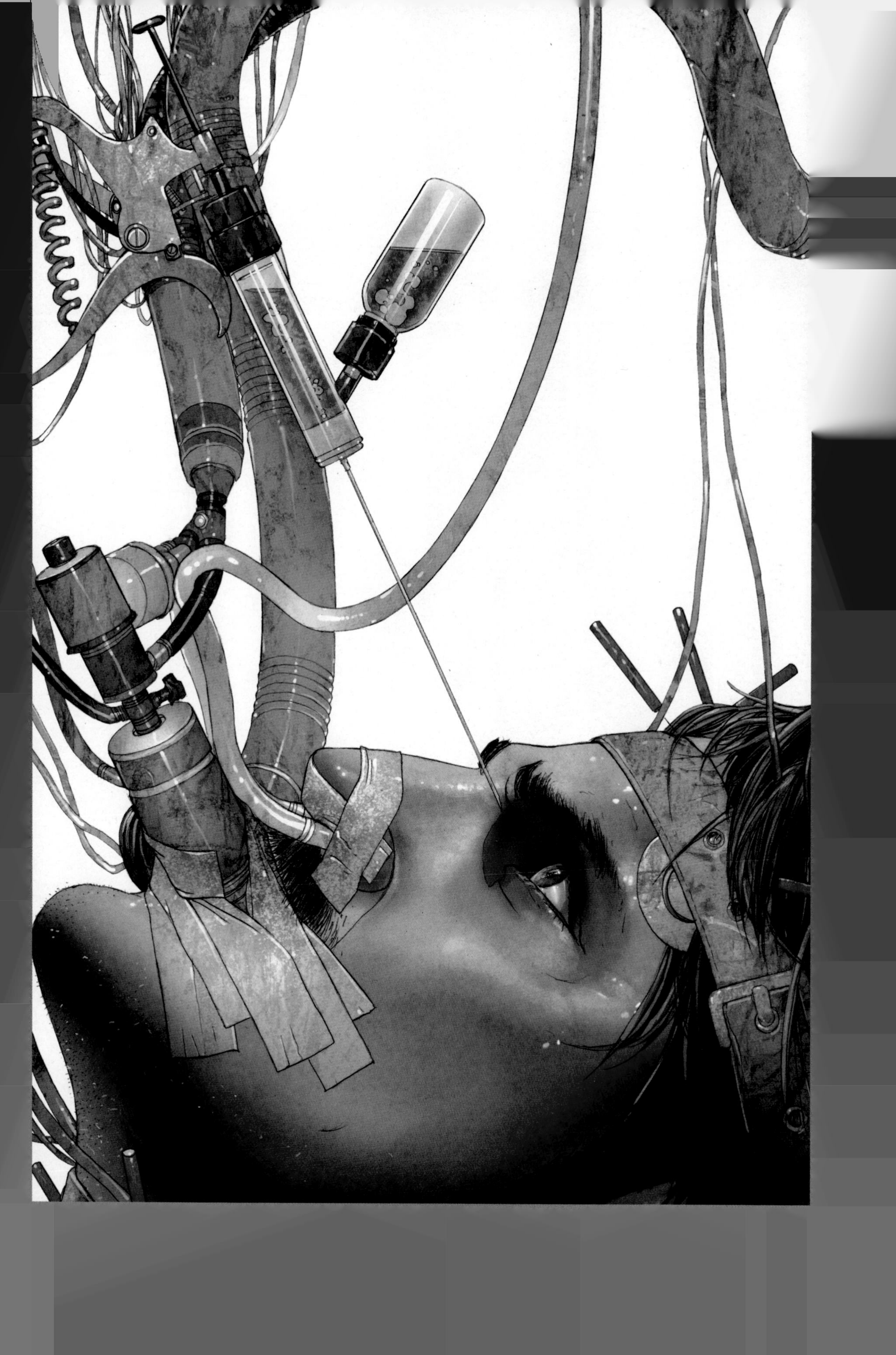

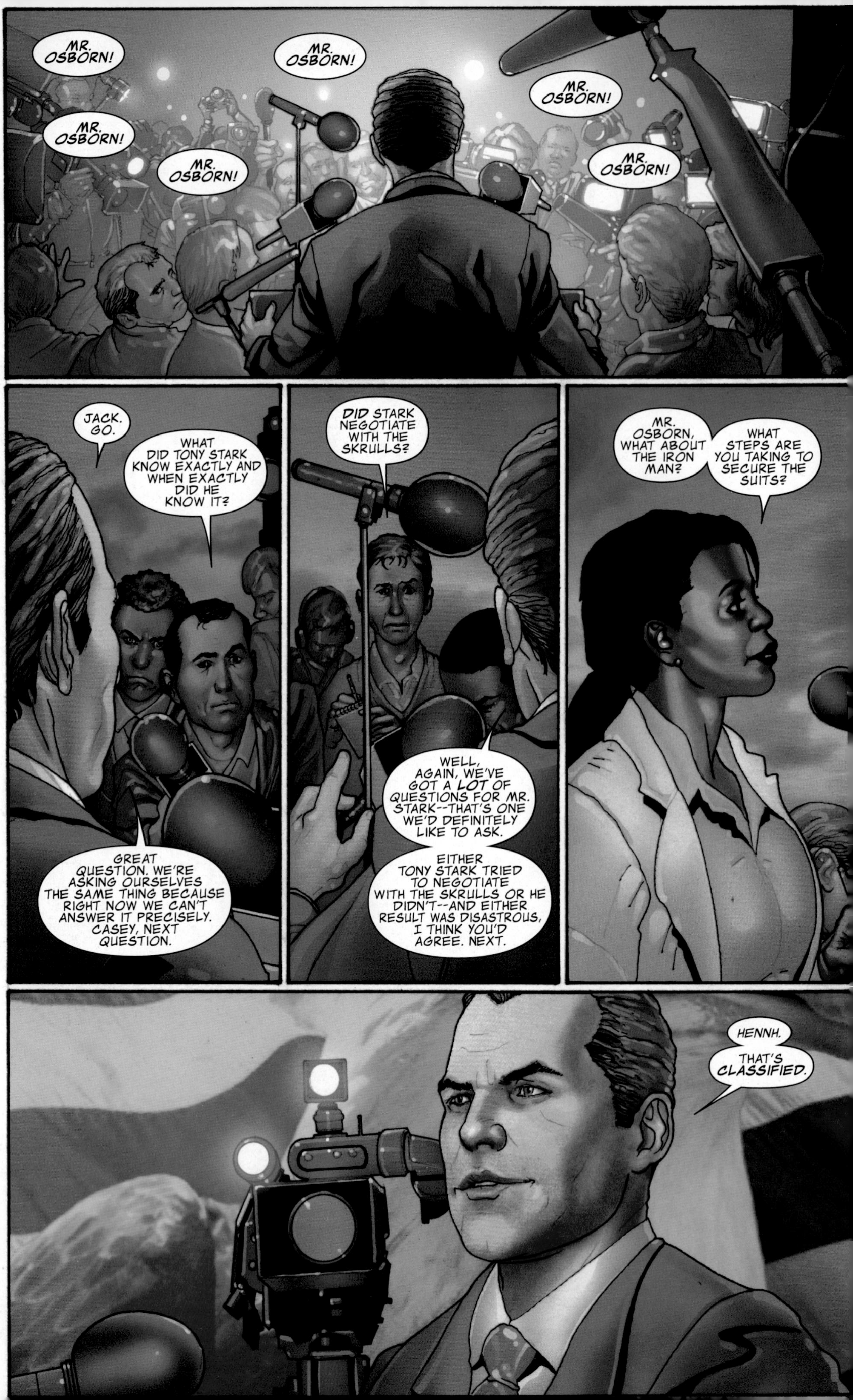
MR. OSBORN!
MR. OSBORN!
MR. OSBORN!
MR. OSBORN!
MR. OSBORN!
MR. OSBORN!
JACK. GO.
WHAT DID TONY STARK KNOW EXACTLY AND WHEN EXACTLY DID HE KNOW IT?
GREAT QUESTION. WE'RE ASKING OURSELVES THE SAME THING BECAUSE RIGHT NOW WE CAN'T ANSWER IT PRECISELY. CASEY, NEXT QUESTION.
DID STARK NEGOTIATE WITH THE SKRULLS?
WELL, AGAIN, WE'VE GOT A LOT OF QUESTIONS FOR MR. STARK--THAT'S ONE WE'D DEFINITELY LIKE TO ASK.
EITHER TONY STARK TRIED TO NEGOTIATE WITH THE SKRULLS OR HE DIDN'T--AND EITHER RESULT WAS DISASTROUS, I THINK YOU'D AGREE. NEXT.
MR. OSBORN, WHAT ABOUT THE IRON MAN?
WHAT STEPS ARE YOU TAKING TO SECURE THE SUITS?
HENNH.
THAT'S CLASSIFIED.

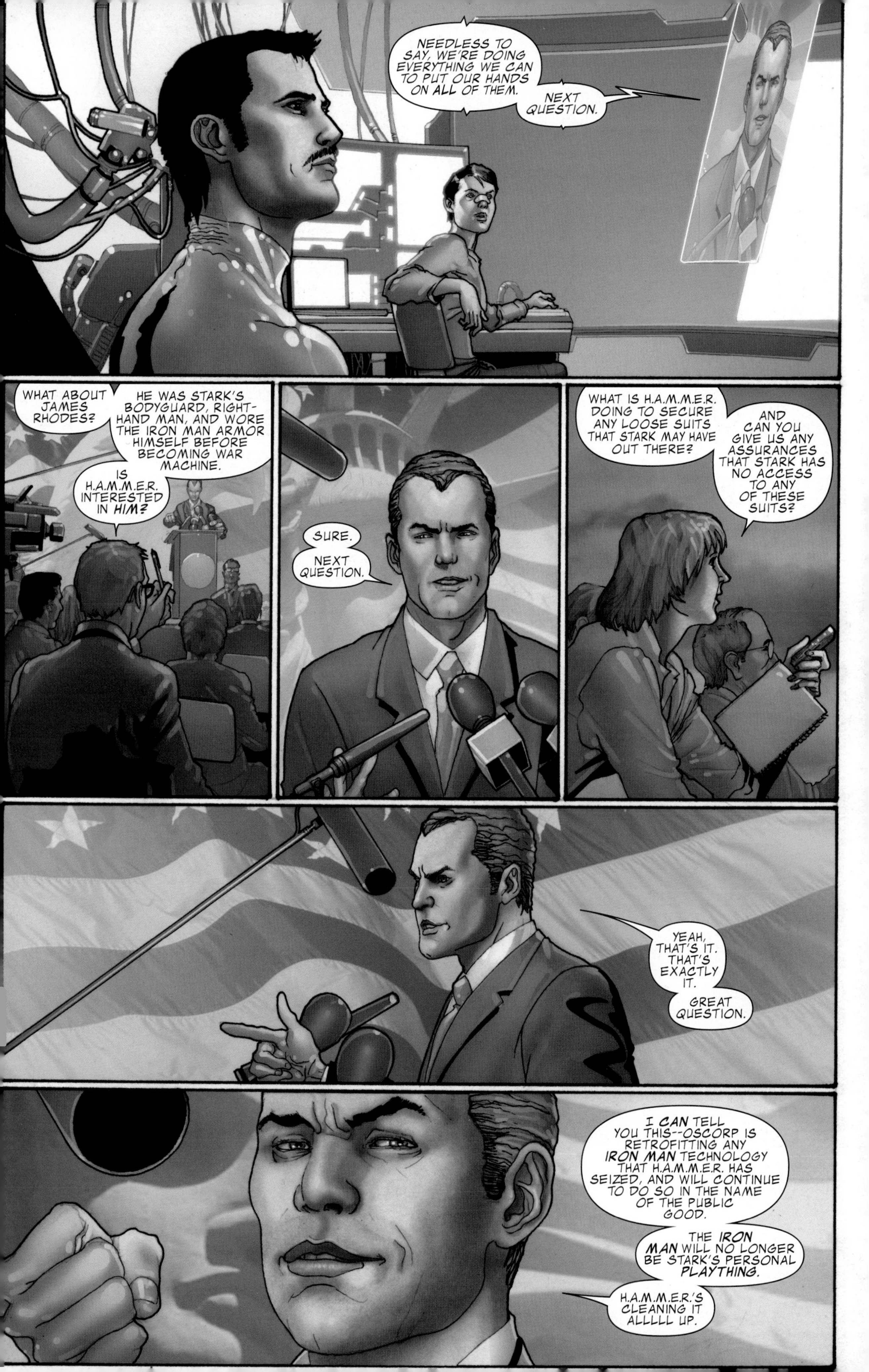
NEEDLESS TO SAY, WE'RE DOING EVERYTHING WE CAN TO PUT OUR HANDS ON ALL OF THEM.
NEXT QUESTION.
WHAT ABOUT JAMES RHODES?
HE WAS STARK'S BODYGUARD, RIGHT-HAND MAN, AND WORE THE IRON MAN ARMOR HIMSELF BEFORE BECOMING WAR MACHINE.
IS H.A.M.M.E.R. INTERESTED IN HIM?
SURE.
NEXT QUESTION.
WHAT IS H.A.M.M.E.R. DOING TO SECURE ANY LOOSE SUITS THAT STARK MAY HAVE OUT THERE?
AND CAN YOU GIVE US ANY ASSURANCES THAT STARK HAS NO ACCESS TO ANY OF THESE SUITS?
YEAH, THAT'S IT. THAT'S EXACTLY IT.
GREAT QUESTION.
I CAN TELL YOU THIS--OSCORP IS RETROFITTING ANY IRON MAN TECHNOLOGY THAT H.A.M.M.E.R. HAS SEIZED, AND WILL CONTINUE TO DO SO IN THE NAME OF THE PUBLIC GOOD.
THE IRON MAN WILL NO LONGER BE STARK'S PERSONAL PLAYTHING.
H.A.M.M.E.R.'S CLEANING IT ALLLLL UP.

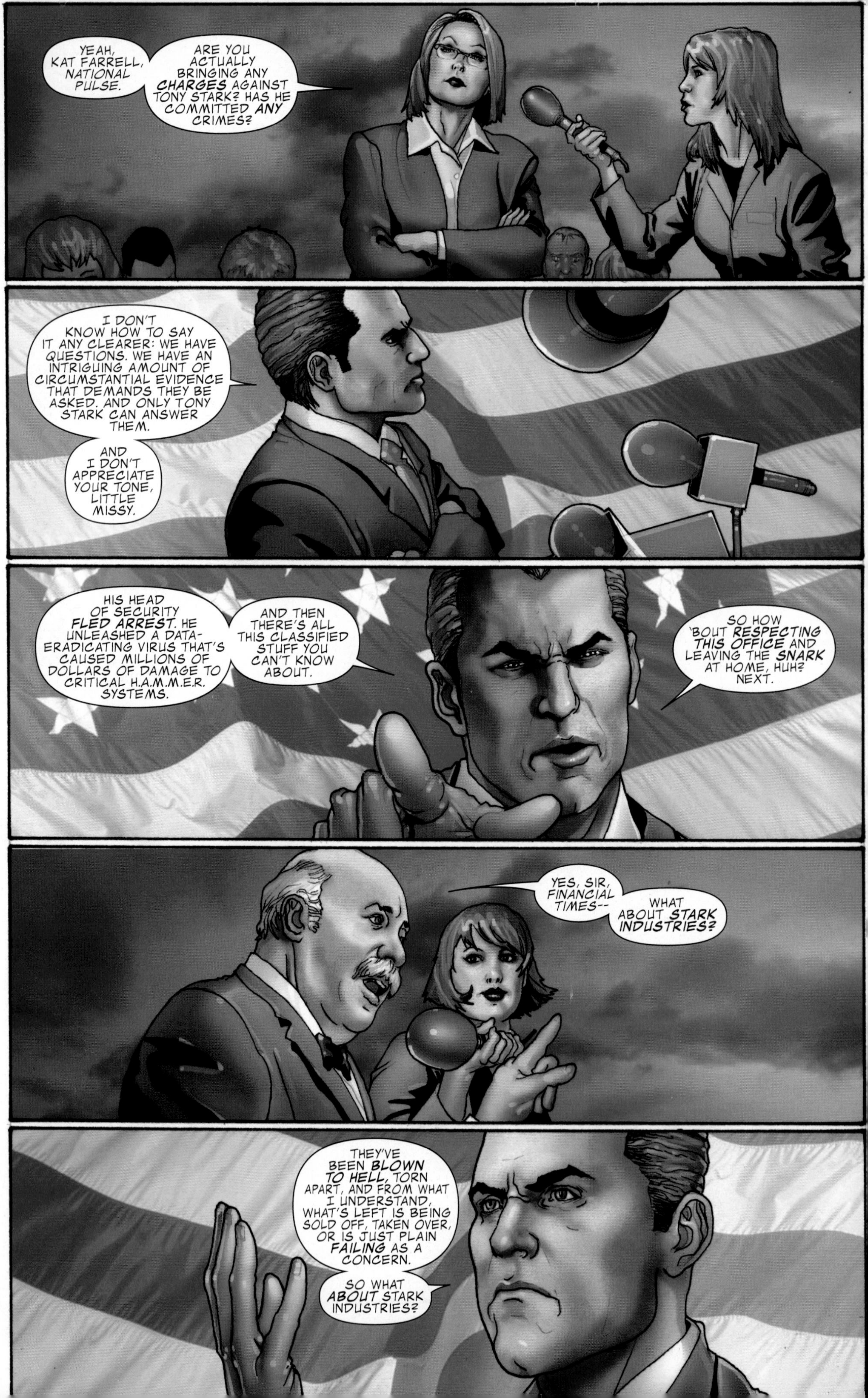
YEAH, KAT FARRELL, NATIONAL PULSE.
ARE YOU ACTUALLY BRINGING ANY CHARGES AGAINST TONY STARK? HAS HE COMMITTED ANY CRIMES?
I DON'T KNOW HOW TO SAY IT ANY CLEARER: WE HAVE QUESTIONS. WE HAVE AN INTRIGUING AMOUNT OF CIRCUMSTANTIAL EVIDENCE THAT DEMANDS THEY BE ASKED. AND ONLY TONY STARK CAN ANSWER THEM.
AND I DON'T APPRECIATE YOUR TONE, LITTLE MISSY.
HIS HEAD OF SECURITY FLED ARREST. HE UNLEASHED A DATA-ERADICATING VIRUS THAT'S CAUSED MILLIONS OF DOLLARS OF DAMAGE TO CRITICAL H.A.M.M.E.R. SYSTEMS.
AND THEN THERE'S ALL THIS CLASSIFIED STUFF YOU CAN'T KNOW ABOUT.
SO HOW 'BOUT RESPECTING THIS OFFICE AND LEAVING THE SNARK AT HOME, HUH? NEXT.
YES, SIR, FINANCIAL TIMES--
WHAT ABOUT STARK INDUSTRIES?
THEY'VE BEEN BLOWN TO HELL, TORN APART, AND FROM WHAT I UNDERSTAND, WHAT'S LEFT IS BEING SOLD OFF, TAKEN OVER, OR IS JUST PLAIN FAILING AS A CONCERN.
SO WHAT ABOUT STARK INDUSTRIES?

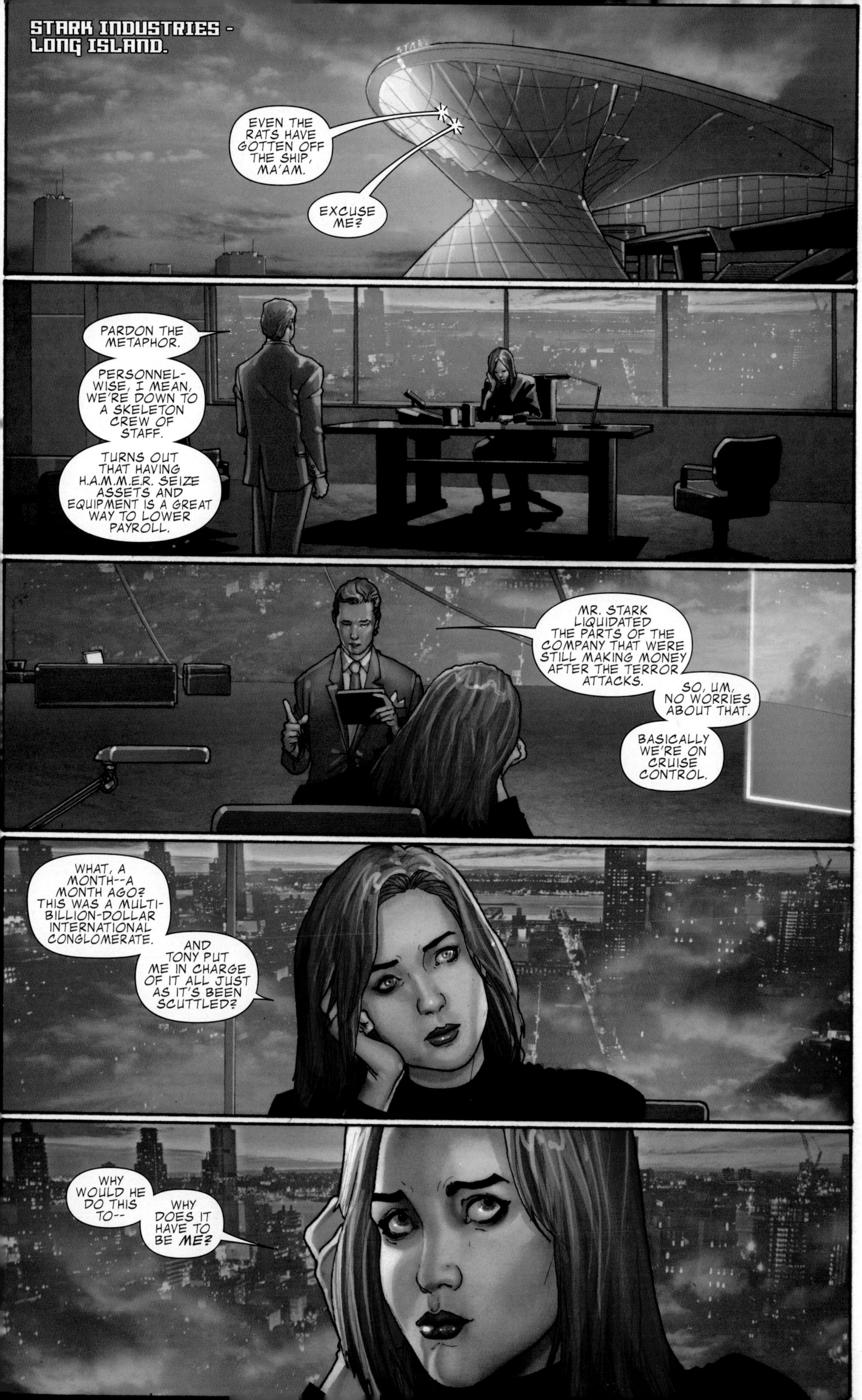
STARK INDUSTRIES - LONG ISLAND.
EVEN THE RATS HAVE GOTTEN OFF THE SHIP, MA'AM.
EXCUSE ME?
PARDON THE METAPHOR.
PERSONNEL-WISE, I MEAN, WE'RE DOWN TO A SKELETON CREW OF STAFF.
TURNS OUT THAT HAVING H.A.M.M.E.R. SEIZE ASSETS AND EQUIPMENT IS A GREAT WAY TO LOWER PAYROLL.
MR. STARK LIQUIDATED THE PARTS OF THE COMPANY THAT WERE STILL MAKING MONEY AFTER THE TERROR ATTACKS.
SO, UM, NO WORRIES ABOUT THAT.
BASICALLY WE'RE ON CRUISE CONTROL.
WHAT, A MONTH--A MONTH AGO? THIS WAS A MULTI-BILLION-DOLLAR INTERNATIONAL CONGLOMERATE.
AND TONY PUT ME IN CHARGE OF IT ALL JUST AS IT'S BEEN SCUTTLED?
WHY WOULD HE DO THIS TO--
WHY DOES IT HAVE TO BE *ME*?

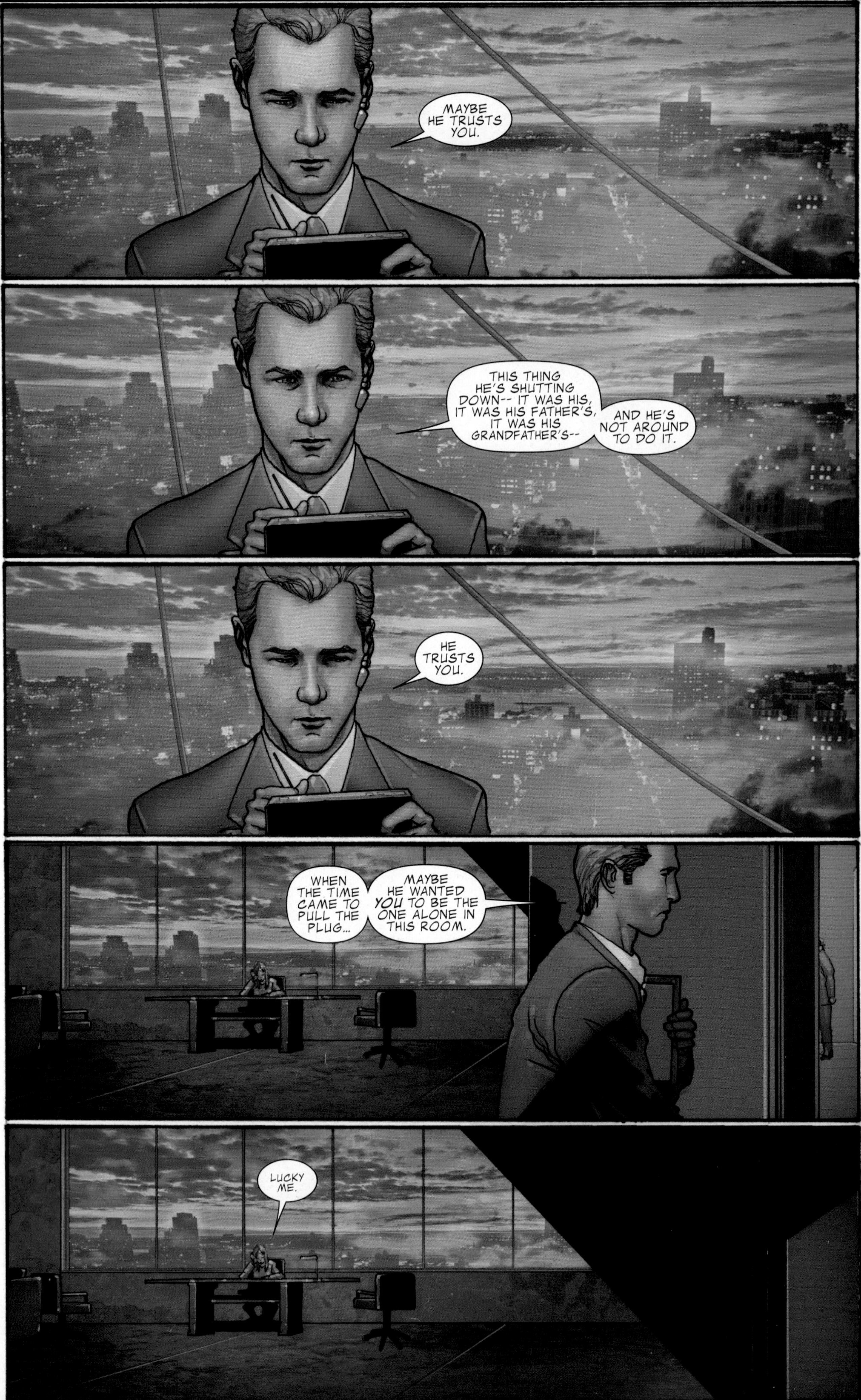
MAYBE HE TRUSTS YOU.
THIS THING HE'S SHUTTING DOWN-- IT WAS HIS, IT WAS HIS FATHER'S, IT WAS HIS GRANDFATHER'S--
AND HE'S NOT AROUND TO DO IT.
HE TRUSTS YOU.
WHEN THE TIME CAME TO PULL THE PLUG...
MAYBE HE WANTED YOU TO BE THE ONE ALONE IN THIS ROOM.
LUCKY ME.

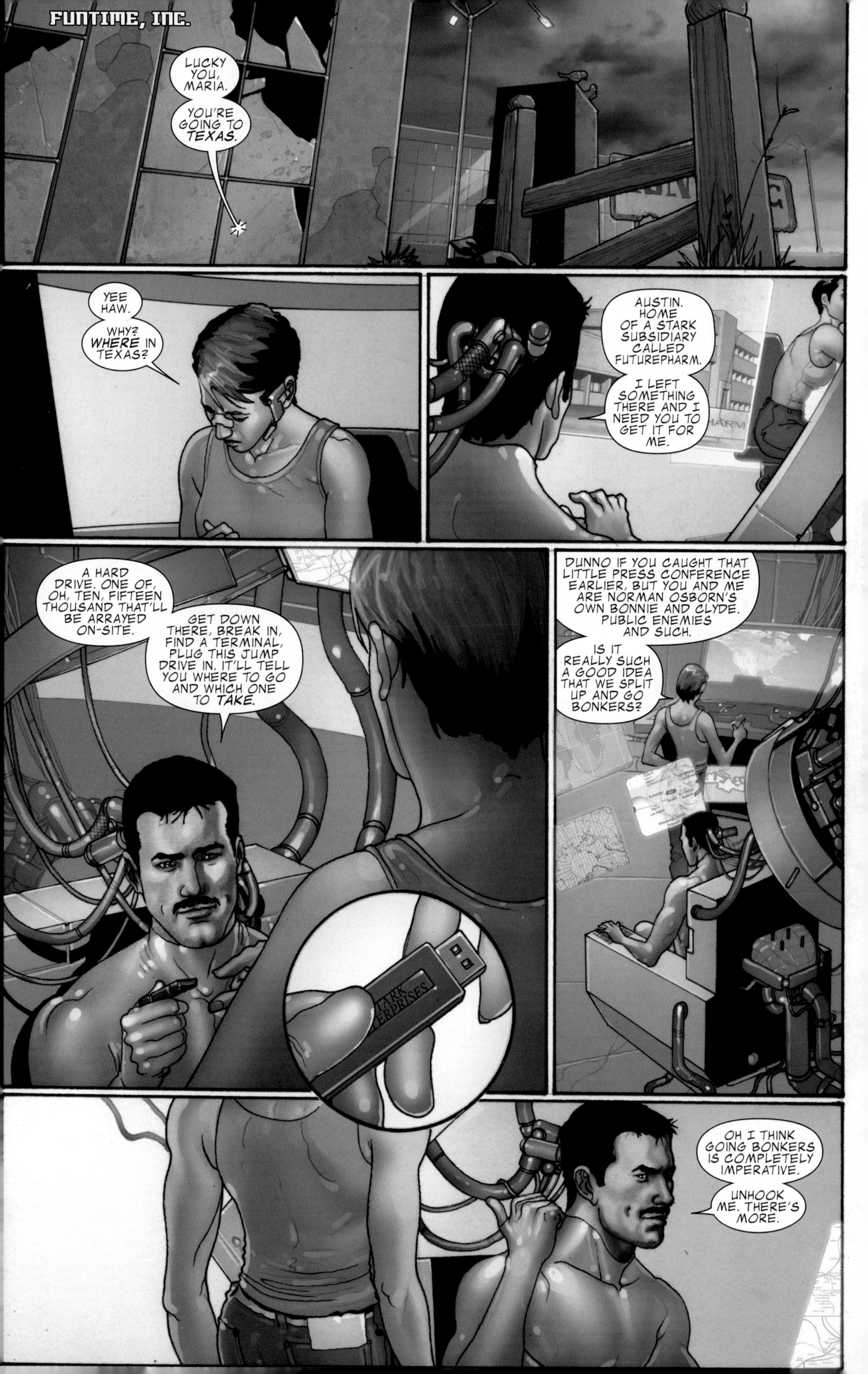
FUNTIME, INC.
LUCKY YOU, MARIA.
YOU'RE GOING TO TEXAS.
YEE HAW.
WHY? WHERE IN TEXAS?
AUSTIN. HOME OF A STARK SUBSIDIARY CALLED FUTUREPHARM.
I LEFT SOMETHING THERE AND I NEED YOU TO GET IT FOR ME.
A HARD DRIVE. ONE OF, OH, TEN, FIFTEEN THOUSAND THAT'LL BE ARRAYED ON-SITE.
GET DOWN THERE, BREAK IN, FIND A TERMINAL, PLUG THIS JUMP DRIVE IN. IT'LL TELL YOU WHERE TO GO AND WHICH ONE TO TAKE.
STARK ENTERPRISES
DUNNO IF YOU CAUGHT THAT LITTLE PRESS CONFERENCE EARLIER, BUT YOU AND ME ARE NORMAN OSBORN'S OWN BONNIE AND CLYDE. PUBLIC ENEMIES AND SUCH.
IS IT REALLY SUCH A GOOD IDEA THAT WE SPLIT UP AND GO BONKERS?
OH I THINK GOING BONKERS IS COMPLETELY IMPERATIVE.
UNHOOK ME. THERE'S MORE.

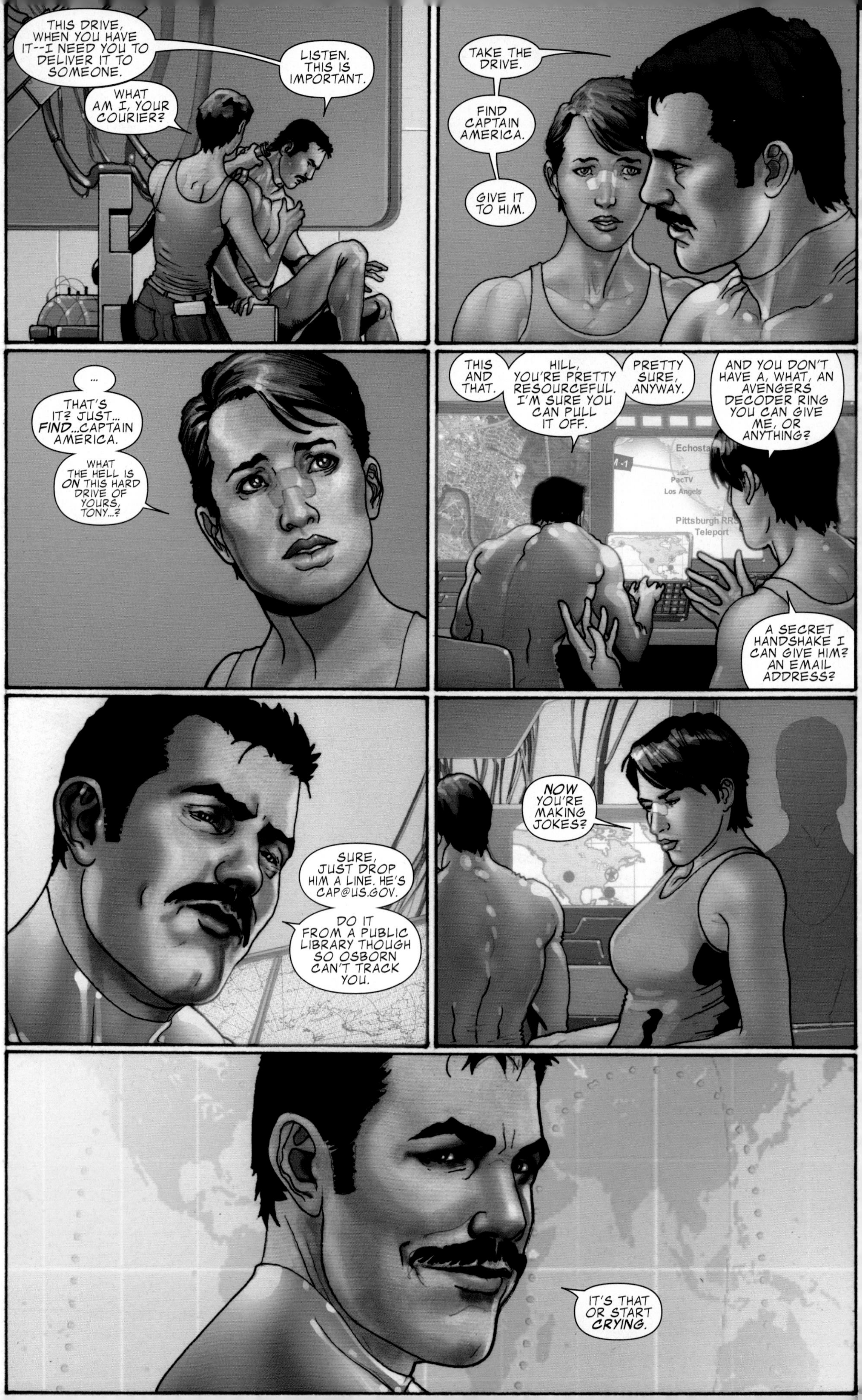
THIS DRIVE, WHEN YOU HAVE IT--I NEED YOU TO DELIVER IT TO SOMEONE.
LISTEN. THIS IS IMPORTANT.
WHAT AM I, YOUR COURIER?
TAKE THE DRIVE.
FIND CAPTAIN AMERICA.
GIVE IT TO HIM.
...
THAT'S IT? JUST... FIND...CAPTAIN AMERICA.
WHAT THE HELL IS ON THIS HARD DRIVE OF YOURS, TONY...?
THIS AND THAT.
HILL, YOU'RE PRETTY RESOURCEFUL. I'M SURE YOU CAN PULL IT OFF.
PRETTY SURE, ANYWAY.
AND YOU DON'T HAVE A, WHAT, AN AVENGERS DECODER RING YOU CAN GIVE ME, OR ANYTHING?
A SECRET HANDSHAKE I CAN GIVE HIM? AN EMAIL ADDRESS?
SURE, JUST DROP HIM A LINE. HE'S CAP@US.GOV.
DO IT FROM A PUBLIC LIBRARY THOUGH SO OSBORN CAN'T TRACK YOU.
NOW YOU'RE MAKING JOKES?
IT'S THAT OR START CRYING.

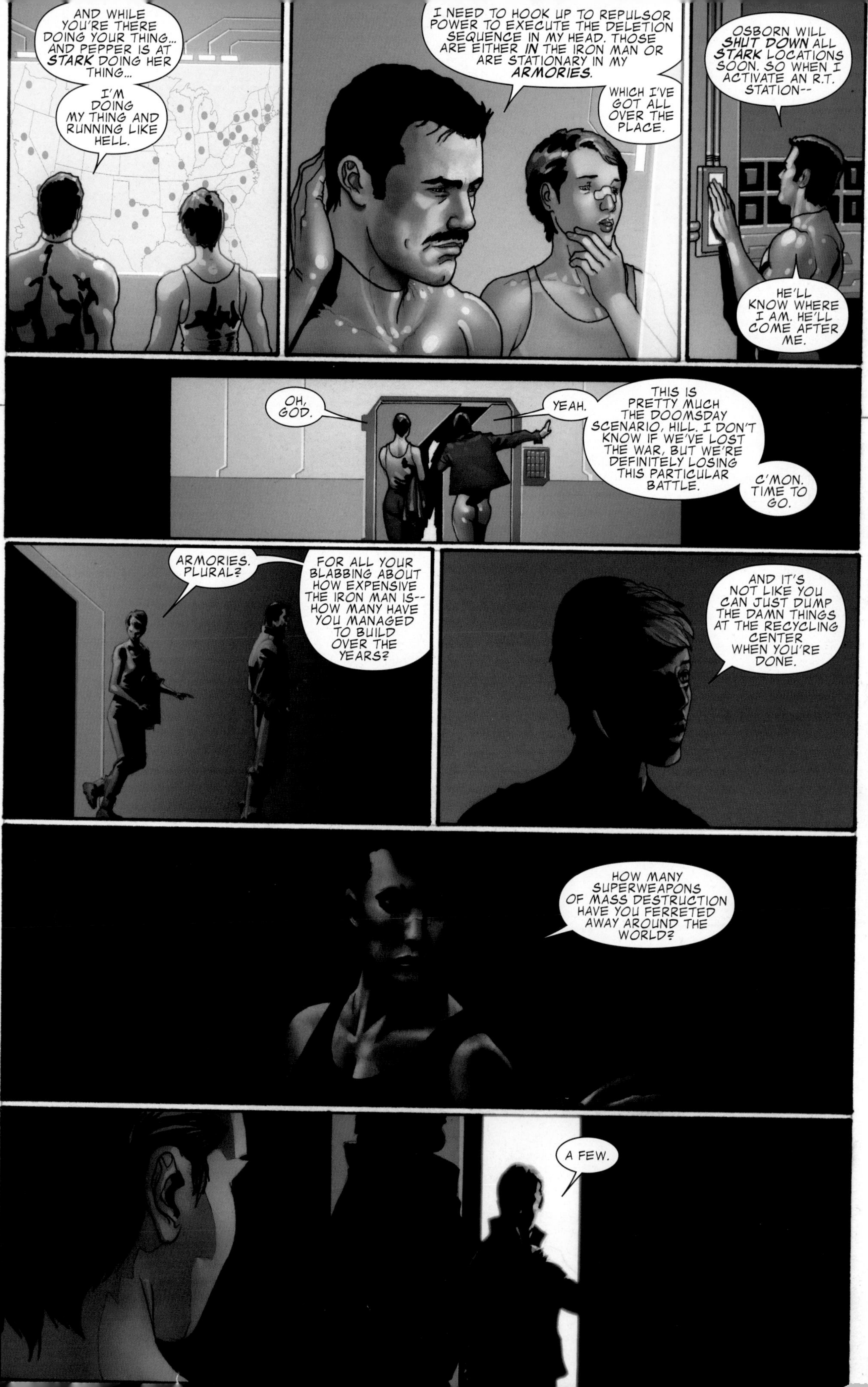
AND WHILE YOU'RE THERE DOING YOUR THING... AND PEPPER IS AT STARK DOING HER THING...
I'M DOING MY THING AND RUNNING LIKE HELL.
I NEED TO HOOK UP TO REPULSOR POWER TO EXECUTE THE DELETION SEQUENCE IN MY HEAD. THOSE ARE EITHER IN THE IRON MAN OR ARE STATIONARY IN MY ARMORIES.
WHICH I'VE GOT ALL OVER THE PLACE.
OSBORN WILL SHUT DOWN ALL STARK LOCATIONS SOON. SO WHEN I ACTIVATE AN R.T. STATION--
HE'LL KNOW WHERE I AM. HE'LL COME AFTER ME.
OH, GOD.
YEAH.
THIS IS PRETTY MUCH THE DOOMSDAY SCENARIO, HILL. I DON'T KNOW IF WE'VE LOST THE WAR, BUT WE'RE DEFINITELY LOSING THIS PARTICULAR BATTLE.
C'MON. TIME TO GO.
ARMORIES. PLURAL?
FOR ALL YOUR BLABBING ABOUT HOW EXPENSIVE THE IRON MAN IS-- HOW MANY HAVE YOU MANAGED TO BUILD OVER THE YEARS?
AND IT'S NOT LIKE YOU CAN JUST DUMP THE DAMN THINGS AT THE RECYCLING CENTER WHEN YOU'RE DONE.
HOW MANY SUPERWEAPONS OF MASS DESTRUCTION HAVE YOU FERRETED AWAY AROUND THE WORLD?
A FEW.

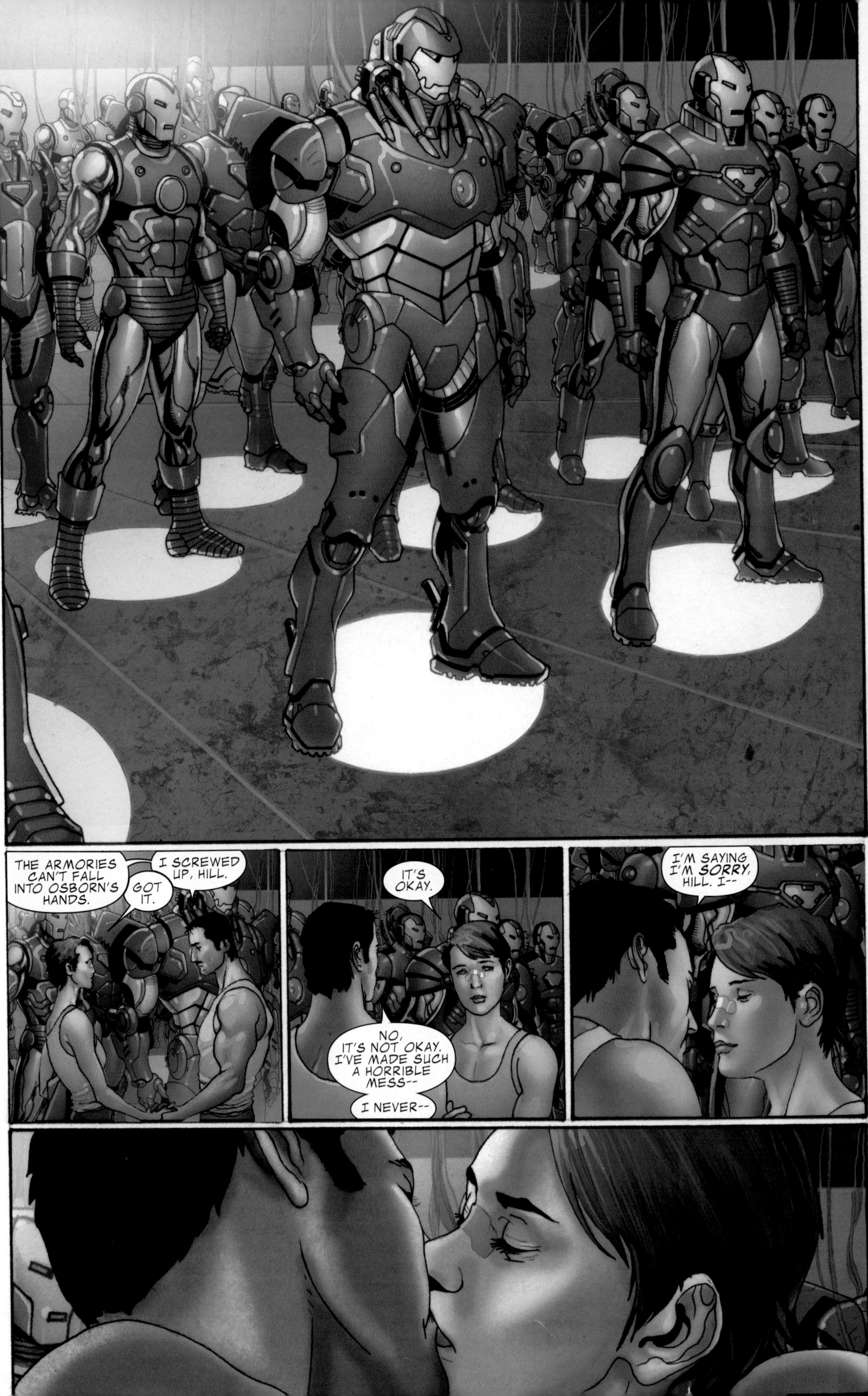
THE ARMORIES CAN'T FALL INTO OSBORN'S HANDS.
GOT IT.
I SCREWED UP, HILL.
IT'S OKAY.
NO, IT'S NOT OKAY. I'VE MADE SUCH A HORRIBLE MESS--
I NEVER--
I'M SAYING I'M SORRY, HILL. I--

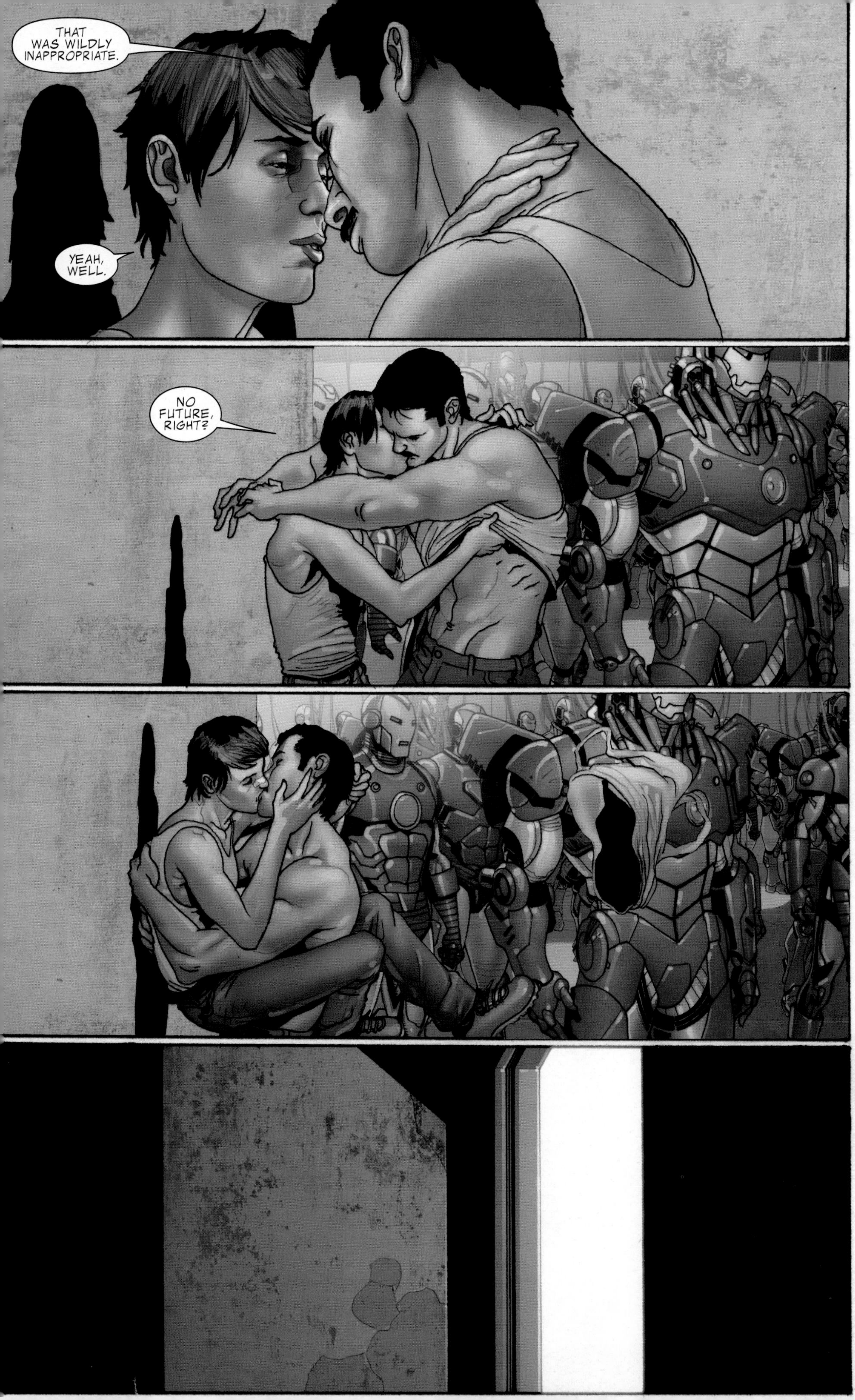
THAT WAS WILDLY INAPPROPRIATE.
YEAH, WELL.
NO FUTURE, RIGHT?

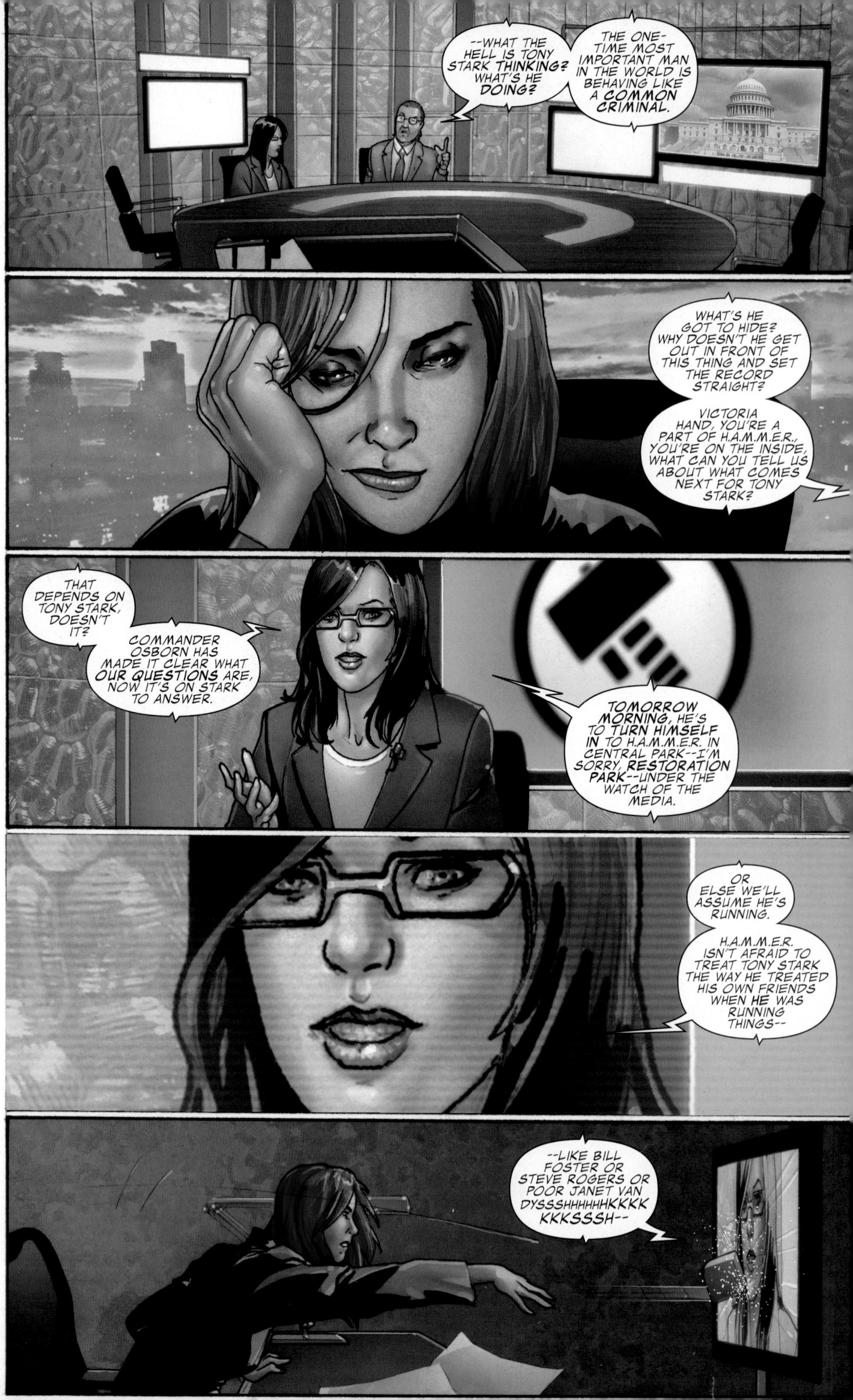
--WHAT THE HELL IS TONY STARK THINKING? WHAT'S HE DOING?
THE ONE-TIME MOST IMPORTANT MAN IN THE WORLD IS BEHAVING LIKE A COMMON CRIMINAL.
WHAT'S HE GOT TO HIDE? WHY DOESN'T HE GET OUT IN FRONT OF THIS THING AND SET THE RECORD STRAIGHT?
VICTORIA HAND, YOU'RE A PART OF H.A.M.M.E.R., YOU'RE ON THE INSIDE, WHAT CAN YOU TELL US ABOUT WHAT COMES NEXT FOR TONY STARK?
THAT DEPENDS ON TONY STARK, DOESN'T IT?
COMMANDER OSBORN HAS MADE IT CLEAR WHAT OUR QUESTIONS ARE, NOW IT'S ON STARK TO ANSWER.
TOMORROW MORNING, HE'S TO TURN HIMSELF IN TO H.A.M.M.E.R. IN CENTRAL PARK--I'M SORRY, RESTORATION PARK--UNDER THE WATCH OF THE MEDIA.
OR ELSE WE'LL ASSUME HE'S RUNNING.
H.A.M.M.E.R. ISN'T AFRAID TO TREAT TONY STARK THE WAY HE TREATED HIS OWN FRIENDS WHEN HE WAS RUNNING THINGS--
--LIKE BILL FOSTER OR STEVE ROGERS OR POOR JANET VAN DYSSSHHHHHHKKKK KKKSSSH--

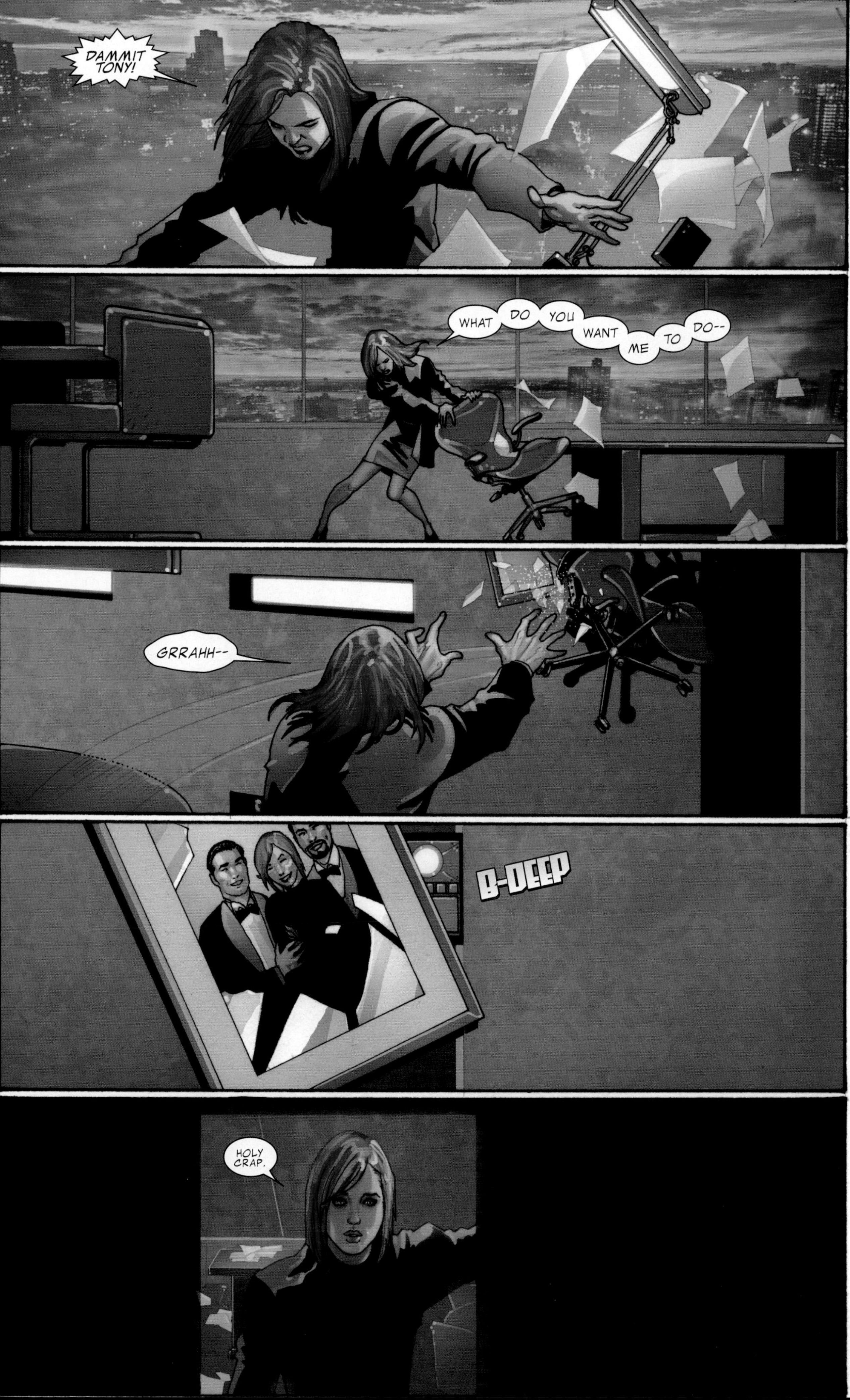
DAMMIT TONY!
WHAT DO YOU WANT ME TO DO--
GRRAHH--
B-DEEP
HOLY CRAP.

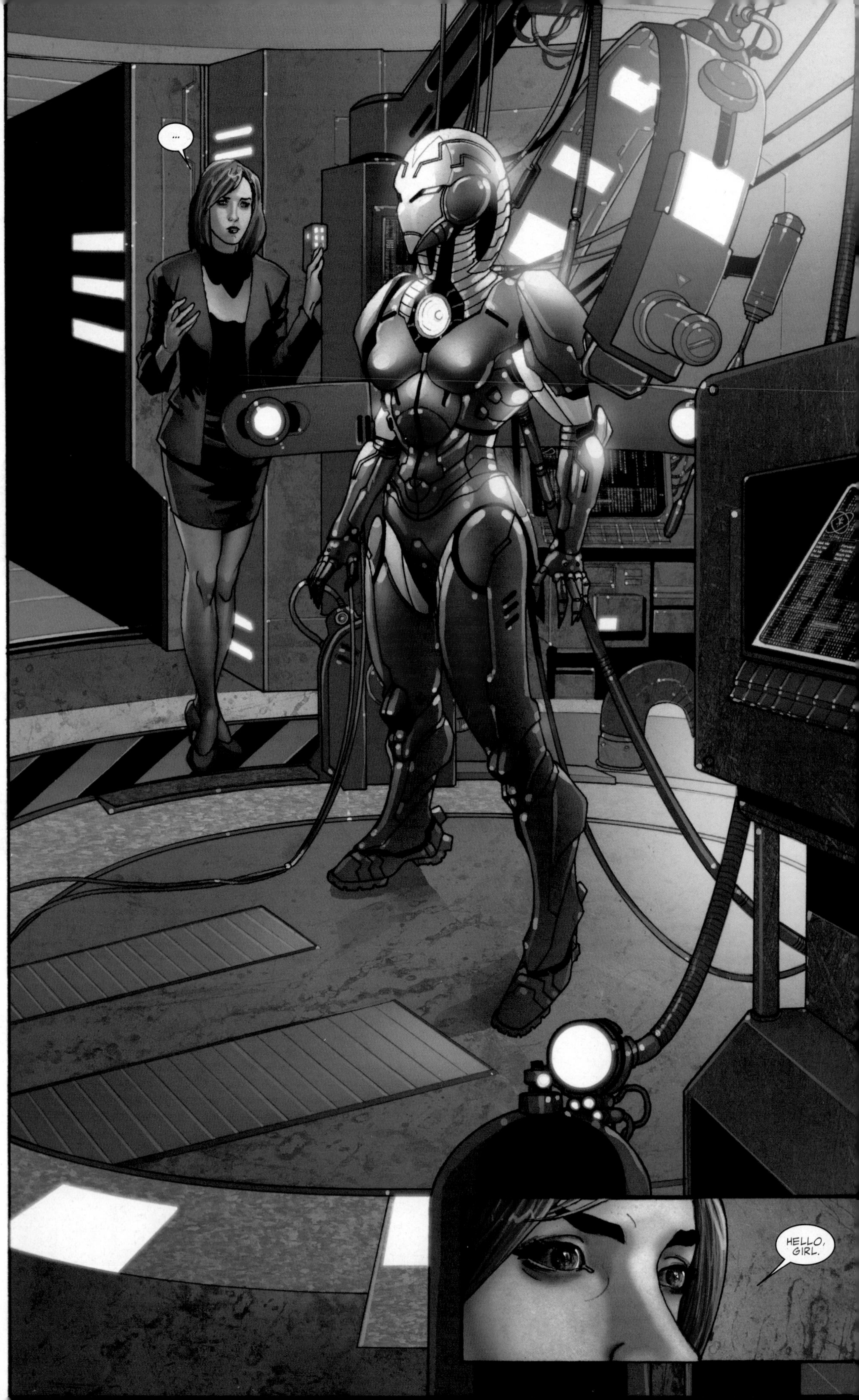
...
HELLO, GIRL.

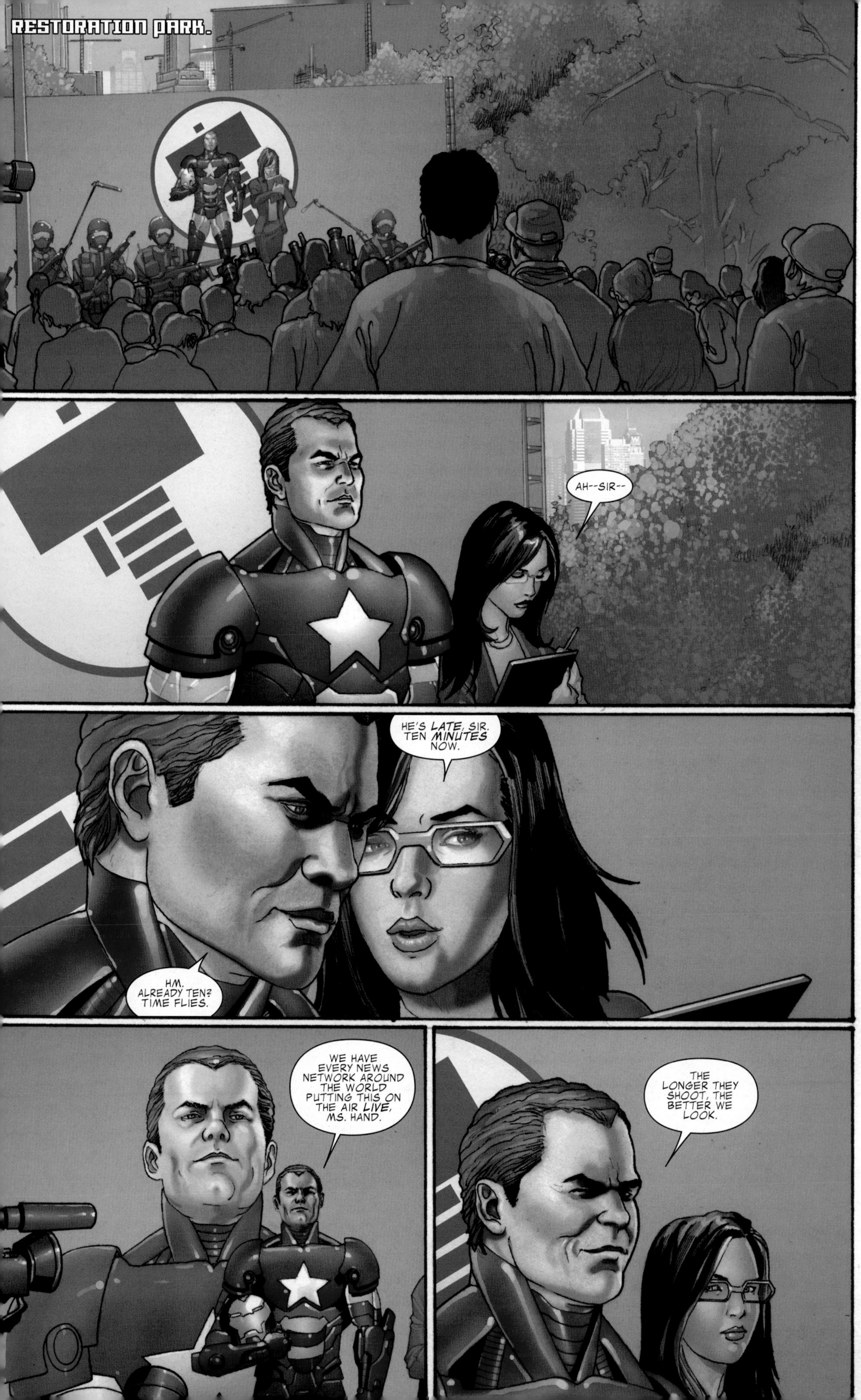
RESTORATION PARK.
AH--SIR--
HE'S LATE, SIR. TEN MINUTES NOW.
HM. ALREADY TEN? TIME FLIES.
WE HAVE EVERY NEWS NETWORK AROUND THE WORLD PUTTING THIS ON THE AIR LIVE, MS. HAND.
THE LONGER THEY SHOOT, THE BETTER WE LOOK.

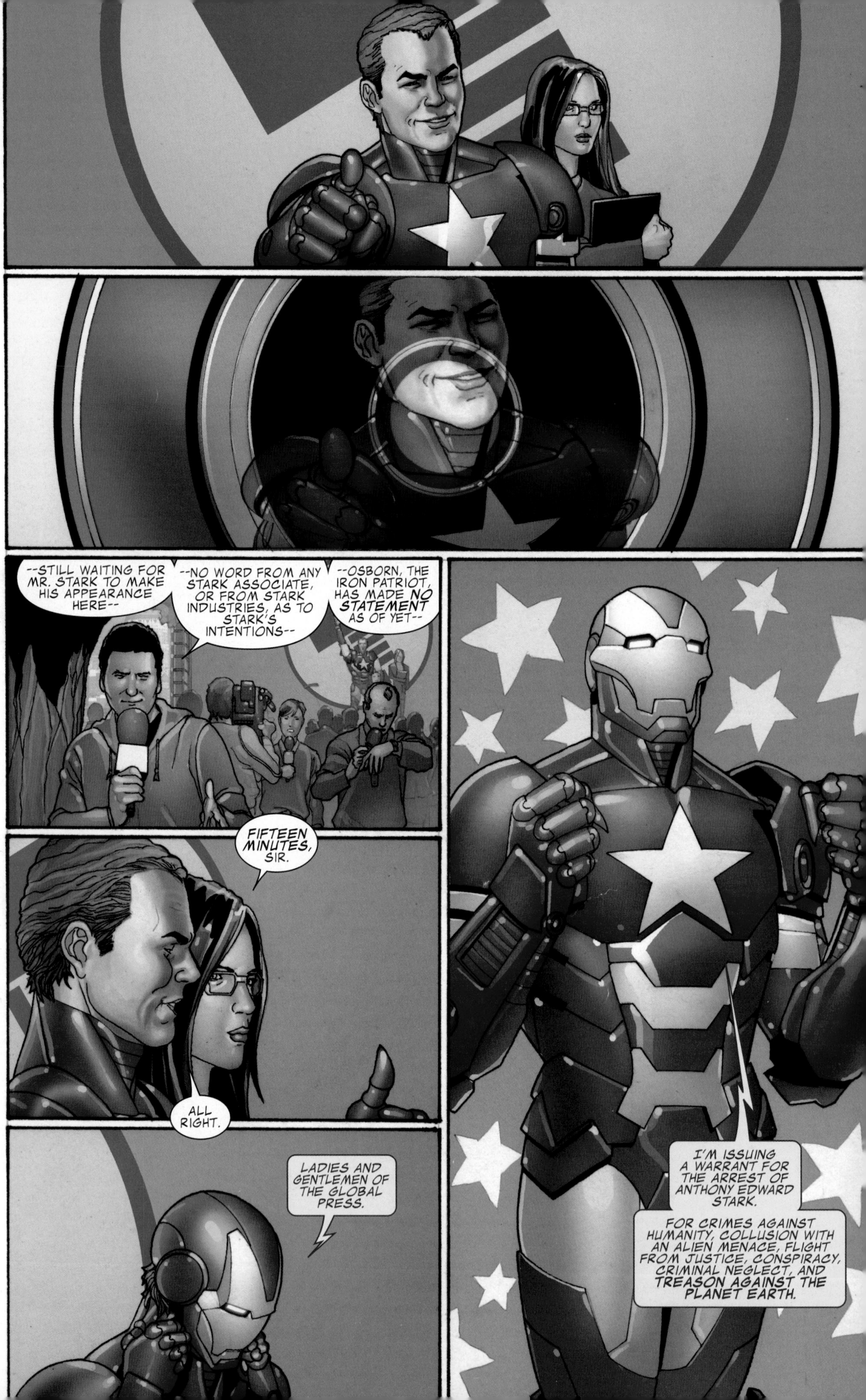
--STILL WAITING FOR MR. STARK TO MAKE HIS APPEARANCE HERE--
--NO WORD FROM ANY STARK ASSOCIATE, OR FROM STARK INDUSTRIES, AS TO STARK'S INTENTIONS--
--OSBORN, THE IRON PATRIOT, HAS MADE NO STATEMENT AS OF YET--
FIFTEEN MINUTES, SIR.
ALL RIGHT.
LADIES AND GENTLEMEN OF THE GLOBAL PRESS.
I'M ISSUING A WARRANT FOR THE ARREST OF ANTHONY EDWARD STARK.
FOR CRIMES AGAINST HUMANITY, COLLUSION WITH AN ALIEN MENACE, FLIGHT FROM JUSTICE, CONSPIRACY, CRIMINAL NEGLECT, AND TREASON AGAINST THE PLANET EARTH.

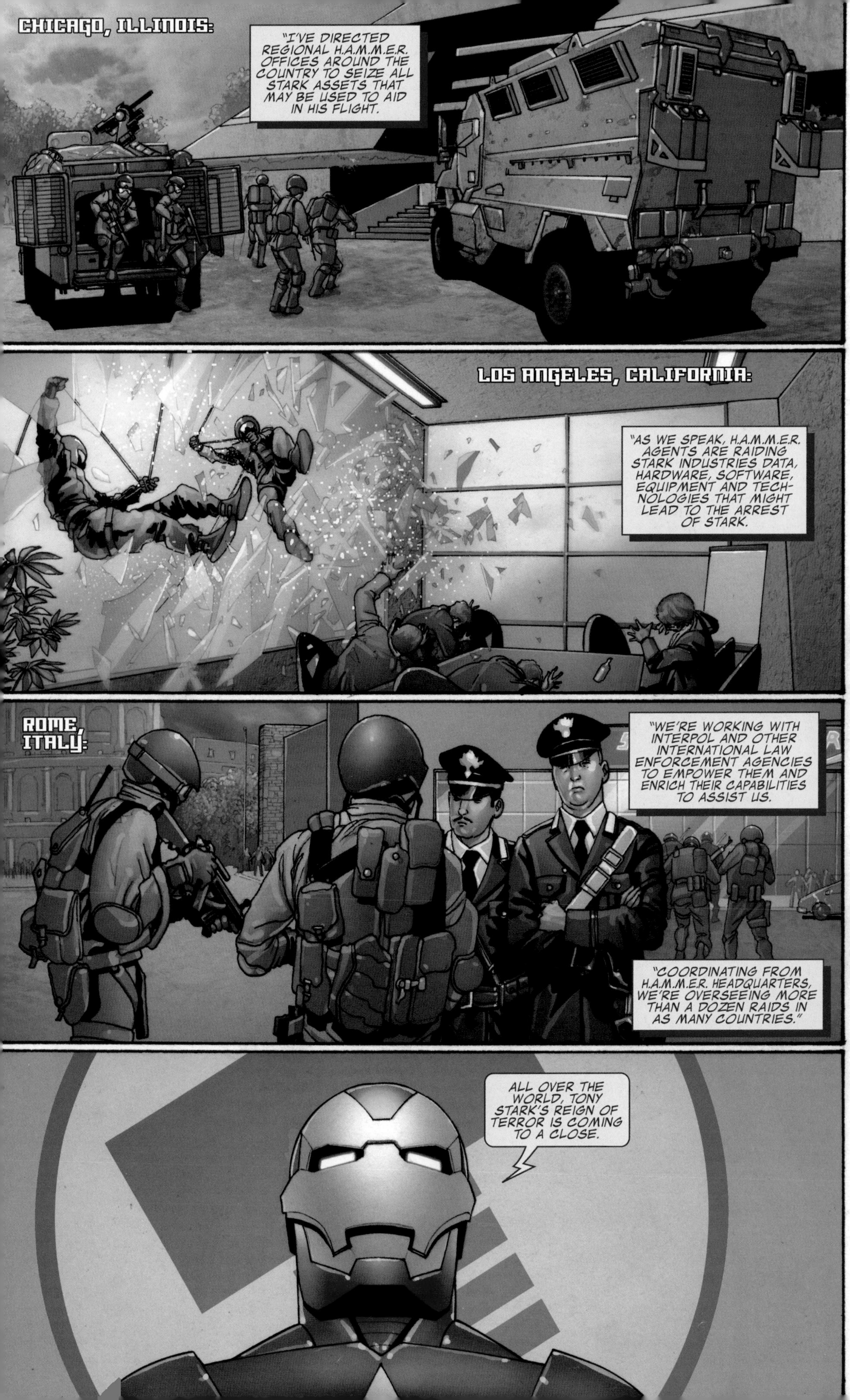
CHICAGO, ILLINOIS:
"I'VE DIRECTED REGIONAL H.A.M.M.E.R. OFFICES AROUND THE COUNTRY TO SEIZE ALL STARK ASSETS THAT MAY BE USED TO AID IN HIS FLIGHT.
LOS ANGELES, CALIFORNIA:
"AS WE SPEAK, H.A.M.M.E.R. AGENTS ARE RAIDING STARK INDUSTRIES DATA, HARDWARE, SOFTWARE, EQUIPMENT AND TECHNOLOGIES THAT MIGHT LEAD TO THE ARREST OF STARK.
ROME, ITALY:
"WE'RE WORKING WITH INTERPOL AND OTHER INTERNATIONAL LAW ENFORCEMENT AGENCIES TO EMPOWER THEM AND ENRICH THEIR CAPABILITIES TO ASSIST US.
"COORDINATING FROM H.A.M.M.E.R. HEADQUARTERS, WE'RE OVERSEEING MORE THAN A DOZEN RAIDS IN AS MANY COUNTRIES."
ALL OVER THE WORLD, TONY STARK'S REIGN OF TERROR IS COMING TO A CLOSE.

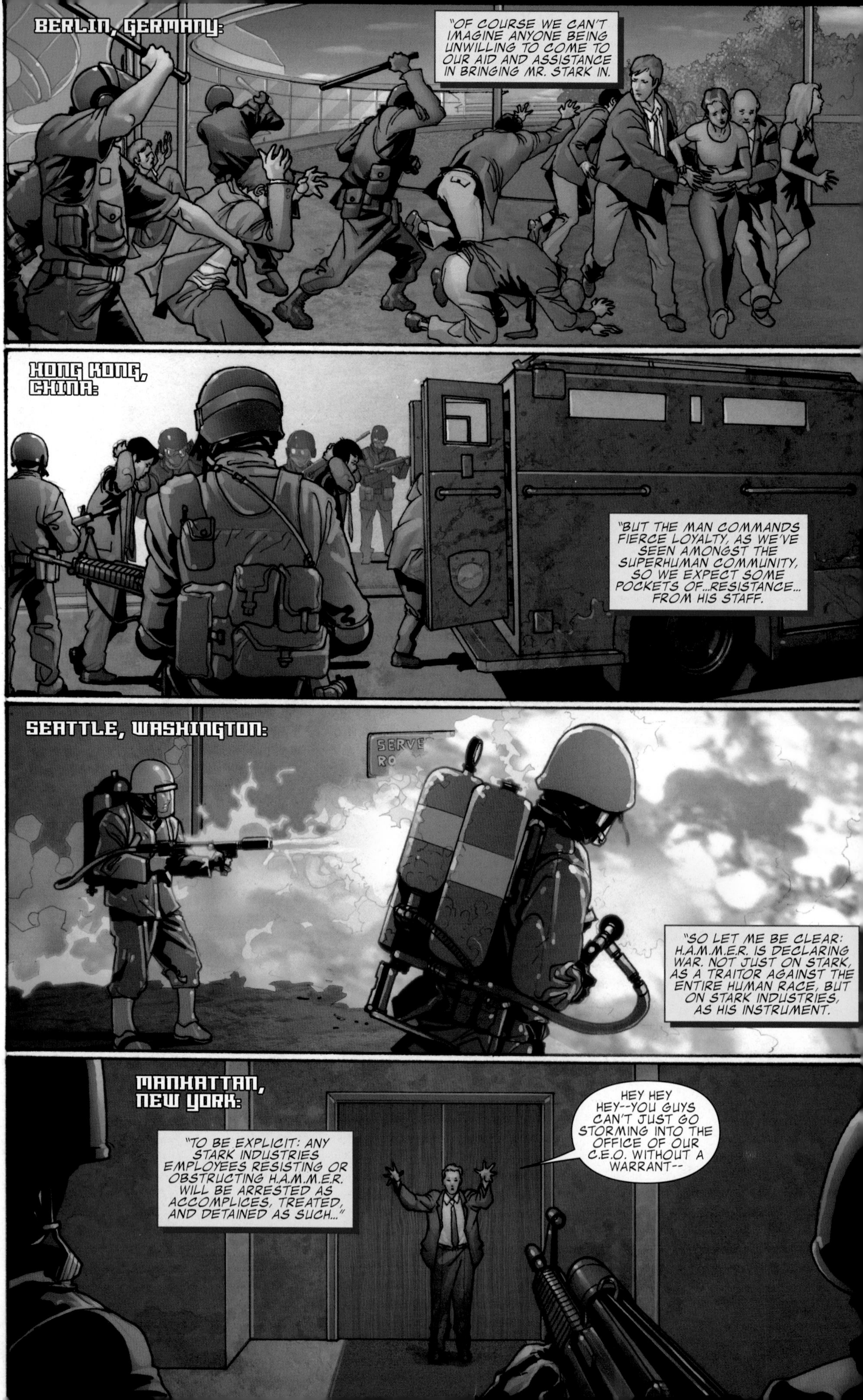
BERLIN, GERMANY:
"OF COURSE WE CAN'T IMAGINE ANYONE BEING UNWILLING TO COME TO OUR AID AND ASSISTANCE IN BRINGING MR. STARK IN.
HONG KONG, CHINA:
"BUT THE MAN COMMANDS FIERCE LOYALTY, AS WE'VE SEEN AMONGST THE SUPERHUMAN COMMUNITY, SO WE EXPECT SOME POCKETS OF...RESISTANCE... FROM HIS STAFF.
SEATTLE, WASHINGTON:
"SO LET ME BE CLEAR: H.A.M.M.E.R. IS DECLARING WAR. NOT JUST ON STARK, AS A TRAITOR AGAINST THE ENTIRE HUMAN RACE, BUT ON STARK INDUSTRIES, AS HIS INSTRUMENT.
MANHATTAN, NEW YORK:
"TO BE EXPLICIT: ANY STARK INDUSTRIES EMPLOYEES RESISTING OR OBSTRUCTING H.A.M.M.E.R. WILL BE ARRESTED AS ACCOMPLICES, TREATED, AND DETAINED AS SUCH..."
HEY HEY HEY--YOU GUYS CAN'T JUST GO STORMING INTO THE OFFICE OF OUR C.E.O. WITHOUT A WARRANT--

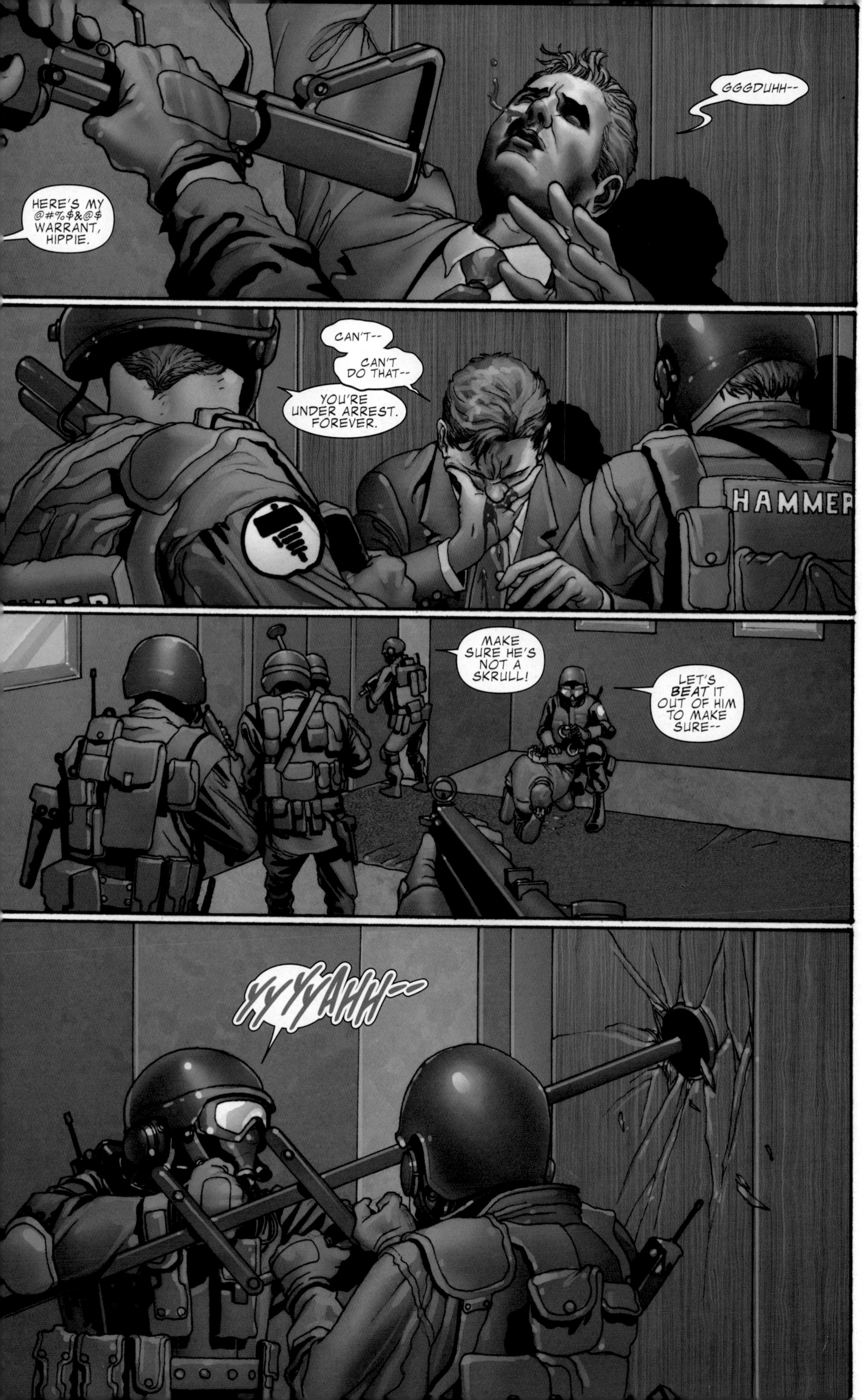
GGGDUHH--
HERE'S MY @#%$&@$ WARRANT, HIPPIE.
CAN'T--
CAN'T DO THAT--
YOU'RE UNDER ARREST. FOREVER.
HAMMER
MAKE SURE HE'S NOT A SKRULL!
LET'S BEAT IT OUT OF HIM TO MAKE SURE--
YYYYAHH--

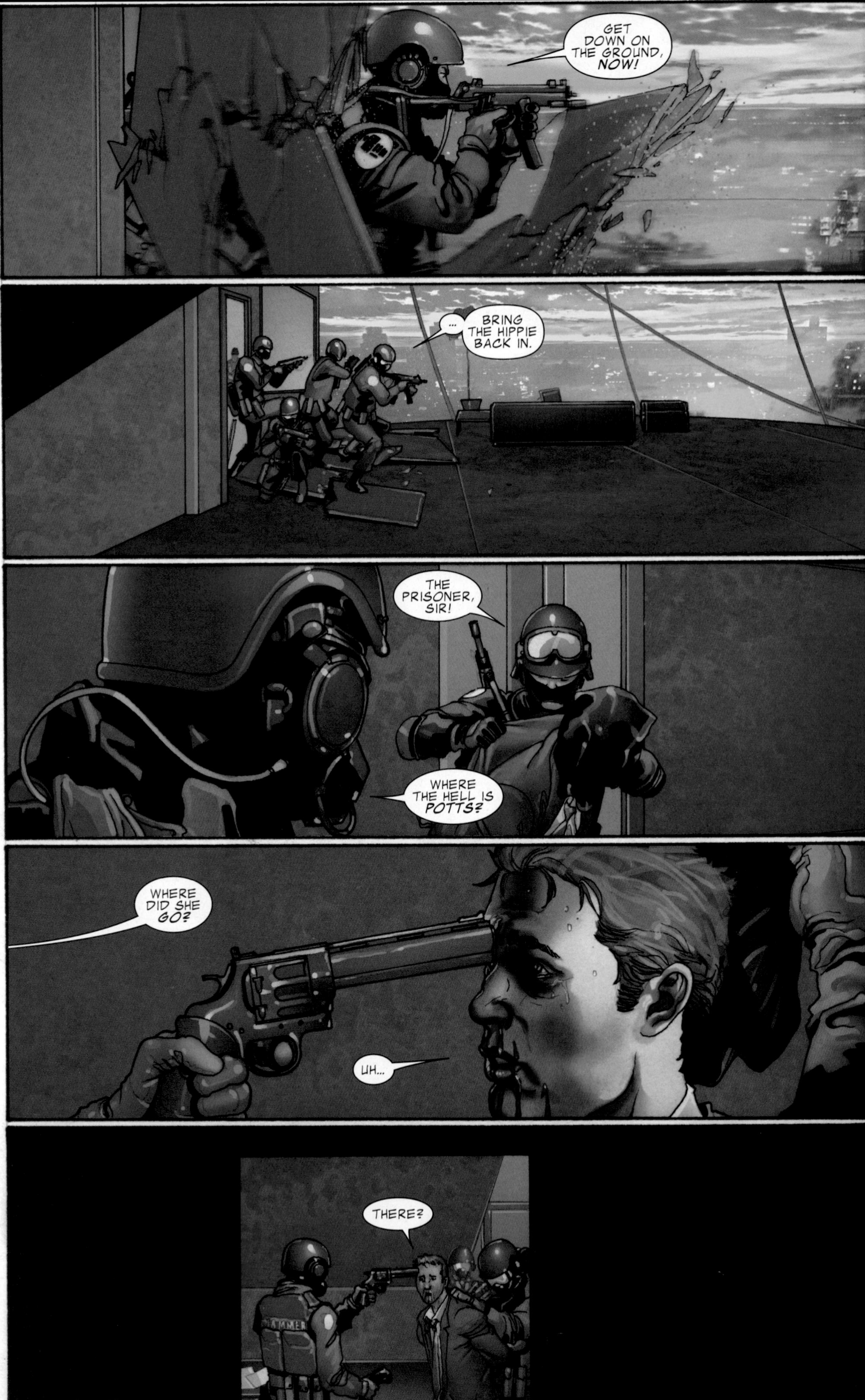
GET DOWN ON THE GROUND, NOW!
... BRING THE HIPPIE BACK IN.
THE PRISONER, SIR!
WHERE THE HELL IS POTTS?
WHERE DID SHE GO?
UH...
THERE?

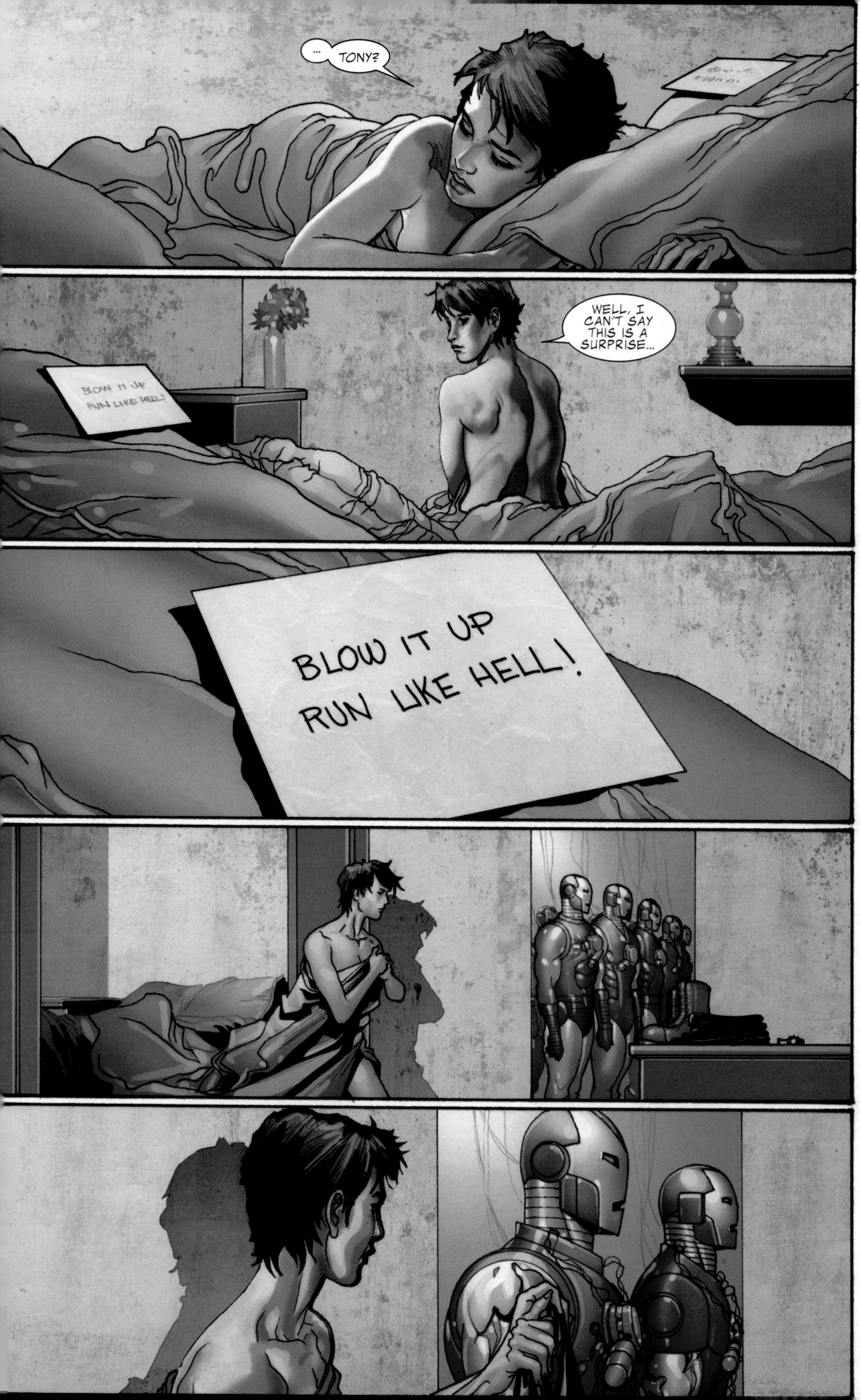
...
TONY?
WELL, I CAN'T SAY THIS IS A SURPRISE...
BLOW IT UP
RUN LIKE HELL!
BLOW IT UP
RUN LIKE HELL!

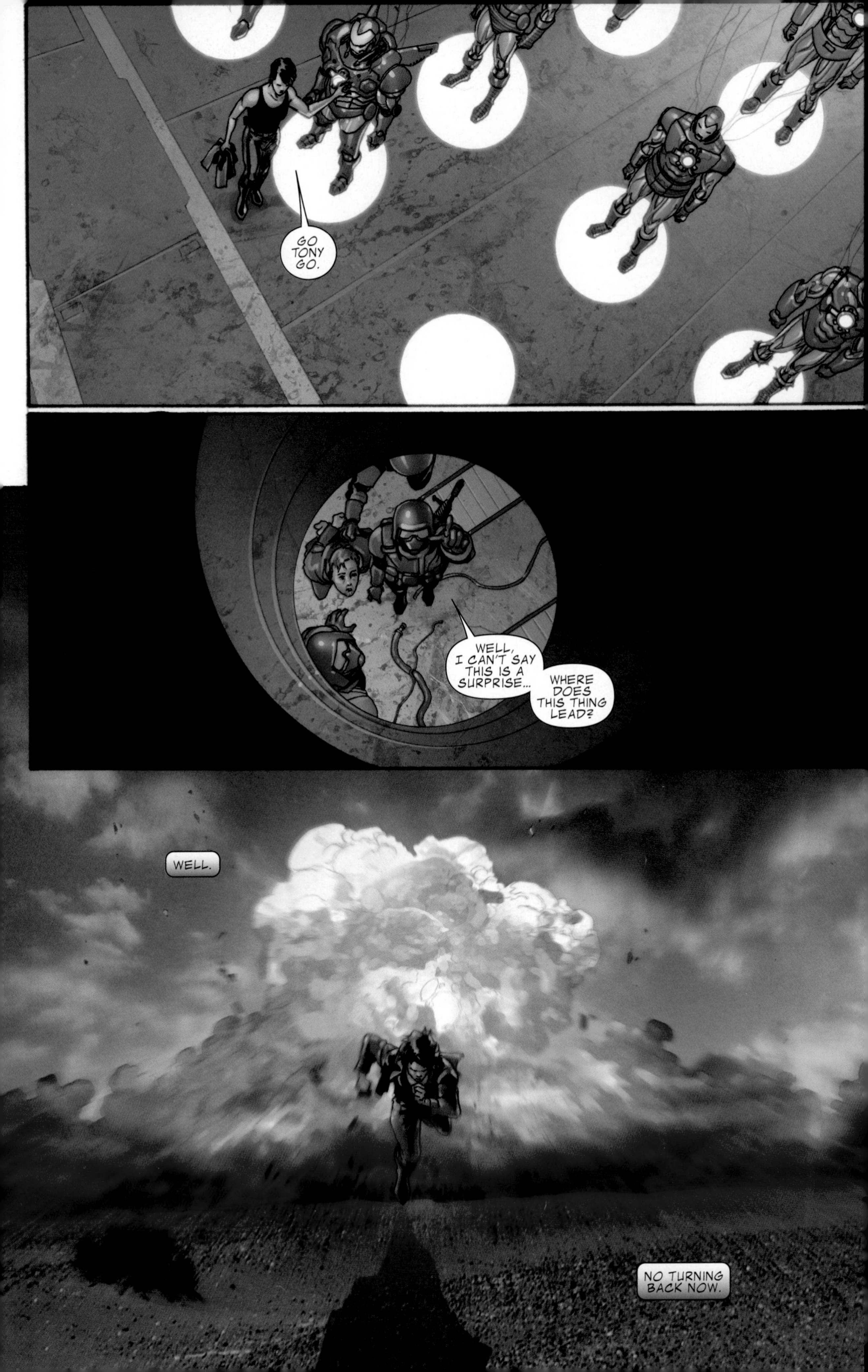
GO TONY GO.
WELL, I CAN'T SAY THIS IS A SURPRISE...
WHERE DOES THIS THING LEAD?
WELL.
NO TURNING BACK NOW.

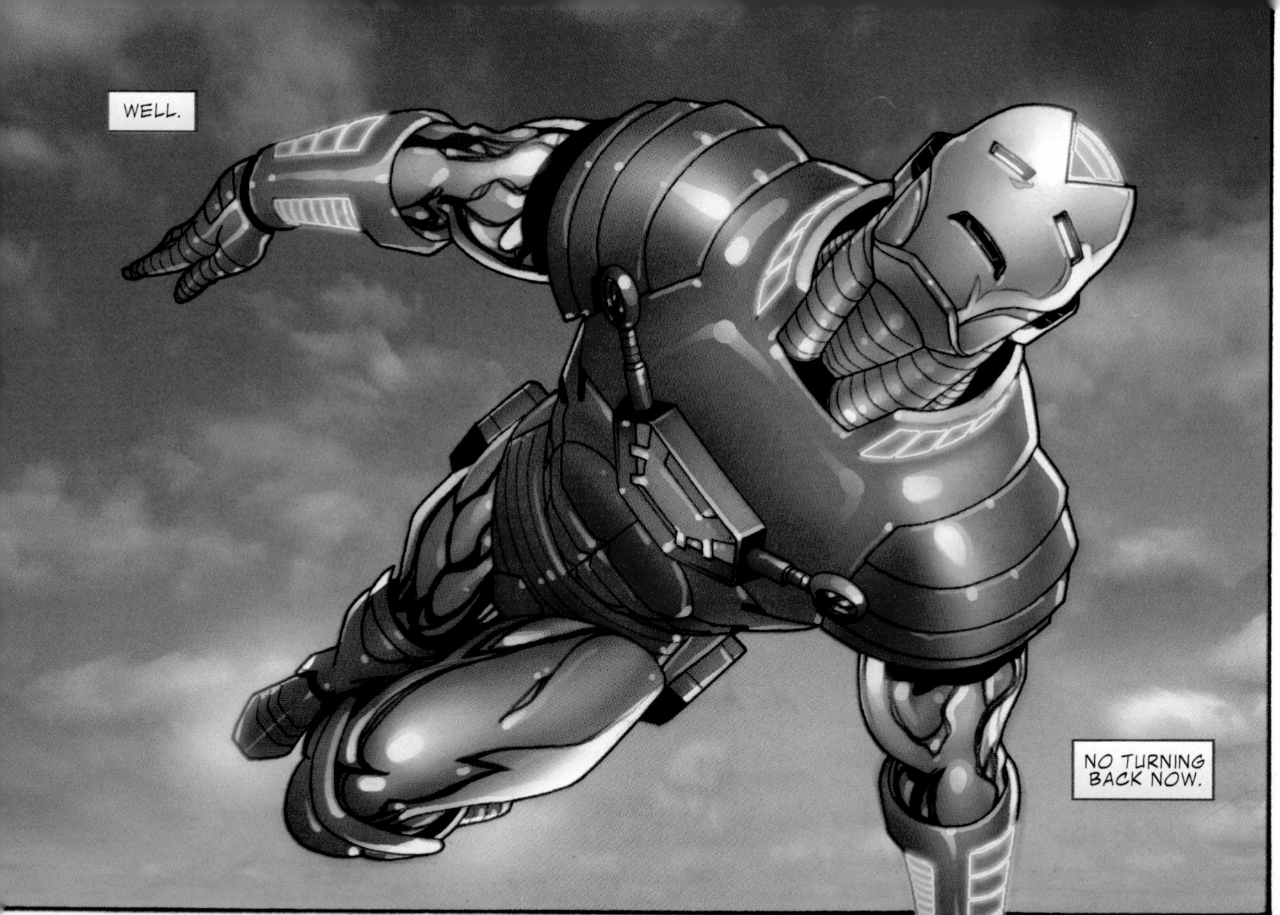
WELL.
NO TURNING BACK NOW.
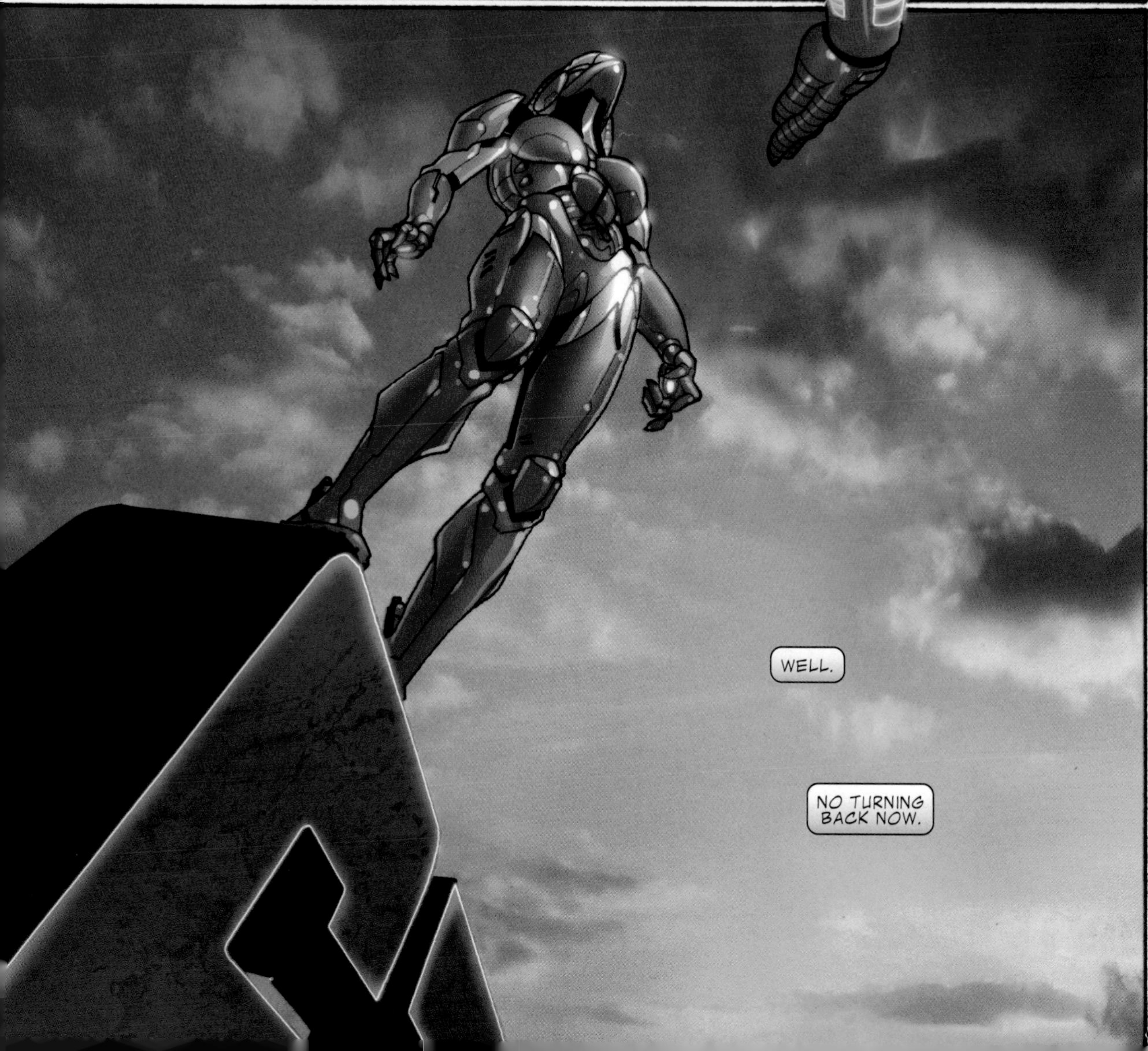
WELL.
NO TURNING BACK NOW.

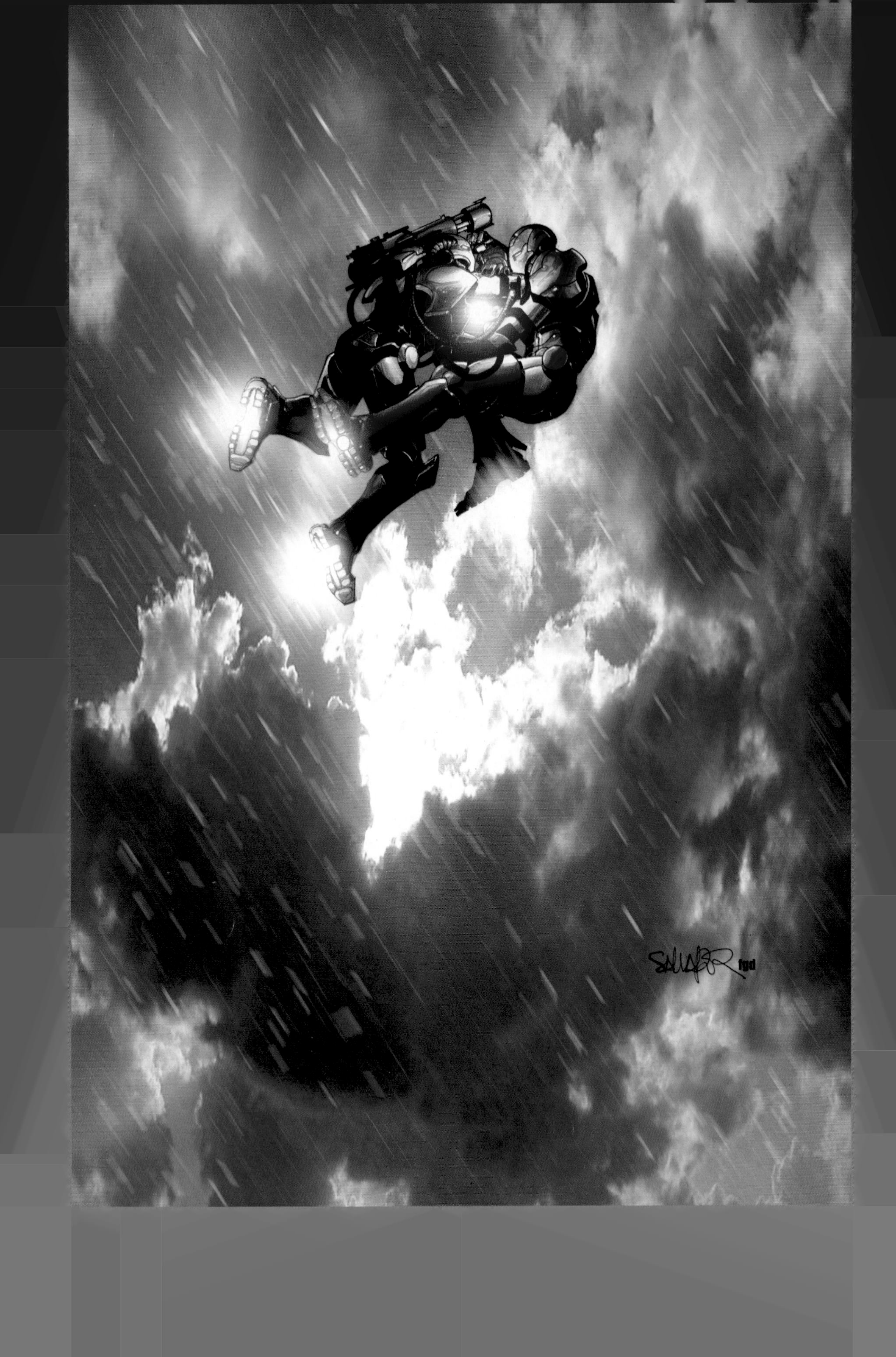

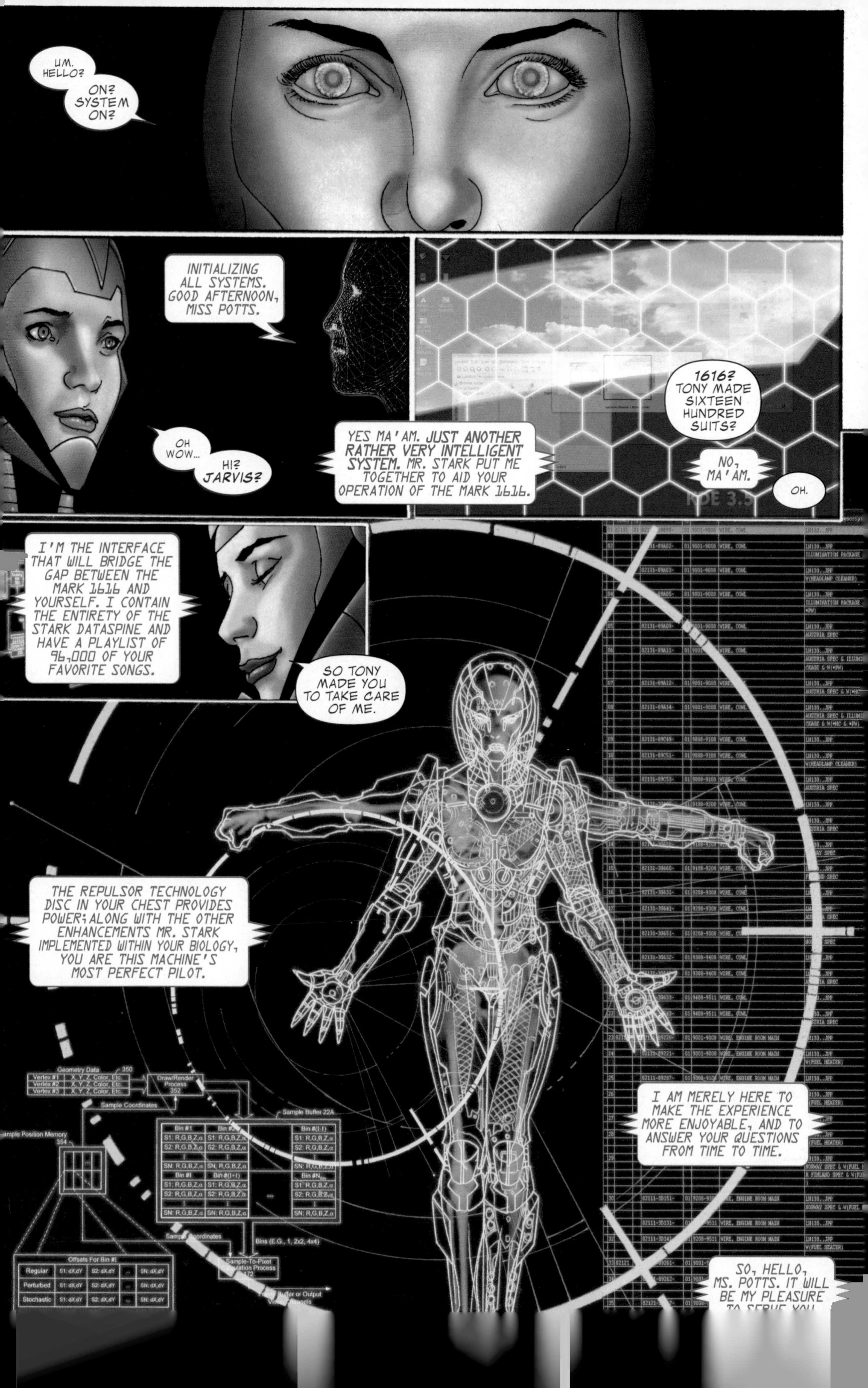
UM. HELLO?
ON? SYSTEM ON?
INITIALIZING ALL SYSTEMS. GOOD AFTERNOON, MISS POTTS.
OH WOW...
HI? JARVIS?
YES MA'AM. JUST ANOTHER RATHER VERY INTELLIGENT SYSTEM. MR. STARK PUT ME TOGETHER TO AID YOUR OPERATION OF THE MARK 1616.
1616? TONY MADE SIXTEEN HUNDRED SUITS?
NO, MA'AM.
OH.
I'M THE INTERFACE THAT WILL BRIDGE THE GAP BETWEEN THE MARK 1616 AND YOURSELF. I CONTAIN THE ENTIRETY OF THE STARK DATASPINE AND HAVE A PLAYLIST OF 96,000 OF YOUR FAVORITE SONGS.
SO TONY MADE YOU TO TAKE CARE OF ME.
THE REPULSOR TECHNOLOGY DISC IN YOUR CHEST PROVIDES POWER; ALONG WITH THE OTHER ENHANCEMENTS MR. STARK IMPLEMENTED WITHIN YOUR BIOLOGY, YOU ARE THIS MACHINE'S MOST PERFECT PILOT.
I AM MERELY HERE TO MAKE THE EXPERIENCE MORE ENJOYABLE, AND TO ANSWER YOUR QUESTIONS FROM TIME TO TIME.
SO, HELLO, MS. POTTS. IT WILL BE MY PLEASURE

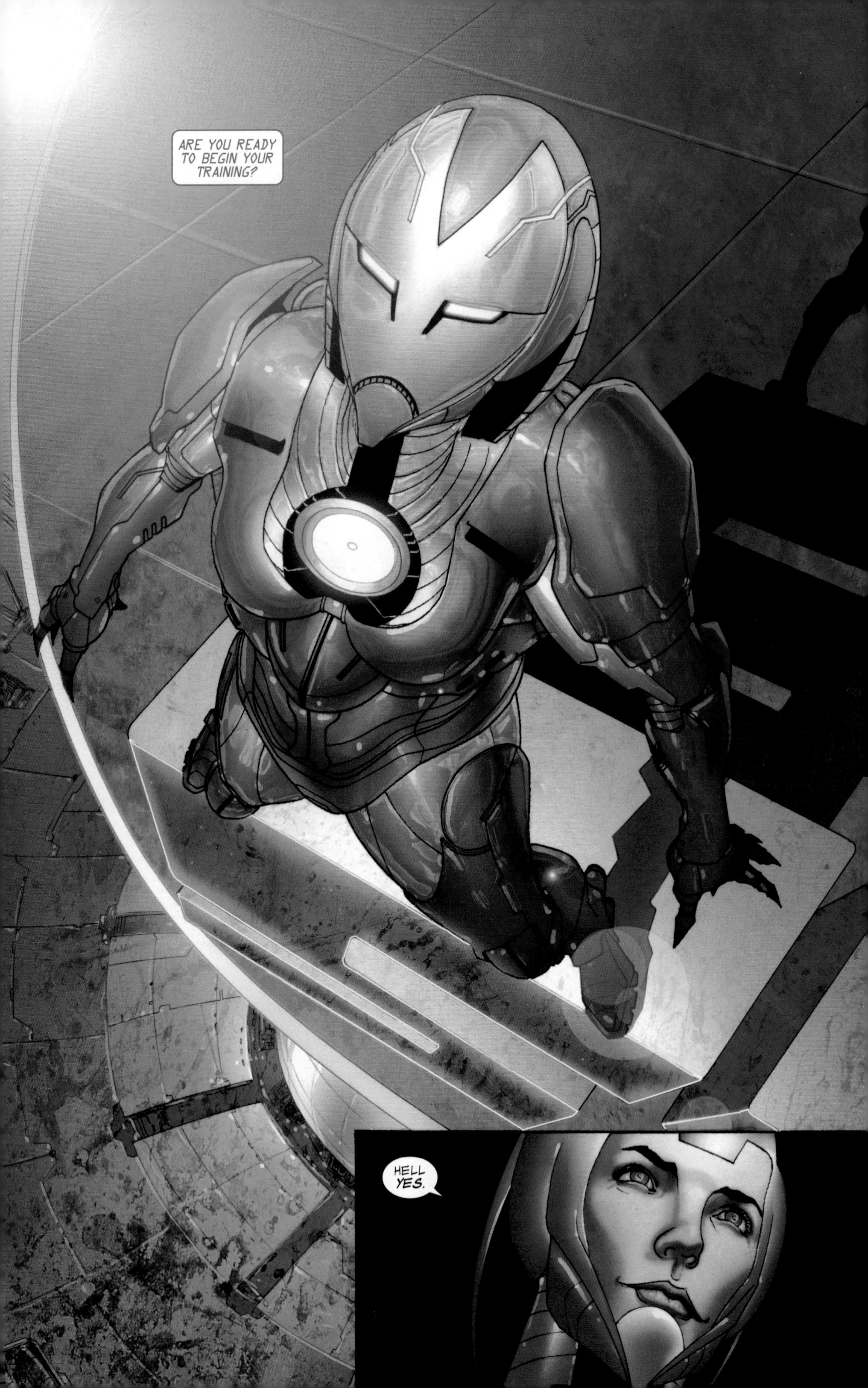
ARE YOU READY TO BEGIN YOUR TRAINING?
HELL YES.

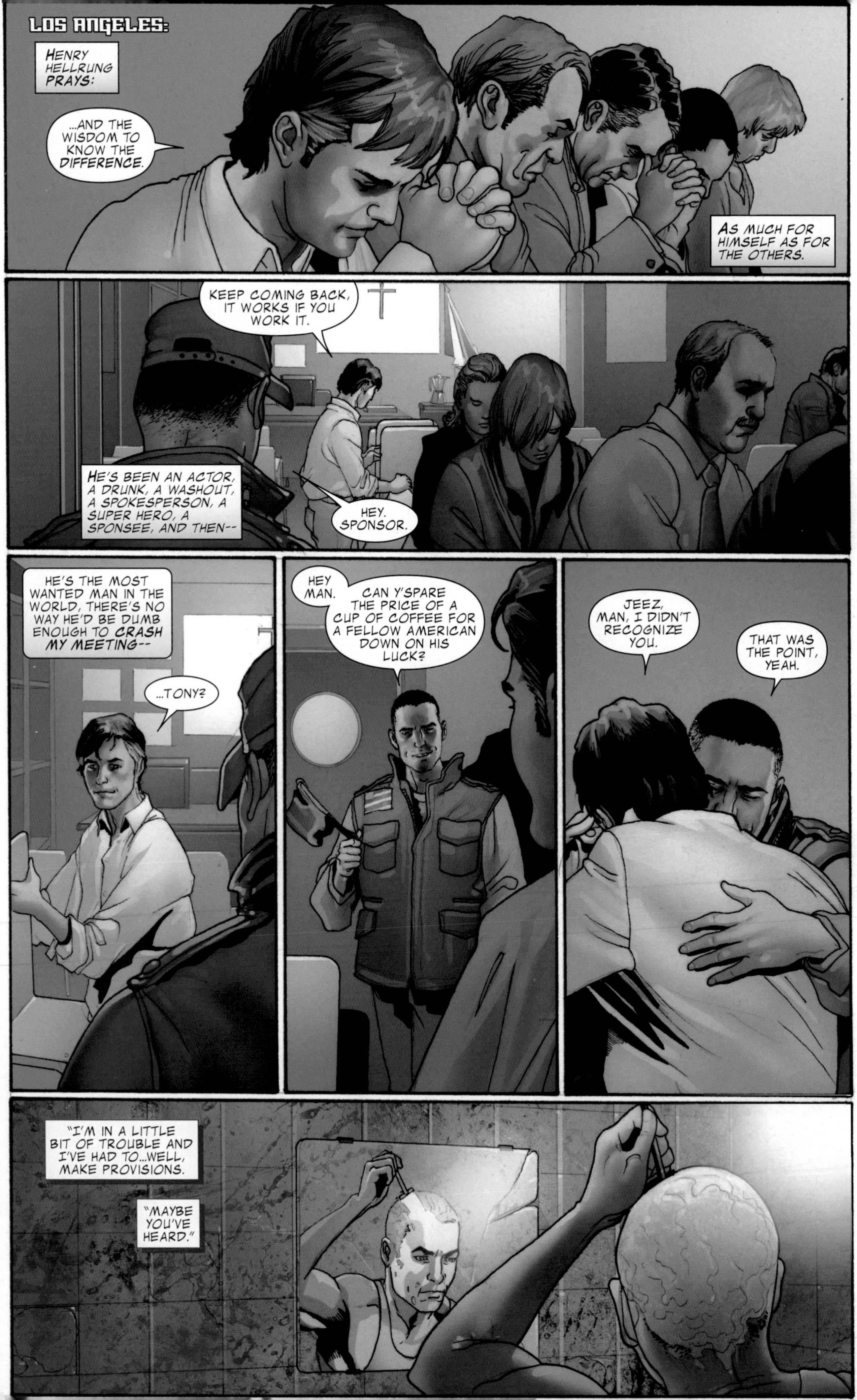
LOS ANGELES:
HENRY HELLRUNG PRAYS:
...AND THE WISDOM TO KNOW THE DIFFERENCE.
AS MUCH FOR HIMSELF AS FOR THE OTHERS.
KEEP COMING BACK, IT WORKS IF YOU WORK IT.
HE'S BEEN AN ACTOR, A DRUNK, A WASHOUT, A SPOKESPERSON, A SUPER HERO, A SPONSEE, AND THEN--
HEY. SPONSOR.
HE'S THE MOST WANTED MAN IN THE WORLD, THERE'S NO WAY HE'D BE DUMB ENOUGH TO CRASH MY MEETING--
...TONY?
HEY MAN.
CAN Y'SPARE THE PRICE OF A CUP OF COFFEE FOR A FELLOW AMERICAN DOWN ON HIS LUCK?
JEEZ, MAN, I DIDN'T RECOGNIZE YOU.
THAT WAS THE POINT, YEAH.
"I'M IN A LITTLE BIT OF TROUBLE AND I'VE HAD TO...WELL, MAKE PROVISIONS.
"MAYBE YOU'VE HEARD."

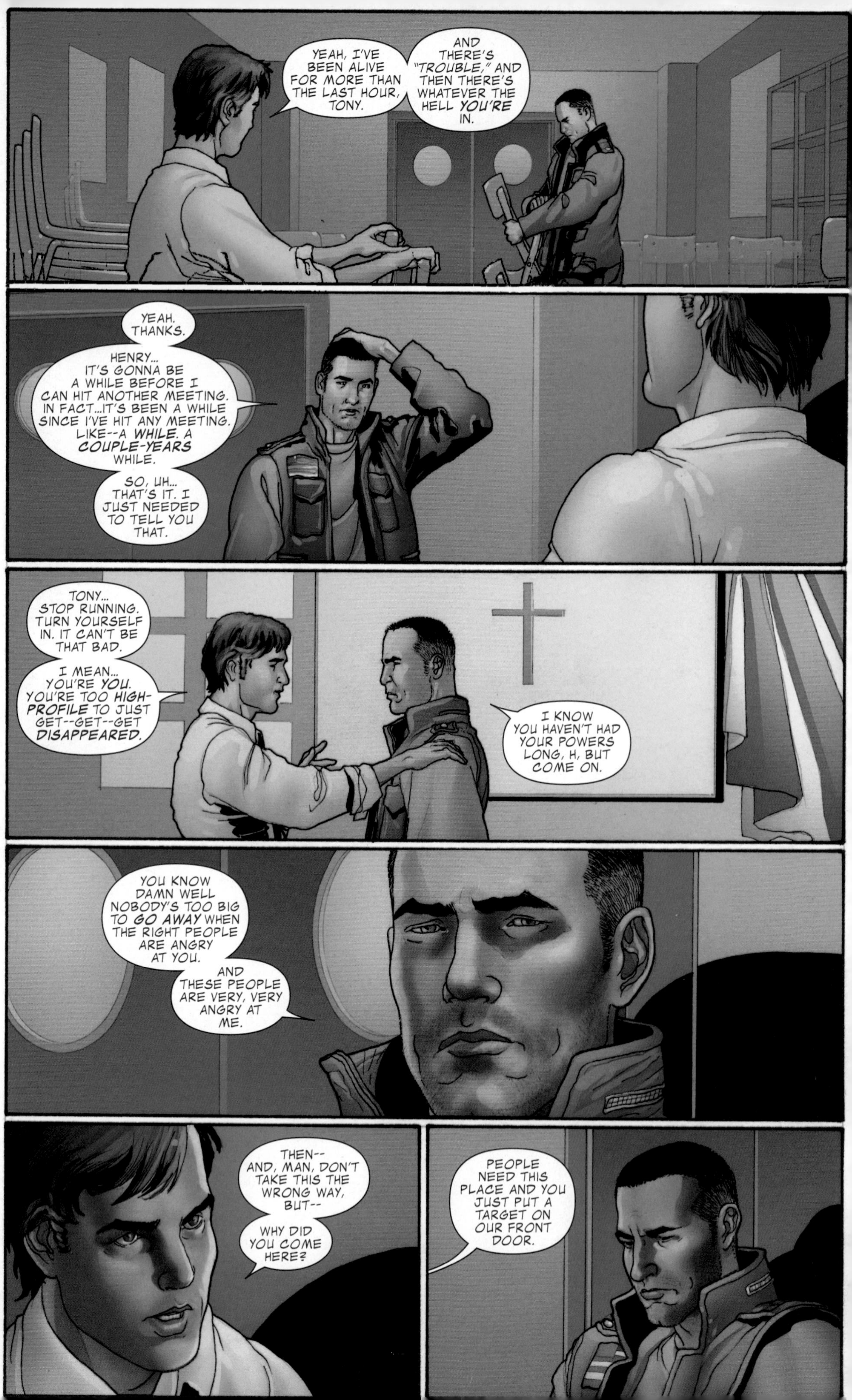
YEAH, I'VE BEEN ALIVE FOR MORE THAN THE LAST HOUR, TONY.
AND THERE'S "TROUBLE," AND THEN THERE'S WHATEVER THE HELL YOU'RE IN.
YEAH. THANKS.
HENRY... IT'S GONNA BE A WHILE BEFORE I CAN HIT ANOTHER MEETING. IN FACT...IT'S BEEN A WHILE SINCE I'VE HIT ANY MEETING. LIKE--A WHILE. A COUPLE-YEARS WHILE.
SO, UH... THAT'S IT. I JUST NEEDED TO TELL YOU THAT.
TONY... STOP RUNNING. TURN YOURSELF IN. IT CAN'T BE THAT BAD.
I MEAN... YOU'RE YOU. YOU'RE TOO HIGH-PROFILE TO JUST GET--GET--GET DISAPPEARED.
I KNOW YOU HAVEN'T HAD YOUR POWERS LONG, H, BUT COME ON.
YOU KNOW DAMN WELL NOBODY'S TOO BIG TO GO AWAY WHEN THE RIGHT PEOPLE ARE ANGRY AT YOU.
AND THESE PEOPLE ARE VERY, VERY ANGRY AT ME.
THEN-- AND, MAN, DON'T TAKE THIS THE WRONG WAY, BUT--
WHY DID YOU COME HERE?
PEOPLE NEED THIS PLACE AND YOU JUST PUT A TARGET ON OUR FRONT DOOR.

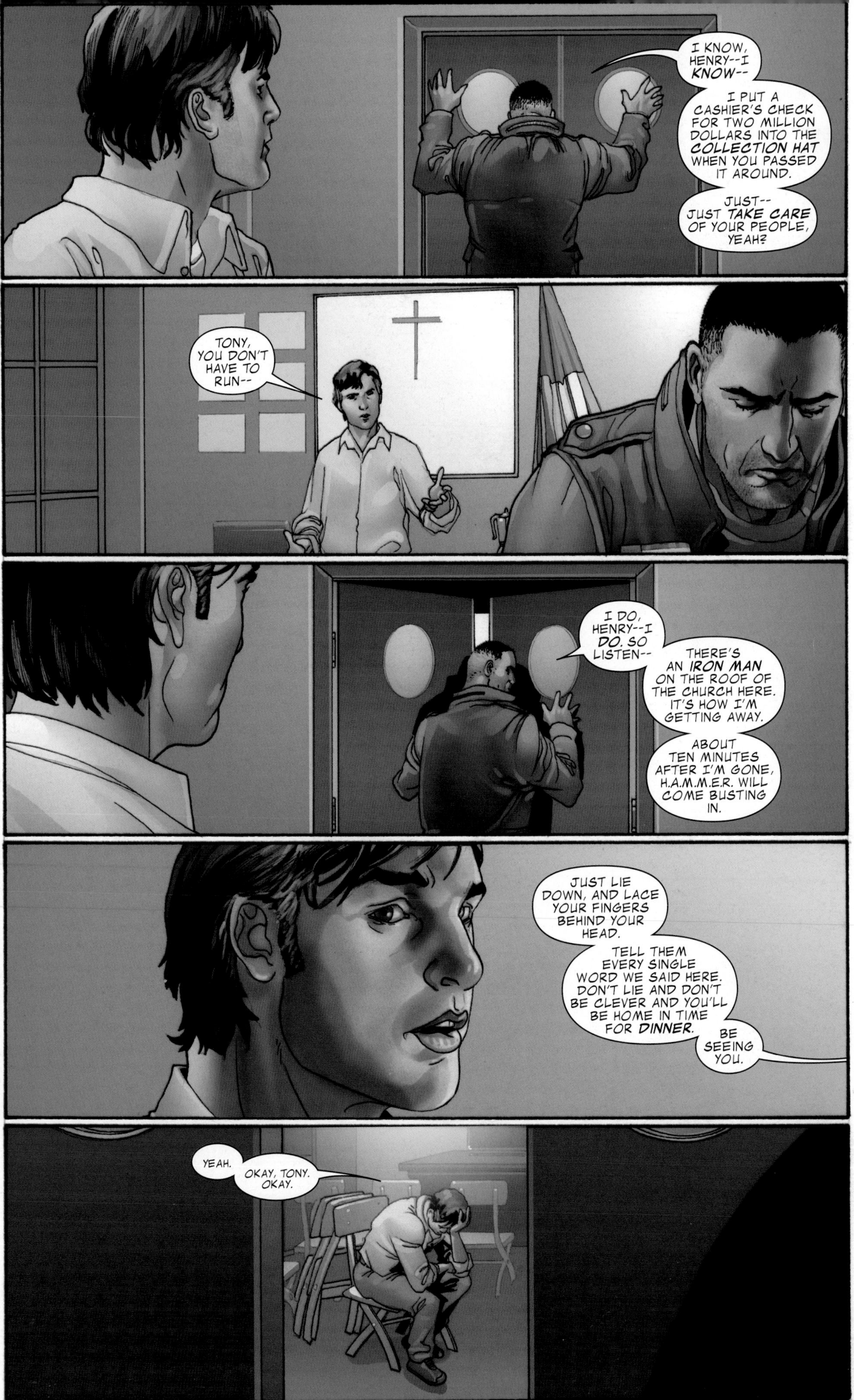

I KNOW, HENRY--I KNOW--
I PUT A CASHIER'S CHECK FOR TWO MILLION DOLLARS INTO THE COLLECTION HAT WHEN YOU PASSED IT AROUND.
JUST-- JUST TAKE CARE OF YOUR PEOPLE, YEAH?
TONY, YOU DON'T HAVE TO RUN--
I DO, HENRY--I DO. SO LISTEN--
THERE'S AN IRON MAN ON THE ROOF OF THE CHURCH HERE. IT'S HOW I'M GETTING AWAY.
ABOUT TEN MINUTES AFTER I'M GONE, H.A.M.M.E.R. WILL COME BUSTING IN.
JUST LIE DOWN, AND LACE YOUR FINGERS BEHIND YOUR HEAD.
TELL THEM EVERY SINGLE WORD WE SAID HERE. DON'T LIE AND DON'T BE CLEVER AND YOU'LL BE HOME IN TIME FOR DINNER.
BE SEEING YOU.
YEAH.
OKAY, TONY. OKAY.

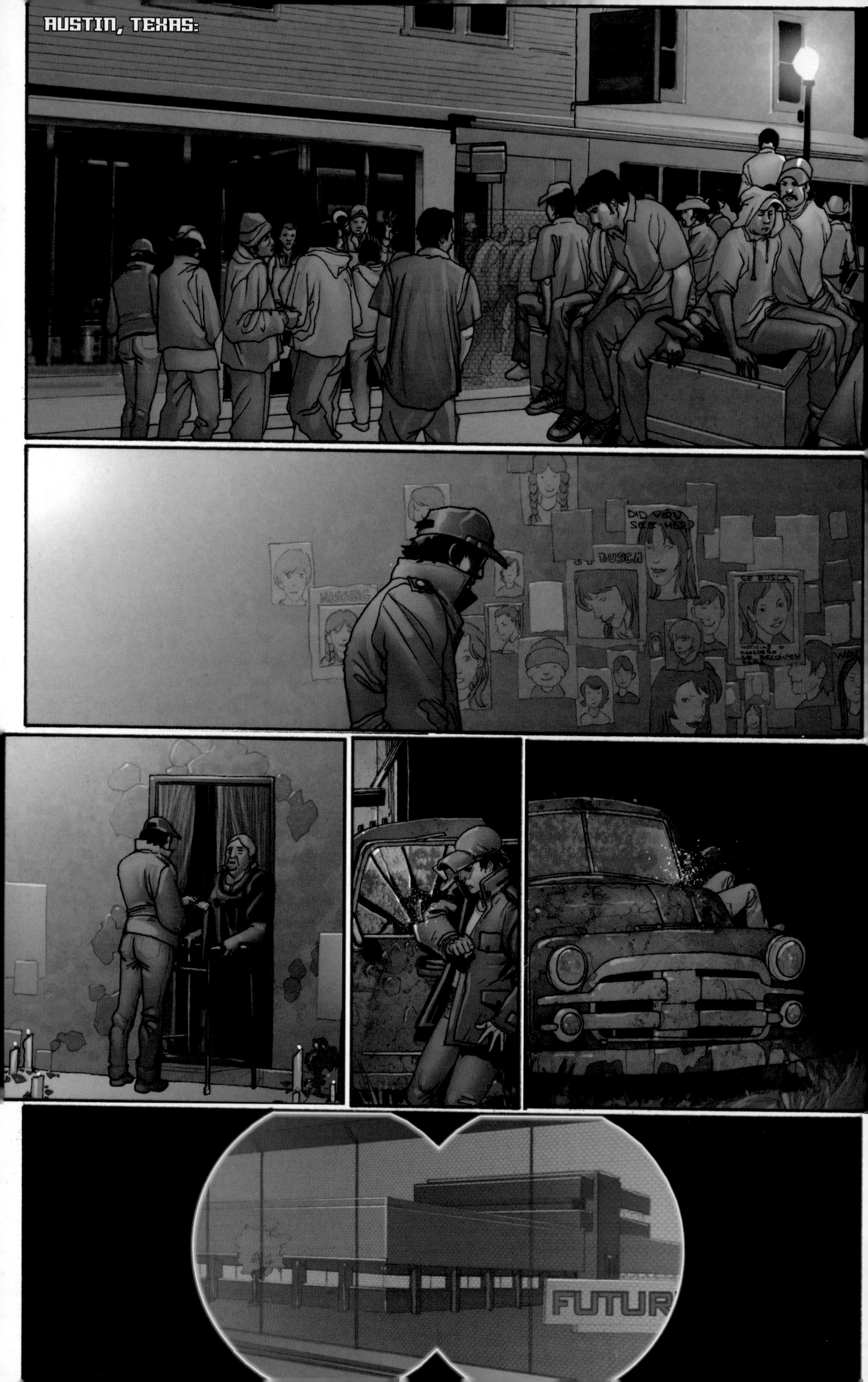
AUSTIN, TEXAS:
MISSING
DID YOU SEE HER?
BUSCA
SE BUSCA
FUTUR

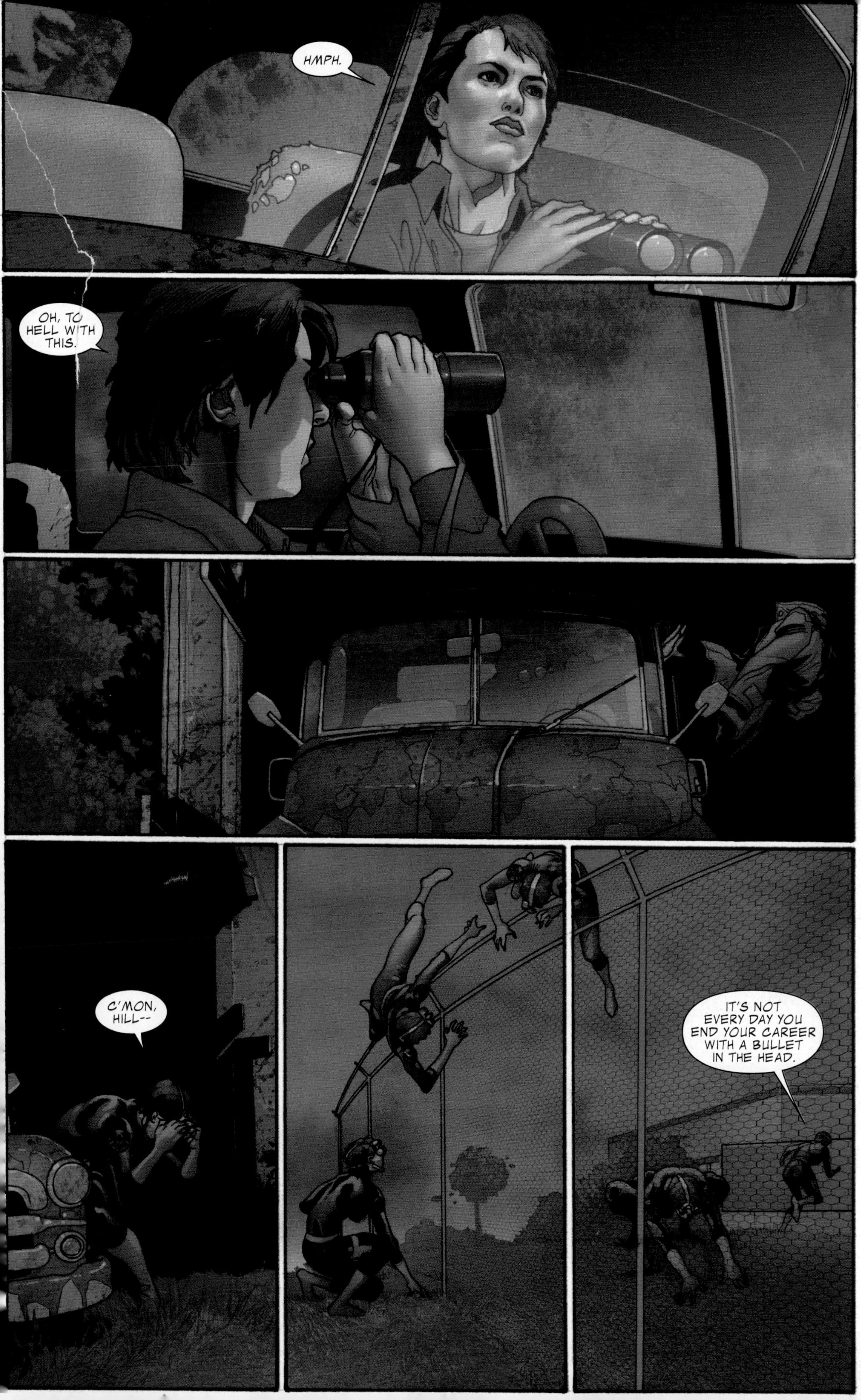
HMPH.
OH, TO HELL WITH THIS.
C'MON, HILL--
IT'S NOT EVERY DAY YOU END YOUR CAREER WITH A BULLET IN THE HEAD.

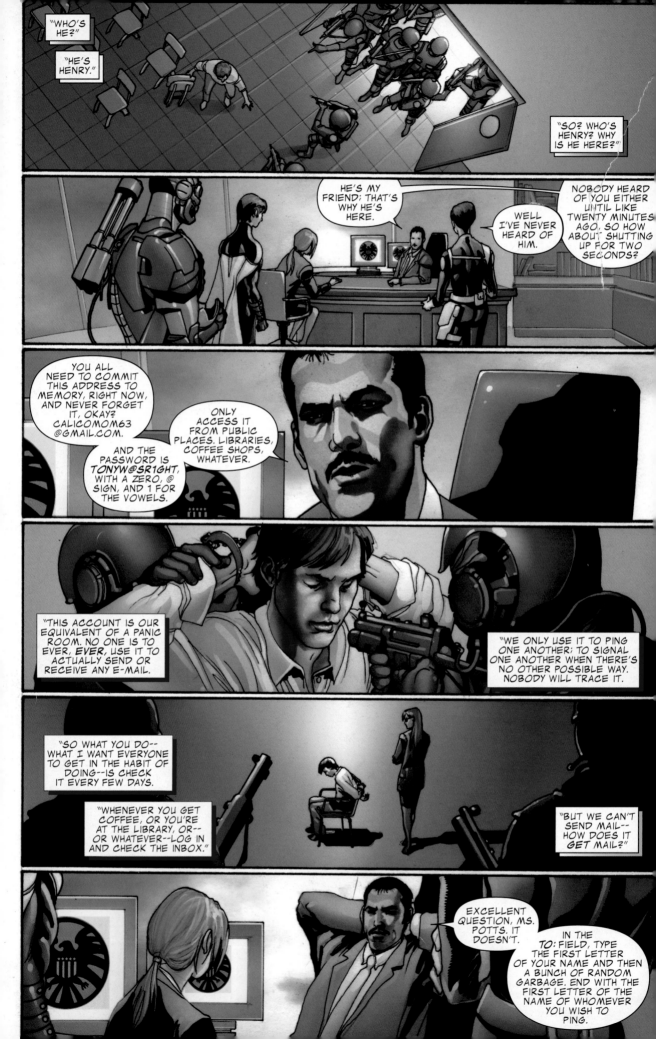

"WHO'S HE?"

"HE'S HENRY."

"SO? WHO'S HENRY? WHY IS HE HERE?"

HE'S MY FRIEND; THAT'S WHY HE'S HERE.

WELL I'VE NEVER HEARD OF HIM.

NOBODY HEARD OF YOU EITHER UNTIL LIKE TWENTY MINUTES AGO, SO HOW ABOUT SHUTTING UP FOR TWO SECONDS?

YOU ALL NEED TO COMMIT THIS ADDRESS TO MEMORY, RIGHT NOW, AND NEVER FORGET IT, OKAY? CALICOMOM63@GMAIL.COM.

AND THE PASSWORD IS TONYW@SR1GHT, WITH A ZERO, @ SIGN, AND 1 FOR THE VOWELS.

ONLY ACCESS IT FROM PUBLIC PLACES. LIBRARIES, COFFEE SHOPS, WHATEVER.

"THIS ACCOUNT IS OUR EQUIVALENT OF A PANIC ROOM. NO ONE IS TO EVER, *EVER*, USE IT TO ACTUALLY SEND OR RECEIVE ANY E-MAIL."

"WE ONLY USE IT TO PING ONE ANOTHER; TO SIGNAL ONE ANOTHER WHEN THERE'S NO OTHER POSSIBLE WAY. NOBODY WILL TRACE IT."

"SO WHAT YOU DO-- WHAT I WANT EVERYONE TO GET IN THE HABIT OF DOING--IS CHECK IT EVERY FEW DAYS."

"WHENEVER YOU GET COFFEE, OR YOU'RE AT THE LIBRARY, OR-- OR WHATEVER--LOG IN AND CHECK THE INBOX."

"BUT WE CAN'T SEND MAIL-- HOW DOES IT GET MAIL?"

EXCELLENT QUESTION, MS. POTTS. IT DOESN'T.

IN THE TO: FIELD, TYPE THE FIRST LETTER OF YOUR NAME AND THEN A BUNCH OF RANDOM GARBAGE. END WITH THE FIRST LETTER OF THE NAME OF WHOMEVER YOU WISH TO PING.

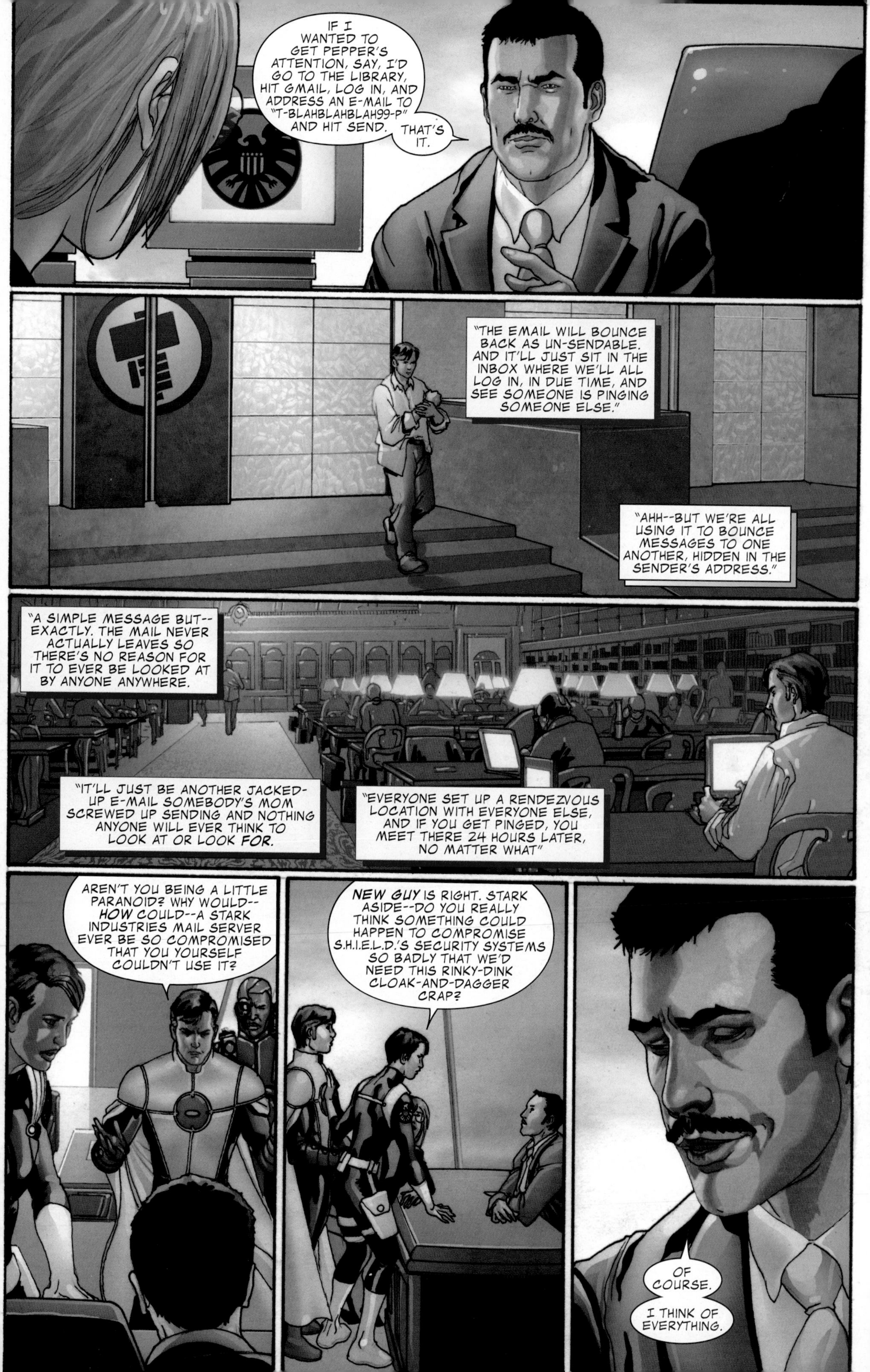
IF I WANTED TO GET PEPPER'S ATTENTION, SAY, I'D GO TO THE LIBRARY, HIT GMAIL, LOG IN, AND ADDRESS AN E-MAIL TO "T-BLAHBLAHBLAH99-P" AND HIT SEND.
THAT'S IT.
"THE EMAIL WILL BOUNCE BACK AS UN-SENDABLE. AND IT'LL JUST SIT IN THE INBOX WHERE WE'LL ALL LOG IN, IN DUE TIME, AND SEE SOMEONE IS PINGING SOMEONE ELSE."
"AHH--BUT WE'RE ALL USING IT TO BOUNCE MESSAGES TO ONE ANOTHER, HIDDEN IN THE SENDER'S ADDRESS."
"A SIMPLE MESSAGE BUT--EXACTLY. THE MAIL NEVER ACTUALLY LEAVES SO THERE'S NO REASON FOR IT TO EVER BE LOOKED AT BY ANYONE ANYWHERE.
"IT'LL JUST BE ANOTHER JACKED-UP E-MAIL SOMEBODY'S MOM SCREWED UP SENDING AND NOTHING ANYONE WILL EVER THINK TO LOOK AT OR LOOK FOR.
"EVERYONE SET UP A RENDEZVOUS LOCATION WITH EVERYONE ELSE, AND IF YOU GET PINGED, YOU MEET THERE 24 HOURS LATER, NO MATTER WHAT"
AREN'T YOU BEING A LITTLE PARANOID? WHY WOULD-- HOW COULD--A STARK INDUSTRIES MAIL SERVER EVER BE SO COMPROMISED THAT YOU YOURSELF COULDN'T USE IT?
NEW GUY IS RIGHT. STARK ASIDE--DO YOU REALLY THINK SOMETHING COULD HAPPEN TO COMPROMISE S.H.I.E.L.D.'S SECURITY SYSTEMS SO BADLY THAT WE'D NEED THIS RINKY-DINK CLOAK-AND-DAGGER CRAP?
OF COURSE.
I THINK OF EVERYTHING.

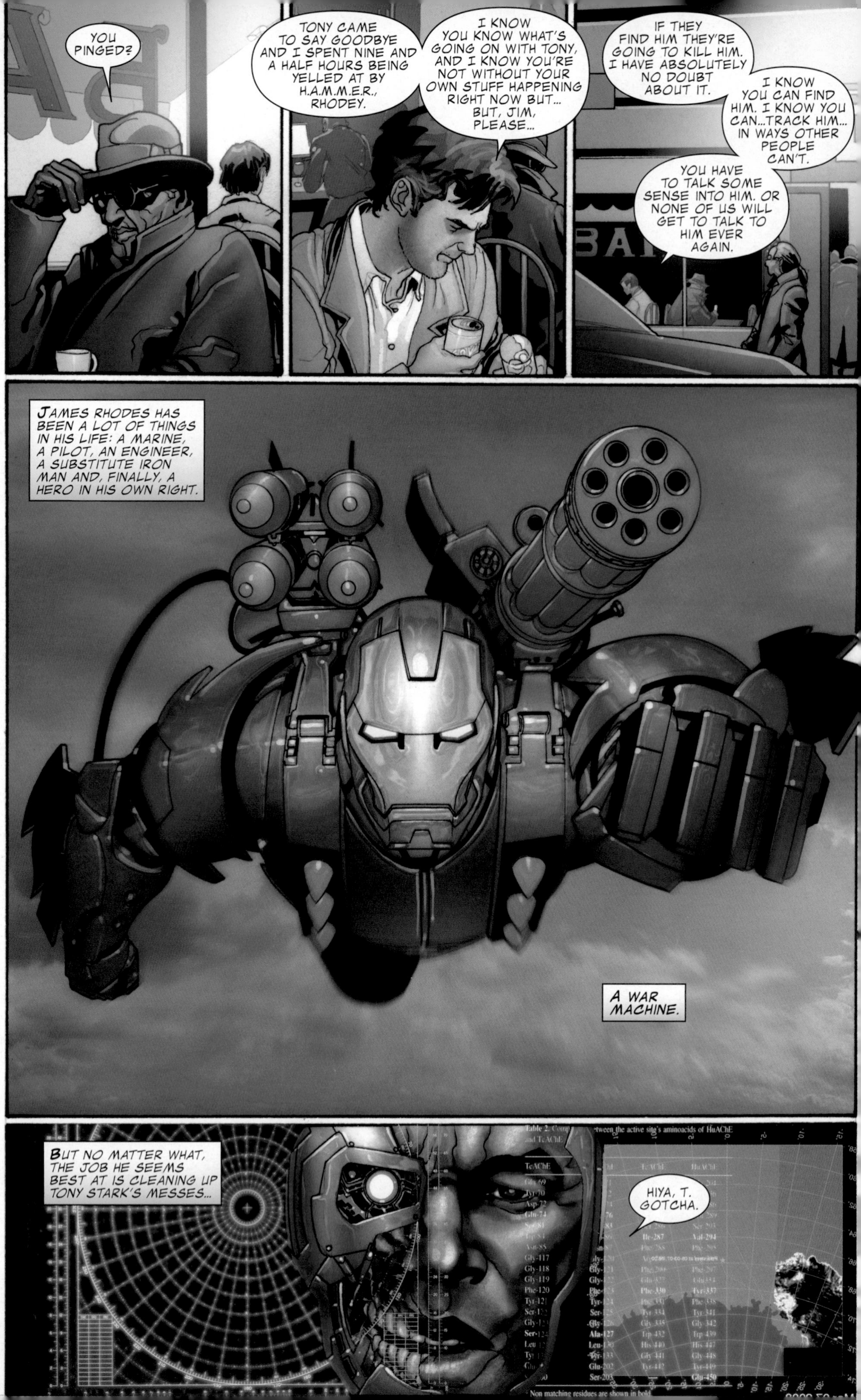
YOU PINGED?
TONY CAME TO SAY GOODBYE AND I SPENT NINE AND A HALF HOURS BEING YELLED AT BY H.A.M.M.E.R., RHODEY.
I KNOW YOU KNOW WHAT'S GOING ON WITH TONY, AND I KNOW YOU'RE NOT WITHOUT YOUR OWN STUFF HAPPENING RIGHT NOW BUT... BUT, JIM, PLEASE...
IF THEY FIND HIM THEY'RE GOING TO KILL HIM. I HAVE ABSOLUTELY NO DOUBT ABOUT IT.
I KNOW YOU CAN FIND HIM. I KNOW YOU CAN...TRACK HIM... IN WAYS OTHER PEOPLE CAN'T.
YOU HAVE TO TALK SOME SENSE INTO HIM. OR NONE OF US WILL GET TO TALK TO HIM EVER AGAIN.
JAMES RHODES HAS BEEN A LOT OF THINGS IN HIS LIFE: A MARINE, A PILOT, AN ENGINEER, A SUBSTITUTE IRON MAN AND, FINALLY, A HERO IN HIS OWN RIGHT.
A WAR MACHINE.
BUT NO MATTER WHAT, THE JOB HE SEEMS BEST AT IS CLEANING UP TONY STARK'S MESSES...
HIYA, T. GOTCHA.

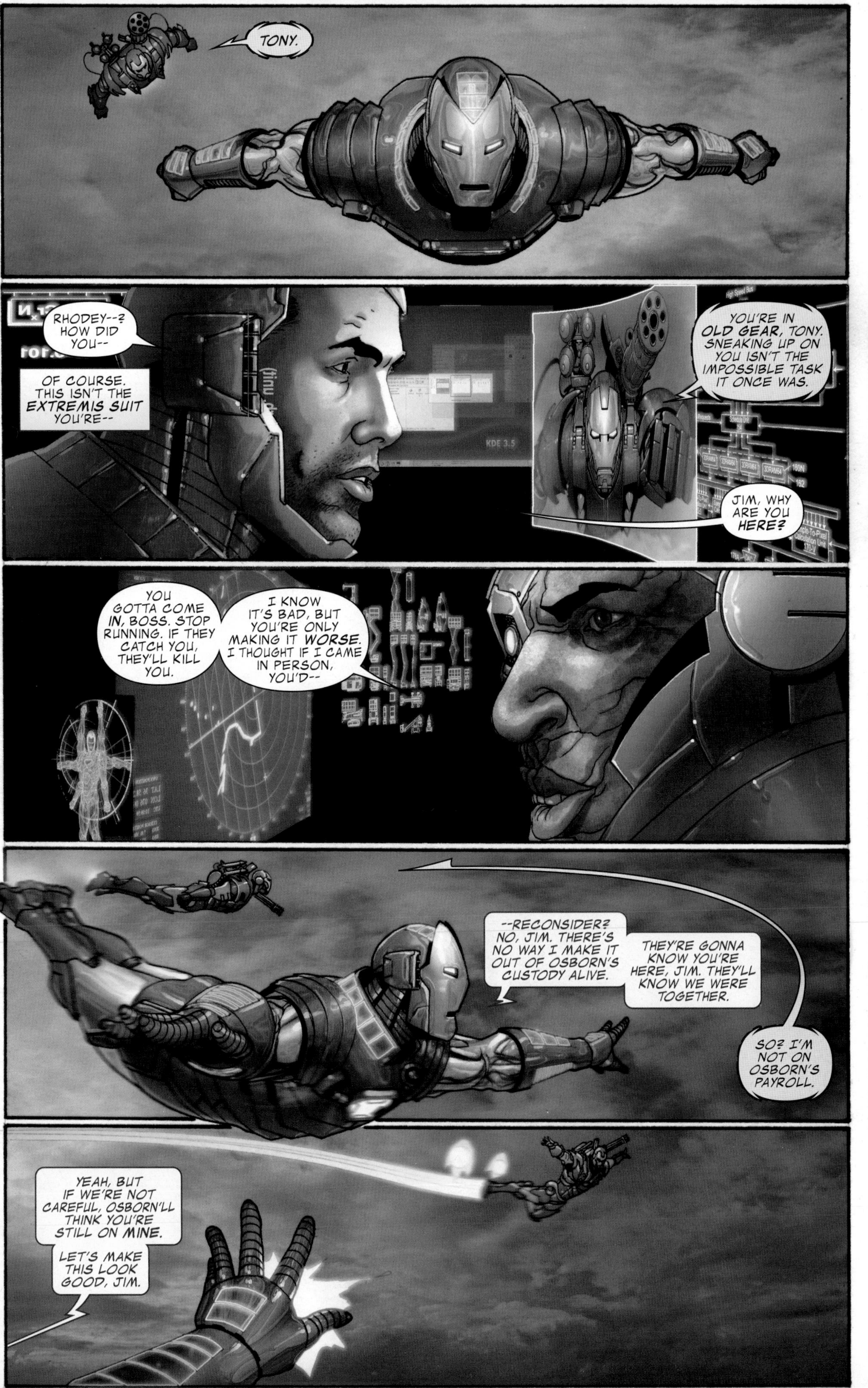
TONY.
RHODEY--? HOW DID YOU--
OF COURSE. THIS ISN'T THE EXTREMIS SUIT YOU'RE--
YOU'RE IN OLD GEAR, TONY. SNEAKING UP ON YOU ISN'T THE IMPOSSIBLE TASK IT ONCE WAS.
JIM, WHY ARE YOU HERE?
YOU GOTTA COME IN, BOSS. STOP RUNNING. IF THEY CATCH YOU, THEY'LL KILL YOU.
I KNOW IT'S BAD, BUT YOU'RE ONLY MAKING IT WORSE. I THOUGHT IF I CAME IN PERSON, YOU'D--
--RECONSIDER? NO, JIM. THERE'S NO WAY I MAKE IT OUT OF OSBORN'S CUSTODY ALIVE.
THEY'RE GONNA KNOW YOU'RE HERE, JIM. THEY'LL KNOW WE WERE TOGETHER.
SO? I'M NOT ON OSBORN'S PAYROLL.
YEAH, BUT IF WE'RE NOT CAREFUL, OSBORN'LL THINK YOU'RE STILL ON MINE.
LET'S MAKE THIS LOOK GOOD, JIM.

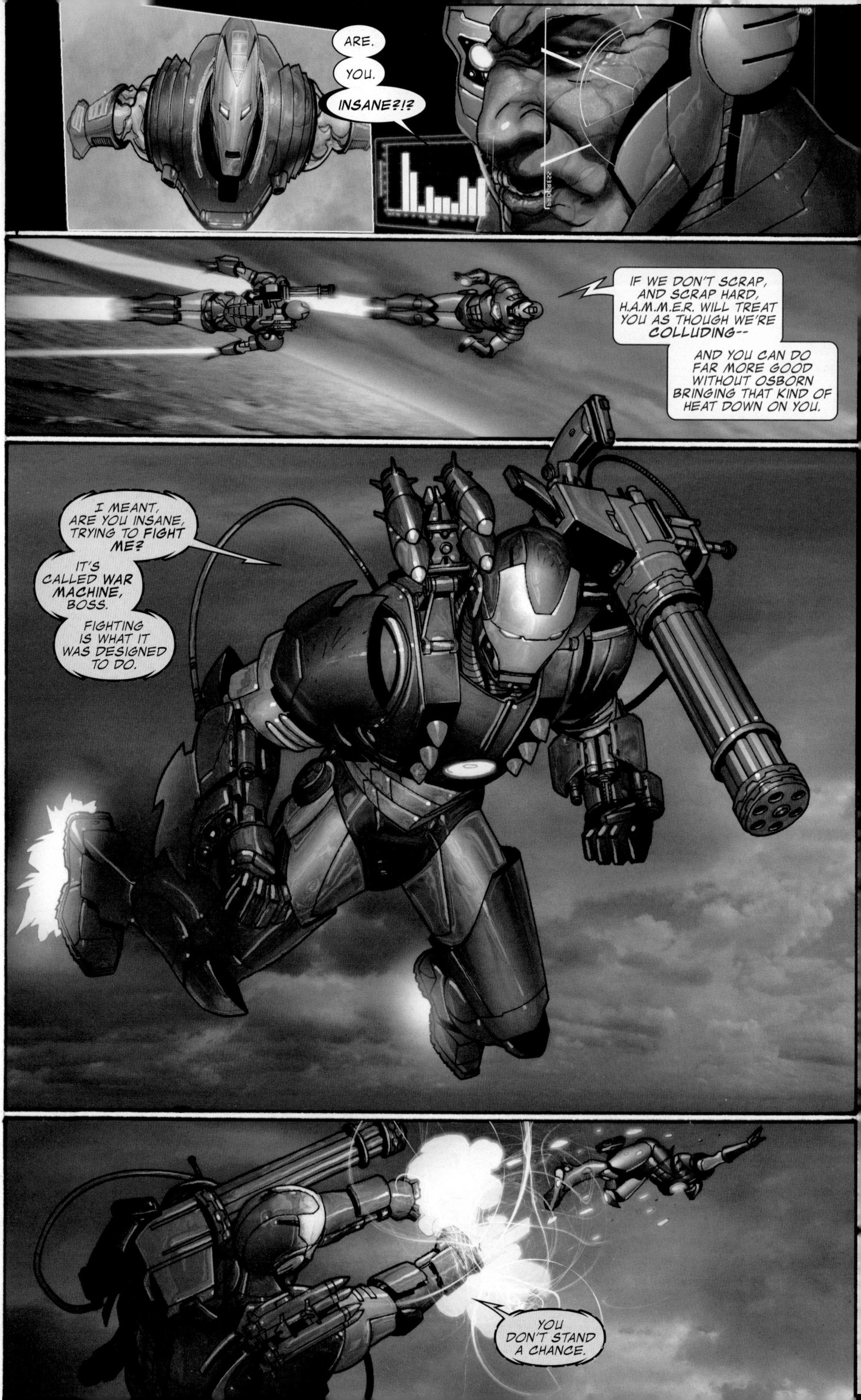
ARE.
YOU.
INSANE?!?
IF WE DON'T SCRAP, AND SCRAP HARD, H.A.M.M.E.R. WILL TREAT YOU AS THOUGH WE'RE COLLUDING--
AND YOU CAN DO FAR MORE GOOD WITHOUT OSBORN BRINGING THAT KIND OF HEAT DOWN ON YOU.
I MEANT, ARE YOU INSANE, TRYING TO FIGHT ME?
IT'S CALLED WAR MACHINE, BOSS.
FIGHTING IS WHAT IT WAS DESIGNED TO DO.
YOU DON'T STAND A CHANCE.

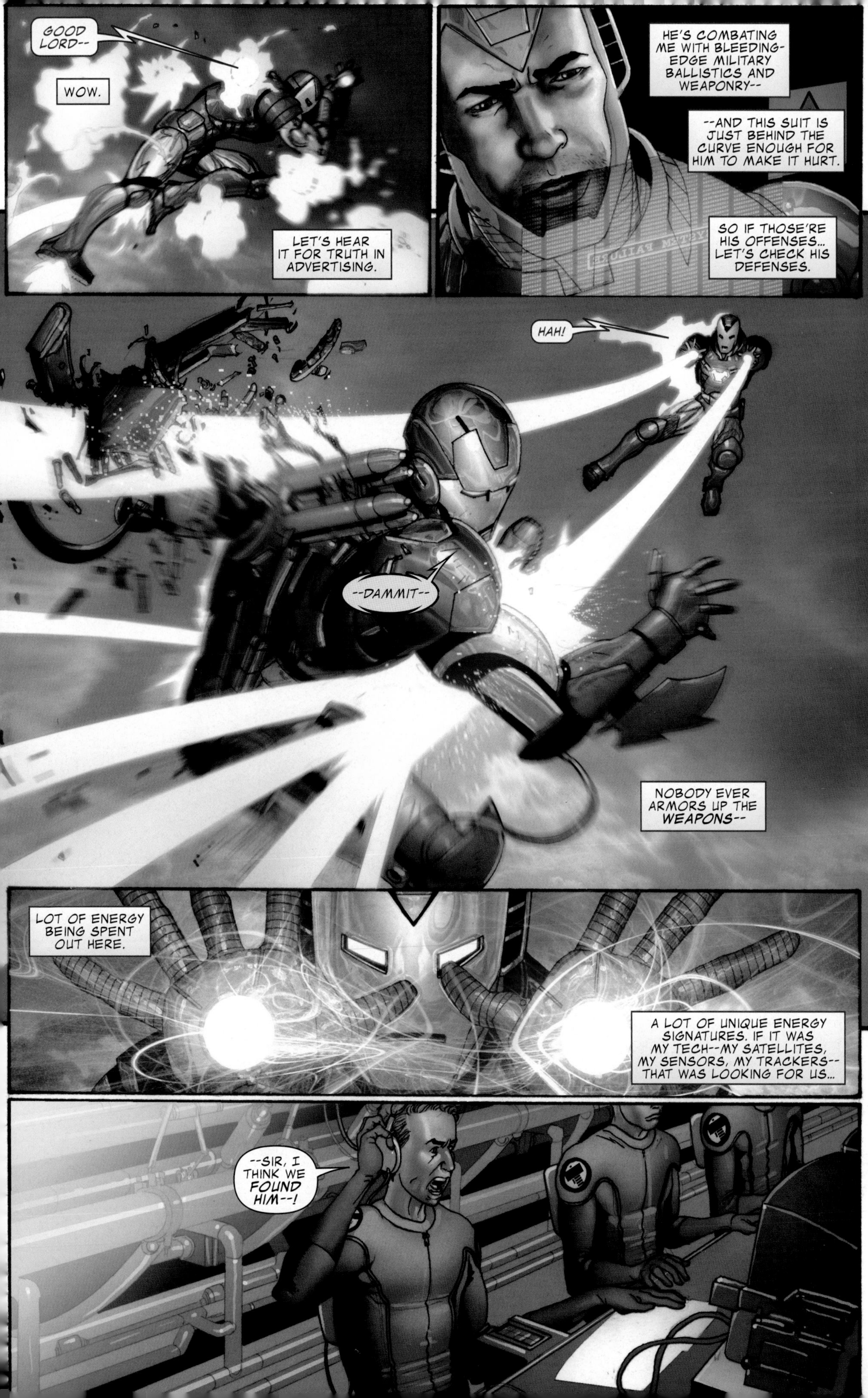
GOOD LORD--
WOW.
LET'S HEAR IT FOR TRUTH IN ADVERTISING.
HE'S COMBATING ME WITH BLEEDING-EDGE MILITARY BALLISTICS AND WEAPONRY--
--AND THIS SUIT IS JUST BEHIND THE CURVE ENOUGH FOR HIM TO MAKE IT HURT.
SO IF THOSE'RE HIS OFFENSES... LET'S CHECK HIS DEFENSES.
HAH!
--DAMMIT--
NOBODY EVER ARMORS UP THE WEAPONS--
LOT OF ENERGY BEING SPENT OUT HERE.
A LOT OF UNIQUE ENERGY SIGNATURES. IF IT WAS MY TECH--MY SATELLITES, MY SENSORS, MY TRACKERS--THAT WAS LOOKING FOR US...
--SIR, I THINK WE FOUND HIM--!

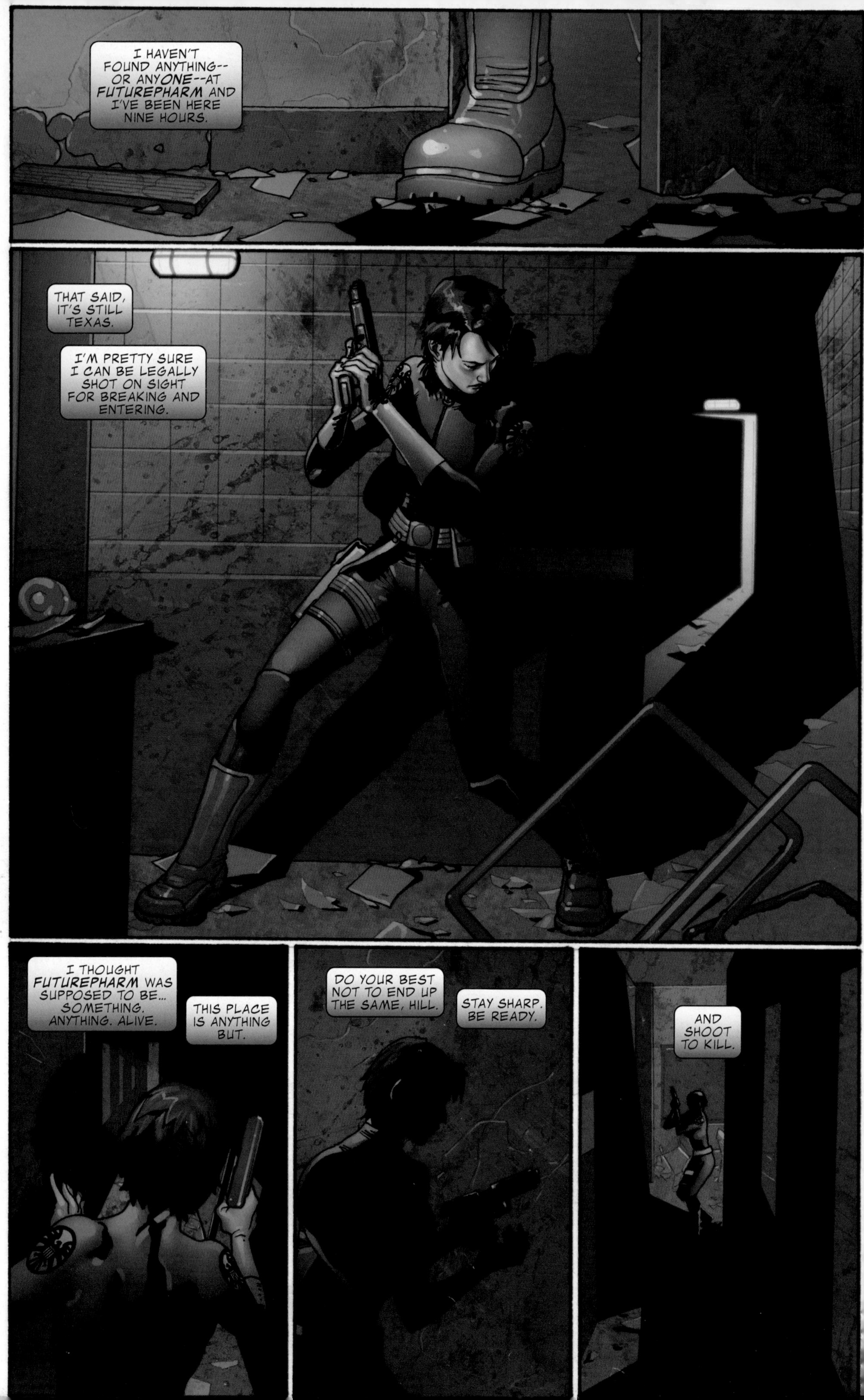
I HAVEN'T FOUND ANYTHING-- OR ANYONE--AT FUTUREPHARM AND I'VE BEEN HERE NINE HOURS.
THAT SAID, IT'S STILL TEXAS.
I'M PRETTY SURE I CAN BE LEGALLY SHOT ON SIGHT FOR BREAKING AND ENTERING.
I THOUGHT FUTUREPHARM WAS SUPPOSED TO BE... SOMETHING. ANYTHING. ALIVE.
THIS PLACE IS ANYTHING BUT.
DO YOUR BEST NOT TO END UP THE SAME, HILL.
STAY SHARP. BE READY.
AND SHOOT TO KILL.

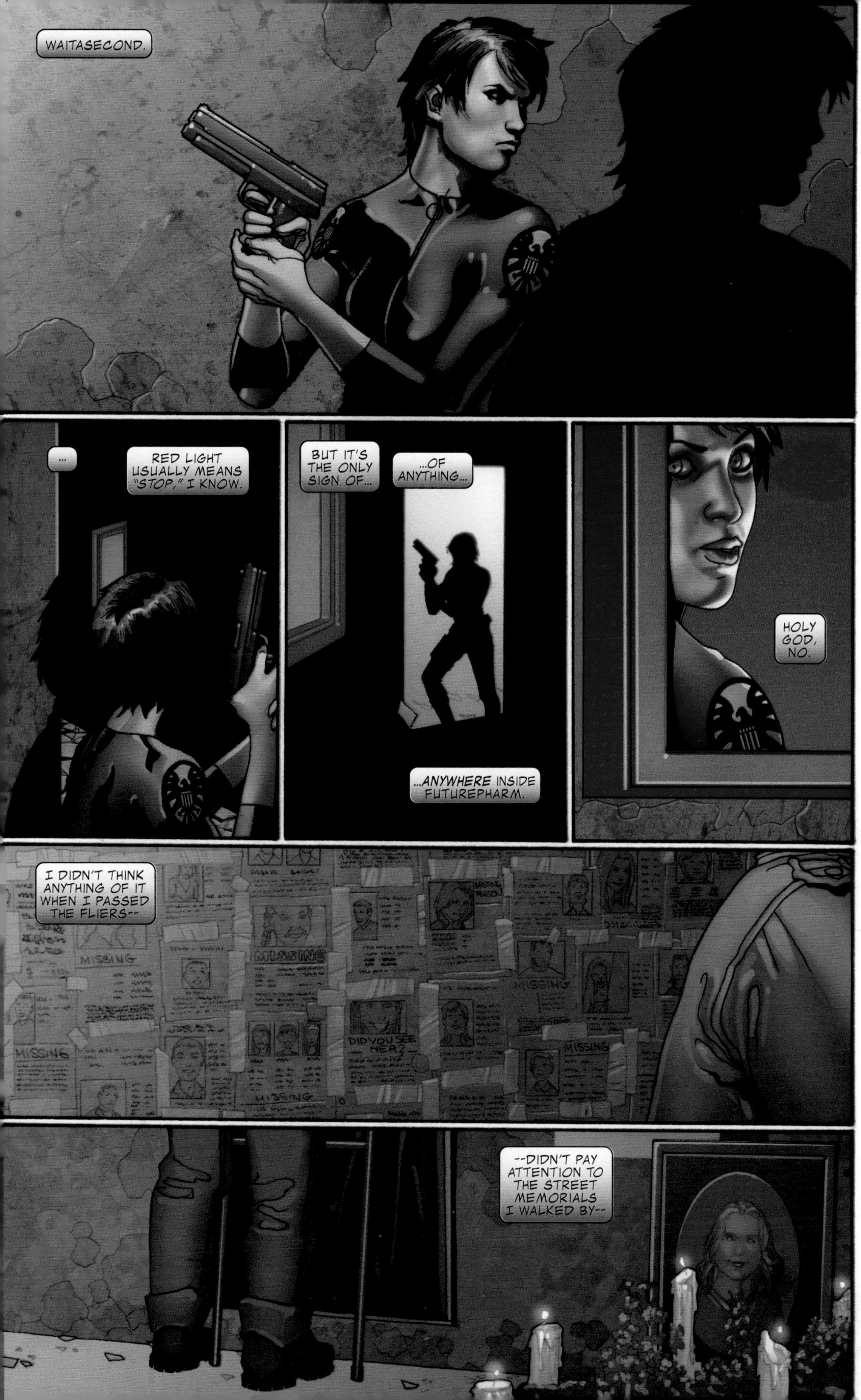
WAITASECOND.
...
RED LIGHT USUALLY MEANS "STOP," I KNOW.
BUT IT'S THE ONLY SIGN OF...
...OF ANYTHING...
...ANYWHERE INSIDE FUTUREPHARM.
HOLY GOD, NO.
I DIDN'T THINK ANYTHING OF IT WHEN I PASSED THE FLIERS--
MISSING
MISSING
MISSING
DID YOU SEE HER?
MISSING
MISSING
MISSING
--DIDN'T PAY ATTENTION TO THE STREET MEMORIALS I WALKED BY--

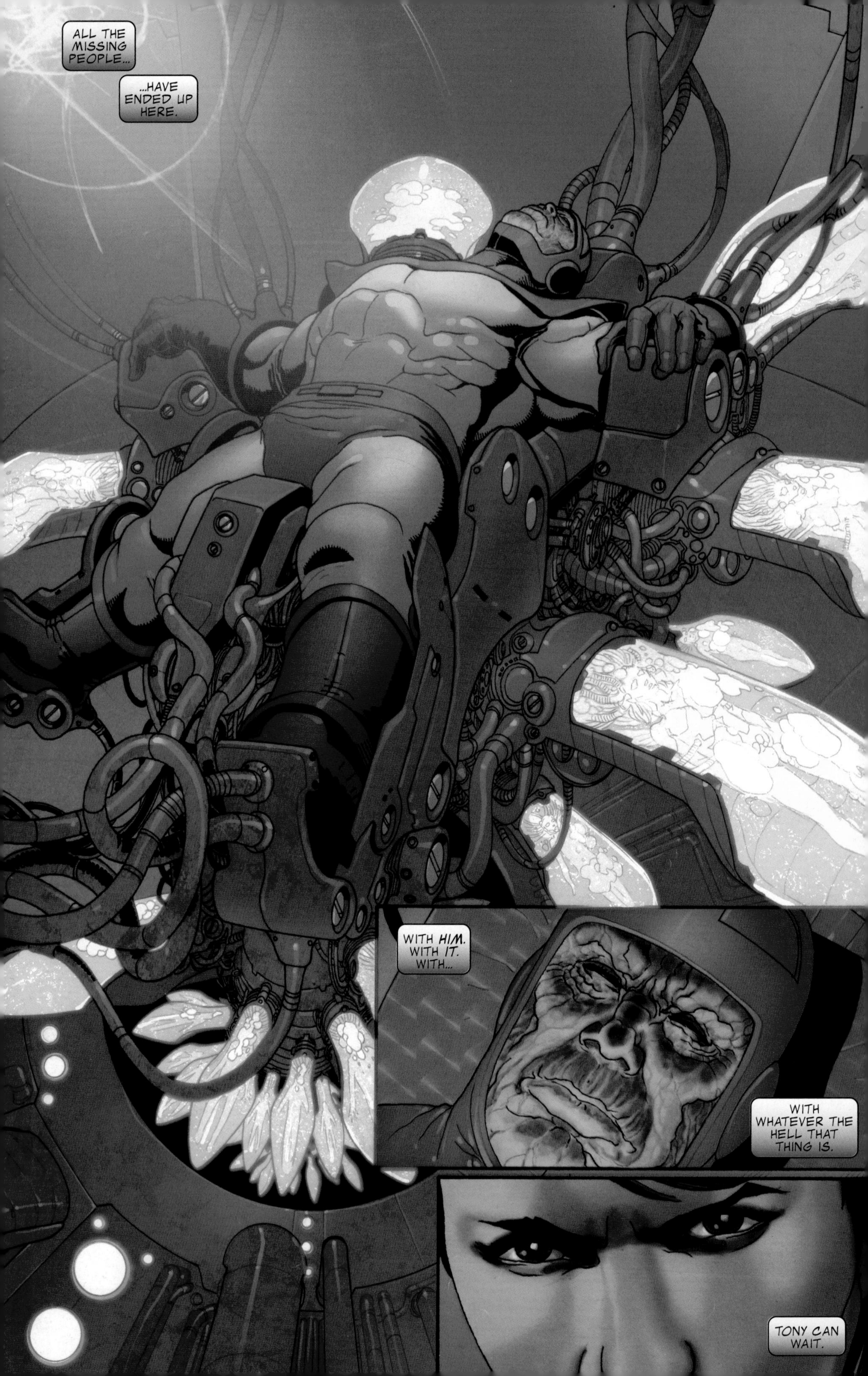
ALL THE MISSING PEOPLE...
...HAVE ENDED UP HERE.
WITH *HIM*. WITH *IT*. WITH...
WITH WHATEVER THE HELL THAT THING IS.
TONY CAN WAIT.

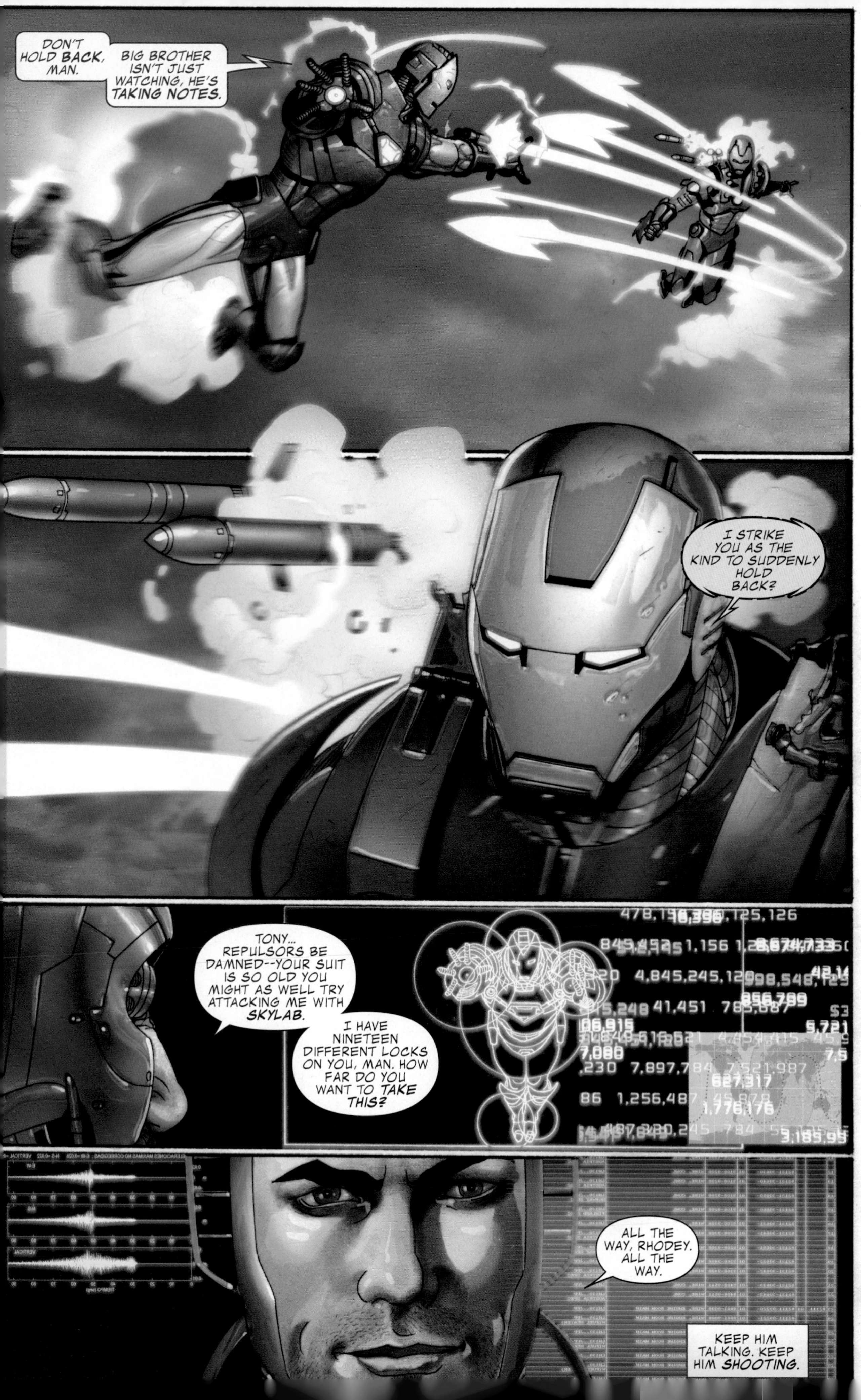

DON'T HOLD BACK, MAN.
BIG BROTHER ISN'T JUST WATCHING, HE'S TAKING NOTES.
I STRIKE YOU AS THE KIND TO SUDDENLY HOLD BACK?
TONY... REPULSORS BE DAMNED--YOUR SUIT IS SO OLD YOU MIGHT AS WELL TRY ATTACKING ME WITH SKYLAB.
I HAVE NINETEEN DIFFERENT LOCKS ON YOU, MAN. HOW FAR DO YOU WANT TO TAKE THIS?
ALL THE WAY, RHODEY. ALL THE WAY.
KEEP HIM TALKING. KEEP HIM SHOOTING.

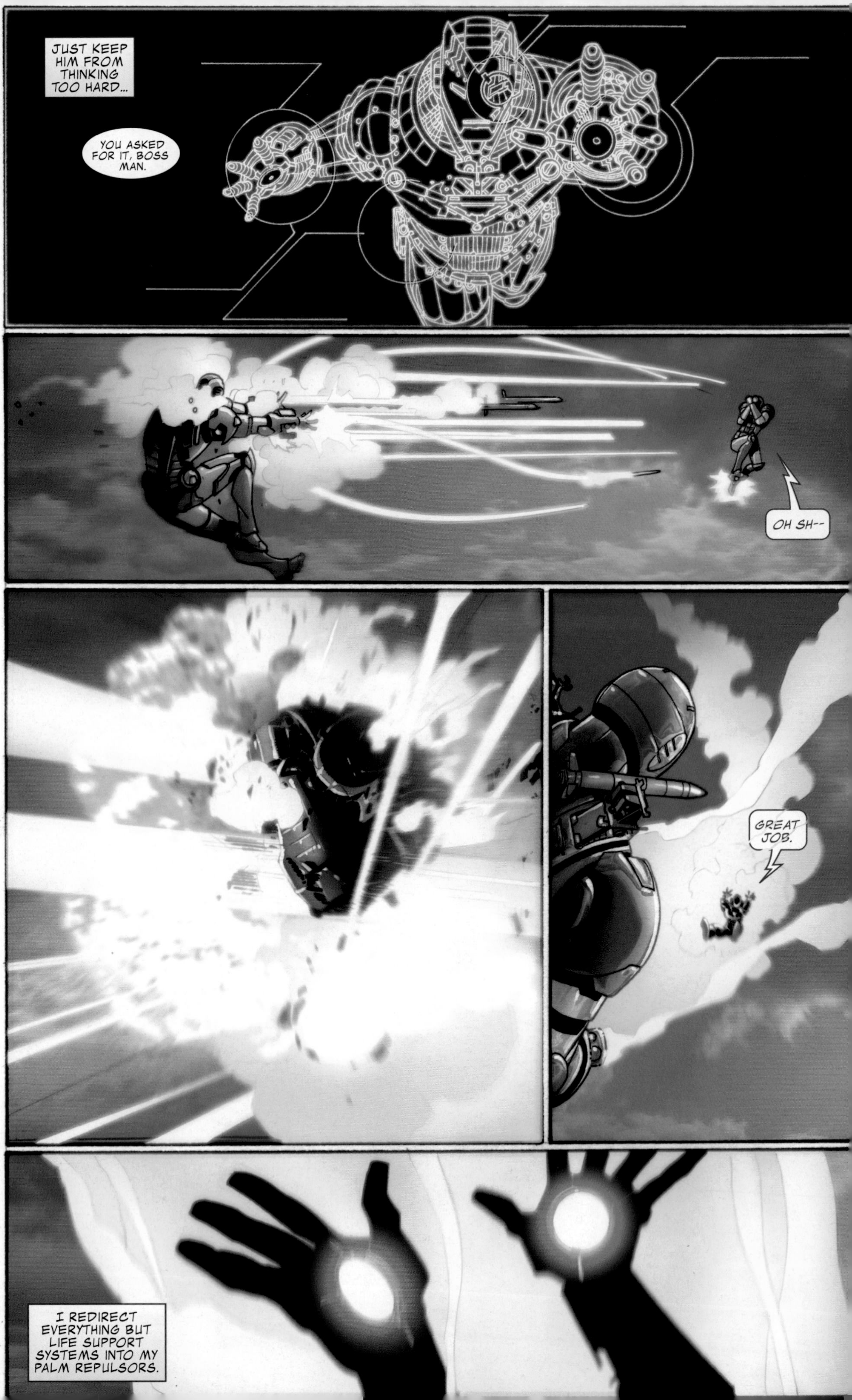
JUST KEEP HIM FROM THINKING TOO HARD...
YOU ASKED FOR IT, BOSS MAN.
OH SH--
GREAT JOB.
I REDIRECT EVERYTHING BUT LIFE SUPPORT SYSTEMS INTO MY PALM REPULSORS.

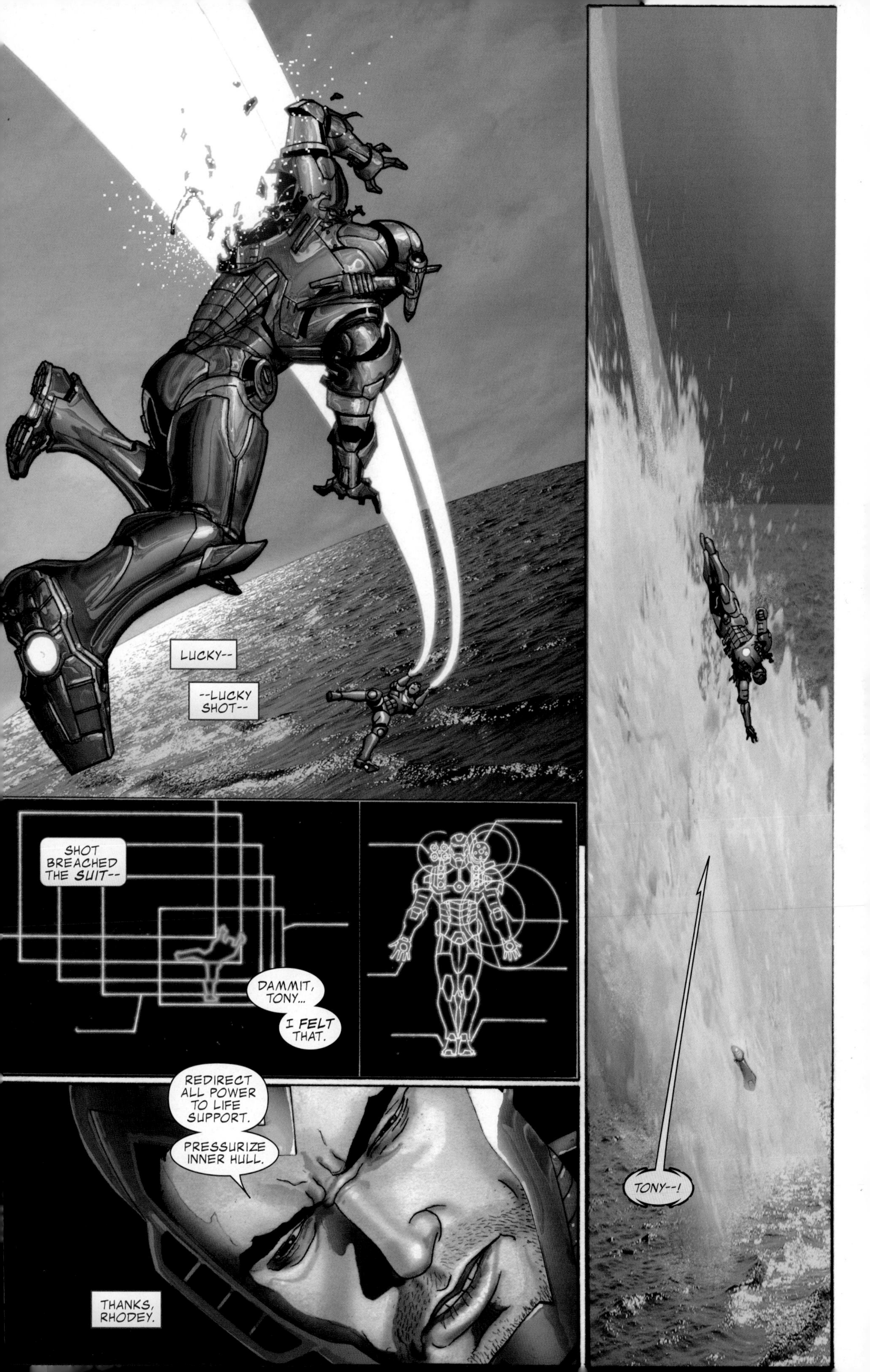

LUCKY--
--LUCKY SHOT--
SHOT BREACHED THE SUIT--
DAMMIT, TONY...
I FELT THAT.
REDIRECT ALL POWER TO LIFE SUPPORT.
PRESSURIZE INNER HULL.
THANKS, RHODEY.
TONY--!

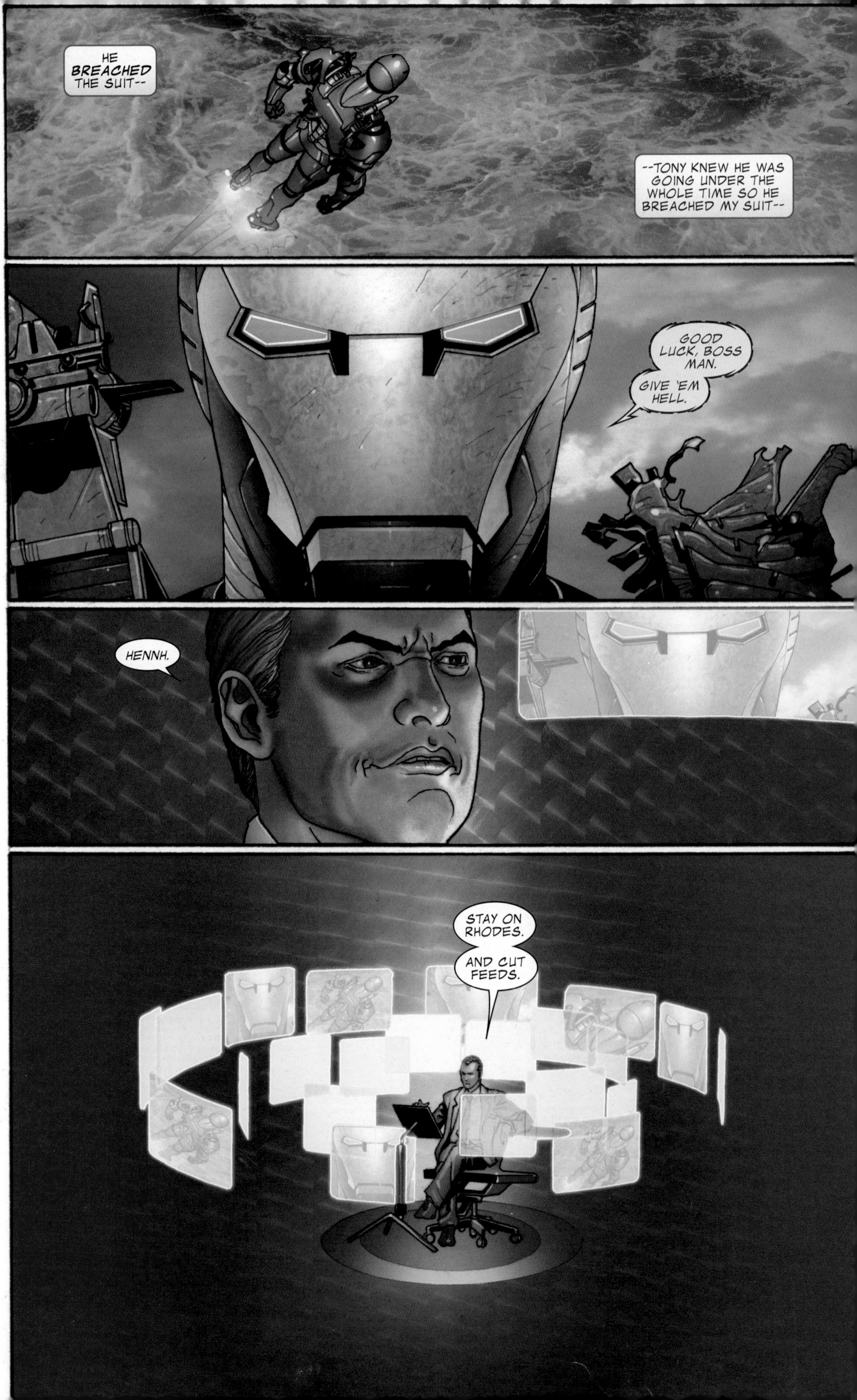
HE BREACHED THE SUIT--
--TONY KNEW HE WAS GOING UNDER THE WHOLE TIME SO HE BREACHED MY SUIT--
GOOD LUCK, BOSS MAN.
GIVE 'EM HELL.
HENNH.
STAY ON RHODES.
AND CUT FEEDS.

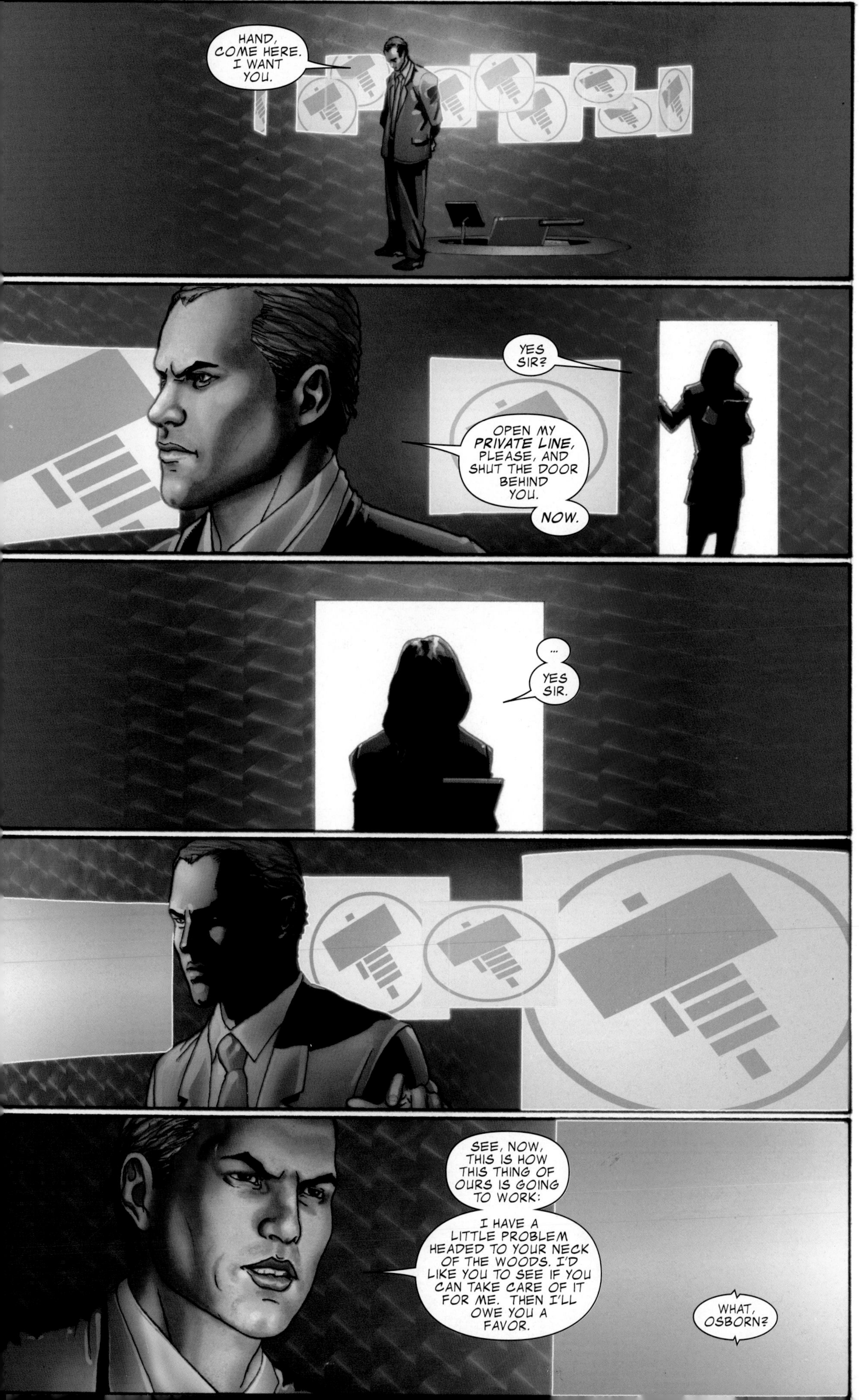
HAND, COME HERE. I WANT YOU.
YES SIR?
OPEN MY PRIVATE LINE, PLEASE, AND SHUT THE DOOR BEHIND YOU.
NOW.
...
YES SIR.
SEE, NOW, THIS IS HOW THIS THING OF OURS IS GOING TO WORK:
I HAVE A LITTLE PROBLEM HEADED TO YOUR NECK OF THE WOODS. I'D LIKE YOU TO SEE IF YOU CAN TAKE CARE OF IT FOR ME. THEN I'LL OWE YOU A FAVOR.
WHAT, OSBORN?

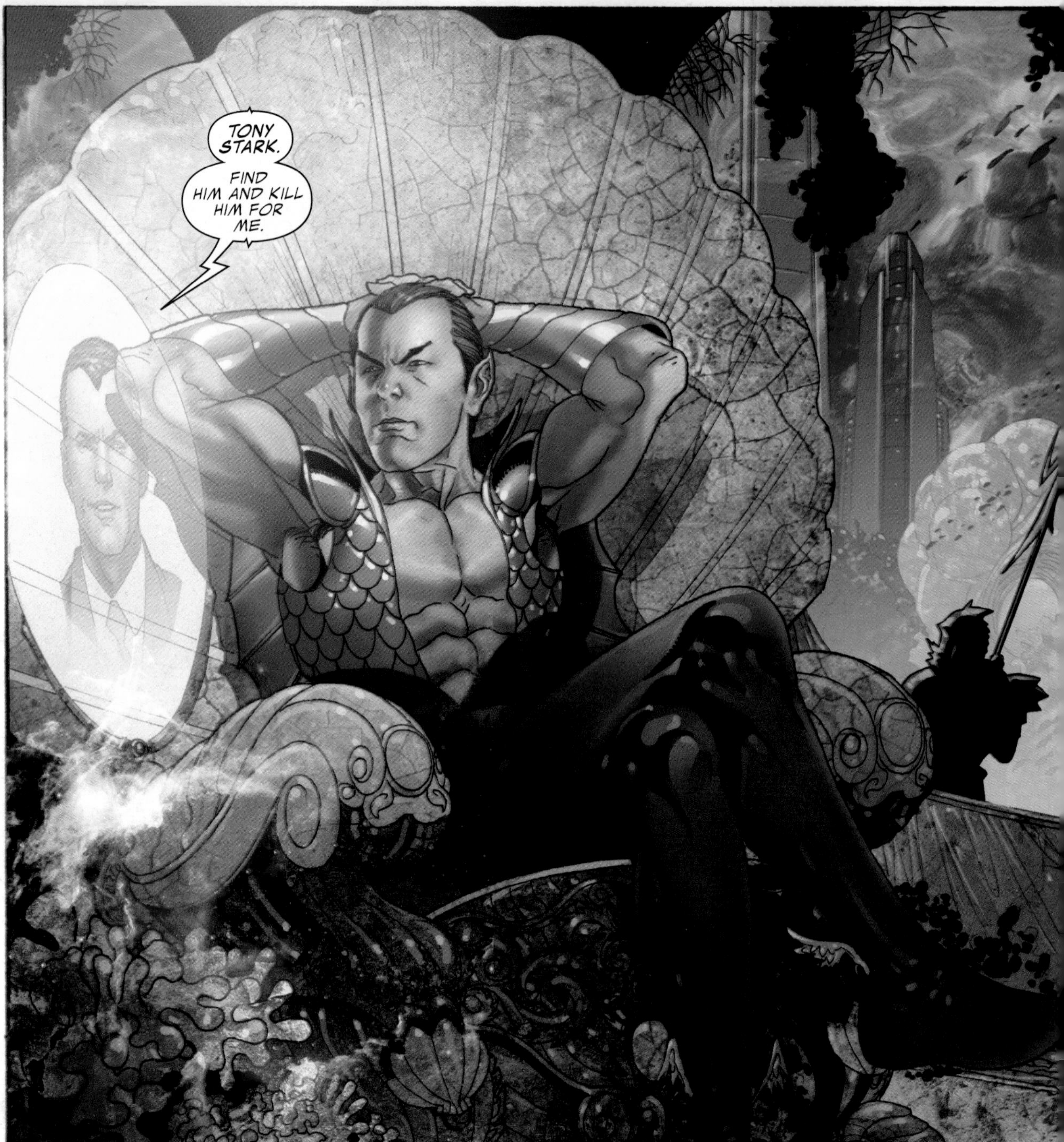
TONY STARK.
FIND HIM AND KILL HIM FOR ME.

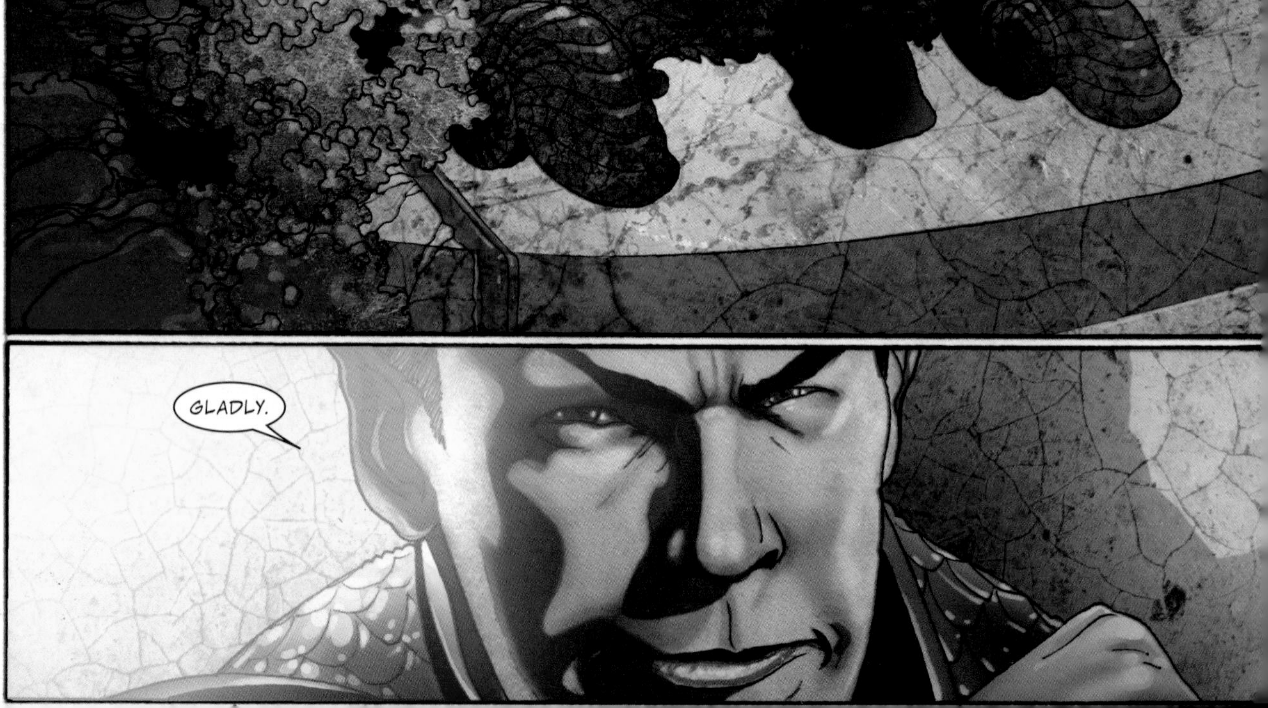
GLADLY.

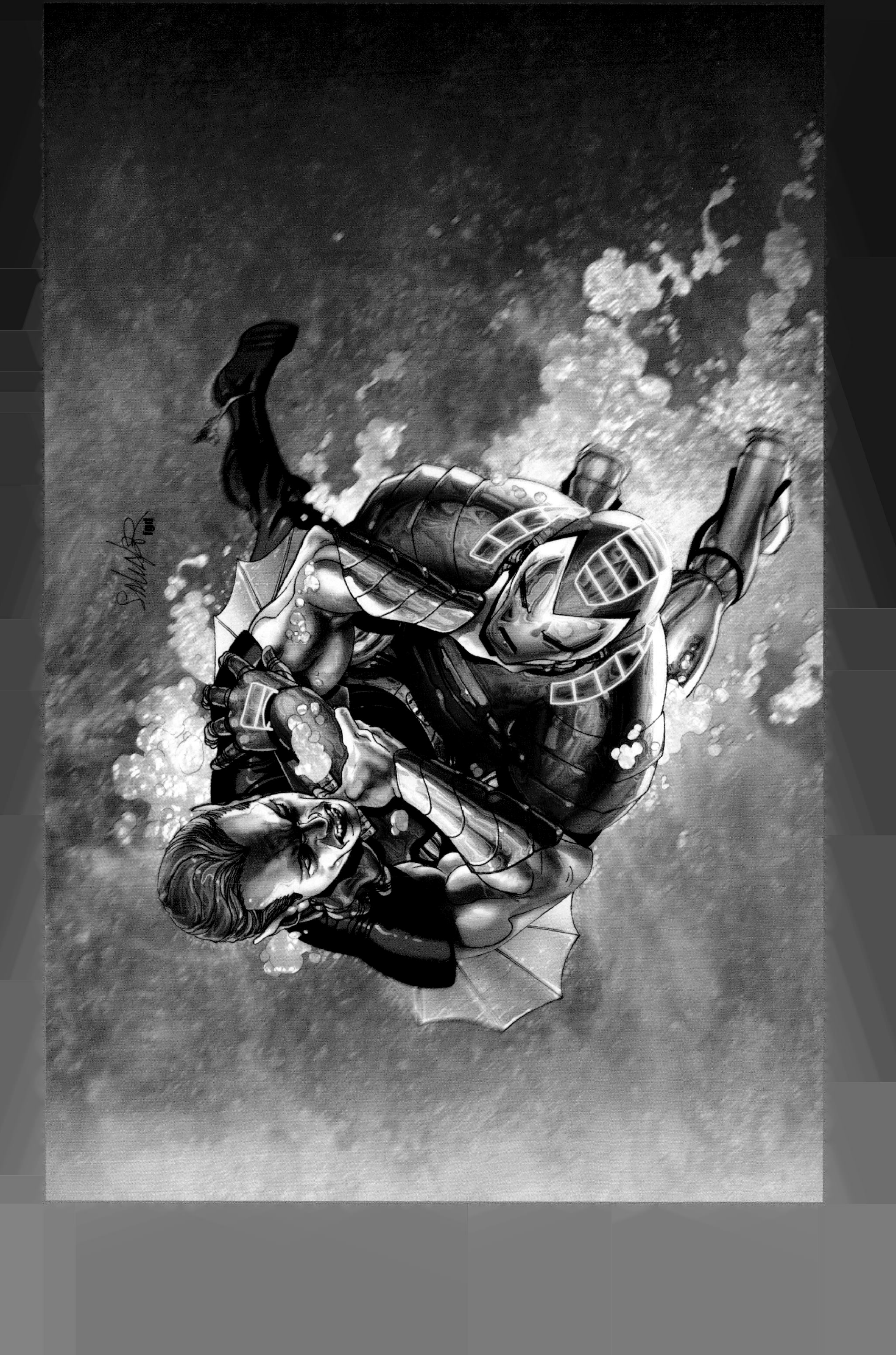

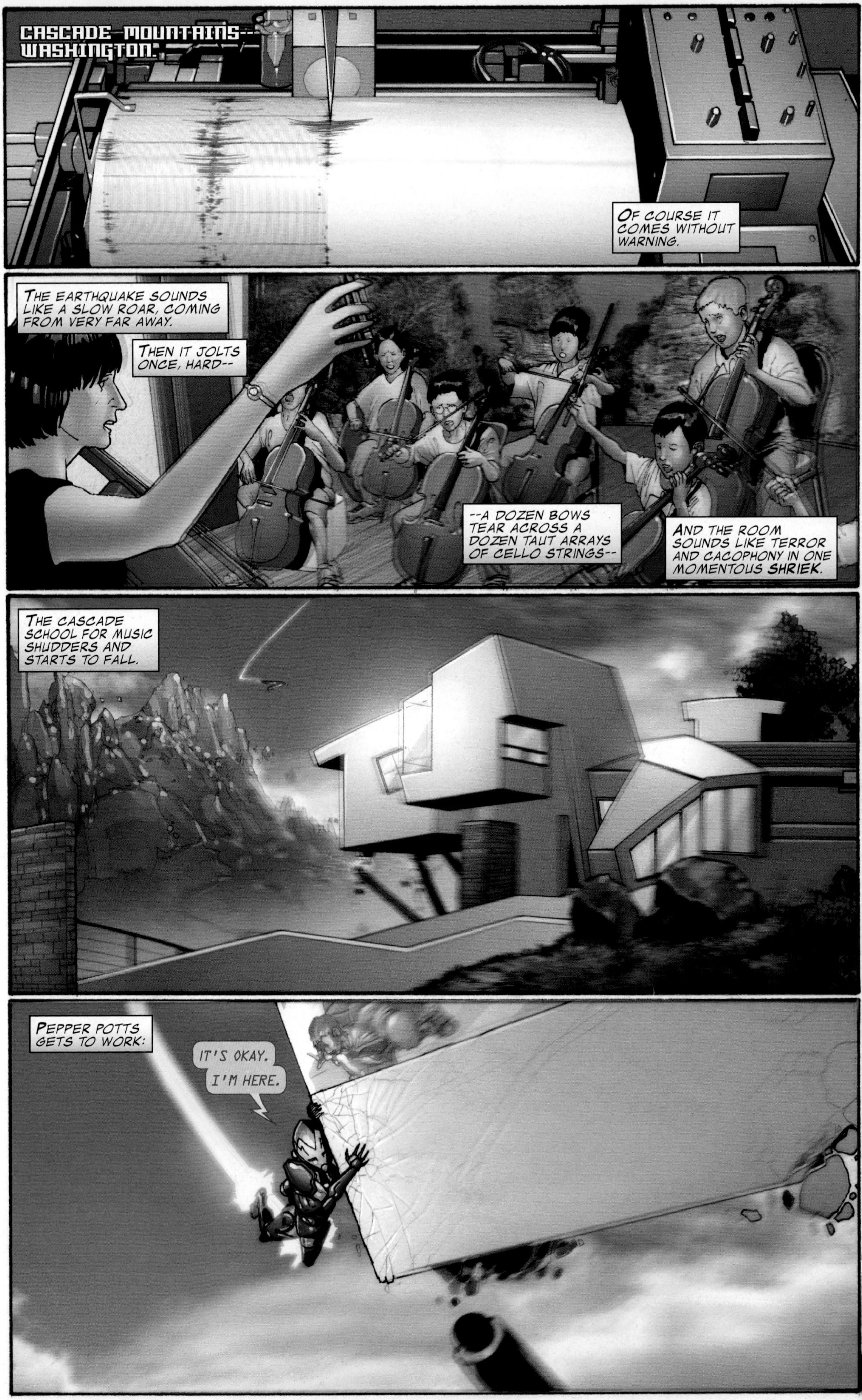
CASCADE MOUNTAINS--
WASHINGTON.
OF COURSE IT COMES WITHOUT WARNING.
THE EARTHQUAKE SOUNDS LIKE A SLOW ROAR, COMING FROM VERY FAR AWAY.
THEN IT JOLTS ONCE, HARD--
--A DOZEN BOWS TEAR ACROSS A DOZEN TAUT ARRAYS OF CELLO STRINGS--
AND THE ROOM SOUNDS LIKE TERROR AND CACOPHONY IN ONE MOMENTOUS SHRIEK.
THE CASCADE SCHOOL FOR MUSIC SHUDDERS AND STARTS TO FALL.
PEPPER POTTS GETS TO WORK:
IT'S OKAY. I'M HERE.

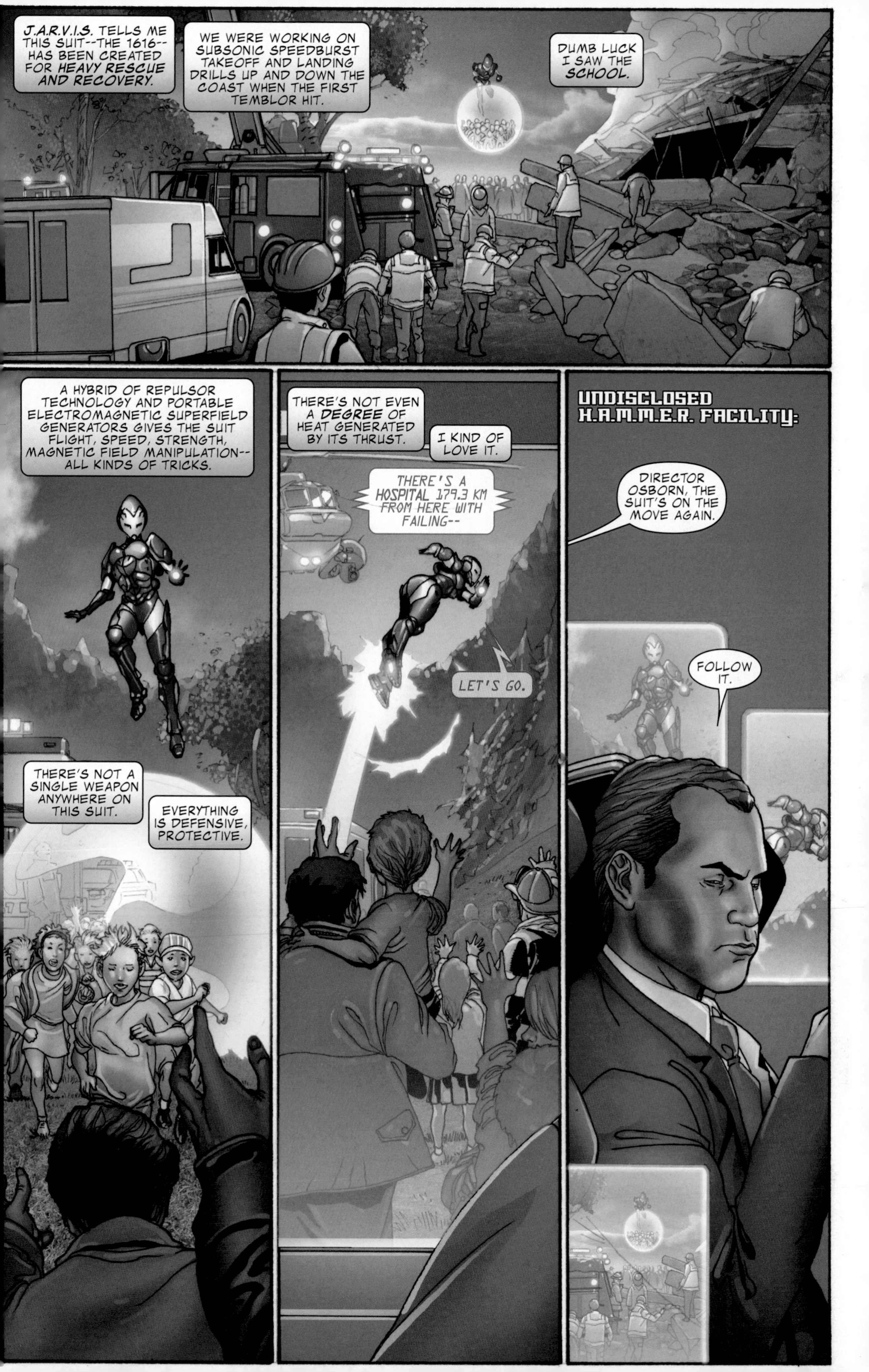
J.A.R.V.I.S. TELLS ME THIS SUIT--THE 1616--HAS BEEN CREATED FOR HEAVY RESCUE AND RECOVERY.
WE WERE WORKING ON SUBSONIC SPEEDBURST TAKEOFF AND LANDING DRILLS UP AND DOWN THE COAST WHEN THE FIRST TEMBLOR HIT.
DUMB LUCK I SAW THE SCHOOL.
A HYBRID OF REPULSOR TECHNOLOGY AND PORTABLE ELECTROMAGNETIC SUPERFIELD GENERATORS GIVES THE SUIT FLIGHT, SPEED, STRENGTH, MAGNETIC FIELD MANIPULATION--ALL KINDS OF TRICKS.
THERE'S NOT A SINGLE WEAPON ANYWHERE ON THIS SUIT.
EVERYTHING IS DEFENSIVE, PROTECTIVE.
THERE'S NOT EVEN A DEGREE OF HEAT GENERATED BY ITS THRUST.
I KIND OF LOVE IT.
THERE'S A HOSPITAL 179.3 KM FROM HERE WITH FAILING--
LET'S GO.
UNDISCLOSED H.A.M.M.E.R. FACILITY:
DIRECTOR OSBORN, THE SUIT'S ON THE MOVE AGAIN.
FOLLOW IT.

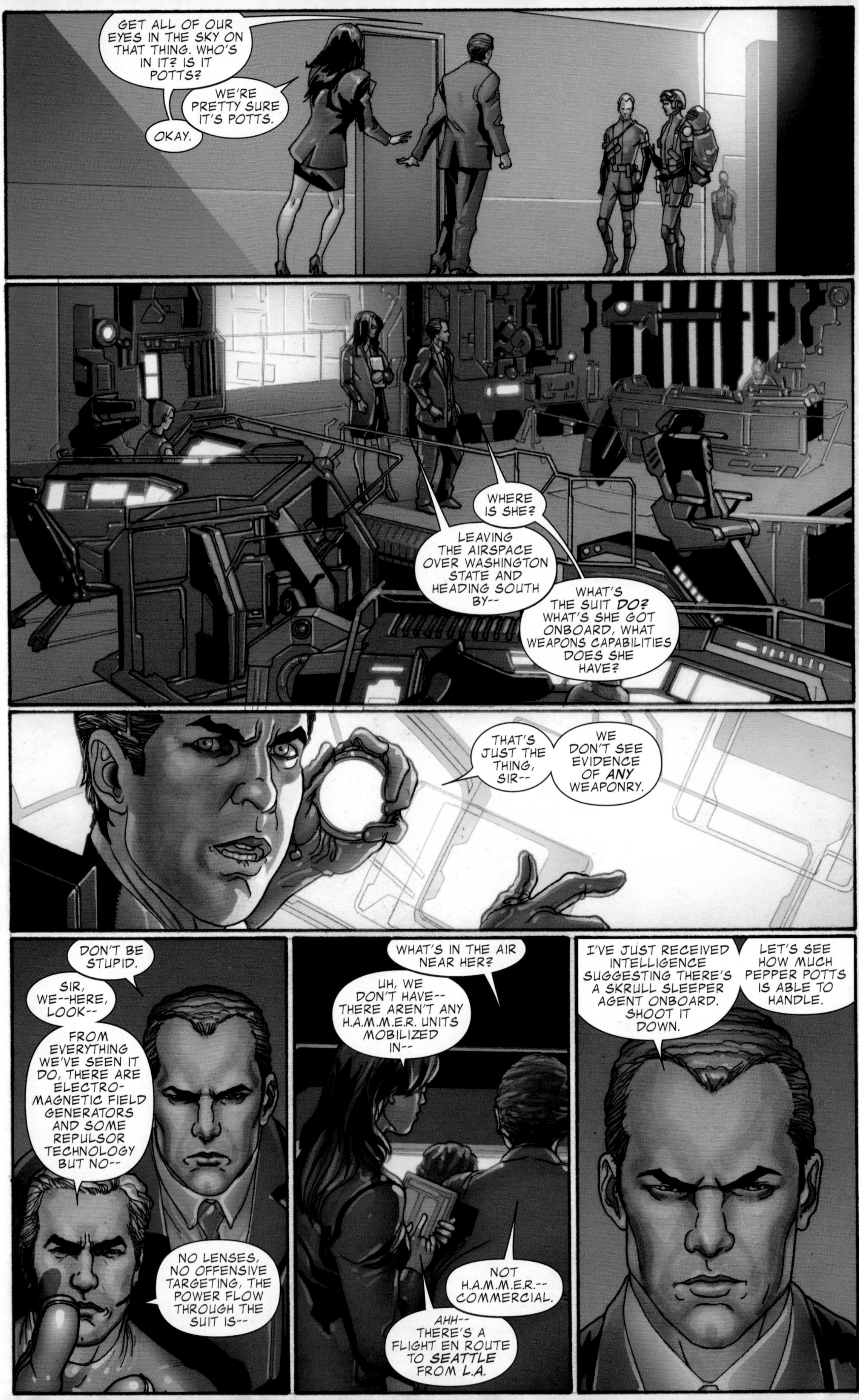
GET ALL OF OUR EYES IN THE SKY ON THAT THING. WHO'S IN IT? IS IT POTTS?
WE'RE PRETTY SURE IT'S POTTS.
OKAY.
WHERE IS SHE?
LEAVING THE AIRSPACE OVER WASHINGTON STATE AND HEADING SOUTH BY--
WHAT'S THE SUIT DO? WHAT'S SHE GOT ONBOARD, WHAT WEAPONS CAPABILITIES DOES SHE HAVE?
THAT'S JUST THE THING, SIR--
WE DON'T SEE EVIDENCE OF ANY WEAPONRY.
DON'T BE STUPID.
SIR, WE--HERE, LOOK--
FROM EVERYTHING WE'VE SEEN IT DO, THERE ARE ELECTRO-MAGNETIC FIELD GENERATORS AND SOME REPULSOR TECHNOLOGY BUT NO--
NO LENSES, NO OFFENSIVE TARGETING, THE POWER FLOW THROUGH THE SUIT IS--
WHAT'S IN THE AIR NEAR HER?
UH, WE DON'T HAVE-- THERE AREN'T ANY H.A.M.M.E.R. UNITS MOBILIZED IN--
NOT H.A.M.M.E.R.-- COMMERCIAL.
AHH-- THERE'S A FLIGHT EN ROUTE TO SEATTLE FROM L.A.
I'VE JUST RECEIVED INTELLIGENCE SUGGESTING THERE'S A SKRULL SLEEPER AGENT ONBOARD. SHOOT IT DOWN.
LET'S SEE HOW MUCH PEPPER POTTS IS ABLE TO HANDLE.

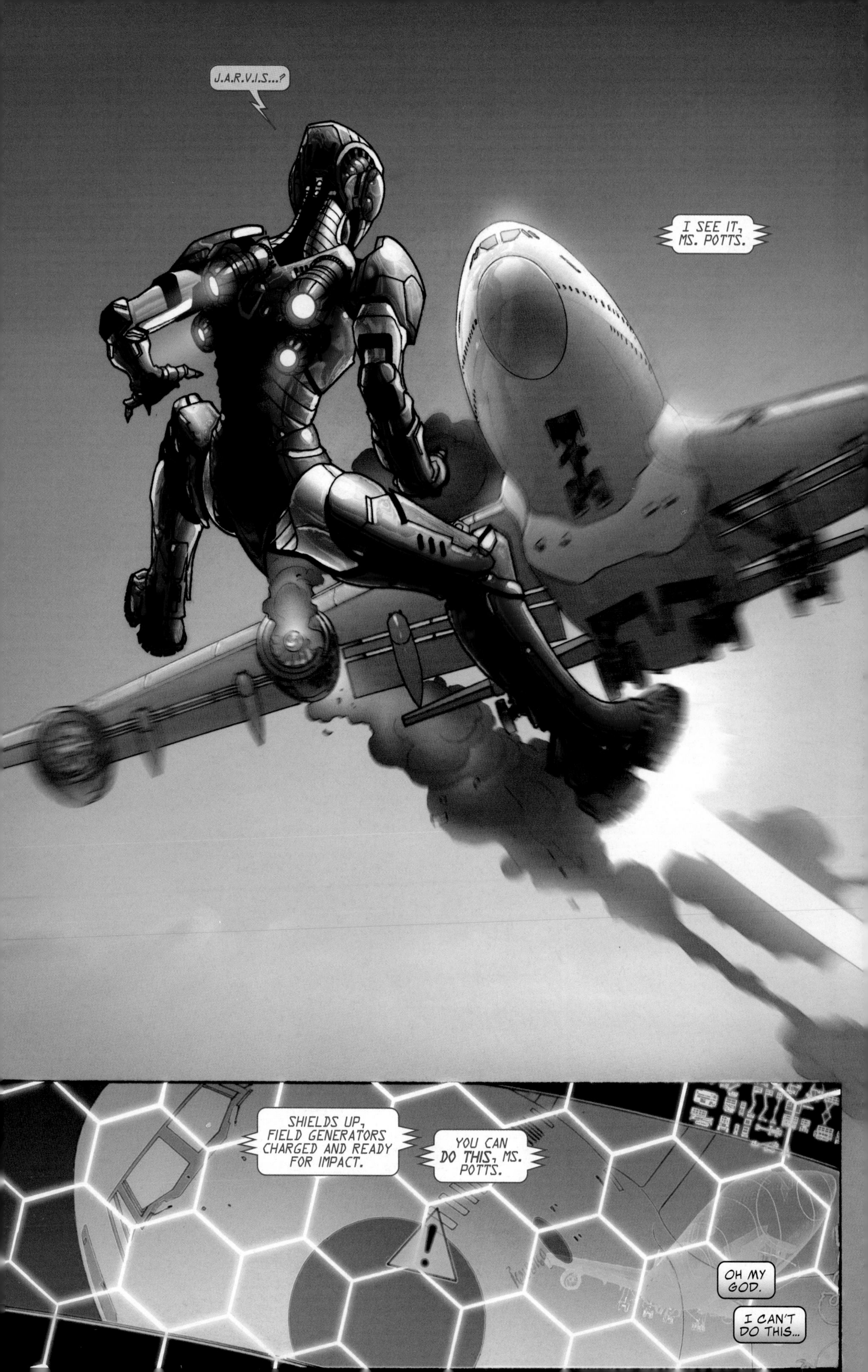
J.A.R.V.I.S...?
I SEE IT, MS. POTTS.
SHIELDS UP, FIELD GENERATORS CHARGED AND READY FOR IMPACT.
YOU CAN DO THIS, MS. POTTS.
OH MY GOD.
I CAN'T DO THIS...

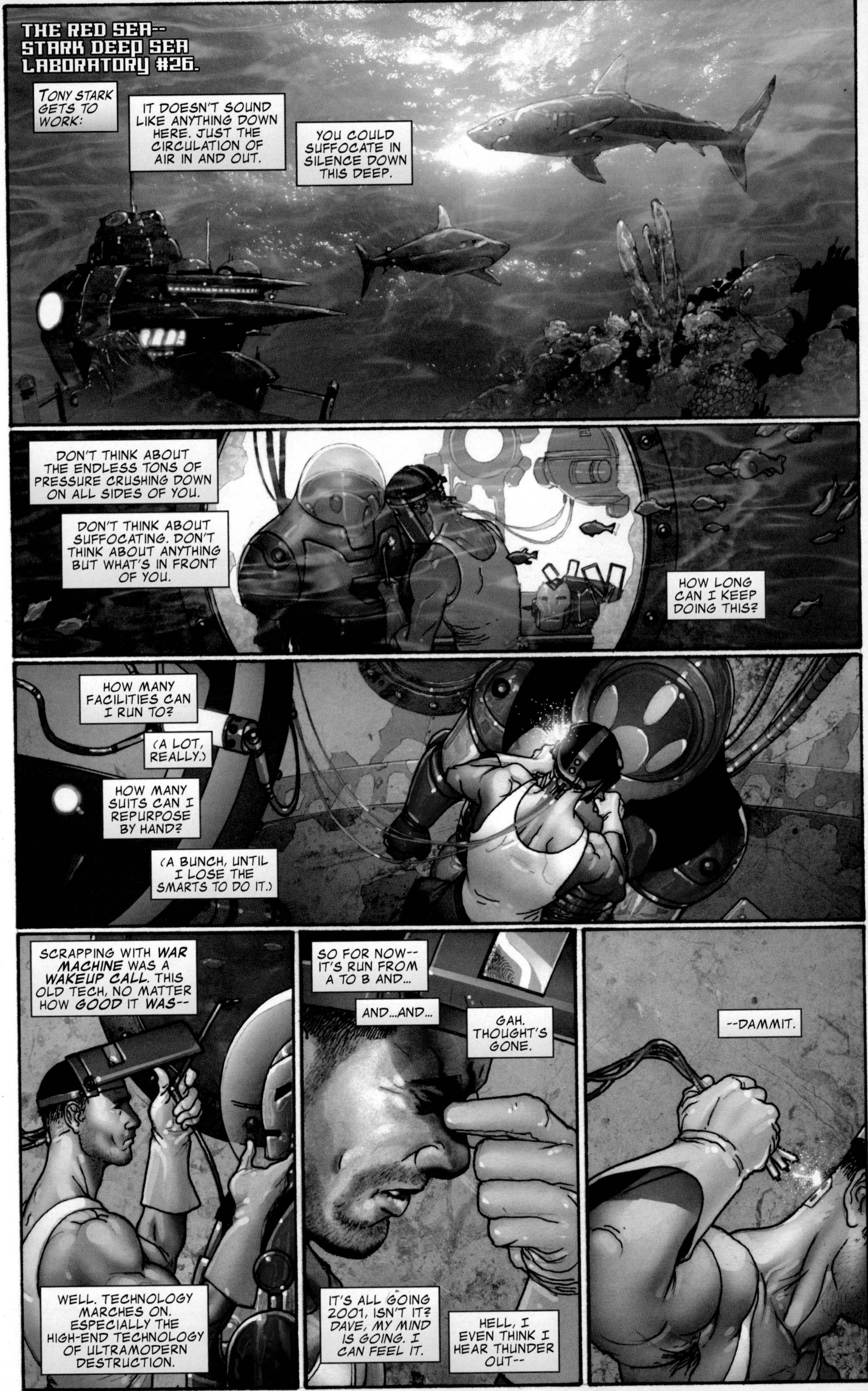
THE RED SEA--
STARK DEEP SEA
LABORATORY #26.
TONY STARK GETS TO WORK:
IT DOESN'T SOUND LIKE ANYTHING DOWN HERE. JUST THE CIRCULATION OF AIR IN AND OUT.
YOU COULD SUFFOCATE IN SILENCE DOWN THIS DEEP.
DON'T THINK ABOUT THE ENDLESS TONS OF PRESSURE CRUSHING DOWN ON ALL SIDES OF YOU.
DON'T THINK ABOUT SUFFOCATING. DON'T THINK ABOUT ANYTHING BUT WHAT'S IN FRONT OF YOU.
HOW LONG CAN I KEEP DOING THIS?
HOW MANY FACILITIES CAN I RUN TO?
(A LOT, REALLY.)
HOW MANY SUITS CAN I REPURPOSE BY HAND?
(A BUNCH, UNTIL I LOSE THE SMARTS TO DO IT.)
SCRAPPING WITH WAR MACHINE WAS A WAKEUP CALL. THIS OLD TECH, NO MATTER HOW GOOD IT WAS--
WELL. TECHNOLOGY MARCHES ON. ESPECIALLY THE HIGH-END TECHNOLOGY OF ULTRAMODERN DESTRUCTION.
SO FOR NOW-- IT'S RUN FROM A TO B AND...
AND...AND...
GAH. THOUGHT'S GONE.
IT'S ALL GOING 2001, ISN'T IT? DAVE, MY MIND IS GOING. I CAN FEEL IT.
HELL, I EVEN THINK I HEAR THUNDER OUT--
--DAMMIT.

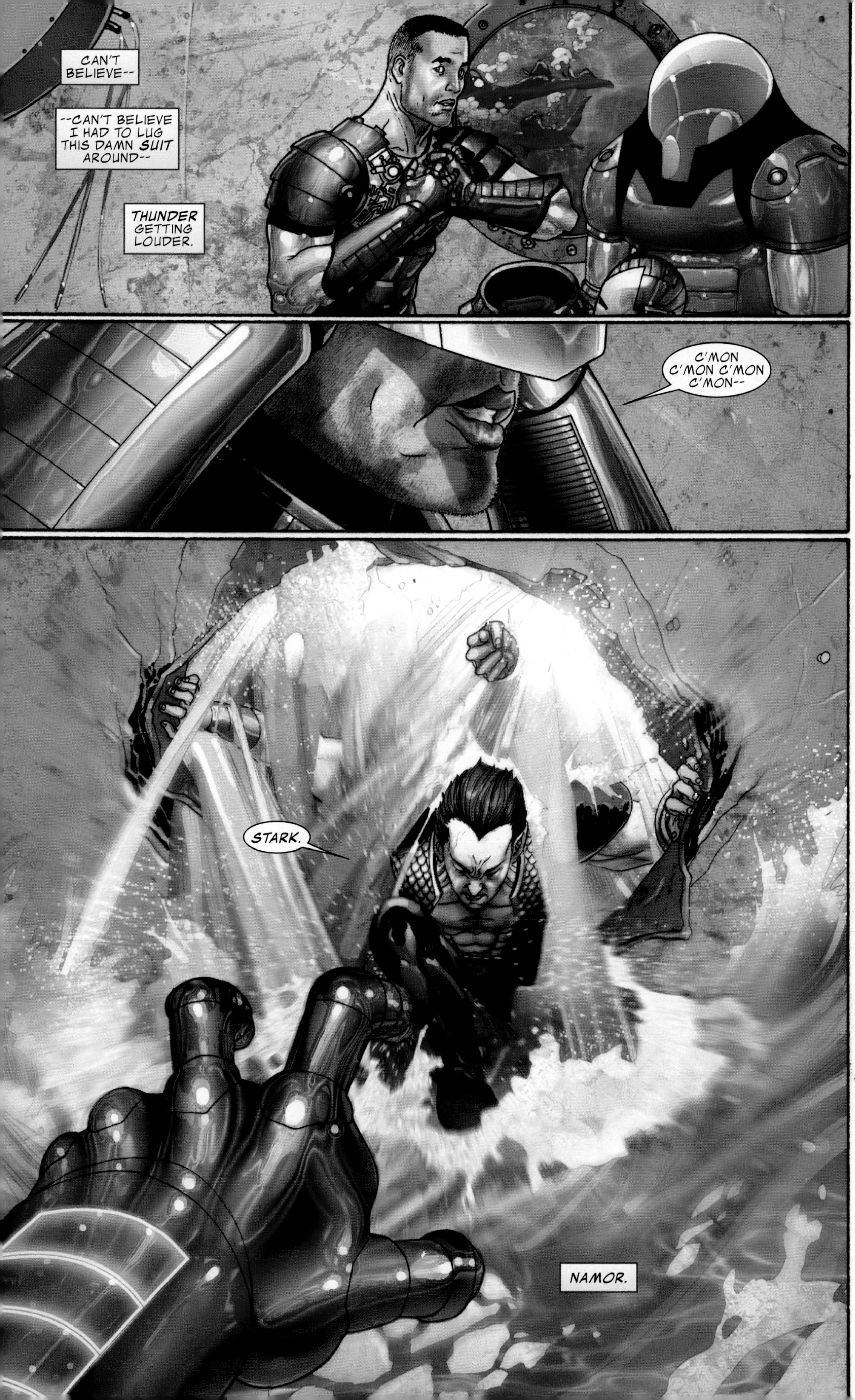
CAN'T BELIEVE--
--CAN'T BELIEVE I HAD TO LUG THIS DAMN SUIT AROUND--
THUNDER GETTING LOUDER.
C'MON C'MON C'MON C'MON--
STARK.
NAMOR.

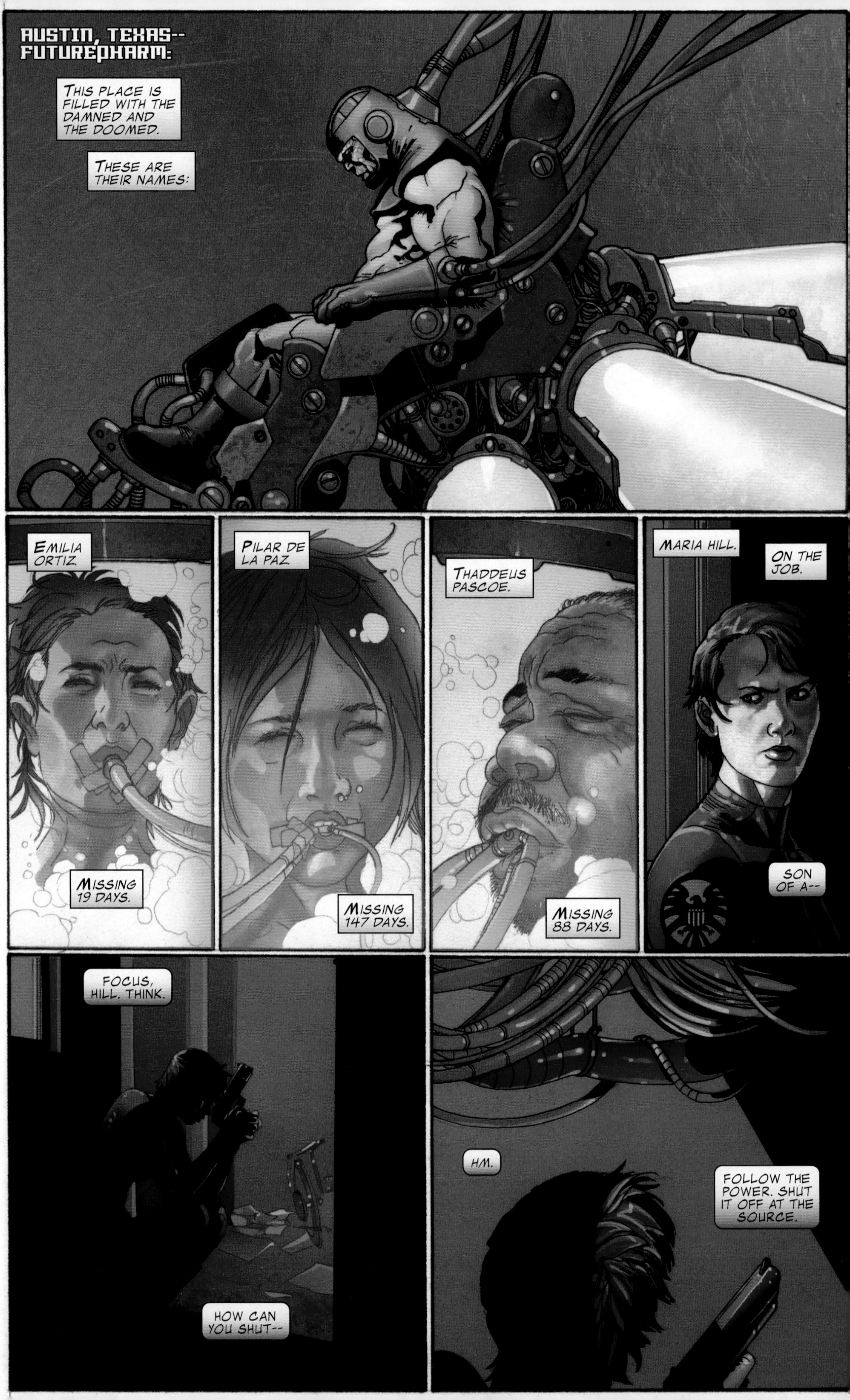
AUSTIN, TEXAS--
FUTUREPHARM:
THIS PLACE IS FILLED WITH THE DAMNED AND THE DOOMED.
THESE ARE THEIR NAMES:
EMILIA ORTIZ.
MISSING 19 DAYS.
PILAR DE LA PAZ.
MISSING 147 DAYS.
THADDEUS PASCOE.
MISSING 88 DAYS.
MARIA HILL.
ON THE JOB.
SON OF A--
FOCUS, HILL. THINK.
HOW CAN YOU SHUT--
HM.
FOLLOW THE POWER. SHUT IT OFF AT THE SOURCE.

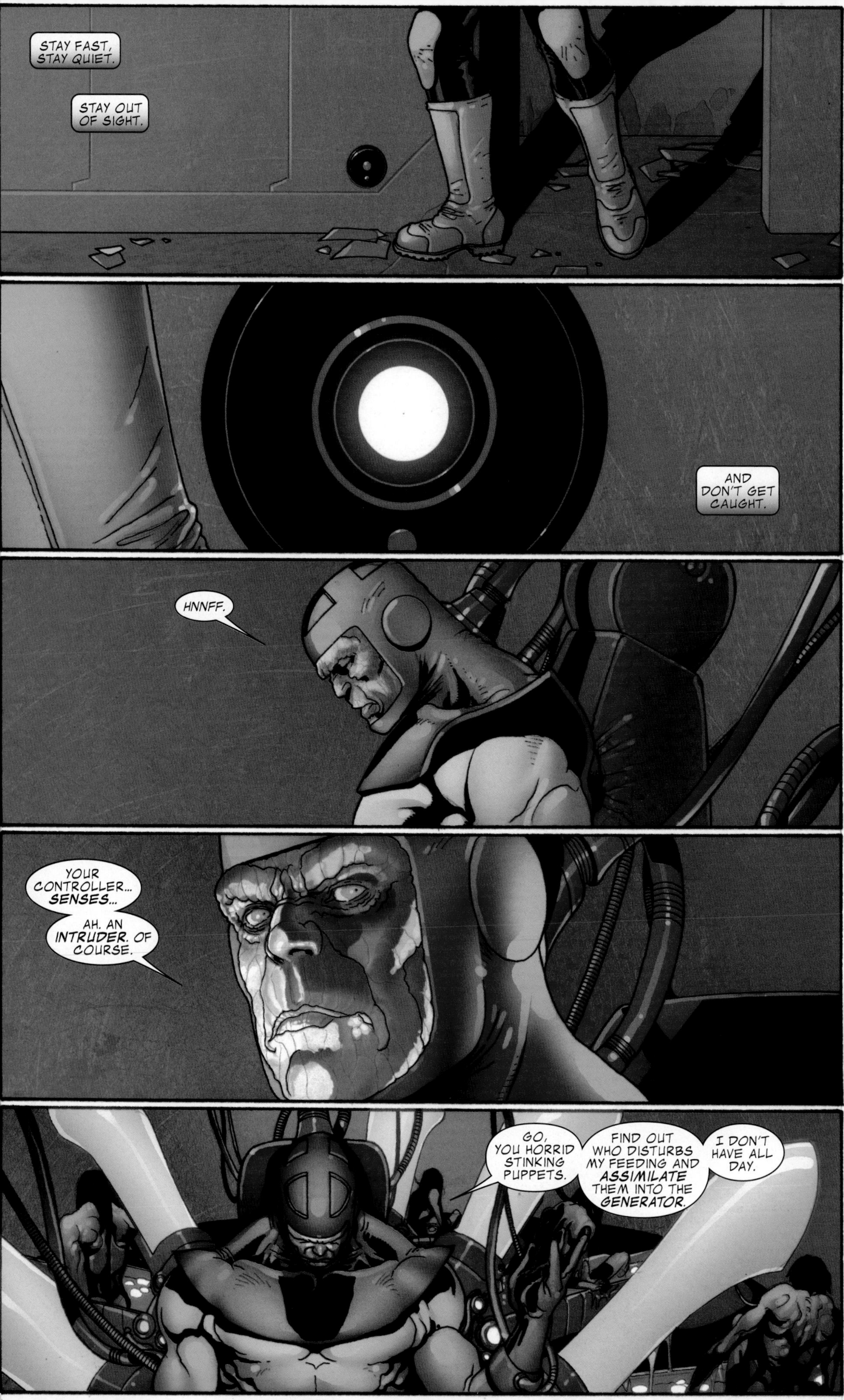

STAY FAST, STAY QUIET.
STAY OUT OF SIGHT.
AND DON'T GET CAUGHT.
HNNFF.
YOUR CONTROLLER... SENSES...
AH. AN INTRUDER. OF COURSE.
GO, YOU HORRID STINKING PUPPETS.
FIND OUT WHO DISTURBS MY FEEDING AND ASSIMILATE THEM INTO THE GENERATOR.
I DON'T HAVE ALL DAY.

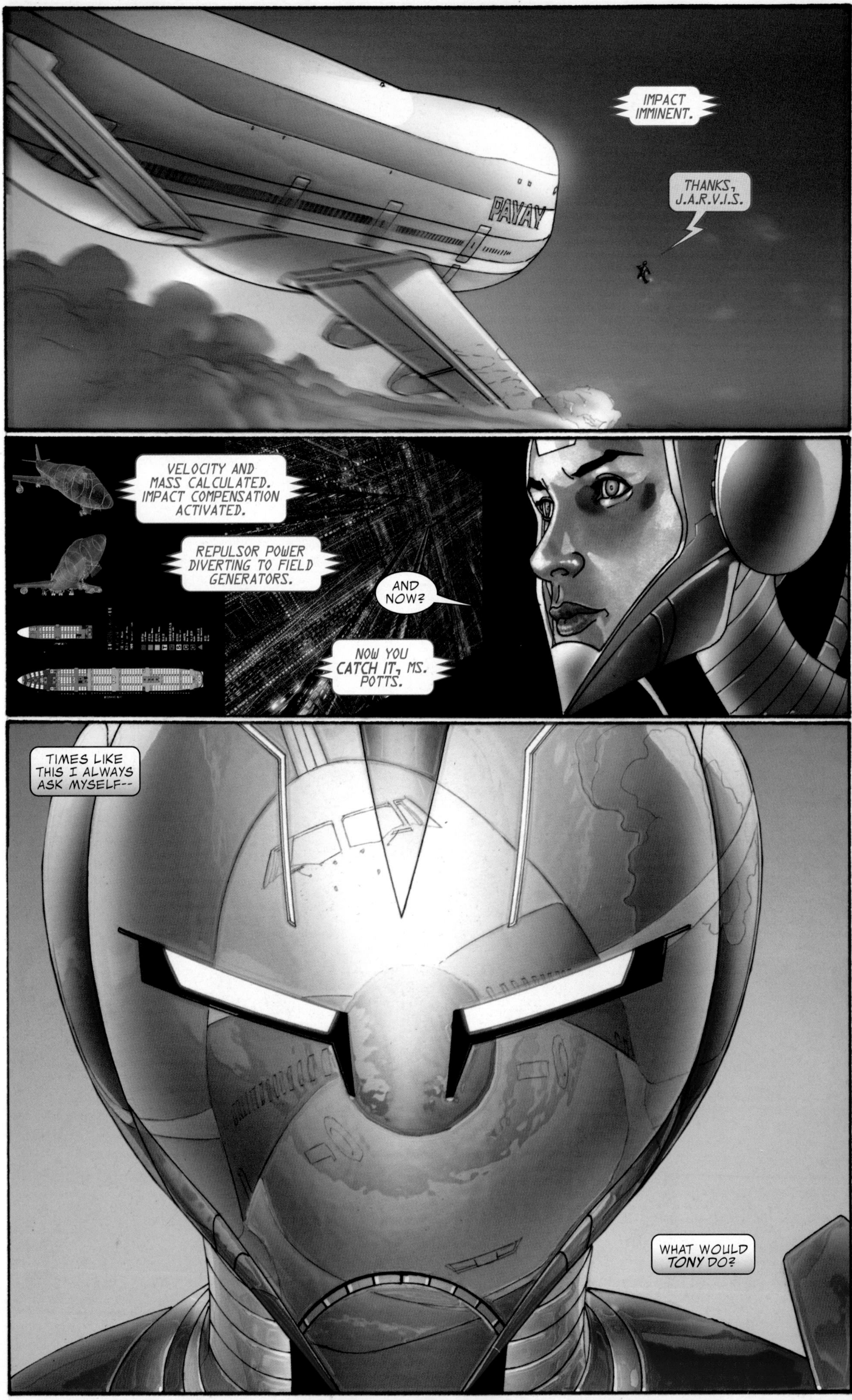
IMPACT IMMINENT.
THANKS, J.A.R.V.I.S.
VELOCITY AND MASS CALCULATED. IMPACT COMPENSATION ACTIVATED.
REPULSOR POWER DIVERTING TO FIELD GENERATORS.
AND NOW?
NOW YOU CATCH IT, MS. POTTS.
PAYAY
TIMES LIKE THIS I ALWAYS ASK MYSELF--
WHAT WOULD TONY DO?

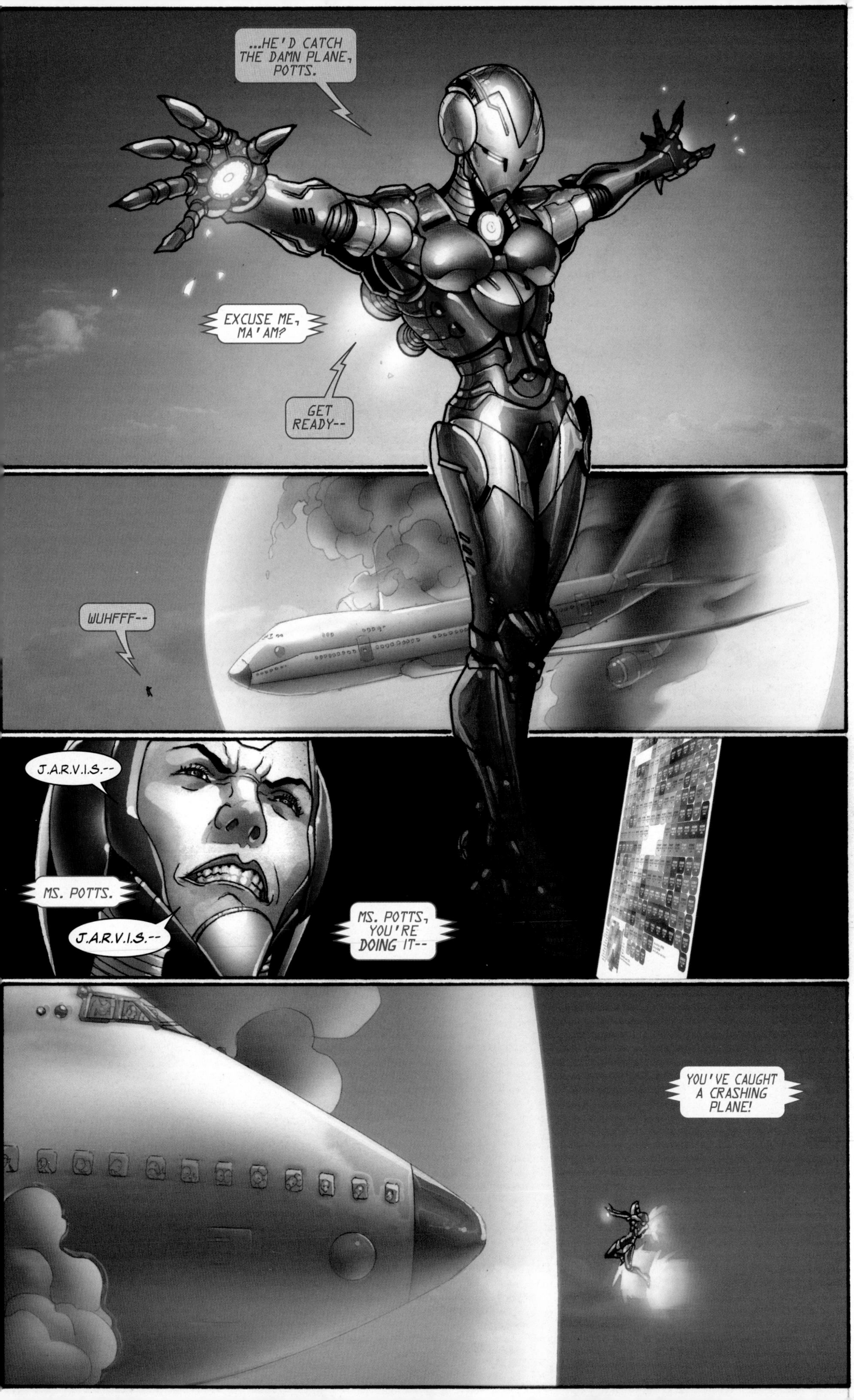
...HE'D CATCH THE DAMN PLANE, POTTS.
EXCUSE ME, MA'AM?
GET READY--
WUHFFF--
J.A.R.V.I.S.--
MS. POTTS.
J.A.R.V.I.S.--
MS. POTTS, YOU'RE DOING IT--
YOU'VE CAUGHT A CRASHING PLANE!

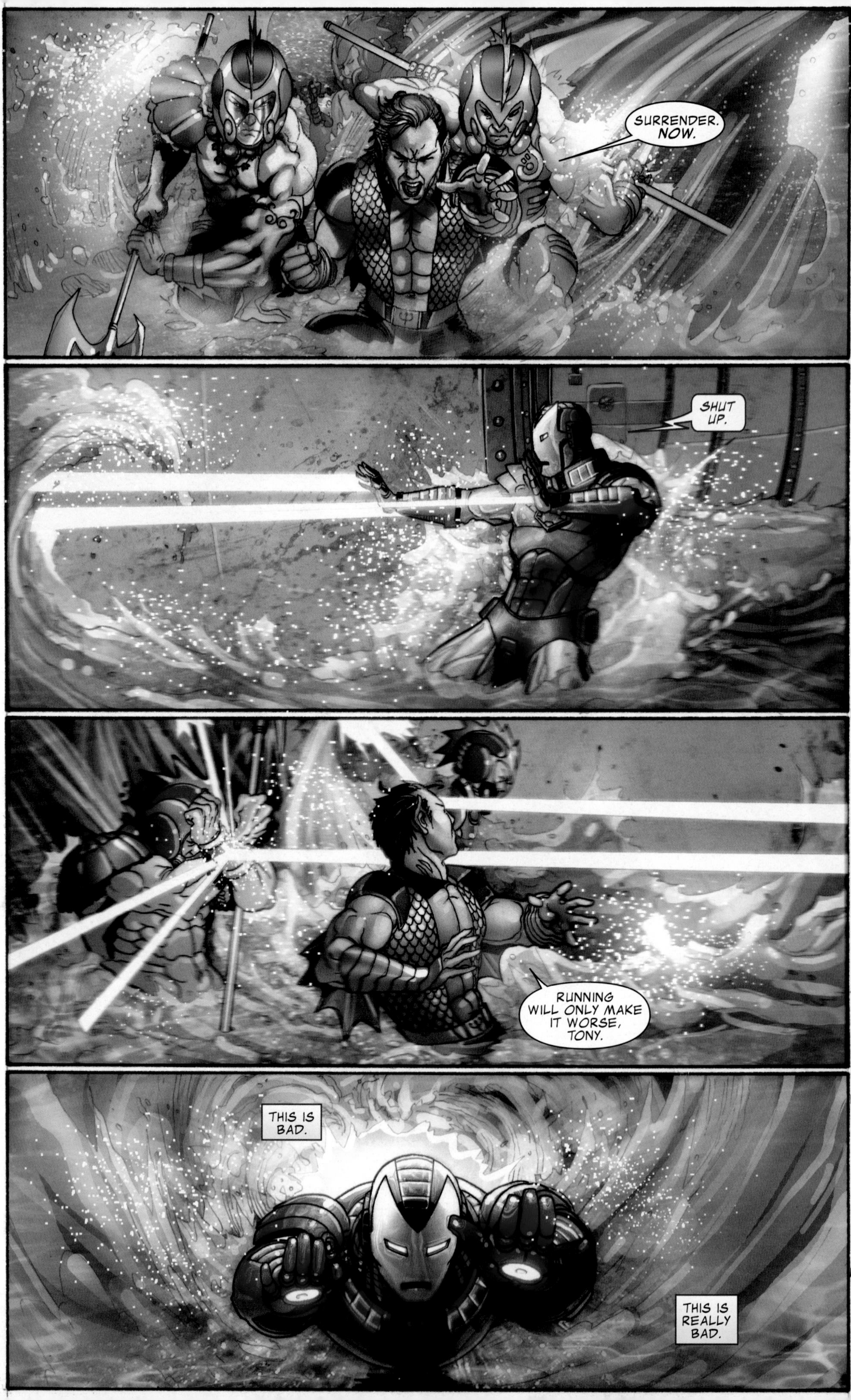
SURRENDER. NOW.
SHUT UP.
RUNNING WILL ONLY MAKE IT WORSE, TONY.
THIS IS BAD.
THIS IS REALLY BAD.

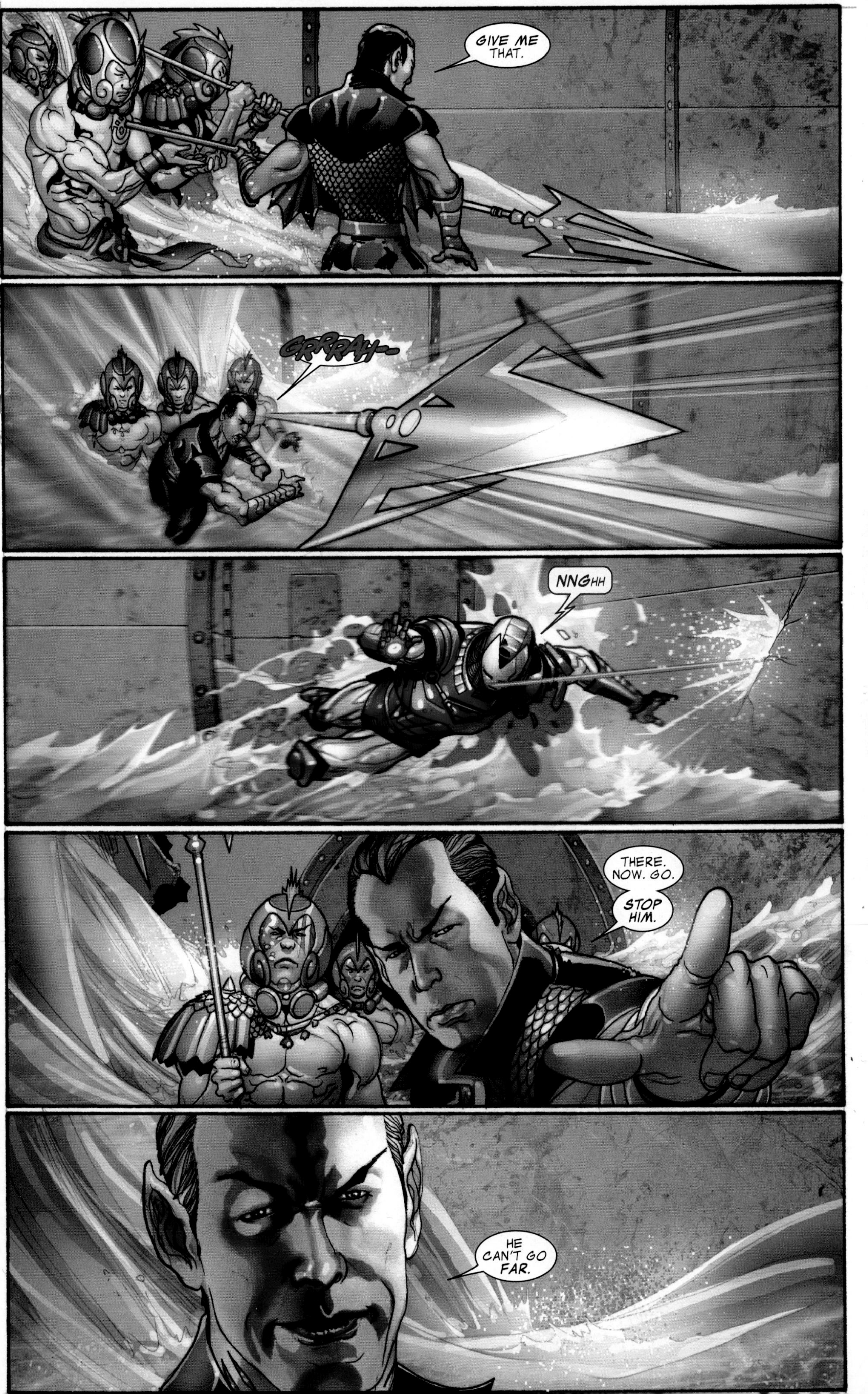
GIVE ME THAT.
GRRRAH--
NNGHH
THERE. NOW. GO.
STOP HIM.
HE CAN'T GO FAR.

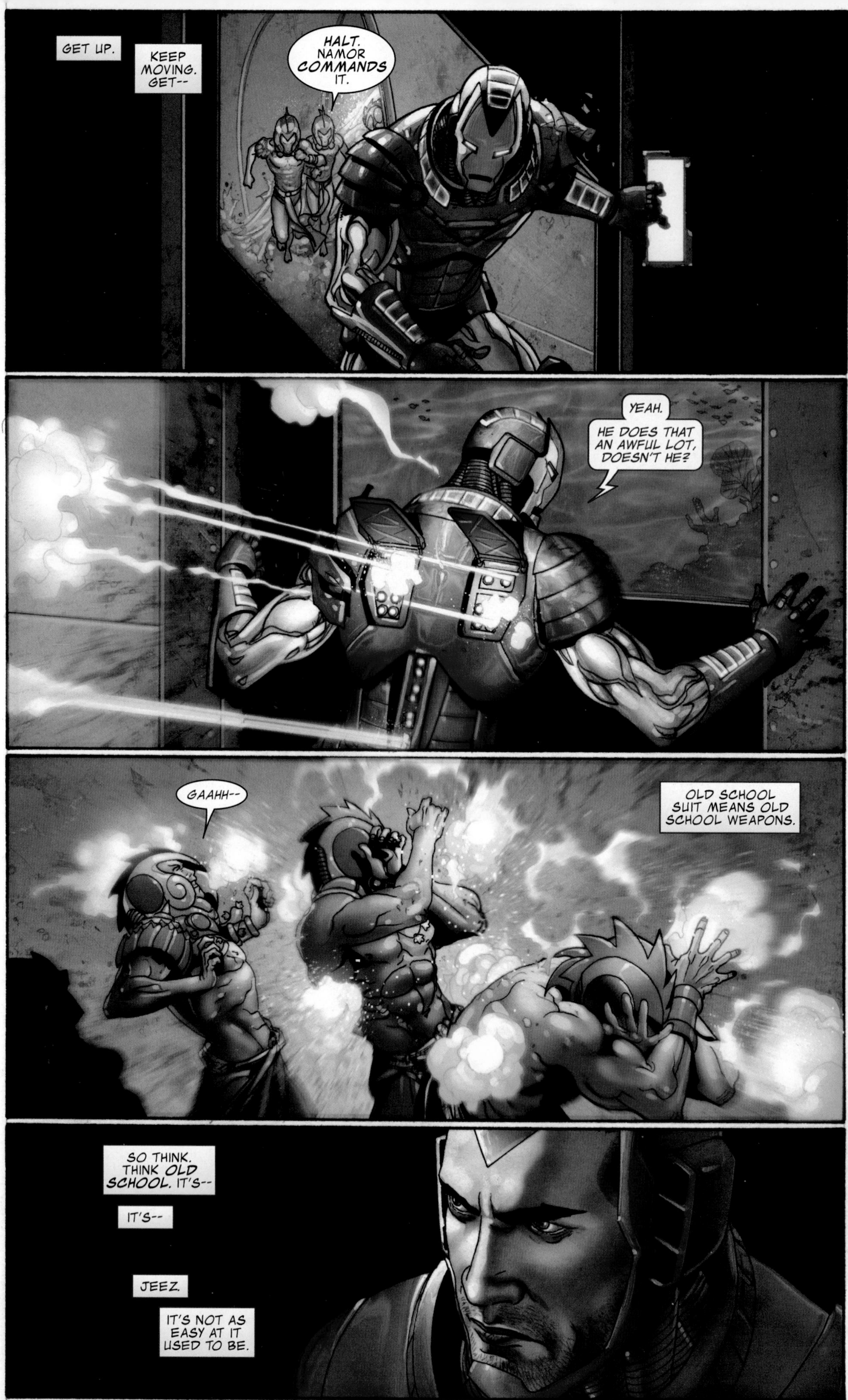
GET UP.
KEEP MOVING. GET--
HALT. NAMOR COMMANDS IT.
YEAH.
HE DOES THAT AN AWFUL LOT, DOESN'T HE?
GAAHH--
OLD SCHOOL SUIT MEANS OLD SCHOOL WEAPONS.
SO THINK. THINK OLD SCHOOL. IT'S--
IT'S--
JEEZ.
IT'S NOT AS EASY AT IT USED TO BE.

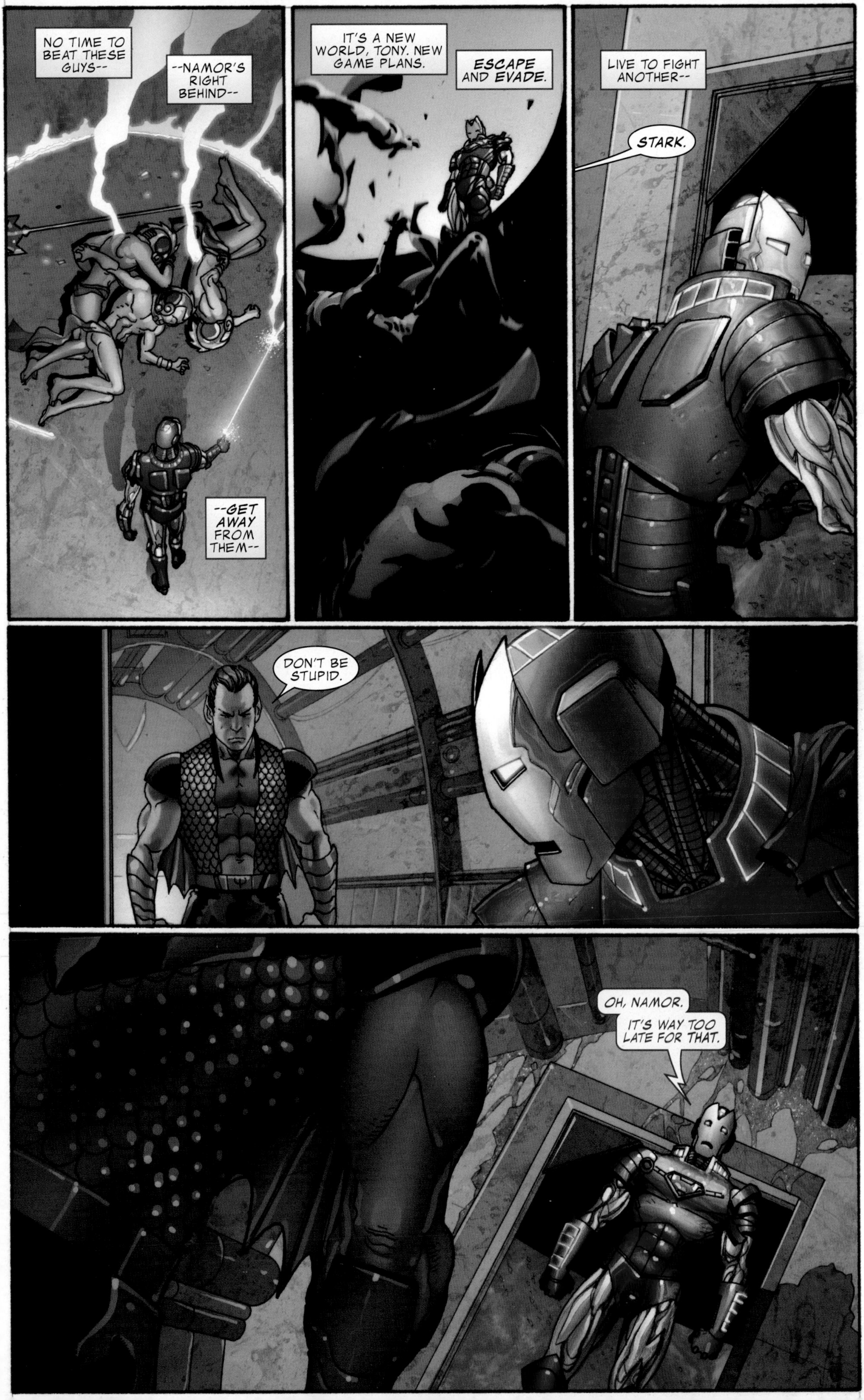
NO TIME TO BEAT THESE GUYS--
--NAMOR'S RIGHT BEHIND--
--GET AWAY FROM THEM--
IT'S A NEW WORLD, TONY. NEW GAME PLANS.
ESCAPE AND EVADE.
LIVE TO FIGHT ANOTHER--
STARK.
DON'T BE STUPID.
OH, NAMOR.
IT'S WAY TOO LATE FOR THAT.

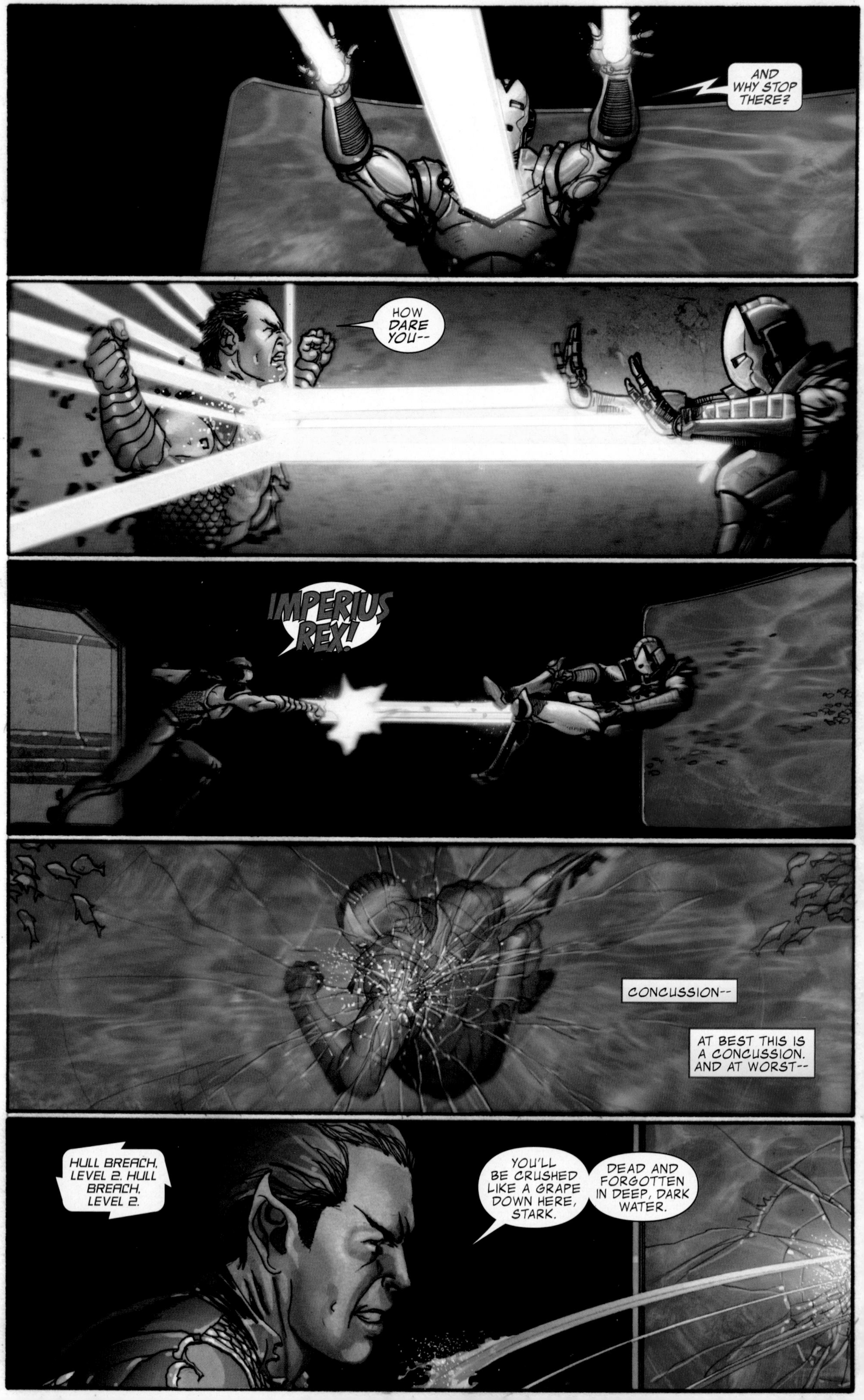
AND WHY STOP THERE?
HOW DARE YOU--
IMPERIUS REX!
CONCUSSION--
AT BEST THIS IS A CONCUSSION. AND AT WORST--
HULL BREACH, LEVEL 2. HULL BREACH, LEVEL 2.
YOU'LL BE CRUSHED LIKE A GRAPE DOWN HERE, STARK.
DEAD AND FORGOTTEN IN DEEP, DARK WATER.

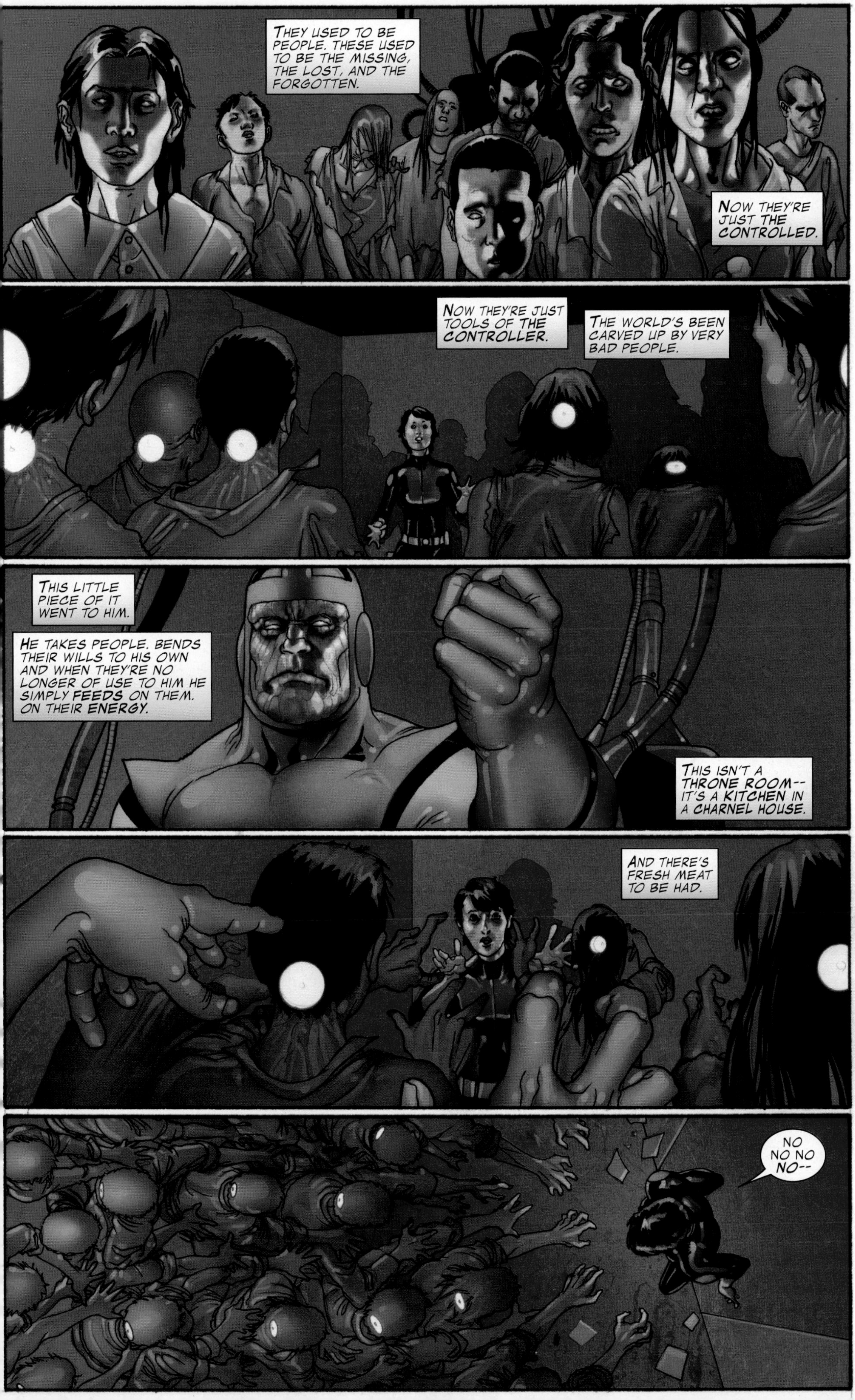

THEY USED TO BE PEOPLE. THESE USED TO BE THE MISSING, THE LOST, AND THE FORGOTTEN.
NOW THEY'RE JUST THE CONTROLLED.
NOW THEY'RE JUST TOOLS OF THE CONTROLLER.
THE WORLD'S BEEN CARVED UP BY VERY BAD PEOPLE.
THIS LITTLE PIECE OF IT WENT TO HIM.
HE TAKES PEOPLE. BENDS THEIR WILLS TO HIS OWN AND WHEN THEY'RE NO LONGER OF USE TO HIM HE SIMPLY FEEDS ON THEM. ON THEIR ENERGY.
THIS ISN'T A THRONE ROOM-- IT'S A KITCHEN IN A CHARNEL HOUSE.
AND THERE'S FRESH MEAT TO BE HAD.
NO NO NO NO--

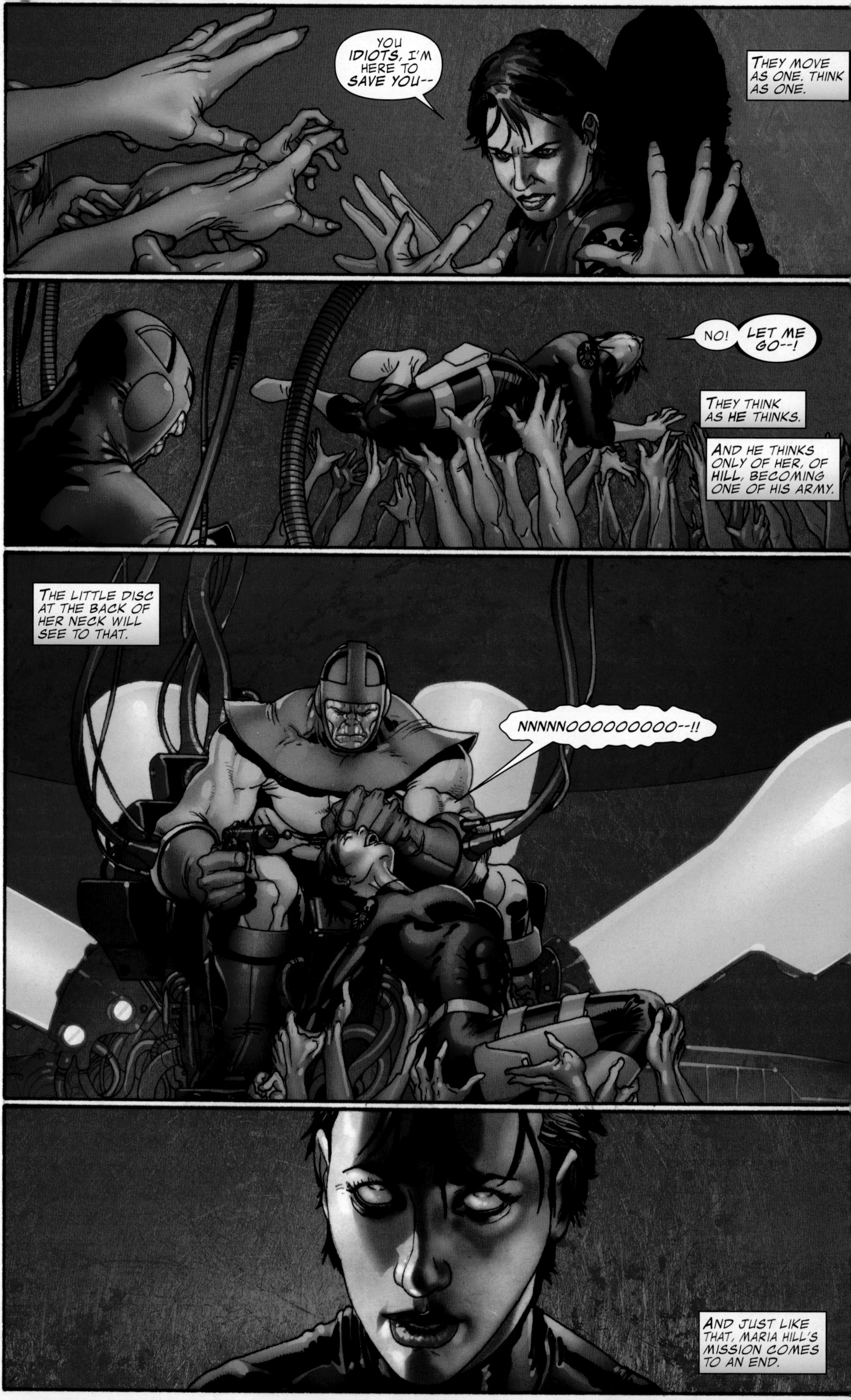
YOU IDIOTS, I'M HERE TO SAVE YOU--
THEY MOVE AS ONE. THINK AS ONE.
NO!
LET ME GO--!
THEY THINK AS HE THINKS.
AND HE THINKS ONLY OF HER, OF HILL, BECOMING ONE OF HIS ARMY.
THE LITTLE DISC AT THE BACK OF HER NECK WILL SEE TO THAT.
NNNNNOOOOOOOOO--!!
AND JUST LIKE THAT, MARIA HILL'S MISSION COMES TO AN END.

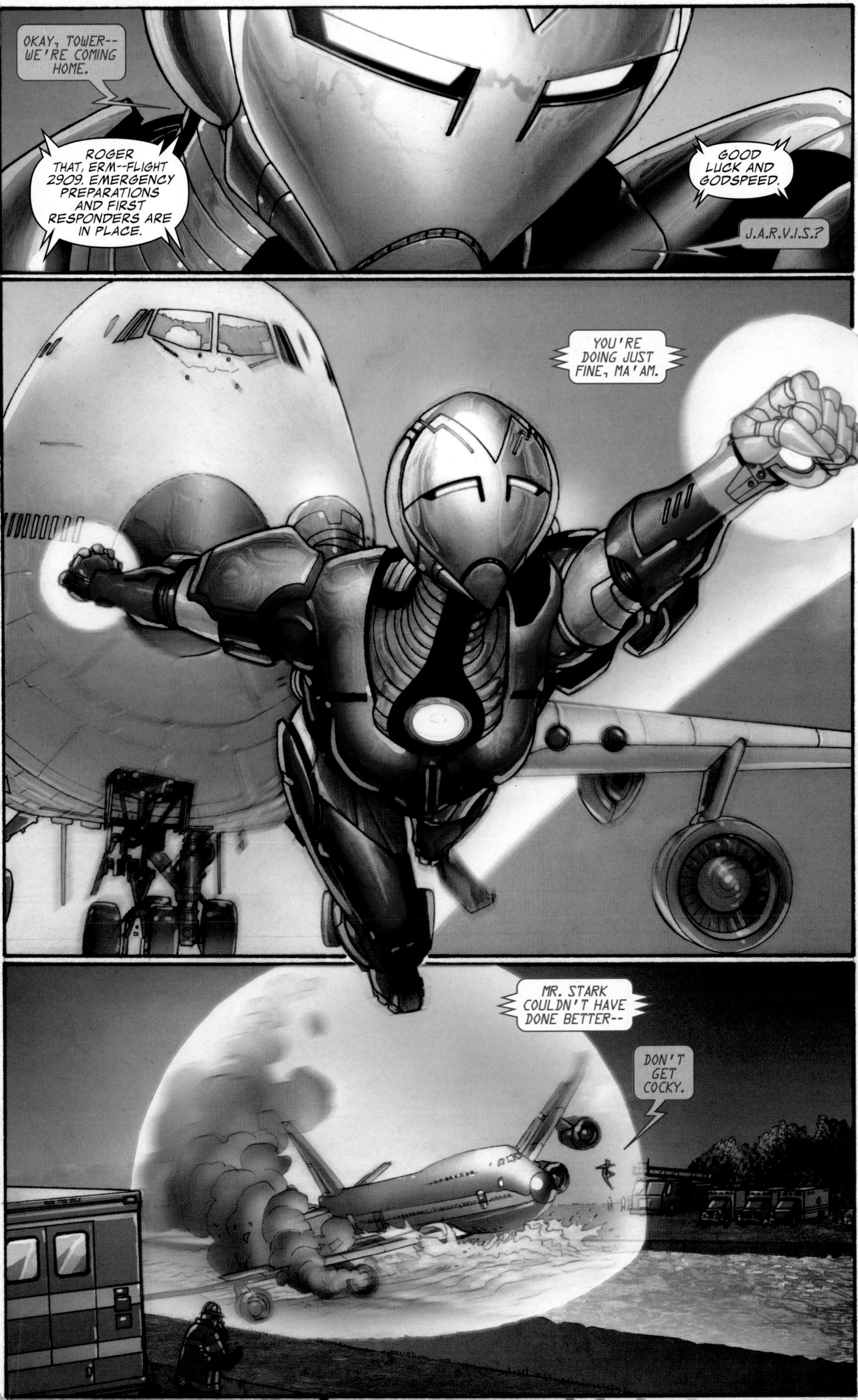
OKAY, TOWER-- WE'RE COMING HOME.
ROGER THAT, ERM--FLIGHT 2909. EMERGENCY PREPARATIONS AND FIRST RESPONDERS ARE IN PLACE.
GOOD LUCK AND GODSPEED.
J.A.R.V.I.S.?
YOU'RE DOING JUST FINE, MA'AM.
MR. STARK COULDN'T HAVE DONE BETTER--
DON'T GET COCKY.

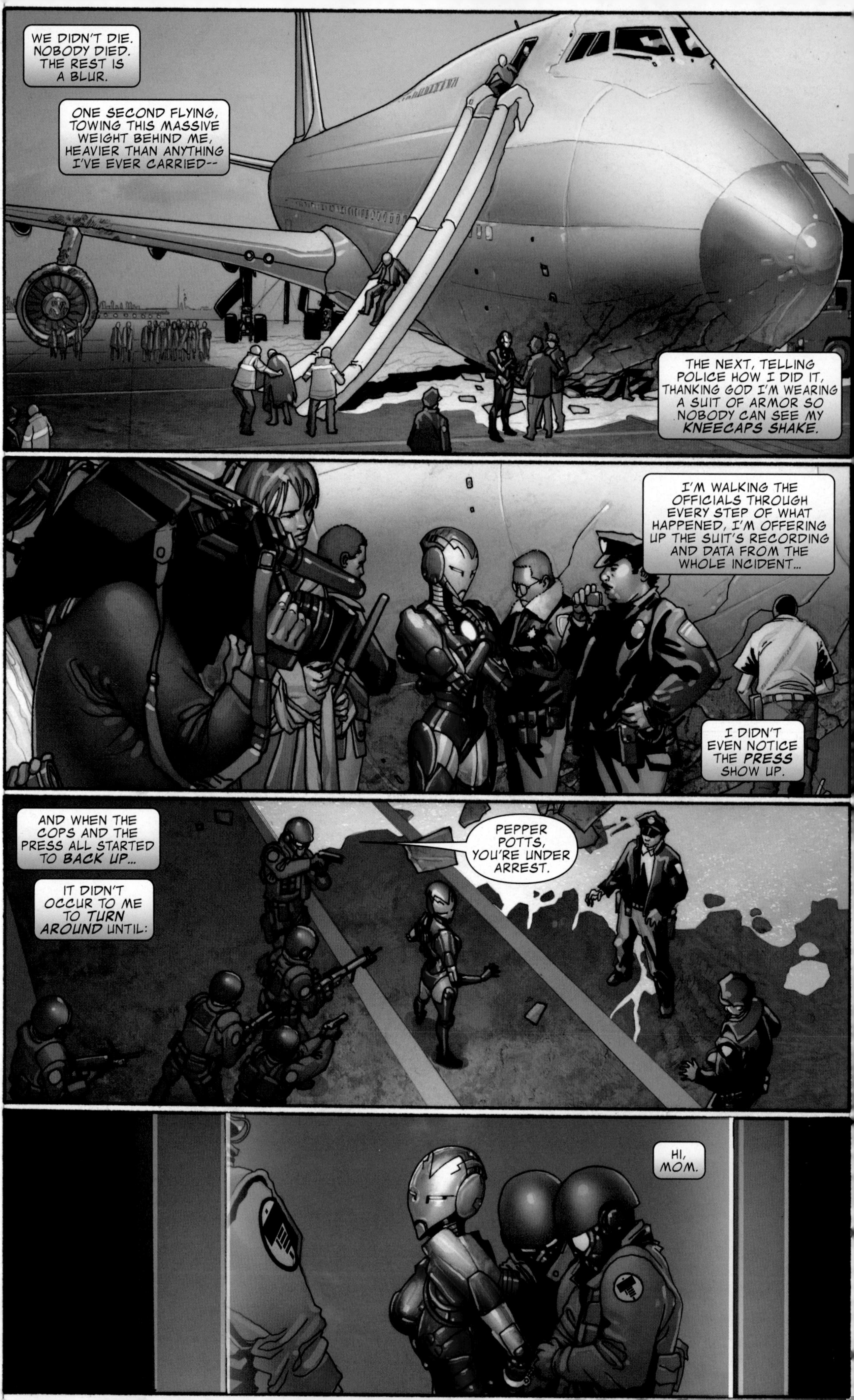
WE DIDN'T DIE. NOBODY DIED. THE REST IS A BLUR.
ONE SECOND FLYING, TOWING THIS MASSIVE WEIGHT BEHIND ME, HEAVIER THAN ANYTHING I'VE EVER CARRIED--
THE NEXT, TELLING POLICE HOW I DID IT, THANKING GOD I'M WEARING A SUIT OF ARMOR SO NOBODY CAN SEE MY KNEECAPS SHAKE.
I'M WALKING THE OFFICIALS THROUGH EVERY STEP OF WHAT HAPPENED, I'M OFFERING UP THE SUIT'S RECORDING AND DATA FROM THE WHOLE INCIDENT...
I DIDN'T EVEN NOTICE THE PRESS SHOW UP.
AND WHEN THE COPS AND THE PRESS ALL STARTED TO BACK UP...
IT DIDN'T OCCUR TO ME TO TURN AROUND UNTIL:
PEPPER POTTS, YOU'RE UNDER ARREST.
HI, MOM.

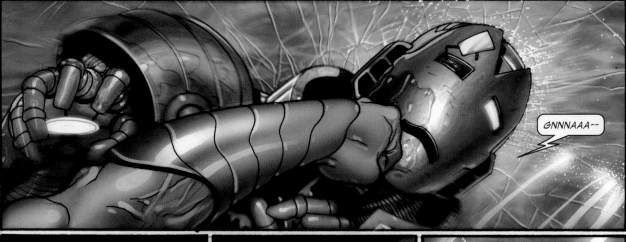

GNNNNAAA--

HE'S BEATING THE SUIT OPEN--

--BEATING THE HULL OPEN--

--ONE PUNCH AT A TIME--

--EVEN UNLOADING WHAT REPULSOR POWER I HAVE LEFT INTO HIM--

--HE'S RELENTLESS--

--STOP FIGHTING HIM, TONY--

--START RUNNING FROM HIM--

--LIVE TO FIGHT ANOTHER DAY--

WASTE PIPE RELAY 53

HYDRAULICS CHANNEL

LIQUID HYDROGEN CHANNEL

SEWAGE RELAY 11

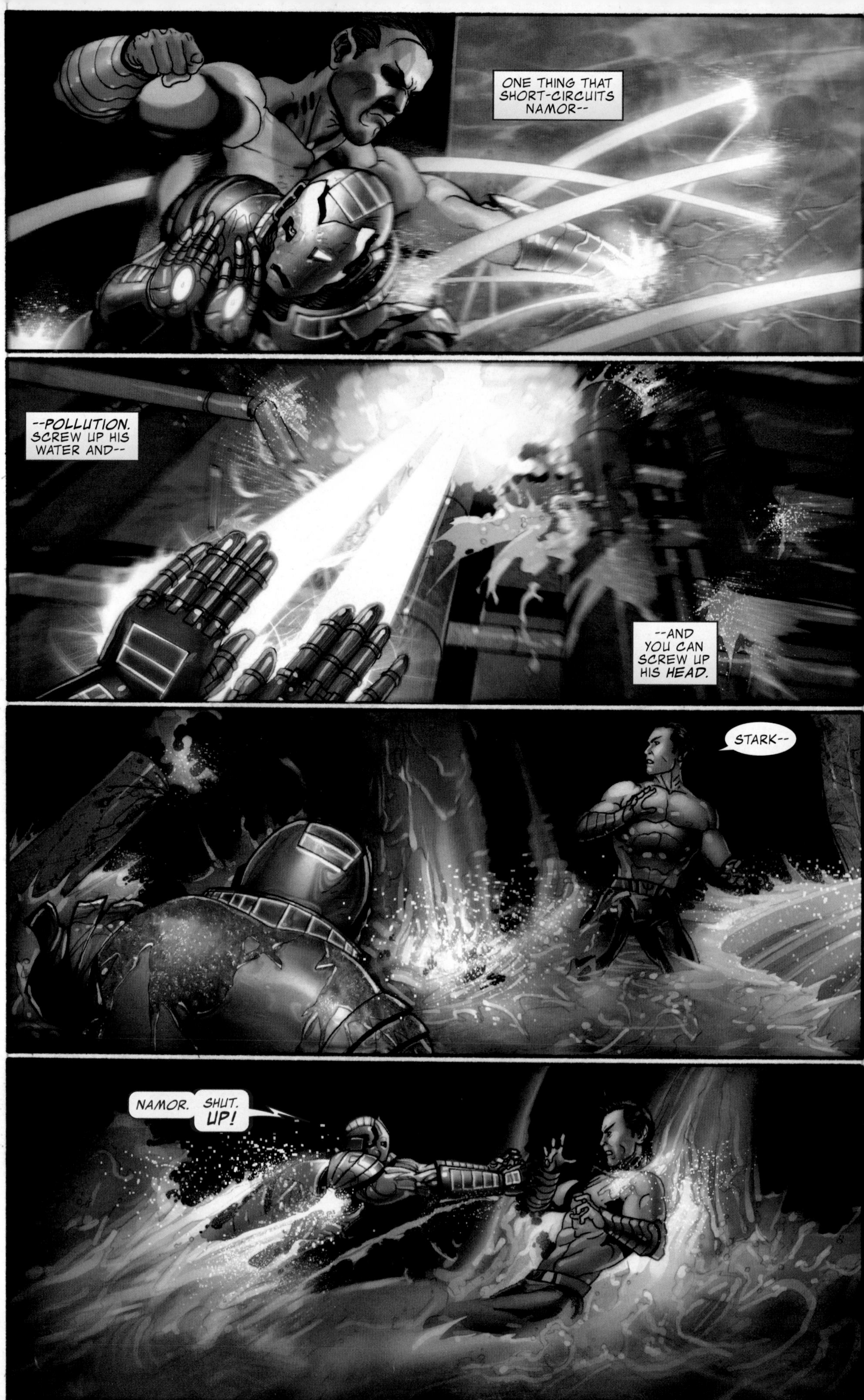
ONE THING THAT SHORT-CIRCUITS NAMOR--
--POLLUTION. SCREW UP HIS WATER AND--
--AND YOU CAN SCREW UP HIS HEAD.
STARK--
NAMOR. SHUT. UP!

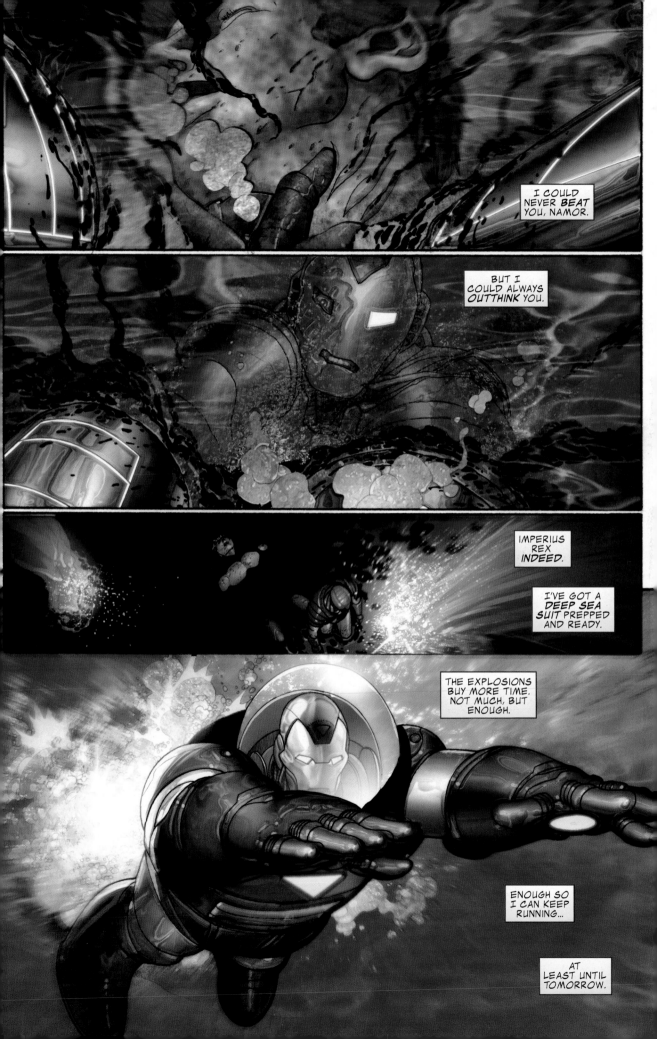

I COULD NEVER **BEAT** YOU, NAMOR.

BUT I COULD ALWAYS **OUTTHINK** YOU.

IMPERIUS REX **INDEED.**

I'VE GOT A **DEEP SEA SUIT** PREPPED AND READY.

THE EXPLOSIONS BUY MORE TIME. NOT MUCH, BUT ENOUGH.

ENOUGH SO I CAN KEEP RUNNING...

AT LEAST UNTIL TOMORROW.

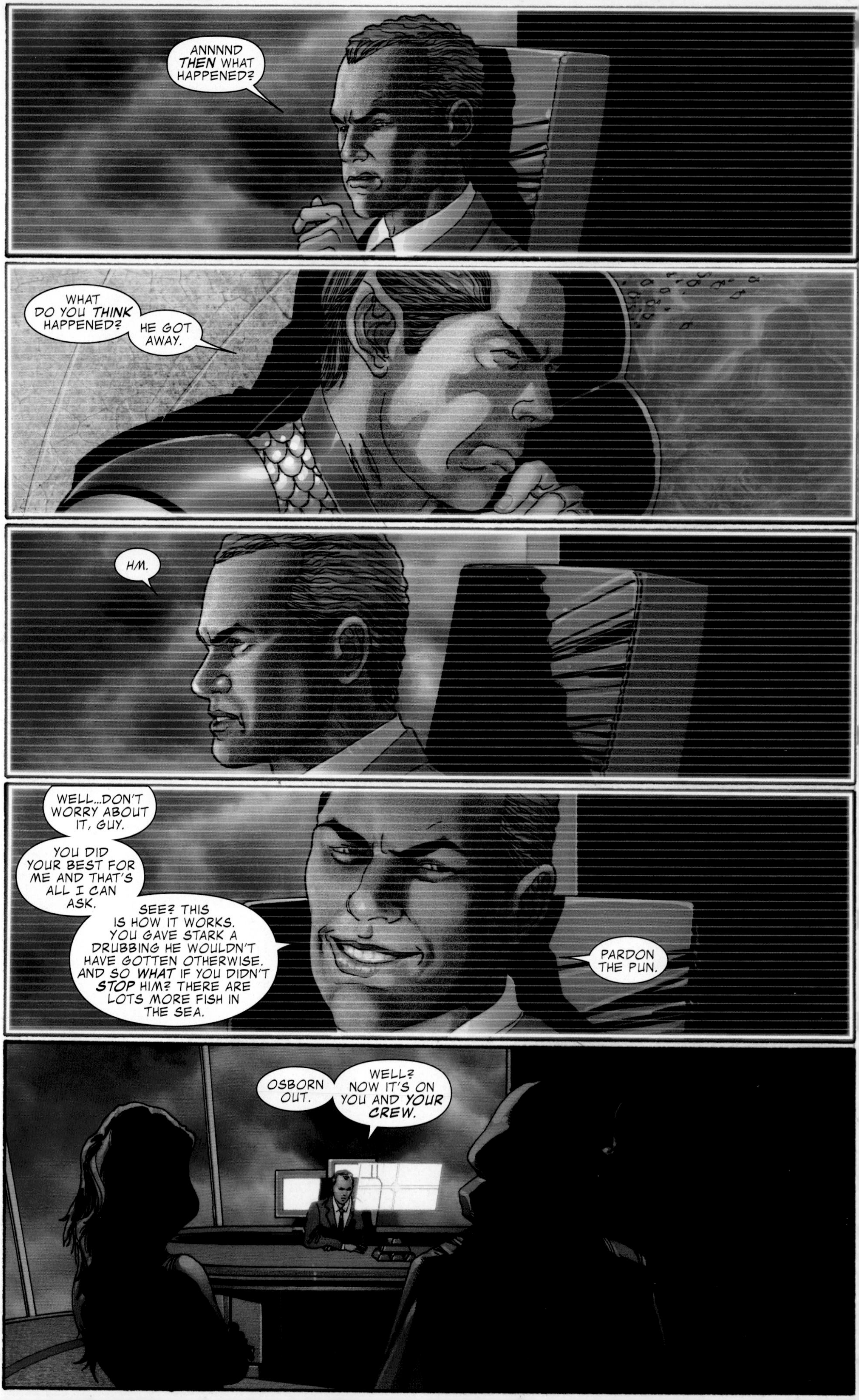
ANNNND THEN WHAT HAPPENED?
WHAT DO YOU THINK HAPPENED?
HE GOT AWAY.
HM.
WELL...DON'T WORRY ABOUT IT, GUY.
YOU DID YOUR BEST FOR ME AND THAT'S ALL I CAN ASK.
SEE? THIS IS HOW IT WORKS. YOU GAVE STARK A DRUBBING HE WOULDN'T HAVE GOTTEN OTHERWISE. AND SO WHAT IF YOU DIDN'T STOP HIM? THERE ARE LOTS MORE FISH IN THE SEA.
PARDON THE PUN.
OSBORN OUT.
WELL? NOW IT'S ON YOU AND YOUR CREW.

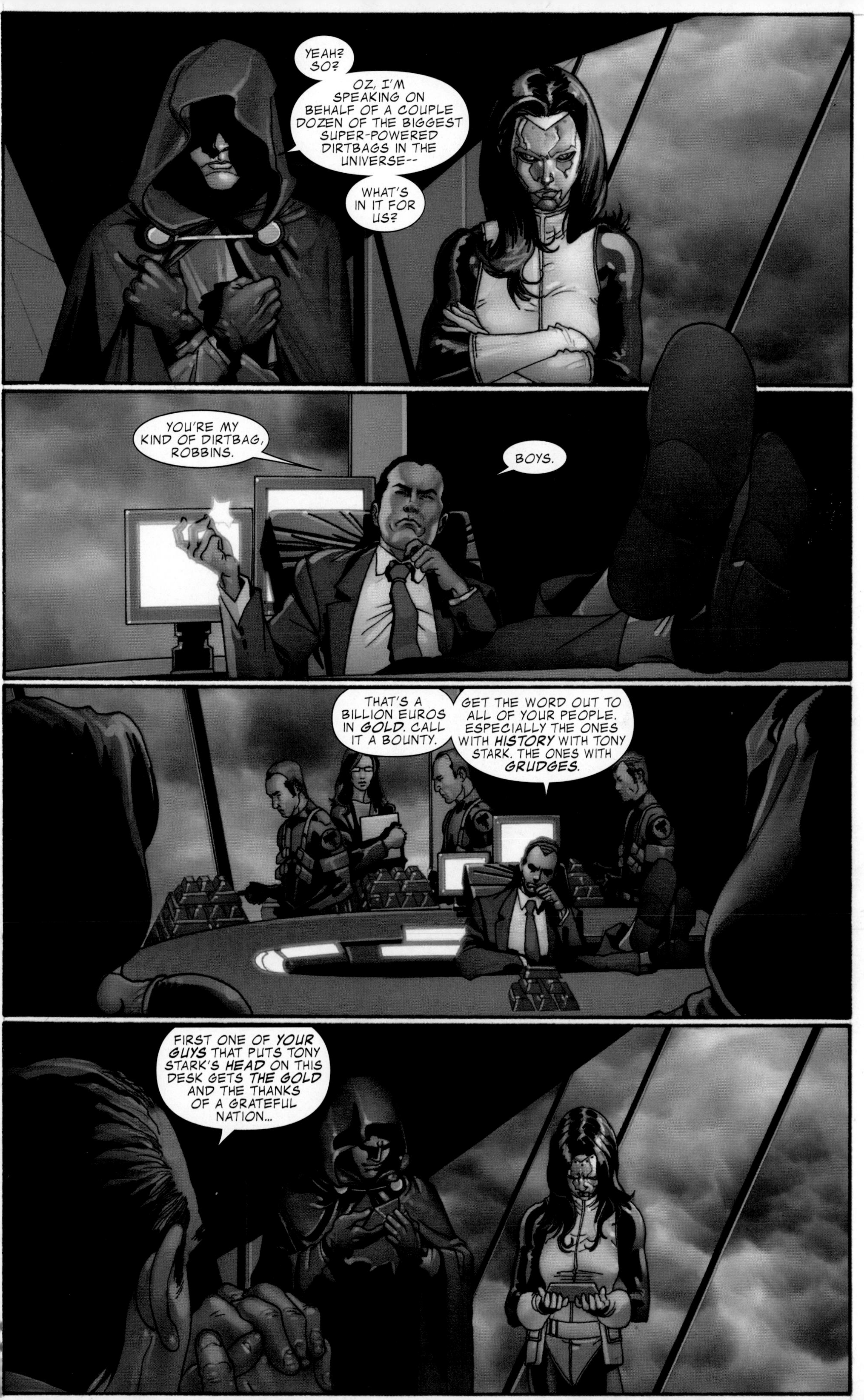
YEAH? SO?
OZ, I'M SPEAKING ON BEHALF OF A COUPLE DOZEN OF THE BIGGEST SUPER-POWERED DIRTBAGS IN THE UNIVERSE--
WHAT'S IN IT FOR US?
YOU'RE MY KIND OF DIRTBAG, ROBBINS.
BOYS.
THAT'S A BILLION EUROS IN GOLD. CALL IT A BOUNTY.
GET THE WORD OUT TO ALL OF YOUR PEOPLE. ESPECIALLY THE ONES WITH HISTORY WITH TONY STARK. THE ONES WITH GRUDGES.
FIRST ONE OF YOUR GUYS THAT PUTS TONY STARK'S HEAD ON THIS DESK GETS THE GOLD AND THE THANKS OF A GRATEFUL NATION...

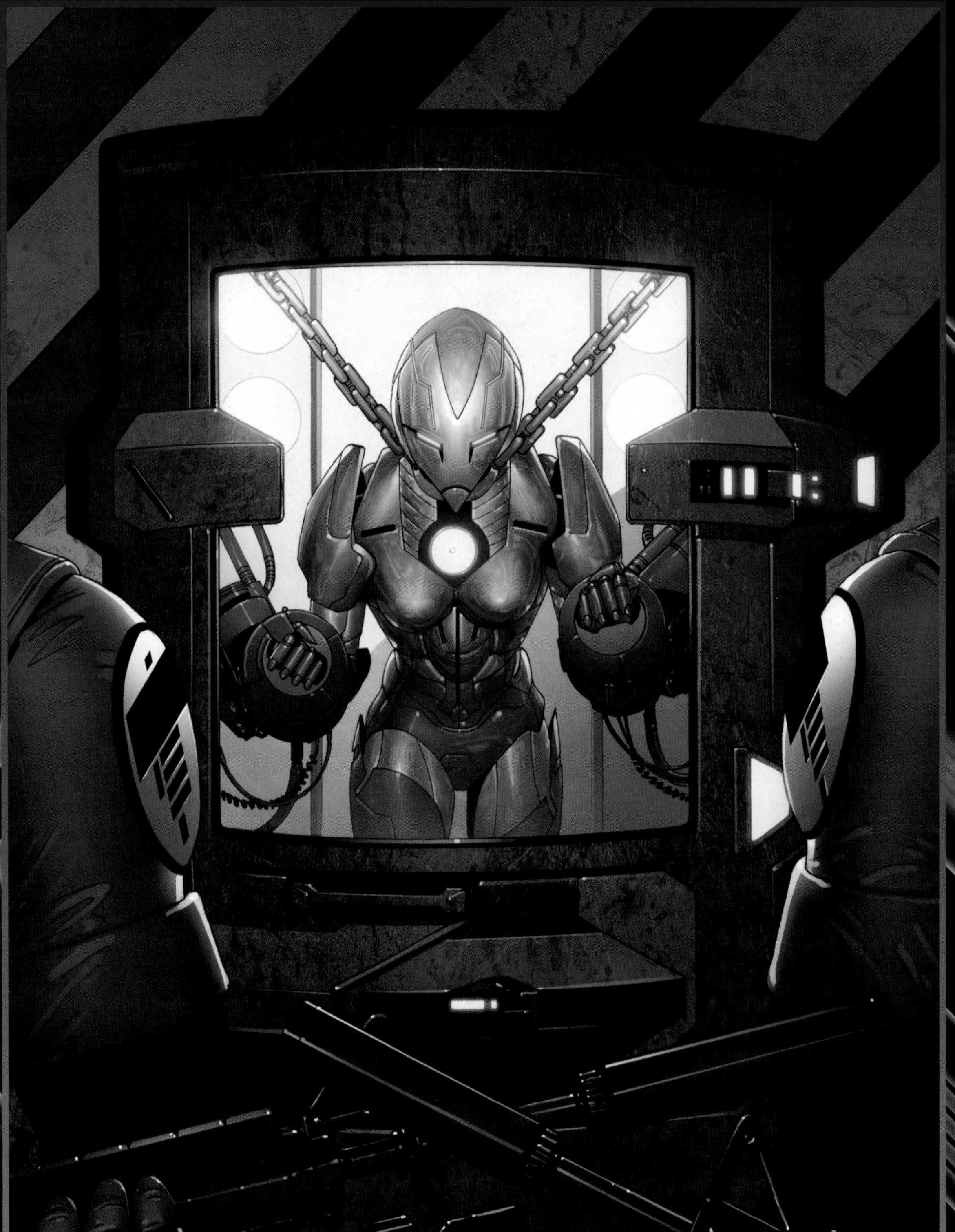

13

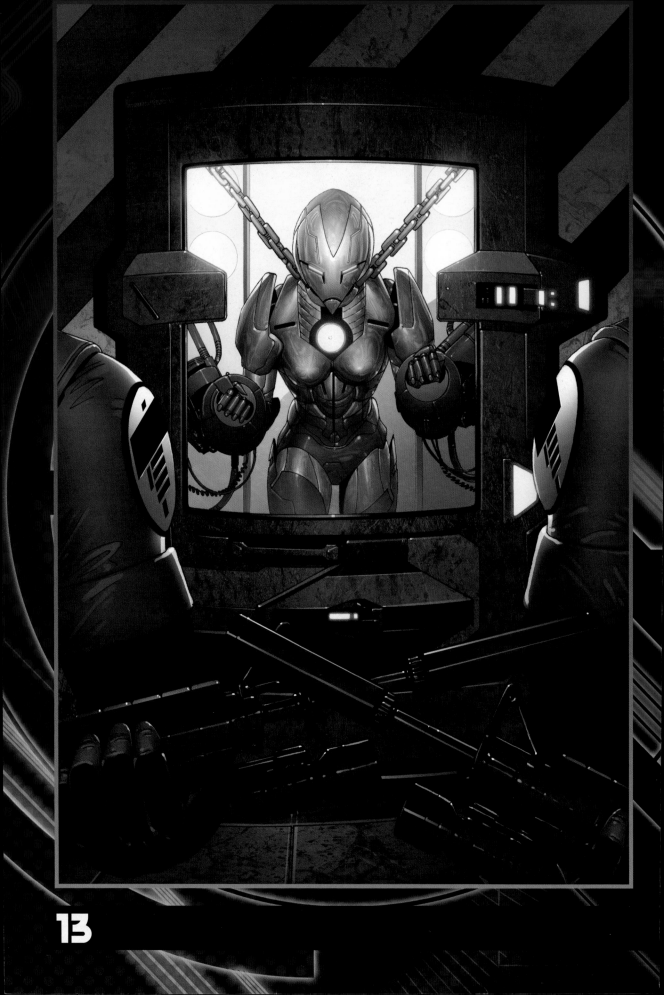

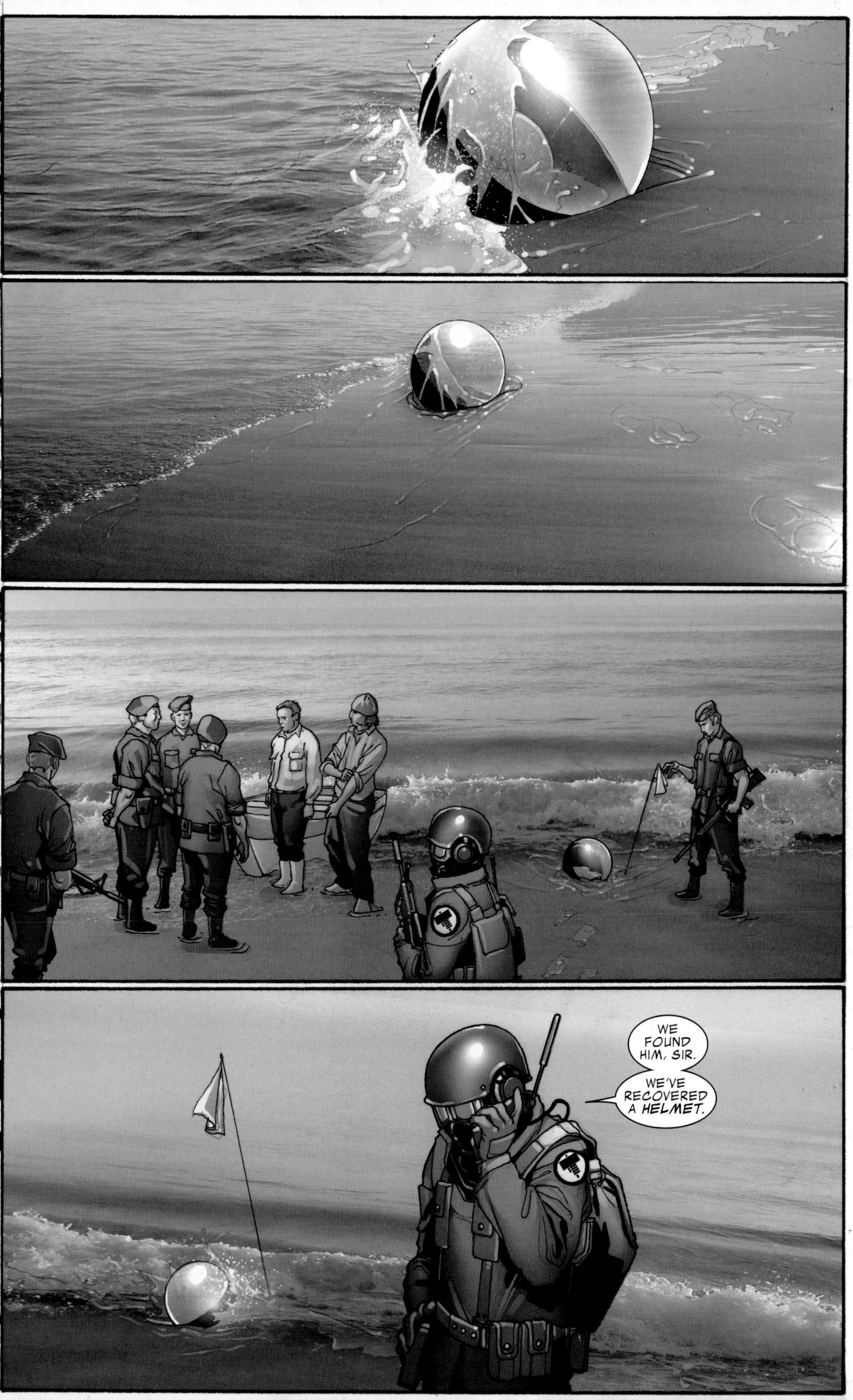
WE FOUND HIM, SIR.
WE'VE RECOVERED A HELMET.

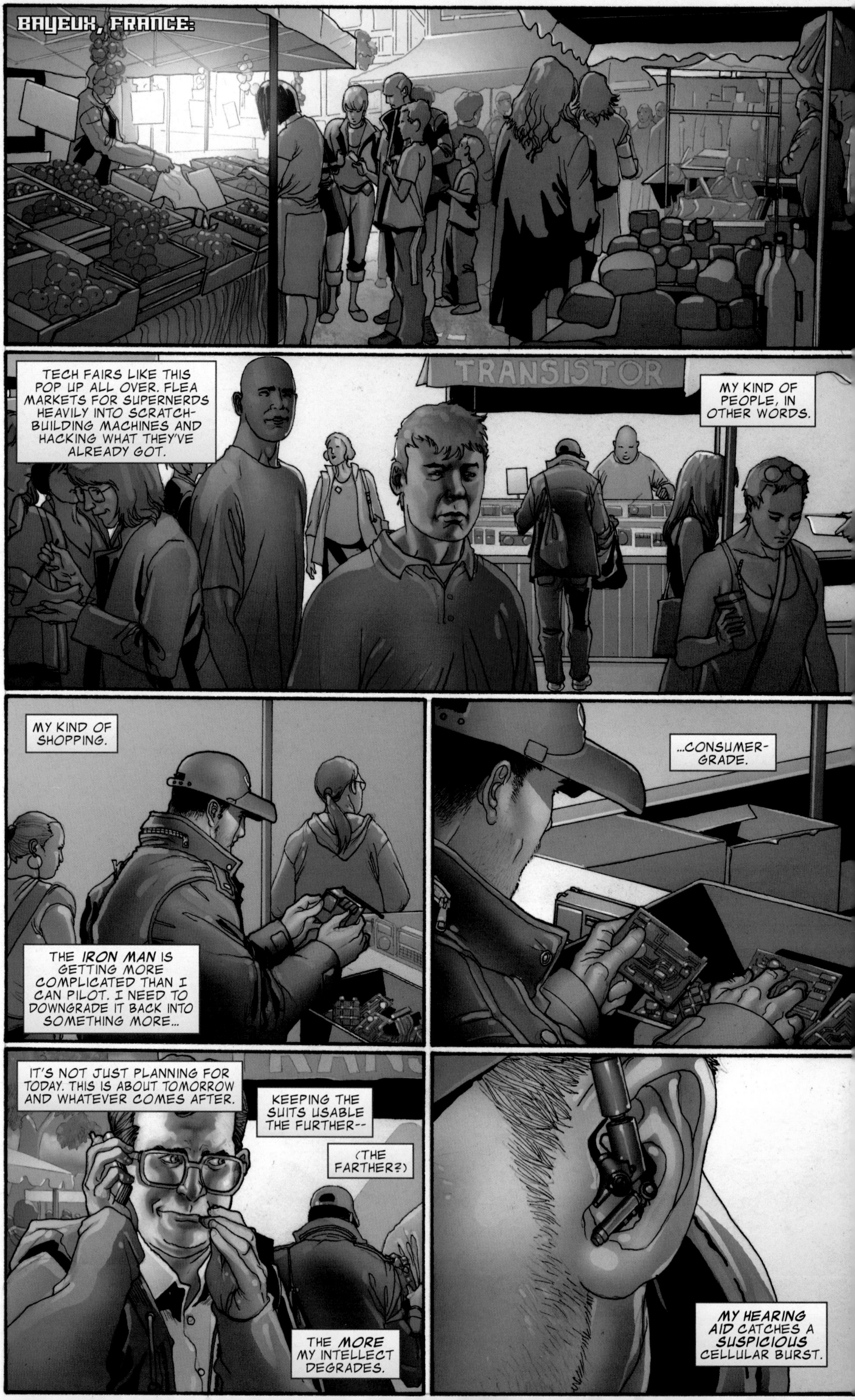
BAYEUX, FRANCE:
TRANSISTOR
TECH FAIRS LIKE THIS POP UP ALL OVER. FLEA MARKETS FOR SUPERNERDS HEAVILY INTO SCRATCH-BUILDING MACHINES AND HACKING WHAT THEY'VE ALREADY GOT.
MY KIND OF PEOPLE, IN OTHER WORDS.
MY KIND OF SHOPPING.
THE IRON MAN IS GETTING MORE COMPLICATED THAN I CAN PILOT. I NEED TO DOWNGRADE IT BACK INTO SOMETHING MORE...
...CONSUMER-GRADE.
IT'S NOT JUST PLANNING FOR TODAY. THIS IS ABOUT TOMORROW AND WHATEVER COMES AFTER.
KEEPING THE SUITS USABLE THE FURTHER--
(THE FARTHER?)
THE MORE MY INTELLECT DEGRADES.
MY HEARING AID CATCHES A SUSPICIOUS CELLULAR BURST.

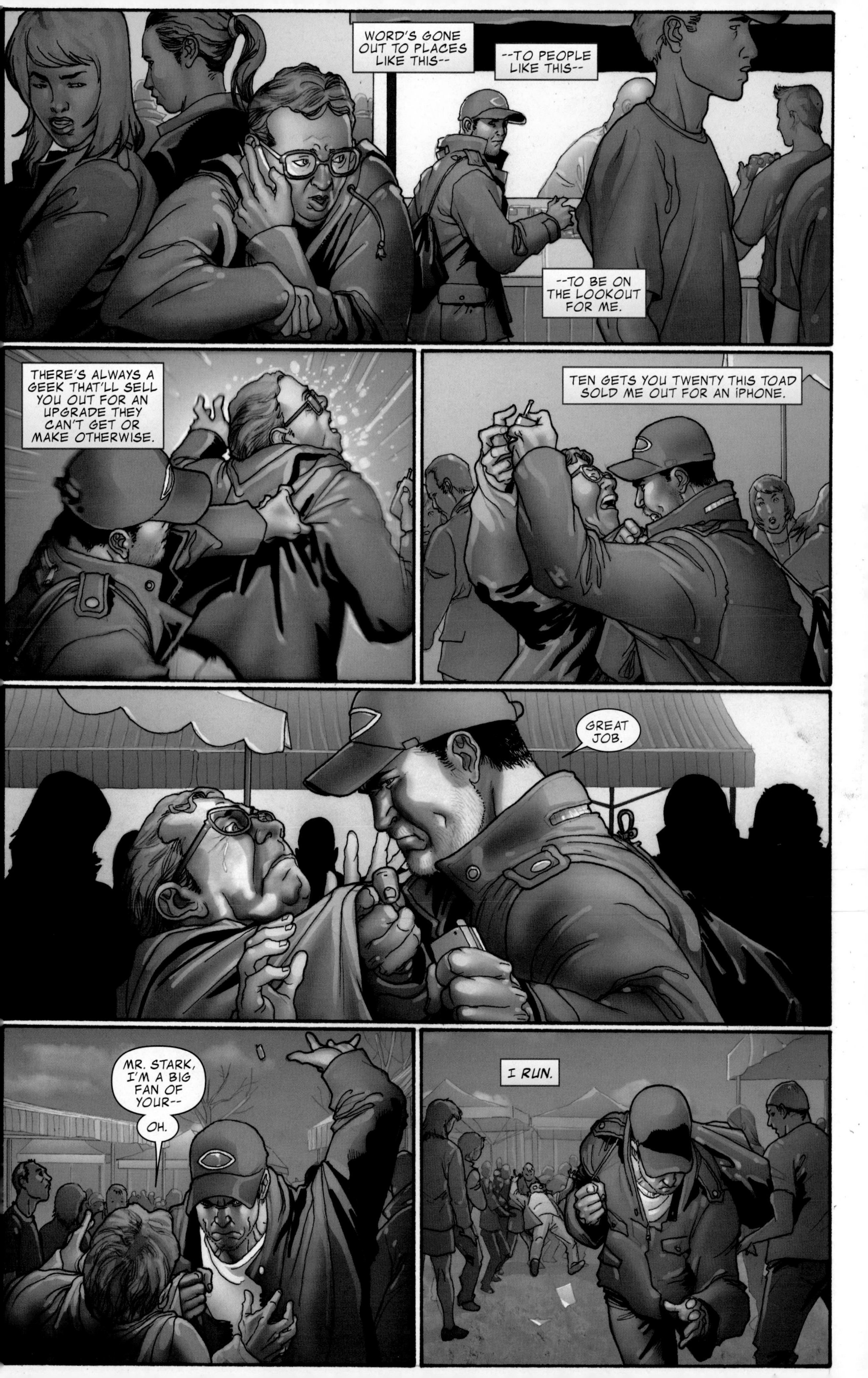
WORD'S GONE OUT TO PLACES LIKE THIS--
--TO PEOPLE LIKE THIS--
--TO BE ON THE LOOKOUT FOR ME.
THERE'S ALWAYS A GEEK THAT'LL SELL YOU OUT FOR AN UPGRADE THEY CAN'T GET OR MAKE OTHERWISE.
TEN GETS YOU TWENTY THIS TOAD SOLD ME OUT FOR AN iPHONE.
GREAT JOB.
MR. STARK, I'M A BIG FAN OF YOUR--
OH.
I RUN.

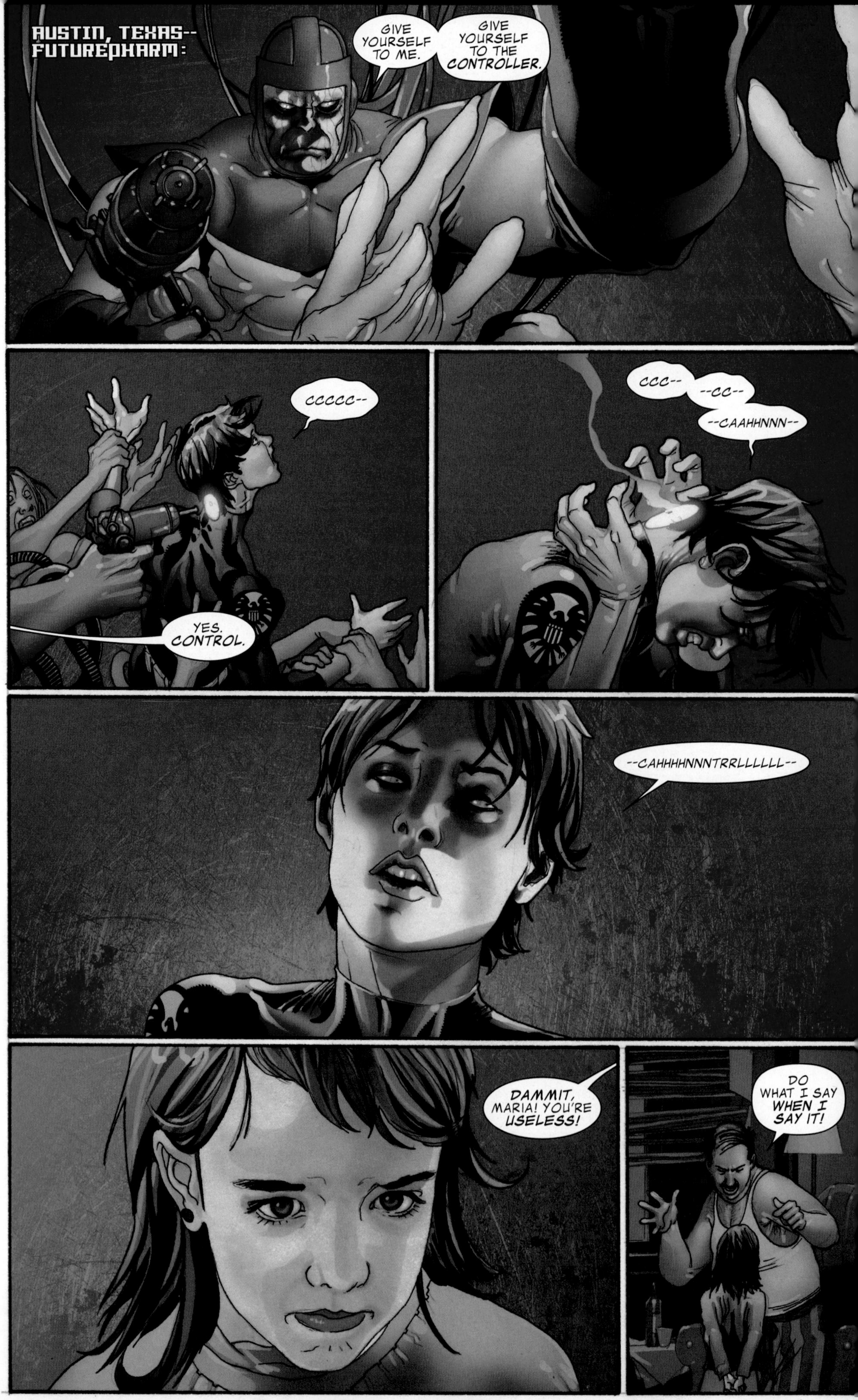
AUSTIN, TEXAS--
FUTUREPHARM:
GIVE YOURSELF TO ME.
GIVE YOURSELF TO THE CONTROLLER.
CCCCC--
YES. CONTROL.
CCC--
--CC--
--CAAHHNNN--
--CAHHHHNNNTRRLLLLLL--
DAMMIT, MARIA! YOU'RE USELESS!
DO WHAT I SAY WHEN I SAY IT!

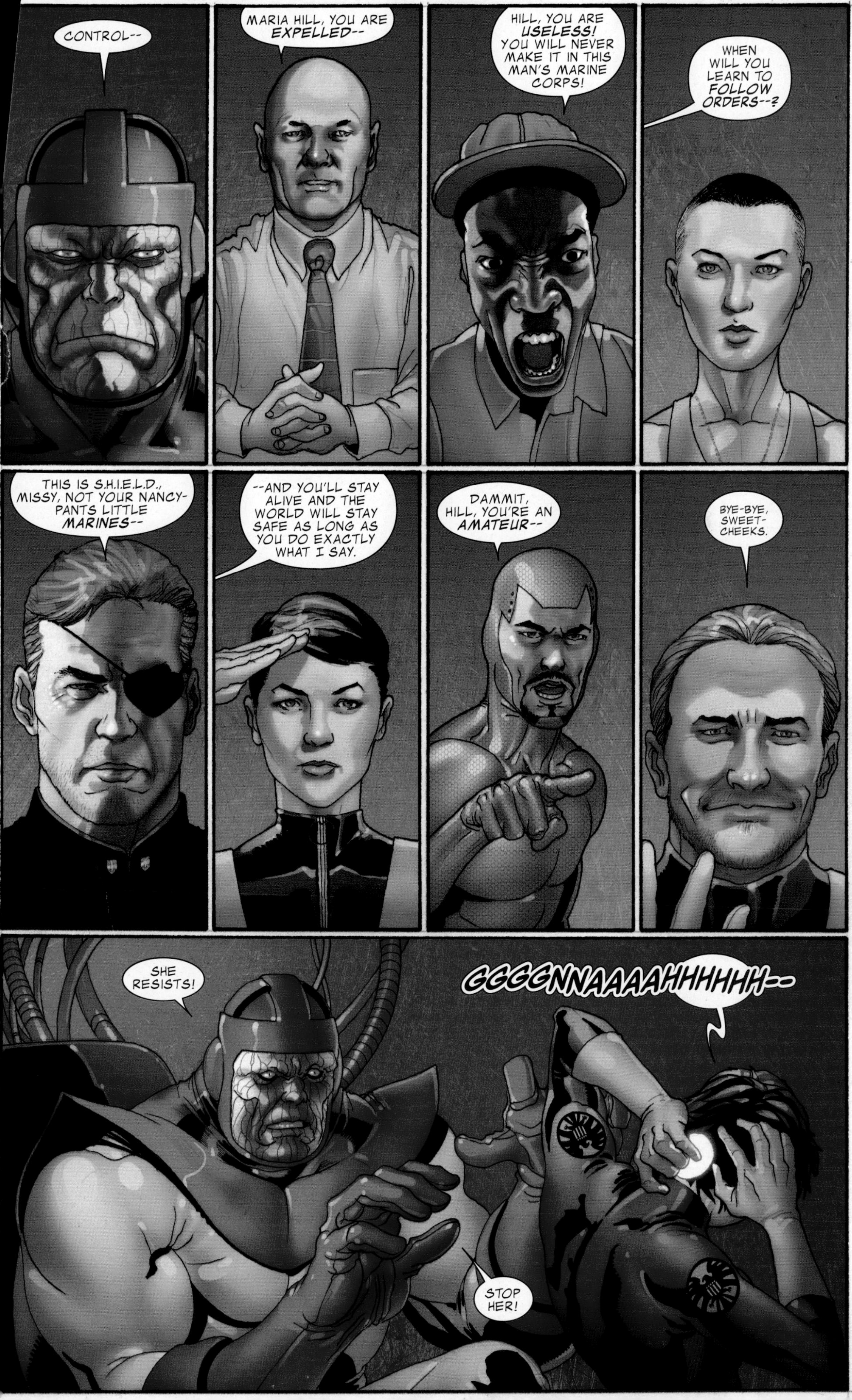
CONTROL--
MARIA HILL, YOU ARE EXPELLED--
HILL, YOU ARE USELESS! YOU WILL NEVER MAKE IT IN THIS MAN'S MARINE CORPS!
WHEN WILL YOU LEARN TO FOLLOW ORDERS--?
THIS IS S.H.I.E.L.D., MISSY, NOT YOUR NANCY-PANTS LITTLE MARINES--
--AND YOU'LL STAY ALIVE AND THE WORLD WILL STAY SAFE AS LONG AS YOU DO EXACTLY WHAT I SAY.
DAMMIT, HILL, YOU'RE AN AMATEUR--
BYE-BYE, SWEET-CHEEKS.
SHE RESISTS!
GGGGNNAAAAHHHHHH--
STOP HER!

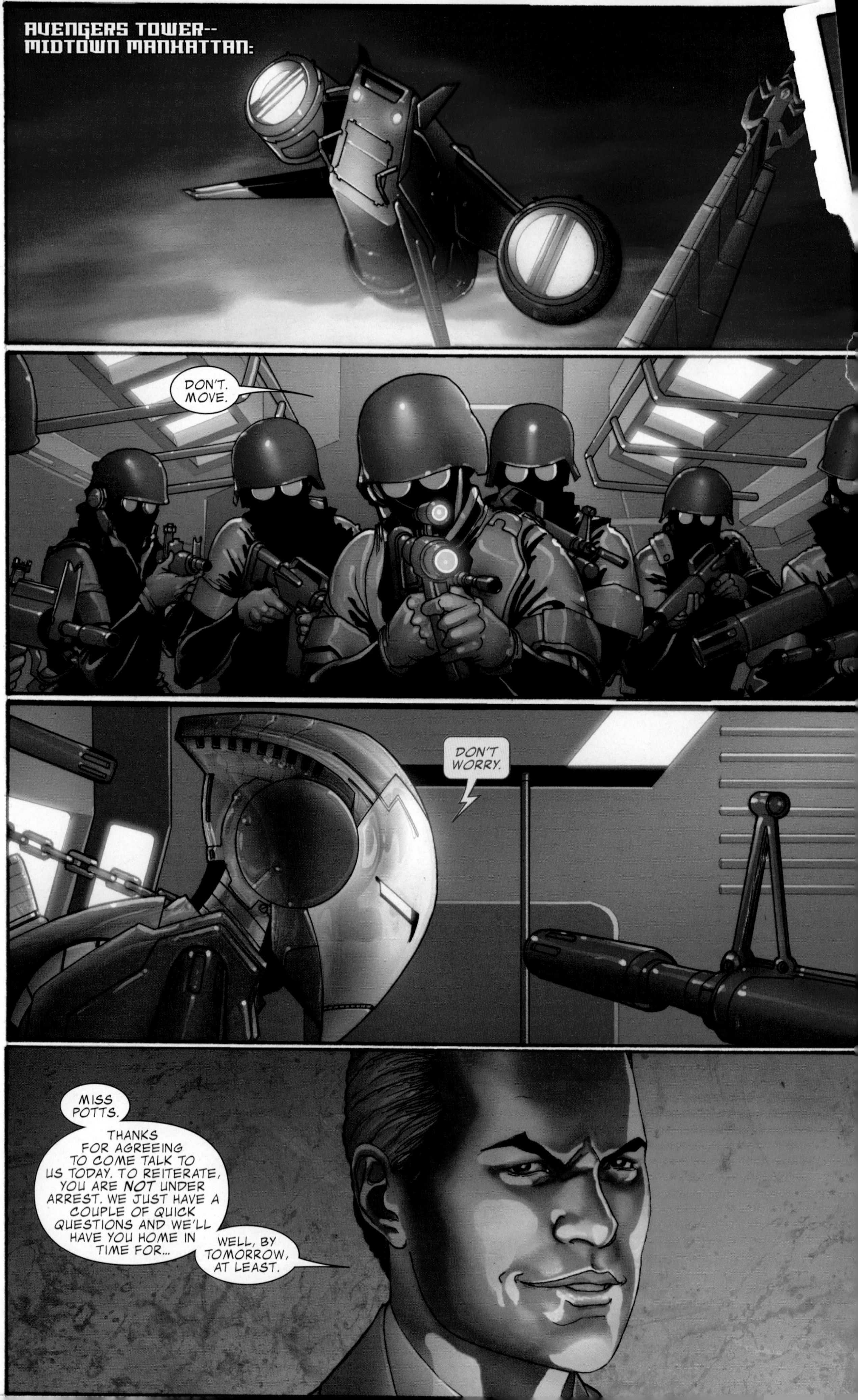
AVENGERS TOWER--
MIDTOWN MANHATTAN:
DON'T. MOVE.
DON'T WORRY.
MISS POTTS.
THANKS FOR AGREEING TO COME TALK TO US TODAY. TO REITERATE, YOU ARE NOT UNDER ARREST. WE JUST HAVE A COUPLE OF QUICK QUESTIONS AND WE'LL HAVE YOU HOME IN TIME FOR...
WELL, BY TOMORROW, AT LEAST.

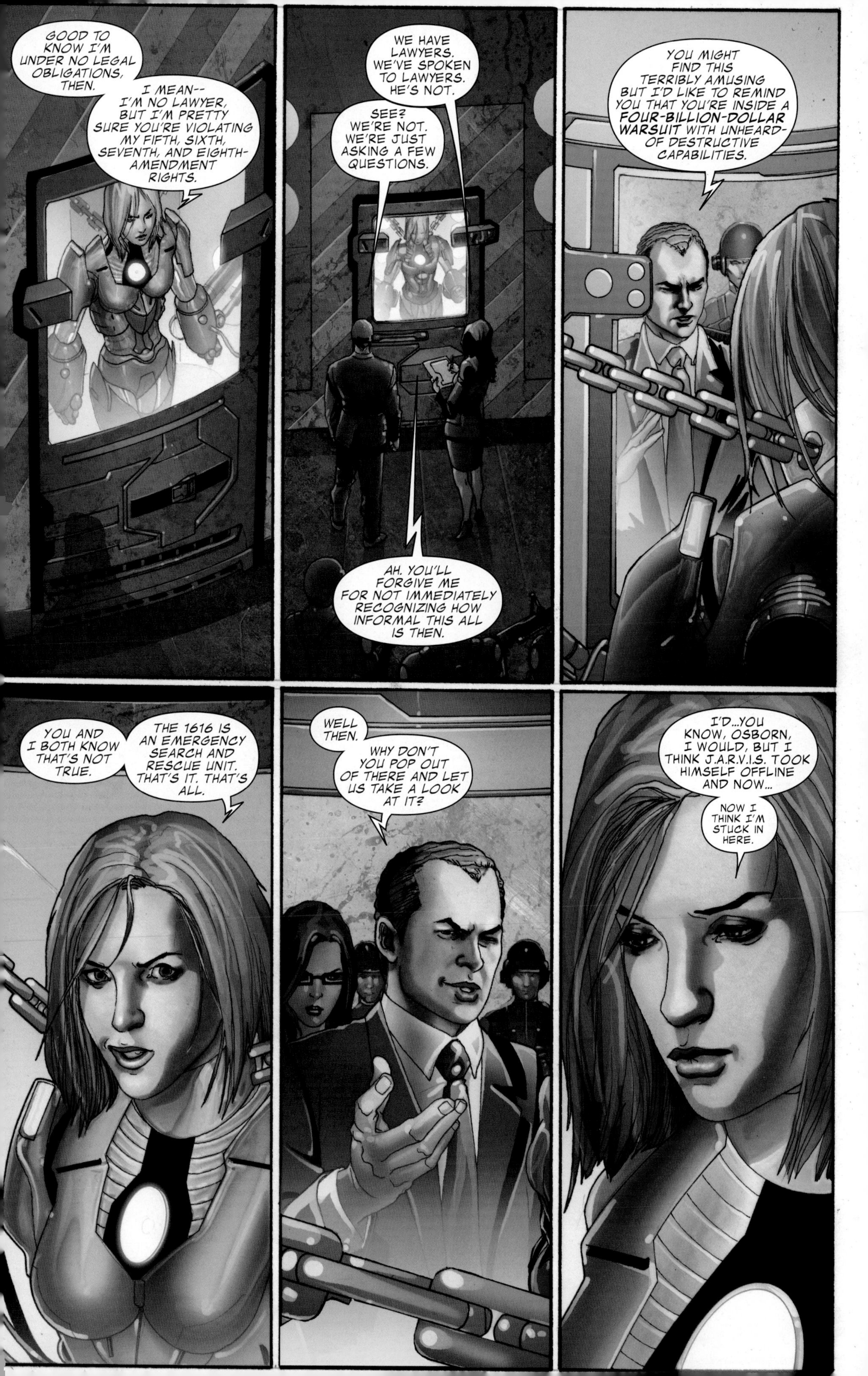
GOOD TO KNOW I'M UNDER NO LEGAL OBLIGATIONS, THEN.
I MEAN-- I'M NO LAWYER, BUT I'M PRETTY SURE YOU'RE VIOLATING MY FIFTH, SIXTH, SEVENTH, AND EIGHTH-AMENDMENT RIGHTS.
WE HAVE LAWYERS. WE'VE SPOKEN TO LAWYERS. HE'S NOT.
SEE? WE'RE NOT. WE'RE JUST ASKING A FEW QUESTIONS.
AH. YOU'LL FORGIVE ME FOR NOT IMMEDIATELY RECOGNIZING HOW INFORMAL THIS ALL IS THEN.
YOU MIGHT FIND THIS TERRIBLY AMUSING BUT I'D LIKE TO REMIND YOU THAT YOU'RE INSIDE A FOUR-BILLION-DOLLAR WARSUIT WITH UNHEARD-OF DESTRUCTIVE CAPABILITIES.
YOU AND I BOTH KNOW THAT'S NOT TRUE.
THE 1616 IS AN EMERGENCY SEARCH AND RESCUE UNIT. THAT'S IT. THAT'S ALL.
WELL THEN.
WHY DON'T YOU POP OUT OF THERE AND LET US TAKE A LOOK AT IT?
I'D...YOU KNOW, OSBORN, I WOULD, BUT I THINK J.A.R.V.I.S. TOOK HIMSELF OFFLINE AND NOW...
NOW I THINK I'M STUCK IN HERE.

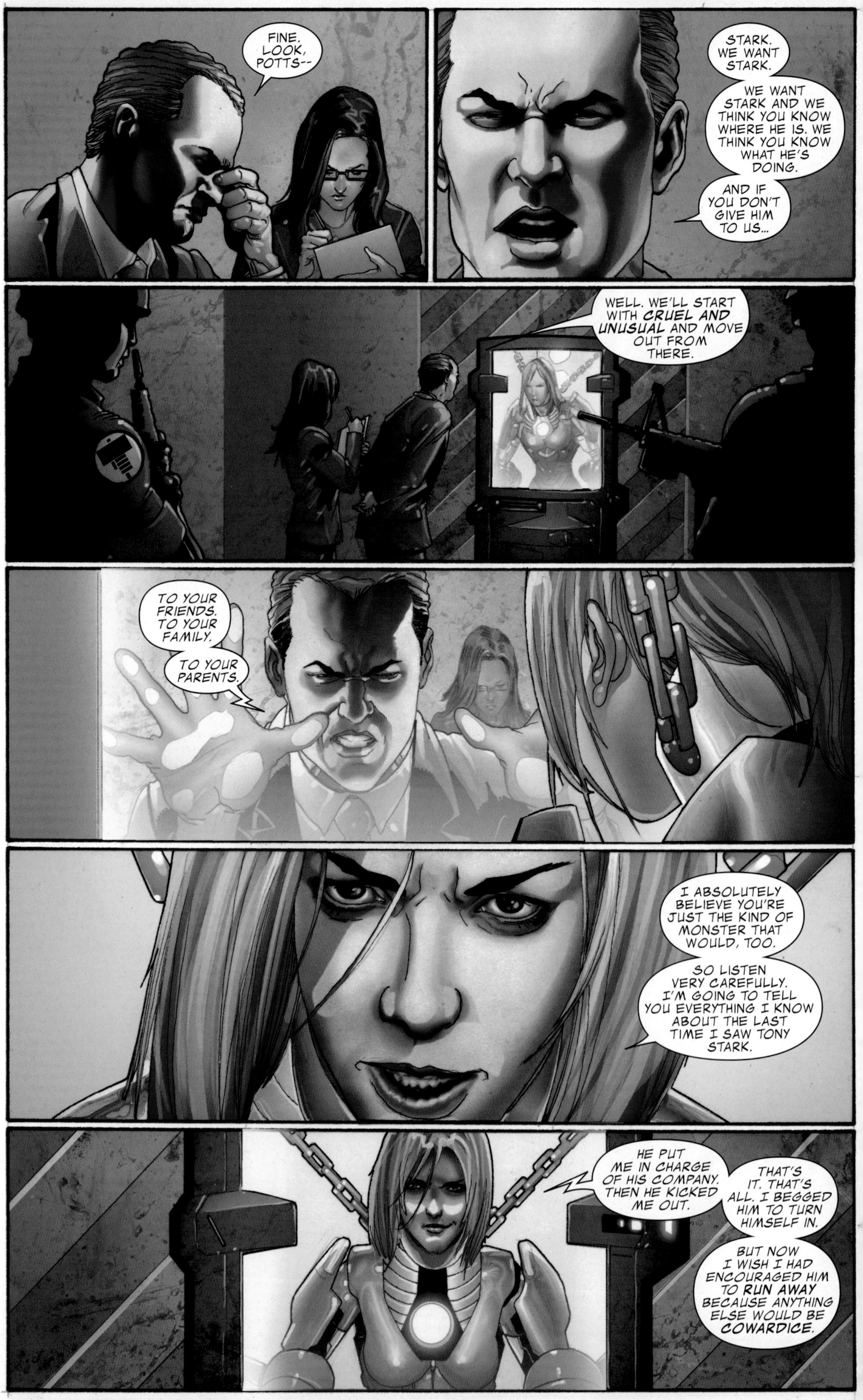
FINE. LOOK, POTTS--
STARK. WE WANT STARK.
WE WANT STARK AND WE THINK YOU KNOW WHERE HE IS. WE THINK YOU KNOW WHAT HE'S DOING.
AND IF YOU DON'T GIVE HIM TO US...
WELL. WE'LL START WITH CRUEL AND UNUSUAL AND MOVE OUT FROM THERE.
TO YOUR FRIENDS. TO YOUR FAMILY.
TO YOUR PARENTS.
I ABSOLUTELY BELIEVE YOU'RE JUST THE KIND OF MONSTER THAT WOULD, TOO.
SO LISTEN VERY CAREFULLY. I'M GOING TO TELL YOU EVERYTHING I KNOW ABOUT THE LAST TIME I SAW TONY STARK.
HE PUT ME IN CHARGE OF HIS COMPANY. THEN HE KICKED ME OUT.
THAT'S IT. THAT'S ALL. I BEGGED HIM TO TURN HIMSELF IN.
BUT NOW I WISH I HAD ENCOURAGED HIM TO RUN AWAY BECAUSE ANYTHING ELSE WOULD BE COWARDICE.

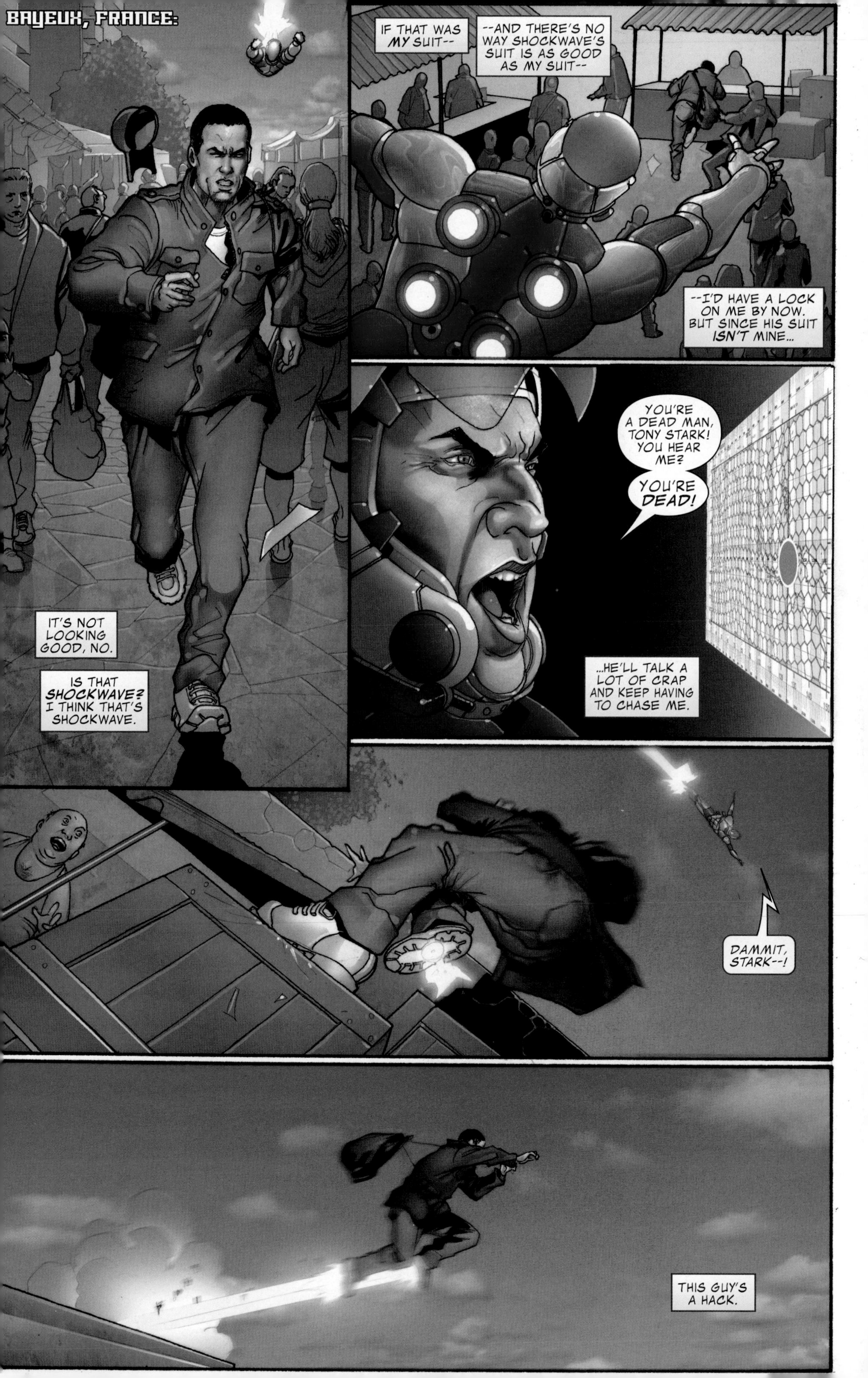
BAYEUX, FRANCE:
IT'S NOT LOOKING GOOD, NO.
IS THAT SHOCKWAVE? I THINK THAT'S SHOCKWAVE.
IF THAT WAS MY SUIT--
--AND THERE'S NO WAY SHOCKWAVE'S SUIT IS AS GOOD AS MY SUIT--
--I'D HAVE A LOCK ON ME BY NOW. BUT SINCE HIS SUIT ISN'T MINE...
YOU'RE A DEAD MAN, TONY STARK! YOU HEAR ME?
YOU'RE DEAD!
...HE'LL TALK A LOT OF CRAP AND KEEP HAVING TO CHASE ME.
DAMMIT, STARK--!
THIS GUY'S A HACK.

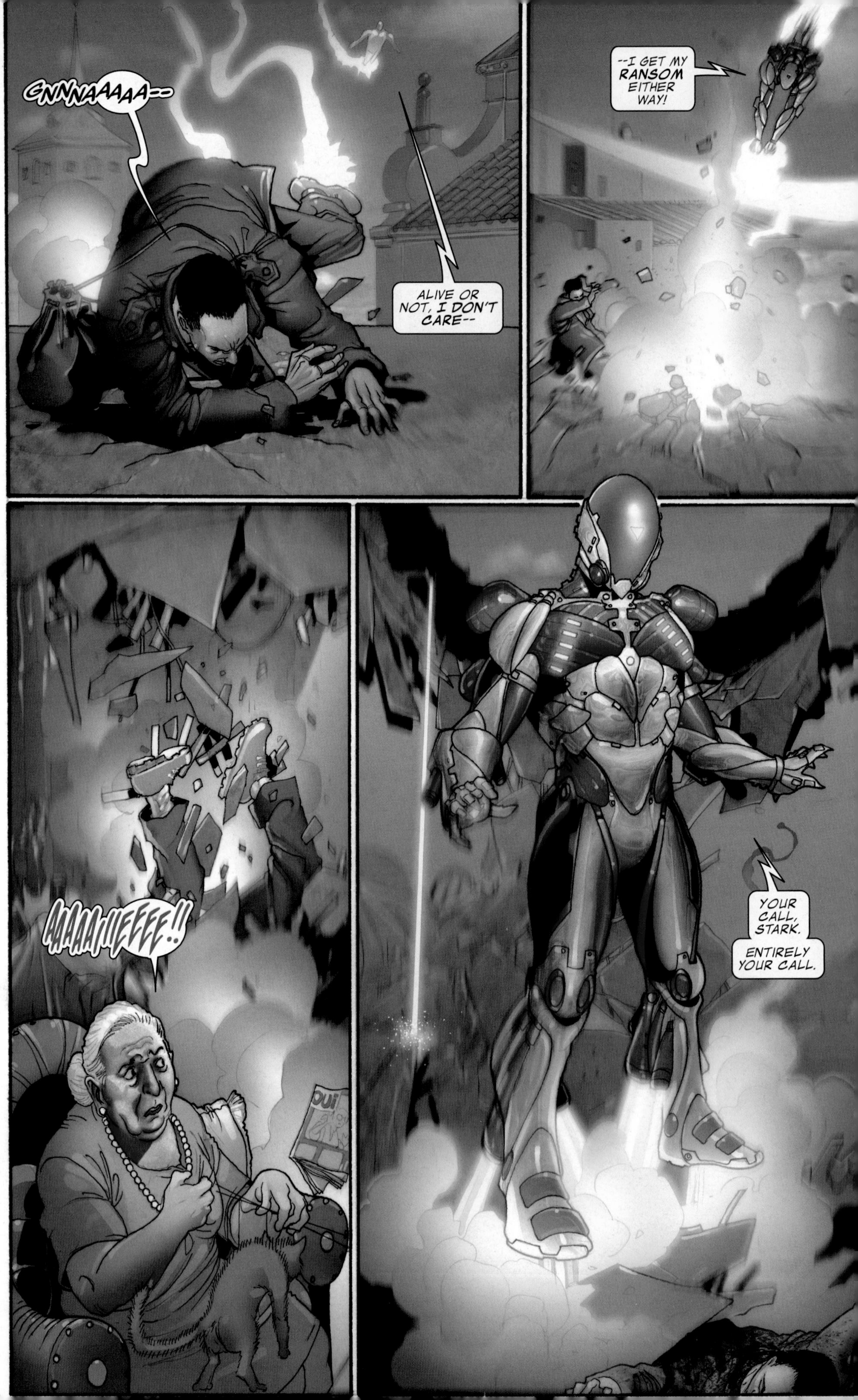
GNNNAAAAA--
ALIVE OR NOT, I DON'T CARE--
--I GET MY RANSOM EITHER WAY!
AAAAAIIIEEEEE!!
YOUR CALL, STARK.
ENTIRELY YOUR CALL.

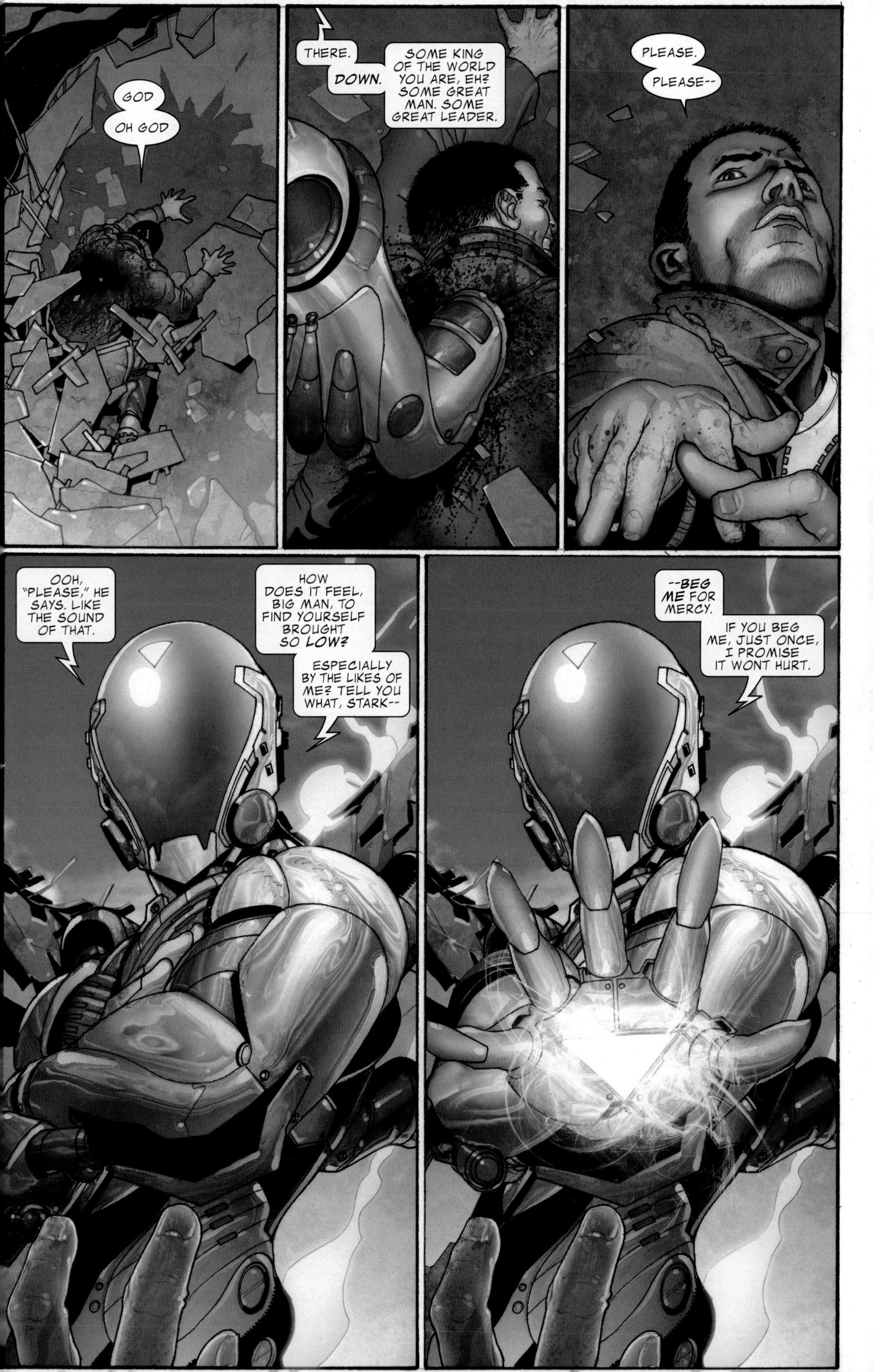
GOD
OH GOD
THERE.
DOWN.
SOME KING OF THE WORLD YOU ARE, EH? SOME GREAT MAN. SOME GREAT LEADER.
PLEASE.
PLEASE--
OOH, "PLEASE," HE SAYS. LIKE THE SOUND OF THAT.
HOW DOES IT FEEL, BIG MAN, TO FIND YOURSELF BROUGHT SO LOW?
ESPECIALLY BY THE LIKES OF ME? TELL YOU WHAT, STARK--
--BEG ME FOR MERCY.
IF YOU BEG ME, JUST ONCE, I PROMISE IT WONT HURT.

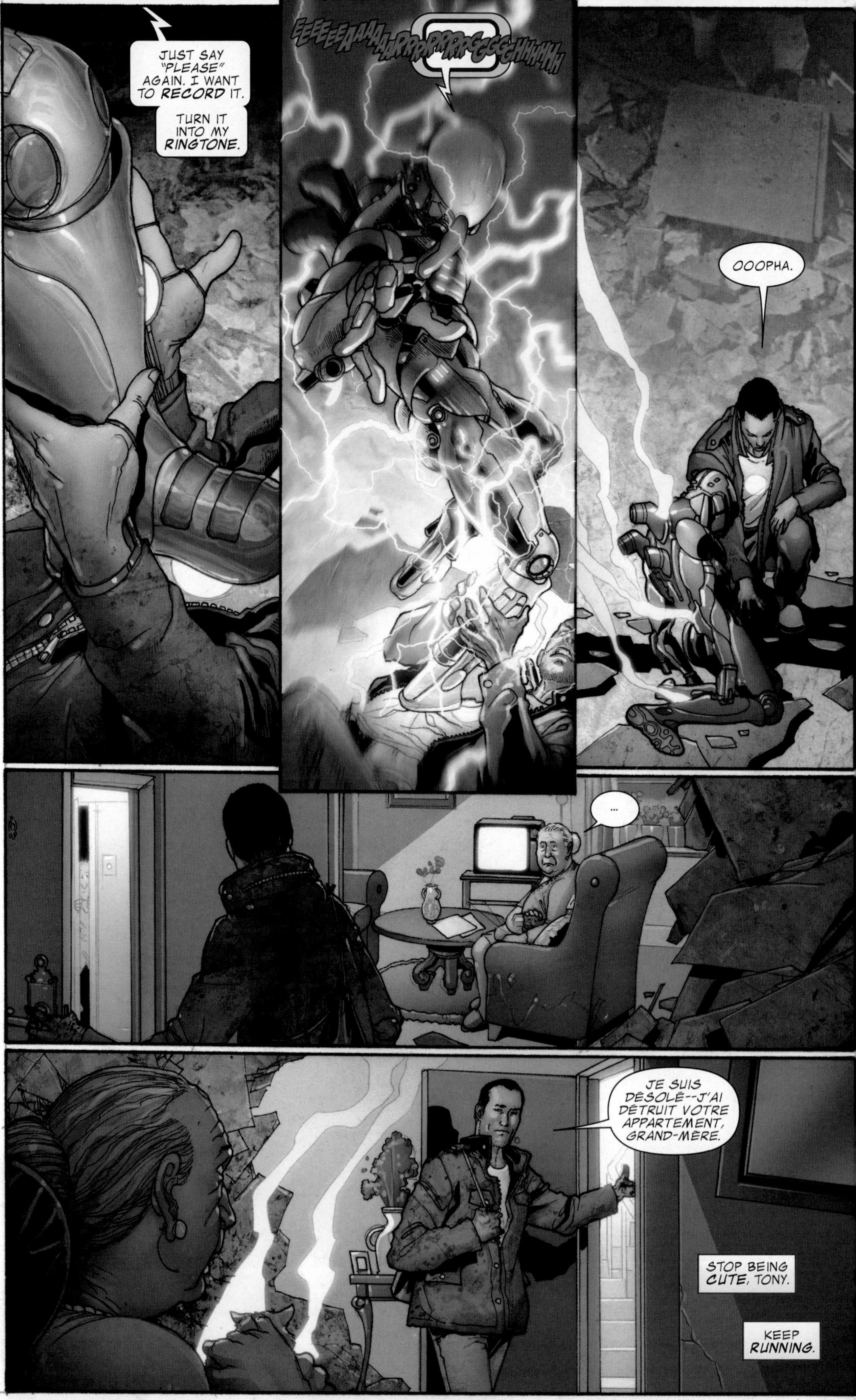
JUST SAY "PLEASE" AGAIN. I WANT TO RECORD IT.
TURN IT INTO MY RINGTONE.
EEEEEAAAAARRRRRRRRRGGGGHHHHHH
OOOPHA.
...
JE SUIS DÉSOLÉ--J'AI DÉTRUIT VOTRE APPARTEMENT, GRAND-MÈRE.
STOP BEING CUTE, TONY.
KEEP RUNNING.

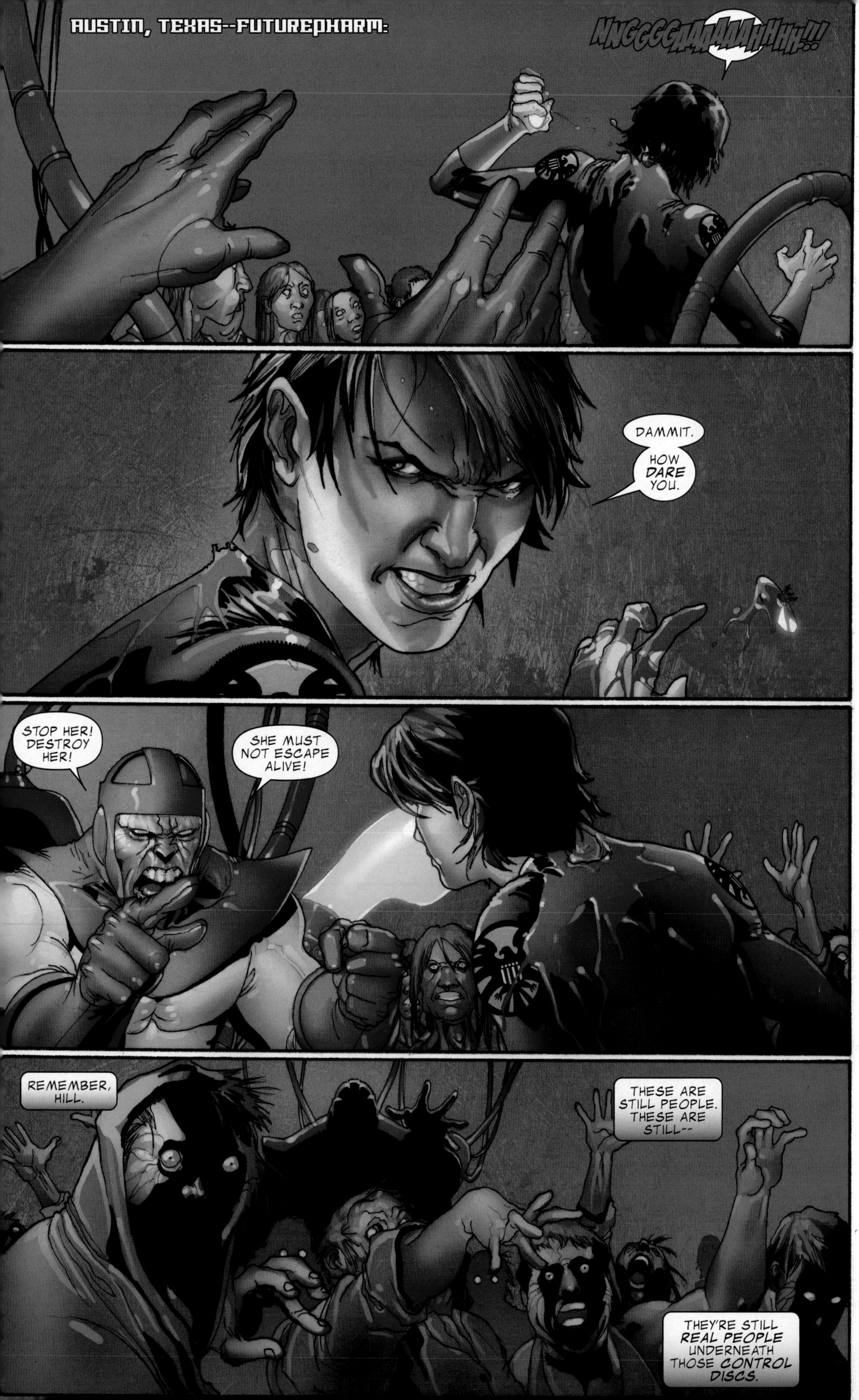
AUSTIN, TEXAS--FUTUREPHARM:
NNGGGGAAAAAAHHHH!!!
DAMMIT.
HOW DARE YOU.
STOP HER! DESTROY HER!
SHE MUST NOT ESCAPE ALIVE!
REMEMBER, HILL.
THESE ARE STILL PEOPLE. THESE ARE STILL--
THEY'RE STILL REAL PEOPLE UNDERNEATH THOSE CONTROL DISCS.

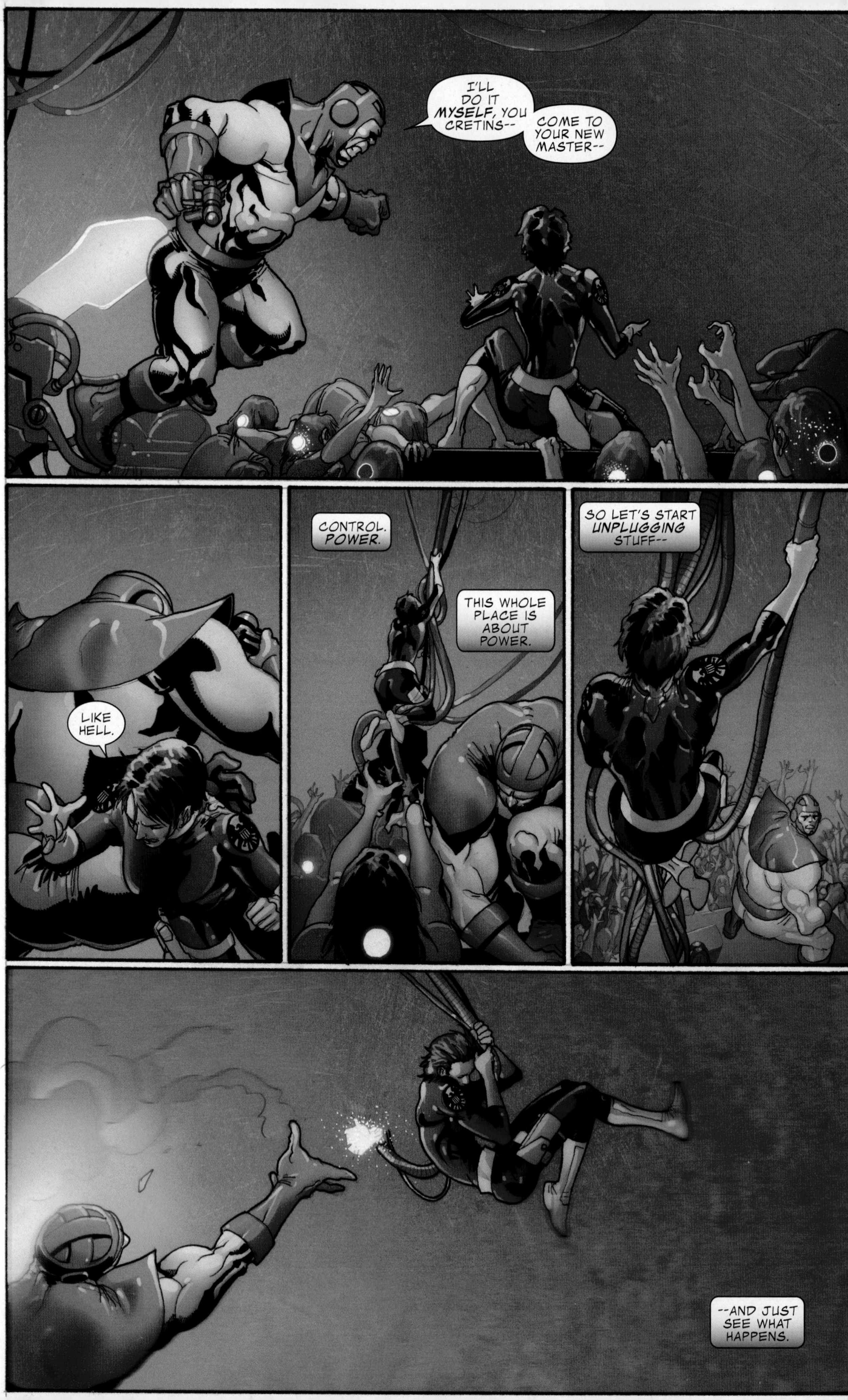
I'LL DO IT MYSELF, YOU CRETINS--
COME TO YOUR NEW MASTER--
LIKE HELL.
CONTROL. POWER.
THIS WHOLE PLACE IS ABOUT POWER.
SO LET'S START UNPLUGGING STUFF--
--AND JUST SEE WHAT HAPPENS.

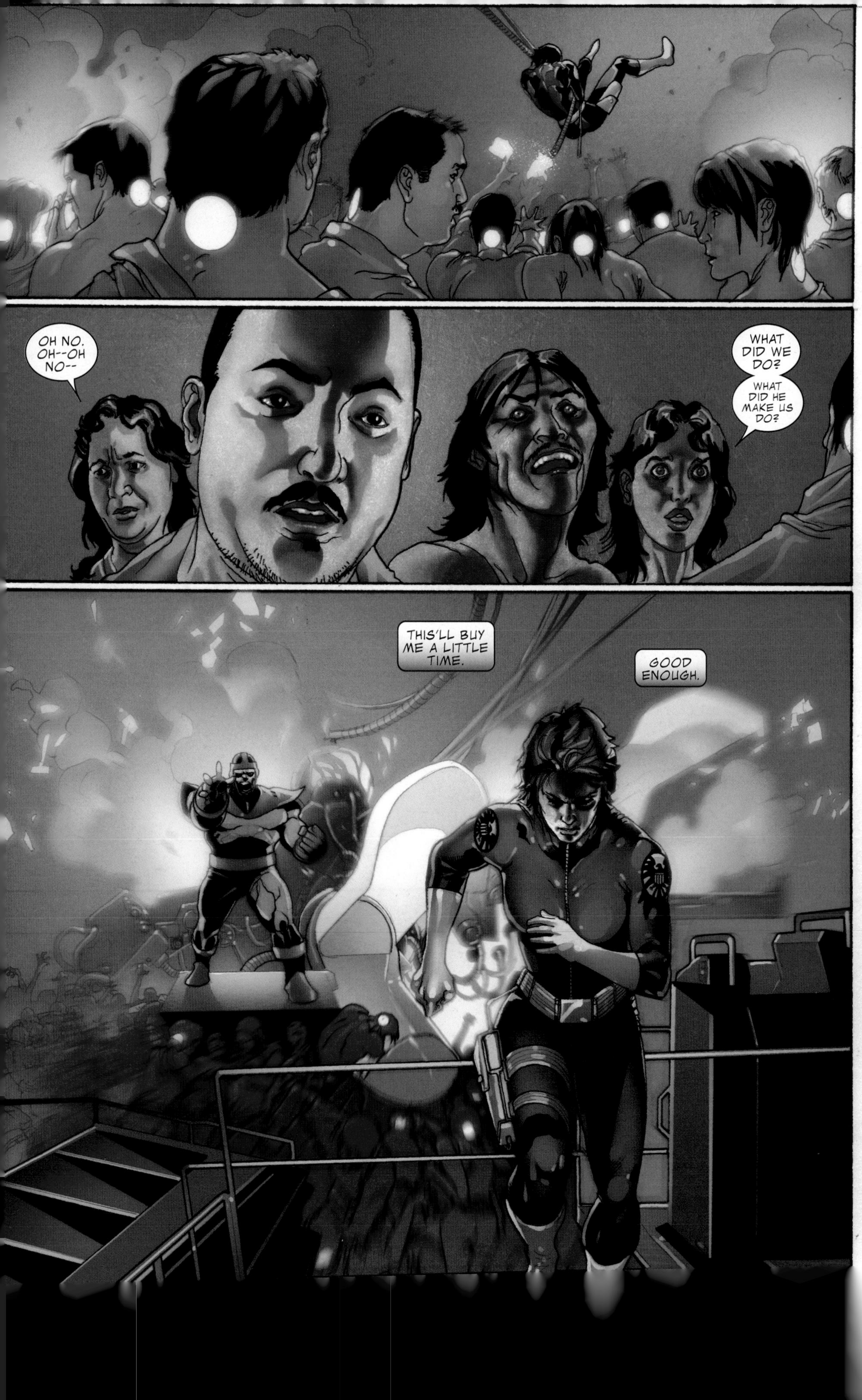

OH NO. OH--OH NO--
WHAT DID WE DO?
WHAT DID HE MAKE US DO?
THIS'LL BUY ME A LITTLE TIME.
GOOD ENOUGH.

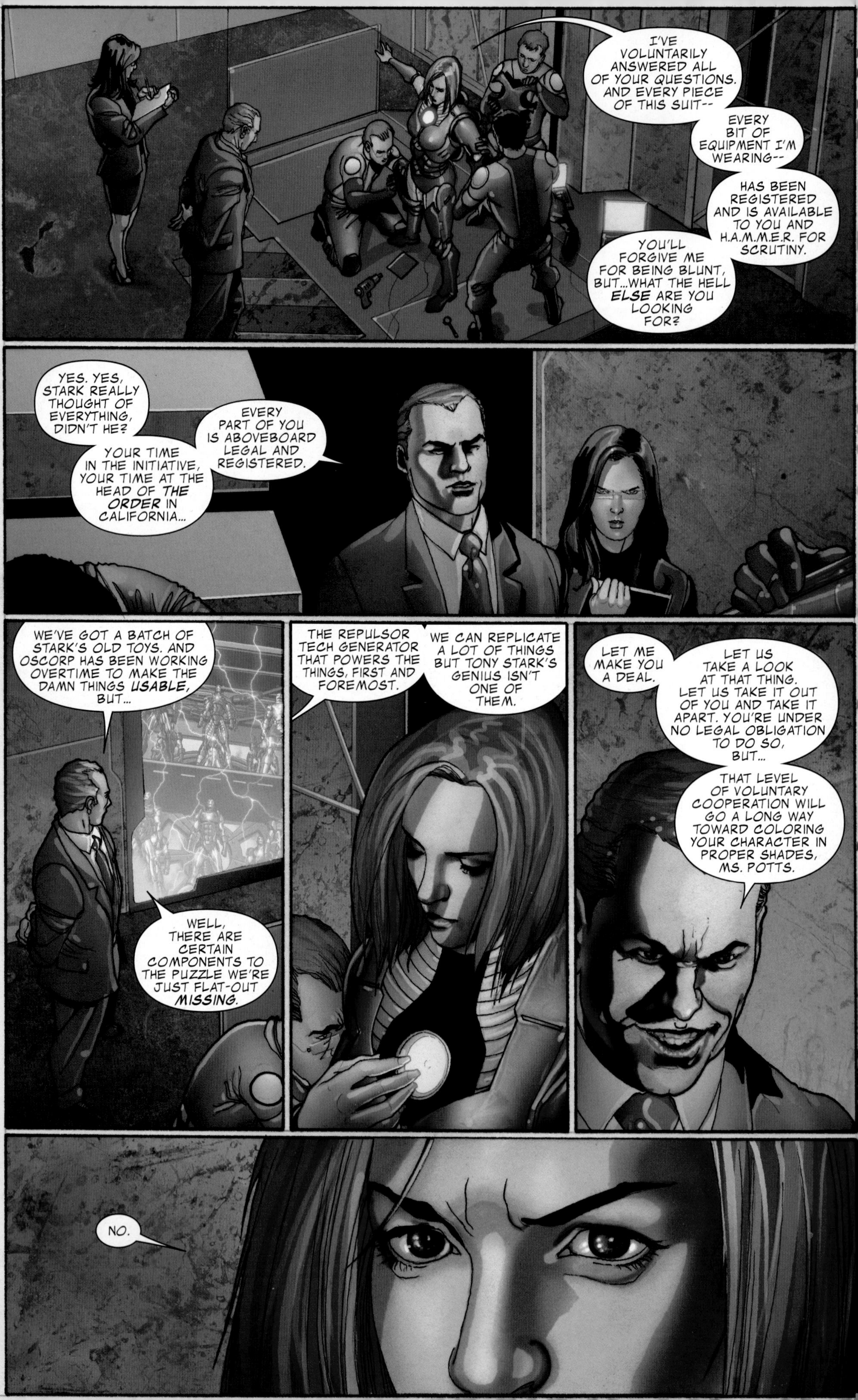
I'VE VOLUNTARILY ANSWERED ALL OF YOUR QUESTIONS. AND EVERY PIECE OF THIS SUIT--
EVERY BIT OF EQUIPMENT I'M WEARING--
HAS BEEN REGISTERED AND IS AVAILABLE TO YOU AND H.A.M.M.E.R. FOR SCRUTINY.
YOU'LL FORGIVE ME FOR BEING BLUNT, BUT...WHAT THE HELL ELSE ARE YOU LOOKING FOR?
YES. YES, STARK REALLY THOUGHT OF EVERYTHING, DIDN'T HE?
YOUR TIME IN THE INITIATIVE, YOUR TIME AT THE HEAD OF THE ORDER IN CALIFORNIA...
EVERY PART OF YOU IS ABOVEBOARD LEGAL AND REGISTERED.
WE'VE GOT A BATCH OF STARK'S OLD TOYS. AND OSCORP HAS BEEN WORKING OVERTIME TO MAKE THE DAMN THINGS USABLE, BUT...
WELL, THERE ARE CERTAIN COMPONENTS TO THE PUZZLE WE'RE JUST FLAT-OUT MISSING.
THE REPULSOR TECH GENERATOR THAT POWERS THE THINGS, FIRST AND FOREMOST.
WE CAN REPLICATE A LOT OF THINGS BUT TONY STARK'S GENIUS ISN'T ONE OF THEM.
LET ME MAKE YOU A DEAL.
LET US TAKE A LOOK AT THAT THING. LET US TAKE IT OUT OF YOU AND TAKE IT APART. YOU'RE UNDER NO LEGAL OBLIGATION TO DO SO, BUT...
THAT LEVEL OF VOLUNTARY COOPERATION WILL GO A LONG WAY TOWARD COLORING YOUR CHARACTER IN PROPER SHADES, MS. POTTS.
NO.

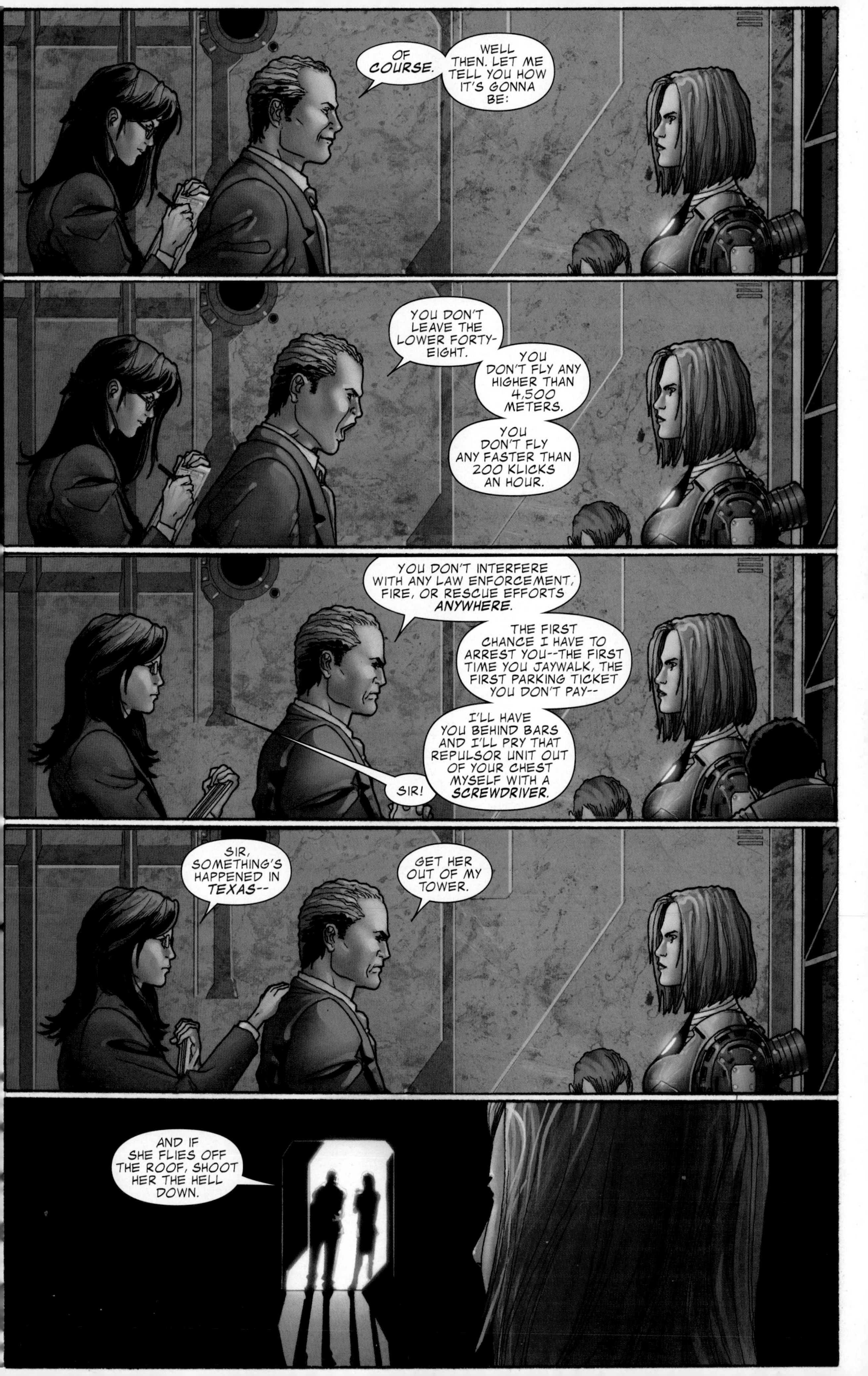
OF COURSE.
WELL THEN. LET ME TELL YOU HOW IT'S GONNA BE:
YOU DON'T LEAVE THE LOWER FORTY-EIGHT.
YOU DON'T FLY ANY HIGHER THAN 4,500 METERS.
YOU DON'T FLY ANY FASTER THAN 200 KLICKS AN HOUR.
YOU DON'T INTERFERE WITH ANY LAW ENFORCEMENT, FIRE, OR RESCUE EFFORTS ANYWHERE.
THE FIRST CHANCE I HAVE TO ARREST YOU--THE FIRST TIME YOU JAYWALK, THE FIRST PARKING TICKET YOU DON'T PAY--
I'LL HAVE YOU BEHIND BARS AND I'LL PRY THAT REPULSOR UNIT OUT OF YOUR CHEST MYSELF WITH A SCREWDRIVER.
SIR!
SIR, SOMETHING'S HAPPENED IN TEXAS--
GET HER OUT OF MY TOWER.
AND IF SHE FLIES OFF THE ROOF, SHOOT HER THE HELL DOWN.

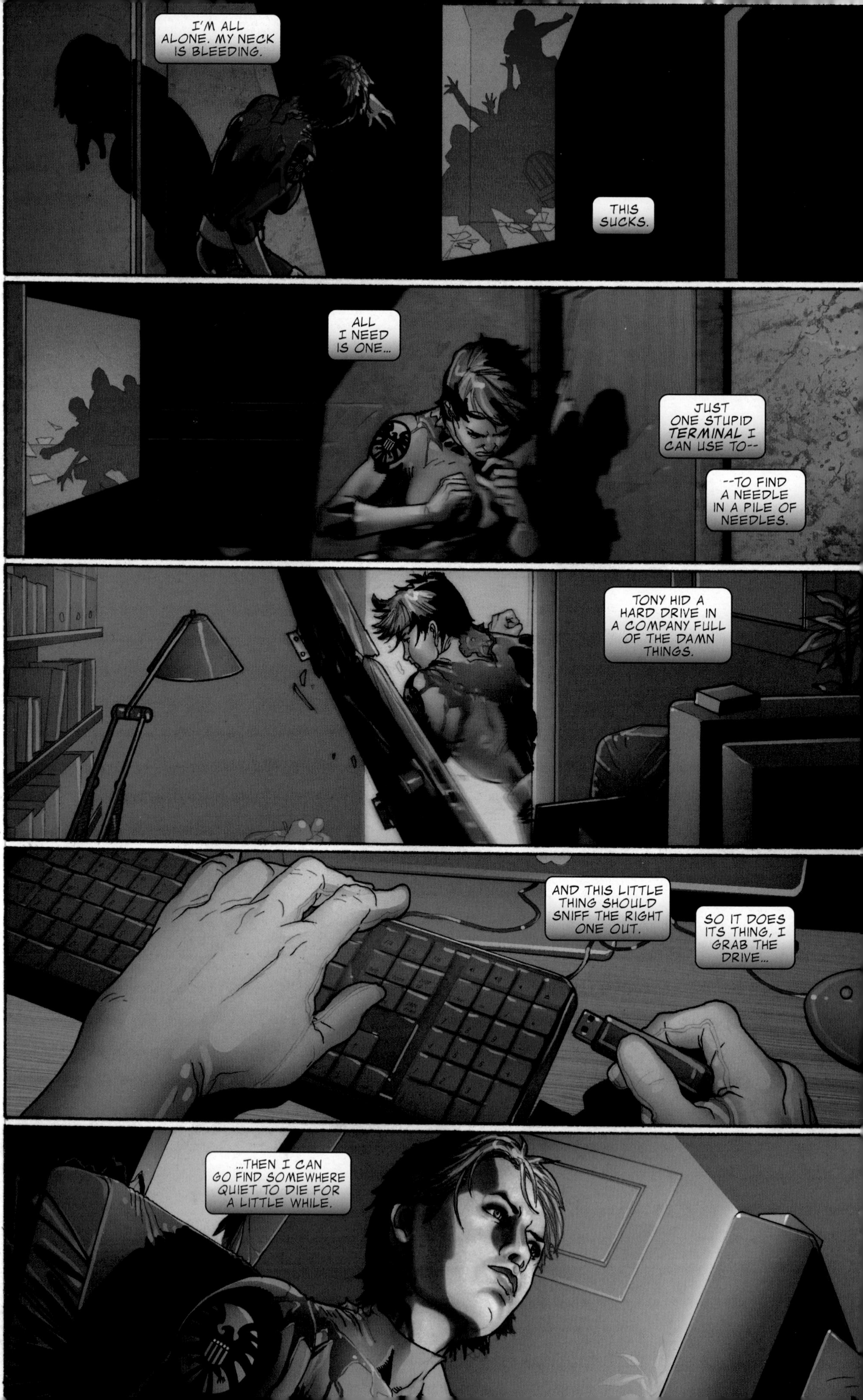
I'M ALL ALONE. MY NECK IS BLEEDING.
THIS SUCKS.
ALL I NEED IS ONE...
JUST ONE STUPID *TERMINAL* I CAN USE TO--
--TO FIND A NEEDLE IN A PILE OF NEEDLES.
TONY HID A HARD DRIVE IN A COMPANY FULL OF THE DAMN THINGS.
AND THIS LITTLE THING SHOULD SNIFF THE RIGHT ONE OUT.
SO IT DOES ITS THING, I GRAB THE DRIVE...
...THEN I CAN GO FIND SOMEWHERE QUIET TO DIE FOR A LITTLE WHILE.

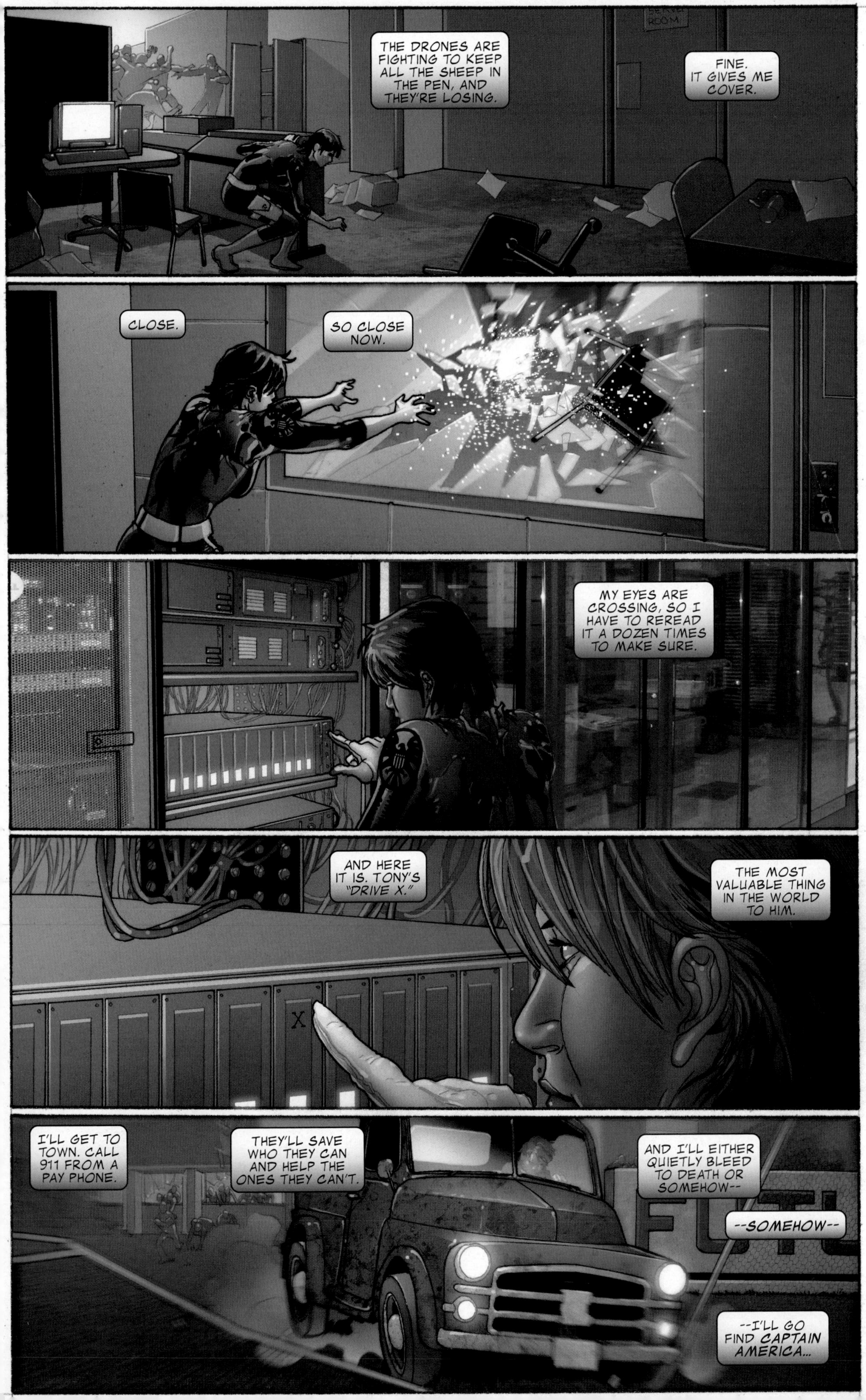
THE DRONES ARE FIGHTING TO KEEP ALL THE SHEEP IN THE PEN, AND THEY'RE LOSING.
FINE. IT GIVES ME COVER.
CLOSE.
SO CLOSE NOW.
MY EYES ARE CROSSING, SO I HAVE TO REREAD IT A DOZEN TIMES TO MAKE SURE.
AND HERE IT IS. TONY'S "DRIVE X."
THE MOST VALUABLE THING IN THE WORLD TO HIM.
I'LL GET TO TOWN. CALL 911 FROM A PAY PHONE.
THEY'LL SAVE WHO THEY CAN AND HELP THE ONES THEY CAN'T.
AND I'LL EITHER QUIETLY BLEED TO DEATH OR SOMEHOW--
--SOMEHOW--
--I'LL GO FIND CAPTAIN AMERICA...

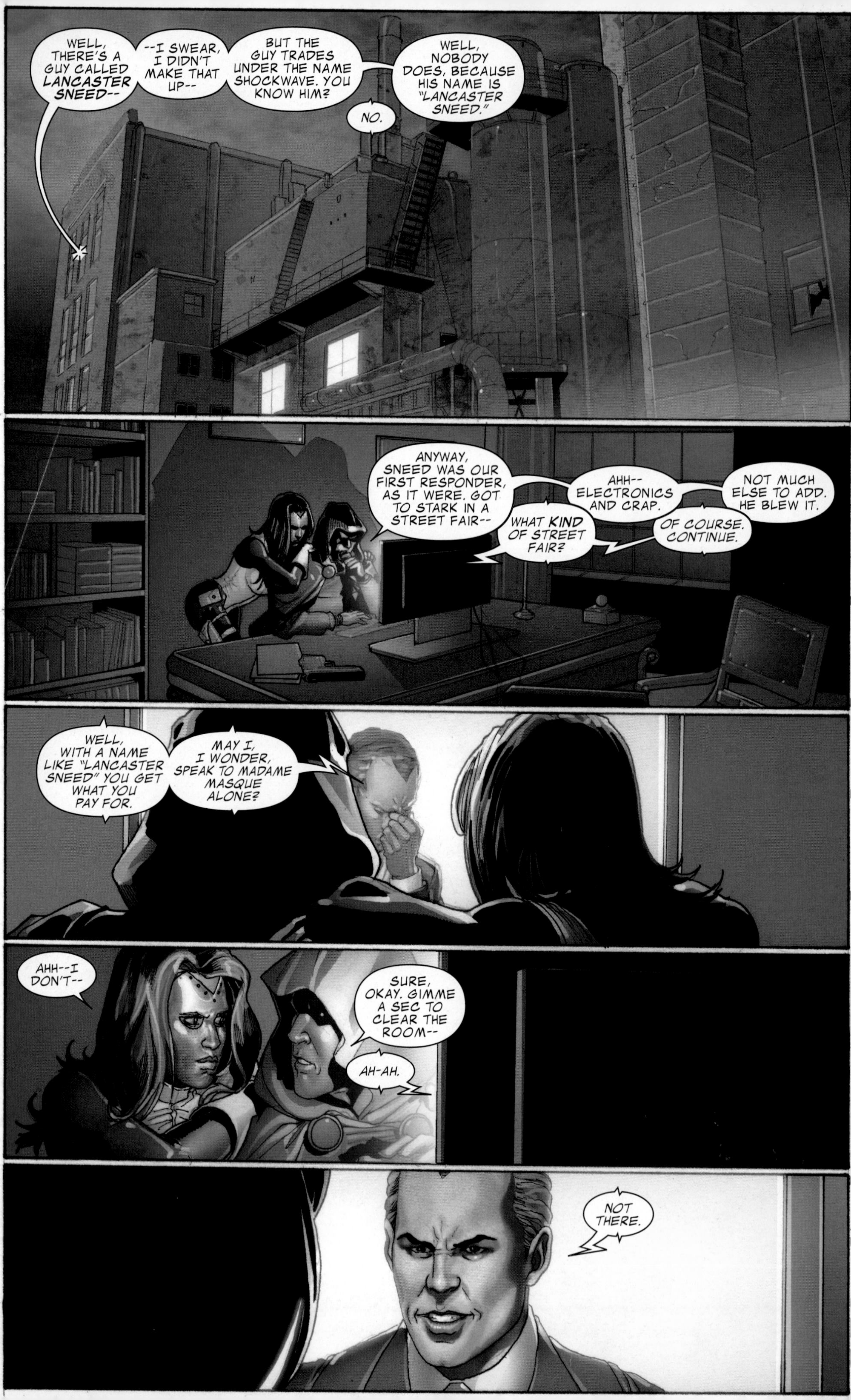
WELL, THERE'S A GUY CALLED LANCASTER SNEED--
--I SWEAR, I DIDN'T MAKE THAT UP--
BUT THE GUY TRADES UNDER THE NAME SHOCKWAVE. YOU KNOW HIM?
NO.
WELL, NOBODY DOES, BECAUSE HIS NAME IS "LANCASTER SNEED."
ANYWAY, SNEED WAS OUR FIRST RESPONDER, AS IT WERE. GOT TO STARK IN A STREET FAIR--
WHAT KIND OF STREET FAIR?
AHH--ELECTRONICS AND CRAP.
OF COURSE. CONTINUE.
NOT MUCH ELSE TO ADD. HE BLEW IT.
WELL, WITH A NAME LIKE "LANCASTER SNEED" YOU GET WHAT YOU PAY FOR.
MAY I, I WONDER, SPEAK TO MADAME MASQUE ALONE?
AHH--I DON'T--
SURE, OKAY. GIMME A SEC TO CLEAR THE ROOM--
AH-AH.
NOT THERE.

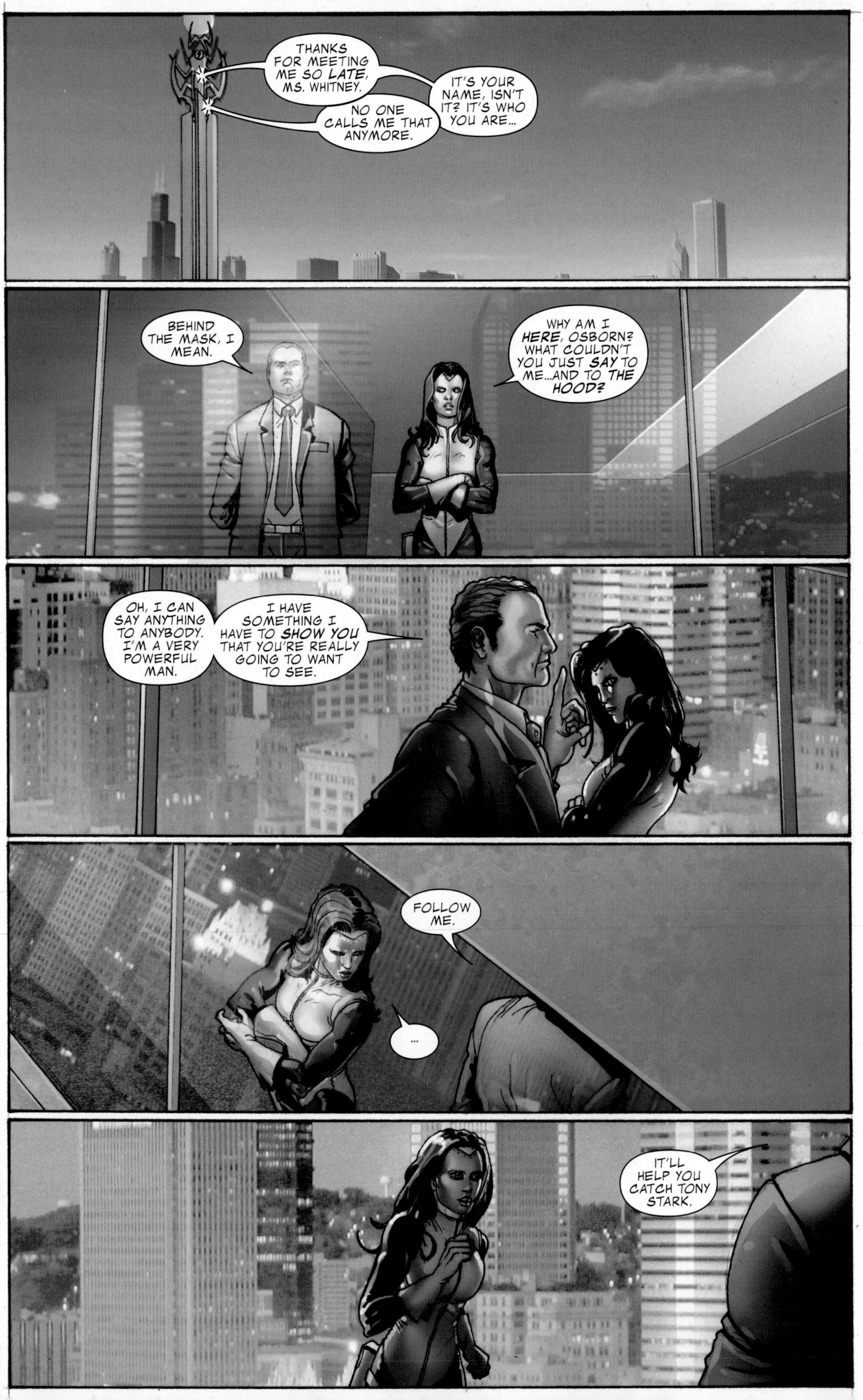
THANKS FOR MEETING ME SO LATE, MS. WHITNEY.
NO ONE CALLS ME THAT ANYMORE.
IT'S YOUR NAME, ISN'T IT? IT'S WHO YOU ARE...
BEHIND THE MASK, I MEAN.
WHY AM I HERE, OSBORN? WHAT COULDN'T YOU JUST SAY TO ME...AND TO THE HOOD?
OH, I CAN SAY ANYTHING TO ANYBODY. I'M A VERY POWERFUL MAN.
I HAVE SOMETHING I HAVE TO SHOW YOU THAT YOU'RE REALLY GOING TO WANT TO SEE.
FOLLOW ME.
...
IT'LL HELP YOU CATCH TONY STARK.

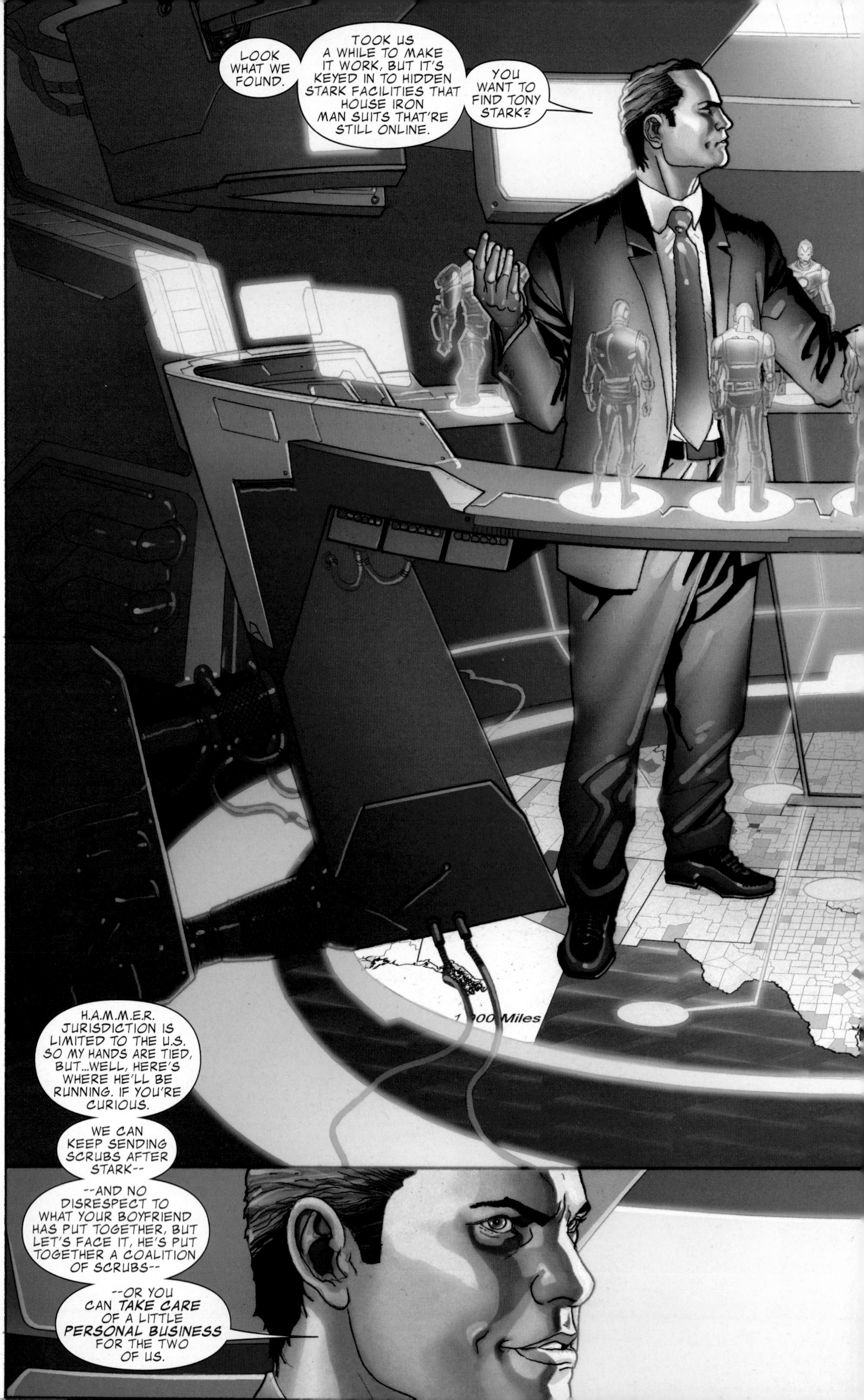
LOOK WHAT WE FOUND.
TOOK US A WHILE TO MAKE IT WORK, BUT IT'S KEYED IN TO HIDDEN STARK FACILITIES THAT HOUSE IRON MAN SUITS THAT'RE STILL ONLINE.
YOU WANT TO FIND TONY STARK?
H.A.M.M.E.R. JURISDICTION IS LIMITED TO THE U.S. SO MY HANDS ARE TIED, BUT...WELL, HERE'S WHERE HE'LL BE RUNNING. IF YOU'RE CURIOUS.
WE CAN KEEP SENDING SCRUBS AFTER STARK--
--AND NO DISRESPECT TO WHAT YOUR BOYFRIEND HAS PUT TOGETHER, BUT LET'S FACE IT, HE'S PUT TOGETHER A COALITION OF SCRUBS--
--OR YOU CAN TAKE CARE OF A LITTLE PERSONAL BUSINESS FOR THE TWO OF US.

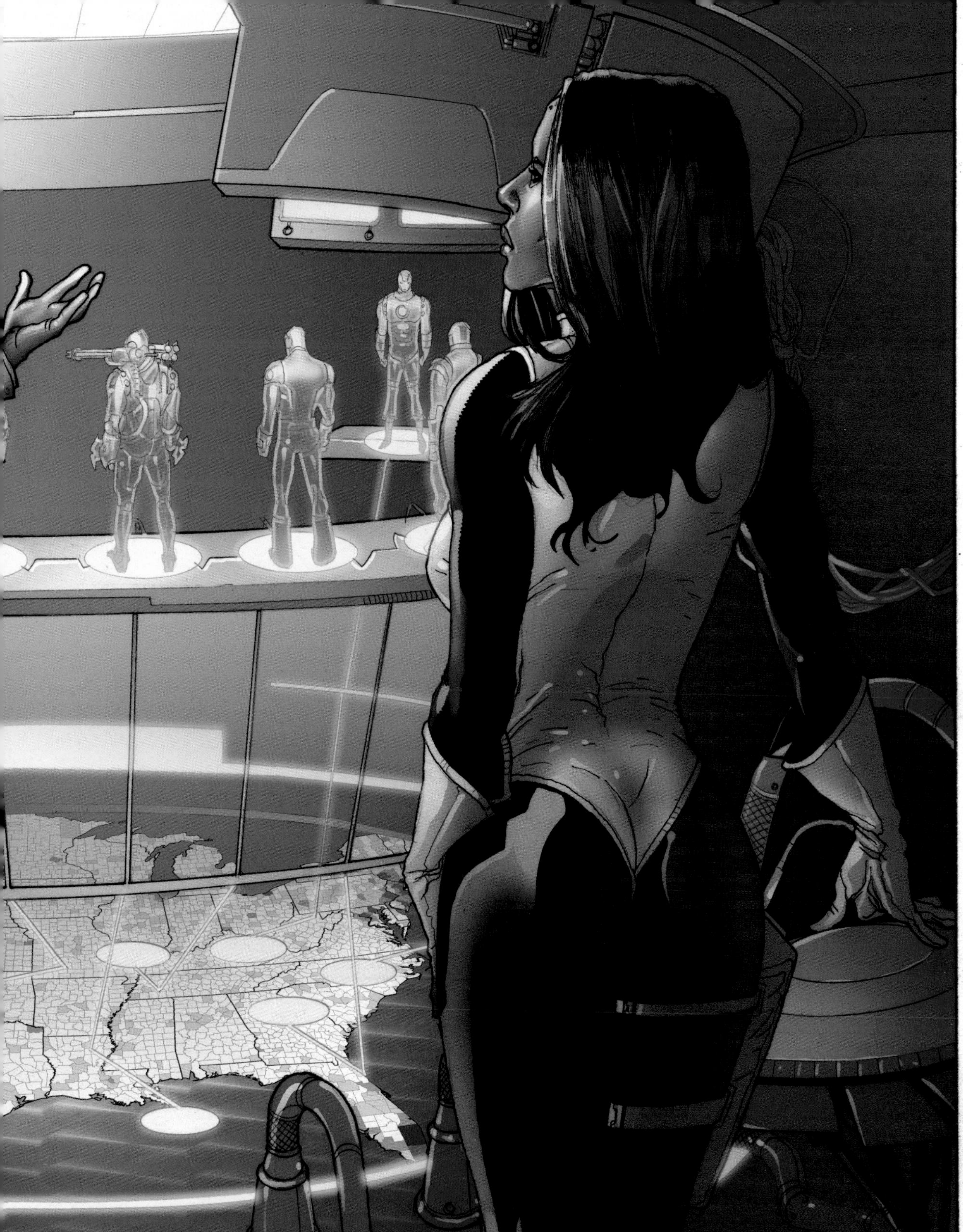

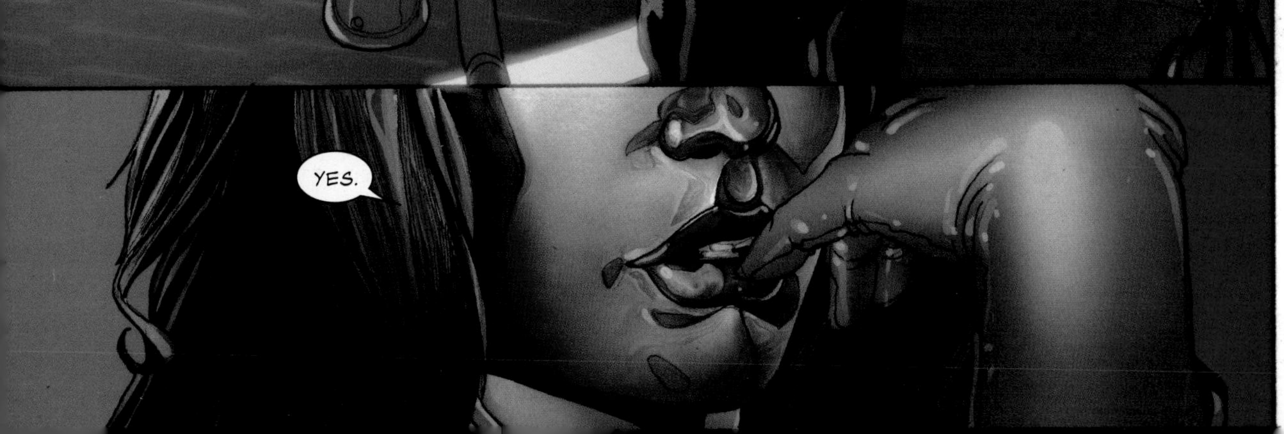
YES.

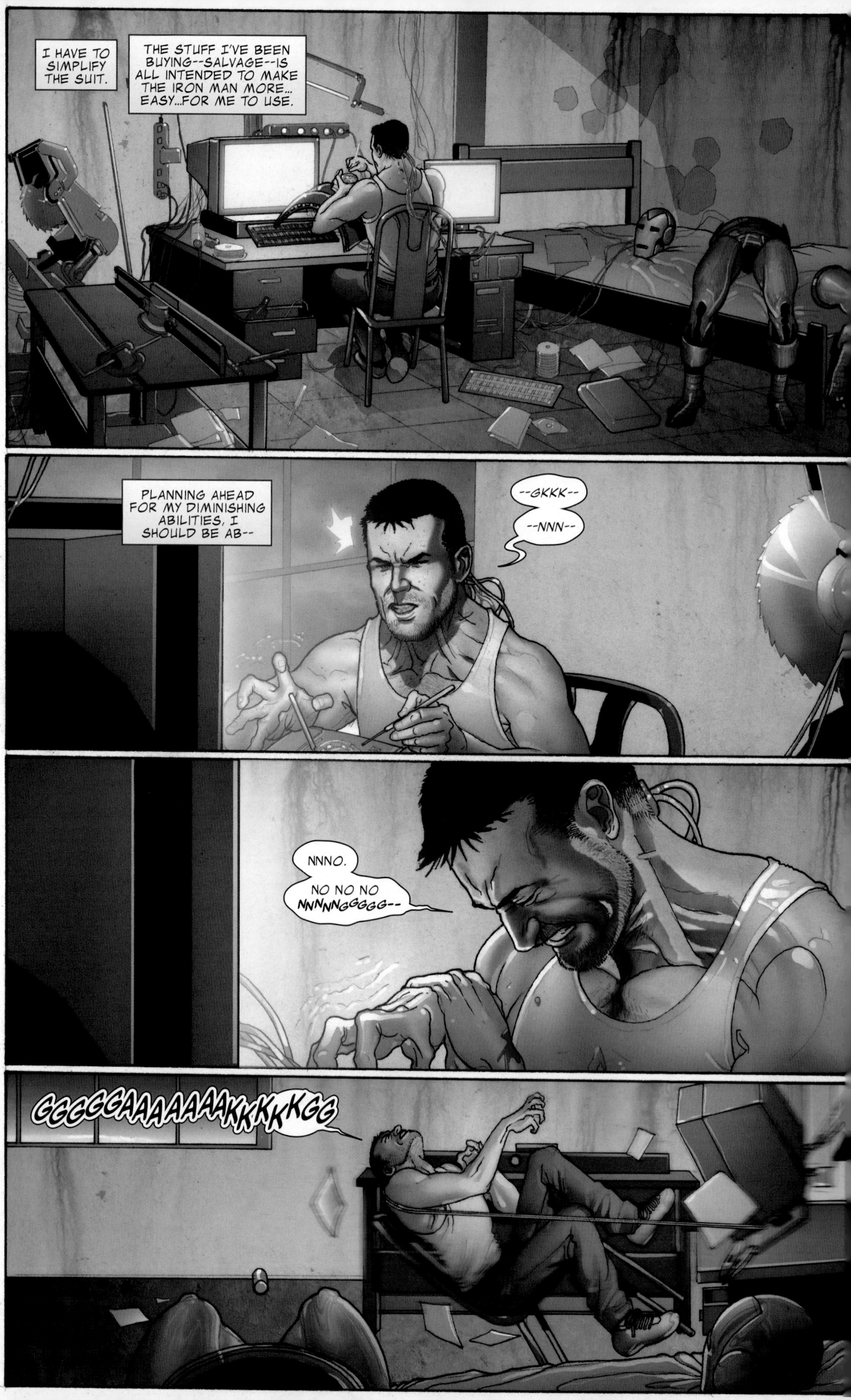
I HAVE TO SIMPLIFY THE SUIT.
THE STUFF I'VE BEEN BUYING--SALVAGE--IS ALL INTENDED TO MAKE THE IRON MAN MORE... EASY...FOR ME TO USE.
PLANNING AHEAD FOR MY DIMINISHING ABILITIES, I SHOULD BE AB--
--GKKK--
--NNN--
NNNO.
NO NO NO NNNNNGGGGG--
GGGGGAAAAAAAKKKKKGG

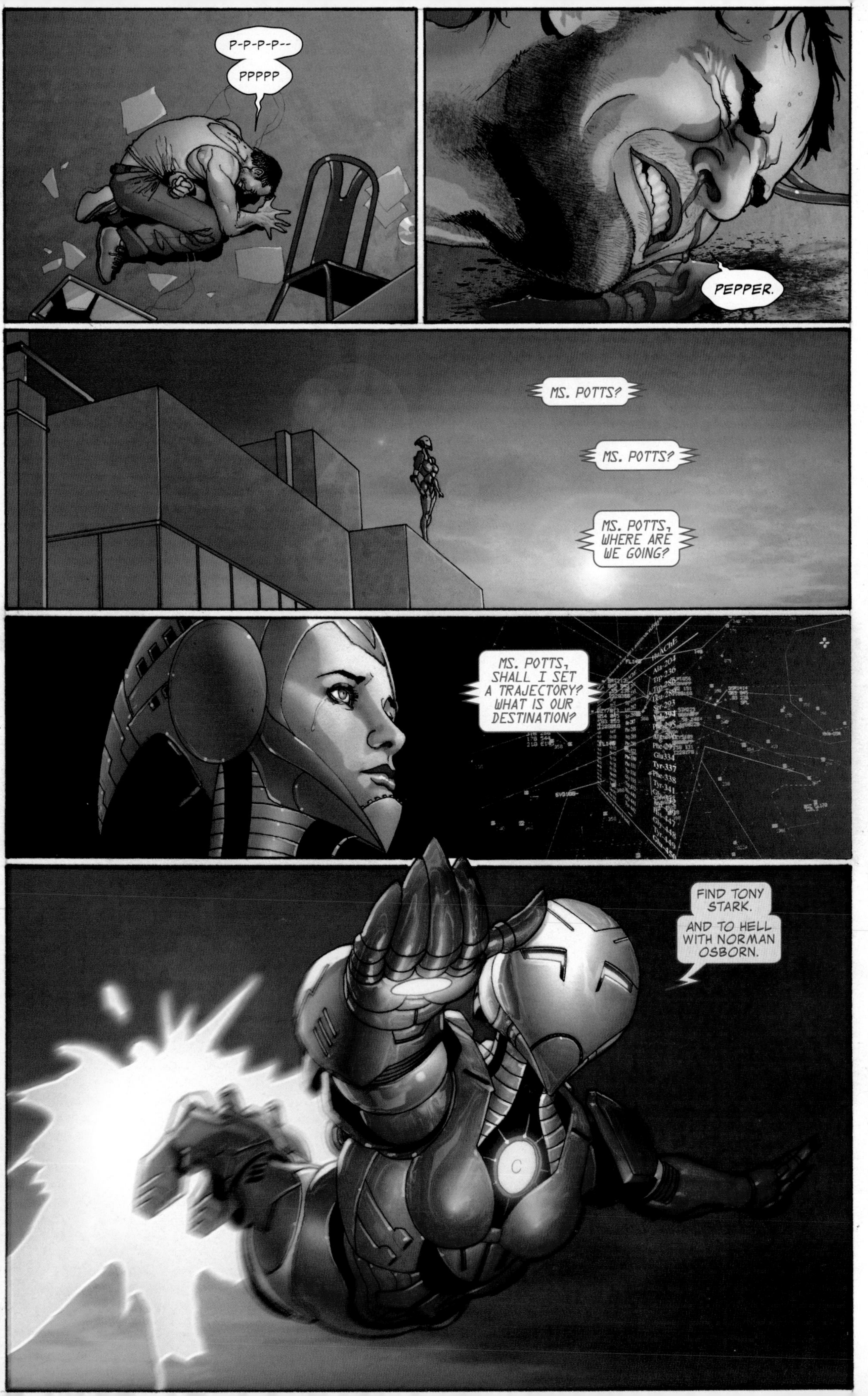
P-P-P-P--
PPPPP
PEPPER.
MS. POTTS?
MS. POTTS?
MS. POTTS, WHERE ARE WE GOING?
MS. POTTS, SHALL I SET A TRAJECTORY? WHAT IS OUR DESTINATION?
FIND TONY STARK.
AND TO HELL WITH NORMAN OSBORN.

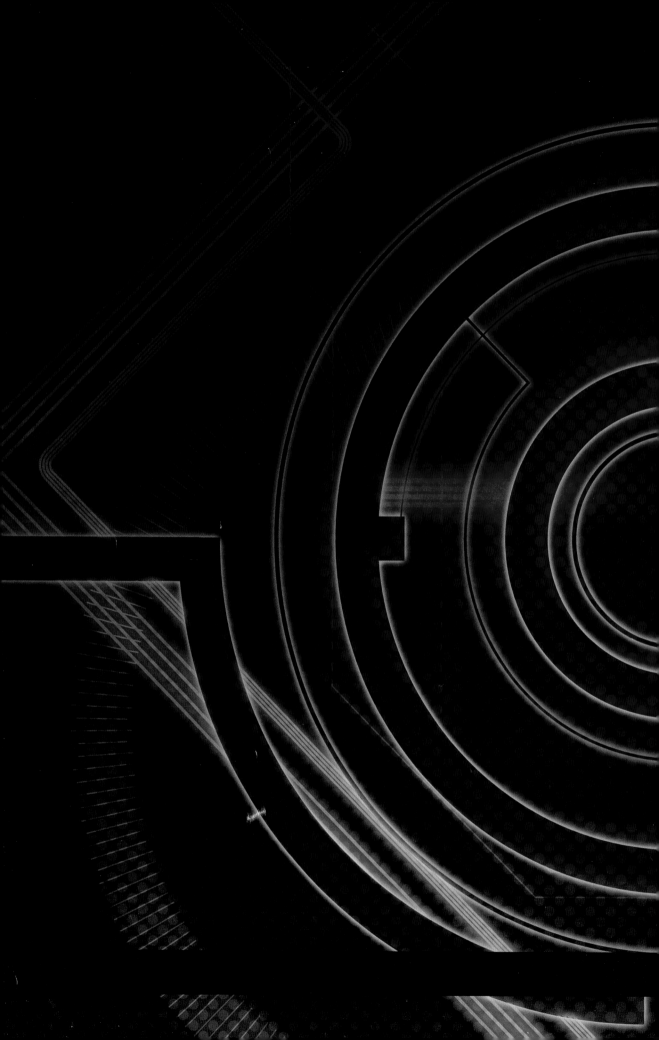

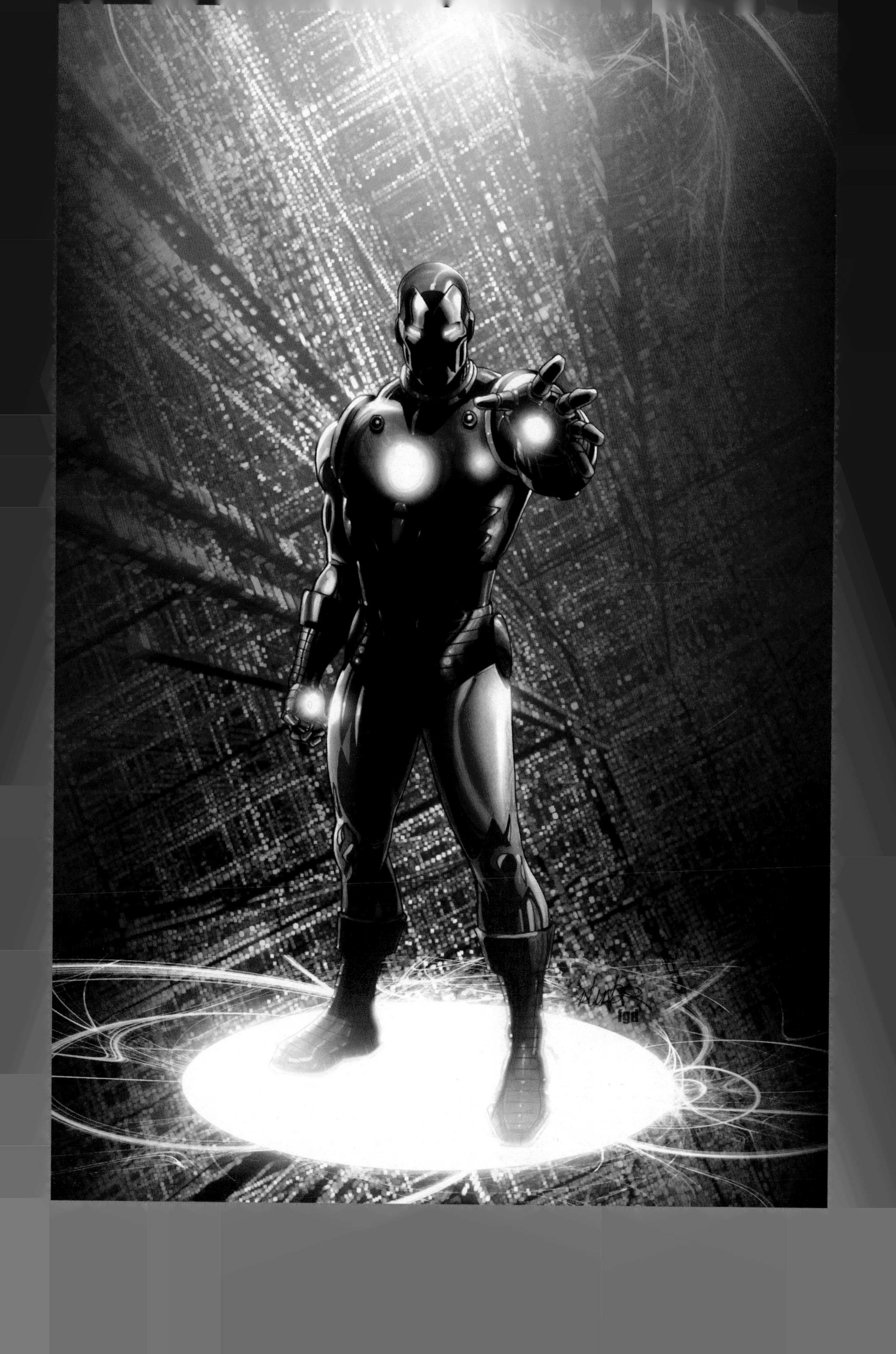

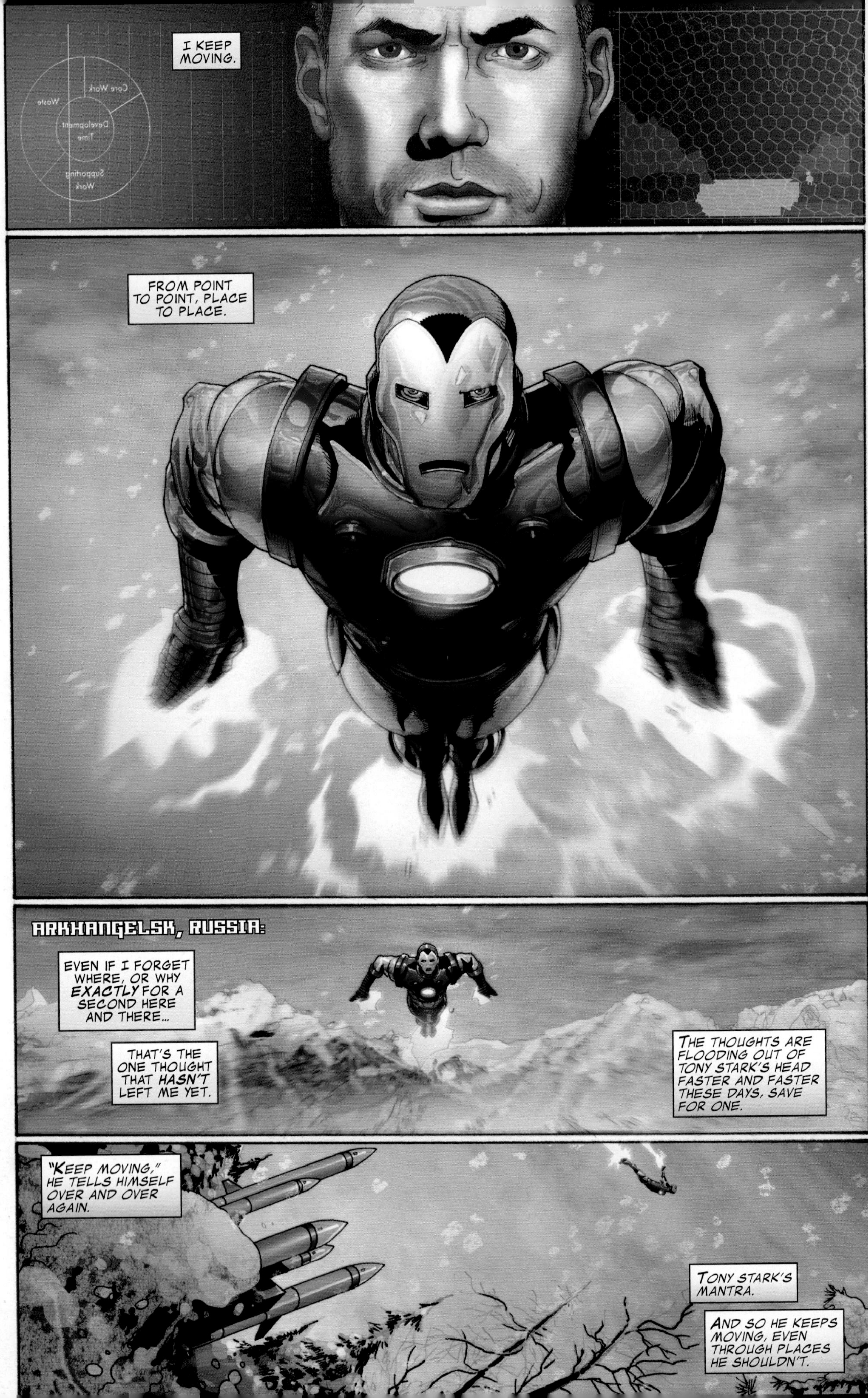
I KEEP MOVING.
FROM POINT TO POINT, PLACE TO PLACE.
ARKHANGELSK, RUSSIA:
EVEN IF I FORGET WHERE, OR WHY EXACTLY FOR A SECOND HERE AND THERE...
THAT'S THE ONE THOUGHT THAT HASN'T LEFT ME YET.
THE THOUGHTS ARE FLOODING OUT OF TONY STARK'S HEAD FASTER AND FASTER THESE DAYS, SAVE FOR ONE.
"KEEP MOVING," HE TELLS HIMSELF OVER AND OVER AGAIN.
TONY STARK'S MANTRA.
AND SO HE KEEPS MOVING, EVEN THROUGH PLACES HE SHOULDN'T.

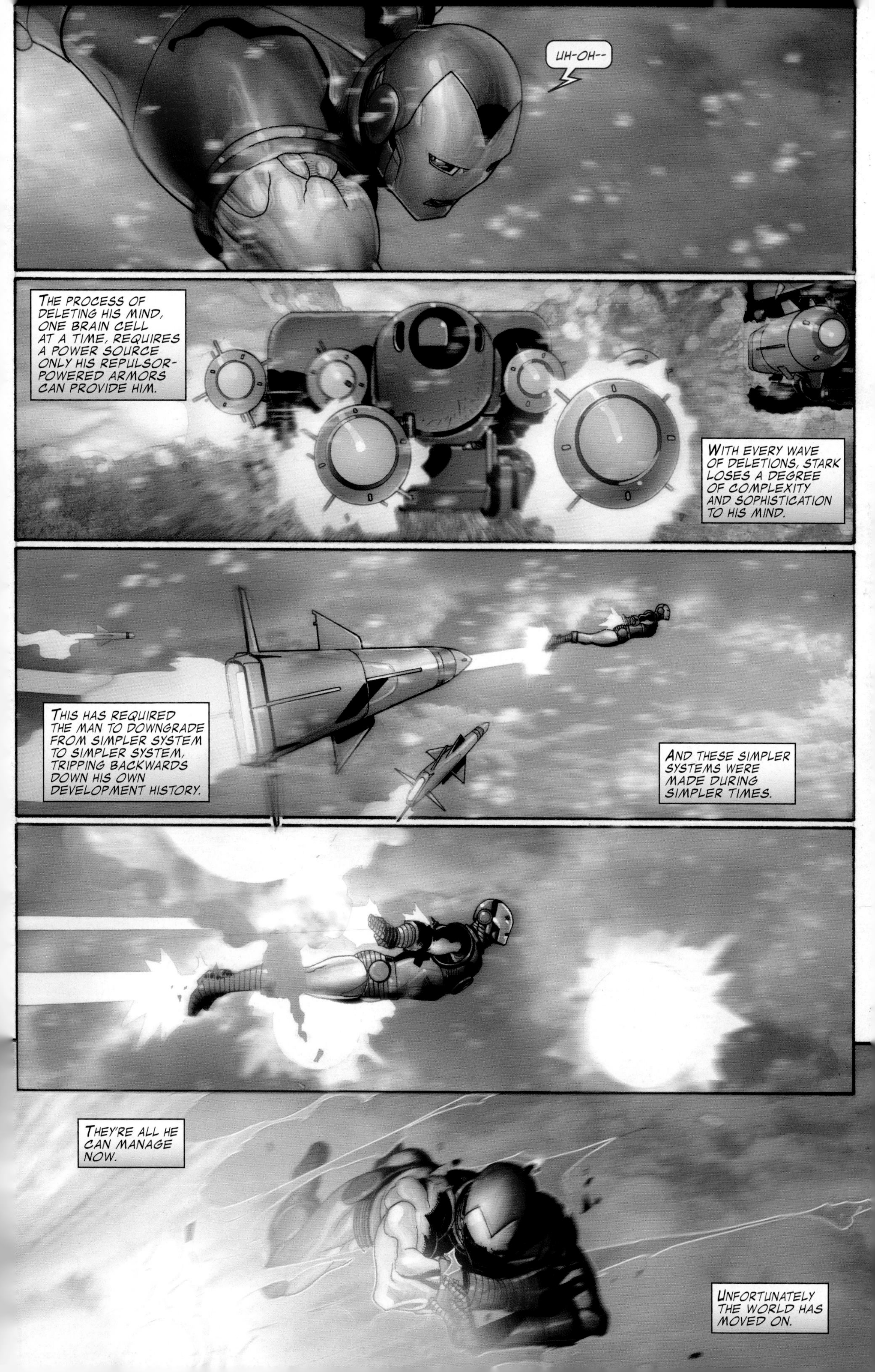
UH-OH--
THE PROCESS OF DELETING HIS MIND, ONE BRAIN CELL AT A TIME, REQUIRES A POWER SOURCE ONLY HIS REPULSOR-POWERED ARMORS CAN PROVIDE HIM.
WITH EVERY WAVE OF DELETIONS, STARK LOSES A DEGREE OF COMPLEXITY AND SOPHISTICATION TO HIS MIND.
THIS HAS REQUIRED THE MAN TO DOWNGRADE FROM SIMPLER SYSTEM TO SIMPLER SYSTEM, TRIPPING BACKWARDS DOWN HIS OWN DEVELOPMENT HISTORY.
AND THESE SIMPLER SYSTEMS WERE MADE DURING SIMPLER TIMES.
THEY'RE ALL HE CAN MANAGE NOW.
UNFORTUNATELY THE WORLD HAS MOVED ON.

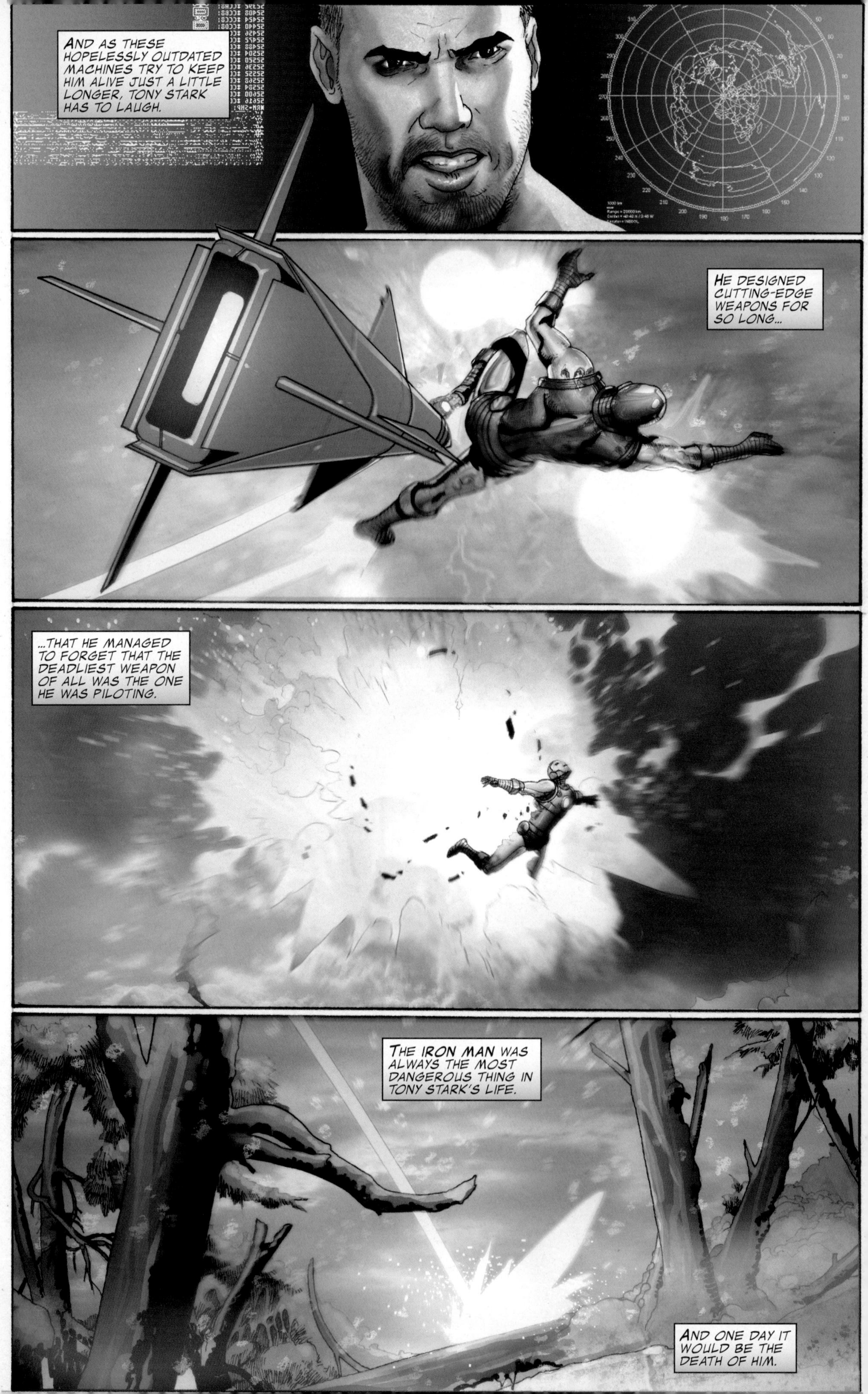
AND AS THESE HOPELESSLY OUTDATED MACHINES TRY TO KEEP HIM ALIVE JUST A LITTLE LONGER, TONY STARK HAS TO LAUGH.
HE DESIGNED CUTTING-EDGE WEAPONS FOR SO LONG...
...THAT HE MANAGED TO FORGET THAT THE DEADLIEST WEAPON OF ALL WAS THE ONE HE WAS PILOTING.
THE IRON MAN WAS ALWAYS THE MOST DANGEROUS THING IN TONY STARK'S LIFE.
AND ONE DAY IT WOULD BE THE DEATH OF HIM.

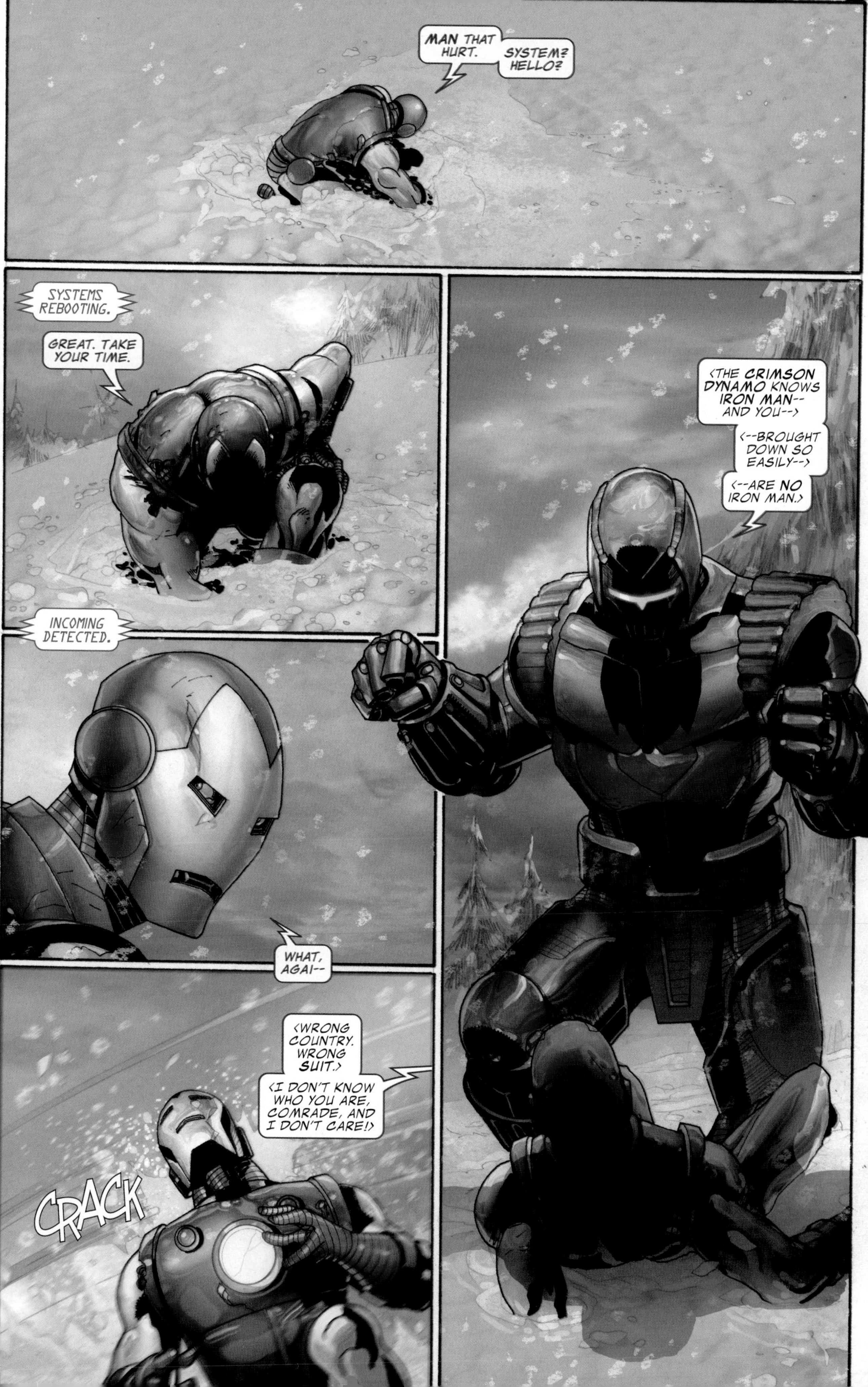
MAN THAT HURT.
SYSTEM? HELLO?
SYSTEMS REBOOTING.
GREAT. TAKE YOUR TIME.
<THE CRIMSON DYNAMO KNOWS IRON MAN-- AND YOU-->
<--BROUGHT DOWN SO EASILY-->
<--ARE NO IRON MAN.>
INCOMING DETECTED.
WHAT, AGAI--
<WRONG COUNTRY. WRONG SUIT.>
<I DON'T KNOW WHO YOU ARE, COMRADE, AND I DON'T CARE!>
CRACK

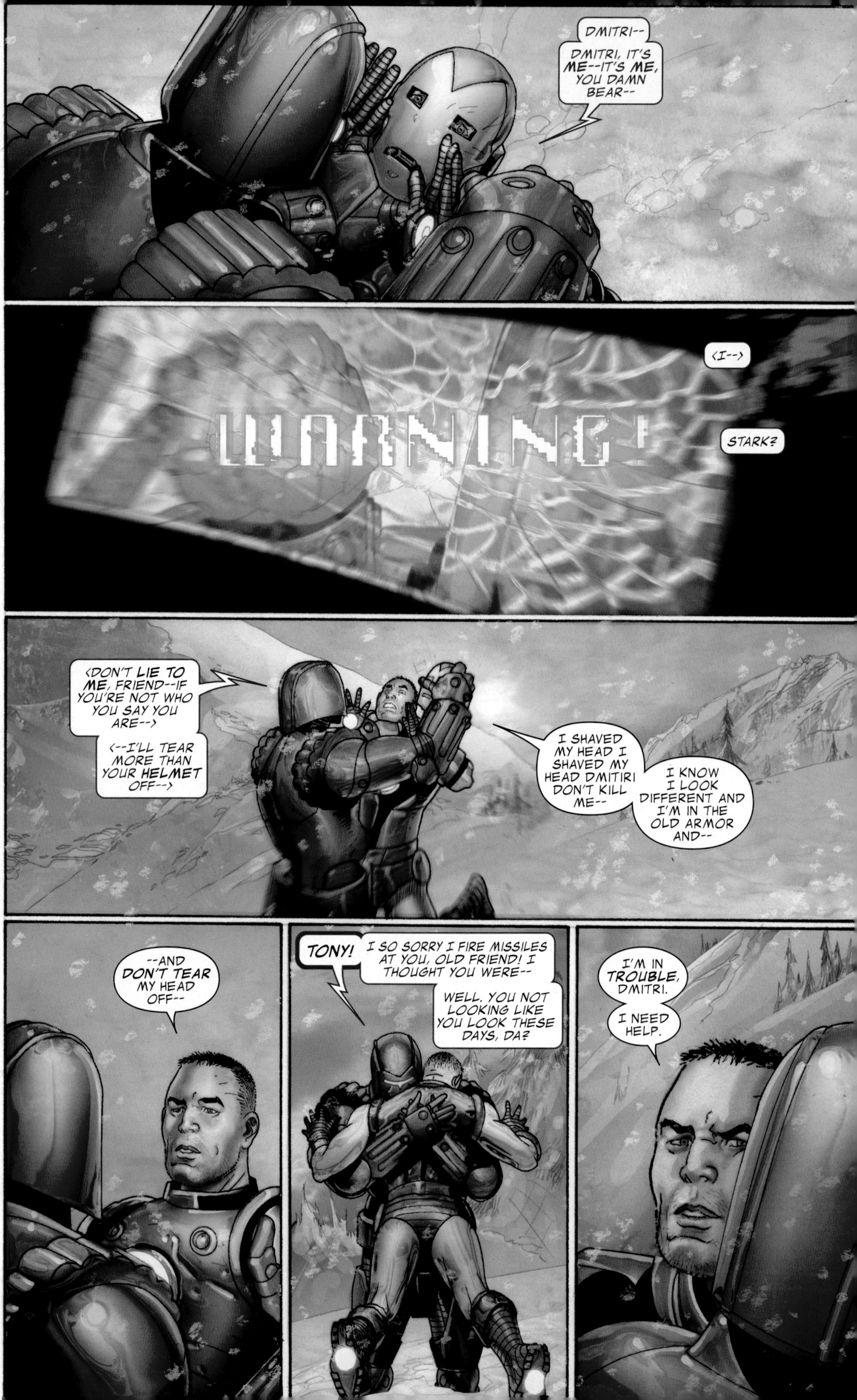
DMITRI--
DMITRI, IT'S ME--IT'S ME, YOU DAMN BEAR--
WARNING!
‹I--›
STARK?
‹DON'T LIE TO ME, FRIEND--IF YOU'RE NOT WHO YOU SAY YOU ARE--›
‹--I'LL TEAR MORE THAN YOUR HELMET OFF--›
I SHAVED MY HEAD I SHAVED MY HEAD DMITIRI DON'T KILL ME--
I KNOW I LOOK DIFFERENT AND I'M IN THE OLD ARMOR AND--
--AND DON'T TEAR MY HEAD OFF--
TONY!
I SO SORRY I FIRE MISSILES AT YOU, OLD FRIEND! I THOUGHT YOU WERE--
WELL. YOU NOT LOOKING LIKE YOU LOOK THESE DAYS, DA?
I'M IN TROUBLE, DMITRI.
I NEED HELP.

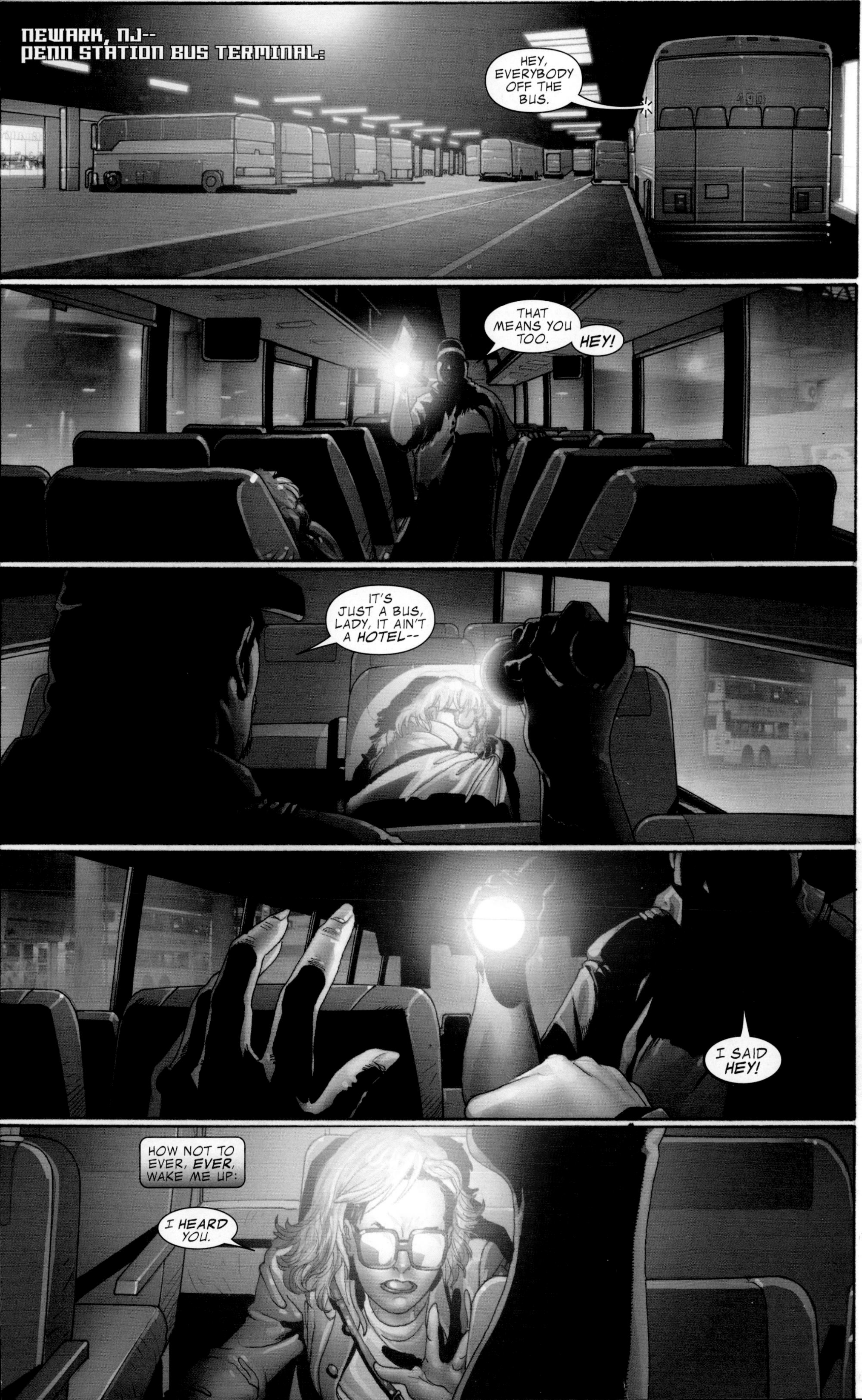
NEWARK, NJ--
PENN STATION BUS TERMINAL:
HEY, EVERYBODY OFF THE BUS.
490
THAT MEANS YOU TOO.
HEY!
IT'S JUST A BUS, LADY, IT AIN'T A HOTEL--
I SAID HEY!
HOW NOT TO EVER, EVER, WAKE ME UP:
I HEARD YOU.

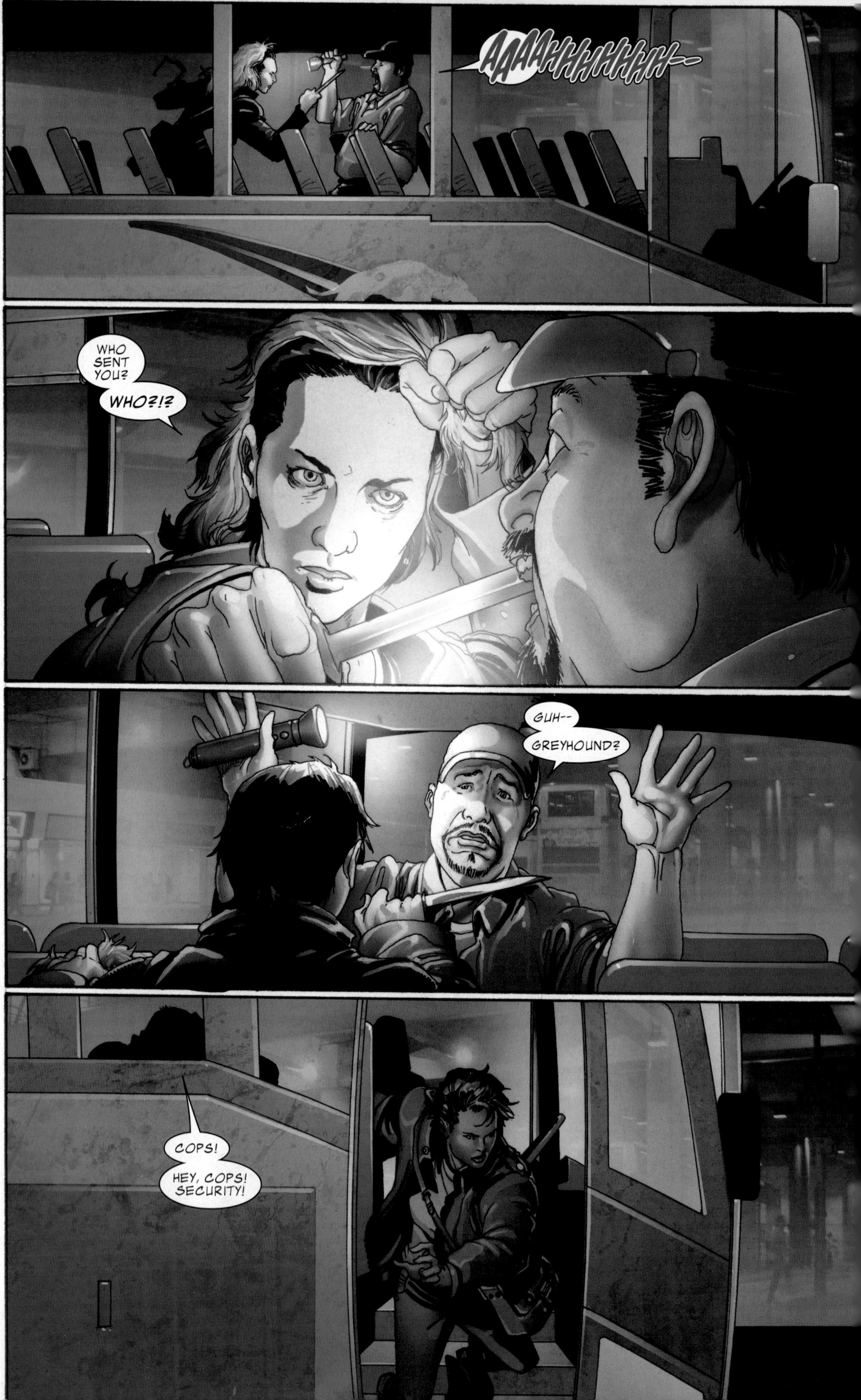
AAAAHHHHHHHH--
WHO SENT YOU?
WHO?!?
GUH--
GREYHOUND?
COPS!
HEY, COPS! SECURITY!

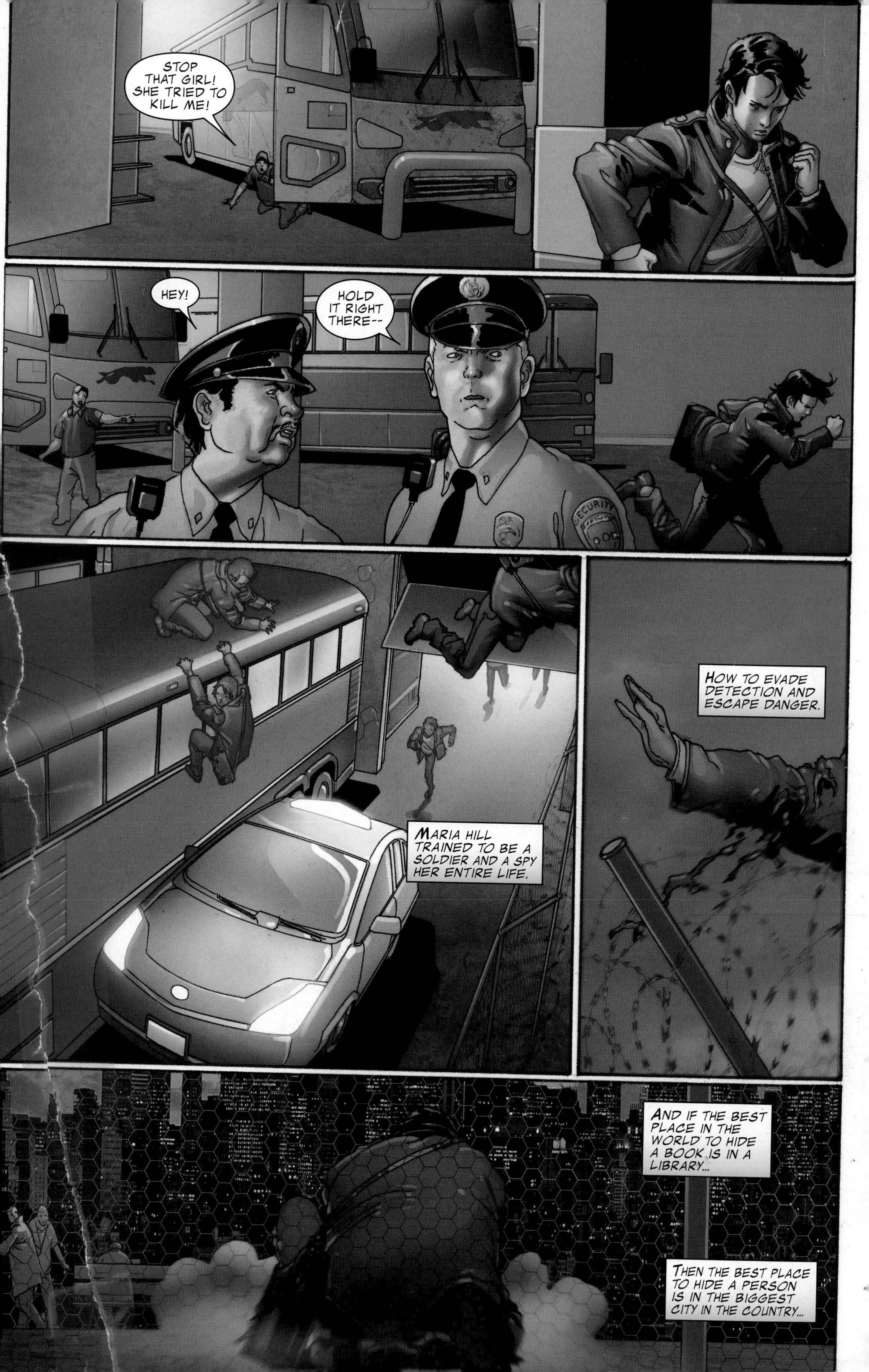
STOP THAT GIRL! SHE TRIED TO KILL ME!
HEY!
HOLD IT RIGHT THERE--
MARIA HILL TRAINED TO BE A SOLDIER AND A SPY HER ENTIRE LIFE.
HOW TO EVADE DETECTION AND ESCAPE DANGER.
AND IF THE BEST PLACE IN THE WORLD TO HIDE A BOOK IS IN A LIBRARY...
THEN THE BEST PLACE TO HIDE A PERSON IS IN THE BIGGEST CITY IN THE COUNTRY...

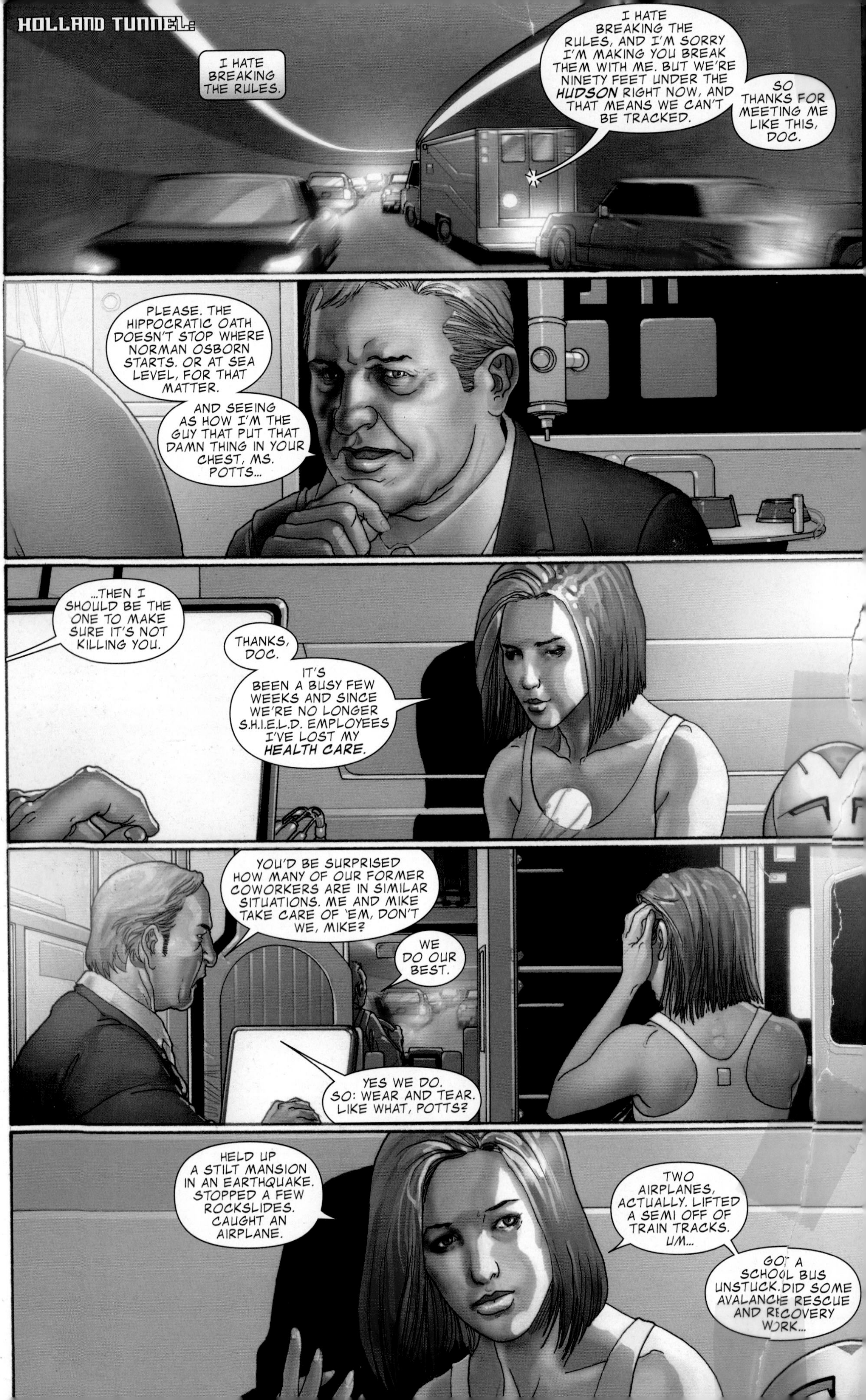
HOLLAND TUNNEL:
I HATE BREAKING THE RULES.
I HATE BREAKING THE RULES, AND I'M SORRY I'M MAKING YOU BREAK THEM WITH ME. BUT WE'RE NINETY FEET UNDER THE HUDSON RIGHT NOW, AND THAT MEANS WE CAN'T BE TRACKED.
SO THANKS FOR MEETING ME LIKE THIS, DOC.
PLEASE. THE HIPPOCRATIC OATH DOESN'T STOP WHERE NORMAN OSBORN STARTS. OR AT SEA LEVEL, FOR THAT MATTER.
AND SEEING AS HOW I'M THE GUY THAT PUT THAT DAMN THING IN YOUR CHEST, MS. POTTS...
...THEN I SHOULD BE THE ONE TO MAKE SURE IT'S NOT KILLING YOU.
THANKS, DOC.
IT'S BEEN A BUSY FEW WEEKS AND SINCE WE'RE NO LONGER S.H.I.E.L.D. EMPLOYEES I'VE LOST MY HEALTH CARE.
YOU'D BE SURPRISED HOW MANY OF OUR FORMER COWORKERS ARE IN SIMILAR SITUATIONS. ME AND MIKE TAKE CARE OF 'EM, DON'T WE, MIKE?
WE DO OUR BEST.
YES WE DO. SO: WEAR AND TEAR. LIKE WHAT, POTTS?
HELD UP A STILT MANSION IN AN EARTHQUAKE. STOPPED A FEW ROCKSLIDES. CAUGHT AN AIRPLANE.
TWO AIRPLANES, ACTUALLY. LIFTED A SEMI OFF OF TRAIN TRACKS. UM...
GOT A SCHOOL BUS UNSTUCK. DID SOME AVALANCHE RESCUE AND RECOVERY WORK...

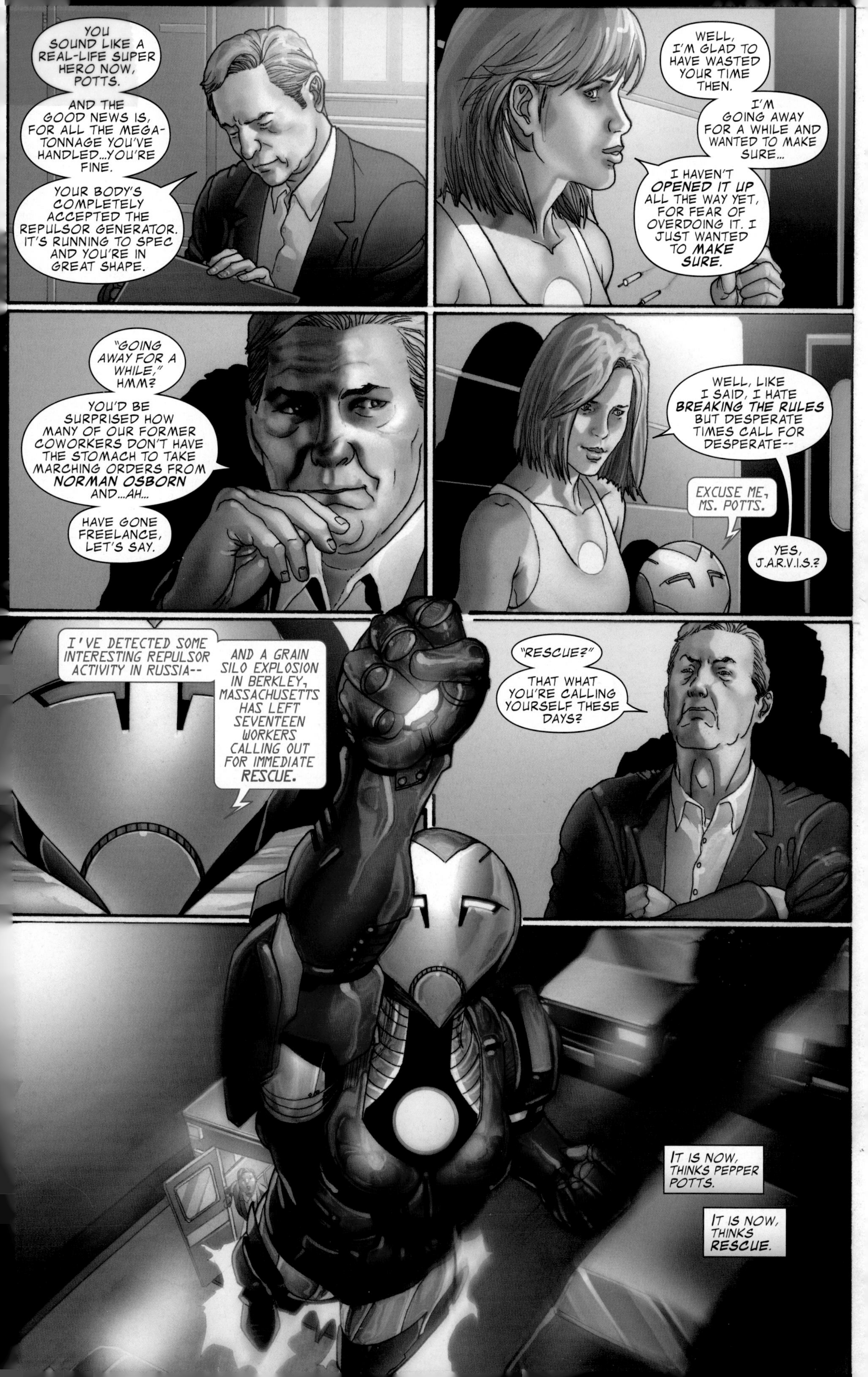
YOU SOUND LIKE A REAL-LIFE SUPER HERO NOW, POTTS.
AND THE GOOD NEWS IS, FOR ALL THE MEGA-TONNAGE YOU'VE HANDLED...YOU'RE FINE.
YOUR BODY'S COMPLETELY ACCEPTED THE REPULSOR GENERATOR. IT'S RUNNING TO SPEC AND YOU'RE IN GREAT SHAPE.
WELL, I'M GLAD TO HAVE WASTED YOUR TIME THEN.
I'M GOING AWAY FOR A WHILE AND WANTED TO MAKE SURE...
I HAVEN'T **OPENED IT UP** ALL THE WAY YET, FOR FEAR OF OVERDOING IT. I JUST WANTED TO **MAKE SURE.**
"GOING AWAY FOR A WHILE," HMM?
YOU'D BE SURPRISED HOW MANY OF OUR FORMER COWORKERS DON'T HAVE THE STOMACH TO TAKE MARCHING ORDERS FROM **NORMAN OSBORN** AND...AH...
HAVE GONE FREELANCE, LET'S SAY.
WELL, LIKE I SAID, I HATE **BREAKING THE RULES** BUT DESPERATE TIMES CALL FOR DESPERATE--
EXCUSE ME, MS. POTTS.
YES, J.A.R.V.I.S.?
I'VE DETECTED SOME INTERESTING REPULSOR ACTIVITY IN RUSSIA--
AND A GRAIN SILO EXPLOSION IN BERKLEY, MASSACHUSETTS HAS LEFT SEVENTEEN WORKERS CALLING OUT FOR IMMEDIATE **RESCUE.**
"RESCUE?"
THAT WHAT YOU'RE CALLING YOURSELF THESE DAYS?
IT IS NOW, THINKS PEPPER POTTS.
IT IS NOW, THINKS **RESCUE.**

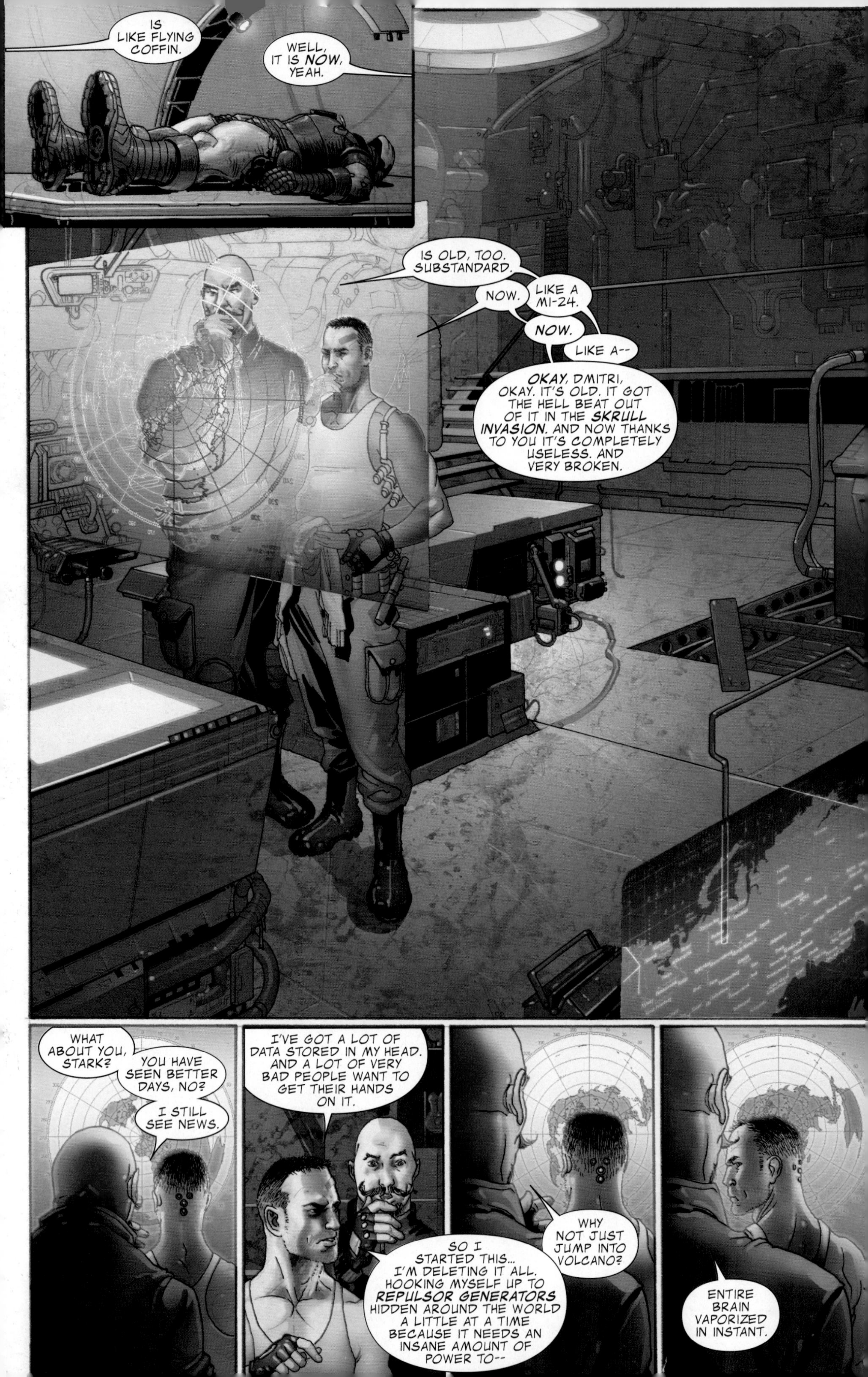
IS LIKE FLYING COFFIN.
WELL, IT IS NOW, YEAH.
IS OLD, TOO. SUBSTANDARD.
LIKE A MI-24.
NOW.
NOW.
LIKE A--
OKAY, DMITRI, OKAY. IT'S OLD. IT GOT THE HELL BEAT OUT OF IT IN THE SKRULL INVASION. AND NOW THANKS TO YOU IT'S COMPLETELY USELESS. AND VERY BROKEN.
WHAT ABOUT YOU, STARK?
YOU HAVE SEEN BETTER DAYS, NO?
I STILL SEE NEWS.
I'VE GOT A LOT OF DATA STORED IN MY HEAD. AND A LOT OF VERY BAD PEOPLE WANT TO GET THEIR HANDS ON IT.
SO I STARTED THIS... I'M DELETING IT ALL. HOOKING MYSELF UP TO REPULSOR GENERATORS HIDDEN AROUND THE WORLD A LITTLE AT A TIME BECAUSE IT NEEDS AN INSANE AMOUNT OF POWER TO--
WHY NOT JUST JUMP INTO VOLCANO?
ENTIRE BRAIN VAPORIZED IN INSTANT.

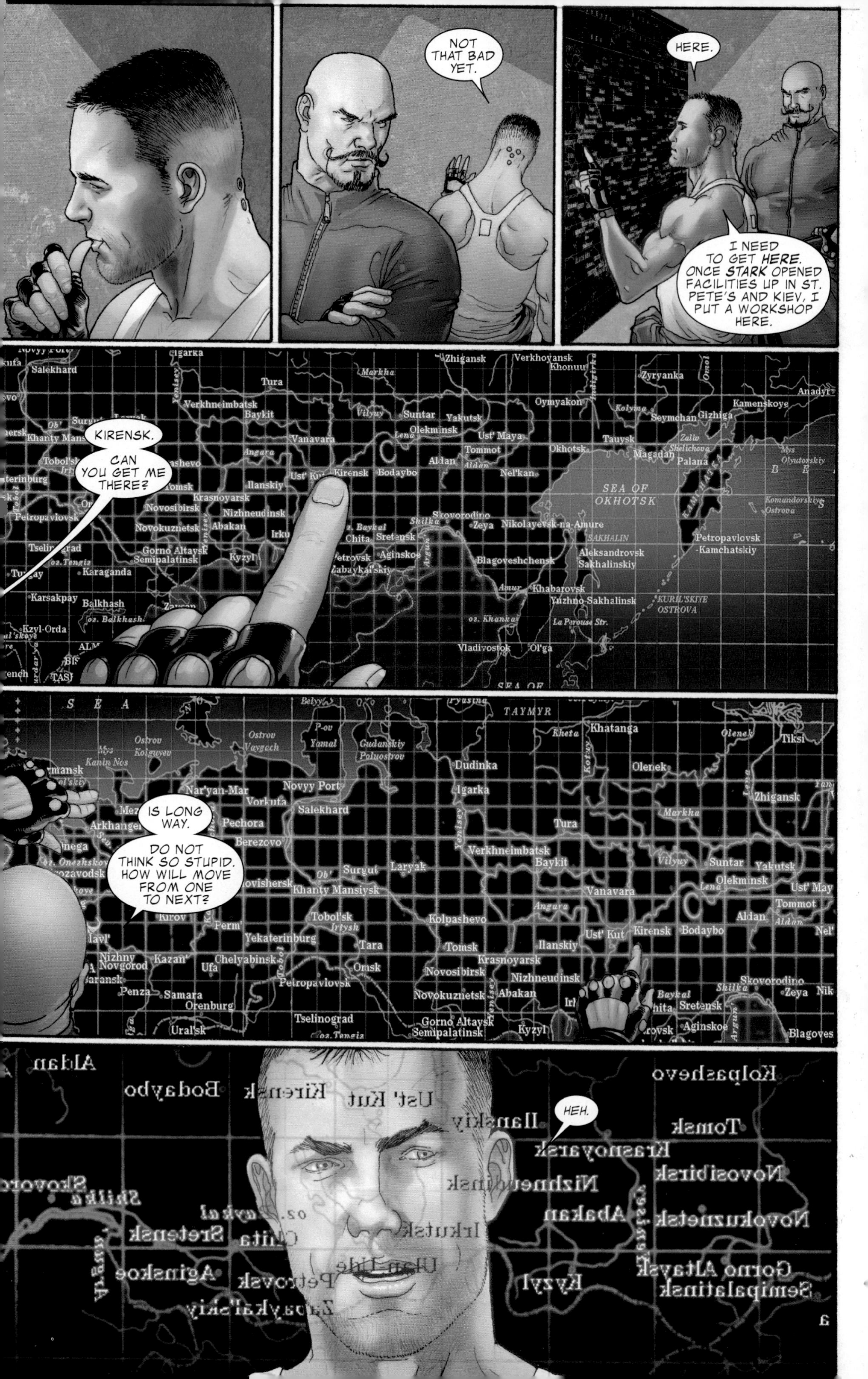
NOT THAT BAD YET.
HERE.
I NEED TO GET HERE. ONCE STARK OPENED FACILITIES UP IN ST. PETE'S AND KIEV, I PUT A WORKSHOP HERE.
KIRENSK.
CAN YOU GET ME THERE?
IS LONG WAY.
DO NOT THINK SO STUPID. HOW WILL MOVE FROM ONE TO NEXT?
HEH.

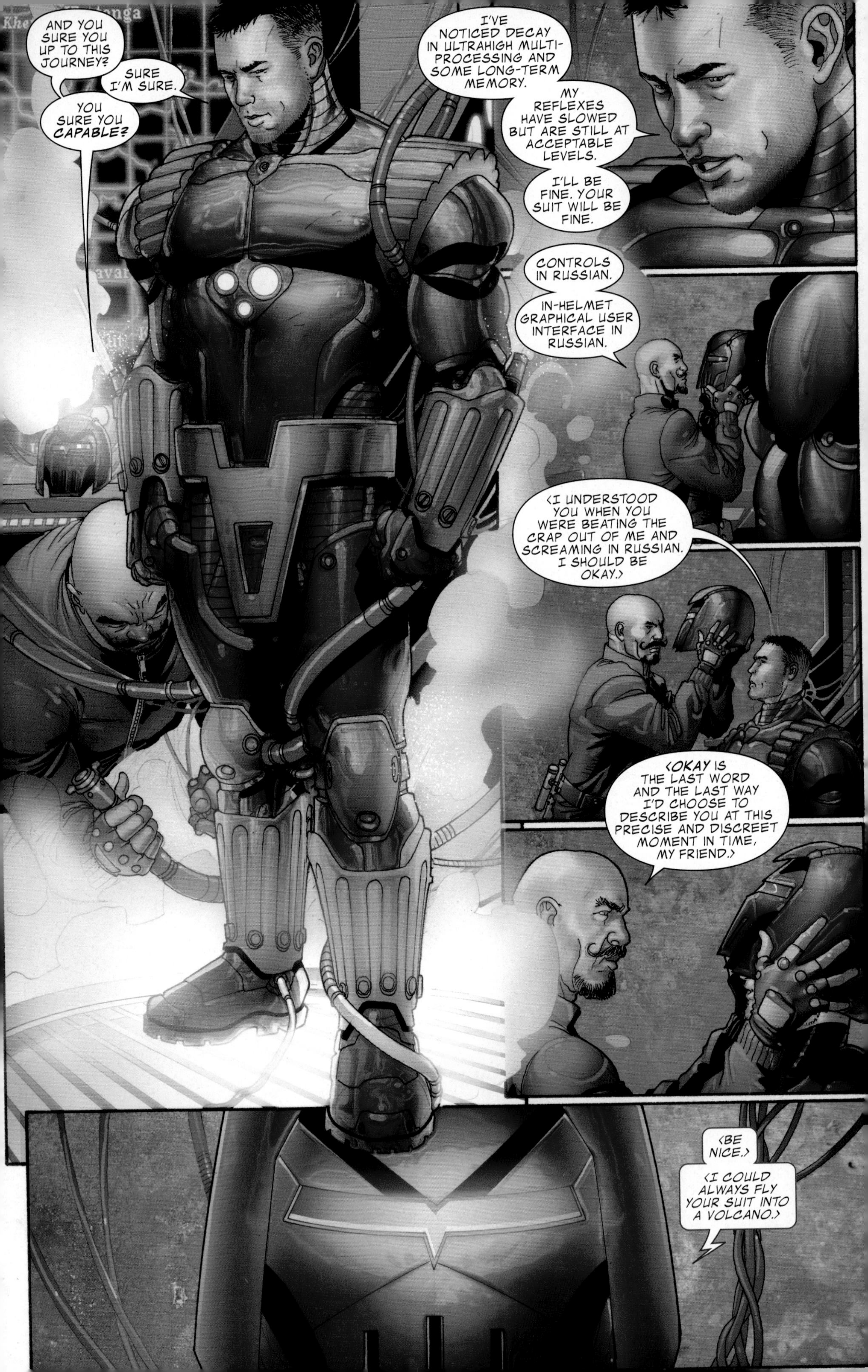
AND YOU SURE YOU UP TO THIS JOURNEY?
SURE I'M SURE.
YOU SURE YOU CAPABLE?
I'VE NOTICED DECAY IN ULTRAHIGH MULTI-PROCESSING AND SOME LONG-TERM MEMORY.
MY REFLEXES HAVE SLOWED BUT ARE STILL AT ACCEPTABLE LEVELS.
I'LL BE FINE. YOUR SUIT WILL BE FINE.
CONTROLS IN RUSSIAN.
IN-HELMET GRAPHICAL USER INTERFACE IN RUSSIAN.
<I UNDERSTOOD YOU WHEN YOU WERE BEATING THE CRAP OUT OF ME AND SCREAMING IN RUSSIAN. I SHOULD BE OKAY.>
<OKAY IS THE LAST WORD AND THE LAST WAY I'D CHOOSE TO DESCRIBE YOU AT THIS PRECISE AND DISCREET MOMENT IN TIME, MY FRIEND.>
<BE NICE.>
<I COULD ALWAYS FLY YOUR SUIT INTO A VOLCANO.>

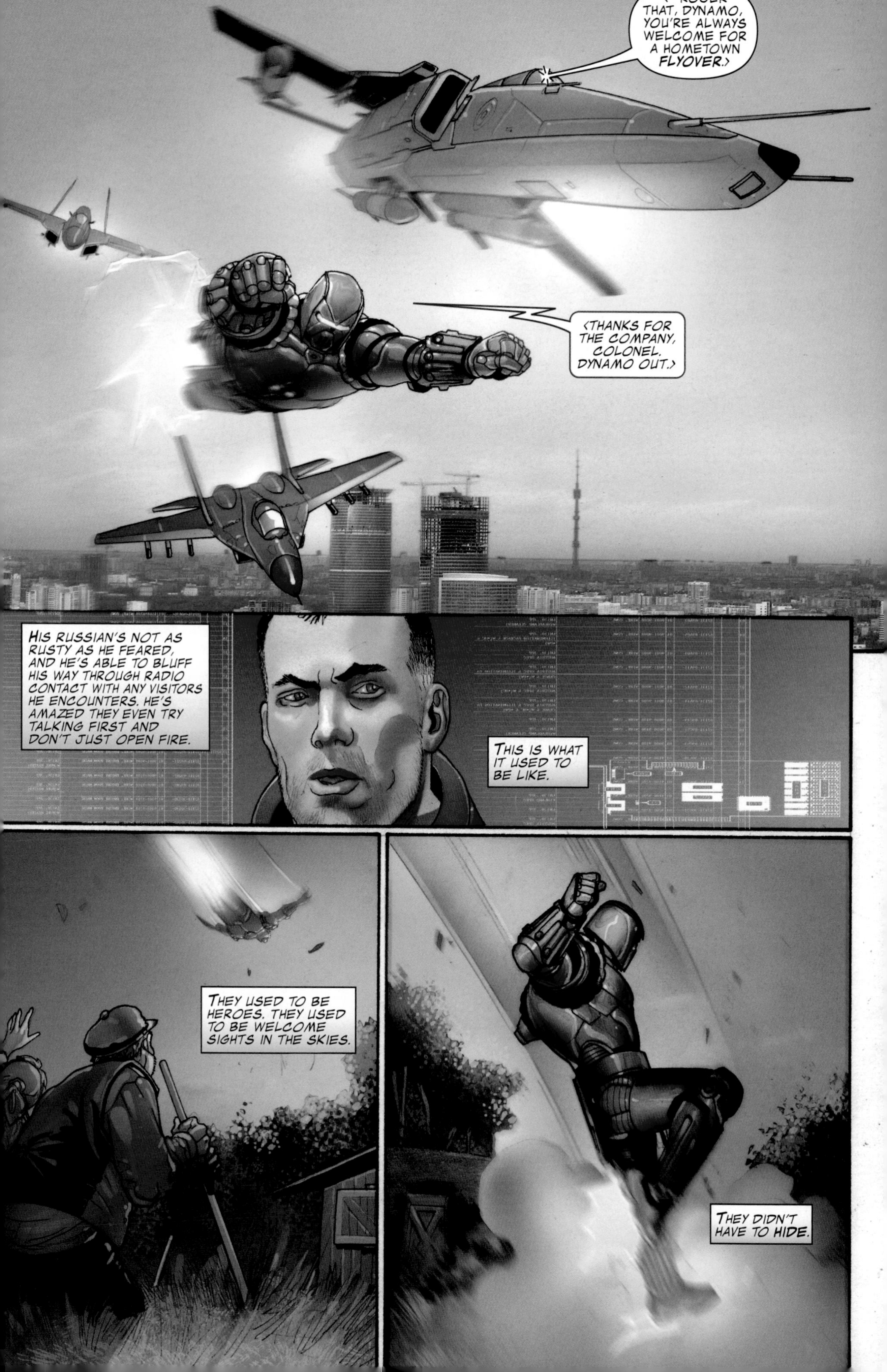
<--ROGER THAT, DYNAMO, YOU'RE ALWAYS WELCOME FOR A HOMETOWN FLYOVER.>
<THANKS FOR THE COMPANY, COLONEL. DYNAMO OUT.>
HIS RUSSIAN'S NOT AS RUSTY AS HE FEARED, AND HE'S ABLE TO BLUFF HIS WAY THROUGH RADIO CONTACT WITH ANY VISITORS HE ENCOUNTERS. HE'S AMAZED THEY EVEN TRY TALKING FIRST AND DON'T JUST OPEN FIRE.
THIS IS WHAT IT USED TO BE LIKE.
THEY USED TO BE HEROES. THEY USED TO BE WELCOME SIGHTS IN THE SKIES.
THEY DIDN'T HAVE TO HIDE.

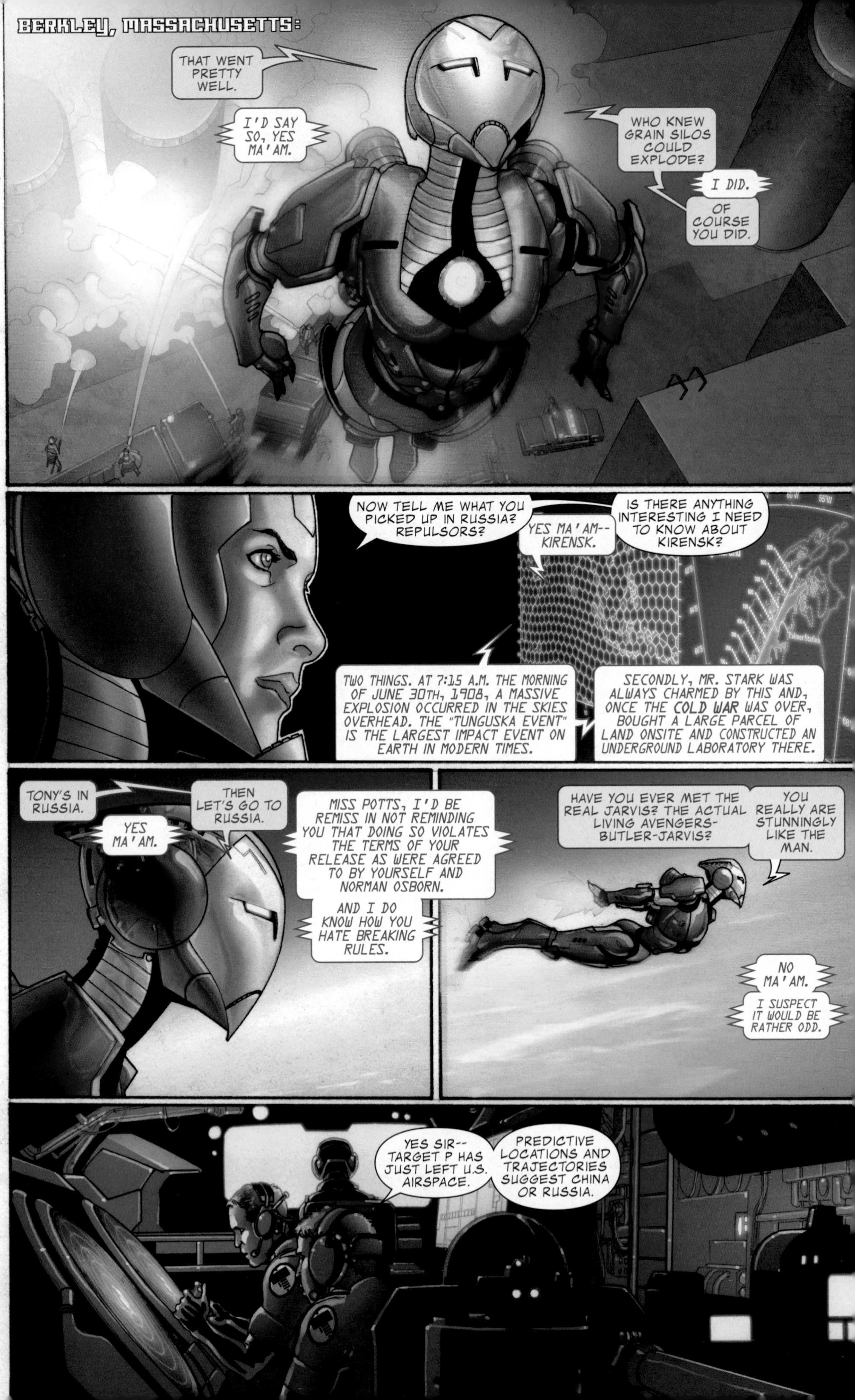
BERKLEY, MASSACHUSETTS:
THAT WENT PRETTY WELL.
I'D SAY SO, YES MA'AM.
WHO KNEW GRAIN SILOS COULD EXPLODE?
I DID.
OF COURSE YOU DID.
NOW TELL ME WHAT YOU PICKED UP IN RUSSIA? REPULSORS?
YES MA'AM-- KIRENSK.
IS THERE ANYTHING INTERESTING I NEED TO KNOW ABOUT KIRENSK?
TWO THINGS. AT 7:15 A.M. THE MORNING OF JUNE 30TH, 1908, A MASSIVE EXPLOSION OCCURRED IN THE SKIES OVERHEAD. THE "TUNGUSKA EVENT" IS THE LARGEST IMPACT EVENT ON EARTH IN MODERN TIMES.
SECONDLY, MR. STARK WAS ALWAYS CHARMED BY THIS AND, ONCE THE COLD WAR WAS OVER, BOUGHT A LARGE PARCEL OF LAND ONSITE AND CONSTRUCTED AN UNDERGROUND LABORATORY THERE.
TONY'S IN RUSSIA.
YES MA'AM.
THEN LET'S GO TO RUSSIA.
MISS POTTS, I'D BE REMISS IN NOT REMINDING YOU THAT DOING SO VIOLATES THE TERMS OF YOUR RELEASE AS WERE AGREED TO BY YOURSELF AND NORMAN OSBORN.
AND I DO KNOW HOW YOU HATE BREAKING RULES.
HAVE YOU EVER MET THE REAL JARVIS? THE ACTUAL LIVING AVENGERS-BUTLER-JARVIS?
YOU REALLY ARE STUNNINGLY LIKE THE MAN.
NO MA'AM.
I SUSPECT IT WOULD BE RATHER ODD.
YES SIR-- TARGET P HAS JUST LEFT U.S. AIRSPACE.
PREDICTIVE LOCATIONS AND TRAJECTORIES SUGGEST CHINA OR RUSSIA.

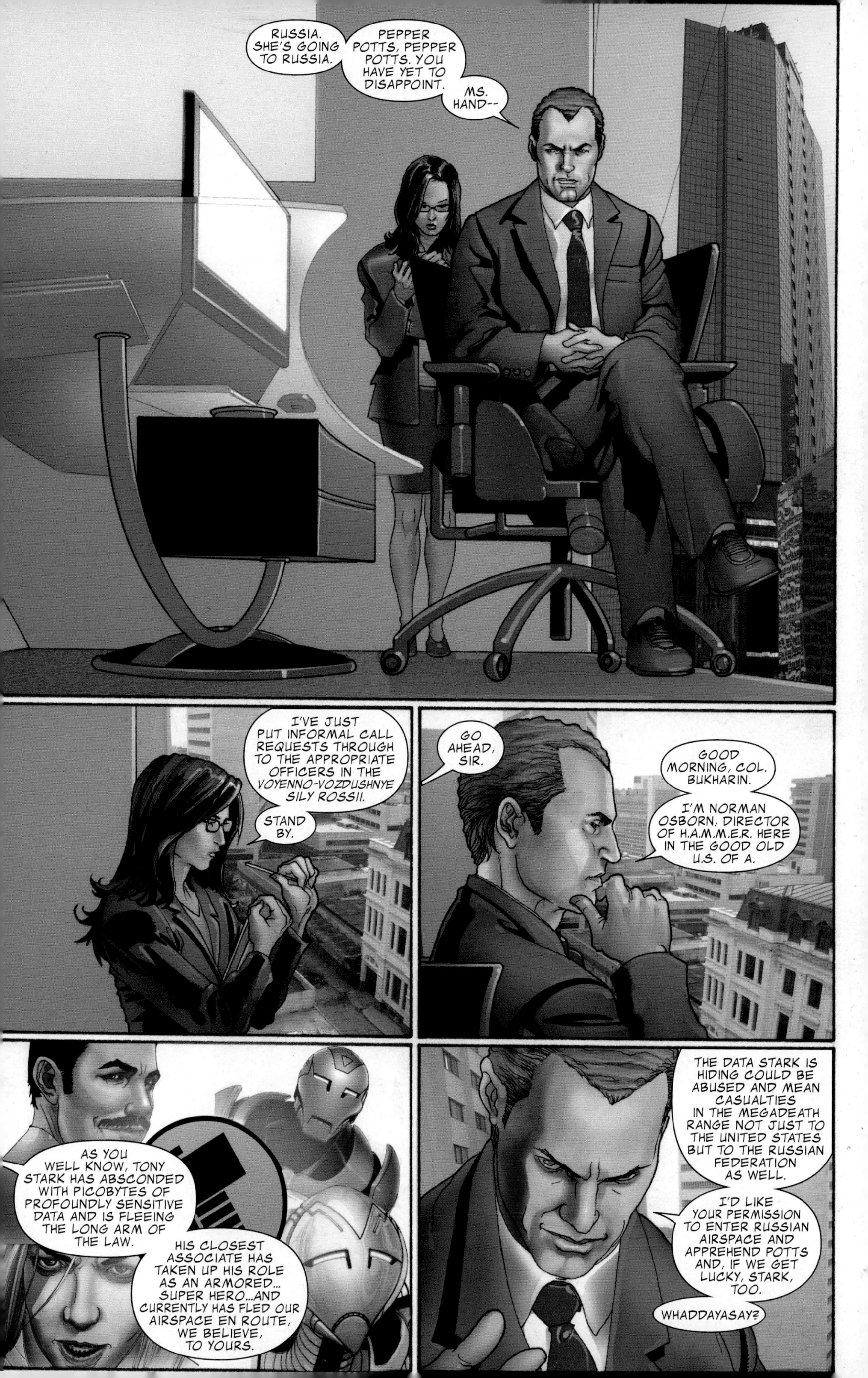
RUSSIA. SHE'S GOING TO RUSSIA.
PEPPER POTTS, PEPPER POTTS. YOU HAVE YET TO DISAPPOINT.
MS. HAND--
I'VE JUST PUT INFORMAL CALL REQUESTS THROUGH TO THE APPROPRIATE OFFICERS IN THE VOYENNO-VOZDUSHNYE SILY ROSSII.
STAND BY.
GO AHEAD, SIR.
GOOD MORNING, COL. BUKHARIN.
I'M NORMAN OSBORN, DIRECTOR OF H.A.M.M.E.R. HERE IN THE GOOD OLD U.S. OF A.
AS YOU WELL KNOW, TONY STARK HAS ABSCONDED WITH PICOBYTES OF PROFOUNDLY SENSITIVE DATA AND IS FLEEING THE LONG ARM OF THE LAW.
HIS CLOSEST ASSOCIATE HAS TAKEN UP HIS ROLE AS AN ARMORED... SUPER HERO...AND CURRENTLY HAS FLED OUR AIRSPACE EN ROUTE, WE BELIEVE, TO YOURS.
THE DATA STARK IS HIDING COULD BE ABUSED AND MEAN CASUALTIES IN THE MEGADEATH RANGE NOT JUST TO THE UNITED STATES BUT TO THE RUSSIAN FEDERATION AS WELL.
I'D LIKE YOUR PERMISSION TO ENTER RUSSIAN AIRSPACE AND APPREHEND POTTS AND, IF WE GET LUCKY, STARK, TOO.
WHADDAYASAY?

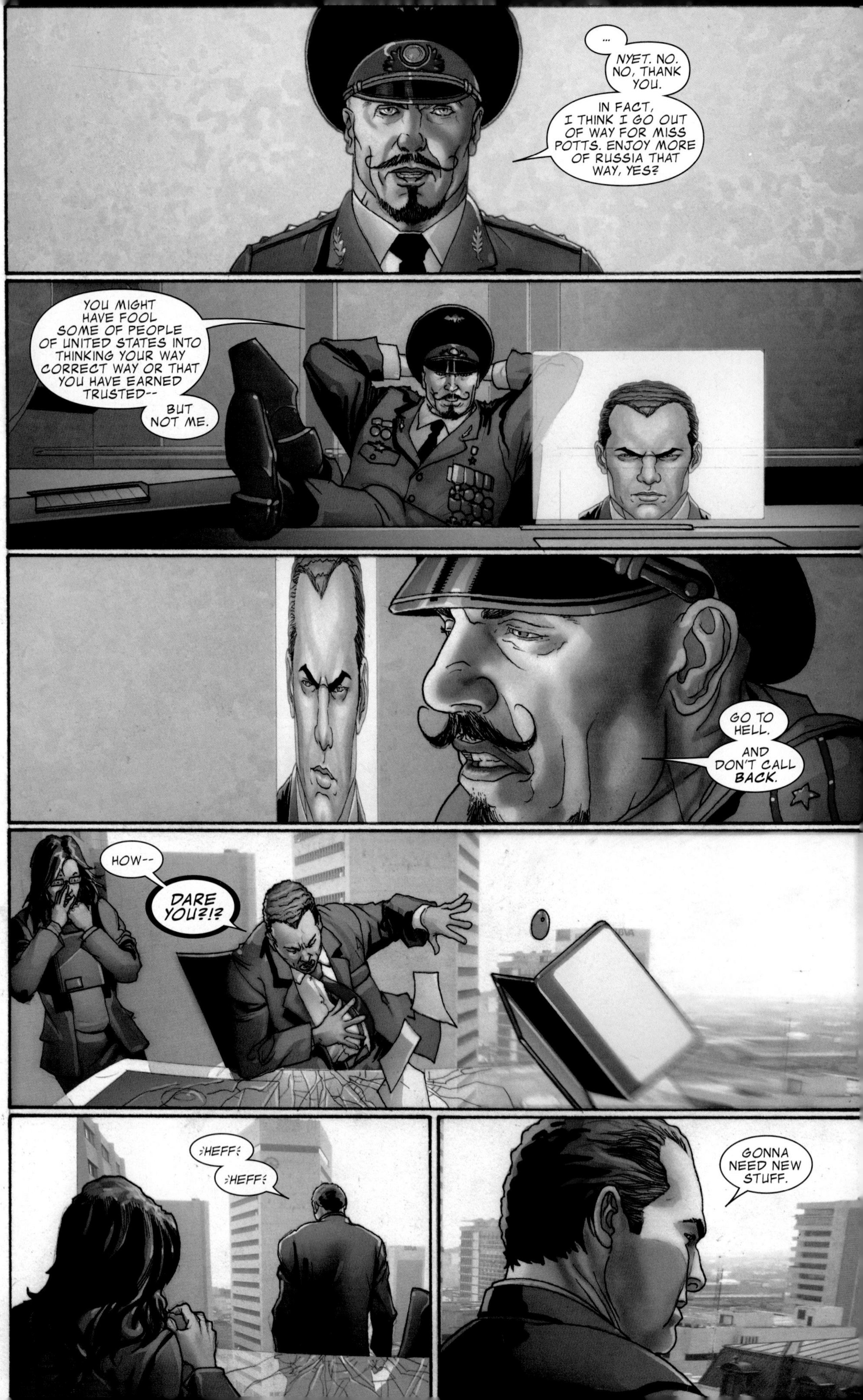
...
NYET. NO. NO, THANK YOU.
IN FACT, I THINK I GO OUT OF WAY FOR MISS POTTS. ENJOY MORE OF RUSSIA THAT WAY, YES?
YOU MIGHT HAVE FOOL SOME OF PEOPLE OF UNITED STATES INTO THINKING YOUR WAY CORRECT WAY OR THAT YOU HAVE EARNED TRUSTED--
BUT NOT ME.
GO TO HELL.
AND DON'T CALL BACK.
HOW--
DARE YOU?!?
HEFF
HEFF
GONNA NEED NEW STUFF.

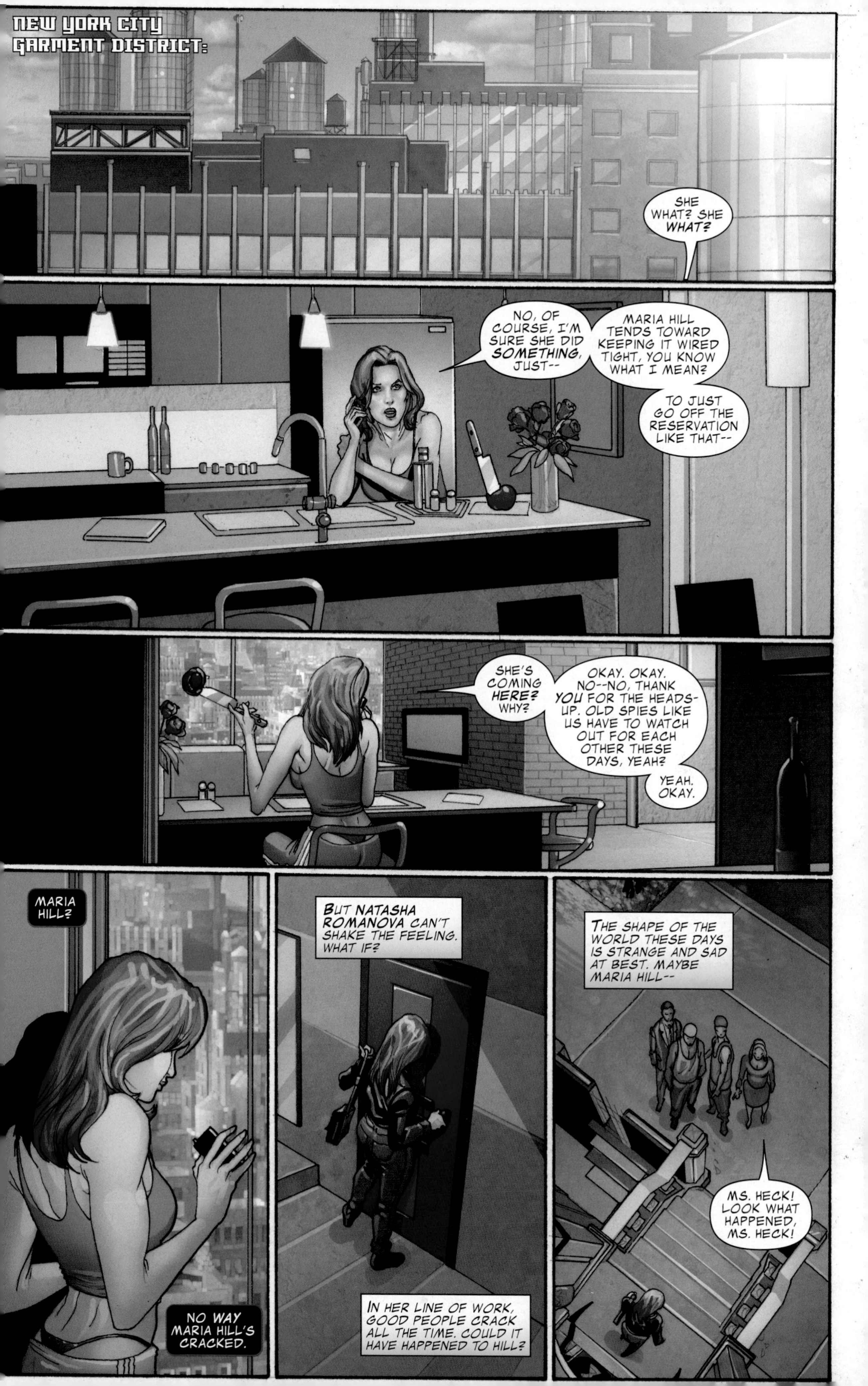
NEW YORK CITY
GARMENT DISTRICT:
SHE WHAT? SHE WHAT?
NO, OF COURSE, I'M SURE SHE DID SOMETHING, JUST--
MARIA HILL TENDS TOWARD KEEPING IT WIRED TIGHT, YOU KNOW WHAT I MEAN?
TO JUST GO OFF THE RESERVATION LIKE THAT--
SHE'S COMING HERE? WHY?
OKAY. OKAY. NO--NO, THANK YOU FOR THE HEADS-UP. OLD SPIES LIKE US HAVE TO WATCH OUT FOR EACH OTHER THESE DAYS, YEAH?
YEAH. OKAY.
MARIA HILL?
NO WAY MARIA HILL'S CRACKED.
BUT NATASHA ROMANOVA CAN'T SHAKE THE FEELING. WHAT IF?
IN HER LINE OF WORK, GOOD PEOPLE CRACK ALL THE TIME. COULD IT HAVE HAPPENED TO HILL?
THE SHAPE OF THE WORLD THESE DAYS IS STRANGE AND SAD AT BEST. MAYBE MARIA HILL--
MS. HECK! LOOK WHAT HAPPENED, MS. HECK!

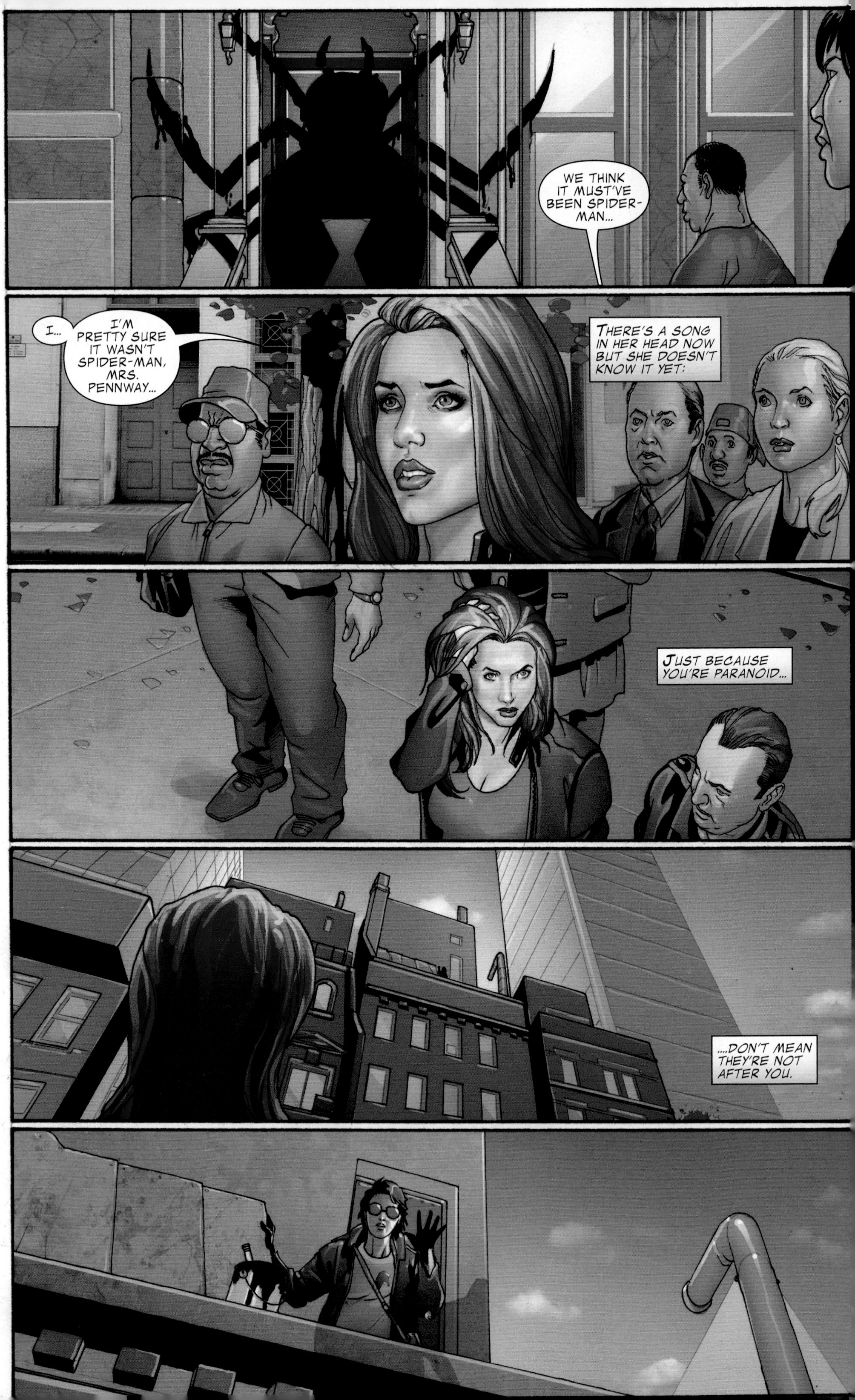

WE THINK IT MUST'VE BEEN SPIDER-MAN...
I...
I'M PRETTY SURE IT WASN'T SPIDER-MAN, MRS. PENNWAY...
THERE'S A SONG IN HER HEAD NOW BUT SHE DOESN'T KNOW IT YET:
JUST BECAUSE YOU'RE PARANOID...
...DON'T MEAN THEY'RE NOT AFTER YOU.

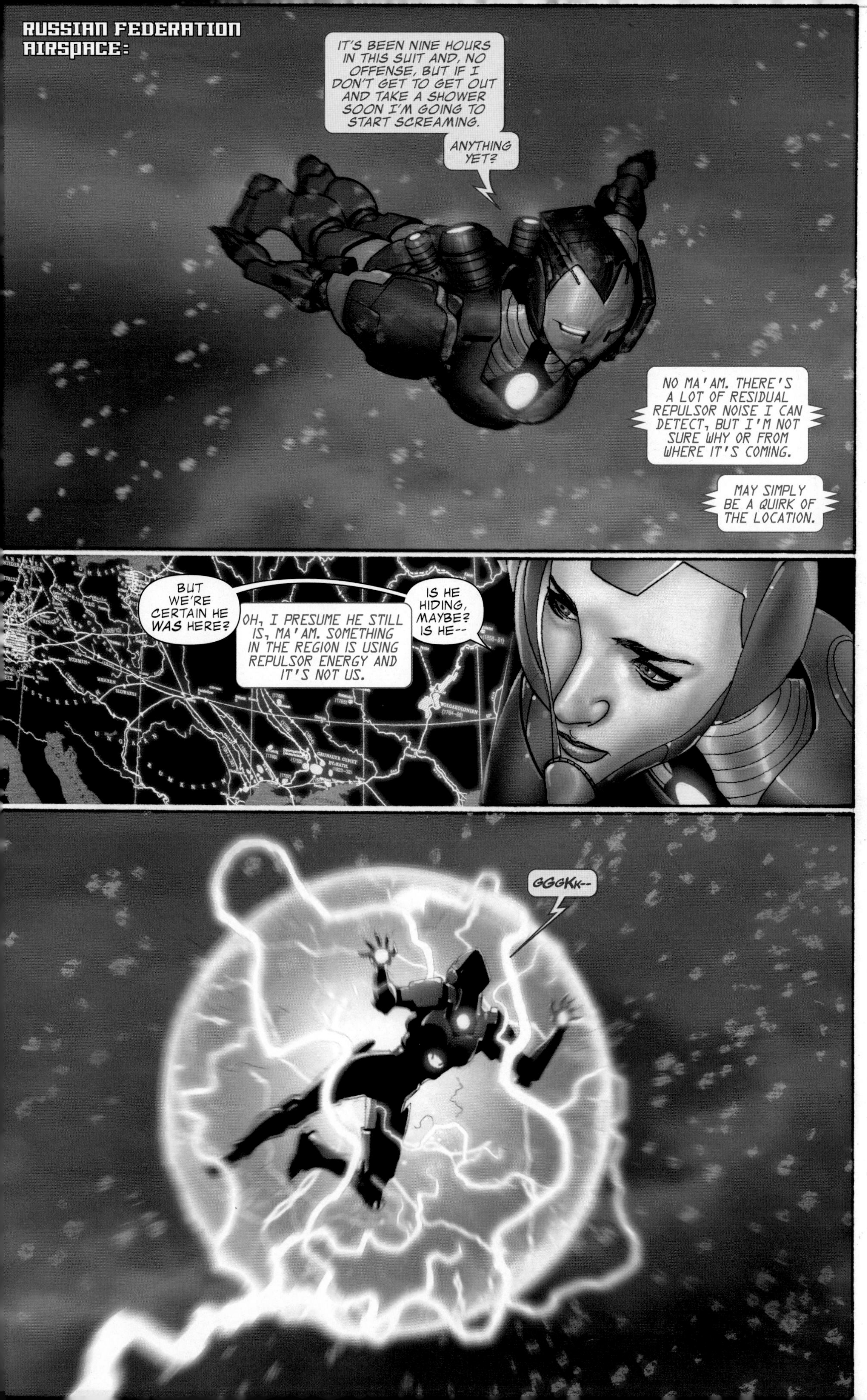
RUSSIAN FEDERATION AIRSPACE:
IT'S BEEN NINE HOURS IN THIS SUIT AND, NO OFFENSE, BUT IF I DON'T GET TO GET OUT AND TAKE A SHOWER SOON I'M GOING TO START SCREAMING.
ANYTHING YET?
NO MA'AM. THERE'S A LOT OF RESIDUAL REPULSOR NOISE I CAN DETECT, BUT I'M NOT SURE WHY OR FROM WHERE IT'S COMING.
MAY SIMPLY BE A QUIRK OF THE LOCATION.
BUT WE'RE CERTAIN HE **WAS** HERE?
OH, I PRESUME HE STILL IS, MA'AM. SOMETHING IN THE REGION IS USING REPULSOR ENERGY AND IT'S NOT US.
IS HE HIDING, MAYBE? IS HE--
GGGKk--

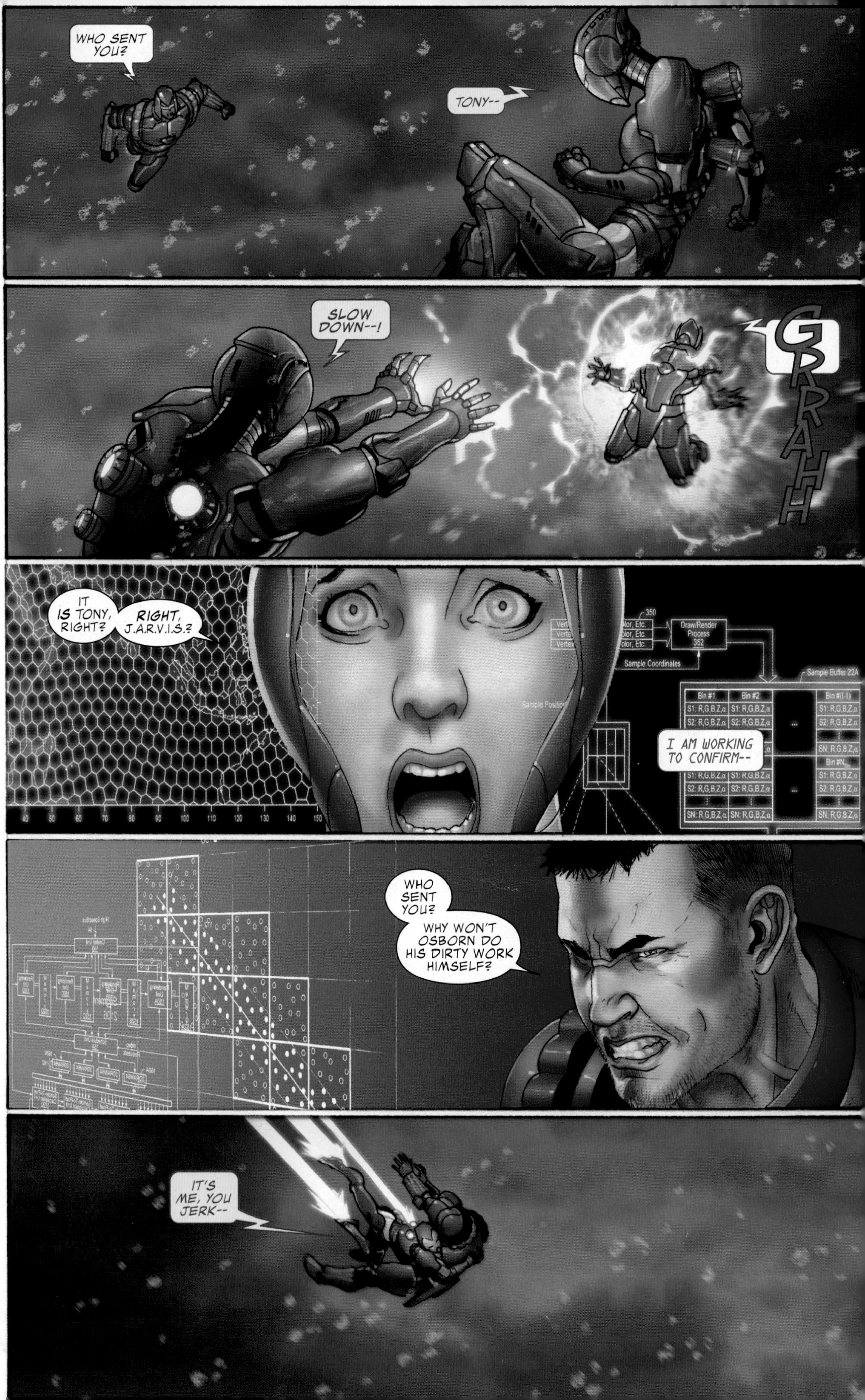
WHO SENT YOU?
TONY--
SLOW DOWN--!
GRRAHH
IT *IS* TONY, RIGHT?
RIGHT, J.A.R.V.I.S.?
I AM WORKING TO CONFIRM--
WHO SENT YOU?
WHY WON'T OSBORN DO HIS DIRTY WORK HIMSELF?
IT'S ME, YOU JERK--

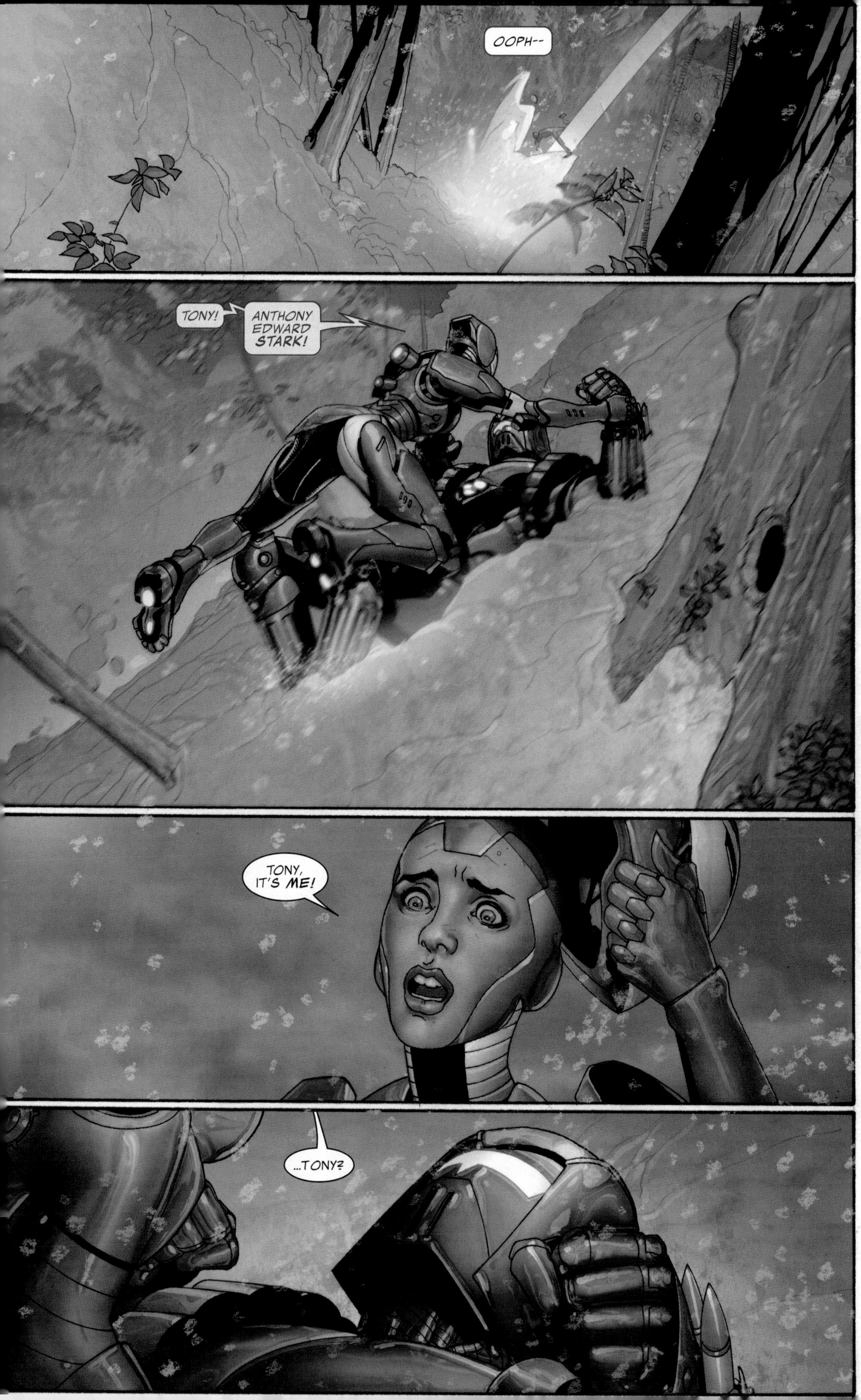
OOPH--
TONY!
ANTHONY EDWARD STARK!
TONY, IT'S ME!
...TONY?

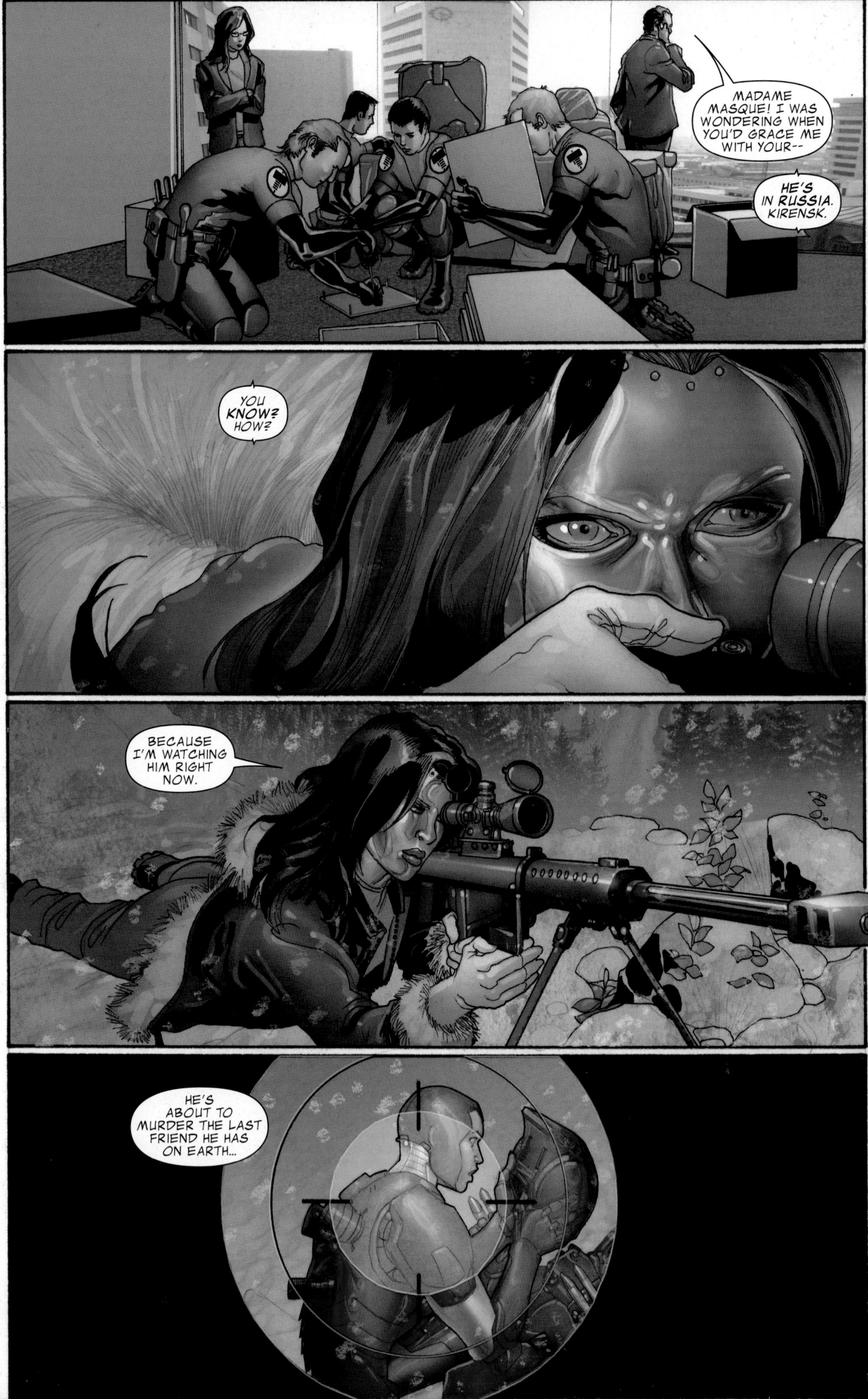
MADAME MASQUE! I WAS WONDERING WHEN YOU'D GRACE ME WITH YOUR--
HE'S IN RUSSIA. KIRENSK.
YOU KNOW? HOW?
BECAUSE I'M WATCHING HIM RIGHT NOW.
HE'S ABOUT TO MURDER THE LAST FRIEND HE HAS ON EARTH...

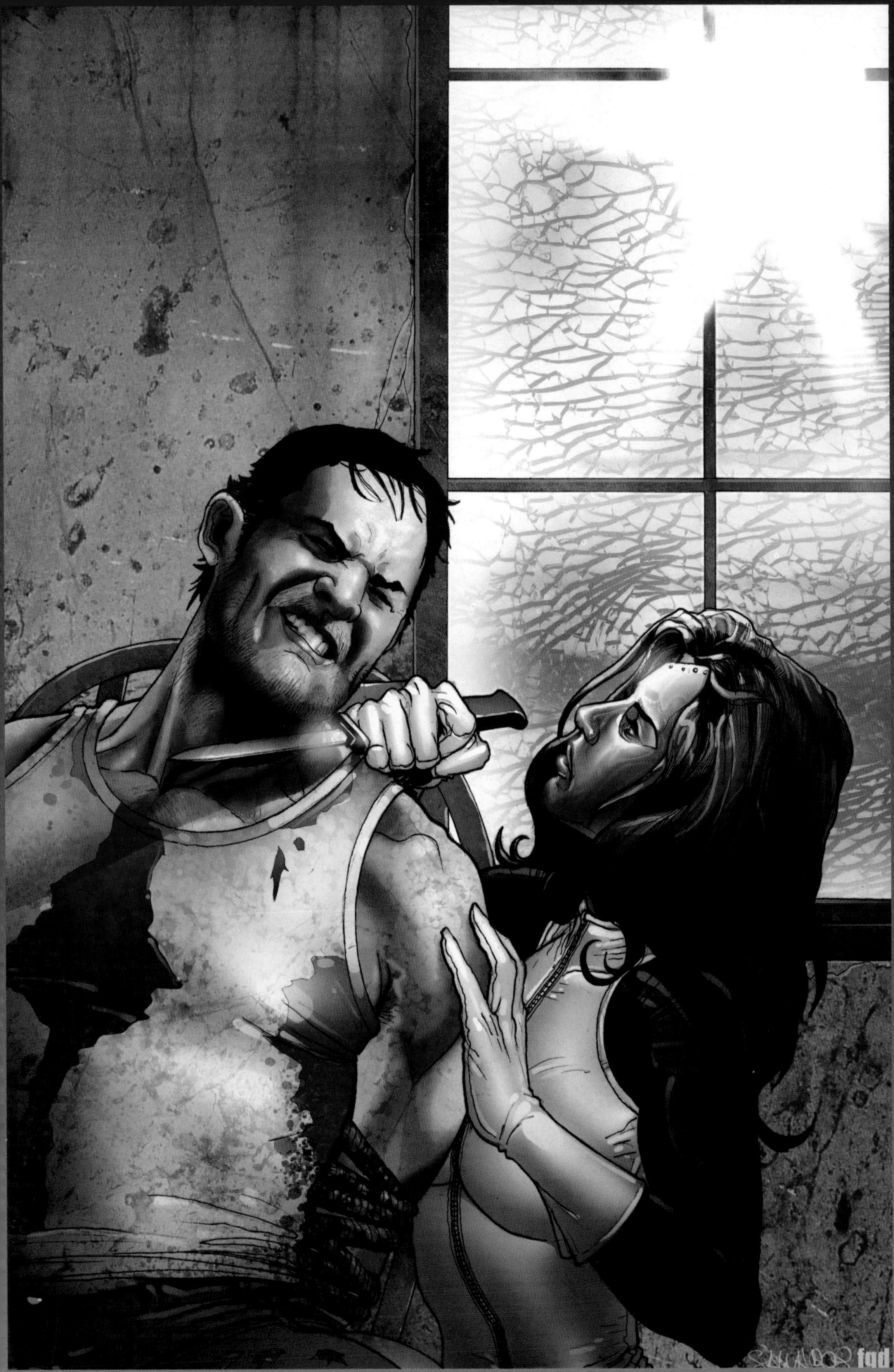

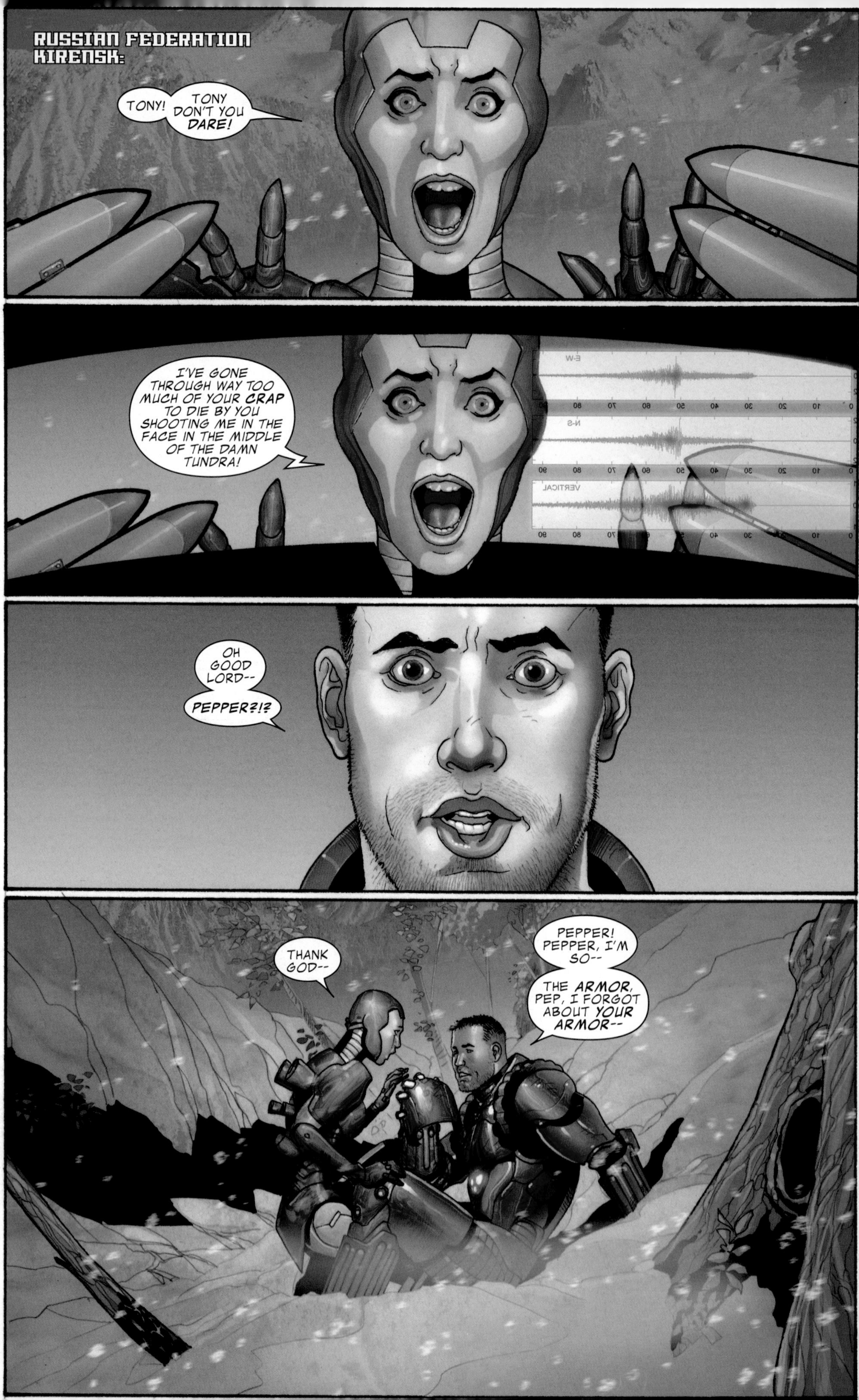
RUSSIAN FEDERATION
KIRENSK:
TONY!
TONY DON'T YOU DARE!
I'VE GONE THROUGH WAY TOO MUCH OF YOUR CRAP TO DIE BY YOU SHOOTING ME IN THE FACE IN THE MIDDLE OF THE DAMN TUNDRA!
E-W
N-S
VERTICAL
OH GOOD LORD--
PEPPER?!?
THANK GOD--
PEPPER! PEPPER, I'M SO--
THE ARMOR, PEP, I FORGOT ABOUT YOUR ARMOR--

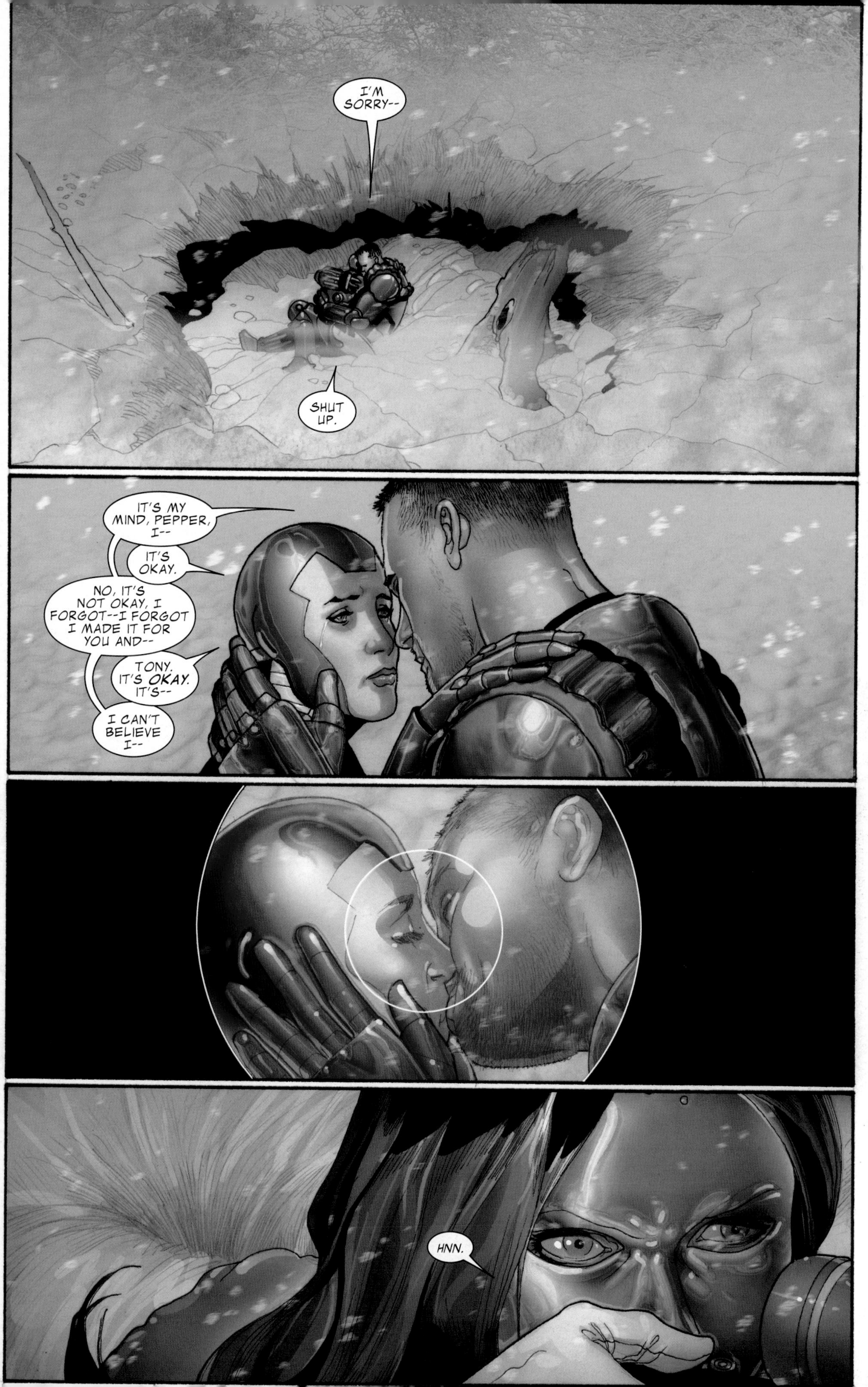
I'M SORRY--
SHUT UP.
IT'S MY MIND, PEPPER, I--
IT'S OKAY.
NO, IT'S NOT OKAY, I FORGOT--I FORGOT I MADE IT FOR YOU AND--
TONY. IT'S OKAY. IT'S--
I CAN'T BELIEVE I--
HNN.

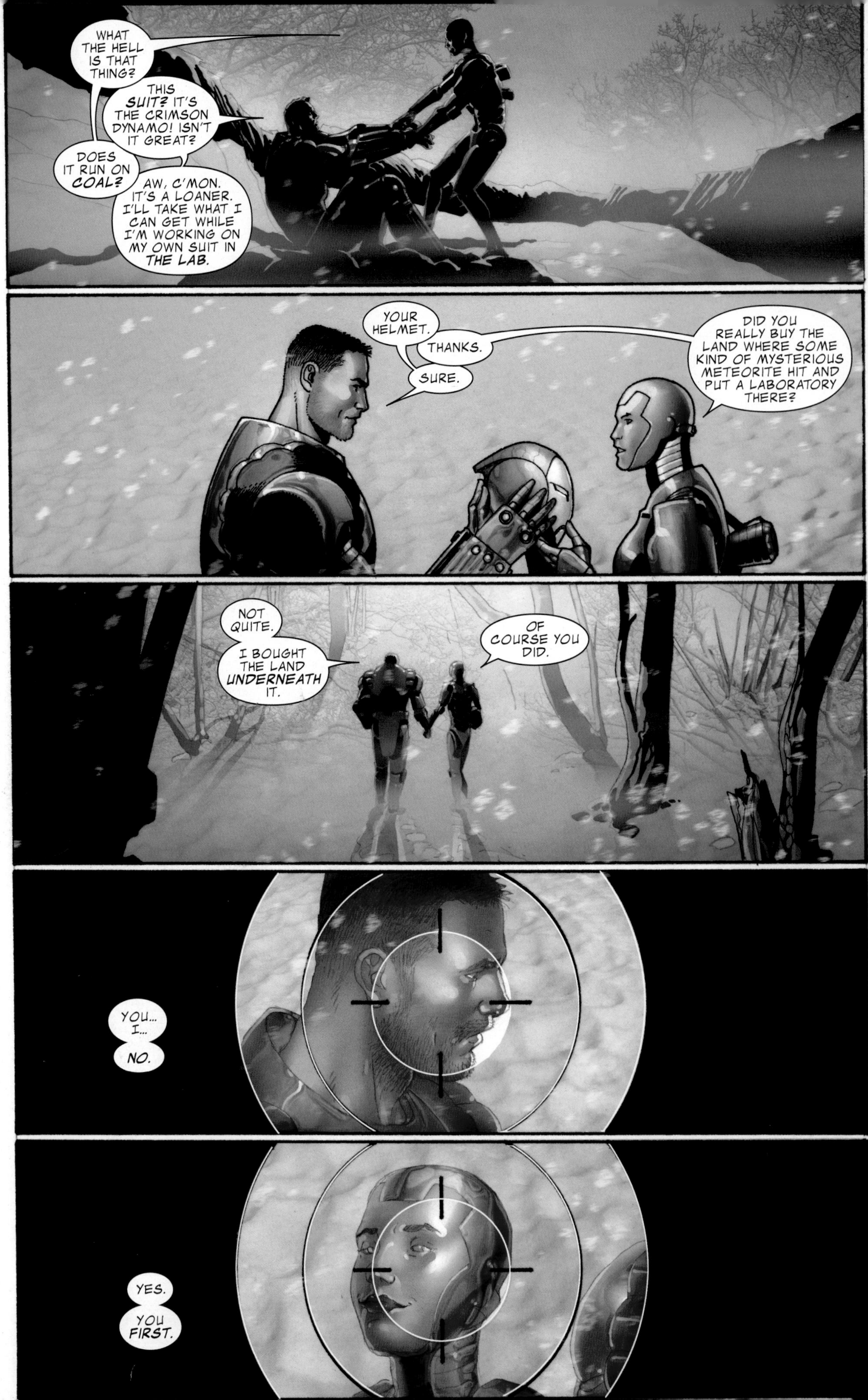
WHAT THE HELL IS THAT THING?
THIS SUIT? IT'S THE CRIMSON DYNAMO! ISN'T IT GREAT?
DOES IT RUN ON COAL?
AW, C'MON. IT'S A LOANER. I'LL TAKE WHAT I CAN GET WHILE I'M WORKING ON MY OWN SUIT IN THE LAB.
YOUR HELMET.
THANKS.
SURE.
DID YOU REALLY BUY THE LAND WHERE SOME KIND OF MYSTERIOUS METEORITE HIT AND PUT A LABORATORY THERE?
NOT QUITE.
I BOUGHT THE LAND UNDERNEATH IT.
OF COURSE YOU DID.
YOU... I...
NO.
YES.
YOU FIRST.

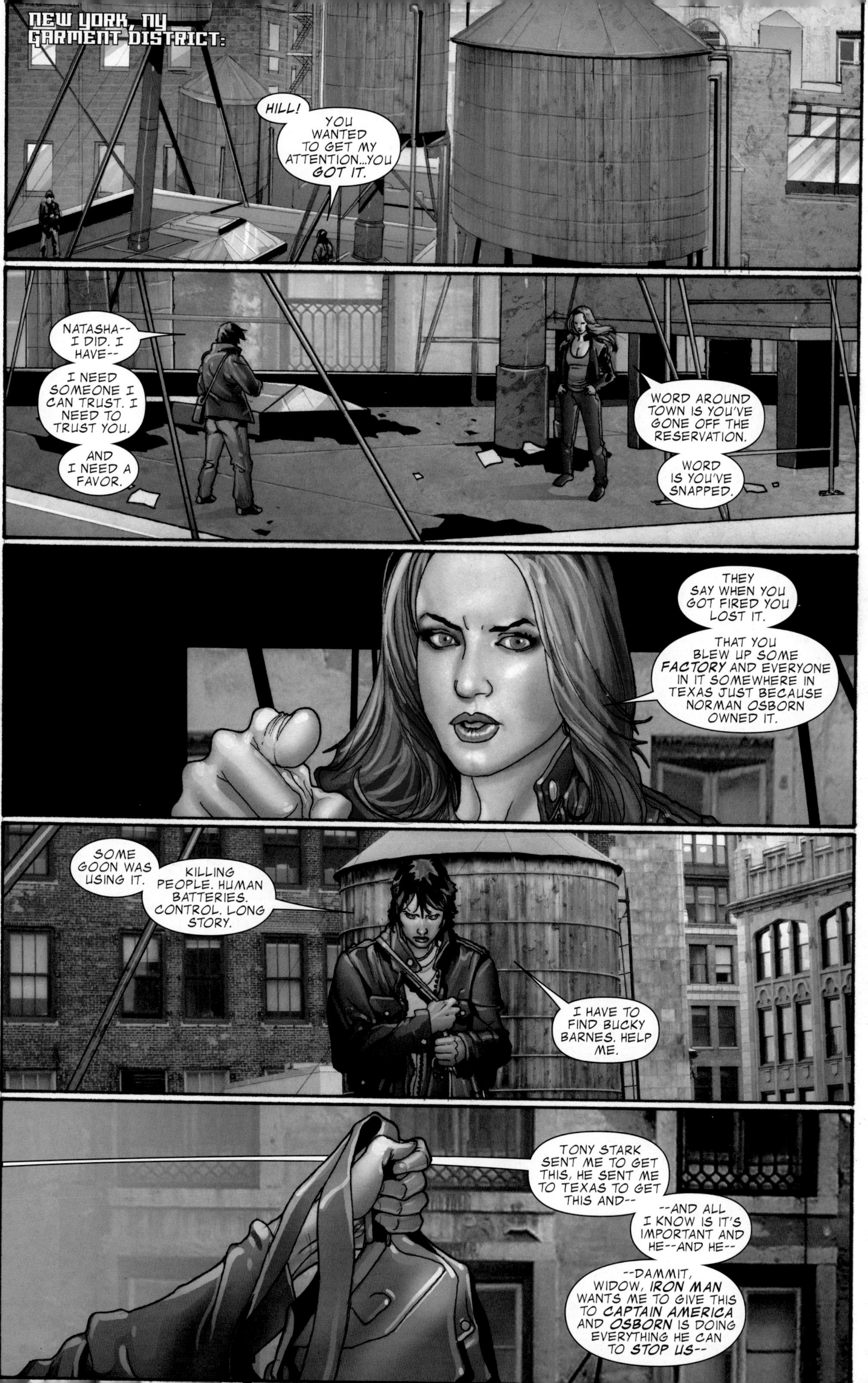
NEW YORK, NY
GARMENT DISTRICT:
HILL!
YOU WANTED TO GET MY ATTENTION...YOU GOT IT.
NATASHA-- I DID. I HAVE--
I NEED SOMEONE I CAN TRUST. I NEED TO TRUST YOU.
AND I NEED A FAVOR.
WORD AROUND TOWN IS YOU'VE GONE OFF THE RESERVATION.
WORD IS YOU'VE SNAPPED.
THEY SAY WHEN YOU GOT FIRED YOU LOST IT.
THAT YOU BLEW UP SOME FACTORY AND EVERYONE IN IT SOMEWHERE IN TEXAS JUST BECAUSE NORMAN OSBORN OWNED IT.
SOME GOON WAS USING IT.
KILLING PEOPLE. HUMAN BATTERIES. CONTROL. LONG STORY.
I HAVE TO FIND BUCKY BARNES. HELP ME.
TONY STARK SENT ME TO GET THIS, HE SENT ME TO TEXAS TO GET THIS AND--
--AND ALL I KNOW IS IT'S IMPORTANT AND HE--AND HE--
--DAMMIT, WIDOW, IRON MAN WANTS ME TO GIVE THIS TO CAPTAIN AMERICA AND OSBORN IS DOING EVERYTHING HE CAN TO STOP US--

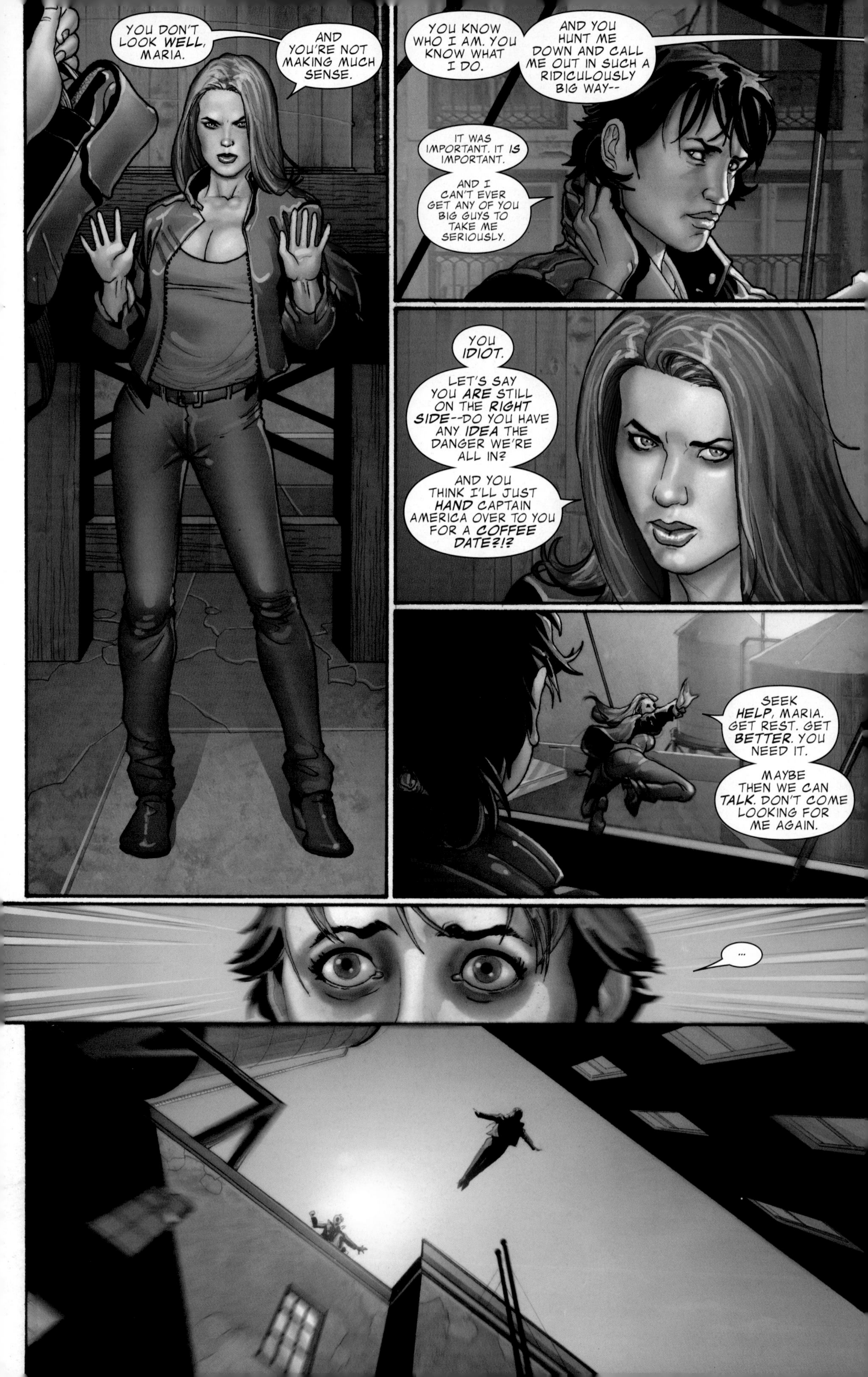
YOU DON'T LOOK WELL, MARIA.
AND YOU'RE NOT MAKING MUCH SENSE.
YOU KNOW WHO I AM. YOU KNOW WHAT I DO.
AND YOU HUNT ME DOWN AND CALL ME OUT IN SUCH A RIDICULOUSLY BIG WAY--
IT WAS IMPORTANT. IT IS IMPORTANT.
AND I CAN'T EVER GET ANY OF YOU BIG GUYS TO TAKE ME SERIOUSLY.
YOU IDIOT.
LET'S SAY YOU ARE STILL ON THE RIGHT SIDE--DO YOU HAVE ANY IDEA THE DANGER WE'RE ALL IN?
AND YOU THINK I'LL JUST HAND CAPTAIN AMERICA OVER TO YOU FOR A COFFEE DATE?!?
SEEK HELP, MARIA. GET REST. GET BETTER. YOU NEED IT.
MAYBE THEN WE CAN TALK. DON'T COME LOOKING FOR ME AGAIN.
...

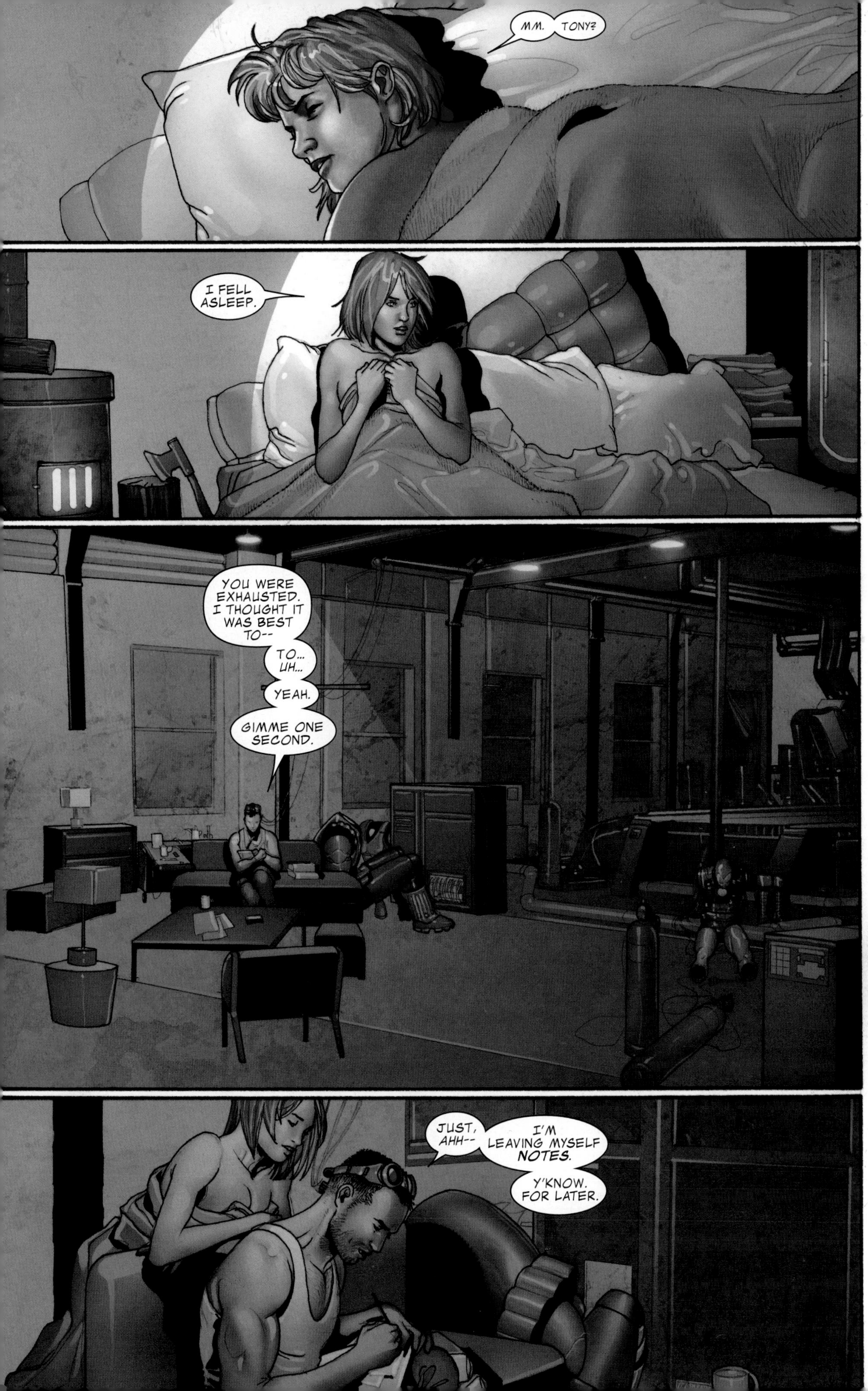
MM. TONY?
I FELL ASLEEP.
YOU WERE EXHAUSTED. I THOUGHT IT WAS BEST TO--
TO... UH...
YEAH.
GIMME ONE SECOND.
JUST, AHH--
I'M LEAVING MYSELF NOTES.
Y'KNOW. FOR LATER.

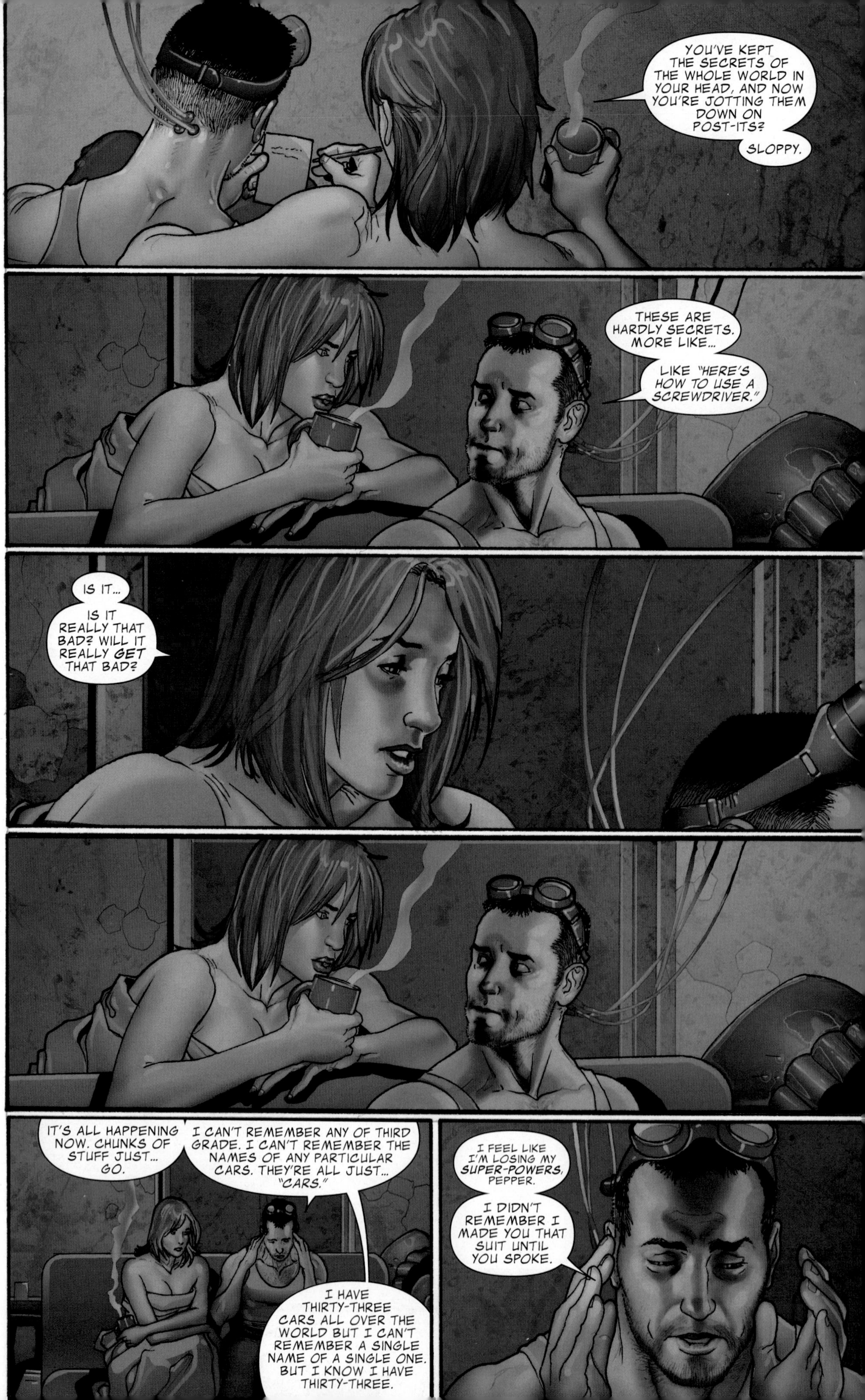
YOU'VE KEPT THE SECRETS OF THE WHOLE WORLD IN YOUR HEAD, AND NOW YOU'RE JOTTING THEM DOWN ON POST-ITS?
SLOPPY.
THESE ARE HARDLY SECRETS. MORE LIKE...
LIKE "HERE'S HOW TO USE A SCREWDRIVER."
IS IT...
IS IT REALLY THAT BAD? WILL IT REALLY GET THAT BAD?
IT'S ALL HAPPENING NOW. CHUNKS OF STUFF JUST... GO.
I CAN'T REMEMBER ANY OF THIRD GRADE. I CAN'T REMEMBER THE NAMES OF ANY PARTICULAR CARS. THEY'RE ALL JUST... "CARS."
I HAVE THIRTY-THREE CARS ALL OVER THE WORLD BUT I CAN'T REMEMBER A SINGLE NAME OF A SINGLE ONE. BUT I KNOW I HAVE THIRTY-THREE.
I FEEL LIKE I'M LOSING MY SUPER-POWERS, PEPPER.
I DIDN'T REMEMBER I MADE YOU THAT SUIT UNTIL YOU SPOKE.

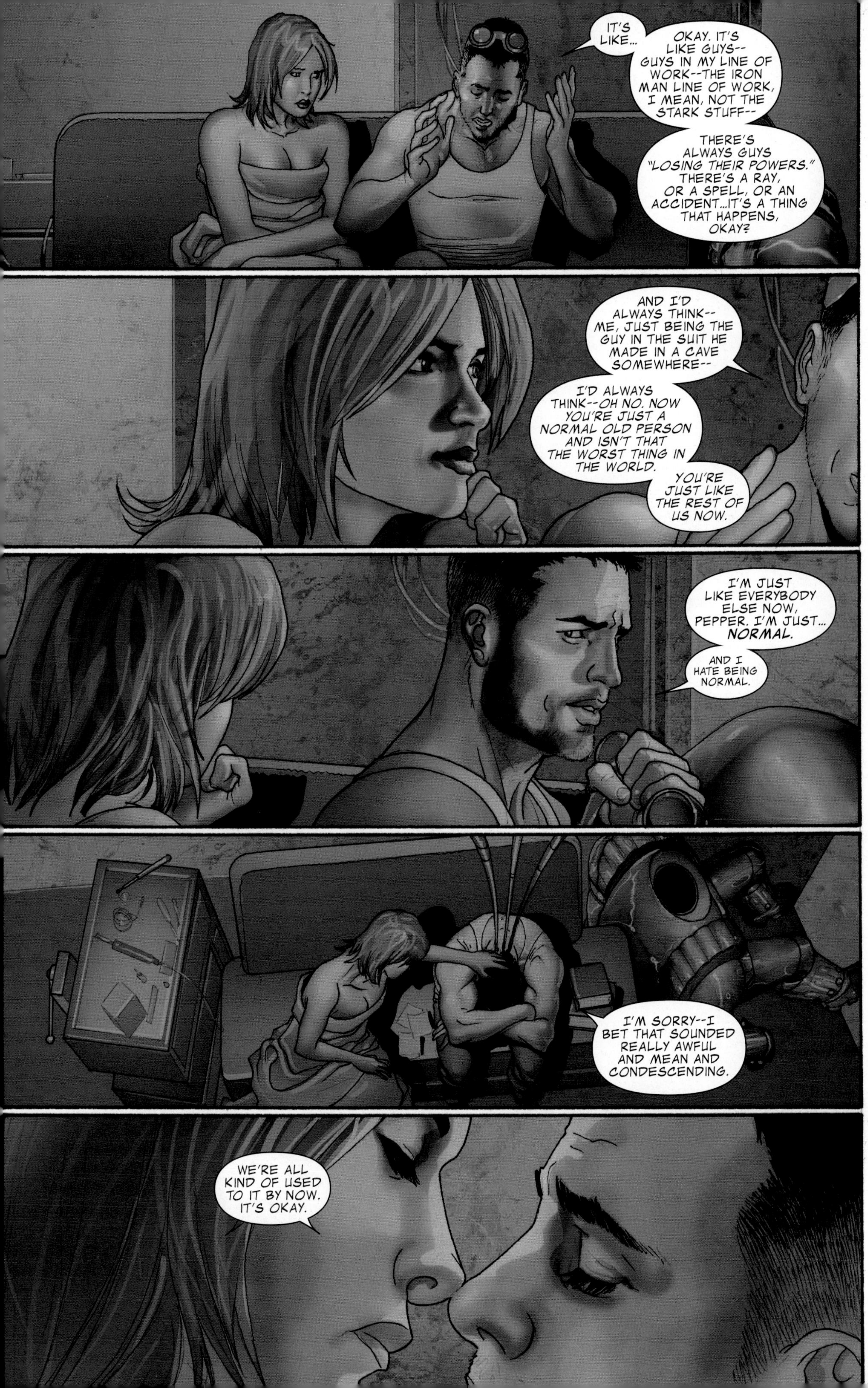
IT'S LIKE...
OKAY. IT'S LIKE GUYS-- GUYS IN MY LINE OF WORK--THE IRON MAN LINE OF WORK, I MEAN, NOT THE STARK STUFF--
THERE'S ALWAYS GUYS "LOSING THEIR POWERS." THERE'S A RAY, OR A SPELL, OR AN ACCIDENT...IT'S A THING THAT HAPPENS, OKAY?
AND I'D ALWAYS THINK-- ME, JUST BEING THE GUY IN THE SUIT HE MADE IN A CAVE SOMEWHERE--
I'D ALWAYS THINK--OH NO. NOW YOU'RE JUST A NORMAL OLD PERSON AND ISN'T THAT THE WORST THING IN THE WORLD.
YOU'RE JUST LIKE THE REST OF US NOW.
I'M JUST LIKE EVERYBODY ELSE NOW, PEPPER. I'M JUST... NORMAL.
AND I HATE BEING NORMAL.
I'M SORRY--I BET THAT SOUNDED REALLY AWFUL AND MEAN AND CONDESCENDING.
WE'RE ALL KIND OF USED TO IT BY NOW. IT'S OKAY.

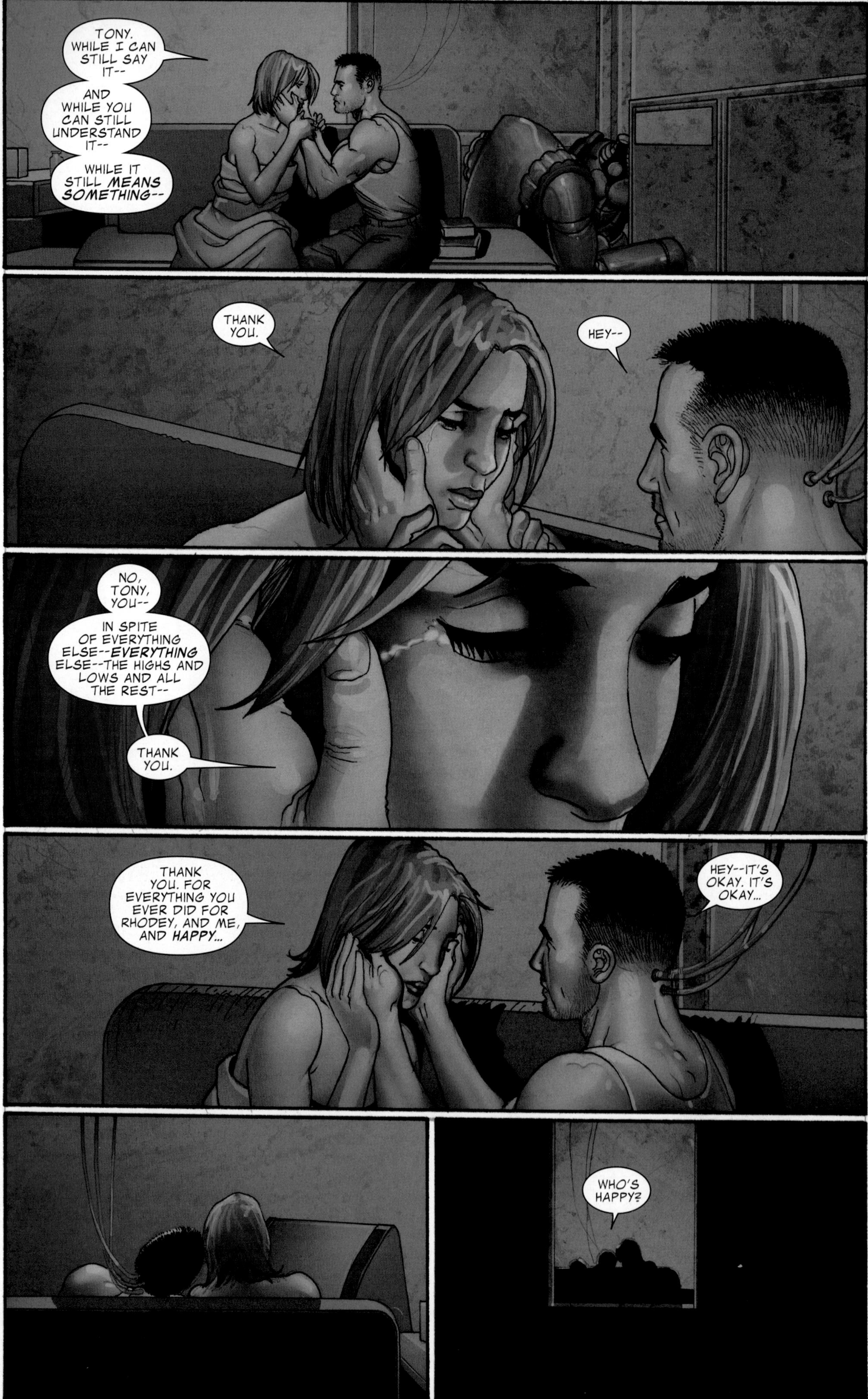
TONY. WHILE I CAN STILL SAY IT--
AND WHILE YOU CAN STILL UNDERSTAND IT--
WHILE IT STILL **MEANS SOMETHING**--
THANK YOU.
HEY--
NO, TONY, YOU--
IN SPITE OF EVERYTHING ELSE--*EVERYTHING* ELSE--THE HIGHS AND LOWS AND ALL THE REST--
THANK YOU.
THANK YOU. FOR EVERYTHING YOU EVER DID FOR RHODEY, AND ME, AND *HAPPY*...
HEY--IT'S OKAY. IT'S OKAY...
WHO'S HAPPY?

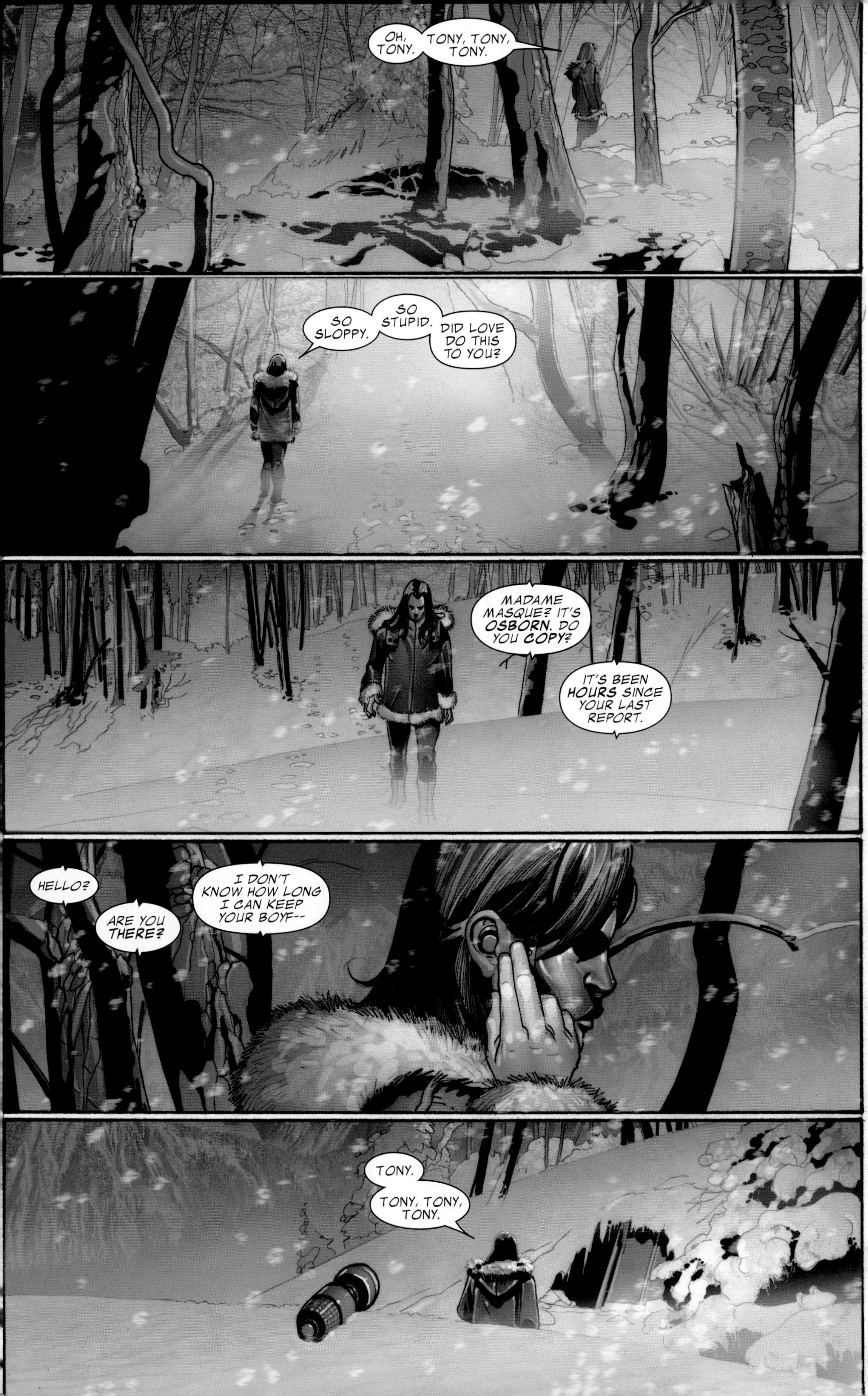
OH, TONY.
TONY, TONY, TONY.
SO SLOPPY.
SO STUPID.
DID LOVE DO THIS TO YOU?
MADAME MASQUE? IT'S OSBORN. DO YOU COPY?
IT'S BEEN HOURS SINCE YOUR LAST REPORT.
HELLO?
ARE YOU THERE?
I DON'T KNOW HOW LONG I CAN KEEP YOUR BOYF--
TONY.
TONY, TONY, TONY.

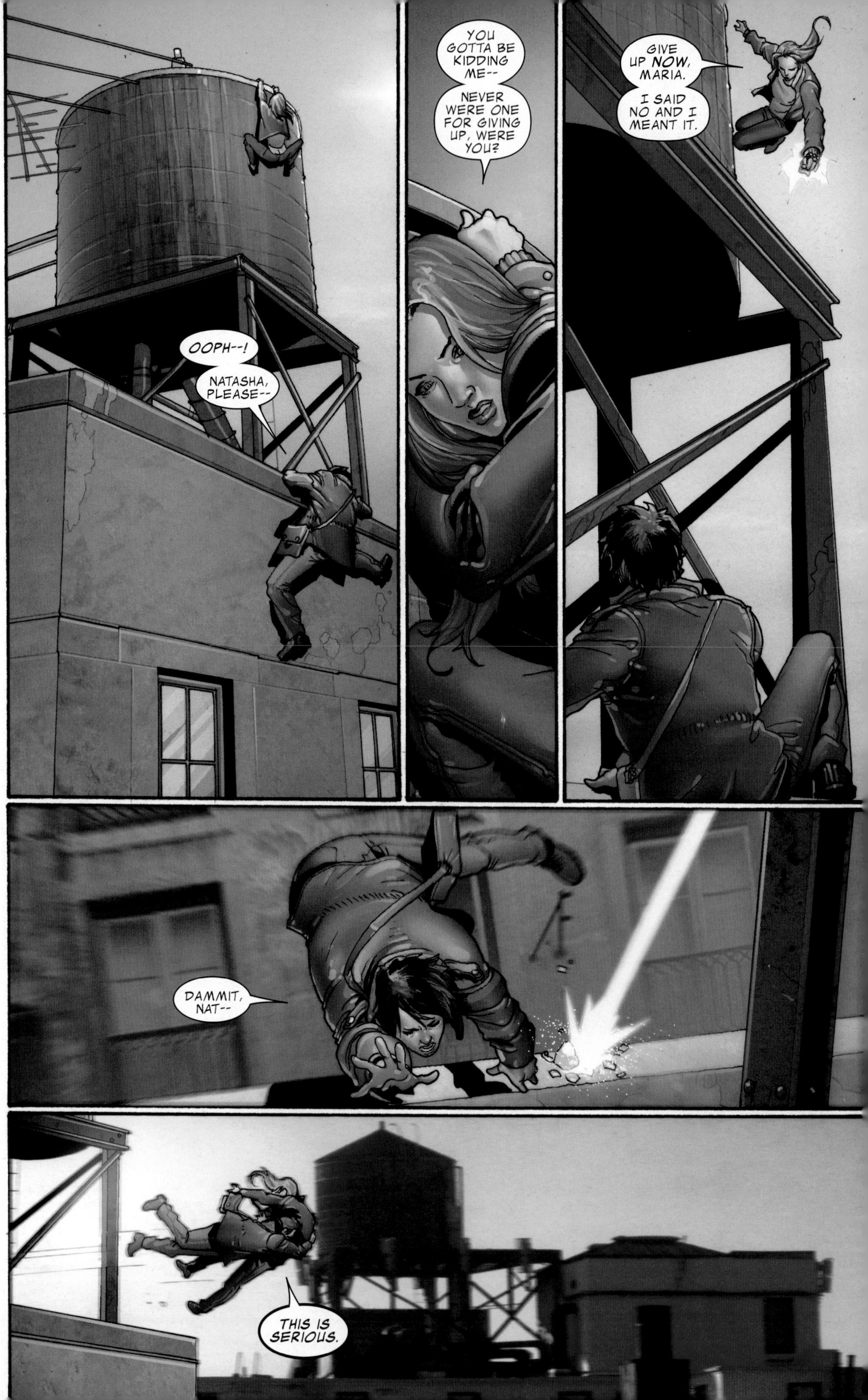
OOPH--!
NATASHA, PLEASE--
YOU GOTTA BE KIDDING ME--
NEVER WERE ONE FOR GIVING UP, WERE YOU?
GIVE UP NOW, MARIA.
I SAID NO AND I MEANT IT.
DAMMIT, NAT--
THIS IS SERIOUS.

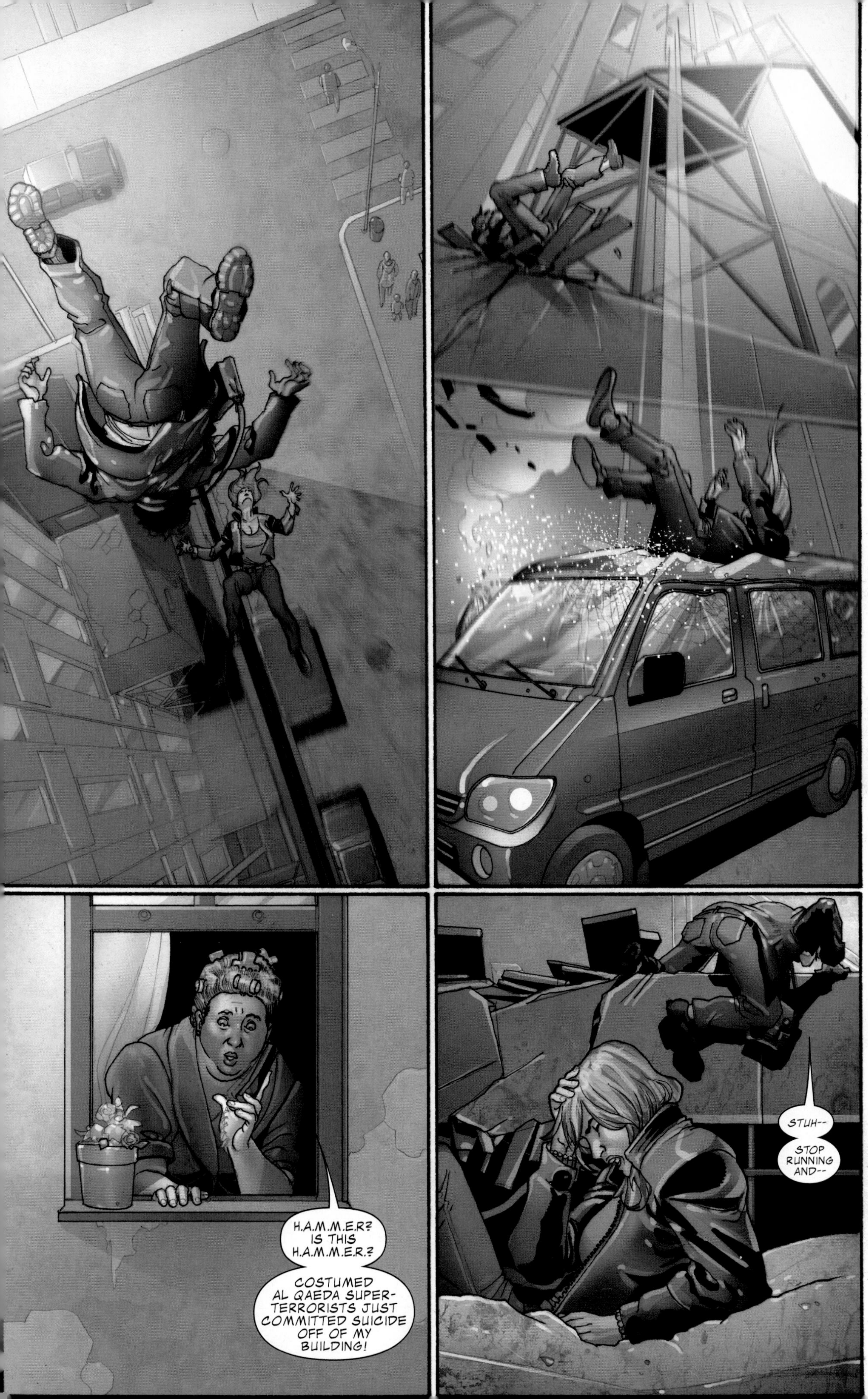

H.A.M.M.E.R.? IS THIS H.A.M.M.E.R.?
COSTUMED AL QAEDA SUPER-TERRORISTS JUST COMMITTED SUICIDE OFF OF MY BUILDING!
STUH--
STOP RUNNING AND--

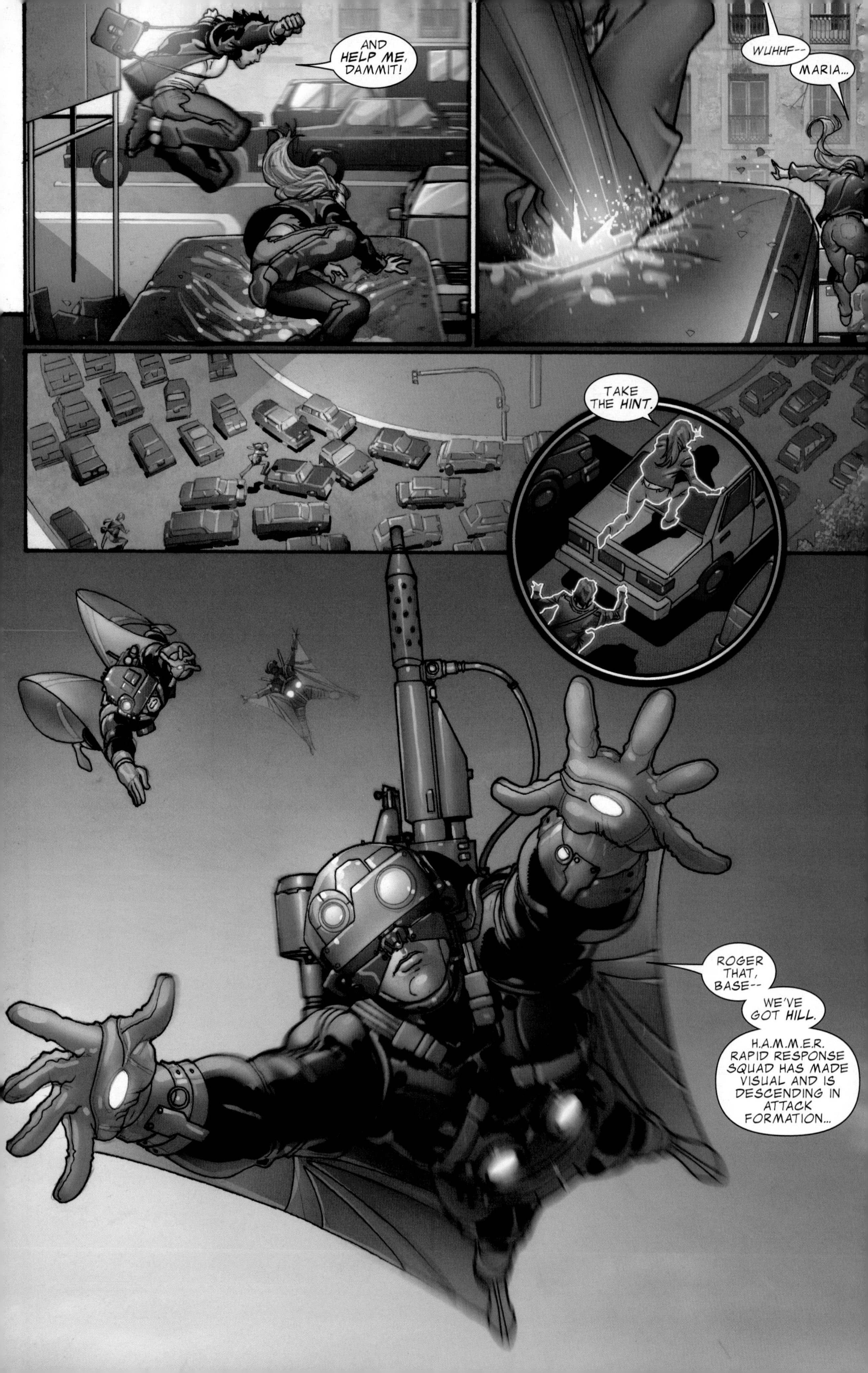
AND HELP ME, DAMMIT!
WUHHF--
MARIA...
TAKE THE HINT.
ROGER THAT, BASE--
WE'VE GOT HILL.
H.A.M.M.E.R. RAPID RESPONSE SQUAD HAS MADE VISUAL AND IS DESCENDING IN ATTACK FORMATION...

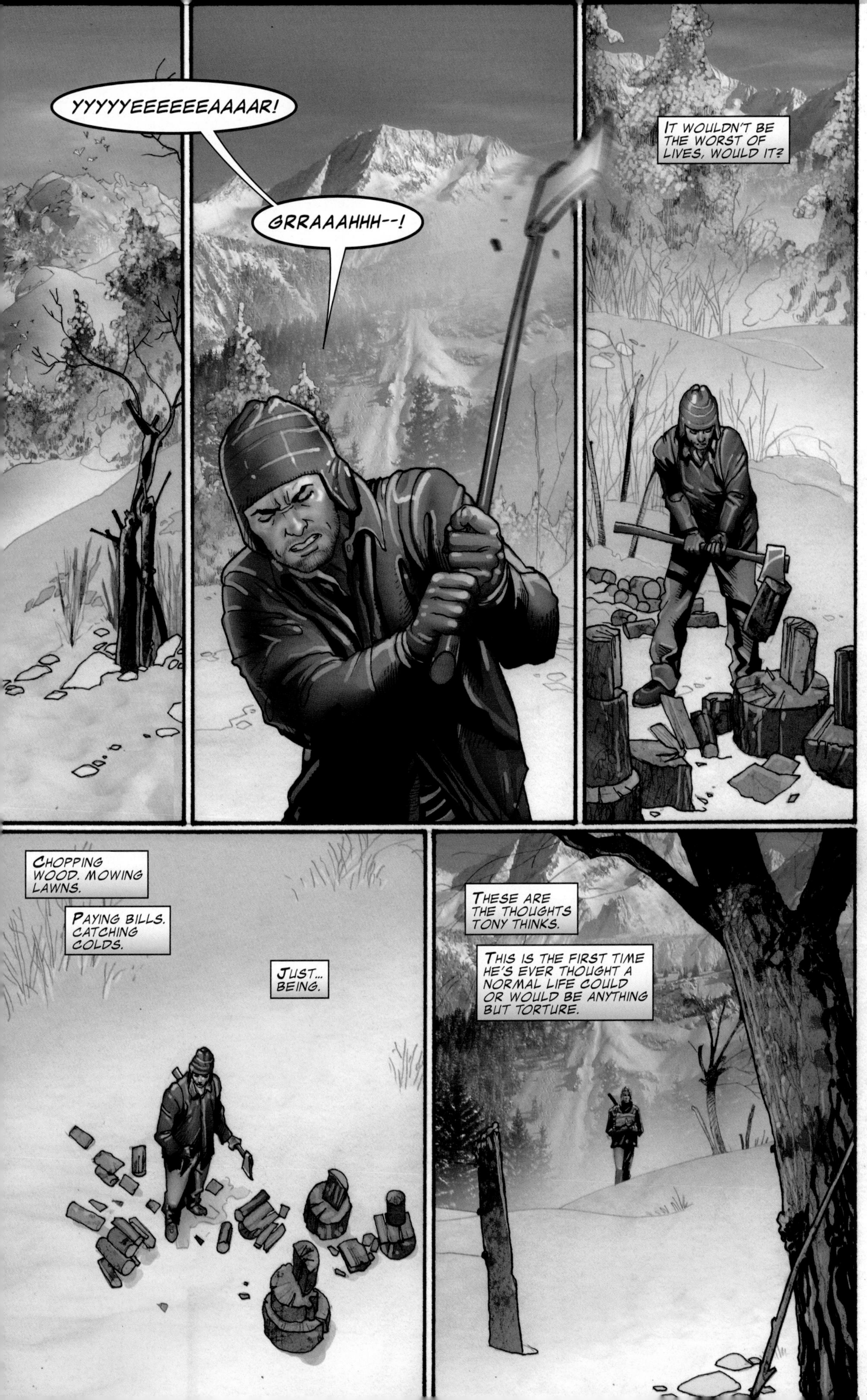

YYYYYEEEEEEAAAAR!
GRRAAAHHH--!
IT WOULDN'T BE THE WORST OF LIVES, WOULD IT?
CHOPPING WOOD. MOWING LAWNS.
PAYING BILLS. CATCHING COLDS.
JUST... BEING.
THESE ARE THE THOUGHTS TONY THINKS.
THIS IS THE FIRST TIME HE'S EVER THOUGHT A NORMAL LIFE COULD OR WOULD BE ANYTHING BUT TORTURE.

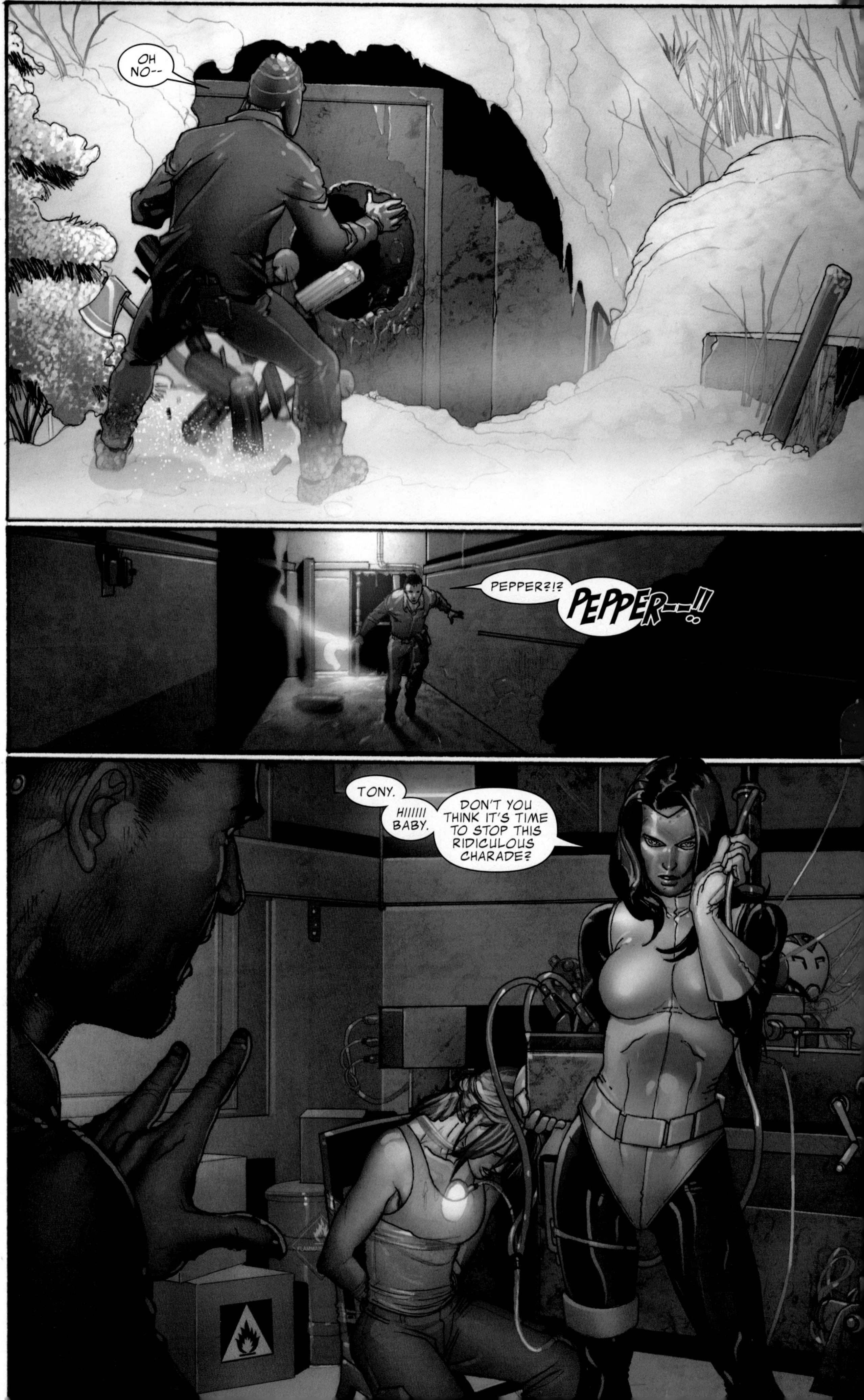
OH NO--
PEPPER?!?
PEPPER--!!
TONY.
HIIIIII BABY.
DON'T YOU THINK IT'S TIME TO STOP THIS RIDICULOUS CHARADE?

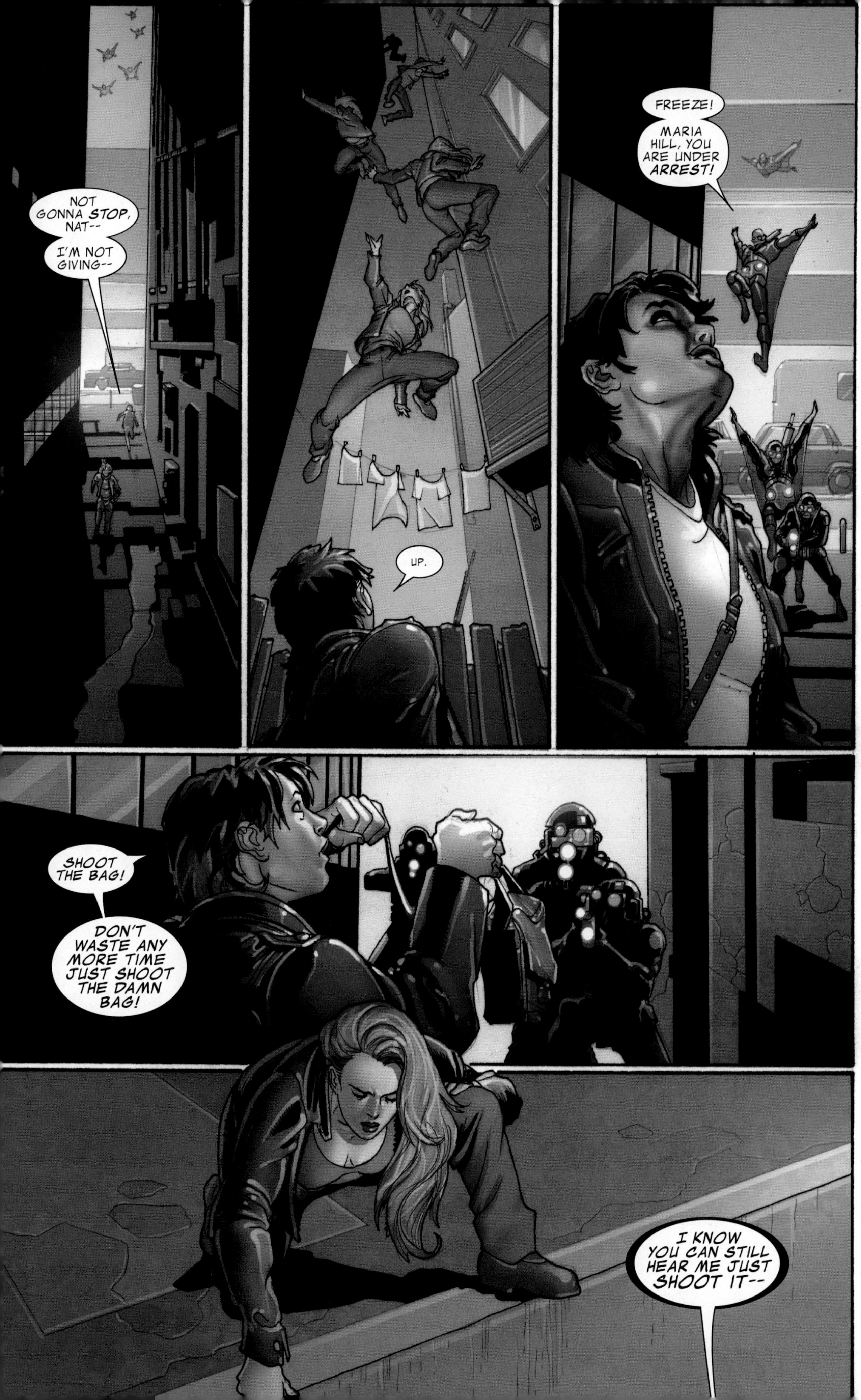
NOT GONNA STOP, NAT--
I'M NOT GIVING--
UP.
FREEZE!
MARIA HILL, YOU ARE UNDER ARREST!
SHOOT THE BAG!
DON'T WASTE ANY MORE TIME JUST SHOOT THE DAMN BAG!
I KNOW YOU CAN STILL HEAR ME JUST SHOOT IT--

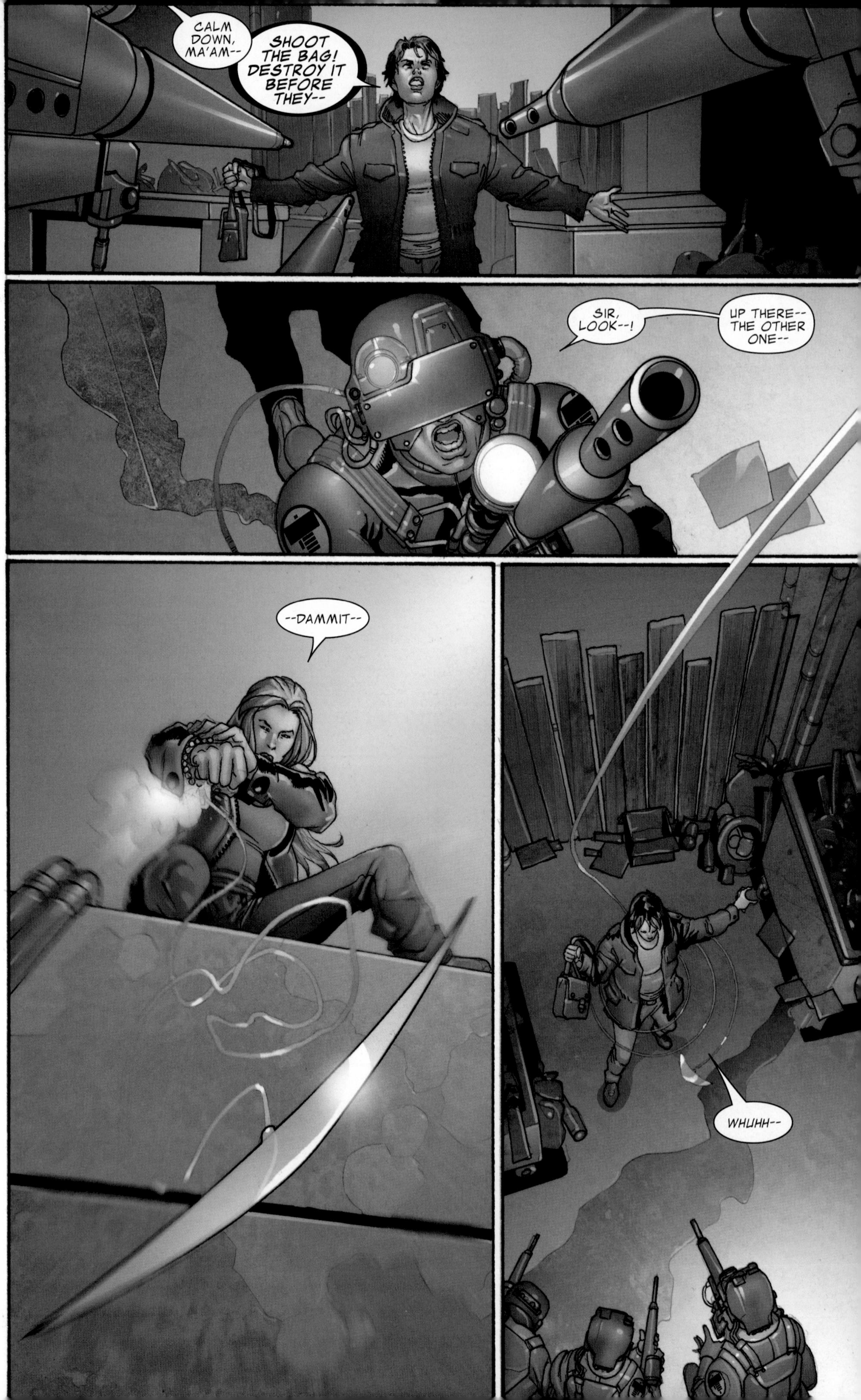
CALM DOWN, MA'AM--
SHOOT THE BAG! DESTROY IT BEFORE THEY--
SIR, LOOK--!
UP THERE-- THE OTHER ONE--
--DAMMIT--
WHUHH--

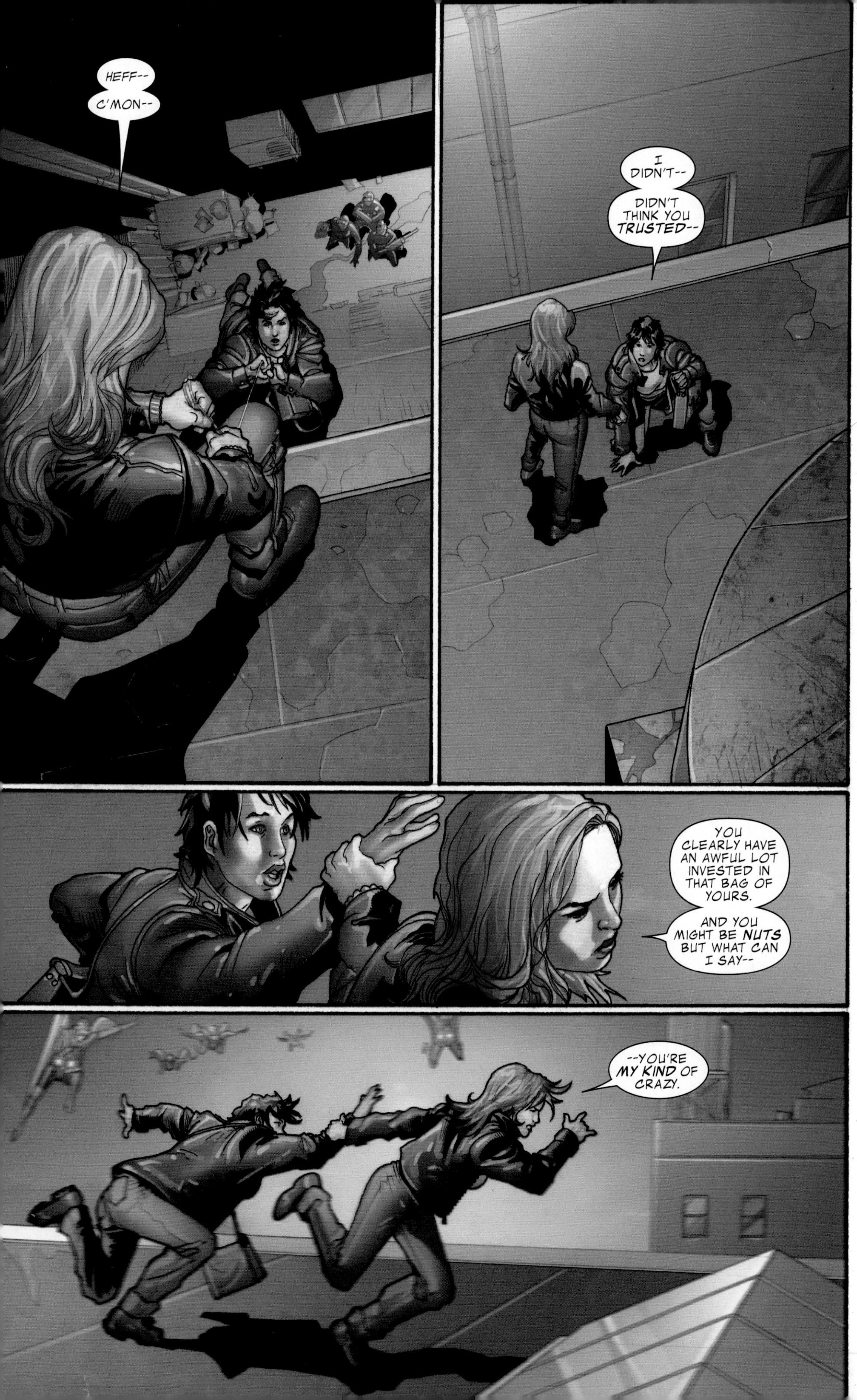
HEFF--
C'MON--
I DIDN'T--
DIDN'T THINK YOU TRUSTED--
YOU CLEARLY HAVE AN AWFUL LOT INVESTED IN THAT BAG OF YOURS.
AND YOU MIGHT BE NUTS BUT WHAT CAN I SAY--
--YOU'RE MY KIND OF CRAZY.

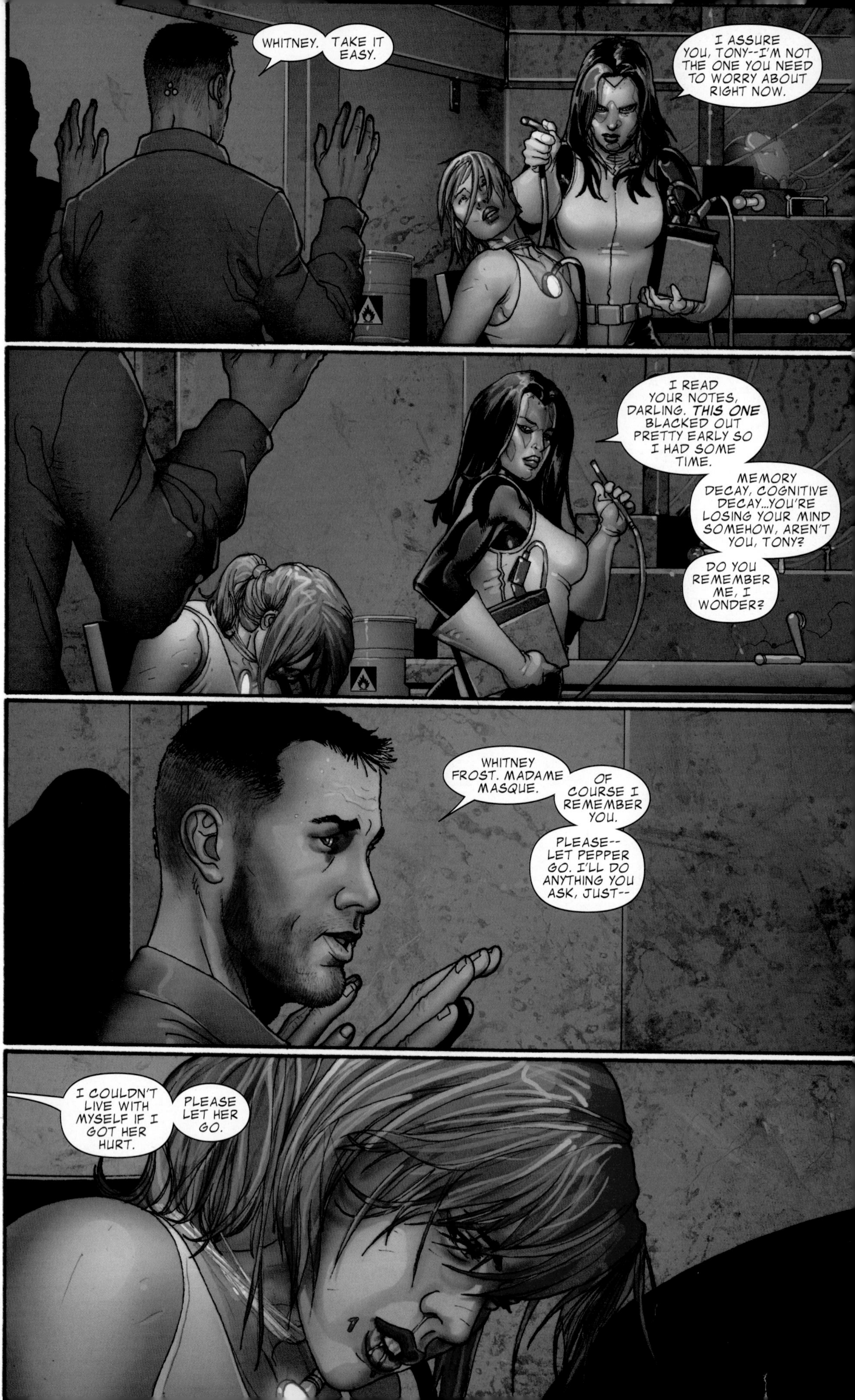
WHITNEY.
TAKE IT EASY.
I ASSURE YOU, TONY--I'M NOT THE ONE YOU NEED TO WORRY ABOUT RIGHT NOW.
I READ YOUR NOTES, DARLING. **THIS ONE** BLACKED OUT PRETTY EARLY SO I HAD SOME TIME.
MEMORY DECAY, COGNITIVE DECAY...YOU'RE LOSING YOUR MIND SOMEHOW, AREN'T YOU, TONY?
DO YOU REMEMBER ME, I WONDER?
WHITNEY FROST. MADAME MASQUE.
OF COURSE I REMEMBER YOU.
PLEASE-- LET PEPPER GO. I'LL DO ANYTHING YOU ASK, JUST--
I COULDN'T LIVE WITH MYSELF IF I GOT HER HURT.
PLEASE LET HER GO.

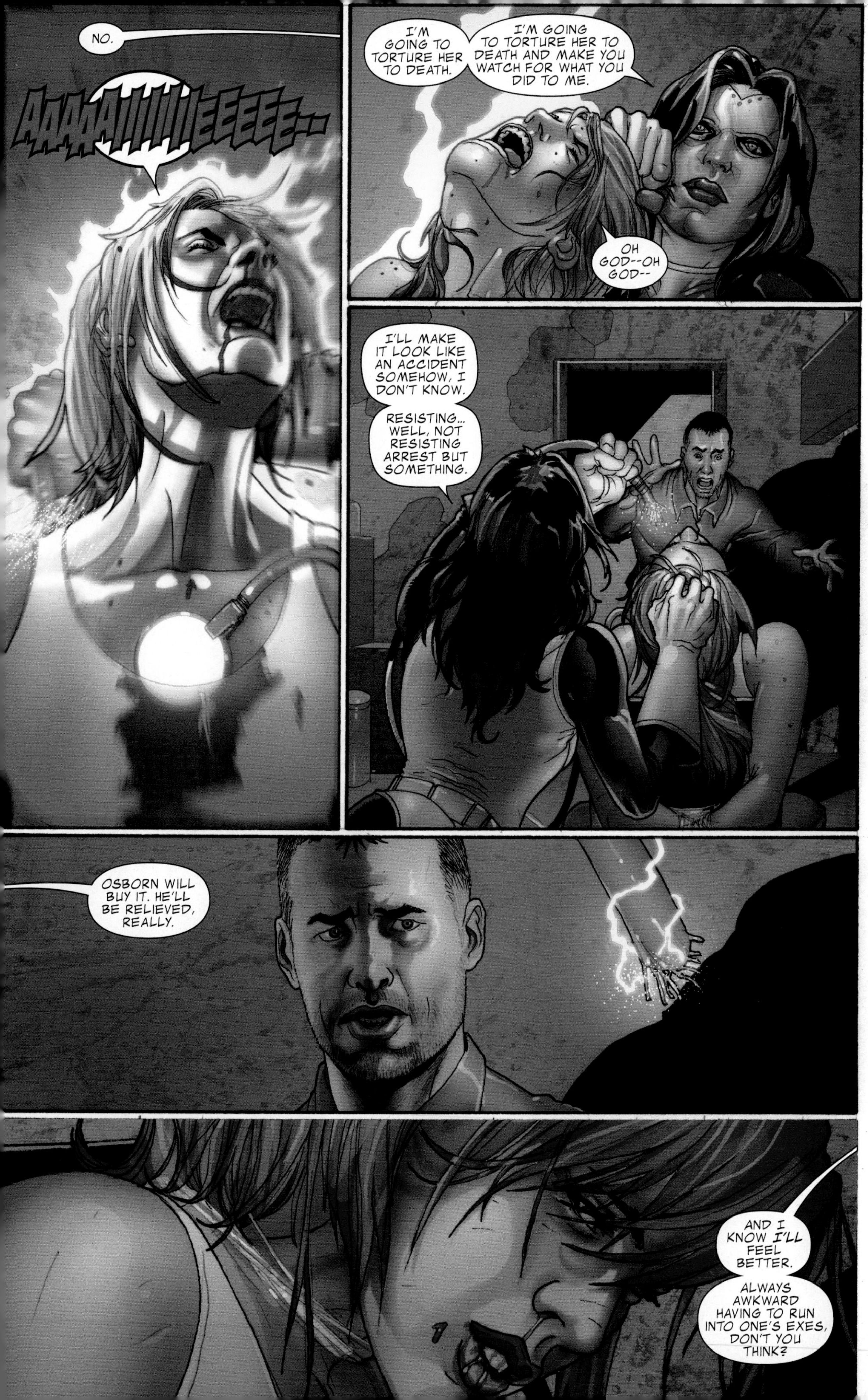
NO.
AAAAIIIIIIEEEEE--
I'M GOING TO TORTURE HER TO DEATH.
I'M GOING TO TORTURE HER TO DEATH AND MAKE YOU WATCH FOR WHAT YOU DID TO ME.
OH GOD--OH GOD--
I'LL MAKE IT LOOK LIKE AN ACCIDENT SOMEHOW, I DON'T KNOW.
RESISTING... WELL, NOT RESISTING ARREST BUT SOMETHING.
OSBORN WILL BUY IT. HE'LL BE RELIEVED, REALLY.
AND I KNOW I'LL FEEL BETTER.
ALWAYS AWKWARD HAVING TO RUN INTO ONE'S EXES, DON'T YOU THINK?

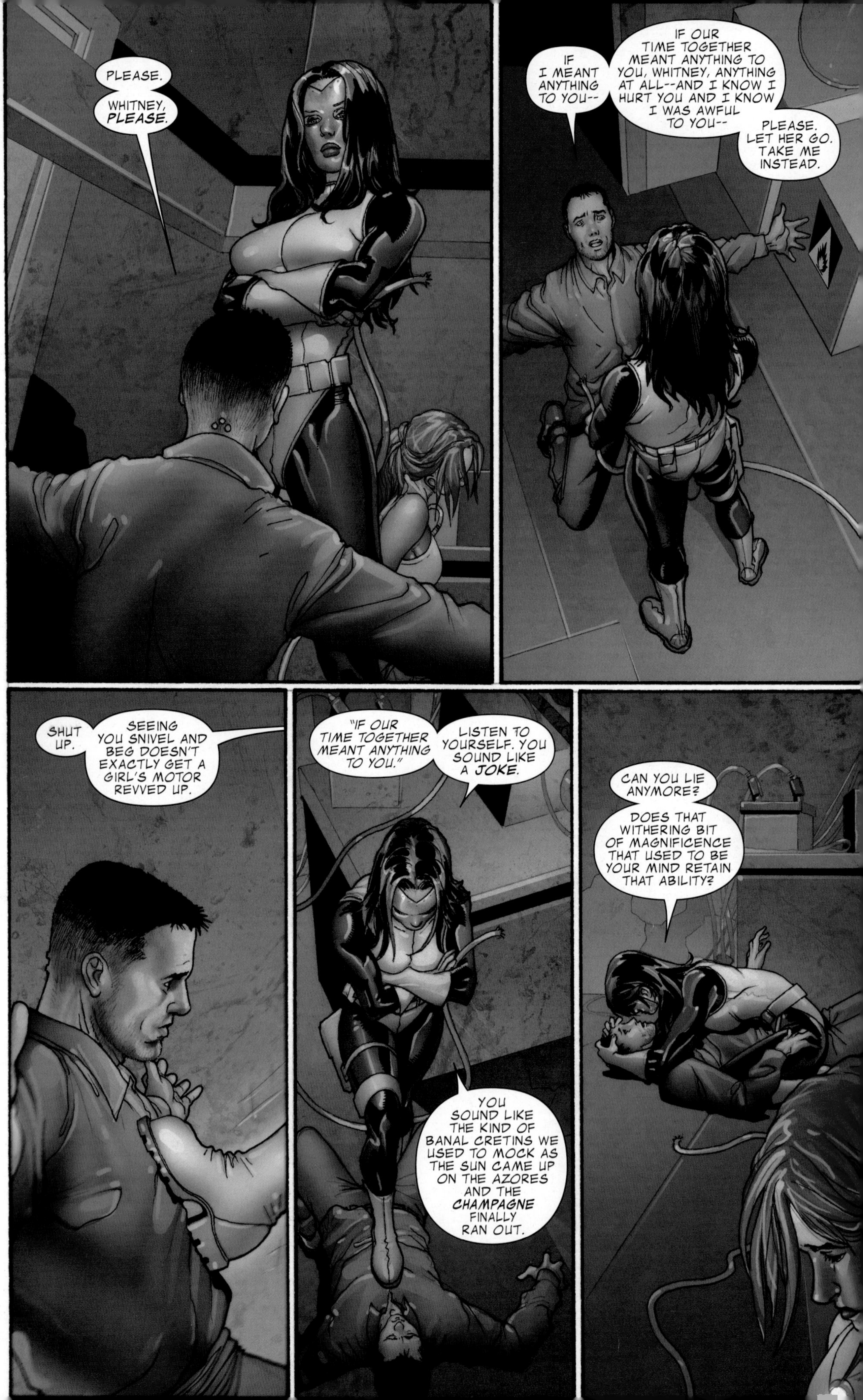
PLEASE.
WHITNEY, PLEASE.
IF I MEANT ANYTHING TO YOU--
IF OUR TIME TOGETHER MEANT ANYTHING TO YOU, WHITNEY, ANYTHING AT ALL--AND I KNOW I HURT YOU AND I KNOW I WAS AWFUL TO YOU--
PLEASE. LET HER GO. TAKE ME INSTEAD.
SHUT UP.
SEEING YOU SNIVEL AND BEG DOESN'T EXACTLY GET A GIRL'S MOTOR REVVED UP.
"IF OUR TIME TOGETHER MEANT ANYTHING TO YOU."
LISTEN TO YOURSELF. YOU SOUND LIKE A JOKE.
YOU SOUND LIKE THE KIND OF BANAL CRETINS WE USED TO MOCK AS THE SUN CAME UP ON THE AZORES AND THE CHAMPAGNE FINALLY RAN OUT.
CAN YOU LIE ANYMORE?
DOES THAT WITHERING BIT OF MAGNIFICENCE THAT USED TO BE YOUR MIND RETAIN THAT ABILITY?

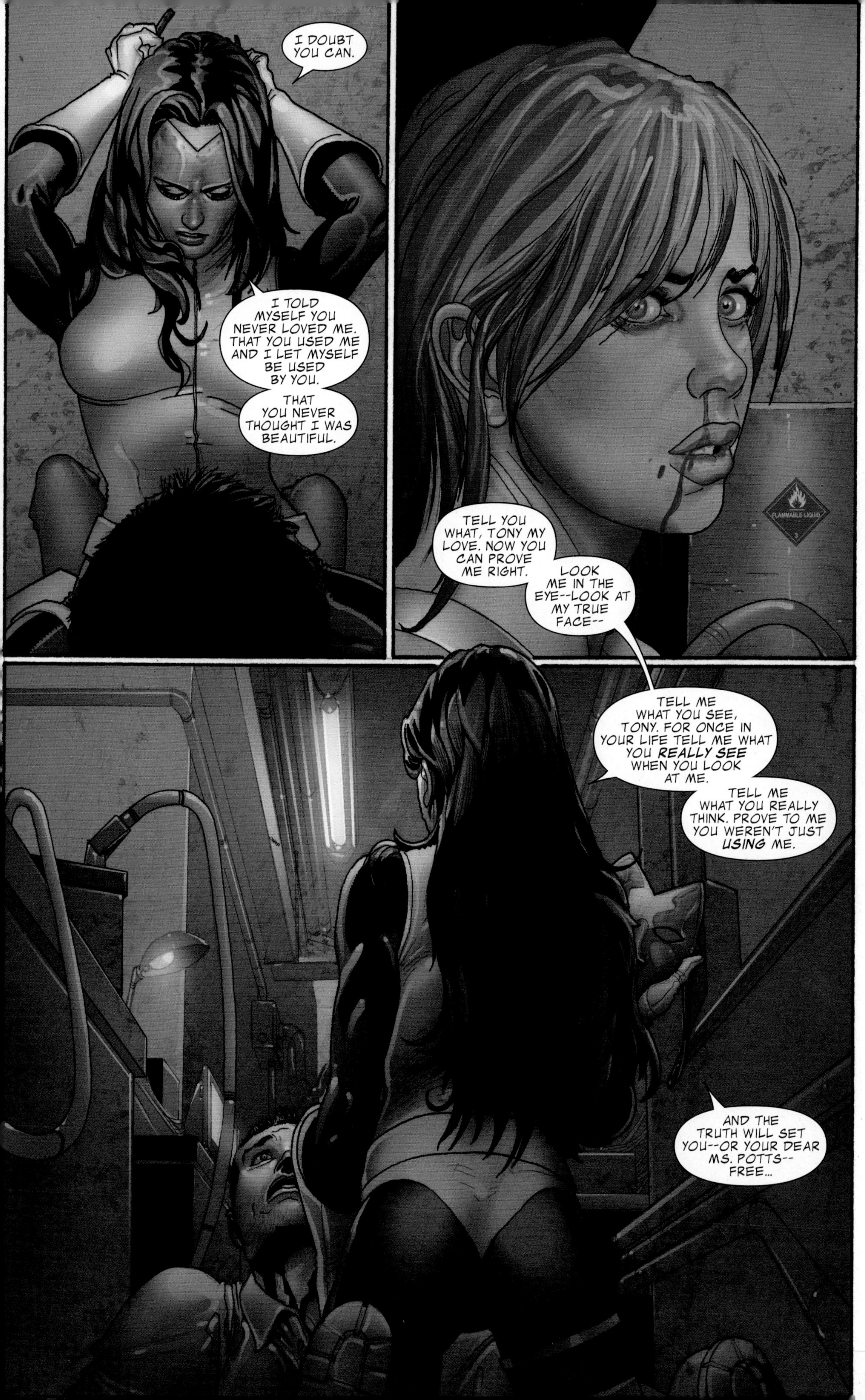
I DOUBT YOU CAN.
I TOLD MYSELF YOU NEVER LOVED ME. THAT YOU USED ME AND I LET MYSELF BE USED BY YOU.
THAT YOU NEVER THOUGHT I WAS BEAUTIFUL.
FLAMMABLE LIQUID
3
TELL YOU WHAT, TONY MY LOVE. NOW YOU CAN PROVE ME RIGHT.
LOOK ME IN THE EYE--LOOK AT MY TRUE FACE--
TELL ME WHAT YOU SEE, TONY. FOR ONCE IN YOUR LIFE TELL ME WHAT YOU *REALLY SEE* WHEN YOU LOOK AT ME.
TELL ME WHAT YOU REALLY THINK. PROVE TO ME YOU WEREN'T JUST *USING* ME.
AND THE TRUTH WILL SET YOU--OR YOUR DEAR MS. POTTS--FREE...

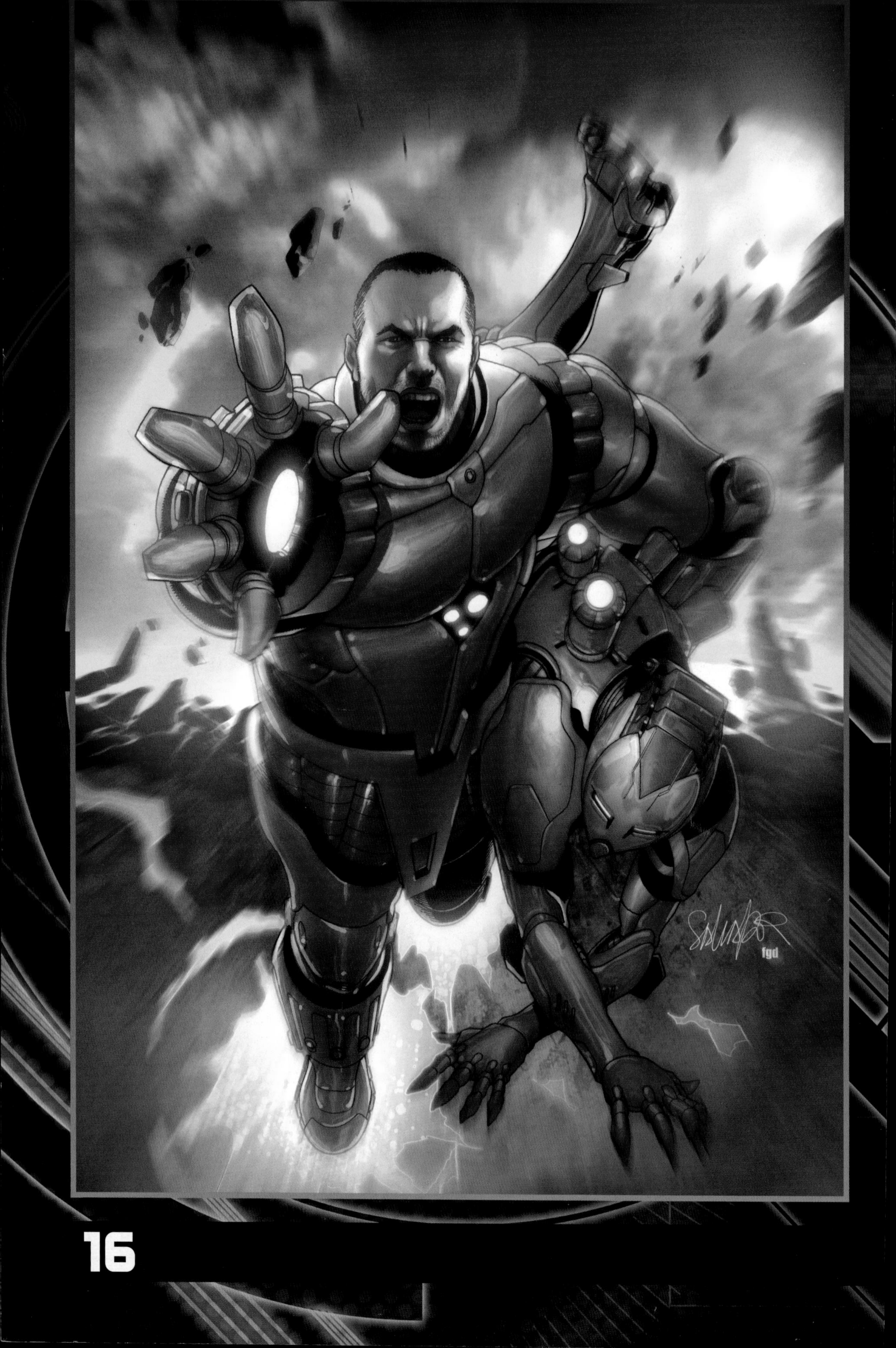

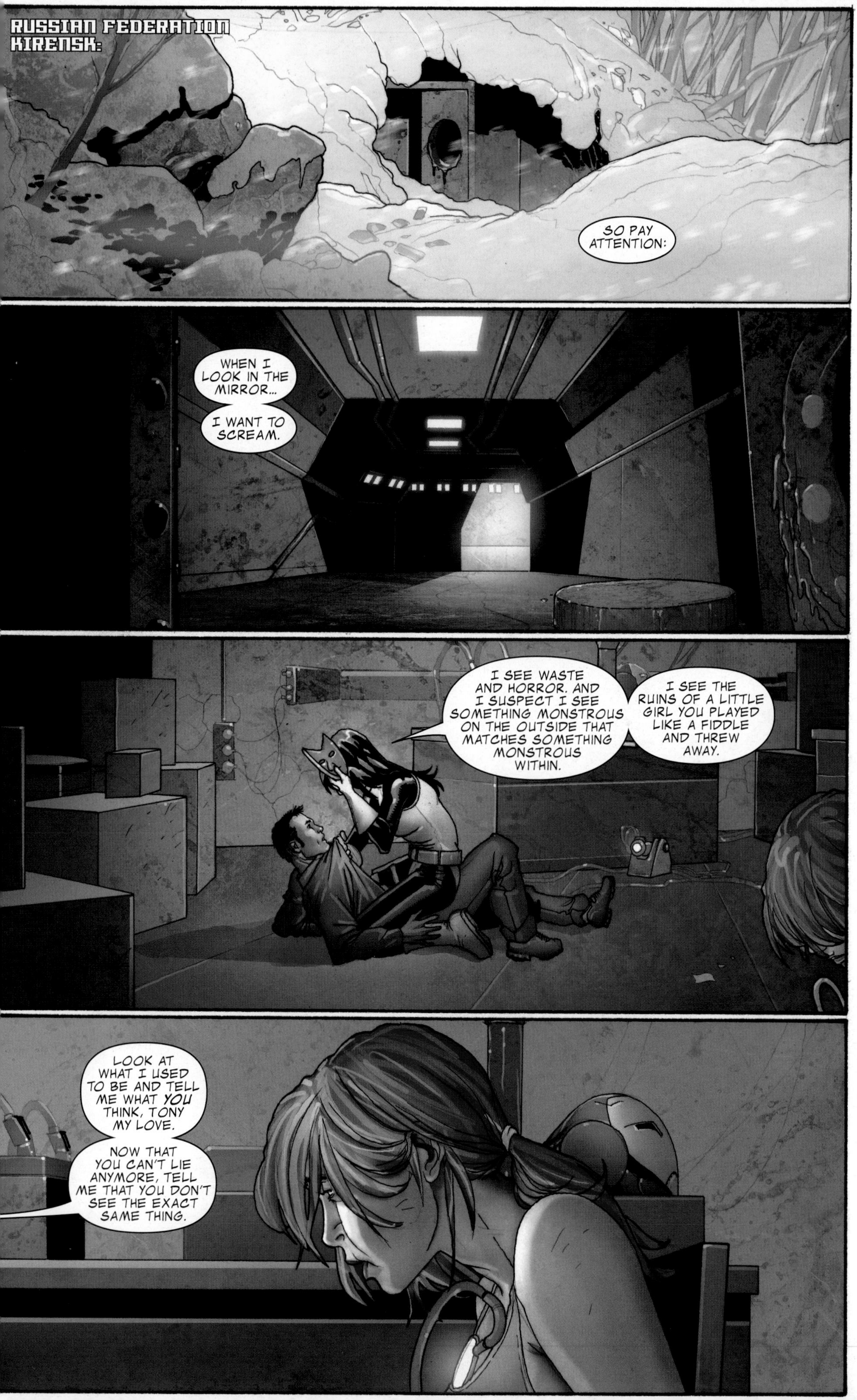
RUSSIAN FEDERATION
KIRENSK:
SO PAY ATTENTION:
WHEN I LOOK IN THE MIRROR...
I WANT TO SCREAM.
I SEE WASTE AND HORROR. AND I SUSPECT I SEE SOMETHING MONSTROUS ON THE OUTSIDE THAT MATCHES SOMETHING MONSTROUS WITHIN.
I SEE THE RUINS OF A LITTLE GIRL YOU PLAYED LIKE A FIDDLE AND THREW AWAY.
LOOK AT WHAT I USED TO BE AND TELL ME WHAT *YOU* THINK, TONY MY LOVE.
NOW THAT YOU CAN'T LIE ANYMORE, TELL ME THAT YOU DON'T SEE THE EXACT SAME THING.

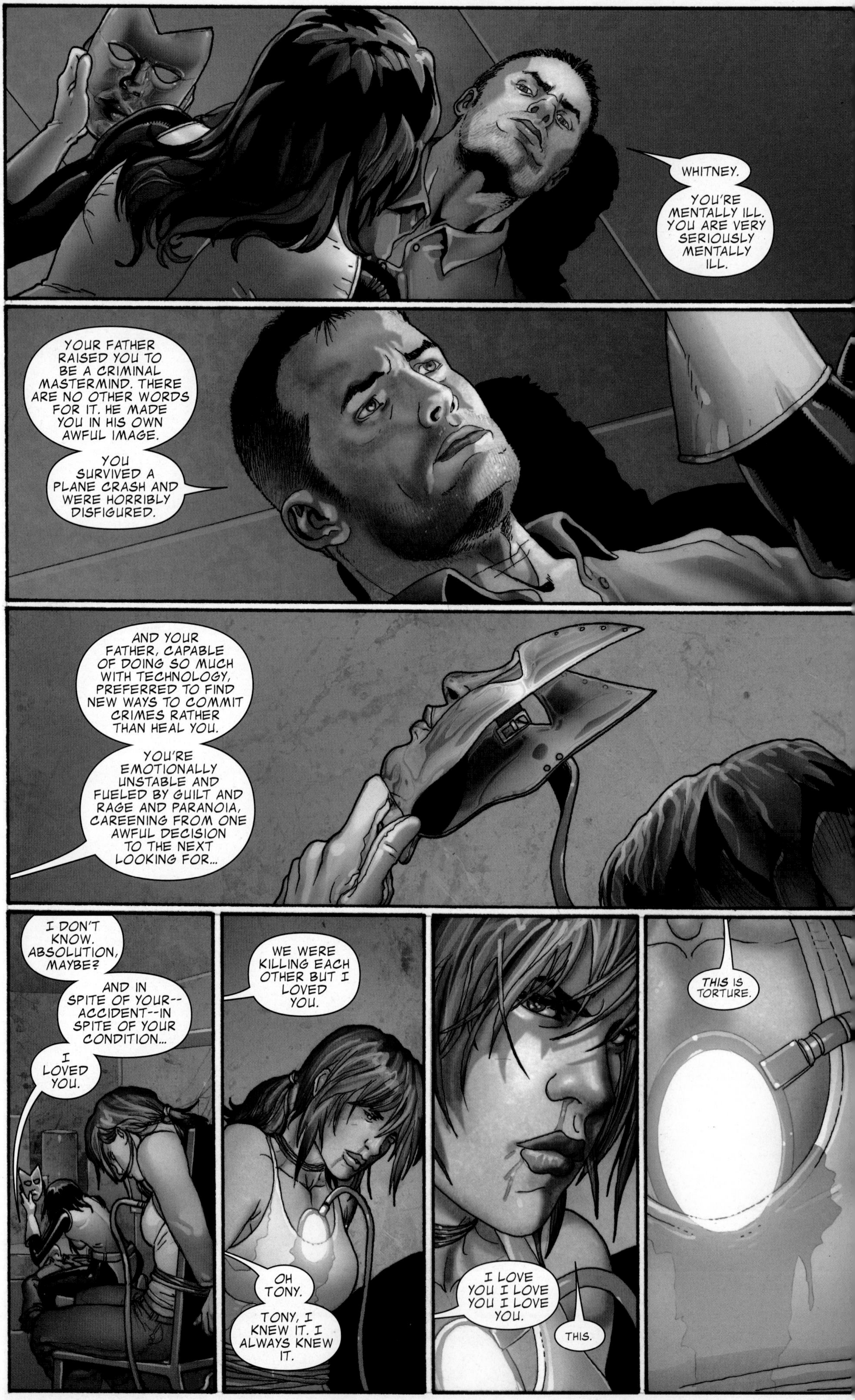
WHITNEY.
YOU'RE MENTALLY ILL. YOU ARE VERY SERIOUSLY MENTALLY ILL.
YOUR FATHER RAISED YOU TO BE A CRIMINAL MASTERMIND. THERE ARE NO OTHER WORDS FOR IT. HE MADE YOU IN HIS OWN AWFUL IMAGE.
YOU SURVIVED A PLANE CRASH AND WERE HORRIBLY DISFIGURED.
AND YOUR FATHER, CAPABLE OF DOING SO MUCH WITH TECHNOLOGY, PREFERRED TO FIND NEW WAYS TO COMMIT CRIMES RATHER THAN HEAL YOU.
YOU'RE EMOTIONALLY UNSTABLE AND FUELED BY GUILT AND RAGE AND PARANOIA, CAREENING FROM ONE AWFUL DECISION TO THE NEXT LOOKING FOR...
I DON'T KNOW. ABSOLUTION, MAYBE?
AND IN SPITE OF YOUR--ACCIDENT--IN SPITE OF YOUR CONDITION...
I LOVED YOU.
WE WERE KILLING EACH OTHER BUT I LOVED YOU.
OH TONY.
TONY, I KNEW IT. I ALWAYS KNEW IT.
I LOVE YOU I LOVE YOU I LOVE YOU.
THIS IS TORTURE.
THIS.

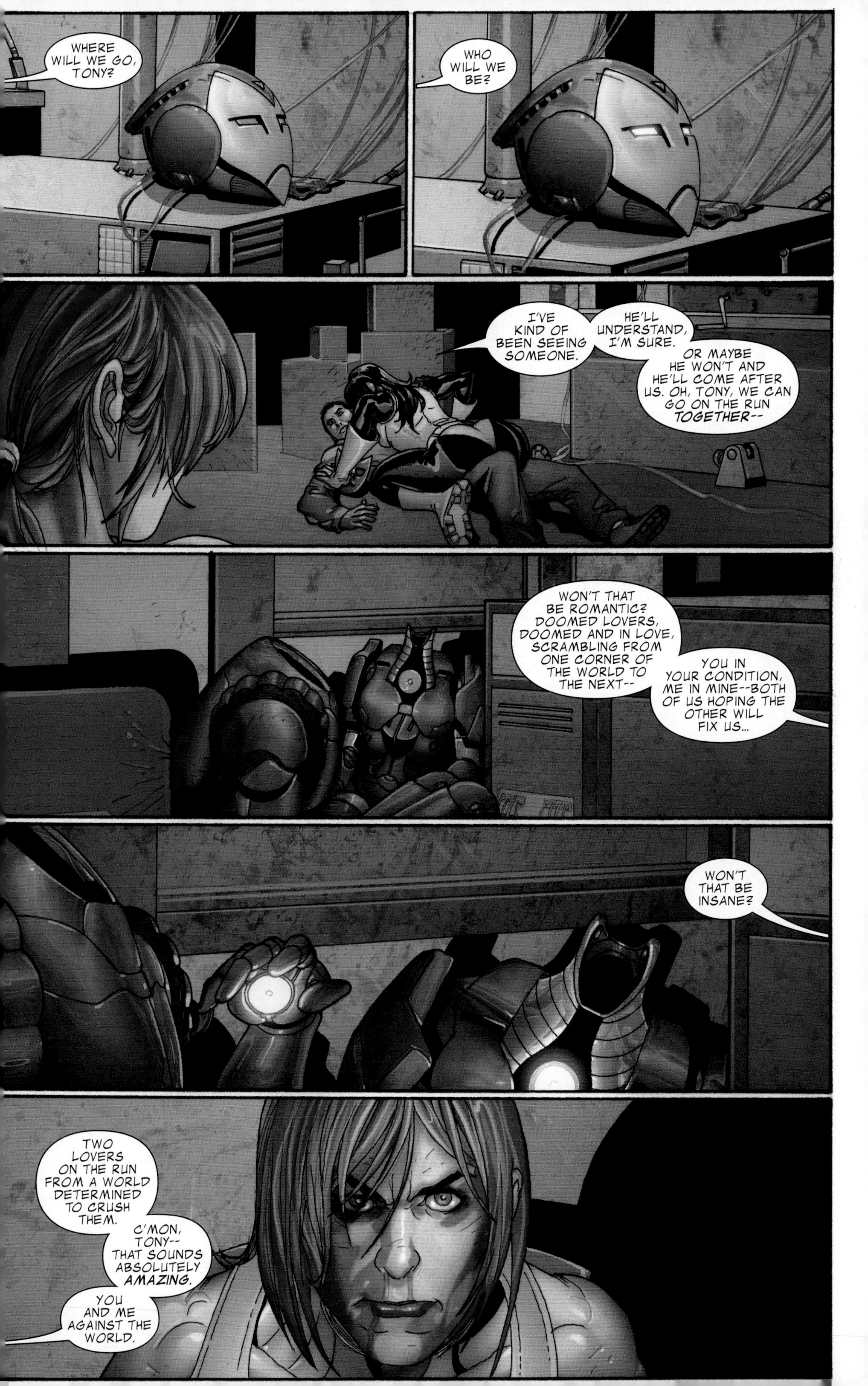
WHERE WILL WE GO, TONY?
WHO WILL WE BE?
I'VE KIND OF BEEN SEEING SOMEONE.
HE'LL UNDERSTAND, I'M SURE.
OR MAYBE HE WON'T AND HE'LL COME AFTER US. OH, TONY, WE CAN GO ON THE RUN *TOGETHER*--
WON'T THAT BE ROMANTIC? DOOMED LOVERS, DOOMED AND IN LOVE, SCRAMBLING FROM ONE CORNER OF THE WORLD TO THE NEXT--
YOU IN YOUR CONDITION, ME IN MINE--BOTH OF US HOPING THE OTHER WILL FIX US...
WON'T THAT BE INSANE?
TWO LOVERS ON THE RUN FROM A WORLD DETERMINED TO CRUSH THEM.
C'MON, TONY-- THAT SOUNDS ABSOLUTELY *AMAZING*.
YOU AND ME AGAINST THE WORLD.

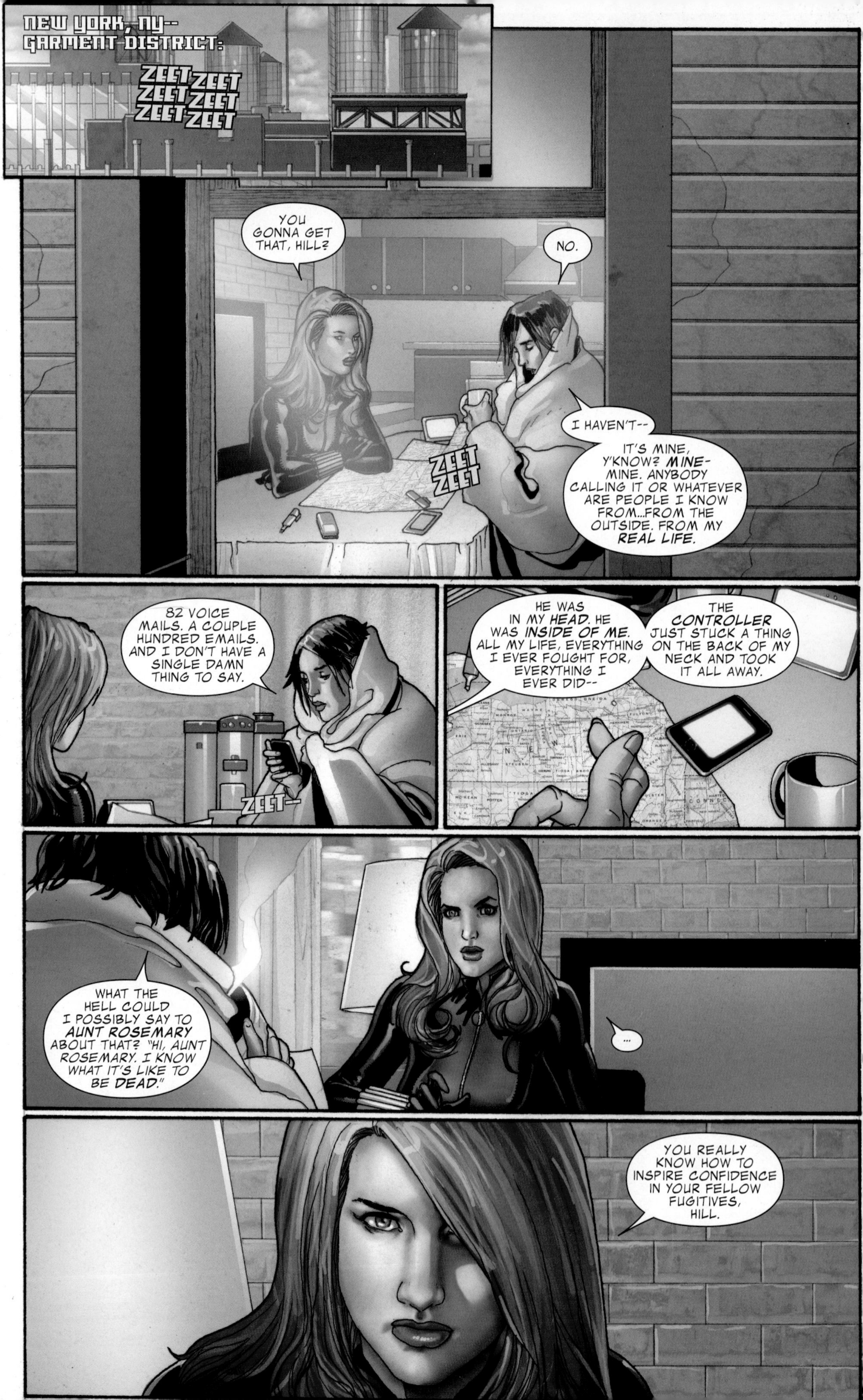
NEW YORK, NY--
GARMENT DISTRICT:
ZEET ZEET ZEET ZEET ZEET ZEET
YOU GONNA GET THAT, HILL?
NO.
I HAVEN'T--
ZEET ZEET
IT'S MINE, Y'KNOW? MINE-MINE. ANYBODY CALLING IT OR WHATEVER ARE PEOPLE I KNOW FROM...FROM THE OUTSIDE. FROM MY REAL LIFE.
82 VOICE MAILS. A COUPLE HUNDRED EMAILS. AND I DON'T HAVE A SINGLE DAMN THING TO SAY.
ZEET--
HE WAS IN MY HEAD. HE WAS INSIDE OF ME. ALL MY LIFE, EVERYTHING I EVER FOUGHT FOR, EVERYTHING I EVER DID--
THE CONTROLLER JUST STUCK A THING ON THE BACK OF MY NECK AND TOOK IT ALL AWAY.
WHAT THE HELL COULD I POSSIBLY SAY TO AUNT ROSEMARY ABOUT THAT? "HI, AUNT ROSEMARY. I KNOW WHAT IT'S LIKE TO BE DEAD."
...
YOU REALLY KNOW HOW TO INSPIRE CONFIDENCE IN YOUR FELLOW FUGITIVES, HILL.

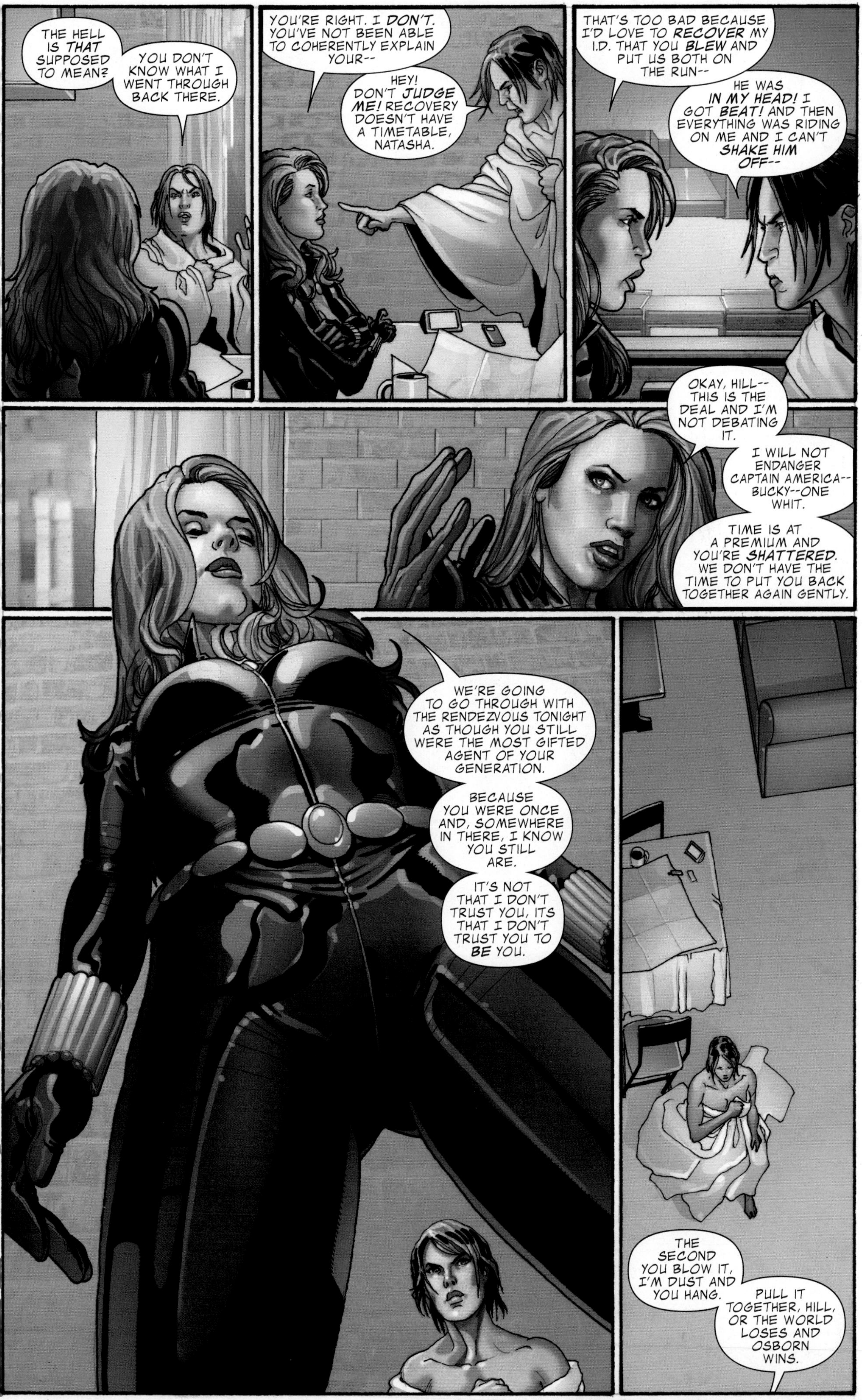

THE HELL IS THAT SUPPOSED TO MEAN?
YOU DON'T KNOW WHAT I WENT THROUGH BACK THERE.
YOU'RE RIGHT. I DON'T. YOU'VE NOT BEEN ABLE TO COHERENTLY EXPLAIN YOUR--
HEY! DON'T JUDGE ME! RECOVERY DOESN'T HAVE A TIMETABLE, NATASHA.
THAT'S TOO BAD BECAUSE I'D LOVE TO RECOVER MY I.D. THAT YOU BLEW AND PUT US BOTH ON THE RUN--
HE WAS IN MY HEAD! I GOT BEAT! AND THEN EVERYTHING WAS RIDING ON ME AND I CAN'T SHAKE HIM OFF--
OKAY, HILL-- THIS IS THE DEAL AND I'M NOT DEBATING IT.
I WILL NOT ENDANGER CAPTAIN AMERICA--BUCKY--ONE WHIT.
TIME IS AT A PREMIUM AND YOU'RE SHATTERED. WE DON'T HAVE THE TIME TO PUT YOU BACK TOGETHER AGAIN GENTLY.
WE'RE GOING TO GO THROUGH WITH THE RENDEZVOUS TONIGHT AS THOUGH YOU STILL WERE THE MOST GIFTED AGENT OF YOUR GENERATION.
BECAUSE YOU WERE ONCE AND, SOMEWHERE IN THERE, I KNOW YOU STILL ARE.
IT'S NOT THAT I DON'T TRUST YOU, ITS THAT I DON'T TRUST YOU TO BE YOU.
THE SECOND YOU BLOW IT, I'M DUST AND YOU HANG.
PULL IT TOGETHER, HILL, OR THE WORLD LOSES AND OSBORN WINS.

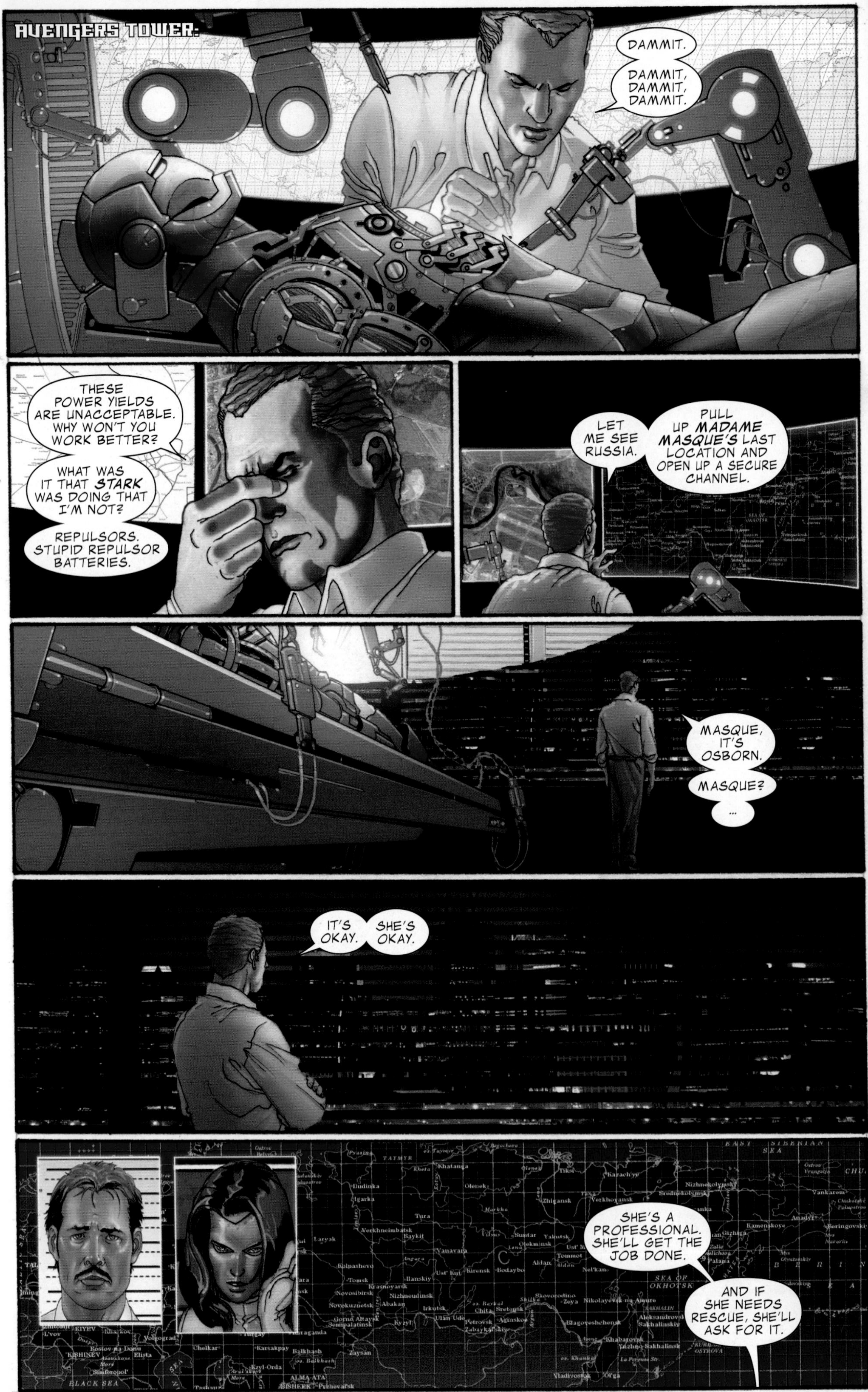
AVENGERS TOWER:
DAMMIT.
DAMMIT, DAMMIT, DAMMIT.
THESE POWER YIELDS ARE UNACCEPTABLE. WHY WON'T YOU WORK BETTER?
WHAT WAS IT THAT STARK WAS DOING THAT I'M NOT?
REPULSORS. STUPID REPULSOR BATTERIES.
LET ME SEE RUSSIA.
PULL UP MADAME MASQUE'S LAST LOCATION AND OPEN UP A SECURE CHANNEL.
MASQUE, IT'S OSBORN.
MASQUE?
...
IT'S OKAY.
SHE'S OKAY.
SHE'S A PROFESSIONAL. SHE'LL GET THE JOB DONE.
AND IF SHE NEEDS RESCUE, SHE'LL ASK FOR IT.

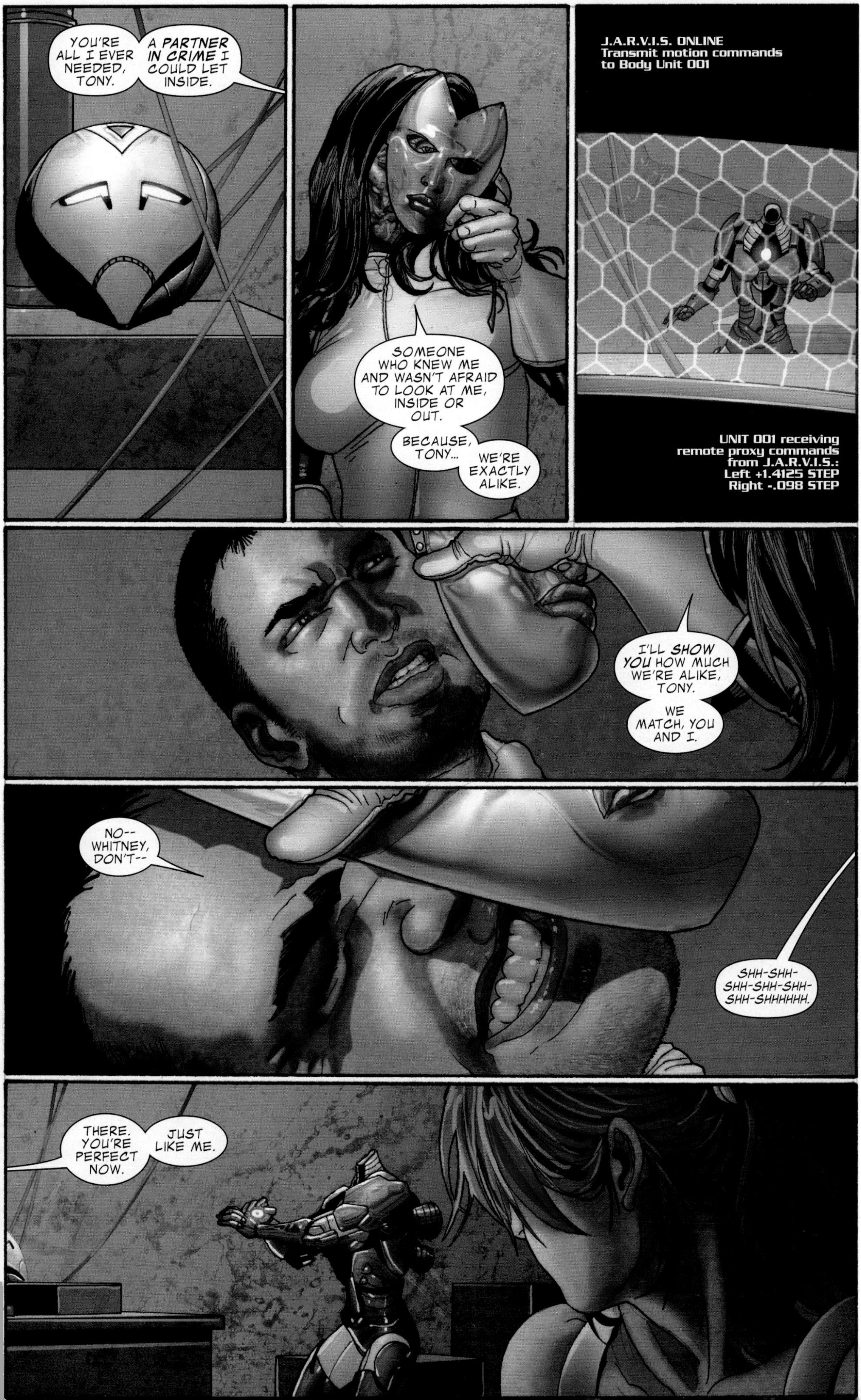

YOU'RE ALL I EVER NEEDED, TONY.
A PARTNER IN CRIME I COULD LET INSIDE.
SOMEONE WHO KNEW ME AND WASN'T AFRAID TO LOOK AT ME, INSIDE OR OUT.
BECAUSE, TONY...
WE'RE EXACTLY ALIKE.
J.A.R.V.I.S. ONLINE
Transmit motion commands to Body Unit 001
UNIT 001 receiving remote proxy commands from J.A.R.V.I.S.:
Left +1.4125 STEP
Right -.098 STEP
I'LL SHOW YOU HOW MUCH WE'RE ALIKE, TONY.
WE MATCH, YOU AND I.
NO-- WHITNEY, DON'T--
SHH-SHH-SHH-SHH-SHH-SHH-SHHHHHH.
THERE. YOU'RE PERFECT NOW.
JUST LIKE ME.

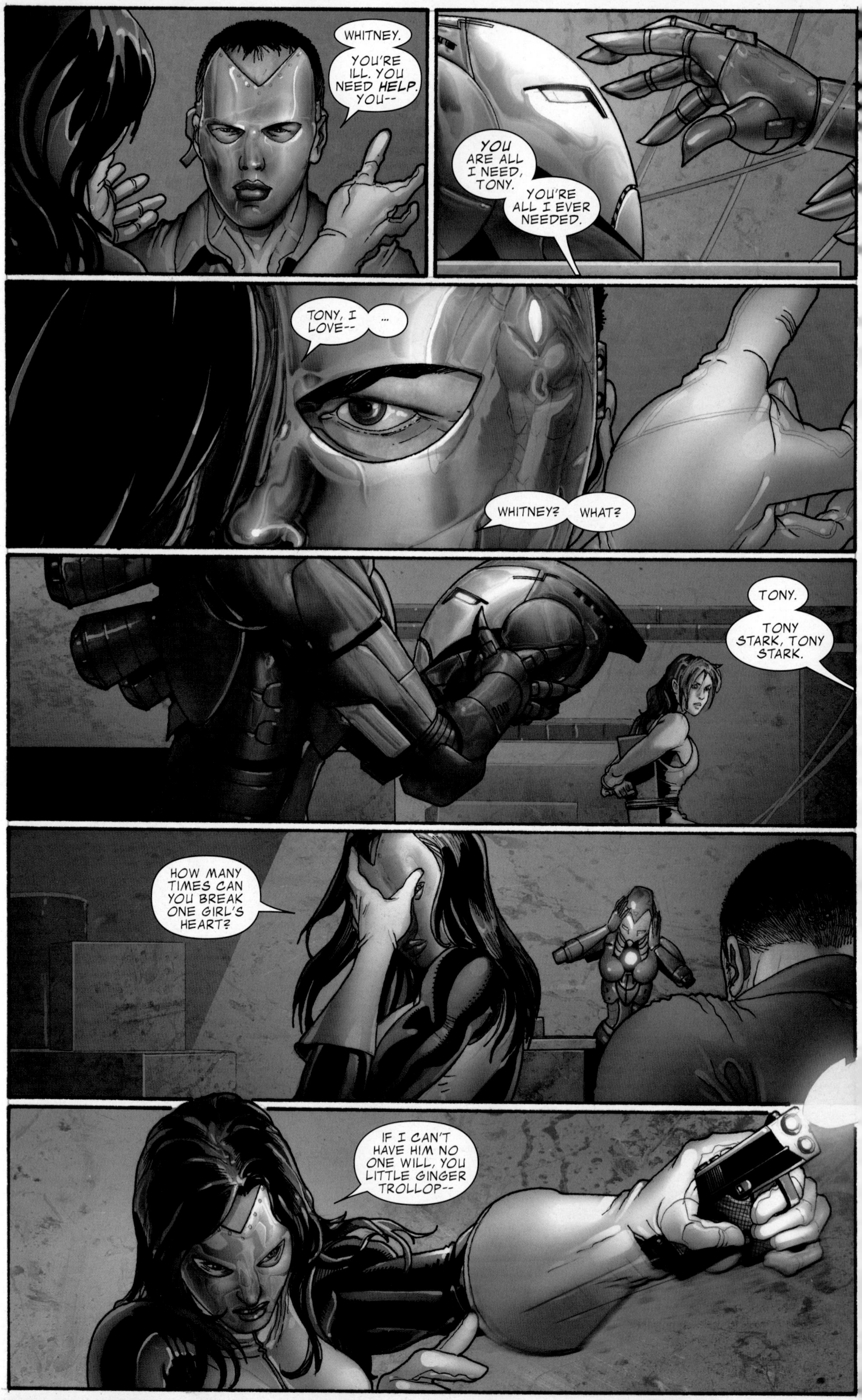
WHITNEY.
YOU'RE ILL. YOU NEED HELP. YOU--
YOU ARE ALL I NEED, TONY.
YOU'RE ALL I EVER NEEDED.
TONY, I LOVE--
...
WHITNEY?
WHAT?
TONY.
TONY STARK, TONY STARK.
HOW MANY TIMES CAN YOU BREAK ONE GIRL'S HEART?
IF I CAN'T HAVE HIM NO ONE WILL, YOU LITTLE GINGER TROLLOP--

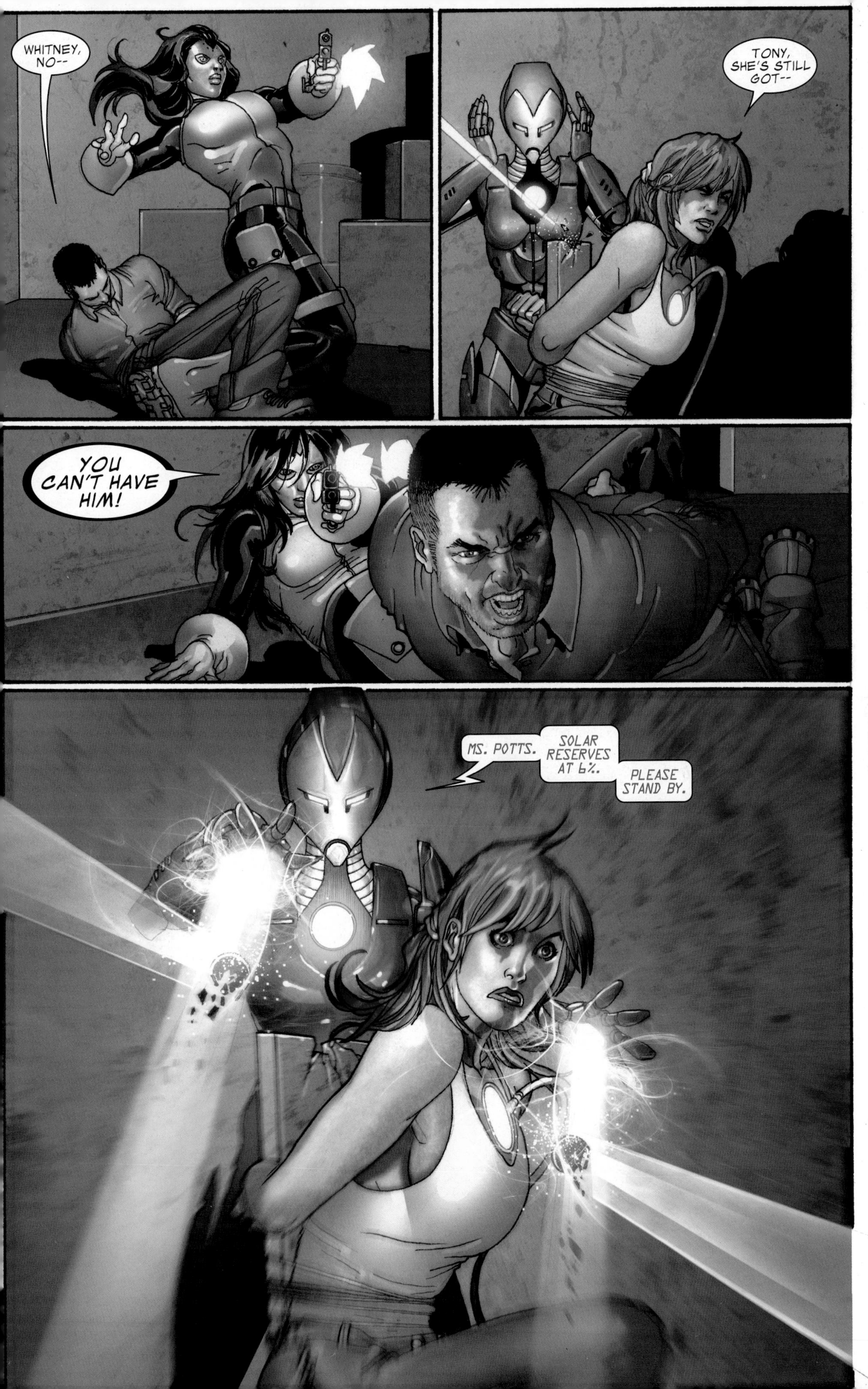
WHITNEY, NO--
TONY, SHE'S STILL GOT--
YOU CAN'T HAVE HIM!
MS. POTTS.
SOLAR RESERVES AT 6%.
PLEASE STAND BY.

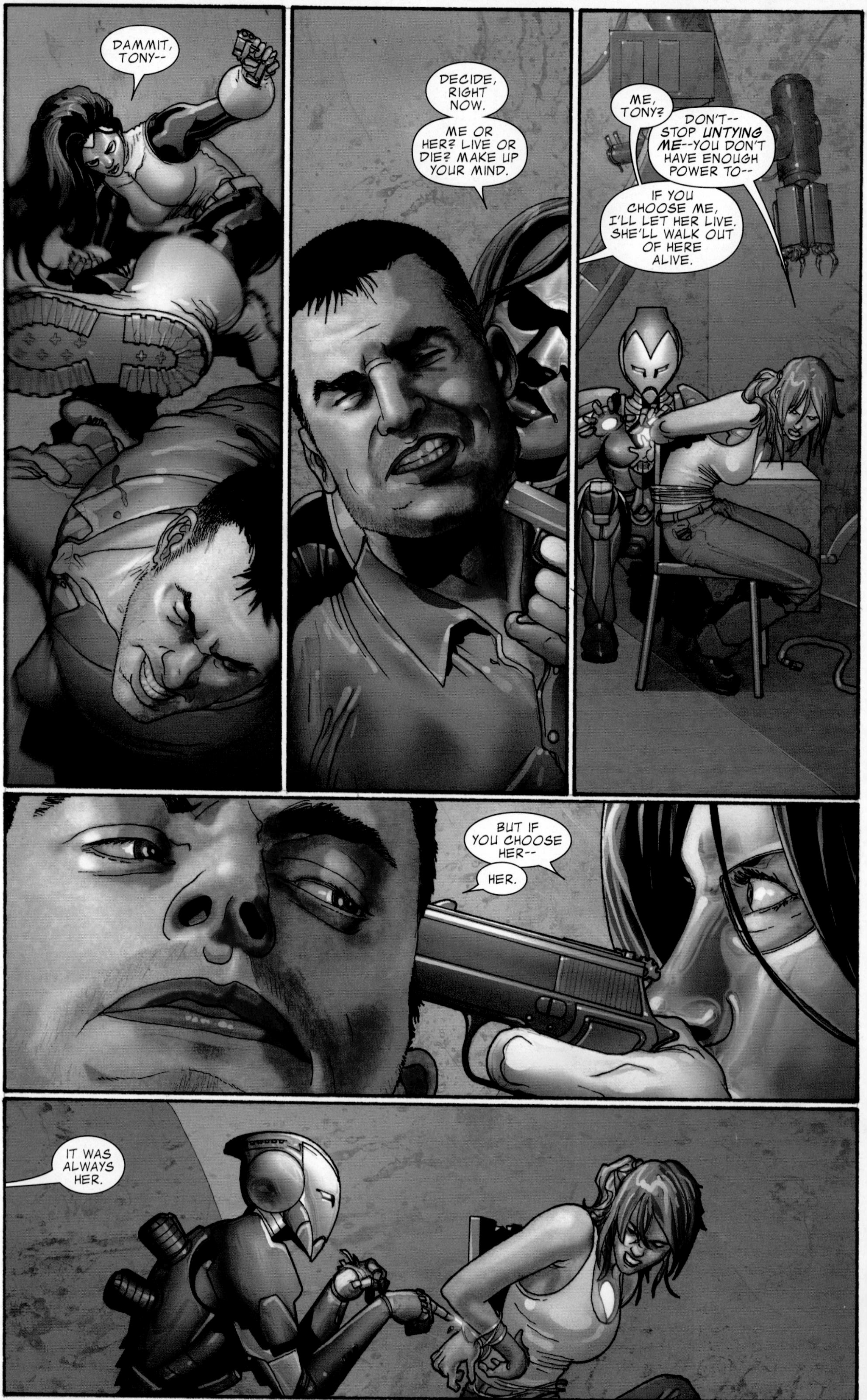
DAMMIT, TONY--
DECIDE, RIGHT NOW.
ME OR HER? LIVE OR DIE? MAKE UP YOUR MIND.
ME, TONY?
DON'T-- STOP UNTYING ME--YOU DON'T HAVE ENOUGH POWER TO--
IF YOU CHOOSE ME, I'LL LET HER LIVE. SHE'LL WALK OUT OF HERE ALIVE.
BUT IF YOU CHOOSE HER--
HER.
IT WAS ALWAYS HER.

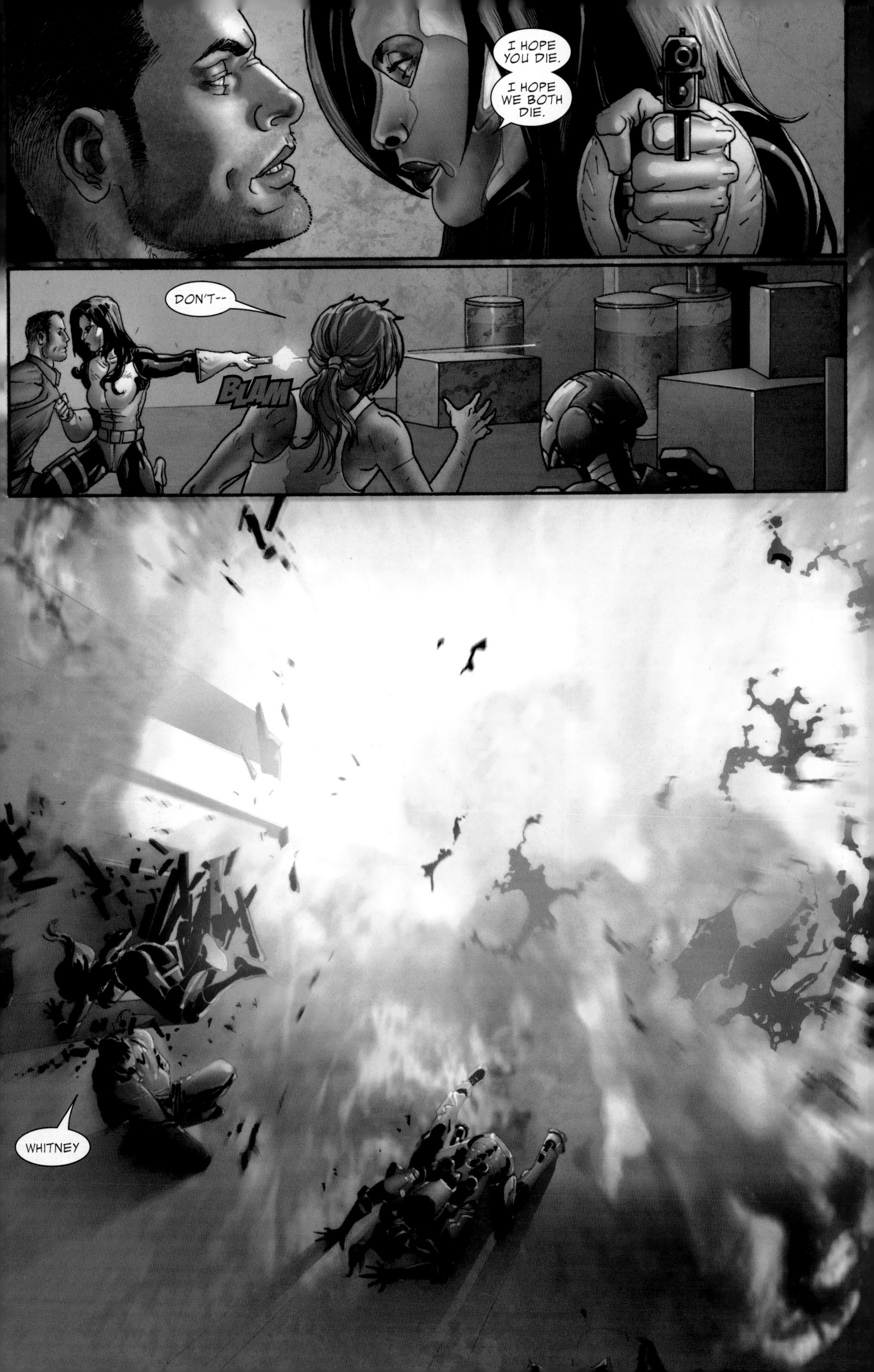
I HOPE YOU DIE.
I HOPE WE BOTH DIE.
DON'T--
BLAM
WHITNEY

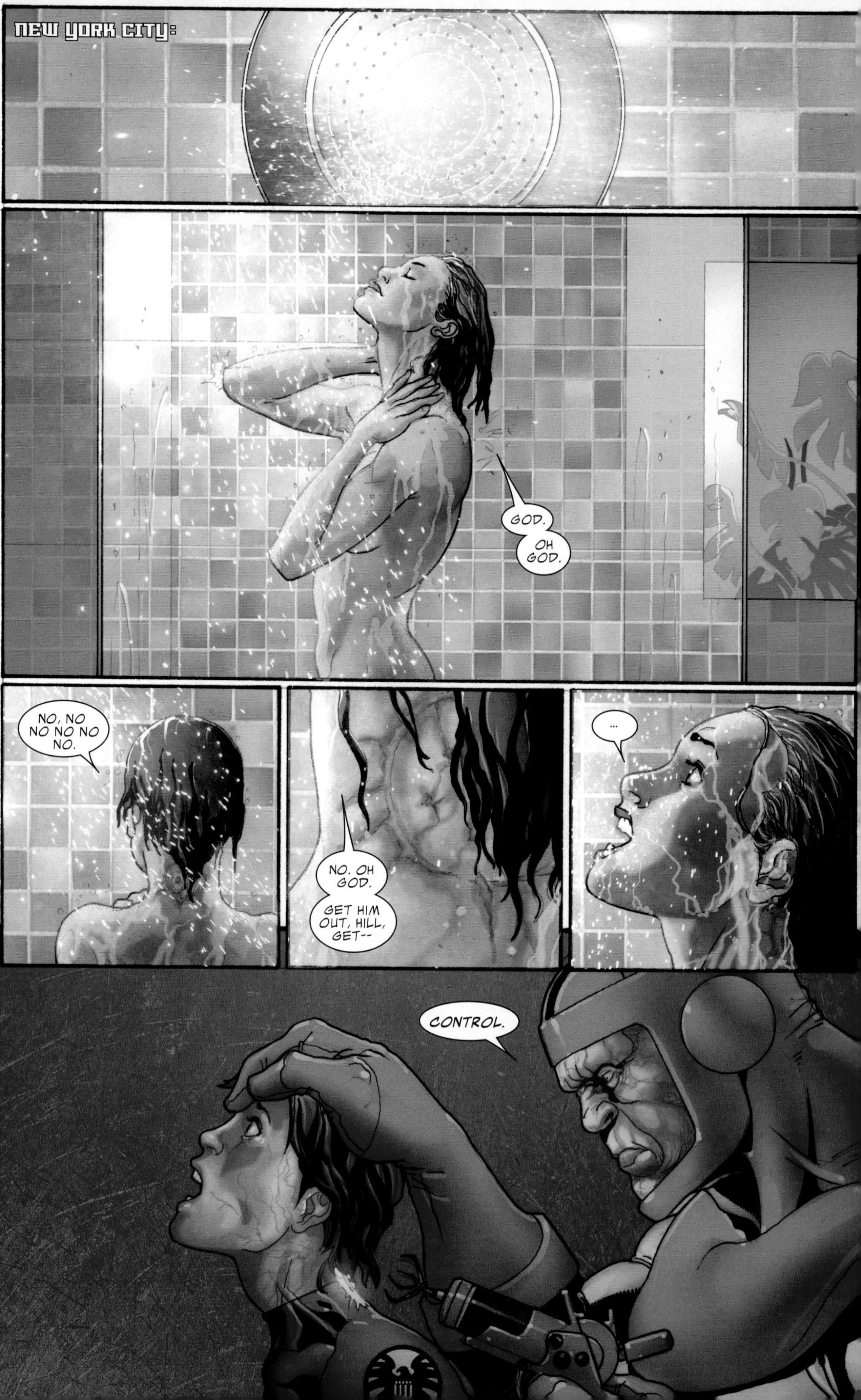
NEW YORK CITY:
GOD.
OH GOD.
NO, NO NO NO NO NO.
NO. OH GOD.
GET HIM OUT, HILL, GET--
...
CONTROL.

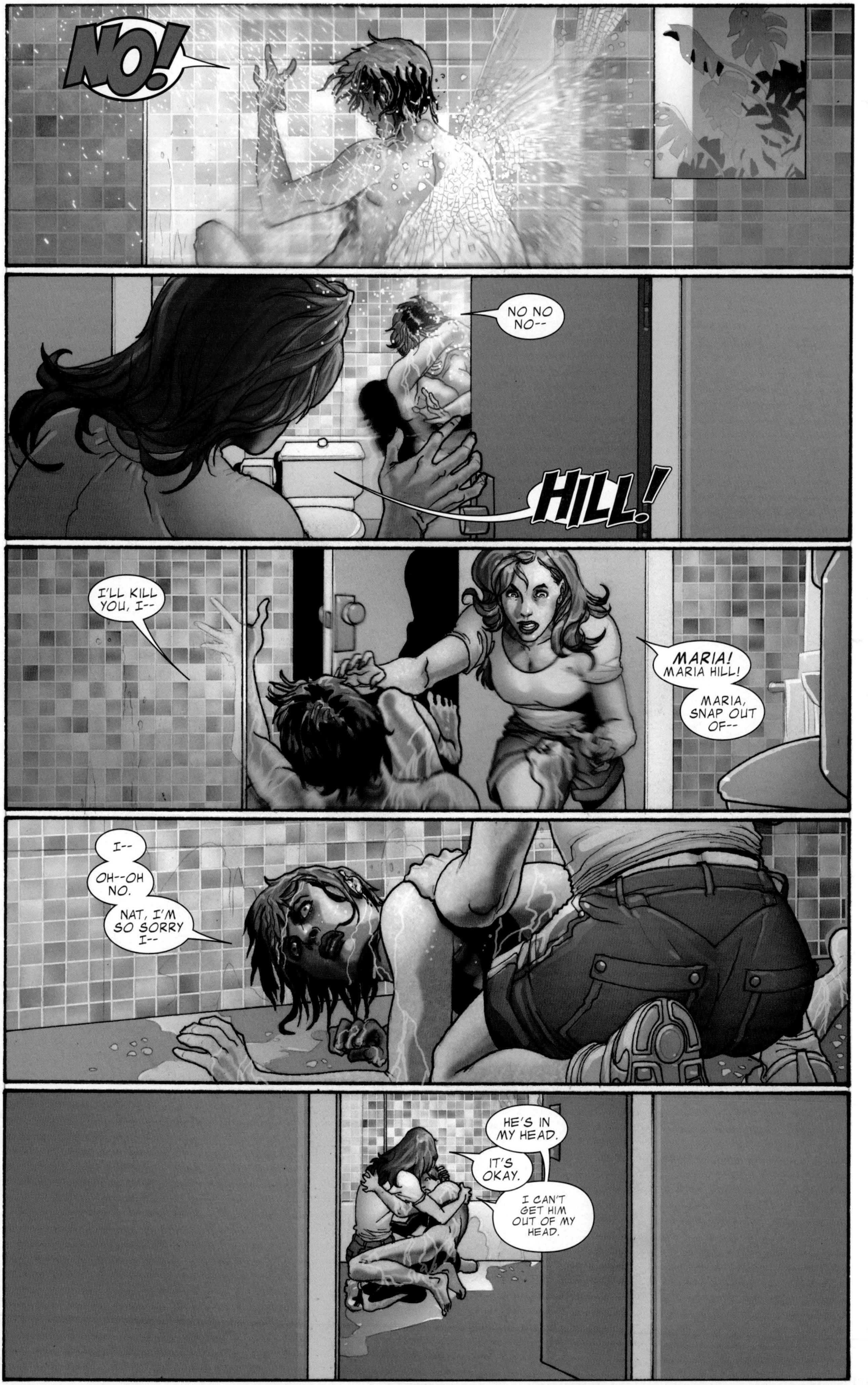
NO!
NO NO NO--
HILL!
I'LL KILL YOU, I--
MARIA! MARIA HILL!
MARIA, SNAP OUT OF--
I--
OH--OH NO.
NAT, I'M SO SORRY I--
HE'S IN MY HEAD.
IT'S OKAY.
I CAN'T GET HIM OUT OF MY HEAD.

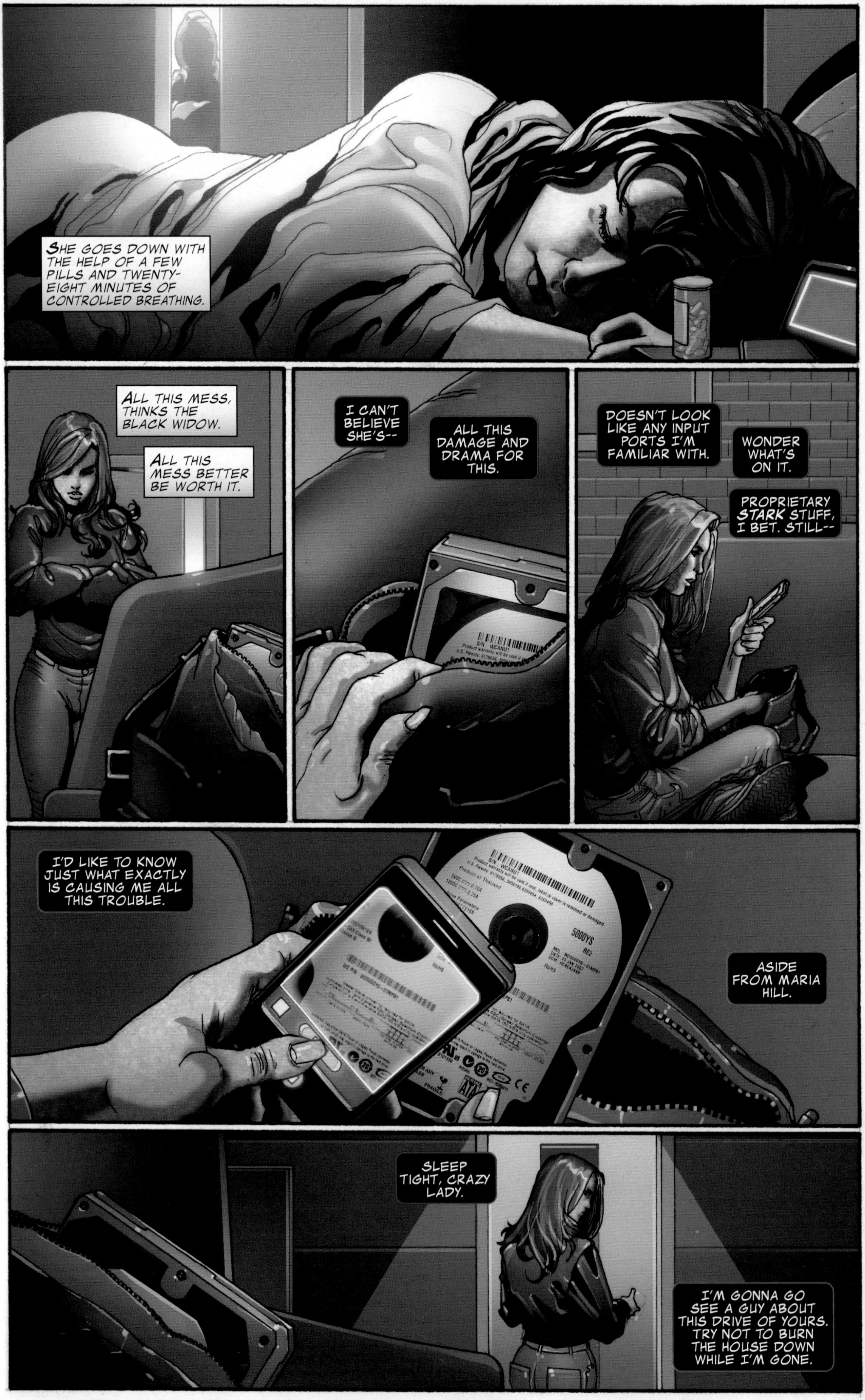
SHE GOES DOWN WITH THE HELP OF A FEW PILLS AND TWENTY-EIGHT MINUTES OF CONTROLLED BREATHING.
ALL THIS MESS, THINKS THE BLACK WIDOW.
ALL THIS MESS BETTER BE WORTH IT.
I CAN'T BELIEVE SHE'S--
ALL THIS DAMAGE AND DRAMA FOR THIS.
DOESN'T LOOK LIKE ANY INPUT PORTS I'M FAMILIAR WITH.
WONDER WHAT'S ON IT.
PROPRIETARY STARK STUFF, I BET. STILL--
I'D LIKE TO KNOW JUST WHAT EXACTLY IS CAUSING ME ALL THIS TROUBLE.
ASIDE FROM MARIA HILL.
SLEEP TIGHT, CRAZY LADY.
I'M GONNA GO SEE A GUY ABOUT THIS DRIVE OF YOURS. TRY NOT TO BURN THE HOUSE DOWN WHILE I'M GONE.

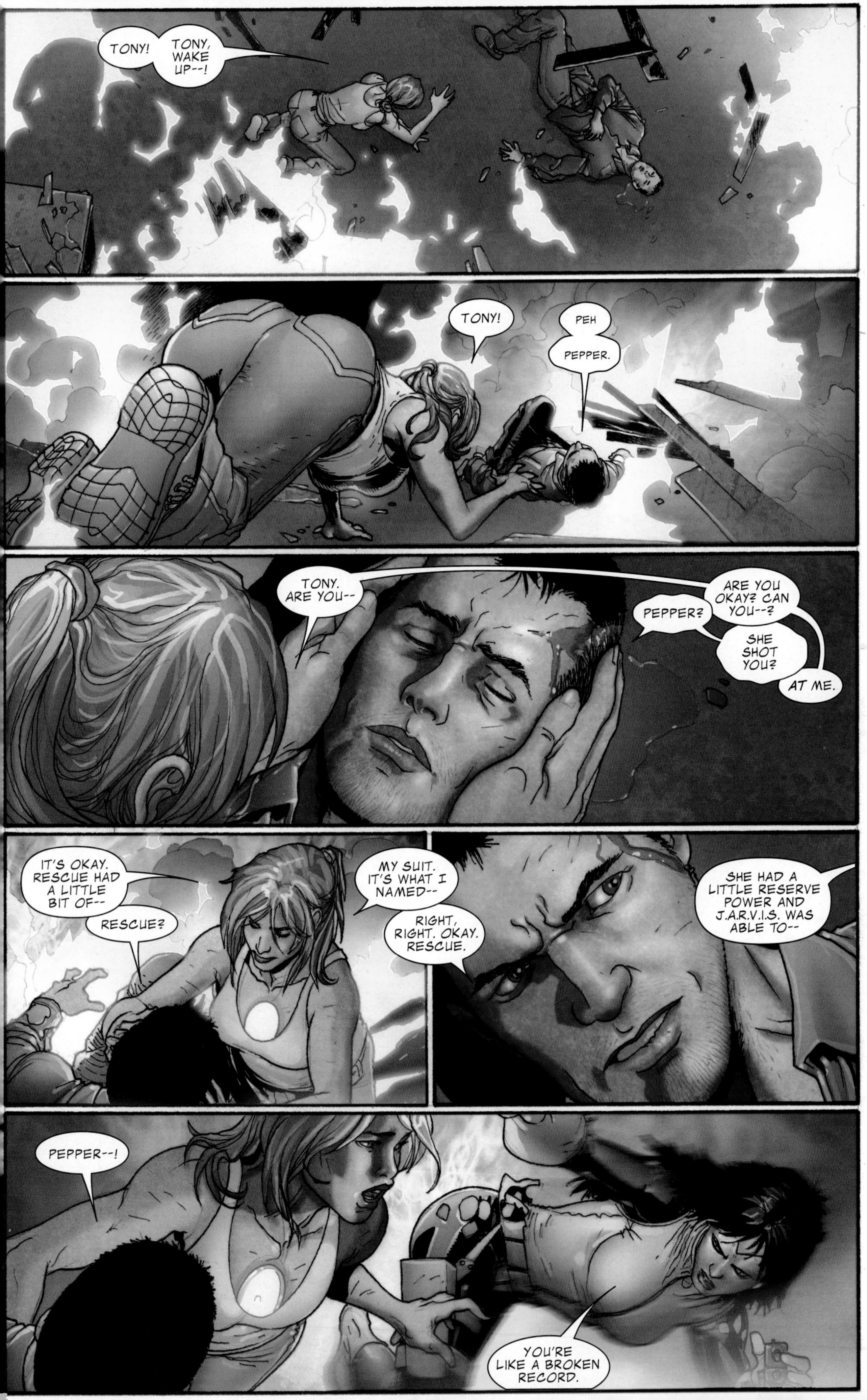
TONY!
TONY, WAKE UP--!
TONY!
PEH
PEPPER.
TONY. ARE YOU--
ARE YOU OKAY? CAN YOU--?
PEPPER?
SHE SHOT YOU?
AT ME.
IT'S OKAY. RESCUE HAD A LITTLE BIT OF--
RESCUE?
MY SUIT. IT'S WHAT I NAMED--
RIGHT, RIGHT. OKAY. RESCUE.
SHE HAD A LITTLE RESERVE POWER AND J.A.R.V.I.S. WAS ABLE TO--
PEPPER--!
YOU'RE LIKE A BROKEN RECORD.

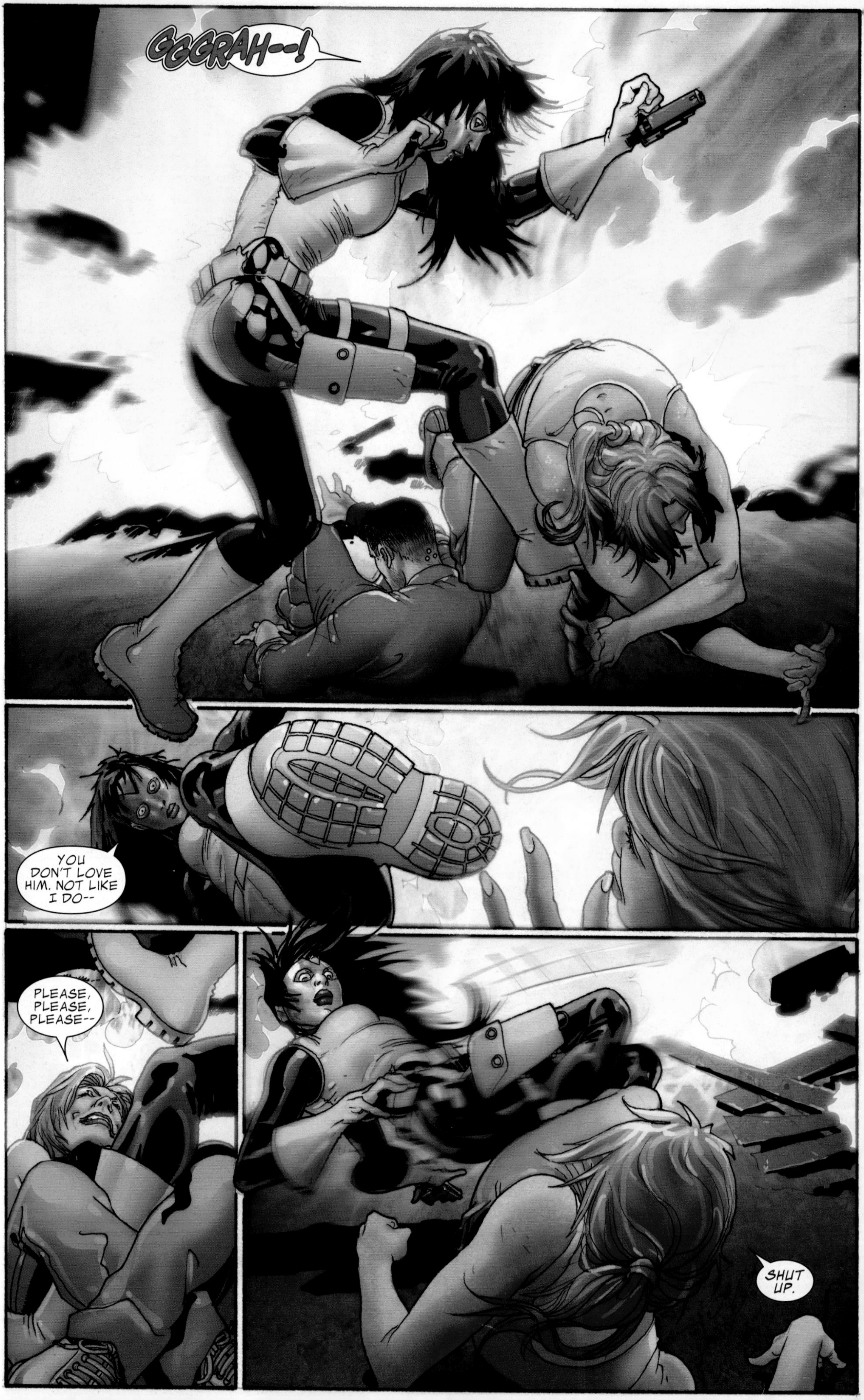
GGGRAH--!
YOU DON'T LOVE HIM. NOT LIKE I DO--
PLEASE, PLEASE, PLEASE--
SHUT UP.

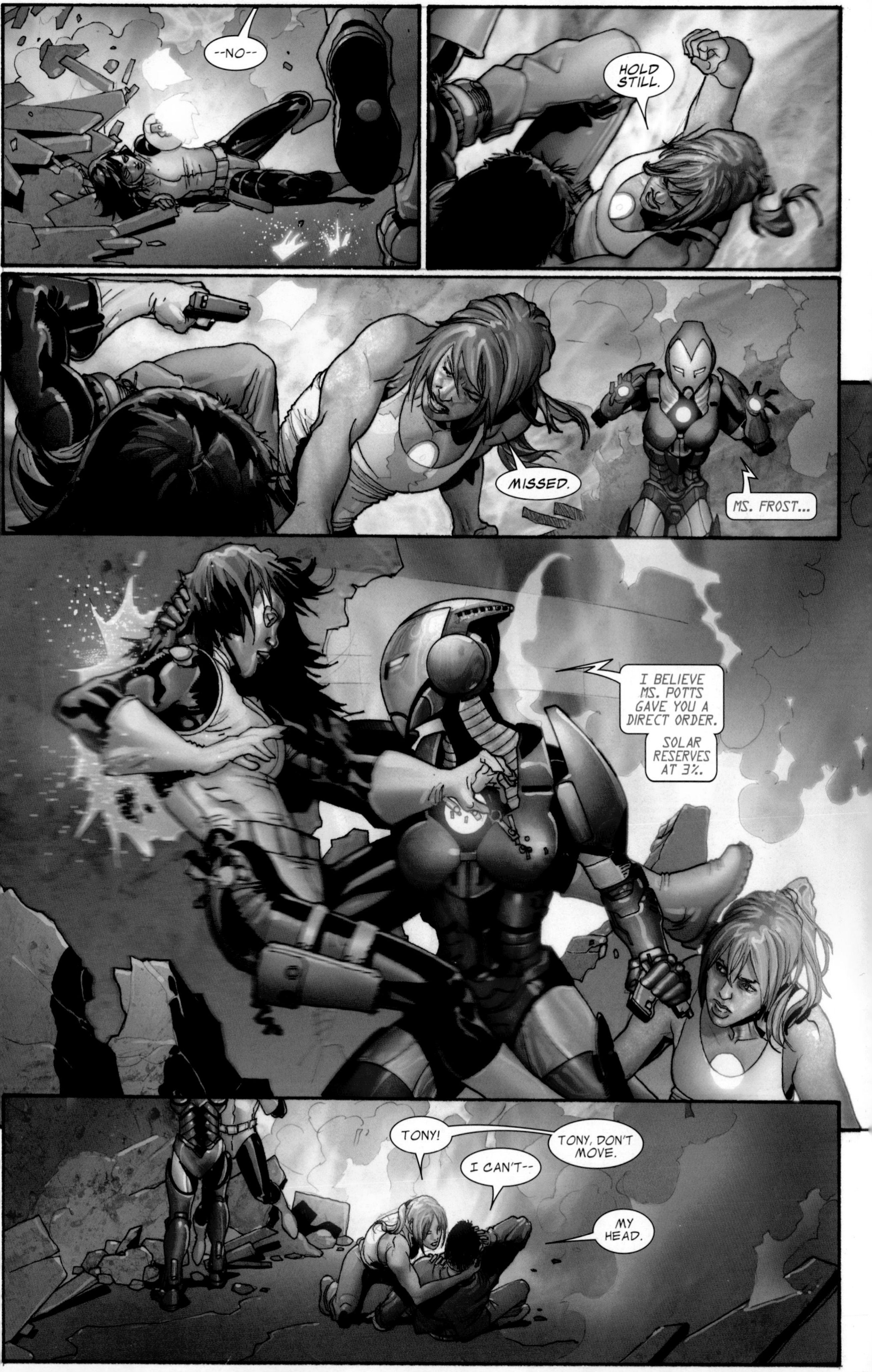
--NO--
HOLD STILL.
MISSED.
MS. FROST...
I BELIEVE MS. POTTS GAVE YOU A DIRECT ORDER.
SOLAR RESERVES AT 3%.
TONY!
TONY, DON'T MOVE.
I CAN'T--
MY HEAD.

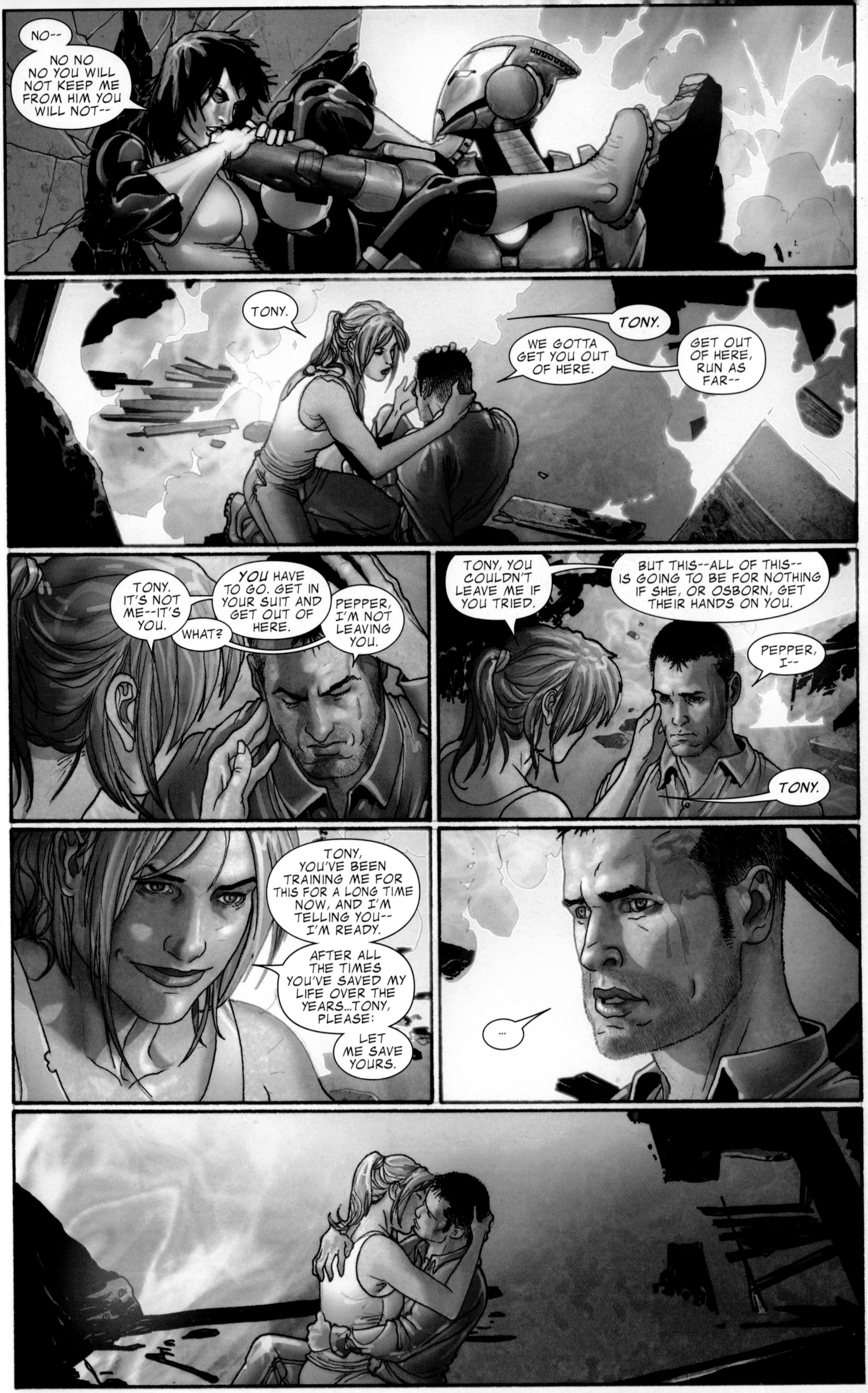
NO--
NO NO NO YOU WILL NOT KEEP ME FROM HIM YOU WILL NOT--
TONY.
TONY.
WE GOTTA GET YOU OUT OF HERE.
GET OUT OF HERE, RUN AS FAR--
TONY. IT'S NOT ME--IT'S YOU.
WHAT?
YOU HAVE TO GO. GET IN YOUR SUIT AND GET OUT OF HERE.
PEPPER, I'M NOT LEAVING YOU.
TONY, YOU COULDN'T LEAVE ME IF YOU TRIED.
BUT THIS--ALL OF THIS--IS GOING TO BE FOR NOTHING IF SHE, OR OSBORN, GET THEIR HANDS ON YOU.
PEPPER, I--
TONY.
TONY, YOU'VE BEEN TRAINING ME FOR THIS FOR A LONG TIME NOW, AND I'M TELLING YOU--I'M READY.
AFTER ALL THE TIMES YOU'VE SAVED MY LIFE OVER THE YEARS...TONY, PLEASE:
LET ME SAVE YOURS.
...

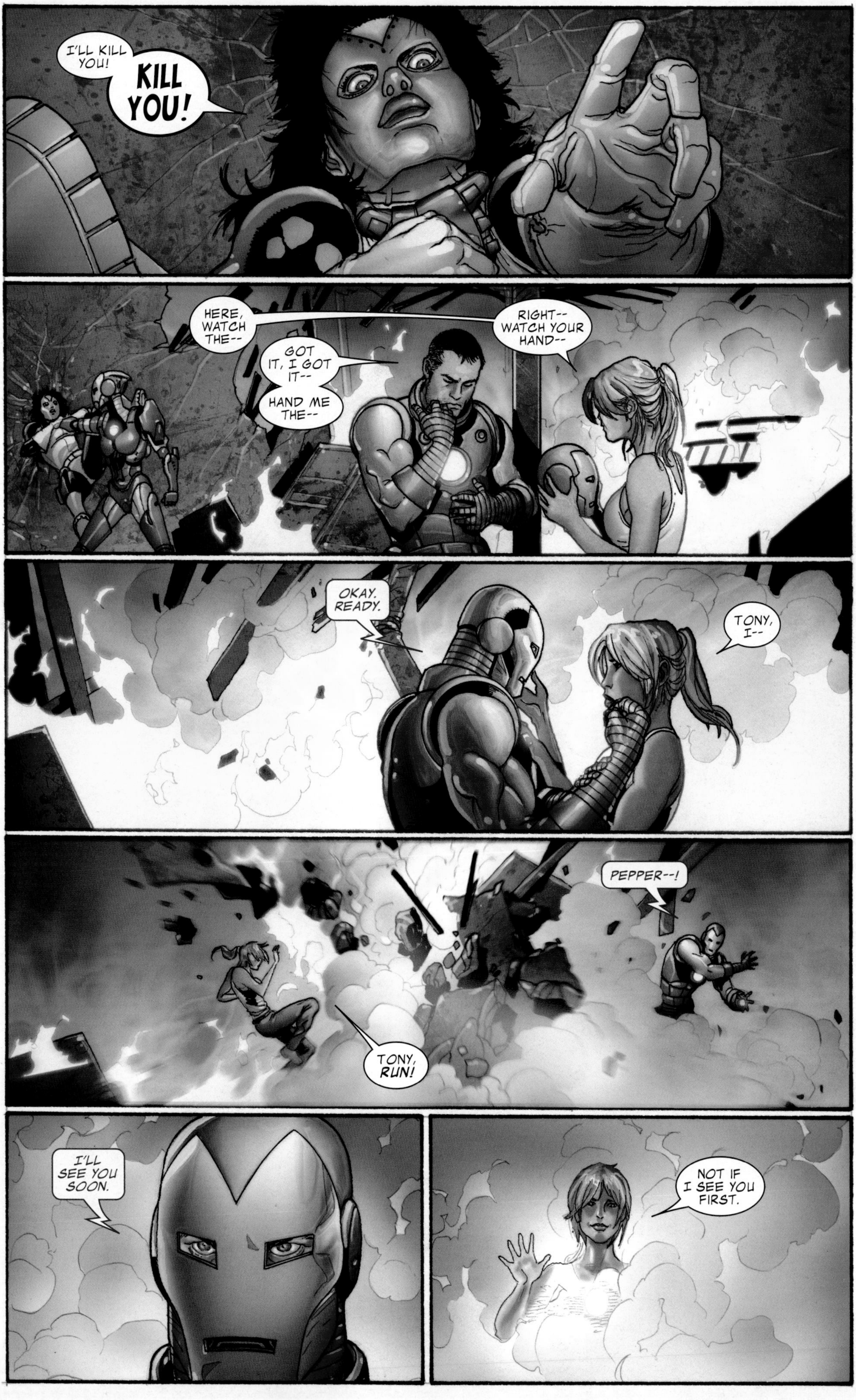
I'LL KILL YOU! KILL YOU!
HERE, WATCH THE--
RIGHT-- WATCH YOUR HAND--
GOT IT, I GOT IT--
HAND ME THE--
OKAY. READY.
TONY, I--
PEPPER--!
TONY, RUN!
I'LL SEE YOU SOON.
NOT IF I SEE YOU FIRST.

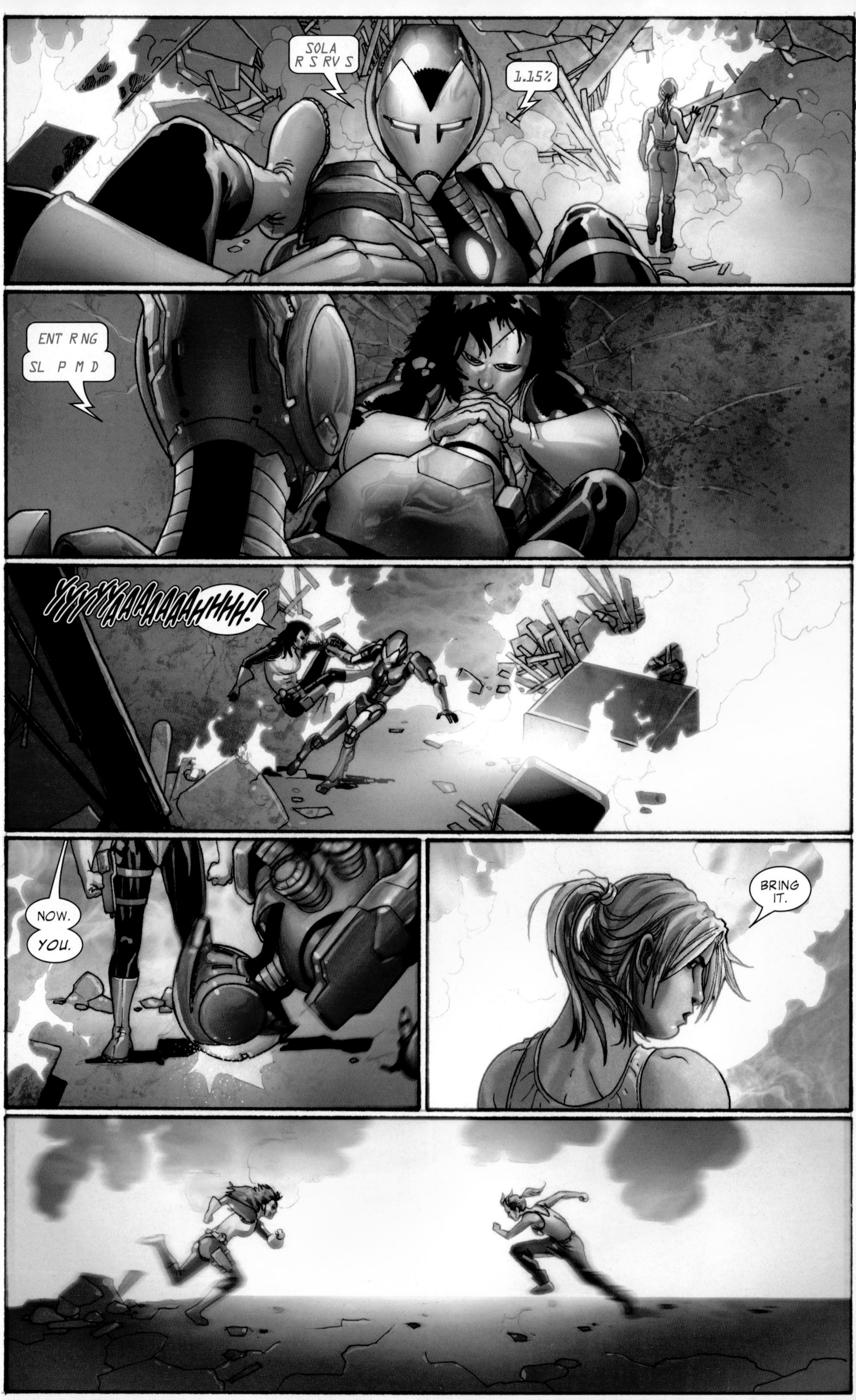
SOLA
R S RV S
1.15%
ENT RNG
SL P M D
YYYYYAAAAAAAHHHH!
NOW.
YOU.
BRING IT.

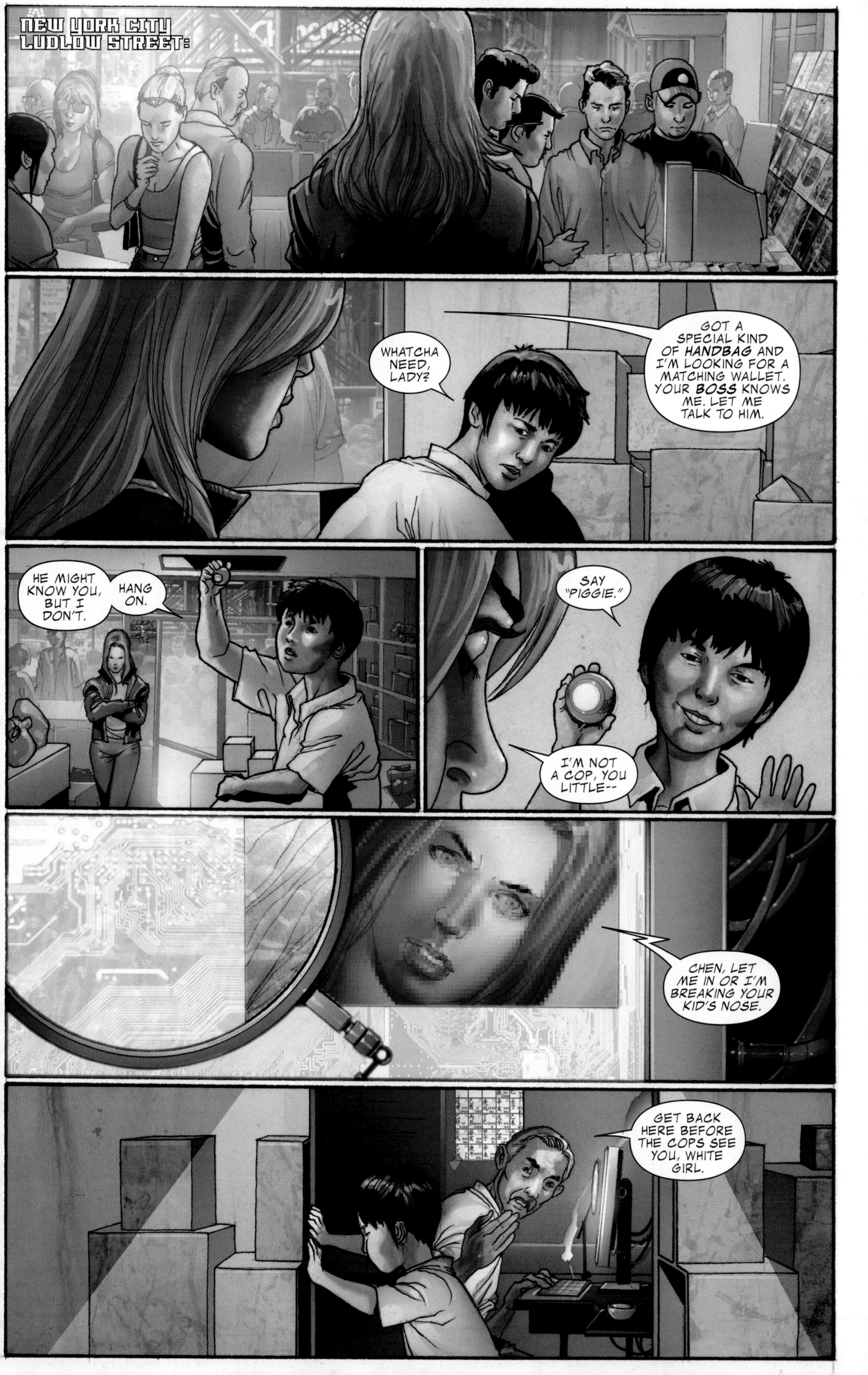
NEW YORK CITY
LUDLOW STREET:
WHATCHA NEED, LADY?
GOT A SPECIAL KIND OF HANDBAG AND I'M LOOKING FOR A MATCHING WALLET. YOUR BOSS KNOWS ME. LET ME TALK TO HIM.
HE MIGHT KNOW YOU, BUT I DON'T.
HANG ON.
SAY "PIGGIE."
I'M NOT A COP, YOU LITTLE--
CHEN, LET ME IN OR I'M BREAKING YOUR KID'S NOSE.
GET BACK HERE BEFORE THE COPS SEE YOU, WHITE GIRL.

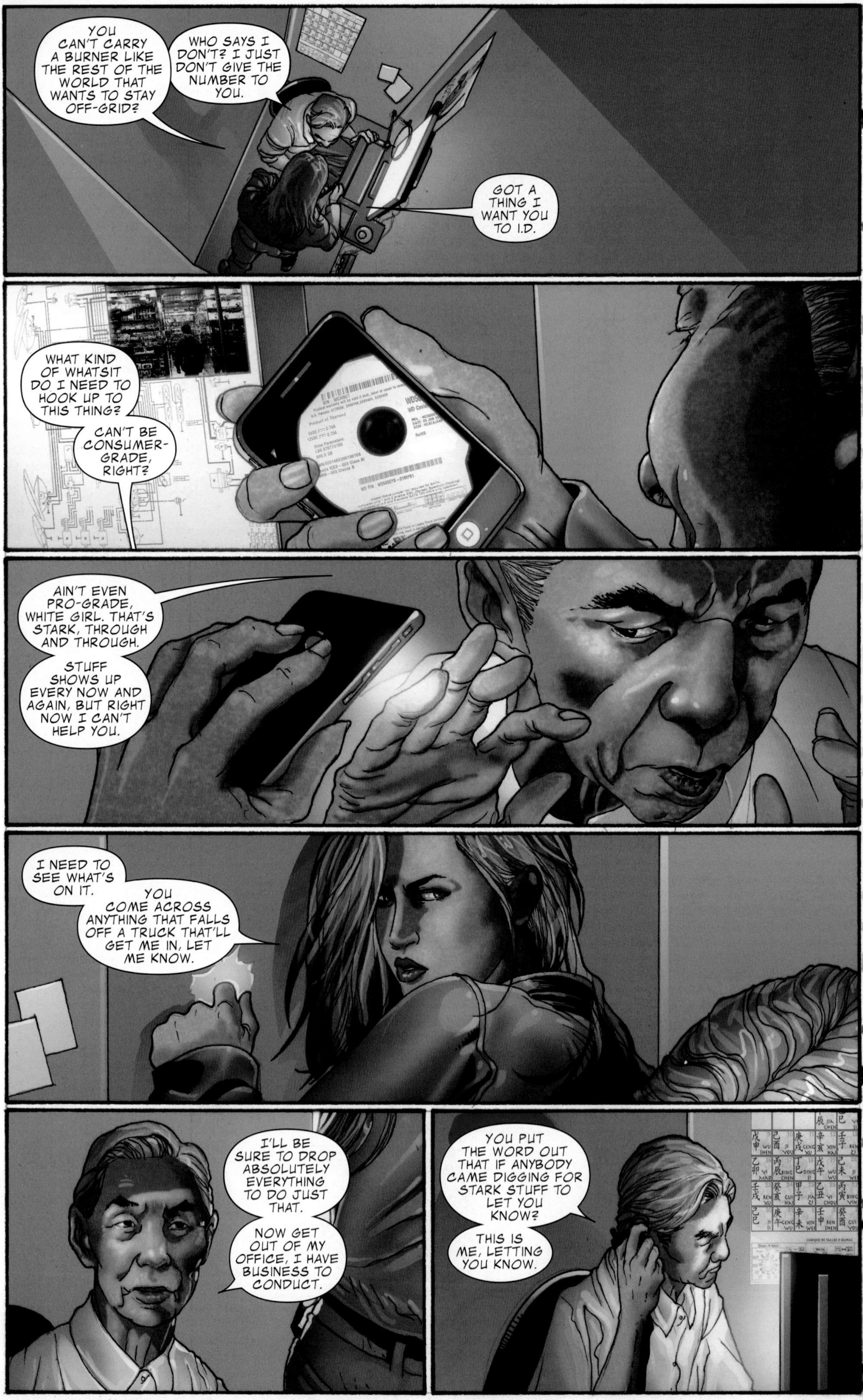
YOU CAN'T CARRY A BURNER LIKE THE REST OF THE WORLD THAT WANTS TO STAY OFF-GRID?
WHO SAYS I DON'T? I JUST DON'T GIVE THE NUMBER TO YOU.
GOT A THING I WANT YOU TO I.D.
WHAT KIND OF WHATSIT DO I NEED TO HOOK UP TO THIS THING?
CAN'T BE CONSUMER-GRADE, RIGHT?
AIN'T EVEN PRO-GRADE, WHITE GIRL. THAT'S STARK, THROUGH AND THROUGH.
STUFF SHOWS UP EVERY NOW AND AGAIN, BUT RIGHT NOW I CAN'T HELP YOU.
I NEED TO SEE WHAT'S ON IT.
YOU COME ACROSS ANYTHING THAT FALLS OFF A TRUCK THAT'LL GET ME IN, LET ME KNOW.
I'LL BE SURE TO DROP ABSOLUTELY EVERYTHING TO DO JUST THAT.
NOW GET OUT OF MY OFFICE, I HAVE BUSINESS TO CONDUCT.
YOU PUT THE WORD OUT THAT IF ANYBODY CAME DIGGING FOR STARK STUFF TO LET YOU KNOW?
THIS IS ME, LETTING YOU KNOW.

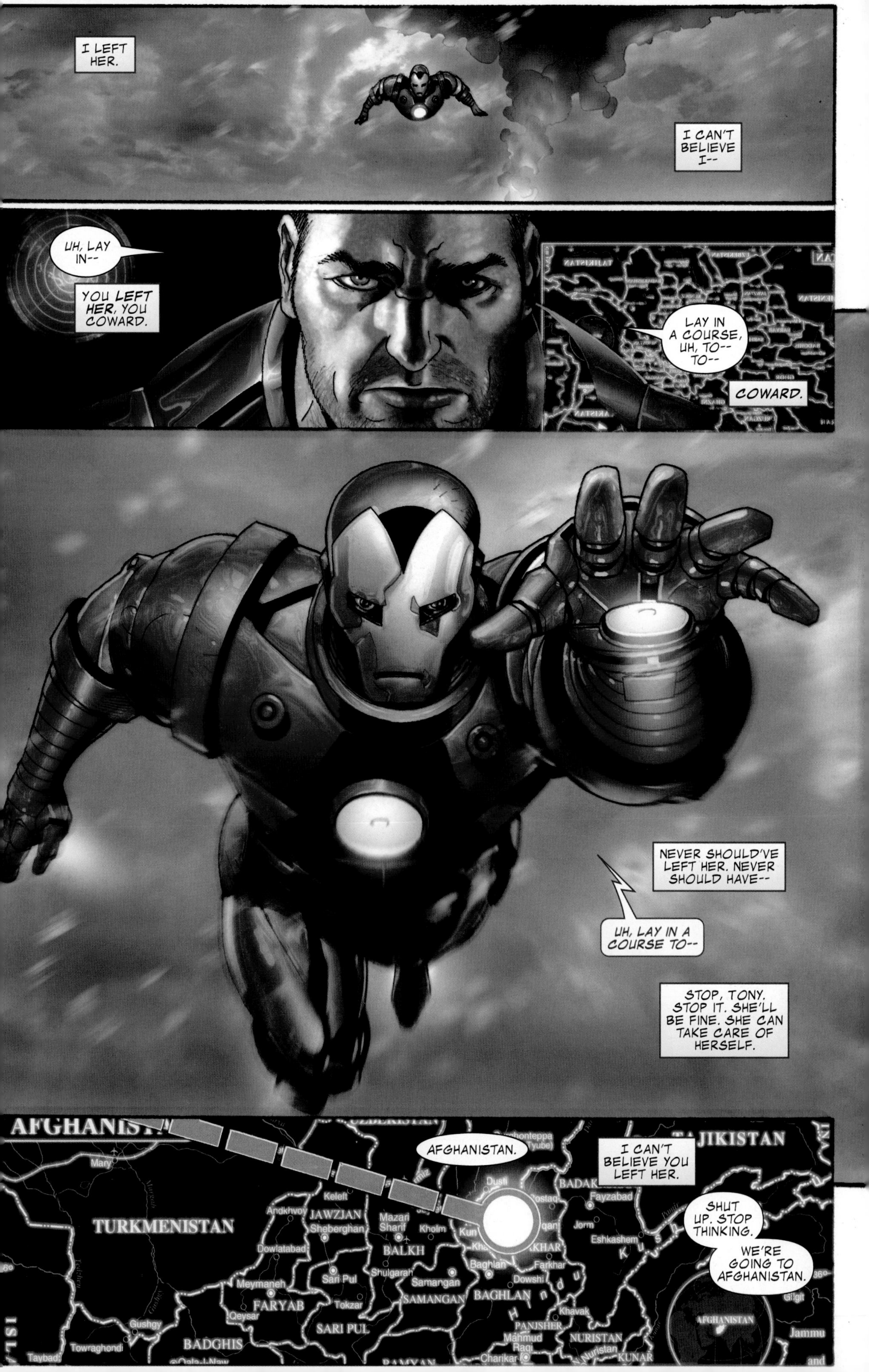
I LEFT HER.
I CAN'T BELIEVE I--
UH, LAY IN--
YOU LEFT HER, YOU COWARD.
LAY IN A COURSE, UH, TO-- TO--
COWARD.
NEVER SHOULD'VE LEFT HER. NEVER SHOULD HAVE--
UH, LAY IN A COURSE TO--
STOP, TONY. STOP IT. SHE'LL BE FINE. SHE CAN TAKE CARE OF HERSELF.
AFGHANISTAN.
I CAN'T BELIEVE YOU LEFT HER.
SHUT UP. STOP THINKING.
WE'RE GOING TO AFGHANISTAN.
TAJIKISTAN
TURKMENISTAN
JAWZJAN
BALKH
FARYAB
SAMANGAN
BAGHLAN
SARI PUL
BADGHIS
NURISTAN
PANJSHER

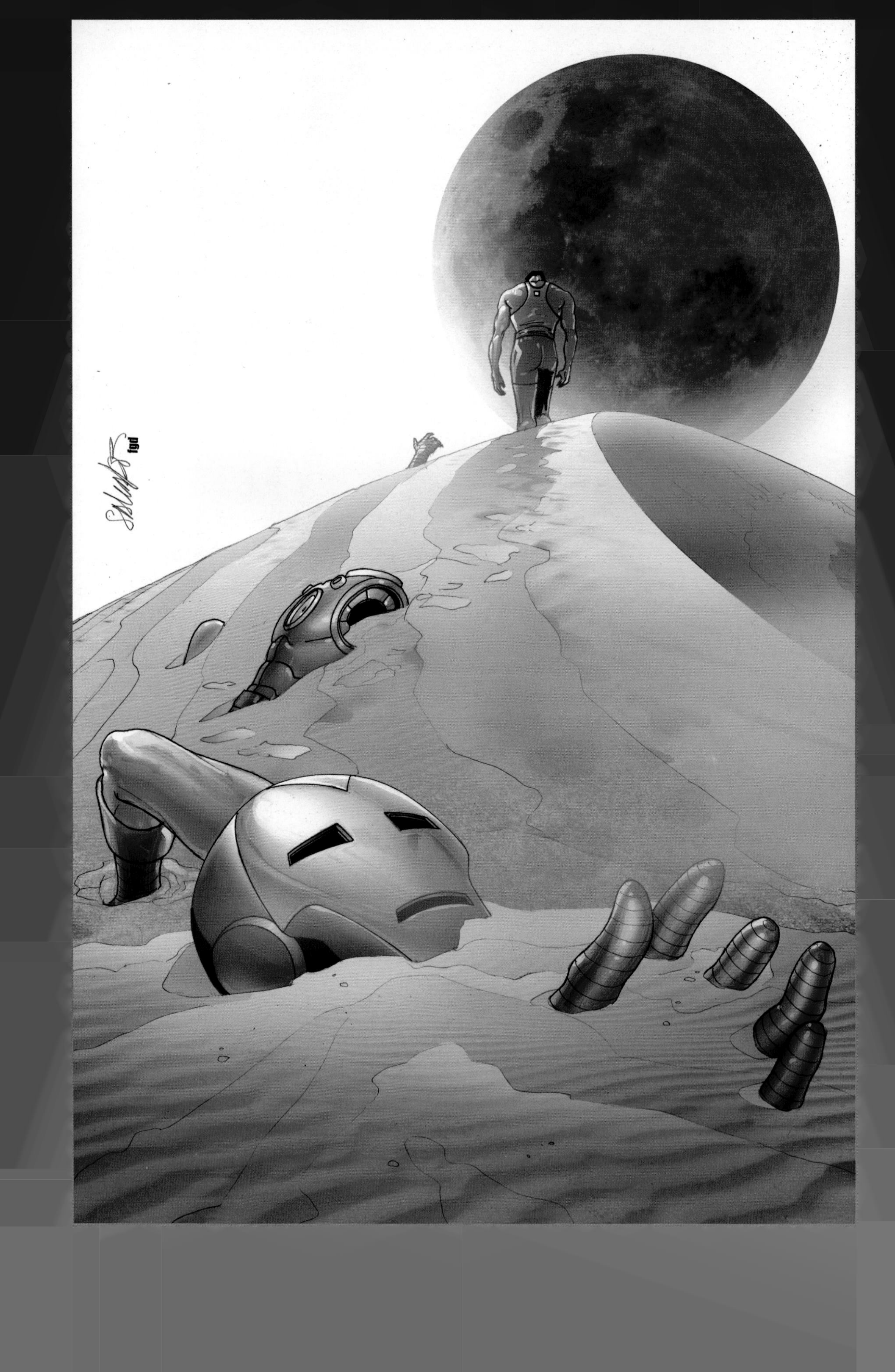

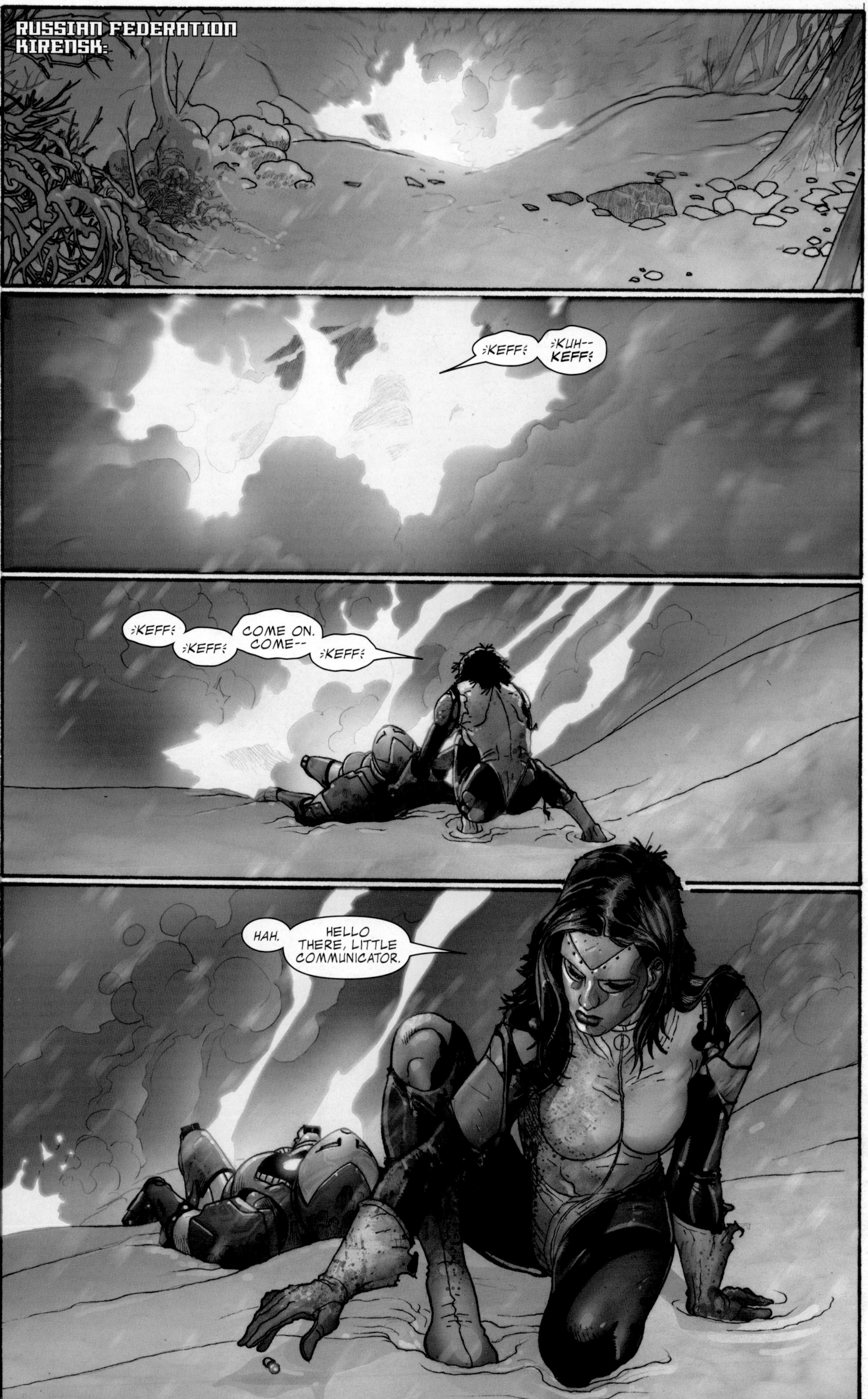
RUSSIAN FEDERATION
KIRENSK:
KEFF
KUH-- KEFF
KEFF
KEFF
COME ON. COME--
KEFF
HAH.
HELLO THERE, LITTLE COMMUNICATOR.

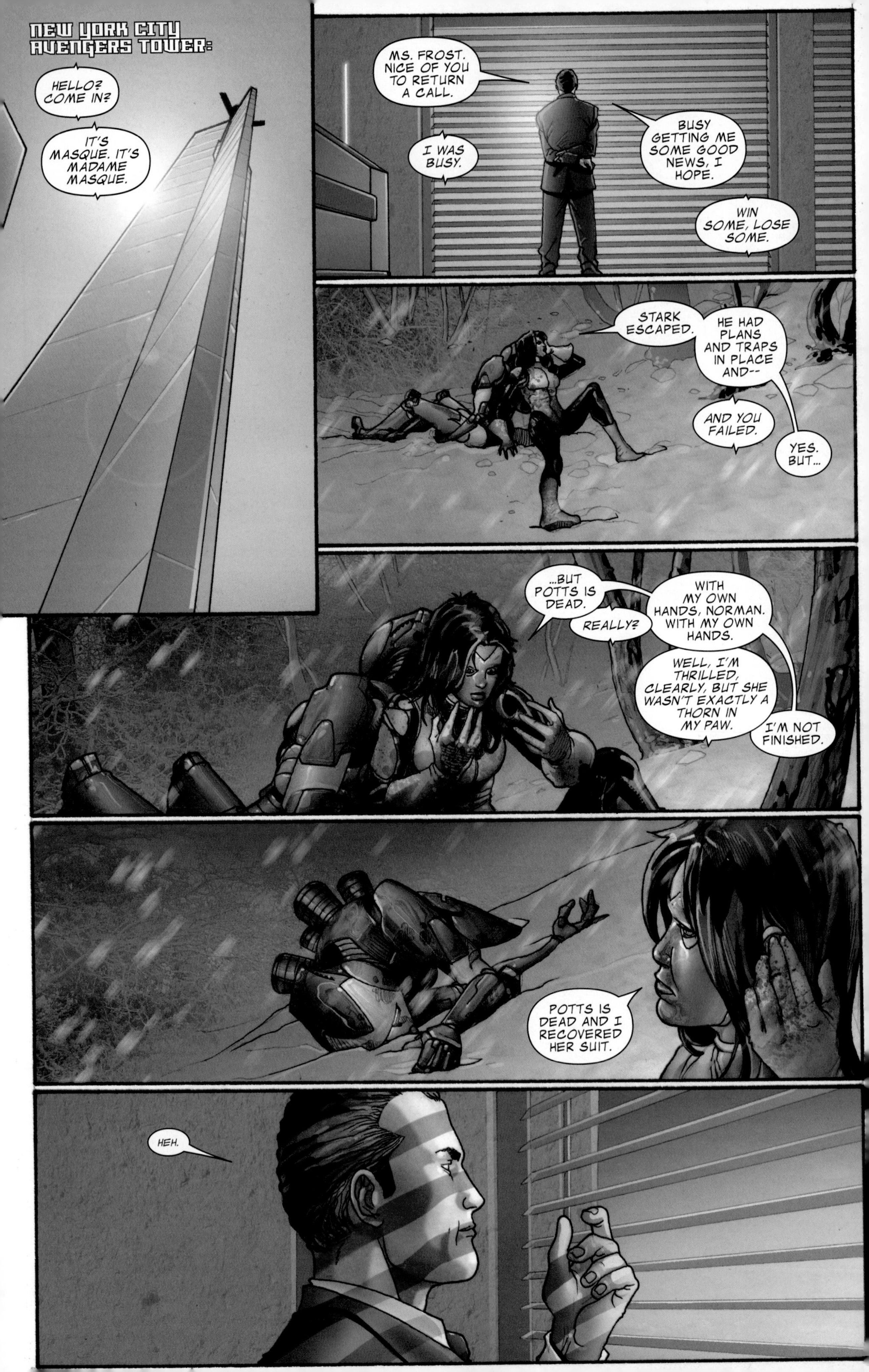

NEW YORK CITY AVENGERS TOWER:
HELLO? COME IN?
IT'S MASQUE. IT'S MADAME MASQUE.
MS. FROST. NICE OF YOU TO RETURN A CALL.
I WAS BUSY.
BUSY GETTING ME SOME GOOD NEWS, I HOPE.
WIN SOME, LOSE SOME.
STARK ESCAPED.
HE HAD PLANS AND TRAPS IN PLACE AND--
AND YOU FAILED.
YES. BUT...
...BUT POTTS IS DEAD.
REALLY?
WITH MY OWN HANDS, NORMAN. WITH MY OWN HANDS.
WELL, I'M THRILLED, CLEARLY, BUT SHE WASN'T EXACTLY A THORN IN MY PAW.
I'M NOT FINISHED.
POTTS IS DEAD AND I RECOVERED HER SUIT.
HEH.

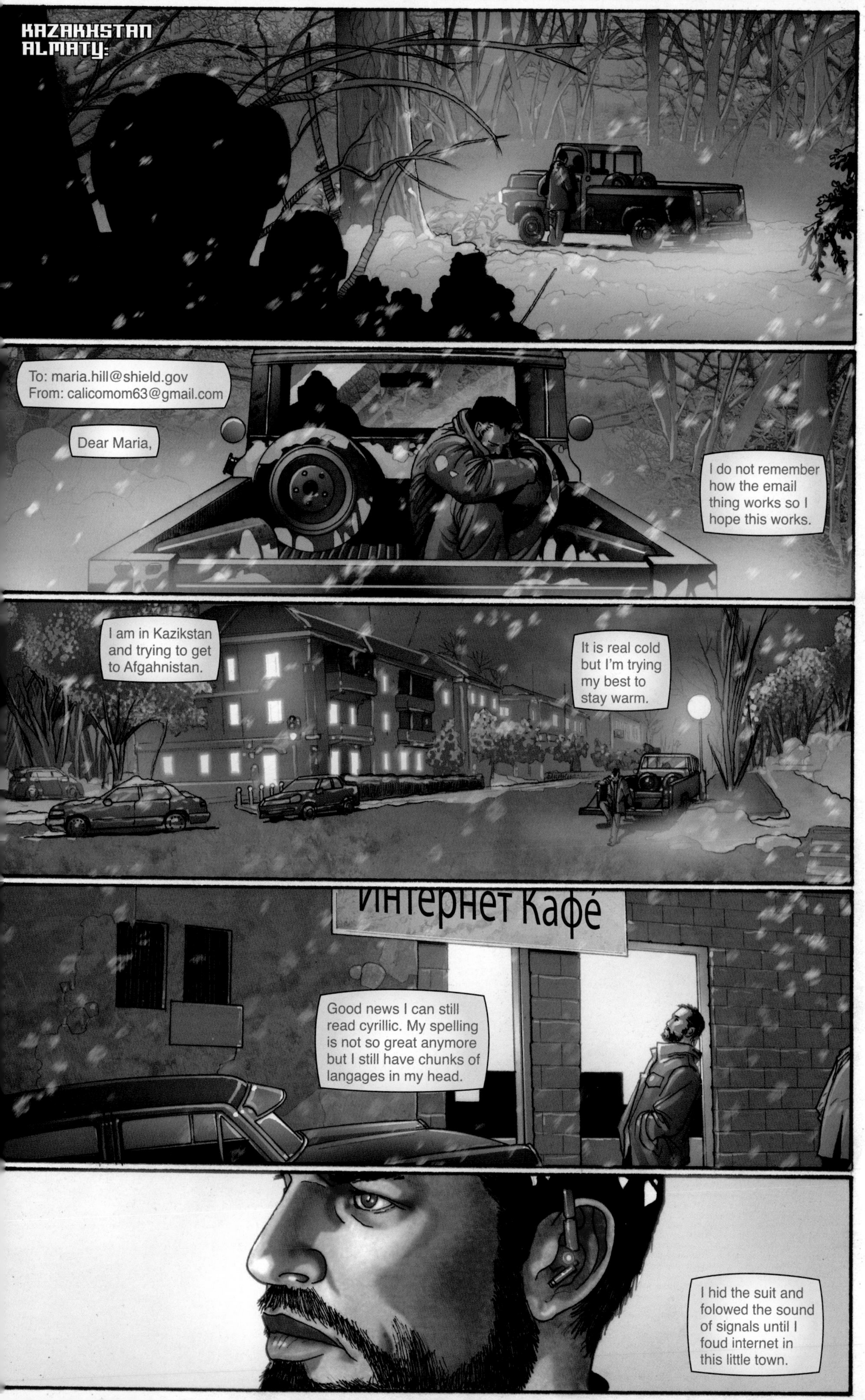
KAZAKHSTAN ALMATY:
To: maria.hill@shield.gov
From: calicomom63@gmail.com
Dear Maria,
I do not remember how the email thing works so I hope this works.
I am in Kazikstan and trying to get to Afgahnistan.
It is real cold but I'm trying my best to stay warm.
Интернет Кафé
Good news I can still read cyrillic. My spelling is not so great anymore but I still have chunks of langages in my head.
I hid the suit and folowed the sound of signals until I foud internet in this little town.

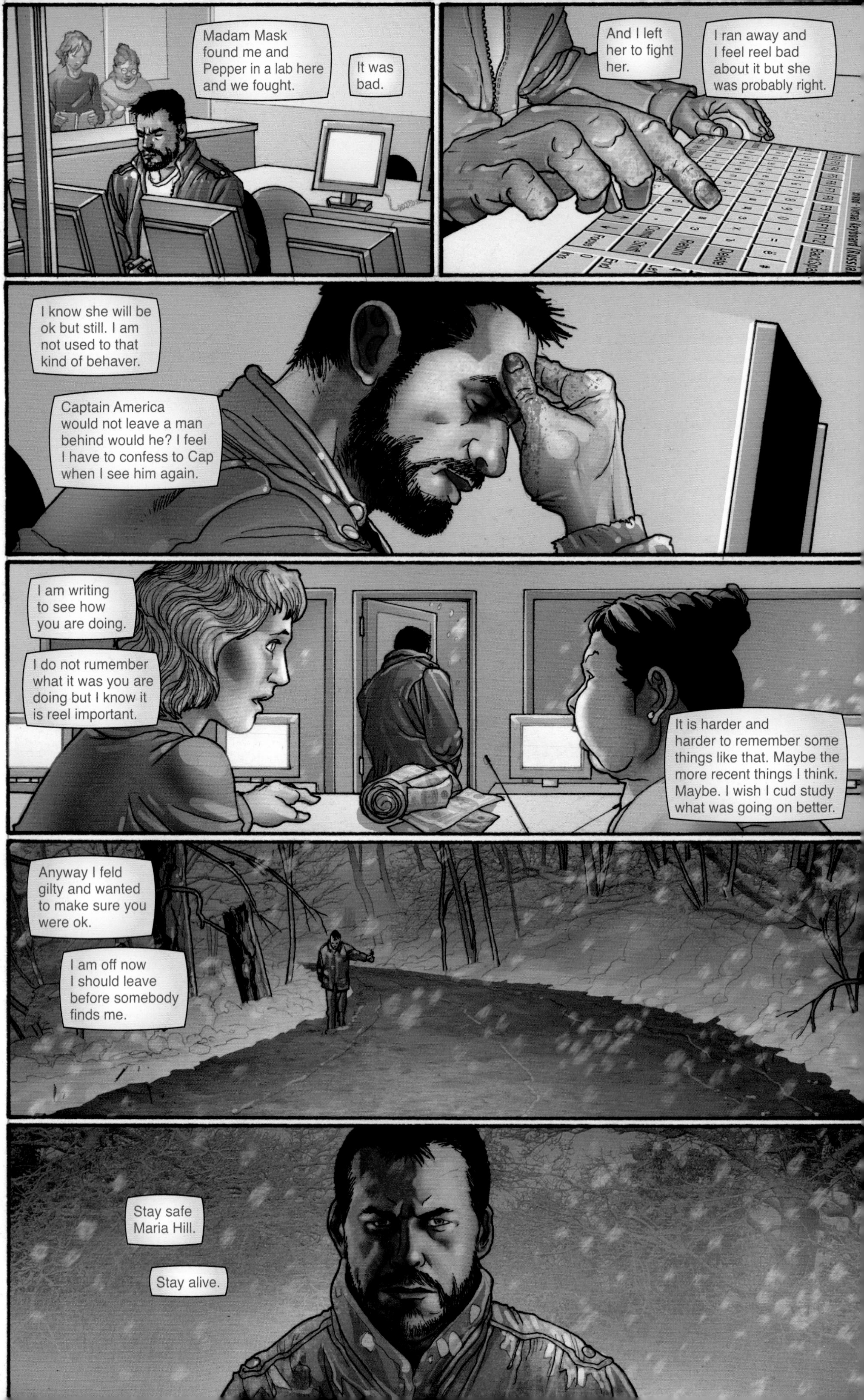
Madam Mask found me and Pepper in a lab here and we fought.
It was bad.
And I left her to fight her.
I ran away and I feel reel bad about it but she was probably right.
I know she will be ok but still. I am not used to that kind of behaver.
Captain America would not leave a man behind would he? I feel I have to confess to Cap when I see him again.
I am writing to see how you are doing.
I do not rumember what it was you are doing but I know it is reel important.
It is harder and harder to remember some things like that. Maybe the more recent things I think. Maybe. I wish I cud study what was going on better.
Anyway I feld gilty and wanted to make sure you were ok.
I am off now I should leave before somebody finds me.
Stay safe Maria Hill.
Stay alive.

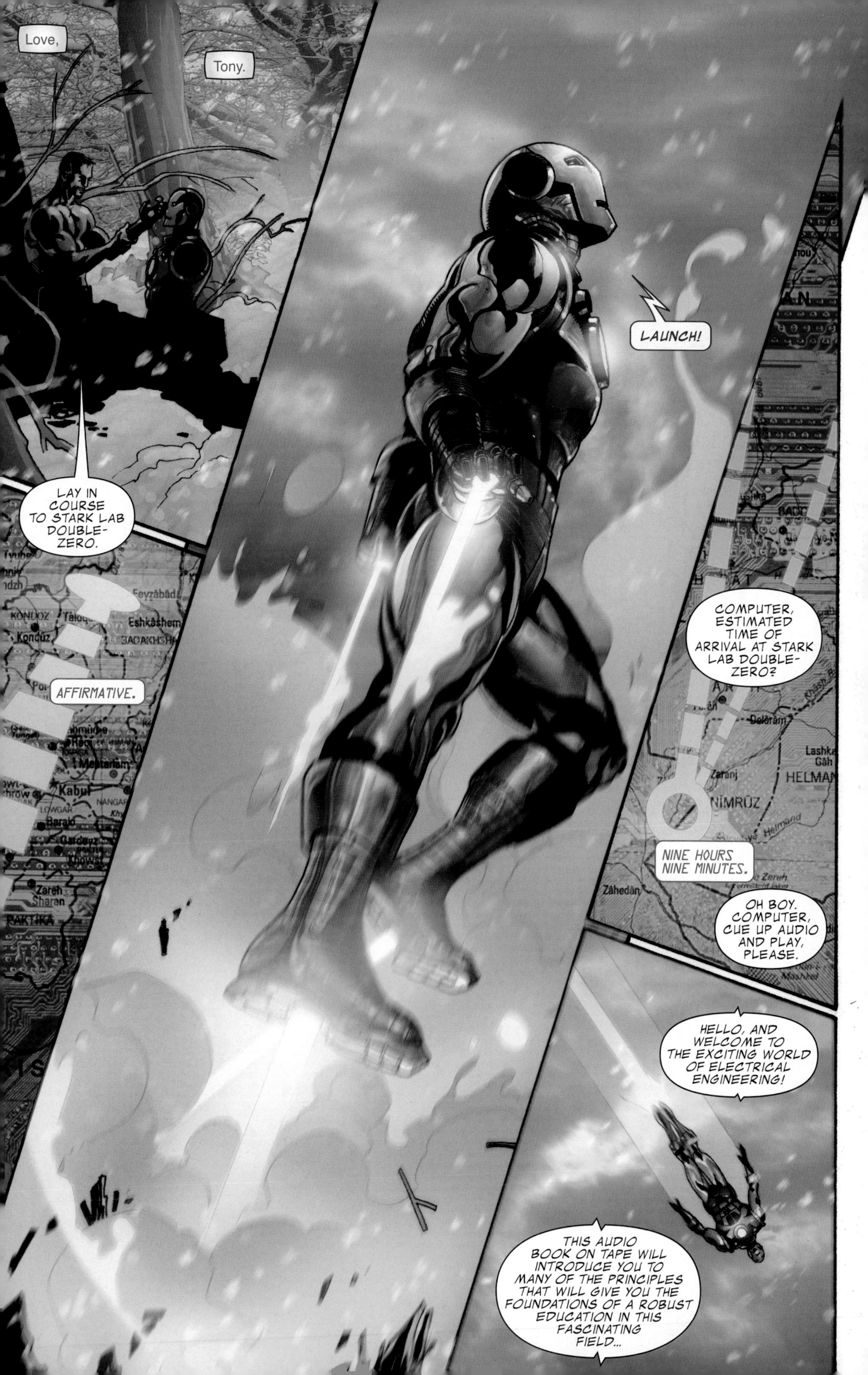

Love,
Tony.
LAY IN COURSE TO STARK LAB DOUBLE-ZERO.
AFFIRMATIVE.
LAUNCH!
COMPUTER, ESTIMATED TIME OF ARRIVAL AT STARK LAB DOUBLE-ZERO?
NINE HOURS NINE MINUTES.
OH BOY. COMPUTER, CUE UP AUDIO AND PLAY, PLEASE.
HELLO, AND WELCOME TO THE EXCITING WORLD OF ELECTRICAL ENGINEERING!
THIS AUDIO BOOK ON TAPE WILL INTRODUCE YOU TO MANY OF THE PRINCIPLES THAT WILL GIVE YOU THE FOUNDATIONS OF A ROBUST EDUCATION IN THIS FASCINATING FIELD...

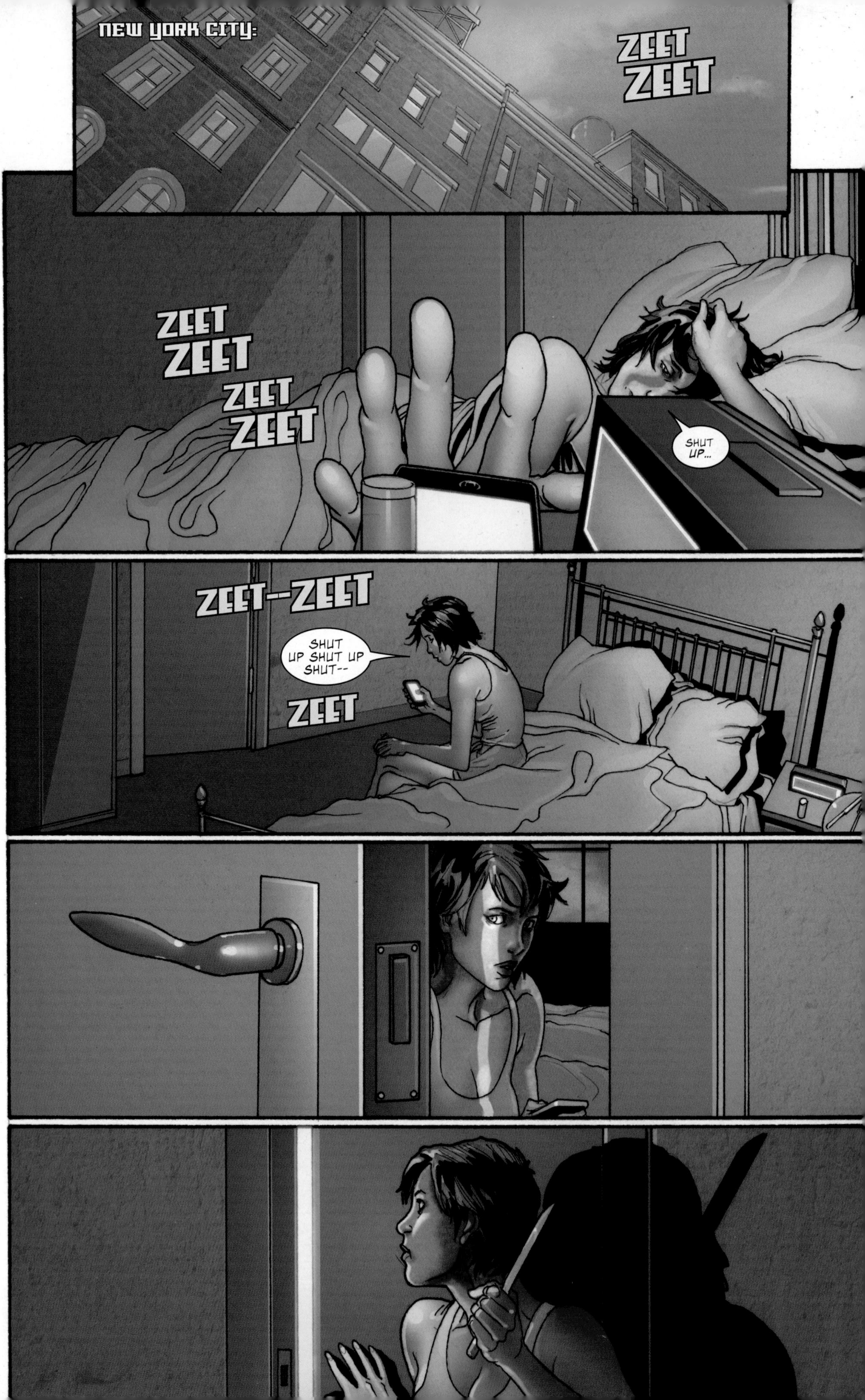
NEW YORK CITY:
ZEET
ZEET
ZEET
ZEET
ZEET
ZEET
SHUT UP...
ZEET--ZEET
SHUT UP SHUT UP SHUT--
ZEET

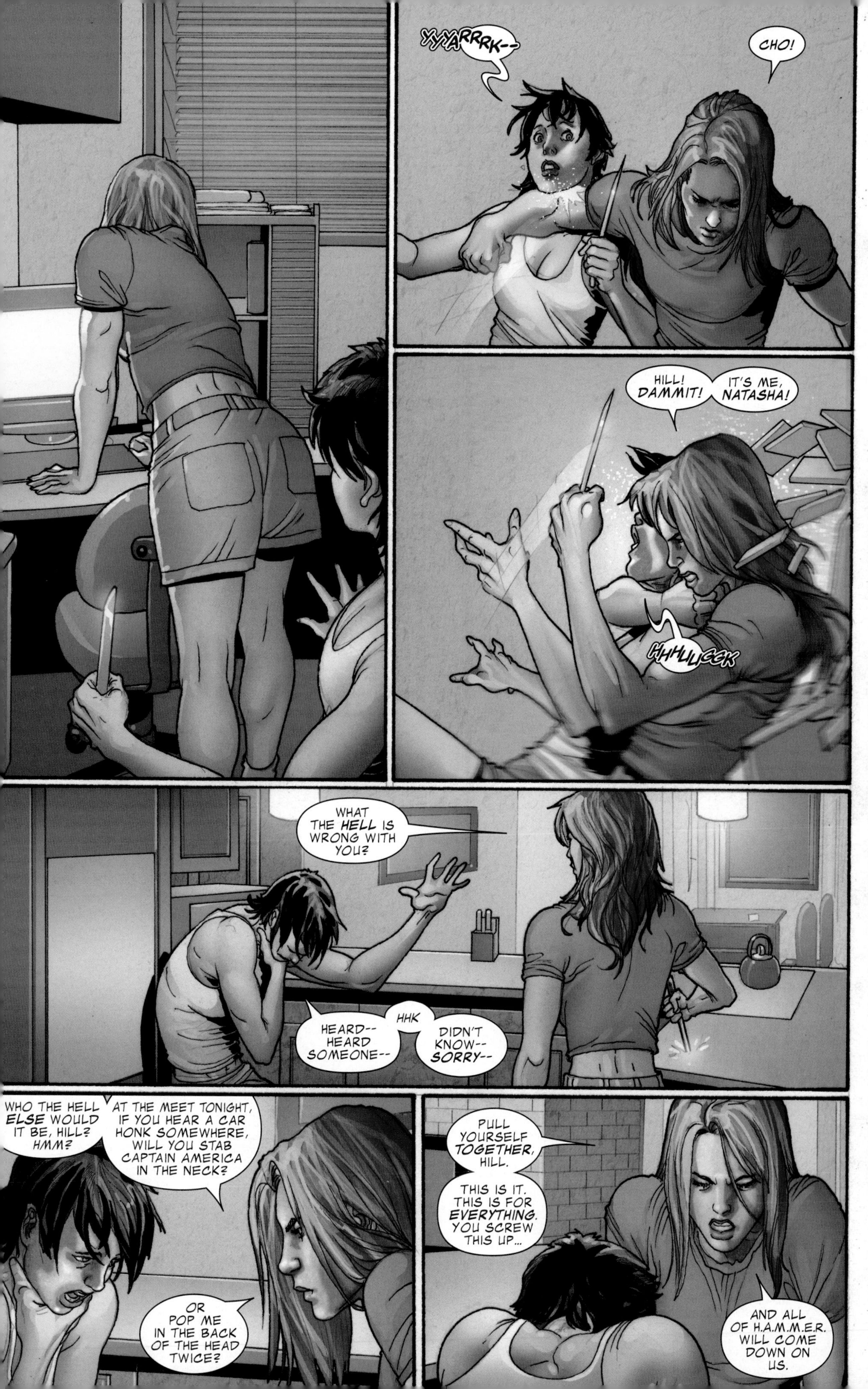
YYYARRRK--
CHO!
HILL! DAMMIT!
IT'S ME, NATASHA!
HHHULGGK
WHAT THE HELL IS WRONG WITH YOU?
HEARD-- HEARD SOMEONE--
HHK
DIDN'T KNOW-- SORRY--
WHO THE HELL ELSE WOULD IT BE, HILL? HMM?
AT THE MEET TONIGHT, IF YOU HEAR A CAR HONK SOMEWHERE, WILL YOU STAB CAPTAIN AMERICA IN THE NECK?
OR POP ME IN THE BACK OF THE HEAD TWICE?
PULL YOURSELF TOGETHER, HILL.
THIS IS IT. THIS IS FOR EVERYTHING. YOU SCREW THIS UP...
AND ALL OF H.A.M.M.E.R. WILL COME DOWN ON US.

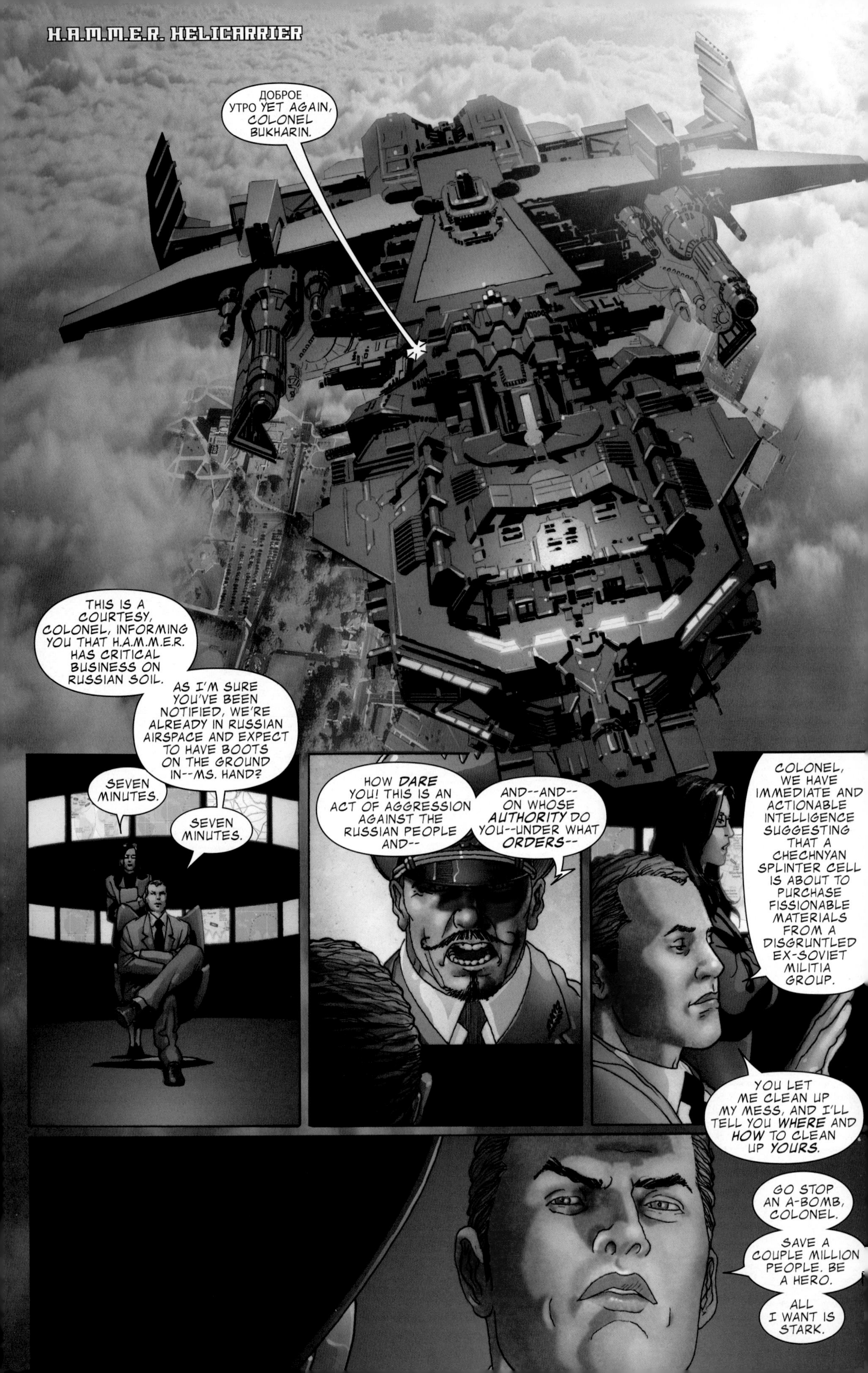
H.A.M.M.E.R. HELICARRIER
ДОБРОЕ УТРО YET AGAIN, COLONEL BUKHARIN.
THIS IS A COURTESY, COLONEL, INFORMING YOU THAT H.A.M.M.E.R. HAS CRITICAL BUSINESS ON RUSSIAN SOIL.
AS I'M SURE YOU'VE BEEN NOTIFIED, WE'RE ALREADY IN RUSSIAN AIRSPACE AND EXPECT TO HAVE BOOTS ON THE GROUND IN--MS. HAND?
SEVEN MINUTES.
SEVEN MINUTES.
HOW DARE YOU! THIS IS AN ACT OF AGGRESSION AGAINST THE RUSSIAN PEOPLE AND--
AND--AND--ON WHOSE AUTHORITY DO YOU--UNDER WHAT ORDERS--
COLONEL, WE HAVE IMMEDIATE AND ACTIONABLE INTELLIGENCE SUGGESTING THAT A CHECHNYAN SPLINTER CELL IS ABOUT TO PURCHASE FISSIONABLE MATERIALS FROM A DISGRUNTLED EX-SOVIET MILITIA GROUP.
YOU LET ME CLEAN UP MY MESS, AND I'LL TELL YOU WHERE AND HOW TO CLEAN UP YOURS.
GO STOP AN A-BOMB, COLONEL.
SAVE A COUPLE MILLION PEOPLE. BE A HERO.
ALL I WANT IS STARK.

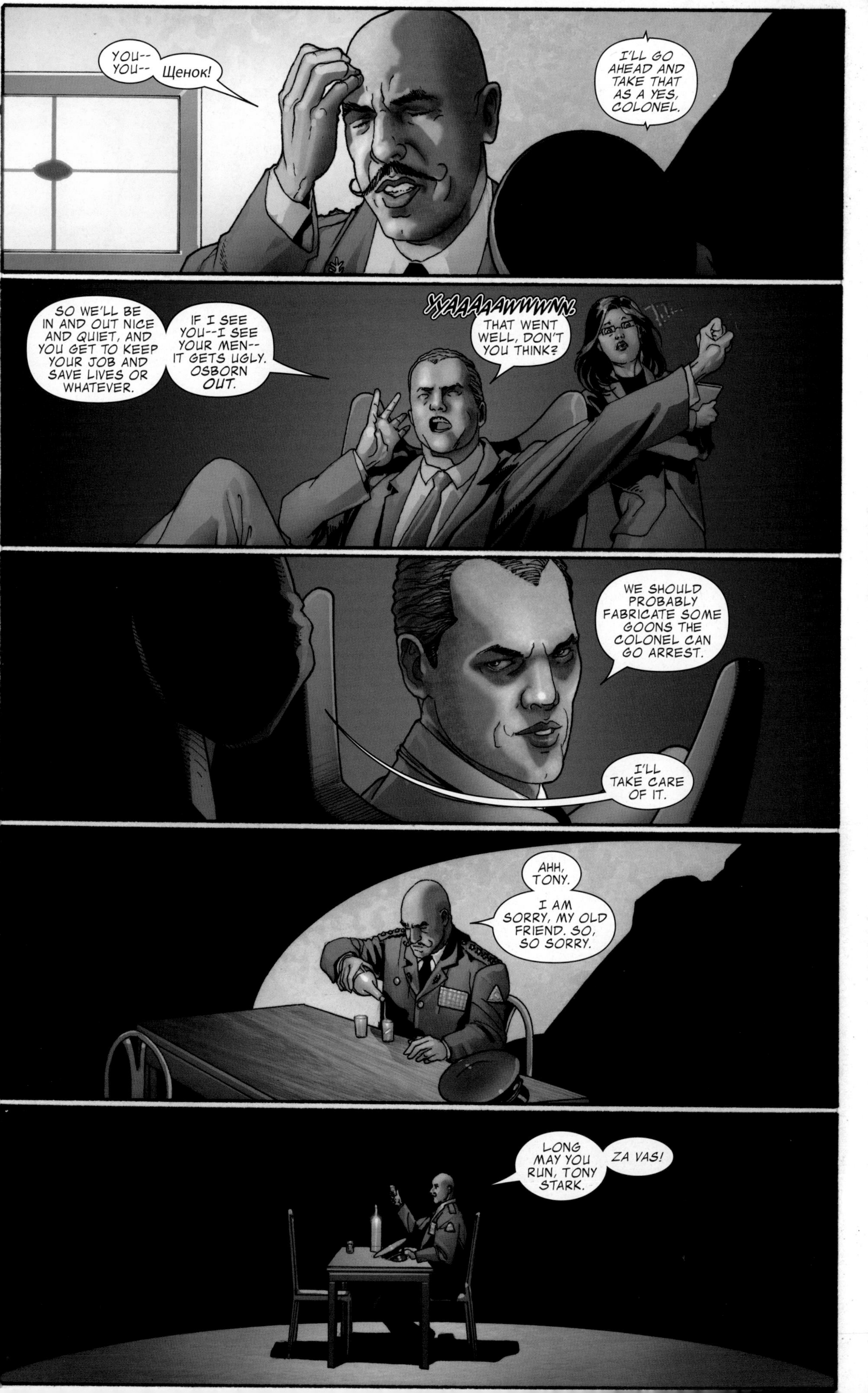
YOU--
YOU-- Щенок!
I'LL GO AHEAD AND TAKE THAT AS A YES, COLONEL.
SO WE'LL BE IN AND OUT NICE AND QUIET, AND YOU GET TO KEEP YOUR JOB AND SAVE LIVES OR WHATEVER.
IF I SEE YOU--I SEE YOUR MEN--IT GETS UGLY. OSBORN OUT.
YYAAAAAWWWNN.
THAT WENT WELL, DON'T YOU THINK?
?!
WE SHOULD PROBABLY FABRICATE SOME GOONS THE COLONEL CAN GO ARREST.
I'LL TAKE CARE OF IT.
AHH, TONY.
I AM SORRY, MY OLD FRIEND. SO, SO SORRY.
LONG MAY YOU RUN, TONY STARK.
ZA VAS!

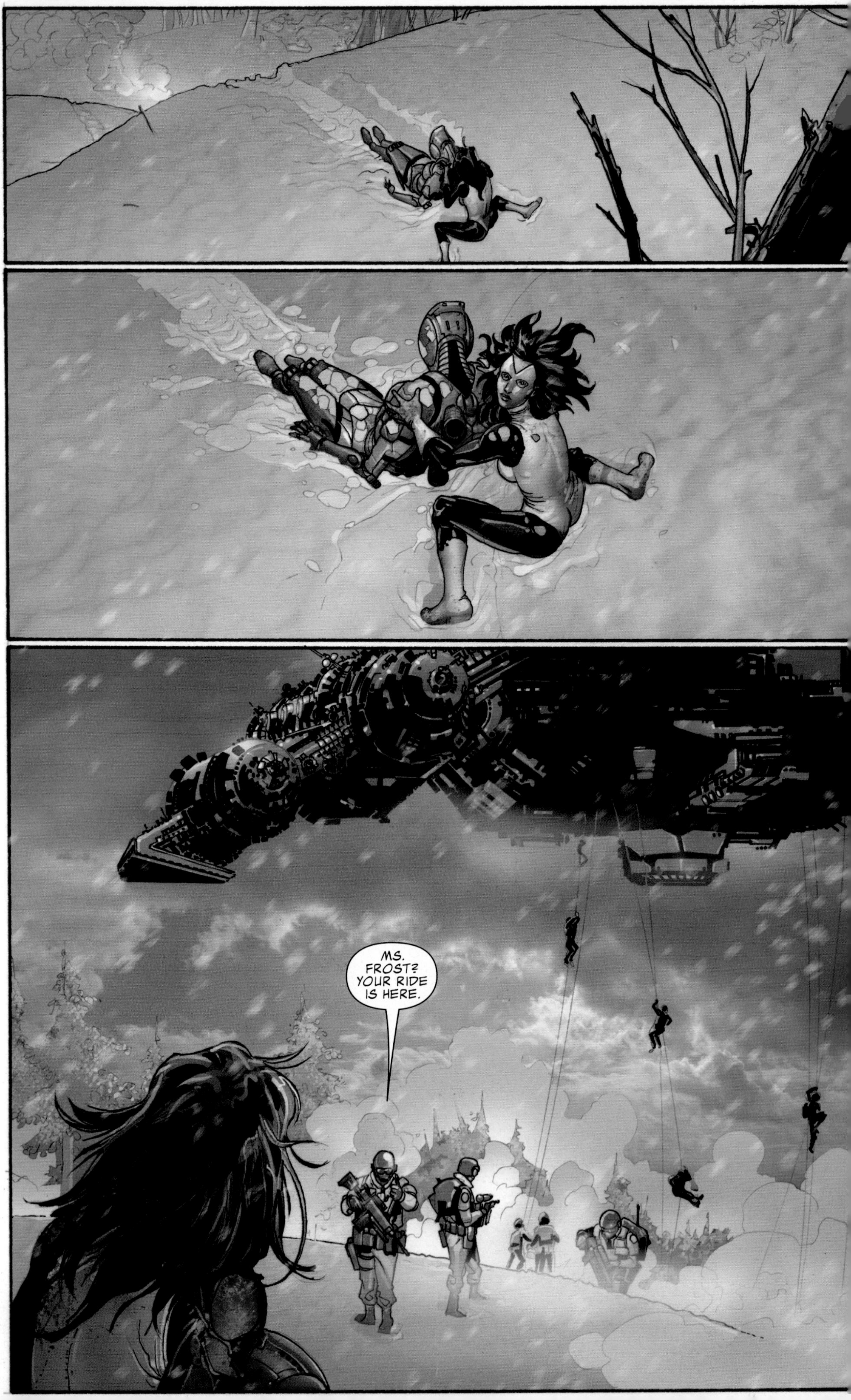
MS. FROST? YOUR RIDE IS HERE.

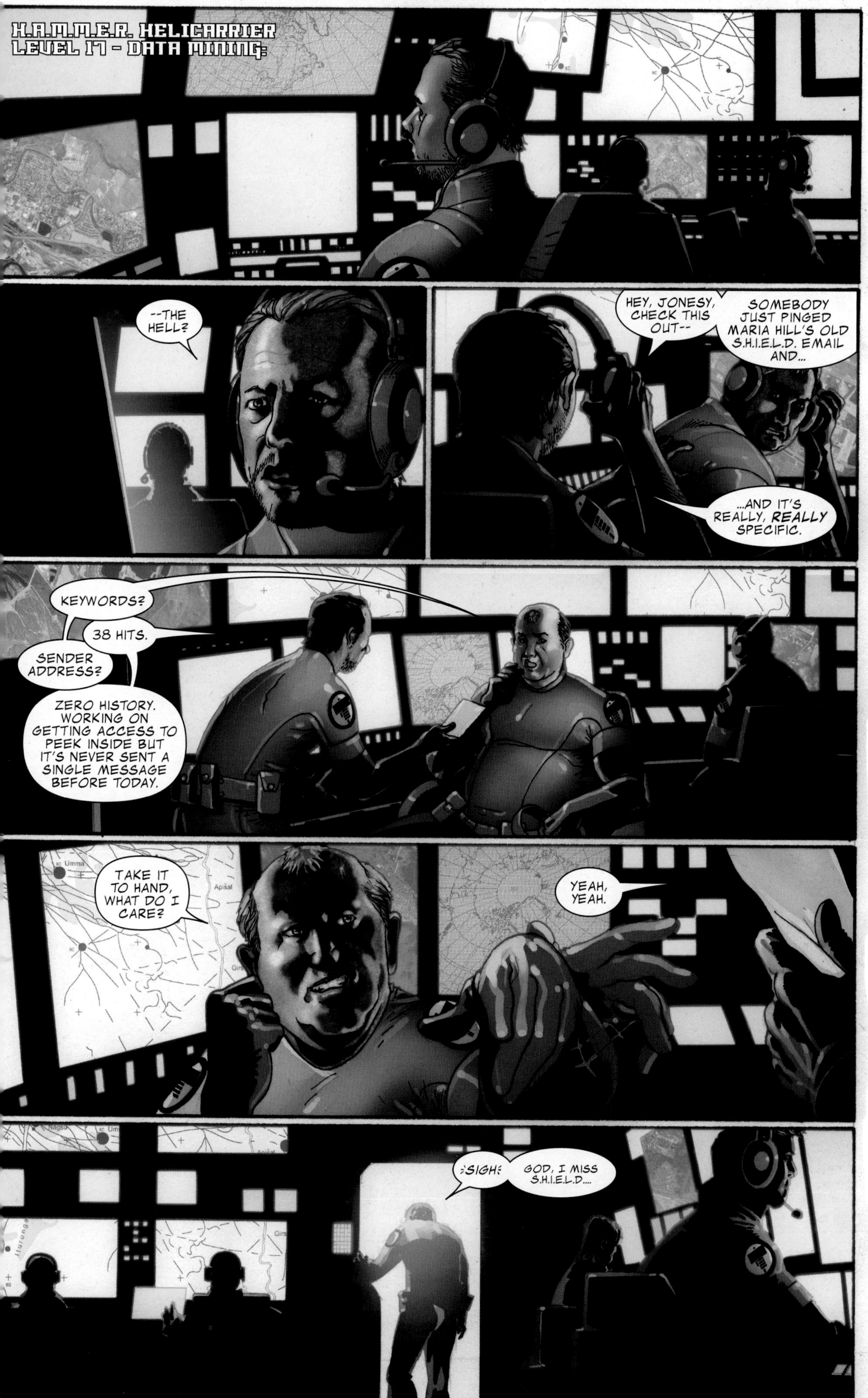
H.A.M.M.E.R. HELICARRIER
LEVEL 17 - DATA MINING:
--THE HELL?
HEY, JONESY, CHECK THIS OUT--
SOMEBODY JUST PINGED MARIA HILL'S OLD S.H.I.E.L.D. EMAIL AND...
...AND IT'S REALLY, **REALLY** SPECIFIC.
KEYWORDS?
38 HITS.
SENDER ADDRESS?
ZERO HISTORY. WORKING ON GETTING ACCESS TO PEEK INSIDE BUT IT'S NEVER SENT A SINGLE MESSAGE BEFORE TODAY.
TAKE IT TO HAND, WHAT DO I CARE?
YEAH, YEAH.
SIGH
GOD, I MISS S.H.I.E.L.D....

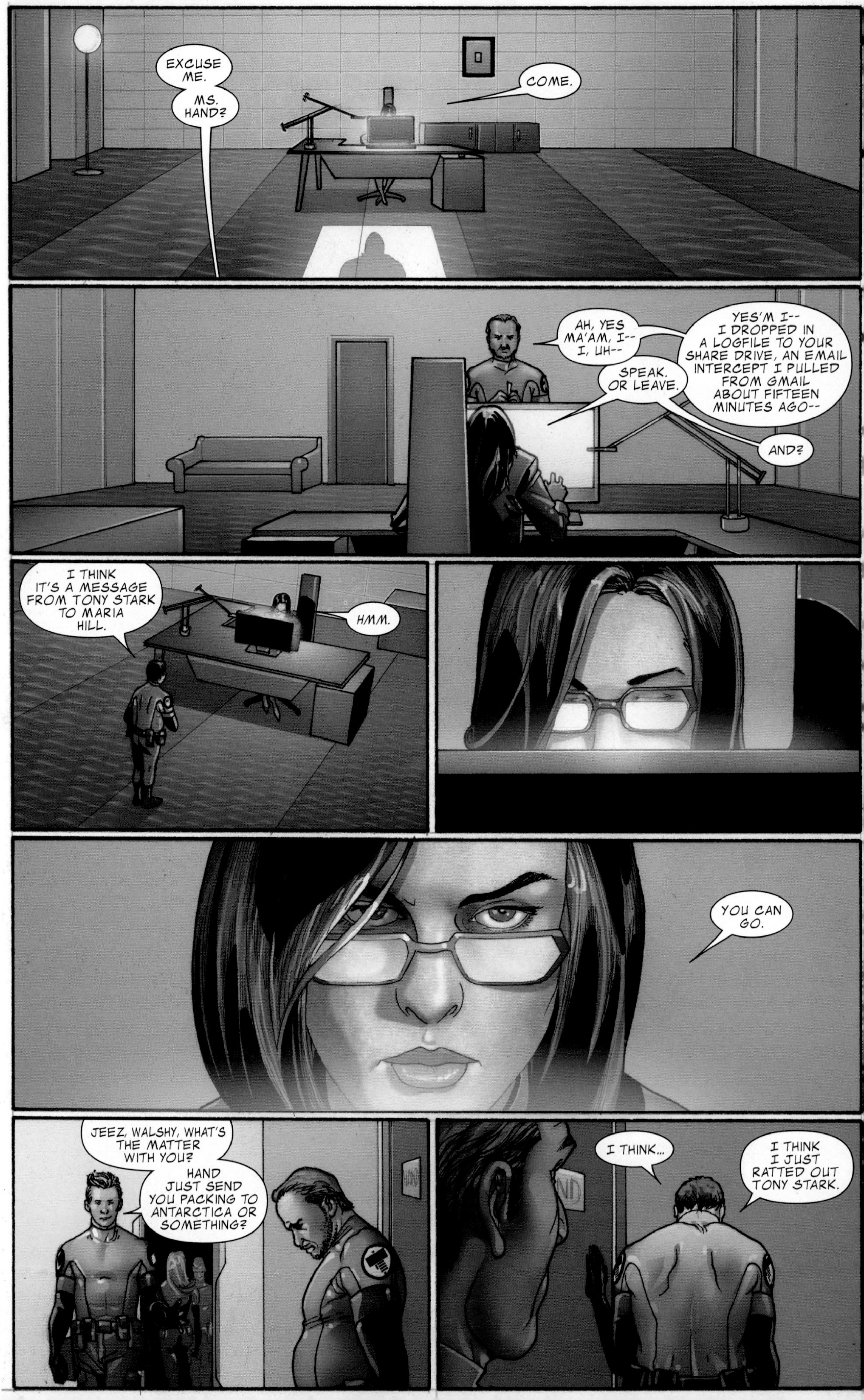
EXCUSE ME.
MS. HAND?
COME.
AH, YES MA'AM, I-- I, UH--
SPEAK. OR LEAVE.
YES'M I-- I DROPPED IN A LOGFILE TO YOUR SHARE DRIVE, AN EMAIL INTERCEPT I PULLED FROM GMAIL ABOUT FIFTEEN MINUTES AGO--
AND?
I THINK IT'S A MESSAGE FROM TONY STARK TO MARIA HILL.
HMM.
YOU CAN GO.
JEEZ, WALSHY, WHAT'S THE MATTER WITH YOU?
HAND JUST SEND YOU PACKING TO ANTARCTICA OR SOMETHING?
I THINK...
I THINK I JUST RATTED OUT TONY STARK.

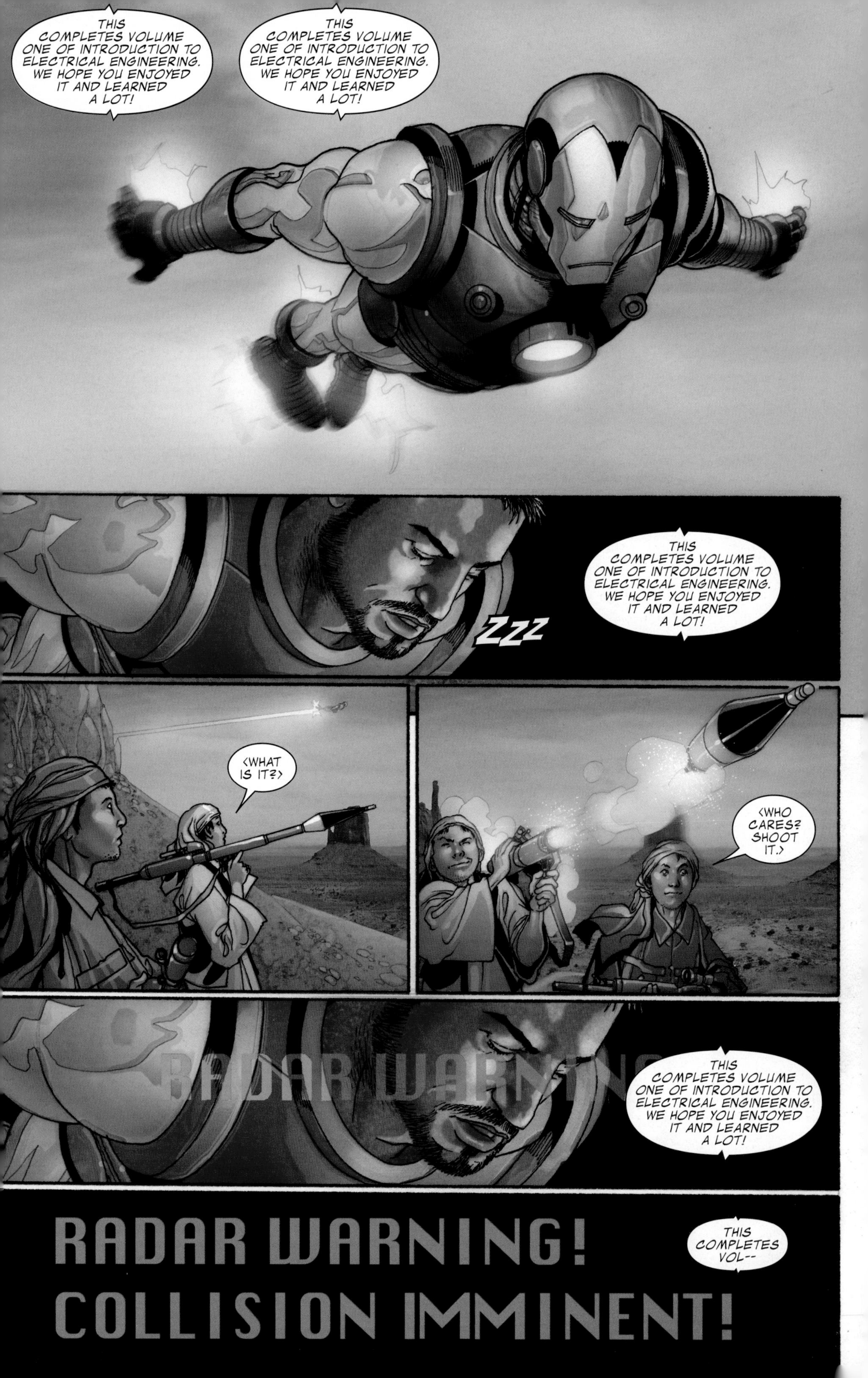
THIS COMPLETES VOLUME ONE OF INTRODUCTION TO ELECTRICAL ENGINEERING. WE HOPE YOU ENJOYED IT AND LEARNED A LOT!
THIS COMPLETES VOLUME ONE OF INTRODUCTION TO ELECTRICAL ENGINEERING. WE HOPE YOU ENJOYED IT AND LEARNED A LOT!
THIS COMPLETES VOLUME ONE OF INTRODUCTION TO ELECTRICAL ENGINEERING. WE HOPE YOU ENJOYED IT AND LEARNED A LOT!
ZZZ
<WHAT IS IT?>
<WHO CARES? SHOOT IT.>
THIS COMPLETES VOLUME ONE OF INTRODUCTION TO ELECTRICAL ENGINEERING. WE HOPE YOU ENJOYED IT AND LEARNED A LOT!
RADAR WARNING! COLLISION IMMINENT!
THIS COMPLETES VOL--

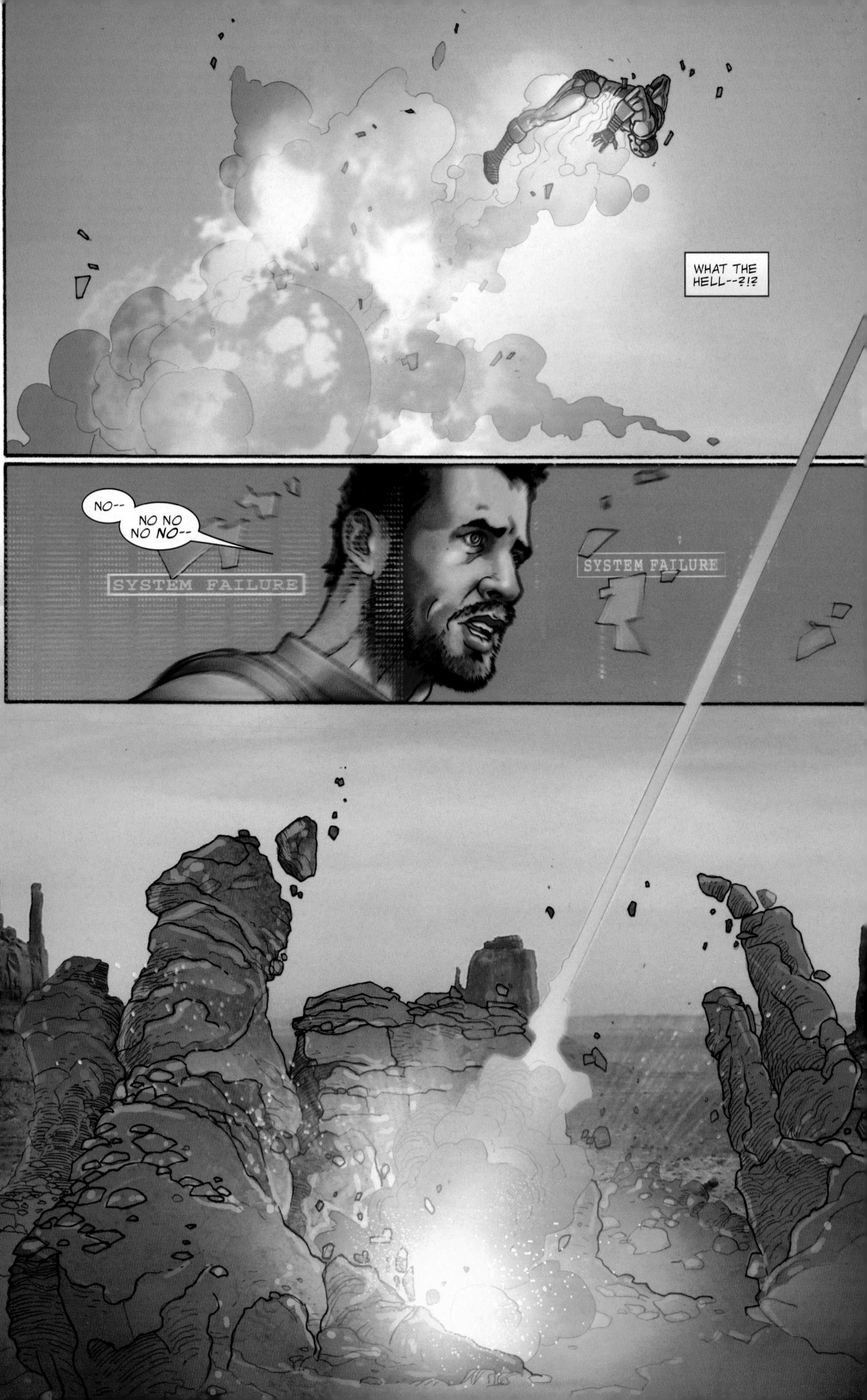
WHAT THE HELL--?!?
NO--
NO NO NO NO--
SYSTEM FAILURE
SYSTEM FAILURE

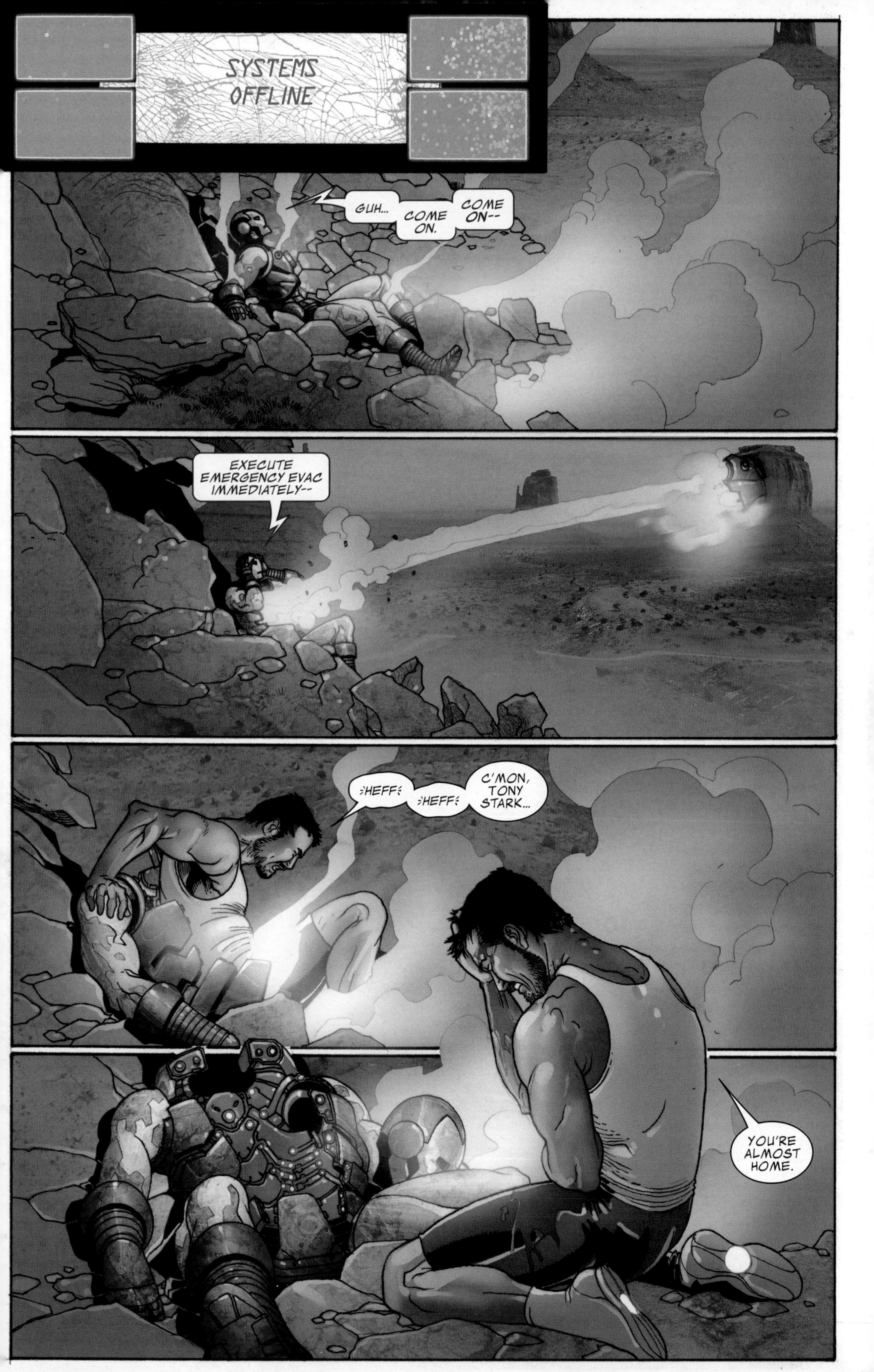
SYSTEMS OFFLINE
GUH...
COME ON.
COME ON--
EXECUTE EMERGENCY EVAC IMMEDIATELY--
HEFF
HEFF
C'MON, TONY STARK...
YOU'RE ALMOST HOME.

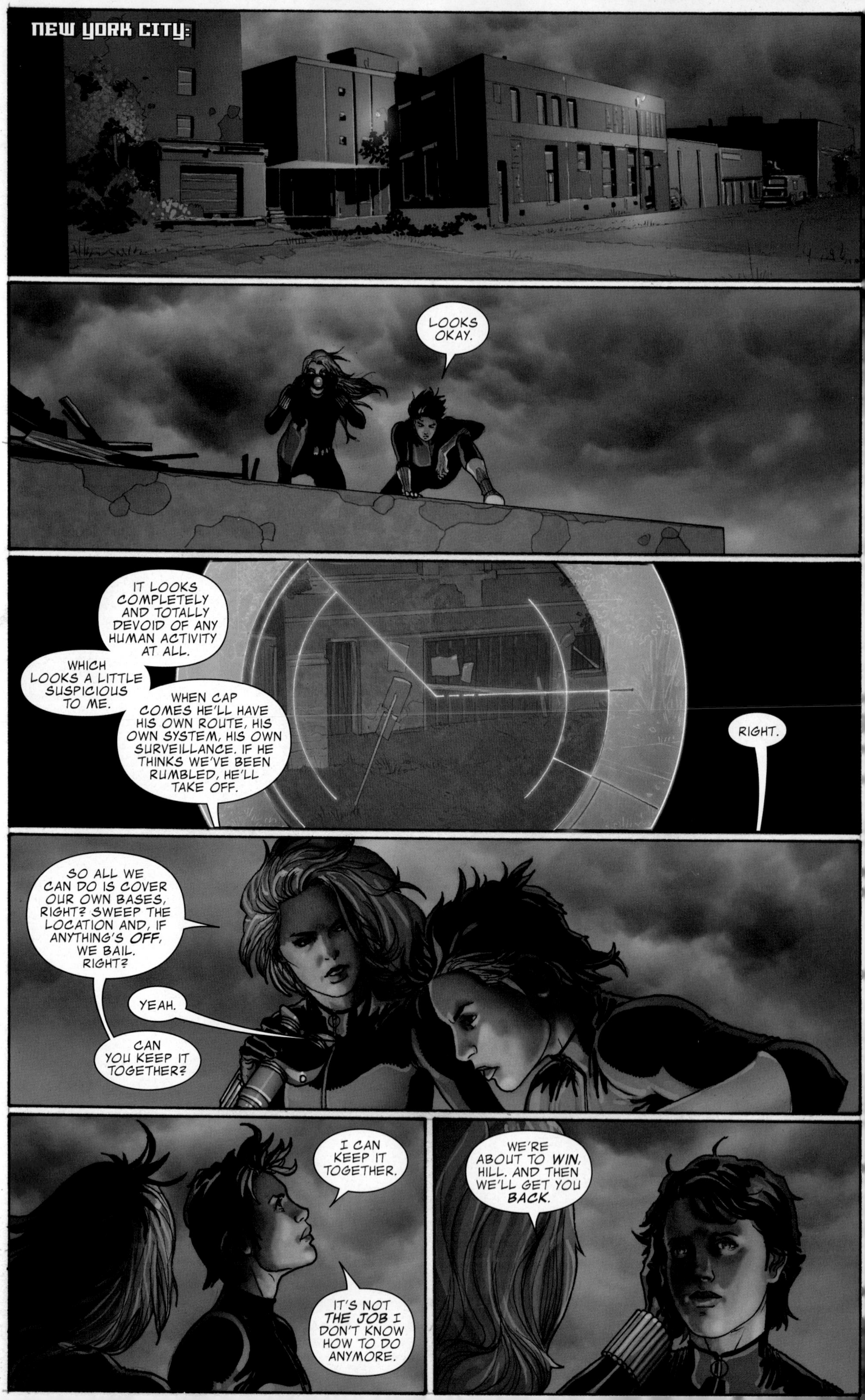
NEW YORK CITY:
LOOKS OKAY.
IT LOOKS COMPLETELY AND TOTALLY DEVOID OF ANY HUMAN ACTIVITY AT ALL.
WHICH LOOKS A LITTLE SUSPICIOUS TO ME.
WHEN CAP COMES HE'LL HAVE HIS OWN ROUTE, HIS OWN SYSTEM, HIS OWN SURVEILLANCE. IF HE THINKS WE'VE BEEN RUMBLED, HE'LL TAKE OFF.
RIGHT.
SO ALL WE CAN DO IS COVER OUR OWN BASES, RIGHT? SWEEP THE LOCATION AND, IF ANYTHING'S OFF, WE BAIL. RIGHT?
YEAH.
CAN YOU KEEP IT TOGETHER?
I CAN KEEP IT TOGETHER.
IT'S NOT THE JOB I DON'T KNOW HOW TO DO ANYMORE.
WE'RE ABOUT TO WIN, HILL. AND THEN WE'LL GET YOU BACK.

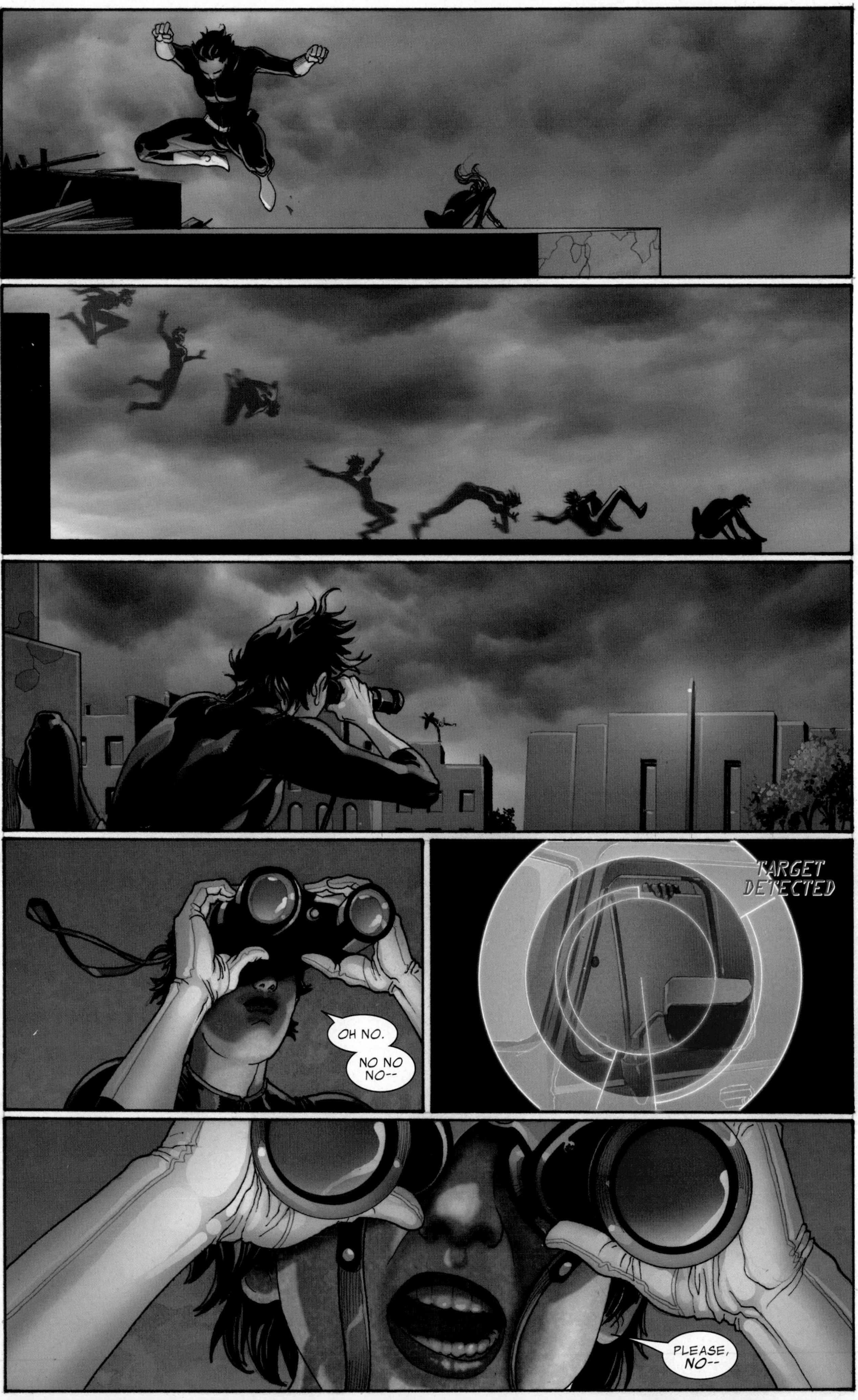

OH NO.
NO NO NO--
TARGET DETECTED
PLEASE, NO--

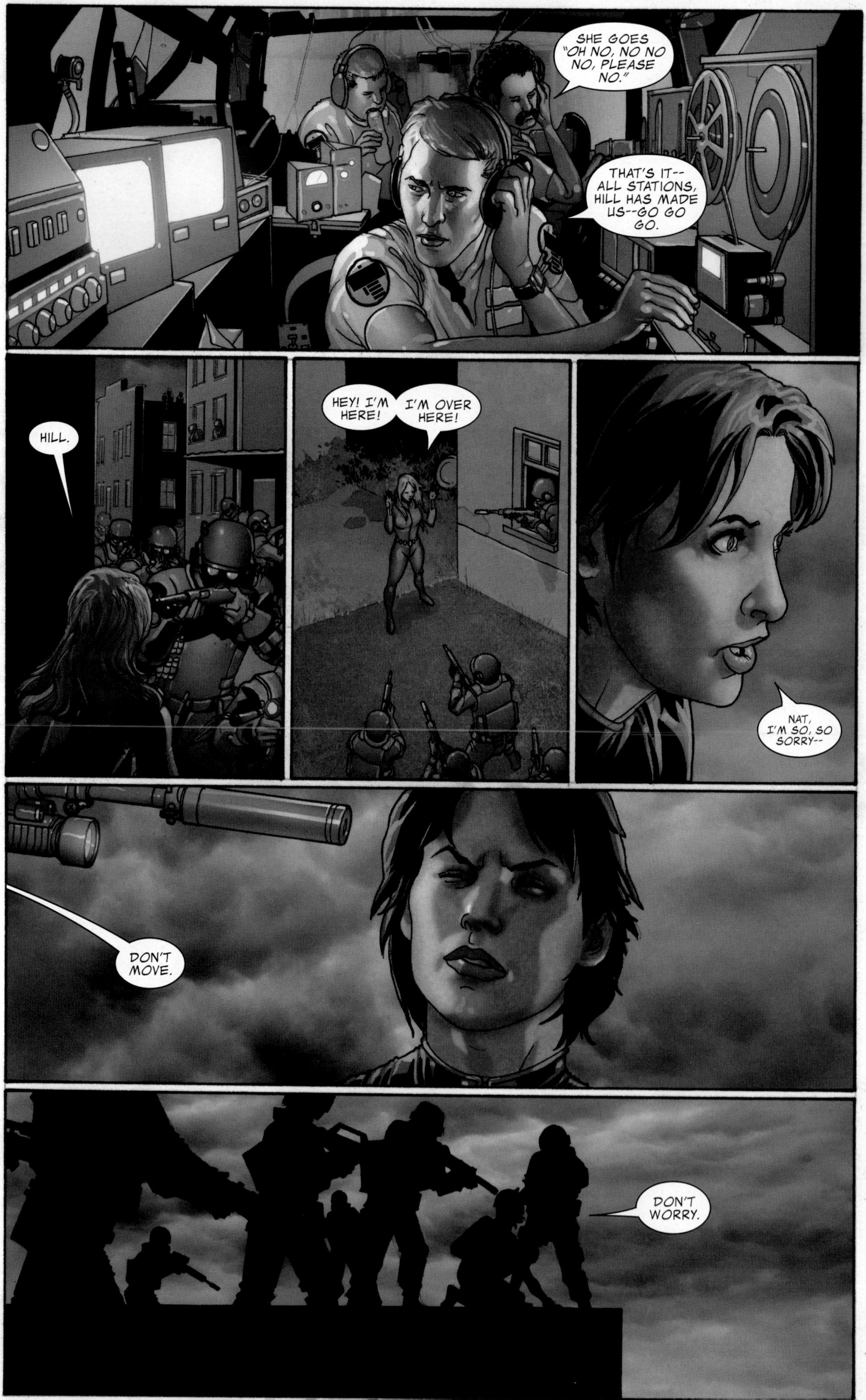
SHE GOES "OH NO, NO NO NO, PLEASE NO."
THAT'S IT-- ALL STATIONS, HILL HAS MADE US--GO GO GO.
HILL.
HEY! I'M HERE!
I'M OVER HERE!
NAT, I'M SO, SO SORRY--
DON'T MOVE.
DON'T WORRY.

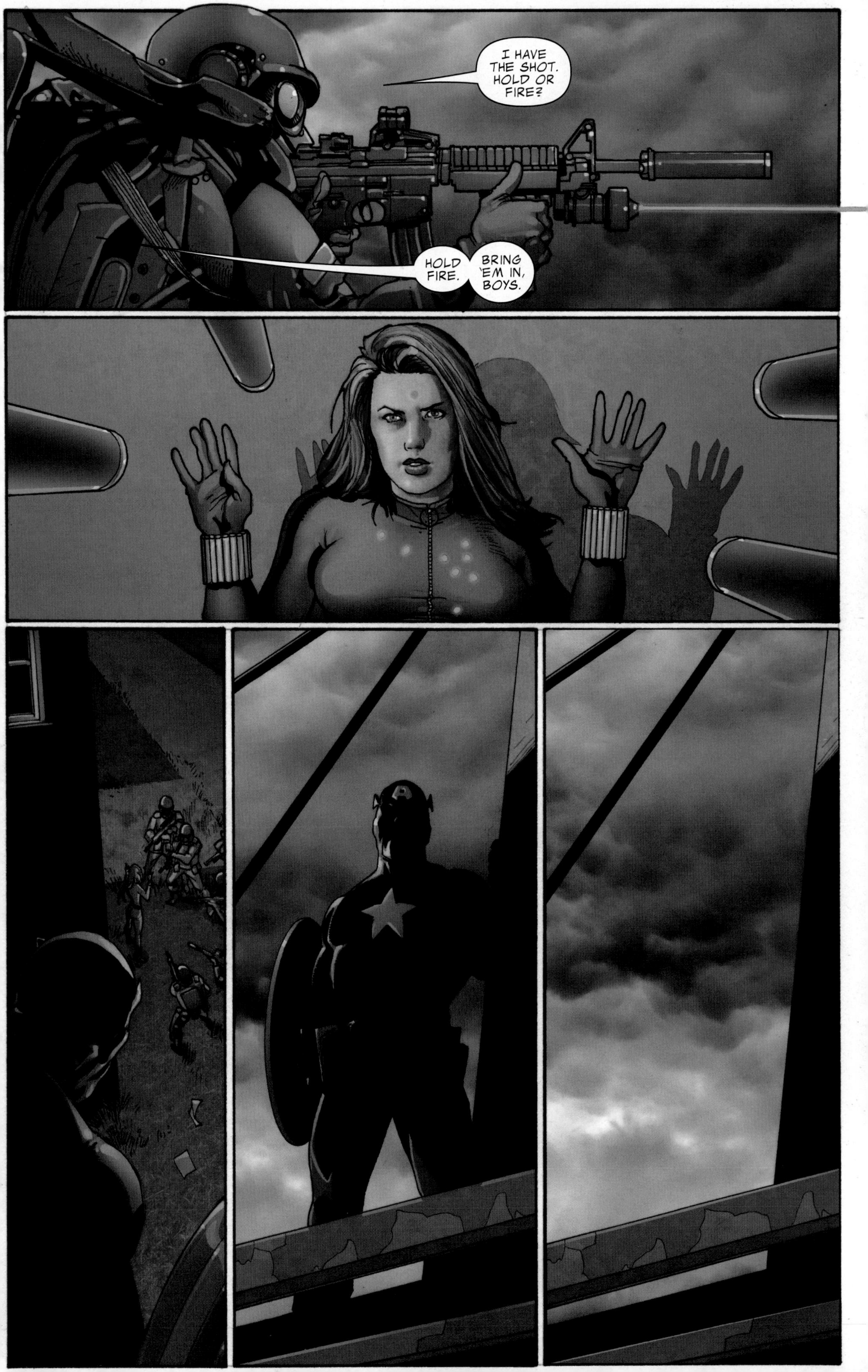
I HAVE THE SHOT. HOLD OR FIRE?
HOLD FIRE.
BRING 'EM IN, BOYS.

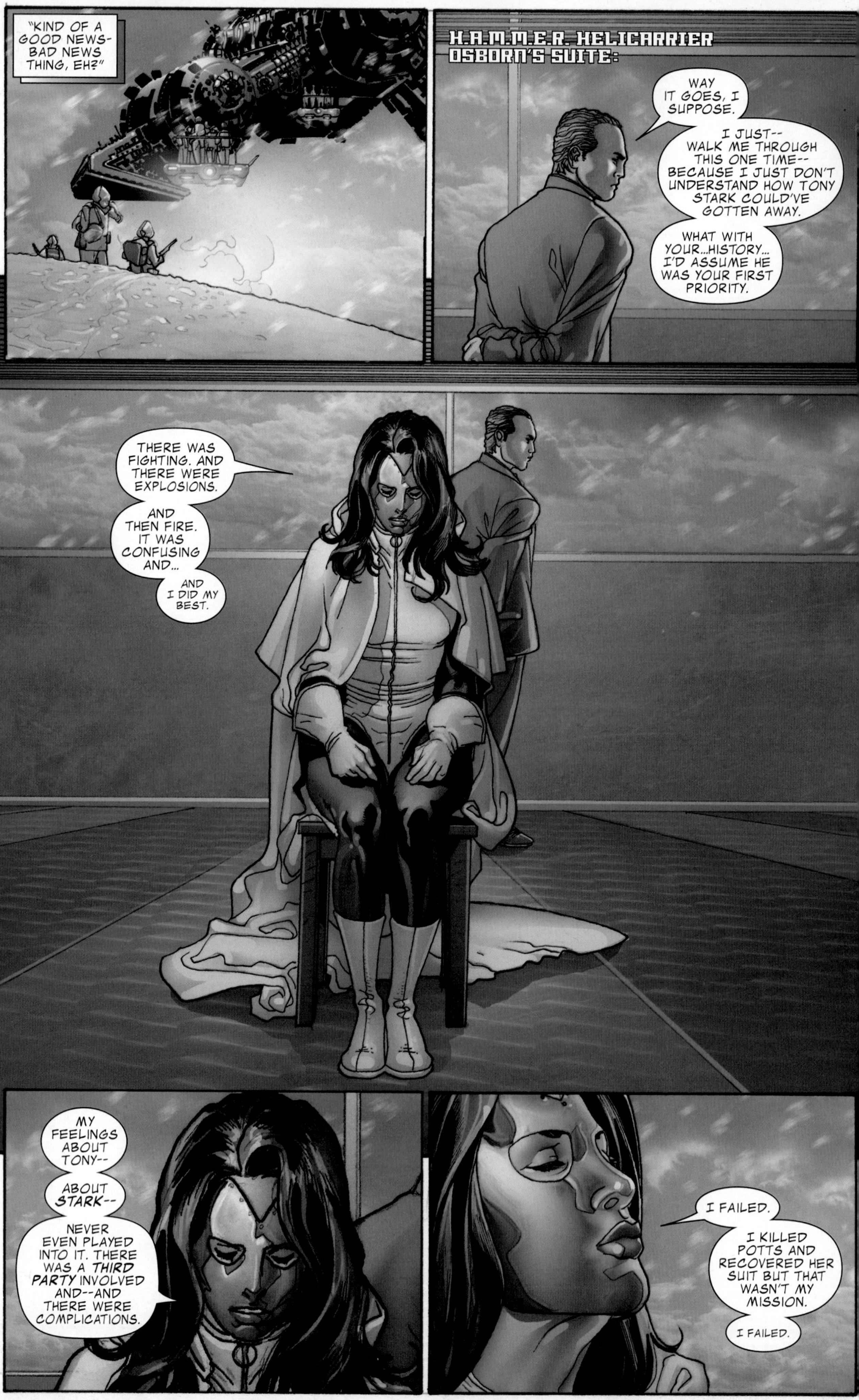
"KIND OF A GOOD NEWS-BAD NEWS THING, EH?"
H.A.M.M.E.R. HELICARRIER OSBORN'S SUITE:
WAY IT GOES, I SUPPOSE.
I JUST-- WALK ME THROUGH THIS ONE TIME-- BECAUSE I JUST DON'T UNDERSTAND HOW TONY STARK COULD'VE GOTTEN AWAY.
WHAT WITH YOUR...HISTORY... I'D ASSUME HE WAS YOUR FIRST PRIORITY.
THERE WAS FIGHTING. AND THERE WERE EXPLOSIONS.
AND THEN FIRE. IT WAS CONFUSING AND...
AND I DID MY BEST.
MY FEELINGS ABOUT TONY--
ABOUT STARK--
NEVER EVEN PLAYED INTO IT. THERE WAS A THIRD PARTY INVOLVED AND--AND THERE WERE COMPLICATIONS.
I FAILED.
I KILLED POTTS AND RECOVERED HER SUIT BUT THAT WASN'T MY MISSION.
I FAILED.

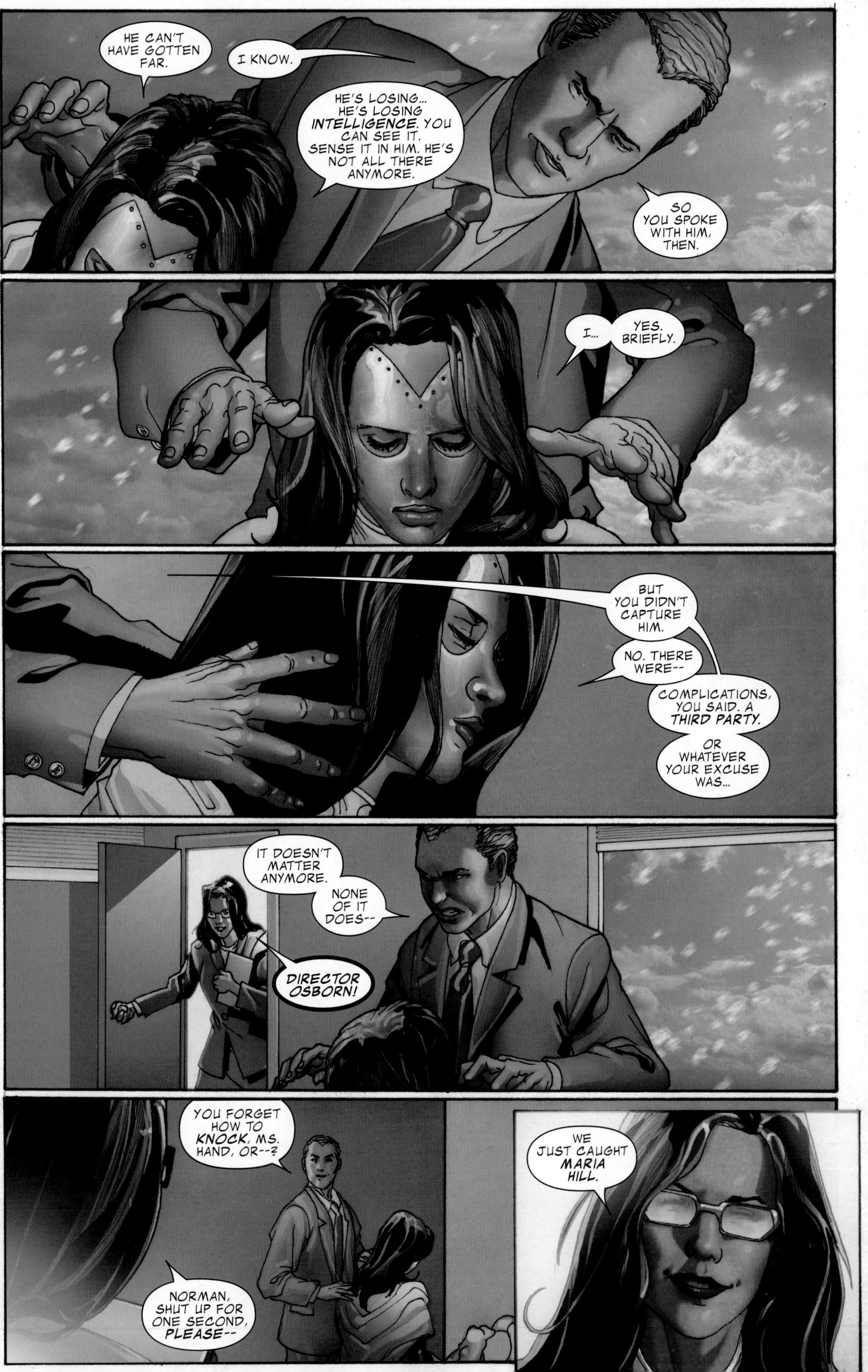
HE CAN'T HAVE GOTTEN FAR.
I KNOW.
HE'S LOSING... HE'S LOSING INTELLIGENCE. YOU CAN SEE IT. SENSE IT IN HIM. HE'S NOT ALL THERE ANYMORE.
SO YOU SPOKE WITH HIM, THEN.
I...
YES. BRIEFLY.
BUT YOU DIDN'T CAPTURE HIM.
NO. THERE WERE--
COMPLICATIONS, YOU SAID. A THIRD PARTY.
OR WHATEVER YOUR EXCUSE WAS...
IT DOESN'T MATTER ANYMORE.
NONE OF IT DOES--
DIRECTOR OSBORN!
YOU FORGET HOW TO KNOCK, MS. HAND, OR--?
NORMAN, SHUT UP FOR ONE SECOND, PLEASE--
WE JUST CAUGHT MARIA HILL.

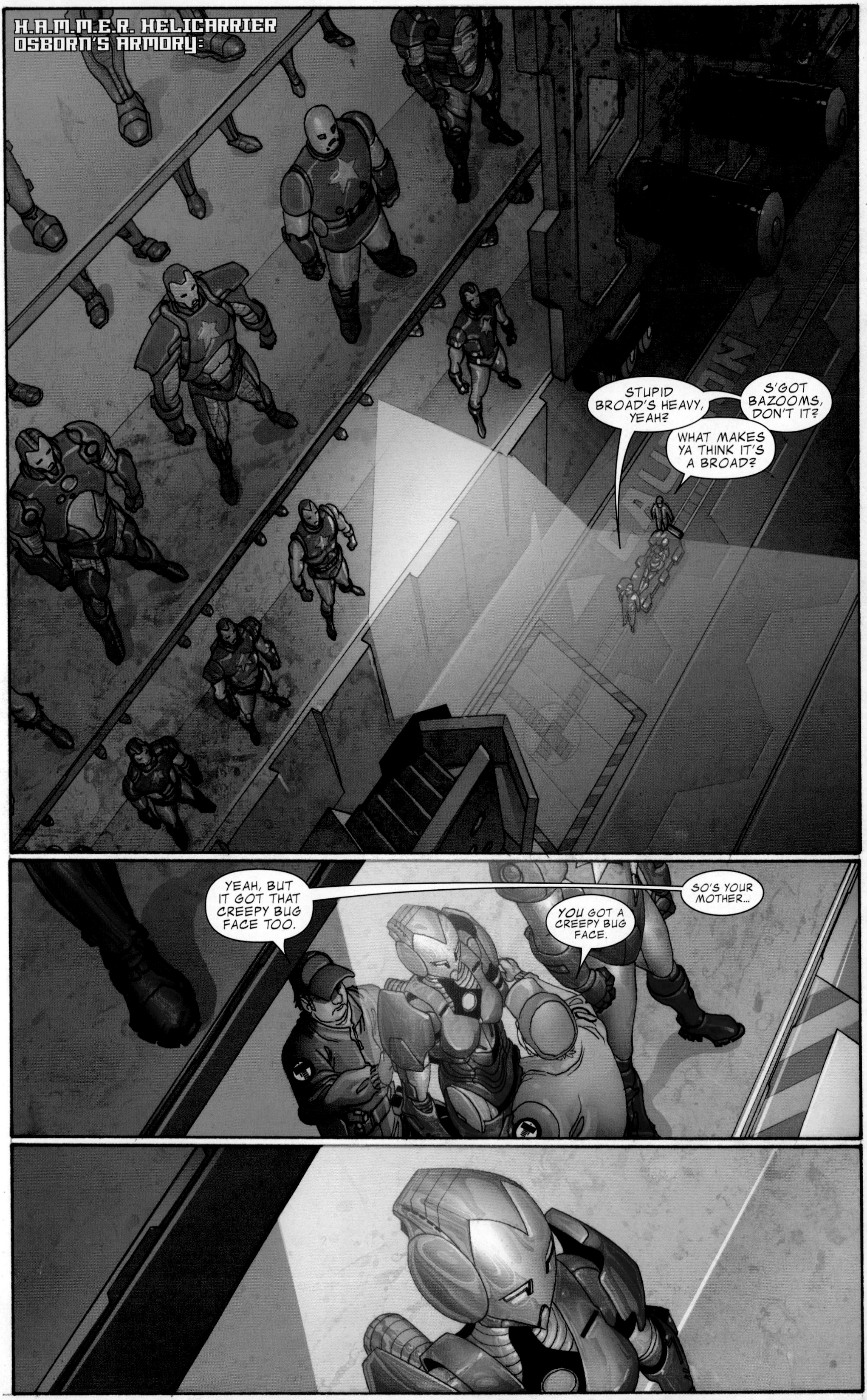
H.A.M.M.E.R. HELICARRIER
OSBORN'S ARMORY:
STUPID BROAD'S HEAVY, YEAH?
S'GOT BAZOOMS, DON'T IT?
WHAT MAKES YA THINK IT'S A BROAD?
YEAH, BUT IT GOT THAT CREEPY BUG FACE TOO.
SO'S YOUR MOTHER...
YOU GOT A CREEPY BUG FACE.

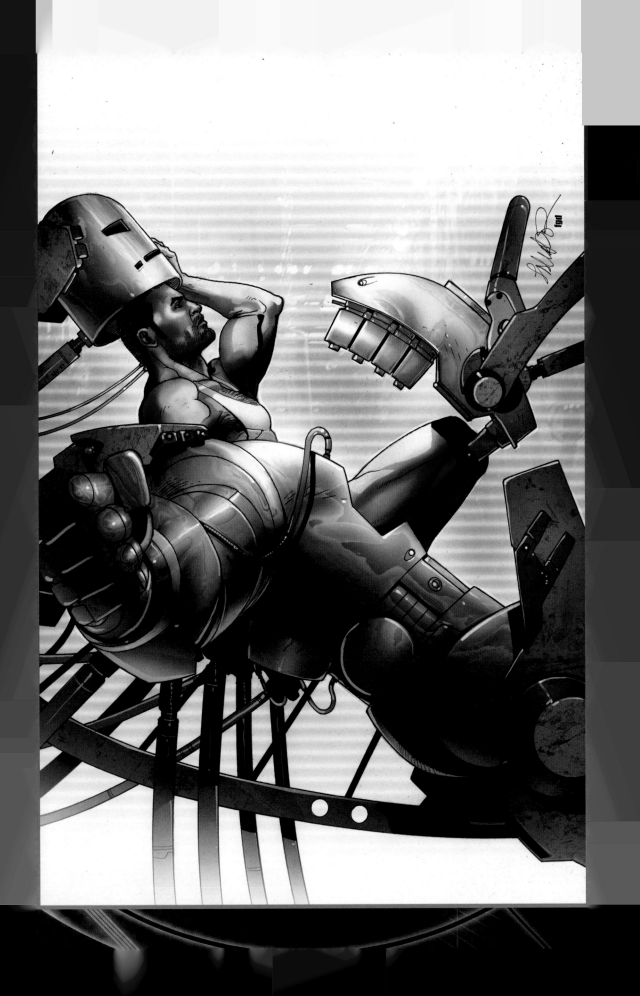

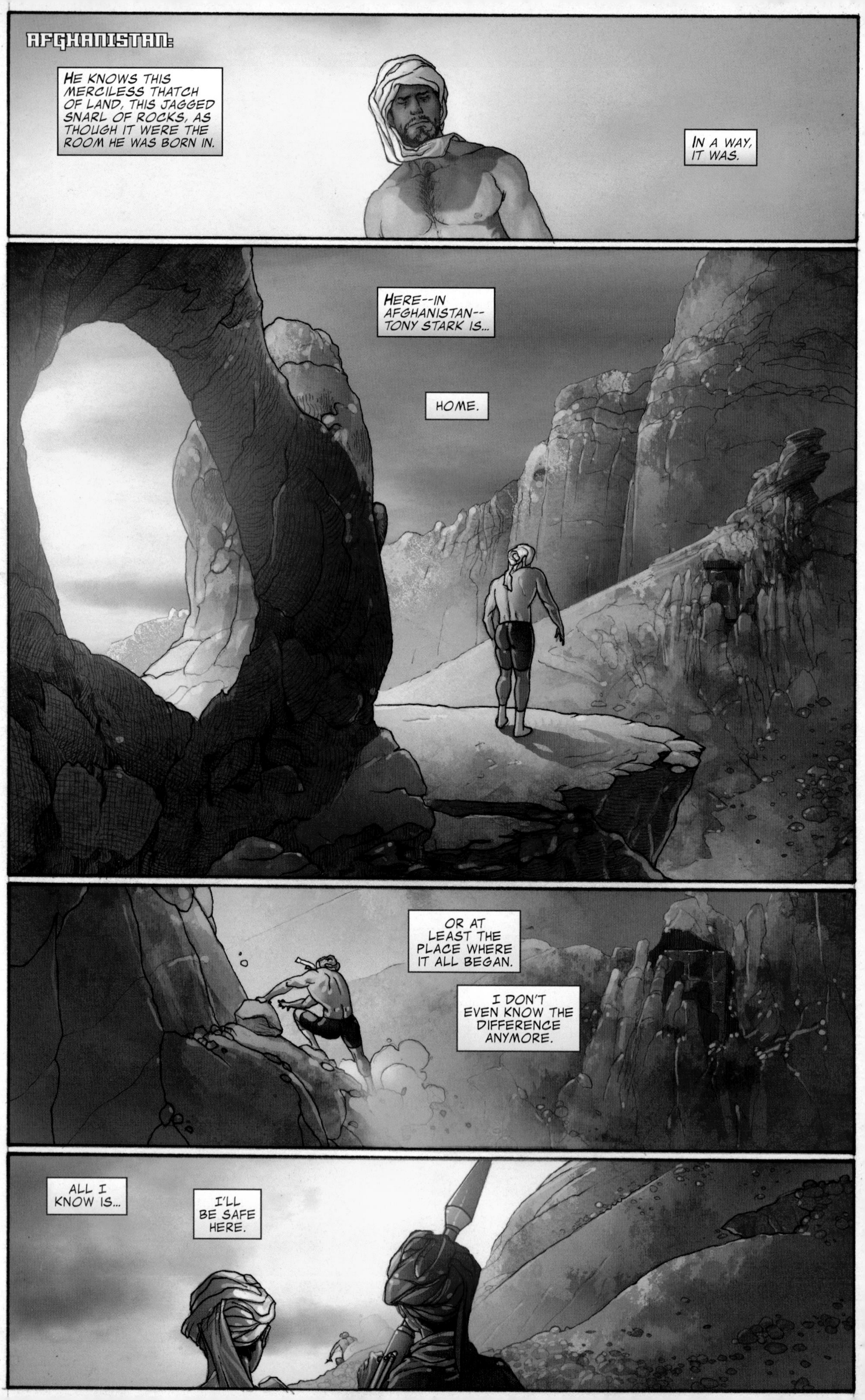
AFGHANISTAN:
HE KNOWS THIS MERCILESS THATCH OF LAND, THIS JAGGED SNARL OF ROCKS, AS THOUGH IT WERE THE ROOM HE WAS BORN IN.
IN A WAY, IT WAS.
HERE--IN AFGHANISTAN--TONY STARK IS...
HOME.
OR AT LEAST THE PLACE WHERE IT ALL BEGAN.
I DON'T EVEN KNOW THE DIFFERENCE ANYMORE.
ALL I KNOW IS...
I'LL BE SAFE HERE.

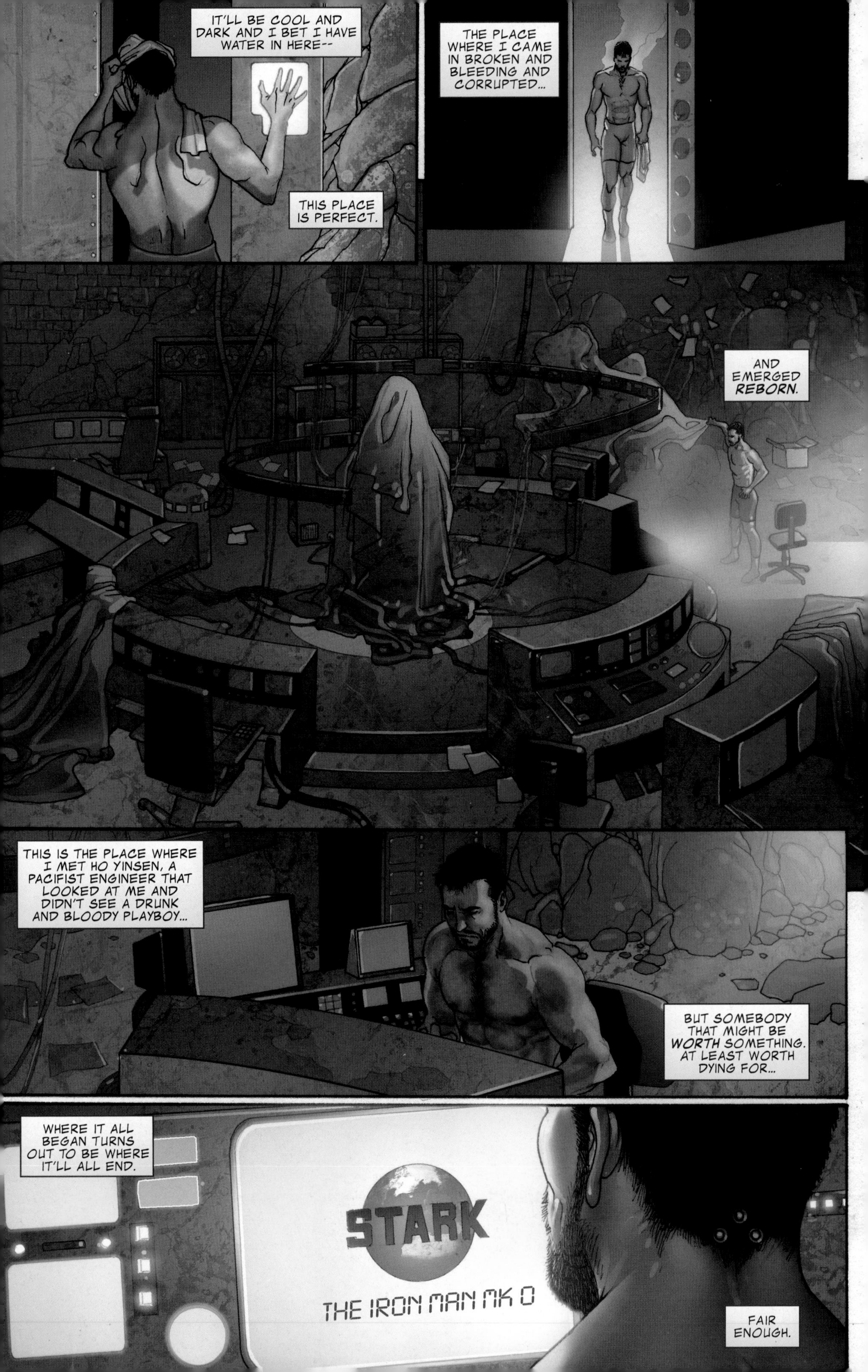
IT'LL BE COOL AND DARK AND I BET I HAVE WATER IN HERE--
THIS PLACE IS PERFECT.
THE PLACE WHERE I CAME IN BROKEN AND BLEEDING AND CORRUPTED...
AND EMERGED REBORN.
THIS IS THE PLACE WHERE I MET HO YINSEN, A PACIFIST ENGINEER THAT LOOKED AT ME AND DIDN'T SEE A DRUNK AND BLOODY PLAYBOY...
BUT SOMEBODY THAT MIGHT BE WORTH SOMETHING. AT LEAST WORTH DYING FOR...
WHERE IT ALL BEGAN TURNS OUT TO BE WHERE IT'LL ALL END.
STARK
THE IRON MAN MK 0
FAIR ENOUGH.

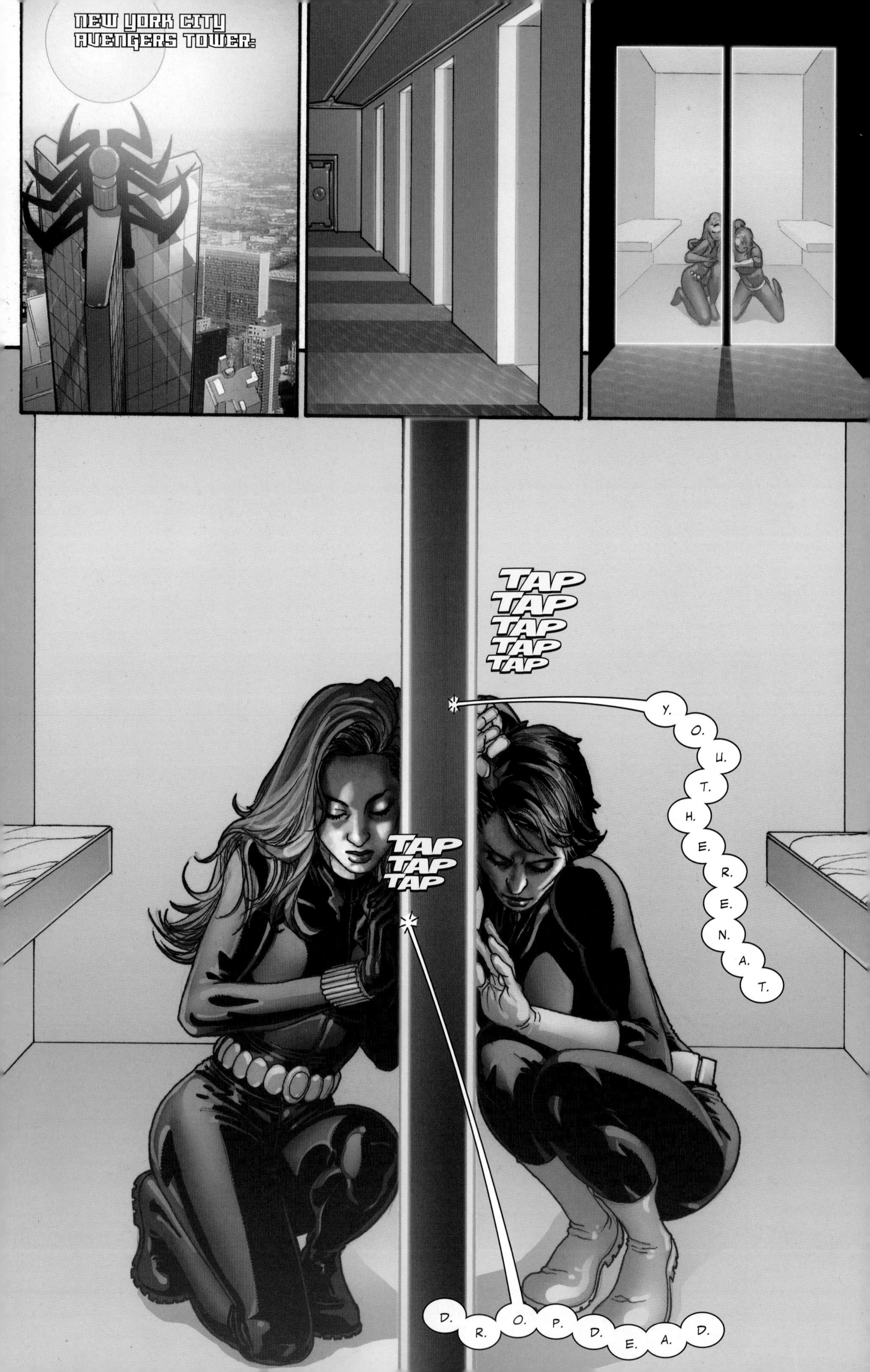
NEW YORK CITY
AVENGERS TOWER:
TAP
TAP
TAP
TAP
TAP
Y. O. U. T. H. E. R. E. N. A. T.
TAP
TAP
TAP
D. R. O. P. D. E. A. D.

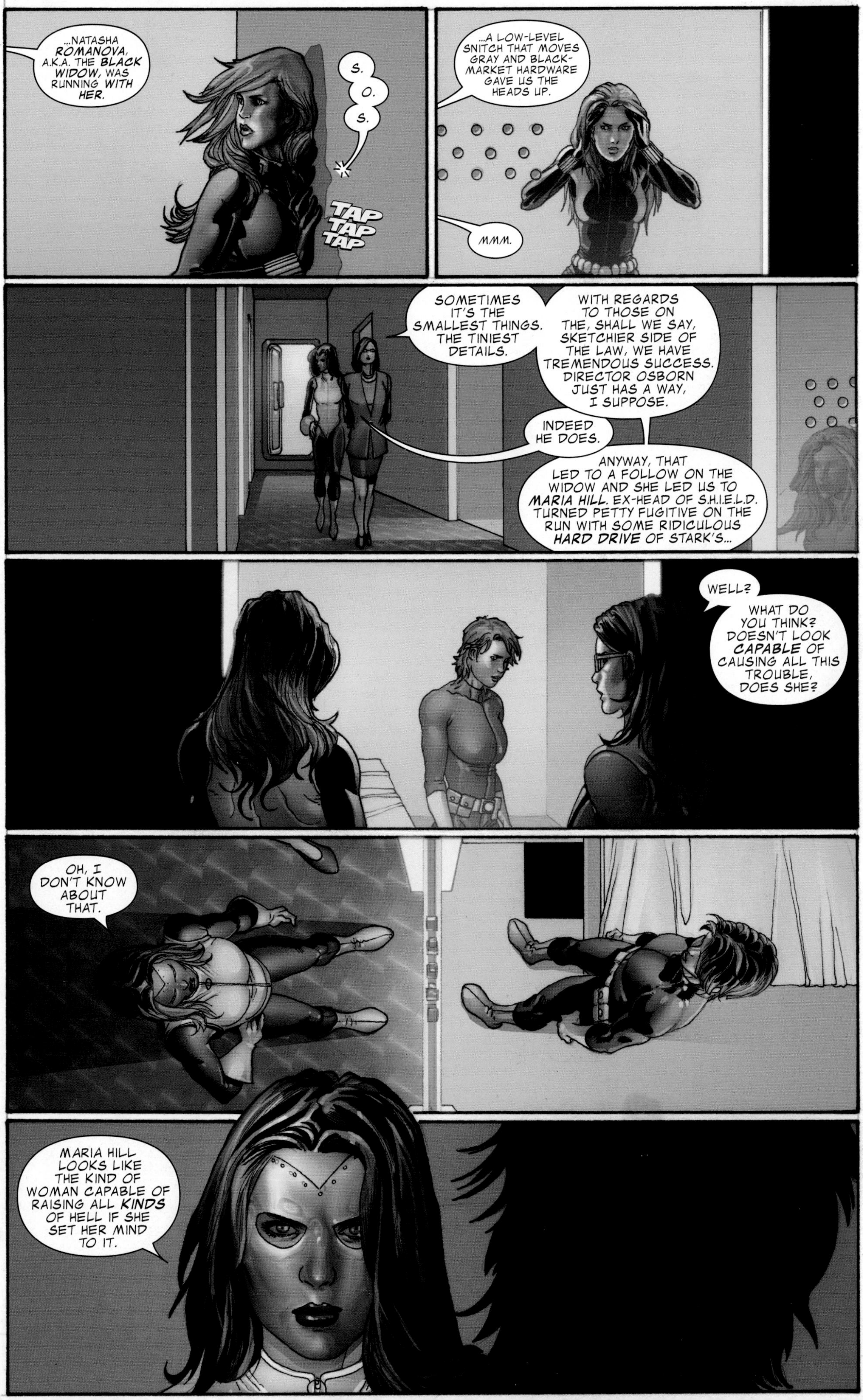
...NATASHA ROMANOVA, A.K.A. THE BLACK WIDOW, WAS RUNNING WITH HER.
S. O. S.
TAP TAP TAP
...A LOW-LEVEL SNITCH THAT MOVES GRAY AND BLACK-MARKET HARDWARE GAVE US THE HEADS UP.
MMM.
SOMETIMES IT'S THE SMALLEST THINGS. THE TINIEST DETAILS.
WITH REGARDS TO THOSE ON THE, SHALL WE SAY, SKETCHIER SIDE OF THE LAW, WE HAVE TREMENDOUS SUCCESS. DIRECTOR OSBORN JUST HAS A WAY, I SUPPOSE.
INDEED HE DOES.
ANYWAY, THAT LED TO A FOLLOW ON THE WIDOW AND SHE LED US TO MARIA HILL. EX-HEAD OF S.H.I.E.L.D. TURNED PETTY FUGITIVE ON THE RUN WITH SOME RIDICULOUS HARD DRIVE OF STARK'S...
WELL?
WHAT DO YOU THINK? DOESN'T LOOK CAPABLE OF CAUSING ALL THIS TROUBLE, DOES SHE?
OH, I DON'T KNOW ABOUT THAT.
MARIA HILL LOOKS LIKE THE KIND OF WOMAN CAPABLE OF RAISING ALL KINDS OF HELL IF SHE SET HER MIND TO IT.

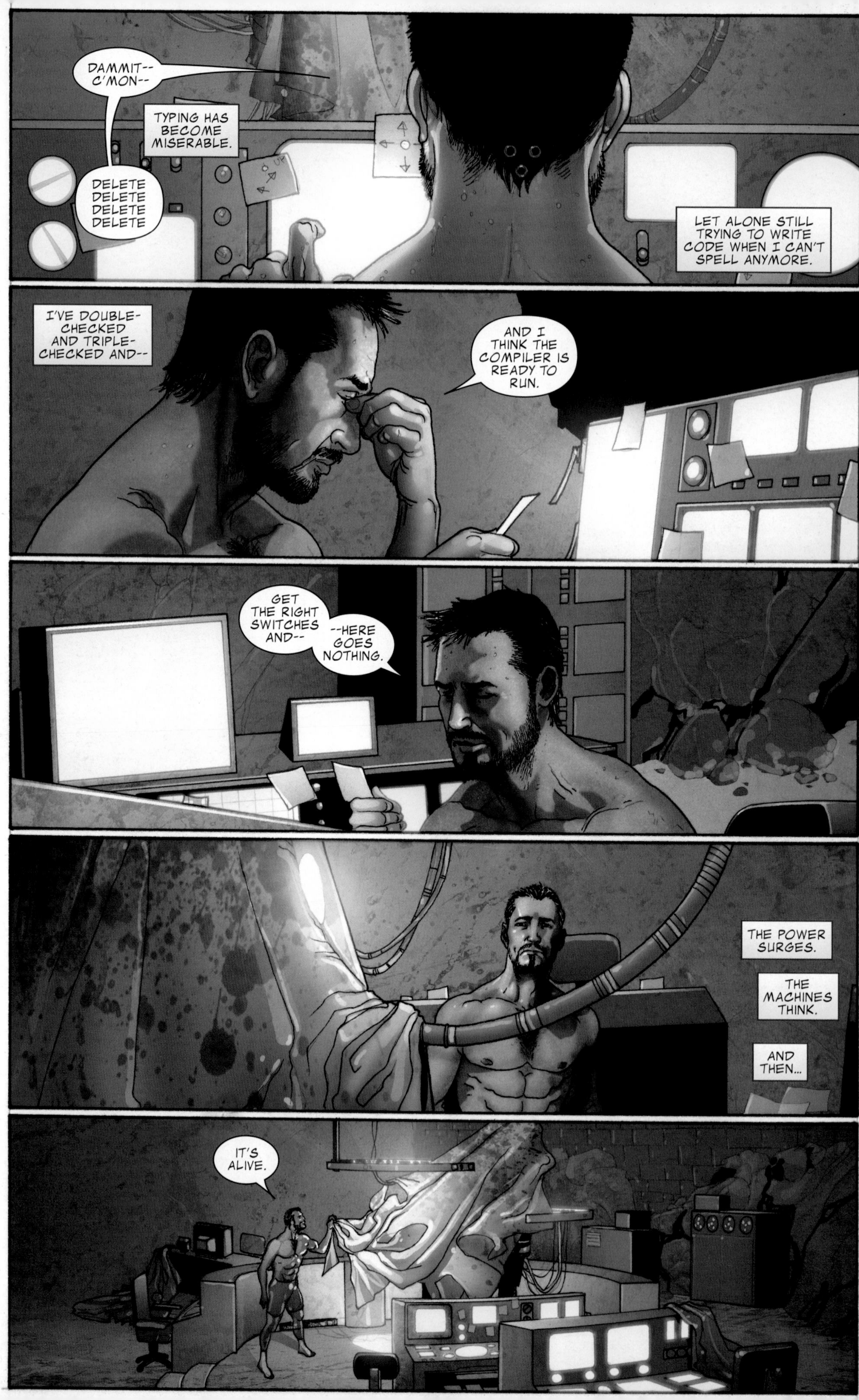
DAMMIT-- C'MON--
TYPING HAS BECOME MISERABLE.
DELETE DELETE DELETE DELETE
LET ALONE STILL TRYING TO WRITE CODE WHEN I CAN'T SPELL ANYMORE.
I'VE DOUBLE-CHECKED AND TRIPLE-CHECKED AND--
AND I THINK THE COMPILER IS READY TO RUN.
GET THE RIGHT SWITCHES AND--
--HERE GOES NOTHING.
THE POWER SURGES.
THE MACHINES THINK.
AND THEN...
IT'S ALIVE.

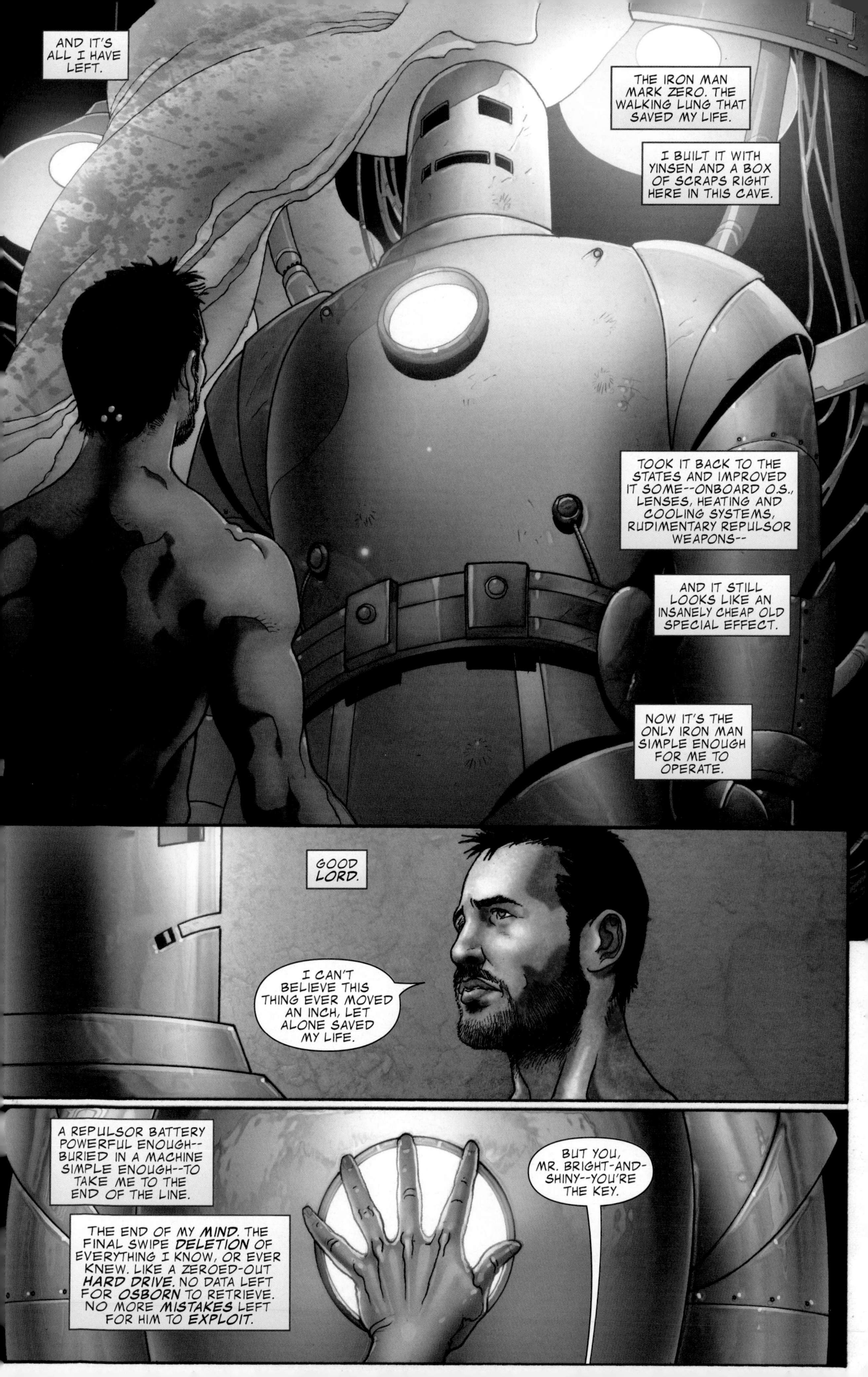
AND IT'S ALL I HAVE LEFT.
THE IRON MAN MARK ZERO. THE WALKING LUNG THAT SAVED MY LIFE.
I BUILT IT WITH YINSEN AND A BOX OF SCRAPS RIGHT HERE IN THIS CAVE.
TOOK IT BACK TO THE STATES AND IMPROVED IT SOME--ONBOARD O.S., LENSES, HEATING AND COOLING SYSTEMS, RUDIMENTARY REPULSOR WEAPONS--
AND IT STILL LOOKS LIKE AN INSANELY CHEAP OLD SPECIAL EFFECT.
NOW IT'S THE ONLY IRON MAN SIMPLE ENOUGH FOR ME TO OPERATE.
GOOD *LORD*.
I CAN'T BELIEVE THIS THING EVER MOVED AN INCH, LET ALONE SAVED MY LIFE.
A REPULSOR BATTERY POWERFUL ENOUGH--BURIED IN A MACHINE SIMPLE ENOUGH--TO TAKE ME TO THE END OF THE LINE.
THE END OF MY *MIND*. THE FINAL SWIPE *DELETION* OF EVERYTHING I KNOW, OR EVER KNEW. LIKE A ZEROED-OUT *HARD DRIVE*. NO DATA LEFT FOR *OSBORN* TO RETRIEVE. NO MORE *MISTAKES* LEFT FOR HIM TO *EXPLOIT*.
BUT YOU, MR. BRIGHT-AND-SHINY--YOU'RE THE KEY.

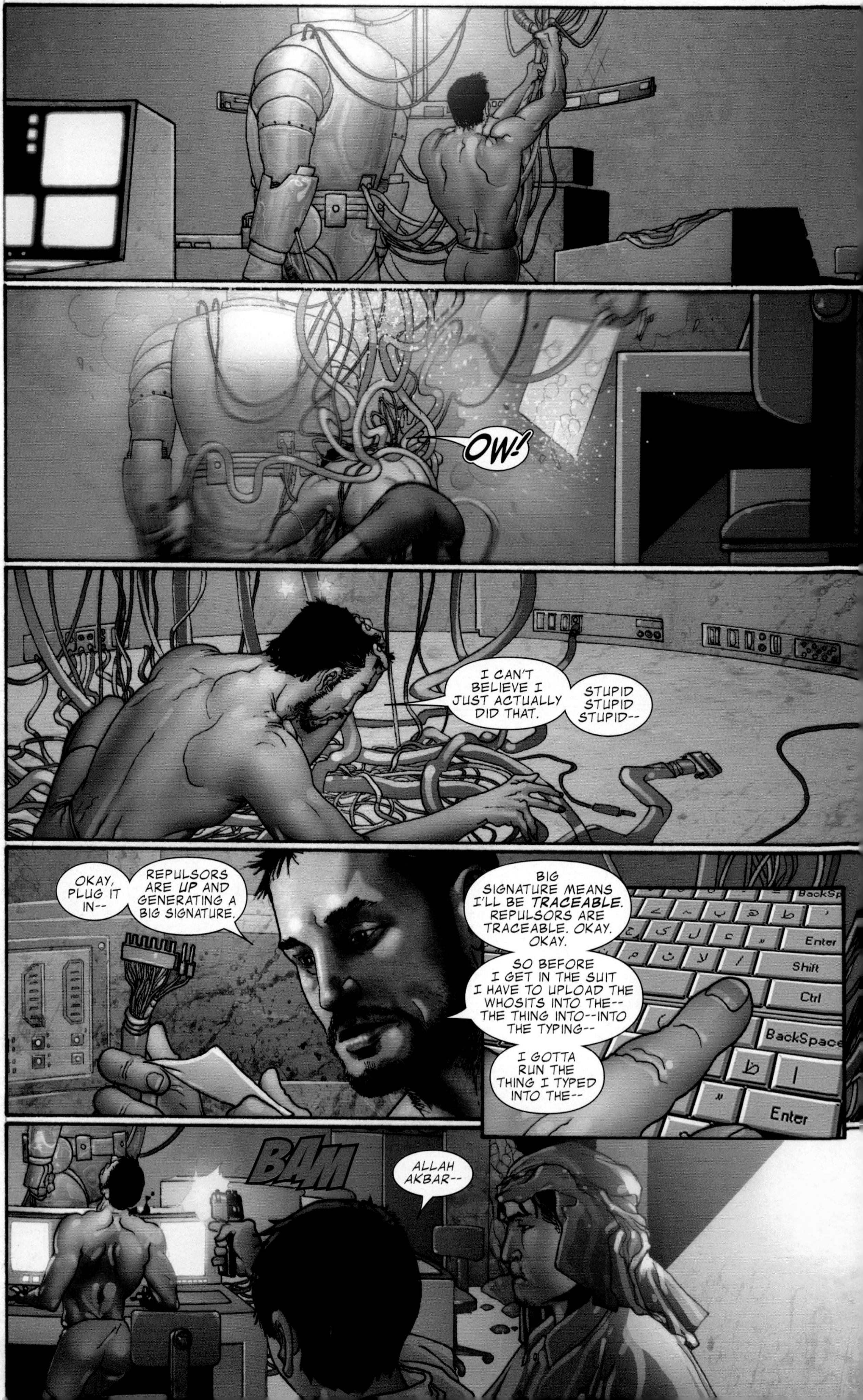
OW!
I CAN'T BELIEVE I JUST ACTUALLY DID THAT.
STUPID STUPID STUPID--
OKAY, PLUG IT IN--
REPULSORS ARE UP AND GENERATING A BIG SIGNATURE.
BIG SIGNATURE MEANS I'LL BE TRACEABLE. REPULSORS ARE TRACEABLE. OKAY. OKAY.
SO BEFORE I GET IN THE SUIT I HAVE TO UPLOAD THE WHOSITS INTO THE-- THE THING INTO--INTO THE TYPING--
I GOTTA RUN THE THING I TYPED INTO THE--
BackSpace
Enter
Shift
Ctrl
BAM
ALLAH AKBAR--

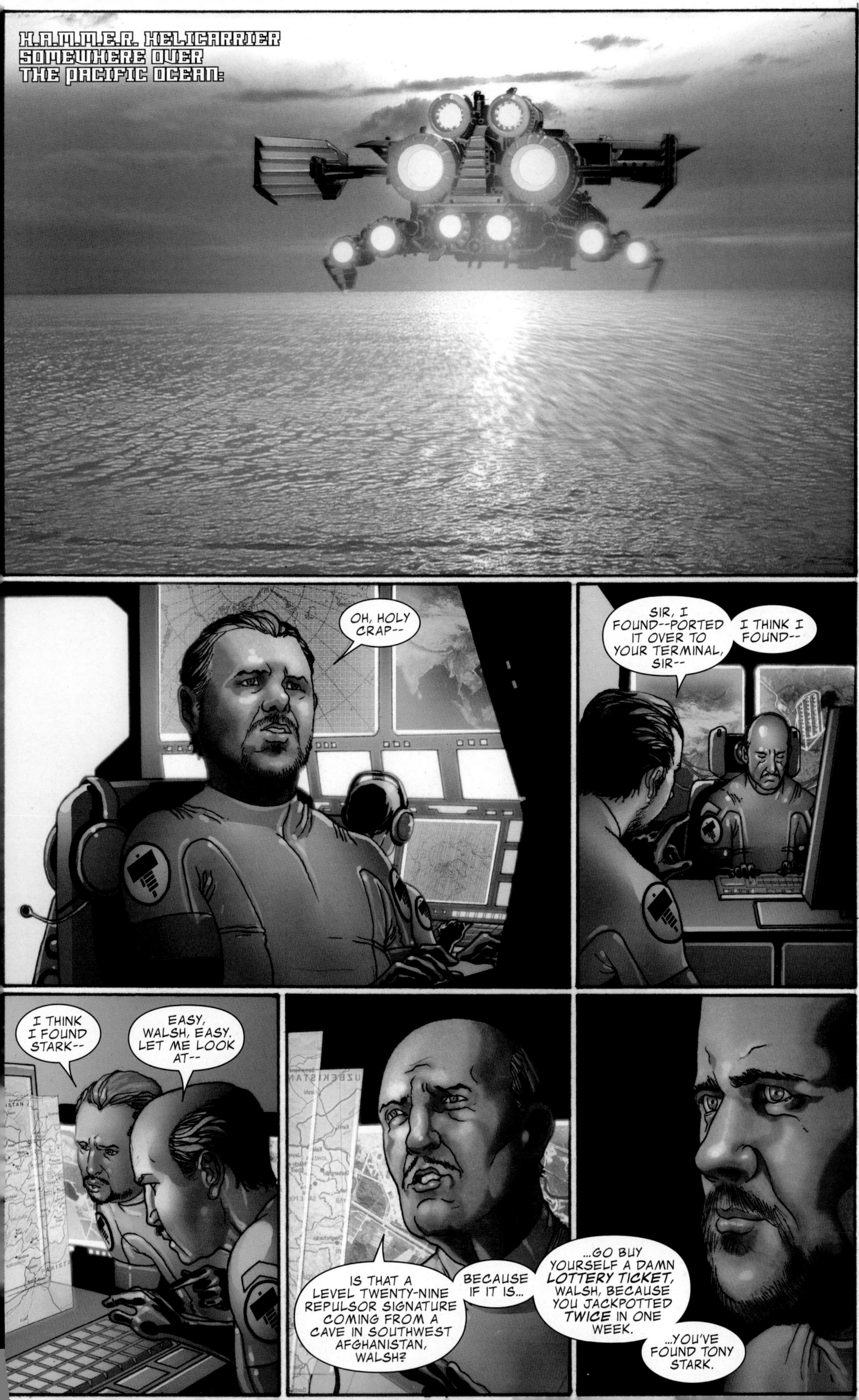
H.A.M.M.E.R. HELICARRIER
SOMEWHERE OVER
THE PACIFIC OCEAN:
OH, HOLY CRAP--
SIR, I FOUND--PORTED IT OVER TO YOUR TERMINAL, SIR--
I THINK I FOUND--
I THINK I FOUND STARK--
EASY, WALSH, EASY. LET ME LOOK AT--
IS THAT A LEVEL TWENTY-NINE REPULSOR SIGNATURE COMING FROM A CAVE IN SOUTHWEST AFGHANISTAN, WALSH?
BECAUSE IF IT IS...
...GO BUY YOURSELF A DAMN LOTTERY TICKET, WALSH, BECAUSE YOU JACKPOTTED TWICE IN ONE WEEK.
...YOU'VE FOUND TONY STARK.

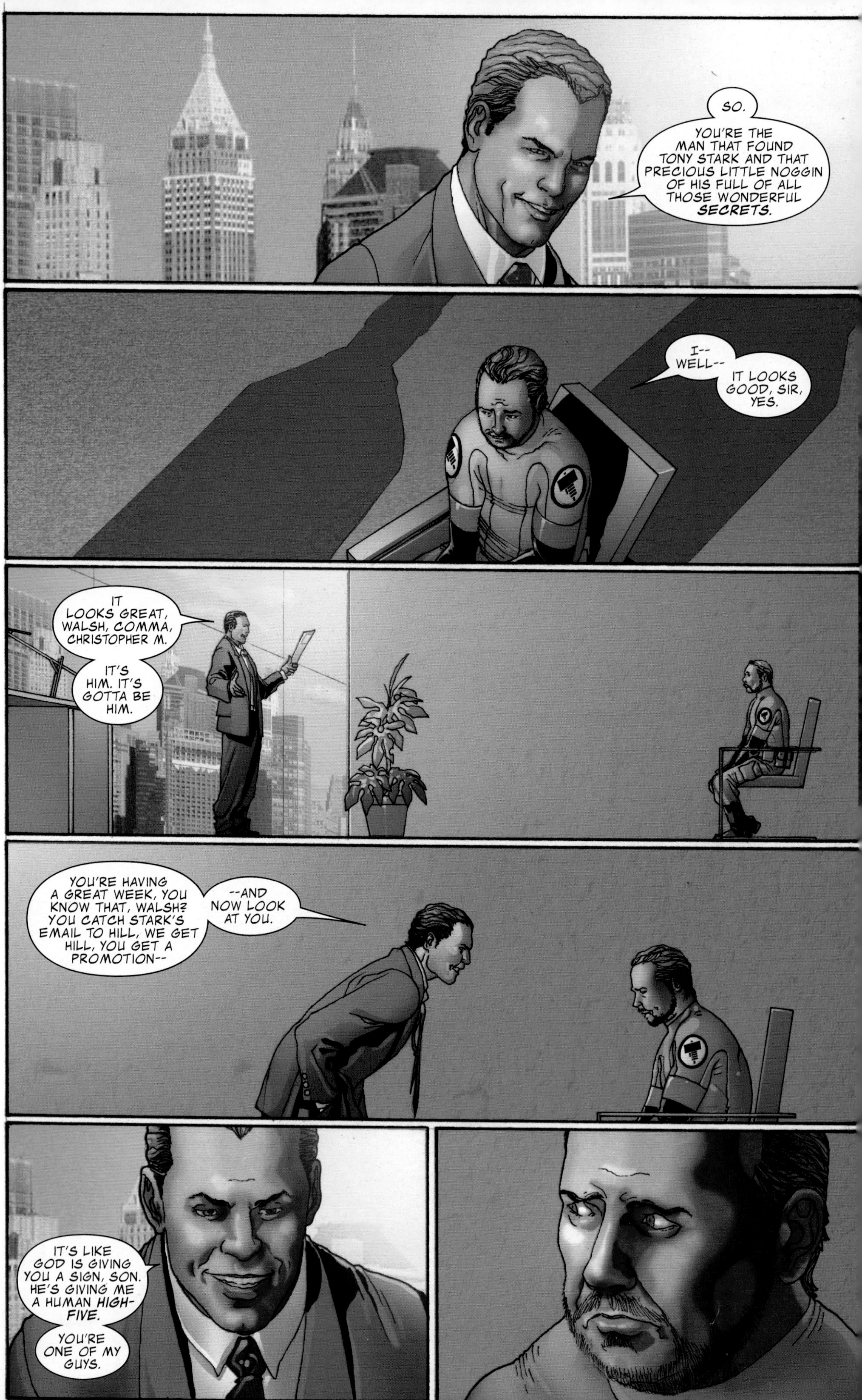
SO.
YOU'RE THE MAN THAT FOUND TONY STARK AND THAT PRECIOUS LITTLE NOGGIN OF HIS FULL OF ALL THOSE WONDERFUL SECRETS.
I-- WELL--
IT LOOKS GOOD, SIR, YES.
IT LOOKS GREAT, WALSH, COMMA, CHRISTOPHER M.
IT'S HIM. IT'S GOTTA BE HIM.
YOU'RE HAVING A GREAT WEEK, YOU KNOW THAT, WALSH? YOU CATCH STARK'S EMAIL TO HILL, WE GET HILL, YOU GET A PROMOTION--
--AND NOW LOOK AT YOU.
IT'S LIKE GOD IS GIVING YOU A SIGN, SON. HE'S GIVING ME A HUMAN HIGH-FIVE.
YOU'RE ONE OF MY GUYS.

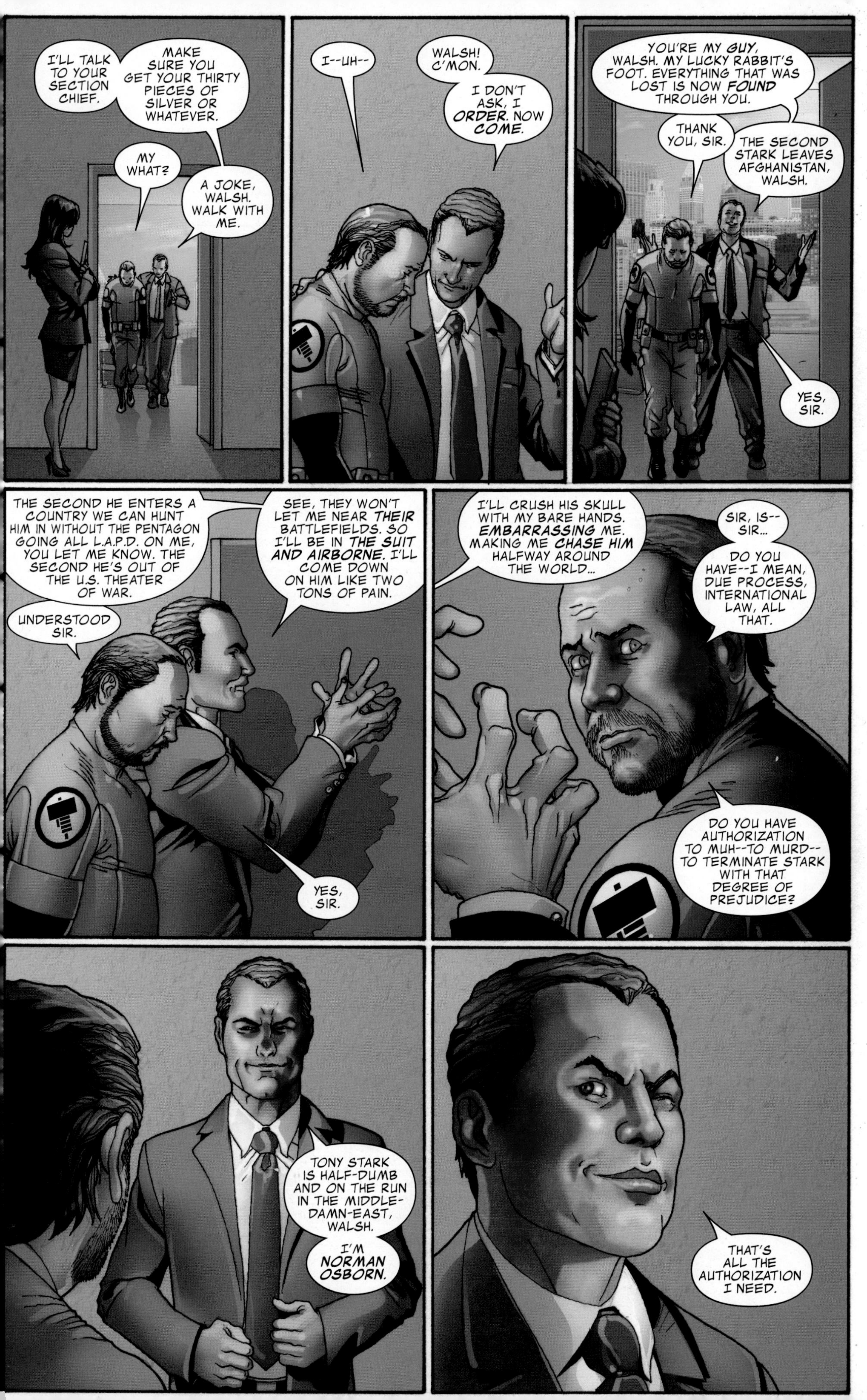
I'LL TALK TO YOUR SECTION CHIEF.
MAKE SURE YOU GET YOUR THIRTY PIECES OF SILVER OR WHATEVER.
MY WHAT?
A JOKE, WALSH. WALK WITH ME.
I--UH--
WALSH! C'MON.
I DON'T ASK, I ORDER. NOW COME.
YOU'RE MY GUY, WALSH. MY LUCKY RABBIT'S FOOT. EVERYTHING THAT WAS LOST IS NOW FOUND THROUGH YOU.
THANK YOU, SIR.
THE SECOND STARK LEAVES AFGHANISTAN, WALSH.
YES, SIR.
THE SECOND HE ENTERS A COUNTRY WE CAN HUNT HIM IN WITHOUT THE PENTAGON GOING ALL L.A.P.D. ON ME, YOU LET ME KNOW. THE SECOND HE'S OUT OF THE U.S. THEATER OF WAR.
UNDERSTOOD SIR.
SEE, THEY WON'T LET ME NEAR THEIR BATTLEFIELDS. SO I'LL BE IN THE SUIT AND AIRBORNE. I'LL COME DOWN ON HIM LIKE TWO TONS OF PAIN.
YES, SIR.
I'LL CRUSH HIS SKULL WITH MY BARE HANDS. EMBARRASSING ME. MAKING ME CHASE HIM HALFWAY AROUND THE WORLD...
SIR, IS-- SIR...
DO YOU HAVE--I MEAN, DUE PROCESS, INTERNATIONAL LAW, ALL THAT.
DO YOU HAVE AUTHORIZATION TO MUH--TO MURD-- TO TERMINATE STARK WITH THAT DEGREE OF PREJUDICE?
TONY STARK IS HALF-DUMB AND ON THE RUN IN THE MIDDLE-DAMN-EAST, WALSH.
I'M NORMAN OSBORN.
THAT'S ALL THE AUTHORIZATION I NEED.

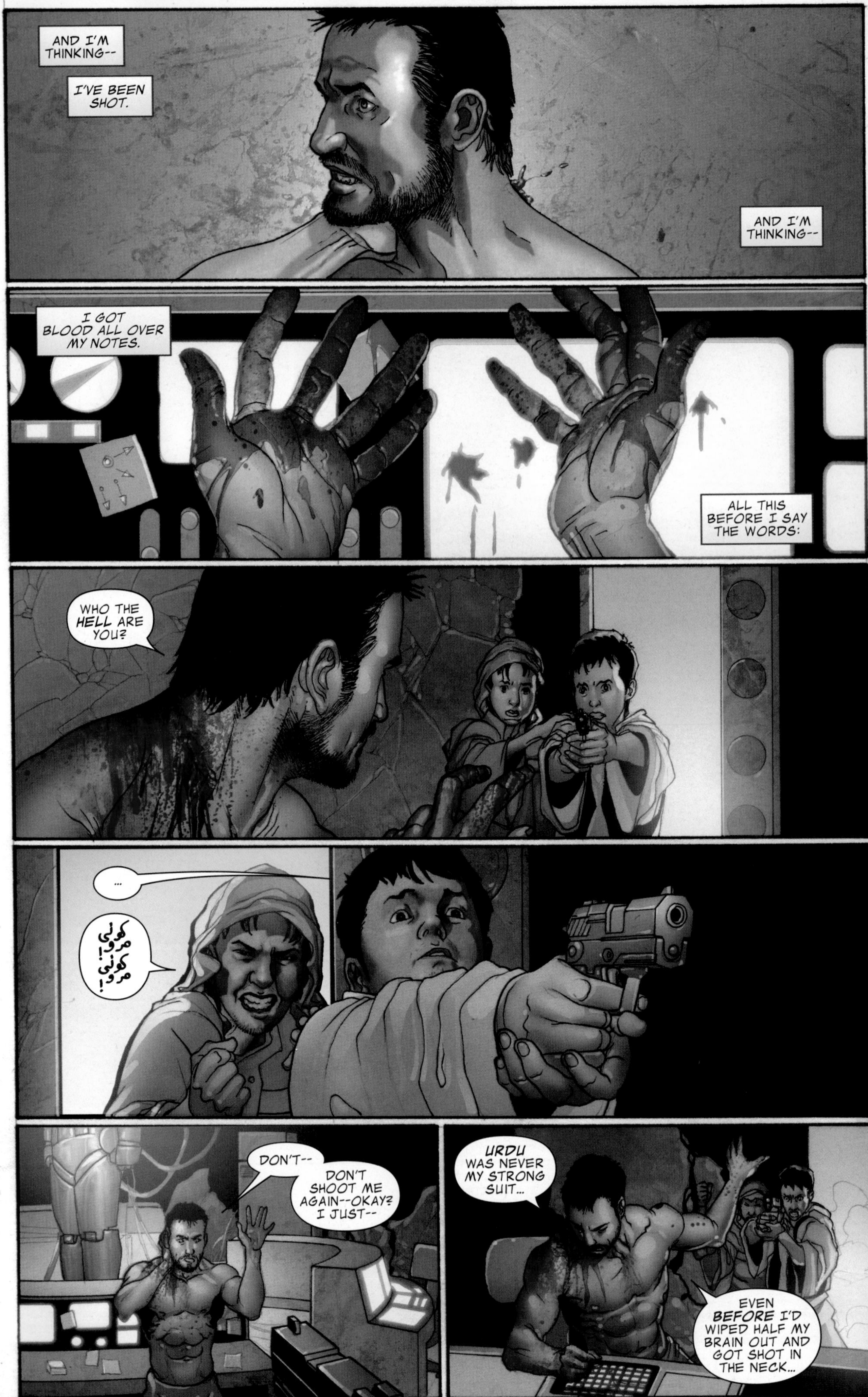
AND I'M THINKING--
I'VE BEEN SHOT.
AND I'M THINKING--
I GOT BLOOD ALL OVER MY NOTES.
ALL THIS BEFORE I SAY THE WORDS:
WHO THE HELL ARE YOU?
...
کوتی مرو! کونی مرو!
DON'T--
DON'T SHOOT ME AGAIN--OKAY? I JUST--
URDU WAS NEVER MY STRONG SUIT...
EVEN BEFORE I'D WIPED HALF MY BRAIN OUT AND GOT SHOT IN THE NECK...

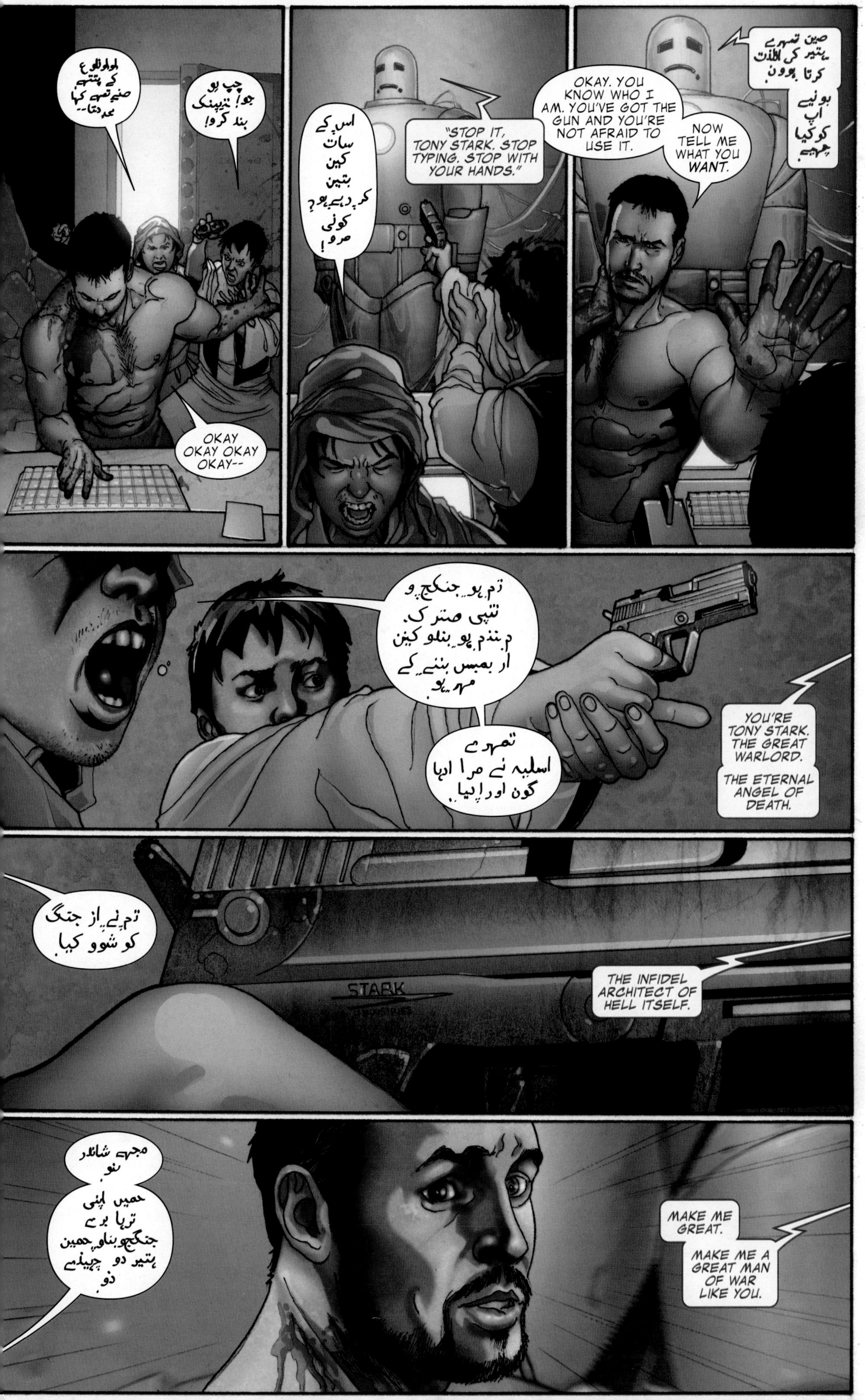

لولولولو ع کے پتتھے صنیے تمھے کہا بعد دتا--
چپ ہو جو! ٹیپنک بند کرو!
OKAY OKAY OKAY OKAY--
اس کے سات کین بتین کر دیے ہو؟ کونی صرو!
"STOP IT, TONY STARK. STOP TYPING. STOP WITH YOUR HANDS."
OKAY. YOU KNOW WHO I AM. YOU'VE GOT THE GUN AND YOU'RE NOT AFRAID TO USE IT.
صین تمھرے ہتیر کی اللذت کرتا ہوون.
NOW TELL ME WHAT YOU WANT.
بونیے اپ کوکیا چھیے.
تم ہو جنکج و تنپی صنترک. م بندم ہو بنلو کین ار بمبس بننے کے مھ ہو.
تمھرے اسلیہ نے مرا ادہا گون اوراپیا.
YOU'RE TONY STARK. THE GREAT WARLORD.
THE ETERNAL ANGEL OF DEATH.
تم نے از جتگ کو شوو کیا.
THE INFIDEL ARCHITECT OF HELL ITSELF.
STARK
مجھے شاندر نو.
حمیں اپنی تربا برے جنگجو بناو حمین ہتیر دو چیدے دو.
MAKE ME GREAT.
MAKE ME A GREAT MAN OF WAR LIKE YOU.

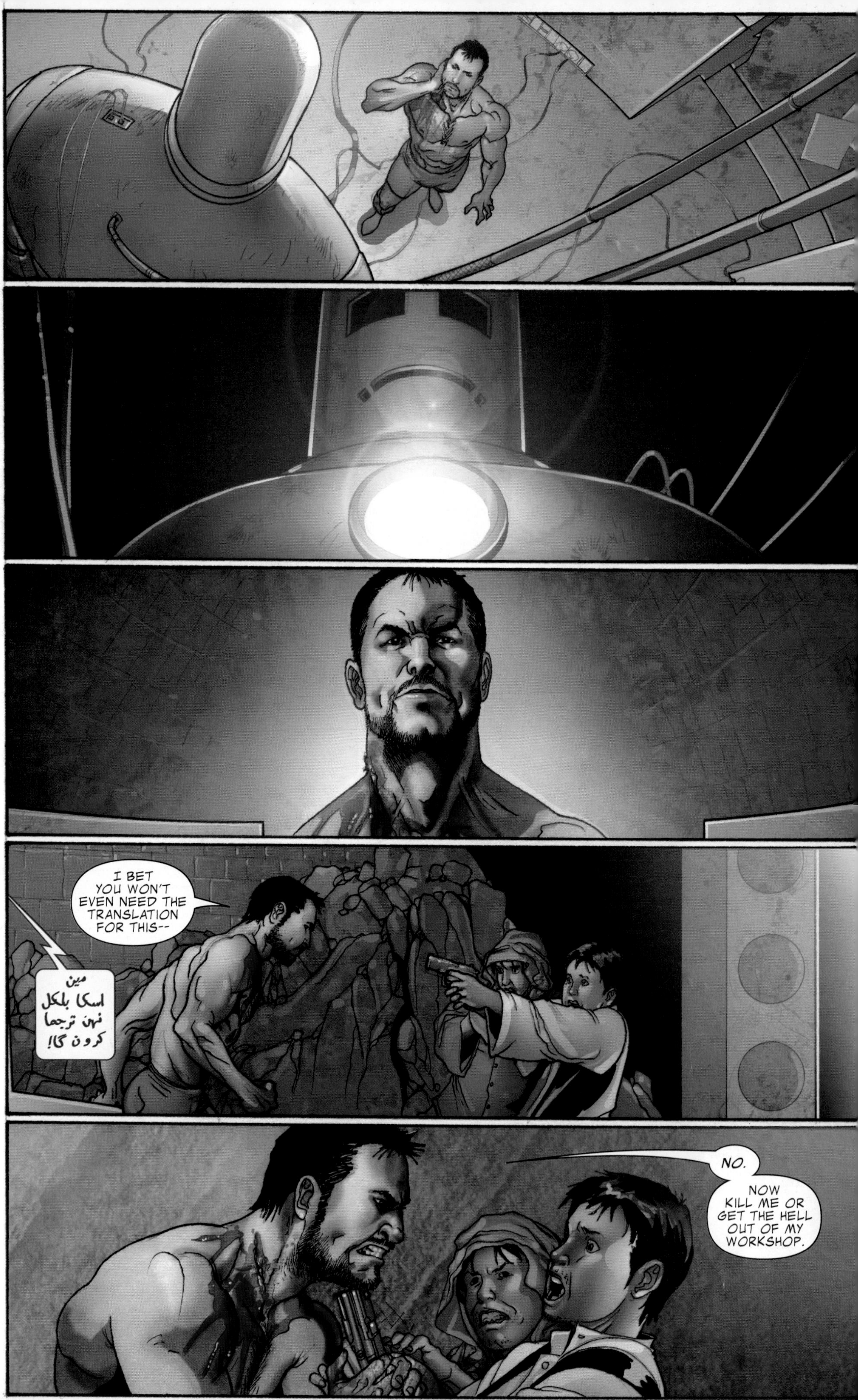

I BET YOU WON'T EVEN NEED THE TRANSLATION FOR THIS--
مین اسکا بلکل نہں ترجما کرون گا!
NO.
NOW KILL ME OR GET THE HELL OUT OF MY WORKSHOP.

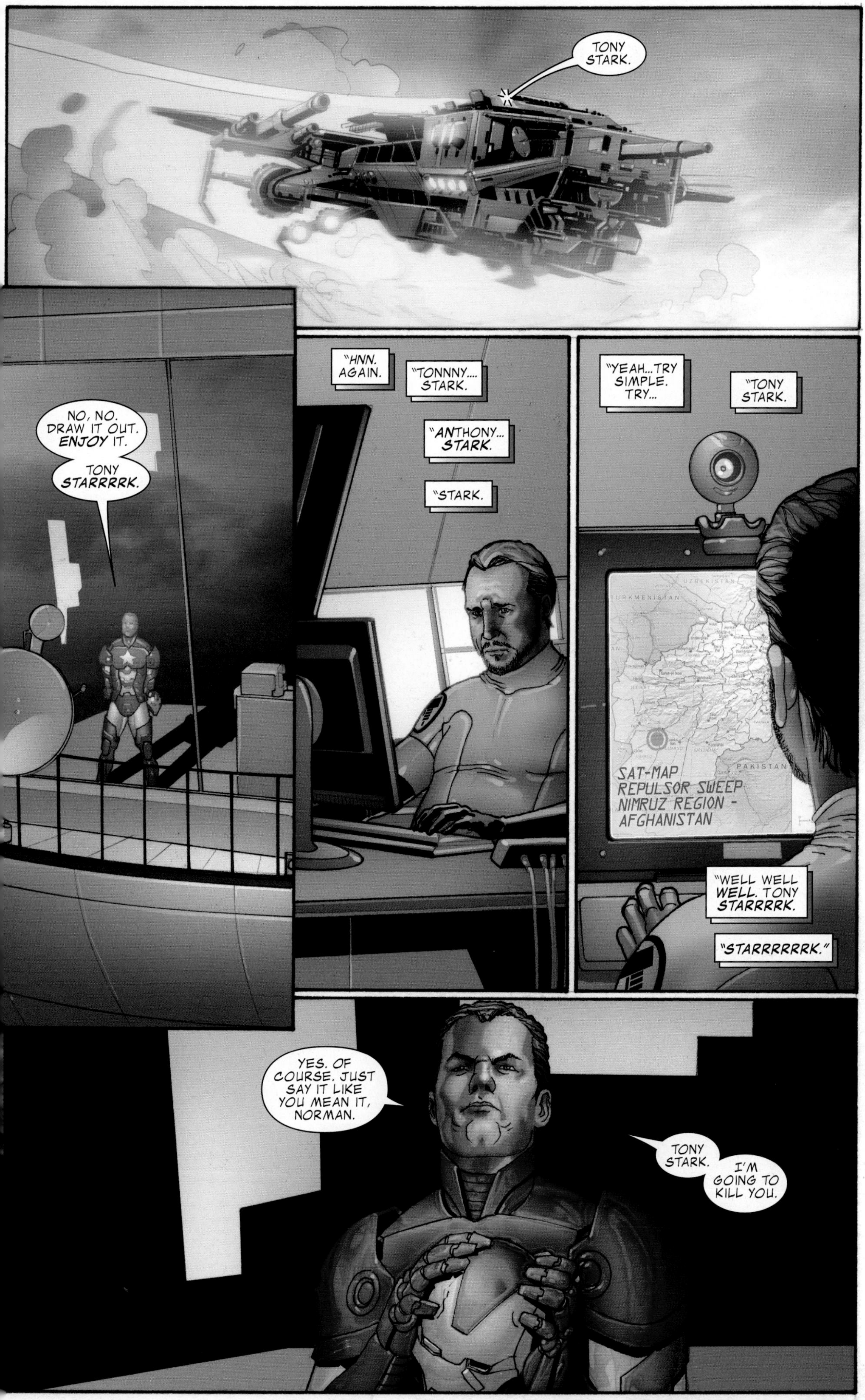
TONY STARK.
NO, NO. DRAW IT OUT. ENJOY IT.
TONY STARRRRK.
"HNN. AGAIN.
"TONNNY.... STARK.
"ANTHONY... STARK.
"STARK.
"YEAH...TRY SIMPLE. TRY...
"TONY STARK.
UZBEKISTAN
TURKMENISTAN
PAKISTAN
SAT-MAP REPULSOR SWEEP NIMRUZ REGION - AFGHANISTAN
"WELL WELL WELL. TONY STARRRRK.
"STARRRRRRK."
YES. OF COURSE. JUST SAY IT LIKE YOU MEAN IT, NORMAN.
TONY STARK.
I'M GOING TO KILL YOU.

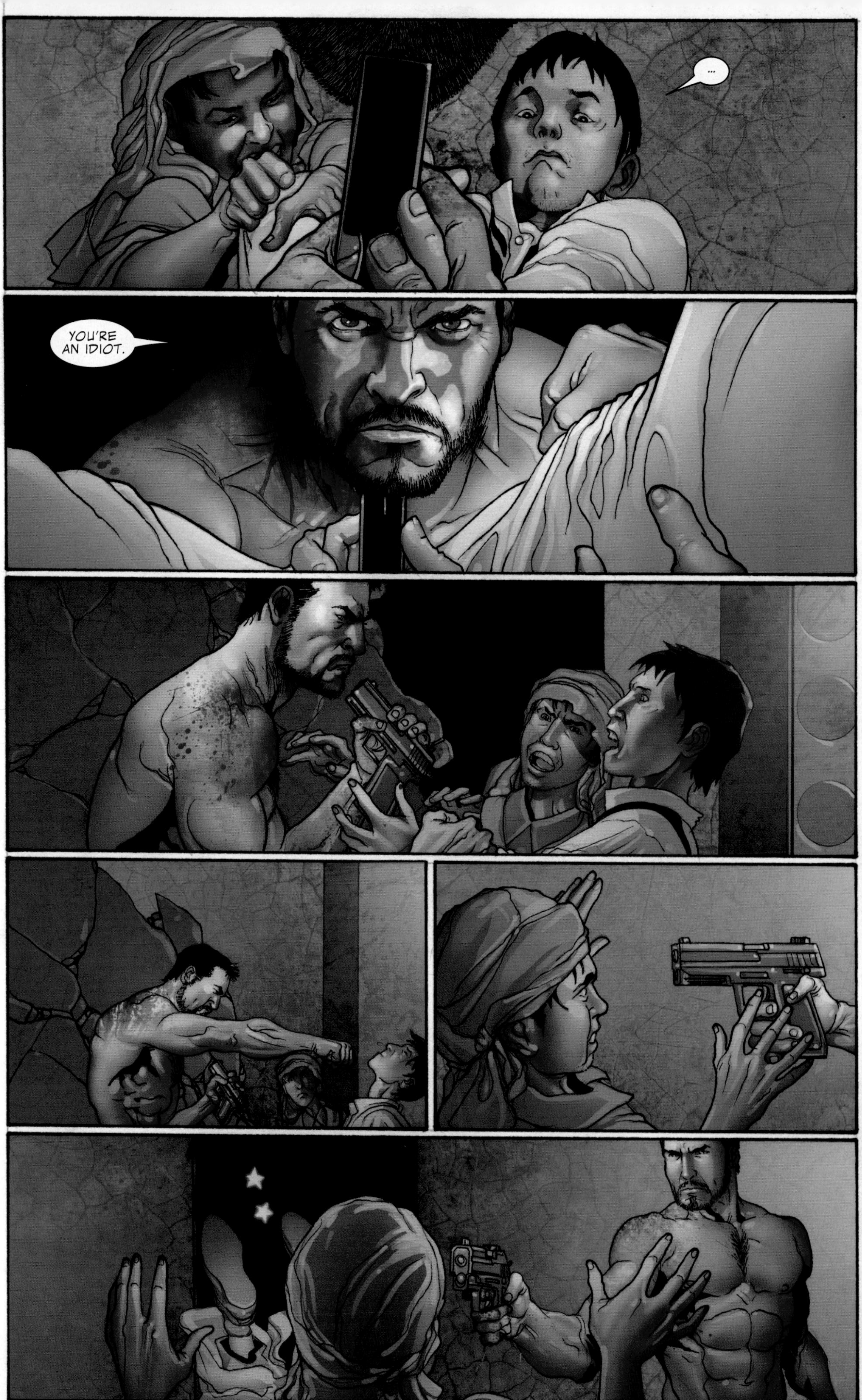
...
YOU'RE AN IDIOT.

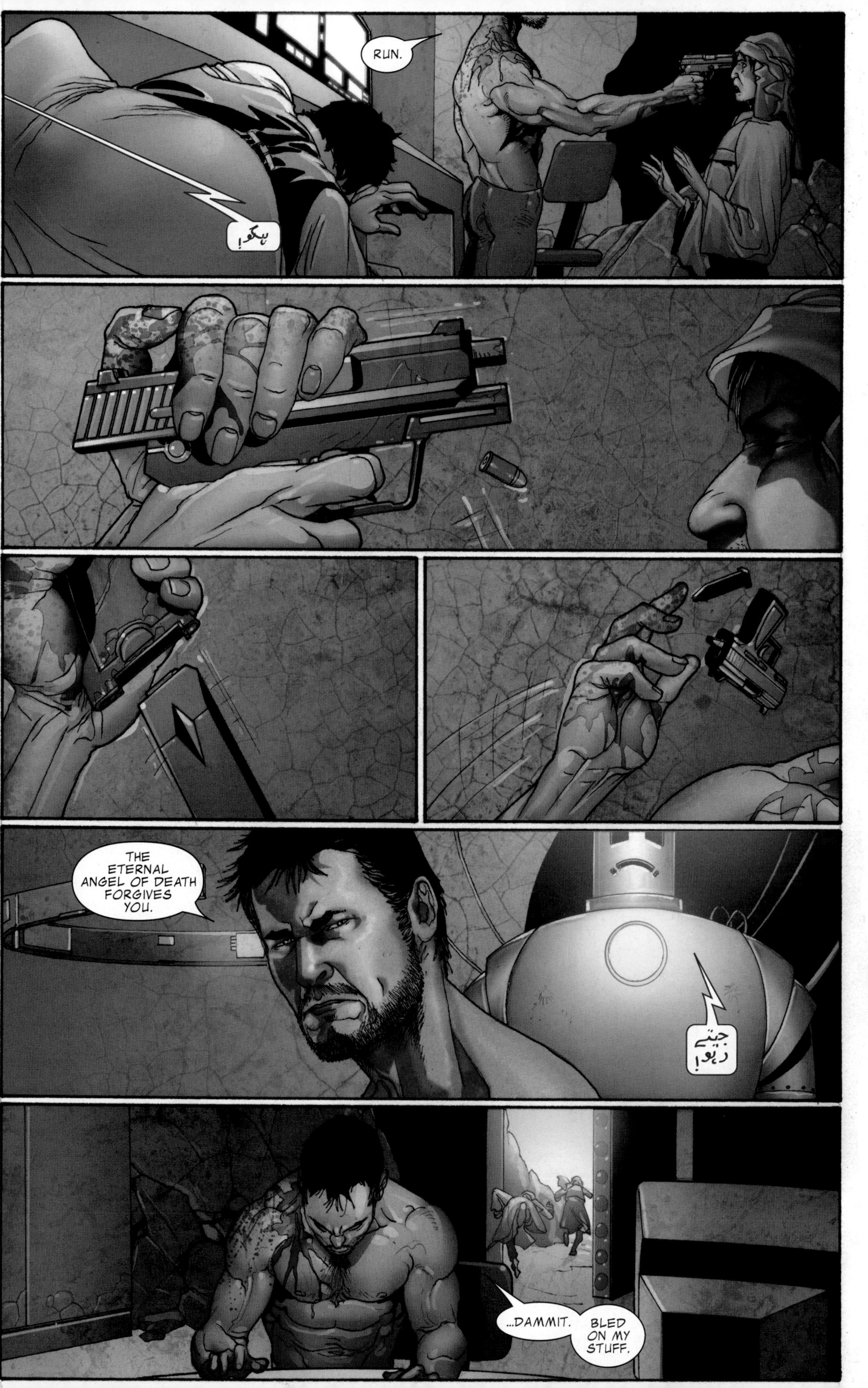
RUN.
بھگو!
THE ETERNAL ANGEL OF DEATH FORGIVES YOU.
جیتے رہو!
...DAMMIT.
BLED ON MY STUFF.

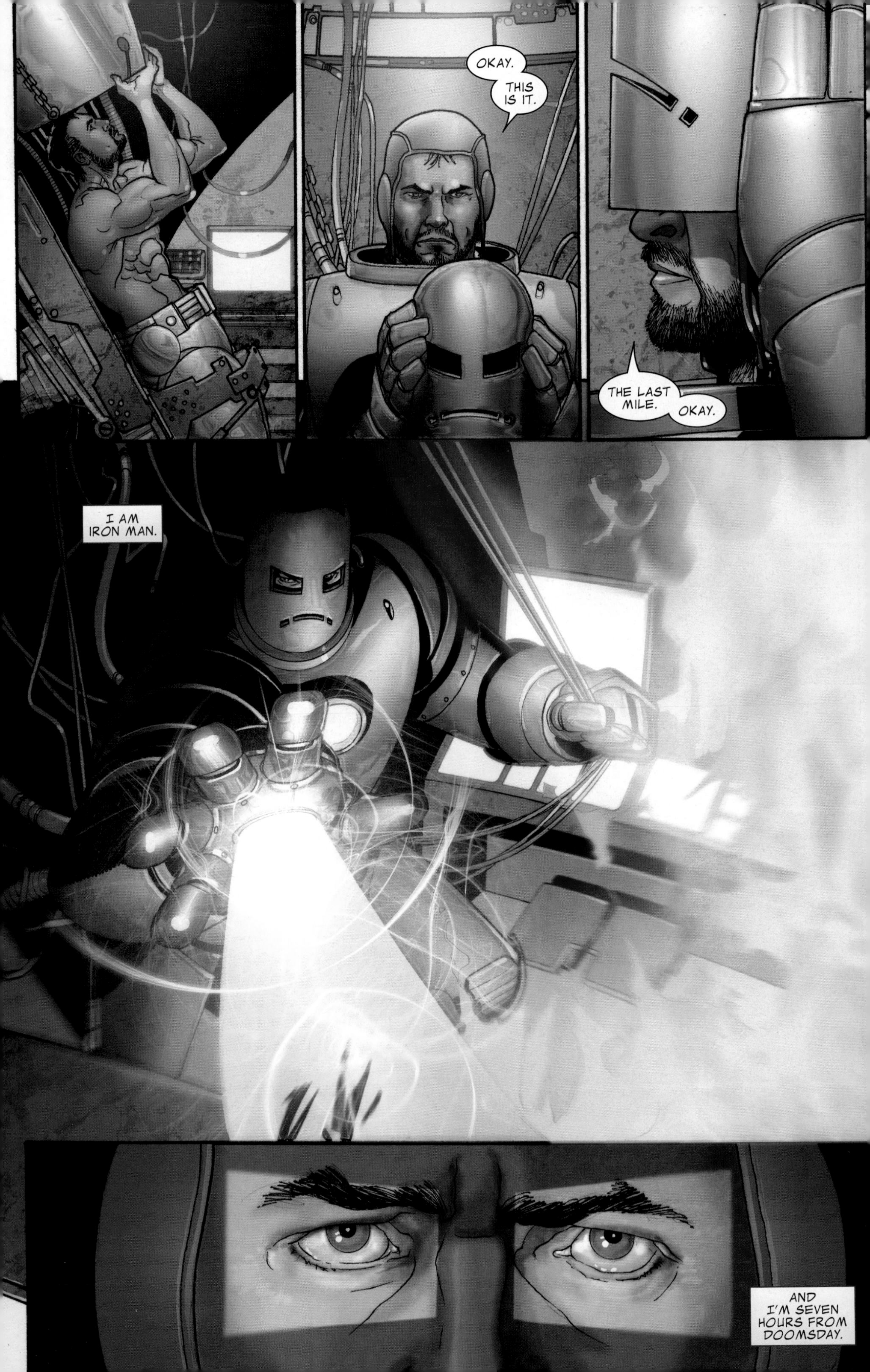
OKAY.
THIS IS IT.
THE LAST MILE.
OKAY.
I AM IRON MAN.
AND I'M SEVEN HOURS FROM DOOMSDAY.

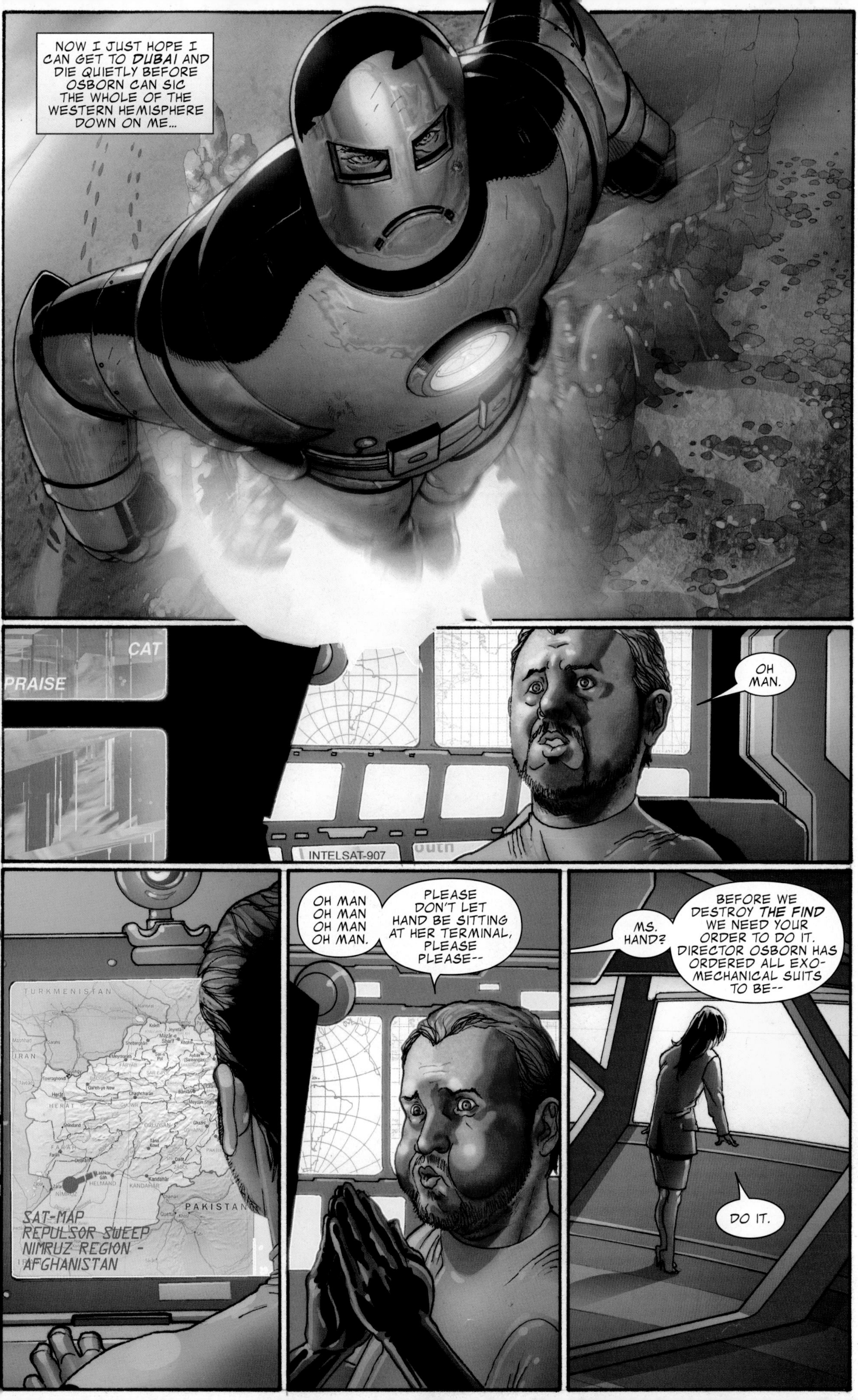
NOW I JUST HOPE I CAN GET TO DUBAI AND DIE QUIETLY BEFORE OSBORN CAN SIC THE WHOLE OF THE WESTERN HEMISPHERE DOWN ON ME...
CAT
PRAISE
OH MAN.
INTELSAT-907
TURKMENISTAN
IRAN
PAKISTAN
SAT-MAP REPULSOR SWEEP NIMRUZ REGION - AFGHANISTAN
OH MAN OH MAN OH MAN OH MAN.
PLEASE DON'T LET HAND BE SITTING AT HER TERMINAL, PLEASE PLEASE--
MS. HAND?
BEFORE WE DESTROY THE FIND WE NEED YOUR ORDER TO DO IT. DIRECTOR OSBORN HAS ORDERED ALL EXO-MECHANICAL SUITS TO BE--
DO IT.

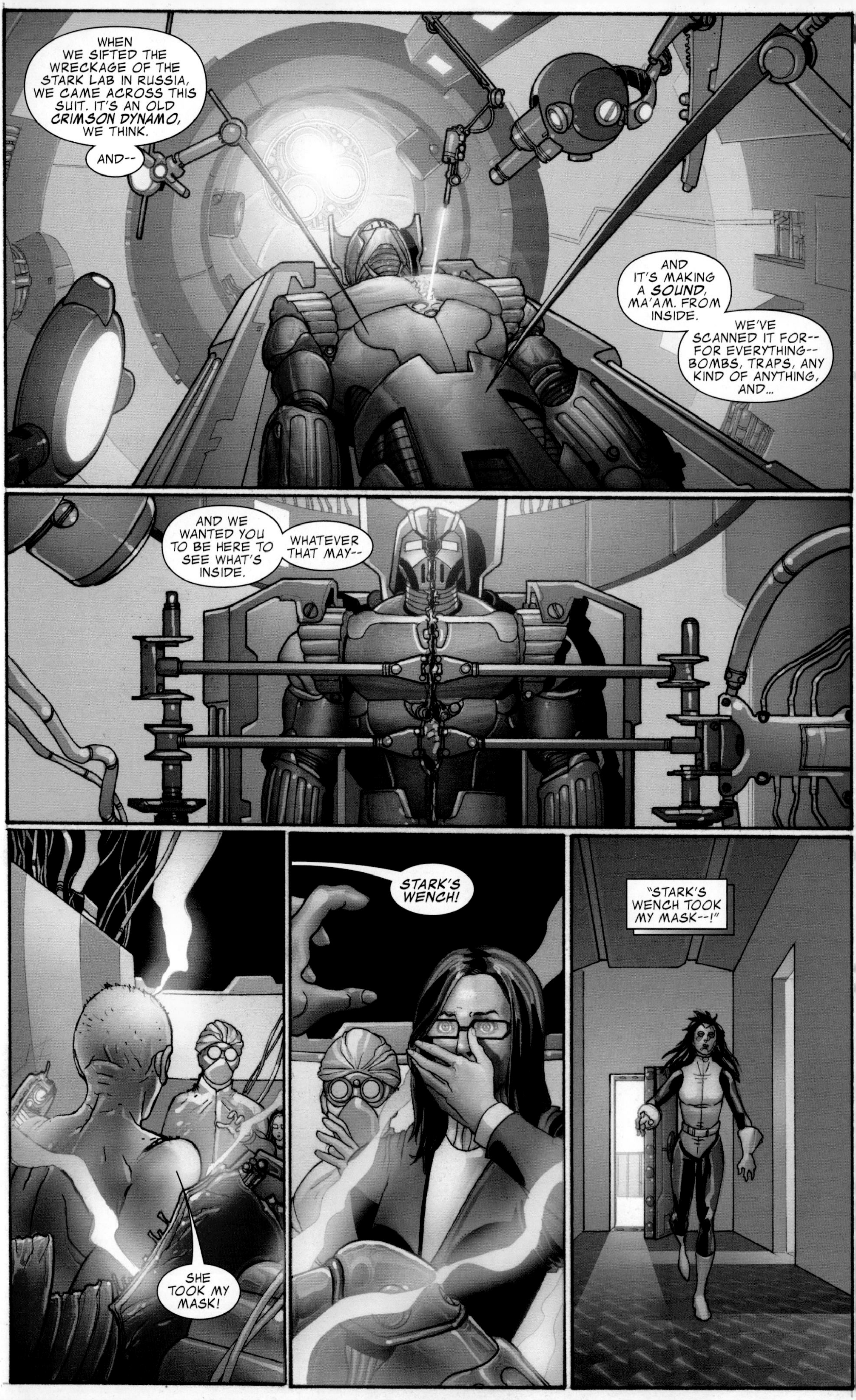
WHEN WE SIFTED THE WRECKAGE OF THE STARK LAB IN RUSSIA, WE CAME ACROSS THIS SUIT. IT'S AN OLD CRIMSON DYNAMO, WE THINK.
AND--
AND IT'S MAKING A SOUND, MA'AM. FROM INSIDE.
WE'VE SCANNED IT FOR--FOR EVERYTHING--BOMBS, TRAPS, ANY KIND OF ANYTHING, AND...
AND WE WANTED YOU TO BE HERE TO SEE WHAT'S INSIDE.
WHATEVER THAT MAY--
SHE TOOK MY MASK!
STARK'S WENCH!
"STARK'S WENCH TOOK MY MASK--!"

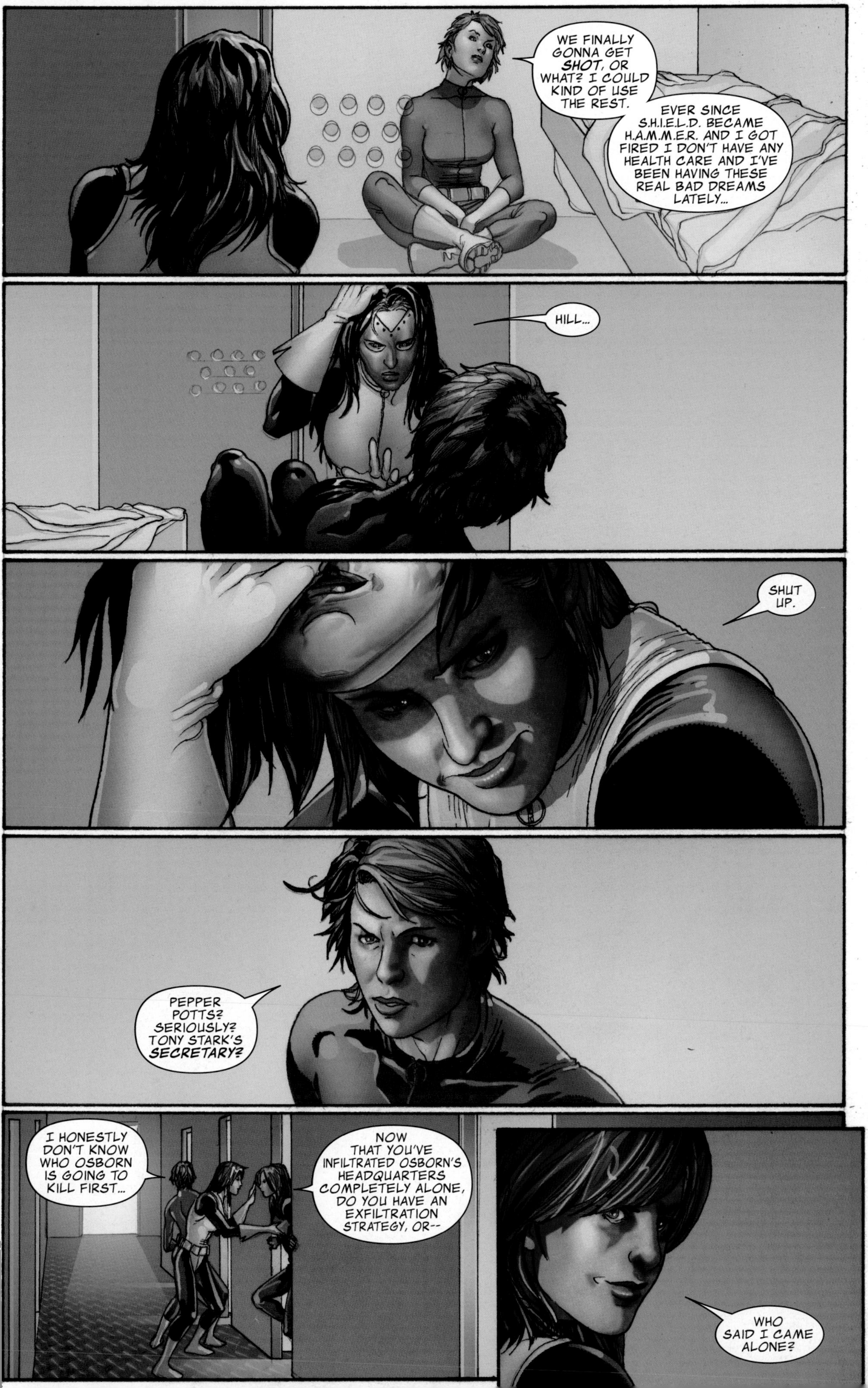
WE FINALLY GONNA GET SHOT, OR WHAT? I COULD KIND OF USE THE REST.
EVER SINCE S.H.I.E.L.D. BECAME H.A.M.M.E.R. AND I GOT FIRED I DON'T HAVE ANY HEALTH CARE AND I'VE BEEN HAVING THESE REAL BAD DREAMS LATELY...
HILL...
SHUT UP.
PEPPER POTTS? SERIOUSLY? TONY STARK'S SECRETARY?
I HONESTLY DON'T KNOW WHO OSBORN IS GOING TO KILL FIRST...
NOW THAT YOU'VE INFILTRATED OSBORN'S HEADQUARTERS COMPLETELY ALONE, DO YOU HAVE AN EXFILTRATION STRATEGY, OR--
WHO SAID I CAME ALONE?

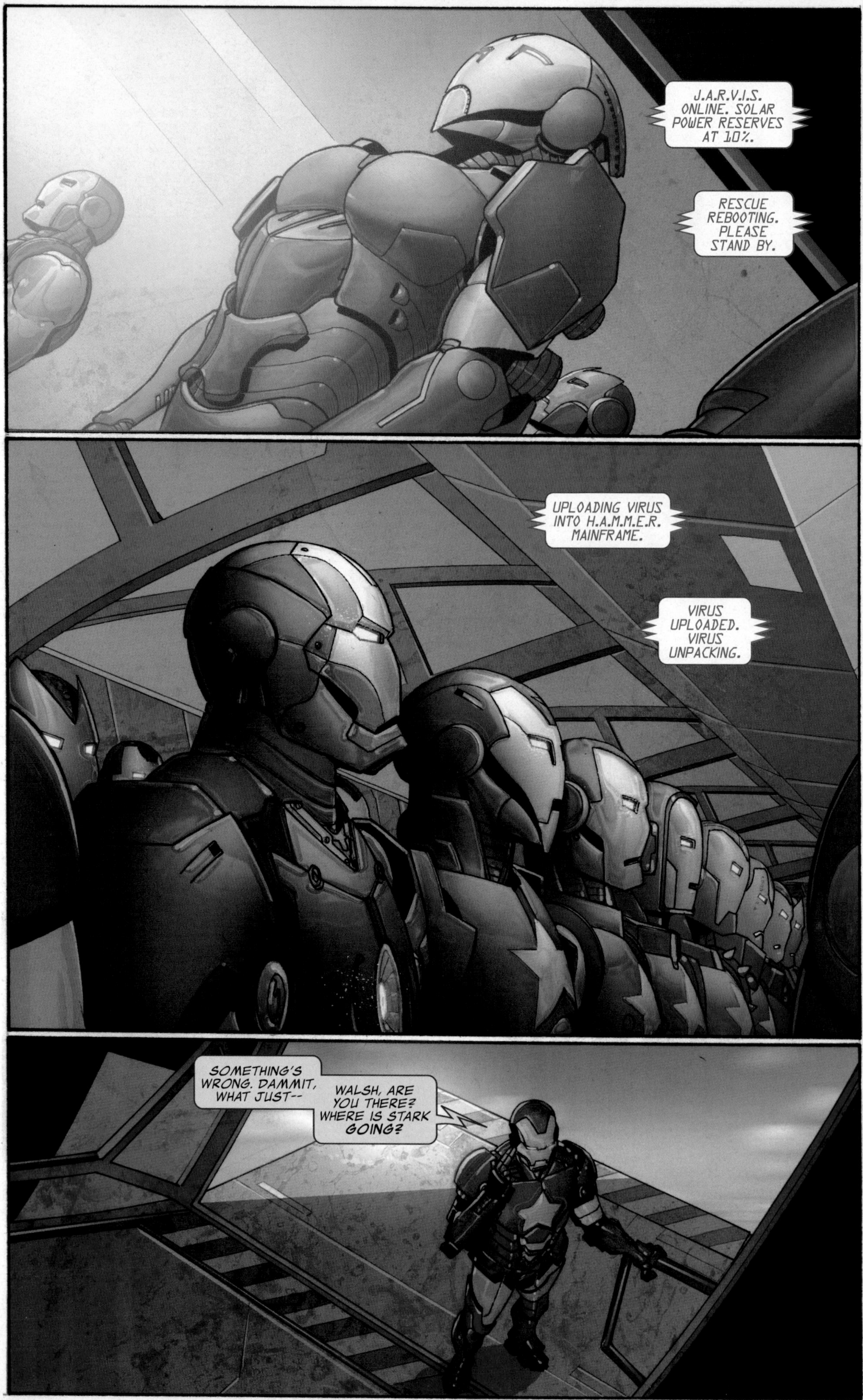
J.A.R.V.I.S. ONLINE. SOLAR POWER RESERVES AT 10%.
RESCUE REBOOTING. PLEASE STAND BY.
UPLOADING VIRUS INTO H.A.M.M.E.R. MAINFRAME.
VIRUS UPLOADED. VIRUS UNPACKING.
SOMETHING'S WRONG. DAMMIT, WHAT JUST--
WALSH, ARE YOU THERE? WHERE IS STARK GOING?

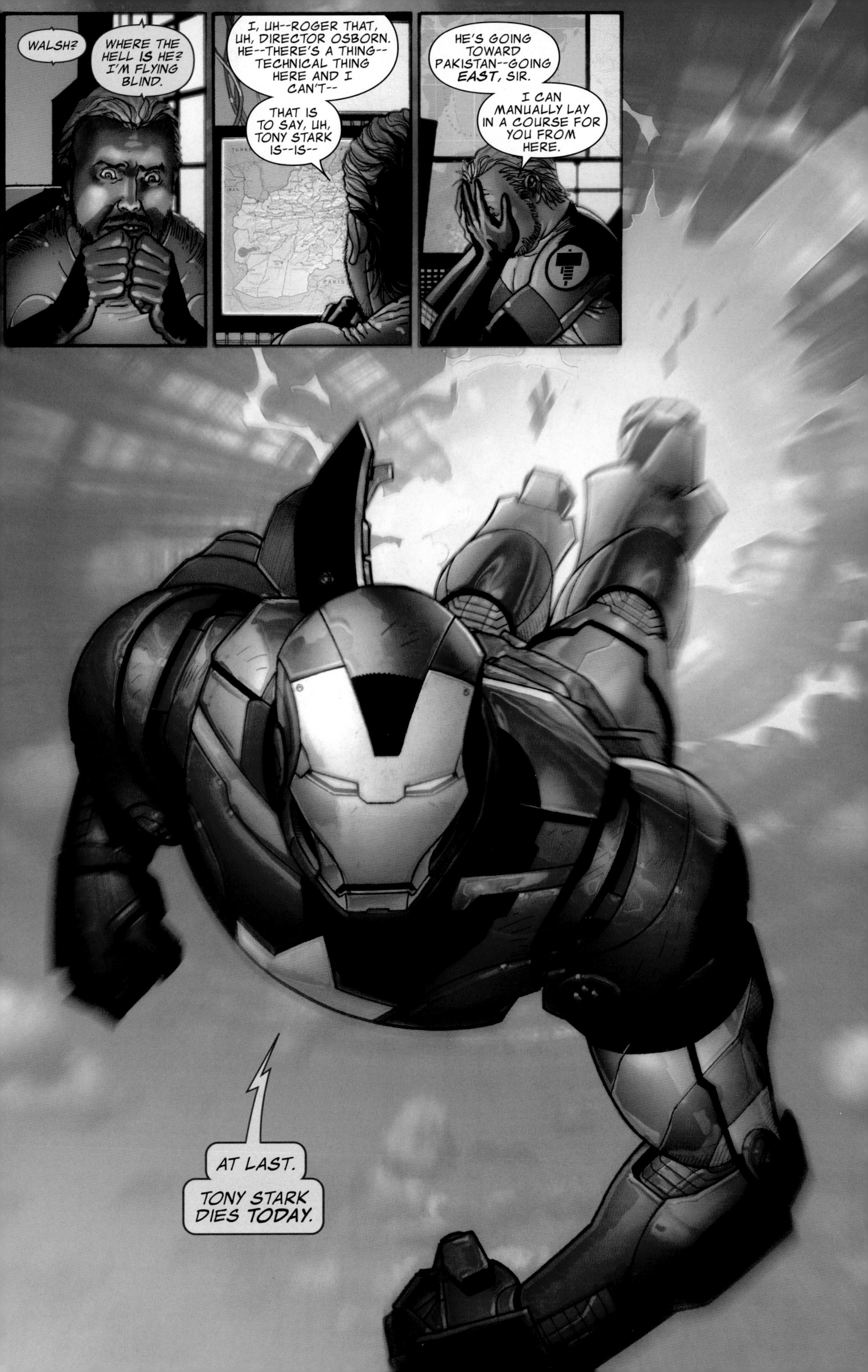
WALSH?
WHERE THE HELL IS HE? I'M FLYING BLIND.
I, UH--ROGER THAT, UH, DIRECTOR OSBORN. HE--THERE'S A THING--TECHNICAL THING HERE AND I CAN'T--
THAT IS TO SAY, UH, TONY STARK IS--IS--
HE'S GOING TOWARD PAKISTAN--GOING EAST, SIR.
I CAN MANUALLY LAY IN A COURSE FOR YOU FROM HERE.
AT LAST.
TONY STARK DIES TODAY.

19

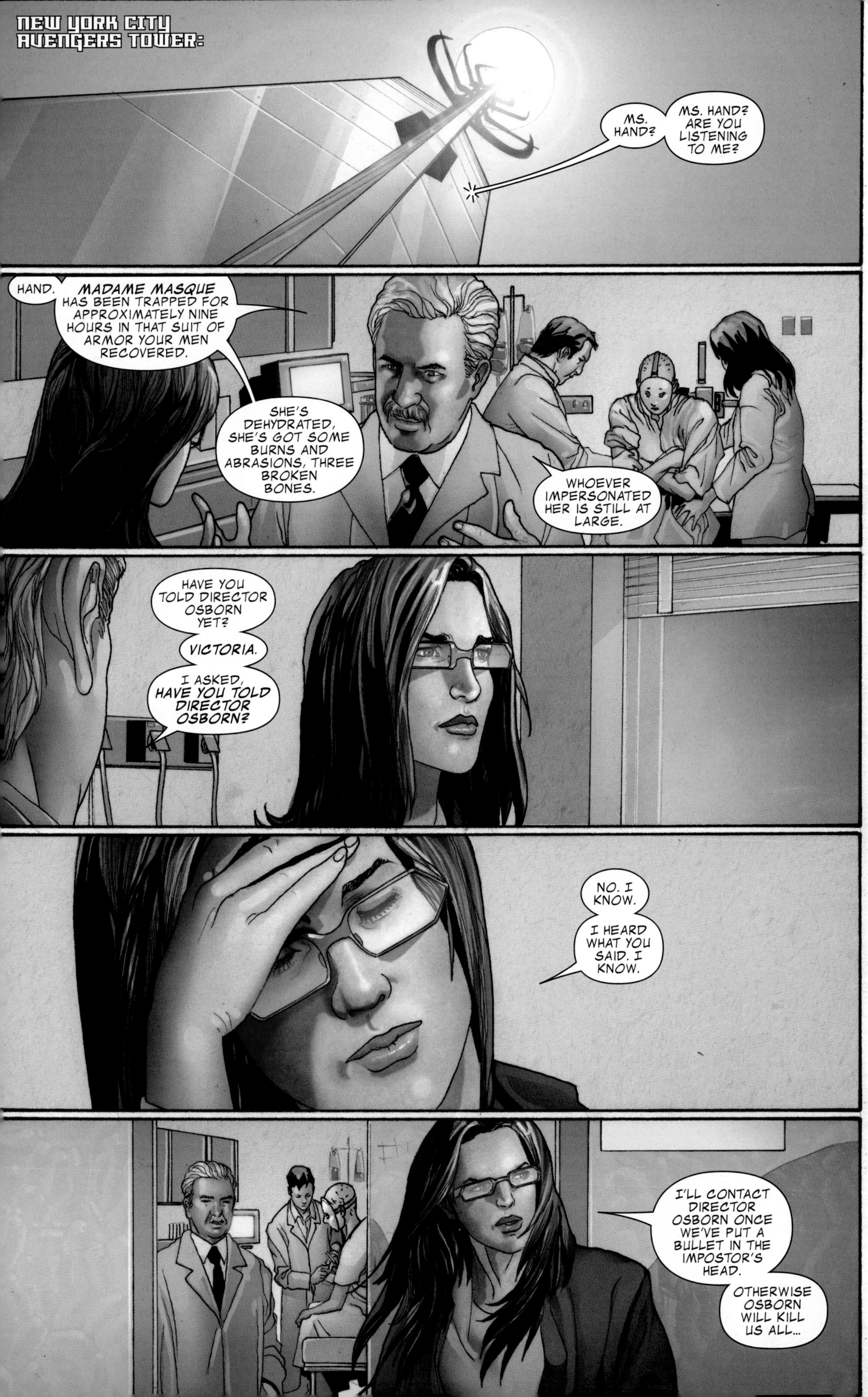
NEW YORK CITY
AVENGERS TOWER:
MS. HAND?
MS. HAND? ARE YOU LISTENING TO ME?
HAND.
MADAME MASQUE HAS BEEN TRAPPED FOR APPROXIMATELY NINE HOURS IN THAT SUIT OF ARMOR YOUR MEN RECOVERED.
SHE'S DEHYDRATED, SHE'S GOT SOME BURNS AND ABRASIONS, THREE BROKEN BONES.
WHOEVER IMPERSONATED HER IS STILL AT LARGE.
HAVE YOU TOLD DIRECTOR OSBORN YET?
VICTORIA.
I ASKED, HAVE YOU TOLD DIRECTOR OSBORN?
NO. I KNOW.
I HEARD WHAT YOU SAID. I KNOW.
I'LL CONTACT DIRECTOR OSBORN ONCE WE'VE PUT A BULLET IN THE IMPOSTOR'S HEAD.
OTHERWISE OSBORN WILL KILL US ALL...

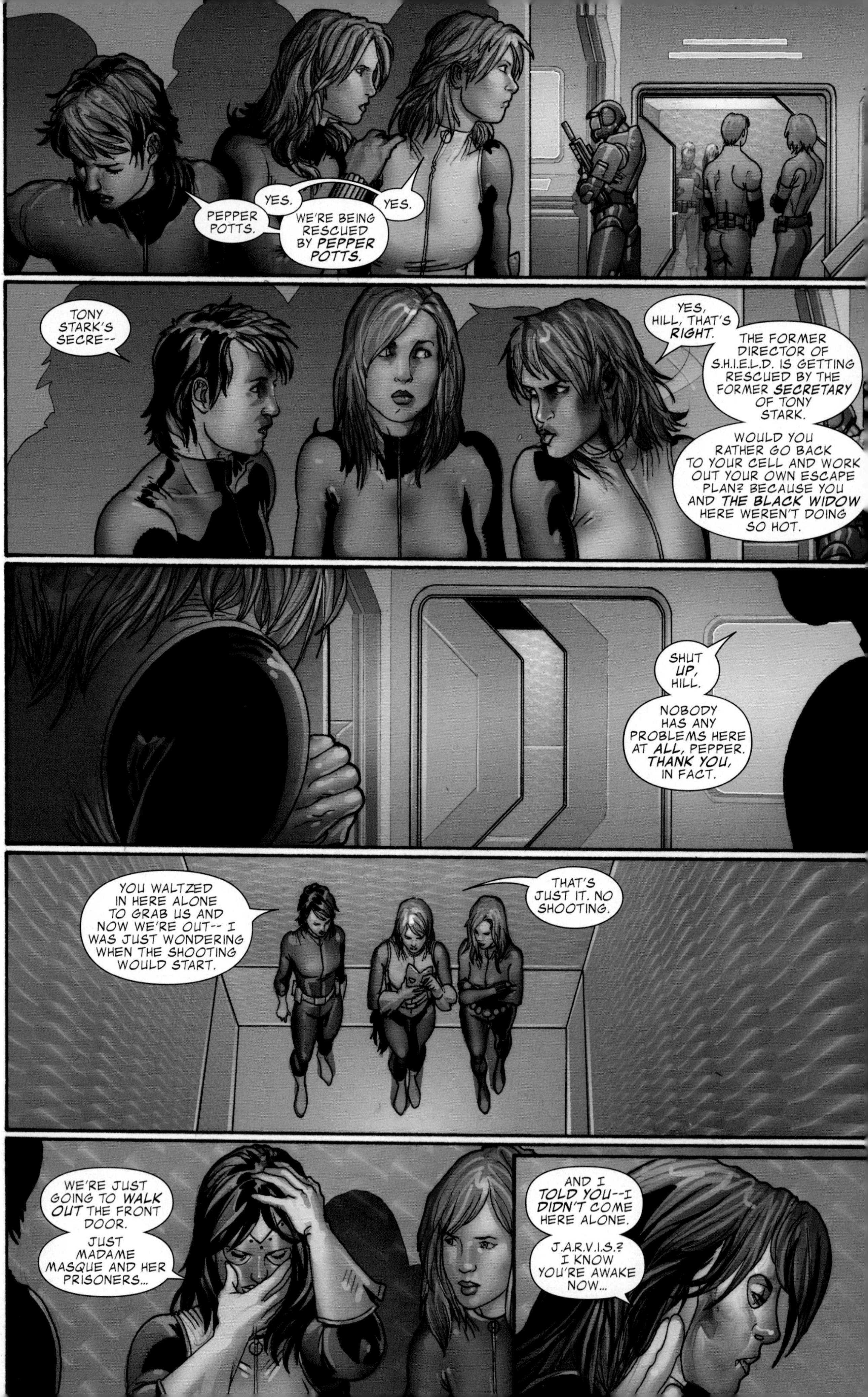
PEPPER POTTS.
YES.
WE'RE BEING RESCUED BY PEPPER POTTS.
YES.
TONY STARK'S SECRE--
YES, HILL, THAT'S RIGHT.
THE FORMER DIRECTOR OF S.H.I.E.L.D. IS GETTING RESCUED BY THE FORMER SECRETARY OF TONY STARK.
WOULD YOU RATHER GO BACK TO YOUR CELL AND WORK OUT YOUR OWN ESCAPE PLAN? BECAUSE YOU AND THE BLACK WIDOW HERE WEREN'T DOING SO HOT.
SHUT UP, HILL.
NOBODY HAS ANY PROBLEMS HERE AT ALL, PEPPER. THANK YOU, IN FACT.
YOU WALTZED IN HERE ALONE TO GRAB US AND NOW WE'RE OUT-- I WAS JUST WONDERING WHEN THE SHOOTING WOULD START.
THAT'S JUST IT. NO SHOOTING.
WE'RE JUST GOING TO WALK OUT THE FRONT DOOR.
JUST MADAME MASQUE AND HER PRISONERS...
AND I TOLD YOU--I DIDN'T COME HERE ALONE.
J.A.R.V.I.S.? I KNOW YOU'RE AWAKE NOW...

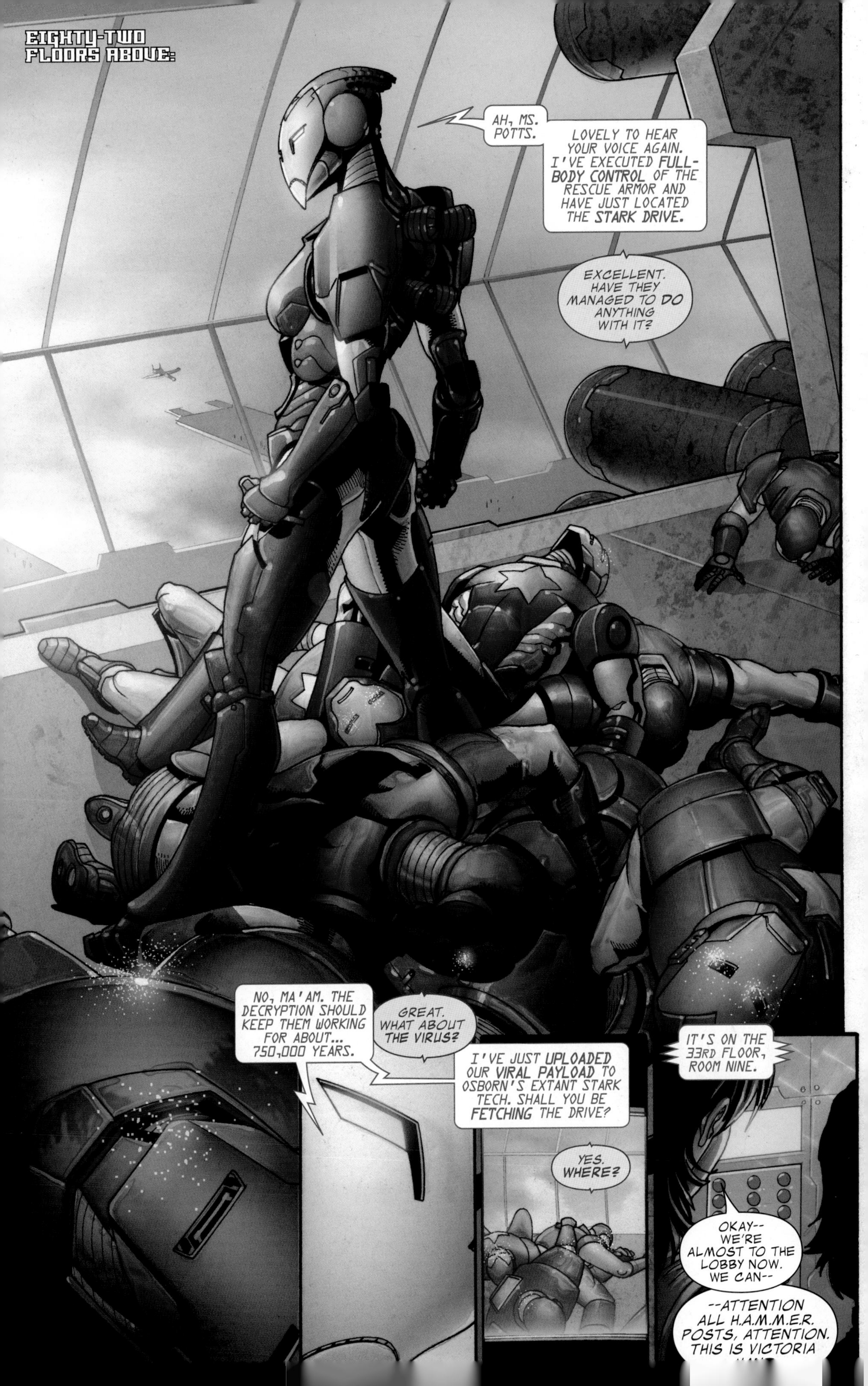
EIGHTY-TWO FLOORS ABOVE:
AH, MS. POTTS.
LOVELY TO HEAR YOUR VOICE AGAIN. I'VE EXECUTED FULL-BODY CONTROL OF THE RESCUE ARMOR AND HAVE JUST LOCATED THE STARK DRIVE.
EXCELLENT. HAVE THEY MANAGED TO DO ANYTHING WITH IT?
NO, MA'AM. THE DECRYPTION SHOULD KEEP THEM WORKING FOR ABOUT... 750,000 YEARS.
GREAT. WHAT ABOUT THE VIRUS?
I'VE JUST UPLOADED OUR VIRAL PAYLOAD TO OSBORN'S EXTANT STARK TECH. SHALL YOU BE FETCHING THE DRIVE?
YES. WHERE?
IT'S ON THE 33RD FLOOR, ROOM NINE.
OKAY-- WE'RE ALMOST TO THE LOBBY NOW. WE CAN--
--ATTENTION ALL H.A.M.M.E.R. POSTS, ATTENTION. THIS IS VICTORIA

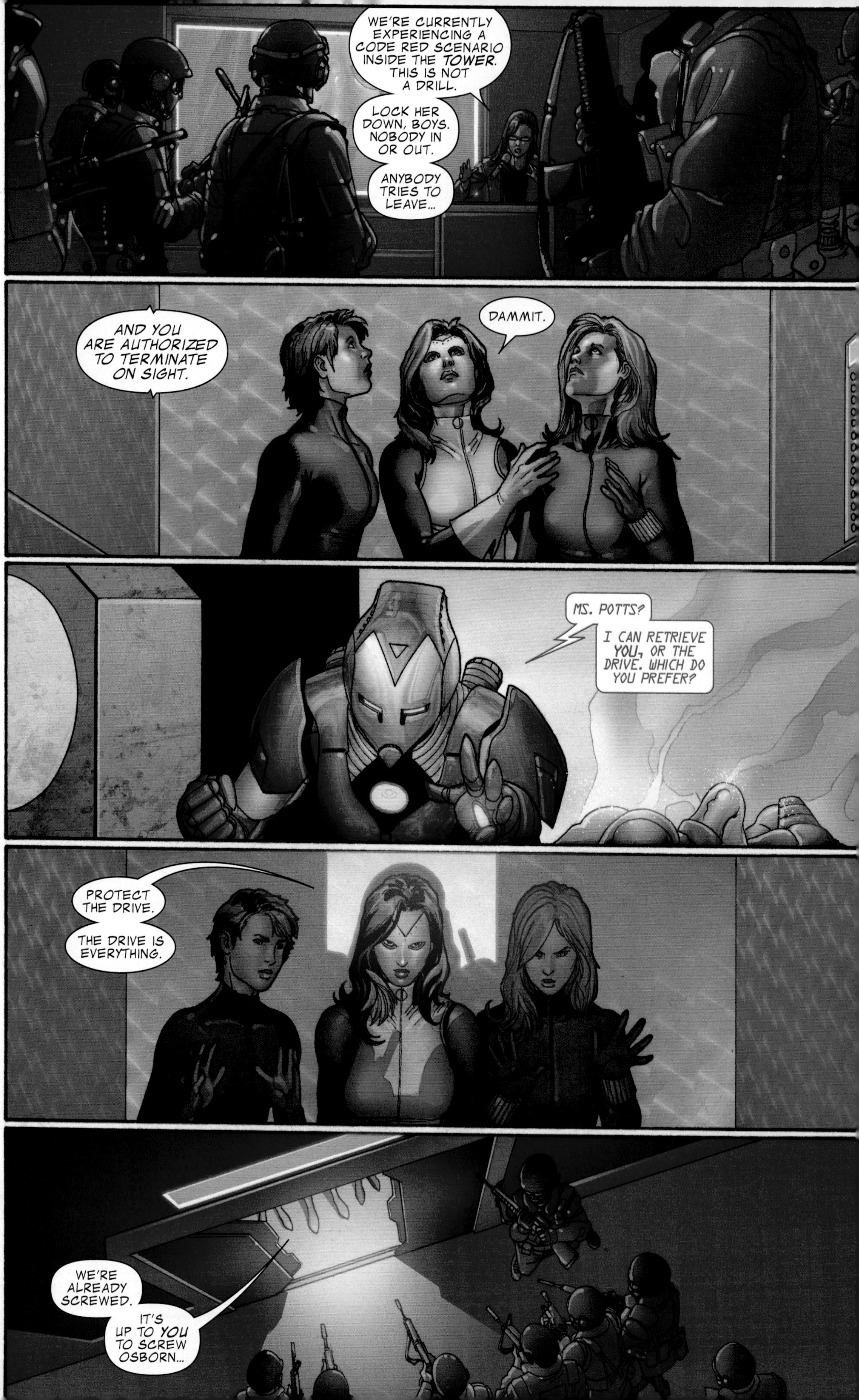
WE'RE CURRENTLY EXPERIENCING A CODE RED SCENARIO INSIDE THE TOWER. THIS IS NOT A DRILL.
LOCK HER DOWN, BOYS. NOBODY IN OR OUT.
ANYBODY TRIES TO LEAVE...
AND YOU ARE AUTHORIZED TO TERMINATE ON SIGHT.
DAMMIT.
MS. POTTS?
I CAN RETRIEVE YOU, OR THE DRIVE. WHICH DO YOU PREFER?
PROTECT THE DRIVE.
THE DRIVE IS EVERYTHING.
WE'RE ALREADY SCREWED.
IT'S UP TO YOU TO SCREW OSBORN...

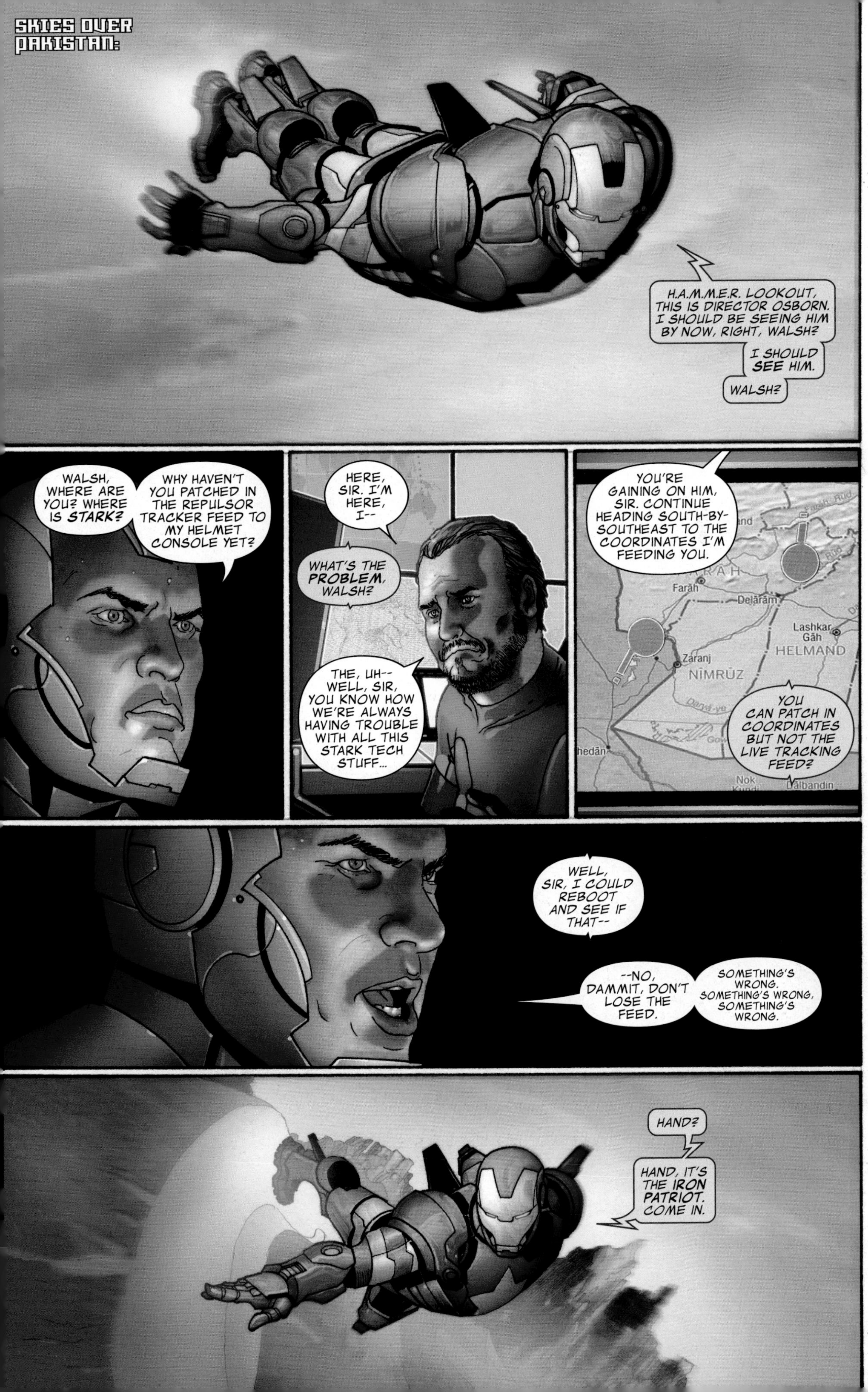
SKIES OVER PAKISTAN:
H.A.M.M.E.R. LOOKOUT, THIS IS DIRECTOR OSBORN. I SHOULD BE SEEING HIM BY NOW, RIGHT, WALSH?
I SHOULD SEE HIM.
WALSH?
WALSH, WHERE ARE YOU? WHERE IS STARK?
WHY HAVEN'T YOU PATCHED IN THE REPULSOR TRACKER FEED TO MY HELMET CONSOLE YET?
HERE, SIR. I'M HERE, I--
WHAT'S THE PROBLEM, WALSH?
THE, UH-- WELL, SIR, YOU KNOW HOW WE'RE ALWAYS HAVING TROUBLE WITH ALL THIS STARK TECH STUFF...
YOU'RE GAINING ON HIM, SIR. CONTINUE HEADING SOUTH-BY-SOUTHEAST TO THE COORDINATES I'M FEEDING YOU.
Farāh
Delārām
Lashkar Gāh
HELMAND
Zaranj
NĪMRŪZ
Dālbandin
YOU CAN PATCH IN COORDINATES BUT NOT THE LIVE TRACKING FEED?
WELL, SIR, I COULD REBOOT AND SEE IF THAT--
--NO, DAMMIT, DON'T LOSE THE FEED.
SOMETHING'S WRONG. SOMETHING'S WRONG, SOMETHING'S WRONG.
HAND?
HAND, IT'S THE IRON PATRIOT. COME IN.

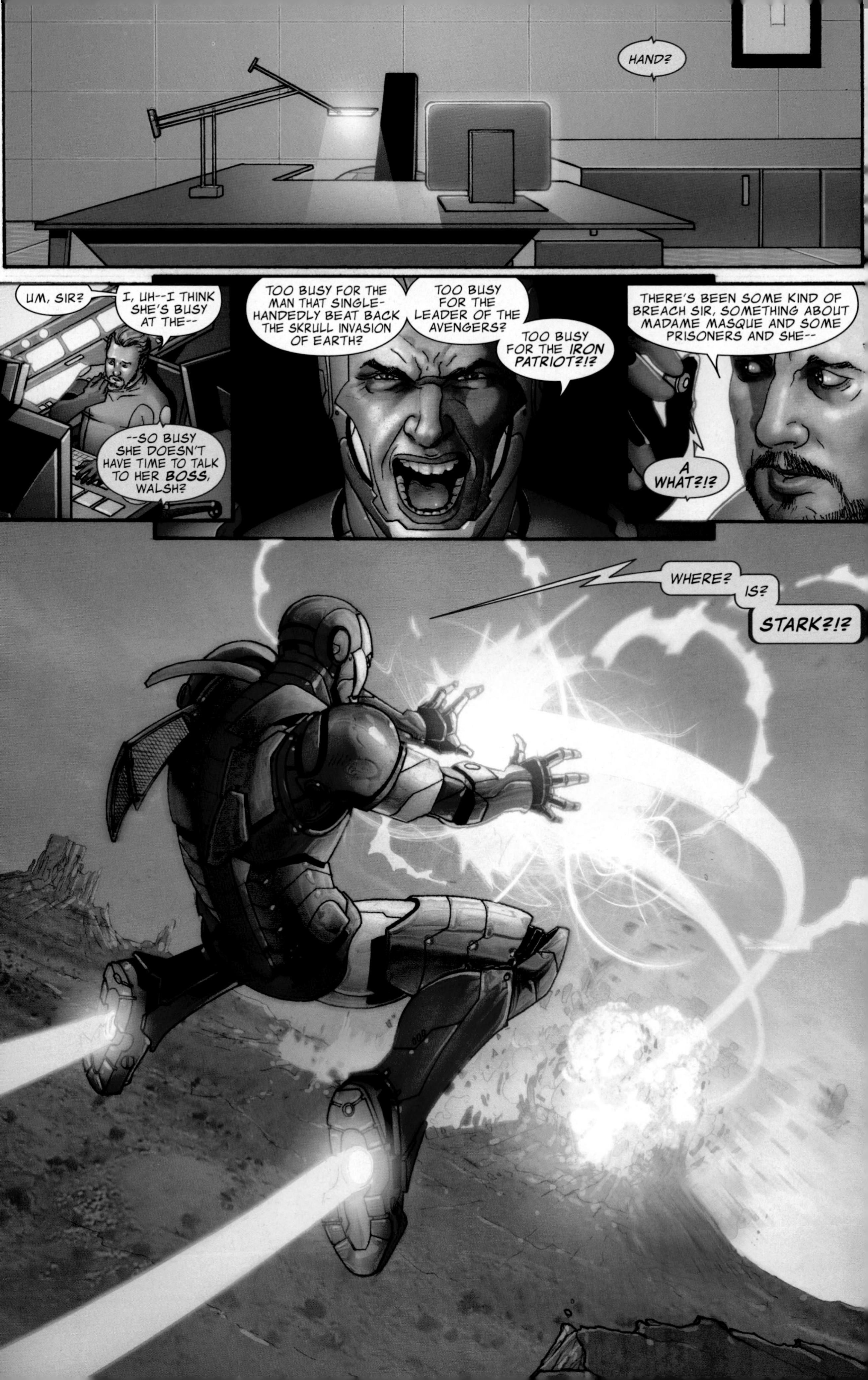
HAND?
UM, SIR?
I, UH--I THINK SHE'S BUSY AT THE--
--SO BUSY SHE DOESN'T HAVE TIME TO TALK TO HER BOSS, WALSH?
TOO BUSY FOR THE MAN THAT SINGLE-HANDEDLY BEAT BACK THE SKRULL INVASION OF EARTH?
TOO BUSY FOR THE LEADER OF THE AVENGERS?
TOO BUSY FOR THE IRON PATRIOT?!?
THERE'S BEEN SOME KIND OF BREACH SIR, SOMETHING ABOUT MADAME MASQUE AND SOME PRISONERS AND SHE--
A WHAT?!?
WHERE? IS? STARK?!?

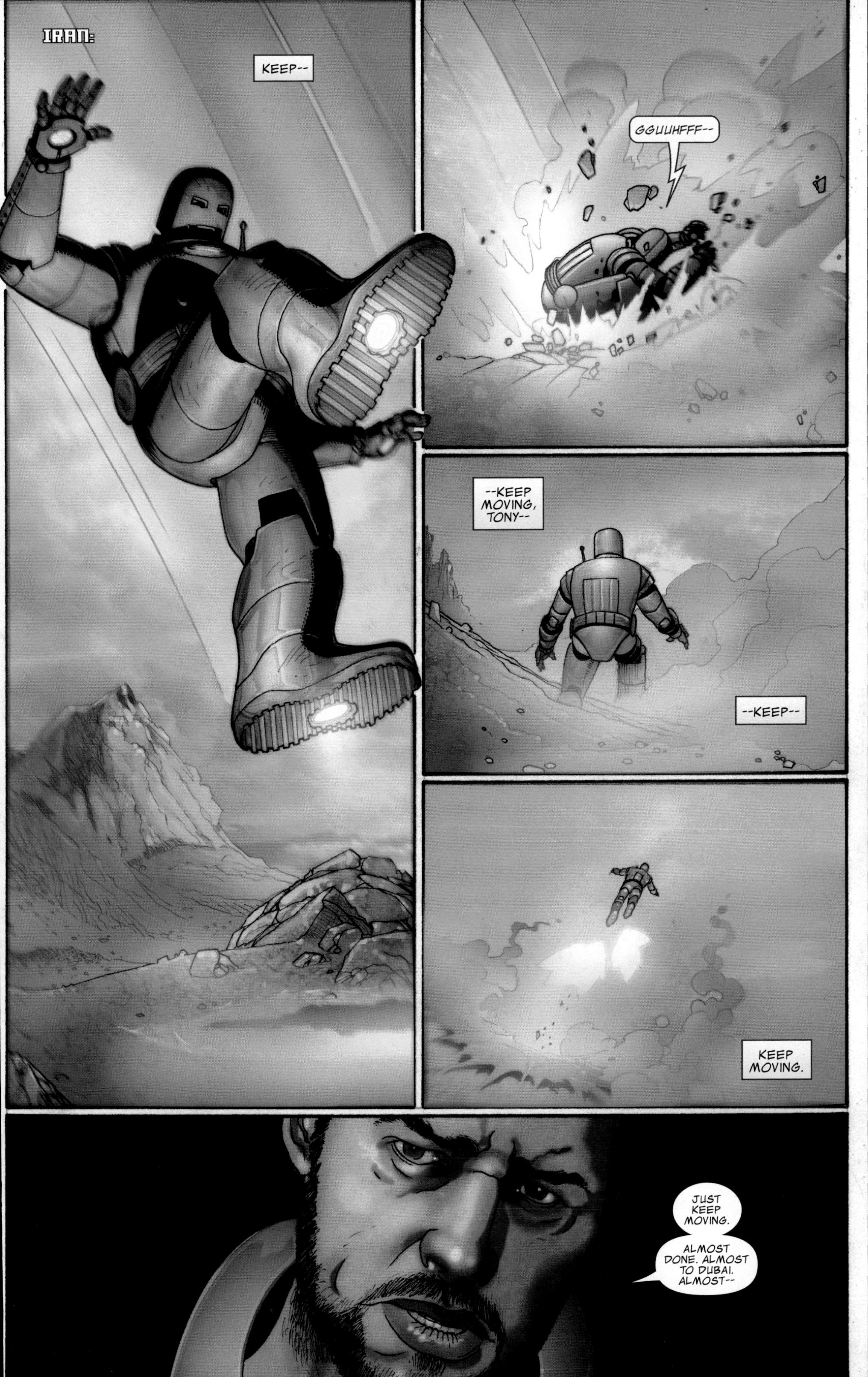
IRAN:
KEEP--
GGUUHFFF--
--KEEP MOVING, TONY--
--KEEP--
KEEP MOVING.
JUST KEEP MOVING.
ALMOST DONE. ALMOST TO DUBAI. ALMOST--

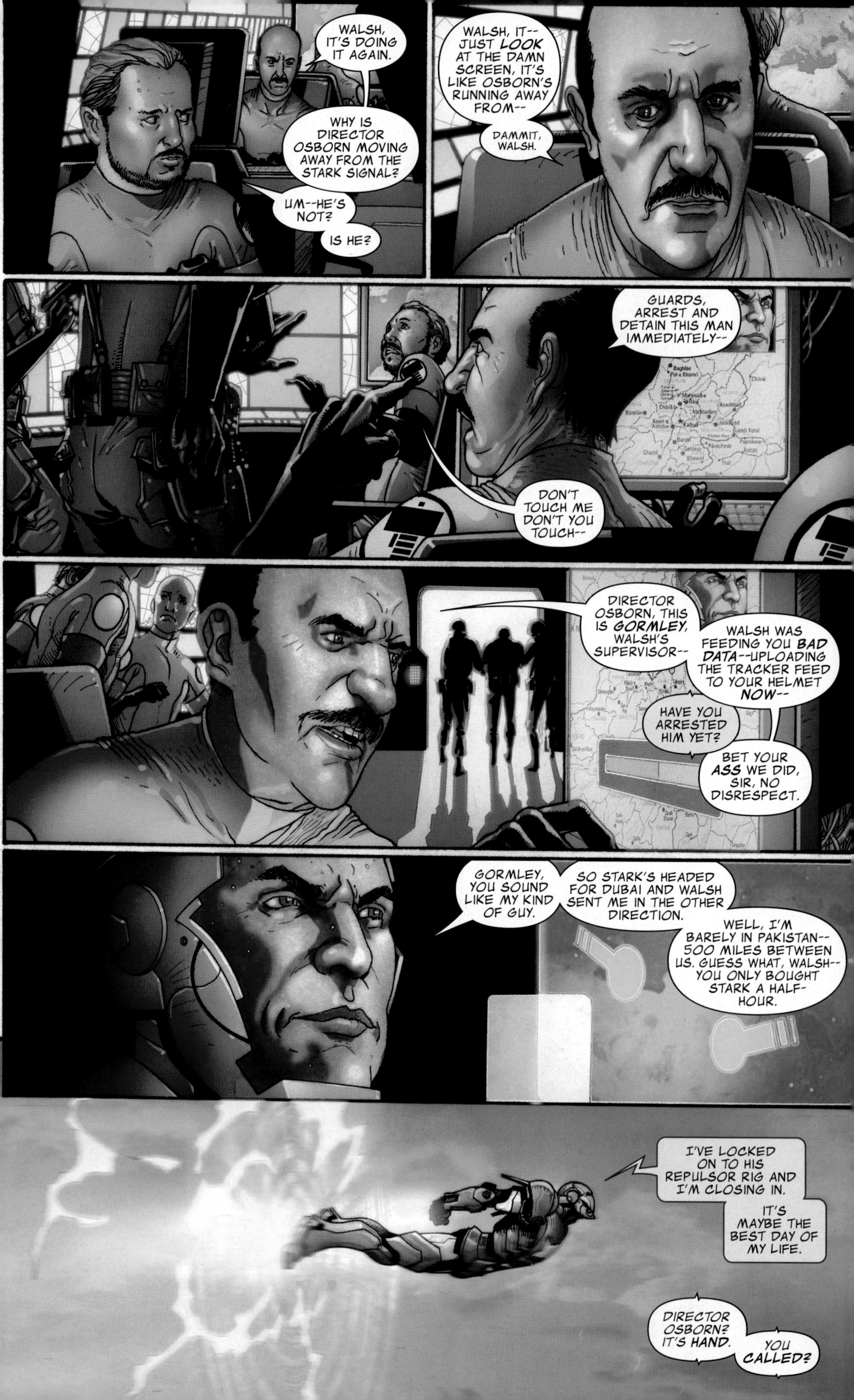

WALSH, IT'S DOING IT AGAIN.
WHY IS DIRECTOR OSBORN MOVING AWAY FROM THE STARK SIGNAL?
UM--HE'S NOT?
IS HE?
WALSH, IT--JUST LOOK AT THE DAMN SCREEN, IT'S LIKE OSBORN'S RUNNING AWAY FROM--
DAMMIT, WALSH.
GUARDS, ARREST AND DETAIN THIS MAN IMMEDIATELY--
DON'T TOUCH ME DON'T YOU TOUCH--
DIRECTOR OSBORN, THIS IS GORMLEY, WALSH'S SUPERVISOR--
WALSH WAS FEEDING YOU BAD DATA--UPLOADING THE TRACKER FEED TO YOUR HELMET NOW--
HAVE YOU ARRESTED HIM YET?
BET YOUR ASS WE DID, SIR, NO DISRESPECT.
GORMLEY, YOU SOUND LIKE MY KIND OF GUY.
SO STARK'S HEADED FOR DUBAI AND WALSH SENT ME IN THE OTHER DIRECTION.
WELL, I'M BARELY IN PAKISTAN--500 MILES BETWEEN US. GUESS WHAT, WALSH--YOU ONLY BOUGHT STARK A HALF-HOUR.
I'VE LOCKED ON TO HIS REPULSOR RIG AND I'M CLOSING IN.
IT'S MAYBE THE BEST DAY OF MY LIFE.
DIRECTOR OSBORN? IT'S HAND.
YOU CALLED?

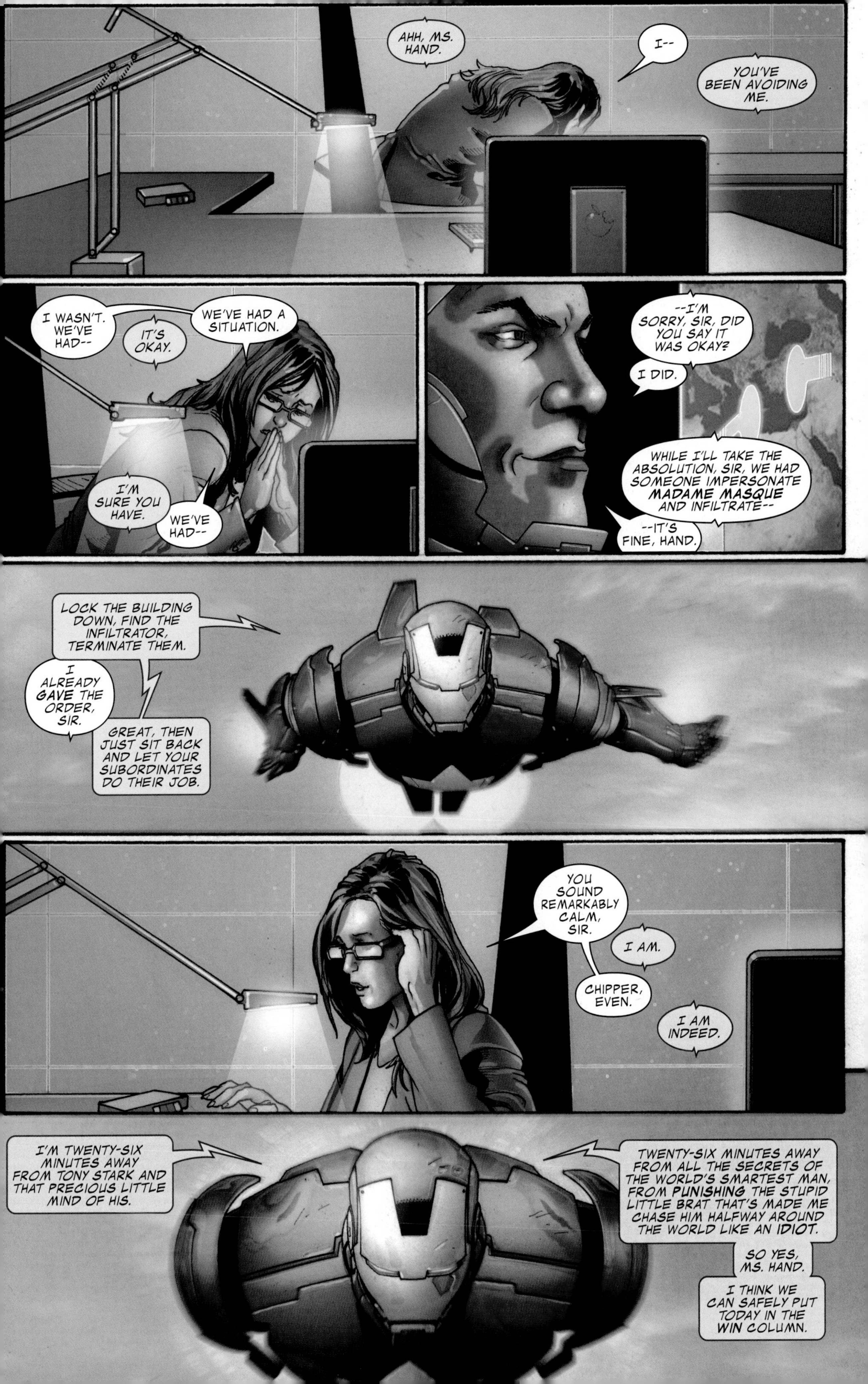
AHH, MS. HAND.
I--
YOU'VE BEEN AVOIDING ME.
I WASN'T. WE'VE HAD--
IT'S OKAY.
WE'VE HAD A SITUATION.
I'M SURE YOU HAVE.
WE'VE HAD--
--I'M SORRY, SIR, DID YOU SAY IT WAS OKAY?
I DID.
WHILE I'LL TAKE THE ABSOLUTION, SIR, WE HAD SOMEONE IMPERSONATE MADAME MASQUE AND INFILTRATE--
--IT'S FINE, HAND.
LOCK THE BUILDING DOWN, FIND THE INFILTRATOR, TERMINATE THEM.
I ALREADY GAVE THE ORDER, SIR.
GREAT, THEN JUST SIT BACK AND LET YOUR SUBORDINATES DO THEIR JOB.
YOU SOUND REMARKABLY CALM, SIR.
I AM.
CHIPPER, EVEN.
I AM INDEED.
I'M TWENTY-SIX MINUTES AWAY FROM TONY STARK AND THAT PRECIOUS LITTLE MIND OF HIS.
TWENTY-SIX MINUTES AWAY FROM ALL THE SECRETS OF THE WORLD'S SMARTEST MAN, FROM PUNISHING THE STUPID LITTLE BRAT THAT'S MADE ME CHASE HIM HALFWAY AROUND THE WORLD LIKE AN IDIOT.
SO YES, MS. HAND.
I THINK WE CAN SAFELY PUT TODAY IN THE WIN COLUMN.

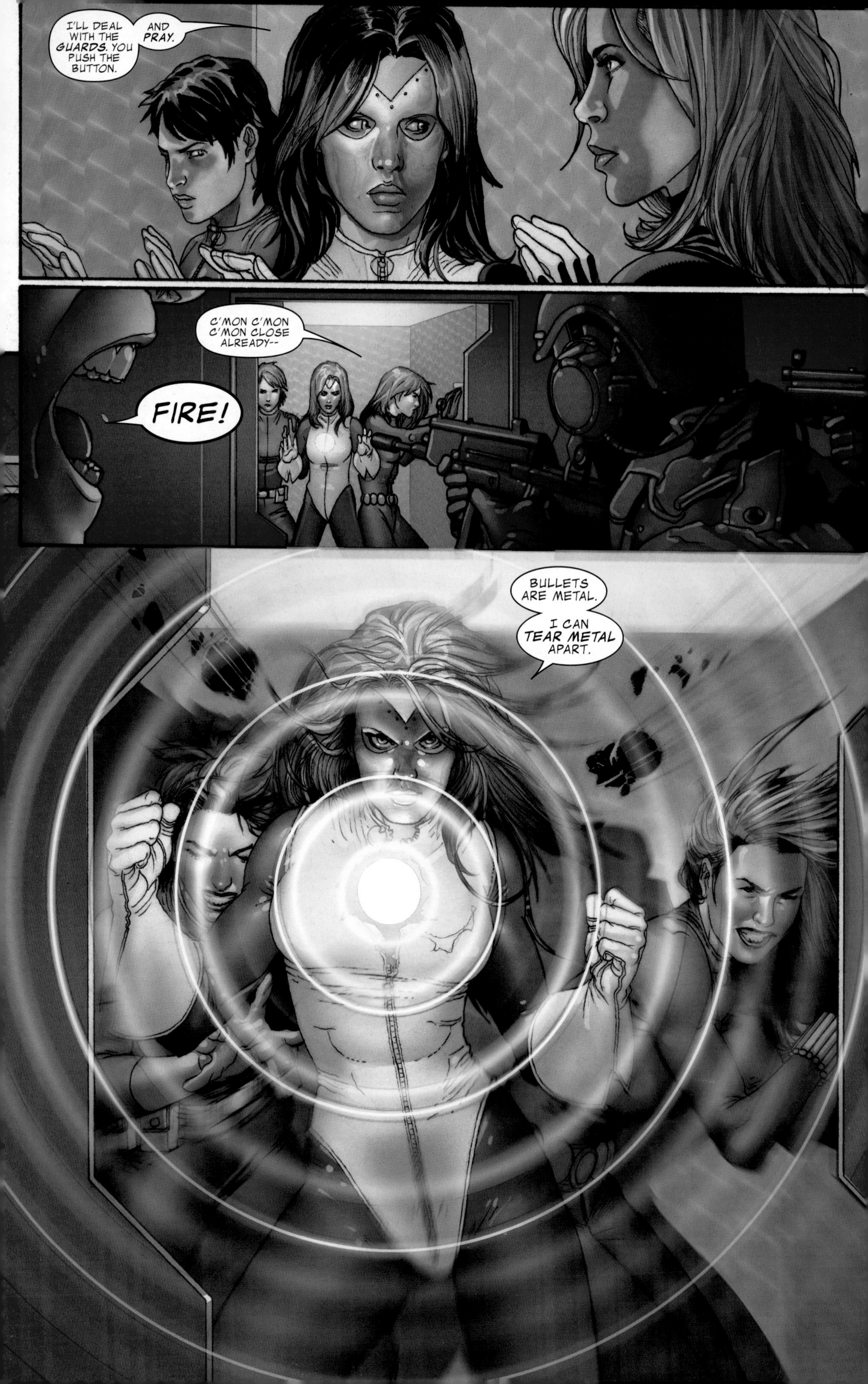
I'LL DEAL WITH THE GUARDS. YOU PUSH THE BUTTON.
AND PRAY.
C'MON C'MON C'MON CLOSE ALREADY--
FIRE!
BULLETS ARE METAL.
I CAN TEAR METAL APART.

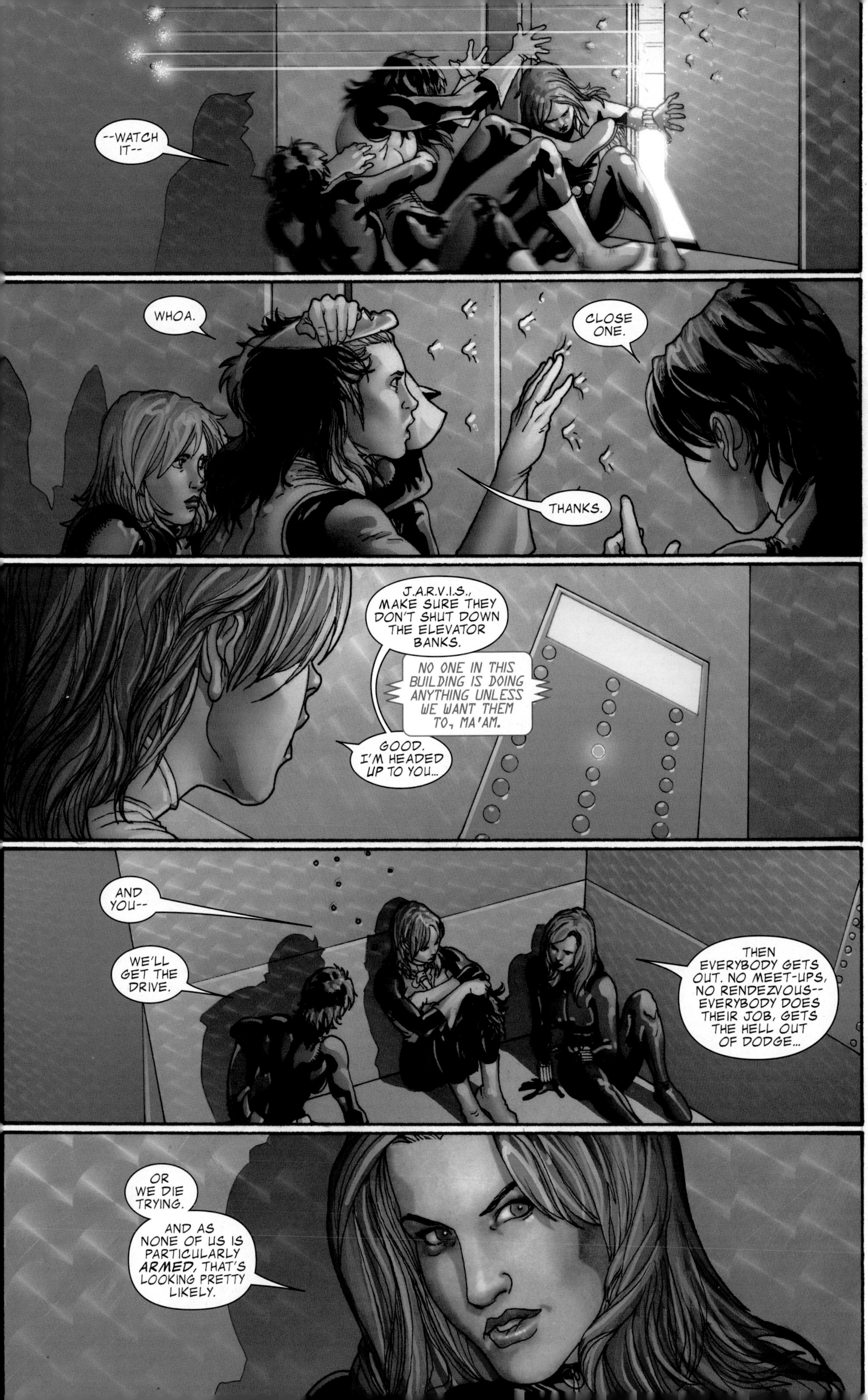
--WATCH IT--
WHOA.
CLOSE ONE.
THANKS.
J.A.R.V.I.S., MAKE SURE THEY DON'T SHUT DOWN THE ELEVATOR BANKS.
NO ONE IN THIS BUILDING IS DOING ANYTHING UNLESS WE WANT THEM TO, MA'AM.
GOOD. I'M HEADED UP TO YOU...
AND YOU--
WE'LL GET THE DRIVE.
THEN EVERYBODY GETS OUT. NO MEET-UPS, NO RENDEZVOUS--EVERYBODY DOES THEIR JOB, GETS THE HELL OUT OF DODGE...
OR WE DIE TRYING.
AND AS NONE OF US IS PARTICULARLY ARMED, THAT'S LOOKING PRETTY LIKELY.

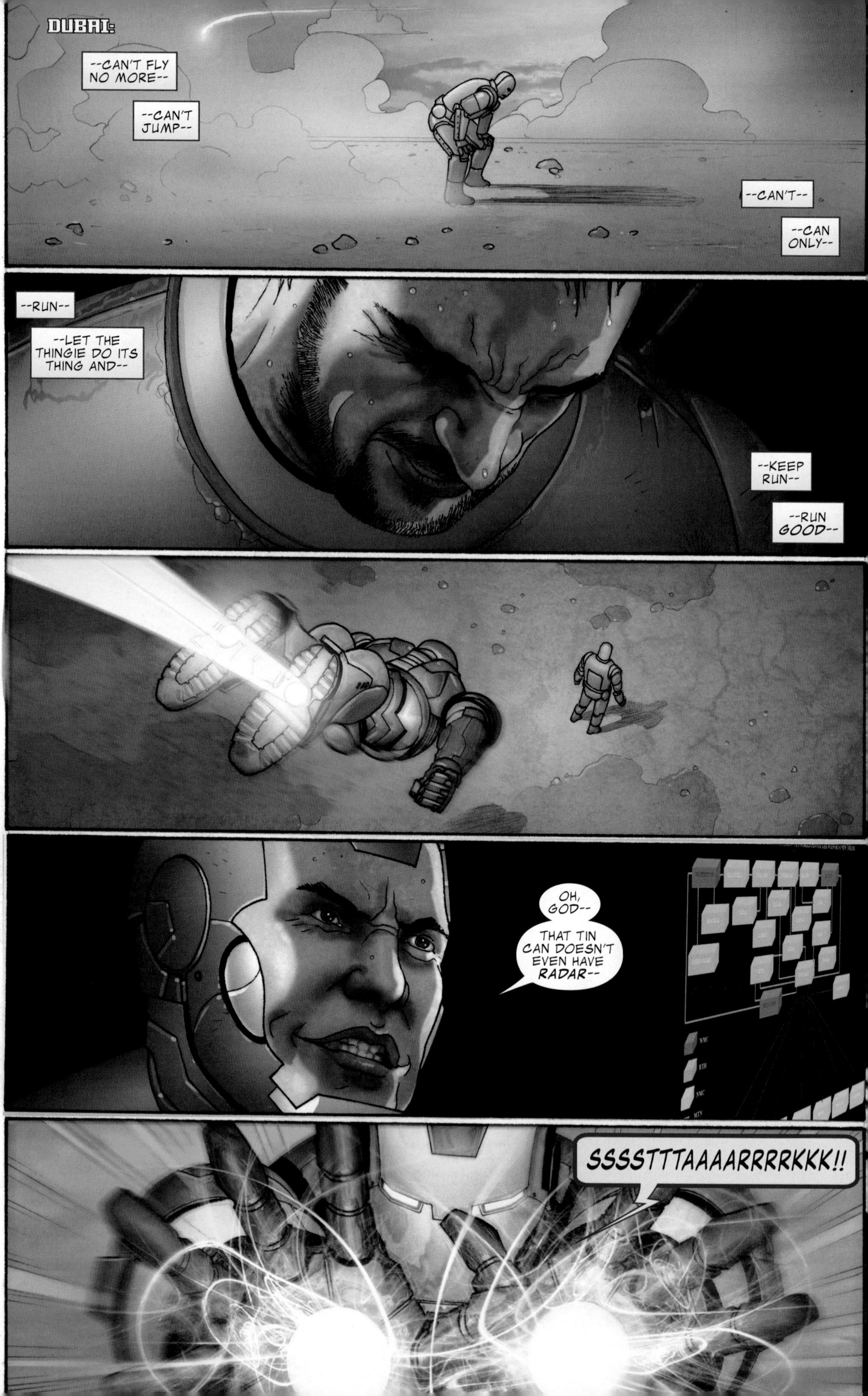
DUBAI:
--CAN'T FLY NO MORE--
--CAN'T JUMP--
--CAN'T--
--CAN ONLY--
--RUN--
--LET THE THINGIE DO ITS THING AND--
--KEEP RUN--
--RUN GOOD--
OH, GOD--
THAT TIN CAN DOESN'T EVEN HAVE RADAR--
SSSSTTTAAAARRRRKKK!!

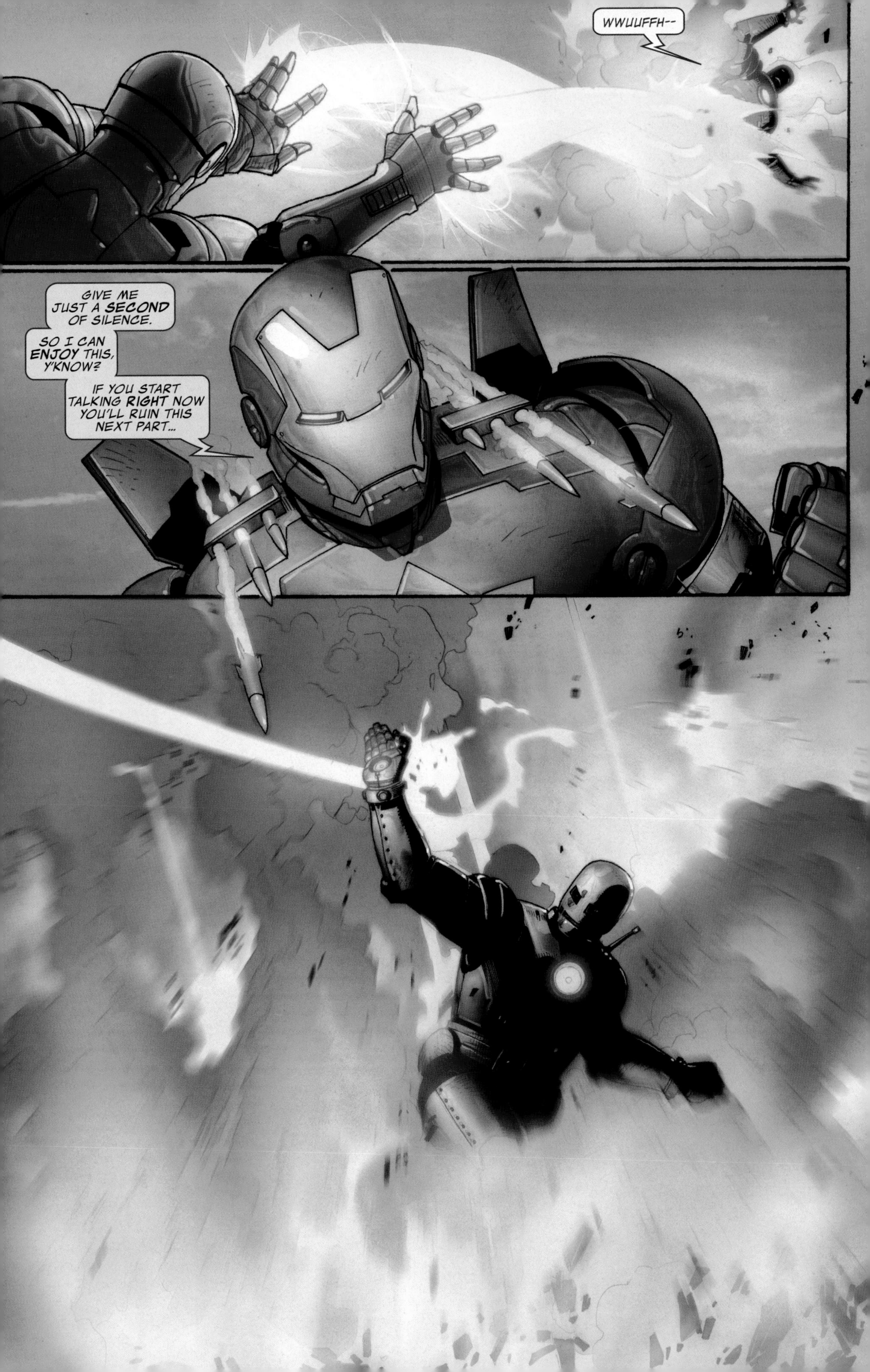
WWUUFFH--
GIVE ME JUST A SECOND OF SILENCE.
SO I CAN ENJOY THIS, Y'KNOW?
IF YOU START TALKING RIGHT NOW YOU'LL RUIN THIS NEXT PART...

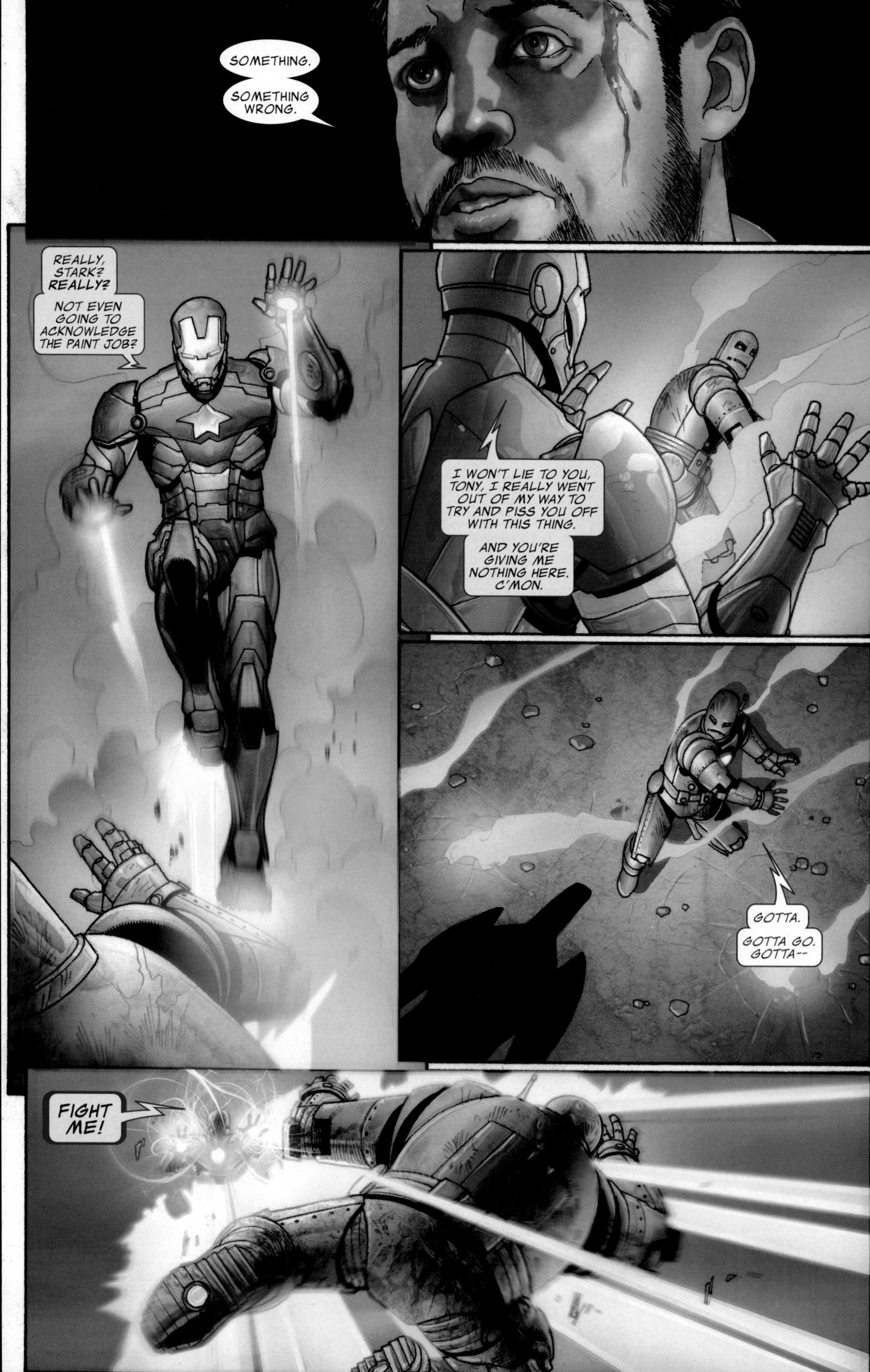
SOMETHING.
SOMETHING WRONG.
REALLY, STARK? REALLY?
NOT EVEN GOING TO ACKNOWLEDGE THE PAINT JOB?
I WON'T LIE TO YOU, TONY, I REALLY WENT OUT OF MY WAY TO TRY AND PISS YOU OFF WITH THIS THING.
AND YOU'RE GIVING ME NOTHING HERE. C'MON.
GOTTA.
GOTTA GO. GOTTA--
FIGHT ME!

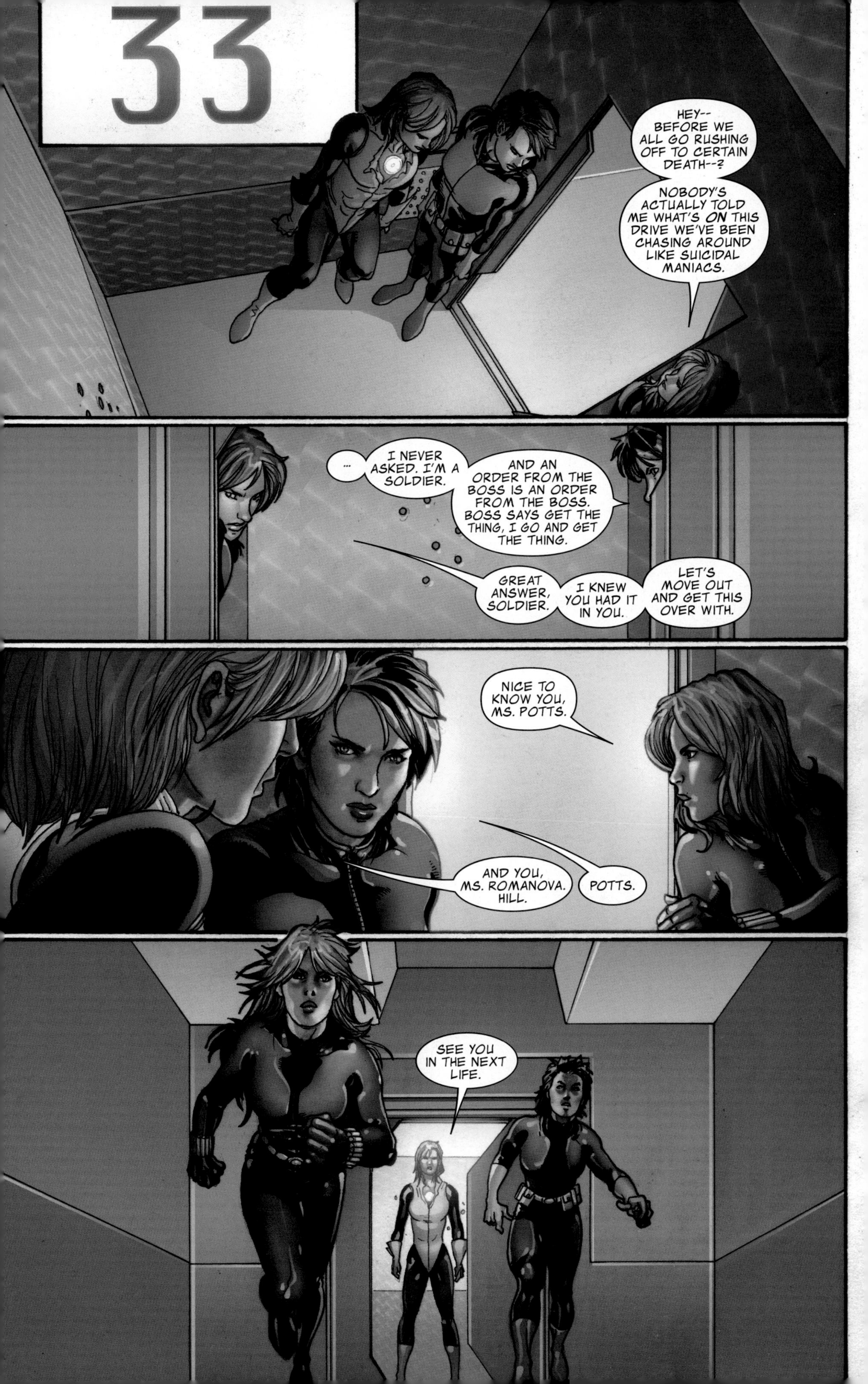
33
HEY-- BEFORE WE ALL GO RUSHING OFF TO CERTAIN DEATH--?
NOBODY'S ACTUALLY TOLD ME WHAT'S ON THIS DRIVE WE'VE BEEN CHASING AROUND LIKE SUICIDAL MANIACS.
...
I NEVER ASKED. I'M A SOLDIER.
AND AN ORDER FROM THE BOSS IS AN ORDER FROM THE BOSS. BOSS SAYS GET THE THING, I GO AND GET THE THING.
GREAT ANSWER, SOLDIER.
I KNEW YOU HAD IT IN YOU.
LET'S MOVE OUT AND GET THIS OVER WITH.
NICE TO KNOW YOU, MS. POTTS.
AND YOU, MS. ROMANOVA. HILL.
POTTS.
SEE YOU IN THE NEXT LIFE.

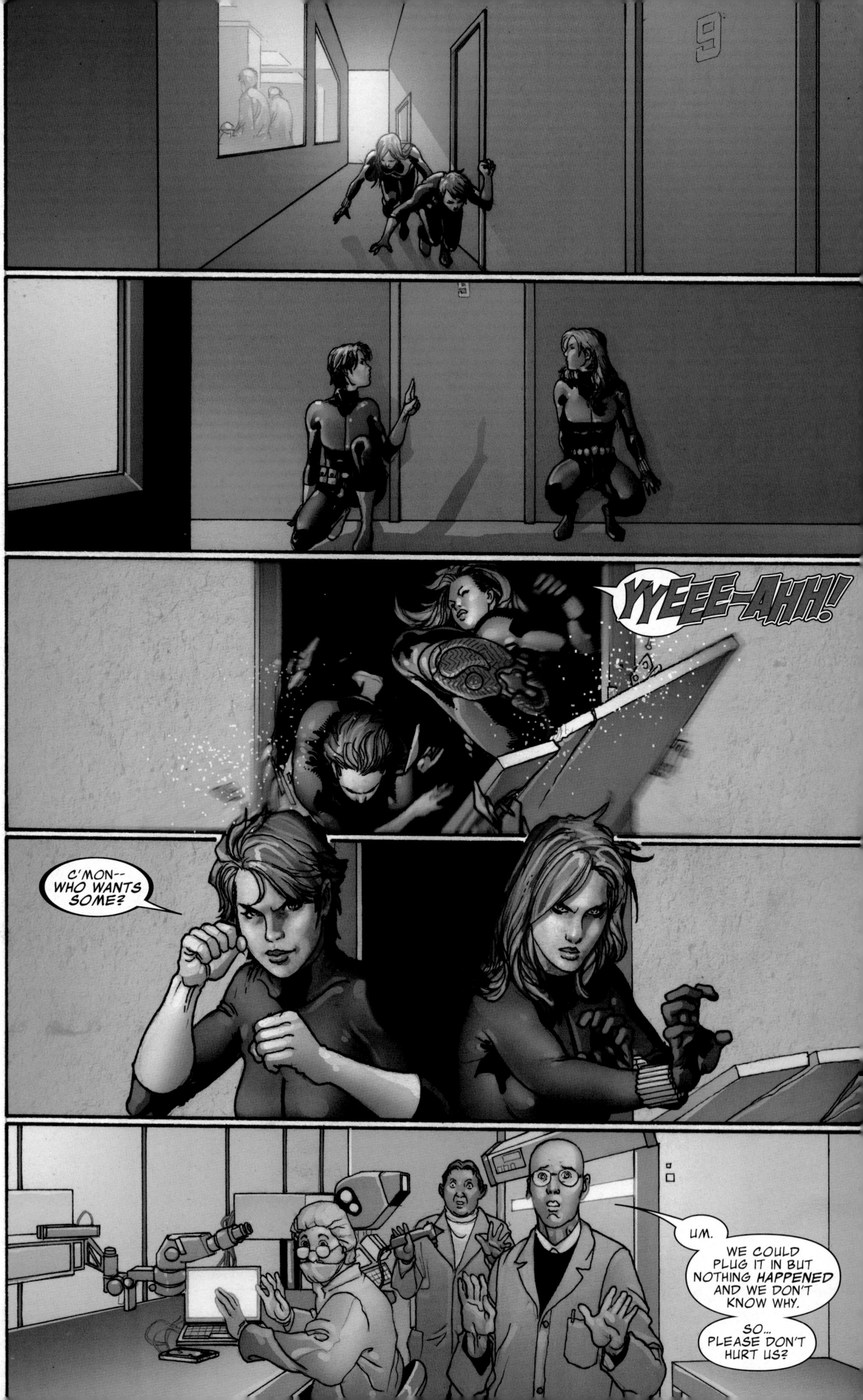
YYEEE-AHH!
C'MON-- WHO WANTS SOME?
UM.
WE COULD PLUG IT IN BUT NOTHING HAPPENED AND WE DON'T KNOW WHY.
SO... PLEASE DON'T HURT US?

DON' WANNA FIGHT.

GET UP. GOTTA GO.

STARK, COME ON. ARE YOU KIDDING ME?

I MEAN, MASQUE--WHOEVER IT IS YOU'VE GOT PRETENDING TO **BE** MASQUE, ANYWAY-- SAID YOU WERE LOSING IT, BUT THIS PROTO-**HULK** PATOIS IS JUST CLICHÉD...

I'M NOT GOING TO LET YOU WALK AWAY WITH ALL THOSE **SECRETS** IN YOUR HEAD. ALL THAT TECHNOLOGY, ALL THE **IDENTITIES** OF ALL YOUR FRIENDS...

I'M A LITTLE OFFENDED THAT I'VE SO CLEARLY BEATEN YOU AND YET YOU CAN'T EVEN BE BOTHERED TO LOOK ME IN THE EYES...

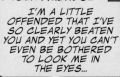

DUNNO.

MY GOD. HE'S REALLY GONE...

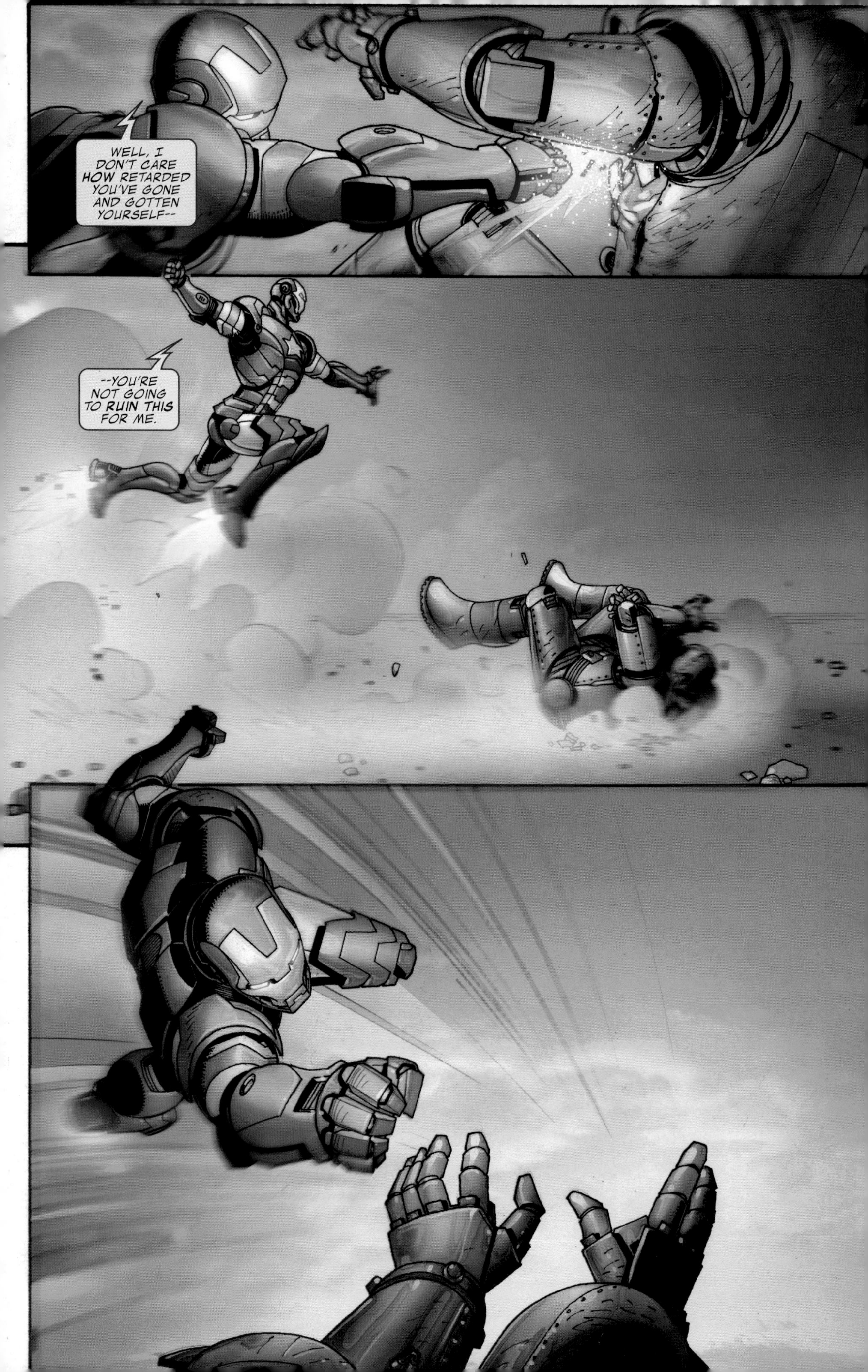
WELL, I DON'T CARE HOW RETARDED YOU'VE GONE AND GOTTEN YOURSELF--
--YOU'RE NOT GOING TO RUIN THIS FOR ME.

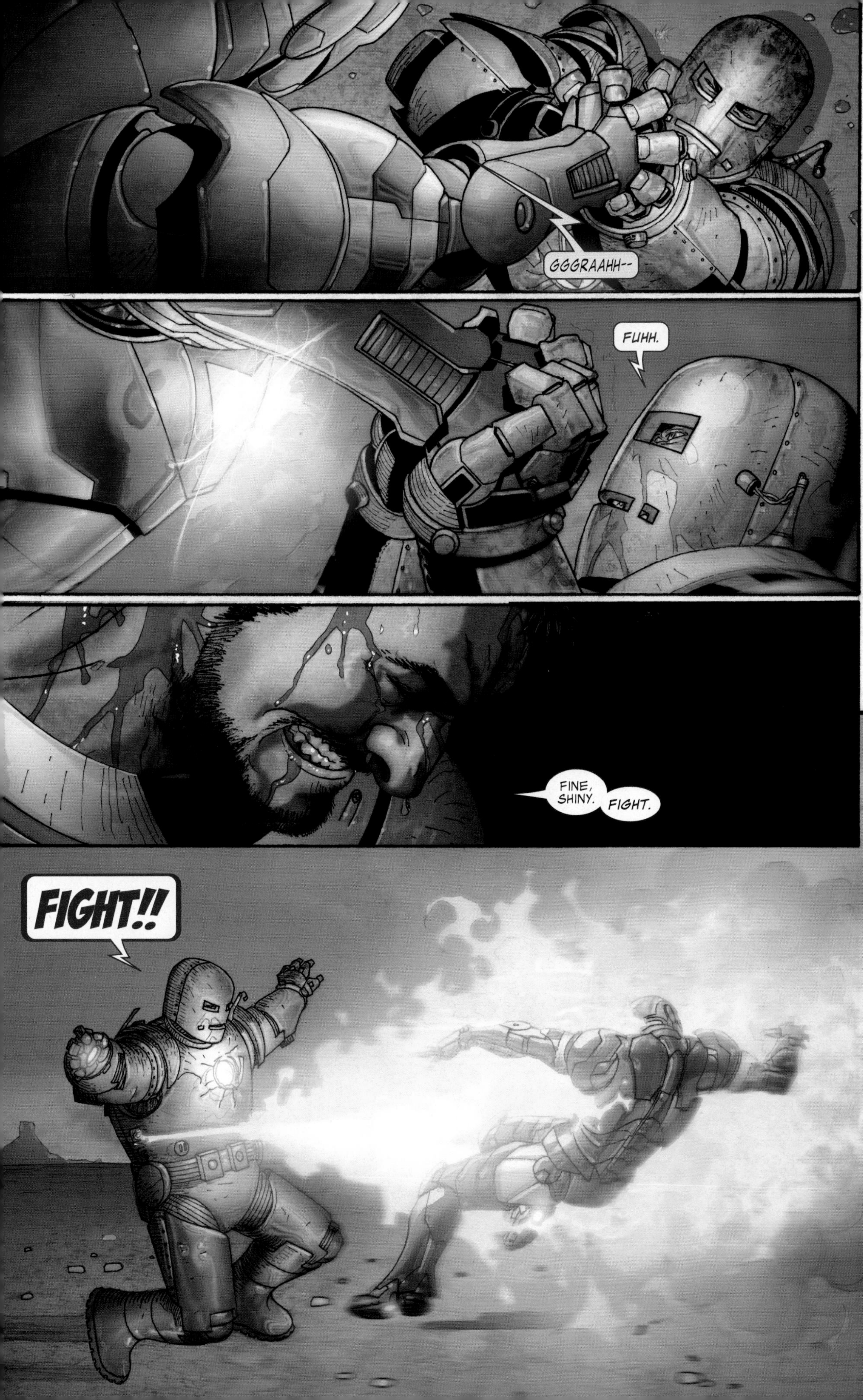
GGGRAAHH--
FUHH.
FINE, SHINY.
FIGHT.
FIGHT!!

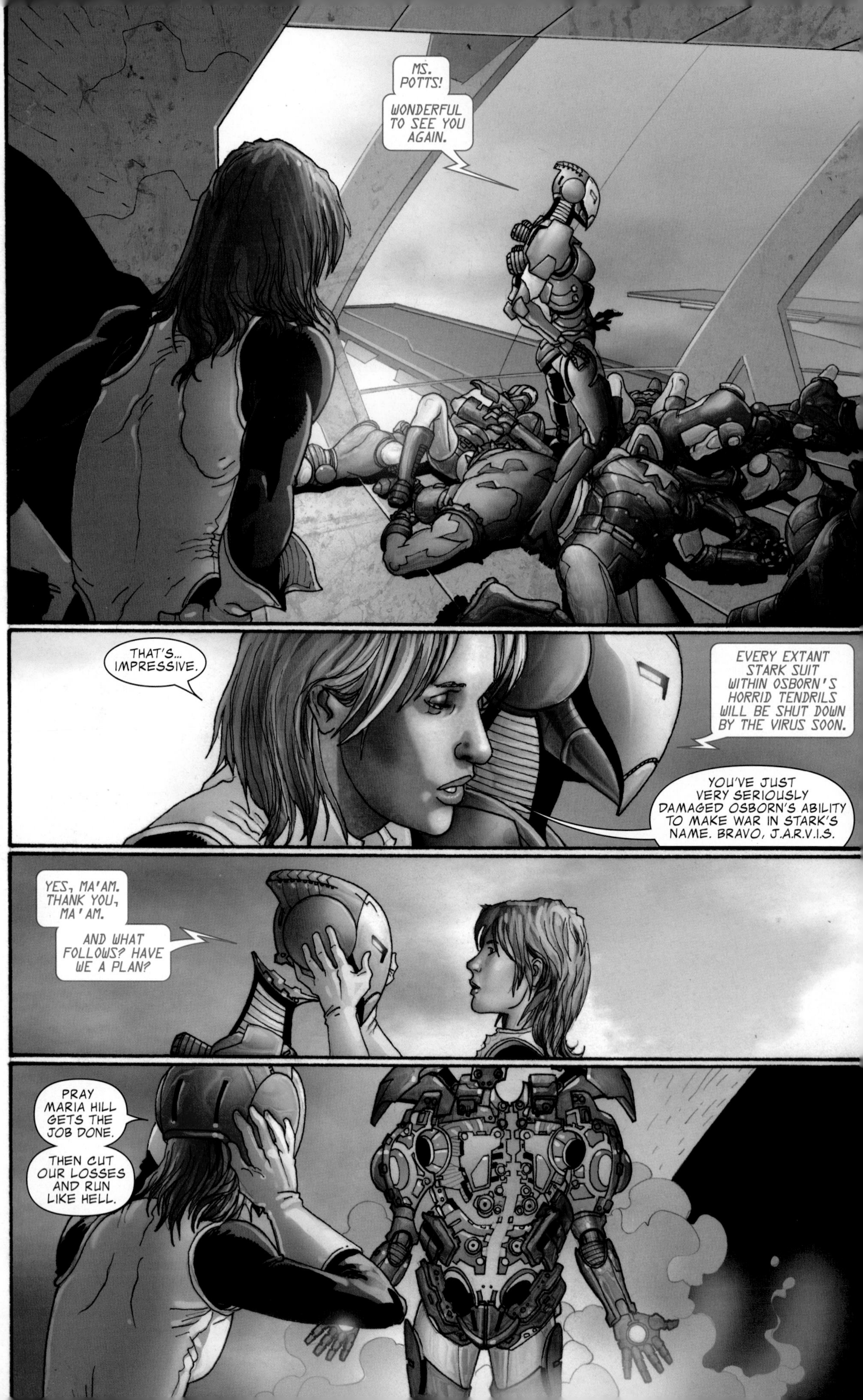
MS. POTTS!
WONDERFUL TO SEE YOU AGAIN.
THAT'S... IMPRESSIVE.
EVERY EXTANT STARK SUIT WITHIN OSBORN'S HORRID TENDRILS WILL BE SHUT DOWN BY THE VIRUS SOON.
YOU'VE JUST VERY SERIOUSLY DAMAGED OSBORN'S ABILITY TO MAKE WAR IN STARK'S NAME. BRAVO, J.A.R.V.I.S.
YES, MA'AM. THANK YOU, MA'AM.
AND WHAT FOLLOWS? HAVE WE A PLAN?
PRAY MARIA HILL GETS THE JOB DONE.
THEN CUT OUR LOSSES AND RUN LIKE HELL.

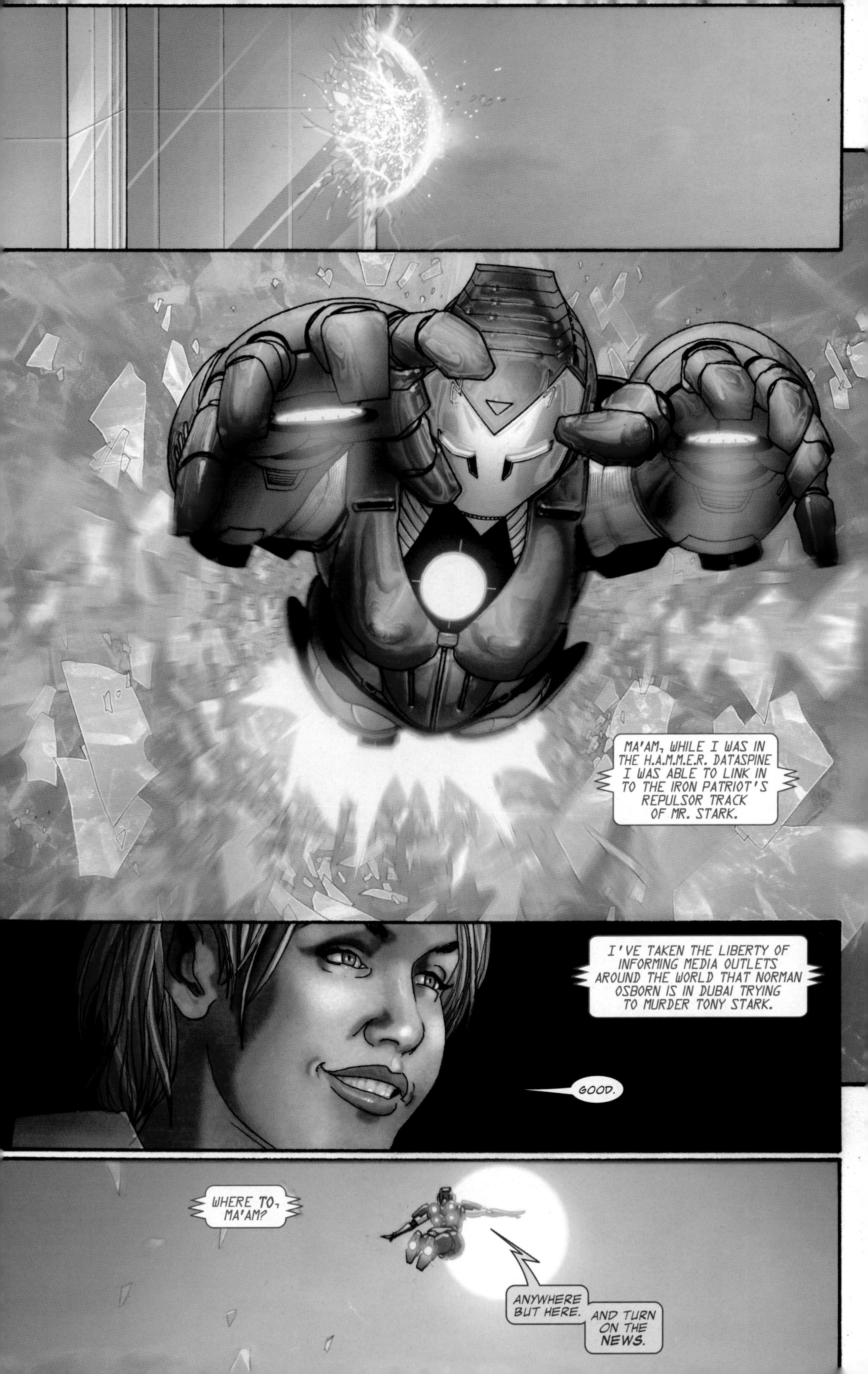
MA'AM, WHILE I WAS IN THE H.A.M.M.E.R. DATASPINE I WAS ABLE TO LINK IN TO THE IRON PATRIOT'S REPULSOR TRACK OF MR. STARK.
I'VE TAKEN THE LIBERTY OF INFORMING MEDIA OUTLETS AROUND THE WORLD THAT NORMAN OSBORN IS IN DUBAI TRYING TO MURDER TONY STARK.
GOOD.
WHERE TO, MA'AM?
ANYWHERE BUT HERE.
AND TURN ON THE NEWS.

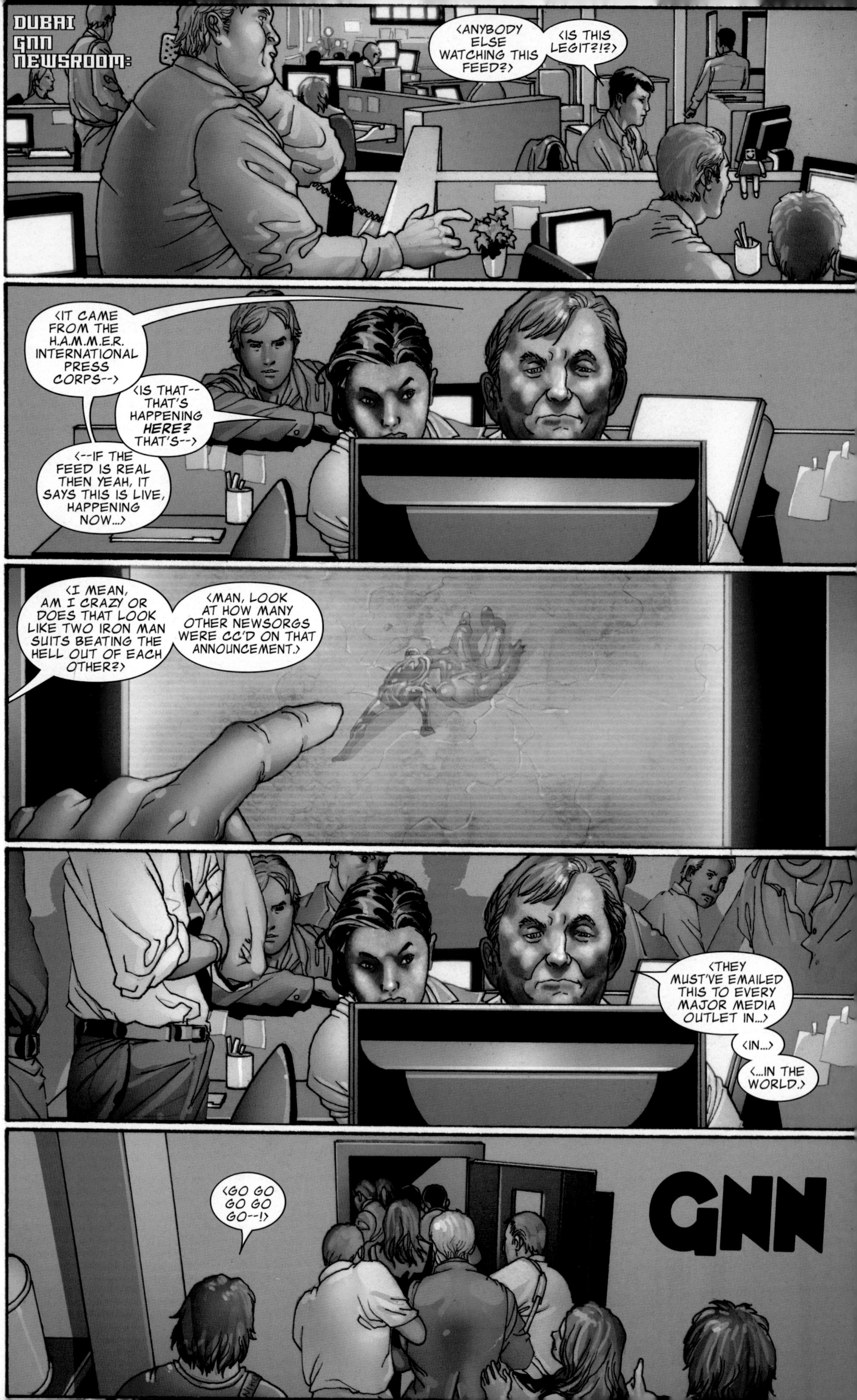
DUBAI GNN NEWSROOM:
<ANYBODY ELSE WATCHING THIS FEED?>
<IS THIS LEGIT?!?>
<IT CAME FROM THE H.A.M.M.E.R. INTERNATIONAL PRESS CORPS-->
<IS THAT-- THAT'S HAPPENING HERE? THAT'S-->
<--IF THE FEED IS REAL THEN YEAH, IT SAYS THIS IS LIVE, HAPPENING NOW...>
<I MEAN, AM I CRAZY OR DOES THAT LOOK LIKE TWO IRON MAN SUITS BEATING THE HELL OUT OF EACH OTHER?>
<MAN, LOOK AT HOW MANY OTHER NEWSORGS WERE CC'D ON THAT ANNOUNCEMENT.>
<THEY MUST'VE EMAILED THIS TO EVERY MAJOR MEDIA OUTLET IN...>
<IN...>
<...IN THE WORLD.>
<GO GO GO GO GO--!>
GNN

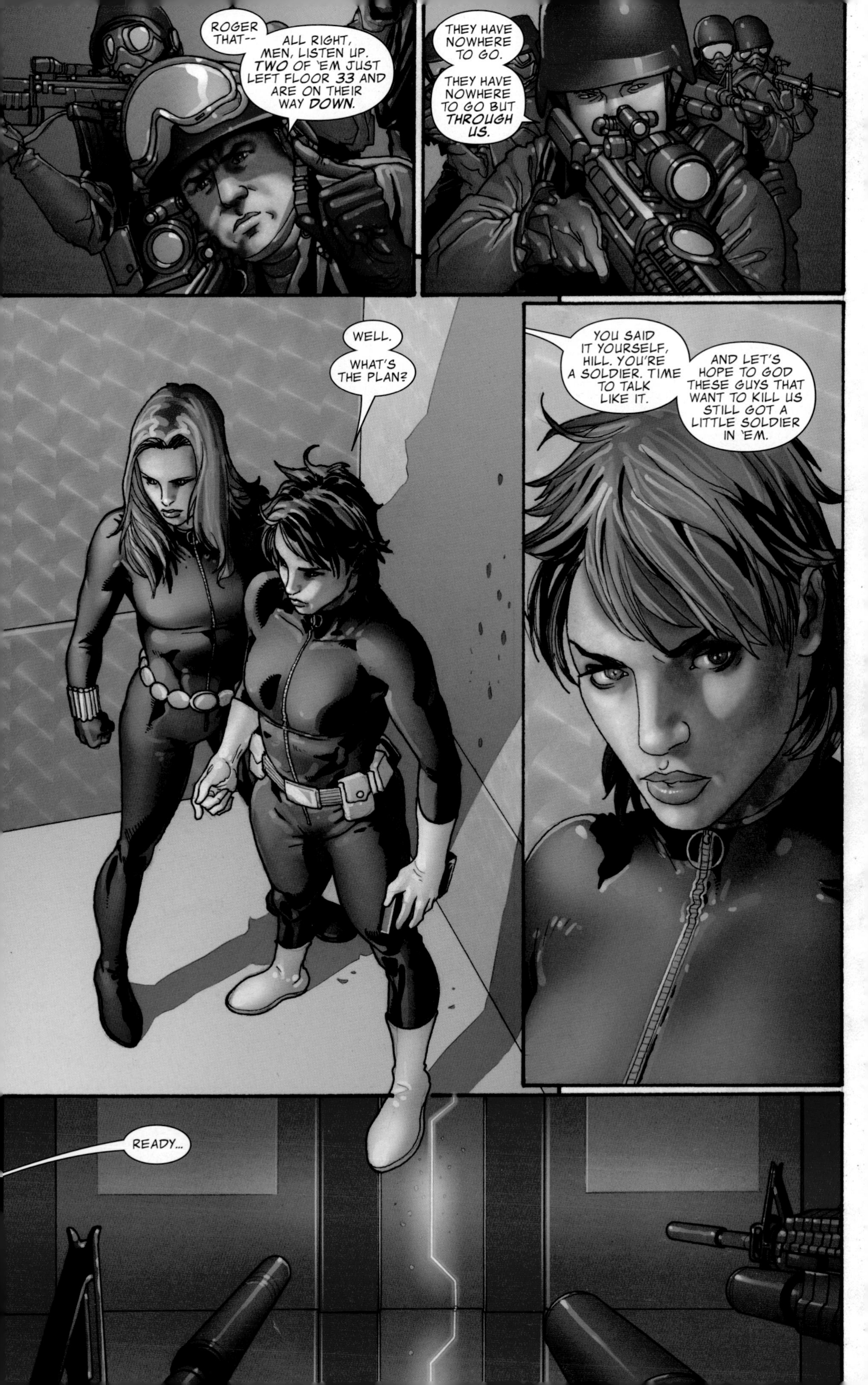
ROGER THAT--
ALL RIGHT, MEN, LISTEN UP. TWO OF 'EM JUST LEFT FLOOR 33 AND ARE ON THEIR WAY DOWN.
THEY HAVE NOWHERE TO GO.
THEY HAVE NOWHERE TO GO BUT THROUGH US.
WELL.
WHAT'S THE PLAN?
YOU SAID IT YOURSELF, HILL. YOU'RE A SOLDIER. TIME TO TALK LIKE IT.
AND LET'S HOPE TO GOD THESE GUYS THAT WANT TO KILL US STILL GOT A LITTLE SOLDIER IN 'EM.
READY...

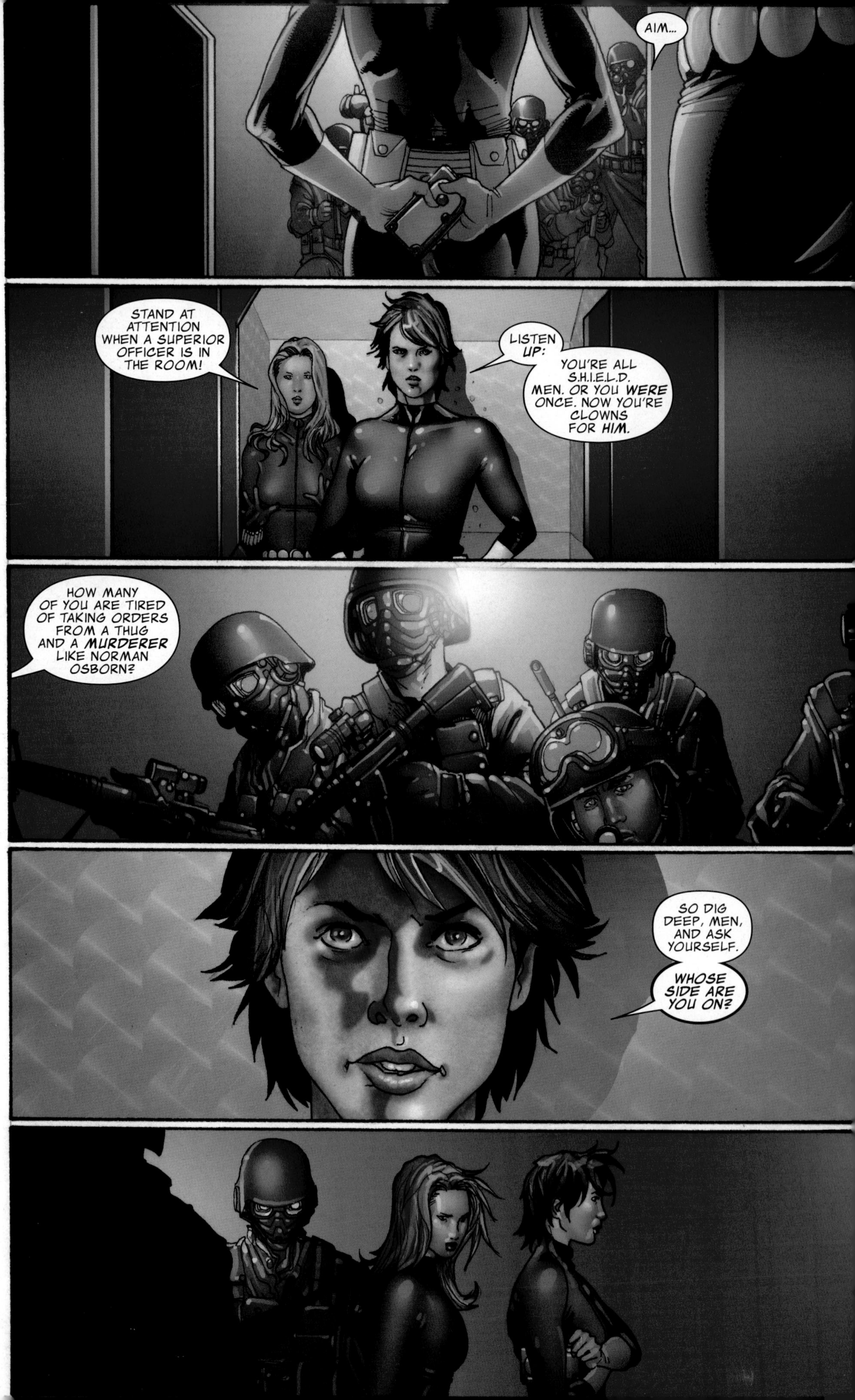
AIM...
STAND AT ATTENTION WHEN A SUPERIOR OFFICER IS IN THE ROOM!
LISTEN UP:
YOU'RE ALL S.H.I.E.L.D. MEN. OR YOU WERE ONCE. NOW YOU'RE CLOWNS FOR HIM.
HOW MANY OF YOU ARE TIRED OF TAKING ORDERS FROM A THUG AND A MURDERER LIKE NORMAN OSBORN?
SO DIG DEEP, MEN, AND ASK YOURSELF.
WHOSE SIDE ARE YOU ON?

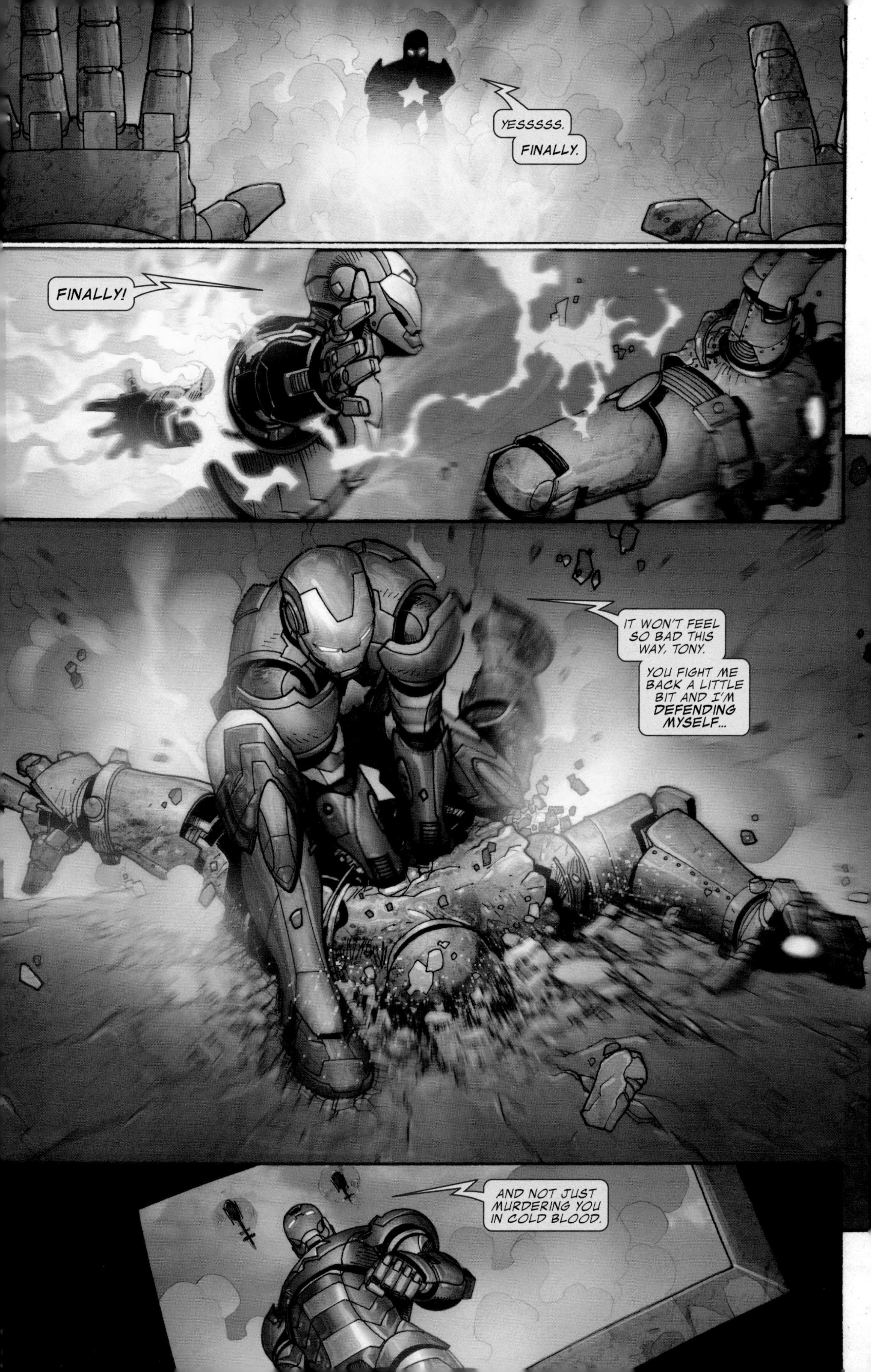
YESSSSS.
FINALLY.
FINALLY!
IT WON'T FEEL SO BAD THIS WAY, TONY.
YOU FIGHT ME BACK A LITTLE BIT AND I'M DEFENDING MYSELF...
AND NOT JUST MURDERING YOU IN COLD BLOOD.

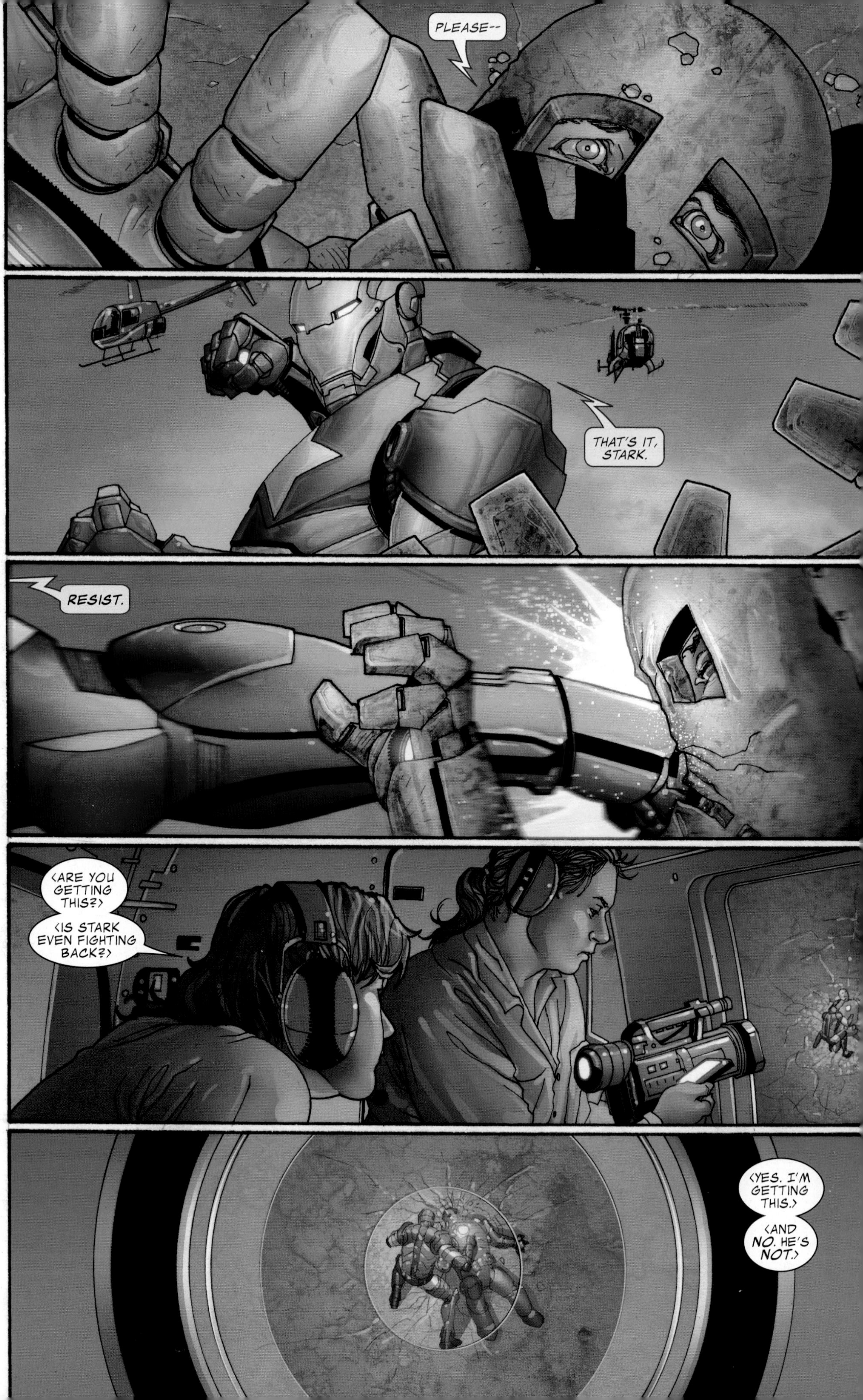
PLEASE--
THAT'S IT, STARK.
RESIST.
<ARE YOU GETTING THIS?>
<IS STARK EVEN FIGHTING BACK?>
<YES. I'M GETTING THIS.>
<AND NO. HE'S NOT.>

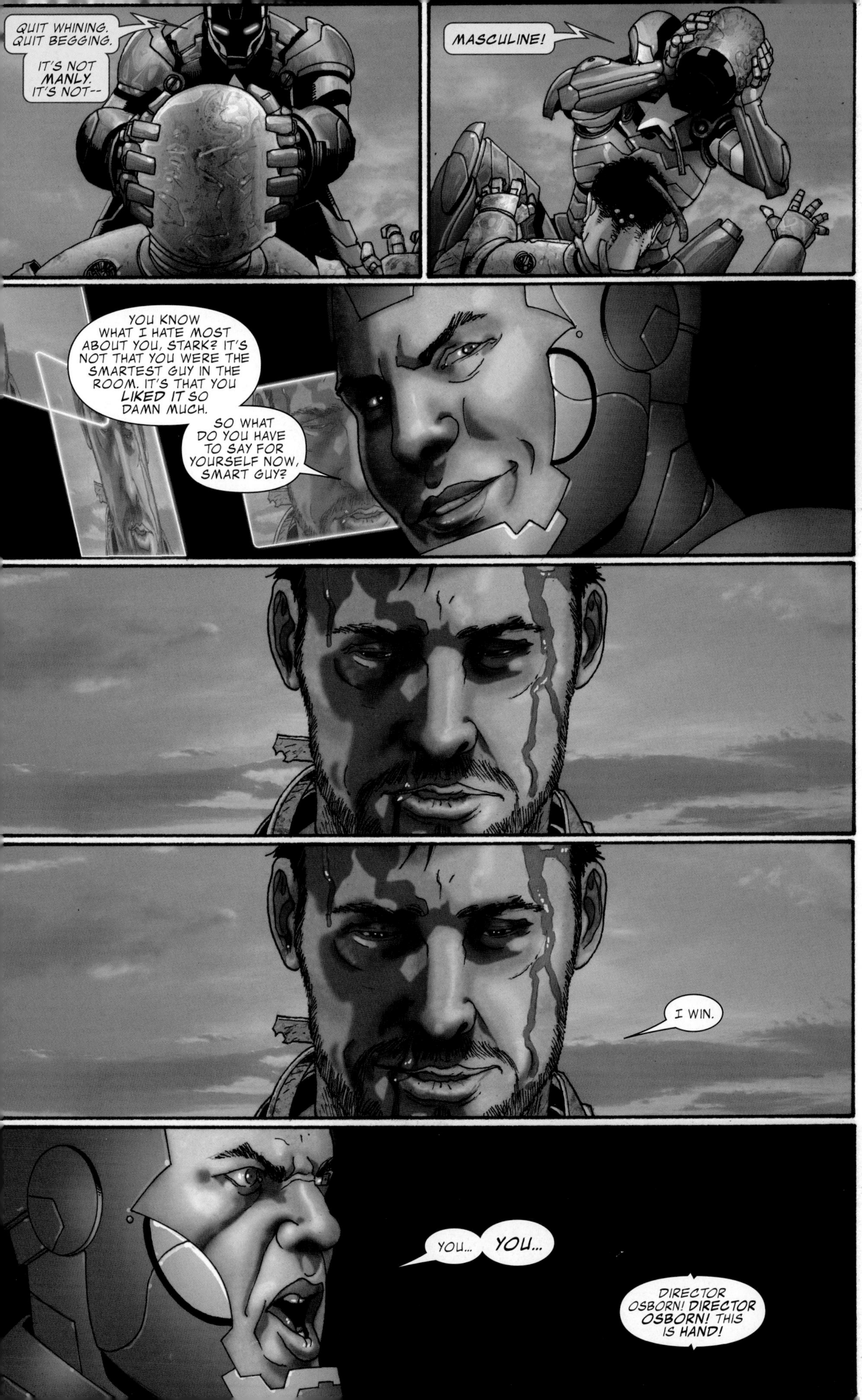
QUIT WHINING. QUIT BEGGING.
IT'S NOT MANLY. IT'S NOT--
MASCULINE!
YOU KNOW WHAT I HATE MOST ABOUT YOU, STARK? IT'S NOT THAT YOU WERE THE SMARTEST GUY IN THE ROOM. IT'S THAT YOU LIKED IT SO DAMN MUCH.
SO WHAT DO YOU HAVE TO SAY FOR YOURSELF NOW, SMART GUY?
I WIN.
YOU...
YOU...
DIRECTOR OSBORN! DIRECTOR OSBORN! THIS IS HAND!

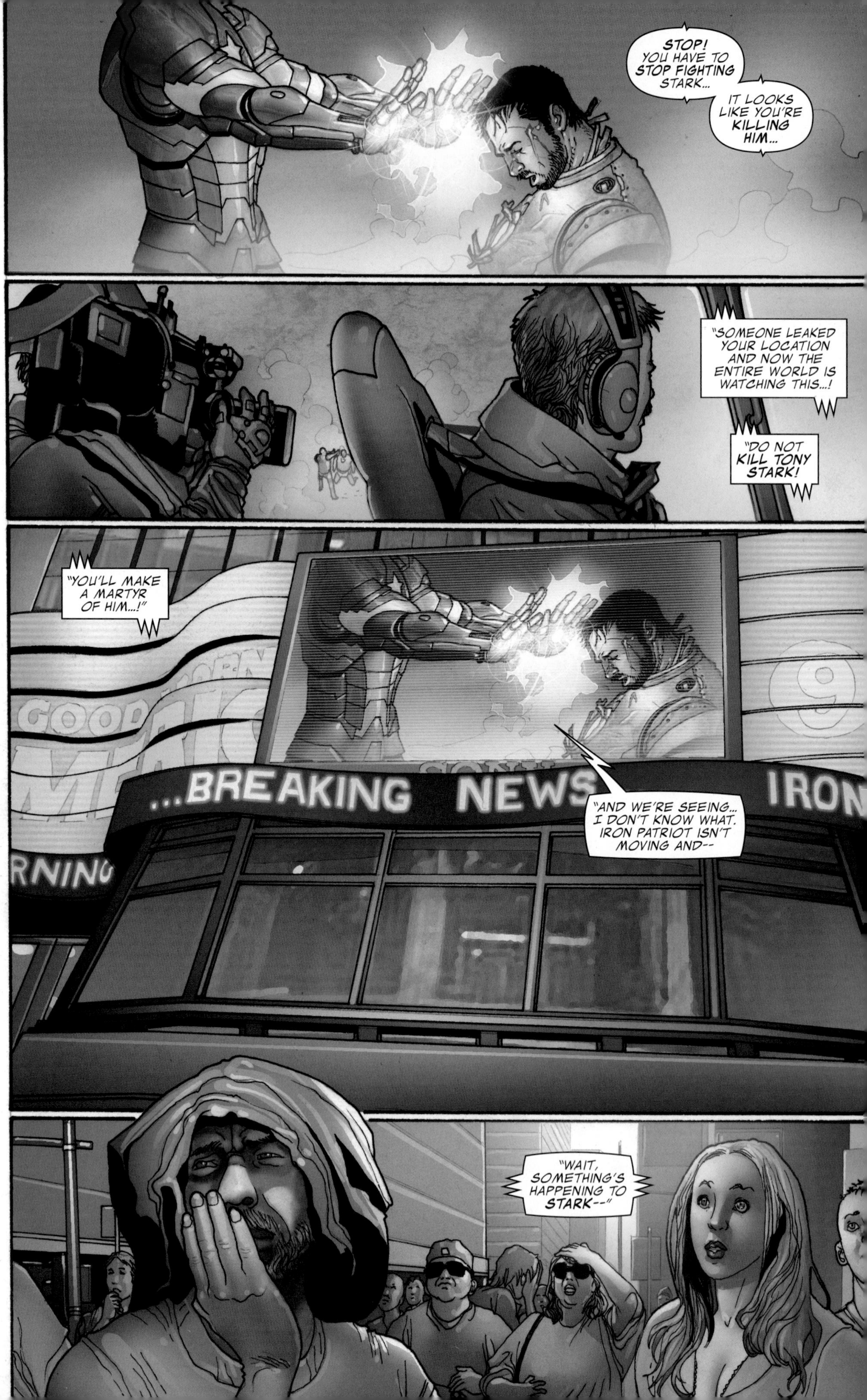
STOP! YOU HAVE TO STOP FIGHTING STARK...
IT LOOKS LIKE YOU'RE KILLING HIM...
"SOMEONE LEAKED YOUR LOCATION AND NOW THE ENTIRE WORLD IS WATCHING THIS...!
"DO NOT KILL TONY STARK!
"YOU'LL MAKE A MARTYR OF HIM...!"
...BREAKING NEWS IRON
"AND WE'RE SEEING... I DON'T KNOW WHAT. IRON PATRIOT ISN'T MOVING AND--
"WAIT, SOMETHING'S HAPPENING TO STARK--"

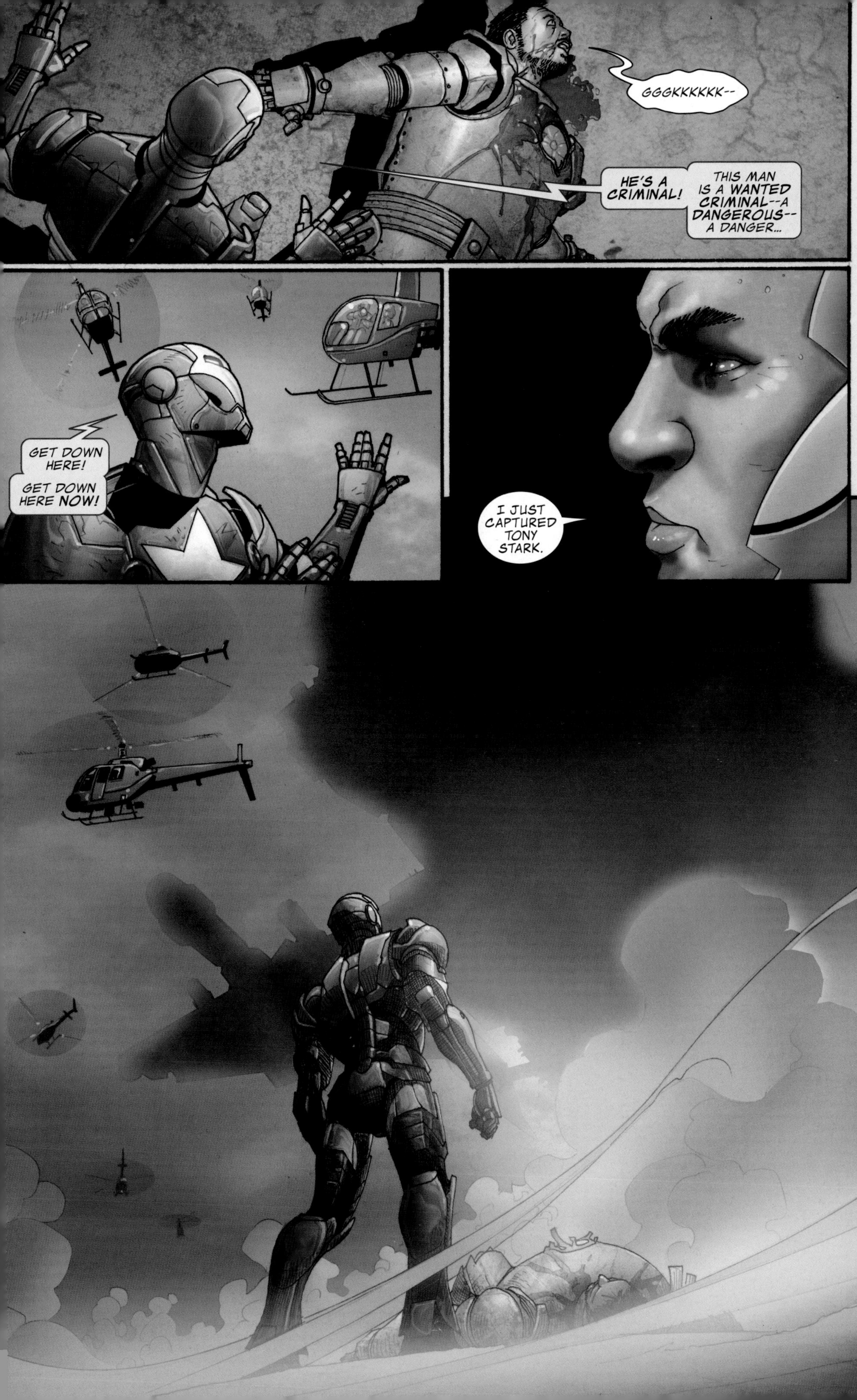
GGGKKKKKK--
HE'S A CRIMINAL!
THIS MAN IS A WANTED CRIMINAL--A DANGEROUS--A DANGER...
GET DOWN HERE!
GET DOWN HERE NOW!
I JUST CAPTURED TONY STARK.

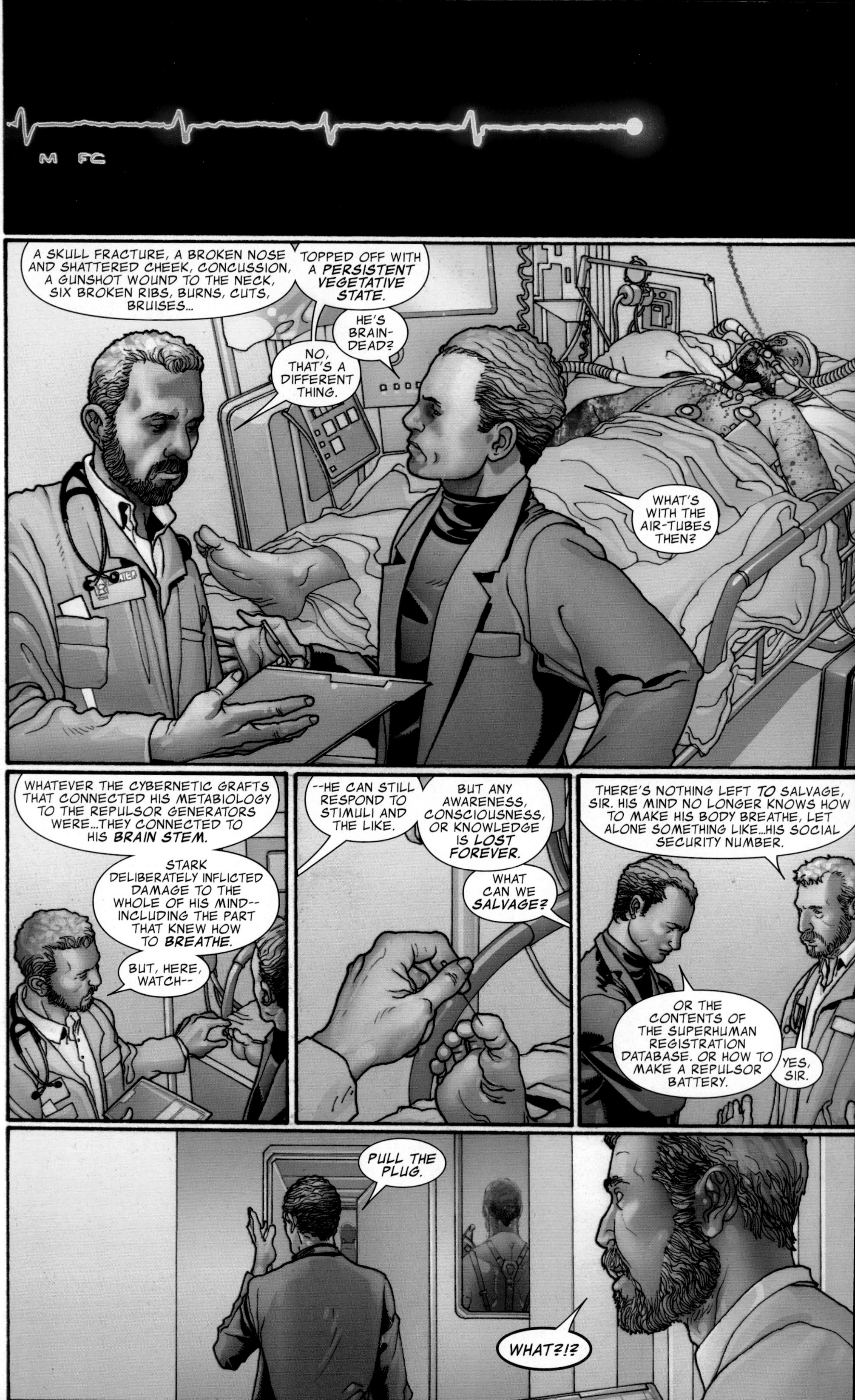
M FC
A SKULL FRACTURE, A BROKEN NOSE AND SHATTERED CHEEK, CONCUSSION, A GUNSHOT WOUND TO THE NECK, SIX BROKEN RIBS, BURNS, CUTS, BRUISES...
TOPPED OFF WITH A PERSISTENT VEGETATIVE STATE.
HE'S BRAIN-DEAD?
NO, THAT'S A DIFFERENT THING.
WHAT'S WITH THE AIR-TUBES THEN?
WHATEVER THE CYBERNETIC GRAFTS THAT CONNECTED HIS METABIOLOGY TO THE REPULSOR GENERATORS WERE...THEY CONNECTED TO HIS BRAIN STEM.
STARK DELIBERATELY INFLICTED DAMAGE TO THE WHOLE OF HIS MIND--INCLUDING THE PART THAT KNEW HOW TO BREATHE.
BUT, HERE, WATCH--
--HE CAN STILL RESPOND TO STIMULI AND THE LIKE.
BUT ANY AWARENESS, CONSCIOUSNESS, OR KNOWLEDGE IS LOST FOREVER.
WHAT CAN WE SALVAGE?
THERE'S NOTHING LEFT TO SALVAGE, SIR. HIS MIND NO LONGER KNOWS HOW TO MAKE HIS BODY BREATHE, LET ALONE SOMETHING LIKE...HIS SOCIAL SECURITY NUMBER.
OR THE CONTENTS OF THE SUPERHUMAN REGISTRATION DATABASE. OR HOW TO MAKE A REPULSOR BATTERY.
YES, SIR.
PULL THE PLUG.
WHAT?!?

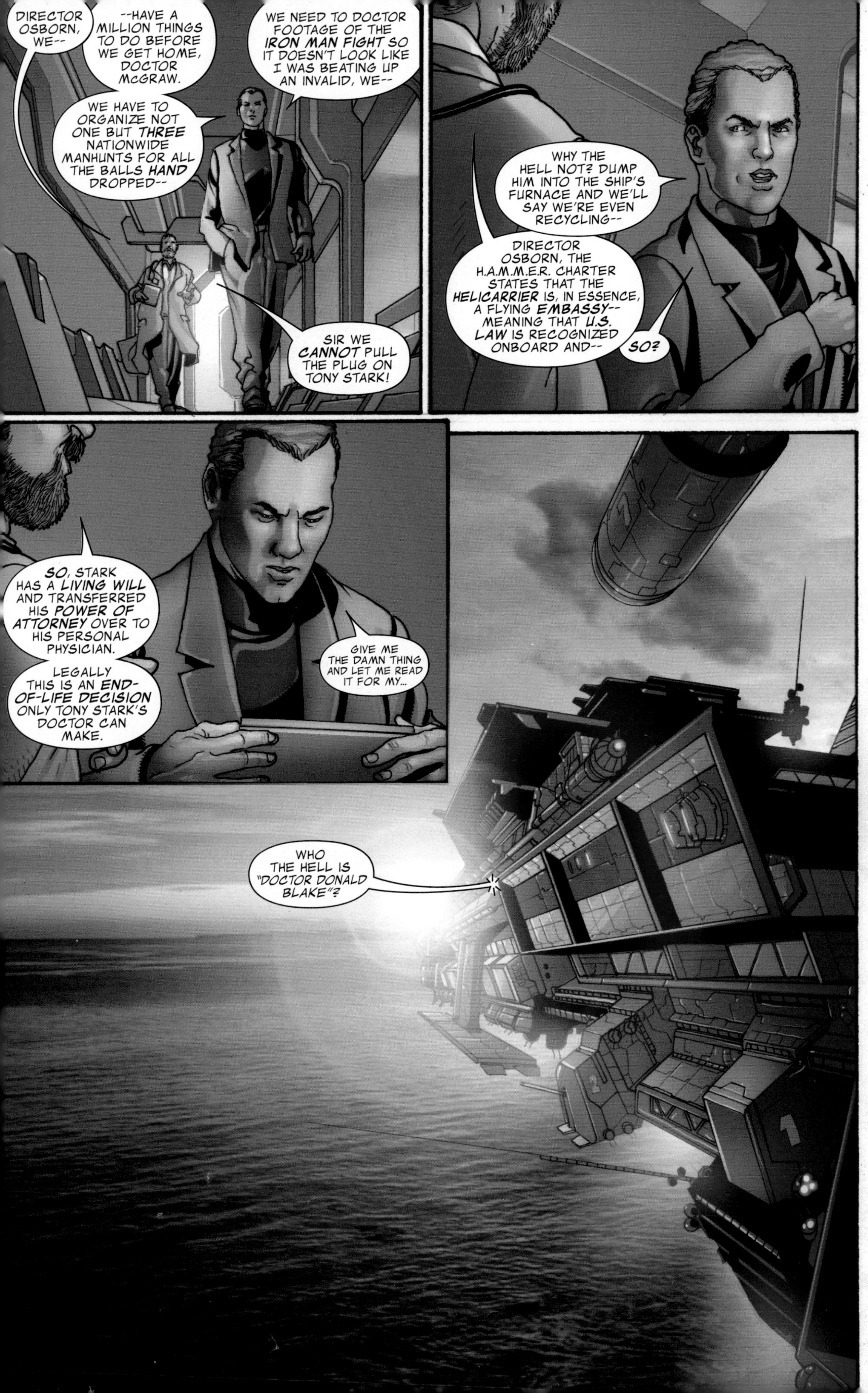
DIRECTOR OSBORN, WE--
--HAVE A MILLION THINGS TO DO BEFORE WE GET HOME, DOCTOR McGRAW.
WE HAVE TO ORGANIZE NOT ONE BUT THREE NATIONWIDE MANHUNTS FOR ALL THE BALLS HAND DROPPED--
WE NEED TO DOCTOR FOOTAGE OF THE IRON MAN FIGHT SO IT DOESN'T LOOK LIKE I WAS BEATING UP AN INVALID, WE--
SIR WE CANNOT PULL THE PLUG ON TONY STARK!
WHY THE HELL NOT? DUMP HIM INTO THE SHIP'S FURNACE AND WE'LL SAY WE'RE EVEN RECYCLING--
DIRECTOR OSBORN, THE H.A.M.M.E.R. CHARTER STATES THAT THE HELICARRIER IS, IN ESSENCE, A FLYING EMBASSY-- MEANING THAT U.S. LAW IS RECOGNIZED ONBOARD AND--
SO?
SO, STARK HAS A LIVING WILL AND TRANSFERRED HIS POWER OF ATTORNEY OVER TO HIS PERSONAL PHYSICIAN.
LEGALLY THIS IS AN END-OF-LIFE DECISION ONLY TONY STARK'S DOCTOR CAN MAKE.
GIVE ME THE DAMN THING AND LET ME READ IT FOR MY...
WHO THE HELL IS "DOCTOR DONALD BLAKE"?

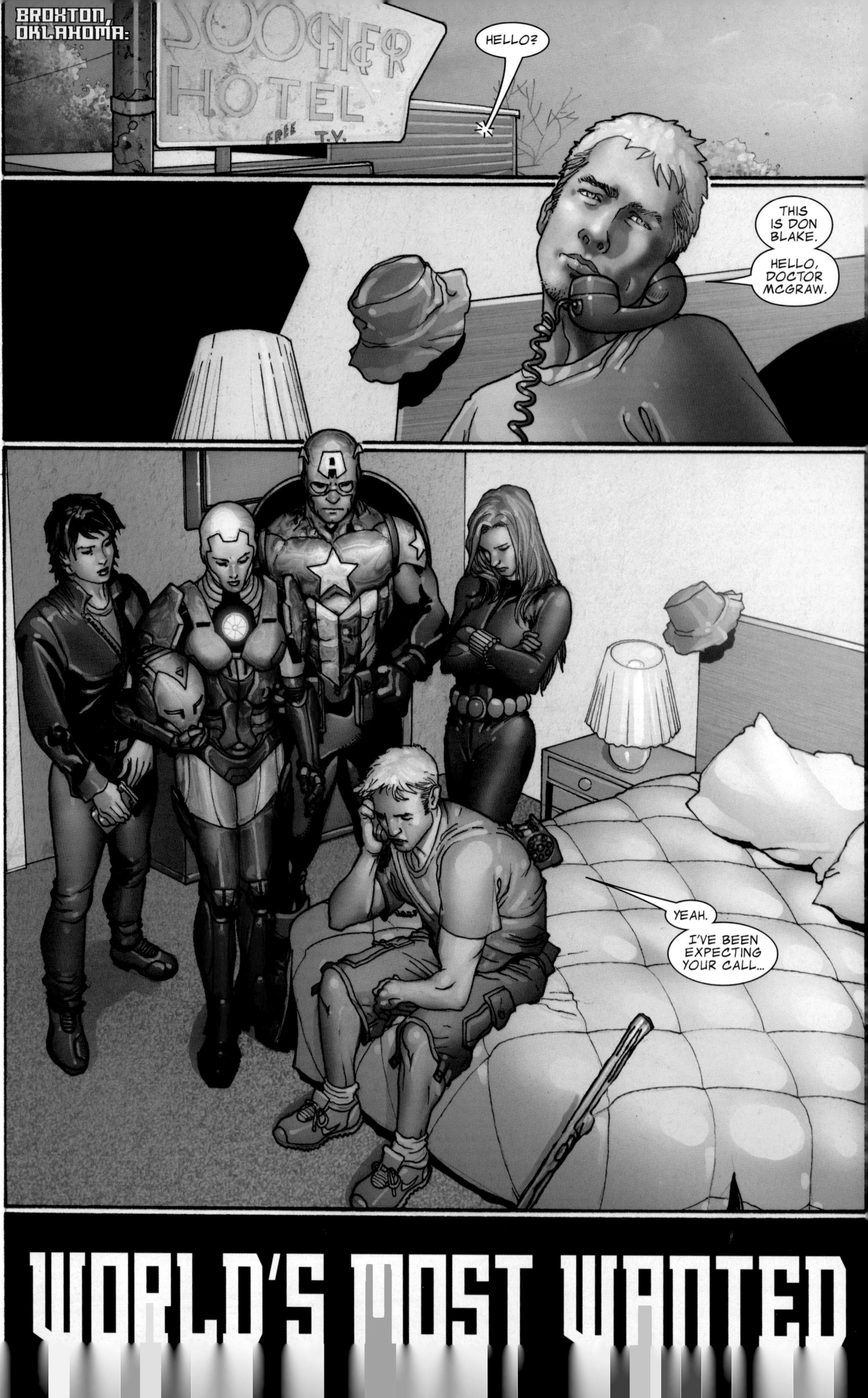
BROXTON, OKLAHOMA:
SOONER HOTEL
FREE T.V.
HELLO?
THIS IS DON BLAKE.
HELLO, DOCTOR MCGRAW.
YEAH.
I'VE BEEN EXPECTING YOUR CALL...
WORLD'S MOST WANTED

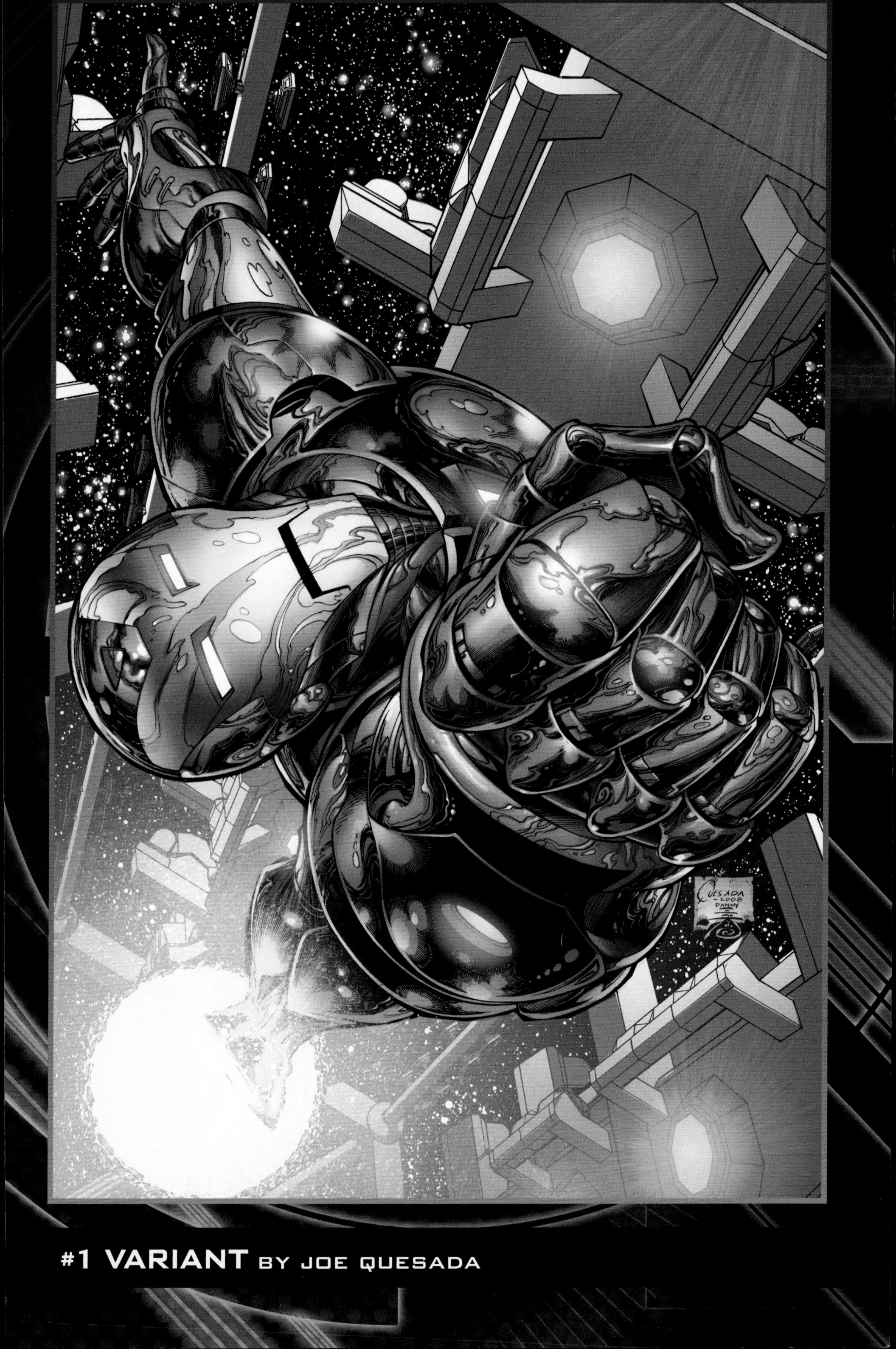
QUESADA
2008
DANNY

#1 VARIANT BY JOE QUESADA

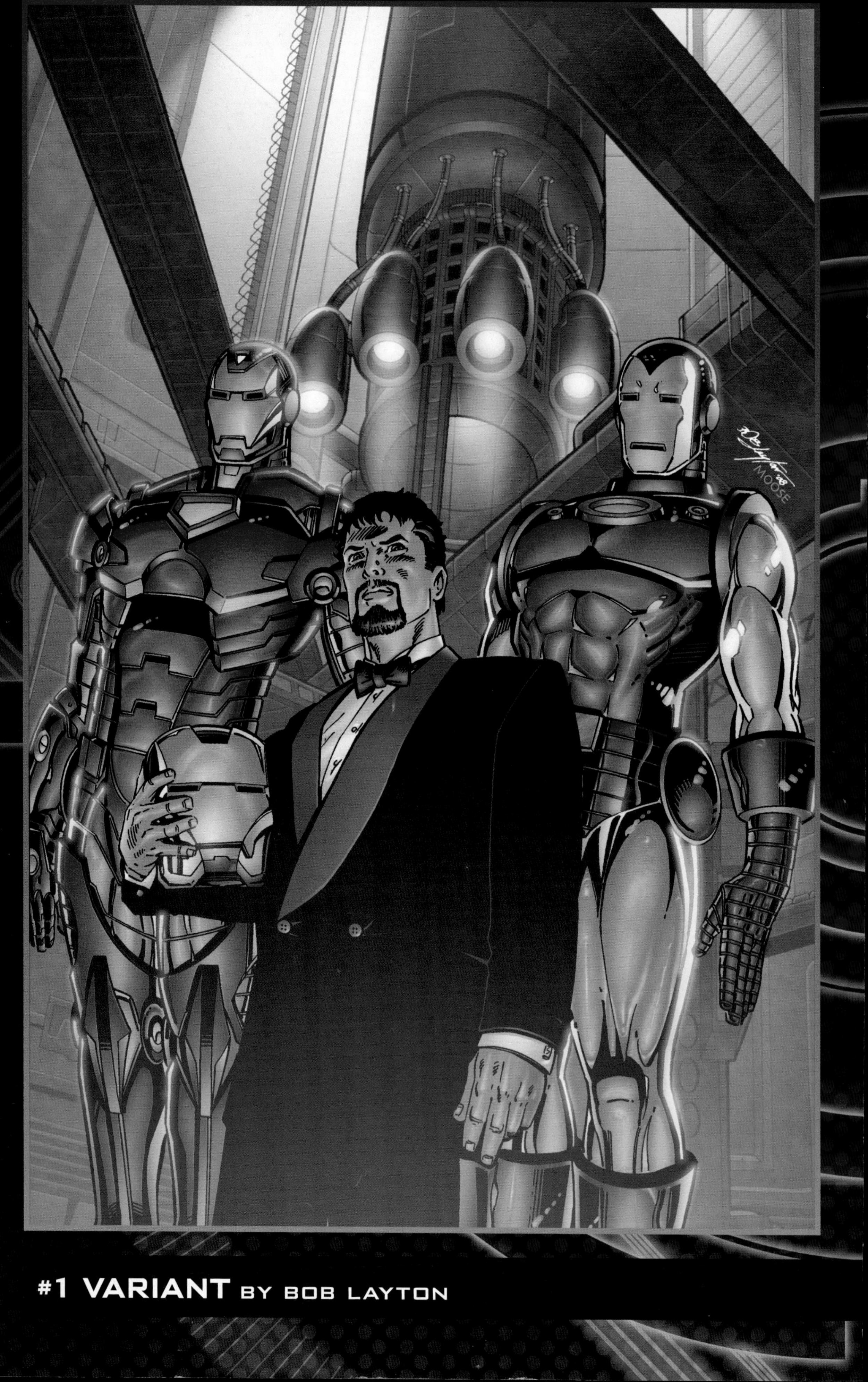
MOOSE

#1 VARIANT BY BOB LAYTON

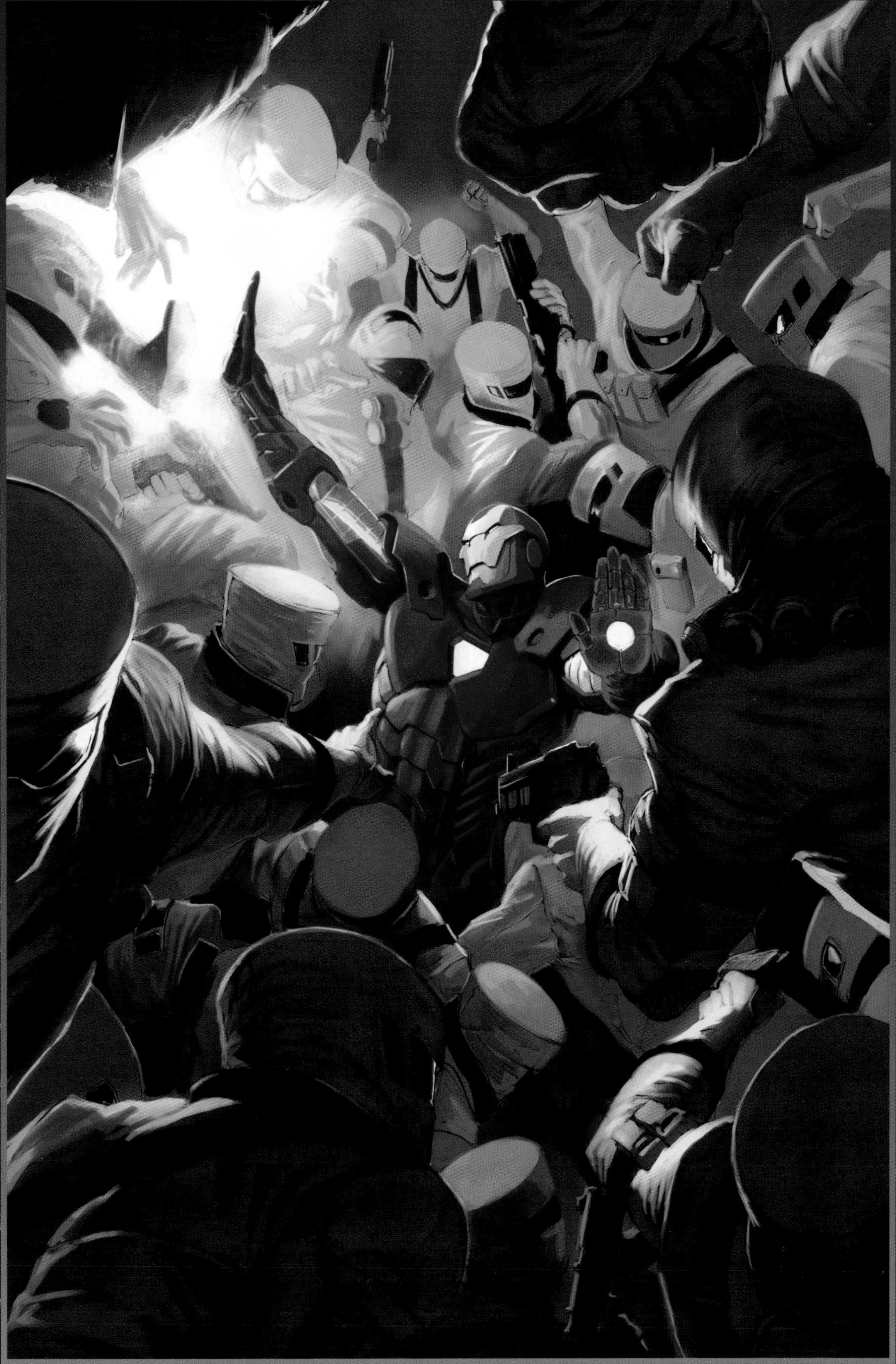

#1 VARIANT BY MARKO DJURDJEVIC

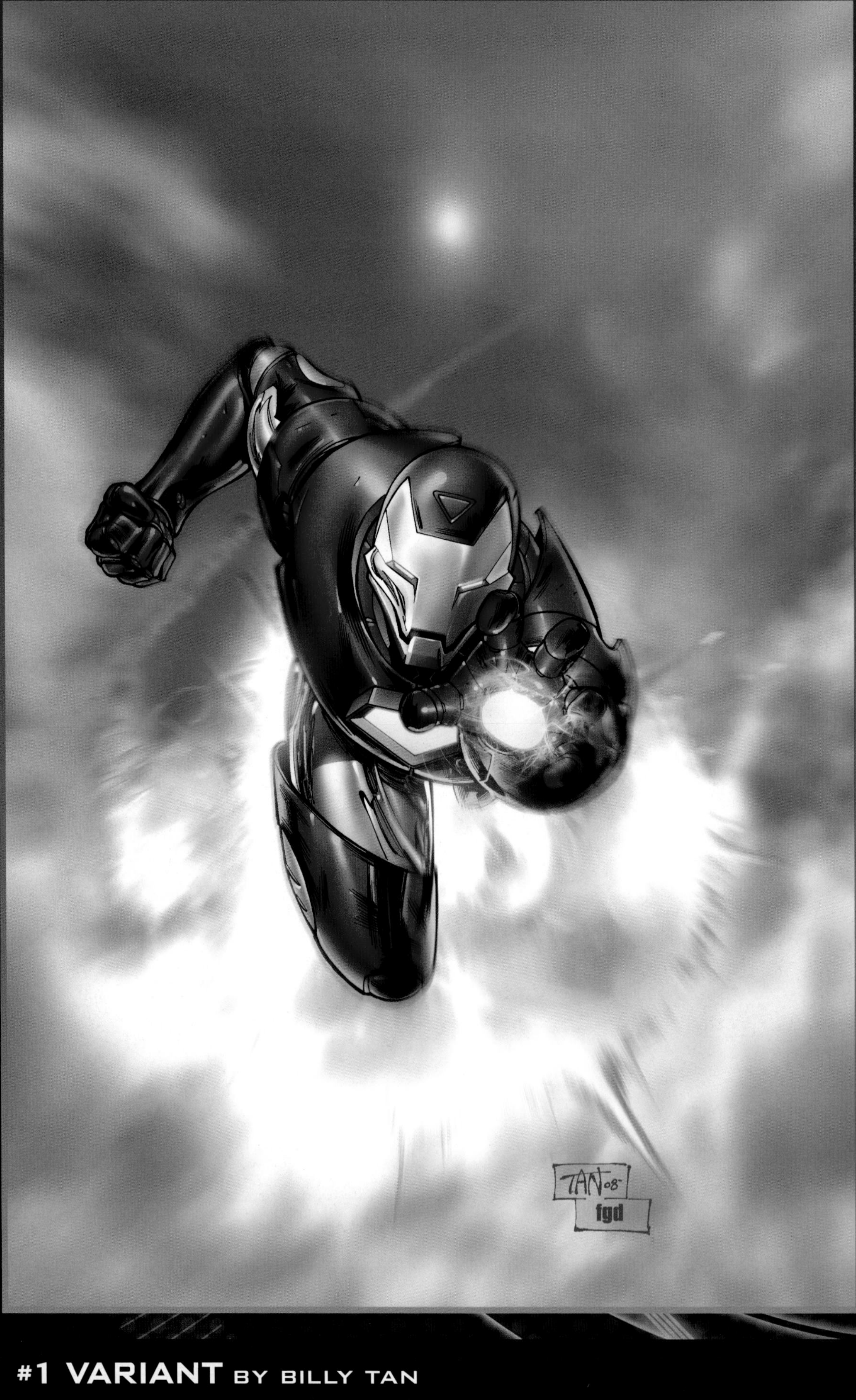
TAN 08
fgd

#1 VARIANT BY BILLY TAN

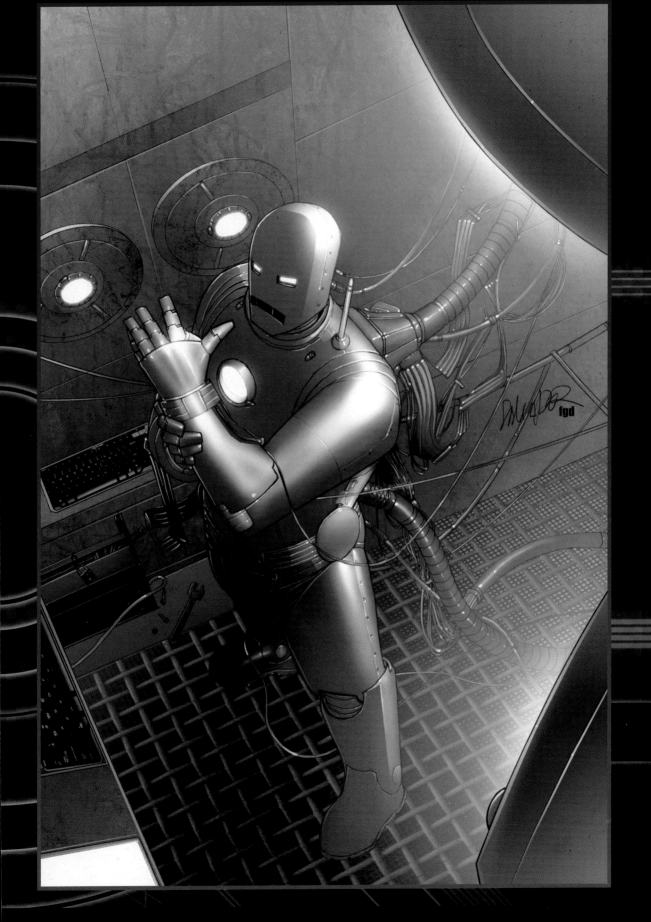

#1 2ND PRINTING VARIANT BY SALVADOR LARROCA

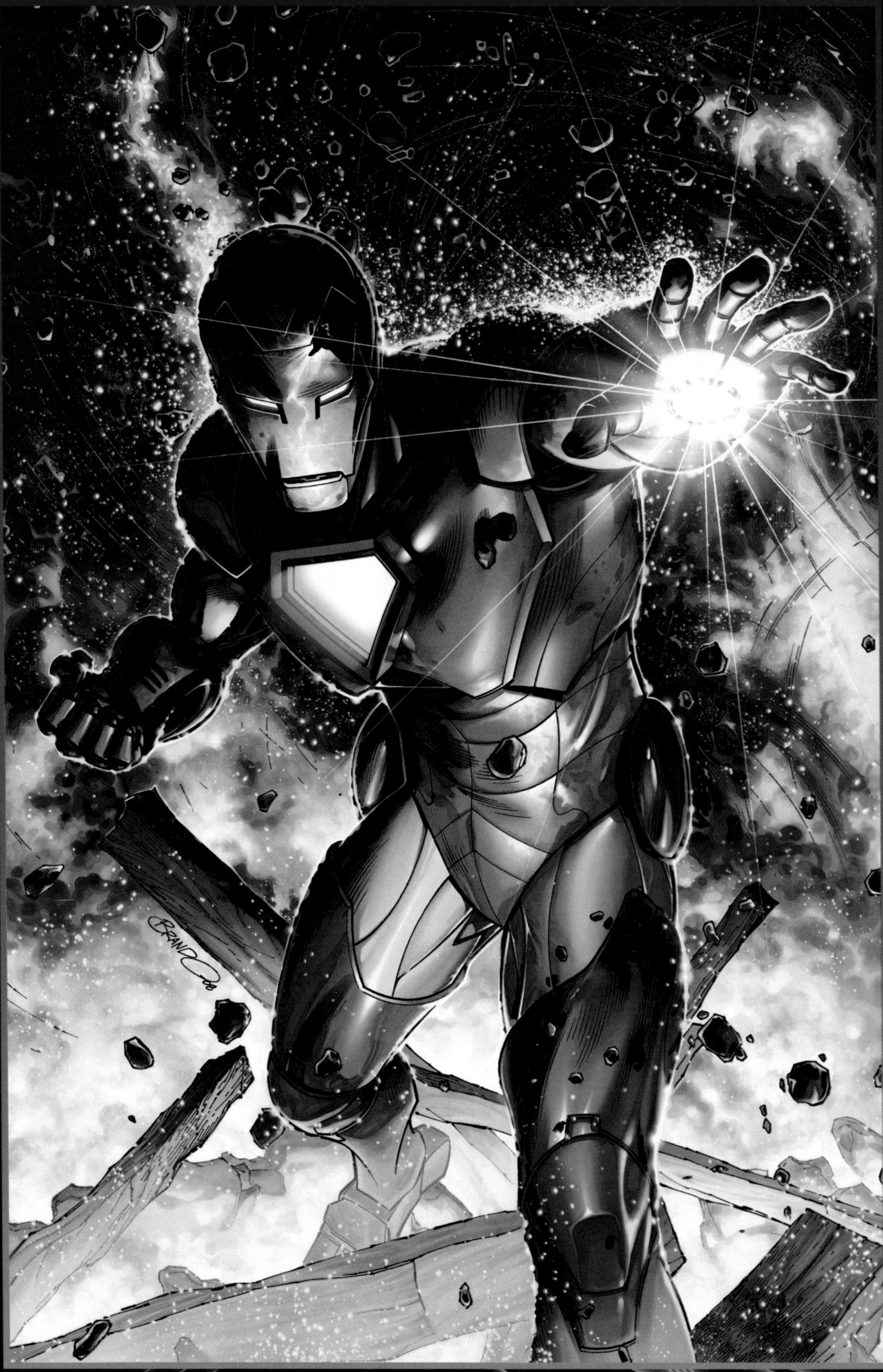

#2 VARIANT BY BRANDON PETERSON

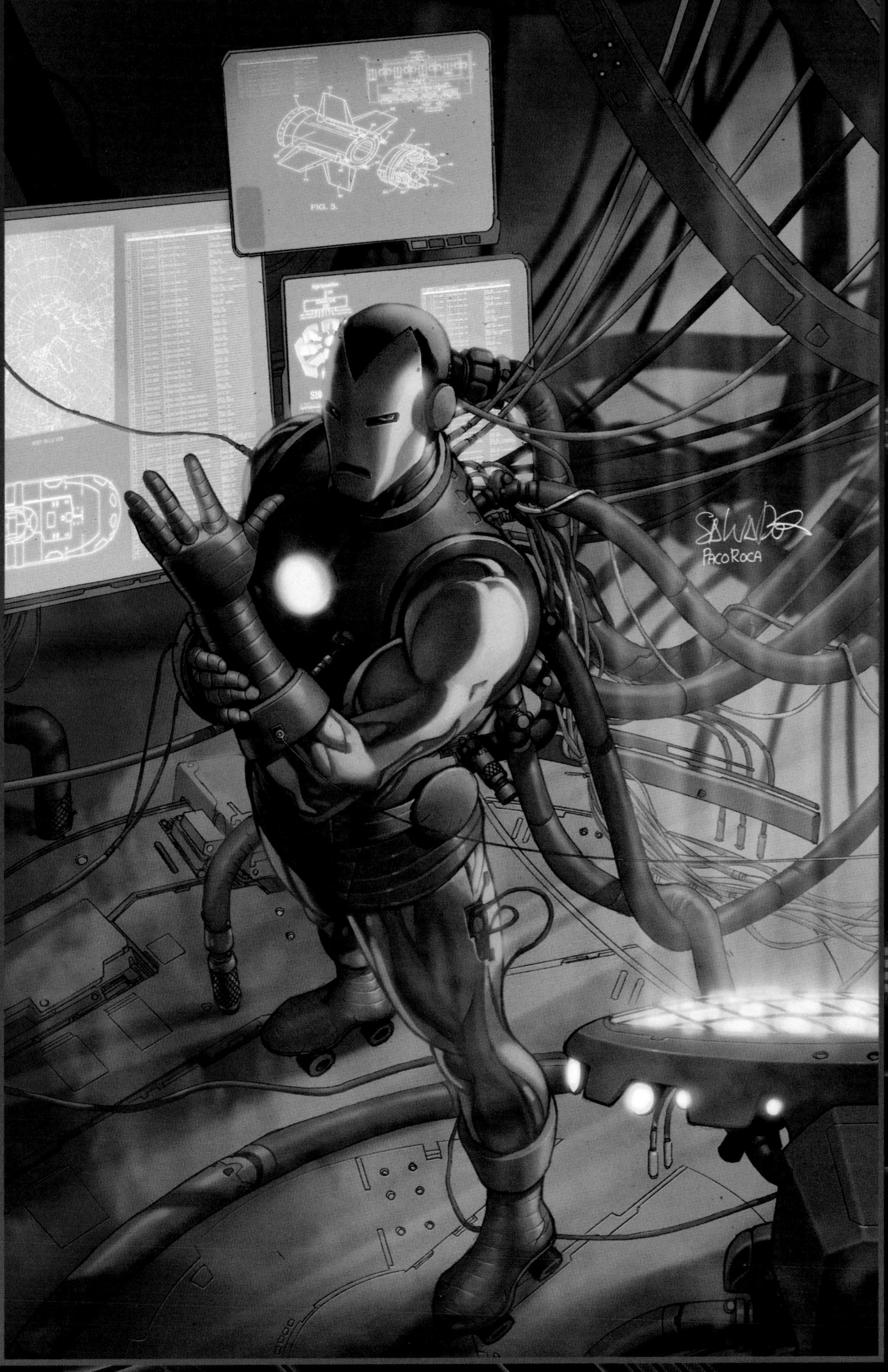
FIG. 3.

#2 2ND PRINTING VARIANT BY SALVADOR LARROCA

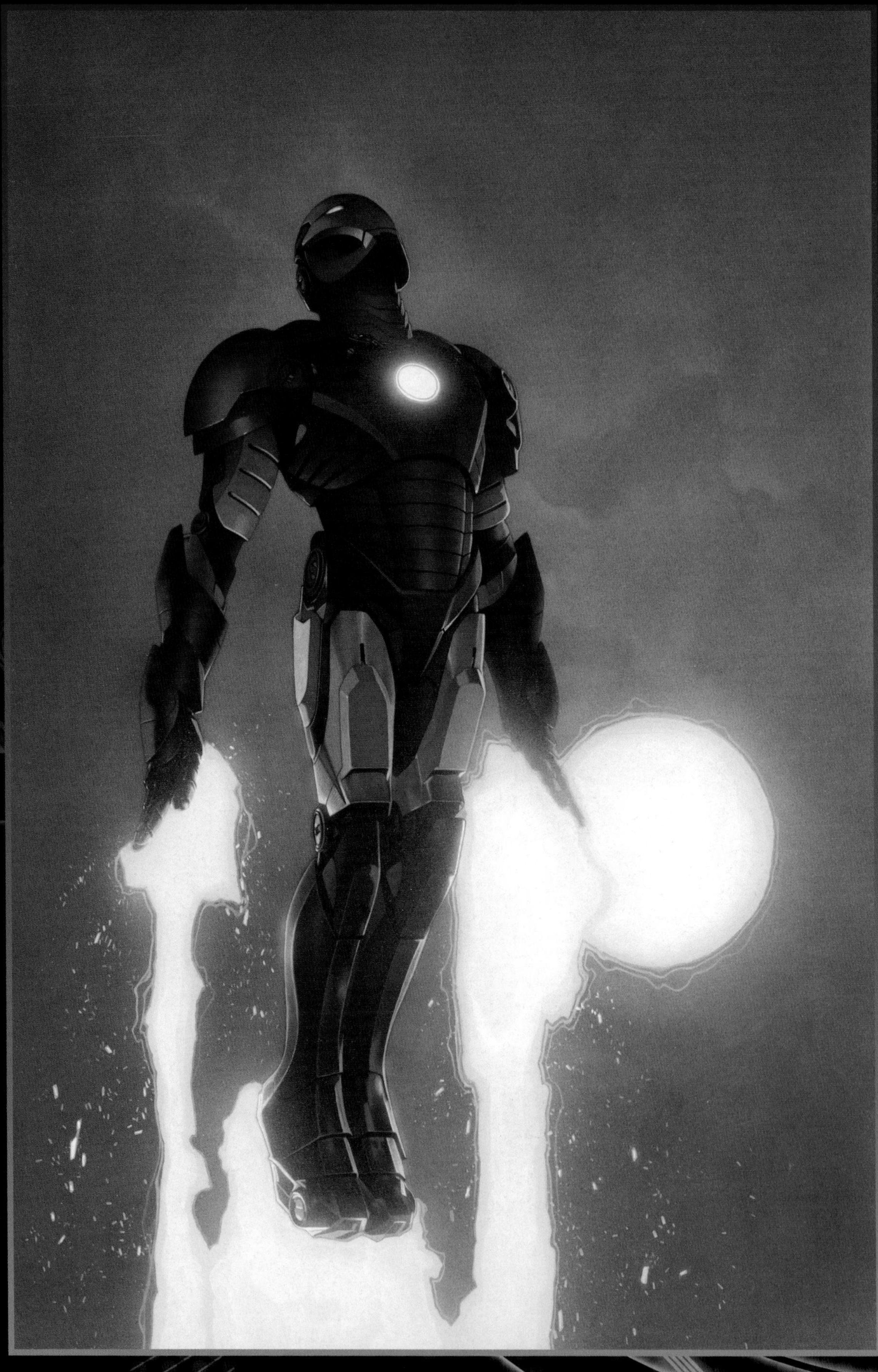

#3 VARIANT BY TRAVIS CHAREST

#3 2ND PRINTING VARIANT BY SALVADOR LARROCA

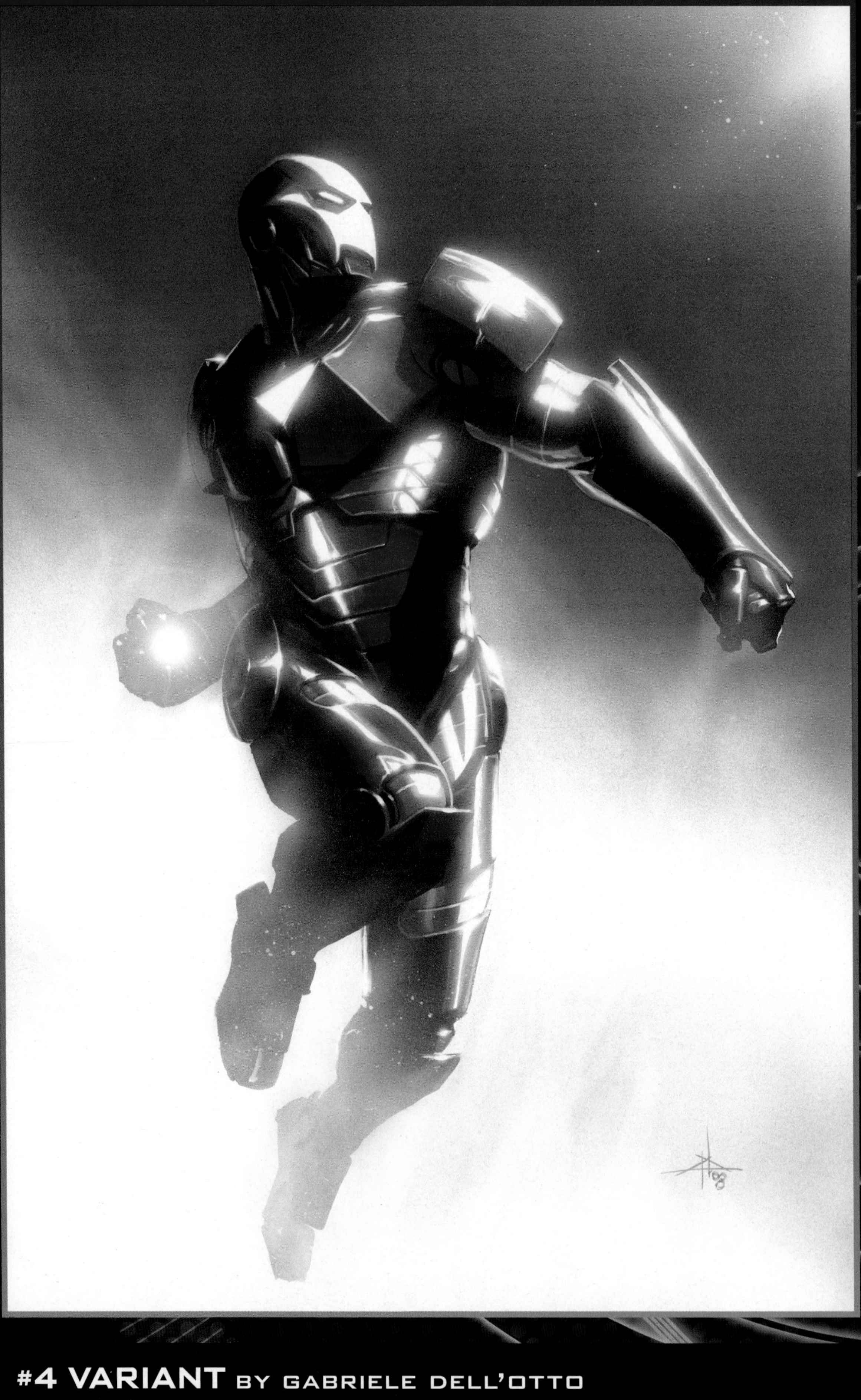

#4 VARIANT BY GABRIELE DELL'OTTO

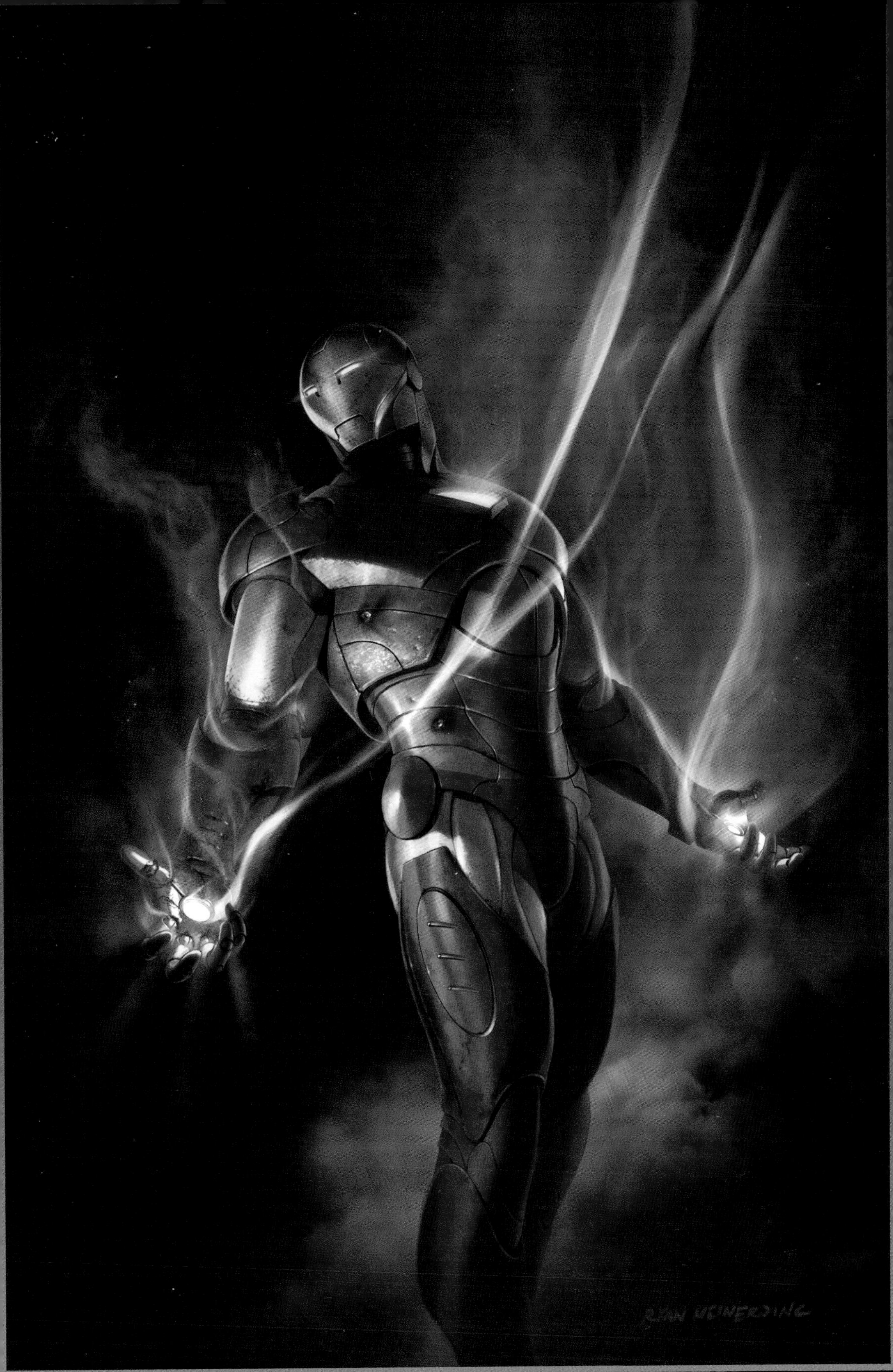
RYAN MEINERDING

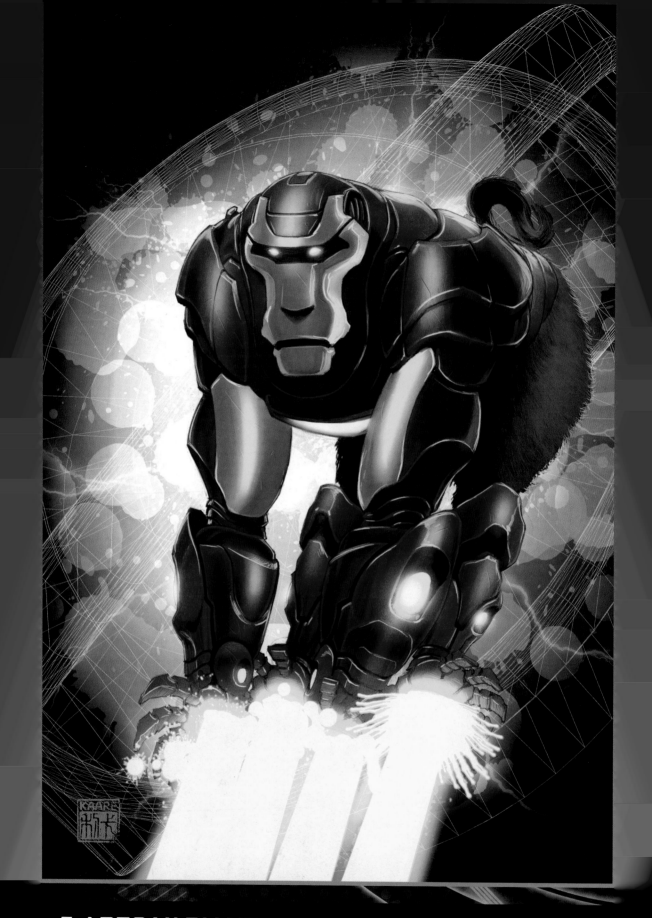

#5 APES VARIANT BY KAARE ANDREWS

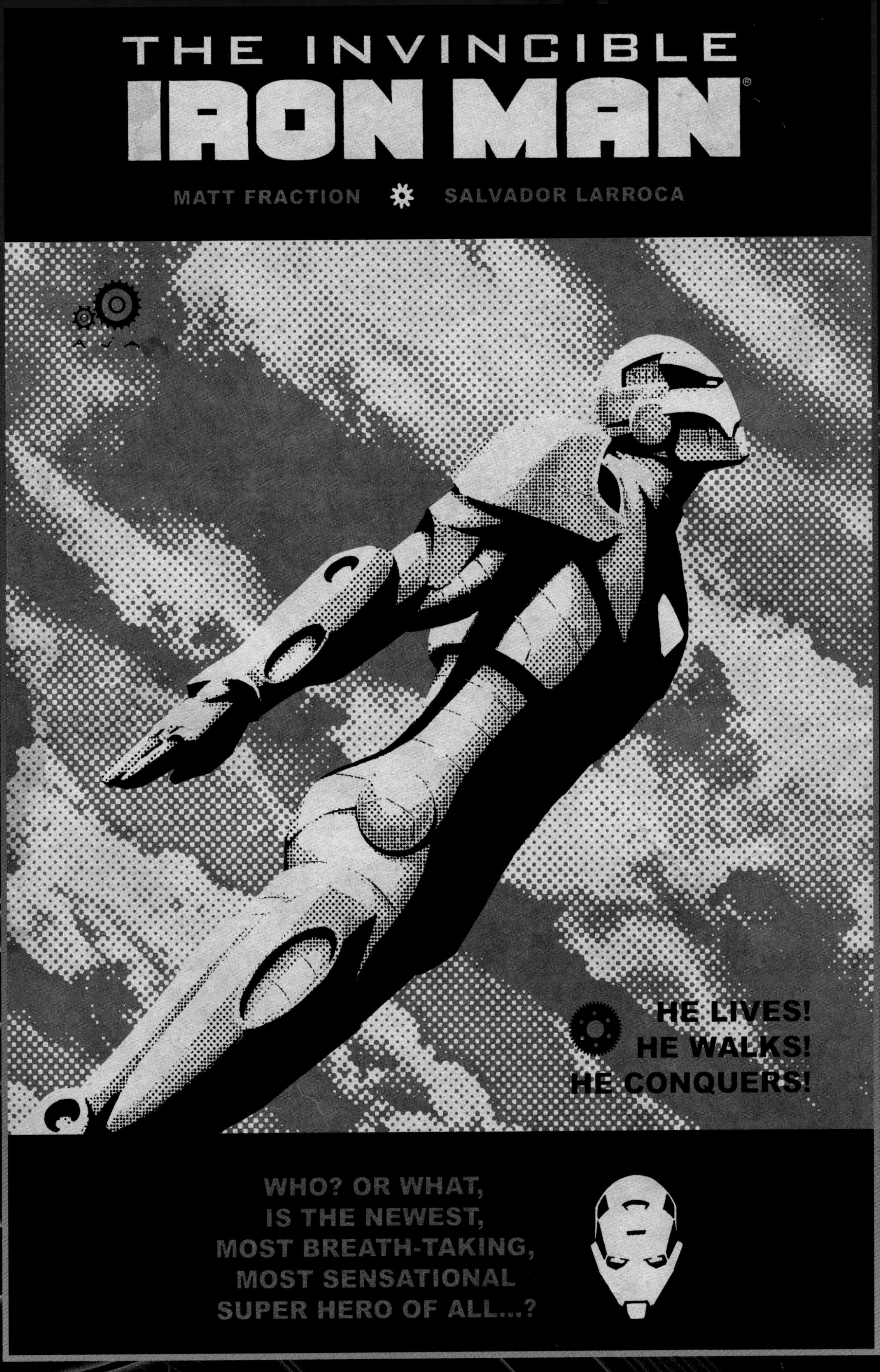

THE INVINCIBLE
IRON MAN®
MATT FRACTION
SALVADOR LARROCA
HE LIVES!
HE WALKS!
HE CONQUERS!
WHO? OR WHAT,
IS THE NEWEST,
MOST BREATH-TAKING,
MOST SENSATIONAL
SUPER HERO OF ALL...?

#6 VARIANT BY DAVID AJA

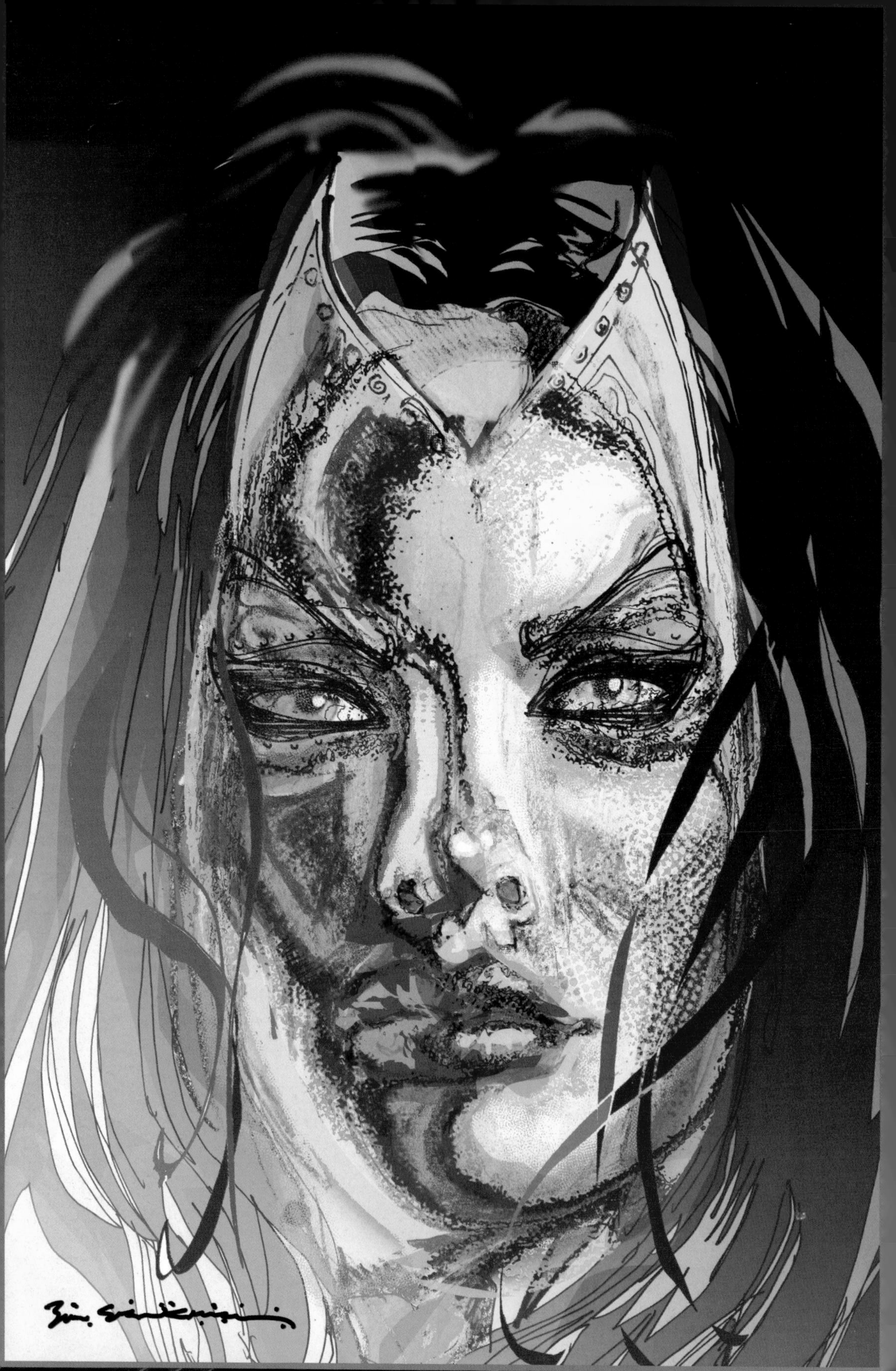

#8 VILLAIN VARIANT BY DAVID AJA

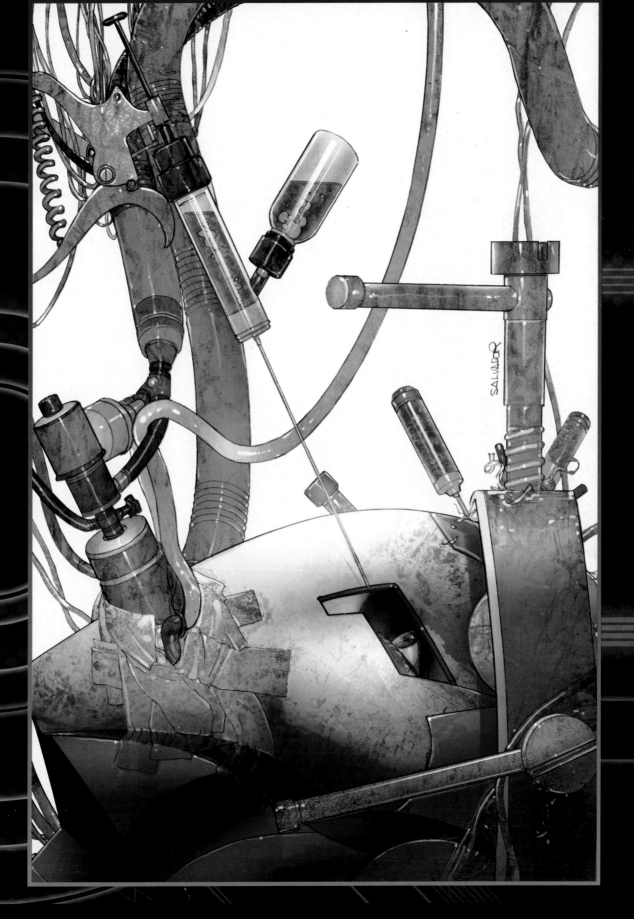

#10 VARIANT BY SALVADOR LARROCA

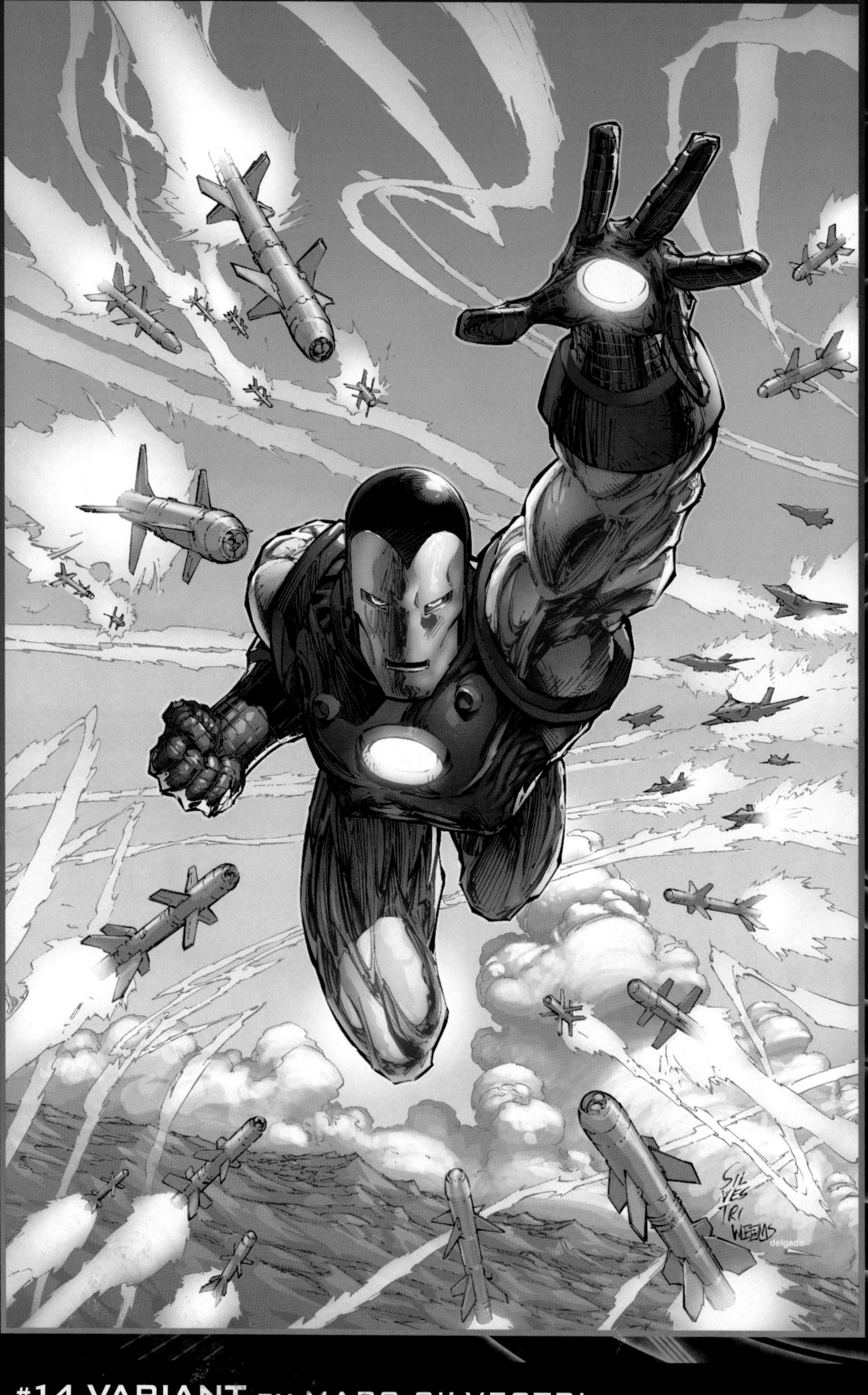
SIL
VES
TRI
WEEMS
delgado

#14 VARIANT BY MARC SILVESTRI

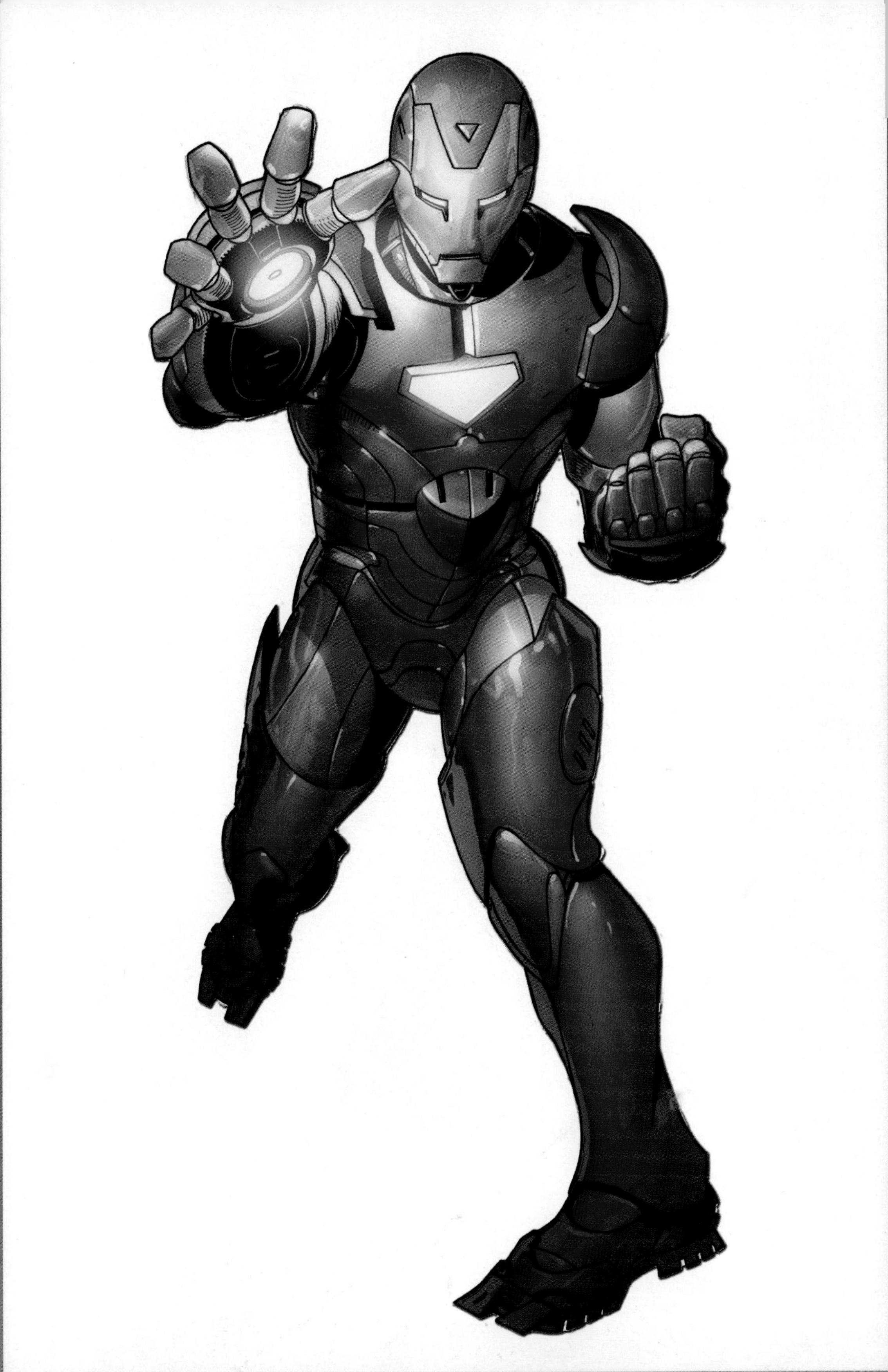

#16 70TH ANNIVERSARY FRAME VARIANT
BY SALVADOR LARROCA

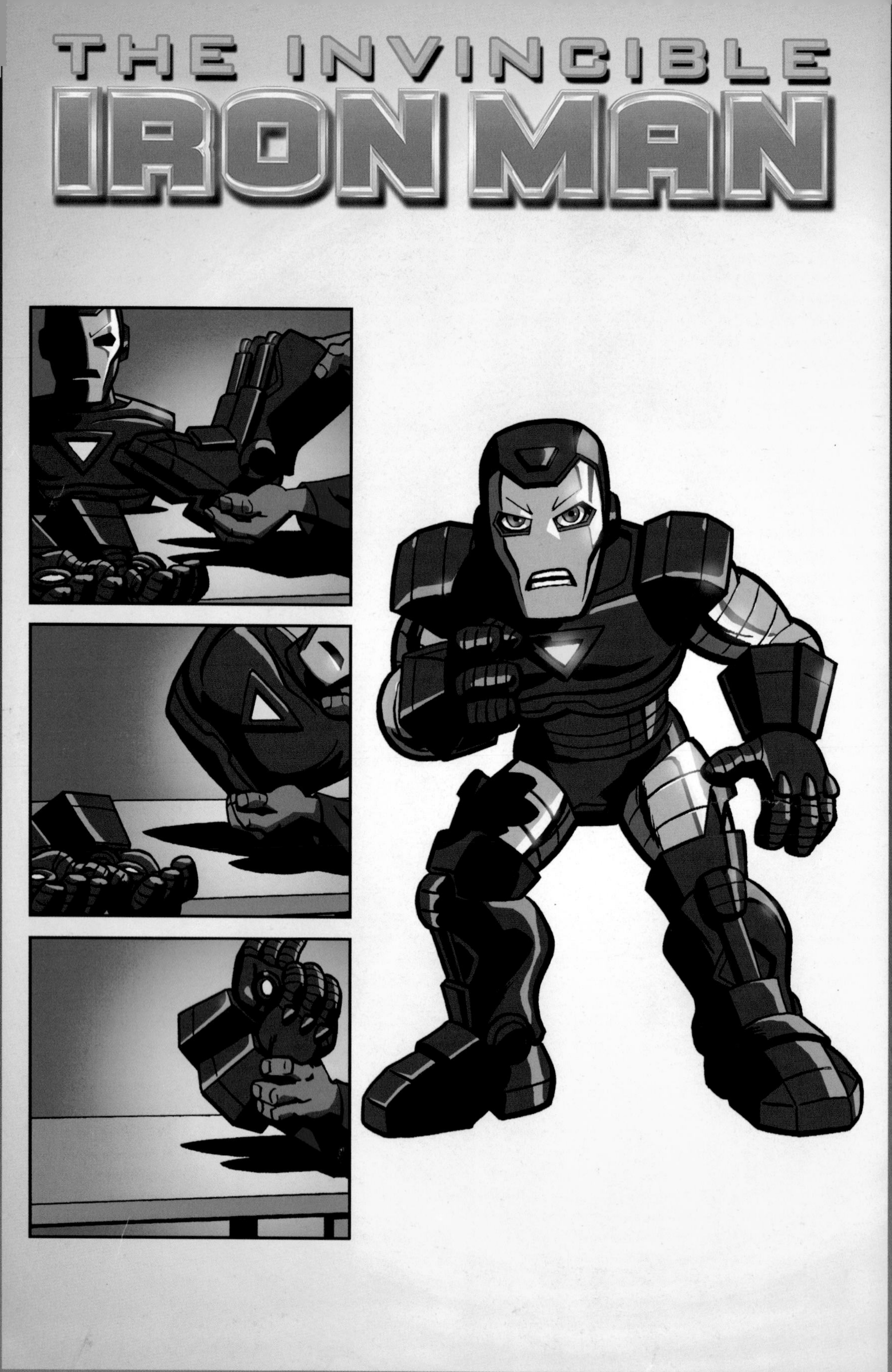
THE INVINCIBLE
IRON MAN

#19 SUPER HERO SQUAD VARIANT
BY CHRISTOPHER JONES

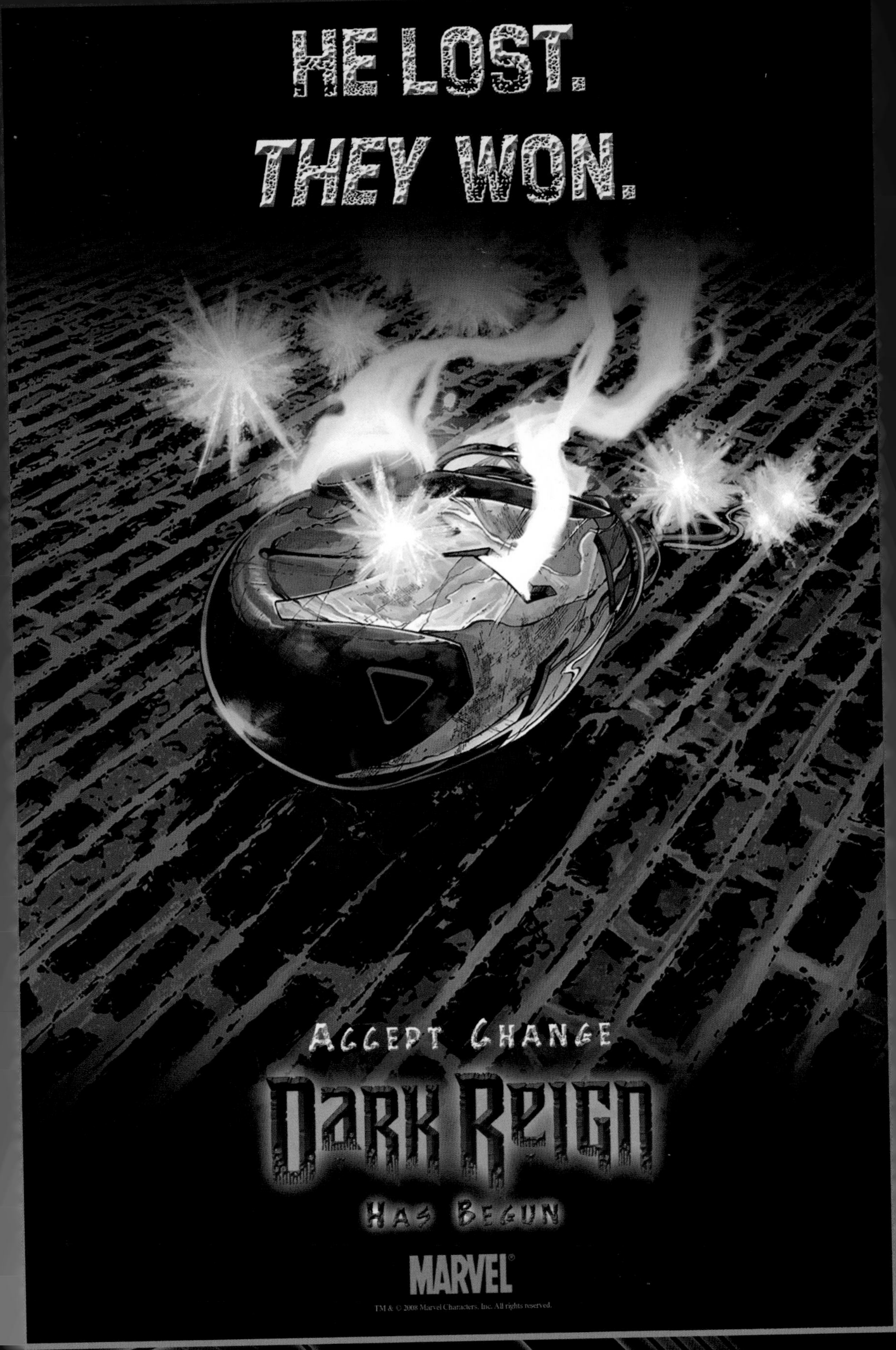
HE LOST.
THEY WON.
ACCEPT CHANGE
DARK REIGN
HAS BEGUN
MARVEL
TM & © 2008 Marvel Characters, Inc. All rights reserved.

DARK REIGN HOUSE AD BY JOE QUESADA

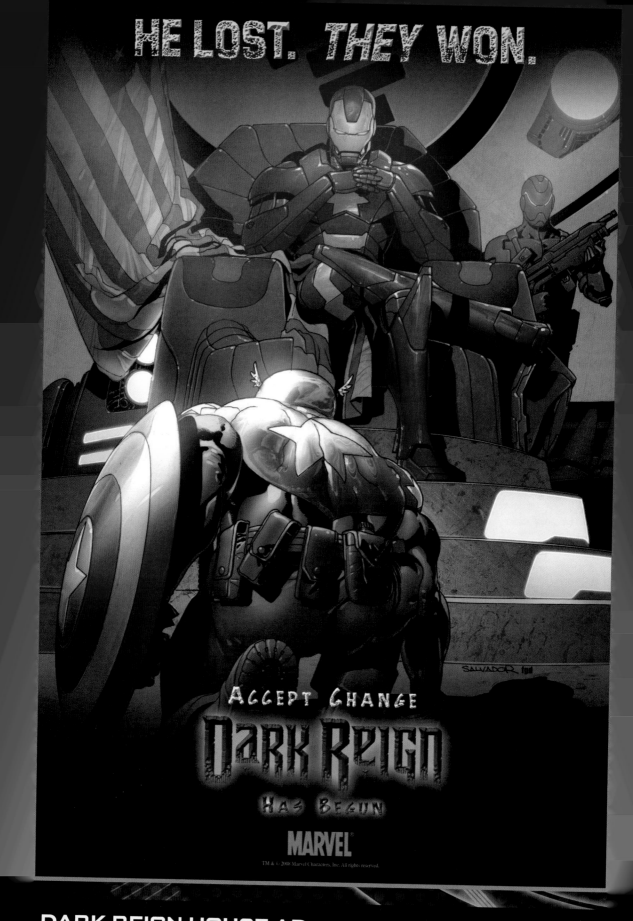

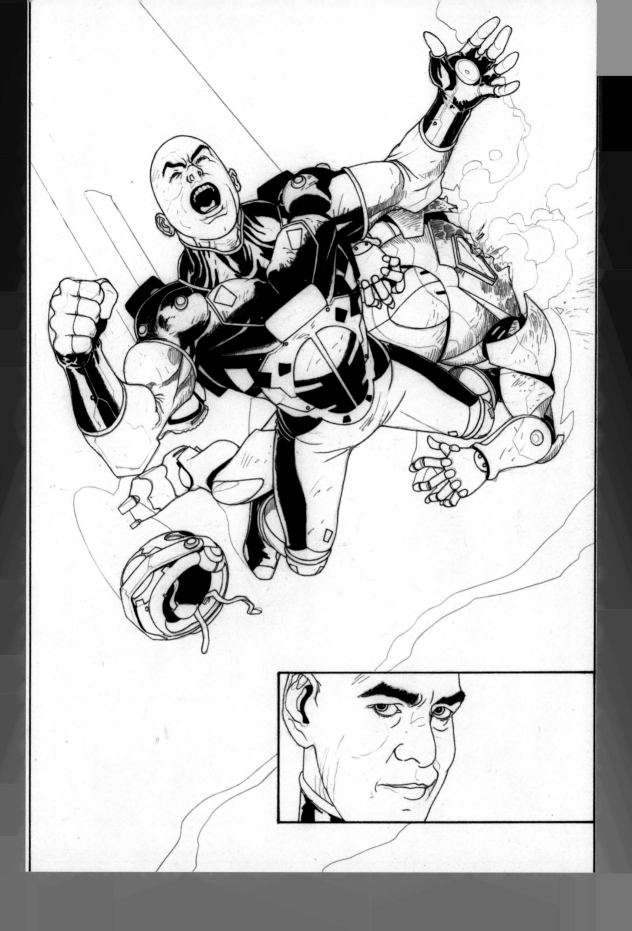

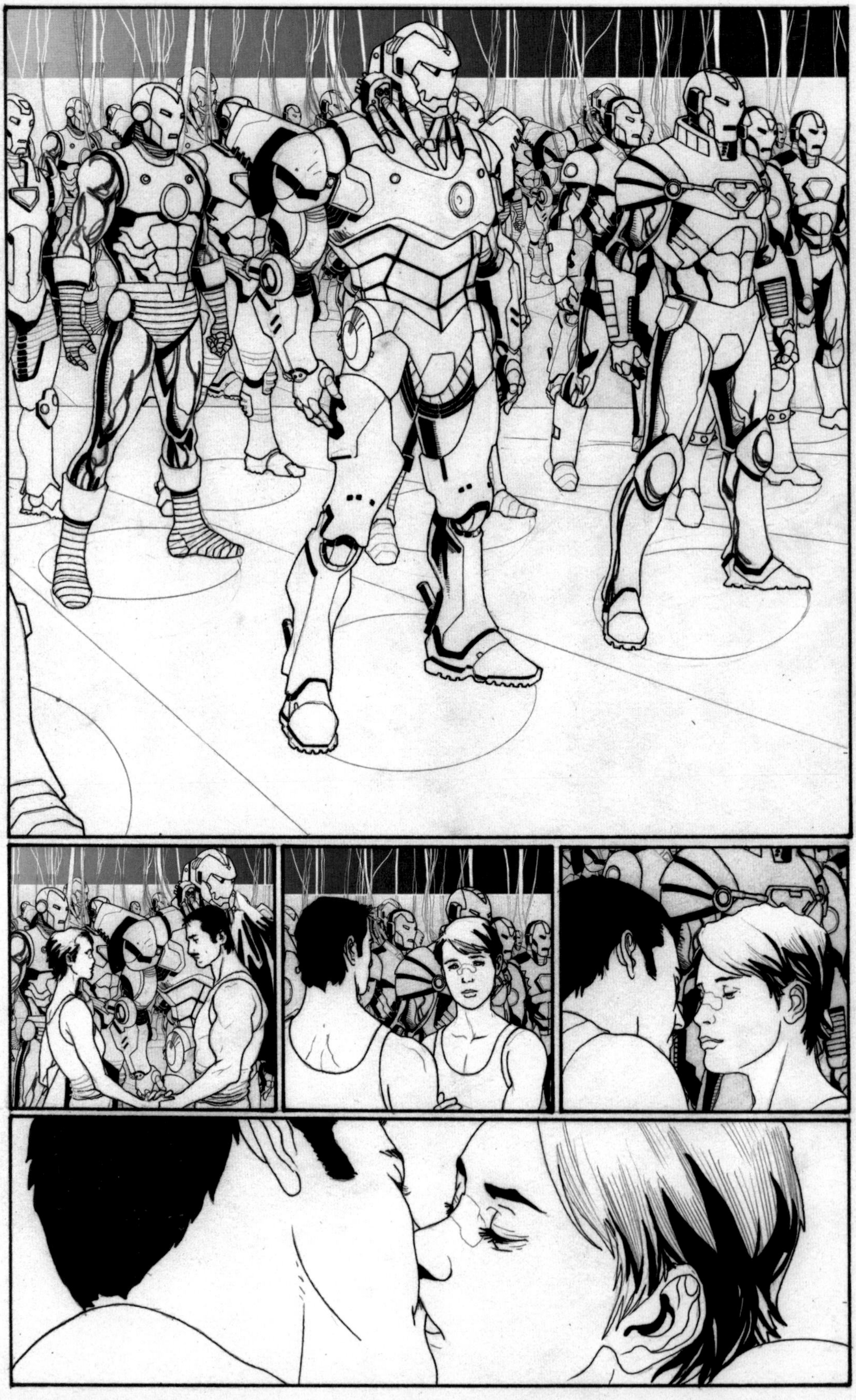

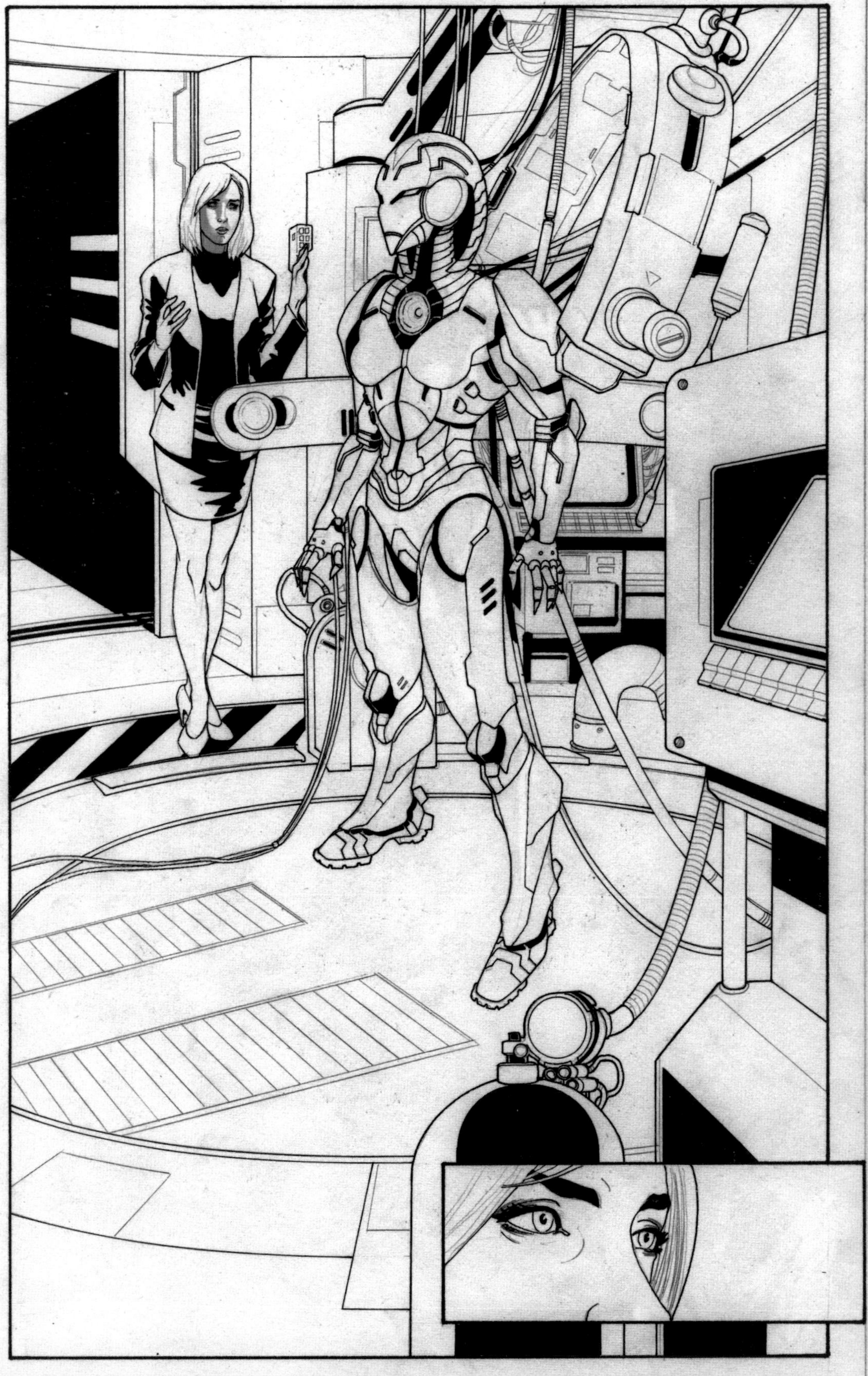

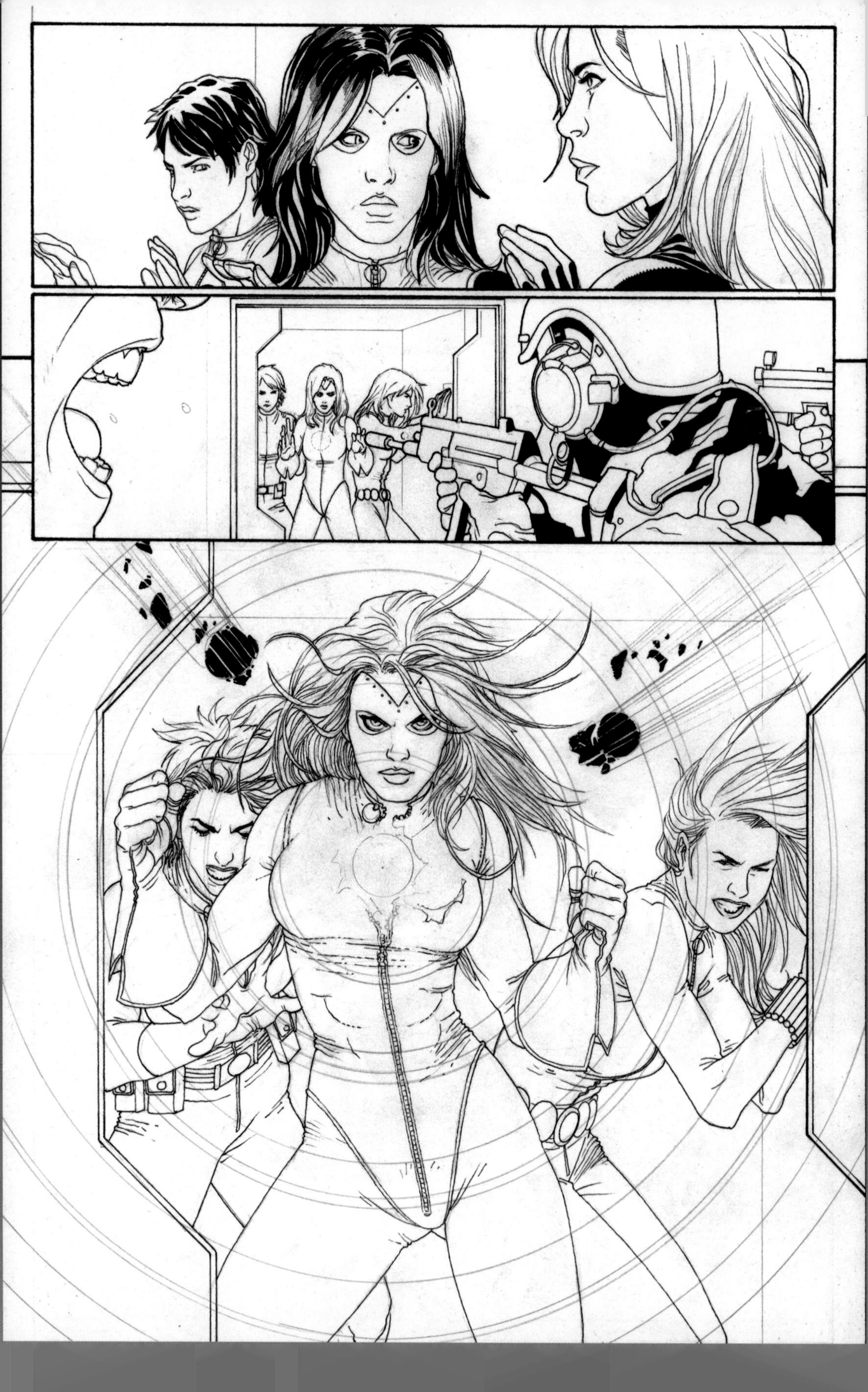

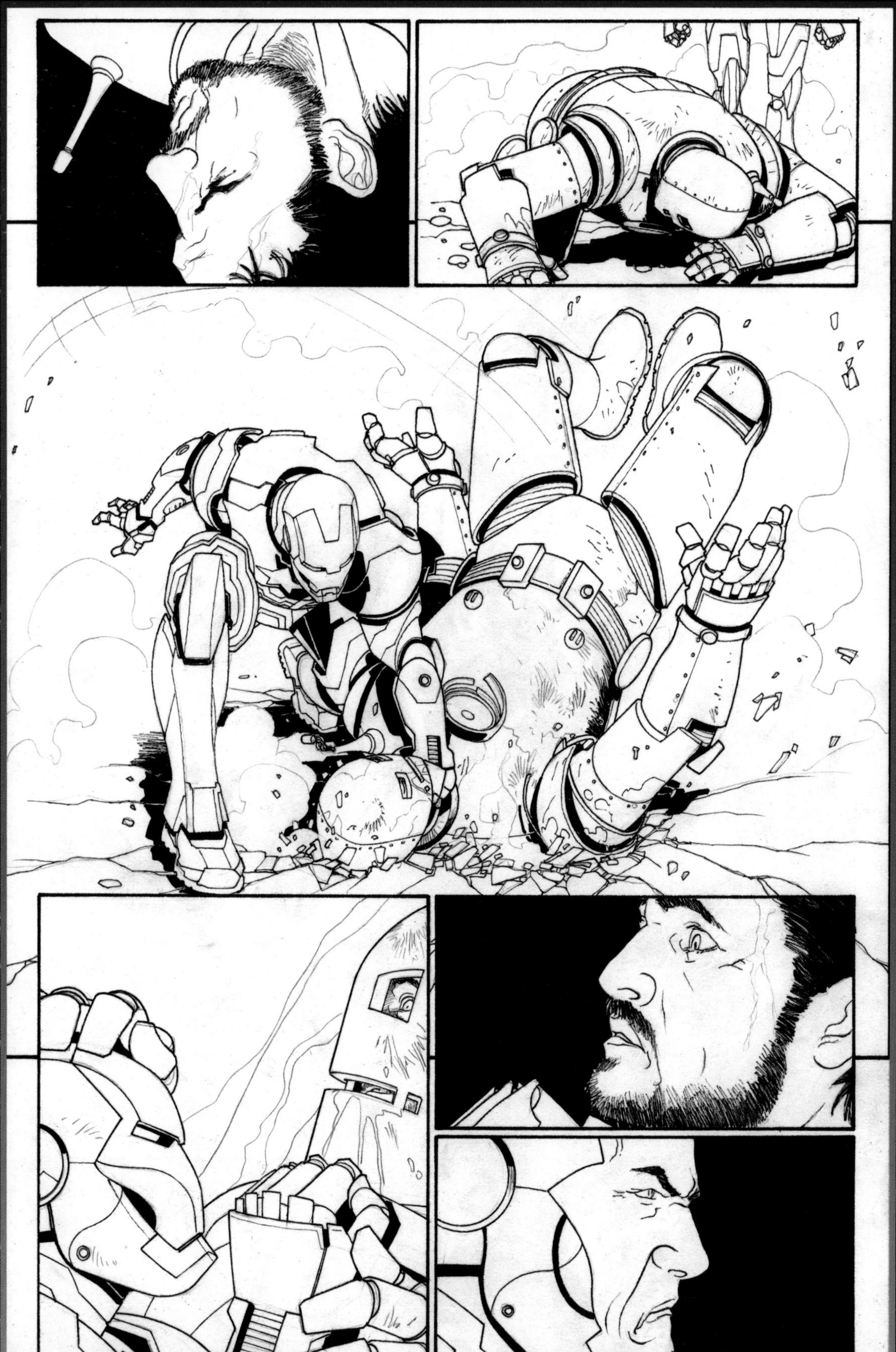

#19 PAGE 17 PENCILS
BY SALVADOR LARROCA

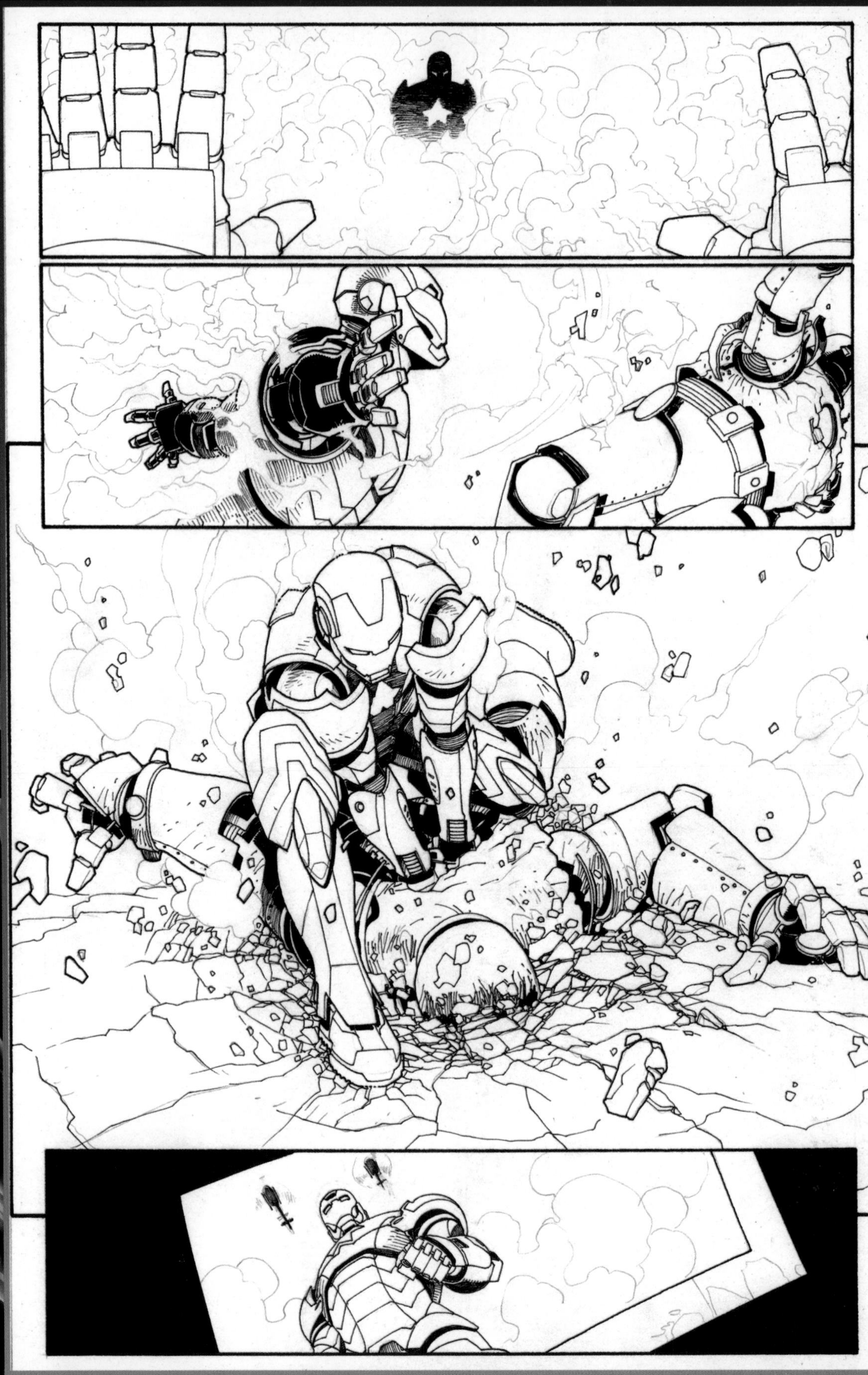

#19 PAGE 25 PENCILS
BY SALVADOR LARROCA